African American Cemeteries in Harford County, Maryland

Henry C. Peden, Jr.

HERITAGE BOOKS
2022

HERITAGE BOOKS
AN IMPRINT OF HERITAGE BOOKS, INC.

Books, CDs, and more—Worldwide

For our listing of thousands of titles see our website
at
www.HeritageBooks.com

Published 2022 by
HERITAGE BOOKS, INC.
Publishing Division
5810 Ruatan Street
Berwyn Heights, Md. 20740

Copyright © 2022 Henry C. Peden, Jr.

All rights reserved. No part of this book may be reproduced or transmitted in any form or by any means, electronic or mechanical, including photocopying, recording or by any information storage and retrieval system without written permission from the author, except for the inclusion of brief quotations in a review.

International Standard Book Number
Paperbound: 978-0-7884-1942-3

INTRODUCTION

There are twenty-three African American cemeteries in Harford County, Maryland, namely Asbury Cemetery (formerly Asbury United Methodist Church Cemetery), Barnhill Cemetery, Berkley Memorial Cemetery (Hosanna A. M. E. Church), Cedars Chapel Cemetery (St. James U. A. M. E. Church), Chestnut Grove A. M. E. Church Cemetery (formerly LaGrange Cemetery at Rocks), Clark's U. M. Church Cemetery, Community Baptist Church Cemetery, Fairview A. M. E. Church Cemetery, Foster's Hill Cemetery (John Wesley Methodist Episcopal Church), Gravel Hill Cemetery (St. James A. M. E. Church), Green Spring United Methodist Church Cemetery, Hill-Johnson Cemetery, Hendon Hill Cemetery, John Wesley United Methodist Church Cemetery (Abingdon Colored Cemetery), Mt. Calvary U. A. M. E. Church Cemetery, Mt. Zion United Methodist Church Cemetery (Mountain Cemetery near McComas Institute), Old Union Chapel Methodist Episcopal Church (on Aberdeen Proving Ground), Skinner Cemetery, St. James United Cemetery, William C. Rice Memorial Cemetery (St. James United Methodist Church, Federal Hill), Tabernacle Mount Zion United Methodist Church Cemetery, Union United Methodist Church Cemetery, and West Liberty Church Cemetery.

Some of the tombstones and grave markers were copied by various people at times since the 1960s and the information was filed with the Historical Society of Harford County. Realizing these lists were incomplete and an update was needed, I visited the African American cemeteries between May and December of 2018 and copied every tombstone and grave marker I could find. Interestingly, some of the markers copied previously were not found and I discovered others that had been overlooked. I also realized that many of those interred did not have a tombstone and while some had temporary funeral home markers, others had handmade wooden crosses and even a few were handwritten on flat cement slabs. Many inscriptions included nicknames, Biblical quotes, poetic verses, photographs, images, and family relationships.

Thousands were buried without any markers of any kind being placed on their graves. To compensate for this lack of information, I conducted additional research and found more burials in some death certificates, some obituaries, some extant funeral home records, namely J. A. Pennington in Havre de Grace and E. G. Kurtz in Jarrettsville, and a few monuments made by the J. C. Taylor Marble Co. This kept me quite busy during the COVID-19 pandemic and my efforts resulted in 6,854 burials being identified and collected for this book. Obviously, there are many more interments that could be found in privately held church records and newspaper obituaries, but I leave that project for another interested person to pursue. Be that as it may, the book that I have compiled is more than a listing of names and dates since most contain family relationships and biographical information, including civic and military service in many cases. It is arranged alphabetically, which precludes the need for a separate index, and at the end of each entry the name of the cemetery is indicated in brackets. Names that appear on the same tombstone or obelisk are noted within the text. Descriptions of the cemeteries follow.

Asbury Cemetery (formerly Asbury United Methodist Church Cemetery)
Located at 114 Asbury Road in Churchville, this old church was initially known as "Big Asbury Methodist Church" when it was organized in 1838. "Big Asbury Colored Methodist Episcopal Church" is mentioned in a deed from the Kennedy family in 1868. It has two cemeteries, the older one situated on the north side across the road and the newer cemetery on the south side of the road near the church. The Methodist congregation no longer exists and a church called "Thy Kingdom Come Ministry" has taken its place. Several tombstones were toppled over in the old cemetery and others that were copied in 1987 were not found in 2018. Additional burials were compiled from other extant sources, such as death certificates and obituaries.

Barn Hill Cemetery
This small cemetery is located in a wooded area in the Norrisville area of northwestern Harford County known as the Long Corner. There is a dearth of information about how it got its name, but the 1878 Martenet Map shows "Barn Hill Col'd. Church" on the west side of what is now Long Corner Road, north of Duncan Road. This cemetery has apparently not been used for over 100 years and only three grave markers have survived that were copied by Jon Harlan Livezey in the 1960s. The church no longer exists, but it was probably organized some time after the Civil War.

Berkley Memorial Cemetery (Hosanna A. M. E. Church)
This church and cemetery are located at 2418 Castleton Road in the community of Berkley near Darlington. It

traces its roots to a log structure built around 1835 on land provided by Robert Paca. The congregation later moved their church services to the Hosanna School in 1867 and remained there until 1880 when a new church was built. It was incorporated on July 15, 1882. Hosanna A. M. E. Church and Berkley Memorial Cemetery have both been well maintained over the years. The tombstones were copied in September 1987, but a number of them had been overlooked or copied incorrectly and some were not found when I recopied them in 2018.

Cedars Chapel Cemetery (St. James U. A. M. E. Church)
This church and cemetery are located at 3345 Cedar Church Road, less than a mile from Route 1 (Conowingo Road), between Dublin and Darlington. Services have been held at this location since 1868 and the existing building was constructed in 1942. Tombstones were copied in 1987 and I recopied this well-kept cemetery in 2018, adding additional information from other sources.

Chestnut Grove A. M. E. Church Cemetery (formerly LaGrange Cemetery at Rocks)
This church and cemetery are located at 828 Coen Road near Street, Md., just north of Rocks State Park. The congregation organized under the name of Chestnut Grove Chapel in 1891. Meetings were held at the Old Rocks School until 1893 at which time Martha J. Rutledge, Grace A. Rogers and Mary C. Rogers, for $80, sold to Moses Rice, Louis Rainbow, Alexander Rice, Charles Densen and Calvin Densen, the trustees of Chestnut Grove Chapel, 158 perches of land, part of the tract *Woods Intent* "beginning at a stone marked 'T' set in the ground on the northeast corner of a lot of ground known as LaGrange Church lot, west of the public schoolhouse and running thence … to the center of the public road leading from Rocks to Streett's Mill." (Information gleaned from Harford County Land Records). Some of the earliest death certificates called it LaGrange Cemetery. The tombstones were copied in 1987 and I recopied them in 2018 and added information from obituaries, death certificates, J. C. Taylor Marble Co. records and a few Kurtz Funeral Home records.

Clark's U. M. Church Cemetery
This church and cemetery are located at 2001 Kalmia Road, east of Conowingo Road (Route 1) and Forge Hill Road, on land in Kalmia conveyed to the trustees of the church by Henry Clark in 1855. It is shown on the 1858 Jennings & Herrick Map of Harford Co. and was originally known as "Clark's Chapel." In 1883 a gable-roofed stucco-over-stone building with pointed-arch windows was built and it became known as Clark's Methodist Episcopal Church. The present Clark's United Methodist Church was constructed in 1972-1973. It stands on a ridge above the 1883 church. The cemetery is adjacent to both of them. (Information from Maryland Historical Trust Survey HA-48, by Walter Smothers, 1977) Tombstones were copied over 30 years ago, several have since toppled over and some are illegible due to weathering. Many graves have no markers. Additions and corrections from other sources to the earlier listing were made when I visited the cemetery in August 2018.

Community Baptist Church Cemetery
This church and cemetery are located at 303 Philadelphia Road in Joppa. The church was built in 1946 and was once known as Mandyville Baptist Church and Magnolia Baptist Church. I copied the tombstones on September 12, 2018 and included additional information from some obituaries.

Fairview A. M. E. Church Cemetery
This church and cemetery are located at 2328 High Point Road and Jarrettsville Road, west of Forest Hill. The church was built in 1909, but a congregation existed before 1897 and they once worshipped in tents. Some information found in obituaries, death certificates and funeral home records has been included. Some tombstones that were copied in 1987 were not found in 2018.

Foster's Hill Cemetery (John Wesley Methodist Episcopal Church)
This cemetery at 508 Foster Branch Road in the Joppa-Magnolia area has been known as Foster's Hill Cemetery, Foster Hill Cemetery, Ebenezer Baptist Church Cemetery, Magnolia Colored Cemetery, Magnolia Baptist Cemetery and John Wesley Methodist Church Cemetery. This latter church was located less than a mile away at the corner of Trimble Road and Dembytown Road, but did not have a cemetery at that location. The land for the church was acquired by trustees of the John Wesley Methodist Episcopal Church on November 14, 1919 and stated, in part, "that no part of the property shall at any time be used as a cemetery or burying ground under any circumstance." This is in reference to the land at 800 Trimble Road. A deed in 1935 from Estella and John F.

Ennis to the Trustees of Ebenezer Baptist Church, regarding the new Joppa Wood Subdivision, included a survey that mentioned "an old cemetery" located at 508 Foster Branch Road. Members of the John Wesley Methodist Church (congregation no longer exists and the church is now occupied by the Nazarene Apostolic Church) were buried at 508 Foster Branch Road. This is evident by the burial of Jennie Belle Demby in 1969 whose obituary stated her "interment was in the John Wesley Methodist Cemetery, Magnolia," yet her tombstone is in the cemetery next to Ebenezer Baptist Church at 508 Foster Branch Road. The obituary of Myra S. Norton in 1984 stated that her "interment was in the John Wesley Cemetery," yet her tombstone is also at 508 Foster Branch Road. In 1954 M. Estella and John F. Ennis conveyed the land next to Ebenezer Baptist Church "to be used as a burying ground for the members of said [John Wesley Methodist] church." The present church building was built circa 1955, but the congregation was in existence long before then. The tombstones were copied in 1987 and I recopied them in 2018. The earliest tombstone is inscribed with the death year 1950, but there were burials as early as 1914 as shown in death certificates, but prior to 1911 these certificates do not indicate places of burial.

Gravel Hill Cemetery (St. James A. M. E. Church)
Located at 4139 Gravel Hill Road at Stewartsville in Harford County's District No. 2, this cemetery is also known as Gravelly Hill or Gravelly Hills and adjoins St. James A. M. E. Church. The church became the centerpiece of the community when James Peaker brought residents together to worship in his home. In 1850 they built the first church that they called the Mount Zion Meeting House. After a series of name changes the church settled on St. James A. M. E. Church in 1868, naming the parish after its founder James Peaker. The church purchased more land in 1881. This information is from the vertical files of the Historical Society of Harford County. An unidentified newspaper in those vertical files reported this cemetery had been added to the register of Harford County landmarks. Tombstones were copied in 1987 and 2002, but many were not found when I visited in the summer of 2018. It appears that due to the lack of tombstones some of the names of those buried here came from sources known only to the copyists. I have inserted more information from other sources.

Green Spring United Methodist Church Cemetery
This church and cemetery are located at the corner of Old Level Road and Green Spring Road just west of the community of Level. For a brief history see "Green Spring Church" by James R. Dorsey in *Harford Historical Bulletin No. 47* (Winter 1991). An old sign above the front door, mounted up near the roof line, states "Level Church of Jesus Christ." The tombstones were copied in the 1980s, updated by James R. Dorsey in 1991 and I recopied them in 2018. I also added some information from extant obituaries and death certificates. Several tombstones were toppled over, some were illegible, and many graves had no markers.

Hendon Hill Cemetery
This cemetery is located about two miles west of Bel Air near Watervale at 1014 Vale Road between Red Pump Road and Grafton Shop Road. An African American school and church building (which no longer exists) had its beginnings here when Benjamin Hendon (1817-1874), a white farmer, conveyed part of his property on February 8, 1869 to George Daugherty, Edward Hall, William Ruff and William Morgan for the purpose "of allowing to be erected a school house for the benefit and education of the Colored People of Harford County forever." Hendon later conveyed a half-acre on September 1, 1873 to the trustees of Ames Methodist Church, namely George Daugherty, William Morgan, James Taylor, Alfred Bond and Lewis Butler "for the purpose of a cemetery for the Colored People of Harford County." These deeds are described in Harford County Land Records Deed Book ALJ, No. 22, page 329, and Deed Book ALJ, No. 29, p. 281. The earliest known burial was for Martha Preston who died on November 21, 1872 and the last burial was for Harriet Smith Burns who died on March 8, 1976. The cemetery has since been closed and the Ames United Methodist Church in Bel Air maintains the property. There are 45 grave markers of which 23 are inscribed, 22 have no markings whatsoever, and some are damaged and weathered. Altogether 160 burials have been identified through existing tombstones, obituaries and death certificates, including eight more burials probably in this cemetery. About 70 percent of the burial lots are unmarked. There are undoubtedly more burials in this cemetery since death certificates that began in 1898 did not indicate the place of burial until 1911 and I did not have access to death certificates after mid-1951. Newspapers were also searched between 1911 and 1976 and a few more burials were found. Many did not have obituaries. Additional information about the deceased has also been included when available from other sources, namely a few from early Kurtz Funeral Home records and J. C. Taylor Marble Co. records. James E. Chrismer,

teacher, historian and volunteer at the Historical Society of Harford County, kindly provided images of the tombstones that he had photographed which aided greatly in deciphering some of the old weathered inscriptions. In the summer of 2018 I visited the cemetery and recopied the inscriptions that had been initially copied in 1986-1987, finding that some old grave markers had been overlooked at that time while a few others were not located at this time. The cemetery was rededicated on October 17, 2021 by Joan Wiggins and members of the Ames United Methodist Church in Bel Air. I was honored to contribute to and be part of this historic event.

Hill-Johnson Family Cemetery
This burial ground is located in a wooded area on the north side of Chapel Road about one-half mile east of the intersection of Chapel Road and Earlton Road and west of Havre de Grace. The grave markers were copied by Jon Harlan Livezey in the 1960s and he noted the stones were widely dispersed through the woods. There were many stone markers without inscriptions and it was likely that many stones may have fallen and had become covered by leaves and brush. In February 2019 James E. Chrismer went to the area and verified the same condition, stating the burial ground was actually located on East Chapel Road directly across from where Blenheim Farm Road joined Chapel Road. I also did additional research on two of the people buried there.

John Wesley United Methodist Church Cemetery (Abingdon Colored Cemetery)
This old church and cemetery are located at 3817 Philadelphia Road between Abingdon and Bush. It reportedly "was given to the Blacks by the Quakers in 1868," according to an undated photo and clipping in the Historical Society of Harford County Archives. The cemetery has been known as John Wesley Cemetery and Abingdon Colored Cemetery. The tombstones were copied in 1987 and I recopied them in 2018 and included additional information from death certificates, obituaries, and various other records.

Mt. Calvary U. A. M. E. Church Cemetery
This church and cemetery are located at 123 Mt. Calvary Church Road in Aberdeen. The tombstones were copied in the 1980s and I recopied them on October 6, 2018 and was perplexed that many of those copied back then were not found today. It is probable that some graves had temporary markers that would only state name and years of birth and death, but several had complete dates, thus implying permanent stone markers. On the day I visited the cemetery a funeral was taking place and I later met Charles Warfield, an elderly gentleman and trustee, who allowed me to copy a plan of the cemetery lot holders in 1951 and a second plan that was not dated. Many of the lots were not filled in on both plans, so there must be another plan or record of burials for the past 70 years. The church was built in September 1868, re-erected in October 1918 and again in 1986, as noted on several markers displayed on the lower left of the building near the church entrance.

Mt. Zion United Methodist Church Cemetery (Mountain Cemetery near McComas Institute)
This old church and cemetery at 1915 Singer Road are located next to historic McComas Institute. It was also known as Mountain Cemetery, Mountain Methodist Cemetery, Mountain Colored Cemetery, Mountain Memorial Cemetery and McComas Chapel on the Mountain. Many tombstones were difficult to read when someone copied them in 1987 and such was the case when I recopied and made several additions and corrections in 2018. I have supplemented the burials with information from some death certificates and obituaries.

Old Union Chapel Methodist Episcopal Church (cemetery now on Aberdeen Proving Ground)
In 1846 several white men called together African American residents of Michaelsville to build a church for them and in 1849 a one-acre lot was purchased for $25 from Ethan Michael, for whom the village was named. (Land Records DHG 35, p. 145) In the spring of 1849 Robert Brown hauled the first material and set up the foundation. The following spring a 28 x 40 x 16 feet building was begun. A short time later Father Maxfield was the first to be buried in the cemetery. For many years to follow the church was known simply as the "New Meeting House." Following a succession of ministers Rev. William Gwynn proposed the name of Union Chapel for the church and it was accepted unanimously. In 1894 a second church was built at a site known as Sidney Park. This church was erected by members of Union Chapel who resided too far away to travel each week to services in the Michaelsville area. The combining of these two churches to form the present-day [1968] Union Methodist Church at Swan Creek followed the sale of their Michaelsville property to the federal government circa 1917. Earlier, about 1900, Rev. Charles A. H. Matthews, pastor of Union Chapel, recorded that there were

nearly 1,500 burials in the old church cemetery that was now on Aberdeen Proving Ground. Residents were forced to move away and it was then that approximately 500 of the graves were removed to cemeteries near Aberdeen. The foregoing information was gleaned from an article in *The Harford Democrat – Upper Bay Citizen – APG News (MD),* March 28, 1968. In 1999 the federal government photographed all of the gravestones on Aberdeen Proving Ground and created two volumes titled *The Silent Sentinels of Aberdeen Proving Ground,* of which a copy is available at the Historical Society of Harford County. They are labeled in Volume 1 as Private Cemetery P-2. The gravestones are not available to general public access, but the pictures speak for themselves. I annotated some with information gleaned from extant death certificates. Also see the comments under Union United Methodist Church Cemetery as some noted in that cemetery may actually be buried here.

Skinner Cemetery
This family cemetery is located in a wooded area between 622 and 624 Chapel Terrace in Havre de Grace. Due to its location to the north of the train tracks it is thought to have been also known as the B & O Cemetery and/or Zion Hill Cemetery. It was the site of the original St. James AME Church on Zion Hill in 1849 and "the first cemetery which is still there (is) called the Skinner Cemetery," according to the late Mrs. Geraldine W. Cox, of Aberdeen, in 2001. The present St. James United Cemetery is located next to Mt. Erin Cemetery near Graceview Road. There are only a few tombstones in Skinner Cemetery and they were copied by Reggie Bishop, an African American researcher, a few years ago. I also found additional burials in some death certificates.

St. James United Cemetery
This cemetery is located next to Mt. Erin Cemetery near Graceview Drive in Havre de Grace and situated on Gover's Hill above the railroad tracks. The tombstones were copied by Herbert H. Holland, Jr. and family in June 1987, but some of them were overlooked and a number of markers were not found when I copied the inscriptions in October 2018. I have made additions from other sources.

William C. Rice Memorial Cemetery (St. James United Methodist Church, Federal Hill)
This church and well-maintained cemetery with a black wrought iron fence are located at 4003 Federal Hill Road, north of Jarrettsville. The cemetery has been named in honor of "William C. Rice, 5/21/1915 – 2/26/2008" as noted on a sign mounted on the fence. I copied the tombstones in the summer of 2018. A sign at the entrance to the church states "St. James / West Liberty United Methodist Church."

Tabernacle Mount Zion United Methodist Church Cemetery
This church and cemetery are located on Connolly Road at Smith Lane in Benson. On February 19, 1867 trustees of the Methodist Episcopal Society bought the Tabernacle Cemetery ground of 92 square perches (0.58 acres) for $120 from Jonas Scott to be used for "religious, burial and School purposes." (Harford County Land Records Book WHD 18, p. 235). However, the church was apparently not built until about nine years later since "Tabernacle M. E. Church 1876-1938. Rev. J. H. Carter." is inscribed on the date stone. The cemetery was subsequently expanded through land acquisitions in the early 1900s. The tombstones were copied in May 1987 and I recopied them in May 2018 and added additional information from some other sources.

Union United Methodist Church Cemetery
On December 21, 1917 *The Aegis* reported "The government has awarded Mr. George T. Pennington, an undertaker at Havre de Grace, the contract for the removal of the cemetery, nearly 100 years old, connected with Union Chapel African M. E. Church, Michaelsville, containing the bodies of about 450 colored people, to the farm recently occupied by Frank H. Morgan near Aberdeen. The church property was among those taken over by the U. S. Proving Grounds and being compelled to move the burying ground Mr. Morgan's property was purchased on which the trustees anticipate building a church adjoining the cemetery." This is now the location of the Union United Methodist Church and cemetery on Swan Creek at 700 Old Post Road (Route 7) south of Aberdeen, near Perryman. The tombstones were copied circa 1993 and in November and December 2018 I recopied most of them (some were toppled over and many more were illegible). I also made many additions and corrections from obituaries, death certificates and Pennington & Son Funeral Home Records. Some of the early death certificates identified burials at Swan Creek Cemetery, Sydney Park Church (erected in 1894), Union Chapel (which existed prior to 1887 when the old colored church was taken down and rebuilt near the former

site, as noted in *The Aegis* on October 21, 1887) and Union United Methodist Church. It should be noted that Sydney Park Church and Union Chapel were once located near Michaelsville which is now part of the Aberdeen Proving Ground. How many graves were actually reinterred as reported in the newspaper in 1917 at this church or some other location are unknown since the funeral home records for that time period are not extant. An article in *The Harford Democrat – Upper Bay Citizen – APG News (MD)* on March 28, 1968 reported that about the year 1900 Rev. Charles A. H. Matthews, pastor of Union Chapel, recorded there were nearly 1,500 burials in the cemetery. After the property was purchased by the government "approximately 500 graves were removed to cemeteries near Aberdeen." It is possible that some of the people listed below could be re-interments from the Old Union Chapel at Michaelsville or they could be buried there in the old churchyard without tombstones. Records are not extant in that regard.

West Liberty Church Cemetery
This church and cemetery are located at 3004 Fallston Road near Upper Cross Roads. The church is no longer in use, but the cemetery is and the latest burial was in 2007. The cemetery is in bad shape landscaping-wise, several tombstones have been toppled over and one was even found lying in the adjoining woods. The tombstones were copied by Christopher T. Smithson in July 2000 and I recopied them in August 2018. I also made additions from some death certificates, obituaries and Kurtz Funeral Home records.

In closing, it is obvious that this book by no means contains all of the burials in the African American cemeteries in Harford County, Maryland for the reasons stated, but it goes a long way in helping to identify many of the people who are buried here. It has been compiled as a research tool to be used in assisting family history researchers in locating the graves and learning more about their departed ancestors.

Henry C. Peden, Jr.
Bel Air, Maryland

January 6, 2022

African American Cemeteries in Harford County, Maryland

Abraham, Harry 1962-2014 (small metal funeral home marker) [St. James United Cemetery]

Adams, Cordelia I., "Beloved Mother and Grandmother" June 4, 1943 – April 20, 1998 (inscribed "Forever In Our Hearts" and with her photo; James Dorsey Card File, African American Obituaries, that is maintained at the Historical Society of Harford County, has a card with obituary from an unidentified newspaper on April 29, 1998 stating Cordelia Idella Adams was born in Elkton, the daughter of the late Robert Marshall Jenifer and Florence Flora Fields, and she worked as an accountant and office manager for HDM Graphics in Detroit, MI; she later lived in Darlington and died at home, survived by a son Craig L. Jones, a daughter Marlise A. Jones, three brothers, two sisters and six grandchildren) [Berkley Memorial Cemetery]

Adams, Enoch died December 27, 1907, age about 50 (no tombstone; death certificate stated he was the son of Samuel Adams and Matilda Gilbert, and all were born in Harford Co.; he died near Mountain; informant was his wife Mary Adams; place of burial not given [probably Mt. Zion U. M. Church Cemetery]

Adams, James May 15, 1873 – August 18, 1917 (no tombstone; death certificate stated he was the son of Samuel Adams and Sarah Preston, all born in Maryland; he was married, worked as a laborer, died in Joppa and was buried in Mountain Colored Cemetery; informant was Edward Scott, of Joppa, and David Davidson, of Upper Falls, was the undertaker) [Mt. Zion U. M. Church Cemetery]

Adams, Lelia R. February 2, 1882 – September 10, 1964 (inscribed "In His Will Is Our Peace") [John Wesley U. M. E. Church Cemetery in Abingdon]

Adams, Lisbin died in October 1912 (no tombstone; no death certificate; death notice in *The Aegis* on October 11, 1912 stated he was an aged and respected colored man who died at the home of Josh Hall, also colored, last week; the notice was published in the "Jarrettsville Letter" section of the newspaper; place of burial not given [possibly William C. Rice Memorial Cemetery, St. James U. M. Church]

Adams. Jefferson died February 27, 1935, age about 65 (no tombstone; death certificate stated he was the unmarried son of Jesse Adams and Harriet Dawson, all born in Danville, VA, and he died in Havre de Grace Hospital) [St. James United Cemetery]

Addison, Annie Christy 1929-1983 (small metal funeral home marker; obituary in *The Aegis* on March 3, 1983 stated she was born in Aberdeen, the daughter of the late Nelson Christy and Edith Ringgold (but her husband was not mentioned); she lived in Aberdeen, retired from the Edgewood Arsenal and died on February 23, 1983 at the Harford Memorial Hospital, survived by a daughter, a brother, 2 sisters, and 4 grandchildren) [Mt. Calvary U. A. M. E. Church Cemetery]

Addison, Calvin B. September 19, 1870 – October 8, 1915 (death certificate; no tombstone; death certificate stated he was born in West Virginia, son of William Addison and Mary Ann DeHaven, both born in Maryland; he was married and a crossing tender at Perryman; informant was Mary Addison) [St. James United Cemetery]

Aikens, Annie died September 22, 1931, age about 55 (no tombstone; death certificate stated Annie "Aikins" was the daughter of Joseph Moore and Eliza Moore, all born in Maryland; she died in Darlington and was married at the time of her death; informant was Granville "Aikins") [Green Spring U. M. Church Cemetery]

Aikens, Christina August 22, 1916 – September 18, 1916 (no tombstone; death certificate stated she was the daughter of Granville Aikens and Flora Christie, all born in Maryland, and she died in Darlington; informant was her father) [Green Spring U. M. Church Cemetery]

Aikens, Clarence April 28, 1920 – June 22, 1920 (no tombstone; death certificate stated he was the son of Clinton Aikens and Eleanor Hopkins, of Castleton, all born in Maryland; he was a premature twin of Clinton Aikens and lived for 1 month and 25 days) [Berkley Memorial Cemetery]

Aikens, Clinton April 28, 1920 – June 12, 1920 (no tombstone; death certificate stated he was the son of Clinton Aikens and Eleanor Hopkins, of Castleton, all born in Maryland; he was a premature twin of Clarence Aikens and lived for 1 month and 15 days) [Berkley Memorial Cemetery]

Aikens, Flora died December 3, 1916, age 36 (no tombstone; death certificate stated she was the daughter of Robert Christie and Elizabeth Moore, all born in Maryland, and was married at the time of her death in Darlington; informant was Granville Aikens, of Darlington) [Green Spring U. M. Church Cemetery]

Aikens, George William March 29, 1858 – May 14, 1917 (no tombstone; death certificate stated he was the son of William Henry Aikens and Grace Ann Presberry, all born in Maryland; he was married, not employed and died near Darlington; informant was Granville Aikens, of Darlington) [Green Spring U. M. Church Cemetery]

Aikens, Gertrude Irene March 10, 1951 – April 22, 1951 (no tombstone; death certificate stated she was born in Harford Co., daughter of Joseph and Gertrude Aikens who lived in Darlington) [Green Spring U. M. Church Cemetery]

Aikens, Granville March 16, 1883 – March 29, 1950 (no tombstone; death certificate stated he was born in Harford Co., the son of Henry Aikens and Grace Ann Presbury; he lived and worked as a farm laborer in rural Darlington and died a widower; informant was Mrs. Pearl Dorsey) [Green Spring U. M. Church Cemetery]

Aikens, Henry died September 10, 1909, age 80 (no tombstone; death certificate stated he was a laborer and widower who lived near Darlington, but his place of birth and names of his parents were not known to informant Granville Aikens who was the same informant when Annie Aikens died in 1931 and was buried at Green Spring) [Green Spring U. M. Church Cemetery]

Aikens, Joseph E. January 6, 1906 – September 30, 1974 [Berkley Memorial Cemetery]

Aikens, Susanna April 15, 1904 – April 22, 1919 (no tombstone; death certificate stated "Susanna Aiken" was the daughter of "George Aiken" and Annie Moore, all born in Maryland; she was single and died in Havre de Grace; informant was H. S. Bailey, Undertaker) [Green Spring U. M. Church Cemetery]

Aikens, Violet Beatrice February 10, 1917 – May 9, 1919 (no tombstone; death certificate stated she was the daughter of Clinton Aikins *(sic)* and Eleanor Hopkins, of Darlington, all born in Maryland) [Berkley Memorial Cemetery]

Aikens, Walter July 16, 1915 – October 14, 1915 (no tombstone; death certificate stated Walter "Aikins" was the son of Granville Aikins and Florence Christy, and all were born in Maryland and lived in Darlngton; informant was his father) [Green Spring U. M. Church Cemetery]

Aikins, William March 6, 1872 – May 11, 1940 (no tombstone; death certificate stated he was born near Trappe Church, Harford Co., the son of William Aikins, born in Harford Co., but his mother's name was not known to informant Francis Green, of Fawn Grove, MD *(sic)*; he was single, worked as a laborer in Fawn Grove, PA, died at the Harford County Home in Bel Air and buried at Rocks) [Chestnut Grove A. M. E. Church Cemetery, formerly LaGrange Cemetery at Rocks]

Akens, Gertrude 1911-   (on same tombstone with Joseph E. Akens and William J. Akens) [Green Spring U. M. Church Cemetery]

Akens, Joseph E. 1906-   (on same tombstone with Gertrude Akens and William J. Akens) [Green Spring U. M. Church Cemetery]

Akens, William J. 1928-1956 (on same tombstone with Joseph E. Akens and Gertrude Akens) [Green Spring U. M. Church Cemetery]

Akins, ---- stillborn male on August 28, 1924 (no tombstone; death certificate stated he was the son of James Akins and Mary Stewart, all born in Maryland, and lived at Street) [Clark's U. M. Church Cemetery]

Akins, Anna M. died December 5, 1983, age 73 (no tombstone; obituary in *The Aegis* on December 8, 1983 stated she was born at Kalmia, was the wife of the late Charles E. Akins, lived for more than 50 years in Street and died at Harford Memorial Hospital in Havre de Grace; she was a member of the Chestnut Grove African Methodist Church for 40 years and was a member of the church choir and Missionary Society) [Chestnut Grove A. M. E. Church Cemetery, formerly LaGrange Cemetery at Rocks]

Akins, Charles May 3, 1893 – February 20, 1978, Pvt., U.S. Army, World War I (tombstone; military record stated he was born May 2, 1895 at Street and was a private in the 154th Dep. Brig.; obituary in *The Aegis* on

March 2, 1978 stated he was born at Rocks, married A. Mabel Lewis, and died at Bel Air; his parents were Charles Akins and Emma Smith; he joined Chestnut Grove A. M. E. Church in 1943 and was an active member until his illness) [Chestnut Grove A. M. E. Church Cemetery, formerly LaGrange Cemetery at Rocks]

Akins, Dora 1913-1981 (tombstone; obituary in *The Aegis* on November 12, 1981 stated Dora Etta Akins, of Bel Air, died November 3, 1981, age 68, at Union Hospital in Elkton, the wife of the late James Edward Akins; she was the daughter of Ed Presbury and Annie Christy; she was survived by 3 sons, 3 daughters, 17 grandchildren and 6 great-grandchildren; her funeral card stated she was born on January 13, 1913 and buried on November 7, 1981) [Clark's U. M. Church Cemetery]

Akins, Elmer R. September 10, 1910 – December 26, 1984, Pvt., U. S. Army, World War II (tombstone; obituary in *The Aegis* on January 3, 1985 stated he was born in Street, the son of Emma and Brook Akins, served in World War II, married Helen --- of Bel Air, retired from Aberdeen Proving Ground after 33 years, served as custodian, trustee and usher at Clark's Chapel and died at the Perry Point VA Medical Center) [Clark's U. M. Church Cemetery]

Akins, Eloise R. F. 1944-2017 (small metal funeral home marker) [Berkley Memorial Cemetery]

Akins, Emma (on same tombstone with Mary V. Akins and Emma A. Watters; no dates when copied in 1987 and not found in 2018) [Clark's U. M. Church Cemetery]

Akins, Ethel P. 1903-1976 (on same tombstone with William Akins; obituary in *The Aegis* on August 5, 1976 stated Ethel Pinkney Akins was born on March 10, 1903, in Harford Co., the daughter of Nathan and Hattie Pinkney; she was the widow of William Akins and died on July 30, 1986 in Churchville) [Asbury Cemetery]

Akins, Everhart Estella July 25, 1925 – June 15, 2008 (tombstone; obituary in *The Aegis* on June 18, 2008 stated she was born in Benson, the daughter of Lilbon and Ellen Brown and wife of the late John Finney Akins, Sr.; she was self-employed at 208 Hayes St. in Bel Air, working with mentally challenged clients; she was a lay leader at Tabernacle and served on the PPR Committee, and trustee and president of United Methodist Women; she was survived by 4 children, 8 grandchildren, 12 great-grandchildren, and 7 great-great-grandchildren, and she was predeceased by a daughter, Toni Marie Thurston) [Tabernacle Mount Zion U. M. Church Cemetery]

Akins, Frances A. September 6, 1922 – April 16, 1923 (no tombstone; death certificate stated she was the daughter of James Akins and Mary Smothers, all born in Maryland, and lived at Street; informant was Mary Akins, his mother, of Street, MD) [Clark's U. M. Church Cemetery]

Akins, Gertrude February 10, 1910 – July 15, 1997 (tombstone; obituary and photo in *The Aegis* on July 30, 1997 stated she was born in Darlington, the daughter of Grandville and Florence Akins, and wife of the late Joseph Akins, Sr.; she worked for the Jordan Cannery and then at Aberdeen Proving Ground in the 1950s; she was a member of Hosanna A. M. E. Church for 40 years and was known as "Mother Akins;" she died at Harford Memorial Hospital, survived by 3 sons, 10 daughters, 47 grandchildren, 77 great-grandchildren, 3 great-great-grandchildren and was predeceased by 1 grandson and 1 great-grandson) [Berkley Memorial Cemetery]

Akins, Gloria D., "Loving Wife and Mother" August 23, 1945 – August 20, 2001 [Clark's U. M. Church Cemetery]

Akins, Hamilton A. May 27, 1960 – November 11, 1988 [Tabernacle Mount Zion U. M. Church Cemetery]

Akins, Helen B. November 19, 1941 -   (on same tombstone with Herbert R. Akins and inscribed with their marriage date of July 28, 1962) [Berkley Memorial Cemetery]

Akins, Herbert R. November 26, 1939 – December 31, 2011 (on same tombstone with Helen B. Akins and inscribed with their marriage date of July 28, 1962) [Berkley Memorial Cemetery]

Akins, James E. II June 8, 1921 – November 29, 2004 [Tabernacle Mount Zion U. M. Church Cemetery]

Akins, John Finney September 9, 1923 – June 2, 2002, TEC 5, U.S. Army, World War II [Tabernacle Mount Zion U. M. Church Cemetery]

Akins, Joseph Jr. 1937-2015 (small metal funeral home marker) [Berkley Memorial Cemetery]

Akins, L. Marlaina June 17, 1969 – April 8, 1999 (inscribed "Loving Daughter and Sister"; obituary in *The*

Aegis on April 14, 1999 stated she was born in Baltimore, daughter of Lewis Elvin Akins, Sr., of York, PA, and Rev. Doritha Elizabeth Collins Henry, of Street, MD, and granddaughter of John W. and Edna E. Cevis, of Street, MD; she lived her entire life in Harford Co. and sang with the Golden Echoes) [Cedars Chapel Cemetery]

Akins, Mary K. December 25, 1888 – June 1, 1917 (no tombstone; death certificate stated she was born in Harford Co., the daughter of Charles Akins, born in Harford Co., and Emma Smith, born in Chestertown, MD; she was single and lived at Street; informant was Emma Johnson) [Clark's U. M. Church Cemetery]

Akins, Mary V. 1901-1928 (on same tombstone with Emma Akins and Emma A. Watters when copied in 1987, but not found in 2018; death certificate stated she was born on May 2, 1901 and died at Kalmia on November 4, 1928 after being struck by an automobile; her parents were ---- (blank) Stewart and Mary Smothers and they were all born in Maryland; she was married and a cook; informant was James Akins, of Bel Air) [Clark's U. M. Church Cemetery]

Akins, Norman "Ike" 1912-2001 (inscribed "Family & Friends Love You") [Berkley Memorial Cemetery]

Akins, Shirley C. July 15, 1945 – December 24, 2014 (inscribed "Forever In Our Hearts") [Mt. Zion U. M. Church Cemetery]

Akins, Thelma S. February 11, 1923 – February 24, 1997 (tombstone; obituary in *The Aegis* on February 26, 1997 stated Thelma Sarah Elizabeth Akins was born in Bel Air, the daughter of George Robert Jones and Mary Elizabeth Hackett; she joined Ames United Methodist Church and was a member of the choir and women's society and senior Bible class; she died at the Bel Forest Nursing and Rehabilitation Center and was survived by 3 children, 18 grandchildren and 6 great-grandchildren; and, 2 sons and a daughter predeceased her) [Tabernacle Mount Zion U. M. Church Cemetery]

Akins, Walter August 30, 1895 – January 20, 1964, Maryland, Pvt., U.S. Army, 154 Depot Brigade, World War I (tombstone mistakenly inscribed "Walter Atkins," but military records stated "Walter Aikens" was born on August 31, 1886 at Street, was inducted on August 23, 1918, served in the 153 *(sic)* Depot Brigade and was honorably discharged on December 16, 1918) [Clark's U. M. Church Cemetery]

Akins, William 1897-1971 (on same tombstone with Ethel P. Akins; obituary in *The Aegis* on July 1, 1971 stated he was born in Harford Co., son of the late Charles Akins and Emma Smith; he married Ethel Pinkney, lived on Rt. 1, Thomas Run Road, worked as a handyman for Richardson's Drug Store and died June 29, 1971, age 74, at Mt. Wilson State Hospital; was a Trustee and former Treasurer of Asbury United Methodist Church in Churchville) [Asbury Cemetery]

Akins, William Albert 1951-2013, U.S. Army, Vietnam (inscribed William A. Akins; obituary in *The Aegis* on January 16, 2013 stated he lived in Edgewood and died suddenly at the Upper Chesapeake Medical Center in Bel Air on January 12, 2013, age 61) [Cedars Chapel Cemetery]

Alcald, Ellen L. 1955-1996 (small metal funeral home marker) [John Wesley U. M. E. Church Cemetery in Abingdon]

Aldrich, Charles died April 21, 1922, age about 58 (no tombstone; death certificate stated he was a laborer and died in Havre de Grace, parents unknown to informant N. K. Beal) [St. James United Cemetery]

Alexander, Barbara Bond, "Beloved Mother" August 12, 1937 – April 30, 1991 [St. James United Cemetery]

Alexander, Lloyd September 20, 1846 – July 12, 1912 (tombstone; death certificate stated he died 2 Jul 1912, age about 64, son of Lloyd Alexander and Sallie Hosier, all born in Harford Co.) [St. James United Cemetery]

Alexander, Mamie March 1, 1908 – February 26, 1931 (no tombstone; death certificate stated she was born in North Carolina, married, and died at home near Street P. O.; her parents were Luther Thompson, born in North Carolina, and Cora Hampton, born in Virginia; informant was George Choat, of Street, MD) [Chestnut Grove A. M. E. Church Cemetery, formerly LaGrange Cemetery at Rocks]

Alexander, Ruth A. 1947-2005 (small metal funeral home marker) [St. James United Cemetery]

Allen, Anna B. Stinson February 4, 1925 – March 15, 1997 [St. James United Cemetery]

Allen, Audrum D. 1969-1995 (handwritten cement slab inscribed "Love Always") [St. James United Cemetery]

Ambush, Eleanor R. January 30, 1950 – September 25, 1983 (tombstone; James Dorsey Card File, African American Obituaries, maintained at the Historical Society of Harford County, has a card for "Mrs. Leanor Rebecca Cain Ambush, see Obit.," but none was found in *The Aegis* newspaper) [Berkley Memorial Cemetery]

Ambush, Franklin C. Sr. August 15, 1903 – March 20, 1993 (inscribed "In Loving Memory;" obituary in *The Aegis* on March 31, 1993 stated Franklin Cornelious Ambush, Sr. was born in Frederick, the son of Robert J. Ambush and Rosetta Russell, married Lealer Peacker, worked as a farmer, lived in Aberdeen and died at Harford Memorial Hospital in Havre de Grace, survived by his wife, 4 children, 11 grandchildren and 7 great-grandchildren) [William C. Rice Memorial Cemetery, St. James U. M. Church]

Ambush, Lealer B. March 24, 1917 – December 17, 2012 (on same tombstone with Sarah J. Gaither and inscribed "Mom, Mighty Matriarch, and Jane, Selfless Sister, Our Blessed Treasure, Rest In Everlasting Love Where The Shadows Fall;" obituary and photo in *The Aegis* on December 21, 2012 stated she was born in Emmorton, the daughter of Walter Thomas Peaker and Mazie Deliverance Gibson, and widow of Franklin C. Ambush, Sr.; she lived in Randallstown, died at Keswick Multi-Care Center in Baltimore, survived by 2 sons, 2 daughters, a brother, a sister, a goddaughter, many grandchildren, great-grandchildren, and 2 great-great-grandchildren, and preceded in death by a daughter and two brothers) [Mt. Zion U. M. Church Cemetery]

Ames, Elsie W., "Mother" November 17, 1908 – June 23, 1978 (inscribed "Forever In Our Hearts") [Union U. M. Church Cemetery]

Ames, Jamica M. 1976-2018 (small metal funeral home marker) [Berkley Memorial Cemetery]

Ames, John A. 1936-1958 [Union U. M. Church Cemetery]

Amos, Abraham (no tombstone, but Kurtz Funeral Home records stated Abraham Amos was buried in a nice walnut coffin on June 25, 1880 from George W. Cairens' tenant house) [West Liberty Church Cemetery]

Amos, Albert B. August 19, 1910 – August 31, 1952, Pvt, U.S. Army, World War II [Fairview A. M. E. Church Cemetery]

Amos, Audra July 9, 1916 – Mary 27, 1990 (on same tombstone with Wilson Lee Amos) [Fairview A. M. E. Church Cemetery]

Amos, Blanch E. 1900-1948 (one of six names on the Amos Monument) [Fairview A. M. E. Church Cemetery]

Amos, Effie E. 1895-1973 (one of six names on the Amos Monument) [Fairview A. M. E. Church Cemetery]

Amos, Emma Louise 1908-2000 (small metal funeral home marker; obituary in *The Aegis* on May 17, 2000 stated she was born June 11, 1908, the daughter of Walter H. Taylor and Mary Smothers, lived in Cooptowm, married W. Elwood Amos, worked as a domestic and died at Lorien Riverside Nursing Home, survived by 9 grandchildren, 14 great-grandchildren, 6 great-great-grandchildren, and predeceased by husband and son Nathaniel M. Washington) [Fairview A. M. E. Church Cemetery]

Amos, Euna 1902-1970 (small metal funeral home marker) [Fairview A. M. E. Church Cemetery]

Amos, Gertrude Evelyn 1892 – February 3, 1981 (obituary in *The Aegis* on February 12, 1981 stated Gertrude Evelyn Amos, of Baltimore, a domestic cook, died at Franklin Square Hospital (in Baltimore County) and was survived by sister-in-law Mary W. Amos, of Coopstown, and a cousin; one of six names on the Amos Monument) [Fairview A. M. E. Church Cemetery]

Amos, James died March 19, 1967, age 93 (no tombstone, obituary in *The Aegis* on March 23, 1967 stated he was the husband of the late Jane Evan Amos, of Forest Hill, and was survived by 5 sons, 29 grandchildren, 43 great-grandchildren, 3 nieces and 1 nephew) [Fairview A. M. E. Church Cemetery]

Amos, Jane Rebecca June 13, 1883 – February 13, 1944 (no tombstone; death certificate stated she was the daughter of March Evans and Susie Woods, all born in Maryland; she married James Amos (age 70 in 1944), lived in Jarrettsville and died at Harford Memorial Hospital in Havre de Grace; informant was "patient, Jarrettsville, Md.") [Fairview A. M. E. Church Cemetery]

Amos, Lillian J. 1902-1971 (one of six names on the Amos Monument) [Fairview A. M. E. Church Cemetery]

Amos, Mary F. August 2, 1865 – December 22, 1923 (death certificate stated Mary Frances Amoss was born in Harford Co., the daughter of Lewis Jenkins and Fannie Turner whose birth places were not known to informant, her husband, Thomas H. Amoss, of near Sharon; he was one of six names on the Amos Monument) [Fairview A. M. E. Church Cemetery]

Amos, Mary W. 1902-1986 (on same tombstone with Warren E. Amos; obituary in *The Aegis* on December 25, 1986 stated Mary Amos was the daughter of Thomas and Sarah Wilson and widow of Warren Amos; she lived in Forest Hill and died on December 4, 1986 at Harford Memorial Hospital in Havre de Grace, survived by nieces, nephews and cousins) [Fairview A. M. E. Church Cemetery]

Amos, Milton 1901-1972 (copied in 1987, but not found in 2018, possibly a temporary marker that is now gone; obituary in *The Aegis* stated he was formerly of Jarrettsville, the son of Alex Muarry *(sic)* and Katie Amos, and died at home at 119 Aisquith St. in Baltimore on February 19, 1972, age 70, survived by several cousins) [Fairview A. M. E. Church Cemetery]

Amos, Rebecca Jane June 7, 1883 – February 13, 1944 (no tombstone; Kurtz Funeral Home Record Book 1944-1949, p. 11, stated she was born in Madonna, married James Amos and died at Harford Memorial Hospital in Havre de Grace; her parents' names were not given) [Fairview A. M. E. Church Cemetery]

Amos, Robert Andrew 1918-1973 (copied in 1987, but not found in 2018, so possibly a temporary marker that is now gone; obituary in *The Aegis* stated he died at home in Jarrettsville on February 20, 1973, age 54, and was survived by three brothers) [Fairview A. M. E. Church Cemetery]

Amos, Thomas H. 1870-1965 (one of six names on the Amos Monument) [Fairview A. M. E. Church Cemetery]

Amos, Warren E. 1898-1967 (on same tombstone with Mary W. Evans) [Fairview A. M. E. Church Cemetery]

Amos, Wayne M. Sr. 1947-1994 (tombstone in section 33) [Mt. Calvary U. A. M. E. Church Cemetery]

Amos, William E. died October 4, 1978, age 80 (no tombstone; obituary in *The Aegis* stated William Elwood Amos was the husband of Emma L. Amos, lived on Cooptown Road in Cooptown, worked as a furniture repairman, was a trustee and treasurer of Fairview AME Church and died at Baltimore City Hospital, survived by his wife, stepson Rev. Nathaniel Washington, of Bel Air, and a brother James H. Amos, Sr., of Cooptown) [Fairview A. M. E. Church Cemetery]

Amos, Wilson Lee May 28, 1905 – April 27, 1975 (on same tombstone with Audra Amos; obituary in *The Aegis* on May 1, 1975 stated he lived in Baltimore and was employed by Baltimore City; he died at the Greater Baltimore Medical Center, survived by his wife Audra B. Amos, 2 daughters, 2 brothers, 14 grandchildren and 2 great-grandchildren) [Fairview A. M. E. Church Cemetery]

Amoss, James died December 20, 1915, age about 75 (no tombstone; death certificate stated he was born in Jarrettsville, the son of Abram Amoss and Grace Wann, both born in Harford Co., he was married, worked as a farmer and died in Jarrettsville; informant was his son, Thomas H. Amoss, of Sharon RFD) [West Liberty Church Cemetery]

Amoss, Marshal Lee December 22, 1921 – January 1, 1923 (no tombstone; death certificate stated he was the son of James Amoss, Jr. and Rebecca Jane Evans, all born in Harford Co.; he died near Jarrettsville and informant was his father, of Sharon RFD) [West Liberty Church Cemetery]

Amoss, Mary Ann December 23, 1846 – August 4, 1934 (no tombstone; death certificate stated she was the daughter of Louisa Hall, both born in Harford Co., but her father's name and place of birth were not known to informant Thomas Amoss, of Sharon; she married James Amoss and died a widow at home at Jarrettsville; Kurtz Funeral Home Records stated the same information and added that "Tom and Jim Amoss" authorized the funeral) [West Liberty Church Cemetery]

Amoss, Sarah Cathrine August 7, 1875 – September 26, 1928 (no tombstone; death certificate stated she was the daughter of James Amoss and Mary Ann Hall, all born in Harford Co.; she was single, unemployed and died in Jarrettsville; informant was James Amoss, of White Hall) [West Liberty Church Cemetery]

Amous, George August 31, 1886 – April 16, 1932 (no tombstone; death certificate stated he was born in Harford Co., son of William Amous, born in Fallston, and Effie Curtis, born in Harford Co.; he married Beaula

Smith, worked as a day laborer until February 1931 and died at home in Bel Air where he had lived for 25 years; informant was Effie Brown, of Bel Air) [Mt. Zion U. M. Church Cemetery]

Anderson, A. November 25, 1921 – July 5, 1992, SFC, U.S. Army, World War II [St. James United Cemetery]

Anderson, Alexander 1876-1944 (tombstone; death certificate stated Alec Anderson October 15, 1876 – May 13, 1944 was the son of Stephen Anderson and Carolina Murphy, all born in North Carolina; he was a widowed cook and died in Harford Memorial Hospital in Havre de Grace) [St. James United Cemetery]

Anderson, Annabell F. 1930-2017 (small metal funeral home marker) [St. James United Cemetery]

Anderson, Annie Rebecca died September 5, 1899, age 1 year and 3 months (no tombstone; death certificate stated she was the daughter of James Bishop and Clara A. Anderson and she died at Mountain; place of burial not given [probably Mt. Zion U. M. Church Cemetery]

Anderson, Caroline died November 3, 1926, age 83 (no tombstone; death certificate stated she was a widow and daughter of A. Wilson and C. Bond; informant was William Anderson, of Bel Air) [Hendon Hill Cemetery]

Anderson, Charles R. February 20, 1890 – July 22, 1969, Pvt, U.S. Army, World War I (tombstone; military records state Charles Ruben Anderson was born in Abingdon, was inducted as a private on August 2, 1918, served in Hq 1 Prov Dep Bn, Camp Sevier, SC and then Co D, 401 Res Lab Bn on September 21, 1918, and was honorably discharged on April 24, 1919) [John Wesley U. M. E. Church Cemetery in Abingdon]

Anderson, Chloe Ann 1841 – December 17, 1929 (no tombstone; death certificate stated she was single, born in Maryland, performed house duties, and died in Havre de Grace Hospital; her parents' names were not known to informant Judge William H. Harlan, of Bel Air) [Gravel Hill Cemetery]

Anderson, Clara S. May 9, 1894 – May 12, 1984 (tombstone; obituary in *The Aegis* on May 24, 1984 stated Clara Stansbury Anderson, wife of the late William Anderson, was born in Perryman, the daughter of the late James and Marion Stansbury; she lived in Havre de Grace and was once employed by the Pennington family, the McLhinney family, and Mrs. Grace Stines; she died in Harford Memorial Hospital and was survived by a sister Anna Robinson) [Union U. M. Church Cemetery]

Anderson, Elizabeth died January 15, 1933, age about 56 (no tombstone; death certificate stated she was the wife of Jacob Anderson, of Havre de Grace, and daughter of Lida Bond, but her father was unknown to informant Harry Rumsey) [St. James United Cemetery]

Anderson, Eva M. April 28, 1930 – September 13, 1936 (no tombstone;death certificate stated she was born in Havre de Grace, the daughter of Elzie Carroll, of Chester, PA, and Evelyn Anderson,of Philadelphia, PA) [St. James United Cemetery]

Anderson, Howard died 13 Mar 1908, age 7 (no tombstone; death certificate stated he died from a gunshot wound; parents were James Anderson and Salle Peve *(sic)*, both born in Maryland) [Hendon Hill Cemetery]

Anderson, James died June 4, 1935, no age given (inscribed "This Man Was A Child's Friend;" obituary in the *Bel Air Times* on June 7, 1935 stated he was age 65 (66?) and son of the late Georgeanna Anderson; he worked for Mr. and Mrs. Harry Hanna, of Roland Park) [Tabernacle Mount Zion U. M. Church Cemetery]

Anderson, Laura December 15, 1841 – March 29, 1925 (no tombstone; death certificate stated she was the daughter of Abraham Cooper and Emily Hayes, all born in Maryland; she was a widow who died in Kalmia; informant was Charles Dutton, of Bel Air) [Clark's U. M. Church Cemetery]

Anderson, Laura V. December 3, 1934 – November 23, 1993 (tombstone; "Laura Anderson" owned a lot in section 8 some time after 1951) [Mt. Calvary U. A. M. E. Church Cemetery]

Anderson, Leonard (no dates recorded in 1987, not listed in 2002, and not found in 2018) [Gravel Hill Cemetery]

Anderson, Lorretta V. October 6, 1911 – December 3, 1911 (no tombstone; death certificate stated she was the daughter of Carvel Wescott and Ida Anderson, all born in Maryland, and they lived in Bel Air) [Tabernacle Mount Zion U. M. Church Cemetery]

Anderson, Martha died January 27, 1931, age about 95 (no tombstone; death certificate stated she was a widow and the daughter of Henry Hall, but informant Mitchell Brown, of Bel Air, did not know where her father was born and he did not know the name of her mother) [Tabernacle Mount Zion U. M. Church Cemetery]

Anderson, Martha died March 28, 1918, age 36 (no tombstone; death certificate stated she was married and worked as a servant in Bel Air; her parents were Mina Scott and Maria Rose and they were all born in Virginia, according to informant Sarah Goyns, 144 Ruth St., Baltimore) [Hendon Hill Cemetery]

Anderson, Milcah died July 11, 1910, age 88 (tombstone; death certificate stated Milcha E. Anderson died in Havre de Grace on July 11, 1910, age 91 years and 3 months, widow of Thomas Anderson; her parents were Jacob Hughes and Sarah White, all born in Harford County) [St. James United Cemetery]

Anderson, Nellie Belle March 30, 1915 – November 21, 1921 (no tombstone; death certificate stated she was the daughter of Robert Anderson and Maud Beasley, born in Maryland; she died in Creswell) [John Wesley U. M. E. Church Cemetery in Abingdon]

Anderson, Robert A. May 4, 1898 – October 26, 1918 (no tombstone; death certificate stated he was the son of Robert A. Anderson and Maud Beasley, all born in Maryland; he died in Abingdon; informant was his mother) [John Wesley U. M. E. Church Cemetery in Abingdon]

Anderson, Robert Albert Flood September 2, 1894 – October 6, 1918 (no tombstone; death certificate stated he was the son of Ruben Anderson, birth place unknown, and Agness Armstrong, born in Maryland; he was married, worked as a laborer for the government and died in Abingdon; informant was Edward Washington, of Abingdon) [John Wesley U. M. E. Church Cemetery in Abingdon]

Anderson, Sallie Mae 1939-2010 (small metal funeral home marker) [Berkley Memorial Cemetery]

Anderson, Sarah Ann March 20, 1880 – August 8, 1925 (no tombstone; death certificate stated she was the daughter of John Pevey and Rachel McComas, all born in Maryland; she was married at the time of her death in Forest Hill; the inform was James Anderson, of Forest Hill) [Asbury Cemetery]

Anderson, Sidonia C. 1872-1955 [Clark's U. M. Church Cemetery]

Anderson, Tanser W., 1910-1977 (copied in 1987, but not found in 2018) [Asbury Cemetery]

Archer, Casandra "Cassie" March 11, 1835 – January 11, 1921 (no tombstone; death certificate stated she was the daughter of Moses Warfield, both born in Maryland, but informant Ady Warfield did not know her mother's name; she was married at the time of her death in Darlington; the 1929 obituary of William J. "Uncle Billy" Archer stated his wife was Cassie Warfield) [Berkley Memorial Cemetery]

Archer, Garrison c.1780-c.1878 (no tombstone; probably buried here since his wife Rachael is buried here) [Hendon Hill Cemetery]

Archer, Rachael died October 12, 1889, age 108 (no tombstone; *The Aegis* on October 18, 1889 stated her husband Garrison Archer died about 10 or 12 years ago and "Aunt Rachael" belonged to the Taylor family in her younger days and subsequently to the late Thomas A. Hays; she was "set free with the rest of her race during the war" and was a cook at the Eagle Hotel for many years; 1860 Harford Co. Census stated Rachel Archer, age about 60 and born in Maryland, was a servant to Otho Scott in Bel Air) [Hendon Hill Cemetery]

Archer, William J. "Uncle Billy" died January 22, 1929, age about 92 (no tombstone; death certificate stated he was born in Maryland, the son of Cassie Archer, but informant Addie Warfield did not know his father's name; he had worked as a laborer and died a widower at home in Darlington; obituary in *The Aegis* on 1 Feb 1929 stated he was known as "Uncle Billy Archer" and was born a slave; his early life was spent near Churchville; he died near Darlington) [Berkley Memorial Cemetery]

Armstead, Carmen G., Beloved Daughter, Mother, Grandmother and Friend, November 11, 1950 – April 13, 2002 (inscribed "To know you is to love you. We miss you Mommy") [St. James United Cemetery]

Armstrong, Carrie M. April 2, 1890 – August 13, 1974 (on same tombstone with Leonard Armstrong; obituary in *The Aegis* stated Mrs. Carrie Moore Armstrong, of 276 N. Harris St., Princeton, N.J., died at Princeton Hospital, the widow of Leonard Armstrong of Harford County; she was the daughter of Isabelle and Marcus

Westley Moore, of Bel Air, and spent her early life in Bel Air and Baltimore before moving to Princeton to care for her ailing brother John E. Moore; she was survived by a sister, Mrs. Bertha Hall Gray, of Perryman) [Mt. Zion U. M. Church Cemetery]

Armstrong, Grace died May 23, 1934, age about 50 (no tombstone; death certificate stated she lived in Bel Air and died in Havre de Grace Hospital; informant was an unnamed person at the hospital who did not know the names and birth places of her husband and her parents) [Hendon Hill Cemetery]

Armstrong, Isaac I. died June 5, 1909, age 11 (no tombstone; death certificate stated he was the son of Lewis and Jennie Armstrong, all born in Maryland; he died in Bel Air and on the back of death certificate is written "The Mountain Church") [Mt. Zion U. M. Church Cemetery]

Armstrong, Jennie November 17, 1865 – November 9, 1927 [Mt. Zion U. M. Church Cemetery]

Armstrong, Leonard January 7, 1887 – July 19, 1966 (on same tombstone with Carrie M. Armstrong) [Mt. Zion U. M. Church Cemetery]

Armstrong, Louis S. died August 10, 1932, age 64 (no tombstone; death certificate stated he was born in Abingdon, the son of John Armstrong and Tresa ---- (unknown), both born in Maryland; he married Lellee ----, worked as a laborer for 40 years until 1931 and died at home in Abingdon; informant was Nelle Armstrong, of Abingdon) [Mt. Zion U. M. Church Cemetery]

Armstrong, Matilda February 15, 1876 – March 26, 1930 (no tombstone; death certificate stated she was the daughter of George Talbot and Jeebe Anderson, all born in Maryland; she was married at the time of her death in Van Bibber; informant was Lewis Armstrong, of Edgewood) [Mt. Zion U. M. Church Cemetery]

Armstrong, Rachel October 12, 1825 – November 9, 1912 (no tombstone; death certificate stated she was born in Cecil Co., MD and was the widowed daughter of James Stewart, but her mother's name unknown; she died in Havre de Grace; informant was Mrs. Tob Skinner) [St. James United Cemetery]

Ash, Abraham died May 24, 1931, age about 60 (no tombstone; death certificate stated born in Maryland and died in Bel Air, bur informant Carrie Brown, of Bel Air, did not know the names and birth places of his parents; James Dorsey Card File, African American Obituaries, maintained at the Historical Society of Harford County, has a card for Abraham Ash, age 72, of Bel Air, died on May 24, 1931 of injuries in an auto accident) [Tabernacle Mount Zion U. M. Church Cemetery]

Ash, Carolyn L. 1896-1987 (on same tombstone with husband William Walter Ash) [Gravel Hill Cemetery]

Ash, Mary F. October 10, 1853 – June 20, 1925 (no tombstone; death certificate stated she was born in Maryland and her parents' names were not known to informant Walter Ash, of Havre de Grace RFD; she died a widow near Havre de Grace) [Gravel Hill Cemetery]

Ash, Nathaniel died November 17, 1947, age 65 (no tombstone; death certificate stated he was the son of Lewis Ash and Mary Presberry, all born in Maryland; he was single, a laborer, and lived at Havre de Grace RFD #1; informant was William Walter Ash at the same address) [Gravel Hill Cemetery]

Ash, Rachel 1777   January 7, 1881 (no tombstone; two death notices appeared in *The Aegis* on January 21, 1881 and one stated she was a mulatto, age 104, while the other stated she was a colored woman at least age 104, died near Hopewell Cross Roads and was buried at "Gravelly Hill burying ground" on January 12, 1881, further noting "According to Wm. B. Stephenson she was born in the year 1777. She was a servant of his ancestors and spent her whole life in his immediate neighborhood.") [Gravel Hill Cemetery]

Ash, Toad (no dates recorded in 1987, not listed in 2002, and not found in 2018) [Gravel Hill Cemetery]

Ash, William Walter 1882-1967 (on same tombstone with wife Carolyn L. Ash) [Gravel Hill Cemetery]

Ashton Georgia August 7, 1876 – September 28, 1939 (no tombstone; death certificate stated she was the daughter of James Smith and Mary Warfield, all born in Harford Co.; she died at home in Street RFD, the widow of George Ashton; informant was Mrs. Daniel Webster) [Berkley Memorial Cemetery]

Ashton, ---- stillborn infant on August 12, 1919, sex not indicated (no tombstone; death certificate stated the infant was the child of Geneva S. Ashton, of Poole, but informant Albert S. Dorsey, of Street, MD, did not know the name of the father) [Berkley Memorial Cemetery]

Ashton, George February 19, 1868 – September 12, 1916 (no tombstone; death certificate stated he was born in Maryland, the son of Thomas Ashton, birth place unknown, and Annie Cornish, born in Maryland; he worked as a laborer and was married at the time of his death at home in Poole; informant was Georgie A. Ashton, of Street, MD) [Berkley Memorial Cemetery]

Ashton, William David November 20, 1911 – July 9, 1928 (no tombstone; death certificate stated he was the son of George Ashton and Georgia Warfield and all were born in Maryland; he worked as a farm laborer in Darlington and accidentally drowned; informant was Georgia Ashton) [Berkley Memorial Cemetery]

Atkins, Walter – see Walter Akins [Clark's U. M. Church Cemetery]

Atkinson, Elizabeth 1916-1982 [St. James United Cemetery]

Aunt Clara died February 19, 1892, age about 90 (no tombstone; obituary in *The Aegis*, February 26, 1892, stated for a great many years she was a servant with Mrs. S. M. Shepherd's family) [Hendon Hill Cemetery]

Aunt Mahala, see Mahala Brown [Berkley Memorial Cemetery]

Avery, Willie April 27, 1912 – March 14, 1987, Sgt., U.S. Army, World War II [Berkley Memorial Cemetery]

Bailey, Andrew May 8, 1860 – June 20, 1924 (no tombstone; death certificate stated he was born in Richmond, VA, the son of Thomas Bailey and Eliza Johnson, both born in Virginia; he was married, worked as a laborer, died in Bel Air and was buried in "Mountain Colored Cemetery;" informant was Elwood Bailey, of Fallston) [Mt. Zion U. M. Church Cemetery]

Bailey, Doris B. died July 6, 1988, age 50 (no tombstone; James Dorsey Card File, African American Obituaries, maintained at the Historical Society of Harford County, has a card for death stating she died in Abingdon, but it did not cite the newspaper) [John Wesley U. M. E. Church Cemetery in Abingdon]

Bailey, Harlen Lester 1956-2015 (small metal funeral home marker) [John Wesley U. M. E. Church Cemetery in Abingdon]

Bailey, Helen D. W. 1954-2018 (small metal funeral home marker) [Berkley Memorial Cemetery]

Bailey, M. 1903-1966 [Berkley Memorial Cemetery]

Bailey, Mary E. February 14, 1916 – April 2, 1917 (no tombstone; death certificate stated she was born in Harford Co., the daughter of Elwood Bailey, born in Harford Co., and Annie Ruff, born in Baltimore City; she died at home near Wilna with burial in "The Mountain Cemetery;" informant was Elwood Bailey, of Fallston) [Mt. Zion U. M. Church Cemetery]

Baines, Charles 1950-2008 (small metal funeral home marker) [Berkley Memorial Cemetery]

Ball, China Mitchell January 13, 1894 – January 11, 1937, Virginia, Pvt., U.S. Army, Battery E, 351 Field Artillery, World War I [Hendon Hill Cemetery]

Banks, ---- stillborn male on April 11, 1939, a 6-month birth (no tombstone; death certificate stated he was born at Magnolia, the son of George Banks, born in Florida, and Mary L. Charity, born in Virginia; informant was his father) [Foster's Hill Cemetery]

Banks, Adelaide Eloise, "Puddin" January 28, 1957 – October 29, 2004 (obituary and photo in *The Aegis* on November 3 and 5, 2004 stated she was born in Havre de Grace, the only daughter of 4 children of the late William and Bessie Tildon; she married Gary D. Banks and worked as a correctional officer for the Baltimore Correctional System and as a security guard for Harford Community College and Cardillo & Sons; she was an active member of Hosanna A. M. E. Church and died at home in Darlington, survived by 3 children and 4 grandchildren) [Berkley Memorial Cemetery]

Banks, Adeline P. December 20, 1881 – October 1, 1935 (on same tombstone with William Banks; death certificate stated "Adline" Banks was wife of William Banks and daughter of Eli Parrott and Hanna Chambers, all born in Maryland; she was born December 20, 1883 and lived at Churchville; informant was Hanna Banks, of Bel Air RFD) [Asbury Cemetery]

Banks, Bertha Richardson 1877-1986 (tombstone; obituary in *The Record* on July 30, 1986 stated she born in Havre de Grace, the daughter of John and Vernie Richardson, and married first to Nelson Taylor and second to Albert Banks; she died on July 21, 1986, age 109, at the Brevin Nursing Home in Havre de Grace and was preceded in death by two husbands and two children; *The Aegis* on February 10, 1977 reported she was age 100 and born on January 21, 1877) [St. James United Cemetery]

Banks, Bessie August 9, 1901 – June 9, 1915 (no tombstone; death certificate stated she was the daughter of Lilly Banks, father unknown; informant was James Fletcher, of Havre de Grace) [St. James United Cemetery]

Banks, Beulah Elizabeth June 7, 1916 – April 18, 1917 (no tombstone; death certificate stated she was born in Aberdeen, the daughter of Charles Turner and Eva Banks, both born in Harford Co.; informant was Eva Banks, of Aberdeen) [Mt. Calvary U. A. M. E. Church Cemetery]

Banks, Cassie A. October 27, 1837 – November 5, 1919 (no tombstone; death certificate stated she was born in Harford Co., daughter of Sandie Richardson, but mother's name was unknown to informant George W. Banks, of Aberdeen; she was a widow who lived near Aberdeen) [Asbury Cemetery]

Banks, Catherine, "Baby" 1909-1911 ("Baby Catherine" buried next to "Baby Rosa;" no last name was on her small, flat and rather modern granite tombstone; death certificate stated Catherine Irene Banks was born in Chester, PA, the daughter of Clarence Banks and Martha J. Hollins, both born in Harford Co., and lived near Michaelsville; she was born on May 14, 1909 and died on November 14, 1911) [Union U. M. Church Cemetery]

Banks, Charles H. (dates on tombstone are below ground level), Maryland, Pvt, 333 Labor Bn, QMC, World War II [Mt. Calvary U. A. M. E. Church Cemetery]

Banks, Clarence E. Sr. March 16, 1946 – October 12, 1976 (no tombstone; obituary in *The Aegis* on October 21, 1976 stated "Clarence E. Banks, Sr. (Larry Haskins)" was the son of Richard Haskins and Florence Banks, of Aberdeen; he married Sarah Turner, resided at 109 Hamilton Place, Washington Park, Aberdeen, and died at Harford Memorial Hospital in Havre de Grace; he was survived by his wife, his parents, a son, a daughter, 3 brothers, and 2 sisters) [Mt. Calvary U. A. M. E. Church Cemetery]

Banks, Clarence H. 1912-1981 (copied in 1987, but not found in 2018; obituary in *The Aegis* on February 26, 1981 stated Clarence Herbert Banks was a lifelong resident of Aberdeen, the son of Robert Smith and Emma Banks, and married Roberta Dallam; he retired from the Board of Education as a custodian, resided at 450 Washington Street and died at Harford Memorial Hospital in Havre de Grace on February 17, 1981, survived by his wife, 4 sons, 5 daughters and 4 grandchildren) [Mt. Calvary U. A. M. E. Church Cemetery]

Banks, Clarence H. 1957-   (on same tombstone with Martha J. Banks) [Union U. M. Church Cemetery]

Banks, Clarence R. May 25, 1938 – July 9, 2014, PFC, U.S. Army [Berkley Memorial Cemetery]

Banks, Danny Elvis 1964-2006 (small metal funeral home marker) [Berkley Memorial Cemetery]

Banks, Delfone Clarence August 18, 1969 – July 27, 2007 (obituary in *The Aegis* on August 8, 2007 stated born in Aberdeen, son of Clarence Banks and Roberta Dallam; he lived in Aberdeen and died at Laurelwood Nursing Home in Elkton, survived by his five siblings and other family, and predeceased by his parents, a sister and a brother; inscribed "Delphone C. Banks, 1969-2007") [Berkley Memorial Cemetery]

Banks, Edward 1899-1963 (on same tombstone with Mable Banks) [Mt. Calvary U. A. M. E. Church Cemetery]

Banks, Eliza Irene August 17, 1914 – March 9, 1915 (no tombstone; death certificate stated she was the daughter of John A. Banks and Nettie Stansbury, all born in Harford Co.) [Union U. M. Church Cemetery]

Banks, Evelyn died October 8, 1991, age 91 (no tombstone; obituary in *The Aegis* on October 16, 1991 stated she was a native of Perryman, lived in Aberdeen and was the widow of Roylan Banks; she died at the Brevin Nursing Home in Havre de Grace and was survived by a daughter-in-law Molly C. Banks) [Mt. Calvary U. A. M. E. Church Cemetery]

Banks, Florence 1918-1982 (copied in 1987, but not found in 2018; "F. Banks" owned a lot in section 42 some time after 1951; obituary in *The Aegis* on January 6, 1983 stated she was born in Aberdeen, the daughter of the late Roy Taylor and Eva Banks, lived in Aberdeen and died at Holy Cross Hospital in Silver Spring; she was survived by 3 sons, Robert Giles, Bernard Dorsey and Richard D. Banks, and 2 daughters, Hilda Giles and Thelma Morgan, 13 grandchildren and 5 great-grandchildren) [Mt. Calvary U. A. M. E. Church Cemetery]

Banks, Frederick died December 29, 1916, age 67 years, 6(?) months (inscribed "In Memory of") [Asbury Cemetery]

Banks, George J. January 19, 1897 – April 10, 1959, Maryland, Pvt., 15th Co., 154 Dep. Brig., World War I (military record stated George Julian Banks was born on January 19, 1898 at Swan Creek near Aberdeen, was inducted on September 26, 1918, served in the 154th Depot Brigade and was honorably discharged December 5, 1918) [Asbury Cemetery]

Banks, George W. October 29, 1873 – January 16, 1935 (no tombstone; death certificate stated he was born at Oakington, the son of Anda Banks and Cassie Richardson, both born in Harford Co.; he was a farm day laborer who lived on Post Road near Aberdeen and was the widower of Sallie Banks; informant was Edward Banks, of Aberdeen RFD) [Asbury Cemetery]

Banks, George Washington October 4, 1836 – September 7, 1919 (no tombstone; death certificate stated he was the son of James Banks and Provie Frisby, all born in Harford Co.; he was a farmer near Bel Air and died a widower; informant was Virginia Brown, of Bel Air) [Asbury Cemetery]

Banks, Harry T. July 14, 1901 – June 20, 1917 (no tombstone; death certificate stated he was the son of George Banks and Sarah McGaw, all were born in Harford Co.; he was single, a day laborer, and died in Havre de Grace Hospital; informant was Lena Banks, of Aberdeen) [Asbury Cemetery]

Banks, Hattie A., wife of William A. Banks April 25, 1883 – September 20, 1919 (inscribed "Asleep In Jesus") [Union U. M. Church Cemetery]

Banks, Hester C. October 14, 1878 – March 6, 1940 (no tombstone; death certificate stated she was the daughter of George Cooper and Elibath *(sic)* Hooper, all born in Churchville; she married H. Banks and died a widow at home near Churchville where she had lived for 60 years; informant was Elibath *(sic)* Williams of "622 Green Hill Road, Pa.;" she was buried at "John Wesley near Abingdon" according to her death certificate, but obituary in the *Bel Air Times* on March 22, 1940 stated she was buried at Asbury Church in Churchville; James Dorsey Card File, African American Obituaries, maintained at the Historical Society of Harford County, has an obituary card that stated she lived at Asbury and was survived by several children [probably Asbury Cemetery]

Banks, Hezekiah, "Husband" died June 26, 1913, age 46 years, 4 months and 11 days (inscribed "It is the Lord let Him / Do what seemth Him good." death certificate stated he was born on February 15, 1867, the son of George Banks and Julia A. Cooper, all born in Harford Co.; he worked as a laborer, married and died at Churchville; informant was Hester C. Banks, of Churchville) [Asbury Cemetery]

Banks, Jane 1881-1967 (copied in 1987, but not found in 2018; obituary in *The Aegis* on July 20, 1967 stated Jane M. Banks was the daughter of the late George Matthews and Sarah Reed, and the widow of Santa Banks, of Aberdeen; she died at Mt. Wilson State Hospital in Baltimore County on July 14, 1967) [Mt. Calvary U. A. M. E. Church Cemetery]

Banks, John April 10, 1875 – July 14, 1937 (no tombstone; death certificate stated he was the son of Susan Green, both born in Harford Co., but the name of his father was not known to informant, his wife, Mrs. Elizabeth S. Banks; he was a day laborer for 40 years, married Elizabeth Snowden and lived on Bush Chapel Road near Aberdeen) [Asbury Cemetery]

Banks, John A. 1894-1952 (inscribed "R.I.P.") [Asbury Cemetery]

Banks, John A. January 4, 1877 – January 2, 1931 (no tombstone; death certificate stated he was the son of John A. Banks and Martha Johnson; informant was Mrs. Nettie Banks) [Union U. M. Church Cemetery]

Banks, Johnny April 5, 1901 – May 15, 1934 (no tombstone; death certificate stated he was the son of Pearce Jones and Rosie Woods, all born in Virginia, according to informant, his wife, Mrs. Lillian Banks, of Aberdeen RFD; since he had a different last name this could be in error; he worked as a day laborer in Aberdeen and died at Havre de Grace Hospital) [Mt. Calvary U. A. M. E. Church Cemetery]

Banks, Julia died April 6, 1928, age 45 (no tombstone; death certificate stated she was married and born in Virginia, the daughter of John Chalmers, born in Virginia, but her mother was unknown to informant Alfred Banks, of Havre de Grace) [Union U. M. Church Cemetery]

Banks, Julia A., wife of George Banks, died February 17, 1910, age 63 (tombstone verse illegible, began "For I am now ready;" death certificate stated she was born in Churchville, the daughter of William Cooper and Lucinda Hays, both born in Maryland; informant was her daughter Virginia Brown) [Asbury Cemetery]

Banks, Lillian Mae 1907-1968 (tombstone; obituary in *The Aegis* on February 8, 1968 stated Lillian Mae Banks was born in Aberdeen, the daughter of the late Lloyd and Rosa Parker, and died at Harford Memorial Hospital in Havre de Grace on January 30, 1968, widow of Johnnie Banks, and was survived by two brothers and five sisters) [Mt. Calvary U. A. M. E. Church Cemetery]

Banks, M., "Mom" 1900-1973 [St. James United Cemetery]

Banks, Mable 1899-1964 (on same tombstone with Edward Banks; "M. Banks" owned a lot in section 42 some time after 1951) [Mt. Calvary U. A. M. E. Church Cemetery]

Banks, Martha J. August 10, 1842 – August 11, 1915 (no tombstone; death certificate stated she was born in Harford Co., the daughter of James Banks and Provie(?) Rodes, birth places not known to informant Lizzie Gibson, of Bel Air; Martha was a widow and laundress) [Asbury Cemetery]

Banks, Martha J. September 8, 1884 – October 15, 1975 (on same tombstone with Clarence H. Banks) [Union U. M. Church Cemetery]

Banks, Mary died February 24, 1922, age 68 (no tombstone; death certificate stated she was the daughter of Hampton Washington, both born in Maryland, but the name of her mother was not known to informant Mary East, of Aberdeen; she died near Aberdeen) [Mt. Calvary U. A. M. E. Church Cemetery]

Banks, Mary Alice 1913-2005 (small metal funeral home marker) [Asbury Cemetery]

Banks, Norman 1907-1998 (tombstone; obituary in *The Aegis* on November 11, 1998 stated he was born in Perryman, the son of John Banks and Nettie Stansbury, and was once employed as a railroad worker; he died on November 9, 1998 at St. James Hospital in Newark, NJ, survived by one niece, Joanette Sconion, and two nephews, Charles and Lloyd Sconion) [Union U. M. Church Cemetery]

Banks, Robert November 9, 1915 – July 11, 1939 (no tombstone; death certificate stated he was the son of Ryland Banks and Evelyn Dorsey, all born in Aberdeen; he was single, a dishwasher, and died in Harford Memorial Hospital; informant was Mrs. Evelyn Banks, of Aberdeen) [Asbury Cemetery]

Banks, Rosa, "Baby" 1908-1909 ("Baby Rosa" buried next to "Baby Catherine;" no last name inscribed on her small, flat and rather modern granite tombstone, but death certificate stated Rosie Slenora Jane Banks was the daughter of Clarance H. Banks and Martha J. Holland and all born in Maryland; informant was Charlotte B. Holland, her grandmother; she died at home in Michaelsville on April 20, 1909, age 1 year, 1 month and 3 days) [Union U. M. Church Cemetery]

Banks, Sadie V. January 3, 1875 – February 21, 1932 (no tombstone; death certificate stated she was the daughter of Aquilla McGaw and Sarah Ringgold, all born in Havre de Grace; she was the wife of George W. Banks and lived in Aberdeen; informant was Lena E. Watters, of 123 Alice Ann St., Bel Air) [Asbury Cemetery]

Banks, Santa died August 28, 1947, age 67 years, 8 months, 28 days (no tombstone; death certificate stated he was the son of Santa Banks and Jannie Matthews, all born in Aberdeen; he lived on Bush Chapel Road and worked as a railroad laborer; informant was Mrs. Mary Banks, of Aberdeen) [Mt. Calvary U. A. M. E. Church Cemetery]

Banks, Susan June 20, 1859 – July 30, 1921 (no tombstone; death certificate stated she was the daughter of James Banks, both born in Maryland, but her mother's name was not known to informant John Banks, of Aberdeen, and she died a widow near Aberdeen) [Asbury Cemetery]

Banks, Walter October 2, 1877 – June 17, 1941 (no tombstone; death certificate stated he was the son of George Brown Banks and Jane Cooper, all born in Churchville; he was single, worked as a laborer and lived on

Churchville Road; informant was Edward Banks, of Bel Air RFD) [Asbury Cemetery]

Banks, Walter George October 11, 1918 – October 4, 1994, MOMM3, U.S. Navy, World War II (tombstone; obituary in *The Aegis* on October 12, 1994 stated he served in World War II, married Maudeline ----, was a teacher, a landscaper, retired from the First National Bank and died at the Perry Point Veterans Administration Medical Center, he was also a founder of the National Association for the Advancement of Colored People in Harford County) [Asbury Cemetery]

Banks, William December 28, 1878 – June 21, 1955 (on same tombstone with Adeline P. Banks) [Asbury Cemetery]

Banks, William March 11, 1888 – May 11, 1933 (no tombstone; death certificate stated he was born in Aberdeen, the son of Isaac Banks, born in Churchville, and Mary J. Washington, born in Washington, D.C.; he was single, worked as a laborer in Aberdeen and died at Havre de Grace Hospital; information from hospital records by Tarring & Sons Funeral Home) [Mt. Calvary U. A. M. E. Church Cemetery]

Banks, William died April 10, 1892, age 52 [Asbury Cemetery]

Banks, William A. 1911-1988 (small temporary marker; obituary in *The Aegis* on April 14, 1988 stated he was born in Bel Air, the son of William and Adeline Banks; he married Mary ---- and served as treasurer, trustee and a member of the choir of Asbury AME Church; he was a retired civil servant from Edgewood Arsenal and died at the Laurelwood Nursing Home in Elkton on April 10, 1988, age 76) [Asbury Cemetery]

Banks, William Harry July 20, 1926 – January 17, 1989, STM1, U.S. Navy, World War II (tombstone; obituary in *The Aegis* on January 25, 1989 stated he was born in Aberdeen, the son of Evelyn Dorsey Banks of Havre de Grace and the late Roland Banks; he served in the U.S. Navy during World War II, worked as an ammunition worker at Aberdeen Proving Ground, lived in Aberdeen and died at Harford Memorial Hospital in Havre de Grace; he was survived by his mother, his wife Molly V. Banks, 3 sons, 4 daughters, 8 grandchildren and 3 great-grandchildren]

Baptist, William T. March 1, 1848 – March 3, 1911 (no tombstone; death certificate stated he was born in Harford Co., the son of William Baptist, but his mother's name was not known by informant G. T. Pennington; he worked as a laborer and died near Havre de Grace) [Green Spring U. M. Church Cemetery]

Barber, Frances November 27, 1893 – June 5, 1932 (no tombstone; death certificate stated she was the daughter of Richard Ward and Eliza Rumsey, and "probably married" to Percy Barber; informant was her father) [St. James United Cemetery]

Barclay, Ruth Ione May 21, 1917 – January 28, 1995 (tombstone; James Dorsey Card File, African American Obituaries, maintained at the Historical Society of Harford County, has a card with obituary from *The Aegis* stating she had received her formal education at the Nanticoke Colored Elementary and High Schools and attended what is now Dover State University; she came to Aberdeen to live with her youngest sister Irene Barclay Nutter and she made quilts, Afghans and Lap Throws; followed by a short stay in the Citizens Nursing Home in Havre de Grace she died at Harford Memorial Hospital) [Berkley Memorial Cemetery]

Barnes, ---- stillborn male on July 28, 1916 (no tombstone; death certificate stated he died in Poole, the son of John Barnes and Mamie White, all born in Maryland) [Clark's U. M. Church Cemetery]

Barnes, Anna Lucretia June 3, 1935 -   (on same tombstone with Russell Barnes Sr.) [St. James United Cemetery]

Barnes, Baby Boy stillborn on October 31, 1977 (no tombstone; Pennington Funeral Home records stated he was the son of Charles O'Neal Barnes and Marion Virginia Davis of 212 Asbury Road in Churchville; he died at Harford Memorial Hospital and was buried in "grave space on top of grandfather") [Asbury Cemetery]

Barnes, Bernice E. 1939-1993 (handwritten on a flat cement slab) [St. James United Cemetery]

Barnes, Blanche Ames 1926-1983 (tombstone; obituary in *The Aegis* on February 17, 1983 stated she was born in Washington, D.C. and married Albert Ross Barnes; she lived in Aberdeen and died at Harford Memorial Hospital 4`on February 6, 1983, age 56, survived by her husband, a son, 6 daughters, 4 brothers, 7 sisters, 26 grandchildren and 5 great-grandchildren) [Berkley Memorial Cemetery]

Barnes, Catherine R., "Ma" June 8, 1908 – January 28, 1998 (tombstone inscribed with a poem) [St. James United Cemetery]

Barnes, Charles Edward October 28, 1911 – May 18, 1912 (no tombstone; death certificate stated he died near Kalmia, the son of John Barnes and Mary White, all born in Harford Co.; informant was James Barnes, of Bel Air) [Clark's U. M. Church Cemetery]

Barnes, Doris Elizabeth "Tootie" July 29, 1936 – January 15, 1998 (no tombstone; James Dorsey Card File, African American Obituaries, maintained at the Historical Society of Harford County, has a card with her obituary from *The Aegis* stating she was born in Bel Air, the daughter of the late Florence P. Barnes and the late Harvey B. Smith, and she received her formal education from the Maryland School for the Colored Blind and Deaf; she died at Fallston General Hospital, survived by a son, a grandson, a brother and other relatives) [Clark's U. M. Church Cemetery]

Barnes, Dorothy 1921-1995 "Pentecostal Pond" (handwritten on flat cement slab) [St. James United Cemetery]

Barnes, Elizabeth C. 1906-1964 (on same tombstone with husband William D. Barnes) [West Liberty Church Cemetery]

Barnes, Emma J., "Loving Mother" 1912-1984 [St. James United Cemetery]

Barnes, Estelle, "Sister" 1924-1960 [Berkley Memorial Cemetery]

Barnes, Eva W. April 22, 1894 – May 20, 1979 (copied in 1987, but not found in 2018; obituary in *The Aegis* on May 31, 1979 stated her maiden name was Brown and she was the widow of John W. Barnes, of Havre de Grace, and died at Harford Memorial Hospital, survived by a son, a daughter, 5 step-daughters, 3 step-sons, 33 grandchildren, 42 great-grandchildren, 7 great-great-grandchildren and 3 brothers) [St. James United Cemetery]

Barnes, Florence 1909-1985 (no tombstone; James Dorsey Card File, African American Obituaries, maintained at the Historical Society of Harford County, has a card for her stating she was buried in "Clarks Cemetery," but did not cite the source nor give more details about her life) [Clark's U. M. Church Cemetery]

Barnes, Florence R. July 12, 1931 – March 18, 1975 (copied in 1987, but not found in 2018; obituary in *The Aegis* on March 27, 1975 stated she was the daughter of Howard and Viola Mae Jackson, and the wife of Clarence J. Barnes, of Aberdeen; she died at home, survived by her husband, a son, 3 daughters, 11 brothers and 8 sisters) [Berkley Memorial Cemetery]

Barnes, Frank Wolbert September 15, 1937 – November 7, 1942 (no tombstone; death certificate stated he was the son of James Barnes, of Havre de Grace, and Mary Swann, of Rockville, MD) [St. James United Cemetery]

Barnes, Henrietta 1923-1986 (handwritten on flat cement slab) [St. James United Cemetery]

Barnes, Henry W. February 25, 1926 – January 13, 2003 (on same tombstone with M. Madeline Barnes and inscribed "I will meet you in the morning. Psalms 130") [Clark's U. M. Church Cemetery]

Barnes, J. Edward died February 22, 1932, age about 61 (no tombstone; death certificate stated he was the son of George Barnes and Kasiah Harris, all born in Berkley; he married Josephine ---- and worked as a farmer in Berkley; informant was Wayman Barnes, of Darlington) [Berkley Memorial Cemetery]

Barnes, John, "Father" February 28, 1882 – November 28, 1960 [Clark's U. M. Church Cemetery]

Barnes, John D. May 7, 1913 – March 28, 1981, U. S. Army, World War II (tombstone; obituary in *The Aegis* on April 2, 1981 stated he was born in Dublin, MD, the son of John D. Barnes and Mary White, and married Sarah Watters; he served in the Army from 1943 to 1945 and retired as a mason helper at Edgewood Arsenal about two years ago; he lived at 3107 Anna Drive in Street and died at the Perry Point VAMC, survived by his wife, 5 sons, 5 sisters and 5 grandchildren) [Clark's U. M. Church Cemetery]

Barnes, John H., "Beloved Son and Brother" November 10, 1941 – March 11, 1993 (tombstone; obituary in *The Aegis* on March 17, 1993 stated John Henry Barnes was born in Street, son of the late John D. Barnes and Sarah Waters, was a pipefitter for Price Brothers Co. in Perryman and died at Fallston General Hospital, survived by four brothers) [Clark's U. M. Church Cemetery]

Barnes, Josepha died March 13, 1932, age about 55 (no tombstone; death certificate stated she died a widow in Bel Air, but informant Wayman Barnes, of Darlington, did not know her parents nor date of birth) [Berkley Memorial Cemetery]

Barnes, Kaziah August 12, 1825 – September 7, 1923 (no tombstone; death certificate stated she was the daughter of George Harris and Elizabeth Prigg, all born in Maryland; she died a widow in Berkley; informant was Wayman Barnes, of Berkley) [Berkley Memorial Cemetery]

Barnes, M. Madeline February 12, 1928 -   (on same tombstone with Henry W Barnes and inscribed "I will meet you in the morning. Psalms 130") [Clark's U. M. Church Cemetery]

Barnes, Malcolm 1938-2017 (small metal funeral home marker) [Clark's U. M. Church Cemetery]

Barnes, Marie H. 1910-2007 (on same tombstone with Warren H. Barnes) [West Liberty Church Cemetery]

Barnes, Mary E., "Mother" March 17, 1892 – July 12, 1970 [Clark's U. M. Church Cemetery]

Barnes, Pauline September 5, 1930 – December 9, 1930 (no tombstone; death certificate stated she was the daughter of Katherine Barnes, father unknown to informant who was her mother) [St. James United Cemetery]

Barnes, Pearl Rebecca Giles September 3, 1928 – October 13, 1974 (no tombstone; Pennington Funeral Home records stated she was the married daughter of William Alexander Giles and Isabella Stansbury, but the name of her husband was not given; she died in Harford Memorial Hospital in Havre de Grace and was buried in "Union Methodist Cemetery, Swan Creek in Aberdeen") [Union U. M. Church Cemetery]

Barnes, Rose B. 1880-1959 (on same tombstone with Wayman W. Barnes) [Berkley Memorial Cemetery]

Barnes, Russell Sr. July 10, 1934 – February 27, 2016 (on same tombstone with Anna Lucretia Barnes) [St. James United Cemetery]

Barnes, Sarah I., "Beloved Wife and Mother" December 25, 1913 – February 10, 1991 [Clark's U. M. Church Cemetery]

Barnes, Stephen E. "Rock" December 21, 1942 – July 14, 2005 [Clark's U. M. Church Cemetery]

Barnes, Warren H. 1905-1991 (on same tombstone with Marie H. Barnes) [West Liberty Church Cemetery]

Barnes, Wayman W. 1878-1969 (on same tombstone with Rose B. Barnes) [Berkley Memorial Cemetery]

Barnes, William D. 1904-1961 (on same tombstone with Elizabeth C. Barnes) [West Liberty Church Cemetery]

Barnett, Hannah died in March 1933, age 85 (no tombstone; James Dorsey Card File, African American Obituaries, maintained at the Historical Society of Harford County, has a card with obituary from the *Bel Air Times* on March 17, 1933 stating she lived in Bel Air and was survived by 3 daughters and a number of grandchildren; however, no death certificate was found in Harford County records) [Hendon Hill Cemetery]

Barrett, Annie T., wife of George W. Barrett – see Tabitha A. Barrett [Asbury Cemetery]

Barrett, Edward T., son of George and Annie Barrett, died December 17, 1916, age 46 (inscribed "At Rest" on same tombstone with Thomas O. Barrett; death certificate stated he was born on September 4, 1870 in Harford Co., a son of George Barrett, born in Kent Co., MD, and Annie Hall, born in Harford Co.; he lived and worked as a barber in Bel Air and was married; informant was Annie Barrett, of Bel Air) [Asbury Cemetery]

Barrett, Ella V. ---- 1887? ----? (marker illegible) [Mt. Zion U. M. Church Cemetery]

Barrett, George M. August 14, 1881 – December 14, 1965 [Berkley Memorial Cemetery]

Barrett, George Washington died November 21, 1900, age 76 years, 3 months and 9 days (copied in 1987 as "In Memory Of" and "Asleep in Jesus / Blessed sleep / From which none ever" *(sic)*, but was not found in 2018 and may have been toppled over) [Asbury Cemetery]

Barrett, Lillian Viola March 10, 1931 – October 4, 1931 (no tombstone; death certificate stated her parents were Harry Barrett and Hester Waters, all born in Maryland, and lived at Rocks; informant was Charles Dunsen, of Street, MD) [Chestnut Grove A. M. E. Church Cemetery, formerly LaGrange Cemetery at Rocks]

Barrett, Olivia M. February 28, 1906 – December 26, 1967 [Berkley Memorial Cemetery]

Barrett, Tabitha A. died January 6, 1941 (inscribed Annie T. Barrett, wife of George W. Barrett, April 18, 1843 – January 6, 1941 "At Rest;" her death notice in *The Aegis* on January 10, 1941 stated she was 97, probably the oldest colored woman in the Asbury section; death certificate stated Tabitha A. Barrett was born April 18, 1858 and died January 6, 1941, age 82, in Harford Co.; she was the widow of George W. Barrett and lived in rural Bel Air; informant was Mrs. Laura V. Oliver, of Bel Air RFD #1) [Asbury Cemetery]

Barrett, Thomas O., son of George and Annie Barrett, died August 20, 1916, age 33 (inscribed "At Rest" on same tombstone with Edward T. Barrett) [Asbury Cemetery]

Barton, Sarah (no tombstone found, but J. C. Taylor Marble Co. records state "Sarah Barton (col.) tomb. was put up Nov 10th 1888 Col. Church near X Roads" (Upper Cross Roads) [West Liberty Church Cemetery]

Basknight, Arliss E. October 7, 1913 – November 11, 1971, New Jersey, Pvt., Army Air Force, World War II

Basknight. Lillian M. 1927-2002 (small metal funeral home marker) [Berkley Memorial Cemetery]

Bason, Georgia A. H. 1888-1959 (on same tombstone with "Sister" Mary E. H. Morgan) [Chestnut Grove A. M. E. Church Cemetery, formerly LaGrange Cemetery at Rocks]

Bassey, Phyllis F. 1954-1995 (inscribed "An Inspiration To All Who Knew Her") [St. James United Cemetery]

Batson, Hilda M. 1911-1993 (on same tombstone with John W. Batson; James Dorsey Card File, African American Obituaries, maintained at the Historical Society of Harford County, has a card with obituary from *The Aegis* on July 7, 1993 stating Hilda Marie Warfield Batson, a native of Perryman, died on June 22, 1993 at Harford Memorial Hospital; she had worked for the F. O. Mitchell Cannery and during World War II she was a civilian employee at Edgewood Arsenal and retired in the 1950s from the Aberdeen Proving Ground Service Club; she married the late John W. Batson in 1929 and was survived by a sister-in-law Alean Warfield and many nieces and nephews) [Union U. M. Church Cemetery]

Batson, James Wesley, son of Shelton S. and Martha Batson, June 15, 1906 – January 27, 1931 (tombstone; death certificate also stated he was the son of Sheton *(sic)* Batson and Martha Barrett, all born in Maryland; he was single, worked as a chauffeur and lived in Churchville; informant was Virginia Turner, of Churchville; J. C. Taylor Marble Co. records stated "James Wesley Batson's Marble head stone was put up Oct 3rd 1931 Asbury Cemetery, ordered by Mrs. Annie Barrett, Bel Air RFD #1) [Asbury Cemetery]

Batson, John W. 1907-1973 (on same tombstone with Hilda M. Batson) [Union U. M. Church Cemetery]

Batson, Martha J. December 18, 1887 – May 24, 1911 (no tombstone; death certificate stated she was born in Harford Co., the daughter of George D. Barrett, born in Kent Co., MD, and T. Annie Hall, born in Baltimore Co., and was married and lived in Bel Air at the time of her death; informant was T. Annie Barrett, of Bel Air) [Asbury Cemetery]

Battle, Alfred April 1, 1895 – June 13, 1957, North Carolina, Pvt., U.S. Army, World War I [Mt. Calvary U. A. M. E. Church Cemetery]

Battle, Bertha Dorsey January 24, 1889 – February 10, 1941 (no tombstone; death certificate stated she was the daughter of Fred Dorsey and Mary Gibson, all born in Harford Co.; she married Alford Batttle (age 46 in 1941) and died near Aberdeen where she had lived for 12 years; informant was her husband) [Mt. Calvary U. A. M. E. Church Cemetery]

Battle, Catherine Virginia February 28, 1918 – August 13, 2008 (no tombstone; owner of a lot in section 20 some time after 1951; obituary in *The Aegis* on August 20, 2008 stated she was born in Aberdeen, the daughter of Rosetta and Lloyd Parker, was a cosmetologist for more than 30 years and she also obtained her nursing and real estate certifications; she was the widow of Alfred Battle and obituary contains many other of her achievements in the community and included a long list of surviving and predeceased relatives; she resided in Aberdeen and died at Harford Memorial Hospital) [Mt. Calvary U. A. M. E. Church Cemetery]

Baxter, Betty Jane October 19, 1933 – June 22, 1937 (no tombstone; death certificate stated she was the daughter of Edward Baxter and Hannah M. Hewitt, all born in Harford Co. and lived at Street, MD; informant was her father; she was buried at Rocks) [probably Chestnut Grove A. M. E. Church Cemetery, formerly LaGrange Cemetery at Rocks]

Baxter, Charlotte Ann died March 5, 1905, age 82 (no tombstone; death certificate stated she was born in Harford Co., married William Baxter and died a widow at Rocks; her mother was Charlotte Hall, but her father's name was not given) [Chestnut Grove A. M. E. Church Cemetery, formerly LaGrange Cemetery at Rocks]

Baxter, Ettyle M. January 14, 1926 – March 12, 1928 (no tombstone; death certificate stated she was the daughter of Ed Baxter and Hannah M. Hewett, all born in Maryland; she lived and died at Rocks; informant was her father) [Chestnut Grove A. M. E. Church Cemetery, formerly LaGrange Cemetery at Rocks]

Baxter, Herbert H. November 22, 1937 – January 2, 1938 (no tombstone; death certificate stated he was the son of William E. Baxter and Hannah Hewitt, all born in Harford Co.; informant was Hannah Baxter, of Pylesville; buried at Rocks) [Chestnut Grove A. M. E. Church Cemetery, formerly LaGrange Cemetery at Rocks]

Baxter, Walter July 25, 1896 – September 18, 1914 (no tombstone; death certificate stated he was single, worked as a laborer and died at Rocks; his parents were Alfred Baxter, born at Rocks, and Lizzie Johnson, born at Pylesville; informant was Charles C. Hall, of Rocks) [Chestnut Grove A. M. E. Church Cemetery, formerly LaGrange Cemetery at Rocks]

Baxter, William died April 18, 1895, age 78 years and 2 months (inscribed "To My Husband") [Chestnut Grove A. M. E. Church Cemetery, formerly LaGrange Cemetery at Rocks]

Beach, Kattie May May 30, 1926 – September 11, 1926 (no tombstone; death certificate stated she was born in Maryland, the daughter of Henry Beach, born in South Carolina, and Barbara Waters, born in Maryland, and died in Van Bibber; she was buried in "Mountain Col. Cemetery;" informant was her father, of Edgewood RFD) [Mt. Zion U. M. Church Cemetery]

Beale, Mildred H. 1927-1992 [Clark's U. M. Church Cemetery]

Beard, Baby Boy stillborn on October 3, 1979, son of James M. Beard and Joan E. Beard; survived by brother Michael C. Beard; informant was his mother Joan E. Beard-Wiggins in March, 2020) [Asbury Cemetery]

Beard, James Michael November 3, 1953 – February 18, 2001, SPEC4, U.S. Army (tombstone inscription; obituary in *The Aegis* on February 23, 2001 stated he was born in Morehead City, NC, the son of Rufus B. Beard, Sr. and Nancy Henry, served in the Army during the Vietnam War and was employed at Perry Point Veterans Hospital as an environmental maintenance man; he was a member of Ames United Methodist Church in Bel Air and died at Richland Memorial Hospital in Columbia, SC, survived by his mother, 2 sons, 1 daughter, 3 brothers, 6 sisters, his former wife Joan E. Beard, of Belcamp, and his fiancé Denise Tate, of SC) [John Wesley U. M. E. Church Cemetery in Abingdon]

Beard, Nancy Henry November 7, 1931 – July 5, 2012 (inscribed "You will always be in our thoughts and forever in our hearts;" her death notice in *The Aegis* on July 13, 2012 stated she was formerly of Havre de Grace and died at Manor Health Care in Towson, MD) [John Wesley U. M. E. Church Cemetery in Abingdon]

Beasley, Betty Jean Gilliam July 21, 1957 – September 12, 1985 (inscribed "In Loving Memory Of Family") [St. James United Cemetery]

Beasley, Charles May 25, 1866 – January 21, 1911 (no tombstone; death certificate stated he was the son of Edward Beasley and Maria Johnson, all born in Virginia; he was married, worked as a farmer and died in Abingdon; informant was Laura Johnson, of Abingdon) [John Wesley U. M. E. Church Cemetery in Abingdon]

Beasley, Clarence November 15, 1907 – July 26, 1923 (no tombstone; death certificate stated he was born in Maryland, the son of Charles Beasley and Laura Beasley, all born in Maryland; he was a school boy who died in Abingdon; informant was his mother) [John Wesley U. M. E. Church Cemetery in Abingdon]

Beasley, Conrad Howard July 8, 1901 – February 1, 1922 (no tombstone; death certificate stated he was born in Maryland, the son of Charles Beasley, born in Virginia, and Louisa Morgan, born in Maryland; he was married, worked as a laborer and died at home in Abingdon; informant was his wife, Leuisa Beasley) [John Wesley U. M. E. Church Cemetery in Abingdon]

Beck, Veronica Y. 1951-2018 (small metal funeral home marker) [St. James United Cemetery]

Beckett, William H. January 12, 1869 – December 5, 1914 (no tombstone; death certificate stated he was born in Virginia, but his parents were not known to informant Isaac Gills, of Aberdeen; he was single, worked as a laborer and died in Aberdeen) [Mt. Calvary U. A. M. E. Church Cemetery]

Bell, Frances B. October 16, 1840 – November 30, 1916 (no tombstone; death certificate stated she was the daughter of Isaac Briscoe and Miria Addison, all born in Maryland; she was married and died at Poole; informant was Carrie Gwynn, of Street RFD #1) [Clark's U. M. Church Cemetery]

Bell, Lloyd May 10, 1866 – November 21, 1921 (no tombstone; death certificate stated he was the son of Daniel Bell, both born in Maryland, but his mother's name was not known to informant Mrs. Lena Preston, of Street; he was a laborer and died a widower at Poole) [Clark's U. M. Church Cemetery]

Bennett, Roland S., "Husband" October 19, 1905 – February 19, 1977 [Berkley Memorial Cemetery]

Benns, Charles L. died March 22, 1904, age 28 (tombstone; death certificate stated he was the son of Edward Harris and Sadonia Benns, all born in Maryland, and he died aged 27 years, 11 months and 22 days; he was single, worked as a laborer and lived in Churchville; informant was his uncle Lewis Benns) [Asbury Cemetery]

Benns, James died April 2, 1921, age 47 (no tombstone; death certificate stated he was the son of Thomas Benns and Alice Dorsey, both of Harford Co., was married, worked as a laborer and died at his home in Churchville; informant was Harriet Kennard, of Aberdeen RFD) [Asbury Cemetery]

Benns, Louis A. died April 12, 1909, aged 62 years, 1 month and 2 days (tombstone also contained a long illegible verse; death certificate stated "Lewis Benns" was the son of Thomas Benns and ---- (unknown) and all were born in Virginia; it also stated he died April 12, 1909, "age 60 years and 28 days" at Churchville; he worked as a laborer and was married at the time of his death; informant was Dr. W. S. Gorsuch, of Churchville) [Asbury Cemetery]

Benns, Mary J., wife of Louis A. Benns, died December 12, 1913, age 62 (inscribed "In Memory of" and "She is not dead, only asleep;" death certificate stated "Mary J. Bends" was born at Creswell, but her parents' names and places of birth were not known to informant Mrs. Margaret Welsh, of Chester, PA; she lived in Churchville and died a widow) [Asbury Cemetery]

Benson, Sidney O. November 10, 1940 – October 25, 1919 (no tombstone; death certificate stated she was the daughter of William Green and Heryett Stump, all born in Maryland; informant was Mollie Preston, of 1408 N. Carey St., Baltimore) [Clark's U. M. Church Cemetery]

Benson, William H. November – (blank), 1837 – May 20, 1942 (no tombstone; death certificate stated he was born in Harford Co., the son of Henry Giles and Mary Benson, both born in Maryland; he married Mamie ---- and died at Gibson where he had resided for 50 years; the informant was Sarah E. Trustry, of Bel Air RFD #1) [Clark's U. M. Church Cemetery]

Bentley, William A. December 20, 1870 – December 16, 1924 (inscribed "God Wanted So Called Him Away") [St. James United Cemetery]

Bently, James E. December 19, 1921 – June 23, 2006, SSgt., U.S. Army, WW II [Berkley Memorial Cemetery]

Berkely, Clyde B. October 16, 1874 – February 19, 1927 (no tombstone; death certificate stated he was born in Virginia and was married, but parents unknown to Clyde A. Berkely, of MA) [Union U. M. Church Cemetery]

Berry, ---- stillborn male on June 25, 1915 (no tombstone; death certificate stated he was the son of Marshel Berry, born at Conowingo, and Fannie E. Washington, born in Castleton) [Berkley Memorial Cemetery]

Berry, Albert October 7, 1845 – February 26, 1931 (on same tombstone with Martha A. Berry; death certificate stated he was born in Harford Co., worked as a farmer, and was a widower; his father was not known to informant, but his mother was Eliza Berry who was born in Harford Co.; informant was Edith Berry, of Rocks) [Chestnut Grove A. M. E. Church Cemetery, formerly LaGrange Cemetery at Rocks]

Berry, Albert H. 1892-1985 (on same tombstone with Edith J. Berry) [Chestnut Grove A. M. E. Church Cemetery, formerly LaGrange Cemetery at Rocks]

Berry, Albert H. Jr. July 20, 1938 – January 24, 1941 (no tombstone; death certificate stated he was born in Baltimore and died near Rocks; his parents were Albert H. Berry, born at Rocks, and Edith R. Johnson, born in Delta, PA; informant was Albert H. Berry, Sr., of Rocks; Kurtz Funeral Home Record Book 1937-1943, p. 174, gave the same information) [Chestnut Grove A. M. E. Church Cemetery, formerly LaGrange Cemetery at Rocks]

Berry, Alexander died May 3, 1901, age 84 (no tombstone; death certificate stated he was the son of John Berry and ---- (blank) and husband of Annie Peaco and Amelia Moore; he was a farmer and died at Berkley; place of burial was not indicated, but was probably in this cemetery since both of his wives were buried here) [Berkley Memorial Cemetery]

Berry, Amelia Moore died September 26, 1918, age 45 years, 6 months and 20 days (no tombstone) [Berkley Memorial Cemetery]

Berry, Anna A., wife of Alexander Berry, died September 29, 1894, age 72 years and 8 months) [Berkley Memorial Cemetery]

Berry, Cassandra died October 7, 1879, age 92 (no tombstone; obituary in *The Aegis* on October 17, 1879 stated she was a servant of the Nelson family in the 4th District and died at the residence of John N. Nelson; she formerly belonged to Admiral William H. Nelson, then to his son Nicholas H. Nelson and subsequently to John N. Nelson; place of burial was not given [possibly William C. Rice Memorial Cemetery, St. James U. M. Church]

Berry, Cynthia Denise July 27, 1957 – September 29, 2001 (inscribed "In God's Care") [Berkley Memorial Cemetery]

Berry, Edith J. 1897-1979 (on same tombstone with Albert H. Berry; obituary in *The Aegis*, August 16, 1979, reported Edith Johnson Berry was born at Peach Bottom, PA, the daughter of George and Julia Johnson, married Albert Henry Berry, of Rocks, and died August 10, 1979 at Citizens Nursing Home in Havre de Grace) [Chestnut Grove A. M. E. Church Cemetery, formerly LaGrange Cemetery at Rocks]

Berry, George H. November 11, 1925 – March 28, 2004 (on same tombstone with Mary B. Berry) [Fairview A. M. E. Church Cemetery]

Berry, Gwendolyn T. Townley February 8, 1951 – October 13, 2007 [Berkley Memorial Cemetery]

Berry, Harriet W. March 8, 1883 – May 6, 1911(no tombstone; death certificate stated she was the daughter of Samuel Wilson and Priscilla Presbury, all born in Harford Co.; she married Thomas Berry, who was informant, and lived and died in Darlington) [Berkley Memorial Cemetery]

Berry, Henry Wheeler August 27, 1873 – April 3, 1947 (tombstone inscribed Henry W. Berry 1873-1947; death certificate stated he was born at Federal Hill on August 27, 1873, the son of Harry Berry and Sallie Billingsley, both born in Harford Co; he married Mary Ellen ---- (age 65 in 1947), worked as a farmer, and lived and died in rural Shawsville on April 3, 1947; informant was Mary E. Berry, of White Hall; burial was in St. James, Federal Hill, Rocks RFD, and his name is on the same tombstone with Mary E. Berry; Kurtz Funeral Home Record Book 1944-1949, p. 148, stated his wife/widow was Mary Ellen Johnson Berry) [William C. Rice Memorial Cemetery, St. James U. M. Church]

Berry, Joshua died February 22, 1942, age about 83 (no tombstone; Kurtz Funeral Home Record Book 1937-1944, p. 216, stated he was single, worked as a farm laborer and died at home near Jackson's Corner; the names of his parents and their places of birth were not known; death certificate added he was probably born in Baltimore Co. and lived near Jackson's Corner for 2 years and 3 months; informant was Wheeler Berry, of White Hall) [William C. Rice Memorial Cemetery, St. James U. M. Church]

Berry, Kenneth Albert, "Loving Father and Pop Pop" July 27, 1948 – April 16, 2005 [Berkley Memorial Cemetery]

Berry, Kenneth C. 1908-1964 [William C. Rice Memorial Cemetery, St. James U. M. Church]

Berry, Martha A. January 1, 1854 – February 14, 1931 (on same tombstone with Albert Berry; death certificate stated Martha Ann Berry was born in Camden, NJ, the daughter of Hiram Cornish and Nancy O. Laws who were both born in Virginia; she was married and died at Rocks; informant was Albert H. Berry, Jr., of Rocks)

[Chestnut Grove A. M. E. Church Cemetery, formerly LaGrange Cemetery at Rocks]

Berry, Mary died in mid-November 1889, age 80 (no tombstone; obituary in *The Aegis*, November 22, 1889, stated she died at the home of her son Joshua Berry, near Forest Hill; she formerly belonged to and was a highly esteemed servant of the late William Glenn, of Federal Hall) [Hendon Hill Cemetery]

Berry, Mary B. April 5, 1925 -   (on same tombstone with George H. Berry; obituary and photo in *The Aegis* stated Mary Frances Bond Berry died July 1, 2016, age 91, the widow of George H. Berry; she was born in Forest Hill, the daughter of Winfield Marion Bond and Clara Kell, taught school for 51 years beginning in 1946 and became the librarian of the newly named Hickory Elementary School in 1965; she was survived by a son, a daughter, two grandchildren, one nephew, two nieces, other relatives and a special sister Mary Paschall) [Fairview A. M. E. Church Cemetery]

Berry, Mary F. 1880-   (on same tombstone with Henry W. Berry) [William C. Rice Memorial Cemetery, St. James U. M. Church]

Berry, Perry died July 31, 1917, age about 58 (no tombstone; death certificate stated he was the married son of Perry Berry, but mother was unknown; wife not named; informant was Will Jones) [St. James United Cemetery]

Berry, Roosevelt Nelson died October 24, 1990, age 85 (no tombstone; James Dorsey Card File, African American Obituaries, maintained at the Historical Society of Harford County, has a card with his obituary from *The Aegis* on October 31, 1990 stating he was a native of White Hall and the son of John W. Berry and Mary Johnson; he lived in Edgewood and was the husband of the late Ida Christy Berry; he died at Evergreen Nursing Home in Baltimore and was survived by a son, a daughter, three sisters, 10 grandchildren and 18 great-grandchildren) [Clark's U. M. Church Cemetery]

Berry, Rose Ester D. November 10, 1936 – April 9, 1937 (no tombstone; death certificate stated she was born in White Hall, Harford Co., the daughter of N. Rosevelt Berry, born in White Hall, and An *(sic)* Ida Christy, born in Gibson; she died at Thomas Run; informant was her father) [Clark's U. M. Church Cemetery]

Berry, Thomas Irvin January 4, 1907 – August 23, 1934 (no tombstone; death certificate stated he was the son of Henry W. Berry, born at Shawsville and Mary E. Johnson, born at Federal Hill; Martin G. Kurtz Funeral Directors Pocket Memo Book stated he was single, worked as a farm laborer and died at home near Shawsville) [William C. Rice Memorial Cemetery, St. James U. M. Church]

Berry, Victoria Chapman, "Beloved Sister, Mother and Grandmother" February 3, 1952 – February 18, 2014 (inscribed "I fought the good fight, I have finished the course, I have kept my faith. 2 Timothy 4:7;" funeral notice and photo in *The Aegis* on February 26, 2014 stated she died at home in Port Deposit) [Berkley Memorial Cemetery]

Berry, William Edward April 16, 1923 – December 16, 1923 (no tombstone; death certificate stated he was the son of Roosevelt Berry and Ida Cecilia Christy, all born in Maryland, and they lived near Shawsville, White Hall P. O., Maryland; informant was not named on the death certificate) [Clark's U. M. Church Cemetery]

Bessex, Margaret July 24, 1860 – August 29, 1912 (no tombstone; death certificate stated she was the daughter of Samuel Bessex and Sarah Webster, and they all were born in Maryland; she died a widow in Berkley; informant was George Bessex, of Ardmore, PA) [Berkley Memorial Cemetery]

Bessix, Lena died January 16, 1896, age not given (no tombstone; death notice in *The Aegis* on January 24, 1896 stated the girl died at her home near the Rocks, apparently from the effects of poison; her place of burial was not reported, but it was possibly at Chestnut Grove) [Chestnut Grove A. M. E. Church Cemetery, formerly LaGrange Cemetery at Rocks]

Bethea, Clifton E. died August 25, 1990, age not given (no tombstone; James Dorsey Card File, African American Obituaries, maintained at the Historical Society of Harford County, has a card with obituary from *The Aegis* stating he was formerly of Harford County and served in Vietnam from 1969-1971; he died in Baltimore and was survived by his wife Annette J. Bethea, his mother Jessie Bethea, one daughter, one stepdaughter, one sister, two brothers and other relatives) [Tabernacle Mount Zion U. M. Church Cemetery]

Bibbs, Mary Bertha July 4, 1880 – January 29, 1940 (no tombstone; death certificate stated she was born in

Cecil Co., the daughter of Augustus Stokes, born in Cecil Co., mother unknown, and was a widow at death, husband not named; buried in "Union Cemetery, Swan Creek, Md.") [Union U. M. Church Cemetery]

Biggett, Nancy M. (Rev.) died February 5, 1979 age 52 (obituary in *The Aegis* on February 15, 1979 stated Rev. Nancy Marie Divers Bennett, formerly of Jarrettsville, was the wife of Frederick Biggett, of Brooklyn, NY, and died at Coney Island Hospital; she was survived by her husband, two sons, eight grandchildren, three brothers and a sister) [Fairview A. M. E. Church Cemetery]

Biggs, Daniel W. 1921-2004 (small metal funeral home marker) [St. James United Cemetery]

Biggs, Eva M. March 11, 1945 – October 1, 2002 (on same tombstone with Ralph L. Biggs) [St. James United Cemetery]

Biggs, Gertrude E. 1925-1986 (handwritten on a flat cement slab) [St. James United Cemetery]

Biggs, Millicent E. 1926-2014 (small metal funeral home marker) [St. James United Cemetery]

Biggs, Ralph L. November 8, 1947 – April 27, 2005 (on same tombstone with Eva M. Biggs) [St. James United Cemetery]

Billingslea, Caroline, wife of Jacob, died June 11, 1885, age 57 years, 2 months, 29 days [Barn Hill Cemetery]

Billingslea, Jacob died November 18, 1887 in his 65th year [Barn Hill Cemetery]

Billingslea, Jacob September 20, 1843 – January 9, 1926 (no tombstone; death certificate stated he was the son of Samuel Billingslea and Caroline Cole, all born in Maryland; he was single, wroked as a laborer, and died near Bel Air; informant was Mary A. Johnson, of Bel Air RFD #1) [Asbury Cemetery]

Billingslea, Sarah A. July 3, 1853 – November 10, 1935 (no tombstone; death certificate stated she was the daughter of Samuel Billingslea and Caroline Cook, all born in Maryland; she was single, lived near Bel Air and died in Havre de Grace Hospital; informant was Mrs. Winfield Harward, of Bel Air [Asbury Cemetery]

Bishop, ---- premature birth on August 8, 1945, lived only 25 minutes (no tombstone; death certificate stated she was born in Havre de Grace, the daughter of Russel Brinkley, born in Detroit, MI, and Geraldine Bishop, born in Philadelphia, PA; informant was Miss Geraldine Bishop, of 1184 4th St., Perry Point, Cecil Co.; she died in Harford Memorial Hospital) [Gravel Hill Cemetery]

Bishop, Bertha C. February 20, 1886 – August 12, 1943 (on same tombstone with Janice A. Terrell when copied in 1987, but inexplicably not found in 2018; death certificate stated she was the daughter of Isaac Jackson, of Virginia, and Charolet Brown of Forest Hill, MD, and the wife of James H. Bishop, of Havre de Grace; informant was Mrs. Ida Bell Terrell, of Havre de Grace [St. James United Cemetery]

Bishop, Carvel B. February 8, 1925 – October 4, 1954, Maryland, TEC5, 598 QM Laundry Co., World War II [Mt. Zion U. M. Church Cemetery]

Bishop, Derwin Maurice "Reesie" died May 25, 1994, age 27 (no tombstone; obituary and photo in *The Aegis* on June 8, 1994 stated he died unexpectedly in Aberdeen and was survived by his parents George and Anne Bishop, a brother Reginald Bishop, a sister Nerissa Bishop, and a niece) [St. James United Cemetery]

Bishop, Edrie Donald June 14, 1936 – April 16, 1996, SP5, U.S. Army [St. James United Cemetery]

Bishop, Eugene W. died May 15, 2014, age 78 (no tombstone; funeral notice and photo in *The Aegis* on May 21, 2014 stated he lived in Aberdeen and died at Harford Memorial Hospital) [Gravel Hill Cemetery]

Bishop, Faith 1923-1983 (copied in 1987, but not found in 2018) [Mt. Zion U. M. Church Cemetery]

Bishop, George P. 1891-1952 (on same tombstone with George P. Preston) [John Wesley U. M. E. Church Cemetery in Abingdon]

Bishop, George W. April 9, 1940 – October 3, 1995, U.S. Army (tombstone; obituary in *The Aegis* on October 11, 1995 stated George Wesley Bishop was the son of the late Oscar and Sarah Bishop and he worked for Baltimore Gas and Electric for 20 years, retiring in 1992; he loved singing and was member of "The Silvertones" and several church choirs as well as the Gravel Hill Performance Club; he died at home in Havre de Grace and was survived by his wife Ann Bishop, son Reginald Bishop, daughter Nerissa Bishop, six sisters, four brothers, a granddaughter and a host of relatives and friends) [St. James United Cemetery]

Bishop, Hilda M. February 12, 1910 (copied in 1987, but not found in 2018) [St. James United Cemetery]

Bishop, Hortence Irene May 2, 1945 – June 16, 1945 (no tombstone; death certificate stated she was born in Harford Co., the daughter of Oscar Bishop and Sarah Bond, both born in Maryland; informant was Mrs. Oscar Bishop, of Havre de Grace RFD #1) [Gravel Hill Cemetery]

Bishop, Jacob February 20, 1861 – September 9, 1945 (no tombstone; death certificate stated he was retired, born in Maryland and died at Harford Memorial Hospital in Havre de Grace; his parents were unknown to informant Katie Bishop, of Bel Air) [Hendon Hill Cemetery]

Bishop, Jacob A. June 6, 1832 – February 2, 1917 (no tombstone; death certificate stated he was the son of Frank Norton and Cassandra Bishop, and all were born in Maryland; he was married, a retired laborer and died at Mountain; informant was Martha Bishop, of Joppa RFD) [Mt. Zion U. M. Church Cemetery]

Bishop, James I. February 6, 1907 – January 19, 1968, Maryland, PFC, 690 Port Co. TC, World War II [St. James United Cemetery]

Bishop, John Albert February 8, 1941 – September 7, 1941 (no tombstone; death certificate stated he was the son of James Thomas Holland, born in Maryland, and Marion Elizabeth Bishop, born in Cecil Co., and died at home in Havre de Grace) [St. James United Cemetery]

Bishop, John Robert January 13, 1915 – January 25, 1915 (no tombstone; death certificate stated he was the son of William Bishop and Octavia Brown, all born in Harford Co., and died in Bel Air) [Mt. Zion U. M. Church Cemetery]

Bishop, Katie January 1, 1872 – October 13, 1949 (no tombstone; death certificate stated she was born in Harford Co., the daughter of Wesley Moore and Jane Sprigg; she lived at 211 Bond St. in Bel Air and died a widow at 115 Hays St.; informant was Mrs. Fannie Jackson; obituary in *The Aegis* on October 28, 1949 stated she was the wife of the late Jacob Bishop and they were employed for years at the summer home of the late Dr. John M. T. Finney in Bel Air; also stated Katie Bishop placed flowers in the Ames M. E. Church for 25 years and she died at the home of her niece Fanny M. Jackson) [Hendon Hill Cemetery]

Bishop, Martha Jane April 27, 1867 – June 12, 1928 (no tombstone; obituary in *The Aegis* on December 30, 1971 stated Martha Jane Bishop was the daughter of George and Jane Bishop and she had a son "Charles Henry Williams (Jr. Bishop);" her death certificate stated she was born in Maryland, the daughter of Jane Washington, born in Maryland, but her father was not known to the informant Robert Bishop, of Joppa; she died a widow in Harford Memorial Hospital and buried in "Mountain Colored Cemetery") [Mt. Zion U. M. Church Cemetery]

Bishop, Mary 1882 – March 22, 1942 (no tombstone; death certificate stated she was the daughter of Harriet Stump and ---- (blank) Bishop, all born in Maryland; she was single and died in Bel Air where she lived for 20 years; informant was Lillian Bishop, of Havre de Grace) [John Wesley U. M. E. Church Cemetery in Abingdon]

Bishop, Melvin Bernard October 13, 1943 – December 6, 1943 (no tombstone; death certificate stated he was the son of Geraldine Bishop, both born in Harford Co., but his father was not known to informant Mrs. Sarah Bishop, of Havre de Grace RFD # 1) [Gravel Hill Cemetery]

Bishop, Oscar A. Jr. December 26, 1928 – February 17, 2005, U.S. Army (military marker; obituary and photo in *The Aegis* on February 23, 2005 stated Oscar Arnold Bishop was born in Havre de Grace, son of Oscar Jerome Bishop and Sarah Bond, married first to Geraldine Sturdivant, of South Hill, VA, in 1953 and after her passing he married Sarah Nowell; he worked as a nurse technician at the Perry Point VAMC and later was a truck driver and lived in Aberdeen; he died at Perry Point and was survived by his wife, 3 daughters, 2 sons, 1 step-son, 1 step-daughter, 1 step-grandson, 3 sisters, 3 brothers, 12 grandchildren, 4 great-grandchildren, his mother-in-law Carrie B. Sturdivant, and many other relatives) [Gravel Hill Cemetery]

Bishop, Oscar Sr. died August 1, 1979, age 80 (no tombstone; obituary in *The Aegis* on August 16, 1979 stated he was a lifelong resident of Harford County and husband of the late Sarah Bond; he lived in Havre de Grace, worked as a plumber for 26 years, was bass singer for the Silver Tone Quartet, and died at Harford Memorial

Hospital, survived by five sons, six daughters, a sister, a brother and 31 grandchildren) [Gravel Hill Cemetery]

Bishop, Oscar J. March 31, 1899 – August 1, 1979 (on same tombstone with wife Sarah A. Bishop) [Gravel Hill Cemetery]

Bishop, Paul (no dates recorded in 1987, not listed in 2002, and not found in 2018) [Gravel Hill Cemetery]

Bishop, Ralph R. October 11, 1859 – March 9, 1929 (no tombstone; death certificate stated he was a laborer and died in Havre de Grace; parents not known to informant James H. Bishop) [St. James United Cemetery]

Bishop, Richard A. January 16, 1914 – July 30, 1914 (no tombstone; death certificate stated he was the son of Agustus Bishop and Hester Durbin, of Havre de Grace) [St. James United Cemetery]

Bishop, Sarah A. November 28, 1902 – November 14, 1966 (on same tombstone with husband Oscar) [Gravel Hill Cemetery]

Bishop, Viola February 14, 1916 – September 9, 1916 (no tombstone; death certificate stated she was the daughter of Agustus Bishop and Celesta Durbin, of Havre de Grace) [St. James United Cemetery]

Black, Ella August 6, 1877 – February 6, 1941 (no tombstone; death certificate stated she was born in Darlington, did not marry, and died in Harford Memorial Hospital in Havre de Grace, but her parents were unknown) [St. James United Cemetery]

Black, Emma A. February 14, 1885 – April 2, 1922 (no tombstone; death certificate stated she was the married daughter of Edward Rice and "Charlett McCommas," all born in Maryland; informant was Charles W. Dennison, of Perryman) [Union U. M. Church Cemetery]

Black, Hester C., "Wife" April 27, 1918 – November 8, 1975 (tombstone; obituary in *The Aegis* on November 13, 1975 stated she was born in Churchville, the daughter of John and Carrie Smith, and wife of Buddie Lee Black; she later lived in Pennsauken, NJ and died at the University of Pennsylvania Hospital, survived by her husband and her sister Rebecca Pounds, of Churchville [Asbury Cemetery]

Black, Hollis 1914-1979 (copied in 1987, but not found in 2018; he was the lot owner some time after 1951; obituary in *The Aegis* on February 22, 1979 stated he was born in Perryman and retired from Aberdeen Proving Ground, Department of the Army; he lived in Havre de Grace, was married to the late Mary Giles Black, and died at Harford Memorial Hospital, survived by two sisters) [Mt. Calvary U. A. M. E. Church Cemetery]

Black, Sarah F. 1881-1956 [Mt. Calvary U. A. M. E. Church Cemetery]

Blackmon, Thome(?) November 13(?), 1971 – January 17(?), 2005 (a shiny and faded tombstone difficult to read) [Berkley Memorial Cemetery]

Blackwell, Amelia died April 7, 1917, age about 80 (no tombstone; death certificate stated she was a widow when she died at Vale; her parents were unknown to informant Maud Quigley, of Vale) [Tabernacle Mount Zion U. M. Church Cemetery]

Blaine, Charles June 28, 1883 – September 6, 1945 (no tombstone; death certificate stated he was the son of Donald Blaine, both born in Virginia, but his mother's name was not known to informant, his wife, Bessie Blaine (maiden name Lipscomb, born 1876), of Havre de Grace RFD #1; he was a day laborer and lived near Green Spring for the past 16 years) [Green Spring U. M. Church Cemetery]

Blainey, Frank died March 29, 1924, age 76 (no tombstone; death certificate stated he was born in Maryland, married, worked as a laborer and lived at Rocks; his father was James Blainey, born in Maryland; mother's name was unknown to informant Wallice Govens, of Rocks) [Chestnut Grove A. M. E. Church Cemetery, formerly LaGrange Cemetery at Rocks]

Blake, Helmsley died July 26, 1911, age 89 (no tombstone; death certificate stated he was born in Kent Co., MD and worked as a farm laborer near Churchville, but informant Joshua Cooper, of Churchville, did not know his parents' names or places of birth; obituary in *The Aegis* on August 18, 1911 stated "Hemsley Blake" died at the home of his daughter Martha Cooper in Churchville on July 27 *(sic)*, 1911 where he had lived for 2 years; he was the sexton of Grace Episcopal Church in Darlington for many years; he and wife Temperance for 20 years lived at *Meadow Farm*, the summer home of Mr. & Mrs. William Silver, above Darlington, and they took charge of the place in the absence of the family) [Asbury Cemetery]

Blake, Herman, "Husband" November 28, 1923 – August 5, 1989 (on same tombstone with Louisa Blake) [Community Baptist Church Cemetery]

Blake, Herman A. September 3, 1947 – October 14, 1973, Maryland, Sgt., U.S. Air Force, Vietnam [Community Baptist Church Cemetery]

Blake, Louisa, "Wife" February 15, 1927 -   (on same tombstone with Herman Blake) [Community Baptist Church Cemetery]

Blake, Temperance died February 9, 1916, age about 84 (no tombstone; death certificate stated she was the daughter of Abraham Brown and Julia Brown, and they all were born in Maryland; she died a widow in Churchville; informant was Mrs. William Silver, of Aberdeen) [Asbury Cemetery]

Blevins, Ethel Allen January 30, 1920 – May 19, 1997 (no tombstone; The James Dorsey Card File, African American Obituaries, that is maintained at the Historical Society of Harford County, has a card with obituary from an unidentified newspaper on June 4, 1997 stating she was born in Birmingham, AL, the seventh of eight children born to John and Martha Allen; she married James Blevins and after his death she married the late Deacon Jesse Huff, Sr. in 1951; she moved to Maryland and lived in Aberdeen and died at Harford Memorial Hospital, survived by 4 sons, 2 sisters, a daughter-in-law, a son-in-law, 22 grandchildren, 38 great-grandchildren and two special friends Martha Williams and Ann Streeter) [St. James United Cemetery]

Blevins, Willie James August 19, 1941 – March 1, 1985, Pvt., U.S. Army, Vietnam [St. James United Cemetery]

Blocker, Bobby (owner of a lot in section 2 some time after 1951) [Mt. Calvary U. A. M. E. Church Cemetery]

Blume, Harold Jr. June 19, 1951 – May 1, 2015 (inscribed "In Loving Memory Of My Husband") [St. James United Cemetery]

Blume, Melanie N., "Our Loving Daughter and Sister" November 21, 1975 – September 6, 1992 (image of a dog named "Chew" was inscribed on her tombstone) [St. James United Cemetery]

Boanes, Leroy F. 1918-2017 (on same tombstone as Mildred Boanes) [Chestnut Grove A. M. E. Church Cemetery, formerly LaGrange Cemetery at Rocks]

Boanes, Mildred 1917-1998 (on same tombstone as Leroy F. Boanes; obituary of Bessie A. Onely in 1971 indicated she was the mother of Mrs. Mildred Boanes with whom she resided near Delta; obituary on May 6, 1998 of Mildred B. Boanes stated she was born October 25, 1917 in Pylesville, the daughter of Leroy Brown and Bessie Peaco, and married Leroy F. Boanes on December 30, 1940; she retired in 1980 from the Army and Air Force Exchange at Aberdeen Proving Ground, moved to Delta and died at York Hospital on April 30, 1998, survived by her husband, a daughter, a brother, a sister, nine grandchildren seven great-grandchildren and two great-great-grandchildren) [Chestnut Grove A. M. E. Church Cemetery, formerly LaGrange Cemetery at Rocks]

Boddy, Akilah Y. March 20, 1989 – May 10, 2006 ("In Our Hearts Always") [St. James United Cemetery]

Boddy, Arthur H. 1895 – February 5, 1976, U.S. Army (tombstone; military records stated "Arthur Henry Bodder" lived at RFD1, Port Deposit, Cecil Co., was inducted into the service as a pvt. at Conowingo on August 2, 1918, age 24, served in 4 Co. Prov. Dep. Bn. at Camp Sevier, S.C. and in Co. D, 401 Res. Lab. Bn. and was honorably discharged on April 15, 1919) [Berkley Memorial Cemetery]

Boddy, Daisy Agnes died September 3, 1995, age 87 (no tombstone; James Dorsey Card File, African American Obituaries, maintained at the Historical Society of Harford County, has a card with obituary from *The Aegis* on September 13, 1985 stating she was the daughter of George W. Owens and Daisy Tidon (Tildon?) and the widow of Cecil Phillip Boddy; she was an honorary member of the Cecil County Branch of the NAACP and died at home in Port Deposit, survived by a niece, a sister, a godchild, two great-nieces, a great-nephew, four great-great-nieces and two great-great-nephews) [Berkley Memorial Cemetery]

Boddy, Darlene H. 1954-2016 (small metal funeral home marker) [St. James United Cemetery]

Boddy, Elizabeth W. December 27, 1920 – December 18, 1994 (on same tombstone with Horace C. Boddy) [Berkley Memorial Cemetery]

Boddy, Georgianna C. 1888-1970 [Berkley Memorial Cemetery]

Boddy, Horace C. September 20, 1923 -   (on same tombstone with Elizabeth W. Boddy) [Berkley Memorial Cemetery]

Boddy, Horace J. Sr. April 25, 1890 – November 5, 1975 [Berkley Memorial Cemetery]

Boddy, Louise L. "Mother" 1894-   (silver letters mounted on a flat cement slab) [St. James United Cemetery]

Boddy, Sherry S. 1985-2010 (small metal funeral home marker) [St. James United Cemetery]

Bolden, Justin E. Sr. "Loving Son, Brother, Father and Friend" June 24, 1982 – May 30, 2008 (also with a picture of him that is inscribed at the bottom "Kan't Get Right") [Asbury Cemetery]

Bolden, Margaret E. 1894-1958 (copied in 1987, but not found in 2018) [Mt. Calvary U. A. M. E. Church Cemetery]

Bolling, Dayvon D'Baz October 6, 2000 – November 8, 2000 (bear-shaped tombstone) [St. James United Cemetery]

Bolling, Lisa 1963-1986 [St. James United Cemetery]

Bond, ---- (female) June 28, 1945 – July 6, 1945, a premature birth (no tombstone; Kurtz Funeral Home Record Book 1944-1949, p. 70, stated she was born in Jarrettsville and died at University Hospital in Baltimore, but the names of her parents were not given) [Fairview A. M. E. Church Cemetery]

Bond, ---- stillborn female on February 15, 1930 (no tombstone; death certificate stated she was the daughter of Harrison Horsey, born in Maryland, and Linda Bond, born in Aberdeen; she died in Havre de Grace Hospital; informant was George Bond, of Aberdeen) [Mt. Calvary U. A. M. E. Church Cemetery]

Bond, ---- stillborn male on May 28, 1941 (no tombstone; death certificate stated he was born at Magnolia, the son of Joseph Leon Bond, born in Bel Air, and Mary Charlotte Chase, born in Magnolia; informant was his father) [Community Baptist Church Cemetery]

Bond, ---- stillborn male on May 28, 1941 (no tombstone; death certificate stated he was born in Magnolia, the son of Joseph Leon Bond, born in Bel Air, and Mary Charlotte Chase, born in Magnolia, and he was buried by his father in the Baptist Cemetery in Magnolia) [Foster's Hill Cemetery]

Bond, A. Elizabeth November 2, 1863 – March 2, 1927 (no tombstone; death certificate stated she was the daughter of William Dorsey and Linda Jamison, all born in Maryland; she was a widow who died near Carsins Run; informant was Ella Harris Warfield, of Havre de Grace) [Asbury Cemetery]

Bond, Adam died on April 25, 1927, "date of birth don't know, 1840," age 87 (no tombstone; death certificate stated he was a widower who was a laborer and lived in Pylesville; his parents' names and birth places were not known to informant Frank Buchanan, of Pylesville) [Chestnut Grove A. M. E. Church Cemetery, formerly LaGrange Cemetery at Rocks]

Bond, Agnes Gertrude February 21, 1924 – May 14, 2006 (tombstone contains her picture; obituary in *The Aegis* on May 17, 2016 stated she lived in Darlington and was survived by a brother Earl Wilson, Sr. and a sister Marian Davis, both of Baltimore) [Cedars Chapel Cemetery]

Bond, Albert January 21, 1921 – March 14, 1929 (no tombstone; death certificate stated he was the son of David Bond and Helen B. Taylor, all were born in Maryland, and he died in Havre de Grace Hospital; informant was David Bond, of Aberdeen) [Mt. Calvary U. A. M. E. Church Cemetery]

Bond, Alexander died June 9, 1943 (no tombstone; obituary in *The Aegis* on June 18, 1943 stated he died on June 9, 1943, age 81, and had been a faithful employee on the farm of former Judge W. W. Preston for the past 41 years; survived by his wife Alice J. Bond; death certificate stated he died "June 9, 1943, aged 70, born 1866" *(sic)* in Emmorton; his parents were Joshua Bond and Alice Bond) [Hendon Hill Cemetery]

Bond, Alice J. May 5, "1869? age 76?" *(sic)* – May 27, 1946 (no tombstone; death certificate stated she was a widow, born in Harford Co., and lived near Bel Air for 42 years; her parents were Ratt Collins and Jane Archer, both born in Maryland; informant was Lucy Johnson, of Bel Air) [Hendon Hill Cemetery]

Bond, Amelia A. "Mother" 1870-1947 (on same tombstone with George W. Bond, which states she was born in 1870, but her death certificate stated Amelia Armstrong Bond was born on November 28, 1872, the daughter of Lawson Harris and Margaret ---- (unknown), all born in Harford County; she died a widow on January 12, 1947; informant was Miss Lucy A. Bond, of Havre de Grace RFD #1) [Gravel Hill Cemetery]

Bond, Ananias "Niah" died in late October, 1884, at a good old age (no tombstone; death notice in *The Aegis* on November 7, 1884 stated he died one day last week on the farm of William Hopkins, Jr., near Glenville; he had never been a slave and was the son of the well-known Prush Bond of the Big Woods; place of burial was not given [possibly Asbury Cemetery]

Bond, Anita A. 1916-1970 (on same tombstone with Webster Bond) [Berkley Memorial Cemetery]

Bond, Anna Bell stillborn on July 21, 1926 (no tombstone; death certificate stated she was born and died at home near Aberdeen, the daughter of George Bond and May Thomas, both were born in Maryland; informant was her father) [Mt. Calvary U. A. M. E. Church Cemetery]

Bond, Annie April 3, 1901 – February 28, 1923 (no tombstone; death certificate stated she was the daughter of Howard Stewart and Ada May Kell, all born in Maryland; she was married and died at Forest Hill; informant, her father, made his "X" mark on the death certificate) [Fairview A. M. E. Church Cemetery]

Bond, Annie B. February 23, 1914 – October 1, 1914 (no tombstone; death certificate stated she was the daughter of Walter H. Bond and Millie Dorsey, all born in Harford Co.; she died at home in Bel Air; informant was Walter H. Bond, of Bel Air) [Hendon Hill Cemetery]

Bond, Arthur died January 22, 1975, age 70 (no tombstone; obituary in *The Aegis* on January 30, 1975 stated he was born in Van Bibber, the son of Grover Bond and Alice Waters, and lived his entire life in the Edgewood area, lately at 1209 Van Bibber Road; he died at Harbor View Nursing Home in Baltimore, survived by five sisters) [Community Baptist Church Cemetery]

Bond, Asbury E. 1928-2011 (small metal funeral home marker) [Mt. Calvary U. A. M. E. Church Cemetery]

Bond, Bella B. 1901-1989 (on same tombstone with husband C. Leon Bond) [Gravel Hill Cemetery]

Bond, Beulah Thompson died August 20, 1972, age 66 (no tombstone; obituary in *The Aegis* on August 24, 1972 stated she was born in Harford Co., the daughter of Mabel Brown Thompson Dallam, of Brooklyn, NY, and the late Charles Thompson; she was the widow of William Bond, of 413 Hanover St., Aberdeen, and was survived by her mother and two sisters) [Green Spring U. M. Church Cemetery]

Bond, Burns McKinley May 4, 1897 – October 1, 1970, Maryland, PFC, 1st Aviation Sq., AAF, World War II (tombstone; military records stated he was born at Churchville where he was inducted into World War I on September 26, 1918; he was a private in the 154th Dep. Brig., the 333 Aux Rmt Dep 10, the 354th Field Rmt Sq., and honorably discharged on May 17, 1919; obituary in *The Aegis* on October 8, 1970 stated he was the son of Elizabeth Bond, of Glenville Road in Churchville, served in World War I and World War II, was a retired employee of the Board of Education and died at Harford Memorial Hospital) [Asbury Cemetery]

Bond, C. Leon 1902-1967 (on same tombstone with wife Bella B. Bond; copied as Carl Bond in 1987]

Bond, Carl Allen March 2, 1945 – September 28, 1945 (no tombstone; death certificate stated he was born in Baltimore, the son of Harry Philmore Bond and Lida Taylor, both born in Maryland; he died in Harford Memorial Hospital and his usual residence was in Perry Point, Cecil Co.; informant was his father who lived at 11834 4th Street, Perry Point) [Gravel Hill Cemetery]

Bond, Carolyn M. January 1, 1964 – December 4, 2012 (inscribed "Jesus Love Me This I Know") [Berkley Memorial Cemetery]

Bond, Carroll S. May 15, 1917 – March 14, 1961, Maryland, Pvt., Co B, 1323 Engr. GS Regt, World War II [Mt. Calvary U. A. M. E. Church Cemetery]

Bond, Celeste (owner of a lot in section 24 some time after 1951) [Mt. Calvary U. A. M. E. Church Cemetery]

Bond, Charles July 19, 1919 – April 10, 1929 (no tombstone; death certificate stated he was the son of David Bond and Helen Taylor, all were born in Maryland, and he died in Havre de Grace Hospital; informant was

David Bond, of Aberdeen) [Mt. Calvary U. A. M. E. Church Cemetery]

Bond, Charles "Brother Pew" 1909-1983 (tombstone; obituary in *The Aegis* on June 23, 1983 stated "Charles (Brother Pugh) Albert Bond" was born in New York City and resided in Maryland for the past 60 years; he was a self-employed tax driver in Havre de Grace for the past 20 years and died on June 15, 1983 at Harford Memorial Hospital, survived by his wife Marie Bond, 14 children, 43 grandchildren and 40 great-grandchildren) [St. James United Cemetery]

Bond, Charles Elsworth died June 26, 1995, age 66 (no tombstone; James Dorsey Card File, African American Obituaries, maintained at the Historical Society of Harford County, has a card with obituary from *The Aegis* July 7, 1995 stating he was the son of John L. Bond and Olivia Cole and served in the Army for 22 years, retiring in 1968; he lived in Bel Air and died at Fort Howard VA Medical Center, survived by a sister, three nieces and two nephews) [Mt. Calvary U. A. M. E. Church Cemetery]

Bond, Charles H. died August 25, 1906, age 2 months (no tombstone; death certificate stated he was the son of Harriet Bond, both born in Maryland, but his father was unknown to informant Jane Bond, his grandmother; he died in Bel Air and on the back of death certificate it is written "Hendon Hill") [Hendon Hill Cemetery]

Bond, Charles W. 1910-1977 (inscribed "Rest in Peace"; obituary in *The Aegis* on August 4, 1977 stated Charles Wesley Bond was born in Harford Co., son of George and Amelia Bond, married Mary H. ----; he retired from the Harford County Board of Education, lived in Baltimore and died on July 31, 1977 at John L. Deaton Medical Center, survived by his wife, a brother Harry Bond, and 3 sisters Josephine Hilton, Estella Jones and Lucy Bond) [Gravel Hill Cemetery]

Bond, Charlotte October 21, 1826 – November 1, 1876 [Tabernacle Mount Zion U. M. Church Cemetery]

Bond, Clara V. 1884-1954 (inscribed "At Rest With God") [Fairview A. M. E. Church Cemetery]

Bond, Daisey February 14, 1906 – November 22, 1928 (no tombstone; death certificate stated she was born in Maryland, the daughter of Edward Wright, born in North Carolina, and Josephine ----, born in Maryland; she married ---- and died in Havre de Grace; informant was her father) [St. James United Cemetery]

Bond, David April 7, 1916 – November 20, 1916 (no tombstone; death certificate stated he was the son of Layton Kyler and Agnes Bond, and died in Havre de Grace; mother was informant) [St. James United Cemetery]

Bond, Della died January 22, 1927, age about 50 (no tombstone; death certificate stated she was a widow and cook who did housework in Bel Air; her father was William Johnson, but her mother was unknown to informant Lucy Brown; they were all born in Maryland) [Hendon Hill Cemetery]

Bond, Doris "Leona" Stevenson December 3, 1946 – June 19, 2003 (inscribed "Father I Stretch My Hand To Thee. Psalm 88:9") [Union U. M. Church Cemetery]

Bond, Dorothy V. September 17, 1923 – January 16, 1978 [Berkley Memorial Cemetery]

Bond, Dortha July 13, 1928 – April 4, 1929 (no tombstone; death certificate stated she was the daughter of David Bond and Helen Taylor, all were born in Maryland, and she died in Havre de Grace Hospital; informant was David Bond, of Aberdeen) [Mt. Calvary U. A. M. E. Church Cemetery]

Bond, Douglas stillborn male on April 5, 1932 (no tombstone; death certificate stated he was the son of Harry Clark, born in Maryland, and Linda M. Bond, born in Harford Co.; he died at home near Aberdeen; informant was May Bond, of Aberdeen) [Mt. Calvary U. A. M. E. Church Cemetery]

Bond, E. Marie March 19, 1914 – November 28, 2000 (no tombstone; obituary in *The Aegis* on December 1, 2000 stated she was born in Bel Air, the daughter of Eugene and Ollie Brown and the youngest of two children; she was raised by her grandmother because her mother died when she was 6 years old; she married the late Herbert Winfield Bond and had two sons; she sang soprano in the Fairview Church choir, was a Sunday School teacher and trained children for the Tot's Choir which she organized; she was survived by two sons, three grandchildren, six great-grandchildren and one great-great-grandchild) [Fairview A. M. E. Church Cemetery]

Bond, Edna July 17, 1904 – August 31, 1925 (no tombstone; death certificate stated she was the daughter of Charles Thompson and Mabel Brown, all born in Maryland; she was married and died in the Havre de Grace

Hospital; informant was Allie Bond, of Aberdeen) [Green Spring U. M. Church Cemetery]

Bond, Eleanor (no dates recorded in 1987, not listed in 2002, and not found in 2018) [Gravel Hill Cemetery]

Bond, Eliza 1907-1978 [Gravel Hill Cemetery]

Bond, Eliza died January 16, 1917, age about 37 (no tombstone; death certificate stated she was the daughter of Samuel and Ellen Turner, all born in Harford County; she was married and lived and died near Havre de Grace; informant was John Bond, of Havre de Grace) [Asbury Cemetery]

Bond, Elizabeth born about July 1840 – October 24, 1930 (no tombstone; death certificate stated she was born in Maryland, the daughter of Basil C. Kell, born in Maryland, but her mother's name was not known to informant Jehu Nelson Johnson, of 2514 Oak St., Baltimore; she was a widow at the time of her death at home at Grafton Shops) [Fairview A. M. E. Church Cemetery]

Bond, Ella May March 25, 1941 – August 30, 1942 (no tombstone; death certificate stated she was the daughter of Charles Bond and Catherine Barnes, of Havre de Grace) [St. James United Cemetery]

Bond, Ellanora March 18, 1871 – April 27, 1911 (no tombstone; death certificate stated she was born in Harford Co., the daughter of Lewis Tillman, born on the Eastern Shore of Maryland, and Delia Wilson, born in Harford Co.; she was married (husband was not named) and died at home in Fallston; informant was Julia Cephas, of 20 W. Lafayette Ave. in Baltimore) [Fairview A. M. E. Church Cemetery]

Bond, Ellen (no dates recorded in 1987, not listed in 2002 and not found in 2018; death certificate stated Ellen E. Bond was born January 7, 1898 and died September 24, 1924; she was the daughter of Albert Stokes and Rachel Gibson, all born in Maryland; she died near Havre de Grace; informant was Harry Bond, of Gravelly Hill; marriage certificate stated Ellen Elizabeth Stokes married Harry Fillmore Bond in 1917) [Gravel Hill Cemetery]

Bond, Emma February –, 1826 – December 26, 1893 ("In Memory Of") [Union U. M. Church Cemetery]

Bond, Emma Howard died January 16, 1971, age 98 (no tombstone; obituary in *The Aegis* stated she was born in Emmorton, the daughter of Stephen Peaker and Eliza Bishop, and was the widow of Walter Bond, of 131 Alice Anne St., Bel Air; she was a lifetime member of Mt Zion Methodist Church in Joppa and was employed by the Boyd Bell family at Windy Walls Farm in Emmorton for over 50 years; she died at the Brevin Nursing Home in Havre de Grace, survived by one son, Calvin Miles Bond, and a number of nieces and nephews) [Mt. Zion U. M. Church Cemetery]

Bond, Emma July 17, 1914 – March 18, 1969 [Mt. Calvary U. A. M. E. Church Cemetery]

Bond, Ethel E. January 3, 1901 – July 30, 1911 (no tombstone; death certificate stated she was born in Philadelphia, PA, the daughter of William Henry Bond, of Glenville, Harford Co., and Margaret E. Mann, of Harford Co.; she died in Darlington; informant was her father) [Green Spring U. M. Church Cemetery]

Bond, Ethel Marie March 19, 1914 – November 8, 2000 (on same tombstone with Herbert W. Bond) [Fairview A. M. E. Church Cemetery]

Bond, Florence A. "Sister" 1916-1965 (on same tombstone with John E. Bond when copied in 1987, but not found in 2018) [Fairview A. M. E. Church Cemetery]

Bond, Frances "Tootsie" December 10, 1934 – September 29, 1997 (no tombstone; James Dorsey Card File, African American Obituaries, that is maintained at the Historical Society of Harford County, has a card with obituary from an unidentified newspaper on October 8, 1997 stating she was born in Havre de Grace, the daughter of Catherine Barnes, of Aberdeen, and the late Charles Bond, and in the early 1960s she moved to New York City where she worked for the Department of Parks and Recreation; she married (husband's name was not given), lived in Manhattan and died at Cabrini Hospital, survived by her mother, four daughters, two sons, two brothers, 8 sisters, 13 grandchildren and 2 great-grandchildren) [St. James United Cemetery]

Bond, Frances L. January 20, 1935 -   (on same tombstone with William H. Bond inscribed "In Loving Memory" with their photos and images of a tractor and a teddy bear) [Berkley Memorial Cemetery]

Bond, Frances Olivia January 1, 1863 – January 3, 1947 (no tombstone; death certificate stated she was born in

Ohio, parents unknown, and she married William Bond and later divorced; informant was James E. Williams, of Havre de Grace) [St. James United Cemetery]

Bond, Franklin December 1, 1932 – January 10, 1933 (no tombstone; death certificate stated he was the son of David Bond and Helen Taylor, all were born in Maryland, and he died at home in Aberdeen RFD; informant was David Bond, of Aberdeen) [Mt. Calvary U. A. M. E. Church Cemetery]

Bond, George born "about 14 Oct 18—," died June 2, 1932, age 79 years, 7 months (no tombstone; death certificate stated he was the son of Phoebe Hall, father unknown, and the wife of informant Elizabeth Bond; he died at the County Home in Bel Air) [Union U. M. Church Cemetery]

Bond, George died November 10, 1912, age 6 (no tombstone; death certificate stated he was the son of George E. Bond and L. Moore, all born in Harford Co.; died in Aberdeen) [Mt. Calvary U. A. M. E. Church Cemetery]

Bond, George D. died July 7, 1888, in his 18th year [Hendon Hill Cemetery]

Bond, George E. died February 9, 1928, age about 75 (no tombstone; death certificate stated he was born in Harford Co., the son of George and Rachel Bond, and was married, worked as a shoemaker and lived near Bel Air; informant was Wesley Bond, of Fallston) [Tabernacle Mount Zion U. M. Church Cemetery]

Bond, George Henry July 10, 1872 – April 1, 1916 (tombstone; death certificate stated he was the son of Henry Watters and Harriett Bond and all were born in Harford Co.; he was married, worked as a day laborer and died in Benson; informant was Harriett Bond, of Benson) [Tabernacle Mount Zion U. M. Church Cemetery]

Bond, George Herbert died May 20, 1968, age 79 (obituary in *The Aegis* stated he was the husband of Ella Smith Bond of Churchville and died at Harford Memorial Hospital in Havre de Grace) [Asbury Cemetery]

Bond, George W. "Father" 1867-1944 (on same tombstone with Amelia A. Bond, but death certificate stated George Washington Bond was born March 5, 1873 *(sic)*; he was the son of Harry Bond and "Sarah Bond unk." and all were born in Pennsylvania; he was a farmer near Havre de Grace, married Amelia A. ---- and died July 9, 1944; informant was his wife Amelia A. Bond, of Havre de Grace RFD #1) [Gravel Hill Cemetery]

Bond, Gladys L. 1917-1996 (on same tombstone with Howard S. Bond and inscribed "Asleep In Jesus;" James Dorsey Card File, African American Obituaries, that is maintained at the Historical Society of Harford County, has a card with obituary from an unidentified newspaper on June 5, 1996 stating Gladys Louise Bond was born in Jarrettsville, the daughter of the late Mattie Virginia Turner and the wife of the late Howard Bond; she died at her home in Bel Air on May 29, 1996, survived by a son, an aunt and several nieces and nephews) [Fairview A. M. E. Church Cemetery]

Bond, Glucas died December 22, 1921, age 2 months (no tombstone; death certificate stated he was the son of Alex and Elenor Bond, all born in Maryland and lived near Bel Air; informant was Graham Brown, of Forest Hill) [Tabernacle Mount Zion U. M. Church Cemetery]

Bond, Gover February 28, 1911 – October 10, 1989 (on same tombstone with Pauline Bond; obituary in *The Aegis* on October 18, 1989 stated he was born in Churchville, the son of the late Martha Bond Prigg and Steve Dorsey; he married Pauline E. ---- and worked for the Penn Central Railroad Co. for 35 years; he died at home in Darlington and was survived by his wife, three sons, five daughters, twelve grandchildren and two great-grandchildren) [Berkley Memorial Cemetery]

Bond, Harriet B. December 12, 1915 – September 21, 1916 (no tombstone; death certificate stated she died in Bel Air, the daughter of John L. Bond and Olivia V. Bond, both born in Harford Co.) [Hendon Hill Cemetery]

Bond, Harriett Ellen February 15, 1859 – August 25, 1946 (no tombstone; death certificate stated she was born at Perryman, was a widow, and had lived in Bel Air for 70 years; her parents were Henry and Eliza Hollingsworth, both born in Maryland; informant was John Bond, of Bel Air) [Hendon Hill Cemetery]

Bond, Harry September 14, 1894 – June 11, 1990, U.S. Army, World War I (tombstone; military records stated Harry Fillmore Bond lived at Havre de Grace RFD #1, was inducted on June 19, 1918, served in the 45th Co., 154 Dep. Brig. and Co. A, 371st Inf., was overseas at Meuse-Argonne and Bonhomme Sector, and was honorably discharged on February 27, 1919; obituary in *The Aegis* on June 13, 1990 stated Harry F. Bond, Sr. was a lifelong resident of Harford Co., the son of George William Bond and Amelia Harris; he married Eliza Taylor, who predeceased him, and he died at Perry Point VAMC, survived by 8 children, 57 grandchildren, 55 great-grandchildren and 8 great-great-grandchildren) [Gravel Hill Cemetery]

Bond, Helen April 22, 1896 – January 8, 1939 (no tombstone; death certificate stated she was born in Harford Co., the daughter of John Taylor, born in Harford Co., and Martha Rumsey, born in Maryland, married David Bond, lived and died at Stepney, Aberdeen RFD where she had lived for 25 years; informant was her husband David Bond) [Mt. Calvary U. A. M. E. Church Cemetery]

Bond, Helen August 13, 1946 – February 4, 1950 (no tombstone; death certificate stated she was born in Bel Air, daughter of Joseph Bond and Mary Chase; she was burned at home when her clothes caught on fire in Emmorton and died at Harford Memorial Hospital in Havre de Grace after a 9 hour stay; informant was her mother Mary Bond; she was buried in "Mountain Colored Cemetery, Joppa") [Mt. Zion U. M. Church Cemetery]

Bond, Henrietta Mae died April 19, 1970, age not given (no tombstone; obituary in *The Aegis* on April 23, 1970 stated she lived at Bel Air RFD #1, Box 370A, and died at Harford Memorial Hospital in Havre de Grave; she was a Smith and the widow of Herbert Bond and she was survived by 1 daughter, 1 brother, 6 grandchildren and 10 great-grandchildren) [Asbury Cemetery]

Bond, Henry died July 15, 1916, age 72 (no tombstone; death certificate stated Henry (possibly W. Henry) Bond was the son of Joshua Bond and Charlotte DeCourcy, all born in Harford Co.; he was a widower and a laborer when he died in Bel Air; informant was Ella Scott) [Tabernacle Mount Zion U. M. Church Cemetery]

Bond, Herbert W. January 29, 1907 – July 26, 1992 (Masonic symbol inscribed on the same tombstone with Ethel Marie Bond; James Dorsey Card File, African American Obituaries, maintained at the Historical Society of Harford County, has a card with the obituary of Herbert Winfield Bond from *The Aegis* on July 29, 1992 stating he was born in Pleasantville, near Pleasantville Road in Fallston, the son of Winfield M. Bond and Clara Kell, and married Marie Brown in 1929; he was formerly of Jarrettsville, lived in Darlington, worked as farmer and was also employed at the old Richardson Pharmacy in Bel Air for 16 years; he died at Harford Memorial Hospital in Havre de Grace, survived by his wife, two sons, two sisters, three grandchildren and five great-grandchildren) [Fairview A. M. E. Church Cemetery]

Bond, Howard S. 1912-1970 (on same tombstone with Gladys L. Bond inscribed "Asleep In Jesus;" obituary in *The Aegis* on April 23, 1970 stated Howard Stanley Bond, husband of Gladys Louise Turner Bond, of 119 Archer St., Bel Air, died April 19, 1970 at Harford Memorial Hospital; he was a mason and was survived by his wife, one brother, Herbert W. Bond, and two sisters, Margaret Robinson and Mary Berry) [Fairview A. M. E. Church Cemetery]

Bond, Isabella Rebecca died April 3, 1974, age 84 (no tombstone; James Dorsey Card File, African American Obituaries, maintained at the Historical Society of Harford County, has a card with an obituary from *The Aegis* on April 13, 1974 stating she was the second of seven daughters born to Mabel E. Fleet, of Baltimore, and George H. Thompson, and the widow of Norvel "Shimmy" Bond; a native of Havre de Grace she retired after 25 years as a nursing assistant at the Perry Point VA Medical Center; she was survived by 4 sons, 4 daughters, 13 grandchildren and 12 great-grandchildren) [St. James United Cemetery]

Bond, Jerry Lewis died January 18, 1990, age 56 (obituary in *The Aegis* on January 31, 1990 stated he was the son of the late David Bond and Helen Taylor, and husband of Evelyn Bond; he served in the U.S. Army during the Korean War, worked as a mechanic at Aberdeen Proving Ground., lived in Darlington and died at Perry Point Veterans Administration Hospital; he was survived by his wife, two sons, three daughters, two brothers and one sister) [Berkley Memorial Cemetery]

Bond, John died January 19, 1917, age about 40 (no tombstone; death certificate stated he was the son of George Bond and both born in Harford Co., but informant Augustus Johnson, of Havre de Grace, did not know John's mother's name; he was a laborer and widower) [Asbury Cemetery]

Bond, John stillborn male on November 3, 1930 (no tombstone; death certificate stated he was the son of Harry Clark and Linda Bond, all were born in Maryland; he died at home near Aberdeen; informant was Mrs. John Horner, of Aberdeen) [Mt. Calvary U. A. M. E. Church Cemetery]

Bond, John E. May 30, 1922 – April 9, 1989, U.S. Army, WW II [Mt. Calvary U. A. M. E. Church Cemetery]

Bond, John E. "Brother" 1920-1965 (on same tombstone with Florence A. Bond when copied in 1987, but not found in 2018) [Fairview A. M. E. Church Cemetery]

Bond, John H. died January 3, 1933, age not given (no tombstone; James Dorsey Card File, African American Obituaries, maintained at the Historical Society of Harford County, has a card with obituary from the *Bel Air Times* on January 27, 1933 stating he spent the greater part of his life at Benson and died at the home of his daughter in Towson) [Mt. Zion U. M. Church Cemetery]

Bond, John H. October 29, 1848 – September 3, 1928 (no tombstone; death certificate stated he was the son of Moses Bond and Lydia Bachlor, all born in Maryland; he was married and worked as a farmer in Castleton; informant was Moses A. Bond of 3111 Barclay St., Baltimore) [Berkley Memorial Cemetery]

Bond, John Henry died July 24, 1976, age not given (no tombstone; obituary in *The Aegis* on July 29, 1976 stated he married Alice Felter, lived at 853 Erie St. in Havre de Grace, managed the Little Wonders Quartet in Havre de Grace for 37 years, and died at Union Hospital in Elkton, survived by his wife, 3 sons, 4 daughters, 4 brothers, and 1 sister) [Mt. Calvary U. A. M. E. Church Cemetery]

Bond, John L. 1884-1966 [Mt. Calvary U. A. M. E. Church Cemetery]

Bond, John T. February 14, 1862 – January 16, 1923 (no tombstone; death certificate stated he was the son of Marca Bond and both were born in Harford Co., but his mother's name was not known to informant John W. Bond, Jr., of Bel Air RFD #1; he was married and worked as a laborer in Churchville) [Asbury Cemetery]

Bond, John W. died December 27, 1926, age 51 (no tombstone; death certificate stated he was married, worked as a laborer, committed suicide at Pylesville and buried in Lagrange Cemetery; he was the son of John Bond Sr. and Hannah Morgan, and all were born in Maryland; informant was Millie Smith, of Cardiff) [Chestnut Grove A. M. E. Church Cemetery, formerly LaGrange Cemetery at Rocks]

Bond, John W. September 20, 1864 – January 19, 1938 (no tombstone; death certificate stated he was born in Pennsylvania, the son of Henry Bond and Sarah Cole, both born in Harford Co.; he married Sarah Cole who had predeceased him; he was a laborer near Level and died near Havre de Grace; informant was Joshua Bond, of Aldino) [Green Spring U. M. Church Cemetery]

Bond, John Westly August 28, 1889 – May 23, 1937 (no tombstone; death certificate stated he was the son of John H. Bond and Sarah Prigg, all born in Harford Co.; he was single, worked as a farm laborer until June 1936 and died in Darlington; informant was Diana James, 48 E. Penn St., Germantown, Philadelphia, PA) [Berkley Memorial Cemetery]

Bond, Joseph Leon died September 4, 1996, age 75 (no tombstone; obituary and photo from *The Aegis* on September 11, 1996 stating he was born in Bel Air, the son of Grover Bond and Emma Smart; he worked for Robert J. Magness for 35 years and was a custodial worker at Southampton Middle School for 16 years; he married (wife's name was not given), lived in Bel Air and died at the Bel Air Nursing and Rehabilitation Center, survived by 3 sons, 3 daughters, 12 grandchildren, 11 great-grandchildren) [Mt. Zion U. M. Church Cemetery]

Bond, Josephine September 8, 1867 – August 4, 1934 (no tombstone; death certificate stated she was the daughter of Abraham Prigg and Jane Stansberry, all born in Harford Co.; she married Joshua Bond and lived and died at Aberdeen RFD #2; informant was Joshua Bond) [Asbury Cemetery]

Bond, Joshua died December 18, 1919, age 62 (no tombstone; death certificate stated he was born in Maryland and was a widower and laborer when he died in Bel Air; his parents were not known to informant William Buckannan, of Bel Air) [Tabernacle Mount Zion U. M. Church Cemetery]

Bond, Joshua March 15, 1855 – January 16, 1942 (no tombstone; death certificate stated he was the son of Harry Bond and Sarah ----, all born in Pennsylvania; married Josephine ----, worked as a farmer near Darlington and died at Harford Memorial Hospital in Havre de Grace; informant was Mr. Verden Bond, of Darlington RFD) [Asbury Cemetery]

Bond, Julia, "Mother of Charles & James Bond" (no dates on tombstone; death certificate stated Julia Ann Bond died on March 19, 1907, age 89; she was born in Harford County, married William Henry Bond and died in Forest Hill; her father was Charles Williams, born in Harford County, but her mother's name was not known to informant James Bond, her son) [Fairview A. M. E. Church Cemetery]

Bond, Larry Wynfield June 18, 1952 – March 2, 1990 (inscribed with an image of a car and "We Love You, But Jesus Loves You Best;" obituary in *The Aegis* on March 7, 1990 stated he was born in Havre de Grace, son of William H. Bond and Frances Hall, of Darlington; he was credit manager for General Electric, lived in Darlington, and died in Fallston General Hospital as the result of an automobile accident; he was survived by his parents, a brother Keith Bond, a sister Kathy Butler, his paternal grandparents Herbert and Marie Bond, his maternal grandparents Losin and Katherine Hall, and five nieces) [Fairview A. M. E. Church Cemetery]

Bond, Laura died December 29, 1892, age 50 (inscribed "In Memory Of") [Union U. M. Church Cemetery]

Bond, Leander October 3, 1905 – February 15, 1976 (no tombstone; obituary in *The Aegis* on February 19, 1976 stated he was the son of David Bond and Mary Baty, lived with his cousin Miss Lucy Bond at 4140 Gravel Hill Road, was a retired custodian for the Board of Education and died at Harford Memorial Hospital in Havre de Grace) [Gravel Hill Cemetery]

Bond, Linda M. 1907-2005 (tombstone; obituary and photo in *The Aegis* on January 19, 2005 stated Linda May Bond was born in Aberdeen, the daughter of George Edward Bond and May M. Thomas; she was self-employed, lived in Aberdeen and was a member of the Stewardess Board and Willing Workers at Mt. Calvary UAME Church; she died at Citizens Care Center in Havre de Grace, survived by a son John H. Bond, 3 daughters Rebecca V. Lucas, Alice M. Walker and Bertha A. Watkins, a brother Ashbury E. Bond, 15 grandchildren, and several great-grandchildren and great-great-grandchildren) [Mt. Calvary U. A. M. E. Church Cemetery]

Bond, Lindsay A. died September 24, 1989, age 61 (no tombstone; obituary in *The Aegis* on October 4, 1989 stated he was the son of Harry F. Bond, Sr. and the late Eliza Taylor, and husband of Barbara Bond, of Joppatowne; he served in the U.S. Army from 1947 to 1950, was a licensed practical nurse for the Veterans Adminstration at Perry Point, MD and Palo Alto, CA, and in 1983 he became minister of music at St. James AME Church in Gravel Hill) [Gravel Hill Cemetery]

Bond, Lisa Marie September 4, 1968 – November 27, 2006 [Fairview A. M. E. Church Cemetery]

Bond, Lizzie E. died October 5, 1902, age 62 (no tombstone; death certificate stated she was the wife of Elias Bond, but her parents were unknown; she was born in Harford County and died at Mountain; place of burial not given [probably Mt. Zion U. M. Church Cemetery]

Bond, Lucy Alberta 1906-1991 (tombstone; obituary in *The Aegis* on November 13, 1991 stated she was the daughter of George W. and Amelia Bond, was a lifelong resident of Havre de Grace, retired from the dietetic area of the Perry Pont VA Medical Center, was the organist at St. James AME Church in Gravel Hill for 50 years, and raised her nephew Charles Jamison) [Gravel Hill Cemetery]

Bond, Lucy Jane November 6, 1876 – September 8, 1926 (no tombstone; death certificate stated she was the daughter of Lewis Jenkins and Fannie Turner, all born in Maryland; she was married and died at home in Bel Air; informant was Gorge W. Bond) [Fairview A. M. E. Church Cemetery]

Bond, Lydia A. died January 2, 1917, age about 90 (no tombstone; death certificate stated she was born in Maryland, the daughter of Stephen Bachler, born in Pennsylvania, but informant John H. Bond, of Castleton, did not know her mother's name; she died a widow in Castleton) [Berkley Memorial Cemetery]

Bond, Malinda (owner of a lot in section 45 some time after 1951) [Mt. Calvary U. A. M. E. Church Cemetery]

Bond, Malinda August 2, 1869 – April 27, 1935 (no tombstone; death certificate stated she was the daughter of Henry Moore and Elizabeth Dorsey, all were born in Harford Co.; she was the widow of George Wesley Bond and worked at "house duties" for 45 years; she lived at 225 S. Strawberry Alley and died at 117 Strawberry Alley in Havre de Grace; informant was Roy Bond, of Havre de Grace) [Asbury Cemetery]

Bond, Marion Reedy August 25, 1924 – July 28, 1926 (no tombstone; death certificate stated she was the daughter of Norvel Bond and Daisy Wright, all born in Maryland, and she died at home at 119 Strawberry Alley in Havre de Grace; informant was her father Norvel Bond) [Asbury Cemetery]

Bond, Marjorie May 7, 1933 – November 13, 1933 (no tombstone; death certificate stated she was the daughter of Harry Clark and Linda Bond, all born in Aberdeen; she died at home near Aberdeen; informant was Mrs.

Linda Bond, of Aberdeen) [Mt. Calvary U. A. M. E. Church Cemetery]

Bond, Martha died March 7, 1916, age 64 (no tombstone; death certificate stated she was born in Richmond, VA, died at Churchville and was married, but her husband's name was not stated; her parents' names were unknown to informant Nellie Lee) [Green Spring U. M. Church Cemetery]

Bond, Martha, wife of William H. Bond March 17, 1863 – June 8, 1902 (tombstone , but death certificate stated she died at home in Fallston on August 8, 1902, age 38, wife of Henry Bond and the daughter of Thomas Perkins(?) and Harriett Bond; she was born in Harford Co.) [Tabernacle Mount Zion U. M. Church Cemetery]

Bond, Mary A. May 2, 1863 – May 10, 1927 (no tombstone; death certificate stated she was the daughter of James Prigg and Sarah J. Shields, all born in Maryland; she died a widow in Castleton; informant was Janie Webster, of Castleton) [Berkley Memorial Cemetery]

Bond, Mary E. November 1, 1889 – September 26, 1911 (no tombstone; death certificate stated she was the daughter of William Buchanan and Lizzie Ailes(?), all born in Harford Co.; she was married (husband was not named) and died in Bel Air; informant was her father) [Fairview A. M. E. Church Cemetery]

Bond, Mary Frances died May 5, 1930, age about 65 (no tombstone; death certificate stated she was born in Maryland, single, and died in Bel Air; her parents were Bruce Bond and Susan Hall; informant was Olivia Brown, of Bel Air; obituary in *The Aegis*, May 9, 1930, stated she was employed by Mr. & Mrs. P. H. McCormick for 29 years, died at their home and during the past ten years it is doubtful she had been off the property ten times; J. C. Taylor Marble Co. records stated "Mary F. Bond's col. Marble head stone was put up Aug 3rd 1831 Hendon Hill, Bel Air, ordered by Mrs. P. H. McCormick, Bel Air, MD) [Hendon Hill Cemetery]

Bond, Mary K. 1904-   [Mt. Calvary U. A. M. E. Church Cemetery]

Bond, Matilda died March 30, 1901, age 90 (no tombstone; death certificate stated she died in Bel Air and was a widow; it did not state where she was buried[possibly at Hendon Hill Cemetery

Bond, Mintie J. died December 8, 1912, age 69 (no tombstone; incomplete death certificate stated she was born in Maryland and worked as a servant in Havre de Grace; informant was not named, but some of the information was provided by the undertaker Herbert S. Bailey) [Green Spring U. M. Church Cemetery]

Bond, Nelson (owner of a lot in section 16 some time after 1951) [Mt. Calvary U. A. M. E. Church Cemetery]

Bond, Norvel "Shimmy" 1902-1975 (tombstone copied in 1987, but not found in 2018; obituary in *The Aegis* on 11 Sep 1975 stated he was born in Aldino, the son of Joshua Bond and Josephine Prigg, and husband of Isabella Bond; he died in Harford Memorial Hospital and was survived by his wife, sons Edward Bond, Joseph Bond, Robert Jackson, Jr. *(sic)*, Theodore Bond, George Bond, and Cecil Bond, daughter Lois Bond Wallace, and 16 grandchildren) [St. James United Cemetery]

Bond, Olivia January 7, 1878 – May 14, 1931 (no tombstone; death certificate stated she was the daughter of Barney Butler and Julia Grinage, all born in Maryland; she married John Bond, lived in Aberdeen and died in Havre de Grace; informant was her husband) [Mt. Calvary U. A. M. E. Church Cemetery]

Bond, Pauline (no dates recorded in 1987, not listed in 2002, and not found in 2018) [Gravel Hill Cemetery]

Bond, Pauline April 12, 1918 – December 23, 2003 (on same tombstone with Gover Bond) [Berkley Memorial Cemetery]

Bond, Pearl E. July 18, 1900 – July 9, 1920 (no tombstone; death certificate stated she was the daughter of Charles Wilson and Addie Warfield, all born in Maryland; she was married and died in Darlington; informant was Rufus Bond, of Darlington) [Berkley Memorial Cemetery]

Bond, Prush A. (no tombstone found, but J. C. Taylor Marble Co. records state "Prush A. Bond's tombstone was put up Oct 14th 1884 Collard church yard near Fallston") [Tabernacle Mount Zion U. M. Church Cemetery]

Bond, Prush A. December 7, 1854 – October 3, 1879 [Asbury Cemetery]

Bond, Raymond F. May 9, 1916 – May 19, 1918 (no tombstone; death certificate stated he was the son of Grover Bond and Emma Smart, all born in Harford Co.; he died at Wheel and was buried in "Mountain Colored

Cemetery;" informant was his mother, Emma Smart, of Joppa) [Mt. Zion U. M. Church Cemetery]

Bond, Rebecca, wife of George Bond March 30, 1844 – November 11, 1892 [Tabernacle Mount Zion U. M. Church Cemetery]

Bond, Rebecca E. August 22, 1877 – March 14, 1938 (no tombstone; death certificate stated she was the widow of George Bond and the daughter of George Gibson and Betsy Mitchell) [Union U. M. Church Cemetery]

Bond, Richard James January 3, 1904 – August 4, 1924 (no tombstone; death certificate stated he was married and employed as a cook in Bel Air; his parents were Walter Bond and Millia Dorsey and they all were born in Maryland and lived in Bel Air; informant was Etta A. Bond) [Hendon Hill Cemetery]

Bond, Richard James Jr. March 1, 1924 – March 5, 1924 (no tombstone; death certificate stated he was the son of Richard James Bond and Etta A. Buchanan, of Bel Air, and they were all born in Harford Co.; informant was Richard Bond, of Bel Air) [Hendon Hill Cemetery]

Bond, Roy February 27, 1925 – February 28, 1925 (no tombstone; death certificate stated he was the son of George Bond and Mary Thomas, all born in Harford Co.; informant was George Bond, of Aberdeen) [Mt. Calvary U. A. M. E. Church Cemetery]

Bond, Roy Lee 1921-1981 (copied in 1987, but not found in 2018) [Fairview A. M. E. Church Cemetery]

Bond, Rudolph (no dates recorded in 1987, not listed in 2002 and not found in 2018) [Gravel Hill Cemetery]

Bond, Rufus L. Jr. died July 20, 1980, age 54 (no tombstone; obituary in *The Aegis* on July 31, 1980 stated he was the son of Rev. and Mrs. Rufus L. Bond of Aberdeen, lived in Elkton, was married to Bernice ----, of Baltimore, and died at the Perry Point VAMC at Perry Point) [Gravel Hill Cemetery]

Bond, Rufus L. Sr. (no dates recorded in 1987, not listed in 2002, and not found in 2018; obituary of his son Rufus L. Jr., in 1980 stated Rev. Rufus L. Sr. was then living in Aberdeen) [Gravel Hill Cemetery]

Bond, Samuel W. died January 17, 1890, age 71 (inscribed "I have fought a good fight;" death notice in *The Aegis* on January 24, 1890 stated he had worked as a wagoner on the farm of Hon. Henry D. Farnandis, near Bel Air, for many years) [Asbury Cemetery]

Bond, Sarah A. died March 26, 1917, age about 8 (no tombstone; death certificate stated she was born in Maryland, the daughter of Neddie Cole, born in Port Deposit, MD, but her mother's name was unknown to informant John Bond, of Aberdeen RFD #2; she was a widow and lived at Webster) [Green Spring U. M. Church Cemetery]

Bond, Sarah F. August 22, 1851 – May 9, 1934 (no tombstone; death certificate stated she was born in Castleton, the daughter of Henry Prigg, born in Harford Co., and Harriett Haines, born in Cecil Co.; she married John H. Bond and died a widow in Castleton; informant was Moses Bond, 3111 Barclay St., Baltimore) [Berkley Memorial Cemetery]

Bond, Thomas R., son of Rev. John T. and Laura M. Bond, 1897-1919 (tombstone; death certificate stated he was born October 7, 1897, the son of John T. Bond and Laura M. Smith, and all born in Maryland; he was single, worked as a laborer and died in Darlington on January 18, 1919; informant was his father) [Berkley Memorial Cemetery]

Bond, Verden August 5, 1883 – March 28, 1950 (no tombstone; death certificate stated he was born in Maryland, the son of Joshua Bond and Josephine Prigg, lived in Havre de Grace and died at Harford Memorial Hospital; informant was his brother Norvel Bond who lived with him) [Asbury Cemetery]

Bond, Walter died August 2, 1997, age 79 (no tombstone; James Dorsey Card File, African American Obituaries, that is maintained at the Historical Society of Harford County, has a card with obituary from an unidentified newspaper on August 6, 1997 stating he was born in Aberdeen, the son of George Bond and May Thomas; he lived in Aberdeen, retired as a road worked for Harford County Public Works and died at Citizens Nursing Home; he was survived by a brother and a sister) [Mt. Calvary U. A. M. E. Church Cemetery]

Bond, Walter H. October 14, 1881 – March 18, 1915 (no tombstone; death certificate stated he was born in Harford Co., married, and worked as a laborer in Bel Air; his parents were Richard H. Bond and Jeannette J.

Brown, both born in Harford Co.; informant was Jeannette J. Jackson, of 122 Balmar St., West Chester, PA) [Hendon Hill Cemetery]

Bond, Webster 1910-1983 (on same tombstone with Anita A. Bond; obituary in *The Aegis* on March 10, 1983 stated Webster Franklin Bond was maintenance supervisor for the Hamilton Court Apartments, now Washington Park Apartments, in Aberdeen for 39 years; he married (wife not named in obituary) and died at Harford Memorial Hospital in Havre de Grace, survived by 3 daughters, 1 sister, 3 brothers, 9 grandchildren and 9 great-grandchildren) [Berkley Memorial Cemetery]

Bond, Webster Wayne 1954-1956 (copied in 1987, but not found in 2018) [Mt. Calvary U. A. M. E. Church Cemetery]

Bond, William (Rev.) 1840-1895 (inscribed "And Family") [Berkley Memorial Cemetery]

Bond, William died April 19, 1915, age about 60 (no tombstone; death certificate stated he was the son of John Bond, both born in Harford Co.,but the name of his mother was not known to informant E. Dean & Son Funeral Home; he was a laborer, died in Havre de Grace and was buried in Bel Air, but the cemetery was not named [possibly Hendon Hill]

Bond, William died February 26, 1918, age 85 (no tombstone; death certificate stated he was the son of Benjamin Bond, both born in Maryland, but his mother's name and place of birth were not known to informant Charles T. Vain, of Forest Hill; William was married, worked as a laborer and died at Forest Hill) [Fairview A. M. E. Church Cemetery]

Bond, William February 15, 1857 – May 12, 1917 (no tombstone; death certificate stated he was the son of Harry Bond, both born in Pennsylvania, but his mother's name and place of birth were not known to informant Jane Bond, of Churchville; he was widowed, worked as a farm hand and died in Churchville) [Green Spring U. M. Church Cemetery]

Bond, William probably died April 12, 1889, age 72 (no tombstone; *The Aegis* on April 19, 1889 stated he was buried on Sunday, April 14th, so he probably died two days earlier on April 12th) [Hendon Hill Cemetery]

Bond, William Cornelius August 7, 1922 – March 21, 1924 (no tombstone; death certificate stated he was born in Aberdeen, the son of George Bond and May Thomas, both born in Maryland; informant was May Bond, of Aberdeen) [Mt. Calvary U. A. M. E. Church Cemetery]

Bond, William H. November 13, 1932 – June 1, 2006 (on same tombstone with Frances L. Bond inscribed "In Loving Memory" with their photos and images of a tractor and a teddy bear; obituary and photo in *The Aegis* on June 7, 2006 stated William Henry Bond was born in Forest Hill, a son of the late Herbert W. Bond and Marie Brown, and husband of Frances Hall; he worked for the former Harco Electronics and recently for Clark's Sales and Service; he lived in Darlington and died at Upper Chesapeake Medical Center in Bel Air, survived by his wife, 1 son, 1 daughter, 6 grandchildren, 2 great-grandchildren, 1 brother and 2 aunts; he was predeceased by his parents and 1 son) [Berkley Memorial Cemetery]

Bond, William H. Sr. March 18, 1936 – October 18, 1999, U.S. Air Force (military marker) [Gravel Hill Cemetery]

Bond, William Henry December 3, 1922 – April 16, 1924 (no tombstone; death certificate stated he was the son of David Bond and Helen Taylor, all born in Maryland; informant was his father, of Aberdeen) [Mt. Calvary U. A. M. E. Church Cemetery]

Bond, William M. October 9, 1946 – December 3, 2010, U.S. Navy (tombstone; funeral notice in *The Aegis* on December 8, 2010 stated William Monroe "Bill" Bond lived in Belcamp and died at Harford Memorial Hospital in Havre de Grace) [Berkley Memorial Cemetery]

Bond, Winfield M. 1887-1954 (inscribed "Thine Is A Perfect Rest") [Fairview A. M. E. Church Cemetery]

Booker, Bernice 1921-1982 [Berkley Memorial Cemetery]

Booker, Edward April 9, 1896 – January 3, 1972, Virginia, PFC, U.S. Army, World War I (tombstone; Harkins Funeral Home Records stated he was born in Cumberland, VA, son of Frederick Booker and Louisa Trent; he was a World War I veteran and his wife was Lucy B. Booker; they lived at R. D. #1, Delta, PA and attended Trinity AME Zion Church) [Berkley Memorial Cemetery]

Booker, George E. February 20, 1924 – November 16, 1994 [Berkley Memorial Cemetery]

Boone, ---- stillborn female, premature birth, died 1 Feb 1928 (no tombstone; death certificate stated she was born near Wilna, the daughter of John Gwynn and Lucie Boone, both born in Maryland; she was buried by her grandfather Denis *(sic)* Boone; informant was Lucie Boone, of Fallston P. O.) [Tabernacle Mount Zion U. M. Church Cemetery]

Boone, Augustus August 18, 1875 – December 28, 1917 (tombstone was mistakenly inscribed Samuel Augusta Boom; death certificate stated his name was C. Augustus Boone, born 1878, died aged 39, "no history" of birth date; he was married, worked as a farmer in Fallston and was the son of William Boone and Catherine Oliver; they were all born in Maryland; informant was Ida Aquilla who lived at 223 W. Preston Street in Baltimore) [Hendon Hill Cemeteyr]

Boone, Caroline died July 12, 1912, age about 55 (no tombstone; death certificate stated she was the daughter of George Bond and Rachel Bond, and they were all born in Maryland; she was married and a house keeper in Fallston; informant was Augustus Boone, of Fallston RFD) [Hendon Hill Cemetery]

Boone, Dennis May 20, 1878 – January 2, 1934 (no tombstone; death certificate stated he was the son of Daniel Boone, both were born in Maryland, but his mother's name was not known to informant Sarah Boone, of Fallston; he was married and worked as a laborer in Fallston) [Tabernacle Mount Zion U. M. Church Cemetery]

Boone, Eugene H. May 8, 1888 – December 21, 1957, Maryland, MA 2, U.S. Navy [Clark's U. M. Church Cemetery]

Boone, Hester died in October 1879, age 100 (no tombstone; 1880 MD Mortality Schedule reported she was born in Maryland and died in the Fallston Precinct) [probably Hendon Hill Cemetery]

Boone, James died July 21, 1928, age about 42 (no tombstone; death certificate stated he was the son of James Brown and Annie Boone, all born in Maryland; he was married, worked as a farm laborer and died at Reckordville; informant was Dennis Boone, of Fallston) [Tabernacle Mount Zion U. M. Church Cemetery]

Boone, Lizzie died in May 1880, age 9 (no tombstone; 1880 Maryland Mortality Schedule reported she was born in Maryland and died in the Fallston Precinct) [probably Hendon Hill Cemetery]

Boone, Martha M. 1889-1979 [John Wesley U. M. E. Church Cemetery in Abingdon]

Boone, Mary Frances died May 5, 1930, age 65 (no dates inscribed on tombstone and her name was misspelled Boom on the same tombstone with husband Augustus; death certificate stated her date of birth was unknown, but her parents were Bruce Bond and Susan Hall; they were all born in Maryland and lived in Bel Air; informant was Olivia Brown, of Bel Air) [Hendon Hill Cemetery]

Boone, Morris D. April 1, 1926 – October 18, 1952, Maryland, PFC, TC, World War II [Tabernacle Mount Zion U. M. Church Cemetery]

Boone, Moses died before 1901 (no tombstone; see Rachel Boone and William Boone) [probably Hendon Hill Cemetery]

Boone, Nellie R. March 14, 1925 – February 18, 1926 (no tombstone; death certificate stated she was the daughter of Denis *(sic)* Boone and Sarah Bradley, all were born in Maryland and lived in Fallston; informant was Sarah Boone, of Fallston) [Tabernacle Mount Zion U. M. Church Cemetery]

Boone, Rachel died October 11, 1901, age about 95 (no tombstone; death certificate stated she was the widow of Moses Boone and daughter of Joshua Britton and Esther Dorsey; she was born in Maryland, was once a servant, and died at Fallston, but the certificate did not state where she was buried [possibly Hendon Hill Cemetery]

Boone, Sarah died October 8, 1920, age 83 (no tombstone; death certificate stated she was the daughter of Moses Boone, both born in Baltimore Co., but her mother's name was not known to informant Annie Goens, of Fallston; she was a widow and died at Reckord) [Tabernacle Mount Zion U. M. Church Cemetery]

Boone, William died February 8, 1930, age about 52 (no tombstone; death certificate stated he was the son of William Boone and Caroline Bond, all born in North Carolina; he was married and died at Havre de Grace Hospital; informant Dr. C. Foley from hospital records) [Tabernacle Mount Zion U. M. Church Cemetery]

Boone, William died November 19, 1924, age about 90 (no tombstone, but there is a small marker with W. B. inscribed on the top; death certificate stated he was a laborer and widower who lived and died near Bel Air; his father was Moses Boone, both born in Harford Co., but his mother was not known to informant, his father Moses, of Upper Falls) [Hendon Hill Cemetery]

Bosley, Elizabeth June 14, 1911 – July 25, 1911 (no tombstone; death certificate stated she was born at Rocks, the daughter of Thomas W. Bosley, born at Rayville, MD, and Rhoda Flowers, born in MD; buried at Lagrange Church; informant was Thomas E. Bosley, of Rocks) [Chestnut Grove A. M. E. Church Cemetery, formerly LaGrange Cemetery at Rocks]

Bosley, Stephen A. died November 2, 1907, age 17 years, 4 months, 2 days (no tombstone; death certificate stated he was born at Mountain, the son of Andrew J. Bosley, of Richmond, VA, and Annie Ruff, of Baltimore Co.; he worked as a farm hand and died at Mountain; informant was his mother Annie Bosley; place of burial was not indicated) [possibly Mt. Zion U. M. Church Cemetery]

Boston, Charles died October 5, 1894, age not given (no tombstone; death notice in *The Aegis* on October 12, 1894 stated he resided near Clayton post office and was buried "in the cemetery at the colored church on the Mountain;" he had been sent by Gen. Frank Bond several years ago to wait on the late Capt. Webster, of Calvary (i.e., Capt. John Adams Webster, U.S.N., of War of 1812 fame), and after the death of Capt. Webster he made Harford Co. his home) [Mt. Zion U. M. Church Cemetery]

Boston, Elizabeth died November 23, 1914, age 52 (no tombstone; death certificate stated she was the daughter of Isaiah Johnson and Delia Johnson, all born in Harford Co,; she was a cook and a widow who lived in Churchville; informant was H. Spalding, of Aberdeen) [Asbury Cemetery]

Bouldin, Henry June 4, 1876 – March 22, 1923 (no tombstone; death certificate stated he was born in Harford Co., the son of Wilson Bouldin, born in Cumberland Co., VA, and Cassandra Pierson, born in Harford Co.; he died at The Mountain and was buried in "The Mountain Colored Cemetery;" informant was his mother Cassandra Pierson, of Joppa) [Mt. Zion U. M. Church Cemetery]

Bouldin, Wilson died January 31, 1926, age about 70 (no tombstone; death certificate stated he was born in Virginia, but the names of his parents were not known to informant Cassandra Bouldin, of Joppa; he was married, worked as a laborer, died at The Mountain and buried in "The Mountain Colored Cemetery") [Mt. Zion U. M. Church Cemetery]

Bowen, Colonel Henry Jr., "Beloved Son" May 11, 1953 – April 1, 2008 (on same tombstone with Lillian F. Bowen and photo) [Berkley Memorial Cemetery]

Bowen, Lillian F., "Beloved Mother" August 1, 1929 -   (on same tombstone with Colonel Henry Bowen, Jr. and photo) [Berkley Memorial Cemetery]

Bowman, Bill 1902-1977 (copied as Browman in 1987, but marker not found in 2018; obituary in *The Aegis* on December 8, 1977 stated Bill Bowman was born in Paris, TN, son of the late Albert and Sally Bowman; he married Florence S. ----, lived in Havre de Grace, was a self-employed shoe shine and died at Harford Memorial Hospital on December 3, 1977) [St. James United Cemetery]

Bowman, David died June 1, 1930, age about 40 (no tombstone; death certificate stated he was born in Virginia and married, but his parents were unknown to informant Mrs. Bertha Bowman) [Union U. M. Church Cemetery]

Bowser, Carl July 29, 1915 – August 21, 1915 (no tombstone; death certificate stated he was the son of Cread Smith and Vera Bowser, of Havre de Grace; informant was Jacob Waters) [St. James United Cemetery]

Bowser, Caroline died November 11, 1904, age 66 (tombstone; death certificate stated she was a servant and died near Fulford, age 75; parents not known to informant Frank H. Jacobs [Asbury Cemetery]

Bowser, Caroline K. December 15, 1890 – September 7, 1948 (no tombstone; death certificate stated she was daughter of Jacob Monk and Elsie Williams, and widow of Robert F. Bowser) [Union U. M. Church Cemetery]

Bowser, Edith Ella November 14, 1892 – April 30, 1982 (no tombstone; obituary in *The Aegis* on May 20, 1982 stated she was born in Harford County, the daughter of Richard and Ella Bowser, and died at Sinai Hospital in Baltimore, "survived by many relatives and friends;" she had been a member of Hosanna AME Church, but later changed to Asbury AME Church where she was very active, so she is probably buried in Asbury Cemetery]

Bowser, Elizabeth (no dates recorded in 1987, not listed in 2002 and not found in 2018) [Gravel Hill Cemetery]

Bowser, Ella E. January 10, 1908 – August 13, 1912 (no tombstone; death certificate stated she was the daughter of Robert F. Bowser and Caroline K. Monk, all born in Harford Co.) [Union U. M. Church Cemetery]

Bowser, Ellen June 15, 1849 – April 19, 1917 (no tombstone; death certificate stated she was born in Baltimore, the daughter of James Brown and Jane Parson, both born in Maryland; she married Richard Bowser and died in Darlington; informant was Richard Bowser) [Berkley Memorial Cemetery]

Bowser, George E. Sr. July 12, 1927 – August 28, 1978, Cpl., U.S. Army, Korea (tombstone; obituary in *The Aegis* stated George Edward Brown, Sr. was born in Aberdeen, the son of the late Robert and Caroline Bowser, and was the husband of Hilda Bowser; he lived in Aberdeen, was a retired government employee of Edgewood Arsenal APG; died at Perry Point VA Hospital, survived by his wife, 6 sons, 2 daughters, 3 sisters, 2 brothers, 5 grandchildren) [Union U. M. Church Cemetery]

Bowser, George E., "Father" 1883-1945 (on same tombstone with Helen F. Bowser; death certificate stated Edward George Bowser was born on March 7, 1883, the son of Joseph Bowser and Semelia Clark, married Helen Johnson and died on June 27, 1945) [Union U. M. Church Cemetery]

Bowser, Helen F., "Mother" 1892-19__ (blank) (on same tombstone with George E, Bowser; obituary in *The Aegis* stated she lived in Perryville and died on December 13, 1970, age not given, at Harford Memorial Hospital in Havre de Grace; she was survived by one brother and one niece) [Union U. M. Church Cemetery]

Bowser, Henry L. October 23, 1840 – February 24, 1913 (no tombstone; death certificate stated he was born near Havre de Grace, son of Stephen Preston and Harriet Bowser, birth places unknown to informant Robert Bowser, of Havre de Grace; Henry was a laborer who lived at Swan Creek near Aberdeen and was a widower at the time of his death) [Gravel Hill Cemetery]

Bowser, Hollis Jr. stillborn on July 1, 1927 (no tombstone; death certificate spelled his name "Holis" and stated he was the son of Holis *(sic)* Bowser and Emma Harris; informant was Mary S. Talbott, of Perryman) [Union U. M. Church Cemetery]

Bowser, I. Marie 1903-1944 (on the same tombstone with R. Nettie Christy, Martha C. Bowser, I. Marie Bowser and Hazel T. Dunn) [St. James United Cemetery]

Bowser, Iccie M. April 19, 1921 – May 25, 1981 [Berkley Memorial Cemetery]

Bowser, John W. 1922-1982, Cpl., U.S. Army, World War II (tombstone; obituary in *The Aegis* stated John Washington Bowser was born in Perryman, the son of the late Robert Bowser and Caroline Monk, and husband of the late Helen Banks Bowser; he served in the Army in World War II, was a building contractor in Aberdeen and died at the Loch Raven VA Medical Center in Baltimore on June 7, 1982, survived by his brother and three sisters) [Union U. M. Church Cemetery]

Bowser, Joseph March 18, 1855 – September 23, 1932 (no tombstone; death certificate stated he was the son of William Bowser, mother unknown, and the husband of Simelia Bwser) [Union U. M. Church Cemetery]

Bowser, Joseph E., Beloved Husband of Catharine M. Bowser October 11, 1869 – June 30, 1908 (inscribed with a verse) [St. James United Cemetery]

Bowser, Joseph I. 1919-1982, Sgt., U.S. Army, World War II (tombstone; obituary in *The Aegis* on December 30, 1982 stated Joseph I. Bowser was born in Aberdeen, the son of the late Robert Bowser and Caroline Monks; he married Nancy K. Murphy, served in World War II from 1941 to 1945 and was maintenance supervisor for U.S. Post Office in Aberdeen for over 30 years; he died at Harford Memorial Hospital in Havre de Grace on December 24, 1982 and was survived by his wife, 3 sons, 1 daughter, 3 sisters, and 3 grandchildren) [Mt. Calvary U. A. M. E. Church Cemetery]

Bowser, Joseph Lee 1948-1979 (on same tombstone with Ida V. Murphy; obituary in *The Aegis* on February 15, 1979 stated he was born in Havre de Grace, the son of Joseph I. Bowser and Nancy Murphy, lived at 434 Baltimore St. in Aberdeen, died at Arundel General Hospital in Annapolis on February 5, 1979 and was survived by his parents, 3 brothers and a sister) [Mt. Calvary U. A. M. E. Church Cemetery]

Bowser, Keith A. Sr. June 23, 1960 – July 13, 2009 [Berkley Memorial Cemetery]

Bowser, Lewis (no tombstone; an unidentified newspaper in the vertical files of the Historical Society of Harford County stated he was one of four Civil War soldiers buried in this cemetery; Lewis and Santa Bowser walked to Philadelphia to enlist in the Union Army; he was one of the trustees in 1881 when the church acquired more land) [Gravel Hill Cemetery]

Bowser, Martha C. 1866-1930 (on the same tombstone with R. Nettie Christy, I. Marie Bowser and Hazel T. Dunn; death certificate stated she was born December 12, 1874 and died May 22, 1930) [St. James United Cemetery]

Bowser, Mary died July 23, 1896, age 60 (copied in 1987, but not found in 2018) [Gravel Hill Cemetery]

Bowser, Mary L. died December 20, 1992, age 61 (no tombstone; obituary in *The Aegis* on December 23, 1992 stated she was born in Baltimore, daughter of the late Robert Stevenson and Mary Tolliver, and widow of William T. Bowser; she lived in Aberdeen and died at Harford Memorial Hospital, survived by 2 sons, 2 daughters, 10 grandchildren and 2 sisters) [Union U. M. Church Cemetery]

Bowser, Nancy 1926-2013 (small metal funeral home marker) [Mt. Calvary U. A. M. E. Church Cemetery]

Bowser, Richard M. September 4, 1847 – June 1, 1933 (no tombstone; death certificate stated he was born in Darlington, the son of Isaiah Bowser and Henrietta Dutton, both born in Maryland; he married Ellen J. ----, worked as a farm laborer in Darlington until December 1928 and died a widower at Aldino where he had lived for 8 months; informant was Edith Bowser) [Berkley Memorial Cemetery]

Bowser, Robert Daniel Jr. December 22, 1912 – September 15, 1936 (no tombstone; death certificate stated he was the son of Robert D. Bowser, Sr. and Caroline Monk, and he died after being struck by a struck on Aberdeen Proving Ground Road) [Union U. M. Church Cemetery]

Bowser, Robert Franklin February 28, 1887 – October 27, 1947 (no tombstone; death certificate stated he was the son of Joseph Bowser and Semelia Christy, and husband of Caroline Monk) [Union U. M. Church Cemetery]

Bowser, Robert J. died February 8, 1919, age about 55 (no tombstone; death certificate stated he was the son of George Bowser and Eliza Lisby, all born in Maryland, and he died a widower) [Union U. M. Church Cemetery]

Bowser, Robert Lewis September 5, 1949 – June 28, 2013, SP5, U.S. Army, Vietnam [Mt. Calvary U. A. M. E. Church Cemetery]

Bowser, Santa (no dates recorded in 1987, but not found in 2018; an unidentified newspaper in the vertical files of the Historical Society of Harford County stated he was one of four Civil War soldiers who are buried in this cemetery; Santa and Lewis Bowser walked to Philadelphia to enlist in the Union Army) [Gravel Hill Cemetery]

Bowser, Semilia May 21, 1862 – January 31, 1933 (no tombstone; death certificate stated she was the widow of Joseph Bowser and the daughter of Jacob Christy and Sarah Clarke) [Union U. M. Church Cemetery]

Bowser, Timothy Owen, "Our Beloved Timmy" November 13, 1954 – December 8, 2008, SP4, U.S. Army (tombstone; obituary in *The Aegis* on December 17, 2008 stated he was born in Havre de Grace, the son of Joseph I. Bowser and Nancy Murphy, but Aberdeen was his hometown; he was discharged from the Army in 1982 and served in the National Guard until honorably discharged in 1986; he married Monica Neumann and had 2 daughters who survived him when he died at his mother's home in Aberdeen, along with 4 grandchildren, 1 sister and 2 brothers) [Mt. Calvary U. A. M. E. Church Cemetery]

Bowser, Tonisha July 31, 1980 – March 20, 2009 (inscribed "In God's Care") [Berkley Memorial Cemetery]

Bowser, Wayne A. 1958-2009 (small metal funeral home marker) [Berkley Memorial Cemetery]

Bowser, William E. August 8, 1865 – August 20, 1917 (no tombstone; death certificate stated he was born in

Harford Co., the son of Santa Bowser, born in Harford Co., but his mother's name was not known' he was carpenter in Havre de Grace and was married at the time of his death; informant was Mrs. Martha Bowser, of Havre de Grace) [Gravel Hill Cemetery]

Bowser, William Thomas March 14, 1928 – March 7, 1985, Private, U.S. Army, Korea [Union U. M. Church Cemetery]

Boyd, ---- (owner of a lot in section 10 some time after 1951) [Mt. Calvary U. A. M. E. Church Cemetery]

Boyd, Catherine Barbara died August 22, 2012, age not given (no tombstone; death notice in *The Aegis* on August 29, 2012 stated she had passed away on Wednesday and the family will receive friends on Saturday at the Aberdeen Bible Church [Community Baptist Church Cemetery]

Boyd, Clifton March 2, 1903 – April 12, 1905 (no tombstone; death certificate stated he was born in Maryland and was the son of Daniel F. Boyd and Lydia M----, and he died at Fulford) [Mt. Zion U. M. Church Cemetery]

Boyd, Ella C. June 29, 1865 – July 18, 1932 (tombstone; death certificate stated she was born in Havre de Grace, daughter of James H. Cooper, born in Baltimore, and Mary Ramsay, born in Bel Air, and wife of John Boyd, of Havre de Grace; informant was Robert Cooper, of Baltimore, MD) [St. James United Cemetery]

Boyd, Russell 1883 – March 28, 1929 (no tombstone; death certificate stated he was born in Virginia and was a laborer in Havre de Grace; parents unknown to informant John Richardson) [St. James United Cemetery]

Boyd, William February 26, 1919 – April 18, 1957, SP3, 2232 2nd Area Service Unit, World War II (tombstone; Pennington Funeral Home records stated he was born in Arkansas, the son of John Boyd and "Elizabeth ?" *(sic)*, both deceased; he lived on Bush Chapel Road, Aberdeen RFD #1, and died at Perry Point Veterans Administration Hospital; his wife Alice B. Boyd paid the funeral bill and Julia Boyd of Pensacola, FL was mentioned) [Mt. Calvary U. A. M. E. Church Cemetery]

Boyden, Bessie G., "Beloved Mother" April 5, 1901 – June 25, 1973 [Berkley Memorial Cemetery]

Boyden, Earl 1923-1977 [Berkley Memorial Cemetery]

Boyden, Geraldine 1924-1981 [Berkley Memorial Cemetery]

Boyden, Jake W. July 8, 1893 – May 16, 1965, North Carolina, Pvt., U.S. Army, Co. B, 304 Svc. Bn., QMC [Berkley Memorial Cemetery]

Boyer, ---- stillborn male died February 3, 1915 (no tombstone; death certificate stated he was born in Bel Air, the son of Charles Boyer, born in Baltimore Co., and Effie Parker, born in Harford Co., and they lived in Bel Air; informant was his mother Effie Boyer) [Hendon Hill Cemetery]

Boyer, Harriet died October 11, 1877, age 68 ("In Memory Of") [Old Union Chapel M. E. Church Cemetery]

Boyer, Mary Caroline died April 7, 1945, age 98 (no tombstone; Kurtz Funeral Home Record Book 1944-1949, p. 62, stated she was born in Baltimore Co., but her parents' names were not known to informant, her niece, Ida Robinson, of Rocks, who also paid the funeral bill; Mary was a retired mill worker and died a widow at home at Rocks; death certificate added she was retired from Woodbery Mills and lived at Federal Hill for 1 year and 2 months) [William C. Rice Memorial Cemetery, St. James U. M. Church]

Boyer, Sophia February 17, 1836 – January 17, 1927 (no tombstone; death certificate stated she was the daughter of Harry Pinion, both born in Maryland, but the name of her mother was not known to informant Malcolm W. Mitchell, of Aberdeen, yet he knew she was born in Maryland; Sophia died a widow in Bel Air) [Mt. Calvary U. A. M. E. Church Cemetery]

Bradford, Annie E. died April 28, 1899, aged 80 years (inscribed "At Rest") [Berkley Memorial Cemetery]

Bradford, Benjamin July 21, 1931, PA, Pvt., U.S. Army, 366 Eng., 92 Division [Berkley Memorial Cemetery]

Bradford, Caroline died October 5, 1909, age 80 (no tombstone; death certificate stated she was the daughter of Santa James, but mother unknown to informant Maria Smart, her daughter; she was the widow of Jacob Bradford and died at Mountain; place of burial was not indicated [probably Mt. Zion U. M. Church Cemetery]

Bradford, Edna died October 20, 1895, age 5 months (on same tombstone with Sarah W. Bradford) [Berkley Memorial Cemetery]

Bradford, Ella H. 1873-1958 (copied in 1987 as being on the same tombstone with Joshua J. Bradford, but the marker was not found in 2018) [Fairview A. M. E. Church Cemetery]

Bradford, Jacob died November 14, 1898, age not given (no tombstone; death certificate stated he worked as a laborer, was married and died at Mountain; his parents' names and wife's name were not given; place of burial was not indicated) [probably Mt. Zion U. M. Church Cemetery]

Bradford, Jacob July 2, 1851 – May 18, 1920 (no tombstone; death certificate stated he died at Kalmia and was the son of Jacob Bradford and Julia Hail, all born in Maryland; informant was Julia Stewart, of Bel Air) [Clark's U. M. Church Cemetery]

Bradford, James died December 30, 1907, age 70 years, 4 months, 2 days (no tombstone; death certificate stated he was born in Abingdon, the son of Jacob Bradford and Ann Bond, both born in Harford Co.; he was single, worked as a farm hand and died at Mountain; informant was Charles Boulden, a non-relative; place of burial was not indicated) [probably Mt. Zion U. M. Church Cemetery]

Bradford, Joseph died February 3, 1901, aged 52 (tombstone; death certificate stated Jos. E. Bradford died in Darlington, parents not known, and his wife was Eliza Spriggs) [Berkley Memorial Cemetery]

Bradford, Joshua James September 23, 1874 – December 26, 1941 (copied in 1987 as being on the same tombstone with Ella H. Bradford, but the marker was not found in 2018; death certificate stated he was born in Maryland, son of Jacob Bradford and Mary Jane Barnes; he married and worked as a farmer at Cooptown; informant was Ella Bradford, of Forest Hill; Kurtz Funeral Home Record Book 1937-1943, p. 210, stated he was born at Kalmia, the son of Jacob Bradford, born at Kalmia, and Mary Jane Barnes, born in Germantown, PA; he married Ella Bradford, worked as a farmer and died at home at Cooptown) [Fairview A. M. E. Church Cemetery]

Bradford, Martha A. November 11, 1924 – October 20, 1999 [Fairview A. M. E. Church Cemetery]

Bradford, Mary Jane February 16, 1848 – February 9, 1923 (no tombstone; death certificate stated she was the daughter of William Bond and Pris Barnes, all born in Maryland; she died a widow at Street; the informant was Richard Williams, of Street, MD) [Clark's U. M. Church Cemetery]

Bradford, Robert A. February 27, 1885 – July 21, 1919 (no tombstone; death certificate stated he was the son of Jacob Bradford and Mary J. Bond, all born in Harford County; he was married, worked as a farmer and died in Fallston; informant was Lillie M. Bradford, of Fallston) [Fairview A. M. E. Church Cemetery]

Bradford, Sarah W. died April 5, 1881, age 2 months (on same tombstone with Edna Bradford) [Berkley Memorial Cemetery]

Bradford, William O. June 5, 1912 – May 14, 1918 (no tombstone; death certificate stated he was Robert Bradford and Lillie M. Robinson, all born in Maryland; informant was his mother Lillie M. Bradford, of Fallston) [Fairview A. M. E. Church Cemetery]

Bradford, Wilson October 24, 1896 – February 18, 1906 (tombstone incsription; death certificate stated Wilson McKinley Bradford was born in Darlington, the son of Joseph Bradford, born in Harford Co., and Eliza Spriggs, born in Baltimore Co., and he died in Berkley) [Berkley Memorial Cemetery]

Bradley, Claud E. January 15, 1919 – May 7, 1919 (no tombstone; death certificate stated he was the son of William Bradley, both born in Maryland, and Helen Lee, born in Pennsylvania, and died in Bel Air; informant was his father) [Tabernacle Mount Zion U. M. Church Cemetery]

Bradley, Dudley January 26, 1875 – April 8, 1930 (no tombstone; death certificate stated he was the son of Arthur Bradley and Elizabeth Jones, all born in Virginia; he was married and died at Vale; informant was Sarah Bradley, of Vale) [Tabernacle Mount Zion U. M. Church Cemetery]

Bradley, Dudley Lloyd Leroy September 27, 1936 – August 13, 1937 (no tombstone; death certificate stated he was born in Emmorton, the son of William Bradley, born in Benson, and Eliza Peaker, born in Wheel; he died at home in Emmorton and was buried in "Mountain Cemetery") [Mt. Zion U. M. Church Cemetery]

Bradley, Eliza M. February 28, 1899 – March 29, 1967 (on same tombstone with William H. Bradley) [Mt. Zion U. M. Church Cemetery]

Bradley, John died March 6, 1924, age about 90 (no tombstone; death certificate stated he died a widower in Havre de Grace; parents not known to informant Maria Luster) [St. James United Cemetery]

Bradley, Lingham died May 26, 1929, age 64 (no tombstone; death certificate stated he was born in Harford Co., the son of Samuel Bradley, born in Maryland, but his mother was not known to informant Lula Kane, of Benson; he married, worked as a dairyman, became a widower, married again, was divorced, died in Benson and was buried in "Abingdon Col. Cem.;" Harford Co. marriage license stated Lingan Bradley, age 47, widower, married Lucy Matthews circa October 19, 1895; Equity Court Case 5955 stated he filed for a divorce on January 21, 1903 and it was granted on April 21, 1903) [John Wesley U. M. E. Church Cemetery in Abingdon]

Bradley, Louise July 17, 1909 – October 22, 1911 (no tombstone; death certificate stated she was born in Harford Co., the daughter of Joseph Bradley and Mary Stokes, both born in Maryland; informant was Eulalia Bradley, of Havre de Grace) [St. James United Cemetery]

Bradley, Raymond H. died July 7, 2017, age 78 (no tombstone; obituary and photo in *The Aegis* stated he was the son of William Henry Bradley and Eliza Meldenia Peaker and was employed at the Olney Pony Farm in Joppa for 58 years where his sidekick dog Monday went to work with him every day; he lived in Fallston and died at the Greater Baltimore Medical Center in Towson, survived by his wife Elizabeth Estella Bradley, 3 sons, 1 daughter, 13 grandchildren and many great-grandchildren and great-great-grandchildren) [Tabernacle Mount Zion U. M. Church Cemetery]

Bradley, Spencer died January 31, 1924, age 70 (no tombstone; death certificate stated he was the married son of Smith Bradley, both born in Virginia; his mother was not known to informant Dudley Bradley, of Benson, but he stated she was born in Virginia; he worked as a laborer and died at Reckord) [Tabernacle Mount Zion U. M. Church Cemetery]

Bradley, William H. January 23, 1897 – July 9, 1978 (on same tombstone with Eliza M. Bradley) [Mt. Zion U. M. Church Cemetery]

Brady, Charlotte died July 5, 1888 at a very advanced age, for many years a well known and respected resident of Bel Air (no tombstone; *Harford Democrat*, July 13, 1888) [Hendon Hill Cemetery]

Brady, Helen November 7, 1918 – March 2, 1920 (no tombstone; death certificate stated she was the daughter of Davis Brady, of North Carolina, and Hilda Tasco, of Maryland; informant was Harry Tasco, of Havre de Grace) [St. James United Cemetery]

Branch, Baby (female) January 28, 1922 – January 30, 1922, a premature birth (no tombstone; death certificate stated she was born in Harford Co., the daughter of Edward Branch and Mary Dawson, both born in North Carolina; she died in Aberdeen and informant was her father) [Mt. Calvary U. A. M. E. Church Cemetery]

Branch, Baby (male) born and died on January 18, 1948 (no tombstone; death certificate stated he died at home on Strawberry Alley in Havre de Grace, the son of Edward Leroy Branch, of Bridgeville, DE, and Mary Irene Deshields, of Winston-Salem, NC); he was premature and lived only five minutes [St. James United Cemetery]

Branch, Catherine 1922-2004 (small metal funeral home marker; she owned a lot in section 2 some time after 1951) [Mt. Calvary U. A. M. E. Church Cemetery]

Branch, Catherine October 10, 1927 – April 28, 2002 (inscribed "In Loving Memory") [St. James United Cemetery]

Branch, Charles E. January 4, 1913 – July 2, 1913 (no tombstone; death certificate stated he was the son of Edward Branch and Mary Dawson, both of North Carolina; he died at home in Oakington near Havre de Grace; informant was his father) [St. James United Cemetery]

Branch, Hilda May March 22, 1927 – April 10, 1928 (no tombstone; death certificate stated she was born in Maryland, the daughter of Edward Branch and Mary Dawson, both were born in North Carolina; she died at home and informant was Edward Branch, of Aberdeen RFD) [Mt. Calvary U. A. M. E. Church Cemetery]

Branch, Louis H. July 4, 1920 – October 2, 1947, Maryland, Pvt, U.S. Army, World War II [Mt. Calvary U. A. M. E. Church Cemetery]

Branch, Mary J. July 4, 1889 – January 27, 1932 (no tombstone; death certificate stated she was born in Greenwell, NC, the daughter of Laura Dorsow, but her father was not known to informant, her husband, Edward Branch, of Aberdeen; she died at home near Aberdeen) [Mt. Calvary U. A. M. E. Church Cemetery]

Branch, Mary Jane September 7, 1914 – December 25, 1928 (no tombstone; death certificate stated she was born in Harford Co., the daughter of Edward Branch and Mary Dawson, both born in North Carolina; she died at home and informant was Mary J. Branch, of Aberdeen) [Mt. Calvary U. A. M. E. Church Cemetery]

Branch, Morgan II 1963-2000 (handwritten on a flat cement slab) [St. James United Cemetery]

Branch, Randolph Jr. 1952-2011, U.S. Army [St. James United Cemetery]

Branch, Randolph Sr. November 11, 1911 – January 30, 2003, U.S. Army, World War II [St. James United Cemetery]

Branch, Viola February 3, 1917 – July 18, 1917 (no tombstone; death certificate stated she was born in Aberdeen, the daughter of Edward Branch and Mary Jane Dawson, both born in North Carolina; informant was her father) [Mt. Calvary U. A. M. E. Church Cemetery]

Branch, William Franklin June 8, 1950 – December 27, 1950 (no tombstone; death certificate stated he was born in Bel Air, the son of Michael William Branch and Frances Elizabeth Daugherty, and died at home at 17 Churchville Road, Bel Air; informant was his mother Frances Branch) [Clark's U. M. Church Cemetery]

Bransford, Evelyn G. August 3, 1880 – February 6, 1941 (no tombstone; death certificate stated she was born at Rock Run, the daughter of Henry Hilton and Eliza Stansbury, both born in Harford Co.; she was married to Hugh L. Bransford, born 1884, and lived at 840 Erie Street, Havre de Grace; informant was her husband) [Green Spring U. M. Church Cemetery]

Bransford, Hugh L. Jr. September 9, 1907 – September 19, 1969, Maryland, STM1, U.S. Navy, World War II (obituary in *The Aegis* on September 25, 1969 stated Hugh Lawson Bransford, Jr. was born in Boston, worked at Perry Point VA, and died at Fort Howard VA Hospital near Baltimore; his wife was the former Aurora Dingus, of Taft, OK, now of Havre de Grace) [Green Spring U. M. Church Cemetery]

Branson, Kathrine April 17, 1919 – September 26, 1919 (no tombstone; death certificate stated she was born in Harford Co., the daughter of Lonza Branson, born in Harford Co., and Mary Williams, born in St. Mary's Co.; she died at home near Aberdeen; informant was her father) [Mt. Calvary U. A. M. E. Church Cemetery]

Branson, William C. 1920-1976, Pfc, Army Air Force, World War II [Mt. Calvary U. A. M. E. Church Cemetery]

Brant, Edward B. died August 30, 1911, age 72 (no tombstone; death certificate stated he was a widower and was born in Virginia, but parents were unknown to informant Garrie Warfield) [Union U. M. Church Cemetery]

Braswell, Anthony March 13, 1923 – December 1, 1947 (no tombstone; death certificate stated he was born in White Springs, FL, but no record of his parents, and he married Bernice ----) [St. James United Cemetery]

Braxton, Allen December 23, 1906 – September 25, 1984 [John Wesley U. M. E. Church Cemetery in Abingdon]

Braxton, Edna August 18, 1905 – April 8, 1926 (no tombstone; death certificate stated she was the daughter of Elijah White and Hannah Harris, all born in Maryland; she was married and died at Dublin; the informant was Elijah White, of Street, MD) [Clark's U. M. Church Cemetery]

Braxton, Isabell January 24, 1925 – December 18, 1979 (on same tombstone with James L. Braxton, Ruth Ann Presberry and Anthony J. Presberry) [Berkley Memorial Cemetery]

Braxton, James L. June 22, 1922 – October 11, 1996 (on same tombstone with Isabell Braxton, Ruth Ann Presberry and Anthony J. Presberry; James Dorsey Card File, African American Obituaries, maintained at the Historical Society of Harford County, has a card with obituary from *The Aegis* on October 23, 1996 stating

James Leroy Braxton was born in Harford County, the son of the late Edna White and husband of the late Isabell Presberry; he later married the late Veora Hawthorne of Alabama; he retired from the Sparrows Point Steel Mill and died at home in Perryville, survived by a son, a sister-in-law, a brother-in-law, two grandchildren and four great-grandchildren) [Berkley Memorial Cemetery]

Braxton, John April 8, 1926 – April 9, 1926 (no tombstone; death certificate stated he was premature birth who lived one day in Dublin; he was the son of Taylor Braxton, born in Virginia, and Edna White, born in Maryland; the informant was Elijah White, of Street, MD) [Clark's U. M. Church Cemetery]Braxton, Keziah "Mother" 1870-1958 [John Wesley U. M. E. Church Cemetery in Abingdon]

Braxton, Samuel "Son" 1903-1952 [John Wesley U. M. E. Church Cemetery in Abingdon]

Braxton, Thomas "Father" 1861-1961 [John Wesley U. M. E. Church Cemetery in Abingdon]

Braxton, Thomas Jr. "Son" 1900-1947 (tombstone; death certificate stated he was born July 11, 1900 at Bay View in Baltimore Co., the son of Thomas Braxton, born in King William Co., VA, and Keziah Fountain, born at Churchton, Anne Arundel Co., MD; he was single, worked as a farmer and died on May 13, 1947 in Abingdon where he had lived for 5 years; informant was Keziah Braxton, of Abingdon) [John Wesley U. M. E. Church Cemetery in Abingdon]

Bridgeforth, Portee Edmund January 20, 1948 – January 29, 1948 (no tombstone; death certificate stated he was the son of Edmund R. Bridgeforth, born in Kinbridge, VA, and Mary Thompson, born in Harford Co., and he died in Darlington; informant was his father who lived at Street, MD) [Clark's U. M. Church Cemetery]

Brightful, Eva A. 1897-1984 (on same tombstone with James D. Brightful) [Berkley Memorial Cemetery]

Brightful, James D. 1899-1984 (on same tombstone with Eva A. Brightful) [Berkley Memorial Cemetery]

Briley, Jacob February 3, 1825 – December 18, 1915 (no tombstone; death certificate stated he was born in Virginia, but his parents' names and birth places were unknown to informant William Briley, of Edgewood; he was a farmer and died a widower in Edgewood; the undertaker, Howard K. McComas, of Abingdon, stated he was buried at "Brick Church" (probably meant "black church" and buried at Foster's Hill where his son John is buried) [Foster's Hill Cemetery]

Briley, John William April 2, 1870 – December 22, 1948 (no tombstone; death certificate stated he was born in Baltimore County, the son of Jacob Briley, born in Shenandoah Valley, VA, and Mary Waters, born in Harford Co.; he married Ada Jane ---- (age 72 in 1948) and died at home in Magnolia where he had lived for 30 years; informant was Mrs. Ada J. Briley; burial was in Magnolia Methodist Cemetery) [Foster's Hill Cemetery]

Brison, Alberta December 14, 1930 – December 15, 1930, premature birth, lived one day (no tombstone; death certificate stated she was born at Street, daughter of Ray Brison, born in Virginia, and Florence? Edlers? (illegible), born in North Carolina; informant was her father) [Chestnut Grove A. M. E. Church Cemetery, formerly LaGrange Cemetery at Rocks]

Britton, Charles died August 2, 1906, age 61 (no tombstone; death certificate stated he was married to Louisa Britton, but his parents' names were blank; he was born in Maryland, worked as a laborer and died in Bel Air; on the back of the death certificate it is written "Tabernacle") [Tabernacle Mount Zion U. M. Church Cemetery]

Britton, Chatman September 15, 1841 – September 20, 1925 (no tombstone; death certificate stated he was the son of Joshua Brittan *(sic)* and Mary Lyons, all born in Maryland; he had worked as a farm hand and died a widower in Rutledge; informant was Henry Brittan *(sic)*, of Jarrettsville) [West Liberty Church Cemetery]

Britton, Emma Olevia November 23, 1912 – June 11, 1913 (no tombstone; death certificate stated she was born in Harford Co., the son of Joshua J. Britton and Eliza J. Gordon, both born in Maryland; she died at Rutledge; informant was her father, of Monkton) [West Liberty Church Cemetery]

Britton, Isaac S., son of M. J. Britton died October 18, 1860 (1869?), age 18 months (on same tombstone with Laura Britton) [Mt. Zion U. M. Church Cemetery]

Britton, Jacob, "Father" and "Husband" died July 5, 1901, age not given (on same obelisk with Rosa H. Britton, Joshua E. Britton, Jesse Ruff, David Ruff and Martha Ruff) [Mt. Zion U. M. Church Cemetery]

Britton, Joshua August 20, 1871 – December 19, 1935 (no tombstone; death certificate stated he was born in Harford Co., son of Chatman Britton, born in Harford Co., and Jane Suell, born in Virginia; he married Jane Gorden, worked as a farm laborer, lived near Lancaster's Corner and died at Fallston RFD where he had lived for 4 years; informant was Henry Britton, of Monkton; Kurtz Funeral Home Records stated similar information) [West Liberty Church Cemetery]

Britton, Joshua E. died December --, 1892 (partly illegible; on same obelisk with Jacob Britton, Rosa H. Britton, David Ruff, Jesse Ruff and Martha Ruff) [Mt. Zion U. M. Church Cemetery]

Britton, Laura, daughter of M. J. Britton age 5 years (dates not given; on same tombstone with Isaac S. Britton) [Mt. Zion U. M. Church Cemetery]

Britton, Mary died September 28, 1883, age 82 (tombstone laying flat on the ground) [West Liberty Church Cemetery]

Britton, Rosa H. (illegible dates; on same obelisk with Jacob Britton, David Ruff, Jesse Ruff and Martha Ruff) [Mt. Zion U. M. Church Cemetery]

Britton, Sarah died August 17, 1888 in her 61st year (inscribed "Blessed are the dead which die in the Lord") [West Liberty Church Cemetery]

Britton, W. Henry 1893-1998 (temporary Kurtz Funeral Home metal funeral home marker noted in 2000 was not found in 2018; obituary in *The Aegis* on November 25, 1998 stated William Henry Britton, of Cooptown, was born in Fallston, the son of John Joshua Britton and Janie Gordon, died November 17, 1998, age 95, at Franklin Square Hospital; he was a farm worked for the Ed Rahll family of Fallston and was survived by 3 sisters, Esther Spencer of Baltimore, Katherine Hall of Cooptown, and Mable Brown of Edgewood) [West Liberty Church Cemetery]

Britton, William Henry Jr. died September 9, 1985, age not given (no tombstone; obituary in *The Aegis* on September 14, 1985 stated he was the son of the late Rev. Henry Britton, Sr. and Louella Holand and died at home in Sparks, MD, survived by his wife Valerie I. Britton, one son William Britton III, one daughter Valerie N. Johnson, two grandsons William H. Britton IV and Howard M. Johnson, foster son Tony M. Smith, mother-in-law Priscilla M. Smith, son-in-law Howard M. Johnson, Sr., three sisters-in-law and six brothers-in-law) [West Liberty Church Cemetery]

Broadway, Joseph died March 19, 1911, age not given (no tombstone; death certificate stated he was a laborer at Van Bibber, died a widower and buried at Mountain; informant was Clara Turner, of Van Bibber who did not know where he was born and did not know his parents names) [Mt. Zion U. M. Church Cemetery]

Brodie, Martha September 21, 1899 – July 31, 1990 [Clark's U. M. Church Cemetery]

Brookes, Annie died August 23, 1938, age about 40 (no tombstone; death certificate stated she was born in Aiken, SC, but her parents were not known to her husband, Benjamin Brookes) [St. James United Cemetery]

Brooks, ---- stillborn male died on March 26, 1940 (no tombstone; death certificate stated he died at Harford Memorial Hospital in Havre de Grace, the son of William Edward Brooks, born in Darlington, and Blanch Sanoria Williams, born in Kalmia, and they lived near Bel Air; informant was his father) [Clark's U. M. Church Cemetery]

Brooks, ---- stillborn male on March 4, 1942 (no tombstone; death certificate stated he died at Harford Memorial Hospital in Havre de Grace, the son of Edward Brooks, born in Darlington, and Blanche Williams, born in Bel Air, and they lived near Bel Air; the information on death certificate was gleaned by an unidentified person from the hospital records) [Clark's U. M. Church Cemetery]

Brooks, Alfred A. April 5, 1936 – July 2, 1961, Maryland, SP4, U.S. Army, Btry C, 1st Artillery [Clark's U. M. Church Cemetery]

Brooks, Benjamin September 16, 1893 – November 19, 1947 (death certificate; on the same tombstone with Minnie Brooks, but the bottom of the small tombstone is completely eroded away) [St. James United Cemetery]

Brooks, Beulah W. February 23, 1933 – January 9, 2010 (inscribed "Forever in our hearts;" death notice in *The*

Aegis on January 13, 2010 stated she died at Upper Chesapeake Medical Center in Bel Air) [Clark's U. M. Church Cemetery]

Brooks, Blanche C. April 7, 1910 – April 23, 2003 (inscribed "In Loving Memory;" her picture is on the tombstone and in her obituary in *The Aegis* on April 30, 2002; she was born in Harford Co., the daughter of John Wesley Williams and Druescella Williams, and married Edward Brooks who predeceased her; she was survived by 1 daughter, 2 sons (2 other sons predeceased her), 2 sisters (1 sister predeceased her as did 4 brothers), 3 daughters-in-law, 20 grandchildren, 31 great-grandchildren, and 10 great-great-grandchildren) [Clark's U. M. Church Cemetery]

Brooks, Charity V. died December 29, 1972, age 52 (no tombstone; obituary in *The Aegis* on January 4, 1973 stated she was the wife of Edward Brooks, of 618 Giles Street in Aberdeen, and died at Harford Memorial Hospital in Havre de Grace, survived by her husband, son Harrison, 3 sisters, and 3 brothers; she had worked for attorney A. Freeborn Brown for 20 years) [Mt. Calvary U. A. M. E. Church Cemetery]

Brooks, Charles December 25, 1882 – February 13, 1947 (no tombstone; death certificate stated he was born in Darlington, the son of Charles H. Brooks, born in Maryland, and Becky Bond, born in Churchville; he married Ella --- (age 59 in 1947), worked "house duties and store help," lived in Bel Air and died at Harford Memorial Hospital in Havre de Grace; informant was his wife Mrs. Ella Brooks, of Bel Air) [Asbury Cemetery]

Brooks, Clinton May 3, 1894 – July 4, 1966, Maryland, Bn, Sgt. Maj., U.S. Army, World War I (on same tombstone with C. Madelaine Brooks, neé Gibson; obituary in *The Aegis* on July 7, 1966 stated he lived at Cedar, MD and died at Perry Point VA Hospital, survived by his wife Madelaine Brooks, 4 daughters, 3 sons, 2 sisters, 3 brothers and 15 grandchildren; military records stated he was born in Darlington and lived at Forest Hill when inducted into the U.S. Army on October 27, 1917; he served overseas from June 19, 1918 to February 21, 1919 and was honorably discharged on March 10, 1919) [Clark's U. M. Church Cemetery]

Brooks, Courtney Madelaine May 20, 1904 – April 12, 2000 (inscribed C. Madelaine Brooks neé Gibson; obituary and photo in *The Aegis* on April 19, 2000 stated she was the eldest of 13 children born to John H. Gibson and Sarah E. Whittington; she married Clinton Brooks on October 17, 1923, had seven children, worked as a caregiver for the Ruby Nottage family for nearly two decades and served on Clark's Chapel Usher Board for over 50 years; she was survived by two sons, four daughters, 15 grandchildren, 2 great-grandchildren, 8 great-great-grandchildren, 3 daughters-in-law, 3 sons-in-law, an aunt and an uncle, and was predeceased by 6 sisters, 3 brothers, and a son Sturgis Brooks who died in July 1984) [Clark's U. M. Church Cemetery]

Brooks, Dilcie 1849-1940 (tombstone inscription, but death certificate stated Dilcy Ann Brooks was born on December 3, 1857 and died on January 15, 1940) [St. James United Cemetery]

Brooks, Edward February 5, 1896 – April 15, 1978, Pvt., U.S. Army, World War I (tombstone; military records stated he was born in Darlington and lived at Bel Air RFD #3 when inducted into the U.S. Army on August 23, 1918; he was a private in the 153 Dep Brig. and Co. A., 811 Pioneer Inf., served overseas from October 20, 1918 to July 24, 1919 and was honorably discharged on July 28, 1919) [Clark's U. M. Church Cemetery]

Brooks, Edward March 4, 1835 – April 1, 1926 (no tombstone; death certificate stated he was born in Maryland, but his parents were not known to the informant James E. Brooks, of Bel Air; he was a farmer and widower who lived at Kalmia) [Clark's U. M. Church Cemetery]

Brooks, Edward B. August 5, 1880 – June 7, 1936, E----(?) Company I, 25th Infantry (tombstone; death certificate stated he was a veteran of the Spanish American War and World War I, but service was not found in published Maryland military records) [Tabernacle Mount Zion U. M. Church Cemetery]

Brooks, Elizabeth December 12, 1913 – February 25, 1913 (no tombstone; death certificate stated she was the daughter of Charles E. Brooks and Ella Butler, all were born in Maryland, and they lived in Bel Air; informant was her father) [Hendon Hill Cemetery]

Brooks, Ella Butler June 19, 1895 – December 28, 1950 (no tombstone; death certificate stated she was born in Churchville, the daughter of John and Mary Butler; she lived in Bel Air for 40 years and died a widow; informant was Ocela B. Hewett, of Bel Air) [Asbury Cemetery]

Brooks, Ella E. October 14, 1916 – August 19, 1917 (no tombstone; death certificate stated she was the daughter of Charles Brooks and Ella E. Butler, all were born in Harford Co. and they lived in Bel Air; informant was Ella E. Brooks, of Bel Air) [Hendon Hill Cemetery]

Brooks, Ham April 28, 1920 – May 1, 1920 (no tombstone; death certificate stated he was the son of Charles Brooks and Ella Butler and they were all born in Maryland and lived in Bel Air) [Hendon Hill Cemetery]

Brooks, Hattie Queen August 17, 1937 – June 5, 2002 (obituary in *The Aegis* on June 28, 2002 stated she was born in Harford County, the daughter of the late Jacob A. Giles, Sr. and the late Eva D. Giles Warfield, and the wife of the late James Brooks; she lived in Aberdeen and died at University of Maryland Hospital in Baltimore, survived by a son Donald Clark, daughter Muriel King, 3 grandchildren, 2 sisters, 1 brother, 4 aunts, and many other relatives) [Berkley Memorial Cemetery]

Brooks, Helen Katherine died March 7, 1993, age 58 (no tombstone; James Dorsey Card File, African American Obituaries, maintained at the Historical Society of Harford County, has a card with obituary with a photo from *The Aegis* on March 24, 1993 stating she was born in Darlington, daughter of the late Howard and Martha Gray, and was survived by husband Perry Joseph Brooks, of Bel Air, 4 daughters, a brother and 6 grandchildren) [Berkley Memorial Cemetery]

Brooks, Ida Mae stillborn on June 27, 1937 (no tombstone; death certificate stated she was born and died near Bel Air, the daughter of Clinton and Madeline Brooks, both born in Maryland; informant was her father) [Clark's U. M. Church Cemetery]

Brooks, James Monroe 1931-1994, U.S. Army, Korea [Clark's U. M. Church Cemetery]

Brooks, James W. 1943-2011 (small metal funeral home marker) [Berkley Memorial Cemetery]

Brooks, James Wesley died April 2, 2011, age 67 (funeral notice and photo in *The Aegis* on April 6, 2011 stated he lived in Havre de Grace and died at the University of Maryland Hospital in Baltimore) [Berkley Memorial Cemetery]

Brooks, Jo'Van Lamar November 2, 1983 – May 26, 2001 (inscribed "Beloved Son and Friend to Many" and included his photo) [Foster's Hill Cemetery]

Brooks, Lillian L. died December 7, 1969, age not given (no tombstone; obituary in *The Aegis* on December 11, 1969 stated she was the daughter of the late Charles and Ella Brooks, of 1316 N. Eutaw St. in Baltimore and she died at Bolton Hill Nursing Home in Baltimore) [Asbury Cemetery]

Brooks, Mary died August 10, 1912, age 84 (no tombstone; death certificate stated she was the daughter of Peter and Mary E. Wallice, and they were all born in Talbot Co., MD; she died a widow in Aberdeen; informant was William Mitchell, of Aberdeen) [Mt. Calvary U. A. M. E. Church Cemetery]

Brooks, Minnie Anderson October 1, 1891 – February 8, 1949 (death certificate; on same tombstone with Benjamin Brooks, but the bottom of their small tombstone was completely eroded away) [St. James United Cemetery]

Brooks, Perry A. June 25, 1902 – November 26, 1920 (no tombstone; death certificate stated he was the son of James E. Brooks and Laura J. Thompson, all born in Maryland; he was a laborer who died at Kalmia; informant was his mother Laura J. Brooks, of Bel Air) [Clark's U. M. Church Cemetery]

Brooks, Phillip January 14, 1913 – February 27, 1913 (no tombstone; death certificate stated he was the son of Charles Brooks and Elizabeth E. Butler, of Bel Air; all were born in Harford Co.) [Hendon Hill Cemetery]

Brooks, Rosalie C. February 2, 1932 – May 7, 1993 (on same tombstone with William E. Brooks; James Dorsey Card File, African American Obituaries, maintained at the Historical Society of Harford County, has a card with her obituary from *The Aegis* on May 19, 1993 stating she was born in Baltimore, the daughter of the late Mildred Gibson and James Hall, and moved to Harford County as a child; she was employed at Bata Shoe Company for 12 years and worked for awhile at Daneker's clock factory in Benson; she lived in Bel Air and died at Fallston General Hospital, survived by her husband of 43 years William E. Brooks, and 4 children, 7 grandchildren, 2 sisters and 2 brothers) [Clark's U. M. Church Cemetery]

Brooks, Seranna May 10, 1924 – January 2, 1925 (no tombstone; death certificate stated she was born in

Maryland, the daughter of Benjamin Brooks and Annie Spand, both of South Carolina, and died in Havre de Grace) [St. James United Cemetery]

Brooks, Theodore September 27, 1911 – December 24, 1911 (no tombstone; death certificate stated he was born in Bel Air, the son of Charles E. Brooks and Ella E. Butler, all born in Harford Co.) [Hendon Hill Cemetery]

Brooks, William Bernard May 16, 1951 – May 17, 1951 (no tombstone; death certificate stated he was born and died at Harford Memorial Hospital in Havre de Grace; he was the son of William Edward Brooks and Rosalie Catherine Hall who lived at Bel Air RFD #1) [Clark's U. M. Church Cemetery]

Brooks, William E. April 16, 1929 -   (on same tombstone with Rosalie C.) [Clark's U. M. Church Cemetery]

Brooks-Taylor, Mary M. September 3, 1933 – July 6, 2012 (no tombstone; obituary in *The Aegis* on July 11, 2013 indicated her name was Mary M. Brooks, but then stated Mary M. Brooks-Taylor, of Bel Air, died at Manor Care Nursing Home on Rossville, MD; she was the daughter of Edward and Blanche Brooks and resided in Darlington with her life-companion, the late Charles (Billy) Townley; she was survived by 3 daughters, 6 grandchildren, 11 great-grandchildren, 5 great-great-grandchildren, and 3 brothers (2 others had predeceased her) [Clark's U. M. Church Cemetery]

Brown, ---- (no tombstone, but Kurtz Funeral Home records stated Henry Brown's wife was buried in a nice cherry coffin on August 7, 1880 from near Denbo Shop) [Hendon Hill Cemetery]

Brown, ---- (no tombstone; death notice in *The Aegis* on January 8, 1897 reported a little adopted child of Thadeus Brown, near Bagley, fell down stairs a few days ago, suffered a con-cussion and died about six hours later; burial place not reported [most likely Tabernacle Mount Zion U. M. Church Cemetery]

Brown, ---- stillborn male died March 20, 1926 (no tombstone; death certificate stated he was the son of Daniel Brown, born in Harford Co, and Mary Hayman, born in Annapolis; informant was Daniel Brown, of Benson) [Tabernacle Mount Zion U. M. Church Cemetery]

Brown, ---- stillborn male died October 19, 1939, premature birth at 4 months (no tombstone; death certificate stated "Baby Brown" was the son of Perry Brown and Louise Quickley, of Joppa, and all were born in Maryland) [Tabernacle Mount Zion U. M. Church Cemetery]

Brown, Aaron N. Sr. "Beloved Son & Father" November 29, 1954 – August 17, 1989 [Berkley Memorial Cemetery]

Brown, Addie C., daughter of E. J. and Ella Brown, died August 29, 1888, age 9 years and 5 months [Asbury Cemetery]

Brown, Adeline May 16, 1882 – April 7, 1938 (no tombstone; death certificate stated she was born in Harford Co, the daughter of William Taylor and Susan Hopkins, both born in Maryland; she was a widow and died at Harford Memorial Hospital in Havre de Grace; informant was Miss Pearley Brown, of Havre de Grace, who did not know her husband's name) [Asbury Cemetery]

Brown, Agnes T., neé Griffin, "Mom" November 10, 1925 – April 20, 2009 (on same tombstone with Vernon W. Brown) [Union U. M. Church Cemetery]

Brown, Albert 1907-1982 (copied in 1987, but not found in 2018; obituary in *The Aegis* on August 5, 1982 stated he was born in Miami, FL, the son of the late Jim and Bertha Brown, and husband of Annie Bowser Hollis Brown; he lived in Aberdeen, died at the Bel Air Convalescent Center, survived by his wife, 2 daughters, 2 step-sons, 1 step-daughter, and 3 grandchildren; buried in section 39) [Mt. Calvary U. A. M. E. Church Cemetery]

Brown, Alexander died August 15, 1947, age about 60 (no tombstone; death certificate stated he was born in Georgia, parents unknown; he was unmarried and worked as a laborer on Greenway's farm near Havre de Grace; informant was William McComas) [St. James United Cemetery]

Brown, Alice 1920-2016 (small metal funeral home marker) [St. James United Cemetery]

Brown, Amanda August 15, 1857 – February 11, 1928 (no tombstone; death certificate stated she was the daughter of Henry Hall and Mary Norton, all born in Maryland; she was a widow and died in Bel Air; informant was Mitchell Brown, of Bel Air) [Tabernacle Mount Zion U. M. Church Cemetery]

Brown, Annie M. January 19, 1866 – June 11, 1936 (no tombstone; death certificate stated she was the unmarried daughter of Robert W. Brown and Dihon Christy, all born in Perryman; she died near Aberdeen and the informant was Mrs. Hattie S. Hollingsworth, of Aberdeen) [Union U. M. Church Cemetery]

Brown, Annie M. July 15, 1889 – March 17, 1966 [Union U. M. Church Cemetery]

Brown, Antoine L. Sr. 1968-2011 [St. James United Cemetery]

Brown, Armistead Junius died May 7, 1912, age 73 (no tombstone; death certificate stated he was born in Ohio, married, and died in Joppa, but the names of his parents and their places of birth were not known to informant William A. Bishop, of Joppa P. O.; see Junius A. Brown) [Mt. Zion U. M. Church Cemetery]

Brown, Arthur August 1, 1903 – August 24, 1917 (no tombstone; death certificate stated he was born in Harford Co., the son of Arthur Brown and Adeline Taylor, both born in Maryland and lived in Havre de Grace; informant was Mrs. Adeline Brown, of Havre de Grace) [Asbury Cemetery]

Brown, Augusta A. 1864 – 1908 (on same tombstone with Francis O. Brown) [St. James United Cemetery]

Brown, Baby – see Baby (Brown) Warfield [Union U. M. Church Cemetery]

Brown, Benjamin McClennan March 11, 1863 – October 18, 1950 (no tombstone; death certificate stated he was born in Fallston, the son of Edward Brown and Susanna Moore; he was a farm hand who died a widower in rural Joppa where he lived for 10 years; informant was Isabelle Robinson) [Tabernacle Mount Zion U. M. Church Cemetery]

Brown, Bertha B. June 11, 1914 – October 11, 1927 (no tombstone; death certificate stated she was the daughter of George Whims and Ida May Brown, all born in Maryland; they lived in Havre de Grace; informant was Nellie Lee, of Havre de Grace) [Green Spring U. M. Church Cemetery]

Brown, Brenton W. "BB" July 31, 1949 – December 13, 2012 (inscribed "In God's Care" with an image of a golfer and another of golf clubs; funeral notice and photo in *The Aegis* on December 19, 2012 stated he died in Havre de Grace) [Berkley Memorial Cemetery]

Brown, C. W. E. 1879-1924 (on same tombstone with E. O. Brown and M. E. Brown Reed) [Union U. M. Church Cemetery]

Brown, Carl U. September 24, 1926 – June 15, 1990, Pvt., U.S. Army, World War II (on same tombstone with Dorothy M. Brown; James Dorsey Card File, African American Obituaries, maintained at the Historical Society of Harford County, has a card with obituary from *The Aegis* on June 27, 1990 stating "Collie" was born in Harford County, the son of the late Walter and Mamie Brown; he married Dorothy Marie Peaco, was employed at Aberdeen Proving Grounds and started his own upholstering business after his retirement; he lived in Havre de Grace and died at Harford Memorial Hospital, survived by his wife, a son, 3 daughters, a brother, 2 sisters and 5 grandchildren) [Union U. M. Church Cemetery]

Brown, Carolyn J. July 2, 1943 – January 3, 2002 (on same tombstone with Myrtle L. Spates, mother, and the tombstone is inscribed with a poem titled "Just One Heart") [St. James United Cemetery]

Brown, Carrie L. November 18, 1895 – November 13, 1972 (on same tombstone with John W. Brown) [Asbury Cemetery]

Brown, Carrie Vivian August 3 – November 21, 1931 (no tombstone; death certificate stated she was born in Bel Air, the daughter of Mitchell Brown, born near Bel Air, and Mattie K. Robinson, born in Virginia; informant was her father) [Tabernacle Mount Zion U. M. Church Cemetery]

Brown, Cecelia I. December 6, 1928 – November 5, 2014 (small temporary plastic marker with her photo) [Union U. M. Church Cemetery]

Brown, Charles A. March 25, 1907 – January 20, 1912 (no tombstone; death certificate stated he was the son of Graham Brown and Blanche Turner, all born in Harford Co.; he died at Forest Hill; informant was Graham Brown, of Bel Air) [Tabernacle Mount Zion U. M. Church Cemetery]

Brown, Charles H., husband of Ida M. Brown, died July 13, 1918 ("Asleep In Jesus;" death certificate stated he was the married son of Charles H. Brown, both born in Virginia, but his mother was unknown to informant Mrs. C. H. Brown, of Havre de Grace; Charles died at about age 56) [Union U. M. Church Cemetery]

Brown, Charles W. B. October 24, 1922 – January 13, 1923 (no tombstone; death certificate stated he was born in Philadelphia and died at Kalmia, the son of Jannie Bounis, but the name of his father and their places of birth were not known to the informant Charlotte Brown, of Bel Air) [Clark's U. M. Church Cemetery]

Brown, Corine M. August 2, 1924 – April 22, 1935 (no tombstone; death certificate stated she was the daughter of Graham Brown and Blanch Turner, and they all were born in Harford Co.) [Tabernacle Mount Zion U. M. Church Cemetery]

Brown, D. 1948 (tombstone next to F. W. Brown) [Berkley Memorial Cemetery]

Brown, Daisy R. 1908-2001 (on same tombstone with Thos. O. Brown; obituary and photo in *The Aegis* on June 27, 2001 stated she was born September 12, 1908 in Perryman, the daughter of John I. and Bessie V. Hoke, and worked over 27 years as a shift food supervisor at the Kirk Army Hospital for the exchange snack bar; she died June 24, 1001, age 91, and was survived by a daughter Marie Christy, a son-in-law Bernard Christy, Sr., 5 grandchildren, 2 step-grandsons, 12 great-grandchildren and 12 great-great-grandchildren) [Union U. M. Church Cemetery]

Brown, Daniel Q. March 27, 1879 – April 20, 1951 (no tombstone; death certificate stated he was born in Maryland, the son of Louis G. Brown and Elizabeth Heath, worked as a day laborer on a farm and died at home on Washington St. in Aberdeen; he was married and informant was Mrs. Minnie L. Brown) [Union U. M. Church Cemetery]

Brown, David 1873-1965 (on same tombstone with Mary Lou Brown; obituary in *The Aegis* on October 21, 1965 stated he was a highly regarded Negro and Republican leader and died October 16, 1965 at his home on Reckord Road in Fallston, survived by 2 sons and 2 daughters) [Tabernacle Mount Zion U. M. Church Cemetery]

Brown, Dorothy Attee June 21, 1914 – May 1, 2007 (inscribed "In Memory" and "Loving Mother and Grandmother;" obituary and photo in *The Aegis* on May 4, 2007 stated she was the daughter of John Westly McMullen and Lula Etta Ann Johnson and lived in Port Deposit, moving there when 4 years old after her mother had accepted a teaching position; she was the widow of Ernest Washington Brown and died at Union Hospital in Elkton, survived by 3 sons, 4 daughters, 32 grandchildren, 43 great-grandchildren, 8 great-great-grand-children, an adopted grandson, 2 nephews and predeceased by 3 sons and 2 brothers) [Berkley Memorial Cemetery]

Brown, Dorothy M., "Beloved Wife and Mother" March 13, 1931 – September 11, 1992 (on same tombstone with Carl U. Brown; tombstone had complete information about her birth and death at the time of her passing, but when copied in 2018 it was noticed the date of death plate was removed) [Union U. M. Church Cemetery]

Brown, E. O. 1876-1917 (on same tombstone with C. W. E. Brown and M. E. Brown Reed) [Union U. M. Church Cemetery]

Brown, Edna E. July 24, 1909 – December 12, 1955 [St. James United Cemetery]

Brown, Edward J. July 8, 1873 – August 30, 1925 (no tombstone; death certificate stated he was the son of John W. Brown, both born in Maryland, but his mother's name was not known to informant Ester Brown, of Bel Air; he was married and a farmer near Bel Air) [Asbury Cemetery]

Brown, Edward J. September 8, 1837 – March 10, 1904 (inscribed "Asleep in Jesus blessed sleep;" death certificate stated he was the son of Benjamin Brown and Matilda Cooper, all born in Maryland; he was a farmer at Churchville; informant was his wife Elenora) [Asbury Cemetery]

Brown, Eleanor E. died July 29, 1982 (no tombstone; obituary in *The Aegis* on August 12, 1982 stated she was the widow of Gram *(sic)* Brown and survived by 2 brothers, 2 sisters, 6 sons, 4 daughters, 18 grandchildren, and 6 great-grandchildren; see Graham A. Brown, Jr.) [Tabernacle Mount Zion U. M. Church Cemetery]

Brown, Eliza died July 3, 1910, age 38 (no tombstone; death certificate stated she was born in Harford Co, the daughter of Daniel Spencer and Mary Johnson, was married and then divorced, worked as a servant and died at Mountain; informant was her brother Aaron Johnson Spencer; her place of burial was not indicated, but it may have been in this cemetery; Harford County divorce records stated that Thaddeus Stephens Brown and Frances Eliza Spencer were married in 1892, she filed for divorce in 1905 and it was granted in 1906) [Mt. Zion U. M. Church Cemetery]

Brown, Elizabeth E. died January 17, 1967, age not given (no tombstone; obituary in *The Aegis* on February 2, 1967 stated she was the wife of Robert E. Brown and she died in Citizens Nursing Home in Havre de Grace) [Asbury Cemetery]

Brown, Elizabeth H. March 7, 1842 – June 28, 1916 (no tombstone; death certificate stated she died a widow and was the daughter of Isaac Heath and Harriet Boyer, all born in Maryland) [Union U. M. Church Cemetery]

Brown, Elizabeth Hall March 23, 1898 – January 17, 1967 (on same tombstone with Charles W. Hall) [Asbury Cemetery]

Brown, Ella died January 23, 1992, age 75 (no tombstone; obituary in *The Aegis* on February 12, 1992 stated she was the daughter of Newton and Lizzy Anderson and resided in the Fallston area for 40 years; she was the widow of Robert Brown) [Tabernacle Mount Zion U. M. Church Cemetery]

Brown, Ella C. 1873-1931 (on same tombstone with Isaac W. Brown; death certificate stated she was born April 21, 1876, married, and died January 9, 1931; she was the daughter of Kailer Reed and Harriett Harris; informant was Isaac Brown, of Perryman) [Union U. M. Church Cemetery]

Brown, Ella May October 20, 1910 – January 22, 1911 (no tombstone; death certificate stated she was the daughter of David Brown and Flora Berry, of Havre de Grace) [St. James United Cemetery]

Brown, Ellen died February 2, 1893, age not given (no tombstone; her death notice in *The Aegis* on February 10, 1893 stated she was the wife of Joseph Brown, of Fallston, and was buried in a meadow in front of Patrick Maynes' house on Bel Air Road, but the following week the newspaper corrected it to report she was buried "at the Tabernacle") [Tabernacle Mount Zion U. M. Church Cemetery]

Brown, Ellen A. June 23, 1898 – April 5, 1933 (no tombstone; death certificate stated she was born in West Chester, PA, daughter of Martha Pitt, father unknown, and she was divorced) [Union U. M. Church Cemetery]

Brown, Elsie M. Quickley died June 30, 1990, age 70 (no tombstone; obituary in *The Aegis* on July 11, 1990 stated she was formerly of Harford Co. and died in Washington, DC at Capitol Hill Hospital; she was the daughter of Amelia and Isaac Quickley, married Edwin Brown in 1942, moved to Washington, DC and retired from the federal government) [Tabernacle Mount Zion U. M. Church Cemetery]

Brown, Emily Williams, daughter of Edward and Susanna Brown, died July 20, 1909, age 4 years [Tabernacle Mount Zion U. M. Church Cemetery]

Brown, Emmett A. 1936-2016 (small metal funeral home marker) [Berkley Memorial Cemetery]

Brown, Eugene April 13, 1887 – November 24, 1947 (no tombstone; death certificate stated he was born in Bel Air, the son of William Brown, born in Baltimore Co., and Amanda Hall, born in Harford Co.; he married Ollie Curry, worked as a day laborer and died in Bel Air by accidentally drowning in a small stream; informant was Mrs. Herbert Bond, of Jarrettsville; Kurtz Funeral Home Record Book 1944-1949, p. 177, stated the same and added that he was a widower and funeral services were held at Ames Methodist Church) [Tabernacle Mount Zion U. M. Church Cemetery]

Brown, Evelyn 1913-2011 (small metal funeral home marker; funeral notice and photo in *The Aegis* on July 22, 2011 stated Evelyn E. Brown lived in Havre de Grace and died at Stella Maris in Timonium, MD on July 19, 2011, age 98) [Berkley Memorial Cemetery]

Brown, F. W. 1930 (tombstone next to D. Brown) [Berkley Memorial Cemetery]

Brown, Flora M. September 1, 1891 – October 18, 1914 (no tombstone; death certificate stated she was the married daughter of William Jones and Emma Flitcher, all born in Harford Co., informant was David Brown, of Havre de Grace) [St. James United Cemetery]

Brown, Frances Ann November 23, 1933 – March 18, 2017 (no tombstone; obituary in *The Aegis* stated she was born in Charlottesville, VA and relocated with her family to Havre de Grace; she was "a dedicated member of St. James A. M. E. Church of Gravel Hill where she served as steward, missionary, treasurer, trustee, choir member and usher, among many other hats") [Gravel Hill Cemetery]

Brown, Francis Leroy November 7, 1946 – March 16, 1987, U.S. Army [Union U. M. Church Cemetery]

Brown, Francis O. 1859-1951 (on same tombstone with Augusta A. Brown) [St. James United Cemetery]

Brown, Freda E. 1929-2016 (Order of the Eastern Star symbol on tombstone; a brief obituary in *The Aegis* stated Freda Eleanora Brown, of Bel Air, died on January 7, 2016 at the Citizens Nursing Home in Havre de Grace) [Clark's U. M. Church Cemetery]

Brown, George born and died February 19, 1946, lived only 9 hours (no tombstone; death certificate stated he was the son of George Brown and Mildred Hawkins, all born in Maryland, and they lived in Fallston; informant was his father) [Tabernacle Mount Zion U. M. Church Cemetery]

Brown, George H. October 26, 1906 – July 16, 1983 (on the same tombstone with Mildred O. Brown; obituary in *The Aegis*, July 21, 1983, reported George Henry Brown was the husband of the late Mildred O. Brown, of Street, MD, and son of David and Mary Lou Brown) [Chestnut Grove A. M. E. Church Cemetery, formerly LaGrange Cemetery at Rocks]

Brown, Grace Mae 1927-2016 (small metal funeral home marker) [St. James United Cemetery]

Brown, Graham A., Jr. January 17, 1920 – November 8, 1964, STM2, USNR, World War II (tombstone; see Eleanor E. Brown) [Tabernacle Mount Zion U. M. Church Cemetery]

Brown, Gwendolyn Geneva November 3, 1924 – October 25, 1997 (tombstone; James Dorsey Card File, African American Obituaries, maintained at the Historical Society of Harford County, has a card with obituary from *The Aegis* on October 29, 1997 stating she was born in Perryman, daughter of Walter Brown and Mamie Kennard; she was an assembly line worker at Bata Shoe Company, lived in Aberdeen and died at Harford Memorial Hospital in Havre de Grace, survived by sons Charles H., Jr., Brian K., and Anthony O. Williams, five daughters, a brother, a sister, 11 grandchildren and 17 great-grandchildren; she was predeceased by son Lawrence L. Ringgold, Jr. (died 1966) and son David M. Williams) [Union U. M. Church Cemetery]

Brown, Hanson J. L. 1895-1962 [Tabernacle Mount Zion U. M. Church Cemetery]

Brown, Hardy February 15, 1921 – May 10, 1945, Maryland, PFC, 24th Inf., World War II, PH [Tabernacle Mount Zion U. M. Church Cemetery]

Brown, Harold 1964-2016 (small metal funeral home marker) [Berkley Memorial Cemetery]

Brown, Harold April 22, 1922 -   (on same tombstone with Iona Brown) [Union U. M. Church Cemetery]

Brown, Harold M. 1941-20_3 (small metal funeral home marker with a number missing) [St. James United Cemetery]

Brown, Harriett Odessa July 28, 1888 – August 3, 1932 (no tombstone; death certificate stated she was the daughter of Nathaniel Durbin and Hester Dennis, all born in Havre de Grace, and wife of Robert Brown [St. James United Cemetery]

Brown, Harry stillborn on July 13, 1940 (no tombstone; death certificate stated he was the son of Harold A. Brown and Ann P. Christy) [Union U. M. Church Cemetery]

Brown, Harry L. April 20, 1886 – April 10, 1913 (no tombstone; death certificate stated he was the son of Joseph H. Brown and Ella V. Garnet, all born in Maryland; he was farm hand who lived and died at Creswell; informant was his father) [Asbury Cemetery]

Brown, Harry Walter November 22, 1935 – December 4, 1992, U.S. Air Force, Korea (Harry W. Brown, born 1935, is also on the same tombstone with Meta Brown, James H. Brown, Stewart C. Brown and Meta G. Clark) [St. James United Cemetery]

Brown, Harvey J. June 6, 1913 – September 7, 1913 (no tombstone; death certificate stated he was the son of Davie Brown, born in Harford Co., and Flora Pinion, born in Cecil Co.); informant was his father [St. James United Cemetery]

Brown, Harvey L. March 20, 1922 – February 5, 1985, U.S. Navy World War II (tombstone; obituary in *The Aegis* stated Harvey Lilbon Brown, of Edgewood, died at home; he was born in Benson, the son of Lilbon Brown and Ellen Lowery, married Mable Britton, and was survived by his wife, 6 sons, 4 daughters, 35 grandchildren, 16 great-grandchildren) [Tabernacle Mount Zion U. M. Church Cemetery]

Brown, Henry September 22, 1888 – January 2, 1929 (no tombstone; death certificate stated he was the son of Zacriah Brown and Elizabeth Parker, all born in Maryland; he was married, worked as a laborer at Edgewood Arsenal and died in an automobile accident with a B&O express train at Joppa station; informant was Simon Brown, of Bradshaw, MD) [Asbury Cemetery]

Brown, Henry E. March 23, 1921 – December 15, 1988, Maryland, PFC, U.S. Army [Union U. M. Church Cemetery]

Brown, Hester A. died January 13, 1918, age about 70 (no tombstone; death certificate stated she was the daughter of Hollinger Rochester, both born in Maryland; her mother was unknown to informant Isaac Brown, of Havre de Grace RFD; she was married; died at Gravelly Hill) [Gravel Hill Cemetery]

Brown, Houston F. June 17, 1923 – January 5, 1963, MD, Pfc., U.S. Army [Union U. M. Church Cemetery]

Brown, Imman 1999-2004 (small metal funeral home marker) [St. James United Cemetery]

Brown, Iona April 12, 1920 – May 16, 1979 (on same tombstone with Harold Brown) [Union U. M. Church Cemetery]

Brown, Isaac died April 4, 1918, age about 52 (no tombstone; death certificate stated he was the son of John Brown, both born in Maryland, but the name of his mother was not known to informant Mrs. Sarah Taylor, of Havre de Grace; he was a laborer and died a widower in Havre de Grace) [Gravel Hill Cemetery]

Brown, Isaac March 4, 1868 – March 13, 1938 (no tombstone; death certificate stated he was born in Darlington, but his parents were not known to informant Mrs. Effie Brown, of Bel Air; he married Effie ----, worked as a day laborer for 45 years until December 1936 and died at home at 32 Howard St. where he had lived for 50 years; buried in "Mountain Cemetery") [Mt. Zion U. M. Church Cemetery]

Brown, Isaac W. 1874-1966 (on same tombstone with Ella C. Brown) [Union U. M. Church Cemetery]

Brown, Jacqueline M. July 21, 1951 – September 3, 1976 [Union U. M. Church Cemetery]

Brown, James B. January 13, 1945 – August 19, 1997 (tombstone; James Dorsey Card File, African American Obituaries, that is maintained at the Historical Society of Harford County, has a card with obituary from an unidentified newspaper on August 27, 1997 stating he was born in Orangeburg, SC, the son of James and Albertha Brown, and was raised by his grandparents Appie and Ida Ferrell in Branchville, SC; in 1962 he moved to Atlantic City, NJ where he worked as an autopsy assistant at the Atlantic City Medical Center; in 1968 he moved to Havre de Grace where he married Audrey Brown and in 1993 he married Drema Brown; "J. B." lived in Aberdeen where he worked as a chauffeur-laborer for the Harford County Department of Public Works and he died at the University of Maryland Medical Center in Baltimore; he was survived by his second wife, three sons, four daughters, a sister, his mother-in-law Susie Mitchell, and 15 grandchildren) [St. James United Cemetery]

Brown, James E. 1937-   [Clark's U. M. Church Cemetery]

Brown, James H. 1940-   (on same tombstone with Meta Brown, Harry W. Brown, Stewart C. Brown and Meta G. Clark) [St. James United Cemetery]

Brown, James W. 1851-1923 (on same tombstone with Martha K. Brown; death certificate stated he was born June 16, 1855, the son of Robert Brown and Dinah Christy, all born in Maryland, and informant was Mrs. James Brown, of Perryman) [Union U. M. Church Cemetery]

Brown, Jessie H. 1920-2001 (small metal funeral home marker) [Union U. M. Church Cemetery]

Brown, John A. August 27, 1951 – December 9, 2011 [Tabernacle Mount Zion U. M. Church Cemetery]

Brown, John E. January 15, 1912 – May 6, 1913(?) (no tombstone) [St. James United Cemetery]

Brown, John Henry October 1, 1897 – December 28, 1916 (no tombstone; death certificate stated he was the son of Ephraim Brown and Mary J. Bordley, all born in Maryland) [Union U. M. Church Cemetery]

Brown, John W. died February 27, 1893, age – (tombstone partially underground) [Asbury Cemetery]

Brown, John W. January 21, 1892 – November 13, 1978 (on same tombstone with Carrie L. Brown; also a military marker: Pvt., U.S. Army, World War I; military record stated he was born at Churchville and inducted on August 23, 1918, served in 59 Co., 15 Bn., 153 Dep. Brig., and was honorably discharged on December 12, 1918) [Asbury Cemetery]

Brown, Joseph died after February 1893 (no tombstone, but wife Ellen is buried here so he probably is also) [Tabernacle Mount Zion U. M. Church Cemetery]

Brown, Joseph H. died November 1, 1919, age 50 (no tombstone; death certificate stated he was born in Maryland, was married, worked as a laborer and died in Abingdon; names and places of birth of his parents were not known to informant Hamm(?) S. Brown, of Towsend) [John Wesley U. M. E. Church Cemetery in Abingdon]

Brown, Joseph H. July 18, 1929 – March 23, 1930 (no tombstone; death certificate stated he died in Bel Air and was the son of T. H. Brown and Amelia G. Booker; they were all born in Maryland; informant was Joseph Booker, of Bel Air) [Hendon Hill Cemetery]

Brown, Junius A. died May 7, 1912, age 77 (no tombstone; death certificate stated he was married and worked as a farm laborer at Bradshaw, but his place of birth and names and places of birth of his parents were not known to informant S. G. Rawlings, of Bradshaw; see Armistead Junius Brown) [Mt. Zion U. M. Church Cemetery]

Brown, Kenneth Jehu July 7, 1924 – November 28, 1963, Maryland, STM1, USNR, World War II [Tabernacle Mount Zion U. M. Church Cemetery]

Brown, Kenneth Lewis May 3, 1944 – May 19, 1944 (no tombstone; death certificate stated he died near Benson, the son of Harvey Brown and Mable Britton, all born in Maryland) [Tabernacle Mount Zion U. M. Church Cemetery]

Brown, L. Philip August 1, 1854 – August 15, 1912 (no tombstone; death certificate stated he was married and the son of Philip Brown, both born in Baltimore, mother not known, and wife not named; he was struck and killed by a train in Havre de Grace) [St. James United Cemetery]

Brown, Lawrence Leroy November 7, 1940 – March 16, 1987, U.S. Army [Union U. M. Church Cemetery]

Brown, Lillian O., "Beloved Mother" September 19, 1905 – November 15, 1976 [St. James United Cemetery]

Brown, Lillie M. 1876-1954 ("Rest In Peace") [Asbury Cemetery]

Brown, Lois Ann July 18, 1940 – June 30, 2000 (inscribed "From Your Boys") [Union U. M. Church Cemetery]

Brown, Mabel O. 1928-2018 (small metal funeral home marker; funeral notice and photo in *The Aegis* stated she lived in Aberdeen and died at Citizens Nursing Home on May 7, 2018, age 90) [Berkley Memorial Cemetery]

Brown, Mable E. September 11, 1886 – May 29, 1925 (no tombstone; death certificate stated she was the widowed daughter of William E. Brown and Mary E. Holland) [Union U. M. Church Cemetery]

Brown, Mable M. January 29, 1921 – January 26, 2009 (tombstone; obituary in *The Aegis* on January 30, 2009 stated Mable Brown, of Edgewood, died at Upper Chesapeake Medical Center in Bel Air; she was born in Benson, the daughter of Joshua and Janie Britton, and married Harvey L. Brown who predeceased her; she was a member of Tabernacle U. M. Church for 70 years; she was survived by 6 sons, 3 daughters, 17 grandchildren, 40 great-grandchildren, and 7 great-great-grandchildren) [Tabernacle Mount Zion U. M. Church Cemetery]

Brown, Mahala died September 25, 1905, age 120 (death certificate stated she was single, had worked as a servant and died at home in Darlington; her place of birth and the names of her parents were blank; a small, badly weathered tombstone states she died in 1905, age about 110 years; her death notice in the *Bel Air Times* on September 29, 1905 stated, "She was considered to be the oldest person in this county, her age being authentically stated at considerably over a century.") [Berkley Memorial Cemetery]

Brown, Mamie R. 1903-1961 (on same tombstone with Walter F. Brown) [Union U. M. Church Cemetery]

Brown, Martha K. 1855-1937 (on same tombstone with James W. Brown; death certificate stated she was the widow of James W. Brown and the daughter of John Brown, but her mother was not known; she was born on March 1, 1865 and died on October 22, 1937) [Union U. M. Church Cemetery]

Brown, Martha Rebecca July 31, 1865 – September 15, 1924 (no tombstone; death certificate stated she was the daughter of Sol Norris and Louiza Turner, all born in Maryland; she died a widow at Joppa and was buried in "Mountain Cemetery;" informant was William Bishop, of Joppa) [Mt. Zion U. M. Church Cemetery]

Brown, Mary (no tombstone; death certificate stated she was born on June 9, 1850, the daughter of Charles Jones and Harriet Jones, all born in Harford Co.; she worked as a washerwoman at Carsins and was a widow at the time of her death on April 23, 1917; informant was Mable Thompson, of Aberdeen) [Green Spring U. M. Church Cemetery]

Brown, Mary A. died May 25, 1878, age 68 [Asbury Cemetery]

Brown, Mary Ann, granddaughter of Mary Johnson, died January 23, 1871, age 6 months, 19 days [Hill-Johnson Cemetery]

Brown, Mary Eliza died July 4, 1901, age 73 years, 2 months, 21 days (no tombstone; death certificate stated she was the daughter of Benjamin and Sophia Tildon, and the wife of Robert W. Brown; she worked as a nurse and died at Michaelsville, survived by her husband and 5 children; place of burial was not indicated, but probably in the Old Union Chapel Cemetery at Michaelsville; possibly reinterred in Union Chapel Cemetery near Aberdeen) [Union U. M. Church Cemetery]

Brown, Mary Ella 1965-2003 (small metal funeral home marker) [Foster's Hill Cemetery]

Brown, Mary L. April 27, 1886 – October 21, 1931 (inscribed "At Rest") [Union U. M. Church Cemetery]

Brown, Mary Lou 1877-1946 (on same tombstone with David Brown) [Tabernacle Mount Zion U. M. Church Cemetery]

Brown, Mary Luverne December 18, 1884 – November 18, 1931 (no tombstone; death certificate stated she was the daughter of Burnert Shorter and Annie Woodland, and died a widow in Havre de Grace; informant was Mary Jane Smith, of Mechaniscville, MD) [St. James United Cemetery]

Brown, Mattie K. January 21, 1890 – May 10, 1937 (tombstone also inscribed "Baby Caroline") [Tabernacle Mount Zion U. M. Church Cemetery]

Brown, Mazie A. February 8, 1886 – March 2, 1926 (no tombstone; death certificate stated she was the married daughter of James Priggs and Cora Stansbury; informant was Robert Brown) [Union U. M. Church Cemetery]

Brown, Melvin K. March 24, 1922 – March 10, 1972, Maryland, Sgt., 386 Port Bn, TC, World War II [Union U. M. Church Cemetery]

Brown, Meta 1906-1972 (on same tombstone with James H. Brown, Harry W. Brown, Stewart C. Brown and Meta G. Clark) [St. James United Cemetery]

Brown, Mildred O. October 26, 1909 – October 19, 1982 (on same tombstone with George H. Brown; obituary in *The Aegis*, October 21, 1982, stated she was the wife of George H. Brown, of Street, MD, and she was "born in T. B., a daughter of the late Clifton and Verbena Hawkins;" she served Chestnut Grove A. M. E. Church as a trustee, steward, stewardess, missionary and member of the choir; she died in Fallston General Hospital, survived by her husband, 4 daughters, 7 grandchildren, a brother, and a sister) [Chestnut Grove A. M. E. Church Cemetery, formerly LaGrange Cemetery at Rocks]

Brown, Minnie, beloved daughter of Richard J. & Eleanora Brown, February 17, 1888 – March 19, 1904 (illegible verse on her tombstone) [Asbury Cemetery]

Brown, Nellie December 18, 1906 – October 24, 1917 (no tombstone; death certificate stated she was born in Havre de Grace, the son of John Brown, of Perryman, and Adeline Taylor, of Churchville; informant was Adeline Brown, of Havre de Grace) [Asbury Cemetery]

Brown, Nellie "Mother" died October 6, 1968 [John Wesley U. M. E. Church Cemetery in Abingdon]

Brown, Olethia O. (Rev.) December 15, 1923 – November 26, 1974 [Berkley Memorial Cemetery]

Brown, Olie C. May 1, 1892 – January 1, 1916 (no tombstone; death certificate stated she was the daughter of Samuel Curry and Martha Smith, and all were born in Howard Co., MD; she was married and died in Bel Air; informant was Martha Taylor, of Sweet Air, MD) [Tabernacle Mount Zion U. M. Church Cemetery]

Brown, Oliver A. April 8, 1911 – March 5, 1956, Maryland, PFC, Co. E, 41st Engineer Bn., World War II [Union U. M. Church Cemetery]

Brown, Pearl S. 1898-   (on same tombstone with William V. Brown) [Union U. M. Church Cemetery]

Brown, Percy E. October 24, 1919 – October 24, 1920 (no tombstone; death certificate stated he was the son of Herbert Brown and Mary M. Monk, of Havre de Grace) [St. James United Cemetery]

Brown, Phoebe E. February 5, 1875 – February 8, 1945 (no tombstone; death certificate stated she was the daughter of James and Erma Bond, all born in Maryland; she married Thadious Brown, worked as a domestic and died a widow in Benson where she had lived all her life; informant was Mrs. Nora Brown, of Benson) [Tabernacle Mount Zion U. M. Church Cemetery]

Brown, Phoebe Sophia, wife of John Brown, died April 26, 1882, age 33 (tombstone was copied in 1987 and the copyist noted "This stone pushed into woods beside graveyard.") [Mt. Zion U. M. Church Cemetery]

Brown, Rachel April 10, 1850 – October 31, 1923 (no tombstone; death certificate stated she was born in Maryland, the daughter of Orange Brooks and Harriett Brooks) [Union U. M. Church Cemetery]

Brown, Robert December 7, 1876 – December 10, 1945 (no tombstone; death certificate stated he was the son of Zechariah Brown and Casie White, and husband of Lillian ----, the informant) [St. James United Cemetery]

Brown, Robert Edward died October 26, 1978, age 41 (no tombstone; obituary in *The Aegis* stated he was born in Baltimore and died there; he was the son of Eleanor Elizabeth Brown, of Baltimore, and the late Graham A. Brown; he was survived by his mother, 4 sisters, 6 brothers) [Tabernacle Mount Zion U. M. Church Cemetery]

Brown, Robert Eugene died January 3, 1984, no age given (no tombstone; obituary in *The Aegis* on January 5, 1984 also did not state his age; he was the husband of Margaret Ellen Brown, of Fallston, and was survived by his wife, 2 brothers, 1 sister, and 2 godchildren) [Tabernacle Mount Zion U. M. Church Cemetery]

Brown, Robert R. November 5, 1904 – June 2, 1965, Maryland, Sgt., 547 QM Depot Sup Co., World War II [Tabernacle Mount Zion U. M. Church Cemetery]

Brown, Roy H. Jr. 1987-2009 (small metal funeral home marker) [Berkley Memorial Cemetery]

Brown, Ruth A. July 19, 1937 – July 10, 1991 (inscribed "Who Did So Much With So Little") [Community Baptist Church Cemetery]

Brown, Sarah Ann April 2, 1877 – November 19, 1982 (no tombstone; obituary in *The Aegis* on December 2, 1982 stated she died at the Lafayette Convalescent Center in Baltimore and was the widow of Oliver Brown, of Bel Air; she was born in Harford Co., the daughter of the late Georgeanna Lee, and was the oldest member of Ames United Methodist Church, Bel Air)

Brown, Sarah J. (no tombstone; death certificate stated she was born December 16, 1851, the daughter of Emory Brown and Harriett Hill, and all were born in Harford Co.; she was unmarried, worked as a servant at Churchville and died on October 2, 1915; informant was David E. Brown, of 2309 Fawn Road, Philadelphia, PA) [Green Spring U. M. Church Cemetery]

Brown, Sherman January 25, 1895 – February 26, 1922 (no tombstone; death certificate stated he was the son of Junius Brown and Martha Henson, all born in Maryland; he was single, worked as a laborer, died in Joppa and was buried in "Mountain Cemetery;" informant was Samuel Brown) [Mt. Zion U. M. Church Cemetery]

Brown, Solomon F. July 16, 1848 – March 20, 1889 [Green Spring U. M. Church Cemetery]

Brown, Solomon J. March 2, 1857 – October 25, 1916 (no tombstone; death certificate stated he died a widower and was the son of Charles and Sabina Brown, all born in Harford Co.) [Union U. M. Church Cemetery]

Brown, Stewart C. 1933-   (on same tombstone with Meta Brown, James H. Brown, Harry W. Brown and Meta G. Clark) [St. James United Cemetery]

Brown, Susanna died December 20, 1918, age 86 (no tombstone; death certificate stated she was the daughter of Perry Moore and Elizabeth Bodely, all born in Baltimore Co.; she was a widow and died in Fallston; informant was Jeroline Johnson, of Fallston) [Tabernacle Mount Zion U. M. Church Cemetery]

Brown, Susie Agnes September 23, 1893 – May 23, 1915 (no tombstone; death certificate stated she was the daughter of Solomon Brown and Annie Kell, all born in Maryland) [Union U. M. Church Cemetery]

Brown, Thaddeus Stephens May 15, 1868 – July 3, 1924 (no tombstone; death certificate stated Thadeus S. Brown was born in Harford Co., the son of Edward Brown, born in Annapolis, and Susanna Moore, born in Baltimore Co.; he was married, worked as a laborer and died in Benson; informant was Jeroline Johnson, of Fallston; Brown family information indicates his full name was Thaddeus Stephens Brown) [Tabernacle Mount Zion U. M. Church Cemetery]

Brown, Thomas Edward February 4, 1894 – March 25, 1911 (no tombstone; death certificate stated he was the son of David Brown and Mary "Coehn" (Cohen), all were born in Harford Co.; he was single, worked as a laborer and died near Fallston; informant was his father) [Tabernacle Mount Zion U. M. Church Cemetery]

Brown, Thomas M. February 2, 1891 – February 1, 1968 (tombstone gave his year of death as 1967, but obituary in *The Aegis* on February 8, 1968 stated Thomas Mitchel Brown died February 1, 1968, age 77, and was in the 371st Army band during World War I; military records stated he was inducted as a private on June 19, 1918, served overseas in the Meuse-Argonne and Bonhomme Sector, and was honorably discharged on March 11 1919; he lived in Bel Air, retired from Civil Service in 1956 and died at Cherokee Nursing Home in New Castle, DE; survived by 1 daughter, 2 sons, 8 grandchildren; he was a member of Ames United Methodist Church and a founding member of American Legion Post 55) [Tabernacle Mount Zion U. M. Church Cemetery]

Brown, Thomas O. 1889-1971 (on same tombstone with Daisy R. Brown) [Union U. M. Church Cemetery]

Brown, Tyre`e Eugene Sr. October 18, 1984 – December 31, 2008 (no tombstone; small metal funeral home marker states Tyree E. Brown, Sr., 1984-2007; obituary and photo in *The Aegis* on January 11, 2008 stated he was born in Havre de Grace, son of Beverly Polston and Douglas Brown, and grandson of John and Beatrice Polston and James and Mary Brown; he was shot to death in Edgewood and was survived by a daughter, a son, 2 brothers, 3 sisters, 4 aunts, 4 uncles, stepfather Howard Taylor, stepmother Nicki Brown, and was predeceased by his grandparents, a brother, an uncle and an aunt, but a wife was not named;) [Berkley Memorial Cemetery]

Brown, Vernon W. III July 28, 1972 – November 13, 2009 (inscribed "A Teacher Affects Eternity") [Union U. M. Church Cemetery]

Brown, Vernon W. Sr., "Dad" July 17, 1926 – December 23, 2015 (on same tombstone with Agnes T. Brown) [Union U. M. Church Cemetery]

Brown, Vivian 1953-2009 (small metal funeral home marker) [St. James United Cemetery]

Brown, Wade Albert Jr. October 8, 1941 – October 9, 1941 (no tombstone; death certificate stated he was born in Aberdeen, MD, the son of Albert Brown, Sr., born in Florida, and Alice Bowman, born in North Carolina, and he was buried in "Union Cemetery, Swan Creek. Maryland") [Union U. M. Church Cemetery]

Brown, Walter E. November 25, 1915 – March 27, 1916 (no tombstone; death certificate stated he was the son of Graham A. Brown and Blanch L. Turner, all born in Harford Co.; informant her father, of Bynum) [Fairview A. M. E. Church Cemetery]

Brown, Walter F. 1893-1972 [Union U. M. Church Cemetery]

Brown, William January 12, 1904 – July 15, 1940 (no tombstone; death certificate stated he was the unmarried son of James Brown, of North Carolina, mother unknown in hospital records; he was born in Tennessee, worked in construction and died in Harford Memorial Hospital in Havre de Grace) [St. James United Cemetery]

Brown, William June 30, 1835 – November 13, 1855 ("Sacred to the Memory of" and "The Lord is righteous in all His ways, and Holy in all His works. Psalm 145 V. 17") [Old Union Chapel M. E. Church Cemetery]

Brown, William March 2, 1848 – August 15, 1921 (no tombstone; death certificate stated he was the son of Zachary Brown and Lizzie Johnson, all born in Maryland; he worked as a laborer and died a widower in Bel Air; informant was Adele Moore, of Bel Air) [Tabernacle Mount Zion U. M. Church Cemetery]

Brown, William Elbert August 23, 1898 – July 7, 1919 (no tombstone; death certificate stated he was born in Harford Co., the son of Elbert Brown, born in South Carolina, and Nellie Bond, born in Maryland; he was single, worked as a day laborer and was stabbed to death in Havre de Grace; informant was Nellie Lee, of Aberdeen) [Green Spring U. M. Church Cemetery]

Brown, William H. 1877 – 1930 (tombstone; *www.findagrave.com* posted the complete dates of October 17, 1877 – December 11, 1930; no death certificate was found in Harford Coumty) [Tabernacle Mount Zion U. M. Church Cemetery]

Brown, William T. 1939-1981, Pvt., U.S. Army [William C. Rice Memorial Cemetery, St. James U. M. Church]

Brown, William V. 1885-1967 (on same tombstone with Pearl S. Brown; obituary in *The Aegis* on June 15, 1967 stated he died on June 11, 1967 and was the son of James and Martha K. Brown, and husband of Pearl S. Brown, of 719 S. Union St., Havre de Grace; he was a church trustee, a Mason and was active in civil and political affairs; he died at Citizens Nursing Home, survived by a daughter, 4 grandchildren, 2 foster sons, a sister and 4 brothers) [Union U. M. Church Cemetery]

Brown, Willie Edward 1905-1973 (Masonic symbol on tombstone) [Clark's U. M. Church Cemetery]

Browne, Beatrice Hoff May 12, 1890 – May 10, 1971 (on same tombstone with Leon Browne; death certificate in *The Aegis* on May 13, 1971 stated she was born in Washington, NJ, the daughter of John and Sarah Hoff, and the wife of Leon Browne, of Route 1, Bel Air, and she died at Harford Memorial Hospital in Havre de Grace) [Asbury Cemetery]

Browne, Daisy Virginia November 18, 1882 – February 17, 1918 (no tombstone; death certificate stated she was born in Churchville, the daughter of Edward J. Browne and Elenora Douglass, both born in Maryland; she was single, a "housekeeper, domestic science" and died at home in Churchville; informant was Elenora Chambers, of Churchville) [Asbury Cemetery]

Browne, Leon February 13, 1890 – January 8, 1962 (on same tombstone with Beatrice) [Asbury Cemetery]

Brue, Mildred December 21, 1913 – September 3, 1914 (no tombstone; death certificate stated she was the daughter of William Brue, of Virginia, and Henrietta Dorsey, of Harford County) [St. James United Cemetery]

Brummer (Brumer), Nancy August 15, 1836 – July 26, 1901 (no tombstone; death certificate stated Nancy "Brumer" was the wife of John "Brumer" and died at Clayton; death notice in *The Aegis* on August 6, 1901 stated Nancy "Brummer" was an old resident of the Mountain; her place of burial was not mentioned in either source, but it was probably John Wesley Methodist Church) [probably Mt. Zion U. M. Church Cemetery]

Bryan, Edgar September 15, 1891 – February 25, 1940 (no tombstone; death certificate stated he was the son of Lowman Bryan and Ann Baker, all born in North Carolina; he worked as a laborer, married Maggie Robinson, lived in Bel Air, and died a widower at Harford Memorial Hospital in Havre de Grace; informant was Carrie Armstrong, of Bel Air) [Tabernacle Mount Zion U. M. Church Cemetery]

Bryan, Lois Alice Jane March 10, 1910 – March 4, 1949 (no tombstone; death certificate stated she was born in North Carolina, the daughter of Edgar Bryan and Ann Baker, and she died in Bel Air unmarried; informant was William L. Bryan) [Tabernacle Mount Zion U. M. Church Cemetery]

Bryan, Margaret Irene 1914-1968 (tombstone; no obituary, but *The Aegis* on April 4, 1968 published "Card of Thanks" from the family signed by Earnestine Bryan Beasley) [Tabernacle Mount Zion U. M. Church Cemetery]

Bryan, Raymond E. April 6, 1913 – October 18, 1977, TEC 5, U.S. Army, World War II (tombstone; obituary in *The Aegis* on October 27, 1977 stated Raymond Edgar Bryan died in Bel Air on October 18, 1977, age 65, but did not mention his service; he was born in Sparta, NC, the son of Edgar Bryan and Ann Baker; survived by 2 brothers 2 sisters and other family) [Tabernacle Mount Zion U. M. Church Cemetery]

Bryan, Willie 1910-1987 [Tabernacle Mount Zion U. M. Church Cemetery]

Bryant, Flora B., "Mother" 1922-1968 [Mt. Zion U. M. Church Cemetery]

Bryd, Eleanor Parker January 9, 1913 – June 27, 1950 (no tombstone; death certificate stated she was born in Virginia and the daughter of Mose Fighter(?) and Susan Minor; she died in Harford Memorial Hospital and was separated from her husband at the time; informant was Mrs. Dora Jenkins) [St. James United Cemetery]

Bryson, Frances 1909-2000 (inscribed "In Loving Memory") [St. James United Cemetery]

Buchanan, ---- stillborn male died December 21, 1925 (no tombstone; death certificate stated he was the son of Milton Waters and Etta Aretha Buchanan of Bel Air and they all were born in Maryland; informant was William Buchanan, of Bel Air) [Hendon Hill Cemetery]

Buchanan, ----, unnamed female, December 25 – December 26, 1917 (no tombstone; death certificate stated she was "born before term, before 8 months, near Jarrettsville" and was the daughter of William Thomas Buchanan and Bessie Irene Evans, both born in Harford Co.; she was buried at Lagrange Cemetery and informant was her father, of Sharon) [Chestnut Grove A. M. E. Church Cemetery, formerly LaGrange Cemetery at Rocks]

Buchanan, Caleb "Cale" 1840 – March 8, 1912 (no tombstone; death certificate stated "Cale" was born in Harford Co., the son of Ned Buchanan, of Harford Co., but his mother's name was not known to informant Frank Buchanan, of Pylesville; he was a laborer at Pylesville and died a widower; death notice stated Caleb Buchanan, an aged and respected colored man, died at home near Five Forks and was buried "at the Rocks in the Afro M. E. cemetery") [Chestnut Grove A. M. E. Church Cemetery, formerly LaGrange Cemetery at Rocks]

Buchanan, Carnell N. December 29, 1927 – February 26, 1949, Maryland, TEC 4, 28th Truck Co., TC, World War II (tombstone; death certificate stated Carnell Nicholas Buchanan was born in White Hall, MD, on December 20, 1926 *(sic)*, the son of Richard Buchanan and Violet Christy; he married, worked at Edgewood Arsenal, was injuted in an auto accident on Route 146 near Jarrettsville and died at Harford Memorial Hospital; informant was Mrs. Carnell N. Buchanan, of Darlington) [Green Spring U. M. Church Cemetery]

Buchanan, Dorothy (owned a lot in section 31 some time after 1951) [Mt. Calvary U.A.M.E. Church Cemetery]

Buchanan, Frank November 5, 1874 – November 13, 1949 (no tombstone; death certificate stated he was born in Pylesville, the son of Cail Buchanan and Jennie Blainy; farmer near Pylesville and died a widower; informant was Luella Buchanan) [Chestnut Grove A. M. E. Church Cemetery, formerly LaGrange Cemetery at Rocks]

Buchanan, Harold G. September 3, 1945 – December 11, 2002 (on same tombstone with Vivian A. Buchanan and inscribed "Our Father Who Art In Heaven") [Asbury Cemetery]

Buchanan, Harriet died October 20, 1892, age not given (no tombstone; death notice in *The Aegis* on October 21, 1892 stated she was fatally burned while making apple butter at Fendall farm near Bel Air; place of burial was not reported [possibly Hendon Hill)

Buchanan, Harry 1919-1985 (copied in 1987, not found in 2018) [Mt. Calvary U. A. M. E. Church Cemetery]

Buchanan, Hattie, daughter of Raymond and Ada Buchanan, 1911-1917 (also inscribed "At Rest;" however, death certificate stated Hattie C. Buchanan was born on January 29, 1910, died on July 10, 1918 and her parents were Raymond Buchanan and Ida Brown, all born in Maryland; informant was her father) [Union U. M. Church Cemetery]

Buchanan, Hattie V., daughter of Thomas and Frances Buchanan, July 3, 1885 – March 9, 1919 (inscribed "In Memory Of") [Union U. M. Church Cemetery]

Buchanan, Henry Ralph died February 9, 1936, age about 54 (no tombstone; death certificate stated he was the son of Kale Buchanan and Jennie Blainie and all were born in Maryland; he was a single farm laborer and burned to death at Street; informant was Frank Buchanan, of Pylesville) [Chestnut Grove A. M. E. Church Cemetery, formerly LaGrange Cemetery at Rocks]

Buchanan, James E. 1848 – June 6, 1933 (no tombstone; death certificate stated he was the son of Edward Buchanan, both born in Harford Co., but the name of his mother was not known to informant John H. Buchanan; he was single, worked as a laborer, lived in Jarrettsville and died at Havre de Grace Hospital; Kurtz Funeral Home records mistakenly stated he was buried at Chestnut Hill Colored Cemetery [Chestnut Grove A. M. E.

Church Cemetery, formerly LaGrange Cemetery at Rocks]

Buchanan, James Thomas May 8, 1930 – June 16, 1930 (no tombstone; death certificate stated he was the son of Leon Buchanan and Mary Dorsey, all born in Maryland; he died at Rocks; informant was Leon Buchanan, of Pylesville) [Chestnut Grove A. M. E. Church Cemetery, formerly LaGrange Cemetery at Rocks]

Buchanan, Jane died June 14, 1896, age not given (no tombstone; death notice in *The Aegis* on June 19, 1896 stated she died at her home in Bel Air and was a very well-known colored woman) [Hendon Hill Cemetery]

Buchanan, John Henry died November 12, 1936, age about 71 (no tombstone; death certificate stated he was the son of Susan Ann Buchanan, father unknown; he married Amanda Lee and died in Federal Hill; informant was Edna Rice, of Baltimore) [William C. Rice Memorial Cemetery, St. James U. M. Church]

Buchanan, Laura died May 2, 1895, age not given (no tombstone; her death notice in *The Aegis* on May 10, 1895 stated she was the wife of Thomas Buchanan, resided near Federal Hill, and was "buried at LaGrange burying ground") [Chestnut Grove A. M. E. Church Cemetery, formerly LaGrange Cemetery at Rocks]

Buchanan, Laura September 10, 1881 – October 10, 1941 (no tombstone; death certificate stated she was born at Rocks and was the wife of Frank Buchanan, of Pylesville, who was born in 1881; her parents were Thomas Maxfield and Fannie Rice, both born in Maryland; she died at Harford Memorial Hospital in Havre de Grace) [Chestnut Grove A. M. E. Church Cemetery, formerly LaGrange Cemetery at Rocks]

Buchanan, Mary M. February 17, 1870 – May 18, 1966 [Union U. M. Church Cemetery]

Buchanan, Mazie Rebecca February 6, 1886 – October 6, 1971 [Union U. M. Church Cemetery]

Buchanan, Millard 1916-1986 (copied in 1987, but not found in 2018; buried in section 31) [Mt. Calvary U. A. M. E. Church Cemetery]

Buchanan, Myron Alan died June 21, 2006, age 25 (no tombstone; obituary in *The Aegis* on June 28, 2006 stated he was born in Rossville and lived in Joppa, the son of Philip Alexander Buchanan and Sheila Denise Cohen, the grandson of Samuel and Betty Miller, of Edgewood, and great-grandson of Louise Harris, of Abingdon; he died in a motorcycle accident in Joppa and was survived by his fianceé Pamela Bristow, of Baltimore, 4 children and other relatives) [Tabernacle Mount Zion U. M. Church Cemetery]

Buchanan, Raymond S. September 10, 1890 – October 29, 1935 (no tombstone; death certificate stated he was the husband of Ada I. Buchanan and the son of Thomas Buchanan and Frances E. Tinson) [Union U. M. Church Cemetery]

Buchanan, Samuel February 24, 1877 – November 8, 1978 [Mt. Zion U. M. Church Cemetery]

Buchanan, Theresa M. August 7, 1978 – 10 Aug 1978 (copied and noted in 1986 as "stone toppled," but not found in 2018) [Mt. Zion U. M. Church Cemetery]

Buchanan, Thomas August 25, 1855 – December 14, 1943 (no tombstone; death certificate stated he was the son of John Pitt and Sofia Buchanan, and the husband of Mary M. Buchanan) [Union U. M. Church Cemetery]

Buchanan, Vivian A. September 9, 1948 -   (on same tombstone with Harold G. Buchanan and inscribed "Our Father Who Art In Heaven") [Asbury Cemetery]

Buchanan, William Oscar Henry died March 11, 1907, age 1 year, 4 months, 4 days (no tombstone; death certificate stated he was born and died at Federal Hill, the son of J. H. Buchanan and Amanda Lee; place of burial was not given [possibly William C. Rice Memorial Cemetery, St. James U. M. Church]

Buchanan, William Wilson July 22, 1919 – August 17, 1919 (no tombstone; death certificate stated he was the son of William W. Buchanan and Laura A. Bond, all born in Harford Co.; he died at home at Cooptown; informant was his mother, Laura Alma Bond, of RFD Forest Hill) [Fairview A. M. E. Church Cemetery]

Buckham, Samuel died June 18, 1945, "age 60?" *(sic)* (no tombstone; death certificate stated he was the son of Robert Buckham and Matilda Mathews, all born in Harford Co.; he was single, worked as a laborer, lived in Fallston and died at Harford Memorial Hospital in Havre de Grace; the information was gleaned by an unidentified person from the hospital records) [Tabernacle Mount Zion U. M. Church Cemetery]

Buckhanna, Harry stillborn on August 23, 1940 (no tombstone; death certificate stated he was the son of Miller Buckhanna and Dorothy Hardy) [Union U. M. Church Cemetery]

Buckhannan, Harriett age 75 (no dates inscribed) [Mt. Zion U. M. Church Cemetery]

Buckingham, James 1935-2011, MSG, U. S Army [Mt. Calvary U. A. M. E. Church Cemetery]

Bueford, Alma J., "Mother" August 23, 1915 – June 18, 1989 [Chestnut Grove A. M. E. Church Cemetery, formerly LaGrange Cemetery at Rocks]

Bugg, Elvina 1908-1994 (on same tombstone with Pink Bugg) [Berkley Memorial Cemetery]

Bugg, Pink 1899-1973 (on same tombstone with Elvina Bugg) [Berkley Memorial Cemetery]

Buggs, Baby Girl stillborn on September 14, 1977 at Harford Memorial Hospital, the daughter of Charles R. Buggs and Sharoon I. Gales, of Aberdeen [St. James United Cemetery]

Bulloch, Elmer E. "Bus" 1913-1973 (on same tombstone with Otelia J. Bulloch) [St. James United Cemetery]

Bulloch, Otelia J. 1919 - (on same tombstone with Elmer E. Bulloch) [St. James United Cemetery]

Bunce, James February – (blank), 1853 – September 28, 1912 (no tombstone; death certificate stated he was born in Pennsylvania and died at Kalmia; he was married and worked as a laborer, but his parents were unknown to informant Sarah E. Bunce, of Forest Hill) [Clark's U. M. Church Cemetery]

Bunn, Kelly August 21, 1976 – July 9, 1998 (no tombstone; obituary in *The Aegis* on July 22, 1998 stated she was born in Baltimore City, the daughter of Sharon Byrd-Thomas and Steven Arizmendi; she died in Baltimore, survived by her mother and father, her adoptive father Richard Bunn, a brother Derek Bunn, sisters Stevy Nicole Bradley, Genai Bunn and Melissa Badilla, step-sisters Shannon and Jeanna Thomas, grandmothers Ann Byrd-Williams, Cecilia Bunn, Velora Broussard and Beatrice Byrd, grandfathers William C. Byrd, Sr. and William Bunn, great-grandmother Lois Byrd, great-grandfather Cornelius J. Smith and great-great-grandmother Annie Dennison) [Union U. M. Church Cemetery]

Burgess, Ethel E. 1944-2015 (small metal funeral home marker) [Berkley Memorial Cemetery]

Burke, Alma Louisa 1945-2014 (small metal funeral home marker) [Berkley Memorial Cemetery]

Burke, Brock Sanchez, "Our Beloved Son" November 24, 1990 – October 16, 1995 [St. James United Cemetery]

Burke, Carl VanBuren March 5, 1946 – December 19, 1946 (no tombstone; death certificate stated he was the son of William O. Burke, of Cecil Co., and Ernestine Durbin, of Harford Co.) [St. James United Cemetery]

Burke, John February 2, ---- (?) – February 21, 1928 (no tombstone; death certificate stated he was senile and a widower, and did not give wife's name nor his birth year and age; he was born in PA, the son of Samuel Burke and mother's name was not known to informant Clarence Burke, of Perryville, MD) [St. James United Cemetery]

Burks, James H. 1930-2012 (small metal funeral home marker) [Berkley Memorial Cemetery]

Burlark, William Henry April 7, 1897 – June 17, 1945 (no tombstone; death certificate stated he was the son of George Burlark (also spelled Burlock on the death certificate), born in Illinois, and ---- mother's name unknown, and he was the husband of Frances Monk) [Union U. M. Church Cemetery]

Burnett, Betty Lou Tharp, "Loving Wife and Mother" December 7, 1933 – January 12, 2010 [St. James United Cemetery]

Burnett, Dorsey Duane April 18, 1955 – June 21, 1976 [St. James United Cemetery]

Burnette, John died September 10, 1922, age about 55 (no tombstone; death certificate stated he was single and born in Detroit, MI, parents' names unknown to informant Kimball Patterson) [St. James United Cemetery]

Burns, Charles died September 28, 1927, no age given (no tombstone and no death certificate; obituary in *The Aegis* on October 6, 1927 stated "Charlie" Burns was employed by A. M. Fulford in Bel Air for many years and died in Baltimore; he was a very skillful fitter and handler of blooded horses, and "was uniformly courteous to everyone") [Tabernacle Mount Zion U. M. Church Cemetery]

Burns, Clorinda E. January 17, 1898 – July 27, 1986 [Tabernacle Mount Zion U. M. Church Cemetery]

Burns, Harriet Smith died March 8, 1976, no age given (tombstone copied in 1986) [Hendon Hill Cemetery]

Burns, John B. Jr. 1956-1996 (small metal funeral home marker) [John Wesley U. M. E. Church Cemetery in Abingdon]

Burry, Betty A. September 25, 1946 - June 9, 2015 (inscribed "Loved by her husband, daughter and son") [Clark's U. M. Church Cemetery]

Burry, Ida C. November 6, 1906 – August 4, 1980 [Clark's U. M. Church Cemetery]

Bush, William March 26, 1906 – May 13, 1940 (no tombstone; death certificate stated he was born in Georgia and a single farmer in rural Aberdeen; his parents were not known to informant Samuel Walker, of Aberdeen RFD, and he died in an auto accident near Havre de Grace) [Green Spring U. M. Church Cemetery]

Butler, Annie R. November 25, 1856 – February 3, 1923 (no tombstone; death certificate stated she was born in Harford Co., the daughter of Isaac Harris, born in Abingdon, Harford Co., and Charlotte Lingham, born in Harford Co., and died a widow near Fulford; informant was David R. Kennard, of Bel Air) [Asbury Cemetery]

Butler, Catherine Reid Osborne 1921-2002 [St. James United Cemetery]

Butler, Edward Sydney November 1, 1879 – February 17, 1936 (no tombstone; death certificate stated he was single and born at Elk Neck, Cecil Co., the son of Sydney Butler, of Harford Co, and Elizabeth Carroll, of Wicomico Co., MD; informant was Laura Harris, of Havre de Grace) [St. James United Cemetery]

Butler, Elizabeth December 1, 1861 – October 2, 1927 (no tombstone; death certificate stated she was the unmarried daughter of Sydney Butler and Elizabeth Carroll, of Havre de Grace) [St. James United Cemetery]

Butler, Elizabeth J. died October 10, 1919, age about 86 (no tombstone; death certificate stated she was a widow and the daughter of Charles and Easter Carroll, of Havre de Grace) [St. James United Cemetery]

Butler, Ernest M. June 15, 1892 – June 7, 1975 (no tombstone; obituary in *The Aegis* on June 12, 1975 stated he was born in Charles Co., MD and died at home on Loflin Road in Aberdeen, survived by a sister, Mrs. Etta Kenley, and a brother Joseph H. Shivers) [Mt. Calvary U. A. M. E. Church Cemetery]

Butler, Gertrude "19?7 – 1972" (copied in 1986, but not found in 2018) [St. James United Cemetery]

Butler, Hannah (no dates given; copied in 1986, but not found in 2018) [Hendon Hill Cemetery]

Butler, Henrietta December 9, 1893 – December 4, 1914 (no tombstone; death certificate stated she was the daughter of Charles Butler and Mary Webster, all born in Maryland; she was single, worked as a servant and died in Castleton) [Berkley Memorial Cemetery]

Butler, Henry 6 October 1855 – August 11, 1945 (no tombstone; death certificate stated he was single, born in Maryland, resided in Bel Air and died in Havre de Grace Hospital; parents unknown, according to hospital; however, Harford County Alms House Book 1, 1909-1944, stated Henry Butler was received on October 17, 1939, removed on November *(sic)* 16, 1945 and buried in Watervale. Unless there was another Henry Butler this is a mistake in the Alms House book since the death certificate appears to be correct.) [Hendon Hill Cemetery]

Butler, John W. October 14, 1867 – October 22, 1932 (no tombstone; death certificate stated he was the son of Barnie Butler and Julie Grinage, all born in Harford Co.; he married Ida ----, worked as a day laborer and died at home in Aberdeen RFD where he had lived for 3 years; informant was Mrs. Sadie F. Black, of Aberdeen) [Mt. Calvary U. A. M. E. Church Cemetery]

Butler, Maggie May 12, 1880 – July 19, 1949 [Hendon Hill Cemetery]

Butler, William H. March 10, 1863 – March 2, 1917 (no tombstone; death certificate stated he was born in Washington, D. C., but his parents were not known to informant Eley Hanson, of Abingdon; he was married, worked as a farm hand and died in Abingdon) [Green Spring U. M. Church Cemetery]

Byrd, Harrison 1903-1979 (handwritten on a flat cement slab with Sallie Byrd) [St. James United Cemetery]

Byrd, Sallie 1946-1995 (handwritten on a flat cement slab with Harrison Byrd) [St. James United Cemetery]

Cage, Barbara A. April 13, 1961 – July 11, 2006 [Berkley Memorial Cemetery]

Cage, Marion A. November 23, 1931 – January 27, 1977 (inscribed "With Love Hawkins Families Also Son Daughter" (Marion Cage owned a lot in section 14 some time after 1951; obituary in *The Aegis* on February 3, 1977 stated Marion Alberta Cage was born in Havre de Grace, the daughter of Howard S. and Julia R. Hawkins (still living), and married first to Francis E. Draper and second to Albert C. Cage; she lived at 709 Girard Street in Havre de Grave, worked as a beautician, and died at Maryland General Hospital in Baltimore) [Mt. Calvary U. A. M. E. Church Cemetery]

Cahl, Ida May February 4, 1889 – March 21, 1986 (tombstone; obituary in *The Aegis* on March 27, 1986 stated she was born in Harford Co., the daughter of James Gilbert and Charlotte Robinson and widow of William A. Cahl; she died at Franklin Square Hospital(Baltimore Co.) and was survived by a daughter Ida V. Williams and two sisters and eight grandchildren) [Foster's Hill Cemetery]

Cahl, Janie Marie died July 14, 1981, age 68 (obituary in *The Aegis* on July 30, 1981 stated she was born in Perryman, the daughter of Walter and Nellie Stansbury, and the widow of John W. Cahl; she was very active in the church, choir and NAACP; she died at her home in Havre de Grace, survived by a son Grafton Sconion, 6 grandchildren and 13 great-grandchildren) [Berkley Memorial Cemetery]

Cahl, John W. 1912-1975, S1, U.S. Navy, World War II (tombstone; obituary in *The Aegis* on 4 Nov 1975 stated John Wesley Cahl, husband of Janie Marie Cahl, of Havre de Grace, died in Baltimore on 31 Oct 1975 and he was the son of Ida M. Cahl and the late William Cahl) [Berkley Memorial Cemetery]

Cahl, Martina May 16, 1925 – September 1, 1925 (no tombstone; death certificate stated she was the daughter of William Cahl and Ida Gilbert, all born in Maryland, and lived in Edgewood) [Foster's Hill Cemetery]

Cahl, Mary J. April 11, 1911 – April 16, 1911 (no tombstone; death certificate stated she was born in Harford Co., the daughter of Frances Cahl, born in Harford Co., but her father was not known to informant who was her mother Frances Cahl, of Edgewood) [John Wesley U. M. E. Church Cemetery in Abingdon]

Cahl, William A. February 3, 1875 – December 18, 1925 (no tombstone; death certificate stated he was the son of Bond Cahl, both born in Maryland, but his mother's name was not known to informant Ida Cahl, of Edgewood; he was married, worked as a laborer, died at home in Edgewood) [Foster's Hill Cemetery]

Cain, ---- March 23, 1922 – March 25, 1922 (no tombstone; death certificate stated she was the daughter of Edward Cain and Sarah Lawson, of Berkley, all born in Maryland) [Berkley Memorial Cemetery]

Cain, ---- stillborn female on December 24, 1914 (no tombstone; death certificate stated she was the daughter of Edward Cain and Flora Christy, of Darlington, all born in Harford County) [Berkley Memorial Cemetery]

Cain, Benjamin H. November 12, 1888 – June 8, 1962 (on same tombstone with Pearline B. Cain) [Berkley Memorial Cemetery]

Cain, David 1905-1973 (on same tombstone with Florence L. Cain) [Berkley Memorial Cemetery]

Cain, David April 11, 1872 – December 21, 1924 (no tombstone; death certificate stated he was the son of Solomon Cain and Fannie Cox, and all were born in Harford Co.; he was married and worked as a laborer in Benson; informant was Lula Cain, of Benson) [Berkley Memorial Cemetery]

Cain, Donald Edward died March 13, 2016, age 64 (funeral notice in *The Aegis* stated he lived in Aberdeen and died at Harford Memorial Hospital in Havre de Grace) [Berkley Memorial Cemetery]

Cain, Edna F. 1902-1985 (on same tombstone with Olethia R. Whitfield) [Berkley Memorial Cemetery]

Cain, Edward H. 1910-1964 (on same tombstone with Marguerite I. Cain) [Berkley Memorial Cemetery]

Cain, Edward H. 1910-1990 (on same tombstone with Elva P. Cain) [Berkley Memorial Cemetery]

Cain, Edward Harrison "Pete" November 11, 1937 – February 4, 1989 (tombstone; obituary in *The Aegis* on February 9, 1989 stated he was the son of Marguerite I. Cain and the late Edward H. Cain, Sr., lived in Darlington and died at Harford Memorial Hospital in Havre de Grace, survived by his mother, one sister, one brother, three sons, four daughters and six grandchildren) [Berkley Memorial Cemetery]

Cain, Elizabeth March 31, 1914 – April 2, 1918, premature birth, lived only 3 days (no tombstone; death certificate stated she was the daughter of William Webster and Cora Cain, of Darlington; informant was her mother) [Berkley Memorial Cemetery]

Cain, Ellen 1872-1944 (handwritten on small flat cement slab) [Union U. M. Church Cemetery]

Cain, Elva P. 1915-2008 (on same tombstone with Edward H. Cain; her picture appeared in *A Journey Through Berkley*, p. 10; obituary in *The Aegis* on July 9, 2008 stated Elva Natalie Presberry Cain was born April 30, 1915, the daughter of Kenton and Dora Presberry, and the widow of Edward Hayes Cain; she taught school in Baltimore County and later in Harford County at Cedars and then at Hosanna; she was secretary for Hosanna AME Church for 27 years and also secretary of the missionary and ushering boards for 50 years; she died on July 5, 2008 at the Citizens Care and Rehabilitation Center in Havre de Grace, survived by 3 stepchildren, 8 step-grandchildren, 2 sisters, 2 nieces, 2 nephews, 1 cousin, and was predeceased by two brothers Earl O. Presberry and Russell Presberry) [Berkley Memorial Cemetery]

Cain, Florence L. 1907-1974 (on same tombstone with David Cain; obituary in *The Aegis* stated she was born in Baltimore, the daughter of Robert and Florence Maddox, married David Cain, who predeceased her, lived at 517 Gerard St., Havre de Grace, and died at the Brevin Nursing Home on April 4, 1974, survived by two brothers Robert and Edward Maddox) [Berkley Memorial Cemetery]

Cain, Frances B. died July 18, 2013, age 84 (no tombstone; funeral notice and photo in *The Aegis* stated she died at home in Aberdeen) [Berkley Memorial Cemetery]

Cain, Frances M. July 4, 1930 – September 13, 1997 (tombstone; The James Dorsey Card File, African American Obituaries, that is maintained at the Historical Society of Harford County, has a card with obituary from an unidentified newspaper on September 17, 1997 stating Frances Mahailia Cain was born in Port Deposit, the daughter of the late Benjamin H. Cain and Pearline Boddy; she became a teacher, never married, traveled extensively, and professionally researched the Cain family history; she lived in Havre de Grace and died at Harford Memorial Hospital, survived by two brothers, five sisters, and other relatives) [Berkley Memorial Cemetery]

Cain, Frederick Douglas December 31, 1866 – August 28, 1920 (no tombstone; death certificate stated he was the son of Solomon Cain and Annie Cox, all born in Harford Co.; he was married, worked as a day laborer and died in Darlington; informant was Eddie Cain, of Darlington) [Berkley Memorial Cemetery]

Cain, Georgia July 11, 1870 – February 24, 1912 (no tombstone; death certificate stated she was born in Harford Co., the daughter of William Parker, born in Cecil Co., and Rebecca Prigg, born in Harford Co.; she was married and lived in Darlington; informant was James Parker) [Berkley Memorial Cemetery]

Cain, Howard Edward "Howdy" August 22, 1955 – September 13, 1995 (tombstone; obituary in *The Record* on September 22, 1995 stated he was known as "Howdie" and was the son of Susie Cain Green and the late Edward Harrison Cain, Jr.; he died in Havre de Grace, survived by his mother, a son Thomas Head, four sisters, two brothers and grandmother Marguerite Cain) [Berkley Memorial Cemetery]

Cain, Isabora V., "Mother" 1921-2007 [Berkley Memorial Cemetery]

Cain, James Albert August 25, 1919 – July 13, 1967, SSgt., U.S. Army, World War II [Berkley Memorial Cemetery]

Cain, James D. June 22, 1916 – July 11, 1955 [Berkley Memorial Cemetery]

Cain, Jean, "His Wife" 1911-1938 (dates on the same tombstone with Marcellus Cain that is also inscribed "At Rest," but death certificate stated she was born on August 27, 1912, the daughter of Nelson Presbury and Louise Webster, all born in Maryland; she married Marcellis *(sic)* Cain, lived near Darlington and died on October 27, 1938 at Harford Memorial Hospital; informant was Richard Cain, of Darlington) [Berkley Memorial Cemetery]

Cain, Jerry Lewis October 10, 1933 – January 18, 1990, Pvt., U.S. Army, Korea [Berkley Memorial Cemetery]

Cain, Leon F. December 31, 1915 – March 10, 1980, Pvt., World War II (tombstone; obituary in *The Aegis* on March 13, 1980 stated he was born in Darlington, the son of the late Cora Cain Christy; he lived in Aberdeen, served in the Army, retired from the Aberdeen Proving Ground and died at the Loch Raven Veterans Hospital in

Baltimore, survived by uncles Edward H. Cain and Edward Presberry and aunts Margaret Lisby and Agnes Presberry) [Berkley Memorial Cemetery]

Cain, Lisa M. April 24, 1961 – April 29, 2000 (tombstone; obituary in *The Aegis* on May 3, 2000 stated Lisa Mae Cain was born in Harford Memorial Hospital in Havre de Grace, the daughter of Susie Green and the late Edward H. Cain, Jr., and died in the place she was born, survived by her mother, two children named Murphy, two children named Johnson, one grandson, two brothers, three sisters, three aunts, three uncles, three great-aunts, special friend Eric Johnson, other relatives and was predeceased by a brother Howard E. Cain) [Berkley Memorial Cemetery]

Cain, Lula H. August 17, 1917 – April 2, 1988 [Berkley Memorial Cemetery]

Cain, Mabel Lulu February 29, 1887 – July 21, 1948 (no tombstone; death certificate stated she was the daughter of Lingan Bradley and Jennie Britton, all born in Maryland; she married David Cain and died a widow in Benson; informant was Charlotte Hall, of Fallston) [Tabernacle Mount Zion U. M. Church Cemetery]

Cain, Marcellus 1903-1977 (on same tombstone with Jean Cain inscribed "At Rest;" a military marker stated he was born on August 27, 1903, died on December 5, 1977 and was a Pvt., U.S. Army, World War II); obituary in The Aegis stated he was born in Darlington, the son of Thomas and Georgia Cain, and died at Citizens Nursing Home in Havre de Grace, survived by a stepdaughter Lillie Mae Basknight, three brothers Roland Cain, Edward Cain and Edward J. Presberry, three sisters Margaret Lisby, Agnes E. Presberry and Isabelle Braxton, two grandchildren and three great-grandchildren) [Berkley Memorial Cemetery]

Cain, Marguerite I. 1910-   (on same tombstone with Edward H. Cain) [Berkley Memorial Cemetery]

Cain, Mary F. June 24, 1867 – January 23, 1940 (no tombstone; death certificate stated she was the daughter of Henry Aikens and Grace A. Presberry, all born in Harford Co.; she married Thomas Cain and died at home in Darlington; informant was Alexander Webster) [Berkley Memorial Cemetery]

Cain, Minnie Hawkins 1934-1983 (tombstone; obituary in *The Aegis* on September 29, 1983 stated she lived in Aberdeen, married Ernest Cain and died September 16, 1983, age 49, at Fallston General Hospital, survived by husband, six sons, five daughters, four grandchildren, four sisters, six brothers) [Berkley Memorial Cemetery]

Cain, Nelson A. December 30, 1899 – November 16, 1955, Maryland, PFC, Co. B, 811 Pioneer Infantry, World War I (tombstone; military records stated Nelson Albert Cain was born on December 31, 1894 *(sic)* and lived in Darlington; he was inducted into the service on August 23, 1918, served overseas from October 20, 1918 to July 4, 1919 and was honorably discharged on July 10, 1919) [Berkley Memorial Cemetery]

Cain, Pearline B. February 2, 1898 – May 15, 1968 [Berkley Memorial Cemetery]

Cain, Priscilla 1818 – December 21, 1893 (inscribed "In Memory Of") [Union U. M. Church Cemetery]

Cain, Roberta D. On Earth 1935 – In Heaven 2007 [Berkley Memorial Cemetery]

Cain, Roland F. December 11, 1898 – March 9, 1978 (tombstone; obituary in *The Aegis* stated he was born in Darlington, son of Thomas Cain and Georgia Parker, and lived on Dorsey Avenue in Aberdeen, worked for the Tarring Funeral Home over 26 years and died at the Citizens Nursing Home in Havre de Grace, survived by two brothers and three sisters) [Berkley Memorial Cemetery]

Cain, Thomas January 13, 1869 – March 18, 1941 (no tombstone; death certificate stated he was the son of John Cain and Mary Cox, all born in Harford Co.; he married Georgia ----, worked as a farm laborer and died at home in Darlington; informant was Samuel Cain, of Aberdeen) [Berkley Memorial Cemetery]

Cain-Ringgold, Michelle Renee October 22, 1952 – April 21, 2018 (small temporary non-funeral marker) [Berkley Memorial Cemetery]

Caine, Adeline November 21, 1882 – January 28, 1938 (no tombstone; death certificate spelled her name Cane and stated she was born in Maryland, parents unknown, and married Thomas Cane; she lived near Joppa, died at Havre de Grace Hospital and was buried in "Mt. A. M. E. Cem.;" informant was Hornberger & Gross, Undertakers, Benson, MD; James Dorsey Card File, African American Obituaries, maintained at the Historical Society of Harford County, has a card with obituary from the *Bel Air Times* on "August 20, 1937" (an obvious mistake) stating Addie Cain was widow of Thomas Cain, of near Mountain, and died January 29 *(sic)* "with funeral services at the M. E. Church. Interment adjoining cemetery.") [Mt. Zion U. M. Church Cemetery]

Caine, Thomas May 1, 1880 – May 12, 1934 (no tombstone; death certificate stated he was born in Harford Co., the son of Charles H. Caine and Harriett Akins, both born in Maryland; he was married, worked as a farm laborer, died at home in Joppa where he had lived all his life and was buried in "Mountain Col. Cem.;" informant was Mrs. Addie Caine, of Joppa) [Mt. Zion U. M. Church Cemetery]

Caines, William H. (Right Rev.) 1865-1921 (inscribed "Asleep In Jesus") [Union U. M. Church Cemetery]

Caldwell, Duke Lewis October 26, 1937 – May 3, 2011 [Tabernacle Mount Zion U. M. Church Cemetery]

Calm, Joan L. February 1, 1949 – July 22, 2012 [Berkley Memorial Cemetery]

Cameron, Vanessa, "Beloved Daughter and Mother" January 28, 1959 – January 8, 2001 ("May God Bless. We Will Always Love You.") [St. James United Cemetery]

Cannon, Solomon February 13, 1861 – November 23, 1926 (inscribed "Soloman H. Cannon, 1860-1927, Gone But Not Forgotten," but death certificate stated he was born in 1861 and "Solomon" was the son of Dennis Cannon and Levinia Bradley, all born in Delaware; he was married and worked as a farmer at Level; informant was Georgia Cannon, of Havre de Grace; inscribed on same obelisk with Susia A. Cannon and Henrietta Chew) [Green Spring U. M. Church Cemetery]

Cannon, Susia A. 1861-1923 (tombstone; death certificate stated "Susie" Cannon was born on July 1, 1863, the daughter of George Chew and Henrietta Washington, all born in Maryland; she was married at the time of death on May 15, 1923 at home at Level; informant was Solomon Cannon, of Havre de Grace; inscribed on same obelisk with Soloman H. Cannon and Henrietta Chew) [Green Spring U. M. Church Cemetery]

Capleton, Leon, "Husband" 1903-1976 [Union U. M. Church Cemetery]

Carey (Garey?), Helen M. 1903-1986 (hand written on a flat cement marker) [St. James United Cemetery]

Carey, ---- stillborn male on September 7, 1917 (no tombstone, death certificate stated he was the son of Jesse Carey, born in Virginia, and Mollie Holland, born in Maryland, and he died at Federal Hill; informant was Jesse Carey, of Rocks) [William C. Rice Memorial Cemetery, St. James U. M. Church]

Carey, Charles 1900-197_ (small metal funeral home marker with last number missing) [William C. Rice Memorial Cemetery, St. James U. M. Church]

Carey, Charles Franklin April 2, 1925 – August 25, 1925 (no tombstone; death certificate stated he was the son of Robert S. Carey and Rosie Thomas, all born in Harford County; he died at Federal Hill, was buried in "Federal Hill Church Cem." and informant was his grandmother Mollie Carey, of Rocks) [William C. Rice Memorial Cemetery, St. James U. M. Church]

Carey, Ella D. February 14, 1943 – October 30, 1991 [St. James United Cemetery]

Carey, George Franklin February 2, 1912 – April 13, 1927 (no tombstone; he was born in Harford Co., the son of Jesse Carey, born in Kent Co., VA *(sic)* and Molly Holland, born in Baltimore Co.; he was a school boy employed at times as a farm hand and lived and died at Federal Hill, Rocks RFD; informant was Molly Carey, of Rocks) [William C. Rice Memorial Cemetery, St. James U. M. Church]

Carey, James A. (Rev.) (There are three lots in this cemetery that are designated as such on small, rectangular, thin metal plates mounted on small, flat, round stones.) [Cedars Chapel Cemetery]

Carey, Jesse March 16, 1884 – May 2, 1944 (no tombstone; Kurtz Funeral Home Record Book 1944-1949, p. 22, stated he was born in New Kent Co., VA, son of Lott Carey, but the name of his mother was not known; he worked as a farm laborer and died a widower at home at Rocks; death certificate added that he lived in rural Jarrettsville for 50 years and informant was Mrs. Frank Thomas, of Rocks) [William C. Rice Memorial Cemetery, St. James U. M. Church]

Carey, Louise (blank) – 1965 (small metal funeral home marker, birth year numbers missing) [William C. Rice Memorial Cemetery, St. James U. M. Church]

Carey, Martha died October 18, 1918, age 21 years and 2 months (no tombstone; death certificate stated she was born in Maryland, the daughter of Jesse Carey, born in Virginia, and Mollie Holland, born in Maryland; she was single, worked as a servant and died at Rocks; informant was Henry Holland, of Rocks) [William C. Rice Memorial Cemetery, St. James U. M. Church]

Carey, Mary Louise June 22, 1923 – October 13, 1923 (no tombstone; death certificate stated she was born in Harford Co., the daughter of Charles A. Carey, born in Harford Co., and Louise Johnson, born in Baltimore Co.; she died at Rutledge; informant was her grandmother Mollie Carey, of Rocks RFD) [William C. Rice Memorial Cemetery, St. James U. M. Church]

Carey, Mollie P. January 1, 1879 – July 23, 1942 (no tombstone; Kurtz Funeral Home Record Book 1937-1944, p. 240, stated she was born in White Hall, Baltimore Co., the daughter of Henry Holland, born in White Hall, and Martha Evans, born in Harford Co.; she was married and died at home in Federal Hill, funeral ordered by children; death certificate added her husband was Jesse Carey (age 71 in 1942) and she lived at Federal Hill for 37 years) [William C. Rice Memorial Cemetery, St. James U. M. Church]

Carey, Rebecca November 7, 1914 – May 13, 1943 (no tombstone; Kurtz Funeral Home Record Book 1944-1949, p. 274, stated she was born at Federal Hill, the daughter of Jesse Carey, born in Maryland, and Mollie Carey, born at Federal Hill; she was single and died at Mercy Hospital in Baltimore) [William C. Rice Memorial Cemetery, St. James U. M. Church]

Carey, Viola 1911-1975 (inscribed "In Loving Memory" and "The Lord Is My Shepherd;" obituary in *The Aegis* on April 17, 1975 stated she lived at 43 Grace St. in Port Deposit and died at Harford Memorial Hospital in Havre de Grace on April 6, 1975, survived by 7 children, but no names were given) [Cedars Chapel Cemetery]

Carey-Gordon, Ruby E. died April 3, 1998, age 65 (no tombstone; James Dorsey Card File, African American Obituaries, maintained at the Historical Society of Harford County, has a card with obituary from an unidentified paper dated April 8, 1998 stating she lived in Aberdeen and died at University Hospital in Baltimore, survived by three sons and two daughters) [Berkley Memorial Cemetery]

Carey-Hall, Joyce Lynn June 18, 1959 – December 21, 2005 (obituary and photo in *The Aegis* on December 28, 1959 stated she was born in Baltimore, the daughter of the late Willard C. Carey and Fannie Carey Taylor; she lived in Aberdeen, worked as an accountant and died at Stella Maris Hospice Care in Timonium, MD, survived by a son Anthony M. Stansbury, Jr., one granddaughter, her stepfather Willie Taylor, a sister-in-law, 2 uncles, 6 aunts, and others) [Berkley Memorial Cemetery]

Carlton, Alonzo M. III February 27, 1976 – December 27, 2009 (buried in section 47; tombstone is inscribed "Loving Son and Brother" and there is also a small metal funeral home marker with his photo on it) [Mt. Calvary U. A. M. E. Church Cemetery]

Carly, Allen C. 1948-2017 (small metal funeral home marker) [William C. Rice Memorial Cemetery, St. James U. M. Church]

Carly, Dorothy 1937-1983 (small metal funeral home marker) [William C. Rice Memorial Cemetery, St. James U. M. Church]

Carr, Luretta C. October 27, 1908 – August 27, 1973 [Union U. M. Church Cemetery]

Carr, Mary L. August 27, 1884 – September 4, 1974 [Berkley Memorial Cemetery]

Carr, Robert Dudley May 4, 1916 – November 11, 1973, TEC5, U.S. Army, World War II [Union U. M. Church Cemetery]

Carrington, Elizabeth M., "Beloved Wife and Mother" 1910-1980 [Community Baptist Church Cemetery]

Carrington, Isabel B. Dennison September 18, 1925 – September 20, 2012 [Union U. M. Church Cemetery]

Carrington, Johnnie, "Son" 1947-1973 [Community Baptist Church Cemetery]

Carry, Ida February 3, 1864 – October 17, 1937 (no tombstone; death certificate stated she was the wife of Charles Carry and daughter of David Timbers, but her mother was unknown) [Union U. M. Church Cemetery]

Carry, Lottie January 29, 1874 – June 17, 1924 (no tombstone; death certificate stated she was the married daughter of David Nickinson and Sarah E. Stansbury; informant was Charles S. Carry, of Havre de Grace RFD) [Union U. M. Church Cemetery]

Carter, Albert C. died May 16, 1922, age about 47 (no tombstone; death certificate stated he was born in Vrginia and died a widow, but his parents were unknown to informant Mrs. Sarah Taylor, of Havre de Grace) [St. James United Cemetery]

Carter, Charles died February 6, 1919, age about 35 (no tombstone; death certificate stated he was born in Virginia and died a widower, but his parents were unknown to John G. Tarring, of Havre de Grace; death certificates of wife Pearl and son Jesse gave his name as Charles H. Carter) [Union U. M. Church Cemetery]

Carter, Jessie M. June 21, 1916 – October 1, 1918 (no tombstone; death certificate stated he was the son of Charles H. Carter and Pearl Oliver, all born in Virginia; died in Havre de Grace) [St. James United Cemetery]

Carter, JoAnne M. died January 21, 1996, age 39 (no tombstone; James Dorsey Card File, African American Obituaries, maintained at the Historical Society of Harford County, has a card with obituary from *The Aegis* on January 31, 1996 stating she was the daughter of the late William T. Cooper and Laura Alice Peaker, grew up in Abingdon and lived in Chase in Baltimore County; she married Winslow Carter and died at Franklin Square Hospital in Rosedale, survived by her husband, a son, two daughters, stepmother Connie Barber, adopted sister Chrystal Wainwright Reed and many other relatives) [John Wesley U. M. E. Church Cemetery in Abingdon]

Carter, Leroy July 14, 1949 – November 4, 2011, Cpl., U.S. Marine Corps [Berkley Memorial Cemetery]

Carter, Pearl May 8, 1898 – October 25, 1918 (no tombstone; death certificate misspelled her name Peril and stated she was the daughter of George Ford, of Virginia, but mother's name not known to informant Charles H. Carter, of Havre de Grace) [St. James United Cemetery]

Carter, Thomas E July 10, 1931 – July 21, 1996, U.S. Army, Korea (buried in section 33) [Mt. Calvary U. A. M. E. Church Cemetery]

Carwell, Cheryl L. Boddy 1954-2002 (on same tombstone with John H. Carwell inscribed "Love Is Forever" and includes their photo) [St. James United Cemetery]

Carwell, John H., "Pete" 1942-   (on same tombstone with Cheryl L. Boddy Carwell inscribed "Love Is Forever" and includes their photo) [St. James United Cemetery]

Carwell, Vera Alice September 25, 1925 – May 1, 1948 (no tombstone; death certificate stated she was the daughter of Howard Richardson, of Harford Co., and Ame Jean Collins, of Philadelphia, PA, and wife of Donald Carwell; informant was Mrs. Ame Jean Richardson, of Havre de Grace) [St. James United Cemetery]

Casey, C. Louise 1941-2010 (small metal funeral home marker) [Berkley Memorial Cemetery]

Cash, Lonnie October 10, 1921 – October 24, 2001, PFC, U.S. Army, WW II [Berkley Memorial Cemetery]

Cash, Pauline G. 1924-2010 (small metal funeral home marker) [Berkley Memorial Cemetery]

Cathey, Charles A. August? *(sic)* 1900 – November 17, 1953 (no tombstone, Pennington Funeral Home records stated he was born in North Carolina, the son of Thomas Cathey and Elizabeth Bryson; he served in World War I and died in Havre de Grace; informant was Bertie Dixon, of Washington, D.C. [St. James United Cemetery]

Cevis, Carrie E. December 20, 1923 – November 11, 1993 (inscribed "In Loving Memory" and "God Bless You;" obituary in *The Aegis* on November 17, 1993 stated Carrie Elizabeth Cevis, a Darlington native, died at Fallston General Hospital; she was the daughter of the late Ralph Tucker and Carrie Price Smith and the wife of Paul L. Cevis for 47 years; she was also a musician for 20 years at Mt. Sinai Church in Arcadia, PA) [Cedars Chapel Cemetery]

Cevis, Edna E. February 4, 1928 – February 21, 2017 (on same tombstone with John W. Cevis, Jr.) [Cedars Chapel Cemetery]

Cevis, John W. Jr. December 23, 1924 – February 8, 2000 (on the same tombstone with Edna E. Cevis; obituary in *The Aegis* on February 11, 2000 stated John William Cevis, Jr. was born in Forest Hill, the son of John W.

Cevis, Sr. and Mary Ethel Wallace; he served in the U.S. Navy from May 1943 to April 1946 and worked for the federal government for 38 years at Aberdeen Proving Ground, Edgewood Area; he was survived by his wife, 5 daughters, 2 sons, 15 grandchildren, 19 great-grandchildren, 3 brothers and 3 sisters, among others) [Cedars Chapel Cemetery]

Cevis, John W. October 1, 1896 – May 1, 1961, Maryland, Pvt., 4th Co., 154th Depot Brigade, World WarI (tombstone; military records state he was born at Street, inducted into service on August 23, 1918 with the "153 Dep Brig" and was honorably discharged on December 12, 1918; "John W. Cevis, 1896-1961" also inscribed on the same tombstone with Mary Ethel Cevis) [Cedars Chapel Cemetery]

Cevis, Joseph Clarence March 7, 1936 – August 25, 1992, U.S. Army (tombstone; obituary in *The Aegis* stated he was born in Street, the son of the late John and Mary Ethel Cevis and the husband of Dorothy Wallace; he lived in Darlington, served in the Army from 1958 to 1965, worked for the State of Maryland and then for Aberdeen Proving Ground and retired in 1987; he was a trustee and musician at St. James Church and was a soloist in the choir and founded the St. James scholarship; he was survived by his wife, a son, a daughter, 4 brothers, 4 sisters, an adopted daughter, an adopted mother, an adopted family, and a granddaughter) [Cedars Chapel Cemetery]

Cevis, Mary Ethel 1899-1978 (on same tombstone with John W. Cevis; obituary in *The Aegis* stated she lived at Street and was the daughter of Joseph and Elizabeth Wallace and the widow of John W Cevis, Sr.; she died at University Hospital in Baltimore on March 28, 1978 and was survived by 6 sons, 5 daughters, 43 grandchildren and 30 great-grandchildren) [Cedars Chapel Cemetery]

Cevis, Melvin E. 1932-2006, U.S. Army, Korea (tombstone; obituary in *The Aegis* on March 29, 2006 stated Melvin Edward "Mel" Cevis was born March 15, 1932 in Street, the son of John and Mary Ethel Cevis, and died March 23, 2006 at University of Maryland Hospital in Baltimore; he had worked for the federal government for 40 years and was survived by his wife Peggy N. Cevis, whom he married June 4, 1964, and 7 children, 7 grandchildren, 12 great-grandchildren, 2 brothers and 1 sister, among others; he served over 25 years as a trustee of St. James Church and sang with the Golden Echoes, both Original and New) [Cedars Chapel Cemetery]

Cevis, Melvin E. II November 2, 1955 – March 29, 1993 (tombstone; obituary in *The Aegis* on April 28, 1993 stated Melvin Edward Cevis, Jr. was survived by his parents, Melvin E. Cevis, Sr. and Peggy Norman Cevis, and 2 sisters and 2 brothers) [Cedars Chapel Cemetery]

Cevis, Peggy N. September 23, 1931 – January 15, 2015 (inscribed "In Loving Memory") [Cedars Chapel Cemetery]

Chalk, Charles Samuel died July 17, 1905, age 44 (no tombstone; death certificate stated "C. Samuel Chalk" was a farmer who died at Frogtown and his wife was Hannah Buchanan; his parents were Abraham Chalk and Rachel Williams; all born in Harford Co.; see Daisy Sophia Chalk) [probably Hendon Hill Cemetery]

Chalk, Daisy Sophia, daughter of Charles and Hannah M. Chalk, died December 27, 1900, age 3 years, 8 months and 17 days (tombstone; death certificate stated "Dasie S. Chalk" was daughter of Samuel Chalk and Hannah Buchanan, of Bel Air; see Charles Samuel Chalk) [Hendon Hill Cemetery]

Chalk, Hannah M., wife of Charles S. Chalk, died April 17, 1919(?), age 60 (inscribed "Mother" on top of marker) [Chestnut Grove A. M. E. Church Cemetery, formerly LaGrange Cemetery at Rocks]

Chalk, Samuel died September 15, 1901, age 70 (no tombstone; death certificate stated he was a huckster in Bel Air and born in Harford Co.; his parents were Samuel and Catherine Chalk) [probably Hendon Hill Cemetery]

Chambers, Eleanor Brown died February 15, 1922, age 67 (tombstone; death certificate stated she was born on February 5, 1855 in Maryland, the daughter of John Douglas and Eliza Williams, both born in Baltimore; she was married and lived in Churchville; informant was Leon Brown) [Asbury Cemetery]

Chambers, Eliza March 31, 1847 – October 28, 1919 (no tombstone; death certificate stated she was the daughter of James Chambers and Eliza Brown, all born in Harford; she was a widow who lived in Bel Air; informant was William N. Johnson, of Bel Air) [Asbury Cemetery]

Chambers, Emory died March 26, 1922, age 83 (tombstone; death certificate stated he was born in May 1839 and was age 82 years, 10 months, 10 days when he died at home near Churchville; he was married and worked as a farmer, but his parents' names and places of birth were not known to informant Emanuel Chambers, of 227 W. Biddle St., Baltimore) [Asbury Cemetery]

Chambers, Florence, daughter of George and Jane Chambers, June 19, 1878 – July 30, 1905 (inscribed "At Rest") [Asbury Cemetery]

Chambers, Fred D. September 12, 1932 – July 8, 1995 (on same tombstone with Virginia C. Chambers; also there is a small concrete slab inscribed Fred D. Chambers, 1932-1994 *(sic)* "One Day at a Time") [Community Baptist Church Cemetery]

Chambers, George (Rev.) January 2, 1842 – December 2, 1916 (inscribed "At Rest" and died on December 2, 1917, age 74," but death certificate stated he was born in Harford Co. on January 2, 1842 and died on December 2, 1916; he was the son of James Chambers, mother's name unknown to informant Jane Chambers, of Bel Air; he was also a farmer at Bel Air and was married at the time of his death) [Asbury Cemetery]

Chambers, Jane, wife of Rev. George Chambers, died January 6, 1924, age 60 (inscribed "At Rest" and death certificate stated she was born in 1864, daughter of George Wells, but her mother's name was unknown to informant Ellen Wells, of Bel Air; she was a widow and died in Churchville) [Asbury Cemetery]

Chambers, Mahala 1873-1955 [Clark's U. M. Church Cemetery]

Chambers, Mary 1845 – October 1, 1917 (no tombstone; death certificate stated she was born in Maryland, the daughter of James Chambers, birth place unknown, and Mary ----, born in Maryland; she was married and died at Fulford; informant was Sarah J. Wilson, of Bel Air) [Asbury Cemetery]

Chambers, Paul May 12, 1868 – May 12, 1926 (no tombstone; death certificate stated he was the son of James Chambers, both born in Maryland, but informant George Chambers, of Bel Air RFD, did not know his mother's name; he was a laborer and widower at Churchville) [Asbury Cemetery]

Chambers, Susanna April 27, 1858 – March 21, 1927 (no tombstone; death certificate stated she was the daughter of Daniel Dalam (Dallam), both born in Harford Co., but her mother's name was not known to informant Richard Chambers, of Fallston; she was a widow who lived and died at Scarff) [Asbury Cemetery]

Chambers, Virginia C. April 24, 1940 – November 30, 2008 (on the same tombstone with Fred D. Chambers; her death notice in *The Aegis* on December 5, 2008 stated she was of Aberdeen and her funeral services were held at the Zion Temple Apostolic Faith Church in Havre de Grace) [Community Baptist Church Cemetery]

Chambers, Wesley died March 28, 1928, age about 70 (no tombstone; death certificate stated he was born in Harford Co., the son of James Chambers, born in Maryland, but mothe not known to informant Walter Parrott, of Bel Air RFD; he was a widower and laborer who died at "Churchville, Bel Air RFD") [Asbury Cemetery]

Chambers, William (no tombstone; death certificate stated he died December 16, 1924, age "probably 86" and was born in Harford Co., but his parents' names were not known to informant William Parrott, of Bel Air; he was a farm hand and widower who lived at Gibson) [Asbury Cemetery]

Chancy, Mary Jane May 18, 1864 – October 4, 1944 (no tombstone; death certificate stated she was born near Bel Air, the daughter of Samuel Chancy, born in Maryland, but her mother's name was not known to informant Miss Bessie Matthews, of Bel Air; she was single and died in Bel Air) [Asbury Cemetery]

Chapman, Daniel L. Sr. April 29, 1941 – May 13, 2010, A2C, U.S. Air Force [Berkley Memorial Cemetery]

Chapman, E. (small stone marker about 5 inches square, lying flat in ground) [Berkley Memorial Cemetery]

Chapman, Eleanor (no dates in 1987, not listed in 2002 and not found in 2018) [Gravel Hill Cemetery]

Chapman, Jeanette Turner 1898-1995 (tombstone; obituary in *The Aegis* on August 30, 1995 misspelled her name as Jeannette Pierce Miller Turner Chatman; she was born at Coney Island, NY, the daughter of Marley and Isabell Pierce, educated at Hampton Institute and taught in Maryland schools for 44 years; Jeanette and her late husband C. B. Miller performed throughout the county singing as a duet; she was also married to Fred Turner, later to Oliver Chapman and died at Rock Spring Village Nursing Home in Forest Hill on August 11, 1995, age 96, survived by a stepson Mark Griffith, daughter-in-law Lillie Miller, granddaughter Melva Miller, and other relatives) [Union U. M. Church Cemetery]

Chapman, Oliver A. 1902-1980 (tombstone; obituary in *The Aegis* on June 26, 1980 stated he was the husband of Jeanette P. Turner Chapman and he died at home at Gravel Hill on June 14, 1980, age 78, survived by his wife, a son Charlton Miller, a brother Addison Chapman, and three sisters, Laura Floyd, Alice Ford and Martha Bellinger) [Union U. M. Church Cemetery]

Chase, ---- stillborn male on April 13, 1914 (no tombstone; death certificate stated "Baby Chase" was the son of Samuel Chase and Hannah Flemings, all born in Maryland, and they lived in Benson; his father buried him) [Tabernacle Mount Zion U. M. Church Cemetery]

Chase, Alfred Douglas died August 5, 1906, age 5 months (no tombstone; death certificate stated he was the son of William Chase and Mary Denison, all born in Maryland, and he died at Michaelsville; his place of burial was not indicated, but probably in the Old Union Chapel Cemetery at Michaelsville; possibly reinterred in Union Chapel Cemetery near Aberdeen) [Union U. M. Church Cemetery]

Chase, Andrew departed this life August 3, 1939 [Union U. M. Church Cemetery]

Chase, Andrew T. 1918-1940 [Union U. M. Church Cemetery]

Chase, Benjamin Franklin (no tombstone, but probably buried here since his wife Helen is buried here) [Community Baptist Church Cemetery]

Chase, Catherine Lillian died March 4, 1990, age 73 (no tombstone; obituary in *The Aegis* on March 7, 1994 stated she was born in Perryman, daughter of the late Raymond Buchanon and Ada Brown, and the widow of Andrew Chase; she worked as a domestic and died at home in Aberdeen, survived by three sisters, Dorothy Parker, Lillian Kenly and Rosie Webster) [Union U. M. Church Cemetery]

Chase, Cierra S., daughter of Pearl and Ryan Chase, November 25, 1992 – January 13, 1993 [Foster's Hill Cemetery]

Chase, David D. December 15, 1890 – January 22, 1960, Maryland, Pvt., Co B, 811 Pioneer Inf, World War I [Foster's Hill Cemetery]

Chase, David Daniel Jr. died October 26, 1972, age 50 (no tombstone; obituary in *The Aegis* stated he was born in Magnolia, the son of David Daniel Chase, Sr. and Lottie Demby, and the husband of the late Charlotte Johnson, of 412 Dembytown Road, Joppa; he died at home, survived by his mother, two daughters, four sons, one brother, two sisters, and nine grandchildren) [Foster's Hill Cemetery]

Chase, George died 1 Jun 1887, age about 20 (no tombstone; death notice in *The Aegis* on June 10, 1887 stated he and another boy were swimming in the dam of Joseph Husband & Sons' Flint Mill on Deer Creek when he drowned; place of burial not given [possibly Clark's U. M. Church Cemetery]

Chase, George died March 8, 1937, age about 38 or 39 (no tombstone; death certificate stated he was the son of William Chase, born in Cecil Co., and Mary Dennison, born in Perryman; also stated he was divorced and his wife was Mrs. Alice Monk; he was struck and killed by a train on the Pennsylvania Railroad in Aberdeen) [Union U. M. Church Cemetery]

Chase, Hannah died 28 Feb 1930, age about 50 (no tombstone; death certificate stated she was born in Harford Co., the daughter of James W. Flemming and Sarah Anderson, both born in Baltimore Co.; she was a widow and died in Bel Air; informant was Albert Chase, of Fallston) [Tabernacle Mount Zion U. M. Church Cemetery]

Chase, Helen C. August 29, 1924 – July 2, 1998 ("In Loving Memory" is inscribed on her tombstone; obituary in *The Aegis* on July 15, 1998 stated Helen Christine Chase was the daughter of Alexander and Gladys Epps, and she married the late Benjamin Franklin Chase in 1970; she was employed as a cook at various restaurants in the surrounding area and was especially known for her crab cake recipe at the Blue Bell Restaurant in Bel Air; she died at the Joseph Richey House in Baltimore, survived by 2 sons, 2 daughters, 2 sisters, 2 brothers, 4 grandchildren, 1 great-grandson, and nieces, nephews, and cousins) [Community Baptist Church Cemetery]

Chase, James March 2, 1929 – January 2, 1989, Cpl., U.S. Army, Korea [Mt. Calvary U. A. M. E. Church Cemetery]

Chase, Lillie (owner of a lot in section 27 some time after 1951) [Mt. Calvary U. A. M. E. Church Cemetery]

Chase, Lottie Virginia died October 1, 1993, age 95 (no tombstone); obituary in *The Aegis* on October 6, 1993 stated she was the daughter of the late William D. Demby and Mary Jane Gilbert, and the widow of David D. Chase; she was a native of Edgewood, lived in Joppa and died at Fallston General Hospital; survived by a son Benjamin F. Chase and 17 grand-children and many great-grandchildren) [Foster's Hill Cemetery]

Chase, Mary E. October 26, 1911 – September 10, 1913 (no tombstone; death certificate stated she was born in Harford Co., the daughter of Samuel Chase, born in Calvert Co., and Hannah M. Flemings, born in Harford Co.; she died in Benson and informant was her mother) [Tabernacle Mount Zion U. M. Church Cemetery]

Chase, Mary M. May 5, 1875 – April 17, 1928 (no tombstone; death certificate stated she was married daughter of Charles W. Dennison and Eliza Morse; informant was William Chase) [Union U. M. Church Cemetery]

Chase, Raymond C. February 22, 1909 – February 8, 1919 (no tombstone; death certificate stated he was born in Harford Co., the son of William Chase, born in Cecil Co. and Mary M. Denison, born in Maryland; informant was William Chase, of Aberdeen) [Union U. M. Church Cemetery]

Chase, Thomas Andrew August 4, 1915 – August 1, 1940 (no tombstone; death certificate stated he was born in Aberdeen, the son of Wm.(?) Andrew Chase and Maggie Harvey, born both in Charles Co., MD, and he was the husband of Catherine Chase) [Union U. M. Church Cemetery]

Chase, William B. May 23, 1897 – October 1, 1933 (no tombstone; death certificate stated he was the son of William Chase, born in Port Deposit, and Mary M. Dennison, born in Perryman, and was single; he died in Havre de Grace Hospital after being struck by a car in Havre de Grace) [Union U. M. Church Cemetery]

Cheatham, Frederick August 14, 1882 – July 11, 1949 (no tombstone; death certificate stated he was born in Kentucky, the son of Paul Cheatham, but mother's name not known to the informant Mary M. Cheatham, wife of Frederick, of Havre de Grace Rt. 1; died in Harford Memorial Hospital) [St. James United Cemetery]

Chesnut, Gussie R. 1903-   (on same tombstone with Flora L. Footman) [Union U. M. Church Cemetery]

Chew, Henrietta 1844-1925 (tombstone; death certificate stated she was born on December 28, 1844, the daughter of Isaac Washington and Maria Dutton, and they all were born in Maryland; she died a widow at home at Level on May 4, 1925; informant was Solomon Cannon, of Havre de Grace; her name and dates are inscribed on the same obelisk with Soloman H. Cannon and Susia A. Cannon)

Choat, Charles November 25, 1930 – January 25, 1931 (no tombstone; death certificate stated he was born in Maryland, the son of Bert Choat and Ome (or Orne?) Eddars, both born in North Carolina; he died at home at Street and was buried by his father in "Rocks Cemetery") [Chestnut Grove A. M. E. Church Cemetery, formerly LaGrange Cemetery at Rocks]

Choate, Gladys Mary – see Gladys Mary Schoate [Fairview A. M. E. Church Cemetery]

Choate, Nora September 23, 1911 – November 21, 1932 (no tombstone; death certificate stated she was the unmarried daughter of Floyd Choate, both born in North Carolina, and Cora Hampton, born in Virginia; she lived in Pylesville, died in Havre de Grace Hospital and buried at Rocks; informant was Herbert P. Harkins, Undertaker, Delta, PA) [Chestnut Grove A. M. E. Church Cemetery, formerly LaGrange Cemetery at Rocks]

Choates, Edward E. February 15, 1938 – March 17, 1998 (inscribed "In Loving Memory;" James Dorsey Card File, African American Obituaries, at the Historical Society of Harford County, has a card with obituary from *The Aegis* on April 8, 1998 stating Edward Eugene "Gene" Choates was born near Rocks, son of the late Alice Choates; he moved to Philadelphia and sang with the Bethlehem Travelers; he served in the Army for two years and worked for the SEPT Transportation Authorities for 21 years; he died at Fitzgerald Mercy Hospital in Upper Darby, PA, survived by his wife Mary, stepson Wilbert Scott, two aunts Beulah Higgins and Hazel Choates Yeoman and dear friend Barbara Green) [Fairview A. M. E. Church Cemetery]

Christ, Charles died October 30, 1918, age about 42 (no tombstone; death certificate stated he was born in North Carolina, worked as a railroad track walker and was killed by a train at Magnolia Station; he was a widower; informant was Tessie Scully, of Van Bibber) [John Wesley U. M. E. Church Cemetery in Abingdon]

Christ, Frances G. February 11, 1879 – October 12, 1918 (no tombstone; death certificate stated she was the daughter of L. Williams and Lizzie Brown, all born in Maryland; she was married and died at Magnolia; informant was Charles Christ, of Magnolia) [John Wesley U. M. E. Church Cemetery in Abingdon]

Christ, Otho April 15, 1916 – February 16, 1918 (no tombstone; death certificate stated he was born in Maryland, the son of Peter Christ, born in North Carolina, and Frances Williams, born in Maryland; he died at home in Magnolia; informant was his mother) [John Wesley U. M. E. Church Cemetery in Abingdon]

Christ, Pearl March 15, 1914 – June 24, 1914 (no tombstone; death certificate stated she was born in Harford Co., the daughter of Charles Chrisst *(sic)* and Frances Williams, both were born in Maryland; she died at home at Van Bibber and was buried in Magnolia Cemetery) [Foster's Hill Cemetery]

Christian, Alice C. 1930-2013 (small metal funeral home marker) [Mt. Calvary U. A. M. E. Church Cemetery]

Christian, Milton L. 1925-2015 (small metal funeral home marker; owned a lot in section 27 some time after 1951) [Mt. Calvary U. A. M. E. Church Cemetery]

Christian, Milton L. Jr. May 17, 1952 – December 28, 1968 (tombstone has a resting lamb mounted on top) [Mt. Calvary U. A. M. E. Church Cemetery]

Christian, Wayne I. June 21, 1953 – January 11, 1995, U.S. Army (tombstone; James Dorsey Card File, African American Obituaries, maintained at the Historical Society of Harford County, has a card for him with an obituary from *The Aegis* stating Wayne Ivan Christian was the son of Milton L. Christian, Sr. and Alice Giles, of Aberdeen, and died at his residence, survived by his parents, his grandmothers Edith V. Giles and Lillian L. Christian, four sisters, four brothers, eleven nieces, nine nephews, two great nieces and a great nephew) [Mt. Calvary U. A. M. E. Church Cemetery]

Christie, Henry L. August 10, 1862 – July 18, 1935 (no tombstone; death certificate stated he was born at Gravelly Hill, worked as a teamster, married Isabelle ---- and died at home in Havre de Grace; informant was Lloyd Christie) [St. James United Cemetery]

Christie, Lloyd A. July 6, 1892 – June 23, 1937 (no tombstone; death certificate stated he was the son of Henry Christie, born in Havre de Grace, and Grace I. Buchanan, born in Stewartstown, PA; he married Grace ---- and died in auto accident on Route 40; military records spelled his name Christy and stated he was inducted into the Army during World War I on June 19, 1918, served overseas from August 26, 1918 to July 30, 1919, attained the rank of corporal, and was honorably discharged on August 5, 1919) [St. James United Cemetery]

Christy, Alex Edward January 3, 1941 – June 20, 1941 (no tombstone; death certificate stated he was the son of Alex Otto Christy and Alma E. Reed) [Union U. M. Church Cemetery]

Christy, Alexander O. October 17, 1918 – November 25, 1978, PFC, U.S. Army, World War II (tombstone; obituary in *The Aegis* on November 30, 1978 stated he was the son of the late Alexander and Hattie Christy, and the husband of Annie M. Christy; he was a retired employee of the Aberdeen Proving Ground and a past commander of VFW Post 6054; he died at Harford Memorial Hospital, survived by his wife, 6 sons, 1 daughter and 2 brothers) [Union U. M. Church Cemetery]

Christy, Alice 1870-1963 (on same tombstone with George W. Christy) [Union U. M. Church Cemetery]

Christy, Alice May 20, 1918 – March 16, 1919 (no tombstone; death certificate stated she was the daughter of William Christy and Fannie Thomas, all born in Maryland; informant was her father William Christy, of Bel Air RFD) [Asbury Cemetery]

Christy, Alma February 26, 1916 – January 25, 2004 (no tombstone; death notice in *The Aegis* on January 28, 2004 stated born in Perryman, daughter of Allen Dorsey and Lillie J. Ringgold) [Union U. M. Church Cemetery]

Christy, Annie L. died February 18, 1919, age about 28 (no tombstone; death certificate stated she was the married daughter of Spot Jones, both born in Virginia, but her mother's name was not known to informant Oscar Christy, of Havre de Grace) [St. James United Cemetery]

Christy, Annie M. Dennison October 21, 1920 – March 11, 1990 (copied in 1992 as Annie Mabel Christy, 1920-1990 but newer tombstone copied in 2018 with more information; obituary in *The Aegis* on March 14,

1990 stated she was born in Perryman and died March 11, 1990 at her home in Aberdeen; she was the daughter of Annie Pinion Dennison and the late Robert A. Dennison; twice widowed, she was first married to Solomon Warfield and then to Alexander Christy; she was survived by her mother and 6 sons, 1 daughter, 3 sisters, 14 grandchildren and 4 great-grandchildren) [Union U. M. Church Cemetery]

Christy, Benjamin died January 22, 1914, age about 50 (no tombstone; death certificate stated he was the married son of Henry Christy and Sarah Christy, all born near Perryman) [Union U. M. Church Cemetery]

Christy, Bernard H. Sr. June 1, 1915 – April 19, 2002 (obituary in *The Aegis* on April 26, 2002 stated he was born in Perryman and was the oldest of 10 children born to Alexander Christy and Hattie Williams; he was married to Hazel Marie Hoke for more than 54 years and retired from Aberdeen Proving Ground after more than 40 years as a boiler and heating engineer; he resided in Aberdeen and was very active with the Boy Scouts; he died at Marine Health Center in Bel Air, survived by 7 children, 14 grandchildren, 16 great-grandchildren and 1 great-great-granddaughter) [Union U. M. Church Cemetery]

Christy, Bertha Lavenia June 13, 1898 – September 27, 1943 (no tombstone; death certificate stated she was the daughter of William Henry Jones and Nell Haycock, and the wife of George O Christy, of Perryman, MD) [St. James United Cemetery]

Christy, Brenda Joyce died June 16, 1996, age 41 (no tombstone; obituary in *The Aegis* on June 26, 1996 stated she was born in Havre de Grace, the daughter of the late Mildred Webster Foster and the late Norman Christy, and died at Fallston General Hospital, survived by a son James Christy, of Waco, TX, three brothers, five sisters, and stepmother Rose Christy) [Union U. M. Church Cemetery]

Christy, Catherine 1935-2007 (small metal funeral home marker) [Union U. M. Church Cemetery]

Christy, Charles died August 29, 1918, age 21 [Union U. M. Church Cemetery]

Christy, Christine Maria "Chris" August 30, 1967 – May 31, 1987 (no tombstone; obituary in *The Record* on June 10, 1987 stated she was the youngest daughter of Catherine and the late Littleton Christy, lived in Havre de Grace and died from injuries received in a car accident on Route 40; she was active in all sports in high school, sang in the Sunbeam Choir at St. Matthew's AUMP Church and lately worked at Pizza Hut; she was survived by her mother, daughter Reiner Bishop, grandmother Frances Bryson, 4 sisters and 4 brothers; "services held at Union United Methodist Church with interment at Swan Creek Cemetery") [Union U. M. Church Cemetery]

Christy, Clarence A. March 6, 1920 – October 4, 1991, Sgt., U.S. Army, World War II [St. James United Cemetery]

Christy, Cleo T. August 20, 1935 – August 30, 1937 (no tombstone; death certificate stated he was the son of William H. Christy and Mary M. Cole) [Union U. M. Church Cemetery]

Christy, Collins D. February – (blank), 1893 – February 21, 1920 (no tombstone; death certificate stated he was the unmarried son of W. H. Christy and Martha Johnson, all born in Maryland) [Union U. M. Church Cemetery]

Christy, Collins E. A. November 27, 1924 – February 18, 1980, SC, U.S. Navy, World War II [Union U. M. Church Cemetery]

Christy, Cora W. 1898-1975 (on same tombstone with John D. Christy; obituary in *The Aegis* stated she was the daughter of the late Thomas and Georgianna Cain, lived at 414 Chestnut Street in Aberdeen and died on April 7, 1975 at Fallston General Hospital, survived by 1 son, 4 brothers and 3 sisters) [Union U. M. Church Cemetery]

Christy, D. O. 1902-1927 [Berkley Memorial Cemetery]

Christy, Darvina Maria December 15, 1966 – March 13, 1987 (tombstone; obituary in *The Record* stated she was born in Havre de Grace, the daughter of William Leroy and Ernestine Christy, and died at Harford Memorial Hospital; she was survived by her parents, 6 brothers and 4 sisters) [Union U. M. Church Cemetery]

Christy, Dorothy M. 1937-1970 (copied in 1987, but not found in 2018; obituary in *The Aegis* on April 23, 1970 stated Dorothy Marie Christy was the daughter of Milton C. Waters and Etta Janett Kenly, and the wife of William Howard Christy, Sr., of 42 Monroe St., Aberdeen; she died at Harford Memorial Hospital in Havre de Grace on April 15, 1970, age 32, survived by her husband, her parents, 4 sons, 3 daughters, 1 brother and 3 sisters) [Mt. Calvary U. A. M. E. Church Cemetery]

Christy, Dorothy May February 20, 1932 – February 21, 1932 (no tombstone; death certificate stated she was born premature and was the daughter of Gideon Warfield and Ida Christy) [Union U. M. Church Cemetery]

Christy, Dorothy R. November 14, 1918 – October 28, 1942 (no tombstone; death certificate stated she was the wife of Bernard H. Christy and daughter of Sherlie Christy and Blanch Tildon) [Union U. M. Church Cemetery]

Christy, Eliza March 4, 1873 – August 2, 1939 (no tombstone; death certificate stated she was the daughter of David Tinker and Lene Stansberry, and the widow of James E. Christy) [Union U. M. Church Cemetery]

Christy, Emma Elizabeth died September 8, 1977, age 83 (no tombstone; obituary in *The Aegis* on September 8, 1977 stated she was born in Havre de Grace, the daughter of Samuel and Emma Johnson, and the widow of Benjamin Christy; she lived in Havre de Grace and died at the Bel Air Convalescent Center, survived by a sister Ella Louise Hawkins and a niece, not named) [St. James United Cemetery]

Christy, Emma July 5, 1863 – April 3, 1920 (no tombstone; death certificate stated she was born in Havre de Grace, the daughter of Edward Sorrell, born in Baltimore, and Frances Skinner, born in Havre de Grace; she was a widow when she died in Havre de Grace; informant was Harry Christy of Havre de Grace) [Skinner Cemetery]

Christy, Ernestine Marie "Teeny" died April 8, 1994, age 68 (obituary in *The Aegis* on April 20, 1994 stated she was born in Dames Quarters, the daughter of the late Robert White and Susie Williams, and died in Oklahoma; she retired from the Harford County Board of Education and was the mother of the late Darvina Christy; she was survived by husband William L. Christy, of Havre de Grace, 4 daughters, 6 sons, 7 grandchildren and many nieces and nephews) [Union U. M. Church Cemetery]

Christy, Ethel Ringgold January 15, 1901 – October 19, 1976 (no tombstone; obituary in *The Aegis* on October 28, 1976 stated she was born in Bush River Neck near Michaelsville, the daughter of William Emory Ringgold and Susan Hollingsworth; she married ---- Christy (name not mentioned) and resided at 1514 Carsins Run Road, Aberdeen, with her daughter Mrs. Annie Addison, where she died, survived by a son, 3 daughters, 1 brother, 2 sisters, 13 grandchildren, and 21 great-grandchildren; was a member of Mt. Calvary UAME Church for over 60 years and previously a member of Sidney Park Methodist Church) [Mt. Calvary U. A. M. E. Church Cemetery]

Christy, Frances O. 1937-2008 (small metal funeral home marker) [St. James United Cemetery]

Christy, Frank died December 15, 1938, age about 82 (no tombstone; death certificate stated he was the son of Ross and Ann Christy and all were born in Maryland; he was single, worked as a farm laborer for 65 years until 1935, and died in Havre de Grace Hospital) [Gravel Hill Cemetery]

Christy, George stillborn on July 6, 1914 (no tombstone; death certificate stated he was the son of Alexander Christy and Hattie C. Williams, all born in Harford Co., and lived at Michaelsville; place of burial was not indicated, but probably in Old Union Chapel Cemetery at Michaelsville; possibly reinterred later in the Union Chapel Cemetery near Aberdeen) [Union U. M. Church Cemetery]

Christy, George Henry March 10, 1870 – August 12, 1914 (no tombstone; death certificate stated he was single and the son of Jacob H. Christy, both born in Harford Co., but his mother was not known to informant Robert Christy, of Perryman, MD) [Union U. M. Church Cemetery]

Christy, George W. 1871-1944 (on same tombstone with Alice Christy; death certificate stated he was born April 25, 1871, the son of Mary Lee Christy, father unknown, and the husband of Alice Gibson Christy, and he died on May 14, 1944) [Union U. M. Church Cemetery]

Christy, Grace died December 4, 1995, age 64 (no tombstone; obituary in *The Aegis* on December 13, 1995 stated she was daughter of Sarah Elizabeth Giles Christy and Walter Alonzo Christy; she lived in Aberdeen and died at Harford Memorial Hospital, survived by daughter, 5 sisters, 2 brothers) [Union U. M. Church Cemetery]

Christy, Gregory A. 1956-1996 (small metal funeral home marker) [St. James United Cemetery]

Christy, Guy March 8, 1892 – May 3, 1919 (no tombstone; death certificate stated he was the son of John Christy and Emma Sorrell, all born in Maryland; he was married, worked as a laborer and died in Havre de Grace; informant was Rebecca Christy, of Havre de Grace) [Berkley Memorial Cemetery]

Christy, Harford Wadsworth "Hardy" February 5, 1933 – July 16, 1996 (inscribed "My guide is but the twilight as it takes me by the hand and leads me to rest." On back of tombstone are his name, dates, and U.S. Army, Korea) [St. James United Cemetery]

Christy, Harriett E. died August 30, 1913, age 40 (no tombstone; death certificate stated she was the daughter of Jarrett Christy and Harriett Birch, all born in Harford Co.; she worked as a cook and servant, and was divorced at the time of her death in Bel Air; informant was Jarrett Christy, of Bel Air; Harford County Equity Court Case 6795 states she married Edward Arthur Draper on November 2, 1888 and he filed for a divorce on May 30, 1910, which was later granted and Harriett assumed her maiden name of Christy) [Asbury Cemetery]

Christy, Harriett E. died January 1, 1972, age not given (inscribed "A Helping Hand" and "born Spesutia Island;" obituary in *The Aegis* on January 6, 1972 stated Miss Harriet (Hattie) Christy, of 718 Old Post Road in Aberdeen, died at Citizens Nursing Home in Havre de Grace; she was born on Spesutia Island, the daughter of the late Jacob Christy and Susie Warfield, and was survived by 1 granddaughter, 2 foster children, 1 brother and 3 sisters) [Union U. M. Church Cemetery]

Christy, Harry July 18, 1902 – February 23, 1941 (no tombstone; death certificate stated he was the son of Jacob F. Christy and Susie Warfield, and the husband of Jannie Chrisry; he was shot on the porch of his house near Havre de Grace and died at Harford Memorial Hospital) [Union U. M. Church Cemetery]

Christy, Harry June 5, 1882 – December 20, 1914 (no tombstone; death certificate stated he was the son of John E. Christy and Emma Sorrell) [Skinner Cemetery]

Christy, Hattie A. April 11, 1912 – June 21, 1918 (no tombstone; death certificate stated she was the daughter of Ephraim and Mary Christy, all born in Maryland) [Union U. M. Church Cemetery]

Christy, Hattie C. July 7, 1889 – January 12, 1971 (inscribed "In Loving Memory;" obituary in *The Aegis* on January 21, 1971 stated she was the widow of Alexander Christy, of 1561 Mitchell Lane in Perryman and died at Harford Memorial Hospital in Havre de Grace; she was born in Perryman, the daughter of the late Solomon and Virgie Williams and was survived by 4 sons, 6 daughters, 2 brothers, 36 grandchildren and 35 great-grandchildren) [Union U. M. Church Cemetery]

Christy, Hazel M. July 12, 1925 -   (on same tombstone with Bernard H.) [Union U. M. Church Cemetery]

Christy, Irwin F. November 27, 1880 – September 13, 1913 (no tombstone; death certificate stated he was single son of William H. Christy and Martha Johnson, all born in Harford Co.) [Union U. M. Church Cemetery]

Christy, Isaac W. August 31, 1893 – September 7, 1962, Maryland, PFC, Co., B, 811 Pioneer Inf., World War I (tombstone; military records stated Isaac Warfield Christy, of Aberdeen RFD #2, was inducted into the service on August 23, 1918, served overseas from October 20, 1918 to July 4, 1919 and was honorably discharged on July 10, 1919) [Union U. M. Church Cemetery]

Christy, J. Ralph November 23, 1904 – February 3, 1925 (no tombstone; death certificate stated he was born in Maryland, the son of Robert L. Christy, born in North Carolina, and Sarah S. Christy, born in Maryland, and he committed suicide near Aberdeen by shooting himself) [Union U. M. Church Cemetery]

Christy, Jacob F. 1850 – October 31, 1917 (no tombstone; death certificate stated he was the son of Jacob Christy, both born in Harford Co., but the name of his mother was not known to informant Isack Christy, of Aberdeen; he was married, worked as a day laborer, died at home near Aberdeen and was buried in "Sidney Park Cemetery") [Union U. M. Church Cemetery]

Christy, James E. March 29, 1865 – October 22, 1936 (no tombstone; death certificate stated he was the son of John Henry Christy and Hetty Reed, and husband of Eliza Christy) [Union U. M. Church Cemetery]

Christy, James Edward died September 17, 1905, age 3 days (no tombstone; death certificate stated he was the son of William Bowser and Mary Christy and he died at Michaelsville; place of burial was not indicated, but probably in Old Union Chapel Cemetery at Michaelsville; possibly reinterred later in Union Chapel Cemetery near Aberdeen) [Union U. M. Church Cemetery]

Christy, James Herbert 1886-1945 [Union U. M. Church Cemetery]

Christy, James Ralph April 18, 1927 – November 5, 1980, PFC, U.S. Army, World War II [St. James United Cemetery]

Christy, Jeffrey Bernard October 19, 1951 – October 27, 1986 [St. James United Cemetery]

Christy, John October 2, 1910 – October 5, 1918 (no tombstone; death certificate stated he was the son of Elsworth Christy and Olevia Richardson, of Havre de Grace) [St. James United Cemetery]

Christy, John D. 1897-1957 (on same tombstone with Cora W. Christy) [Union U. M. Church Cemetery]

Christy, John H. February 8, 1874 – January 14, 1930 (no tombstone; death certificate stated he was the married son of Harriet Schoefield, but father was unknown to informant Annie E. Kenly) [Union U. M. Church Cemetery]

Christy, Joyce Y. died June 19, 1971, age 24 (no tombstone; obituary in *The Aegis* on June 24, 1971 stated she was the wife of Earl O. Christy, of 4 Andover Court, Huntington, Long Island, NY, and died as the result of an automobile accident on the JFK Highway (I-95); she was survived by her husband, her parents William and Cecelia Bunn of Old Stepney Road, Aberdeen, a son, a daughter, five brothers, three sisters, her maternal grandmother Mrs. Hattie Anderson, of Aberdeen, and her mother-in-law Mary Christy Brown, of Perryman) [Union U. M. Church Cemetery]

Christy, Kenfield stillborn on August 4, 1932 (no tombstone; death certificate stated he was born in Havre de Grace, the son of Elmer Christy, born on Spesutia Island, and Blanch Randolph, of Ohio) [Union U. M. Church Cemetery]

Christy, Kenneth B. January 2, 1929 – November 3, 1996, Pvt., U.S. Army, Korea [St. James United Cemetery]

Christy, Lloyd A. June 22, 1937, Maryland, Cpl., 860 Co. Trans. Corps [St. James United Cemetery]

Christy, Luciel E. March 9, 1850 – March 9, 1930 (no tombstone; death certificate stated she was the married daughter of Isaac Hynson, both born in Maryland, but her mother was unknown to informant Lloyd Christy, of Havre de Grace) [St. James United Cemetery]

Christy, Marcelline December 18, 1889 – September 7, 1945 (no tombstone; death certificate stated she was born in Maryland, daughter of William Christy and Martha Clark, both born in Virginia) [Union U. M. Church Cemetery]

Christy, Margaret died March 21, 1907, age 78 years, 6 months (no tombstone; death certificate stated she had one child, husband not named, and was the daughter of Aquilla Holliday and Mary Christy; death notice in *The Aegis* on March 29, 1907 stated "Aunt" Margaret Christy died at her home in Bel Air; for many years she served the family of A. Lingan Jarrett and more recently with the family of S. W. Bradford; her place of burial was not given [possibly Hendon Hill Cemetery where some members of the Holliday family are buried]

Christy, Martha died April 19, 1918, age about 65 (no tombstone; death certificate stated she was the married daughter of William Jones, both born in Virginia, but her mother was not known to informant William Christy, of Aberdeen) [Union U. M. Church Cemetery]

Christy, Martha J. died March 1, 1920, age 36 (no tombstone; death certificate stated she was married and born in Maryland, but her parents were unknown to informant William Christy) [Union U. M. Church Cemetery]

Christy, Mary A. May 30, 1878 – December 29, 1924 (no tombstone; death certificate stated she was the widowed daughter of Jacob Christy, both born in Maryland, but her mother was unknown to informant Charles Holland, of Havre de Grace) [Union U. M. Church Cemetery]

Christy, Mary D. 1888-1952 (on same tombstone with Solomon B. Christy) [Union U. M. Church Cemetery]

Christy, Mary E. August 7, 1882 – April 16, 1963 (inscribed "Absent From Friends But Present With God") [St. James United Cemetery]

Christy, Mary F. May 26, 1870 – September 17, 1927 (no tombstone; death certificate stated she was the married daughter of John Crockson and Sidney Stewart; informant was Frank Crockson) [Union U. M. Church Cemetery]

Christy, Mary M. R., "Mother" November 12, 1898 – January 2, 1971 (tombstone; obituary in *The Aegis* on January 7, 1971 stated she lived at 636 Hickory Circle in Aberdeen, was the widow of William H. Christy, died at Harford Memorial Hospital in Havre de Grace and was survived by 7 sons, 2 brothers and 1 sister) [Union U. M. Church Cemetery]

Christy, Mary Susie died April 24, 1975, age 91 (no tombstone; obituary in *The Aegis* on May 1, 1975 stated she lived in Havre de Grace and died at Harford Memorial Hospital; she was born in Perryman, the daughter of John and Annie Kenly, but her husband was not mentioned; she was survived by two daughters, one sister, five grandchildren, 24 great-grandchildren, and 18 great-great-grandchildren) [Union U. M. Church Cemetery]

Christy, Mattie March 16, 1874 – February 18, 1923 (no tombstone; death certificate stated she was born in Harford Co., the daughter of Isaac Christy and Fannie Robinson, and both were born in Maryland; she was married and informant was Garrow Warfield, of Perryman, MD) [Union U. M. Church Cemetery]

Christy, Mildred V. 1932-1977 (on same tombstone with Mark E. Christy) [Union U. M. Church Cemetery]

Christy, Milvain(?) Alexander March 1, 1894 – September 9, 1915 (no tombstone; death certificate stated he was the son of William and Mary Christy, all born in Harford County; he was single, worked as a laborer and died near Michaelsville; place of burial was not indicated, but probably in Old Union Chapel Cemetery at Michaelsville; possibly reinterred in Union Chapel Cemetery near Aberdeen) [Union U. M. Church Cemetery]

Christy, Myrtle E. 1887-1920 (inscribed "At Rest;" death certificate stated she was born May 24, 1889 and was the married daughter of Robert Griffin and Eliza Stansbury, all born in Harford Co.; she died February 11, 1920; informant was Jacob H. Christy, of Aberdeen) [Union U. M. Church Cemetery]

Christy, Nancy D. August 4, 1942 – November 25, 1942 (no tombstone; death certificate stated she was the daughter of Alexander O. Christy and Alma E. Reed, of Perryman, MD) [Union U. M. Church Cemetery]

Christy, Nelson (owner of a lot in section 7 some time after 1951) [Mt. Calvary U. A. M. E. Church Cemetery]

Christy, Norman C. 1900-1961 [Union U. M. Church Cemetery]

Christy, Norman Oliver April 4, 1930 – August 11, 1978, Pvt., U.S. Army, Korea (tombstone; obituary in *The Aegis* on August 17, 1978 stated he was born in Perryman, the son of the late Alexander and Hattie Christy, and the husband of Rose Marie Christy; he was a Korean War veteran and was a taxi cab driver for the Aberdeen Proving Ground; he died at Harford Memorial Hospital and was survived by his wife, a son, 5 daughters, 3 brothers and 6 sisters) [Union U. M. Church Cemetery]

Christy, Percy L. died March 19, 1971, age not given (no tombstone; obituary in *The Aegis* on March 25, 1971 stated he was the son of the late Robert and Eliza J. Christy, lived at 721 N. Stokes Street in Havre de Grace, worked as a hardware store clerk and was a World War II veteran; he died at the Veterans Hospital in Washington, D. C., and was survived by a daughter Mrs. Susan Marie Smith, three brothers Carl S. Ridgeley, James Ralph Christy and Richard Bernard Christy, two sisters, two grandchildren, four nieces, seven nephews) [Union U. M. Church Cemetery]

Christy, R. Nettie 1889-1936 (on same tombstone with Martha C. Bowser, I. Marie Bowser and Hazel T. Dunn; death certificate stated Nettie Bowser Christy August 28, 1890 – April 23, 1936) [St. James United Cemetery]

Christy, Robert Alexander April 7, 1915 – January 9, 1917 (no tombstone; death certificate stated he was the son of William Christy and Fannie Thomas, all born in Maryland, and lived at Belcamp RFD; informant was William Christy, of Belcamp) [Asbury Cemetery]

Christy, Robert J. October 17, 1895 – March 16, 1967, Maryland, PFC, U.S. Army, World War I (tombstone; military records stated he was born on October 17, 1894 in Aberdeen, was inducted into service on August 23, 1918, served in Co. B, 811 Pion. Inf., was overseas from October 20, 1918 to July 4, 1919 and was honorably discharged on July 10, 1919) [Union U. M. Church Cemetery]

Christy, Robert L. December 12, 1869 – Mat 12, 1945 (no tombstone; death certificate stated he was the son of William A. Christy and Martha Reddick, both born in Virginia, and husband of Sarah Christy who predeceased him) [Union U. M. Church Cemetery]

Christy, Roberta 1933-1984 (copied in 1987 when name and dates were silver letters and numbers mounted on a flat slab, but by 2018 the name was missing and only the years remained) [St. James United Cemetery]

Christy, Rose Marie 1940-2006 (small metal funeral home marker; funeral notice in *The Aegis* on July 19, 2006 stated she lived in Aberdeen, died at the University of Maryland Medical Center in Baltimore on July 16, 2003, age 65; services held on July 22, 2006 at Union Methodist Church in Aberdeen) [Union U. M. Church Cemetery]

Christy, Sabina died September 24, 1900, age 67 (no tombstone; death certificate stated she was the wife of Jacob H. Christy and the daughter of Ephraim Brown and Susan Rumsey; she died at Michaelsville, leaving a husband and seven children; place of burial was not indicated, but probably in the Old Union Chapel Cemetery at Michaelsville; possibly reinterred in Union Chapel Cemetery near Aberdeen) [Union U. M. Church Cemetery]

Christy, Sadie E. April 1, 1917 – August 14, 1926 (no tombstone; death certificate stated she was the daughter of Charles Christy and Ida Coale, of Havre de Grace) [St. James United Cemetery]

Christy, Sadie R. September 12, 1921 – January 28, 1929 (no tombstone; death certificate stated he was the son of Robert J. Christy, Jr. and Eliza J. Harris, of Havre de Grace) [Union U. M. Church Cemetery]

Christy, Sarah Elizabeth June 6, 1909 – September 29, 2000 (no tombstone; obituary in *The Aegis* on October 4, 2000 stated she was born in Aberdeen, the daughter of Sam and Florence Giles, married Walter James Christy and worked many years as a domestic; she had 9 children, of which 2 daughters predeceased her; she resided in Havre de Grace, died at Citizens Care Center and was survived by 5 daughters, 2 sons, 38 grandchildren, 52 great-grandchildren, and 9 great-great-grandchildren) [Union U. M. Church Cemetery]

Christy, Sarah F. June 27, 1888 – April 26, 1916 (no tombstone; death certificate stated she was married and born in Harford Co., the daughter of Josiah Hoke, born in Baltimore, and Martha Stansbury, born in Harford Co.; informant was Herbert Christy, of Perryman) [Union U. M. Church Cemetery]

Christy, Sarah S. died February 14, 1914, age 38 (tombstone; death certificate stated she was born on February 1, 1878, the daughter of Jacob Christy and Susan Johnson, all born in Harford Co.; she married, died on Spesutia Island and was buried in "Sidney Park Cemetery;" informant was Robert Christy, of Aberdeen RFD) [Union U. M. Church Cemetery]

Christy, Savannah 1922-1981 [St. James United Cemetery]

Christy, Shawn M., "Superman Shawn" October 18, 1983 – May 20, 2012 (with his photo; funeral notice in *The Aegis* on May 25, 2012 stated Shawn Marcel Christy, of Havre de Grace, died suddenly and services will be held at, and the funeral from, the Word of Faith International Outreach in Aberdeen; an expression of thanks from the Christy family was printed in *The Aegis* on June 8, 2012) [St. James United Cemetery]

Christy, Shirley Elizabeth March 30, 1950 – September 5, 1950 (no tombstone; death certificate stated she was born in Havre de Grace, daughter of ---- (blank) and Roberta Christy, died at home at 220 N. Ohio St. and was buried at "Swan Creek;" informant was Miss Roberta Christy) [Union U. M. Church Cemetery]

Christy, Solomon B. 1887-1951 (on same tombstone with Mary D. Christy; death certificate stated Solomon Benjamin Christy was born in Perryman, the son of Jacob C. Christy and Harriett Reed, worked as a construction laborer and died at home in Perryman, Aberdeen P. O.; he was married and informant was Mrs. Mary Christy, of Aberdeen P. O.) [Union U. M. Church Cemetery]

Christy, Susan 1861-1961 (white wooden cross, about 3 feet in height, with "Grand" inscribed at the top) [Union U. M. Church Cemetery]

Christy, Susie M., "Mother" 1884-1975 (tombstone' obituary in *The Aegis* stated Mary Susie Christy was born in Perryman, the daughter of John and Annie Kenly; she lived at 118 Strawberry Court in Havre de Grace and died at Harford Memorial Hospital, survived by 2 daughters, 1 sister, 5 grandchildren, 24 great-grandchildren and 18 great-great-grandchildren) [Berkley Memorial Cemetery]

Christy, Viola V. June 6, 1926 – January 12, 2006 (obituary and photo in *The Aegis* on January 20, 2006 stated she was the daughter of the late Walter Alonzo Christy and Sarah Elizabeth Giles; she worked for Aberdeen Proving Ground contractors and retired in 1998; she died at the Citizens Care and Rehabilitation Center in Havre de Grace, survived by four sisters and two brothers; her parents and two sister predeceased her; no tombstone; a small metal funeral home marker states Viola W. Christy, 1926-2006) [Berkley Memorial Cemetery]

Christy, Walter A. April 22, 1909 – December 4, 1946 (no tombstone; death certificate stated he was the son of Robert L. Christy and Sarah Christy, and the husband of Elizabeth Giles) [Union U. M. Church Cemetery]

Christy, Walter Jr. stillborn on February 18, 1937 (no tombstone; death certificate stated he was the son of Walter Christy, Sr. and Sarah E. Giles) [Union U. M. Church Cemetery]

Christy, William May 12, 1872 – December 16, 1925 (no tombstone; death certificate stated he was the son of Jarrett Christy and Harriett Turner, all born in Maryland, and worked as a farmer in Bel Air RFD #2; informant was Fannie Christy, also of Bel Air RFD #2) [Asbury Cemetery]

Christy, William "Son" 1910-1934 (tombstone; death certificate stated William Francis Christy was born on February 13, 1910, the son of William Christy and Fannie A. Thomas, and all were born in Maryland; lived and worked as a laborer at Bel Air RFD #2 and died October 8, 1934) [Asbury Cemetery]

Christy, William A. 1849-1925 (tombstone; death certificate stated he was born December 1, 1849 and died a widower on November 30, 1925 near Aberdeen, but his parents were unknown to informant William A. Christy, of Aberdeen Proving Ground) [Union U. M. Church Cemetery]

Christy, William A. March – (blank), 1949 – January 16, 1951 (no tombstone; death certificate stated he was the son of Percy Christy and Ernestine Starling, of Havre de Grace,but the Pennington Funeral Home records stated he was the son of Leroy Christy and Emiline Starling and the funeral bill was rendered to Ernestine Starling, 339 Strawberry Alley, Havre de Grace) [St. James United Cemetery]

Christy, William A., "Husband" 1869-1924 [Asbury Cemetery]

Christy, William Alexander March 1, 1894 – September 9, 1915 (no tombstone; death certificate stated he was the son of William and Mary Christy and died near Michaelsville; buried in Old Union Chapel Cemetery [reinterred in Union U. M. Church Cemetery near Aberdeen]

Christy, William D. September 25, 1895 – September 1, 1932 (no tombstone; death certificate stated he was the husband of Edna Whims Christy and son of Jacob Christy and Susie Warfield) [Union U. M. Church Cemetery]

Christy, William G. October 17, 1900 – January 16, 1951 (no tombstone; death certificate stated he was born in Maryland, the son of Robert L. Christy and Sarah Christy, worked as day laborer and house trimmer, lived on Post Road Ext. near Aberdeen and died a widower at home; informant was Lizette R. Christy, of Aberdeen RFD #2) [Union U. M. Church Cemetery]

Christy, William H. 1957-1985 (copied in 1987, but not found in 2018) [Mt. Calvary U. A. M. E. Church Cemetery]

Christy, William H. June 6, 1890 – August 22, 1938 (tombstone; military records stated he was born in Michaelsville, lived at 315 Freedom Alley in Havre de Grace, was inducted into service on August 23, 1918, served in Co. B, 811 Pioneer Inf., was overseas from October 20, 1918 to July 4, 1919 and honorably discharged on July 10, 1919; death certificate stated William Christy, Jr. was the husband of Mary Christy and the son of William Christy and Martha Johnson; he was buried in the cemetery at "Sawn (Swan) Creek, Md.") [Union U. M. Church Cemetery]

Christy, William H. Sr. 1931-201_ (small metal funeral home marker with last number missing) [Mt. Calvary U. A. M. E. Church Cemetery]

Christy, William Henry August 22, 1863 – July 20, 1948 (no tombstone; death certificate stated he was son of William Christy and Safinna Brown, and widower of Martha Johnson Christy) [Union U. M. Church Cemetery]

Christy, William L. October 24, 1926 – January 24, 2005, U.S. Army [St. James United Cemetery]

Christy. Charles D. November 25, 1925 – November 28, 1925 (no tombstone; death certificate stated he was the son of William D. Christy and Edna F. Whims) [Union U. M. Church Cemetery]

Christy. John W. November 25, 1887 – August 30, 1945 (no tombstone; death certificate stated he was the son of Jacob F. Christy and Susie Warfield, and was husband of Nettie R. Christy) [Union U. M. Church Cemetery]

Clark, Alfred died May 19, 1923, age 54 (no tombstone; death certificate stated he was the son of Susan Clark, both born in Maryland, but his father was unknown to informant Mrs. Holloway, of Perryman, MD; he was a cook, not married, and died at the Almshouse in Bel Air) [Union U. M. Church Cemetery]

Clark, Annie L. January 31, 1888 – October 23, 1913 (no tombstone; death certificate stated she was the daughter of Jarrett Clark and Lizzie J. Collins, all born in Harford Co.; she was single and died at Kalmia; informant was Lizzie J. Clark, of Bel Air) [Clark's U. M. Church Cemetery]

Clark, Bessie M. March 12, 1878 – May 31, 1944 (no tombstone; death certificate stated she was born in Harford Co., daughter of Sam Way(?), birth place unknown, and Annie Wilson, born in York Co., PA; she died a widow in Bel Air; informant was Gene Dockens, of Pylesville) [Chestnut Grove A. M. E. Church Cemetery, formerly LaGrange Cemetery at Rocks]

Clark, Daniel died May 3, 1964, age 64 (no tombstone; Pennington Funeral Home records stated he was born in British West Indies, parents unknown; he married Susie Spink and lived in Havre de Grace for 60 years [St. James United Cemetery]

Clark, Elizabeth J. July 21, 1866 – November 18, 1916 (no tombstone; death certificate stated she died in Kalmia, the daughter of Semore *(sic)* Collins and Harriett Hall, all wborn in Harford Co.; she was married and the informant was Maggie Rumsey, of Bel Air) [Clark's U. M. Church Cemetery]

Clark, Elsie M. 1921-1984 (on same tombstone with James W. Clark) [Berkley Memorial Cemetery]

Clark, Ester V. January 14, 1886 – December 14, 1912 (no tombstone; death certificate stated she was the daughter of Jarrett Clark and Elizabeth Collins, all born in Harford Co.; she was single and died at Kalmia; informant was Elizabeth Clark, of Bel Air) [Clark's U. M. Church Cemetery]

Clark, Florence Elizabeth Thomas July 9, 1888 – January 9, 1948 (no tombstone; Kurtz Funeral Home Record Book 1944-1949, p. 189, stated she was born at Federal Hill, the daughter of George Edgar Thomas, birth place unknown, and Margaret Ann Jones, born at Rocks; she married Preston Clark and died a widow in Towson; informant was Mrs. Clifton Lewis, of Rocks) [William C. Rice Memorial Cemetery, St. James U. M. Church]

Clark, George Ellsworth June 8, 1949 – June 12, 1949 (no tombstone; death certificate stated he was the son of Glen Clark and Mendora Lehman, of Havre de Grace) [St. James United Cemetery]

Clark, Gertrude F. November 14, 1920 – September 12, 1993 (inscribed Nov 1920 – Sep 1993 and "In Loving Memory Of" and "Psalm 23;" James Dorsey Card File, African American Obituaries, maintained at the Historical Society of Harford County, has a card for her with an obituary from *The Aegis* stating "Gertie" was a native of Havre de Grace and she had worked for the federal government and part-time at the Mitchell Canning House in Perryman in summer; she died at Harford Memorial Hospital and was survived by her husband James W. Clark, 2 sons, 1 daughter. 10 grandchildren and 3 great-grandchildren) [St. James United Cemetery]

Clark, Grace R. March 20, 1925 – September 13, 1972 [Berkley Memorial Cemetery]

Clark, Henry Jarrett 1899-1982 (tombstone; obituary in *The Aegis* on September 9, 1982 stated "Harry Clark, Jr." was born in Baltimore Co., the son of Harry Clark and Annie Berry; he married Edna Fender and retired from Edgewood Arsenal in 1964; he died at Baltimore City Hospital, age 85, survived by his wife, 2 sons, a daughter and a brother [Asbury Cemetery]

Clark, Hezekiah Jr. 1936-2017 (small metal funeral home marker) [Berkley Memorial Cemetery]

Clark, Irene Belle, wife of J. Preston Clark, June 4, 1888 – October 22, 1918 (tombstone did not give her middle name nor give her complete dates of birth and death; death certificate stated "Belle Clark" was the daughter of John Rice and Mary Simms, all born in Maryland, and she was married at the time of her death; informant was Preston Clark, of Rocks; her death notice in *The Aegis* on November 1, 1918 stated she had been in the employ of Mrs. J. Clarence Wilson) [Chestnut Grove A. M. E. Church Cemetery, formerly LaGrange Cemetery at Rocks]

Clark, James L. 1953-2004 (small metal funeral home marker) [Berkley Memorial Cemetery]

Clark, James W. 1918-2001 (on same tombstone with Elsie M. Clark) [Berkley Memorial Cemetery]

Clark, Jarrett June 21, 1856 – September 21, 1918 (no tombstone; death certificate stated he was born in Harford Co., the son of Samuel Collins and Lizzie Collins, both born in Maryland; he was a farmer and died a widower at Kalmia; the informant was Henry Clark, of Bel Air) [Clark's U. M. Church Cemetery]

Clark, John December 4, 1860 – February 5, 1922 (no tombstone; death certificate stated he was the son of Solomon Clark and Mary Chambers, all born in Maryland; he was single and died at Kalmia; informant was Hattie Tyler, of Bel Air) [Clark's U. M. Church Cemetery]

Clark, John E. June 6, 1874 – July 15, 1905 (no tombstone; death certificate stated he was single and born in Harford Co., the son of Joshua and Harriet Clark, both born in Harford Co., and he died at Rocks; his place of burial was not indicated, but it was most likely at Chestnut Grove; informant was his mother Harriet Clark) [Chestnut Grove A. M. E. Church Cemetery, formerly LaGrange Cemetery at Rocks]

Clark, Joseph March – (blank), 1872 – July 20, 1943 (no tombstone; death certificate stated he was the son of Solomon Clark and "Maria – unknown" and all were born in Maryland; he was born at Clark's Chapel and had lived in Bel Air for 60 years; he was married and had no occupation at the time of his death; informant was Mrs. Lucy B. Clark, of Bel Air) [Clark's U. M. Church Cemetery]

Clark, Joshua died May 29, 1904, age 70 (no tombstone; death certificate stated he was born and lived at Rocks in Maryland, worked as a laborer and had four children living at the time of his death; his wife was Harriet ---- and his father was John Clark but his mother's name was unknown; his place of burial was not indicated) [probably Chestnut Grove A. M. E. Church Cemetery, formerly LaGrange Cemetery at Rocks]

Clark, Kenneth September 26, 1947 – September 28, 1947 (no tombstone; death certificate stated he was the son of Glen Clark and Mendora Leaman, of Havre de Grace) [St. James United Cemetery]

Clark, M. Elizabeth 1868-1951 (copied in 1987, but not found in 2018) [Mt. Calvary U. A. M. E. Church Cemetery]

Clark, Mary E. May 5, 1962 – August 30, 2009 [St. James United Cemetery]

Clark, Meta G. 1937-   (on same tombstone with Meta Brown, James H. Brown, Harry W. Brown and Stewart C. Brown) [St. James United Cemetery]

Clark, Mindora March 8, 1919 – May 3, 1961 [Berkley Memorial Cemetery]

Clark, Pauline L. 1925-1988 (tombstone; obituary in *The Record* on December 21, 1988 stated Pauline Lucinda Clark was born in Perryman, the daughter of Robert Bowser and Caroline Monk; she lived in Aberdeen and died at Harford Memorial Hospital in Havre de Grace, widow of Henry Clark; she was survived by a son Haroldine Bowser, a daughter Jennie Mae Elliott, a sister Annie Brown, 8 grandchildren, and 10 great-grandchildren) [Union U. M. Church Cemetery]

Clark, Steven Eugene 1962-2017 (small metal funeral home marker) [Berkley Memorial Cemetery]

Clark, Susie S. August 7, 1901 – March 31, 1969 (no tombstone; Pennington Funeral Home records stated she was born in Pennsylvania, the daughter of George White and Mary Frances, married Daniel Clark, worked as a domestic, lived at 916 Warren St. in Havre de Grace and died at Spring Grove State Hospital in Catonsville, Baltimore County) [Berkley Memorial Cemetery]

Clark, Thomas Clifton August 4, 1911 – November 13, 1912 (no tombstone; death certificate stated he was the illegitimate son of Roberta Clark, both born in Harford Co., and he died at Kalmia; his father's name and place of birth were unknown to the informant Lizzie Clark, of Bel Air) [Clark's U. M. Church Cemetery]

Clark, William 1871-1951 (copied in 1987, but not found in 2018) [Mt. Calvary U. A. M. E. Church Cemetery]

Clark, William McKinley Sr. January 23, 1928 – June 11, 2006 (obituary and photo in *The Aegis* on June 14, 2006 stated he was born in Danville, VA, the son of Charles Clanton Clark and Ella Will Martin, and they resided on a former tobacco plantation; he was a standout high school athlete and was drafted into the Army and sent to Korea; later he was a Harford County educator and coached relay teams, cross country and basketball; he married Meta Brown in 1959 and died at the Forest Hill Health & Rehabilitation Center, survived by his wife, 4 children and 3 grandchildren, and was predeceased by 4 brothers and 1 sister) [St. James United Cemetery]

Clark, Winfield 1890 – August 7, 1936 (no tombstone; death certificate stated he was the son of John Clark, both born in Maryland, but his mother was not known to informant Bessie Clark, his wife; he was a farm laborer, lived near Pylesville and died at Havre de Grace Hospital; place of burial was at Rocks, which was most likely Chestnut Grove) [Chestnut Grove A. M. E. Church Cemetery, formerly LaGrange Cemetery at Rocks]

Clarke, Emily Ann died May 2, 1977, age 81 (no tombstone; obituary in *The Aegis* on May 5, 1977 stated she was the daughter of David and Mary Lou Brown, married William Clarke, and died at Fallston General Hospital, survived by a daughter Sandra L. Bishop and other family) [Tabernacle Mount Zion U. M. Church Cemetery]

Clarke, Henry March 10, 1909 – January 2, 2001 (inscribed "I will say of the Lord He is my refuge and my fortress My God in him will I trust. Psalm 91:2") [Chestnut Grove A. M. E. Church Cemetery, formerly LaGrange Cemetery at Rocks]

Clarke, William N. May 7, 1892 – September 8, 1982, U.S. Army, World War I (tombstone; obituary in *The Aegis* on September 16, 1982 stated he was born in Fort Union, VA, the son of William and Ella Clarke, and served in World War I; he was the husband of the late Emily A. Clarke and died at the Perry Point Veterans Administration Hospital, survived by two sisters, Mary Wood and Hattie Anderson, and an adopted daughter Sandra Bishop) [Tabernacle Mount Zion U. M. Church Cemetery]

Clinton, Henry 1889-1975 (small metal funeral home marker; obituary in *The Aegis* on August 28, 1975 stated he lived at 4090 Federal Hill Road, Jarrettsville, was a retired laborer and died on August 23, 1975, age 85, at Fallston General Hospital; he was the husband of the late Mary Hardy Clinton and was survived by 3 sons James, Acie and Willy, 1 daughter Mary C. Stewart, 13 grandchildren, 3 great-grandchildren and 3 brothers) [William C. Rice Memorial Cemetery, St. James U. M. Church]

Clinton, James Henry 1920-1999 (small metal funeral home marker) [William C. Rice Memorial Cemetery, St. James U. M. Church]

Clouders, Tee N. 1888-1982 [Clark's U. M. Church Cemetery]

Coale, Albert S. August 16, 1915 – October 4, 1915 (no tombstone; death certificate stated he was the son of John Coale and Eulah Wise, of Havre de Grace; informant was Mrs. Thomas Wise) [St. James United Cemetery]

Cobb, Martha Moore died May 29, 1938, age not given (no tombstone; James Dorsey Card File, African American Obituaries, maintained at the Historical Society of Harford County, has a card for her with an obituary from the *Bel Air Times* on June 20, 1938 stating she was the widow of William Cobb and the sister of Steve and Ellsworth Moore and Carrie Moore Armstrong, all of Bel Air; she died at her home in Baltimore) [Tabernacle Mount Zion U. M. Church Cemetery]

Cobbs, James Ernest December 11, 1918 – January 18, 2009 (on same tombstone with Sally Pearl Cobbs) [Foster's Hill Cemetery]

Cobbs, Sally Pearl March 3, 1929 – February 29, 2004 (on same tombstone with James Ernest Cobbs) [Foster's Hill Cemetery]

Cohan, Esther February 14, 1907 – April 26, 1936 (no tombstone; death certificate stated she was the daughter of Sam Norman and Mary Kellem, all born in North Carolina; she married Hollis Cohan, lived near Forest Hill and died at Havre de Grace Hospital; informant was Mr. Hollis P. Cohen *(sic)*, of Forest Hill) [Fairview A. M. E. Church Cemetery]

Cohen, Celia A. died December 21, 1944, age 81 (no tombstone; death certificate stated she was the daughter of Edward Brown and Susanna Moore, all born in Maryland; she married Daniel Cohen, worked as a domestic and died a widow in Fallston; informant was David Brown) [Tabernacle Mount Zion U. M. Church Cemetery]

Cohen, Daniel T. January 28, 1877 – December 24, 1939 (no tombstone; death certificate stated he was born at Benson, the son of Hanson Cohen and Martha Jackson, both born in Maryland; he married Celia --- (age 78 in 1939), worked as a laborer and died at home in Benson; informant was George Collins, of Bel Air) [Tabernacle Mount Zion U. M. Church Cemetery]

Cohen, Hanson May 7, 1849 – December 2, 1917 (no tombstone; death certificate stated Hanson "Coehn" was born in Harford Co., the son of Samuel "Coehn," born in "United States," and Urath Ayers, born in Harford Co.;

he married and worked as a laborer in Benson; informant was Martha "Coehn," of Benson) [Tabernacle Mount Zion U. M. Church Cemetery]

Cohen, J. W. Naaman, beloved son of J. W. and Rosetta Cohen, March 1, 1879 – April 8, 1892 [Tabernacle Mount Zion U. M. Church Cemetery]

Cohen, James W., "Father" October 25, 1851 – January 17, 1929 (on same tombstone with Rosa E. Cohen; death certificate stated his middle name was Wesley and he was born in Harford Co., the son of Samuel Cohen, but his mother's name was not known to informant Rosa Cohen, of Fallston; he was married, worked as a farmer and died in Fallston) [Tabernacle Mount Zion U. M. Church Cemetery]

Cohen, Martha A. died December 18, 1926, age about 80 (no tombstone; death certificate stated Martha A. "Coehn" was t daughter of George Jackson, but her mother's name was not known to informant David Brown, of Fallston; she was a widow and an article on *The Aegis* on December 24, 1926 stated she died in a fire; mentioned her daughter Mary Lou Brown) [Tabernacle Mount Zion U. M. Church Cemetery]

Cohen, Queen April 17, 1882 – June 10, 1913 (no tombstone; death certificate stated Queen "Coehn" was born in Essex Co., VA, the daughter of Henry Brown, born in Prince George's Co., MD, and Mary Barnes, born in Essex Co., VA; she married and died in Benson; informant was Daniel "Coehn," of Benson) [Tabernacle Mount Zion U. M. Church Cemetery]

Cohen, Rosa E. June 30, 1860 – November 22, 1930 (on same tombstone with James W. Cohen; no death certificate was found in Harford County) [Tabernacle Mount Zion U. M. Church Cemetery]

Cohen, Walter 1888-1983 (tombstone; obituary in *The Aegis* on April 14, 1983 stated he was born in Benson, the son of Hanson and Martha Cohen, and died at Citizens Nursing Home in Havre de Grace on April 7, 1983, age 94) [Tabernacle Mount Zion U. M. Church Cemetery]

Cohen, William Albert "Buttons" died May 13, 1974, age not given (no tombstone; obituary in *The Aegis* on May 16, 1974 stated he was born in Harford Co., moved to Baltimore, worked at the Sparrows Point Steel Company (Bethehem Steel) and died at 523 Presman *(sic)* Street in Baltimore, age not given; he was the husband of Belle Virginia Cohen) [Tabernacle Mount Zion U. M. Church Cemetery]

Cohens, William L. April 10, 1913 – February 13, 1914 (no tombstone; death certificate stated he was the son of William Cohens (possibly Cohen) and Alice Bond and all were born in Harford Co.) [Hendon Hill Cemetery]

Cohn, Robert Sr. February 11, 1900 – May 24, 1976, Pvt., U.S. Army, World War I [Berkley Memorial Cemetery]

Coker, Maggie R. July 28, 1886 – April 8, 1966 [Mt. Calvary U. A. M. E. Church Cemetery]

Coker, Patrick H. July 2, 1884 – June 23, 1966 [Mt. Calvary U. A. M. E. Church Cemetery]

Colbert, Baby stillborn male on May 31, 1922 (no tombstone; death certificate stated he was stillborn in Havre de Grace, the son of Robert Colbert and Hattie White, both born in Virginia) [St. James United Cemetery]

Colbert, Mary O. March 19, 1920 – August 7, 1927 (no tombstone; death certificate stated she was the daughter of Benjamin Hill and Mary O. Colbert, all born in Maryland; informant was Mrs. Florence Bond, of Havre de Grace) [St. James United Cemetery]

Cole, Annie 1846 – December 19, 1911 (no tombstone; death certificate stated she was the daughter of Louis and Annie McLane, all born in Maryland; she died a widow; informant was Emma Cole, of Havre de Grace) [St. James United Cemetery]

Cole, Anthony Leon April 4, 1932 – November 29, 1932 (no tombstone; death certificate stated he was son of Robert J. Cole, born in Aberdeen, and Lillie Mae Cromwell, born in Towson) [Union U. M. Church Cemetery]

Cole, Bernard James 1930-2013 (small metal funeral home marker) [Mt. Calvary U. A. M. E. Church Cemetery]

Cole, Ezekiel Co. A, 30th U. S. C. T. (no dates; military records stated he was a private in Co. A., 30th Regiment Infantry, United States Colored Troops, Maryland Volunteers, under Capt. LeRoy E. Baldwin from February 2,

1864 until discharged on June 24, 1865 for disability) [St. James United Cemetery]

Cole, George T. 1950-2014 (small metal funeral home marker) [St. James United Cemetery]

Cole, Isaac 1903 (on same tombstone with Mary W. Cole) [Berkley Memorial Cemetery]

Cole, Isaac stillborn male on December 7, 1921 (no tombstone; death certificate stated he was the son of Isaac Cole and Ellen Lisby, of Havre de Grace) [Skinner Cemetery]

Cole, John October 8, 1886 – May 4, 1912 (no tombstone; death certificate stated he was son of Charles Hoke and Annie Cole, all born in Harford Co.; he was single, worked as a farm hand, died at Perryman and buried in "Sydney Park Cemetery;" informant was Charles Spencer, of Aberdeen) [Union U. M. Church Cemetery]

Cole, John E. May 12, 1893 – September 12, 1942 (no tombstone; death certificate stated he was born in Churchville, the son of Isaac Cole and Julia Blake; he married Beulah V. ---- and died in Havre de Grace; informant was Mrs. Beulah V. Cole, of Lancaster, PA; military records state John Edward Cole served in the U.S. Army from 2 Aug 1918 until honorably discharged on 24 Apr 1919) [St. James United Cemetery]

Cole, Julia Ann October 1, 1875 – March 7, 1945 (no tombstone; death certificate stated she was the daughter of Edward Blake and Mary Blake ? *(sic)* and the widow of Isaac Cole; informant was Mrs. Mary Christy, of Havre de Grace) [St. James United Cemetery]

Cole, Lilly Mae, "Mother" February 16, 1901 – August 7, 1993 (inscribed "Forever In Our Hearts;" "Lillie Cole" owned a lot in section 16 some time after 1951; James Dorsey Card File, African American Obituaries, maintained at the Historical Society of Harford County, has a card for her with an obituary from *The Aegis* on August 11, 1993 stating she was born in Towson, lived in Aberdeen and was the widow of Robert J. Cole who died in 1943; she had been a domestic worker and died at Harford Memorial Hospital, survived by 3 son, 2 daughters, 41 grandchildren and 27 great-grandchildren) [Mt. Calvary U. A. M. E. Church Cemetery]

Cole, Mary W. 1903 (on same tombstone with Isaac Cole) [Berkley Memorial Cemetery]

Cole, Olivia V. 1890-1985 [Mt. Calvary U. A. M. E. Church Cemetery]

Cole, Ralph Leroy January 1, 1897 – October 15, 1958, Maryland, Corporal, 593 Co. MTC, World War I (tombstone; military records stated he was born in Guilford Co., NC, enlisted at Bel Air, MD on 26 Sep 1918 and was honorably discharged on May 24, 1919) [Hendon Hill Cemetery]

Cole, Robert James March 19n, 1889 – April 26, 1943 (no tombstone; death certificate stated he was the son of George Cole and Annie Cole, and the husband of "Mrs. Robert Cole") [Union U. M. Church Cemetery]

Coleman, Arthur died June 30, 1995, age 64 (no tombstone; James Dorsey Card File, African American Obituaries, maintained at the Historical Society of Harford County, has a card for him with an obituary from *The Aegis* on July 12, 1995 stating he was the son of the late Guvis and Catherine Coleman; he was formerly of Georgiana, AL, lived in Aberdeen and died at University Hospital in Baltimore, survived bu his wife Thelma Coleman, three sons, a daughter, a stepson, and five grandchildren) [Clark's U. M. Church Cemetery]

Coleman, B. Clarence May 11, 1911 – September 6, 1911 (no tombstone; death certificate stated he was the son of Henry Coleman and Adeline Brown, all born in Harford Co.) [St. James United Cemetery]

Coleman, Baby (male) March 8, 1917 – March 11, 1917 (no tombstone; death certificate stated he was born in Harford Co., son of Charles Coleman and Dora Bee, both born in Virginia) [St. James United Cemetery]

Coleman, Coara April 5, 1871 – April 24, 1913 (no tombstone; death certificate stated she was the wife of Charles Coleman and daughter of John Waters and Sarah Jones, all of Harford Co.) [St. James United Cemetery]

Coleman, Davon T. 1987-1987 (small metal funeral home marker) [St. James United Cemetery]

Coleman, Eloise J. May 20, 1925 – November 27, 2000 (on same tombstone with William H. Coleman, Sr.) [St. James United Cemetery]

Coleman, Jeffrey W. 1953-2016 (small metal funeral home marker) [St. James United Cemetery]

Coleman, John 1934-2014 (small metal funeral home marker) [Berkley Memorial Cemetery]

Coleman, John E. January 6, 1887 – January 4, 1937 (no tombstone; death certificate stated he was the son of Charles Coleman, of Alexandria, VA, and Cora Harris, of Havre de Grace; informant was his wife Leanna Coleman) [St. James United Cemetery]

Coleman, John T. 1865 – March 8, 1923 (no tombstone; death certificate stated he was born in Virginia and died in Bel Air; he was unmarried, worked as a day laborer, and his parents were unknown to informant George Collins, of Perryman, MD) [St. James United Cemetery]

Coleman, Martha died October 13, 1917, age about 60 (no tombstone; death certificate stated she was born in Maryland and died a widow in Havre de Grace; her parents were not known to the informant Joe Coleman, of Havre de Grace) [St. James United Cemetery]

Coleman, Ronald September 8, 1960 – April 10, 1986 ("Forever In Our Hearts") [St. James United Cemetery]

Coleman, William January 4, 1913 – July 23, 1913 (no tombstone; death certificate stated he was the son of Henry Coalman *(sic)* and Adeline Taylor, of Havre de Grace [St. James United Cemetery]

Coleman, William H. Sr. August 7, 1923 – August 25, 2002 (on same tombstone with Eloise J. Coleman) [St. James United Cemetery]

Coley, Climesto J. Sr. August 27, 1948 – June 12, 1998, U.S. Army, Vietnam (tombstone; James Dorsey Card File, African American Obituaries, that is maintained at the Historical Society of Harford County, has a card with obituary from an unidentified newspaper on June 17, 1998 stating C. J. Coley, Sr. was born in Goldsboro, NC, the son of Henry Lee Coley, Sr. and Hilda Bell Cox; he was a member of the VFW, The American Legion, and the Disabled Veterans of Maryland; he lived in Aberdeen, retired from Aberdeen Proving Ground after many years of military and civil service as a supply clerk, and died at the University of Maryland Medical Systems Hospital; he was survived by his parents, his wife of 29 years Patricia Gittings Coley, seven children, four brothers, four sisters, seven granddaughters and five god-children; he was the brother of the late Hirisa Coley) [John Wesley U. M. E. Church Cemetery in Abingdon]

Collins, ---- premature stillborn male on August 27, 1931 (no tombstone; death certificate stated he was born and died at Havre de Grace Hospital, and was the son of Finnie Collins and Rosie Presbury, both born in Harford Co; informant was his Finnie Collins, of Bel Air) [Clark's U. M. Church Cemetery]

Collins, ---- stillborn female on April 12, 1921 (no tombstone; death certificate stated she was the daughter of Finney Collins and Rose E. Presbury, all born in Harford Co.; she died at Kalmia; informant was Finney Collins, of Bel Air) [Clark's U. M. Church Cemetery]

Collins, ---- stillborn female on December 13, 1916 (no tombstone; death certificate stated she died in Kalmia, the daughter of Catherine Collins, both born in Maryland, but her father's name was not known to the informant Samuel Collins, of Bel Air) [Clark's U. M. Church Cemetery]

Collins, ---- stillborn female on September 20, 1923 (no tombstone; death certificate stated she was the daughter of Finney Collins and Rosa Presberry, of Castleton, all born in Maryland; informant was Henry Presberry, of Darlington; she was buried in cemetery by her father) [Berkley Memorial Cemetery]

Collins, ---- unnamed male born on August 31, 1916 and died on October 19, 1916 at Aldino (no tombstone; death certificate stated he was the son of Robert Collins and Harriet Bond, all born in Maryland; informant was Robert Collins, of Aberdeen RFD) [Green Spring U. M. Church Cemetery]

Collins, Addie B. 1910-1987 (tombstone; obituary in *The Aegis* on February 26, 1987 stated she died at home in street on February 13, 1987, age 76; she was active in the church and served on the Senior Usher Board and the Communion Steward Board and was chaired the Health and Welfare Committee; she was married (husband's name not given) and survived by a daughter, a son, a stepson, 4 stepdaughters, 6 grandchildren, and 7 great-grandchildren) [Clark's U. M. Church Cemetery]

Collins, Addison W. January 25, 1901 – April 6, 1929 (no tombstone; death certificate stated he died at Kalmia, the son of Samuel Collins and Margaret Dutton, all born in Maryland; he was married and worked as a laborer; informant was Finney Collins, of Bel Air) [Clark's U. M. Church Cemetery]

Collins, Alvin A. June 30, 1918 – August 6, 1918 (no tombstone; death certificate stated he was the son of

Arthur Collins and Sylvia Tildon, of Havre de Grace) [St. James United Cemetery]

Collins, Angiline April 24, 1879 – February 12, 1942 (no tombstone; death certificate stated she was daughter of Peter G. Monk and Susanna Christy, and wife of Richard H. Collins) [Union U. M. Church Cemetery]

Collins, Arthur A. February 28, 1926 – April 16, 2004, Cpl., U.S. Marine Corps, World War II [St. James United Cemetery]

Collins, Arthur C. (Rev.), husband of Grace Wescott, May 9, 1885 – March 15, 1979 (on same tombstone with his wife) [Clark's U. M. Church Cemetery]

Collins, Arthur March 30, 1895 – April 24, 1946 (no tombstone; death certificate stated he was the son of George Raymond Collins and Sylvia Whyte, and husband of Sylvia V. Collins) [St. James United Cemetery]

Collins, Baby (female) March 14, 1923 – March 21, 1923 (no tombstone) [St. James United Cemetery]

Collins, Baby (male) stillborn on April 15, 1919 (no tombstone; death certificate stated he was the son of Arthur Collins and Sylvia Tildon, of Havre de Grace) [St. James United Cemetery]

Collins, Betty Jean March 22, 1948 – June 20, 1948 (no tombstone; death certificate stated she was the daughter of John H. Collins and Pauline Robinson, of Havre de Grace) [St. James United Cemetery]

Collins, Caloise May 11, 1915 – May 25, 1917 (no tombstone; death certificate stated he was the son of Catherine Collins, both born in Harford Co., but his father's name and place of birth were not known to the informant Morris Collins, of Bel Air; the infant died in Kalmia) [Clark's U. M. Church Cemetery]

Collins, Caroline died November 12, 1904, age 66 (no tombstone; death certificate stated she was the wife of Leven Collins, Sr. and the daughter of William Ringgold and Hannah Frisby, all born in Harford Co.; she died at Michaelsville and was survived by her husband; informant was her nephew Robert Ringgold) [Old Union Chapel M. E. Church Cemetery; possibly reinterred in Union U. M. Church Cemetery near Aberdeen]

Collins, Charles Alexander January 22, 1890 – November 15, 1957, Maryland, PFC, Co. D, Svc Bn, QMC, World War I (tombstone; military records state he lived in Perryman, was inducted into the service on August 2, 1918, served in SC and VA, last served in Co. D, 431 Serv Bn beginning on January 14, 1919 and was honorably discharged on July 24, 1919) [Union U. M. Church Cemetery]

Collins, Charles Edward October 5, 1874 – July 22, 1912 (no tombstone; death certificate stated he was born in Harford Co., the son of Semour *(sic)* Collins, born in Anne Arundel Co., and Harriet Hall, born in Harford Co.; he was married, worked as a stevedore and died at Kalmia; informant was Elizabeth Clark, of Bel Air) [Clark's U. M. Church Cemetery]

Collins, Charles Wesley February 7, 1873 – June 4, 1932 (no tombstone; death certificate stated he was born in Harford Co., the son of Joseph A. Collins and Sabina Gilbert, both born in Maryland; he was single, worked as a farmer for 45 years, and lived and died at Havre de Grace RFD#2; informant was Mrs. Georgia Cannon, of Havre de Grace RFD #1) [Green Spring U. M. Church Cemetery]

Collins, Eldon Earl January 29, 1897 – June 19, 1967, New Jersey, Sgt, U.S. Army, World War I [Clark's U. M. Church Cemetery]

Collins, Elizabeth A., wife of James H. Collins, August 9, 1849 – September 13, 1903 (no date of death on tombstone; death certificate stated Elizabeth Ann Collins was the daughter of William Kenly and Phoebe Aikens, all were born in Harford Co.; she died at home near Level; informant was her husband James Henry Collins) [Green Spring U. M. Church Cemetery]

Collins, Elwood Smith August 9, 1881 – March 27, 1926 (inscribed "At Rest" on same tombstone with William Daniel Collins, sons of Samuel E. and Margaret L. Collins) [Clark's U. M. Church Cemetery]

Collins, Florence E. May 13, 1920 – June 14, 1920 (no tombstone; death certificate stated she died at Kalmia, the daughter of Finney Collins and Rosa E. Presbury, all born in Harford Co.; informant was Finney Collins, of Bel Air) [Clark's U. M. Church Cemetery]

Collins, Frank A. 1870-1927 (on same tombstone with Leven H. Collins, Jr.) [Union U. M. Church Cemetery]

Collins, George H. 1898-1978 (on same tombstone with Mary E. Collins) [Union U. M. Church Cemetery]

Collins, George R. November 5, 1924 – May 22, 1925 (no tombstone; death certificate stated he was the son of George H. Collins and Marsoline Coleman) [Union U. M. Church Cemetery]

Collins, Grace Wescott July 17, 1892 – October 6, 1959 (inscribed "Death is but an open door to life;" her name is on the same tombstone with her husband Rev. Arthur C. Collins, but an unidentified researcher once noted that she was actually buried in Fairview Cemetery in Philadelphia) [Clark's U. M. Church Cemetery]

Collins, Harriet 1873-1954 [Green Spring U. M. Church Cemetery]

Collins, Hattie Ann April 13, 1908 – February 23, 1975 (no tombstone; obituary in *The Aegis* stated she was born in Harford Co., the daughter of Robert Collins and Harriett Bond; she lived at 140 St. John Street in Havre de Grace and died at Harford Memorial Hospital, survived by brothers Howard and Gilbert Collins and sisters Nellie Giles and Martha Collins) [Green Spring U. M. Church Cemetery]

Collins, James Henry June 18, 1855 – April 27, 1920 (no tombstone; death certificate stated James H. Collins was the son of Joseph A. Collins, both born in Maryland, but his mother's name was not known to informant Annie Morgan, of 3905 Meton St., Philadelphia, PA; he lived in or near Bel Air and was a farming day laborer) [Green Spring U. M. Church Cemetery]

Collins, James Wesley May 5, 1886 – September 22, 1949 (no tombstone; death certificate stated he was born in Maryland, the son of William Collins and Sarah Moore, worked as a railroad crossing watchman, was married and died at home in Perryman, informant was Idella Collins) [Union U. M. Church Cemetery]

Collins, Jane V. died February 1, 1920, age about 92 (no tombstone; death notice in *The Aegis* on February 6, 1920 stated she was "a respected old colored woman in the vicinity of Emmorton" and died at age about 92; death certificate stated she was a widow, age 92, anddaughter of Garrison Archer and Betsy Wilson, all born in Harford Co. and lived in Emmorton; informant was Alice R. Johnson, of Emmorton) [Hendon Hill Cemetery]

Collins, Jennie February 13, 1875 – February 16, 1916 (no tombstone; death certificate stated she died at Thomas Run, the daughter of J. Alexander Colns (Collins?) and Jennie Prigg, all born in Harford Co., and she was married; informant was Leander Collins, of Bel Air) [Clark's U. M. Church Cemetery]

Collins, John A. June 12, 1913 – June 29, 1959, Maryland, PFC, 481st Port Bn, TC, World War II [Green Spring U. M. Church Cemetery]

Collins, John F. 1897-1981 [Clark's U. M. Church Cemetery]

Collins, John Finney stillborn on May 6, 1919 (no tombstone; death certificate stated he was the son of John F. Collins and Rosie Presbery, all born in Maryland; he died at Castleton and was buried in "Kalmia Cemetery;" informant was her father John Collins, of Darlington) [Clark's U. M. Church Cemetery]

Collins, Joseph A. 1830-1903 [Green Spring U. M. Church Cemetery]

Collins, Joseph T. July 4, 1883 – January 29, 1904 (inscribed "One by one life robs us of our treasures, Nothing is our own except our dead") [Clark's U. M. Church Cemetery]

Collins, Latetia A. March 9, 1912 – March 1, 1915 (no tombstone; death certificate stated she died in Bel Air, the daughter of Arthur C. Collins and Grace E. Westcoat, all born in Harford Co.; informant was Arthur C. Collins, of Bel Air) [Clark's U. M. Church Cemetery]

Collins, Lee E. October 26, 1894 – January 15, 1928 (no tombstone; death certificate stated he was the unmarried son of L. H. Collins and Sarah Lee; informant was L. H. Collins) [Union U. M. Church Cemetery]

Collins, Leven H. died January 22, 1913, age "possibly 70" (no tombstone; death certificate stated he was a widower who was born in Maryland, but his parents were unknown to informant Leven H. Collins, Jr., of Perryman) [Union U. M. Church Cemetery]

Collins, Leven H. Jr. 1868-1942 (on same tombstone with Frank A. Collins; death certificate stated Leven Henry Collins, Jr. was the son of Leven H. Collins, Sr. and Mary Welsh, of Perryman) [Union U. M. Church Cemetery]

Collins, Levin died January 22, 1913, age 70 (tombstone; death certificate stated Leven H. Collins was a farm hand who died a widower at Perryman and his age was "possibly 70" according to informant Leven H. Collins, Jr.; he was born in Maryland, but his parents were not known; he was buried in Union Chapel Cemetery by Pennington Funeral Home) [Old Union Chapel M. E. Church Cemetery]

Collins, Margaret August – (blank), 1861 – April 19, 1938 (no tombstone; death certificate stated she was the daughter of William Dutton, born in Harford Co., and Mary Cooper, born in Churchville; she married Samuel Collins and died a widow at Kalmia; informant was Hattie Hill, of Bel Air) [Clark's U. M. Church Cemetery]

Collins, Martha Mary 1918-1980 [Green Spring U. M. Church Cemetery]

Collins, Mary, beloved wife of Len Collins, died October 25, 1880, age 35 (inscribed "In Memory Of"); wife of Levin H. Collins [Old Union Chapel M. E. Church Cemetery]

Collins, Mary E. 1899-1988 (on same tombstone with George H. Collins; obituary in *The Aegis* on January 5, 1989 stated Mary Elizabeth Collins was born in Perryman, the daughter of the late Daniel and Mannie Webster, and the wife of the late George H. Collins; she worked as a domestic and was a member of the Usher Board and Willing Workers of Union United Methodist Church; she lived in Aberdeen and died in Harford Memorial Hospital on December 28, 1988, survived by one step-son Edgar Collins and two step-grandchildren) [Union U. M. Church Cemetery]

Collins, Mary Elizabeth January 2, 1903 – December 23, 1932 (no tombstone; death certificate stated she died at Kalmia, the daughter of Samuel Collins, born at West River, and Margaret Collins, born at Churchville; she was single and the informant was Hattie Hill, address not given) [Clark's U. M. Church Cemetery]

Collins, Mildred L. July 20, 1926 – September 11, 1926 (no tombstone; death certificate stated she was the daughter of George H. Collins and Marsoline Colman, of Perryman, MD) [Union U. M. Church Cemetery]

Collins, Patricia Jean June 25, 1941 – January 6, 1942 (no tombstone; death certificate stated she was the daughter of James Franklin Dade and Mary Catherine Collins, of Havre de Grace) [St. James United Cemetery]

Collins, Robert 1874-1954 [Green Spring U. M. Church Cemetery]

Collins, Robert died December 4, 1919, age 7 months (no tombstone; death certificate stated he was the son of Robert Collins and Harriett Bond, all born in Maryland, and he died at Aldino; informant was Robert Collins, of Aberdeen) [Green Spring U. M. Church Cemetery]

Collins, Robert Howard June 17, 1899 – November 3, 1976 (no tombstone; obituary in *The Aegis* stated he was born in Aldino, the son of Robert Collins and Harriet Bond; he lived at 140 St. John Street in Havre de Grace, was a retired laborer for a sod company and died at Harford Memorial Hospital, survived by his sister Martha Collins of Havre de Grace) [Green Spring U. M. Church Cemetery]

Collins, Robert M. June 4, 1929 – September 28, 1929 (no tombstone; death certificate stated he was the son of George G. Collins, both born in Maryland, and Gladys M. Hander, of Harford, CT; informant was his father George G. Collins, of Aberdeen RFD) [Green Spring U. M. Church Cemetery]

Collins, Rosie P. May 15, 1900 – August 31, 1931 (no tombstone; death certificate stated she was the daughter of Henry Presbery and Susan Washington, all born in Darlington; she married Finnie Collins, lived in Darlington and died at Havre de Grace Hospital; information was gleaned by an unidentified person from the hospital records) [Clark's U. M. Church Cemetery]

Collins, Rudolph Richard April 12, 1972 – July 17, 1982 [Berkley Memorial Cemetery]

Collins, Ruth (no dates when copied in 1987, but not found in 2018) [St. James United Cemetery]

Collins, Samuel F. September 14, 1852 – January 29, 1925 (inscribed "Asleep in Jesus;" death certificate of Samuel Collins stated he was born in April *(sic)*, but the day and year were not given, and he died January 29, 1925, age 72; son of Dan Collins, both born in Maryland, but his mother's name was not known to the informant Elsworth Collins, of Bel Air; married and worked as a farm laborer at Kalmia) [Clark's U. M. Church Cemetery]

Collins, Seymour (name on base, but no dates inscribed) [Clark's U. M. Church Cemetery]

Collins, Sylvia Virginia August 8, 1909 – November 19, 1948 (no tombstone; death certificate stated she was the daughter of Garfield Tildon and Lula Stansbury, of Havre de Grace, and the widow of the late Arthur Collins; informant was Richard M. Collins, of Havre de Grace) [St. James United Cemetery]

Collins, Thomas October – (blank), 1820 – February 7, 1922 (no tombstone; death certificate stated he was the son of Seymore Collins and Katharine Walkins, all were born in Maryland; he died a widower at Kalmia; the informant was John Williams, of Forest Hill; obituary in *The Aegis* on February 19, 1922 stated he died at the home of his daughter near Harkins Shop; "fairly accurate records fix Uncle Tom's age at 102 years, thus making him Harford's oldest man … for many years the old fellow was a servant in the Nelson (Neilson) family at Priestford and later went upwards Kalmia on a little property of his own;" he was survived by a daughter, 6 grandchildren, 8 great-grandchildren, 1 great-great-grandchild) [Clark's U. M. Church Cemetery]

Collins, William Daniel December 6, 1869 – February 17, 1926 "At Rest" (on same tombstone with Elwood Smith Collins, sons of Samuel E. and Margaret L. Collins; death certificate stated he died February 17, 1926, age 43 *(sic)*, was married, worked as a farmer, and died at Indian Spring Farm; informant was Mrs. Hattie Hill, of Darlington) [Clark's U. M. Church Cemetery]

Conley, Washington (no tombstone, but Kurtz Funeral Home records stated he was buried from his home near Rogers forges in an "Im Cherry on P" coffin on June 15, 1883 at Lagrange Church) [Chestnut Grove A. M. E. Church Cemetery, formerly LaGrange Cemetery at Rocks]

Conner, Ann Huston died April 27, 1885, age 76 (no tombstone; her death notice in *The Aegis* on May 15, 1885 stated she died in Philadelphia; for many years she was a domestic for the family of Dr. Harlan in Churchville and went with his family to Philadelphia when he was surgeon at the Naval Asylum in 1864; she usually visited her old home in Churchville twice a year; her remains were brought to Asbury Church for burial on April 29, 1885) [Asbury Cemetery]

Conwell, Edith Evelyn, "Loving Niece" November 25, 1907 – April 7, 1995 [Fairview A. M. E. Church Cemetery]

Conyers, Michele A. 1959-1999 (copied in 1987 and 2002, but not found in 2018) [Gravel Hill Cemetery]

Cook, Charles Sonny 1935-2010 (small metal funeral home marker) [St. James United Cemetery]

Cook, Joseph died November 2, 1930, age about 53 (no tombstone; death certificate stated he was unmarried and his parents were not known to the informant, Clara Stansbury) [St. James United Cemetery]

Cook, Kenyah Lynn 2005-2006 (small metal funeral home marker) [St. James United Cemetery]

Cook, Mary E. 1870-1930 (tombstone; death certificate stated she was born January 1, 1871, the daughter of Isaac Banks and Mary J. Washington, all born in Maryland; she died a widow on August 22, 1930 in Aberdeen; informant was Georgianna Turner, 1453 Mantua Ave., Philadelphia) [Mt. Calvary U. A. M. E. Church Cemetery]

Cook, Mary M. March 27, 1936 – May 23, 2001 [St. James United Cemetery]

Cooper, Abraham June 11, 1850 – December 16, 1914 (no tombstone; death certificate stated he was the son of Abraham Cooper and Lucinda Hays, all born in Maryland; he was a laborer, was married, and lived and died at Fulford; informant was Thomas Fisher, of Churchville) [Asbury Cemetery]

Cooper, Abraham, "Brother" died August 11, 1903, age 68 years, 4(?) months, 20 days (tombstone; death certificate stated he was born in Maryland, the son of Edward Cooper, born in Maryland, and Malinda Fisher, born in Pennsylvania, worked as a laborer, and died on August 11, 1903, age 68, in Bel Air; informant was his brother William Cooper)

Cooper, Benjamin Barnes April 5, 1891 – July 10, 1946 (no tombstone; death certificate stated he was the son of Edward I. Cooper and Susan Boyce, all born in Harford Co.; he was single, worked a farmer in Perryman and died at Harford Memorial Hospital; informant was William E. Cooper, of Perryman) [Asbury Cemetery]

Cooper, Charles E. September 28, 1916 – October 19, 1916 (no tombstone; death certificate stated he was the son of William E. Cooper and Rachel A. Dorsey, all born in Harford Co.; Charles died in Bel Air; informant was Rachel A. Cooper, of Bel Air) [Asbury Cemetery]

Cooper, Charles Raymond November 22, 1891 – May 3, 1975 (no tombstone; an article and obituary in *The Aegis* on May 8, 1875 reported Charles Raymond "Charlie" Cooper, of Washington St., drowned near Tydings Park in Havre de Grace; he was a lifelong resident of Harford Co., a World War I veteran, and a former employee at the Coca-Cola Bottling Works; military records stated he resided at Bel Air RFD #1, when he was inducted on August 2, 1918, served in Co. B, 401 Res Lab Bn., and was honorably discharged on April 23, 1919)

Cooper, Edward August 7, 1852 – February 15, 1912 (no tombstone; death certificate stated he was born in Harford Co., the son of Edward Cooper and Laudia Tasker, married, was a farmer and reverend, and died in Churchville; informant was Delworth Cooper, of Bel Air) [Asbury Cemetery]

Cooper, Edward Franklin November 18, 1854 – March 23, 1927 (no tombstone; death certificate stated he was the son of Franklin Dorsey and Emily J. Cooper, all born in Churchville; he was a widow and farmer who died at Churchville; informant was Barns Cooper, of Bel Air RFD) [Asbury Cemetery]

Cooper, Eliza J. December 2, 1905 – November 7, 1988 (no tombstone; James Dorsey Card File, African American Obituaries, maintained at the Historical Society of Harford County, has a card for her that was prepared by the Tittle Funeral Home in Bel Air) [Berkley Memorial Cemetery]

Cooper, Ellen I. January 6, 1908 – February 7, 1977 [Union U. M. Church Cemetery]

Cooper, Ellsworth 1921-1978 (copied in 1987, but not found in 2018) [Asbury Cemetery]

Cooper, Emily V. 1882-1958 (small metal funeral home marker) [Clark's U. M. Church Cemetery]

Cooper, George L. September 11, 1952 – October 27, 2001, Sgt., U.S. Army [St. James United Cemetery]

Cooper, George W., "Father" died October 2, 1907, age 21 [Asbury Cemetery]

Cooper, Georgeanna died October 18, 1881, age 37 [Asbury Cemetery]

Cooper, John G. July 13, 1850 – October 7, 1917 (no tombstone; death certificate stated he was born in Harford Co., son of Emily J. Cooper, born in Harford Co., but his father's name was not known to the informant Albert S. Dorsey, of Street; he was married, worked as a coachman and died at Street) [Clark's U. M. Church Cemetery]

Cooper, Laura 1913-1986 (copied in 1987, but not found in 2018) [John Wesley U. M. E. Church Cemetery in Abingdon]

Cooper, Louisa March – (blank), 1842 – August 14, 1914 (no tombstone; death certificate stated she was the daughter of Shadrach Cooper and Nellie Stewart, all were born in Harford Co.; she was a widow who died at Fulford; informant was Ellsworth Cooper, of Bel Air) [Asbury Cemetery]

Cooper, Martha Ann died March 8, 1938, "age 89?" *(sic)* (no tombstone; death certificate stated she was the daughter of Hemsley Blake, both born in Maryland, but her mother's name was unknown to informant Thomas Fisher, of Bel Air; she married Abraham Cooper and was a widow) [Asbury Cemetery]

Cooper, Mary E., "Mother" March 3, 1835 – August 6, 1918 (tombstone; death certificate stated she was born March 1, 1835 in Maryland and died in Havre de Grace on August 7, 1918; her husband and mother were not named, but her father was Robert Ramsay; informant was Ella Cooper, of Havre de Grace; she died a widow) [St. James United Cemetery]

Cooper, Mary Rebecca died March 11, 1912, age 64, "Safe in the Arms of Jesus" (tombstone; death certificate stated she was the daughter of Stephen Hooper and Ann Hall, all born in Harford Co., and she died a widow at Churchville; informant was Hester C. Banks, of Churchville) [Asbury Cemetery]

Cooper, Rose Jane February 20, 1873 – March 20, 1943 (no tombstone; death certificate stated she was born in Churchville, the daughter of Nathan Cooper and Georgianna Dorsey, both born in Maryland; she was single and lived and died in rural Bel Air; informant was Ellsworth Cooper, of Bel Air) [Asbury Cemetery]

Cooper, Susan February 19, 1860 – May 9, 1921 (no tombstone; death certificate stated she was born in Maryland, the daughter of Vincen *(sic)* Boyce and Sarah Brown, birth places unknown to informant Edward L.Cooper, of Bel Air; she was married and lived in Churchville) [Asbury Cemetery]

Cooper, Virginia P. October 14, 1851 – February 21, 1944 (no tombstone; death certificate stated she was born in Harford Co., the daughter of John Cooper and Louisa Dutton, both were born in Maryland; she was a widow and died near Street where she had lived for 30 years; informant was John C. Cooper, of Street RFD #1) [Clark's U. M. Church Cemetery]

Cooper, William July 22, 1850 – April 28, 1920 (no tombstone; death certificate stated he was the son of Edward Cooper and Malinda Fisher, all born in Maryland; he was single and worked as a farmer in Churchville; informant was Hester C. Banks, of Bel Air) [Asbury Cemetery]

Cooper, William E. F. November 20, 1895 - June 8, 1957, Maryland, Pvt, U.S. Army, World War I (tombstone; military records state he was born November 20, 1896, lived at Bel Air RFD #1 and was inducted into the service on August 23, 1918; he served in the 154 Dep Brig and 32 Const Co. AS and was honorably discharged on December 10, 1918) [Union U. M. Church Cemetery]

Copeland, ---- 1931-2008 (small metal funeral home marker) [Clark's U. M. Church Cemetery]

Copeland, Eugene 1915-1976 [Clark's U. M. Church Cemetery]

Copeland, Geane Frances July 3, 1948 – June 26, 1949 (no tombstone; death certificate stated she was the daughter of Joseph Harding Copeland and Grace Davis and died at Harford Memorial Hospital) [Union U. M. Church Cemetery]

Copeland, John Edward November 19, 1919 – May 8, 1982, Cpl., U.S. Army, World War II, Korea (tombstone; obituary in *The Aegis* on May 20, 1982 stated he was born in Richmond, VA, lived in Aberdeen and died at Perry Point VA Hospital, survived by 7 daughters, 2 sons, 1 sister, 25 grandchildren and 4 great-grandchildren; his wife was not mentioned in the obituary) [St. James United Cemetery]

Copeland, Margarite V. 1919-   [Clark's U. M. Church Cemetery]

Copeland, Rosa Marie September 17, 1946 – April 6, 1975 (no tombstone; death certificate stated she was born in Newport News, VA, the daughter of John Copeland, Sr. and the late Marie Brown; she lived in Seaside, Monterey Co., CA and died at Belview Nursing Home in Pacific Grove, CA, survived by two sons Raymond Brown and LaMont Frazier, a daughter Regina Frazier, her father John Copeland, two brothers, seven sisters, and maternal grandmother Josephine Brown, of Holland, VA) [Union U. M. Church Cemetery]

Corey, Agnes E. "Mother" March 7, 1903 – February 10, 1993 (on same tombstone with Betty Lee Corey) [Clark's U. M. Church Cemetery]

Corey, Betty Lee "Wife and Mother" January 6, 1933 – July 3, 2000 (on same tombstone with Agnes E. Corey) [Clark's U. M. Church Cemetery]

Corey, Devon O'dell October 8, 2009 – August 2, 2010 (no tombstone; obituary in *The Aegis* on September 8, 2010 stated he was the son of Zakkiya M. Corey and Anthony W. Joseph, Jr. and the grandson of Emery M. Corey, Carol Walker Joseph and Anthony (LaTasha) W. Joseph) [Clark's U. M. Church Cemetery]

Corey, Emery Milton, "Loving Husband, Father and Grandfather" December 15, 1929 – September 6, 2015, U.S. Navy, Korea, Vietnam [Clark's U. M. Church Cemetery]

Corn, William H. 1871-1949 [Clark's U. M. Church Cemetery]

Cornelius, Hazel Osborne August 8, 1921 – January 13, 1982 (no tombstone; James Dorsey Card File, African American Obituaries, maintained at the Historical Society of Harford County, has a card for her from an unidentified newspaper stating she was the daughter of Cecilia Dorsey Osborne and the late Clarence Osborne) [Asbury Cemetery]

Cornish, Ella December 25, 1868 – July 9, 1928 (no tombstone; death certificate stated she was the widowed daughter of Santie Reddick and Martha Reed, all born in North Carolina) [Union U. M. Church Cemetery]

Cornish, George E. August 15, 1868 – January 23, 1926 (no tombstone; death certificate stated he was the married son of George E. Cornish and ----; informant was Ella N. Cornish) [Union U. M. Church Cemetery]

Cornish, Nancy O. December 30, 1828 – April 15, 1906 (tombstone; death certificate stated Nancy Opy Cornish was born in Virginia, daughter of Daniel Laws and Margarett Manns, both born in Virginia; she married

Hiram Cornish, worked as a laundress at Rocks, and died a widow; informant was her daughter Martha Berry) [Chestnut Grove A. M. E. Church Cemetery, formerly LaGrange Cemetery at Rocks]

Corns, Agnes J. June 19, 1881 – February 11, 1921 (no tombstone; death certificate stated she was the daughter of Telitha Wells, father's name unknown, all born in Maryland; she was married and died at Thomas Run; informant was James A. Corns, of Bel Air) [Asbury Cemetery]

Corns, Alexander November 16, 1841 – December 6, 1927 (no tombstone; death certificate stated he was the son of William Corns, both born in Maryland, but mother's name was not known to informant James A. Corns, of Bel Air RFD; a widower and farmer he died at Havre de Grace Hospital) [Clark's U. M. Church Cemetery]

Corns, Carson W. October 21, 1914 – May 18, 1963, Maryland, SSgt, 4226 Qtr Master Co., World War II [Clark's U. M. Church Cemetery]

Corns, Hannah R., "His Wife" 1894-1961 (on same tombstone with James A. Corns) [Clark's U. M. Church Cemetery]

Corns, James A. 1881-1961 (on same tombstone with Hannah R. Corns) [Clark's U. M. Church Cemetery]

Corns, Jennie died February 26, 1926, age 73 (no tombstone; obituary and tribute in *The Aegis* on March 5, 1926 stated she was the wife of Alexander Corns and died at the home of her son James A. Corns in the Thomas Run section; she had been a faithful member of Clark's Chapel for forty years; death certificate stated she was the daughter of A. Prigg and ---- (blank) Presbury, all born in Maryland; she was married, but her birth date was not known to the informant James A. Corns, of Bel Air) [Clark's U. M. Church Cemetery]

Corns, Mary Agnes died June 11, 1972, age not given (no tombstone; obituary in *The Aegis* stated she was the daughter of the late James A. Corns and the late Agnes Corns; she lived at 3723 Nortonia Road in Baltimore and died at Harford Memorial Hospital in Havre de Grace) [Clark's U. M. Church Cemetery]

Cothran, James died January 9, 1928, age about 39 (no tombstone; death certificate stated he was the married son of ---- Cothran and Eliza Moore, all born in North Carolina; informant was Eva Cothran, of Havre de Grace) [St. James United Cemetery]

Cottman, Alonzo died March 1, 1951, age about 65 (no tombstone; death certificate stated he was born in Maryland, lived and worked as a farm laborer near Level, and died a widower; the names of his parents were not known to informant Ernest Cooper, of Level RFD) [Green Spring U. M. Church Cemetery]

Cotton, Belford 1900-1967 (on same tombstone with Jane Cotton and John Cotton; obituary in *The Aegis* on June 15, 1967 stated George Belford Cotton was the son of the late John Cotton and Jane Beckett, and husband of Emma J. Parker; he resided on Mt. Calvary Church Road and died at Greater Baltimore Medical Center in Baltimore on June 11, 1967, age 66) [Mt. Calvary U. A. M. E. Church Cemetery]

Cotton, Emma Jane June 12, 1891 – August 1, 1976 (no tombstone; obituary in *The Aegis* on August 5, 1976 stated she was the daughter of Lloyd Parker and Martha Banks, and the widow of George Belford Cotton; she resided at 23 Bush Chapel Road in Aberdeen, and died at Harford Memorial Hospital in Havre de Grace, survived by a daughter Alverta Hill, 2 brothers, 3 sisters, 7 grandchildren, 20 great-grandchildren, and 2 great-great-grandchildren) [Mt. Calvary U. A. M. E. Church Cemetery]

Cotton, Jane 1870-1966? (on same tombstone with John Cotton and Belford Cotton) [Mt. Calvary U. A. M. E. Church Cemetery]

Cotton, John 1871-1953 (on same tombstone with Jane Cotton and Belford Cotton) [Mt. Calvary U. A. M. E. Church Cemetery]

Cotton, Sarah 1820 – January 14, 1917 (no tombstone; death certificate stated she was born in Virginia and was a widow when she died near Aberdeen; her parents were unknown to informant D. F. Rowe, of Aberdeen) [Mt. Calvary U. A. M. E. Church Cemetery]

Council, Mollie Unita, "Beloved Mother" March 25, 1912 – September 14, 2003 [Community Baptist Church Cemetery]

Couplan, Mary E. died August 6, 1907, age 11 months (no tombstone; death certificate stated she was born in

Baltimore Co., the daughter of James Couplan, born in Harford Co., and Vera Spencer, born in Harford Co.; she died at Mountain and her place of burial was not indicated) [possibly Mt. Zion U. M. Church Cemetery]

Cox, Arethea May 14, 1897 – April 3, 1948 (no tombstone; death certificate stated she was born at "Fitzgerald, Benhill, GA" and lived at 217 Freedom Alley, Havre de Grace; her parents were unknown to informant William Vickers who lived at the same address; she died a widow at Harford Memorial Hospital) [Asbury Cemetery]

Cox, Clara B., "Mother" 1910-1992 (tombstone; James Dorsey Card File, African American Obituaries, that is maintained at the Historical Society of Harford County, has a card for her with an obituary from *The Aegis* on February 5, 1992 stating Clara Bernice Cox was born in Virginia, the daughter of William Divers and N---- (hole punched through card) Price, and she was the widow of Vivian Cox; she was a domestic worker, lived in Street and died at Harford Memorial Hospital in Havre de Grace, survived by a daughter, a son, a brother, and many grandchildren and great-grandchildren) [Fairview A. M. E. Church Cemetery]

Cox, Edmund died May 16, 1907, age 1 year and 3 months (no tombstone; death certificate stated he was the son of David Cox and Eva Lee, all born in Maryland, and he died in Bel Air; on the back of death certificate it is written "Hendon Hill") [Hendon Hill Cemetery]

Cox, George L. March 1, 1874 – February 25, 1933 (no tombstone; death certificate stated he was the son of Levie Cox and Elizabeth Bond, all born in Harford Co.; he was married, worked as a day laborer, died in Bel Air where he had lived all his life and was buried in "Mountain Cemetery, Harford Co.;" informant was Mrs. Lillie M. Cox, of Bel Air) [Mt. Zion U. M. Church Cemetery]

Cox, Geraldine W. 1918-2016 (small metal funeral home marker; funeral notice with photo in *The Aegis* stated she died on January 31, 2016, age 67, with services at St. James A. M. E. Church) [St. James United Cemetery]

Cox, Hannah Toney died December 12, 1928, age 45 years, 10 months (no tombstone; death certificate stated she was the daughter of Joseph Toney and Hannah Guy, all born in Maryland; she was married and died in Bel Air; informant was George Cox, of Bel Air) [Tabernacle Mount Zion U. M. Church Cemetery]

Cox, Virginia October 2, 1873 – January 14, 1937 (no tombstone; death certificate stated she was the daughter of Henry Cox and Frances Hollis, and died a widow in Harford Memorial Hospital; informant was George Cox, of Havre de Grace) [St. James United Cemetery]

Craig, Annie M., wife of William Craig, September 12, 1859 – May 8, 1883 [Tabernacle Mount Zion U. M. Church Cemetery]

Crawford, Emory J. Sr. November 17, 1929 – September 11, 1978, Pvt., U.S. Army, World War II [Union U. M. Church Cemetery]

Crawford, Eria September 16, 1920 – June 23, 2018 (no tombstone yet; Ames United Methodist Church memorial pamphlet contains several pictures and stated she was born in Montpelier, MS, the daughter of Tyson and Willie Ann Lofton, and moved to Blytheville when she was two years old; she lived there until age 95 when she moved in with her only daughter Tyce Rucks (of Baltimore); fondly referred to as "Mama" or "Gran" or "Aunt Eria" she was known for being a strong, faithful and hard-working domestic worker for many years; she was survived by her daughter and two grandchildren) [Tabernacle Mount Zion U. M. Church Cemetery]

Crawford, Herman June 14, 1911 – August 18, 1935 (no tombstone; death certificate stated he was the son of Willie Crawford and Sarah Frye, all born in Maryland; he was single, lived in Aberdeen and died by accidentally drowning; informant was Mrs. Sarah Gunsoliver, of Baltimore) [Mt. Calvary U. A. M. E. Church Cemetery]

Crawford, Pearl R. 1951-2014 (small metal funeral home marker) [Berkley Memorial Cemetery]

Crenshaw, Will 1900-1981 [St. James United Cemetery]

Crockson, Charles Edward February 6, 1882 – November 24, 1943 (no tombstone; death certificate stated he was born in Harford Co., the unmarried son of Bunn Crockson and Rosie Hemore, of Havre de Grace; informant was Dora Louise Miller) [St. James United Cemetery]

Crockson, Frances May 23, 1920 – May 17, 1922 (no tombstone; death certificate stated she was born in Harford Co., daughter of Frank Crockson and Lilly Pitt, born in Maryland) [Union U. M. Church Cemetery]

Crockson, Frank Albert May 16, 1924 – December 15, 1982, Pvt., U.S. Army, World War II (tombstone; buried in section 39; obituary in *The Aegis* on December 23, 1982 stated he was born in Aberdeen, the son of the late Frank P. Crockson and Lillie Pitt; he retired in 1978 from Aberdeen Proving Ground Post Engineers as a cement finisher and died at Loch Raven Veterans Administration Center in Baltimore, survived by two sons, four daughters, two brothers, two sisters and three grandchildren) [Mt. Calvary U. A. M. E. Church Cemetery]

Crockson, Herbert Edward September 23, 1922 – December 19, 1992, TEC4, U.S. Army, World War II (tombstone; buried in section 2; James Dorsey Card File, African American Obituaries, maintained at the Historical Society of Harford County, has a card for him with an obituary from *The Aegis* on December 23, 1992 stating he was born in Aberdeen, son of the late Frank P. Crockson and Lillie A. Pitt, and was a sergeant in the Army; he lived in Aberdeen, retired as an experimental mobile equipment service worker at Aberdeen Proving Ground and died at Perry Point VAMC, survived by two sisters) [Mt. Calvary U. A. M. E. Church Cemetery]

Crockson, Leon C. January 12, 1930 – August 23, 1985, Sgt., U.S. Marine Corps, Korea (tombstone; buried in section 2) [Mt. Calvary U. A. M. E. Church Cemetery]

Crockson, Sallie Bowser June 7, 1873 – December 10, 1903 [St. James United Cemetery]

Crockson, Sidney F. July 7, 1861 – November 7, 1926 (no tombstone; death certificate stated she was the widowed daughter of Charles Stewart and Pollie Lewis; informant was Frank Crockson) [Union U. M. Church Cemetery]

Crockson, William Henry April 2, 1875 – March 11, 1944 (no tombstone; death certificate stated he was the son of John W. Crockson and Sidney Lomis, and husband of the late Sallie Bowser Crockson) [Union U. M. Church Cemetery]

Cromwell, Albert Thompson August 17, 1872 – February 15, 1911 (no tombstone; death certificate stated he was the son of Joshua H. Cromwell and Rosella Berry, all born in Harford Co.; he was married, worked as a laborer and died at Rutledge; informant was Mary Alverta Cromwell) [West Liberty Church Cemetery]

Cromwell, Charlotte 1813 – April 13, 1876 (tombstone; Kurtz Funeral Home records stated "Lotty Cromel" was buried on April 14, 1876)

Cromwell, Dolly M. October 19, 1880 – June 8, 1948 (no tombstone; death certificate stated she was born in Maryland, the daughter of William S. Lee, born in Maryland, but her mother's name was not known to informant, her husband, William S. Lee, of Abingdon; she worked as a domestic servant, lived in Abingdon and died at Harford Memorial Hospital in Havre de Grace after a 13 day stay) [John Wesley U. M. E. Church Cemetery in Abingdon]

Cromwell, Edna L. 1933-1980 (tombstone; obituary in *The Aegis* on November 27, 1980 stated Edna Louise Govans Cromwell, wife of Gene E. Cromwell, of Battle Street in Edgewood, died on November 18, 1980 at Fallston General Hospital, survived by her husband, 3 sons, 2 daughters, 6 grandchildren, 5 sisters and her mother Laura B. Govans) [Chestnut Grove A. M. E. Church Cemetery, formerly LaGrange Cemetery at Rocks]

Cromwell, Edward (Daugherty) February 9, 1911 – May 10, 1949 (no tombstone; death certificate stated he was born in Maryland, the son of Rosa Cromwell Daugherty, but his father's name was not known to informant Edward Cromwell, of Abingdon; he worked as a domestic, lived in Abingdon and died at Harford Memorial Hospital in Havre de Grace after a 1 day stay) [John Wesley U. M. E. Church Cemetery in Abingdon]

Cromwell, Elizabeth V. 1900-1922 (on the same tombstone with parents John H. and Harriet E. Cromwell and siblings G. Ernest Cromwell and Mae C. Wells) [West Liberty Church Cemetery]

Cromwell, Ethel M. 1965-1965 (small white wooden cross grave marker) [Chestnut Grove A. M. E. Church Cemetery, formerly LaGrange Cemetery at Rocks]

Cromwell, Frances, wife of William Cromwell, died December 5, 1879, age not given (copied in 1987, but not found in 2018) [John Wesley U. M. E. Church Cemetery in Abingdon]

Cromwell, Frances Haywood died January 11, 1984, age 88 (no tombstone; obituary in *The Aegis* stated she was born in Annapolis, the daughter of Abraham Dorsey and Rebecca Johnson, and the widow of Philip Nelson Cromwell, of Abingdon; she served as Sunday School Superintendent of John Wesley United Methodist Church and died in Abingdon, survived by one niece, Georgianna Peaker, of Abingdon and many grand-nieces and grand-nephews including Richard Calvin, John Harris, Jerry Harris, Phillip Harris and Hutch Bailey) [John Wesley U. M. E. Church Cemetery in Abingdon]

Cromwell, Frances Joyner August 23, 1920 – January 26, 1999 (inscribed "Great To Thou Faithfulness") [St. James United Cemetery]

Cromwell, G. Ernest 1891-1938 (on same tombstone with parents John H. and Harriet E. Cromwell and sisters Elizabeth V. Cromwell and Mae C. Wells) [West Liberty Church Cemetery]

Cromwell, Harriet A. July 30, 1855 – December 24, 1929 (no tombstone; death certificate stated she was the daughter of Ralph Washington and Sophia Washington *(sic)*, all born in Maryland; she married ----, died a widow in Bel Air and was buried at "John Wesley Church;" informant was Mary Bishop, of Bel Air) [John Wesley U. M. E. Church Cemetery in Abingdon]

Cromwell, Harriet E. 1862-1939 (on same tombstone with husband John H. Cromwell and children G. Ernest Cromwell, Elizabeth V. Cromwell and Mae C. Wells) [West Liberty Church Cemetery]

Cromwell, Hazel died September 30, 1932, age 18 (no tombstone; death certificate stated she was the daughter of Henry Cromwell and Mary Lee, all were born in Abingdon; she was single, worked as a maid, lived in Abingdon and died at Havre de Grace Hospital; informant was Edward Cromwell, of Abingdon) [John Wesley U. M. E. Church Cemetery in Abingdon]

Cromwell, Henry A. died March 26, 1926, age 62 years, 10 months (no tombstone; death certificate stated he was the son of William E. Cromwell and Frances Hilton, all born in Maryland; he worked as a laborer and died a widower in Abingdon; informant was Edna Cromwell) [John Wesley U. M. E. Church Cemetery in Abingdon]

Cromwell, Horace Albert October 22, 1912 – March 21, 1913 (no tombstone; death certificate stated he was the son of Horace Cromwell and Grace Wye, of Taylor near Monkton, MD) [St. James United Cemetery]

Cromwell, Horace E. October 25, 1914 – January 6, 1986, SP2, U.S. Navy, WWII [St. James United Cemetery]

Cromwell, Irene (Mrs.) died July 31, 1938, age about 60 (no tombstone; death certificate stated she was the daughter of Josiah Smith, of Chestertown, MD, and Temperance Doman, of Millington, MD, and wife of Abel Cromwell, of Havre de Grace [St. James United Cemetery]

Cromwell, Jacqueline Johnson February 8, 1947 – January 17, 1948 (no tombstone; death certificate stated she was the daughter of Charles Cromwell and Annetta Johnson [St. James United Cemetery]

Cromwell, James (no tombstone found, but Kurtz Funeral Home records stated "Richard Cromel" was either buried or paid for a funeral on January 12, 1873; burial place not give [probably West Liberty Church Cemetery]

Cromwell, James died September 6, 1917 in his 64th year (tombstone; death certificate stated James Henry Cromwell was born in 1852 and died on September 5, 1917, age 65; he was born in Baltimore Co., the son of James Cromwell, born in Baltimore Co., and Charlota Ayers, born in Harford Co.; he worked as a "day laborer on a farm etc.", was single, and died near Jarrettsville; informant was Jane Hall, of Sharon RFD) [Fairview A. M. E. Church Cemetery]

Cromwell, John F. Jr. March 7, 1953 – September 27, 2000, Sgt., U.S. Army (inscribed" Gone to be with Grandma;" obituary in *The Aegis* on October 4, 2000 stated John Frederick Cromwell, Jr. was born in Harford Co., the son of John Frederick Sr. and Constance G. Cromwell; he joined the Army, served 17 years, and recently returned home to Bel Air as a single parent to be with his parents who survived him as did his 3 sons and 2 daughters) [Chestnut Grove A. M. E. Church Cemetery, formerly LaGrange Cemetery at Rocks]

Cromwell, John Frederick March 23, 1923 – February 1, 2003, U.S. Army Air Force, World War II ("Rest in peace until we join you") [Chestnut Grove A. M. E. Church Cemetery, formerly LaGrange Cemetery at Rocks]

Cromwell, John H. 1855-1925 (on the same tombstone with wife Harriet E. Cromwell and children G. Ernest Cromwell, Elizabeth V. Cromwell and Mae C. Wells) [West Liberty Church Cemetery]

Cromwell, Joshua Hutchins April 1, 1838 – February 23, 1924 (no tombstone; death certificate stated he was the son of Benjamin Cromwell and Amelia Barnes, all born in Harford Co.; he was a day laborer doing general work and died a widower near Rutledge; informant was his daughter-in-law Mollie Jackson, of Fallston RFD) [West Liberty Church Cemetery]

Cromwell, Laura, daughter of J. H. and R. E. Cromwell, died March 22, 1881, age 10 months and 14 days [West Liberty Church Cemetery]

Cromwell, Lelia R. 1942-2014 (small metal funeral home marker) [St. James United Cemetery]

Cromwell, Lillie Jeanette January 8, 1878 – July 15, 1925 (no tombstone; death certificate stated she was born in Baltimore Co., the daughter of Joshua Harris and Rachel Young; she was married at the time of her death in "White Hall, Harford Co." and informant was William Cromwell) [Union U. M. Church Cemetery]

Cromwell, Mary died May 2, 1919, age about 55 (no tombstone; death certificate stated she was born in Maryland, was married, worked as a servant, and was the daughter of Zack Cromwell, born in Maryland, but her mother's name was not known to informant Jost Cromwell, of Fallston RFD) [West Liberty Church Cemetery]

Cromwell, Mary F., wife of Henry Cromwell, died November 19, 1921, age not given (copied in 1987, but not found in 2018; death certificate stated Mary Frances Cromwell was born on March 30, 1860, the daughter of Emanuel Lee and Dorcas Lingham, and they all were born in Maryland; she was married (husband's name not mentioned) and died in Abingdon; informant was Mary Dougherty, of RFD Bel Air) [John Wesley U. M. E. Church Cemetery in Abingdon]

Cromwell, Mary L. died January 6, 1916, age about 24 (not found in 2018) [St. James United Cemetery]

Cromwell, Phillip N. February 9, 1890 – June 26, 1943, Maryland, Pvt, 60 CO 15 BN, 153 Depot Brig, World War I (tombstone; military records state Philip Nelson Cromwell was born in Abingdon, was inducted as a private on August 23, 1918, served in 153 Dep Brig and was honorably discharged on December 16 1918) [John Wesley U. M. E. Church Cemetery in Abingdon]

Cromwell, Richard (no tombstone, but Kurtz Funeral Home records stated "Richard Cromel" was buried or paid for a funeral on September 30, 1874, but burial place not given [probably West Liberty Church Cemetery]

Cromwell, William Henry March 11, 1930 – February 7, 2008 (inscribed "Deer Creek Lodge No, 103, F. & A. M.;" obituary in *The Aegis* on February 6, 2008 stated William Henry Cromwell, Sr. was born in Abingdon, the son of John Albert Harris, Sr. and Hazel Cromwell; known as "Billy" he was a truck driver with the CB handle was "Mulehead" for 40 years; he died at Upper Chesapeake Medical Center in Bel Air, where he lived, and was survived by his wife Alma of 47 years, 5 sons, 4 daughters, 2 brothers, 2 sisters, 23 grandchildren and 24 great-grandchildren, and was predeceased by a granddaughter) [John Wesley U. M. E. Church Cemetery in Abingdon]

Croxen, John Wesley died July 10, 1917, age about 39 (no tombstone; death certificate stated he was the son of Edward Croxen and Annie Brown [St. James United Cemetery]

Croxin, Harrison June 4, 1890 – April 29, 1917 (no tombstone; death certificate stated he was the son of Edward Croxin and Annie Brown) [St. James United Cemetery]

Croxon, Bun 1892 – September 24, 1918 (no tombstone; death certificate stated he was married, but his wife and parents were unknown to informant Frank Croxon, of Havre de Grace [St. James United Cemetery]

Croxsell, Annie E. (Mrs.) died May 20, 1939, age about 82 (no tombstone; death certificate stated she was the daughter of John Brown and Eliza Maxfield, of Gravelly Hill, and widow of Edward Croxsell; informant was Mrs. Pear lHenry, of Havre de Grace) [St. James United Cemetery]

Croxsell, Clara V. (Pastor) February 9, 1898 – January 10, 1993 [Berkley Memorial Cemetery]

Croxsell, Marvin October 8, 1892 – June 16, 1958 (inscribed "In Loving Memory Of My Husband") [Berkley Memorial Cemetery]

Croxson, Laura Virginia February 9, 1878 – November 9, 1934 (no tombstone; death certificate stated she was the wife of Mitchell Croxson and daughter of Edward Leager and Mary Allen) [St. James United Cemetery]

Croxson, Threassa V. died May 29, 1911, age 3 months and 30 days (no tombstone; death certificate stated she was the daughter of Harry Croxson and Stella Ellis) [St. James United Cemetery]

Crumwell, Sherrie 1987-2004 (small metal funeral home marker) [Berkley Memorial Cemetery]

Currie, Florine 1945-2009 (small metal funeral home marker) [St. James United Cemetery]

Currie, Rhetta M. 1938-2009 (small metal funeral home marker) [St. James United Cemetery]

Currington, Mary A. died July 29, 1911, age about 38 (no tombstone; death certificate stated she was the daughter of Robert Lingham and Amanda Norton, all born in Maryland; she was married and died at Abingdon; informant was W. H. Currington, of Wilmington) [John Wesley U. M. E. Church Cemetery in Abingdon]

Curtis, Amelia J. 1857-1950 (tombstone; death certificate stated she was born on May 14, 1857 and died on May 24, 1950, the widowed daughter of James Ramsey and ---- ("no record") ; informant was Mrs. Beatrice Merchant, of Havre de Grace) [St. James United Cemetery]

Curtis, C. W. (no dates recorded in 1987, not listed in 2002 and not found in 2018) [Gravel Hill Cemetery]

Curtis, Caroline March 12, 1873 – December 6, 1935 (no tombstone; death certificate stated she was the daughter of Henry Williamson and Lucy(?) Taska (Tasker?), all born in Maryland; she married Isaac Curtis and lived in Fallston; informant was Earnest Curtis, of Fallston) [Clark's U. M. Church Cemetery]

Curtis, Carrie September 2, 1915 – September 28, 1916 (no tombstone; death certificate stated she was the daughter of Ernest Curtis and Bella Green, all born in Maryland, and died at Street; informant was Ernest Curtis, of Street, MD) [Clark's U. M. Church Cemetery]

Curtis, Ernest January 31, 1922 – March 30, 1923 (no tombstone; death certificate stated he was the son of Ernest Curtis and Bell Green, all born in Maryland; he died and was buried at Rocks, possibly Chestnut Grove; informant was his father; undertaker was Amos Devoe) [Chestnut Grove A. M. E. Church Cemetery, formerly LaGrange Cemetery at Rocks]

Curtis, George A. November 12, 1874 – July 19, 1934 (no tombstone; death certificate stated he was the son of Freeborn Curtis and Josephine Armstrong, and husband of Isabella Jackson) [St. James United Cemetery]

Curtis, George W. died July 22, 1894 (damaged tombstone recorded in 1987 and 2002, but not found in 2018) [Gravel Hill Cemetery]

Curtis, Harriett A. December 6, 1836 – December 31, 1934 (no tombstone; death certificate stated she was the daughter of Effie Kenneth, both born in Maryland, but her father was not known to informant Mrs. Effie Brown, of Bel Air; she married Cornelius Curtis, died a widow at home at 24 Port Deposit Avenue in Bel Air and was buried at "John Wesley Church") [John Wesley U. M. E. Church Cemetery in Abingdon]

Curtis, Helen E September 24, 1909 – August 3, 1919 (no tombstone; death certificate stated she was the daughter of Ernest Curtis and Belle Green, all were born in Harford Co., and she died at Gibson; informant was Ernest Curtis, of Bel Air) [Clark's U. M. Church Cemetery]

Curtis, Isaac S. September 9, 1874 – April 25, 1927 (no tombstone; death certificate stated he was the son of Major Curtis and ---- (blank) Harkins, all born in Maryland, and died at Kalmia; informant was Caroline Curtis, of Bel Air) [Clark's U. M. Church Cemetery]

Curtis, Isabell (Mrs.) died February 8, 1937, age about 66 (no tombstone; death certificate stated she was the daughter of Isaac Jackson, of Charlottesville, VA, and Rebecca Bobb, of Havre de Grace, and widow of George Curtis) [St. James United Cemetery]

Curtis, Jane died March 3, 1917, age about 70 (no tombstone; death certificate stated she was born in Charles Co., MD, parents unknown, and died a widow in Havre de Grace; informant was Miss Clara Stansbury, of Havre de Grace) [St. James United Cemetery]

Curtis, Jane Roberta stillborn, premature 6 month birth, died August 18, 1930 (no tombstone; death certificate stated she was the daughter of Ernest G. Curtis and Mary Isabelle Green, of Rocks) [Chestnut Grove A. M. E. Church Cemetery, formerly LaGrange Cemetery at Rocks]

Curtis, Josephine, wife of Freeborn Curtis, January 31, 1847 – November 10, 1866 [Hill-Johnson Cemetery]

Curtis, Joyce Ann died June 29, 1986, age 45 (no tombstone; obituary in *The Aegis* on July 9, 1986 stated she was born in Baltimore, the daughter of Thomas Holland, of Havre de Grace, and the late Annie Irby; she lived in Aberdeen and died at Harford Memorial Hospital, survived by two sons, two daughters and one brother) [Union U. M. Church Cemetery]

Curtis, Mary L. June 24, 1912 – July 23, 1918 (no tombstone; death certificate stated she was the daughter of Percy Bowser and Beatrice Curtis, of Havre de Grace) [St. James United Cemetery]

Curtis, Rosie May 16, 1894 – August 4, 1928 (no tombstone; death certificate stated she was born in Maryland, the daughter of Neal Curtis, born in Harford Co., and Harriett Hooper, born in Maryland; she was single, occupied as a "house worker" and died in Havre de Grace with burial in "John Wesley Cemetery;" informant was George Amos, of Bel Air) [John Wesley U. M. E. Church Cemetery in Abingdon]

Curtis, William J. April 20, 1888 – July 17, 1935 (no tombstone; death certificate stated he was the son of George W. Curtis and Isabella Jackson, of Havre de Grace, and husband of Emma Poke; he drowned while swimming in the Susquehanna River in Havre de Grace) [St. James United Cemetery]

Dagones, Frank 1884-1979 [William C. Rice Memorial Cemetery, St. James U. M. Church]

Dagons, Eugene May 26, 1902 – March 23, 1950 (no tombstone; death certificate stated he was born in Harford Co., the son of Hall and Bessie Dagons; he was a laborer and lived and died in rural Pylesville, marital status not stated; informant was James Meadows, of Pylesville) [Chestnut Grove A. M. E. Church Cemetery, formerly LaGrange Cemetery at Rocks]

Dagons, Hall died March 30, 1920, age 66 (no tombstone; death certificate stated he was the son of John Dagons and Eliza Jones, all born in Maryland; he worked as a laborer, was married, lived at Pylesville and died a widower; informant was Bessie Dagons, of Pylesville) [Chestnut Grove A. M. E. Church Cemetery, formerly LaGrange Cemetery at Rocks]

Daily, Frantz Augusta December 4, 1950 – December 14, 1950 (no tombstone; death certificate stated he was the son of Jonnie Lee Daily and Mary Edwards, of 28 Hanover St. in Aberdeen) [Union U. M. Church Cemetery]

Daily, Johnnie Ron, "Son, Father, Great Dad and Brother" Sunrise June 1, 1958 – Sunset December 9, 1997 (with photo) [Berkley Memorial Cemetery]

Daily, Mary E. "Deannie" Sunrise January 20, 1920 – Sunset September 20, 2011 (inscribed "In Loving Memory of Our Queen") [Berkley Memorial Cemetery]

Dallam, Albert H. December 18, 1922 – February 25, 1944, Maryland, Pvt., Trans Corps, World War II (tombstone; *The Aegis* reported on March 17, 1944 that he drowned while serving in New Guinea.) [Green Spring U. M. Church Cemetery]

Dallam, Benjamin Webster May 5, 1879 – February 25, 1951 (no tombstone; death certificate stated he was born in Maryland, the son of Jacob J. Dallam and Harriet Tansen; he was a farm day laborer, married, lived at Aberdeen and died at Harford Memorial Hospital in Havre de Grace; informant was Mrs. Mabel Dallam) [Green Spring U. M. Church Cemetery]

Dallam, Benny Jr. February 12, 1920 – February 23, 1920 (no tombstone; death certificate stated he was the son of Benny Dallam and Mabel Brown, all born in Maryland) [Union U. M. Church Cemetery]

Dallam, Jacob J., "Father" 1840-1919 (inscribed "Asleep In Jesus") [Union U. M. Church Cemetery]

Dallam, Louise June 6, 1894 – February 27, 1931 (no tombstone; death certificate stated she was married and daughter of Edward Rice and Charlotte McComas; died in Harford Memorial Hospital; informant was Sidney T. Dallam, of Aberdeen) [Union U. M. Church Cemetery]

Dallam, Robert died May 29, 1890, age about 70 (no tombstone; *The Aegis*, June 6, 1890, reported "Old Bob" died at his home on Charles W. Michael's Bay Shore Farm near Michaelsville and was buried at Union Chapel; he was a former slave of George Nelson and obtained his freedom at the death of his master which occurred several years before the emancipation) [Old Union Chapel M. E. Church Cemetery]

Dallam, Roberta I. 1931-2000 (tombstone; "Roberta Dalium" is buried in section 8) [Mt. Calvary U. A. M. E. Church Cemetery]

Dallam, Sarah C. June 5, 1892 – October 6, 1912 (no tombstone; death certificate stated she was married and the daughter of William A. Pitt and Emma Jones, all born in Harford Co.) [Union U. M. Church Cemetery]

Dallam, Sidney E. September 5, 1916 – October 10, 1924 (no tombstone; death certificate stated he was the son of Sidney T. Dallam and Louisa Rice; informant was his father) [Union U. M. Church Cemetery]

Daniel, Stephen, son of Shadrach and Mary M. Daniel, died November 24, 1911, age 25 years, -- months and 2 days (copied in 1987, but not found in 2018) [Asbury Cemetery]

Daniel, Vivina January 11, 1946 – January 16, 1946 (no tombstone; death certificate stated she was born in Havre de Grace, the daughter of Clarence Daniel and Margaret Brown, both born in Mississippi, and they lived in Edgewood) [St. James United Cemetery]

Daniels, Noah (Rev.) February 15, 1868 – February 13, 1920 (on the same tombstone with Rachael C. Daniels that stated he was born in 1865 and died in 1920; death certificate stated he was the son of Noah Daniels and Mary E. Ash, all born in Maryland; he was married, worked as a preacher and died near Aberdeen; informant was Mrs. Noah L. Daniels) [Mt. Calvary U. A. M. E. Church Cemetery]

Daniels, Rachael C., wife of Noah Daniels October 21, 1873 – March 19, 1920 (on the same tombstone with Rev. Noah Daniels that stated she was born in 1868 and died in 1920; death certificate stated she was the daughter of Joseph Matthews and Mary Frances Wilson, all born in Caroline Co., MD; she was a widow and died at home near Aberdeen; informant was Christine Daniels) [Mt. Calvary U. A. M. E. Church Cemetery]

Daugherty, Annie M. July 2, 1878 – May 13, 1920 (no tombstone; death certificate stated she was the daughter of Henry Hooper and Sarah Howard, all born in Harford Co.; she was married, worked as a domestic and lived in Bel Air; informant was Ella Hooper, of Bel Air) [Asbury Cemetery]

Daugherty, Benjamin – see Benjamin Dougherty [Asbury Cemetery]

Daugherty, Charles Howard December 18, 1913 – November 29, 1918 (no tombstone; death certificate stated he was the son of Ambrose Daugherty and Annie W. Hooper, all born in Maryland, and he died in Bel Air; informant was Ambrose Daugherty, of Bel Air) [Asbury Cemetery]

Daugherty, Edward – see Edward (Daugherty) Cromwell [John Wesley U. M. E. Church Cemetery]

Daugherty, Elizabeth O., beloved wife of George Daugherty died October 31, 1882 in her 62nd year (inscribed "God's finger touched her and she slept.") [Hendon Hill Cemetery]

Daugherty, Ellen Wells March 21, 1887 – July 17, 1976 (no tombstone; obituary in *The Aegis* on July 22, 1976 stated she was born in Harford Co., daughter of Florence Wells and widow of Frank Daugherty; she lived in Churchville and for many years served on the staff of the Lee family in Bel Air; she then moved to Newark, DE where she "worked as a companion;" she returned to Churchville and later died at Maryland General Hospital in Baltimore) [Asbury Cemetery]

Daugherty, Fannie December 25, 1858 – December 23, 1896 (tombstone copied in 1987; James Dorsey Card File, African American Obituaries, that is maintained at the Historical Society of Harford County, has a card for her noting an obituary is in the *Bel Air Times* on January 9, 1897) [Hendon Hill Cemetery]

Daugherty, Finney his wife Fannie *(sic)* (no dates inscribed on tombstone; death certificate stated Finney Daugherty died March 16, 1927, age 73; he was born in January 1854 in Creswell, the son of Samuel Daugherty, born in Maryland, but his mother's name was unknown to informant William Daugherty; Finney was a farmer at Bel Air RFD #2 and was married at the time of his death) [Asbury Cemetery]

Daugherty, Franklin July 8, 1872 – December 6, 1941 (no tombstone; death certificate stated he was born in Churchville, the son of George S. Daugherty, born in Maryland, but his mother's name was not known to informant, his wife, Ellen Daugherty; he was a butler and lived in Bel Air for 50 years) [Asbury Cemetery]

Daugherty, George October 18, 1843 – August 22, 1926 (no tombstone; death certificate stated he was the son of George S. Daugherty and Salie *(sic)* McGaw, all born in Maryland; he was a widower, a laborer and lived in Abingdon; informant was Anne Norton, of Abingdon) [Asbury Cemetery]

Daugherty, George died May 25, 1907, age 81 (no tombstone; death certificate stated he was a laborer who died a widow in Bel Air; the names of his parents were not known to informant, his grandson, George F. Daugherty; obituary in *The Aegis* on May 31, 1907 stated he was a good, rough carpenter and general mechanic and died about age 85; his funeral was held from the home of Miss Jane Kelly, near Bel Air, on May 27; the place of burial was not given, but it was undoubtedly in Hendon Hill where wife Elizabeth was buried in 1882; James Dorsey Card File, African American Obituaries, maintained at the Historical Society of Harford County, has a card for him stating he was born January 27, 1874 and died May 27, 1907, age 85 *(sic)* and he was apparently a trustee at Hendon Hill Church) [Hendon Hill Cemetery]

Daugherty, George F. 1875-1954 (on same tombstone with M. Jennie Daugherty, Charles Turner and George L. Turner; Pennington Funeral Home records stated he was born September 23, 1874 in Harford Co., the son of William Chambers and ---- "unknown;" he worked as a hospital orderly and died on December 7, 1954 in Havre de Grace where he had lived for 42 years; informant was his wife Jennie Lee Daugherty) [Green Spring U. M. Church Cemetery]

Daugherty, George Samuel May 31, 1934 – October 25, 1934 (no tombstone; death certificate stated he was born in Bel Air, the son of George Samuel Daugherty and Blanch Presbury, all born in Harford Co., and he died at Bel Air RFD; informant was Blanch Presbury, of Bel Air; Kurtz Funeral Home Records stated the same) [Clark's U. M. Church Cemetery]

Daugherty, George Samuel November 28, 1910 – January 1, 1934 (no tombstone; death certificate stated he was the son of John Daugherty and Fannie Smothers, all born in Maryland; he was married and a laborer at Forest Hill; he was shot to death at a road side fruit stand near Kalmia; article in *The Aegis* on January 5, 1934 reported a New Year's Eve party at the home of James Bond on Conowingo Road near Kalmia led to drinking cider and wrestling, and a quarrel between George Daugherty and James Akins who shot him in the stomach and later died) [Clark's U. M. Church Cemetery]

Daugherty, Gladys January 13, 1913 – October 11, 1913 (no tombstone; death certificate misspelled her name Glayds and stated she was the daughter of Ambrose Daugherty and Annie M. Hooper, all born in Harford Co.; informant was Annie M. Daugherty, of Bel Air) [Asbury Cemetery]

Daugherty, Harriet V. August 1, 1868 – February 1, 1925 (no tombstone; death certificate stated she was the daughter of Shadrach Johnson and Amelia Dorsey, all born in Maryland, was married at the time of her death in Churchville; informant was Mary A. Johnson, Bel Air RFD #1) [Asbury Cemetery]

Daugherty, Jennie Lee August 30, 1876 – March 26, 1958 (Pennington Funeral Home records stated she was born at Rock Run, the daughter of William S. Lee and Mary Ellen Peaco; she worked as a hospital cook, married George F. Daugherty and died a widow at 136 Baltimore Avenue in Aberdeen where she had lived for 3 years; informant was Mrs. William Dorsey of that same address; Jennie's name is on the same tombstone with George F. Daugherty, Charles Turner and George L. Turner, but the inscription shows her name as "M. Jennie Daugherty, 1875 – 19--" and year of death has not yet been inscribed) [Green Spring U. M. Church Cemetery]

Daugherty, Mary A. September 7, 1904 – September 2, 1913 (no tombstone; death certificate stated she was the daughter of Ambrose D. Daugherty and Annie M. Hooper, all born in Harford Co., and she died in Bel Air; informant was Ambrose D. Daugherty, of Bel Air) [Asbury Cemetery]

Daugherty, Rosia August – (blank), 1882 – April 3, 1922 (no tombstone; death certificate stated she was the daughter of Sippio Delaige and Rose Smothers, and they were all born in South Carolina; she was a widow who died in Bel Air; informant was Hattie Newkirk, 2519 S. Woodstock, Philadelphia, PA) [Asbury Cemetery]

Daugherty, Sam January 5, 1893 – February 6, 1950 (no tombstone; death certificate misspelled his name "Daughtry" and stated he was the son of Finney "Daughtry" and Fannie Ruff; he was a laborer, lived at The Pines, Bel Air RFD #2, divorced and died at Harford Memorial Hospital in Havre de Grace; informant was Will "Daugherty" of Creswell) [Asbury Cemetery]

Daugherty, Samuel died June, 7, 1872, age 52 (copied in 1987, but not found in 2018) [Asbury Cemetery]

Daugherty, Sarah B.(?), wife of Samuel Daugherty, died September 5, 1899 in her 81st year (no death certificate; tombstone inscribed "Her Children will rise up and call her Blessed / Blessed are the dead who died in the Lord.") [Asbury Cemetery]

Daugherty, Susie A. April 27, 1908 – April 24, 1975 (on same tombstone with Hannah E. Johnson; obituary in *The Aegis* on May 1, 1975 stated Susie A. (Banks) Daugherty, of Philadelphia, PA, formerly of Harford County, was the widow of David H. Daugherty and was survived by a son David Daugherty, Jr., a granddaughter, four sisters, two brothers and several nieces and nephews) [Asbury Cemetery]

Daugherty, Thomas died on July 18, 1899, age not given (no tombstone; death notice in *The Aegis* on July 21, 1899 stated he died suddenly in Baltimore and was a brother of Finney Daugherty of Harford Co.; he was "buried at Asbury M. E. (colored) Church near Schuck's Corner") [Asbury Cemetery]

Davis, ---- stillborn male on August 20, 1925, miscarriage at 3½ months, in Bel Air (no tombstone; death certificate stated his mother was Lillian Davis who was born at Loreley, MD, but his father was not known to informant Raymond Ruff, of Bel Air) [Hendon Hill Cemetery]

Davis, Charles Edward December 29, 1937 – September 10, 1938 (no tombstone; death certificate stated he was born in Aberdeen, the son of Isiah R. Davis, born in Virginia, and Hattie Branson, born in St. Mary's Co., MD; he died at home on Bush Chapel Road near Aberdeen; informant was his mother Mrs. Hattie Davis) [Mt. Calvary U. A. M. E. Church Cemetery]

Davis, Curtis Garfield June 5, 1919 – November 2, 1942 [Chestnut Grove A. M. E. Church Cemetery, formerly LaGrange Cemetery at Rocks]

Davis, Edith February 28, 1894 – December 1, 1933 (no tombstone; death certificate stated she was born in Harford Co., the daughter of Charles Rice, born at Rocks, and Jane Chancy, born in Harford Co.; she was the widow of Jordon Davis and died at the Harford County Alms House in Bel Air; informant was James Chancy, of Bel Air) [Asbury Cemetery]

Davis, Edna C., "Wife & Mother" June 30, 1900 – March 30, 1957 [Clark's U. M. Church Cemetery]

Davis, Ernest M. (Rev.), "Beloved Husband, Father and Grandfather" December 1, 1921 – August 1, 2001 [St. James United Cemetery]

Davis, Florie 1910-1970 (tombstone located near the woods and inscribed "In Loving Memory;" obituary in *The Aegis* on July 23, 1970 stated she was formerly of South Carolina and lived in Harford County with Mr. & Mrs. Eugene Bailey; she died on July 13, 1970 at Franklin Square Hospital and was survived by four sisters) [Fairview A. M. E. Church Cemetery]

Davis, Frances March 26, 1914 – September 26, 1914 (no tombstone; death certificate stated she was born in Pennsylvania, the daughter of William Davis and Ada Swann, both were born in Maryland; informant was Alex Swann, of Jarrettsville) [William C. Rice Memorial Cemetery, St. James U. M. Church]

Davis, Glasgow A., "Father" November 15, 1898 – December 25, 1980 (inscribed "In Loving Memory of") [Clark's U. M. Church Cemetery]

Davis, Glasgow C. February 15, 1918 – September 11, 1920 (no tombstone; death certificate stated he was born in Harford Co., the son of Glasgow Davis and Edna Williams, both were born in Maryland; informant was Edna Williams, of Bel Air) [Clark's U. M. Church Cemetery

Davis, Harold Herbert November 8, 1894 – September 29, 1953, Pennsylvania, Cpl., Btry. E, 351 Field Arty, World War I [Fairview A. M. E. Church Cemetery]

Davis, Hazel March 30, 1945 – August 16, 1945 (no tombstone; death certificate stated she was born in Bel Air, daughter of Miller Davis and Lizzie Hamilton, both born in Darlington, SC) [Hendon Hill Cemetery]

Davis, Helen Stills, "Beloved Mother" December 27, 1933 – November 13, 1999 [Foster's Hill Cemetery]

Davis, Iris Alease 1930-2012 (small metal funeral home marker) [Community Baptist Church Cemetery]

Davis, James died September 1, 1927, age about 35 (no tombstone; he was married and worked as a taxi driver in Havre de Grace when he was shot and killed; names of parents and places of birth were not known to informant Wendel J. Dipple, of 300 S. Eden St., Baltimore) [Asbury Cemetery]

Davis, Louise March 16, 1888 – June 11, 1963 [Berkley Memorial Cemetery]

Davis, Lucy May 11, 1899 – May 29, 1935 (no tombstone; death certificate stated she was born in Forest Hill, the daughter of Charles Jenkins and Bessie Hill, both born in Maryland; she married Harold Davis, lived near Aberdeen, was severely burned in a gasoline explosion at home and died at Havre de Grace Hospital; informant was her husband Harold; James Dorsey Card File, African American Obituaries, maintained at the Historical Society of Harford County, has a card for her with an obituary from the *Bel Air Times* on June 7, 1935 stating Lucy J. Davis died at home in Aberdeen on May 30, 1935 *(sic)* and was survived by her husband and ten children) [Fairview A. M. E. Church Cemetery]

Davis, Margaret Marie Lee died on February 17, 1991, aged 67 (no tombstone; James Dorsey Card File, African American Obituaries, maintained at the Historical Society of Harford County, has a card for her with an obituary from *The Aegis* on March 13, 1991 stating she was the daughter of the late James C. and Susie V. Lee; she lived in Havre de Grace and died at Harford Memorial Hospital, survived by her husband Joseph Davis, five brothers and four sisters) [St. James United Cemetery]

Davis, Martha E., "Wife" July 22, 1902 – July 27, 1970 [Clark's U. M. Church Cemetery]

Davis, Martha W. 1894-1966 [Berkley Memorial Cemetery]

Davis, Mary F. September 16, 1936 – September 17, 1936, lived just 12 hours (no tombstone; death certificate stated she was born in Aberdeen RFD, the daughter of Isiah R. Davis, born in Virginia, and Hattie Branson, born in St. Mary's Co., MD; she died at home on Bush Chapel Road near Aberdeen; informant was her mother Hattie Davis) [Mt. Calvary U. A. M. E. Church Cemetery]

Davis, Rachel Catherine June 14, 1937 – June 25, 1937 (no tombstone; death certificate stated she was born and died in Bel Air, the daughter of Glascow *(sic)* Davis and Edna Williams, both born in Maryland; the informant was her father) [Clark's U. M. Church Cemetery]

Davis, Randolph 1922-2006, U.S. Army [St. James United Cemetery]

Davis, Robert E. 1942-2008 (small metal funeral home marker) [Mt. Calvary U. A. M. E. Church Cemetery]

Davis, Ruby 1939-2007 (small metal funeral home marker) [St. James United Cemetery]

Davis, Sabina Davena, "Daughter" December 13, 1989 – March 31, 2002 [St. James United Cemetery]

Davis, Sarah A. died March 24, 1916, age about 50 (no tombstone; death certificate stated she was the married daughter of Merrill Stokes, both born in Harford Co., but her mother was not known to informant George Ringgold, of Perryman) [Union U. M. Church Cemetery]

Davis, Sarah C., "Loving Wife" 1922-2005 [St. James United Cemetery]

Davis, Virginia M. Scott August 30, 1934 – April 23, 2005 (inscribed "Forever In Our Hearts") [St. James United Cemetery]

Dawes, Hariett January 24, 1836 – August 2, 1927 (no tombstone; death certificate stated she was born in Maryland and was a widow who died at home at Harford Furnace; her parents' names and places of birth were unknown to informant Benjamin Snowden, of Bel Air RFD #2) [Asbury Cemetery]

Daws, John Edward September 14, 1875 – October 31, 1894 (inscribed "A precious one from us has gone / A voice we loved is stilled / A place is vacant in our home / Which never can be filled / God in his wisdom has recalled / The boon his love had given / And though the body slumbers here / The soul is safe in heaven.") [Asbury Cemetery]

Day, Shanika 1987-1991 (on same tombstone with Samantha Mann) [Berkley Memorial Cemetery]

Dean, Agnes M. 1918-2014 (small metal funeral home marker) [Berkley Memorial Cemetery]

Dean, Jakiah M. 2007-2007 (small metal funeral home marker) [St. James United Cemetery]

DeCourcey, Isaiah September 12, 1814 – August 17, 1907 (on same tombstone with Sarah Jane DeCoursey) [St. James United Cemetery]

DeCourcey, Joel I. 1844-1926 (tombstone; death certificate stated October 2, 1845 – December 30, 1926) [St.

James United Cemetery]

DeCourcey, Sarah Jane March 25, 1825 – May 2, 1909 (on same tombstone with Isaiah DeCoursey) [St. James United Cemetery]

Delbridge, Sudie Ames, "Loving Mother and Grandmother" July 26, 1932 – September 8, 2007 [Berkley Memorial Cemetery]

Demby (Denby?), ---- stillborn female on March 24, 1940, a 7-month premature birth (no tombstone; death certificate spelled her name Denby and stated she was the daughter of Theodore Peters, Jr. and Mary Denby, all born in Maryland; she died at home in Magnolia and was buried "at Foster's Hill by one of the family;" informant was Belle Denby, of Magnolia) [Foster's Hill Cemetery]

Demby (Denby?), ---- stillborn male on June 9, 1936 (no tombstone; death certificate spelled his name Denby and stated he was the son of Charles Denby, both born in Maryland, and Belle Turner, born in Magnolia; he died at home in Magnolia and was buried at Fosters Hill) [Foster's Hill Cemetery]

Demby, Alexander Jr. died September 3, 1972, age 25 (no tombstone; obituary in *The Aegis* stated he was the husband of Carolyn Norman and died at home on Asbury Road in Churchville, survived by his wife, his father Alexander Demby, his mother Mrs. Evelyn Richardson, a son Alexander Demby III, and 6 sisters, 2 nieces, 2 nephews and a host of aunts and uncles) [Asbury Cemetery]

Demby, Alice Margaret Ann died February 6, 1990, age 70 (no tombstone; obituary in *The Aegis* on February 14, 1990 stated she was born in Magnolia, the daughter of Alex Demby and Blanche Franklin, and worked as a domestic; she lived in Joppa and died at Fallston General Hospital, survived by one sister Patience L. Washington and nieces and nephews and other relatives) [Mt. Zion U. M. Church Cemetery]

Demby, Annie Maria August 1, 1841 – June 18, 1915 (no tombstone; death certificate stated she was the married daughter of Anthony Brooks and Araminta Anderson, all born in Maryland; informant was George W. Demby, of Edgewood) [Union U. M. Church Cemetery]

Demby, Bruce M. Sr. December 6, 1946 – October 21, 2006 (tombstone is on the same base with the tombstone of James H. Demby, Jr. with his picture; obituary and photo in *The Aegis* on October 27, 2016 stated Bruce Medford Demby, Sr. was born in Havre de Grace, the son of James Howard Demby, Sr. and the late Ellen Rebecca Smith, and served in the Army in the Vietnam War; he lived in Edgewood, was a tractor trailer driver and died at the Baltimore Rehabilitation Extended Care, survived by son Bruce "Flip Demby, Jr., girlfriend Tonia Moorehead, a daughter Jamila Demby, a granddaughter Cailen Demby, and three sisters) [Asbury Cemetery]

Demby (Denby?), Charles Henry September 25, 1917 – October 1, 1938 (no tombstone; death certificate spelled his name Denby and stated he was born in Magnolia, the son of Charles M. Denby, born at Still Pond, Kent Co., and Jennie B. Turner, born at Van Bibber; he was single, worked as a laborer in Joppa, was killed by a bus at Joppa and buried in "Magnolia Cemetery;" informant was Charles M. Denby, of Magnolia) [Foster's Hill Cemetery]

Demby (Denby?), Charles Medford September 28, 1882 – December 3, 1939 (no tombstone; death certificate spelled his name Denby and stated he was the son of George W. Denby and Anna M. Brooks, all born in Maryland; he married Jennie B. Turner, worked as a laborer in Magnolia and was buried at "Fosters Hill near Magnolia;" informant was Belle Denby, of Magnolia) [Foster's Hill Cemetery]

Demby, Clara M., "Beloved Sister and Aunt" 1914-2000 (also inscribed "The Lord Is My Light") [Foster's Hill Cemetery]

Demby (Denby?), David Alexander April 15, 1921 – April 17, 1921, a 7½ month premature birth, lived 2 days (no tombstone; death certificate spelled name the Denby and stated he was the son of Alex Denby and Blanche Franklin, all born in Maryland; informant was Alex Denby, of Magnolia) [Foster's Hill Cemetery]

Demby, Edward E., "Son" April 17, 1962 – August 26, 1985 (tombstone; obituary in *The Aegis* on September 12, 1985 stated he was the son of Elsie Lingham, of Edgewood, and James E. Demby, of Joppa, and died in Aberdeen on August 25 *(sic)*, 1985, survived by his parents, two daughters, two sisters, one brother, three step-sisters and three step-brothers) [Community Baptist Church Cemetery]

Demby, George Allen August 13, 1948 – March 11, 1969, Maryland, SP4, Co A, 2 Inf, 25 Inf Div, Vietnam, BSM & OLG-PH (tombstone; obituary in *The Aegis* on March 20, 1969 stated he was the son of Alexander Demby and Mrs. Evelyn Smith Richardson, and was killed in Vietnam, survived by his parents, wife Janice Lynn Demby, his stepfather Henry Richardson, and six sisters) [John Wesley U. M. E. Church Cemetery in Abingdon]

Demby (Denby?), George Washington March 28, 1834 – December 7, 1924 (no tombstone; death certificate spelled his name Denby and stated he was a farmer at Magnolia and died a widow; the names and places of birth of his parents were not known to informant William "Denby," of Magnolia) [Foster's Hill Cemetery]

Demby, James H. Jr. October 18, 1958 – February 13, 2002 (tombstone is on the same base with the tombstone of Bruce M. Demby, Sr. with his picture; obituary and photo in *The Aegis* on March 1, 2002 stated James Howard Demby, Jr., was the son of the late James Howard Demby, Sr. and Ellen Rebecca Smith, and was employed at JCB Manufacturing Co. for 10 years; he lived in Edgewood, survived by 2 daughters Letrisha and Ebony Demby, 2 grandchildren Meleek Demby and Deonte Ferguson, a brother Bruce Demby, Sr., 3 sisters, a niece, a nephew Bruce Demby, Jr. who he adopted as a son, and fiancée Melissa Ann Jones) [Asbury Cemetery]

Demby, Jennie Belle December 15, 1894 – January 16, 1969 (inscribed "Beloved Mother" and "We Love and Miss You;" obituary in *The Aegis* on January 20, 1969 stated she was born at Van Bibber, the daughter of Henry Turner and Clara Broadway, and died at Johns Hopkins Hospital in Baltimore; she was the widow of Charles Demby and lived at 413 Dembytown Road in Joppa; she was active in community organizations and was survived by 6 sons, 4 daughters, 3 brothers, 4 sisters, 43 grandchildren, and 17 great-grand-children; burial was in the John Wesley Methodist Cemetery in Magnolia) [Foster's Hill Cemetery]

Demby, Jennie Belle died January 16, 1969, age 73 (no tmbstone; obituary in *The Aegis* stated she was born in Van Bibber, the daughter of Henry Turner and Clara Broadway, and married Charles Demby who predeceased her; she lived at 415 Dembytown Road in Joppa, died at Johns Hopkins Hospital in Baltimore and was survived by six sons, four daughters, 43 grand-children and 17 great-grandchildren) [Mt. Zion U. M. Church Cemetery]

Demby, Mary E. (Henson) February 22, 1919 – April 24, 2012 (inscribed "Forever In Our Hearts;" her funeral notice and photo in *The Aegis* on April 27, 2012 she lived in Churchville and died at Bel Air Health & Rehabilitation Center) [Mt. Zion U. M. Church Cemetery]

Demby, Mary Jane April 9, 1881 – September 13, 1945 (no tombstone; death certificate stated she was born in Harford Co., daughter of Joseph Robinson and Tamer Evans, both born in Maryland, and married William Demby; she worked as a domestic and died a widow in Magnolia where she lived all her life; she was buried in the Baptist Cemetery at Magnolia; informant was Lottie V. Chase, of Magnolia) [Foster's Hill Cemetery]

Demby, Paul E. March 8, 1928 – March 3, 1955(?) [Foster's Hill Cemetery]

Demby (Denby?), Thomas died September 21, 1918, age about 55 (no tombstone; death certificate stated he was a teamster who died in Edgewood; his place of birth and parents and places of birth not known to informant Howard K. McComas, Undertaker, in Abingdon) [John Wesley U. M. E. Church Cemetery in Abingdon]

Demby, William H. May 2, 1859 – January 3, 1939 (no tombstone; death certificate spelled his name Denby and stated he was the son of George W. Denby and Annie Brooks, all born in Maryland; he married Mary ----, worked as a laborer in Magnolia, died at home in Magnolia where he had lived for 23 years; informant was Mary Denby, of Magnolia) [Foster's Hill Cemetery]

Demby-Smith, Letrisha March 19, 1980 – August 14, 2005 (small metal marker was inscribed Lakewood Funeral Home, Howell, NJ, placed at the foot of the tombstones of Bruce and James Demby) [Asbury Cemetery]

Denis, Albert E. April 10, 1910 – March 13, 1993 (on same tombstone with Anna E. Dennis; obituary and photo in *The Aegis* on March 24, 1993 stated Albert Edward Dennis, Sr. was the son of Benjamin Dennis and Minnie Anderson and he grew up in Holly Hill, SC; he moved to Maryland in the 1930s and married Anna A. Turner, who predeceased him; he was ordained a deacon in Mt. Zion Baptist Church in 1954 and worked for the B&0 Railroad for 37 years; he died at home in Havre de Grace and was survived by 2 daughters, 3 sons, 17 grandchildren and 23 great-grandchildren) [John Wesley U. M. E. Church Cemetery in Abingdon]

Dennis, Alverta Lucinda July 24, 1937 – May 11, 2012 (no tombstone; obituary in *The Aegis* on May 16, 2012 stated she was the daughter of Allen E. Murphy and Ada V. Kennard; she retired from Father Martin's Ashley in

Havre de Grace and worked part-time at Citizens Care Center; she was survived by 2 sons, Ronnie Dennis and Vivan Dennis III, both of Aberdeen, 3 grandchildren, 2 great-grandchildren and 3 sisters) [Mt. Calvary U. A. M. E. Church Cemetery]

Dennis, Anna A. March 11, 1912 – August 12, 1976 (on same tombstone with Albert E. Dennis) [John Wesley U. M. E. Church Cemetery in Abingdon]

Dennis, Gary Leroy Sr. October 19, 1945 – February 15, 2016, U.S. Army, Vietnam [St. James United Cemetery]

Dennis, Helen M. May 1, 1919 – January 14, 1990 (on same tombstone with W. Bishop Dennis inscribed "Together Forever" and "married June 12, 1938") [St. James United Cemetery]

Dennis, Hester August 9, 1917 – February 15, 1929 (no tombstone; death certificate stated she was the daughter of James Suell and Minnie Anderson, all born in South Carolina; informant was Frank Ridgeley, of Havre de Grace) [St. James United Cemetery]

Dennis, W. Bishop September 12, 1911 – October 11, 1984 (on same tombstone with Helen M. Dennis inscribed "Together Forever" and "married June 12, 1938") [St. James United Cemetery]

Dennison, Annie M. November 10, 1892 – July 19, 1999 (tombstone; obituary and photo in *The Aegis* on July 28, 1999 stated she was one of ten children born to Carrie Collins and Louis Pinion and was married to the late Robert Alexander Dennison and they had ten children; she was a cook at Aberdeen Proving Ground and "Miss Mabel" was known throughout Perryman for her homemade rolls and caked, which she made for the family until age 99; the following year she became a member of the Harford County Centenarian Club; she died at Harford Memorial Hospital, survived by three daughters, two sons, one sister, 16 grandchildren, 14 great-grandchildren, and 24 great-great-grandchildren) [Union U. M. Church Cemetery]

Dennison, Arominta E. April 22, 1824 – December 3, 1870 [Old Union Chapel M. E. Church Cemetery]

Dennison, Charles W. March 2, 1845 – June 27, 1924 (no tombstone; death certificate stated he was born in Maryland, died a widower; parents unknown to informant Robert A. Dennison) [Union U. M. Church Cemetery]

Dennison, Charles W. September 12, 1865 – July 21, 1948 (no tombstone; death certificate stated he was the son of Charles W. Dennison and Eliza Webster, and widower of Annie Lewis) [Union U. M. Church Cemetery]

Dennison, Edna L. January 3, 1919 – April 2, 2007 (on same tombstone with Lewis E. Dennison) [St. James United Cemetery]

Dennison, Eliza September 10, 1842 – January 17, 1923 (no tombstone; death certificate stated she was born in Harford Co. and was the married daughter of Tilmen McGommry, but his place of birth and her mother's name were not known to informant Robert A. Dennison) [Union U. M. Church Cemetery]

Dennison, Elizabeth January 20, 1868 – December 24, 1968 (on same tombstone with Isaac L. Dennison and inscribed "At Rest;" yet, obituary in *The Aegis* on January 2, 1969 stated she was the widow of the late Jason Dennison, of Perryman; she was born in Harford Co., daughter of George Webster and Eliza Gibson, and she was survived by several nieces and nephews) [Union U. M. Church Cemetery]

Dennison, Ester Armenta Adelade October 16, 1912 – April 18, 1913 (no tombstone; death certificate stated she was daughter of John Dennison and Jessie Collins, all born in Maryland) [Union U. M. Church Cemetery]

Dennison, Hester A. September 2, 1916 – March 24, 1926 (no tombstone; death certificate stated she was the daughter of John Dennison and Jessie Collison) [Union U. M. Church Cemetery]

Dennison, Hester J. died on May 14, 1933 (on the same tombstone with John C. Dennison inscribed "In Memory Of") [Union U. M. Church Cemetery]

Dennison, Howard Oscar January 1, 1909 – August 21, 1990 (inscribed "Remember O Lord Thy Tender Mercies And Thy Loving Kindness;" obituary in *The Aegis* on September 19, 1990 stated "Denny" was born in Perryman, the son of John T. and Jessie C. Dennison, and for many worked as a truck driver for Siebert's Foodland and for the past 20 years was employed at American Legion Post 47; he died at Harford Memorial Hospital in Havre de Grace and was survived by two sons, two sisters and one granddaughter; his wife Laura

Mills had predeceased him) [St. James United Cemetery]

Dennison, Isaac L. 1862-1938 (on same tombstone with Elizabeth Dennison inscribed "At Rest" with those dates, but death certificate stated he was born October 31, 1863, son of Aaron Dennison and Mary McComas, and the husband of Elizabeth Dennison, and he died May 2, 1936) [Union U. M. Church Cemetery]

Dennison, Isadore Janice October 12, 1929 – February 21, 2006 (no tombstone; obituary in *The Aegis* on February 24, 2006 and anotobituary with her photo on March 10, 2006 stated she was born in Perryman, the daughter of Robert Dennison and Annie Pinion, and removed to New York where she was employed by the Arthur Mansfield family for many years; she returned to Aberdeen to assist her mother in caring for uncles, the late George and Raymond Pinion; she then lived in Havre de Grace and died at Harford Memorial Hospital, survived by two brothers, two sisters, other relatives, and dear friends Cecilia Bunn and Catherine Reed) [Union U. M. Church Cemetery]

Dennison, John C. died on August 8, 1923 (on same tombstone with Hester J. Dennison inscribed "In Memory Of") [Union U. M. Church Cemetery]

Dennison, John L. February 16, 1924 – November 23, 1924 (no tombstone; death certificate stated he was the son of Robert A. Dennison and Annie M. Pinion) [Union U. M. Church Cemetery]

Dennison, John T. died August 17, 1987, age 73 (no tombstone; obituary in *The Record* stated he was born in Havre de Grace, the son of John T. Dennison and Jessie Stansbury, and died at Harford Memorial Hospital, survived by three sisters and two brothers) [St. James United Cemetery]

Dennison, John Thomas July 2, 1874 – August 10, 1947 (no tombstone; death certificate stated he was the son of John Carver Dennison and Hester Tilden, and died a widower in Havre de Grace) [Union U. M. Church Cemetery]

Dennison, Laura Mary Della Mills March 4, 1916 – December 18, 1982 (inscribed "I will lift up mine eyes unto the hills from whence cometh my help. Ps. 121:1;" obituary in *The Aegis* on December 30, 1982 stated she had been affiliated with St. James AME Church Senior Usher Board and Susquehanna Temple No. 196 Elks Lodge; she died at Harford Memorial Hospital in Havre de Grace, survived by her husband Howard, two sons, one brother and one sister) [St. James United Cemetery]

Dennison, Lewis E. August 14, 1910 – December 27, 1984 (on same tombstone with Edna L. Dennison and inscribed "In Loving Memory" with his photo; obituary in *The Aegis* in January 3, 1985 stated he was born in Aberdeen, the son of John and Jessie Dennison, retired from Penn Central Railroad and died at Harford Memorial Hospital, survived by his wife Edna, four sons, five daughters, three brothers, three sisters and 13 grandchildren) [St. James United Cemetery]

Dennison, Lydia M. October 1, 1921 – January 19, 1922 (no tombstone; death certificate stated she was the daughter of Charles W. Dennison and Emlie Rice, all born in Maryland) [Union U. M. Church Cemetery]

Dennison, Manuel E., "Husband, Son, Father, Brother, Uncle" June 13, 1960 – February 13, 1998 (tombstone; The James Dorsey Card File, African American Obituaries, that is maintained at the Historical Society of Harford County, has a card with obituary from an unidentified newspaper on February 18, 1998 stating Manuel Edward Dennison was born in Havre de Grace, the son of Edna Dupree and the late Lewis E. Dennison; he lived in Silver Spring, worked as a heavy equipment operator and died at Bethesda Naval Medical Center; he was survived by his mother, his wife Vivian K. Kelly Dennison, a son Dequinne Guary, a daughter Nicole Dennison, three brothers and five sisters) [St. James United Cemetery]

Dennison, Pearl P. September 20, 1916 – April 21, 1934 (no tombstone; death certificate stated she was the daughter of Robert A. Dennison and Annie M. Pinion) [Union U. M. Church Cemetery]

Dennison, Robert A. March 11, 1885 – August 30, 1973 [Union U. M. Church Cemetery]

Densby, Clara J. September 1, 1878 – August 31, 1930 (no tombstone; death certificate stated she was the married daughter of Edward Webster and Alice Bond; informant was Gilbert Densby) [Union U. M. Church Cemetery]

Densby, Etta Brown 1884 – May 30, 1937, age 52 *(sic)* (no tombstone; death certificate stated she was born in

Pennsylvania, the daughter of Ben Stump, birth place unknown, and her mother's name was not known to the informant, Etta's husband, Gilbert Densby, of Route 2, Fallston) [Clark's U. M. Church Cemetery]

Dew, Martha P. June 16, 1942 – February 5, 2018 [Berkley Memorial Cemetery]

Dewberry, Irene March 13, 1884 – July 23, 1943 [Mt. Calvary U. A. M. E. Church Cemetery]

Dews, Constance M. Perkins Jackson, "Loving Mother" October 7, 1933 – January 22, 1993 [St. James United Cemetery]

Dickerson, Ollie F., "Honey" "Mama" August 8, 1899 – May 25, 1991 (inscribed "The Lord Is My Shepherd") [Union U. M. Church Cemetery]

Dilworth, Jasper May 10, 1921 – April 18, 1922 (no tombstone; death certificate stated he was born in Maryland, the son of Jasper Dilworth and Annie Jones, both born in North Carolina, and they lived near Churchville; informant was Jasper Dilworth, of Aberdeen RFD) [Green Spring U. M. Church Cemetery]

Divers, Clattis M. December 24, 1908 – February 16, 1929 (no tombstone; death certificate stated she was the daughter of William A. Divers and Nancy M. Price, all born in Floyd Co., VA; she was single and died at home in Jarrettsville; informant was her father William) [Fairview A. M. E. Church Cemetery]

Divers, Ernest Edwin 1924-1979 (copied in 1987 and not found in 2018) [Fairview A. M. E. Church Cemetery]

Divers, Nancy Mitildy June 22, 1886 – September 5, 1948 (no tombstone; Kurtz Funeral Home Record Book 1944-1949, p. 231, stated she was the daughter of London Price and Mary Jones, all born in Franklin Co., VA; she married William A. Divers and died near Bel Air where they had lived for 2 years; informant was Mrs. Clara Cox, of Forest Hill; funeral bill was paid in full by William A. Divers, Jr.) [Fairview A. M. E. Church Cemetery]

Divers, Patrick I. April 4, 1945 – June 12, 1979, TEC Sgt, U.S. Air Force [Fairview A. M. E. Church Cemetery]

Divers, Stanford Henry December 4, 1915 – July 11, 1933 (no tombstone; Kurtz Funeral Home Records and death certificate stated he was the son of William A. Divers and Nancie M. Price, all born in Floyd Co., VA; a school boy, he died at home near Sharon; informant was his father) [Fairview A. M. E. Church Cemetery]

Divers, William Anderson June – (blank), 1868 – January 14, 1950 (no tombstone; death certificate stated he was born in Floyd Co., VA, the son of William Anderson Divers, but his mother was not known to informant Mrs. Clara Cox; he was a farm laborer and died a widower at home at Forest Hill where he had lived 1 year) [Fairview A. M. E. Church Cemetery]

Dixon, Emma Mazie Barnes Rumsey died September 6, 1998, age 83 (no tombstone; obituary in *The Aegis* on September 16, 1998 stated she was the daughter of Mary E. Barnes and John D. Barnes, Sr. and was employed by the families of Judge Edward Higinbothom and Dr, Raymond Sedney of Bel Air for many years; she married Charles Seymour Rumsey in 1933 who died in an accident in 1952; they had eight children; she briefly married and then divorced James Dixon; she died at Lorien Nursing and Rehabilitation Center, survived by 4 daughters, 2 sons, 18 grandchildren, 21 great-grandchildren, 10 great-great-grandchildren and 1 sister; she was also mother of the late Alberta Rumsey) [Clark's U. M. Church Cemetery]

Dixon, Jerry (no tombstone, but Kurtz Funeral Home records stated he was buried at Lagrange Church in an "Im Cherry on P" coffin on July 28, 1883 "from Martha Tuter near Chro. H." (Chrome Hill) and noted "John Hopkins took it out") [Chestnut Grove A. M. E. Church Cemetery, formerly LaGrange Cemetery at Rocks]

Dogon, John died in mid-August 1885, age 60 (no tombstone; death notice in *The Aegis* on August 21, 1885 stated he had been assisting in threshing wheat and died suddenly while working in the barn of John T. Smithson near Jarrettsville; his date of death and place of burial were not given [possibly William C. Rice Memorial Cemetery, St. James U. M. Church]

Doles, Lucille Phillips June 12, 1898 – May 30, 1950 (no tombstone; death certificate stated she was born in Ohio, was employed by the government, married, and died in Bel Air where she had lived for 22 years; her father was Miles Bently, but mother unknown to informant Harry Doles) [Hendon Hill Cemetery]

Donaldson, Brittany Grace December 13, 1989 – February 8, 2017 (poem titled "Grace" on tombstone and her photo) [St. James United Cemetery]

Donaldson, Claudia C. June 21, 1935 - November 13, 2003 (on same tombstone with Jack Donaldson, Jr.) [St. James United Cemetery]

Donaldson, Jack Jr. December 18, 1930 - November 7, 2003 (on same tombstone with Claudia C. Donaldson) [St. James United Cemetery]

Donaldson, Kevin E. Sr. August 9, 1959 – September 20, 2007, U.S. Army [St. James United Cemetery]

Donaldson, Terry D. December 25, 1954 – January 25, 2004, U.S. Navy [St. James United Cemetery]

Donmore, Anita October 5, 1944 – October 14, 1944 (no tombstone; death certificate stated she was the daughter of Harry Donmore and Lee Etta Washington, and died of "prematurity") [St. James United Cemetery]

Dorman, Carrie (no tombstone, but probably buried beside her husband Samuel Dorman) [Community Baptist Church Cemetery]

Dorman, Dorothy Virginia "Dottie" March 22, 1949 – July 22, 2001 (no tombstone; obituary in *The Aegis* on July 27, 2001 stated she was born in Joppa, the daughter of the late James Richard and Effie Virginia Dorman, and worked for the Veterans Administration at both Perry Point and Fort Howard; she was survived by two sons, Thante Dorman and Monkeya Dorman, five sisters, two aunts, nine nieces and nephews, but husband not mentioned, and other relatives) [Community Baptist Church Cemetery]

Dorman, Effie V. June 9, 1921 – March 23, 1988 (on same tombstone with James R. Dorman, Sr.; obituary in the *Havre de Grace Record* on April 13, 1988 stated Effie Virginia Dorman was born in Loreley, Baltimore Co., the daughter of Lewis Beard and Dorothy Couplin, and the wife of the late James Richard Dorman, Sr.; she died at University Hospital in Baltimore, survived by four sons, six daughters, and thirteen grandchildren) [Community Baptist Church Cemetery]

Dorman, James R. Sr, March 10, 1910 – December 18, 1979 (on same tombstone with Effie V. Dorman; obituary in *The Aegis* on December 20, 1979 stated James Richard Dorman, Sr. was born in Baltimore, the son of the Frost Dorman and Jennie Trimble; he married Effie Virginia Couplin, worked for Lembach Construction Co. in Baltimore, died at Franklin Square Hospital, survived by his wife Effie, of Joppa, four sons, five daughters, three brothers, three half-brothers, one sister, and nine grandchildren) [Community Baptist Church Cemetery]

Dorman, Samuel 1876 – February 8, 1948 (no tombstone; death certificate stated he was born in Somerset Co., MD, the son of Frost Dorman and Mary Bailey, both born in Maryland; he worked as a laborer in Harford Co., married Carrie ---- and died a widow in rural Joppa where he had lived for one year; informant was Frost Dorman, of Joppa RD) [Community Baptist Church Cemetery]

Dorris, Pennsylvania November 17, 1919 – February 25, 1996 (tombstone inscription; "Penni Dorris" was owner of a lot in section 24 some time after 1951) [Mt. Calvary U. A. M. E. Church Cemetery]

Dorsey, ---- stillborn male on January 22, 1915 (no tombstone; death certificate stated he was the son of Daisy Dorsey, both born in Maryland, but informant Joshua Dorsey, of Darlington, did not know the name of his father) [Berkley Memorial Cemetery]

Dorsey, Albert Jr. 1903-1931 (copied in 1987 and 2002, but not found in 2018) [Gravel Hill Cemetery]

Dorsey, Albert Sydney January 9, 1866 – July 12, 1932 (no tombstone; death certificate stated he was the son of Franklin Dorsey and Emily Jane Cooper, all born in Harford Co.; he was a farmer at Street and the widower of Anna Dorsey; informant was Emma J. Parrott) [Asbury Cemetery]

Dorsey, Alice died August 18, 1894 in the 11th year of her age [Asbury Cemetery]

Dorsey, Allen A. August 18, 1879 – August 30, 1960 (on same tombstone with Lillie J. Dorsey inscribed "Always In Our Hearts") [Mt. Calvary U. A. M. E. Church Cemetery]

Dorsey, Allen July 6, 1906 – January 15, 1939 (no tombstone; death certificate stated he was the son of Henry F. Dorsey and Annie Reed, and was killed by a Pennsylvania Railroad train at Perryman; his widow was Dorothy Dennison) [Union U. M. Church Cemetery]

Dorsey, Allen R. November 1, 1838 – November 4, 1913 (no tombstone; death certificate stated he was the son of James Dorsey, both born in Harford Co., but his mother's name was unknown; he was a laborer who lived at Perryman and informant was Mrs. Allen R. Dorsey) [Gravel Hill Cemetery]

Dorsey, Anna W. 1906-   [Clark's U. M. Church Cemetery]

Dorsey, Annie L. May 18, 1878 – July 21, 1931 (no tombstone; death certificate stated she was the married daughter of John T. Reed and Elizabeth Williams; informant was Mrs. Henry Dorsey, of Perryman,MD) [Union U. M. Church Cemetery]

Dorsey, Avon Thomas June 20, 1915 – September 6, 1915 (no tombstone; death certificate stated he was born in Harford Co., the son of Clinton Akins and Rachel Dorsey, of Harford Co., and informant was Mary Dorsey, of Havre de Grace) [Gravel Hill Cemetery]

Dorsey, Baby (Brown) stillborn male on June 1, 1930 (no tombstone; death certificate stated he was the son of John Brown and Henriette Dorsey, died in Havre de Grace [St. James United Cemetery]

Dorsey, Baby Boy December 19, 1958 – December 20, 1958 (no tombstone; death certificate stated he was born prematurely at Harford Memorial Hospital, the son of David Dorsey and Evelyn Aiken, of Route 1, Box 256, Bel Air, MD; H. S. Bailey, Funeral Director, of Darlington) [Green Spring U. M. Church Cemetery]

Dorsey, Baby Girl 1973 (copied in 1987, but not found in 2018) [John Wesley U. M. E. Church Cemetery in Abingdon]

Dorsey, Bernard C. "Duce" August 11, 1942 – May 13, 2007, AB, U.S. Air Force (tombstone; obituary in *The Aegis* on May 18, 2007 stated he was born in Harford County, the son of Bernard Dorsey and Florence Banks; her served in the U.S. Air Force and retired from Aberdeen Proving Ground commissary in 2006; he was survived by brothers Robert and Richard Dorsey, sister Thelma Morgan, a special friend Dolly Davis, and was predeceased by a brother Clarence Banks and a sister Hilda Banks) [Mt. Calvary U. A. M. E. Church Cemetery]

Dorsey, C. E. 1895-1967 [Berkley Memorial Cemetery]

Dorsey, Carroll Edward January 1, 1945 – June 10, 2016 (on same tombstone with Roland Edward Dorsey and Nine Webster Dorsey and inscribed "In Loving Memory") [Berkley Memorial Cemetery]

Dorsey, Catherine R. 1933-2018 [Berkley Memorial Cemetery]

Dorsey, Charles died July 6, 1939, age 80 (no tombstone; death certificate stated he was born on Gun-powder Neck, but informant William Bradford did not know his parents' names and birth places; he was single, worked as a farm laborer and died at the County Home in Bel Air) [Hendon Hill Cemetery]

Dorsey, Clara Estella (no tombstone, but Kurtz Funeral Home Records stated she was born in Harford Co., the daughter of James Amoss, and died in Mt. Pleasants, NY, age 36 years, 3 months and 20 days; buried at West Liberty on February 14, 1934; informant was husband Edward Dorsey) [West Liberty Church Cemetery]

Dorsey, Clarence E. (no tombstone; death certificate stated he was born on April 14, 1915 and died at Carsins Run on September 3, 1915, the son of Fred Dorsey, Jr. and Mable Brown, and they were all born in Harford Co.; informant was Fred Dorsey, Jr., of Aberdeen RFD) [Green Spring U. M. Church Cemetery]

Dorsey, Clarence E. 1890-1969 (on same tombstone with Margaret K. Dorsey; obituary in *The Aegis* on January 20, 1969 stated he was the son of the late Mr. & Mrs. Fred Dorsey, married Margaret Parker, was a retired baggage agent for the Pennsylvania Railroad and died in Aberdeen on January 18, 1969, age 78, survived by his wife, 3 daughters, 7 grandchildren, and 6 great-grandchildren) [Mt. Calvary U. A. M. E. Church Cemetery]

Dorsey, Cornelius March 22, 1916 – September 4, 1916 (no tombstone; death certificate stated he was the son of Henry Dorsey and Anna Reed, all born in Perryman) [Union U. M. Church Cemetery]

Dorsey, Daisy V., "Mother" April 3, 1901 – November 5, 1980 [Berkley Memorial Cemetery]

Dorsey, Daniel Webster November 17, 1901 – June 5, ____ , Maryland, Pvt., U.S. Army, World War II [Union U. M. Church Cemetery]

Dorsey, David E. "Davey" 1962-1991 (tombstone; obituary in *The Aegis* on January 8, 1992 stated David

Emmanuel Dorsey lived in Edgewood, died at Deaton Medical Center (in Baltimore) on December 26, 1991, age 29, and was survived by his parents, Shirley Akins, of Edgewood, and Frederick A. Dorsey, Sr., of Baltimore, and 2 brothers, 4 sisters, and grandmother Pearl Dorsey, of Darlington) [Mt. Zion U. M. Church Cemetery]

Dorsey, Dorothy February 14, 1910 – December 2, 1918 (no tombstone; death certificate stated she was the wife of Allen Dorsey, daughter of Charles Wesley Dennison and Emma ? *(sic)* and was buried at Swan Creek) [Union U. M. Church Cemetery]

Dorsey, Earl Eugene, "Son" 1932 – February 1, 2015 (on same tombstone with mother Hannah Roberta Dorsey, but it has no date of death; funeral notice and photo in *The Aegis* stated he lived in Aberdeen and died at Upper Chesapeake Medical Center in Bel Air on February 1, 2015, age 82) [Berkley Memorial Cemetery]

Dorsey, Edith T. 1887 – 19— (no date of death; on same tombstone with husband Wesley C. Dorsey) [Gravel Hill Cemetery]

Dorsey, Edward A. March 18, 1971 – May 21, 1980, TEC5, U.S. Army, World War II (tombstone; obituary in *The Aegis* stated Edward Austin Dorsey was born in Perryman, the son of Allen A. Dorsey and Lillie J. Ringgold, served in World War II, married (wife not mentioned), lived in Aberdeen, retired from Aberdeen Proving Ground and died at Harford Memorial Hospital in Havre de Grace, survived by a son, 3 brothers and 3 sisters) [Mt. Calvary U. A. M. E. Church Cemetery]

Dorsey, Edward October 19, 1898 – February 6, 1963, Maryland, 398 Sv. Bn., QMC, World War I [Berkley Memorial Cemetery]

Dorsey, Effie 1911-1997 (on same tombstone with James Dorsey Sr. and Jr.) [Clark's U. M. Church Cemetery]

Dorsey, Elizabeth C. 1888-1964 ("At Rest") [Asbury Cemetery]

Dorsey, Evangeline J. March 23, 1895 – December 10, 1962 (on same tombstone with Maurice S. Dorsey) [Berkley Memorial Cemetery]

Dorsey, Frances Ann March 12, 1840 – September 17, 1917 (no tombstone; death certificate stated she was born in Maryland, the daughter of Cassie Wells, born in Maryland, but her father's name was known to informant Lilly J. Dorsey, of Perryman; she died a widow in Perryman) [Gravel Hill Cemetery]

Dorsey, Frank died November 8, 1881, age 49 [Asbury Cemetery]

Dorsey, Frank March 2, 1921 – November 14, 1935 (no tombstone; death certificate stated he was born in Darlington, the son of George Dorsey and Annie Cevir, both born in Maryland; he was a schoolboy who died at home in Darlington; informant was his father) [Berkley Memorial Cemetery]

Dorsey, Frank E. 1903-1979 (tombstone; obituary in *The Aegis* on September 27, 1979 stated he was the son of Shadrick and Mary Dorsey, married Anna W. ----, worked as a self-employed plumber, lived in Bel Air and died at Fallston General Hospital; survived by his wife, 2 brothers and 2 sisters) [Clark's U. M. Church Cemetery]

Dorsey, Fred died August 1, 1919, age 50 (no tombstone; death certificate stated he was born in Maryland in September (exact date not given), was single and worked as a farm laborer; parents were Jule Dorsey and Mary Daugherty, both born in Maryland; informant was Mary Dorsey, of Bel Air) [Hendon Hill Cemetery]

Dorsey, Frederick April 17, 1883 – October 15, 1937 (no tombstone; death certificate stated he was born in Harford Co., the son of Frederick J. Dorsey, born in Maryland, and Mary Gibson, born in Harford Co.; he was single, worked as a day laborer and died at home on Race Track Lane near Havre de Grace; informant was Mrs. Bertha Battle, of Aberdeen) [Mt. Calvary U. A. M. E. Church Cemetery]

Dorsey, George died December 31, 1968, age 75 (no tombstone; obituary in *The Aegis* stated he was the son of Charles Dorsey and Jane Sconion, and husband of the late Alice Williams Dorsey of Forge Road, Perry Hall; he was a retired trackman for the B & O Railroad and died at the home of his son, Thomas Dorsey, of Abingdon, survived by 3 sons, 14 grandchildren and 17 great-grandchildren) [Asbury Cemetery]

Dorsey, George July 10, 1874 – May 22, 1939 (no tombstone; death certificate stated he was the son of Frederick Dorsey and Cassie Rice, and died a widower, wife not named) [Union U. M. Church Cemetery]

Dorsey, Gloria H. September 19, 1926 – August 11, 1997 (no tombstone; James Dorsey Card File, African American Obituaries, maintained at the Historical Society of Harford County, has a card for her with an obituary from *The Aegis* on August 20, 1997 stating she was born in Perryman, the daughter of the date Robert Hoke, Sr. and the late Gladys Stansbury, and was the widow of Howard Dorsey; she worked many years at Perry Point VAMC and Aberdeen Proving Ground before retiring in 1992; she died at Lorien-Riverside Nursing Home, survived by four sons, Robert Hoke, Jr., James Warfield, Nelson Bond and Gregory Kenly, a brother, Dennis Hoke, four sisters, Mildred Lisby, Arlene Carlton, Shirley Giles and Sandra Raisin, 16 grandchildren and 14 great-grandchildren) [Union U. M. Church Cemetery]

Dorsey, Hannah October 20, 1859 – January 9, 1912 (no tombstone; death certificate stated she was born in York Co, PA, the daughter of Jupiter Dorsey, born in Kent Co., MD, and Annie Householder, born in Lancaster Co., PA, was single, did housework, and lived and died in Pylesville; informant was James Hall, of Pylesville) [Chestnut Grove A. M. E. Church Cemetery, formerly LaGrange Cemetery at Rocks]

Dorsey, Hannah Roberta "Mother" November 16, 1911 – October 1, 1997 ((on same tombstone with son Earl Eugene Dorsey; The James Dorsey Card File, African American Obituaries, that is maintained at the Historical Society of Harford County, has a card with obituary from an unidentified newspaper on October 8, 1997 stating eh was born in Harford County, the daughter of George Nelson Dorsey and Annie Cevis; she lived in Street, later in Aberdeen and died at Harford Memorial Hospital in Havre de Grace; she was survived by a son Earl Dorsey, five sisters, a brother, 9 grandchildren and 11 great-grandchildren) [Berkley Memorial Cemetery]

Dorsey, Harry F. March 4, 1876 – January 27, 1942 (no tombstone; death certificate stated he was the son of Allen Dorsey, of Frederick Co., and Frances C. Hemore, of Harford Co.) [Union U. M. Church Cemetery]

Dorsey, Henrietta, "Mother" 1896-1962 [Berkley Memorial Cemetery]

Dorsey, Howard Clyde died February 22, 1997, age 73 (small metal funeral home marker inscribed Howard C. Dorsey, 1903-1997; obituary in *The Aegis* on March 5, 1997 stated Howard Clyde Dorsey was born in Perryman, son of the late Allen Dorsey and Lillian Ringgold, was married (wife not mentioned by name) and lived in Aberdeen; he was a U.S. Army veteran, worked for the civil service in maintenance at Aberdeen Proving Ground and died at the Lorien Nursing Home in Riverside; he was survived by 3 sons, 1 brother, 3 sisters and 4 grandchildren) [Mt. Calvary U. A. M. E. Church Cemetery]

Dorsey, Infant female born and died March 18, 1922 (no tombstone; death certificate stated she was the daughter of Charles Malory and Henrietta Dorsey, of Havre de Grace) [St. James United Cemetery]

Dorsey, Isaac died September 2, 1912, age 72 (no tombstone; death certificate stated he was married, worked as a farm laborer and lived and died at Rocks; his parents and their places of birth were not known to the informant, his wife, Mary Dorsey, of Rocks) [Fairview A. M. E. Church Cemetery]

Dorsey, Jacob Henry January 6, 1857 – March 3, 1932 (no tombstone; death certificate misspelled his name Darsey and stated born in Maryland, the son of Juniper Dorsey, born in Maryland, and Anna Householder, born in Pennsylvania; he was a laborer who lived and died in Pylesville and was buried at Rocks; informant was John Dorsey, of Pylesville) [Chestnut Grove A. M. E. Church Cemetery, formerly LaGrange Cemetery at Rocks]

Dorsey, Jacob R. December 16, 1851 – April 18, 1923 (no tombstone; death certificate stated he was the son of Frederick Dorsey and Mary J. Miller, all were born in Maryland; he was married, worked as a laborer, died at home in Havre de Grace, his wife predeceased him and he was buried at Gravelly Hill; informant was John Dorsey, of near Havre de Grace) [Gravel Hill Cemetery]

Dorsey, James Garfield July 6, 1918 – November 26, 1982 (no tombstone; obituary in *The Aegis* on December 9, 1982 stated James Garfield Dorsey was born in Aldino, son of the late James Stansbury and Carrie ----; James Dorsey Card File, African American Obituaries, maintained at the Historical Society of Harford County, has a card for him with an obituary abstract; he was the husband of Virginia Dorsey; he was a past commander of American Legion Post 55 in Bel Air and died at the Elsmere V. A. Medical Hospital in Wilmington, DE, survived by his wife, a brother, a sister and stepfather *(sic)* James Stansbury) [Union U. M. Church Cemetery]

Dorsey, James June 17, 1918 – March 3, 1918 (no tombstone; death certificate stated he was the son of George Dorsey and Annie Sefir, of Darlington, all born in Maryland; informant was his father) [Berkley Memorial

Cemetery]

Dorsey, James Jr. 1937-   (on same tombstone with Effie Dorsey and James Dorsey, Sr.) [Clark's U. M. Church Cemetery]

Dorsey, James Sr. 1905-1992 (on same tombstone with Effie Dorsey and James Dorsey, Jr.) [Clark's U. M. Church Cemetery]

Dorsey, Laura died February 20, 1934, age about 50 (no tombstone; death certificate stated she was the daughter of Jane Dorsey, both born in Harford Co., but her father's name was not known to informant Edward Dorsey, of Darlington; she was single and lived in Darlington) [Gravel Hill Cemetery]

Dorsey, Lee Arlington November 7, 1913 – October 13, 1956, Maryland, SSgt, 2028 QM Trk Co, World War II [Mt. Calvary U. A. M. E. Church Cemetery]

Dorsey, Leonard L. July 11, 1934 – December 11, 1934 (no tombstone; death certificate stated he was son of George Dorsey and Annie Cevir, all born in Darlington; informant was his father) [Berkley Memorial Cemetery]

Dorsey, Lillie J. September 8, 1889 – June 6, 1965 (on same tombstone with Allen A. Dorsey inscribed "Always In Our Hearts") [Mt. Calvary U. A. M. E. Church Cemetery]

Dorsey, Lillie Jane died in 1969, age not given (no tombstone; obituary in *The Aegis* on June 2, 1969 stated Mrs. Lillie Jane Dorsey (neé Ringgold) was born in Harford County and died at her home on Spesutia Road in Perryman; she was the widow of Allen A. Dorsey and was survived by 4 sons, 3 daughters, 1 brother, 3 sisters, 8 grandchildren, 8 great-grandchildren and 2 great-great-grandchildren) [Union U. M. Church Cemetery]

Dorsey, Lilly May 11, 1892 – June 10, 1932 (no tombstone; death certificate stated she was the daughter of Joshua Dorsey and Melvina Banks) [Union U. M. Church Cemetery]

Dorsey, Linda died April 4, 1894, age 74 [Asbury Cemetery]

Dorsey, Lloyd died January 4, 1924, age about 35 (no tombstone; death certificate stated he was the son of Al Dorsey, born in Maryland, but the undertaker did not know the name of his mother; he lived in Darlington and supposedly died from dementia and exposure per jury inquest [Berkley Memorial Cemetery]

Dorsey, Lucy died April 12, 1883, age 80 [Asbury Cemetery]

Dorsey, Lula 1883 – September 1, 1911 (no tombstone; death certificate stated she was born in Harford Co., the daughter of George Bond, born in Harford Co., and Sallie Mooe, born in Havre de Grace, and lived near Aberdeen; informant was Arthur Dorsey, of Aberdeen) [Asbury Cemetery]

Dorsey, Malvina November 11, 1867 – July 23, 1921 (no tombstone; death certificate stated she was the daughter of Ambro Banks and Cassy Richardson, all born in Maryland, and she was married and lived near Aberdeen; informant was Evelyn Banks, of Aberdeen) [Asbury Cemetery]

Dorsey, Mamie C. October 4, 1903 – February 8, 1948 (no tombstone; death certificate stated she was the daughter of Henry Dorsey and Malverna Banks, and was divorced at the time of death) [Union U. M. Church Cemetery]

Dorsey, Margaret A. June 11, 1929 – December 28, 1929 (no tombstone; death certificate stated she was the daughter of Allen A. Dorsey and Lilley J. Ringgold, all born in Maryland; she died in Havre de Grace Hospital; informant was Allen J. Dorsey, of Perryman) [Mt. Calvary U. A. M. E. Church Cemetery]

Dorsey, Margaret K. 1904-1979 (on same tombstone with Clarence E. Dorsey; "Margaret Dorsey" owned a lot in section 41 some time after 1951) [Mt. Calvary U. A. M. E. Church Cemetery]

Dorsey, Margaret Marie died October 11, 1996, age 67 (obituary in *The Aegis* on October 16, 1996 stated she was born in Orange Co., VA, daughter of the late Levi Smith and Anna Lucas of Washington, D.C., and was the widow of Nelson G. Dorsey; lived in Aberdeen, died at Franklin Square Hospital in Baltimore Co., and survived by a daughter, 3 brothers, a sister, 5 grandchildren 3 great-grandchildren) [Berkley Memorial Cemetery]

Dorsey, Margaritte April 10, 1928 – April 20, 1930 (no tombstone; death certificate stated she was the daughter of George Dorsey and Annie Sevirs, of Darlington, all born in Maryland) [Berkley Memorial Cemetery]

Dorsey, Mary E. 1871-1936 (on same tombstone with Shadrach Dorsey; death certificate stated she was born August 12, 1871 and died March 10, 1936; she was the widow of Shadrach Dorsey, lived at Thomas Run, and was the daughter of George Wells and Amanda Presco, all born in Harford Co.; informant was Elizabeth C. Dorsey, of Bel Air) [Asbury Cemetery]

Dorsey, Maurice S. August 10, 1898 – February 7, 1959 (on same tombstone with Evangeline J. Dorsey; obituary in *The Democratic Ledger* on February 12, 1959 stated he was the husband of Evangeline Dorsey, of Darlington, and died at University Hospital in Baltimore) [Berkley Memorial Cemetery]

Dorsey, Nellie V. September 20, 1921 – July 4, 1937 (no tombstone; death certificate stated he was the daughter of Samuel Dorsey and Carrie Brown and she was buried at "Swan Creek") [Union U. M. Church Cemetery]

Dorsey, Nelson George February 3, 1916 – October 9, 1977, PFC, U.S. Army, World War II [Berkley Memorial Cemetery]

Dorsey, Nelson R. July 5, 1928 – March 12, 1986, Cpl., U.S. Army, Korea (obituary in *The Aegis* on March 20, 1986 stated Nelson Robert Dorsey, of Darlington, died at Harford Memorial Hospital in Havre de Grace, and was survived by his wife Catherine Rosalie Dorsey, his mother Pearline Dorsey, son Jeffrey Dorsey, daughter Janet Dorsey, four brothers, three sisters, three aunts, three uncles and a host of nieces, nephews and cousins) [Berkley Memorial Cemetery]

Dorsey, Nina Webster January 12, 1923 – December 1, 2016 (on same tombstone with Carroll Edward Dorsey and Roland Edward Dorsey and inscribed "In Loving Memory") [Berkley Memorial Cemetery]

Dorsey, Norman H. 1909-1978 (tombstone; obituary in *The Aegis* on August 10, 1978 stated Norman Henry Dorsey was born in Harford County, the son of Stevenson and Rebecca Dorsey, married Myrtle Taylor, retired from the Wanamaker's Store and died in Philadelphia on July 26, 1978, survived by his wife, a son, a daughter, and 7 grandchildren) [Clark's U. M. Church Cemetery]

Dorsey, Pearlene Maggie, "Beloved Mother" 1902-1992 [Berkley Memorial Cemetery]

Dorsey, Richard died June 9, 1917, age about 60 (no tombstone; death certificate stated he was the son of Rose Dorsey, both born in Harford Co., but his father's name was un known to informant Ellsworth Cooper, of Bel Air RFD #1; he was a widower and farmer at Kalmia) [Clark's U. M. Church Cemetery]

Dorsey, Roland Edward February 2, 1924 – March 8, 2016 (on same tombstone with Carroll Edward Dorsey and Nina Webster Dorsey and inscribed "In Loving Memory") [Berkley Memorial Cemetery]

Dorsey, Shadrach 1872-1924 (on same tombstone with Mary E. Dorsey; death certificate stated he was born on March 4, 1872 and died on July 17, 1924; father was Shadrach Dorsey, but mother's name was unknown to informant Maurice Dorsey, of Bel Air; he was married and a farmer near Bel Air) [Asbury Cemetery]

Dorsey, Shadrach died May 31, 1886, age 82 [Asbury Cemetery]

Dorsey, Stephen Daniel, son of Shadrach and Mary M. Dorsey, died November 24, 1911, age 25 years, 6 months and 20 days [Asbury Cemetery]

Dorsey, Thornton October 10, 1924 – May 23, 1925 (no tombstone; death certificate stated he was the son of Albert Dorsey and Ethel Stansbury, all born in Maryland; she died in Havre de Grace; informant was her father) [Gravel Hill Cemetery]

Dorsey, Viola V. died February 22, 1979, age 73 (no tombstone; obituary in *The Aegis* on March 1, 1979 stated she was born in Darlington, lived in Baltimore, died there at Lutheran Hospital and was survived by a brother William Dorsey, a sister Rachel Cromwell, and nieces and nephews) [Berkley Memorial Cemetery]

Dorsey, Wesley C. 1884-1961 (on same tombstone with wife Edith T. Dorsey) [Gravel Hill Cemetery]

Dorsey, Wilbur Joseph January 2, 1914 – May 6, 1953, Maryland, PFC, Co. D., 224th Engr. Regt., World War II, BSM [Cedars Chapel Cemetery]

Dorsey, William February 23, 1870 – March 4, 1920 (no tombstone; death certificate stated he was the son of William Dorsey and Lindey Jimmison, all born in Maryland; he was a cook and lived in Churchville; informant was John Bond, of Bel Air RFD) [Asbury Cemetery]

Dorsey, William C. September 5, 1909 – February 11, 1951, Maryland, PFC, QMC, World War II [Mt. Calvary U. A. M. E. Church Cemetery]

Dorsey, William H. March 7, 1872 – January 2, 1937 (no tombstone; death certificate stated he was the son of Margaret Dorsey, father unknown, and husband of Melvina Banks who predeceased him) [Union U. M. Church Cemetery]

Dorsey, William H. September 20, 1868 – April 4, 1917 (no tombstone; death certificate stated he was the unmarried son of Abner Dorsey and Harriet French, all born in Maryland; informant was Abraham Henry Peaco, of Havre de Grace [St. James United Cemetery]

Dorsey, William S. died August 12, 2000, age 92 (obituary in *The Aegis* on August 16, 2000 stated he was born in Darlington, married (wife's name not given), retired in 1969 from McCormick Spice Co. and died at the Riverside Nursing and Rehabilitation Center in Belcamp; he was survived by two sons, William Sidney Dorsey and George E. Dorsey; inscribed "William S. Dorsey, Sr., 1907-2000") [Berkley Memorial Cemetery]

Dougherty, Benjamin Franklin, son of Benjamin Franklin Dougherty, died June 2, 1898, age illegible (inscribed "In Memory of") [Asbury Cemetery]

Dougherty, Betsy died October 30, 1882, age not given (no tombstone; her death notice in *The Aegis* on November 3, 1882 stated she was a respectable woman who died at home near Bel Air; place of burial was not given, but it was probably at Asbury Church) [Asbury Cemetery]

Dougherty, Margaret A. March 12, 1841 – July 28, 1882 [Asbury Cemetery]

Douglas, Bessie, "Daughter" 1894-1925 (buried next to Olivia Douglas and Mary Douglas) [Berkley Memorial Cemetery]

Douglas, James H. died October 16, 1937, age about 48, Virginia, Sgt., 155 Depot Brig., World War I (tombstone gave his name, date of death and service; death certificate stated he was born in Parlettsville, VA, parents unknown, and undertaker R. Madison Mitchell stated he was found dead from an apparent heart attack in Thomas Hopkins' cornfield) [St. James United Cemetery]

Douglas, James P. 1848 – February 21, 1919 (no tombstone; death certificate stated he was born in Maryland, was married, worked as a laborer and died at Rocks; the names and places of his parents were not known to informant David St. Clair, of Rocks) [William C. Rice Memorial Cemetery, St. James U. M. Church]

Douglas, Mary, "Daughter" 1898-1919 (buried next to Olivia Douglas and Bessie Douglas) [Berkley Memorial Cemetery]

Douglas, Olivia, "Daughter" 1897-1916 (buried next to Mary Douglas and Bessie Douglas) [Berkley Memorial Cemetery]

Douglass, H. Rena March 25, 1891 – August 10, 1907 [St. James United Cemetery]

Dowery, Perry died February 22, 1935, age about 80 (no tombstone; Kurtz Funeral Home Pocket Memo Book stated he was single, born in Buckeystown, Frederick Co., worked as a laborer in Jarrettville, and died at the County Home in Bel Air; place of burial not indicated, but death certificate stated it was "St. James Colored" cemetery and his parents were not known) [William C. Rice Memorial Cemetery, St. James U. M. Church]

Downing, Dorothy C. Mitchell "Loving Mother, Wife, Mom-mom, Sister" September 25, 1956 – August 31, 2005 [Clark's U. M. Church Cemetery]

Downing, Faith Antoinette December 6, 1953 – March 17, 1975 (tombstone; obituary in *The Aegis* on March 27, 1975 stated she was a daughter of William A. and Nellie Downing and a student at Morgan State College; she lived in Forest Hill and died at Provident Hospital in Baltimore, survived by her mother, 3 brothers and 10 sisters) [Mt. Zion U. M. Church Cemetery]

Downing, Lydia A. July 25, 1955 – May 16, 1998 [Tabernacle Mount Zion U. M. Church Cemetery]

Downing, Nellie R. Bishop September 15, 1917 – October 13, 1991 [Mt. Zion U. M. Church Cemetery]

Downing, Richard A. Sr. October 10, 1942 – December 11, 2008, U.S. Navy [Berkley Memorial Cemetery]

Downing, William September 10, 1909 – October 23, 1964 (inscribed "In Memory Of") [Mt. Zion U. M. Church Cemetery]

Draper, Edgar P. 1893-1957 [Union U. M. Church Cemetery]

Draper, Ethel B. August 7, 1897 – May 7, 1928 [Union U. M. Church Cemetery]

Draper, Harriet A., "Mother" 1847-1930 [Union U. M. Church Cemetery]

Duncan, Charles Saunders Jr., "Our Son CJ" March 30, 1989 – July 15, 1989 [Mt. Calvary U. A. M. E. Church Cemetery]

Dunn, Hazel T. 1893-1950 (on same tombstone with R. Nettie Christy, I. Marie Bowser and Martha C. Bowser) [St. James United Cemetery]

Dunsen, ---- stillborn male on August 7, 1920 (no tombstone; death certificate stated he was born in Maryland, the son of Joe Ray, born in Maryland, and Blanch Dunsen, born in New York, and they lived at Rocks; informant was Mrs. Rose Dunsen, of Rocks) [Chestnut Grove A. M. E. Church Cemetery, formerly LaGrange Cemetery at Rocks]

Dunsen, Annie M. died December 18, 1916, age 70 (no tombstone; death certificate stated she was born in Maryland, lived at Rocks and died a widow; her father was Anthony Gover, who was born in Maryland, but her mother was unknown to informant Charles Dunsen, of Rocks) [Chestnut Grove A. M. E. Church Cemetery, formerly LaGrange Cemetery at Rocks]

Dunsen, Charles C. November 5, 1907 – October 21, 1970 (no tombstone; obituary in *The Aegis* on October 22, 1970 stated he died at Brevin Nursing Home in Havre de Grace and was the husband of Lyda P. Dunsen, of Street, MD; Harkins Funeral Home Records confirm this information and gave his date of birth, stating he was born in White Plains, N.Y., the son of William Dunsen and Rose Marks; informant was his wife Lyda P. Dunsen) [Chestnut Grove A. M. E. Church Cemetery, formerly LaGrange Cemetery at Rocks]

Dunsen, Charles H. May 1, 1868 – April 12, 1929 (tombstone; death certificate stated Charles Henry Dunsen was born in Maryland, married, worked as a farmer and died at Rocks; his parents were Calvin Dunsen, of North Carolina, and Annie M. Gover, of Maryland; informant was Walter Fisher, of Rocks) [Chestnut Grove A. M. E. Church Cemetery, formerly LaGrange Cemetery at Rocks]

Dunsen, Charles M. June 15, 1933 -   (on same tombstone with Roberta C. Dunsen) [Chestnut Grove A. M. E. Church Cemetery, formerly LaGrange Cemetery at Rocks]

Dunsen, Jarrett Francis, son of Calvin and Annie M. Dunsen, May 22, 1871 – June 9, 1885 [Chestnut Grove A. M. E. Church Cemetery, formerly LaGrange Cemetery at Rocks]

Dunsen, John C. Jr. died October 10, 1909, age 31 (no tombstone; death certificate stated he was born in Maryland, married Venie Jordan, worked as a laborer and died a widower at Rocks; his parents were John C. Dunsen, Sr., born in North Carolina, and Annie M. Gover, born in Maryland; informant was his father John C. Dunsen, Sr.) [Chestnut Grove A. M. E. Church Cemetery, formerly LaGrange Cemetery at Rocks]

Dunsen, John Calvin died December 16, 1916, age about 70 (no tombstone; death certificate stated he was born in North Carolina, married, worked as a farmer and died at Rocks; his father was Calvin Dunsen, but his mother was not known to informant, Mrs. Dunsen, of Rocks) [Chestnut Grove A. M. E. Church Cemetery, formerly LaGrange Cemetery at Rocks]

Dunsen, Lavenia Elizabeth died March 30, 1908, age 28 (no tombstone; death certificate stated she was born at Mill Green, married John Dunsen and died at Mill Green; her parents were William Jordan, whose birth place was unknown, and Julia Morgan, who was born in Maryland; informant was her husband John Dunsen) [Chestnut Grove A. M. E. Church Cemetery, formerly LaGrange Cemetery at Rocks]

Dunsen, Lyda P. died March 20, 1989, age 85 (no tombstone; obituary in the *Delta Star* on March 23, 1989 stated she was born in Delta, PA, the daughter of the late Joseph E. Peaco and Laura Murray, and the wife of the late Charles C. Dunsen (who was her second husband as she had been first married to a Lowe); Lyda was of

Aberdeen, formerly of York, and died at Harford Memorial Hospital) [Chestnut Grove A. M. E. Church Cemetery, formerly LaGrange Cemetery at Rocks]

Dunsen, Marcus A. June 5, 1957 – October 30, 1990 (inscribed "Bound for Glory;" obituary in *The Aegis* on November 14, 1990 stated Marcus "Mark" Antonio Dunsen, of Baltimore, formerly of Harford Co., was the son of Charles Dunsen, of Street, MD, and Shirley Dunsen, of Aberdeen, the stepson of Roberta Dunsen, and the husband of Naomi Dunsen; he was survived by his wife, two sons, his mother and father, a stepmother, one brother, four sisters, grandmother Nevada Dunsen and grandfather Matthew Dunsen) [Chestnut Grove A. M. E. Church Cemetery, formerly LaGrange Cemetery at Rocks]

Dunsen, Mary Lavinia, daughter of Calvin and Annie Dunsen, October 5, 1873 – June 15, 1885 [Chestnut Grove A. M. E. Church Cemetery, formerly LaGrange Cemetery at Rocks]

Dunsen, Matthew W., "Beloved father of nine" February 19, 1920 – December 15, 1990 (inscribed "Always in our hearts;" obituary in *The Aegis* on December 19, 1990 stated Matthew William Dunsen, of Street, MD, was the husband of Nevada Dunsen and died at Harford Memorial Hospital; known as "Mr. Matt," he was born in White Plains, NY, the son of the late William Dunsen and Rose Marks, and was survived by his wife Nevada Dunsen, four sons, five daughters, 17 grandchildren and 9 great-grandchildren) [Chestnut Grove A. M. E. Church Cemetery, formerly LaGrange Cemetery at Rocks]

Dunsen, Nevada G. "Loving mom, sister and grandmother" November 4, 1910 – September 18, 1995 (tombsone; obituary in *The Aegis* on September 27, 1995 stated she lived in Street, died at St. Agnes Hospital in Baltimore and was the widow of Matthew W. Dunsen, survived by 4 sons, 5 daughters, a brother Jesse Edwards, 18 grandchildren and 9 great-grandchildren) [Chestnut Grove A. M. E. Church Cemetery, formerly LaGrange Cemetery at Rocks]

Dunsen, Robert Lee May 31, 1931 – April 22, 1996, Pvt., U.S. Army (tombstone; obituary in *The Aegis* on May 1, 1996 stated Robert L. "Bob" Dunsen, of Street, died at the Veterans Hospital in Baltimore; he served in the 101st Airborne during the Korean War and was the son of the late Matthew and Nevada Dunsen; he had been married (wife's name was not given) and was survived by 8 siblings, 6 children, 7 stepchildren, and 20 grandchildren) [Chestnut Grove A. M. E. Church Cemetery, formerly LaGrange Cemetery at Rocks]

Dunsen, Roberta E. July 31, 1941 – August 16, 2015 (on the same tombstone with Charles M. Dunsen; obituary in *The Aegis* states Roberta Elizabeth Dunsen died in Bel Air) [Chestnut Grove A. M. E. Church Cemetery, formerly LaGrange Cemetery at Rocks]

Dunsen, Rose L. 1879-1949 (tombstone inscription, but death certificate stated she was born on January 8, 1880 in Maryland, the daughter of William Marks and "Jean – no record of last name;" she died a widow on September 28, 1949 at Street RFD #1; informant was Mrs. Blanche O. Dunsen) [Chestnut Grove A. M. E. Church Cemetery, formerly LaGrange Cemetery at Rocks]

Dunsen, Shirley E. G. 1934-2016 (small metal funeral home marker) [Berkley Memorial Cemetery]

Dunsen, William A. February 5, 1876 – April 12, 1915 [Chestnut Grove A. M. E. Church Cemetery, formerly LaGrange Cemetery at Rocks]

Dupree, Frances B. May 5, 1909 -   (on same tombstone with Julius Dupree) [Union U. M. Church Cemetery]

Dupree, Jessie B. (Rev.) July 3, 1926 – August 2, 1995 (tombstone; James Dorsey Card File, African American Obituaries, maintained at the Historical Society of Harford County, has a card for her with an obituary from *The Aegis* on August 16, 1995 stating she was born in Cairo, GA, the daughter of the late Evelyn Patterson, and for more than 50 years she had been a resident of both Cecil and Harford Counties, working in the dietetic department at Perry Point VAMC from 1958 until retiring in 1990; she lived in Perryman and began her ministry in 1982; she was survived by 5 sons, 2 sisters, a brother, 5 grandchildren, 4 great-grandchildren and many other relative) [St. James United Cemetery]

Dupree, Joseph January 18, 1925 – January 10, 1991 [Union U. M. Church Cemetery]

Dupree, Joseph Jr., "Big Joe" April 9, 1947 – April 12, 2005 (inscribed "Too well loved to be forgotten") [St. James United Cemetery]

Dupree, Julius C. April 9, 1898 – February 18, 1977 (on same tombstone with Frances Dupree) [Union U. M. Church Cemetery]

Dupree, Minda August 25, 1879 – September 4, 1932 (no tombstone; death certificate stated she was born in Florence, SC, and was the wife of Simon Dupree and the daughter of Wade Patterson, born in Florence, SC, and Florence Cox, born in Red Hill, SC) [Union U. M. Church Cemetery]

Dupree, Simon March 14, 1865 – July 28, 1937 (no tombstone; death certificate stated he was the son of Simon Dupree, mother unknown, all born in South Carolina, and the husband of Minda Dupree who predeceased him; informant was Young Dupree, of Aberdeen) [Union U. M. Church Cemetery]

Durbin, Agnes April 6, 1896 – March 31, 1918 (no tombstone; death certificate stated she was the unmarried daughter of Thomas Durbin and Elizabeth French, of Havre de Grace) [St. James United Cemetery]

Durbin, Alfred died November 21, 1926, age about 64 (no tombstone; death certificate stated he was born in Maryland and died a widower; informant was Mrs. Hannah Beatty) [St. James United Cemetery]

Durbin, Amelia V. 1926-2015 [Mt. Calvary U. A. M. E. Church Cemetery]

Durbin, Anne M. 1908-1996 (handwritten on a flat cement slab and also inscribed "One Day;" obituary in *The Aegis* on December 4, 1996 stated Evangelist Annie Mary Durbin was born May 18, 1908 in Baltimore, the oldest of nine children born to Henry Croxsell and Estella Ellis of Havre de Grace, and married William Durbin on November 16, 1927; she was a charter member of the Zion Temple Church and was very active, holding offices that included Sunday School teacher, church trustee, church clerk, associate pastor, missionary president, Senior Choir member, District Council secretary, missionary secretary and missionary field worker; she died at Harford Memorial Hospital on November 25, 1996, survived by five sons, three daughters, a sister, a god-daughter, 48 grandchildren, 79 great-grandchildren, 3 great-great-grandchildren and a host of nieces, nephews, cousins and other relatives, and preceded in death by five sons and one daughter) [St. James United Cemetery]

Durbin, Arthur October 22, 1916 – May 8, 1918 (no tombstone; death certificate stated he was the son of William Ramsey and Mary Durbin, of Havre de Grace) [St. James United Cemetery]

Durbin, Baby stillborn male on July 13, 1954 (no tombstone; Pennington Funeral Home records stated he was the son of Robert Durbin and Doris Pinion, of Havre de Grace [St. James United Cemetery]

Durbin, Carrie B. 1878-1967 (copied in 1987 and a faded small tombstone was found in 2018) [St. James United Cemetery]

Durbin, Clarence August – (blank), 1884 – September 15, 1940 (no tombstone; death certificate stated he was the son of Thomas Durbin and Rebecca French, of Havre de Grace, and married Eva ----; he died in Harford Memorial Hospital) [St. James United Cemetery]

Durbin, Cynthia F. 1938-2016 [St. James United Cemetery]

Durbin, Ella Jane January 14, 1865 – December 29, 1941 (no tombstone; death certificate stated she was the daughter of James H. Leggar, of Bush River, MD, and Eliza Myers, of Duncannon, PA) [Skinner Cemetery]

Durbin, Ernest O. November 6, 1902 – January 7, 1917 (no tombstone; death certificate stated he was the son of Thomas Durbin and Rebecca French, of Havre de Grace) [St. James United Cemetery]

Durbin, Eva M. July 14, 1887 – June 19, 1940 (no tombstone; death certificate stated she was born in Havre de Grace, the daughter of Peter Moses, born in Virginia, and Julia A. Maxwell, born in Maryland; she married Harry Durbin, born c1888, lived at 569 Girard Street in Havre de Grace and died at 517 Alliance Street where she had lived for about one month; informant was her husband) [Gravel Hill Cemetery]

Durbin, Frank died January 30, 1916, age about 35 (no tombstone; death certificate stated he was the son of Mathew Holmes and Jane Durbin and an "illegitimate child took mother's name") [St. James United Cemetery]

Durbin, Harold A. July 28, 1932 – January 11, 1997, U.S. Army, Korea (tombstone; obituary in *The Aegis* on January 29, 1997 stated Harold Austin Durbin, Sr. was born in Havre de Grace, the son of William and Annie Mary Durbin, served two years in the Army during the Korean War, received the Purple Heart, was discharged, re-enlisted in the Air Force and served three more years; he married Cecelia White on February 28, 1955, retired as a motorman for the New York City Transit Authority and died in Manhattan, survived by his wife, five sons, three daughters, four brothers, three sisters, four uncles, five aunts, one god-daughter, 13 grandchildren and one great-grandchild) [St. James United Cemetery]

Durbin, Hattie M. August 5, 1915 – October 23, 1915 (no tombstone; death certificate stated she was the daughter of Frank Durbin and Mary Johnson, of Havre de Grace) [St. James United Cemetery]

Durbain, Ida died August 3, 1923, age about 50 (no tombstone; death certificate spelled her name Durban and stated she was the daughter of John Watters and Henrietta Bond, all born in Maryland; she died a widow in Abingdon; informant was Aleck Watters, of Abingdon) [Mt. Zion U. M. Church Cemetery]

Durbin, Joseph L. April 25, 1940 – January 11, 1941 (no tombstone; death certificate stated he was the son of William Durbin and Anna May Croxon, of Havre de Grace) [St. James United Cemetery]

Durbin, Kenneth Eugene March 3, 1926 – October 18, 1975, STM2, U.S. Navy, World War II [St. James United Cemetery]

Durbin, Marian Delorise "Sunshine" September 14, 1955 – November 18, 1996 (no tombstone; obituary in *The Aegis* on December 4, 1996 stated she was the daughter of David Durbin, Sr. and Viola Collins and died at Maryland General Hospital in Baltimore, survived by her parents, a son James Ronnie Evans, Jr., five brothers, a sister, two grandchildren, ten nieces and six nephews) [St. James United Cemetery]

Durbin, Milton V. February 14, 1884 – February 21, 1912 (no tombstone; death certificate stated he was the unmarried son of Nathaniel Durbin, born in Havre de Grace, and Hester Dennison, born in Baltimore) [St. James United Cemetery]

Durbin, Nathaniel July 10, 1860 – March 1, 1924 (no tombstone; death certificate stated he was the son of Stephen Durbin and Celesta Skinner, all born in Maryland; informant was Mrs. Nathaniel Durbin, of Havre de Grace) [Skinner Cemetery]

Durbin, Nelson November – (blank), 1858 – August 24, 1943 (no tombstone; death certificate stated he was the unmarried son of Steve Durbin and Vina Richardson and died in Harford Memorial Hospital in Havre de Grace) [St. James United Cemetery]

Durbin, Olivia G., wife of Joseph H. Durbin, 1875-1951 (tombstone; death certificate stated she was born on June 9, 1876, the daughter of John Richardson and ---- (unknown), and died on April 3, 1915 in Havre de Grace) [St. James United Cemetery]

Durbin, Rebecca died January 1, 1950 (no tombstone; death certificate stated she was born about 1874, but Rebecca French was age 18 when she married Thomas Durbin on 25 Jan 1876, thus born about 1857-1858) [St. James United Cemetery]

Durbin, Robert S. June 14, 1912 – August 21, 1914 (no tombstone; death certificate stated he was the son of Frank Durbin and Mary Chambers, of Havre de Grace) [St. James United Cemetery]

Durbin, Thomas June 2, 1853 – July 12, 1927 (inscribed Thomas Durbin and Family, but no other names and dates are on it; he was the husband of Rebecca French Durbin; death certificate stated he was the son of Isaac Durbin and Martha Peaco, of Havre de Grace) [St. James United Cemetery]

Durbin, William A. 1905-1983 (tombstone; obituary in *The Aegis* on April 14, 1982 stated that William A. Durbin, Sr., husband of Anna May Durbin of Havre de Grace, retired from Aberdeen Proving Ground and died at Harford Memorial Hospital, survived by a sister, 7 sons, 49 grandchildren and 29 great-grandchildren) [St. James United Cemetery]

Durbin, William A., "Baby Tad" (no dates; handwritten on a flat cement slab) [St. James United Cemetery]

Duren, Katherine 1920-1997 (flat handwritten cement marker; James Dorsey Card File, African American Obituaries, maintained at the Historical Society of Harford County, has a card for her death notice in *The Aegis* on April 16, 1997 stating Catherine Duren, of Port Deposit, died on April 10, 1997, age 77 at Harford Memorial Hospital) [Berkley Memorial Cemetery]

Durham, Caruso D. April 13, 1952 – April 1, 1991, SP4, U.S. Army, Vietnam [St. James United Cemetery]

Dutton, Albert and Family (no dates; name inscribed on same tombstone with Mary J. Lee and Family) [Mt. Calvary U. A. M. E. Church Cemetery]

Dutton, Charles Daniel February 24, 1915 – January 12, 1916 (no tombstone; death certificate stated he died in Bel Air, the son of John Dutton and Ella Price, all born in Maryland; informant was John Dutton, of Bel Air) [Clark's U. M. Church Cemetery]

Dutton, Charles October 10, 1859 – February 13, 1944 (no tombstone; death certificate stated he was born in Harford Co., the son of William Dutton and Mary Cooper, both born in Maryland; he married Mary ----, who predeceased him, and was a farmer at Kalmia where he had lived all his life; informant was Joshua Dutton, of Oxford, PA) [Clark's U. M. Church Cemetery]

Dutton, Edward died April 16, 1888, age about 51 (no tombstone; his death notice in *The Aegis* on April 20, 1888 stated he died in the Second District after a short illness; "he bore a wound received in the late war (Civil War, 1861-1865) for which he received a pension until his death; he was formerly employed in the Baltimore Custom House;" place of burial was not given [possibly Mt. Calvary M. E. Church Cemetery]

Dutton, Edward John May 11, 1894 – April 30, 1945 (no tombstone; death certificate stated he was born in Harford Co., the son of William R. Dutton and Ruth A. Talbott, both born in Maryland; he married Nellie I. ---- (born 1906) and was a laborer in rural Street where he had lived for the past 3 years; informant was Nellie I. Dutton, of Street, MD) [Clark's U. M. Church Cemetery]

Dutton, Ella N. June 17, 1882 – January 27, 1959 [Clark's U. M. Church Cemetery]

Dutton, Ellen J., "Mother" 1841-1922 (inscribed "Gone But Not Forgotten" and death certificate stated she died March 11, 1922, age about 83) [St. James United Cemetery]

Dutton, Emily L. October 9, 1896 – January 10, 1925 (no tombstone; death certificate stated she was the daughter of John James and Isabel Johnson, all born in Maryland; she was married and lived at Dublin; informant was Edward J. Dutton, of Darlington) [Clark's U. M. Church Cemetery]

Dutton, George died April 28, 1932, age about 55 (no tombstone; death certificate stated he was the son of William Dutton and Mary Cooper, all born in Maryland; he married Janie Hines, was a laborer, and died at Kalmia; informant was Charles H. Dutton, of Bel Air) [Clark's U. M. Church Cemetery]

Dutton, Harold E. July 13, 1929 – December 13, 1929 (no tombstone; death certificate stated he died at Dublin, the son of Edward J. Dutton and Nellie Johnson, and all were born in Maryland; informant was E. J. Dutton, of Street, MD) [Clark's U. M. Church Cemetery]

Dutton, Henry died February 14, 1935, age about 59 (no tombstone; death certificate stated he was born in Harford Co., but his parents were unknown to informant Olivia White, of Street, MD; he was single, worked as a farm laborer and died in Darlington where he had lived 50 years) [Berkley Memorial Cemetery]

Dutton, J. William (no tombstone; death certificate stated he was born March 4, 1885 in Bel Air, the son of John Dutton and Alice Pinion, both born in Harford Co.; he worked as a laborer in Havre de Grace and was married at the time of his death on March 10, 1914; informant was George Dutton, of Havre de Grace) [Green Spring U. M. Church Cemetery]

Dutton, Janie January 10, 1860 – October 11, 1936 (no tombstone; death certificate stated she was the daughter of Dennis Hines, both born in Harford Co., but her mother's name was not known to the informant Susie Adams, 516 E. Haines St., Germantown, Philadelphia, PA; she married George Dutton and died a widow at Kalmia) [Clark's U. M. Church Cemetery]

Dutton, John Edward February 17, 1826 – January 11, 1891 (inscribed "A Faithful Friend") [Clark's U. M. Church Cemetery]

Dutton, Joshua December 15, 1880 – March 31, 1955 [Clark's U. M. Church Cemetery]

Dutton, Joshua Hayward February 27, 1916 – March 12, 1916 (no tombstone; death certificate stated he was the son of Joshua Dutton and Ella Price, all born in Harford Co., and died at Poole; informant was Joshua Dutton, of Street, MD) [Clark's U. M. Church Cemetery]

Dutton, Julia died March 16, 1902, age 17 (no tombstone; death certificate stated she was the daughter of William Dutton and Mary Cooper and died at Kalmia; place of burial not given [probably Clark's U. M. Church Cemetery]

Dutton, Lewis August 6, 1930 – September 4, 1930 (no tombstone; death certificate stated he was the son of Edward Dutton and Nellie Johnson, all born in Maryland, and died at Dublin; informant was Edward Johnson *(sic)*, of Street, MD) [Clark's U. M. Church Cemetery]

Dutton, Louiesa died September 29, 1917, age 98 (no tombstone; death certificate stated she was born in Maryland, the daughter of Seymour Collins, born in Maryland, but her mother's name was not known to the informant John C. Cooper, of Street, MD; she died a widow in Street) [Clark's U. M. Church Cemetery]

Dutton, Louisa F. September 7, 1909 – March 6, 2009 [Clark's U. M. Church Cemetery]

Dutton, Mary August 11, 1866 – November 24, 1940 (inscribed "Blessed are the Pure in Heart for they shall see God") [Clark's U. M. Church Cemetery]

Dutton, Mary E., wife of William R. Dutton, July 20, 1820? – November 17, 1901? (tombstone is badly weathered) [Clark's U. M. Church Cemetery]

Dutton, Nellie February 25, 1939 – March 7, 1939, premature birth, lived 10 days (no tombstone; death certificate stated she was the daughter of Edward Dutton and Nellie Johnson, all born in Harford Co., and they lived at Dublin; informant was Edward Dutton, of Street, MD) [Clark's U. M. Church Cemetery]

Dutton, Ruth A. P. December 3, 1916 – May 27, 1920 (no tombstone; death certificate stated she was the daughter of Edward Dutton and Emily James, all were born in Maryland, and she died at Poole; informant was her father, of Street, MD) [Clark's U. M. Church Cemetery]

Dutton, William R. May – (blank), 1873 – October 24, 1911 (no tombstone; death certificate stated he was the son of William Dutton and Mary Cooper, all were born in Harford Co.; he was single, worked as a laborer, and died at Kalmia; informant was Charles Dutton, of Bel Air) [Clark's U. M. Church Cemetery]

Dutton, William R. May 2, 1852 – January 18, 1936 (no tombstone; death certificate stated he was the son of Edward J. Dutton and Luisa Collins, all born in Harford Co.; he married Ruthann ----, worked as a farm laborer all his life until 1930 and died at Darlington where he had lived for 83 years; the informant was Edward Dutton, of Street; his death notice in *The Aegis* on January 31, 1936 stated he worked many years for the Neilson family at Priestford) [Clark's U. M. Church Cemetery]

Dyson, Clyde L. 1929-1991 (handwritten on a flat cement slab) [St. James United Cemetery]

Dyson, Cora B. January 25, 1926 – June 24, 2002 ("In Loving Memory") [Berkley Memorial Cemetery]

Dyson, Estella V., "Mother" 1892-1984 [Berkley Memorial Cemetery]

Dyson, Harry 1934-   (handwritten on same flat cement slab with Irene Dyson inscribed 1 Corinthians 13) [St. James United Cemetery]

Dyson, Harry L. Sr. December 28, 1943 – April 13, 2000, PFC, U.S. Army [St. James United Cemetery]

Dyson, Irene 1936-1998 (on same flat, handwritten, cement slab with Irene Dyson and 1 Corinthians 13; obituary in *The Aegis* on May 13, 1998 stated Irene Marie Dyson was born May 19, 1936, the daughter of the late Robert Christy and Eliza Harris, and the wife of Harry Lee Dyson, Sr. who she married in 1961; she lived in Havre de Grace and died on April 29, 1998 at Fallston General Hospital; she was survived by her husband, two sons, and adopted daughter and three grandchildren; an adopted son preceded her in death) [St. James United Cemetery]

Dyson, James R. December 5, 1925 – December 5, 1988, U.S. Navy, World War II [St. James United Cemetery]

Dyson, William Sr. June 17, 1923 – March 25, 1995, U.S. Army, World War II [Berkley Memorial Cemetery]

Dyson, William A. January 19, 1947 – October 24, 2014, U.S. Army, Vietnam [Berkley Memorial Cemetery]

Earl, Gayelynn 1864-2015 (small metal funeral home marker) [John Wesley U. M. E. Church Cemetery in

Abingdon]

Eason, Leroy October 17, 1926 – September 14, 1927 (no tombstone; death certificate stated he was the son of George Lee Eason, of North Carolina, and Elmira Bond, of Maryland) [St. James United Cemetery]

East, Clarence April 10, 1912 – December 24, 1971 (copied in 1987, but not found in 2018) [Mt. Calvary U. A. M. E. Church Cemetery]

Edwards (tombstone with no names and no dates) [St. James United Cemetery]

Edwards, Agnes Pauline died July 9, 1992, age 77 (no tombstone; obituary in *The Aegis* on August 5, 1992 stated she was born in Forest Hill, the daughter of Henry and Lillie Robinson, and lived in Edgewood; she died a widow (husband was not named) at Harford Memorial Hospital, survived by 2 sons, 3 daughters, 4 brothers, 16 grandchildren and 10 great-grandchildren) [William C. Rice Memorial Cemetery, St. James U. M. Church]

Edwards, Bruce April 10, 1919 – April 6, 1974, Maryland, TEC 5, U.S. Army, World War II (tombstone; obituary in *The Aegis* on April 11, 1974 stated he was born in Sparta NC, the son of Wiley H. and Estella Edwards, was the husband of Mary Irene Edwards, of 444 Hartman St. in Edgewood, served in World War II, was employed at Edgewood Arsenal and died at Franklin Square Hospital in Baltimore County) [Tabernacle Mount Zion U. M. Church Cemetery]

Edwards, Carolyn Ann July 17, 1953 – November 13, 2013 (tombstone; obituary in *The Aegis* on November 20, 2013 stated Carolyn "Sis" Edwards was born in York, PA, the daughter of Louis Vernon Leonard and Edith Rosella Douglas (who had a large family including five sets of twins); Carolyn was married to Bradford Jay Edwards for 27 years, lived in Delta, PA and later moved to Aberdeen; she died at University of Maryland Hospital in Baltimore) [Tabernacle Mount Zion U. M. Church Cemetery]

Edwards, Clyde Louella 1914-   [Clark's U. M. Church Cemetery]

Edwards, Dorothy E. August 10, 1927 – February 26, 2010 (tombstone; the obituary of her mother Edna A. Walton in *The Aegis* on July 30, 1981 stated Dorothy E. Edwards lived in Aberdeen) [Chestnut Grove A. M. E. Church Cemetery, formerly LaGrange Cemetery at Rocks]Edwards, Emma 1892-1979 (handwritten on a flat cement slab) [St. James United Cemetery]

Edwards, Ethel Marie 1925-1999 (small white wooden cross grave marker) [Chestnut Grove A. M. E. Church Cemetery, formerly LaGrange Cemetery at Rocks]

Edwards, J. Talmadge 1913-1990 (small white wooden cross grave marker) [Chestnut Grove A. M. E. Church Cemetery, formerly LaGrange Cemetery at Rocks]

Edwards, James T. died July 31, 1990, age 82 (no tombstone; James Dorsey Card File, African American Obituaries, maintained at the Historical Society of Harford County, has a card for him with an obituary from *The Aegis* stating he was born in Sparta, N.C., the son of Wiley and Stella Edwards, and moved to Maryland more than 60 years ago, engaged in mushroom farming before becoming a cement mason; he died at home in Churchville, survived by his wife Agnes Robinson Edwards, four daughters, two sons, four sisters, two brothers, 16 grandchildren and 9 great-grandchildren) [William C. Rice Memorial Cemetery, St. James U. M. Church]

Edwards, Jesse Lee Sr. February 23, 1926 – September 18, 2005 (inscribed "In Loving Memory" and "Your Loving Children;" obituary and photo in *The Aegis* on September 23, 2005 stated he was born in Starter, N.C., the son of Wiley Edwards and Ethal Choate, and lived in Fayetteville, N.C. before moving to Harford County where he worked for the federal government for 32 years, retiring in 1989; he subsequently worked for the Almost Family for many years and for the past 8 years he lived with his daughter in Fayetteville, N.C.; he married (wife's name not given in obituary) and was survived by 2 sons, 5 daughters, 3 sisters, 9 grandchildren, 8 great-grandchildren, and a host of other relatives) [Berkley Memorial Cemetery]

Edwards, Rodney Lee, "Dad's No. 1 Son" September 26, 1961 – October 22, 1992 (inscribed "In Loving Memory, Our Son and Brother, We loved you but God loved you best") [Chestnut Grove A. M. E. Church Cemetery, formerly LaGrange Cemetery at Rocks]

Edwards, Wiley Edward December 25, 1884 – December 26, 1962 [Asbury Cemetery]

Ellender, Mary July 5, 1875 –   [Green Spring U. M. Church Cemetery]

Ellis, Daniel May 3, 1935 – November 18, 1935 (no tombstone; death certificate stated he was "Twin #2" of James Ellis and Elonar Richardson, of Havre de Grace) [St. James United Cemetery]

Ellis, Elmira May 9, 1907 – October 4, 1940 (no tombstone; death certificate stated she was the daughter of John Richardson and Harriett Leggar, and married James Ellis, of Havre de Grace) [St. James United Cemetery]

Ellis, James Parker 17 Aug 1890 – June 25, 1944 (no tombstone; death certificate stated he was the son of James Ellis, mother unknown, and the widowed husband of Elmira Ellis; he died at home in Havre de Grace; informant was Miss Rosetta Ellis, of Bel Air; military records stated he was inducted into the Army during World War I on August 23 1918 and was honorably discharged on December 13, 1918) [St. James United Cemetery]

Ellis, John F. Jr. 1951-1981 [St. James United Cemetery]

Ellis, Mary C. January 19, 1874 – October 28, 1924 (no tombstone; death certificate stated she was married and died in Havre de Grace, but her parents were unknown to informant Jerry Ellis) [St. James United Cemetery]

Ellis, Toby, "Beloved Father" 1898-1973 [St. James United Cemetery]

Emanuel, Betty Jean neé Souter May 26, 1930 – February 16, 1992 (inscribed "Sacred to the Memory of" and "Her ways were ways of pleasantness and all her paths were peace;" James Dorsey Card File, African American Obituaries, maintained at the Historical Society of Harford County, has two cards with obituaries from *The Aegis* on February 26, 1992 and March 4, 1992 stating she was born in Pontotoc, MS, married James Emanuel in 1953, lived in Peoria, IL and moved to Harford County about 30 years ago; she lived in Aberdeen and died at Harford Memorial Hospital, survived by three sons, eight brothers and two sisters) [Berkley Memorial Cemetery]

Emproso, Marie Ann April 15, 1947 – March 31, 2008 (inscribed "In Loving Memory" with her photo) [St. James United Cemetery]

Emproso, William Peter May 18, 1935 – March 13, 1985, MSgt., U.S. Army, Vietnam [St. James United Cemetery]

English, Joseph W. 1900-1981 (copied in 1987, but not found in 2018; James Dorsey Card File, African American Obituaries, maintained at the Historical Society of Harford County, has a funeral card for him prepared by the Howard K. McComas III Funeral Home stating Joseph William English was born January 1, 1900 and died December 31, 1981) [Mt. Zion U. M. Church Cemetery]

English, Pearl 1895-1935 [Chestnut Grove A. M. E. Church Cemetery, formerly LaGrange Cemetery at Rocks]

Ennis (tombstone with no names and no dates) [St. James United Cemetery]

Ennis, Samuel J. April – (blank), 1867 – October 28, 1943 (no tombstone; death certificate stated he was born in Mardella Spring, MD, the son of Saul Ennis, mother unknown, and married Annie ----; informant was Annie Ennis, of Havre de Grace) [St. James United Cemetery]

Evans, Clinton E. 1884-1959 (on same tombstone with Mae B. Evans) [Fairview A. M. E. Church Cemetery]

Evans, Elsie R. August 31, 1909 – June 7, 2004 (on same tombstone with Menzo Evans; obituary and photo in *The Aegis* on June 16, 2004 stated she was born in Perryman in what is now part of Aberdeen Proving Ground, the daughter of Ida May Christy and John Edward Reed; "Miss Elsie: operated a mini-laundry specializing in uniforms for the Army, established a kindergarten class at the Masonic Temple in Havre de Grace, graduated from the Apex Beauty School in Baltimore and operated her own hair salon; she lived in Havre de Grace and died at the Citizens Nursing Home, survived by a daughter, eight grandchildren and a godson; she was preceded in death by husband Menzo Evans, a daughter and a grandson) [Union U. M. Church Cemetery]

Evans, Jarrett died December 6, 1888, age not given (an article in *The Aegis* on December 14, 1888 stated he was a respectable colored man who died in a fire at the house of James Amos near Federal Hill; place of burial was not stated [possibly William C. Rice Memorial Cemetery, St. James U. M. Church]

Evans, Mae B. 1900-1984 (on same tombstone with Clinton E. Evans; obituary in *The Aegis* on November 29, 1984 stated Emma Mae Buchanan Evans, of Madonna, died November 25, 1984, age 84, at Harford Memorial

Hospital; she was the widow of Clinton E. Evans and survived by a daughter Mary T. Murray, three grandchildren and a sister Mamie Johnson) [Fairview A. M. E. Church Cemetery]

Evans, Mary Oleta died January 3, 1892, age not given (no tombstone; death notice in *The Aegis* on January 15, 1892 stated she was the wife of David Evans and a member of Ames M. E. Church; she died at the home of Mrs. Elizabeth G. Lee, of Bel Air; buried at Tabernacle Cem.) [Tabernacle Mount Zion U. M. Church Cemetery]

Evans, Menzo February 10, 1906 – January 19, 1985 (on same tombstone with Elsie R. Evans; obituary in The Aegis stated he was the son of Menzo Evans, Sr. and Angronie Evans, and was employed by the Harford County Board of Education; he lived in Havre de Grace and died at Harford Memorial Hospital, survived by his wife, three daughters, a sister, two grandchildren and four great-grandchildren) [Union U. M. Church Cemetery]

Evans, Thelma Watters (dates unknown, but probably buried here because her husband William R. Evans is buried here) [Fairview A. M. E. Church Cemetery]

Evans, William Ralph 1931-1979 (small metal funeral home marker; obituary in *The Aegis* on January 11, 1979 stated he was the husband of Thelma Watters Evans, lived at 5623 Bellgwynn Road, Glen Arm, was employed at Stenersen Corp. in Cockeysville and died at St. Joseph's Hospital on January 5, 1979, survived by his wife, a son William C. Evans, a daughter Veronica Evans, stepmother Emma Evans, his mother Agnes Edwards and a sister Mary Murray) [Fairview A. M. E. Church Cemetery]

Ezell, Robert Eugene September 6, 1927 – November 2, 2004, 1SG, U.S. Army, Vietnam [St. James United Cemetery]

Fairfax, Henry F. May – (blank), 1860 – March 17, 1915 (no tombstone; death certificate stated he was the son of Furton Fairfax and Lucy Block, all born in Virginia; he was married, worked as a laborer and died in Reckord; informant was Jane Fairfax, of Fallston) [Tabernacle Mount Zion U. M. Church Cemetery]

Faison, Keziah August 21, 1879 – February 13, 1949 (no tombstone; death certificate stated she was born in Faison, NC, and was the unmarried daughter of Henry Faison and Susan Bryant) [St. James United Cemetery]

Fauntleroy, Catherine M. November 25, 1905 – July 20, 1996 [William C. Rice Memorial Cemetery, St. James U. M. Church]

Fax, Audrey L. August 4, 1937 – November 4, 1937 (no tombstone; death certificate stated she was born in Aberdeen, the daughter of John H. Fax, born in Baltimore, and Pearl C. Giles, born in Aberdeen; she died at home at Mt. Calvary in Aberdeen RFD; informant was her father) [Mt. Calvary U. A. M. E. Church Cemetery]

Fax, Berkley K. Sr. June 14, 1936 – February 6, 2015 (inscribed "In Loving Memory" and "Rest In Peace" and "When you live in the hearts of those you love, remember then you never die.") [Berkley Memorial Cemetery]

Felder, Margaret Johnson died June 16, 1978, age 52 (no tombstone; obituary in *The Aegis* on June 29, 1978 stated she was the daughter of Joseph and Alice Johnson, lived in Fallston, moved to Baltimore, married Benjamin Felder, worked as an engineering technician at Edgewood Arsenal for over 30 years, died at Johns Hopkins Hospital in Baltimore, and was survived by her mother Alice Johnson and a step-son Ronald Felder) [Tabernacle Mount Zion U. M. Church Cemetery]

Fennell, Esther S. 1916-1992 [Berkley Memorial Cemetery]

Ferdinand, Albertha A. July 21, 1946 – March 1, 1998 (tombstone; "A. Ferdinand" owned a lot in section 8) [Mt. Calvary U. A. M. E. Church Cemetery]

Ferguson, John Rogers February 2, 1945 – August 11, 1977 [John Wesley U. M. E. Church Cemetery in Abingdon]

Ferguson, Neal Douglas May 9, 1943 – October 18, 1987 [John Wesley U. M. E. Church Cemetery in Abingdon]

Ferguson, Neal H. 1916-1974 [John Wesley U. M. E. Church Cemetery in Abingdon]

Ferrell, Mary Bowser 1911-1985 [Union U. M. Church Cemetery]

Fickens, Phillip C. July 1, 1930 – December 3, 2008, U.S. Army [St. James United Cemetery]

Fields, Anna Maria died February 19, 1890 in her 93rd year (no tombstone; obituary in *The Aegis* on February 28, 1890 stated she died at *Rangers' Lodge* where she had a been a devoted servant in the Williams family for half a century and was never known to tell a lie) [Asbury Cemetery]

Fields, Diane November 17, 1945 – November 26, 1945 (no tombstone; death certificate stated she was the premature daughter of Leon Fields and Margaret Black, of Aberdeen) [St. James United Cemetery]

Fields, Ethel T. November 23, 1907 – March 16, 1976 (tombstone; obituary in *The Aegis* on March 26, 1976 stated Ethel Elizabeth (Turner) Fields, of 2412 W. Lombard Sr., Baltimore, died at Maryland Hospital; she was a clerk-typist for Holdtight Manufacturing Co. and was survived by a daughter with whom she made her home (her husband was not mentioned), a brother, a sister, three grandchildren, four great-grandchildren and five nieces) [Fairview A. M. E. Church Cemetery]

Fields, Marie Williams June 2, 1937 – March 23, 1998 (no tombstone; James Dorsey Card File, African American Obituaries, maintained at the Historical Society of Harford County, has a card for her with an obituary from *The Aegis* on April 8, 1998 stating she was born in White Marsh, the daughter of the late Leon and Julia Williams, and married Alvin S. Fields on August 19, 1957; she first worked for the Army Chemical Center in Edgewood, was later employed by the Baltimore County Board of Education and lastly worked for Honeywell, Inc.; she formerly lived in Edgewood, held office in the United Methodist Women's Society and died at her home in Baltimore, survived by two sons, four daughters, eight grandchildren and a host of other family and friends) [Asbury Cemetery]

Fink, Portia November 2, 1950 – February 23, 2011 (inscribed with a quote from John 3:16) [Berkley Memorial Cemetery]

Finney, Pearlis L. January 1, 1928 – December 27, 2019 [Berkley Memorial Cemetery]

Fisher, ---- stillborn female on October 19, 1922 (no tombstone; death certificate stated she died at Magnolia, the daughter of William Fisher and Nettie Gilbert; all born in Maryland) [Foster's Hill Cemetery]

Fisher, ----, November 1, 1923 – November 6, 1923 (no tombstone; death certificate stated he was the son of Jerry Fisher and Mamie Bond, of Benson, all born in Harford Co.; informant was her father) [Tabernacle Mount Zion U. M. Church Cemetery]

Fisher, Allen Joe 1947-2012 (tombstone, but his year of death was not inscribed; obituary and photo in *The Aegis* on January 11, 2012 stated Allen Joseph Fisher was born on October 18, 1947 in Havre de Grace, the son of Roland and Katherine Fisher, lived in Bel Air and died at Upper Chesapeake Medical Center on January 6, 2012, survived by his brother Charles "Ike" Peaker and three sisters Ann Waters, Shirley Akins and Janice Matthews) [Mt. Zion U. M. Church Cemetery]

Fisher, Ancle A. 1918-1980 [Fairview A. M. E. Church Cemetery]

Fisher, Creolia A. October 22, 1917 – January 13, 2016 (on same tombstone with Dunsen C. Fisher) [William C. Rice Memorial Cemetery, St. James U. M. Church]

Fisher, Douglas January 21, 1919 – July 26, 1919 (no tombstone; death certificate stated he was the son of Richard Watters and Stella Fisher, all born in Maryland, and he died at Wilna; informant was his mother Stella Fisher, of Benson) [Tabernacle Mount Zion U. M. Church Cemetery]

Fisher, Dunsen C. August 24, 1916 – August 28, 1989 (on same tombstone with Creolia A. Fisher; obituary in *The Aegis* on August 30, 1989 stated Dunsen Calvin Fisher was born in Rocks, the son of Harry and Laura Fisher, married Creolia Walton, worked as a plumber, and lived in New Park, PA; he died at York Hospital and was survived by one brother, one sister, four grandchildren and ten great-grandchildren) [William C. Rice Memorial Cemetery, St. James U. M. Church]

Fisher, Edward (owned a lot in section 16 some time after 1951) [Mt. Calvary U. A. M. E. Church Cemetery]

Fisher, Elsie O. died August 8, 1991, age 96 (no tombstone; obituary in *The Aegis* on August 14, 1991 stated she was born in Blythedale, daughter of Oliver Fisher and Annie Hines, spent most of her life in Havre de Grace and died at home; there were no immediate survivors) [Asbury Cemetery]

Fisher, Frances K., "Mommo" 1908-1981 (tombstone; obituary and photo in *The Aegis* stated Frances Katherine Fisher was born in Harford Co., the daughter of Stephen Peaker and Sarah White, and was the widow of Roland S. Fisher; she lived in Bel Air and died at Fallston General Hospital, survived by four sons, four daughters, two sisters, a brother, 20 grandchildren and 6 great-grandchildren) [Mt. Zion U. M. Church Cemetery]

Fisher, George died September 23, 1924 (no tombstone; death certificate stated he was the unmarried son of George Fisher and Frances Fisher, both born in Virginia and he was born in Maryland; informant was Sarah Wilmer, of 20 Slong St. (S. Long St.?), Philadelphia, PA) [Union U. M. Church Cemetery]

Fisher, Gladys Pearl 1913-1977 [Chestnut Grove A. M. E. Church Cemetery, formerly LaGrange Cemetery at Rocks]

Fisher, Herbert A. December 22, 1930 – September 13, 1987 [Fairview A. M. E. Church Cemetery]

Fisher, Janie Rebecca August 7, 1904 – September 4, 1943 (no tombstone; death certificate stated she was born in Harford Co., married, divorced, and died at 111 Alice Ann St. in Bel Air; her parents were Samuel Taylor and Adeline Jackson, of Maryland; informant was Adeline Taylor) [Hendon Hill Cemetery]

Fisher, Jeremiah April 28, 1875 – April 17, 1933 (no tombstone; death certificate stated he was born in Harford Co., the son of Charles Fisher and Mary Ellen Kell, both born in Maryland; he married Mamie ----, worked as a laborer and died in Benson; informant was John Waters, of Bel Air) [Tabernacle Mount Zion U. M. Church Cemetery]

Fisher, John Walter died January 23, 1977, age 70 (no tombstone; obituary in *The Aegis* stated he lived in Street, worked as a farmer, was married to Gladys Jones, and died in Baltimore, survived by his wife, his mother Mrs. Laura D. Fisher, three foster sons, three brothers, four sisters, four nieces and a nephew) [Chestnut Grove A. M. E. Church Cemetery, formerly LaGrange Cemetery at Rocks]

Fisher, Joseph 1881-1961 [Union U. M. Church Cemetery]

Fisher, Joshua E. 1905-1969 (on same tombstone with Vella Mae Fisher; obituary in *The Aegis* on May 22, 1969 stated Joshua Eugene Fisher, husband of Vella A. Fisher, died May 16, 1969 and was survived by his wife, one sister, one brother and seven children) [Asbury Cemetery]

Fisher, Laura D. June 4, 1883 – March 21, 1978 (tombstone; obituary in *The Aegis* on March 30, 1978 stated Laura D. Fisher, formerly of Rocks, and widow of Harry W. Fisher, died at the Wallingford Nursing Home, Media, PA, survived by a daughter Margaret Lee, 3 sons Marshall Fisher, Dunsen C. Fisher and Ancle A. Fisher, 6 grandchildren, 3 foster grandchildren and 17 great-grandchildren) [Chestnut Grove A. M. E. Church Cemetery, formerly LaGrange Cemetery at Rocks]

Fisher, Lidia February 21, 1900 – June 16, 1944 (no tombstone; death certificate stated she was the daughter of George Henry Williams and Ellen Gibson, and the wife of Charles Fisher) [Union U. M. Church Cemetery]

Fisher, Louisa, "Mother" January 12, 1837 – June 25, 1902 [Tabernacle Mount Zion U. M. Church Cemetery]

Fisher, Mary Ellen September 27, 1848 – January 31, 1921 (no tombstone; death certificate stated she was born in Harford Co., the daughter of Basil Kell, born in Maryland, and Moriah Bond, born in Harford Co., and she died a widow near Wilna; informant was Thomas Fisher, of Churchville) [Tabernacle Mount Zion U. M. Church Cemetery]

Fisher, Maude Ann died July 20, 1982, age 68 (no tombstone; obituary in *The Aegis* stated she was born in Port Deposit, the daughter of Valentine and Hannah Quomony, and was married (name of husband not given), lived in Havre de Grace and died at Harford Memorial Hospital, survived by a daughter, a brother, two sisters, 7 grandchildren and 2 great-grandchildren) [Berkley Memorial Cemetery]

Fisher, Mildred D. 1920-2005 (tombstone, but her year of death was not inscribed; obituary and photo in *The Aegis* on February 2, 2005 stated Mildred Lucille Fisher was born in Harford County, the daughter of the late Charles Greene and Ida Harris, and she was preceded in death by her husband Ancle A. Fisher; she lived in Cooptown and died at Country View Elder Care on January 28, 2005) [Fairview A. M. E. Church Cemetery]

Fisher, Roland Shadrick September 6, 1942 – February 9, 1993, SP4, U.S. Army, Vietnam (tombstone; James

Dorsey Card File, African American Obituaries, maintained at the Historical Society of Harford County, has a card with obituary from *The Aegis* on February 17, 1993 stating "Dub" was a native of Bel Air and the son of the late Roland S. Fisher, Sr. and Katherine F. Fisher; he was noted for his bass voice and sang with a group called "The Five Lloyds" and with the Asbury Church Choir; he lived in Joppatowne and died at Fallston General Hospital, survived by his good friend Betty Johnson, a daughter, a son, four sisters, three brothers, and a granddaughter) [Mt. Zion U. M. Church Cemetery]

Fisher, Sarah Viola April 1, 1916 – January 31, 1918 (no tombstone; death certificate stated she was the daughter of Jerry Fisher and Mamie Bond, all born in Harford Co., and lived at Wilna; informant was her father) [Tabernacle Mount Zion U. M. Church Cemetery]

Fisher, Shadrach R. Sr. 1902-1959 [Mt. Zion U. M. Church Cemetery]

Fisher, Vella Mae 1930-1971 (on the same tombstone with Joshua E. Fisher; obituary in *The Aegis* on August 5, 1971 stated Vella Moses Fisher was born in Grayson Co., VA, the daughter of the late Fred and Vella Moses, and was the widow of Joshua Eugene Fisher; she lived on Archer St. in Bel Air and died in an automobile accident on July 30, 1971, survived by three sons, six daughters, four grandchildren, three brothers and three sisters) [Asbury Cemetery]

Fisher, Vernon Elmer died July 2, 1990, age 67 (no tombstone; obituary in *The Aegis* stated he was born in Bel Air, the son of Ella Fisher and John Brown, served in the Army in World War II, retired from Edgewood Arsenal as a materials segregator, lived in Cooptown, was formerly married, and died at Fallston General Hospital, survived by a daughter and a sister) [Fairview A. M. E. Church Cemetery]

Fisher, William, "Father" August 17, 1835 – April 8, 1903 (tombstone; death certificate stated he was born in Harford Co., worked as a farmer, married Louisa Fisher and died at Reckord on April 3, 1903, age 66; parents' names were not given; informant was his daughter Mary Fairfax) [Tabernacle Mount Zion U. M. Church Cemetery]

Fleetwood, Arthur 1924-1988 (handwritten on a flat cement slab) [St. James United Cemetery]

Fleming, Clarence September 9, 1896 – August 10, 1912 (no tombstone; death certificate stated he was the son of Eli Fleming and Mary Bond, all born in Maryland; informant was his mother Mary Bond, of Forest Hill) [Fairview A. M. E. Church Cemetery]

Fleming, John H. May 2, 1928 – January 8, 2018, Cpl., U.S. Army, Korea (inscribed "Everlasting Love") [Berkley Memorial Cemetery]

Fleming, Katie E. 1860 – October 26, 1909 (tombstone did not give her age, but death certificate stated she died at Darlington on October 25, 1909, age 49; her maiden name was Bailey and she was born in Chester Co., PA and married Albert Fleming; informant was her son George Fleming) [Berkley Memorial Cemetery]

Fleming, William Howard February 6, 1927 – June 27, 1990 (inscribed "Walk In The Light") [St. James United Cemetery]

Flemming, Melvin February 16, 1931 – June 17, 1931 (no tombstone; death certificate stated he was born in Maryland, the son of John Flemming, born in Washington, D.C., and Hattie Branson, born in Maryland; he died at home near Aberdeen; informant was his father) [Mt. Calvary U. A. M. E. Church Cemetery]

Flemmings, James W. September 4, 1929 – April 6, 1997, Cpl., U.S. Army, Korea [Mt. Calvary U. A. M. E. Church Cemetery]

Flemmings, Sarah T. died February 6, 1919, age 65 (no tombstone; death certificate stated she was born in Baltimore, the daughter of Amous Anderson, born in Maryland, but mother's name was unknown to informant Hannah Chase, of Fallston; she was a widow and died at Benson) [Tabernacle Mount Zion U. M. Church Cemetery]

Flemmings, Simeon D. died August 17, 1907, age 22 years and 1 month (no tombstone; death certificate stated he was born in Harford Co., the son of James Flemmings and Sarah T. Anderson, both born in Baltimore Co., and was a laborer who lived and died at Benson; obituary in *The Aegis* on August 23, 1907 stated "Simeon Fleming" was a highly regarded young man of near Benson who died a few days ago and was buried at the

Tabernacle colored church) [Tabernacle Mount Zion U. M. Church Cemetery]

Fletcher, Infant stillborn female on February 12, 1917 (no tombstone; death certificate stated she was the daughter of Moses Fletcher, born in Havre de Grace, and Martha Parsons, born in Delaware, and they lived in Havre de Grace) [St. James United Cemetery]

Fletcher, Infant stillborn male on May 9, 1927 (no tombstone; death certificate stated he was the son of Moses Fletcher, born in Havre de Grace, and Martha Parsons, born in Delaware, and they lived in Havre de Grace) [St. James United Cemetery]

Fletcher, James March 4, 1847 – September 19, 1942 (no tombstone; death certificate stated he was born in Washington, D.C., the son of John Fletcher and Margaret ----, birth places unknown; he married Annabelle --- and was a local preacher; informant was Walter Fletcher, of Havre de Grace) [St. James United Cemetery]

Fletcher, Margurite May 9, 1918 – June 6, 1918 (no tombstone; death certificate stated she was the daughter of Moses Fletcher, born in Havre de Grace, and Martha Parsons, born in Delaware, and they lived in Havre de Grace) [St. James United Cemetery]

Fletcher, Virginia Ethel Louise July 1, 1931 – December 1, 1931 (no tombstone; death certificate stated she was the daughter of Moses Fletcher, born in Havre de Grace, and Martha Fletcher (actually Parsons), born in Delaware, and they lived in Havre de Grace) [St. James United Cemetery]

Fletcher, Walter 1912-1972 [Union U. M. Church Cemetery]

Flint, Julia A. aged 13 years (no dates) [Old Union Chapel M. E. Church Cemetery]

Flood, Lucinda 1872-1925 (tombstone) [John Wesley U. M. E. Church Cemetery in Abingdon]

Fluitt, Johnnie Robert, "Loving Husband, Father and Grandfather" January 12, 1940 – December 15, 2012, SFC, U.S. Army. Vietnam, Bronze Star Medal [Berkley Memorial Cemetery]

Foarman, Lillie M. May 9, 1914 – September 9, 1915 (no tombstone; death certificate stated she died on September 9, 1915, age 1 year and 4 months, in Bel Air, and was the daughter of Clay Foarman and Frances Bryan; all were born in Harford Co.) [Hendon Hill Cemetery]

Footman, Flora L. 1900-1983 (on same tombstone with Gussie R. Chesnut) [Union U. M. Church Cemetery]

Foreman, Albert J. died March 13, 1914, age about 58 (no tombstone; death certificate stated he was the unmarried son of Jerry Foreman and ---- (unknown), and died in Havre de Grace) [Gravel Hill Cemetery]

Foreman, George died December 9, 1922, age 73 (no tombstone; death certificate stated he was born in Maryland, but his parents' names and places of birth were not known by informant William R. Nixon, of Sewell RFD; he was single, unemployed and died at Sewell) [John Wesley U. M. E. Church Cemetery in Abingdon]

Foreman, Mark died July 18, 1931, age 65 (no tombstone; death certificate stated he was a widower and died in Havre de Grace Hospital; his parents were Stephenson Foreman and Margaret Bond and they were all born in Maryland; informant was Alice Johnson, of Bel Air) [Hendon Hill Cemetery]

Foreman, Philip J. April 11, 1845 – April 11, 1912 (no tombstone; death certificate stated he was a widower and the son of Isaac Foreman and Milky Foreman, all born in Maryland) [Union U. M. Church Cemetery]

Forest, Brian K., "Son, Father, Brother" January 8, 1967 – November 18, 2003 (inscribed "In Loving Memory") [Berkley Memorial Cemetery]

Forman, Frances September 17, 1895 – October 24, 1932 (no tombstone; death certificate stated she was the wife of Clay Forman; she was born in Bel Air and died in Havre de Grace Hospital; her father was Bryan Forman and her mother was unknown, according to informant Clay Forman) [Hendon Hill Cemetery]

Forman, Margaret died August 23, 1918, age about 40 (no tombstone; death certificate stated she was the daughter of Henry Forman and Margaret Forman, all born in Maryland' she was single and died at home in Darlington; informant was S. S. Holloway, of Darlington) [Berkley Memorial Cemetery]

Foster, Anthony C. 1969-1979 [St. James United Cemetery]

Foster, Eugene July 15, 1899 – May 31, 1974, Pvt., U.S. Army (tombstone; obituary in *The Aegis* on June 6, 1974 stated he was born in Christy, VA, the son of George and Ann Foster, and husband of Margaret E. Foster; he served in World War I and worked as a mail carrier for 13 years before coming to Maryland where he was employed at Edgewood Arsenal; he lived at 559 Lewis St., Havre de Grace, and died in Delaware at the Wilmington VAMC, survived by his wife, a step-son Hanson Howard, of Alabama, and four grandchildren) [St. James United Cemetery]

Foster, Mark Edward died January 27, 1982, age 25 (obituary in *The Aegis* on February 4, 1982 stated he was born in Havre de Grace, the son of Louis Foster, of Philadelphia, PA and the late Mildred Webster Foster; he lived in Aberdeen, and died at the John L. Deaton Medical Center in Baltimore, survived by his father, 2 brothers, 2 sisters, maternal grandparents Alvert *(sic)* and Rosia Webster, 4 aunts and 3 uncles) [Union U. M. Church Cemetery]

Foster, Mary December 20, 1903 – January 2, 1919 (no tombstone; death certificate stated she was born in Mississippi, the daughter of George Foster and Mattie Marshall, both born in Alabama, and she died in Havre de Grace Hospital) [St. James United Cemetery]

Fountain, Lena B. March 19, 1910 – June 1, 1988 (on same tombstone with Mary B.) [Asbury Cemetery]

Fraling, Alverta L. 1898-1973 (on same tombstone with Edgar B.) [Mt. Calvary U. A. M. E. Church Cemetery]

Fraling, Edgar B. 1900-   (on same tombstone with Alverta L.) [Mt. Calvary U. A. M. E. Church Cemetery]

Francis, Caroline died – 27(?), 1893(?), age 40(?) (mostly illegible marker broken into three pieces with a large cross inscribed in top half of it; "Erected by her daughter Jane Berry" inscribed at bottom; 1880 Census stated Caroline, mulatto, age 27, was wife of Jacob H. Francis, age 27, black; marriage records indicate Jacob H. Francis married Caroline Evans in 1874) [Hendon Hill Cemetery]

Francis, Eliza Jane 1883-1958 (copied in 1987, but not found in 2018) [Fairview A. M. E. Church Cemetery]

Franklin, James 1920-1974 (on same tombstone with Marion Franklin; obituary in *The Aegis* stated he was the husband of Marion Franklin, lived at 105 N. Washington St., Havre de Grace, and died at Harford Memorial Hospital on May 8, 1974, survived by his wife, two sons, one daughter and eight grandchildren) [St. James United Cemetery]

Franklin, Marion 1923-1975 (on same tombstone with James Franklin; obituary in *The Aegis* stated Marian *(sic)* Elizabeth Franklin was the daughter of the late George Bishop and Jane Dutton, and the widow of James E. Franklin; she lived at 630 S. Freedom Lane, Havre de Grace, was a retired cook from Bainbridge Naval Station and died at Harford Memorial Hospital on January 13, 1975; she was survived by two sons, one daughter, two brothers, four sisters and ten grandchildren) [St. James United Cemetery]

Franklin, Mary Alice December 10, 1875 – May 24, 1945 (no tombstone; death certificate stated she was born in Edgewood, the daughter of Daniel Peters and Missouri Turner, both born in Maryland; she was married to Peter Franklin, lived in Magnolia and died a widow in an institution or hospital in Edgewood after being there only 1 hour and 25 minutes; informant was Blanche Demby, of Magnolia; she was buried in Ebenezer Baptist Cemetery at Magnolia) [Foster's Hill Cemetery]

Franklin, Peter February 27, 1859 – April 6, 1921 (no tombstone; death certificate stated he was born in Maryland, as were his parents, but informant Alice Franklin did not know their names; he lived at Magnolia and worked as a laborer; he was shot and killed near Edgewood and buried in Foster Hill Cemetery at Magnolia; brief articles about the murder appeared in *The Aegis* on April 15, 1921, April 22, 1921 and June 24, 1921) [Foster's Hill Cemetery]

Franklyn, Sarah A. 1880-1952 [Union U. M. Church Cemetery]

Fraser, Charles L. September 23, 1861 – September 8, 1911 (no tombstone; death certificate stated he was the married son of George Fraser and Hester May, all born in Virginia; he worked as a cook and died in Havre de Grace) [St. James United Cemetery]

Frazier, Elezabeth February – (blank), 1853 – August 18, 1912 (no tombstone; death certificate stated she was born in Richmond, VA, the daughter od George Dixon and Elizabeth Smith; she was a school teacher and died a widow in Havre de Grace; informant was Alice Smell) [St. James United Cemetery]

Frederick, Alfred died March 14, 1906, age 80 (no tombstone; death certificate stated he was the son of Washington and Emily Frederick, married Eliza ----, worked as a farmer and died at Mountain; informant was John W. Watters, a non-relative; place of burial not given [probably Mt. Zion U. M. Church Cemetery]

Frederick, Charlotte, "To Our Mother" August 17, 1809 – October 10, 1888 [John Wesley U. M. E. Church Cemetery in Abingdon]

Frederick, Eliza died February 22, 1909, age 70 (no tombstone; death certificate stated she was the daughter of Santa James, both born in Harford Co.; mother's name not known to informant Joseph Smart, her nephew; she was the widow of Alfred Frederick and died at Mountain; place of burial not given [probably Mt. Zion U. M. Church Cemetery]

Freeman, Mary P. P., wife of Alexander Freeman, 1885-1913 (tombstone was also inscribed "Asleep In Jesus;" death certificate stated Mary Freeman was the married daughter of Frederick Tildon and Hattie Ransom, all born in Harford Co.; informant was Benjamin Christy, of Havre de Grace) [Union U. M. Church Cemetery]

Freemen, Thelma August 3, 1924 – August 9, 1925 (no tombstone; death certificate stated she was the daughter of Leonard Freemen and Olivia Skinner, all born in Maryland; informant was her father, of Havre de Grace) [Skinner Cemetery]

French, Harriett January 23, 1853 – October 10, 1911 (no tombstone; death certificate stated she was the married daughter of Harry Kane, but her mother was not known to informant Sarah French, her daughter, of Havre de Grace) [St. James United Cemeter

French, Henretta August 10, 1892 – December 26, 1946 (no tombstone; death certificate stated she was the unmarried daughter of Frank Holmes and Harriett French; informant was Mrs. Esther Barnes, of Havre de Grace) [St. James United Cemetery]

Frisby, Aquilla 1897-1967 (tombstone; buried in section 47; obituary in *The Aegis* on April 27, 1967 stated he was the son of George Frisby and Harriet Green, married Hazel Barnes, lived at 419 Baltimore Street in Aberdeen and died at home on April 24, 1967, survived by his wife, a stepson William Oliver Dorsey, Jr., a brother Charles Frisby and a sister Mrs. Kate Williams) [Union U. M. Church Cemetery]

Frisby, Charles H. 1904-1973 (tombstone; obituary in *The Aegis* stated Charles Henry "Bunny" Frisby was the son of George and Hariett Frisby and was a retired trackman from the Penn-Central Railroad; he died at home at 427 Baltimore St., Aberdeen, and was survived by his wife Hazel V. Frisby, one sister Mrs. Catherine "Kate" Williams, one niece and two nephews) [Union U. M. Church Cemetery]

Frisby, Charles W. August 1, 1872 – May 2, 1912 (no tombstone; death certificate stated he was the married son of Joseph Frisby and Mary A. Clark, all born in Harford Co.) [Union U. M. Church Cemetery]

Frisby, Clarence November 5, 1884 – April 29, 1932 (no tombstone; death certificate stated he was born in Aberdeen, son of George Frisby and Harrett Green, both born in Maryland; he married Blanch Lomax, worked as a day laborer and while employed as a stable man he was injured by a runaway mule and died at Havre de Grace Hospital; informant was his wife) [Mt. Calvary U. A. M. E. Church Cemetery]

Frisby, Ellerie died August 1, 1996, age 81 (no tombstone; James Dorsey Card File, African American Obituaries, maintained at the Historical Society of Harford County, has a card with obituary from *The Aegis* on August 14, 1996 stating she was born in Elizabethtown, NJ, the daughter of John Harris and Emma Harris Matthews, and married Herbert Frisby in 1950, having moved to Havre de Grace in 1945; she died at the Bel Air Rehabilitation Center, survived by a son, a brother, three sisters, a granddaughter and two nieces, two nephews, 18 great-nieces and nephews and great-great-nieces and nephews) [Mt. Calvary U. A. M. E. Church Cemetery]

Frisby, Hazel V. 1909-2003 [Union U. M. Church Cemetery]

Frisby, James Hill died August 16, 1994, age 76 (no tombstone; James Dorsey Card File, African American Obituaries, maintained at the Historical Society of Harford County, has a card with obituary from *The Aegis* on August 31, 1994 stating he was born in Harford County, the son of George Frisby and Margaret Townsend; he worked as a handyman and died at Lorien Riverside Nursing Home, survived by four nephews and many other relatives) [Union U. M. Church Cemetery]

Frisby, Joe Herbert May 14, 1914 – August 28, 1914 (no tombstone; death certificate stated he was the son of Joe Frisby and Virgia *(sic)* Ridgley, all born in Harford Co.; they lived near Aberdeen) [Mt. Calvary U. A. M. E. Church Cemetery]

Frisby, Joseph 1885-1950 (copied in 1987, but not found in 2018) [Mt. Calvary U. A. M. E. Church Cemetery]

Frisby, Olive November 9, 1916 – November 19, 1916 (no tombstone; death certificate stated she was the daughter of Joseph Frizby *(sic)* and Vergis Gibson, all born in Harford Co., and lived near Aberdeen) [Mt. Calvary U. A. M. E. Church Cemetery]

Frisby, William died December 20, 1966, age 76 (no tombstone; obituary in *The Aegis* on December 29, 1966 stated he was the son of the late George Frisby and Harriet Green and died at home at 319 Baltimore St. in Aberdeen; he was survived by 2 brothers and 2 sisters) [Mt. Calvary U. A. M. E. Church Cemetery]

Gaddy, James E. December 27, 1897 – April 17, 1986 [Berkley Memorial Cemetery]

Gaddy, Winnie J. February 1, 1908 – September 22, 1974 [Berkley Memorial Cemetery]

Gaines, Cora 1901-1983 (inscribed "and Family") [Union U. M. Church Cemetery]

Gaines, Harriett 1860 – March 23, 1945 (no tombstone; death certificate stated she was born in Buckingham Co, VA, the daughter of Lee Luckett and Martha ----, both born in Virginia, and the widow of Rev. W. H. Gaines; informant was Mrs. Rosa Gordon, of Havre de Grace RFD 1) [Union U. M. Church Cemetery]

Gaines, William H. (Rev.), "Husband" 1865-1921 ("Asleep In Jesus") [Union U. M. Church Cemetery]

Gaither, Eva February 25, 1897 – December 3, 1924 (no tombstone; death certificate stated she was the married daughter of George Curtis and Belle Jackson, of Havre de Grace) [St. James United Cemetery]

Gaither, Sarah J. (Jane) May 4, 1939 – May 20, 1990 (on the same tombstone with Lealer B. Ambush that is inscribed "Mom, Mighty Matriarch, and Jane, Selfless Sister, Our Blessed Treasure, Rest In Everlasting Love Where The Shadows Fall") [Mt. Zion U. M. Church Cemetery]

Galloway, Alfred December 18, 1906 – August 22, 1988, U.S. Army, World War II [St. James United Cemetery]

Galloway, Alice L. 1905-1982 [St. James United Cemetery]

Galloway, Benjamin April 30, 1882 – January 11, 1936 (no tombstone; death certificate stated he was the unmarried son of Benjamin Galloway and Maria Mitchell, of Havre de Grace, and died in Havre de Grace Hospital; informant was William Galloway) [St. James United Cemetery]

Galloway, Frank died January 27, 1888, age about 18 (no tombstone; death notice in *The Aegis* on February 3, 1888 stated he worked for Mr. Burton at Long Green and was taken ill; he was removed to his mother's house on Silas Baldwin's place near Jarrettsville and died the next day; his place of burial was not given [possibly William C. Rice Memorial Cemetery, St. James U. M. Church]

Galloway, Galdys E. September 14, 1924 -   (inscribed "In Loving Memory") [Berkley Memorial Cemetery]

Galloway, Harriett February 14, 1880 – June 24, 1949 (no tombstone; death certificate stated she was the daughter of Mose Martin and Mary French, of Havre de Grace, and died a widow; informant was Mrs. Eva Malloy) [St. James United Cemetery]

Galloway, Hattie C. July 25, 1873 – July 29, 1933 (no tombstone; death certificate stated she was the daughter of Milton Curtis, of Havre de Grace, but her mother's name was unknown to informant William Galloway, her husband) [St. James United Cemetery]

Galloway, Isaac Benjamin Jr. died July 4, 1907, age 74 (no tombstone; death certificate stated he was born in Baltimore Co., the son of Isaac Benjamin Galloway, birth place unknown, and Annie Ross, born in Havre de Grace; he married Marie ----, worked as a laborer and died in Havre de Grace; informant was his son Wilton Galloway; place of burial not given [probably St. James United Cemetery]

Galloway, James H. "Bo" 1926-1995 (handwritten on a flat cement slab; The James Dorsey Card File, African

American Obituaries, that is maintained at the Historical Society of Harford County, has a card with obituary from an unidentified newspaper on February 22, 1995 stating James Hugh "Bo" Galloway was the son of William Henry Galloway and Alice Lucille Jenkins of Havre de Grace; he served for a short time in the service and later took on many part time jobs in the county, working for Carroll's Cleaners, Tawney's Garage and Vancherie'e Inter-County Bus Lines; he died at Harford Memorial Hospital, survived by his former wife Gladys Galloway, four sisters, and two brothers]

Galloway, Louis (Rev.) 1928-2003 (small metal funeral home marker) [Clark's U. M. Church Cemetery]

Galloway, Martha Fredericks died March 17, 1945, age about 73 (no tombstone; death certificate stated she was born in Annapolis, MD, the daughter of –?-- Frederick and Caroline --?-- *(sic)* and the wife of Charlies Galloway; informant was Ethel Boston, of Havre de Grace) [St. James United Cemetery]

Galoway, Henry Franklin, son of James and Annie Galoway (dates illegible in 1987 and copyist stated the; tombstone was found leaning against a tree on south side edge of cemetery) [West Liberty Church Cemetery]

Galoway, James died March 29, 1892, age 67 (on same broken obelisk with wife Ruth Ann Galoway and inscribed "In Memory of") [West Liberty Church Cemetery]

Galoway, Ruth Ann died March 31, 1892, age 56 (on same broken obelisk with husband James Galoway and inscribed "In Memory of") [West Liberty Church Cemetery]

Gamble, Lionel Andrew June 9, 1944 – February 1, 1949 (no tombstone; death certificate stated he was the son of Robert C. Gamble and Ida May Giles, of Aberdeen Route 2) [Union U. M. Church Cemetery]

Gardner, Mary (owner a lot in section 8 some time after 1951) [Mt. Calvary U. A. M. E. Church Cemetery]

Gardner, William Edwin stillborn on February 7, 1925 (no tombstone; death certificate stated he was born and died in "Monkton, Harford Co.," the son of George Gardner, born in Baltimore Co., and Nettie Bowman, born in Frederick Co.) [Union U. M. Church Cemetery]

Gardner, William T. died April 12, 1912, age about 38 (no tombstone; death certificate stated he was born in Wilmington, DE and was the married son of William T. Gardner, born in Cecil Co., MD, but his mother was unknown to informant Mrs. Mary F. Rice, of Perryman, MD) [Union U. M. Church Cemetery]

Garey (Carey?), Helen M. 1903-1986 (hand written on a flat cement marker) [St. James United Cemetery]

Garland (name on base, but no tombstone) [St. James United Cemetery]

Garland, Clarissa Johnson, "Mother" April 19, 1907 – December 24, 1981 [St. James United Cemetery]

Garland, Susan December 26, 1868 – October 26, 1934 (no tombstone; death certificate stated she was the daughter of Henry Holmes and Mary Lawson, all born in Virginia, and the widow of Noah Garland, of Havre de Grace; informant was Hattie Rector) [St. James United Cemetery]

Garrett, Adelia August 31, 1884 – March 1, 1936 (no tombstone; death certificate stated she was the daughter of George Ridgely and Mary Garrett, all born in Harford Co., was separated from "? Thomas Smith" *(sic)* and lived at 415 Lawrence Street in Havre de Grace; she died in Havre de Grace Hospital; informant was Emma Harris, of Havre de Grace) [Green Spring U. M. Church Cemetery]

Garrett, Elizabeth died January 8, 1942, age 88 (no tombstone; death certificate stated she was the daughter of John Lisby and Ellen Hollingsworth, all born in Harford Co.; she married Henry Garrett, lived at Level RFD #1, Havre de Grace, and died a widow; informant was George R. Lisby, of Philadelphia, PA) [Green Spring U. M. Church Cemetery]

Garrett, Henry October 17, 1865 – February 23, 1921 (no tombstone; death certificate stated he was the son of Charles Garrett and Emma Nelson, all born in Maryland; he was a farmer near Havre de Grace and died in Havre de Grace Hospital; informant was Mrs. Henry Garrett) [Green Spring U. M. Church Cemetery]

Garrison Horace March 25, 1888 – October 30, 1927 (no tombstone; death certificate stated he was the married son of Alex Garrison and Mattie Christie; informant was Alverta Garrison) [Union U. M. Church Cemetery]

Garrison, Alverta O. February 25, 1896 – August 21, 1977 [Foster's Hill Cemetery]

Garrison, Briley O. Sr. 1917-1977, TEC5, U.S. Army, World War II [Foster's Hill Cemetery]

Garrison, Catherine A. January 1, 1023 – August 3, 1983 (inscribed "In Loving Memory of") [Foster's Hill Cemetery]

Garrison, Eliza November 11, 1874 – May 8, 1927 (no tombstone; death certificate stated she was the unmarried daughter of Christy Garrison and Mary Garrison; informant was Mary Garrison) [Union U. M. Church Cemetery]

Garrison, Frances Jeanette died October 26, 1924, age about 61 (no tombstone; death certificate stated she was born in Maryland, but her parents' names and places of death were not known to informant William H. Taylor, of Havre de Grace; she was married and died in Havre de Grace) [Gravel Hill Cemetery]

Garrison, Pamela, Loving Daughter of Briley and Catherine Harrison, April 2, 1947 – July – (blank), 1991 [Foster's Hill Cemetery]

Garrison, Robert June 30, 1865 – July 23, 1932 (no tombstone; death certificate stated he was born in Maryland, married Jeannette ---- and died a widower in Harford Memorial Hospital in Havre de Grace; informant was Irene Taylor, of New York, NY) [St. James United Cemetery]

Garrison, Wallace W. June 9, 1927 – October 21, 1927 (no tombstone; death certificate stated he was the son of Horace Garrison and Alverta Briley, all born in Maryland and lived at Magnolia; informant was his father) [John Wesley U. M. E. Church Cemetery in Abingdon]

Gease, Catherine 1908-1987 (small metal funeral home marker) [John Wesley U. M. E. Church Cemetery in Abingdon]

Geddes, Leander September 1, 1906 – February 7, 1987, SFC, U.S. Army, World War II and Korea [Berkley Memorial Cemetery]

Geddes, Mary A., "Wife, Mother, Sister" 1924-1982 ("In Memory Of") [Berkley Memorial Cemetery]

Gibbs, Barbara Ann 1946-2012 (small metal funeral home marker) [Berkley Memorial Cemetery]

Gibbs, James M. February 28, 1922 – May 7, 1973, Pennsylvania, Cpl., U.S. Army, World War II [St. James United Cemetery]

Gibbs, James R. "Baby" October – November 1972 [St. James United Cemetery]

Gibbs, Lillian M. 1930-2010 ("In Loving Memory") [St. James United Cemetery]

Gibson, A. Wylie, "Husband" November 30, 1910 – January 13, 1937 [Clark's U. M. Church Cemetery]

Gibson, Amos July 13, 1919 – August 30, 1952, Maryland, PFC, 3197 QM Service Co., World War II [Clark's U. M. Church Cemetery]

Gibson, Annie Priscilla stillborn on April 6, 1927 (no tombstone; death certificate stated she died in Bel Air and was the daughter of John H. Gibson and Sarah E. Whittington, all born in Maryland; informant was John H. Gibson, of Bel Air) [Clark's U. M. Church Cemetery]

Gibson, Catherine G. On Earth May 26, 1920 – In Heaven August 5, 1997 (tombstone; obituary in *The Aegis* on August 13, 1997 stated Catherine Geneva Gibson, of Bel Air, died at Harford Memorial Hospital in Havre de Grace; she was born in Bel Air, the daughter of Augustus Hill and Virginia Laura Wilson, and widow of John Carville Gibson; she was retired from Aberdeen Proving Ground, was a life member of Clark's Chapel and sang in the Sanctuary Choir; daughters Phyllis A. and Charlotte E. Gibson predeceased her) [Clark's U. M. Church Cemetery]

Gibson, Edith W. March 10, 1916 – January 3, 1919 (no tombstone; death certificate stated she was the daughter of James H. Gibson and Sarah Whittington, all born in Harford Co.; she died at Kalmia and buried in "Clarks Chapel Cem.;" informant was Mildred Gibson, of Bel Air) [Clark's U. M. Church Cemetery]

Gibson, Edna Richardson April 7, 1910 – July 7, 1940 (no tombstone; death certificate stated she was born in Philadelphia, the daughter of Robert Crouch, of Havre de Grace, and Amy J. Collins, of Philadelphia; informant was her husband John Gibson) [St. James United Cemetery]

Gibson, Elaine M. February 28, 1974 – September 5, 2015 (inscribed "Forever In Our Hearts;" funeral notice in *The Aegis* showed her photo and stated Elaine Marie Gibson was survived by her husband William Gibson, her mother Ruth Taylor and other relatives) [Berkley Memorial Cemetery]

Gibson, Ellen died September 11, 1921 age 65 (no tombstone; death certificate stated she was born in Harford Co., but her parents' names were unknown to informant Walter Parrott, of Bel Air; she was single and lived near Churchville) [Asbury Cemetery]

Gibson, Georgianna died March 1, 1911, age 50 (no tombstone; death certificate stated she was the married daughter of Isaac Welsh and Charlotte Moore, all born in Maryland; informant was Mollie Gould, of Havre de Grace) [St. James United Cemetery]

Gibson, Jane, daughter of Esau and Sarah Morgan, died July 7, 1908, age 78 years, 7 months, and 6 days (inscribed "At Rest") [Clark's U. M. Church Cemetery]

Gibson, John C. Jr. March 2, 1912 – March 3, 1974, STM1, U. S. Navy (tombstone; obituary in *The Aegis* stated John Carvel Gibson, of Thomas Run Road, Bel Air, died suddenly at home; his wife was Catherine Gibson and his daughter was Phyllis Ann Gibson) [Clark's U. M. Church Cemetery]

Gibson, John died June 4, 1837, age about 70 (no tombstone; death certificate stated he was unmarried and his parents were not known to informant Mrs. Annie Johnson, of Perryman; he lived on Hopper's Alley in Havre de Grace and was buried at "Swan Creek") [Union U. M. Church Cemetery]

Gibson, John H. 1877-1854 [Clark's U. M. Church Cemetery]

Gibson, Lizzie August 10, 1860 – June 19, 1922 (no tombstone; death certificate stated she was the daughter of Martha Banks, both born in Maryland, but her father's name was unknown to informant Sadie Gibson, of Bel Air; she was a widow and wash woman at Thomas Run) [Asbury Cemetery]

Gibson, Lucy T. 1896-1979 (on the same tombstone with William Gibson; obituary in *The Aegis* on February 1, 1979 stated Theresa Lucy Gibson, age 82, of Bel Air, widow of William S. Gibson, died on January 27, 1979 at Harford Memorial Hospital in Havre de Grace; she was born in Harford Co. and a member of the Ames United Methodist Church in Bel Air) [Clark's U. M. Church Cemetery]

Gibson, Mary Elizabeth, daughter of William and Jane Gibson, died February 20, 1915 (inscribed "Gone but not forgotten") [Clark's U. M. Church Cemetery]

Gibson, Robert 1879 – January 25, 1931 (no tombstone; death certificate stated Robert Gibson died January 25, 1931, "age 51, born unknown 1879" and was the son of William Gibson and Jane Morgan, all born in Maryland; lived in Bel Air; informant was Ora Howard, of Bel Air) [Clark's U. M. Church Cemetery]

Gibson, Robert, son of William and Jane Gibson, September 6, 1866 -   [Clark's U. M. Church Cemetery]

Gibson, Ruth A. P. December 3, 1916 – May 27, 1920 (no tombstone; death certificate stated she died at Poole and was the daughter of Edward Dutton and Emily James, all born in Maryland; informant was Edward Dutton, of Street, MD) [Clark's U. M. Church Cemetery]

Gibson, Samuel died January 3, 1990, age 93 (death notice in *The Aegis* on January 10, 1990 stated he was born in Gibson, N.C., son of Henry Gibson and Sarah Smith; he lived in Aberdeen, worked as a cook and died at Harford Memorial Hospital in Havre de Grace) [Berkley Memorial Cemetery]

Gibson, Sarah E. 1884-1954 [Clark's U. M. Church Cemetery]

Gibson, Sarah Jane, daughter of William and Jane Gibson, died March 24, 1914, age 56 years and 1 day (inscribed "Died in the Triumph of Faith") [Clark's U. M. Church Cemetery]

Gibson, Shirley Alberta September 14, 1939 – December 16, 1939 (no tombstone; death certificate stated she was born at Johns Hopkins Hospital in Baltimore, daughter of John C. Gibson and Catherine Hill, both born in Harford Co., and died at home near Bel Air; informant was her father) [Clark's U. M. Church Cemetery]

Gibson, Theresa Lucy – see Lucy T. Gibson [Clark's U. M. Church Cemetery]

Gibson, William 1885-1961 (on same tombstone with Lucy T. Gibson) [Clark's U. M. Church Cemetery]

Giddings, ---- stillborn male on March 23, 1920 (no tombstone; death certificate stated he was born in Berkley, the son of Herbert Giddings and Selia Washington, both born in Maryland; informant was Isaac Washington, of Berkley) [Berkley Memorial Cemetery]

Giddings, James Earl August 31, 1942 – March 18, 1943 (no tombstone; death certificate stated he was the son of Samuel Giddings and Helena Mary Rustin, of Havre de Grace) [St. James United Cemetery]

Giddings, Margaret died January 15, 1919, age about 45 (no tombstone; death certificate stated she was born in Maryland, the daughter of William Smith, born in Maryland, and Mollie Johnson, born in Pennsylvania; she died at home in Darlington; Herbert Gittings *(sic)* was the informant [Berkley Memorial Cemetery]

Giddings, Walter E. January 25, 1891 – March 24, 1975, Wagoner, U.S. Army, World War I (Pennington Funeral Home records stated he was the widowed son of Lawson Giddings and Mary Giddings and he died at Perry Point Veterans Hospital in Cecil Co., MD; military records stated he was age 22 years *(sic)* and 9 months when he enlisted in Rockville, MD as a private in the National Guard on 1 Jan 1918; he served on active duty as a wagoner and in the infantry overseas from 30 Mar 1918 until 11 Feb 1919 and was honorably discharged on 3 Mar 1919 [St. James United Cemetery]

Gilbert, ---- July 27, 1947 – August 24, 1947, a premature female who lived "27 days" (no tombstone; death certificate stated "Baby Girl Gilbert" was born in Havre de Grace, the daughter of William W. Peaker, born in Abingdon, and Irene Gilbert, born in Magnolia; she died at Harford Memorial Hospital and was buried in Magnolia Baptist Cemetery in Magnolia by Howard K. McComas & Son Funeral Home; informant was her mother Irene Gilbert, of Magnolia) [Foster's Hill Cemetery]

Gilbert, ---- stillborn male died July 18, 1917 (no tombstone; death certificate stated he was the son of George Gilbert and Mary Wilmer, both born in Maryland, and died at Gunpowder Neck; informant was his mother Mary Gilbert, of Magnolia) [Mt. Zion U. M. Church Cemetery]

Gilbert, ---- stillborn male on January 28, 1924 (no tombstone; death certificate stated he was the son of George W. Gilbert and Mary B. Wilmore, and all were born in Maryland; he died at Magnolia where he was buried by Howard K. McComas, Undertaker, of Abingdon, MD) [Foster's Hill Cemetery]

Gilbert, Alverta stillborn female on December 17, 1929, an 8-month premature birth (no tombstone; death certificate stated she was the daughter of George W. Gilbert and Mary B. Wilmore, all born in Maryland; she died at Magnolia where she was buried by Howard K. McComas, Undertaker, of Abingdon, MD, who misspelled the name of the cemetery as Porter Hill) [Foster's Hill Cemetery]

Gilbert, Clarence Raymond June 22, 1922 – October 16, 1922 (no tombstone; death certificate stated he was the son of Charles Gilbert and Mary M. Stevenson, all born in Maryland, and lived at Joppa; informant was his father) [Foster's Hill Cemetery]

Gilbert, Ernest W. May 11, 1922 – February 13, 1965, TEC5, 296 Port Co., TC, World War II [Foster's Hill Cemetery]

Gilbert, Frank Edward August 3, 1921 – March 24, 1922 (no tombstone; death certificate stated he was the son of Charles Gilbert and Mary M. Stevenson, and they were all born in Maryland and lived at Joppa; informant was his father) [Foster's Hill Cemetery]

Gilbert, George William Isaak August 5, 1913 – December 27, 1913 (no tombstone; death certificate stated he was the son of George Gilbert and Mary B. Wilmer, all born in Harford Co.; died in Abingdon) [John Wesley U. M. E. Church Cemetery in Abingdon]

Gilbert, Henry Burley October 22, 1914 – March 26, 1980, S1, U.S. Navy, World War II (tombstone; obituary in *The Aegis* on April 3, 1980 stated he was born in Abingdon, the son of the late George Gilbert and Mary Wilmer, and husband of Mary Toliver Gilbert; he was a custodian for the Board of Education and worked at Joppatowne Elementary School; he lived in Joppa, died at Fallston General Hospital and was buried at Ebenezer Baptist Church in Joppa; he was survived by his wife, 3 daughters Bernice Shuckey, Edna I. Stevenson and Mary Louise Bowser, 2 sisters, 15 grandchildren, and 9 great-grandchildren) [Foster's Hill Cemetery]

Gilbert, Jim Buck June 11, 1860 – August 17, 1921 (no tombstone; death certificate stated he was the son of Nelson Gilbert and Hannah ---- (maiden name unknown), all born in Maryland; he was married and worked as a laborer in Magnolia; informant was Charlott E. Gilbert) [Foster's Hill Cemetery]

Gilbert, John September 2, 1924 – October 7, 1924 (no tombstone; death certificate stated he was the son of Charles Gilbert and Mary Stevenson; all born in Maryland, and they lived in Joppa) [Foster's Hill Cemetery]

Gilbert, Laura August 1, 1876 – August 31, 1941 (no tombstone; death certificate stated she was the daughter of ---- Lee, born in Maryland, but her mother's name was unknown to informant Adolphs Rouser, of Edgewood; she lived in Edgewood, but died a widow at the County Home near Bel Air, where she had lived for 1 year; burial at "Fosters Hill in Magnolia") [Foster's Hill Cemetery]

Gilbert, Leroy Amos November 8, 1938 – October 19, 1939 (no tombstone; death certificate stated he was born in Joppa, son of Theodore Gilbert and Charlott ---- (blank), both born in Magnolia, and died at home in Joppa; informant was Thomas Gilbert, of Magnolia) [Foster's Hill Cemetery]

Gilbert, Lottie Marie stillborn on September 5, 1911 (no tombstone; death certificate stated she died at Van Bibber, the daughter of George W. Gilbert and May Bertha Welmer, of Harford Co.) [John Wesley U. M. E. Church Cemetery in Abingdon]

Gilbert, Mamie 1892-196__ (small metal funeral home marker) [Foster's Hill Cemetery]

Gilbert, Manley July 19, 1923 – August 28, 1923 (no tombstone; death certificate stated he was the son of Charles Gilbert and Mary Stevenson, all born in Maryland, and they lived in Joppa) [Foster's Hill Cemetery]

Gilbert, Martha B. August 12, 1921 – September 8, 2011 (on same tombstone with Robert L. Gilbert; funeral notice and photo in *The Aegis* on September 14, 2011 stated Martha Jane Gilbert, of Aberdeen, died September 8, 2011, age 90) [Mt. Calvary U. A. M. E. Church Cemetery]

Gilbert, Mary Bertha "Mamie" died September 16, 1969, age 77 (no tombstone; obituary in *The Aegis* stated she was the daughter of Isaac Wilmer and Ida Jones, and the widow of George W. Gilbert; she lived at 603 Dembytown Road in Joppa and was survived by two daughters, one son, one sister, seven grandchildren and 15 great-grandchildren) [Foster's Hill Cemetery]

Gilbert, Mary Ida Margaret August 25, 1912 to September 14, 1912 (no tombstone; death certificate stated she was born in Harford Co., the daughter of George Gilbert and Mary Wilmer, both born in Maryland, and she died at Van Bibber; informant was her father) [John Wesley U. M. E. Church Cemetery in Abingdon]

Gilbert, Matilda June 13, 1885 – August 6, 1918 (no tombstone; death certificate stated she was the unmarried daughter of James Gilbert and Charlotte Robinson, all born in Maryland, and lived in Magnolia; informant was James Gilbert, of Magnolia; she was buried at "Fosters Hill, Joppa") [Foster's Hill Cemetery]

Gilbert, Mildred Irene August 13, 1932 – October 2, 1932 (no tombstone; death certificate stated she was the daughter of Joseph Preston and Blanche Gilbert, all born in Maryland, and they lived in Magnolia; informant was Blanche Gilbert, of Magnolia) [Foster's Hill Cemetery]

Gilbert, Nina 1925-1982 (tombstone; obituary in *The Aegis* on October 14, 1982 stated Nina Lee Gilbert was born in Enfield, NC, the daughter of the late Amoss Bailey and Eva Peterson, and she married Howard Gilbert;, lived in Edgewood and died at Johns Hopkins Hospital on October 9, 1982, age 57; she was survived by her husband, a son Howard Wesley Bailey, two sisters Eula May Coates and Ethel Townes, and five grandchildren) [Foster's Hill Cemetery]

Gilbert, Paul Walter August 2, 1918 – March 4, 1919 (no tombstone; death certificate stated he was the son of George Gilbert and Marie Wilmer, all born in Maryland. and they lived in Magnolia; informant was George Gilbert, of Magnolia) [Foster's Hill Cemetery]

Gilbert, Rhoda Jane June 2, 1922 – October 23, 1983 (tombstone; obituary in *The Aegis* in October 27, 1983 stated she was a lifelong resident of Joppa and died at Fallston General Hospital; she was an active member of John Wesley United Methodist Church and survived by husband Jerry A. Gilbert, 6 children, 20 grandchildren, 6 great-grandchildren, a sister Olean Myers and a brother Horace Garrison; obituary stated services were held at John Wesley United Methodist Church, Joppa, but did not indicate the place of burial) [Foster's Hill Cemetery]

Gilbert, Robert L. May 13, 1913 – March 30, 1992 (on same tombstone with Martha B. Gilbert; obituary in *The Aegis* on April 1, 1992 stating Robert Lee Gilbert was born in Long Island, VA, the son of William Gilbert and Hommie Lovelace; he lived in Aberdeen, was a construction worked and served as president of the Mt. Calvary Church Trustee Board; he died at Harford Memorial Hospital, survived by his wife Martha, a daughter, 10 grandchildren, 5 great-grandchildren, a brother and 3 sisters) [Mt. Calvary U. A. M. E. Church Cemetery]

Gilbert, Rose September 2, 1924 – September 28, 1924 (no tombstone; death certificate stated she was the daughter of Charles Gilbert and Mary Stevenson; they all were born in Maryland and lived in Joppa) [Foster's Hill Cemetery]

Gilbert, Theodore E. February 17, 1910 – November *(sic)* 13, 1959, Maryland, PFC, U.S. Army, World War II (tombstone; an article in *The Aegis* on August *(sic)* 19, 1959 stated Theodore Ellton Gilbert, age 49, of Joppa, was struck by an automobile while attempting to walk across Route 40 at the Joppa Farm Road intersection Friday evening about 5:50 p.m. and was pronounced dead at Harford Memorial Hospital in Havre de Grace) [Foster's Hill Cemetery]

Gilbert, William (no tombstone found, but J. C. Taylor Marble Co. records stated "William Gilbert's Marble Marker was put up May 11th 1935 Colord *(sic)* Cemetery Magnolia, ordered by Mrs. Laura J. Brown, Magnolia, MD") [Foster's Hill Cemetery]

Gilbert, William 1930-1976 (tombstone; obituary in *The Aegis* on April 8, 1976 stated William Alexander Gilbert was born in Magnolia, the son of the late Minty Gilbert Charles, was the stepson of Elbert Charles and was a Korean War veteran; he lived in Baltimore City, married Delores Turner, was employed by the Baltimore City Sanitation Department and died at University Hospital on March 30, 1976, age 45; he was survived by his wife, stepfather, two daughters and three grandchildren) [Foster's Hill Cemetery]

Gilbert, William April 14, 1856 – August 11, 1918 (death certificate stated William Gelburt *(sic)* was the son of "Nelsen Gelburt and Hannah(?)" *(sic)*, all born in Maryland; he was married, worked as a farm laborer and died in Van Bibber; informant was John Raisin, of Van Bibber; he was buried at "Fosters Hill, Joppa;" a notice in *The Aegis* on May 13, 1982 with a picture of a tombstone that was inscribed "William Gilbert, From Club, 1853-1918" and stated "Target of Vandals. Sheriff's Department investigators are looking for information about this tombstone found along Singer road in Joppa during February. The investigators have not been able to locate the cemetery from which the tombstone was taken in early February." In *The Aegis* on May 20, 1982 it was reported "Apparently, vandals stole the tombstone from the John Wesley Cemetery near the Ebenezer Baptist Church in Joppatowne and placed it on the Singer Road driveway this past February. There had been no real progress in the case until Jerry Gilbert, a relative of the deceased, claimed the item Tuesday.") [Foster's Hill Cemetery]

Giles William Alexander "Abby" died August 26, 1985, age 88 (no tombstone; obituary in *The Havre d Grace Record* on September 4, 1985 stated he was born on Spesutia Island and when he reported for duty in World War I he was asked his name and answered nervously "Aberdeen, Maryland sir;" the sergeant laughed and from that time on he was called Abby; he worked 35 years as an Aberdeen Proving Ground oil truck driver, was a cannery pressure cooker operator and delivered prescriptions part-time for City Pharmacy; he died at Perry Point VAMC) [Union U. M. Church Cemetery]

Giles, ---- (owned lots in sections 28 and 39 some time after 1951) [Mt. Calvary U. A. M. E. Church Cemetery]

Giles, ---- stillborn male on March 21, 1916, a premature birth at 7 months (no tombstone; death certificate stated he was the son of Samuel Giles and Helen Pinion, both of Maryland) [Union U. M. Church Cemetery]

Giles, Ada (owned a lot in section 40 some time after 1951) [Mt. Calvary U. A. M. E. Church Cemetery]

Giles, Amelia died December 25, 1930, age about 66? (no tombstone; death certificate stated she was the widowed daughter of Solomon Brown, mother unknown to informant Raymond Giles; marriage record state she married Solomon Giles on 26 Jun 1879 and 1900 Harford County Census stated she was born in March 1857) [Union U. M. Church Cemetery]

Giles, Annie February 6, 1859 – February 6, 1933 (no tombstone; death certificate stated she was the daughter of George Webster and Ann Gibson, all born in Perryman, and the wife of James Giles, of Havre de Grace; informant was Annie E. Johnson, of Perryman) [St. James United Cemetery]

Giles, Aquila birth miscarriage on May 1, 1915 (no tombstone; death certificate stated he was the son of Samuel Giles and Helen Pinion, all born in Maryland) [Union U. M. Church Cemetery]

Giles, Benjamin F. 1885-1968 [Union U. M. Church Cemetery]

Giles, Bennett E. 1912-1990 (small brass marker) [Union U. M. Church Cemetery]

Giles, Beulah F. 1908-1982 (tombstone; obituary in *The Aegis* on July 8, 1982 stated Beulah Frances Giles was born at Clark's Chapel, raised by the late Mary and John Barner and was the widow of Ernest T. Giles and mother of William S. Dorsey and George E. Dorsey; she later joined the Ames Methodist Church in Bel Air and subsequently moved to Joppa) [Clark's U. M. Church Cemetery]

Giles, Chauncey M. February 20, 1895 – March 6, 1941 (no tombstone; death certificate stated he was the son of Solomon Giles and Amelia Brown, and the husband of Rebecca Giles) [Union U. M. Church Cemetery]

Giles, Clara J., "His Wife" 1868-1931 (on same tombstone with William H. Giles) [Union U. M. Church Cemetery]

Giles, Dora stillborn September 4, 1914 (no tombstone; death certificate stated she was the daughter of Samuel Giles and Mabel Pinion, all born in Maryland) [Union U. M. Church Cemetery]

Giles, Dorsey D. August 29, 1916 – December 1, 1966, Maryland, Cpl, 920 AB SCTY, BWAAF, World War II (tombstone; obituary in *The Aegis* on December 8, 1966 stated he was the son of the late Isaac F. Giles and Ann Thompson and the husband of Anna B. Hughes Giles of Route 1, Aberdeen; he was a mechanic at APG and died suddenly at Kirk Army Hospital; he was survived by his wife, 4 brothers and 2 sisters, but his military service was not mentioned) [Mt. Calvary U. A. M. E. Church Cemetery]

Giles, Edith V. 1910-2003 (small metal funeral home marker; obituary in *The Aegis* on August 13, 2003 stated she was born at Oakington on October 6, 1910, the daughter of Rev. Samuel Kelly and Mary Banks, married James Alfred Giles, Sr. and lived in Aberdeen; "family members said Mrs. Giles was called Mother, Aunt Edith, and Mom-Mom;" she died August 3, 2003 at Harford Memorial Hospital in Havre de Grace, survived by a daughter, 16 grandchildren, "a host of great-grandchildren and great-great-grandchildren, nephews, great-nieces and great-nephews, great-great-nieces, great-great-nephews") [Mt. Calvary U. A. M. E. Church Cemetery]

Giles, Eliza J. 1878 – July 7, 1926 (no tombstone; death certificate stated she was born in Harford Co., as was her father, but informant James Giles, of Joppa, did not know the names of his parents or the birth place of her mother; she was married, died at Joppa and was buried in "The Mountain Colored Cemetery") [Mt. Zion U. M. Church Cemetery]

Giles, Elmer "Buck" died October 14, 1971, age 76 (no tombstone; obituary in *The Aegis* stated he was born in Harford Co., the son of Alex Giles and Mary Haycock, lived at 415 Baltimore Street in Aberdeen, was the caretaker of the Mitchell Farm and died at Harford Memorial Hospital in Havre de Grace; he was survived by one brother William A. Giles, of Aberdeen) [Mt. Calvary U. A. M. E. Church Cemetery]

Giles, Ernest T. 1911-1980 (Masonic symbol on tombstone; obituary in *The Aegis* on June 19, 1980 stated Ernest Thomas Giles was born in Churchville and was the husband of Beulah F. Giles; he was a farmer at Findary Farm and a deliveryman for the Kunkle Service Co., both owned by John F. Kunkle, Sr.; he was a gospel singer and member of the Little Wonders Spiritual Quartet and a 32nd degree Mason; obituary stated he died at Harford Memorial Hospital, age 69, and was interred in Bel Air Memorial Gardens, but his tombstone is actually at Clark's Chapel) [Clark's U. M. Church Cemetery]

Giles, Florence Green died March 18, 1978, age 85 (obituary in *The Aegis* stated she was born in Harford Co., the daughter of the late James Green and Laura Monk Green, and wife of the late Samuel Edward Giles; she lived at 2215 Williams Drive, Havre de Grace, and died at Harford Memorial Hospital, survived by 6 daughters, 46 grandchildren, 53 great-grandchildren and 28 great-great-grandchildren) [Union U. M. Church Cemetery]

Giles, George Earl December 31, 1923 – July 20, 1983, S1, U.S. Navy, World War II (tombstone; buried in section 39; obituary in *The Aegis* stated he was born in Aberdeen, son of Isaac and Annie Giles, married Virginia Fisher, lived in Havre de Grace and died at Harford Memorial Hospital, survived by his wife, 2 daughters, 3 brothers, a sister and 3 grandchildren]

Giles, Hannah Pearl December 27, 1900 – September 21, 1944 (no tombstone; death certificate stated she was born in Virginia, the daughter of Crockett Wolf and Elizabeth Canada, both born in North Carolina; she married Ernest Giles and lived and died at 15 Howard St. in Bel Air; informant was her husband) [Tabernacle Mount Zion U. M. Church Cemetery]

Giles, Harry H. Jr. May 30, 1932 – August 16, 1990, Cpl., U.S. Army, Korea [Mt. Calvary U. A. M. E. Church Cemetery]

Giles, Harry Herbert Sr. died September 5, 1998, age 86 (no tombstone; obituary in *The Aegis* on September 9, 1998 stated he was born in Aberdeen, the son of Isaac Franklin Giles and Annie Elizabeth Thompson; he worked at J. Smith Michaels where he was a caretaker and married Martha Parker who predeceased him, as did his son Harry H. Jr.; he died at Harford Memorial Hospital in Havre de Grace and was survived by sons Roger and Robert Giles, daughter Jeanne A. Giles, brother Kessler K. Giles, and 13 grandchildren) [Mt. Calvary U. A. M. E. Church Cemetery]

Giles, Helen E. 1896-1989 (tombstone; obituary in *The Aegis* on November 22, 1989 stated Helen Elizabeth Giles, of Aberdeen, was the daughter of Lewis Pinion and Carrie Collins, and the widow of Samuel Howard Giles; she died at Harford Memorial Hospital in Havre de Grace and was survived by a son, a daughter, 3 grandchildren and 2 sisters) [Union U. M. Church Cemetery]

Giles, Hester 1856-1933 (tombstone; death certificate stated she died February 5, 1933, age about 76, and was the daughter of American Bond and widow of George Giles; her mother's name was not known to the informant Mrs. Virginia Frieze, of Havre de Grace) [St. James United Cemetery]

Giles, Howard Louis April 16, 1911 – April 25, 1973 (no tombstone; obituary in *The Aegis* stated he was born in Perryman, the son of Helen Pinion Giles (with whom he lived at 434 Dorsey Street in Aberdeen) and Samuel H. Giles; he died at University Hospital in Baltimore and was survived by his mother, a brother and a sister) [Union U. M. Church Cemetery]

Giles, Ida J. December 19, 1897 – January 25, 1927 (no tombstone; death certificate stated she was the married and daughter of Randolf Brown and Sadia Stansbury; Alex Giles, informant) [Union U. M. Church Cemetery]

Giles, Jacob Alfred Jr. 1933 – April 26, 1996 (obituary and photo in *The Aegis* on May 1, 1996 stated Jake was born in Perryman, the son of Jacob A. Giles, Sr. and Eva Warfield, and was an Army veteran of the Korean War; he married (wife not named), worked in maintenance at the Aberdeen Post Office and died at Fallston General Hospital; he was survived by 5 sons, 4 daughters, 1 step-daughter, 1 brother, 3 sisters, 25 grandchildren and 1 great-grandchild) [Berkley Memorial Cemetery]

Giles, James A. Jr. June 27, 1929 – August 19, 1998 (tombstone with his photo) [St. James United Cemetery]

Giles, James Alfred May 17, 1910 – April 24, 1949, Maryland, TEC5, 145 Port Co., TC, World War II [Mt. Calvary U. A. M. E. Church Cemetery]

Giles, Jeanine Ann, "Beloved Wife" April 7, 1940 – December 30, 1964 [Mt. Calvary U. A. M. E. Church Cemetery]

Giles, John died September 25, 1910, age 46 (no tombstone; death certificate stated he was the son of Henry Giles, both born in Harford Co., but his mother was not known to informant Mary Giles, his daughter; he worked as a farm hand and died at Michaelsville, survived by his wife Rose Giles and at least one daughter; place of burial was not indicated, but probably in Old Union Chapel Cemetery at Michaelsville; possibly reinterred later in Union Chapel Cemetery near Aberdeen) [Union U. M. Church Cemetery]

Giles, John Theodore August 28, 1941 – October 23, 1961, Maryland, SA, U.S. Navy [Union U. M. Church Cemetery]

Giles, Leroy Chauncey, Sr. May 12, 1928 – January 29, 1975, STM2, U.S. Navy (obituary in *The Aegis* on February 6, 1975 stated he was a son of Chauncey Giles and Rebecca Jane Christy, of Aberdeen, and served in the Navy in World War II; he lived in Aberdeen and worked for Parks and Recreation for 15 years; he died at the Perry Point Veterans Administration Hospital and was survived by his wife Cordelia, his mother, two sons, four daughters, two brothers, two sisters and six grandchildren) [Berkley Memorial Cemetery]

Giles, Lloyd December 28, 1882 – March 3, 1934 (no tombstone; death certificate misspelled his first name as Llyod and stated he was the son of Isaac Giles and Anna Coale, and the husband of Mary Giles who had predeceased him) [Union U. M. Church Cemetery]

Giles, Lorna Mae 1930-1974 (copied in 1987, not found in 2018) [Mt. Calvary U. A. M. E. Church Cemetery]

Giles, Martha Marie died April 16, 1992, age 76 (no tombstone; her obituary in *The Aegis* on April 22, 1992 stated she was the daughter of Samuel Parker and Sadie Butler and wife of Harry H. Giles, Sr.; she was a native of the Bush Chapel area of Aberdeen, worked as cafeteria manager for the Harford County Board of Education for 15 years and died at Harford Memorial Hospital in Havre de Grace; she was survived by her husband, two sons, a daughter, a sister, 4 grandchildren and 4 great-grandchildren; son Harry Jr. died in 1990) [Mt. Calvary U. A. M. E. Church Cemetery]

Giles, Mary June 13, 1851 – May 7, 1932 (no tombstone; death certificate stated she was the daughter of Abraham Prigg and Jane Stansbury, and wife of Lloyd Giles, of Havre de Grace) [St. James United Cemetery]

Giles, Melvin Leroy March 26, 1927 – July 26, 1972 (no tombstone; Pennington Funeral Home records stated he was born in Aberdeen, the brother of Mrs. Ida M. Gamble and the son of William Alexander Giles and Isabell Elizabeth Stansbury; he was unmarried, a veteran, and worked at Harford Memorial Hospital; he died in Havre de Grace and was buried in "Swan Creek Methodist Cemetery") [Union U. M. Church Cemetery]

Giles, Nellie Collins died October 10, 1975, age 73 (no tombstone; obituary in *The Aegis* on October 16, 1975 stated she was born in Aldino, the daughter of Robert Collins and Harriett Bond, and she lived in Havre de Grace; she was the widow of Roy Milford Giles and died at Harford Memorial Hospital, survived by 1 son, 1 brother, 1 sister, 6 grandchildren and 3 great-grandchildren) [Green Spring U. M. Church Cemetery]

Giles, Pauline died on May 17, 1957, age about 69 (no tombstone; Pennington Funeral Home records stated she was born in Harford County, the daughter of John Washington and Jennetta Hoke, married (husband's name not given), lived at Swan Creek, died a widow in Lincoln Memorial Hospital in Baltimore and was buried in Swan Creek Cemetery near Aberdeen; informant was William A. Giles, of Swan Creek; the funeral bill was rendered to William A. Giles and Vernon Brown, of Aberdeen[Union U. M. Church Cemetery]

Giles, Rebecca Jane July 11, 1895 – April 16, 1976 [Union U. M. Church Cemetery]

Giles, Robert M. Jr. 1982-1982 (tombstone; obituary in *The Aegis* on April 15, 1982 stated he was the three month old infant of Robert M. Giles, Sr. and Priscilla Dennison, of Havre de Grace, and he died on April 12, 1982 at Harford Memorial Hospital) [Green Spring U. M. Church Cemetery]

Giles, Roy Milford March 17, 1907 – September 11, 1974 (no tombstone; obituary in *The Aegis* stated he was born in Delta, PA, the son of Clarence and Bertha Kalmia Giles, and married Nellie Collins; he lived on Thomas Run Road near Bel Air, was a retired construction worker, and died at Harford Memorial Hospital in Havre de Grace) [Green Spring U. M. Church Cemetery]

Giles, Ruby Marjorie February 6, 1914 – October 16, 1914 (no tombstone; death certificate stated she was the daughter of Isaac F. Giles and A. E. Thompson, all born in Harford Co.; she died at Mt. Calvary; informant was her father, of Aberdeen) [Mt. Calvary U. A. M. E. Church Cemetery]

Giles, S. 1848-1921 (tombstone; no death certificate; probably Solomon Giles) [Union U. M. Church Cemetery]

Giles, Samuel August 6, 1861 – September 9, 1936 (no tombstone; death certificate stated he was the son of Quila Giles and Fannie Ringel, and the husband of Viola Giles) [Union U. M. Church Cemetery]

Giles, Sarah F. July 23, 1855 – July 4, 1919 (no tombstone; death certificate stated she was the daughter of Mary Stansbury, both born in Harford Co., but the name of her father was not known to informant E. Idella Green, of Aberdeen; she was a widow and died near Aberdeen) [Mt. Calvary U. A. M. E. Church Cemetery]

Giles, Solomon died January 9, 1922, age about 50 *(sic)* (no tombstone; death certificate stated he was the son of Isaac Giles and Rubie Coale, all born in Maryland; informant was Mrs. S. Giles; 1900 Harford County Census states he was born in November 1854, thus age 67 when he died, not 50; marriage record states he married Amelia Brown on 26 Jun 1879) [Union U. M. Church Cemetery]

Giles, William September 20, 1861 – May 14, 1922 (no tombstone; death certificate stated he was the married son of George Giles, both born in Maryland, but his mother was unknown to the informant Mrs. Betty Giles, of Havre de Grace) [St. James United Cemetery]

Giles, William (owner of a lot in section 39 some time after 1951) [Mt. Calvary U. A. M. E. Church Cemetery]

Giles, William Alexander Sr. August 10, 1873 – November 15, 1931 (no tombstone; death certificate stated he was the husband of Charlotte A. Giles and the son of Isaac Giles, mother unknown to informant Mrs. Giles) [Union U. M. Church Cemetery]

Giles, William H. 1870-1918 (on same tombstone with Clara J. Giles; death certificate stated William Henry Giles was born on April 2, 1872 in Harford Co., the son of Alfred Giles and Sarah Frances Iser, both born in Maryland, and he died on September 12, 1918; informant was Clara Giles, of Aberdeen) [Union U. M. Church Cemetery]

Gillespie, Willie B. October 25, 1915 – February 8, 1993, U.S. Army, World War II (tombstone; James Dorsey Card File, African American Obituaries, maintained at the Historical Society of Harford County, has a card with obituary from *The Aegis* on March 3, 1993 stating "Mr. Willie" was born in Hernando, MS, the son of Bessie and Rudolph Gillespie; while serving in the Army and stationed at Aberdeen Proving Ground he met and married the late Jennie Gillespie; upon his retirement from Perry Point VAMC he opened his own business "City Upholstery" for many years; he died at home in Havre de Grace, survived by three daughters, one son, a nephew whom he raised, and 15 grandchildren) [Union U. M. Church Cemetery]

Gilliam, Ethel 1936-2005 (small metal funeral home marker) [St. James United Cemetery]

Gilliam, Hazel V. December 17, 1935 – March 30, 2018 (inscribed "Gone To Be An Angel" with her photo) [St. James United Cemetery]

Gilliam, William M. Jr. January 27, 1955 – December 1, 2001 (inscribed "In Loving Memory" and "I Am Free") [St. James United Cemetery]

Gillven, James April 3, 1868 – December 13, 1932 (no tombstone; death certificate stated he was born in Maryland, son of Richard Gillven and Mary Booker, both born in Kentucky) [Union U. M. Church Cemetery]

Gittings-Dyer, Barbara, "A Devoted and Loving Mother" November 9, 1936 – April 6, 2013 (inscribed "In Loving Memory Of" and "Forever In Our Hearts") [Berkley Memorial Cemetery]

Gittings, ---- female born and died on August 13, 1922 (no tombstone; death certificate stated she died at Poole, the daughter of Herbert Gittings and Marie White, all born in Maryland; the informant was Herbert Gittings, of Street, MD) [Clark's U. M. Church Cemetery]

Gittings, ---- premature stillborn male died on August 10, 1921 (no tombstone; death certificate stated he died at Dublin, the son of Herbert Gittings and Marie White, all born in Maryland; informant was Herbert Gittings, of Street, MD) [Clark's U. M. Church Cemetery]

Gittings, Herbert B. August 14, 1923 – September 29, 1923 (no tombstone; death certificate stated he died at Dublin, the son of Herbert Gittings and Marie C. White, all born in Maryland; informant was Herbert Gittings, of Street, MD) [Clark's U. M. Church Cemetery]

Gittings, Louis H. Sr. August 19, 1928 – December 17, 1995, U.S. Army, Korea [Berkley Memorial Cemetery]

Gittings, Marie White October 2, 1898 – February 5, 1951 (no tombstone; death certificate stated she was born in Harford Co., the wife of Herbert Gittings and the daughter of Elijah White and Hannah Harris; she lived and died in rural Darlington; informant was Herbert Gittings) [Clark's U. M. Church Cemetery]

Gittings, Thomas W. September 30, 1926 – October 13, 1996, ST1, U.S. Navy, World War II [Berkley Memorial Cemetery]

Gittings, William E. October 5, 1925 – October 8, 1926 (no tombstone; death certificate stated he died in Dublin, the son of Herbert Gittings and Marie White, all born in Maryland; informant was H. W. White, of Street, MD) [Clark's U. M. Church Cemetery]

Givens, Charles Lee October 5, 1930 – December 1, 2001, Pfc., U.S.M.C., Korea [St. James United Cemetery]

Givens, Olivia 1880-1954 [St. James United Cemetery]

Givens, Olivia G. 1910-1983 [St. James United Cemetery]

Glasco, Mary Rebeccah November 25, 1933 – February 24, 1934 (no tombstone; death certificate stated she was the daughter of Mary Rebecca Glasco and Jack Cerry, of Havre de Grace) [St. James United Cemetery]

Glover, Charlotte January 20, 1856 – October 17, 1913 (no tombstone; death certificate stated she was the daughter of Asbury and Hettie Sly, all born in Maryland; she died a widow in Aberdeen and was buried in Sydney Park Cemetery; informant was Sallie Harrad, of Aberdeen) [Union U. M. Church Cemetery]

Glover, Robert D. "Smitty" January 11, 1955 – February 6, 1999 [Berkley Memorial Cemetery]

Goins, Charles (owner of a lot in section 24 some time after 1951) [Mt. Calvary U. A. M. E. Church Cemetery]

Goins, Dorah (owner of a lot in section 24 some time after 1951) [Mt. Calvary U. A. M. E. Church Cemetery]

Goins, Edward F. May 4, 1901 – February 24, 1917 (no tombstone; death certificate stated he was the son of Edward Goins and Lydia Jackson, of Havre de Grace) [St. James United Cemetery]

Goins, Lydia 1878-1955 ("Rest In Peace") [St. James United Cemetery]

Goins, Mollie February 1, 1872 – June 16, 1911 (no tombstone; death certificate stated she was born in Anne Arundel Co., the married daughter of William Johnson, born in Anne Arundel Co., and Mary Island, born in Calvert Co.; informant was Philip Brown, of Havre de Grace) [St. James United Cemetery]

Gooding, M. (no dates on grave marker) [Chestnut Grove A. M. E. Church Cemetery, formerly LaGrange Cemetery at Rocks]

Goodman, Lena Ann September 12, 1961 – April 1, 2010 (inscribed "Beautiful memories of you will live in our hearts forever. John 14:2, 3") [St. James United Cemetery]

Gordon, Bennie May 14, 1909 – January 20, 1912 (no tombstone; death certificate stated he was the son of Benjamin Gordon and Sarah Branch, all born in North Carolina) [St. James United Cemetery]

Gordon, Charles L. Sr., "Loving Husband and Father" June 1, 1924 – July 28, 1996 (inscribed "May the work I've done speak for me.") [Union U. M. Church Cemetery]

Gordon, Charles Lewis March 26, 1917 – October 23, 1945, Maryland, PFC, 786 AAF Aviation Squadron, World War II [Berkley Memorial Cemetery]

Gordon, David Gilphin Sr. October 30, 1922 – March 15, 2003 (on same tombstone with Edith Eleanor Gordon and inscribed "In Loving Memory") [Berkley Memorial Cemetery]

Gordon, David Gilpin July 5, 1908 – June 9, 1911 (no tombstone; death certificate stated he was the son of John Gordon and Mary E. James, all born in Harford Co., and he died at home in Darlington) [Berkley Memorial Cemetery]

Gordon, Edith Eleanor April 5, 1924 – January 27, 2010 (on same tombstone with David Gilphin Gordon, Sr, and inscribed "In Loving Memory") [Berkley Memorial Cemetery]

Gordon, James L. 1925-2012 (small metal funeral home marker) [Berkley Memorial Cemetery]

Gordon, John A. April 5, 1934 – September 13, 1987, A1C, U.S. Force, Korea [Union U. M. Church Cemetery]

Gordon, John H. March 26, 1847 – January 4, 1928 (no tombstone; death certificate stated he was born in Maryland, the son of Rachel Chancie(?), born in Maryland, but his father was unknown to informant Mary Gordon, of Darlington; he was married, worked as a laborer and died at home in Darlington) [Berkley Memorial Cemetery]

Gordon, John Robert May 3, 1942 – May 11, 1942 (no tombstone; death certificate stated he was born in Bel Air, the son of Robert Harrison Gordon, born in Darlington, and Edna Mae Nelson, born in Charlestown, WV; he died at home at 6 Bond St., Bel Air; informant was his mother) [Berkley Memorial Cemetery]

Gordon, Queen Esther August 16, 1915 – August 24, 1950 (no tombstone; death certificate stated she was born in Prospect, Prince Edward Co., VA, the daughter of William A. Gordon and Rosetta Lockett, and died at home in Havre de Grace RFD#1; informant was Mrs. Rosetta Gordon) [Union U. M. Church Cemetery]

Gordon, Robert H. July 28, 1914 – October 2, 1968, Maryland, TEC5, 4121 Base Unit, AAF, World War II [Berkley Memorial Cemetery]

Gordon, Ruby E. "Shorty" July 17, 1932 – April 3, 1998 [Berkley Memorial Cemetery]

Gordon, William E.,"Hump" 1936-2000 [Union U. M. Church Cemetery]

Gough, ---- stillborn male on August 24, 1906 (no tombstone; death certificate stated he was the son of Isaac Gough and Seretha James, both born in Harford Co., he died in Bel Air and on the back of death certificate it is written "Hendon Hill") [Hendon Hill Cemetery]

Gough, Matilda died February 2, 1892, age 72 (no tombstone; death notice in *The Aegis* on March 4, 1892 stated she was formerly a servant in the family of the late James Pannell) [Asbury Cemetery]

Gould, Mary died November 1, 1931, age about 56 (no tombstone; death certificate stated she was the daughter of Abraham Lee, but her mother was unknown to informant Annie Frisby; she died a widow in Havre de Grace) [Union U. M. Church Cemetery]

Govans, Clara J. 1888-1981 (on same tombstone with Clinton R. Govans; obituary in *The Aegis* on April 1, 1981 stated she was formerly of Jarrettville, died in Baltimore, widow of Clinton R. Govans, survived by 3 sons, 3 daughters, 20 grandchildren and 12 great-grandchildren) [William C. Rice Memorial Cemetery, St. James U. M. Church]

Govans, Clarence William died June 18, 1996, age 80 (no tombstone; obituary in *The Aegis* on June 26, 1996 stated Rev. Clarence William Govans was born in Jarrettsville, the son of Clinton Reynolds Govans and Clara Jane Johnson; he served in the Army during World War II and retired from Edgewood Arsenal; he ministered at various churches in Harford County and died at the Bel Air Nursing and Rehabilitation Center, survived by a daughter, two brothers, a sister, 14 grandchildren, 10 great-grandchildren, and three daughters predeceased him) [William C. Rice Memorial Cemetery, St. James U. M. Church]

Govans, Clinton R. 1885-1945 (on same tombstone with Clara J. Govans; Kurtz Funeral Home Record Book 1944-1949, p. 79, stated he was born in 1885 at White Hall, the son of Jehu Govans, born in Baltimore Co., and Georgie Berry, born at Rocks; he married ---- (blank), worked as a farm laborer and died on October 7, 1945 at University Hospital in Baltimore) [William C. Rice Memorial Cemetery, St. James U. M. Church]

Govans, Elmer July 27, 1908 – June 28, 1931 (no tombstone; death certificate stated he was born in Baltimore, the son of Clinton Govans, born in Baltimore, and Clara Johnson, born in Maryland; he was single, worked as a farm laborer and died at Havre de Grace Hospital; informant was Clara Govans, of Rocks) [William C. Rice Memorial Cemetery, St. James U. M. Church]

Govans, Georgina August 31, 1864 – July 12, 1928 (no tombstone; death certificate stated she was the married daughter of George Quickley and Dolly Edwards, all born in Baltimore Co.) [Union U. M. Church Cemetery]

Govans, Hattie February 29, 1932 – February 10, 1997 (no tombstone, but she owned a lot in section 12 some time after 1951; obituary in *The Aegis* on February 19, 1997 stated Hattie Elizabeth Osborne "Boots" Govans was born in Havre de Grace, the daughter of the late Herbert Elmer Reid and Etta J. Kenly, and she worked for Madison Mitchell in Havre de Grace where she met and married John Govans in 1954; she also worked for a time as a housekeeper at Aberdeen Proving Ground and was survived by her husband, two adopted children Wayne Parker and Carolyn L. Hawkins, a brother Winfield E. Parker, a sister Mabel O. Brown, three grandchildren, three great-grandchildren, and other relatives) [Mt. Calvary U. A. M. E. Church Cemetery]

Govans, Howard N. 1929-1975 (small white wooden cross grave marker; obituary in *The Aegis* on November 13, 1975 stated Howard Nelson Govans, of Rocks, was born on April 17, 1929 and died on November 6, 1975; he was the son of Wallace and Laura Govans, and was married, but wife not named; he was survived by a son Ronald Govans, a daughter Sharon Robinson, two grandchildren, six sisters and two brothers) [Chestnut Grove A. M. E. Church Cemetery, formerly LaGrange Cemetery at Rocks]

Govans, James Edward January 10, ---- (blank) – September 21, 1943 (no tombstone; Kurtz Funeral Home Record Book 1944-1949, p. 287, stated he was born in Sunnyburn, PA, the son of Clinton Govans, born in White Hall, MD, and Clara Johnson, born in Jarrettsville; he was single, worked as a laborer and died at Henryton Sanitarium) [William C. Rice Memorial Cemetery, St. James U. M. Church]

Govans, Jehu Leroy 1935-1993 (small white wooden cross grave marker; obituary in *The Aegis* on June 23, 1993 stating "Sonny" was born in Rocks, son of Wallace W. Govans and Laura Blaney, lived in Jarrettsville and died at Fallston General Hospital on June 21, 1993, age 58, survived by 3 sisters, 1 brother, nieces and nephews) [Chestnut Grove A. M. E. Church Cemetery, formerly LaGrange Cemetery at Rocks]

Govans, Jessie Rebecca died January 4, 1993, age 80 (no tombstone; obituary in *The Aegis* on January 12, 1993 stated she was born in Delta, PA, the daughter of Stanford Mason and Janie Miller Giles; she lived in Jarrettsville and died at Fallston General Hospital, survived by her husband Clarence W. Govans, a daughter Yvonne M. Williams, a brother, 6 sisters, 13 grand-children, 9 great-grandchildren, and was predeceased by a daughter Theresa L. Moses) [William C. Rice Memorial Cemetery, St. James U. M. Church]

Govans, John J. Sr. 1926-1979 (small metal funeral home marker; no tombstone; obituary in *The Aegis* stated John Joshua Govans, Sr. lived in Jarrettsville, worked as a truck driver for Grimmel Brothers and died on March 23, 1979, age 52, survived by his wife Louise Young Govans, three daughters, 3 sons, 3 brothers, 3 sisters, and mother Clara J. Govans, of Baltimore) [William C. Rice Memorial Cemetery, St. James U. M. Church]

Govans, Laura R. March 28, 1901 – July 15, 1984 (tombstone; obituary and photo in *The Aegis* on July 19, 1984 stated Laura Rebecca Blaney Govans, of Bel Air, formerly of Rocks, and widow of Wallace W. Govans, was survived by 5 daughters, 2 sons and 26 grandchildren) [Chestnut Grove A. M. E. Church Cemetery, formerly LaGrange Cemetery at Rocks]

Govans, Louise Young February 21, 1934 – September 13, 2006 (no tombstone; obituary in *The Aegis* on September 20, 2006 stated she was born in Stewartstown, PA, the daughter of the late Samuel Andrew Young and Nettie Rebecca Mae Wallace, and widow of John J. Govans, Sr.; she worked for three years at the Harford County Public Library and was employed also as a supervisor and telemarketer with Hekin Research and Consumer Pulse in White Marsh; she lived in Edgewood and died at home, survived by 5 children, 1 brother, 2 brothers-in-law, 2 sisters-in-law, 10 grandchildren, and 3 great-grandchildren; she was predeceased by a daughter, a stepdaughter, 2 sisters, 6 brothers) [William C. Rice Memorial Cemetery, St. James U. M. Church]

Govans, Mabel Jane February 25, 1902 – July 8, 1917 (no tombstone; death certificate stated she was born in Baltimore City and was the married daughter of John Whye, born in Baltimore Co., and Bessie Cromwell, born in Harford Co.; informant was Mrs. John Whye, of Monkton) [Union U. M. Church Cemetery]

Govans, Nicholas Simon January 4, 1855 – July 10, 1913 (no tombstone; death certificate stated he was a widower and the son of John Govans, born in Maryland, and Susan Amos, born in Pennsylvania; he was born in Maryland and informant was Dollie Govans, of Monkton) [Union U. M. Church Cemetery]

Govans, Wallace W. February 22, 1898 – April 23, 1970 (tombstone; obituary in *The Aegis* stated Wallace William Govans married Laura R. Blaney, worked as a farm laborer and died at home at 127 Archer Street in Bel Air, survived by his wife, three sons and seven daughters, and was buried at "Rocks AME Church") [Chestnut Grove A. M. E. Church Cemetery, formerly LaGrange Cemetery at Rocks]

Gover, Annie died March 15, 1919, age 94 (no tombstone; death certificate stated she was the daughter of Sam and Dollie Simms, all born in Maryland; she was a widow and died at home at Rocks; informant was Charles Dunsen, of Rocks) [Chestnut Grove A. M. E. Church Cemetery, formerly LaGrange Cemetery at Rocks]

Gover, Edna A. 1889-1992 (on same tombstone with W. Stanley Gover) [Fairview A. M. E. Church Cemetery]

Gover, George H., "Father" February 6, 1854 – January 18, 1915 (inscribed "In Memory of" and "Asleep in Jesus;" death certificate stated George Henry Gover was the son of Jarrett and Susan Gover and they all were born in Harford Co.; he was married, worked as a farmer and died near Pleasantville; informant was Martha A. Gover, of Forest Hill RFD) [West Liberty Church Cemetery]

Gover, Harry March 17, 1844 – November 6, 1913 (no tombstone; death certificate stated he was the son of Toney and Levina Gover, all born in Harford Co.; he was married, worked as a laborer in Bel Air and was buried at Chestnut Grove Cemetery; informant was Maria Dunsen, of Rocks; his death notice in *The Aegis* on November1 14, 1913 stated he died at the Almshouse and was buried in the Rocks colored cemetery; he spent his life among the Wilsons and Streets, of Upper Harford; a number of white people attended his funeral) [Chestnut Grove A. M. E. Church Cemetery, formerly LaGrange Cemetery at Rocks]

Gover, Jarrett, son of George H. and Martha A. Gover, May 4, 1892 – April 28, 1908 (on the same obelisk with Nettie Gover and Sadie Gover; death certificate stated Jarrett Clinton Gover was the son of George Henry Hall and Martha Alverda Hll, all born in Harford Co.; he was single, worked as a farm laborer and died near Pleasantville; informant was his father) [West Liberty Church Cemetery]

Gover, Lucinda A. died December 28, 1952, age 91 (no tombstone; Harkins Funeral Home Record stated she was born in Harford Co., the daughter of Joseph Dorsey and ---- (blank), and she died a widow at Delta; informant was her niece Fannie Griffin, of Oxford, PA) [Chestnut Grove A. M. E. Church Cemetery, formerly LaGrange Cemetery at Rocks]

Gover, Marie Verbena August 19, 1931 – April 21, 1991 (on same tombstone with William F. Gover; obituary and photo in *The Aegis* on May 1, 1991 stated she was the oldest of 5 children born to George Brown and Mildred Hawkins, was the first secretary of the old Consolidated High School at Hickory and worked at Aberdeen Proving Ground from 1965 to 1978; a native of Fallston, she died at St. Joseph Hospital in Towson, survived by her husband of 41 years William Francis Gover, two daughters, one son and three sisters) [Fairview A. M. E. Church Cemetery]

Gover, Martha A., "Mother" March 31, 1859 – October 1, 1934 (inscribed "In Memory of" and "At Rest;" death certificate stated she died October 2, 1934 and was the daughter of Robert Hall and Louisa Berry, all born in Harford Co.; she married George H. Gover and died a widow at Forest Hill; informant was Stanley Gover, of Forest Hill; Kurtz Funeral Home Records stated she died in Forest Hill near the Baptist corner) [West Liberty Church Cemetery]

Gover, Milky died August 3, 1886 in her 77th year [Clark's U. M. Church Cemetery]

Gover, Nettie Irene, daughter of George H. and Martha A. Gover, July 19, 1897 – January 2, 1912 (on same obelisk with Jarrett Gover and Sadie Gover; death certificate stated born in Harford Co., as were her parents, and she died at home near Forest Hill; informant was her father George) [West Liberty Church Cemetery]

Gover, Sadie, daughter of George H. and Martha A. Gover, August 25, 1885 – January 30, 1907 (on the same obelisk with Jarrett Gover and Nettie Gover; also an illegible poem inscribed at the bottom; death certificate stated she was the daughter of George H. Gover and Martha Alverda Gover, all born in Harford Co.; she was single, worked as a domestic and died near Jarrettsville on January 30, 1907 at 7:30 a.m., age 21 years, 5 months, and 5 days; informant was her father George H. Gover) [West Liberty Church Cemetery]

Gover, W. Stanley 1889-1955 (on same tombstone with Edna A. Gover) [Fairview A. M. E. Church Cemetery]

Gover, William A. September 10, 1864 – September 21, 1949 (no tombstone; Harkins Funeral Home Record stated he was born in Harford Co., parents unknown, and he died at home in Delta; informant was his wife Lucy Gover) [Chestnut Grove A. M. E. Church Cemetery, formerly LaGrange Cemetery at Rocks]

Gover, William F. November 17, 1927 -   (on same tombstone with Marie V. Gover) [Fairview A. M. E. Church Cemetery]

Graddick, Vincent C. 1956-2009 [St. James United Cemetery]

Graham, Harry (owned a lot in section 19 some time after 1951) [Mt. Calvary U. A. M. E. Church Cemetery]

Graham, John Henry III died November 18, 1966, age 21 (no tombstone; obituary in *The Aegis* on November 24, 1966 stated he was the son of Harry Graham and Annie Scruggs, of Baltimore, and died in an automobile accident, survived by his parents and 3 siblings) [Mt. Calvary U. A. M. E. Church Cemetery]

Grandmother Ella (no name, no dates; buried between Malinda V. Smith and Lena Waters) [Asbury Cemetery]

Graves, Theodore February 21, 1929 – October 25, 1929 (no tombstone; death certificate stated he was born in Pennsylvania and died in Castleton, MD, the son of Ella Graves, born in Virginia, but informant Bertie Jasper, of

Castleton, did not know his father's name) [Berkley Memorial Cemetery]

Gray, ---- August 9, 1913 – September 28, 1913 (no tombstone; death certificate stated he died at Kalmia, the son of Howard Gray and Kate Collins, all born in Harford Co.; informant was Samuel Collins, of Bel Air) [Clark's U. M. Church Cemetery]

Gray, Bertha G. September 17, 1884 – August 25, 1975 (on the same tombstone with Junious W. Gray; obituary in *The Aegis* on August 28, 1975 stated she was born in Bel Air, the daughter of Marcus and Isabelle Moore, lived in Aberdeen and died at Brevin Nursing Home in Havre de Grace, survived by husband Junious, two nieces and two nephews; James Dorsey Card Files, African-American Obituaries, maintained at the Historical Society of Harford County, stated her middle name was Grace) [Tabernacle Mount Zion U. M. Church Cemetery]

Gray, Grayson A. April 24, 1973 – June 15, 2004, SPC, U.S. Army [Tabernacle Mount Zion U. M. Church Cemetery]

Gray, Howard Rudolph Jr. December 7, 1927 – August 29, 1994 (no tombstone; James Dorsey Card File, African American Obituaries, that is maintained at the Historical Society of Harford County, has a funeral card from the Tarring-Cargo Funeral Home and also obituary from *The Aegis* on September 2, 1994 stating he was born in Darlington, the son of Howard R. Sr. and Martha Gray, and he lived in Aberdeen; he was a dishwasher at the Maryland House Restaurant for 17 years and died at Harford Memorial Hospital, survived by 2 sons, 3 daughters, 1 brother, 1 sister, 4 grandchildren and 1 great-grandchild) [Berkley Memorial Cemetery]

Gray, James Alfred Sr. 1912-1988, Pvt., U.S. Army, World War II [Clark's U. M. Church Cemetery]

Gray, John W. July 10, 1913 – July 19, 1913 (no tombstone; death certificate stated he was the son of Charles Gray and Ethel Morgan, all born in Harford Co., and he died at Poole; informant was Ethel Gray, of Street, MD) [Berkley Memorial Cemetery]

Gray, Julia G. April 28, 1928 – January 7, 1978 (on the same tombstone with James T. Thompson inscribed "In Loving Memory of Mother and Brother") [Asbury Cemetery]

Gray, Junious W. August 9, 1897 -   (on same tombstone with Bertha G. Gray; no date of death, but he died after his wife Bertha who died in 1975) [Tabernacle Mount Zion U. M. Church Cemetery]

Gray, Mary O. 1903 (on same tombstone with Otis I. Gray) [Berkley Memorial Cemetery]

Gray, Nellie M. died April 9, 19---, age 71 (no tombstone; The James Dorsey Card File, African American Obituaries, maintained at the Historical Society of Harford County, has a card with his obituary from *The Aegis* but it is undated, stating she was born in Rocks, the daughter of the late William and Mary Heuitt; she worked at Edgewood Arsenal and retired from Harford Memorial Hospital in 1982; she was the widow of James A. Gray, Sr. (who died on 1988) and she died at Harford Memorial Hospital, survived by a son, eight grandchildren, eleven great-grandchildren and a sister) [Clark's U. M. Church Cemetery]

Gray, Otis I. 1914 (on same tombstone with Mary O. Gray) [Berkley Memorial Cemetery]

Gray, William stillborn male on July 12, 1924 (no tombstone; death certificate stated he was born in Berkley, the son of Howard Gray, born in Pennsylvania, and Martha Presberry, born in Maryland; informant was Howard Gray, of Brekley) [Berkley Memorial Cemetery]

Green, ---- February 9, 1936 – February 13, 1936 (no tombstone; death certificate stated he was born in Sharon, son of Marvin Hall, born in Harford Co., and Mildred Green, born in Sharon; informant was Aquilla Green, of Sharon) [Fairview A. M. E. Church Cemetery]

Green, ---- stillborn female died on June 30, 1921 (no tombstone; death certificate stated she was the daughter of Francis Green and Daisey Buchanan, of Rocks, all born in Maryland) [Chestnut Grove A. M. E. Church Cemetery, formerly LaGrange Cemetery at Rocks]

Green, ---- stillborn female on August 6, 1918 (no tombstone; death certificate stated "Probably tardy delivery of after coming head. It was a breech case;" daughter of David Green and Mattie F. Turner, all born in Maryland; she died at Putnam; informant was her father, of Forest Hill RFD) [West Liberty Church Cemetery]

Green, ---- stillborn male died December 11, 1917 (no tombstone; death certificate stated he was the son of

Jacob Green and Florence Kell, all born in Harford Co., and lived at Forest Hill; informant was F. P. Smithson, of Forest Hill) [Fairview A. M. E. Church Cemetery]

Green, Alex 1885 – December 7, 1927 (no tombstone; death certificate stated he was unmarried and died in Darlington, but his parents were not known) [St. James United Cemetery]

Green, Benjamin March 28, 1875 – February 1, 1934 (no tombstone; Kurtz Funeral Home Records and death certificate stated he was born in Sharon, son of Jacob Green and Mary Presberry, both born in Harford Co.; he married Maggie Kell, worked as a farm laborer until 1933 and died at home in Forest Hill; informant was Maggie Green, of Forest Hill) [Fairview A. M. E. Church Cemetery]

Green, Benjamin A. (no tombstone; military records state he served as a private in Co. F, 4th Regt., U.S.C.T.; death certificate stated he died on March 25, 1913, age about 60, but since he served in the Civil War he would have been closer to age 70; he was single and died at home in Darlington; informant was Ida Ridgely, of Darlington) [Green Spring U. M. Church Cemetery]

Green, Benjamin M. October 16, 1876 –   [Green Spring U. M. Church Cemetery]

Green, Caroline A. August 1849 –   [Green Spring U. M. Church Cemetery]

Green, Charles Millard September 29, 1942 – February 10, 1943 (no tombstone; death certificate stated he was born in Baltimore, the son of William Wilson, born in Fawn Grove, PA, and Mable W. Green, born in Baltimore; he died at home near Tollgate Road in Bel Air; informant was Miss Mable Green, of Fallston) [Tabernacle Mount Zion U. M. Church Cemetery]

Green, Daniel March – (blank), 1901 – March 2, 1918 (no tombstone; death certificate stated he was the son of James Green and Laura Smith, all born in Harford Co.; he was single and died in Havre de Grace; informant was his father, of Aberdeen) [Mt. Calvary U. A. M. E. Church Cemetery]

Green, Darryl J., "Our Darling" 1958-1960 [Union U. M. Church Cemetery]

Green, Dorothy Elizabeth Lee died January 8, 1998, age 64 (no tombstone; James Dorsey Card File, African American Obituaries, maintained at the Historical Society of Harford County, has a card with obituary from *The Aegis* on January 13, 1998 stating she was born in Newport News, VA and was the wife of Douglas W. Green, Sr.; she lived in Aberdeen and died at the Johns Hopkins Hospital in Baltimore, survived by her husband and two sons) [St. James United Cemetery]

Green, Eliza E. 18— (copied in 1992, but not found in 2018) [Union U. M. Church Cemetery]

Green, Eliza J. died August 31, 1926, age about 52 (no tombstone; death certificate stated she was the daughter of Charles Denmore and Josephine Harris, all born in Maryland; she was a widow who lived at Gravelly Hill; informant was Robert Green, of Gravelly Hill) [Green Spring U. M. Church Cemetery]

Green, Hannah J. died March 22, 1902, age 44 (inscribed "In Memory of Our Mother" and J. C. Taylor Marble Co. records stated "Hannah J. Green's colored head stone was put up Sept 1st 1933 Colord Church, Forest Hill") [Fairview A. M. E. Church Cemetery]

Green, Harry E. August 10, 1908 – July 4, 1916 (no tombstone; death certificate he was born in Perryman, the son of Grafton Pitt and Sadie Green, both born in Harford Co.; informant was Charles Taylor, of Havre de Grace) [St. James United Cemetery]

Green, Isaac E. February 27, 1916 – November 19, 1976, SFC, U.S. Army, World War II, Korea, Vietnam [Berkley Memorial Cemetery]

Green, Iva Grace, "Daughter" 1926-1965 [Union U. M. Church Cemetery]

Green, James February 9, 1915 – July 1, 1957, Maryland, PFC, U.S. Army, 216 Port Co., TC, World War II [Mt. Calvary U. A. M. E. Church Cemetery]

Green, John died October 1, 1928, age not given (no tombstone; death certificate he was single, worked as a laborer, and was the son of William Green and Susie Green, of Havre de Grace) [St. James United Cemetery]

Green, Josephine July 21, 1927 – September 9, 1928 (no tombstone; death certificate stated she was born in

Maryland, the daughter of Will Green, born in Maryland, and Georgia A. Mitchell, born in Philadelphia; she died at home in Aberdeen and informant was her father) [Mt. Calvary U. A. M. E. Church Cemetery]

Green, Laura March 15, 1863 – June 22, 1935 (no tombstone; death certificate stated she was the daughter of Joseph Smith and Virginia Brown, all born in Harford Co.; she married James E. Green and died at her home in Aberdeen; informant was Mrs. Charles H. Green, of Aberdeen) [Mt. Calvary U. A. M. E. Church Cemetery]

Green, Maggie Margarete April 1, 1870 – March 27, 1936 (no tombstone; death certificate stated she was born in Forest Hill, the daughter of Frank Kell and Darcus Ann Johnson, both born in Harford Co.; she married Benjamin Green and died a widow at home in Forest Hill; informant was Nathan Kell, of Forest Hill) [Fairview A. M. E. Church Cemetery]

Green, Mary C. June 9, 1855 – April 16, 1916 (no tombstone; death certificate stated she was born in Harford Co., daughter of David Presbury, born in Maryland, but the name of her mother was not known to informant Jacob Green, of Sharon; she was married and died at home in Sharon; undertaker Charles E. Hornberger stated buried at Hickory Cemetery, but there is no such place [probably buried at Fairview A. M. E. Church Cemetery]

Green, Milton February 14, 1904 – September 5, 1932 (no tombstone; death certificate stated he was the son of Sydney and Sarah Green, all born in Maryland; he was single, a laborer at Havre de Grace RFD, and died in Havre de Grace Hospital; information was from their records) [Gravel Hill Cemetery]

Green, Rachel A. 1928 – February 10, 1919, age 90 (no tombstone; death certificate stated she was born in Maryland, but informant Charles H. Webster, of Darlington, did not know her parents' names and birth places; she was a widow and died in Darlington) [Berkley Memorial Cemetery]

Green, Rena July 15, 1881 – June 7, 1915 (no tombstone; death certificate stated she was the daughter of Mark Prigg and Mary Cain, all born in Maryland; she was married (name of husband not given) and died at home in Darlington; informant was Duglas Cain, of Darlington) [Berkley Memorial Cemetery]

Green, Robert December 7, 1929 – March 10, 1930 (no tombstone; death certificate stated he was the son of Will Green and Georgeanna Mitchell, all born in Maryland; he died at home in Aberdeen; informant was his father) [Mt. Calvary U. A. M. E. Church Cemetery]

Green, Susan July 1, 1863 – July 4, 1912 (no tombstone; death certificate she was the unmarried daughter of Samuel Green and Fannie Hoard, of Havre de Grace) [St. James United Cemetery]

Green, Theodore Roosevelt died in May 1989, age 85 (no tombstone; James Dorsey Card File, African American Obituaries, maintained at the Historical Society of Harford County, has a card with some information from *The Record* on May 24, 1989, but not the complete obituary0 [St. James United Cemetery]

Green, Viola R. August 14, 1912 – January 25, 1932 (no tombstone; death certificate stated she was born in Fallston, the daughter of Benjamin Johnson, born in Maryland, and Ethel Buckhanan, born in Pennsylvania; she married William Green, lived at 18 Bond St, in Bel Air and died at home due to rupture during pregnancy; informant was Mrs. Ethel Batson, same address) [Tabernacle Mount Zion U. M. Church Cemetery]

Green, William H. January 27, 1878 –   [Green Spring U. M. Church Cemetery]

Green, Willie March 1, 1901 – May 5, 1951 (no tombstone; Pennington Funeral Home records stated he was born in North Carolina, the son of Marcellus Green and Lucy Gardner, married Georgia Anna ----, and died in Havre de Grace [Mt. Calvary U. M. E. Church Cemetery]

Green, Wilma E., neé Dunsen, December 2, 1915 – January 17, 1980 [Chestnut Grove A. M. E. Church Cemetery, formerly LaGrange Cemetery at Rocks]

Greene Twins 1962-1962 [Fairview A. M. E. Church Cemetery]

Greene, Alice D. 1885-1978 (on same tombstone with David A. Greene; obituary in *The Aegis* on May 4, 1978 stated Alice Dorsey Greene died May 2, 1978 at Key Circle Hospice in Baltimore; she was born in Harford County, the daughter of Shadrick Dorsey and Mary Wells, and was the widow of David Greene; she was survived by a son, 3 brothers and 2 sisters) [Berkley Memorial Cemetery]

Greene, Annie Marie August 28, 1913 – October 12, 2004 (on same tombstone with Jacob Aquilla Greene;

obituary and photo in *The Aegis* on October 15, 2004 stated she was born in Shawsville, daughter of Clarence B. Smith and Annie May Johnson, and was the widow of Rev. J. Aquilla Greene; she was very active in the Fairview AME Cburch and the Mt. Joy AME Church and received several certificates of merit; she also worked for Spencer's and Donald Stubbs Canneries, Harford County Board of Education, John Archer School, and Greene's Garage; she died at home in Forest Hill, survived by a son Calvin A. Greene, a sister-in-law, a daughter-in-law, 7 grandchildren, 16 great-grandchildren, 5 great-great-grandchildren, and was predeceased by a son William E. Greene) [Fairview A. M. E. Church Cemetery]

Greene, Calvin A. 1930-2018 (temporary marker; cement foundation for tombstone was poured on September 27, 2018) [Fairview A. M. E. Church Cemetery]

Greene, Charles E. March 22, 1934 – July 22, 2004, U.S. Marine Corps [St. James United Cemetery]

Greene, Dale T., "Beloved Husband & Father" February 28, 1944 – February 27, 1972 [Fairview A. M. E. Church Cemetery]

Greene, David A. 1889-1973 (on same tombstone with Alice D. Greene; obituary in *The Aegis* on October 4, 1973 stated he was born in Sharon, MD on June 11, 1887, the son of Jacob and Mary Greene; he lived at Route 1, Box 162, Bel Air, married Alice Dorsey and died at Harford Memorial Hospital in Havre de Grace, survived by his wife, two brothers and one sister) [Berkley Memorial Cemetery]

Greene, Delvin L., "Beloved Son and Brother" January 24, 1980 – April 27, 2000 (inscription with photo) [Berkley Memorial Cemetery]

Greene, Florence A. February 22, 1887 – July 25, 1972 (on same tombstone with Jacob H., William A. and Harry R. Greene as copied in 1987, but inexplicably not found in 2018) [Fairview A. M. E. Church Cemetery]

Greene, Glenda L. 1934-2017 (small metal funeral home marker and a small white ceramic cross) [Fairview A. M. E. Church Cemetery]

Greene, Hannah E. September 16, 1907 – January 5, 1991 (on same tombstone with Roy L. Greene; James Dorsey Card File, African American Obituaries, maintained at the Historical Society of Harford County, has a card with obituary from *The Aegis* on January 9, 1991 stating Hannah Elizabeth Greene was the daughter of Howard W. Stewart and Mary Kell and the wife of Roy L. Greene; she lived in Forest Hill and died at Fallston General Hospital, survived by her husband, two sons, five daughters, two sisters, fifteen grandchildren and eight great-grandchildren) [Fairview A. M. E. Church Cemetery]

Greene, Hannah E., "Ralph's Mom" January 11, 1930 – February 23, 2013 [Fairview A. M. E. Church Cemetery]

Greene, Harry R. May 25, 1905 – December 15, 1921 (on same tombstone with Jacob H., Florence A. and William A. Greene when copied in 1987, but inexplicably not found in 2018; death certificate stated Harry Roosevelt Greene was born in Forest Hill, the son of Jacob H. Greene, of Sharon, and Florence A. Kell, of Forest Hill; he was single and worked as a farm laborer at Forest Hill; informant was his father, Jacob H. Greene, of Forest Hill) [Fairview A. M. E. Church Cemetery]

Greene, Ida S. 1884-1969 (copied in 1987, but not found in 2018) [Fairview A. M. E. Church Cemetery]

Greene, Jacob Aquilla January 7, 1909 – July 28, 2004 (on same tombstone with Annie Marie Greene; obituary and photo in *The Aegis* on August 6, 20004 stated Rev. Jacob Aquilla Green was born in Harford Co., the son of Charles and Ida Greene, and was the owner of J. A. Greene and Sons, Inc. Garage, in Cooptown, and was a school bus contractor for 53 years, owning 13 buses; he was a trustee, class leader and secretary of Fairview AME Church, was president of the Colored Voters League, president of the Bel Air Colored High School PTA, and director and bandleader of the Fairview Troop Band; sometime after 1962 he was ordained a local deacon and served several churches; he died at home in Cooptown and was survived by his wife Anne Marie Smith Greene, a son Calvin A. Greene, a sister Mildred Fisher, 7 grandchildren, 16 great-grandchildren, 4 great-great-grandchildren, two daughters-in-law and was preceded in death by a son William E. Greene) [Fairview A. M. E. Church Cemetery]

Greene, Jacob H. January 28, 1886 – January 17, 1960 (on same tombstone with Florence A. Greene, Harry R.

Greene and William A. Greene when copied in 1987, but inexplicably not found in 2018) [Fairview A. M. E. Church Cemetery]

Greene, James Edward September 7, 1914 – December 11, 1971, TEC5, Army Air Force, World War II (copied in 1987, but inexplicably not found in 2018) [Fairview A. M. E. Church Cemetery]

Greene, Laura H. April 8, 1917 – January 15, 1989 (on the same tombstone with Maurice H. Greene inscribed with Psalm 23) [Union U. M. Church Cemetery]

Greene, Marian M. July 14, 1922 – February 20, 1989 [Fairview A. M. E. Church Cemetery]

Greene, Maurice H. June 30, 1913 – Mary 21, 1988 (on the same tombstone with Laura H. Greene inscribed with Psalm 23) [Union U. M. Church Cemetery]

Greene, Robert R., "Our Beloved Brother" February 25, 1925 – January 6, 1994 (tombstone; James Dorsey Card File, African American Obituaries, maintained at the Historical Society of Harford County, has a card with obituary from *The Aegis* on January 12, 1994 stating Robert Roosevelt McKinley Greene was a native of Forest Hill and the son of Roy L. Greene and Hannah Stewart; he lived in Forest Hill, worked as a cook at Aberdeen Proving Ground and also did masonry, and died at Fallston General Hospital, survived by a brother and five sisters) [Fairview A. M. E. Church Cemetery]

Greene, Roy L. July 31, 1905 – April 8, 1994 (on same tombstone with Hannah E. Greene; James Dorsey Card File, African American Obituaries, maintained at the Historical Society of Harford County, has a card with obituary from *The Aegis* on April 13, 1994 stating Roy Linly Greene worked for the John Archer Cemetery Co. and died a widower at home in Forest Hill; his wife was Hannah Stewart and he was survived by a son, 5 daughters, a brother, a sister, 15 grandchildren, 8 great-grandchildren and 3 great-great-grandchildren) [Fairview A. M. E. Church Cemetery]

Greene, William A. July 5, 1910 – July 26, 1965 (on same tombstone with Jacob H., Harry R. and Florence A. Greene when copied in 1987, but inexplicably not found in 2018) [Fairview A. M. E. Church Cemetery]

Greene, William E. Sr. 1933-1967 (small metal funeral home marker and also a small white ceramic cross) [Fairview A. M. E. Church Cemetery]

Greer, Laura Virginia 1879-1961 (inscribed "In God We Trust") [Asbury Cemetery]

Greer, Thomas Garfield October 9, 1885 – December 25, 1962 [Asbury Cemetery]

Gregg, Annie E. September 4, 1914 – February 10, 1957 [Community Baptist Church Cemetery]

Gregg, Betty 1938-2007 (small metal funeral home marker) [John Wesley U. M. E. Church Cemetery in Abingdon]

Gregg, Frank L. December 14, 1934 -   (on same tombstone with Genevieve L. Gregg) [Berkley Memorial Cemetery]

Gregg, Genevieve L. September 22, 1936 – October 6, 2017 (on same tombstone with Frank L. Gregg) [Berkley Memorial Cemetery]

Gregg, Hilda I. January 14, 1917 – January 23, 1969 [Community Baptist Church Cemetery]

Gregg, Robert L. October 15, 1930 – February 28, 2006 (inscribed "In Loving Memory" and "Never To Be Forgotten") [Berkley Memorial Cemetery]

Gregory, Brandon "JC" April 6, 1985 – August 2, 2005 (tombstone with photo and inscribed "In Loving Memory" and "Always In Our Hearts" and "We Miss You So Much" and "Mom, Dad, Pop, Monique, Nicole, Shawn and Krickett") [Berkley Memorial Cemetery]

Grey, Mina March 22, 1899 – February 13, 1915 (no tombstone; death certificate stated she died near Darlington, the daughter of Mamie Gray Harris, both born in Maryland, but her father's name was not known to the informant Mamie Gray Harris, of Street, MD) [Clark's U. M. Church Cemetery]

Grier, Robert Wesley 1926-2017, SDG3, U.S. Navy [Berkley Memorial Cemetery]

Griffin, Barbara A. July 4, 1947 -   (on same tombstone with Ralph E. Griffin inscribed "Till We Meet Again") [Berkley Memorial Cemetery]

Griffin, Cora H. 1938-2014 (small metal funeral home marker) [Berkley Memorial Cemetery]

Griffin, Edna M. 1896-1946 (on same tombstone with Rev. Robert A. Griffin) [Union U. M. Church Cemetery]

Griffin, Eliza E. February 25, 1862 – September 15, 1916 (inscribed "At Rest;" death certificate stated she was the married daughter of William H. Stansbury and Delhia Tildon, all born in Maryland; she died at home near Aberdeen and was buried in "Sydney Park" Cemetery; informant was Robert Griffin, of Aberdeen RFD) [Union U. M. Church Cemetery]

Griffin, Elva A. 1918-1998 (on same tombstone with James E. Griffin) [Berkley Memorial Cemetery]

Griffin, Emerson Newton November 6, 1931 – July 12, 1977, SSgt., U.S. Air Force, Korea [Union U. M. Church Cemetery]

Griffin, George died February 24, 1929, age about 65 (no tombstone; death certificate stated he was born in Maryland and married, but parents not known to informant Samelia Bowser) [Union U. M. Church Cemetery]

Griffin, George B. 1935-2014 (small metal funeral home marker) [Berkley Memorial Cemetery]

Griffin, Isaac C. 1894-1937 (inscribed "In Loving Memory;" death certificate stated he was the husband of Mary E. Griffin and the son of Robert A. Griffin and Eliza Stansbury) [Union U. M. Church Cemetery]

Griffin, James E. 1912-   (on same tombstone with Elva A. Griffin) [Berkley Memorial Cemetery]

Griffin, James E. Jr. October 20, 1940 – March 21, 2007 [Berkley Memorial Cemetery]

Griffin, Mary Elizabeth 1900-1965 (inscribed "Rest In Peace") [Union U. M. Church Cemetery]

Griffin, Norma P. 1937-2014 (small metal funeral home marker; funeral notice and photo in *The Aegis* stated Norma P. "Patsy" Griffin, neé Cromwell, of Forest Heights, MD, died on October 10, 2014, age 77, at Georgetown University Hospital, Washington, D.C., and was buried in St. James United Cemetery in Havre de Grace) [St. James United Cemetery]

Griffin, Ralph E. August 20, 1943 – February 18, 2002 (on same tombstone with Barbara A. Griffin inscribed "Till We Meet Again") [Berkley Memorial Cemetery]

Griffin, Robert A. (Rev.) 1892-1940 (on same tombstone with Edna M. Griffin) [Union U. M. Church Cemetery]

Griffin, Robert A. died May 13, 1931, age about 75 (no tombstone; death certificate stated he was the son of Isaac Griffin and Charlotte Glover; informant was Mrs. Robert A. Glover, of Aberdeen) [Union U. M. Church Cemetery]

Griffin, Robert E. 1856-1931 (inscribed "At Rest") [Union U. M. Church Cemetery]

Griffin, Thomas February 7, 1868 – October 16, 1930 (no tombstone; death certificate stated he was born in Maryland, but his parents were not known to informant Mrs. Lillian Griffin; he was married, worked as a day laborer and died at home near Aberdeen) [Mt. Calvary U. A. M. E. Church Cemetery]

Grimes, Walter July 22, 1926 – August 5, 1926 (no tombstone; death certificate stated he was the son of William Grimes and Florence Jones, all born in Maryland, and lived in Havre de Grace) [Gravel Hill Cemetery]

Grinage, Annie March 6, 1857 – February 24, 1937 (no tombstone; death certificate stated she was born in Harford Co., daughter of Perry Hall, born in Baltimore, but her mother was unknown to informant Mr. Asbry Thomas, of Aberdeen; she married William Grinage and lived and died a widow at home on Bel Air Road in Aberdeen RFD) [Mt. Calvary U. A. M. E. Church Cemetery]

Grinage, Charles Washington died March 25, 1966, age 85 (no tombstone; obituary in *The Aegis* on March 31, 1966 stated he was the son of John Wesley Grinage and Mary Elizabeth Lewis, resided on Route 1, Aberdeen, died in Harford Memorial Hospital in Havre de Grace and was survived by his wife Mabel Lee Grinage, a sister, and two-stepsons and their children) [Mt. Calvary U. A. M. E. Church Cemetery]

Grinage, Mabel F. (Rev.) 1908-1980 (inscribed "In Loving Memory Of" and buried in section 8; obituary in *The Aegis* on September 25, 1980 stated Rev. Mabel Frances Grinage was born near Lexington, VA, the daughter of Mr. & Mrs. Herbert Lee, and was ordained in 1966; she was church superintendent of the Mt. Calvary AME Church for 23 years; she lived on First Street in Aberdeen and died at Harford Memorial Hospital on September 17, 1980; she was the widow of Charles Grinage and was survived by a son Howard L. Scott, a step-son Vernon Brown, 7 grandchildren, and 13 great-grandchildren) [Mt. Calvary U. A. M. E. Church Cemetery]

Grinage, Martha A. died November 21, 1914, age 24 years, 5 months (no tombstone; death certificate stated she was born in Baltimore, the daughter of Finie Furguson, born in Howard Co., but her mother was not known to informant, Eliza A. Hooper, of Aberdeen; she was married, worked as a nurse and died at Calvary) [Mt. Calvary U. A. M. E. Church Cemetery]

Grinage, Mary Elizabeth June 19, 1863 – December 11, 1928 (no tombstone; death certificate stated she was the daughter of William and Julia Lewis and all were born in Maryland; she died a widow in Aberdeen; informant was Charles W. Grinage, of Aberdeen) [Mt. Calvary U. A. M. E. Church Cemetery]

Grinage, Sidney 1864-1925 (copied in 2018, but not on the 1987 and 2002 lists; death certificate stated "Sydney Grinage" was the daughter of Louis Ash and Mary F. Presbury, all born in Maryland; she was married and died on July 25, 1925, age about 60; informant was Nathaniel Ash, of Gravelly Hill RFD) [Gravel Hill Cemetery]

Grinage, Thomas February 23, 1863 – March 2, 1928 (no tombstone; death certificate stated he was the son of William Grinage, both born in Maryland; mother's name was unknown to informant Nathaniel Ash, of Gravelly Hill; he was a widower and laborer near Havre de Grace) [Gravel Hill Cemetery]

Grinage, William H. September 24, 1833 – November 23, 1928 (no tombstone; death certificate stated he was the son of Benjamin Grinage, both born in Maryland, but the name and birth place of his mother was not known to informant Mrs. Annie Grinage, of Aberdeen; William was married, worked as a farmer and died in Aberdeen) [Mt. Calvary U. A. M. E. Church Cemetery]

Grubb, John died January 6, 1884, age 105 (no tombstone; his death notice in *The Aegis* on January 18, 1884 stated he was found dead in his bed on Thomas W. Hall's farm near Abingdon; he had formerly belonged to the Rumsey family of Baltimore Co., but for nearly 40 years had lived in the house where he died; place of burial not given; probably at John Wesley) [John Wesley U. M. E. Church Cemetery in Abingdon]

Guary, Adrian A. February 28, 1964 – June 10, 1970 [Berkley Memorial Cemetery]

Guary, Audrey A. May 8, 1960 – July 12, 2015 (inscribed "Always Loving, Always Loved") [Berkley Memorial Cemetery]

Guary, Moses Jr. November 24, 1924 – July 25, 2004, U.S. Army [Berkley Memorial Cemetery]

Guary, Ora Mae 1921-2004 (small metal funeral home marker) [Berkley Memorial Cemetery]

Guest, Betty L. 1917-2005 (small metal funeral home marker) [Berkley Memorial Cemetery]

Guest, Darvell R. 1979-2005 (small metal funeral home marker) [Berkley Memorial Cemetery]]

Gunter, B. Rosetta August 17, 1938 – October 11, 1990 (on same tombstone with Michael D. Gunter and Hazel E. Jones) [St. James United Cemetery]

Gunter, Michael D. January 10, 1957 -   (on same tombstone with B. Rosetta Gunter and Hazel E. Jones) [St. James United Cemetery]

Guy, Hannah (Mrs.) died January 6, 1917, age 90 (no tombstone; death certificate stated she was a widow when she died in Bel Air, but her parents were not known to informant Joseph Toney) [Tabernacle Mount Zion U. M. Church Cemetery]

Gwynn, ---- stillborn female died July 21, 1918 (no tombstone; death certificate stated she died in Darlington, the daughter of Louis Gwynn and Carrie Elsie Bell, all born in Maryland; the informant was Louis Gwynn, of Darlington) [Clark's U. M. Church Cemetery]

Gwynn, Anna E. May 15, 1877 – February 13, 1927 (no tombstone; death certificate stated she was the daughter of Jessie Snowden and Caroline Gibson, all born in Maryland; she was married and died at McCann's Corner; informant was Elias Gwynn, of Street, MD) [Clark's U. M. Church Cemetery]

Gwynn, Carrie B. 1882-1976 (on same tombstone with Lewis Gwynn; obituary in *The Aegis* on September 23, 1976 stated she was born on November 21, 1882 in Harford Co., the daughter of Lloyd and Barbara Frances Bell, lived at 121 Archer St. in Bel Air and died at Brevin Nursing Home in Havre de Grace; she was survived by 3 sons, 4 daughters, 14 grand- children, 34 great-grandchildren and 2 great-great-grandchildren) [Clark's U. M. Church Cemetery]

Gwynn, Cecelia E. 1903-1970 [Clark's U. M. Church Cemetery]

Gwynn, Lewis 1877-1950 (on same tombstone with Carrie B. Lewis; death certificate stated he was born on August 15, 1877 and died on June 22, 1950, the son of ---- (blank) Gwynn and Julia Brogmenev(?); he was born in Essex, VA, married ----, worked as a farm laborer and lived in rural Forest Hill for 16 years; the informant was Carrie B. Gwynn, of Forest Hill) [Clark's U. M. Church Cemetery]

Gwynn, Lewis L. 1900-1980 (Masonic symbol) [Clark's U. M. Church Cemetery]

Gwynn, Marion C. February 25, 1928 – March 10, 1938 (no tombstone; death certificate stated she was born in Baltimore Co. and died at home at Gibson in Harford Co., the daughter of Corrina Whittington, who was born in Harford Co., but the name of the child's father was not known to the informant Miss Corrina Whittington, of Forest Hill) [Clark's U. M. Church Cemetery]

Hackett, Andrew died November 29, 1893, age 22 (no tombstone; death notice in *The Aegis* on December 8, 1893 stated he died in Bagley; burial place not stated [probably Tabernacle Mount Zion U. M. Church Cemetery]

Hackett, Benjamin Franklin February 7, 1871 – October 4, 1927 (no tombstone; death certificate stated he was born in Baltimore Co., the son of John Hackett, born in Baltimore Co., and Annie Jones, born in Baltimore City; he was married, worked as a farm helper, died at Wilna and was buried in "Mt. Colored Cem.;" informant was Catherine Hackett, of Joppa) [Mt. Zion U. M. Church Cemetery]

Hackett, Katie Anne October 11, 1869 – February 16, 1961 (inscribed "My Beloved Great Grandmother") [Mt. Zion U. M. Church Cemetery]

Hackett, Mary M. July 22, 1888 – February 15, 1963 (Kurtz Funeral Home Records stated she was the daughter of John and Annie Hackett and she lived at Old Bay Farm in Havre de Grace for 40 years; informant was Sen. William S. James who also paid the funeral bill; undertaker noted "Taken from family Bible by grand child Thelma Akins, 11 Bond St., Bel Air.") [Berkley Memorial Cemetery]

Hackett, Moses died February 1, 1873, age 90 [Tabernacle Mount Zion U. M. Church Cemetery]

Hackett, Sarah E. died April 12, 1885, age 96 (no tombstone; obituary in *The Aegis* on April 24, 1885 stated she was born in Little Britain Township, Chester Co., PA, and died at home near Franklinville, survived by 15 children, 46 grandchildren and 21 great-grandchildren; an article in *The Aegis* on March 1, 1889 stated Sarah Hackett was buried at Hendon's Hill) [Hendon Hill Cemetery]

Hagland, Sarah 1877-1929 (copied in 1987, but not found in 2018; perhaps toppled over) [Asbury Cemetery]

Hague, Gertrude B. February 21, 1925 -   (on same tombstone with Herman N. Hague) [Berkley Memorial Cemetery]

Hague, Herman N. October 24, 1922 – August 6, 1997 (on same tombstone with Gertrude B. Hague) [Berkley Memorial Cemetery]

Hague, Julia E. June 13, 1899 – February 6, 1992 (tombstone; obituary in *The Aegis* on February 26, 1992 stated Julia Erby Hague was born in Bluefield, WV, the daughter of Simon and Corena Erby, and she was once a domestic employee of Cab Calloway's sister Ruth in New York City; she lived in Havre de Grace, was the widow of David Hague and died at Brevin Nursing Home, survived by a son, three brothers, four sisters, nine grandchildren and many great-grandchildren) [Berkley Memorial Cemetery]

Haines, Arlene R. "Beloved Wife and Mother" March 19, 1932 – May 11, 2001 [Berkley Memorial Cemetery]

Haines, Betty died June 9, 1920, age about 73 (no tombstone; death certificate she was born in Virginia, parents unknown, and she died in Havre de Grace; informant was James Haines) [St. James United Cemetery]

Haines, David Henry August 15, 1907 – January 16, 1930 (no tombstone; death certificate stated he was the son of David Haines and Molly Harris, all born in Maryland; he was single, worked as a laborer and died in Dublin; informant was Molly Haines, of Stree.t, MD) [Berkley Memorial Cemetery]

Haines, Elzena April 19, 1908 – March 24, 1911 (no tombstone; death certificate stated she was born in Dublin, the daughter of David Harris, born in Harford Co., and Mollie Harris, born in Bel Air, and died in Darlington; informant was her father David Haines, of Street, MD) [Berkley Memorial Cemetery]

Haines, George Nelson January 16, 1913 – March 24, 1913 (no tombstone; death certificate stated he was the son of David Haines and Molly Harris, all born in Maryland; he died at home in Darlington; informant was his father David Haines, of Darlington) [Berkley Memorial Cemetery]

Haines, Helen October 3, 1910 – April 29, 1929 (no tombstone; death certificate stated she was the daughter of David Haines and Mollie Harris, all born in Maryland, and she died at home in Berkley; informant was Mrs. Mollie Haines, of Darlington) [Berkley Memorial Cemetery]

Haines, James A. Sr., "Great Husband and Father" April 13, 1926 – November 20, 1998, U.S. Army, World War II [Berkley Memorial Cemetery]

Haines, James Arthur Jr. May 15, 1952 – May 6, 1978 (inscribed "Always In Our Hearts;" obituary in *The Aegis* on May 11, 1978 stated he was the son of James A. Haines, Sr. and Arlene Haines, of Bel Air, and he worked as a chauffeur for the Chesapeake Cab Company in Havre de Grace and died from injuries sustained when struck by a car on Route 40 at Robin Hood Road; he was survived by his parents, 3 brothers, 3 sisters and grandfather James Presberry, of Darlington) [Berkley Memorial Cemetery]

Haines, John William April 22, 1916 – October 13, 1916 (no tombstone; death certificate stated he was the son of David Haines and Mollie Harris, all born in Maryland; and died at home in Darlington; informant was David Haines, of Darlington) [Berkley Memorial Cemetery]

Haines, Leona Virginia January 16, 1951 – March 5, 1951 (no tombstone; death certificate stated she was the daughter of James Aurthur Haines and Arlene Ellis, of Havre de Grace) [St. James United Cemetery]

Haines, Mary E. died November 26, 1901, age 57 (no tombstone; death certificate stated she was the wife of John Haines and the daughter of Lewis Tillman, but her mother's name was blank; she was born in Pennsylvania and died at Berkley, leaving a husband and one child) [Berkley Memorial Cemetery]

Haines, Phillip H. January 26, 1891 – November 16, 1955, Maryland, Pvt., 53 CO, 153 Depot Brigade, World War I (tombstone; military records stated he was born in Muttonberg, lived in Darlington, was inducted into the service on August 23, 1918, served overseas from October 20, 1918 to July 4, 1919 and was honorably discharged on July 10, 1919) [Berkley Memorial Cemetery]

Hairston, Elaine M. April 14, 1934 –   (on same tombstone with McCoy F. Hairston) [Tabernacle Mount Zion U. M. Church Cemetery]

Hairston, McCoy F. May 26, 1918 – July 14, 1979, CWO III, 3 U.S. Army (on same tombstone with Elaine M. Hairston; obituary in *The Aegis*, July 19, 1979, stated McCoy Fuller Hairston died July 14, 1979, age 61, and his wife Elaine Clay Hairston was still living at that time) [Tabernacle Mount Zion U. M. Church Cemetery]

Hairston, Rashaad Dwayne November 21, 1980 – March 30, 1994 (buried in section 24; tombstone inscribed "In God's Loving Care") [Mt. Calvary U. A. M. E. Church Cemetery]

Hall, ---- (no tombstone, but Kurtz Funeral Home records stated Isaac Hall's son was buried in a plain cherry coffin on August 9, 1880 from near Powel's Mill) [West Liberty Church Cemetery]

Hall, ---- stillborn male on April 10, 1938 (no tombstone; death certificate stated he was born in Fallston, son of Elizabeth Hall, born in Harford Co., but his father's name was not known to informant Abbie Hall, of Fallston; buried in "The Mountain Colored Cemetery") [Mt. Zion U. M. Church Cemetery]

Hall, Abbie Jane December 17, 1888 – October 21, 1971 [Fairview A. M. E. Church Cemetery]

Hall, Alfred H. October 30, 1861 – May 16, 1951 (on same tombstone with wife Martha C. Hall; death certificate stated he was born near Rutledge, the son of Isaac Hall and Charlotte Brown; he was a farm laborer and died a widower in rural Fallston where he had lived for 65 years; informant was Reno E. Hall, of Hyde, MD) [West Liberty Church Cemetery]

Hall, Amanda 1875-1937 (on same tombstone with husband Charles Hall; death certificate stated Amanda Ellen Hall was born August – (blank), 1875 and died September 12, 1937, age 62 years and 1 month; she was the daughter of Richard and Charity Cromwell and they all were born in Harford Co.; she married Charles Hall and died at home in Rutledge where she had lived for 29 years; informant was Charles Hall, of Fallston; Kurtz Funeral Home Record Book 1937-1943, p. 35, stated the same information) [West Liberty Church Cemetery]

Hall, Amelia November 16, 1869 – January 9, 1930 (no tombstone; death certificate stated she was born in Virginia and married, but her parents were unknown to informant Joseph Hall) [Union U. M. Church Cemetery]

Hall, Anna Mae October 12, 1891 or 1893 – October 4, 1931 (tombstone inscribed born in 1891, but death certificate stated born in 1893, daughter of George Clouders and Emma Williams, and all born in Kentucky; she married Edgar D. Hall and died at home in Churchville) [Clark's U. M. Church Cemetery]

Hall, Annie, wife of Joseph Hall, died July 7, 1904, age 92 (inscribed "In Memory of My Dear Mother") [Asbury Cemetery]

Hall, Aquilla (Rev.) died after 1886 (no tombstone; his wife Mary's obituary in *The Aegis* on October 1, 1886 stated he was in charge of a congregation in Washington, D.C., but had been known as a temperance orator in Bel Air and had formerly worked for many years on the farms of Col. E. H. Webster and James McCormick; he was probably buried beside his wife) [Hendon Hill Cemetery]

Hall, Arthur, son of Howard and Maria Hall, January 7, 1895 – August 3, 1961 [West Liberty Church Cemetery]

Hall, Bessie August 25, 1897 – December 18, 1986 [Berkley Memorial Cemetery]

Hall, C. Parker August 21, 1907 – August 1, 1944 (no tombstone; Harkins Funeral Home Records stated he was born in Harford Co., the son of Charles C. Hall, born in Harford Co., and Hattie Parker, born in Philadelphia; he was married (wife's name was not given), worked as a laborer and died at home in Whiteford R. D.; informant was his father) [Chestnut Grove A. M. E. Church Cemetery, formerly LaGrange Cemetery at Rocks]

Hall, Charles 1874-1964 (on same tombstone with wife Amanda Hall) [West Liberty Church Cemetery]

Hall, Charles April 2, 1892 – July 31, 1977, PFC, U.S. Army, World War I (tombstone; military records state he lived in Aberdeen and was inducted into service on September 1, 1918, age 23; he served in Co. C, 811 Pioneer Inf., was overseas from October 20, 1918 to July 4, 1919 and was honorably discharged on July 10, 1919) [Union U. M. Church Cemetery]

Hall, Charles Clark October 1, 1871 – March 25, 1946 (no tombstone; death certificate stated he was born in Harford Co., married Hattie P. ---- (born 1875), worked as a farmer and died at Rocks; his father was James Hall, but mother not known to informant Hattie P. Hall, of Rocks; Harkins Funeral Home Records stated his funeral was authorized by the Welfare Board) [Chestnut Grove A. M. E. Church Cemetery, formerly LaGrange Cemetery at Rocks]

Hall, Charles E. June 7, 1872 – December 2, 1933 (no tombstone; death certificate stated he was the son of Elisha M. Hall and Ruth E. Warin, all born in Maryland; he was single, worked as a laborer in Fallston and died in Havre de Grace Hospital; informant was Daniel Hall) [Tabernacle Mount Zion U. M. Church Cemetery]

Hall, Charles W. September 12, 1888 – January 2, 1959 (on same tombstone with Elizabeth Hall Brown) [Asbury Cemetery]

Hall, Charlotte Ann died March 6, 1888, age 58 years and 10 months [West Liberty Church Cemetery]

Hall, Cynthia Vernice June 11, 1944 – October 26, 2010, "Forever In Our Hearts" (tombstone with her picture) [Asbury Cemetery]

Hall, Dora, daughter of E. Merryman and Ruth E. Hall, died February 5, 1897, age 18 (on same tombstone with Elijah A. Hall; death notice in *The Aegis* on February 12, 1897 stated she was a grown daughter of Merryman Hall and was buried at "Mountain colored church, one of the largest funerals seen for some time") [Mt. Zion U. M. Church Cemetery]

Hall, E. Merryman, "Father" died February 7, 1907, age 58 years and 8 months (on same obelisk with Ruth E. Hall and Sarah C. Wann; death certificate stated Elijah M. Hall was born in Harford Co., the son of Elijah Hall, born in Harford Co., and ---- (blank) Hardy, born in Baltimore; he was a laborer and died at home near Fallston; informant was his wife Ruth Hall]

Hall, Edele Bailey 1912-2000 (small metal funeral home marker) [Fairview A. M. E. Church Cemetery]

Hall, Elijah A., son of E. Merryman and Ruth E. Hall, died November 22, 1897, age 17 years, 2 months and 5 days (on the same tombstone with Dora Hall) [Mt. Zion U. M. Church Cemetery]

Hall, Elizabeth March 16, 1919 – May 5, 1919 (no tombstone; death certificate stated she was the daughter of Fred Cain and Elenor Hall, all born in Harford Co.; she died at home at Madonna; informant was William A. Hall, of White Hall RFD) [Chestnut Grove A. M. E. Church Cemetery, formerly LaGrange Cemetery at Rocks]

Hall, Elizabeth J. October 28, 1904 – October 17, 1968 (on same tombstone with William A. Hall, Jr.) [Fairview A. M. E. Church Cemetery]

Hall, Elizella S. "Beloved Mother and Grandmother" 1923-1998 [Foster's Hill Cemetery]

Hall, Ellsworth, son of Henry Hall, 1894-1932 (tombstone; J. C. Taylor Marble Co. records stated "Ellsworth Hall's Marble head stone was put up June 25th 1932 Hendon Hill, ordered by Otha Hall, Bel Air") [Hendon Hill Cemetery]

Hall, Florence May May 2, 1912 – September 8, 1912 (no tombstone; death certificate stated she was daughter of John T. Hall and Sarah Brown, all born in Harford Co.; she died at home near Perryman and was buried in "Sidney Park Cemetery;" informant was her father) [Union U. M. Church Cemetery]

Hall, George died July 18, 1891, age 96, "At Rest" (tombstone; James Dorsey Card File, African American Obituaries, maintained at the Historical Society of Harford County, has a card with obituary from the *Harford Democrat* on July 24, 1891 stating "Uncle George Hall died on the 17th instant, near Upper Cross Roads, aged about 100 years") [West Liberty Church Cemetery]

Hall, George William died October 23, 1922, age 67 (no tombstone; death certificate stated he was the son of James Hall and Carline Morgan, all born in Harford Co.; he was married, worked as a farmer and died at home in Rocks; informant was his brother Charles Hall, of Forest Hill) [William C. Rice Memorial Cemetery, St. James U. M. Church]

Hall, Harry J. died April 24, 1950, age 66 (no tombstone; death certificate stated he was born in Pennsylania, worked as a farm hand, lived at Pylesville and died a widower in Harford Memorial Hospital in Havre de Grace; father was shown as Jacob Chambers *(sic)*, but his mother's name was not known, according to hospital records) [Chestnut Grove A. M. E. Church Cemetery, formerly LaGrange Cemetery at Rocks]

Hall, Harry W. July 7, 1894 – August 1, 1948 (no tombstone; death certificate stated he was the son of Harry Hall and Annie W. Sims, of Aberdeen, and he was a veteran of World War I) [Union U. M. Church Cemetery]

Hall, Hattie February 12, 1881 – May 31, 1919 (no tombstone; death certificate stated she was the married daughter of Richard Moore and Millie Griffin, all born in Harford County; informant was William P. Wilmore, of Aberdeen RFD) [Union U. M. Church Cemetery]

Hall, Hattie P. died December 18, 1946, age 72 (no tombstone; death certificate stated she was born in Pennsylvania in 1874, parents unknown; she married Charles Hall, lived near Street, and died in Harford Memorial Hospital in Havre de Grace; information from hospital record) [Chestnut Grove A. M. E. Church Cemetery, formerly LaGrange Cemetery at Rocks]

Hall, Henry died November 27, 1901, age 92 years, 10 months and 3 days (no tombstone; death certificate stated he was born in Maryland, the son of Carville and Margaret Hall, worked as a laborer, was married to Mary Hall and Sallie Hall, and died in Bel Air; on the back of death certificate it is written "Abingdon" so he is probably buried at John Wesley) [John Wesley U. M. E. Church Cemetery in Abingdon]

Hall, Henry July 5, 1873 – February 4, 1941 (no tombstone; death certificate stated he was born in Bel Air, married Maggie Hall, worked as a farmer and died at home near Bel Air; his parents were West Hall and ---- (blank) Hill, both born in Bel Air; informant was Otho Hall) [Hendon Hill Cemetery]

Hall, Howard March 25, 1867 – March 26, 1958 (on same tombstone with wife Maria W. Hall) [West Liberty Church Cemetery]

Hall, Howard Jr. died November 18, 1955 [West Liberty Church Cemetery]

Hall, Ida December 12, 1890 – November 12, 1933 (no tombstone; death certificate stated she was born in Harford Co., but her parents were not known to informant Miss Kate Frisby, of Aberdeen; she was single and died at home in Aberdeen) [Mt. Calvary U. A. M. E. Church Cemetery]

Hall, Israel died July 26, 1907, age 75 (no tombstone; death certificate stated he was the son of George Hall, both born in Maryland, but his mother's name not known to informant Benjamin Talbot, his son-in-law; he married Rosa ----, worked as a laborer, and died at Mountain; his place of burial was not indicated) [probably Mt. Zion U. M. Church Cemetery]

Hall, Ivan F. 1936-2000 (inscribed "married August 1, 1959" to Marian E. Hall) [William C. Rice Memorial Cemetery, St. James U. M. Church]

Hall, James H. (no tombstone; death certificate stated he died on November 30, 1930, age 78, was born in Maryland, married, worked as a laborer, and died in Pylesville; his parents were James Hall and Caroline Morgan, born in Maryland; informant was Charles Hall, of Whiteford) [Chestnut Grove A. M. E. Church Cemetery, formerly LaGrange Cemetery at Rocks]

Hall, James Henry May 4, 1851 – November 26, 1927 (no tombstone; death certificate stated he died a widower; parents unknown to informant James F. Hall, of Havre de Grace) [Union U. M. Church Cemetery]

Hall, Jane, wife of Joshua Hall, January 3, 1851 – March 2, 1948 (on same tombstone with Joshua Hall; death certificate and Kurtz Funeral Home Record Book 1944-1949, p. 202, both stated she was born in Jarrettsville, daughter of Lawson Francis and Charity ---- *(sic)*, birth places not known by informant Stanley Gover, of Forest Hill; she died a widow at home in Jarrettsville) [Fairview A. M. E. Church Cemetery]

Hall, John March 15, 1867 – July 16, 1912 (no tombstone; death certificate stated he was a farm labor, married, and the son of James Hall and Henrietta Fields; informant was Lettice Hall; *The Aegis* on May 17, 1912 reported "Old Johnnie Hall" was in declining health and for 60 *(sic)* years he has been recognized second to no gentleman in this community (Bel Air) "for politeness of manner, amiability of disposition and honesty of character;" his death notice in *The Aegis* on July 19, 1912 stated he died at his home in Bel Air, aged about 60, yet he was only 45 years and 4 months old according to death certificate; obituary stated "John's modesty was as unbounded as was his good nature. He was not handsome of feature or comely of form, nor did he possess a brilliant mind, but he possessed those sterling qualities of honesty, loyalty, fidelity and gratitude, which are above price whether found in the humble or the great. John was an honest man.") [Hendon Hill Cemetery]

Hall, John C. (no dates when copied in 1987, but not found in 2018) [Mt. Zion U. M. Church Cemetery]

Hall, John E. March 11, 1885 – March 10, 1930 [West Liberty Church Cemetery]

Hall, John H. (no tombstone; death certificate stated he died on July 6, 1913, age 56, the son of George and Alice Hall, and they were all born in Maryland; he worked as a laborer and was married at the time of his death at The Rocks; informant was William Rice, of Rocks) [Chestnut Grove A. M. E. Church Cemetery, formerly LaGrange Cemetery at Rocks]

Hall, Joseph E. 1868-1949 (on same tombstone with wife Sarah L. Hall and son Lee W. Hall; death certificate stated he was in Harford Co. on August 31, 1868, son of Joseph Hall and Mary ---- (surname unknown); he was a laborer, lived at 133 Archer Street for over 50 years and died a widower on January 16, 1949; information on the death certificate was completed by Elmer E. Bullock, Funeral Director, Havre de Grace) [Asbury Cemetery]

Hall, Joseph E. Jr. July 31, 1889 – February 5, 1977 (tombstone; obituary in *The Aegis* on February 10, 1977 stated Joseph Edward Hall was born July 31, 1889, the son of Joseph and Sarah Hall, lived at 137 Alice Anne St., Bel Air, and died February 5, 1977 at Spring Grove Hospital) [Asbury Cemetery]

Hall, Josephine January 7, 1904 – July 29, 1912 (no tombstone; death certificate stated she was born in Baltimore City, the daughter of Richard Hall and Martha Brown, both of Harford Co.; she died at Benson; informant was Sarah Preston, of Benson) [John Wesley U. M. E. Church Cemetery in Abingdon]

Hall, Josephine B. January 31, 1923 – November 5, 1982 [Berkley Memorial Cemetery]

Hall, Joshua died November 29, 1915, age 62 years, 1 month, 9 days (on same tombstone with Jane Hall inscribed "Dearest husband thou hast left me / Here thy loss I deeply feel / But 'tis God that hath bereft me / He can all my sorrow feel;" death certificate stated Joshua Jarrett Hall was born October 25, 1853 in Harford Co., the son of Robert Hall, born in Baltimore Co., and Louisa Berry, born in Harford Co.; he worked as a farmer and died at Jarrettsville; informant was his wife Jane Hall, of Sharon; his death notice in *The Aegis* on December 3, 1915 stated he was kicked by a horse and died the next day at his home near Cooptown; no family information was reported) [Fairview A. M. E. Church Cemetery]

Hall, Katherine I. August 19, 1916 – August 26, 2007 (on same tombstone with Losin F. Hall; obituary and photo in *The Aegis* on August 29, 2007 stated she was the daughter of Joshua Britton and Janie Gorden and widow of Losin F. Hall; she was a domestic worked for several local families and was an usher at Fairview AME Church for more than 50 years, as well as a Johnson Willing Worker and Missionary; she lived in Fallston, later in Cooptown, and died at Citizens Care and Rehabilitation Center in Havre de Grace, survived by a son, a daughter, 2 sisters, 7 grandchildren, 16 great-grandchildren, 3 great-great-grandchildren) [Fairview A. M. E. Church Cemetery]

Hall, Laura died November 18, 1903, age 40 (no tombstone; death certificate did not give the place of burial, but stated she was born in Maryland, the daughter of Dealia Johns, but her father was not known to the informant, her husband; she died at home in Bel Air; obituary in *The Aegis* on November 27, 1903 stated she was a respected woman and he wife of Wesley Hall) [probably Hendon Hill Cemetery]

Hall, Laura Elizabeth October 9, 1917 – May 10, 1931 (no tombstone; death certificate stated she was born and died in Maryland and her mother was Ada Hall, but her father was not known to informant Ada Hall, of Bel Air, who was also born in Maryland) [Hendon Hill Cemetery]

Hall, Laura Ethel Jane, daughter of William and Alverta Hall, March 31, 1904 – May 31, 1906 (tombstone; death certificate stated Laura Jane Hall was born and died at Madonna, daughter of William Hall and Virginia Gover, both born in Maryland; informant was her brother W. F. Hall) [Chestnut Grove A. M. E. Church Cemetery, formerly LaGrange Cemetery at Rocks]

Hall, Lee W. 1892-1944 (on same tombstone with parents Joseph E. Lee and Sarah L. Lee) [Asbury Cemetery]

Hall, Lizzie died July 17, 1913, age unknown (no tombstone; death certificate stated she was born in Harford Co., but her parents' names were not known to informant Benjamin Johnson, of Bel Air RFD; she was a servant in Bel Air and was single at the time of her death) [Asbury Cemetery]

Hall, Losin F. February 24, 1914 – April 15, 1997 (on same tombstone with Katherine I. Hall; obituary in *The Aegis* on April 23, 1997 stated Losin Franklin Hall was born in Fallston, the son of Walter and Abbie Gail Hall, and husband of the late Kathleen Britton Hall; he lived in Cooptown, worked as a truck driver for Kefauver Lumber Co., and died at Fallston General Hospital; he was a member of Fairview AME Church for over 50 years and served as an usher and trustee and was a member of the male chorus; he was also a member of Deer Creek Masonic Lodge 103; he was survived by a son, a daughter, 7 grandchildren, 12 great-grandchildren and 1 great-great-grandchild) [Fairview A. M. E. Church Cemetery]

Hall, Louisa died October 24, 1925, age 51 (no tombstone; death certificate stated she was the daughter of Henry Hall and Phebe Bond, all born in Maryland; she was married, did laundry work, died in Bel Air and was buried in "Mountain Cemetery;" informant was Olevia Harkins, of Bel Air) [Mt. Zion U. M. Church Cemetery]

Hall, Louisa A. February 28, 1862 – March 20, 1940 (on same tombstone with William A. Hall, Sr. when copied in 1987, but not found in 2018, possibly toppled over; Kurtz Funeral Home Record Book 1937-1943 stated Louisa Alverda Hall was born on February 28, 1865, the daughter of Jarrett Gover and Susan Gover, all born in

Harford Co.; she married William A. Hall and died a widow at home near Jarrettsville) [Fairview A. M. E. Church Cemetery]

Hall, Margarett February 15, 1867 – March 22, 1936 (no tombstone; death certificate stated she was the daughter of Mouse (Monse?) Green, both born in Harford Co., but her mother was not known to informant Mrs. Rose Parker, of Aberdeen RFD; she married Richard Hall and died a widow at home outside Mt. Calvary in Aberdeen RFD) [Mt. Calvary U. A. M. E. Church Cemetery]

Hall, Maria V. "Twiggy" October 16, 1968 – August 19, 1986 [St. James United Cemetery]

Hall, Maria W. April 12, 1870 – May 14, 1948 (on same tombstone with husband Howard Hall) [West Liberty Church Cemetery]

Hall, Marian E. 1940- (inscribed "married August 1, 1959" to Ivan F. Hall) [William C. Rice Memorial Cemetery, St. James U. M. Church]

Hall, Martha September 11, 1863 – May 17, 1938 (no tombstone; death certificate stated she was born in Pennsylvania, the daughter of Jeppardy Dorsey, born in Maryland, and Annie Hansold, born in Pennsylvania, and widow of John Hall; she lived near Pylesville and died in Harford Memorial Hospital; the information was from the hospital records) [Chestnut Grove A. M. E. Church Cemetery, formerly LaGrange Cemetery at Rocks]

Hall, Martha C. August 25, 1885 – February 16, 1928 (on same tombstone with husband Alfred H. Hall) [West Liberty Church Cemetery]

Hall, Mary December 13, 1865 – April 25, 1930 (no tombstone; death certificate stated she was born in Maryland, married, and died a widow at Rocks; her parents were Samuel Simms and Debra Chase, both were born in Maryland; informant was John Rice, of Pylesville) [Chestnut Grove A. M. E. Church Cemetery, formerly LaGrange Cemetery at Rocks]

Hall, Mary December 17, 1893 – September 17, 1916 (no tombstone; death certificate stated she was the unmarried daughter of James Hall and Harriet Moore, all born in Maryland and she died at Michaelsville; informant was Annie Wilmore, of Perryman) [Union U. M. Church Cemetery]

Hall, Mary died at the end of September, 1886, age and date not given (no tombstone; *The Aegis* on October 1, 1886 reported the remains of Mrs. Mary Hall, wife of Rev. Aquilla Hall, of Washington, DC, arrived in Bel Air on Tuesday, September 28, 1886 and was buried on Wednesday, September 29, 1886 at Hendon's Hill; she formerly belonged to and was a faithful servant of the McCormick family in Bel Air) [Hendon Hill Cemetery]

Hall, Mary Christy died May 19, 19--, age 85 (no tombstone; James Dorsey Card File, African American Obituaries, maintained at the Historical Society of Harford County, has a card with obituary from *The Aegis* (undated) stating she was born in Perrryman and was the foster daughter of Alice Christy and her husband was the late Charles H. Hall; she was raised in Chester, PA, moved to Aberdeen in 1921 and was very active in Union United Methodist Church; she died at the Brevin Nursing Home in Havre de Grace where she had lived for the past five years and was survived by a niece, two nephews and a godchild) [Union U. M. Church Cemetery]

Hall, Mary F., wife of Joseph Hall March 4, 1895 – April 8, 1947 (no tombstone; death certificate stated she was born in Aberdeen the daughter of Nelson Gilbert, born in Philadelphia, and Lavina Giles, born in Maryland, and the wife of Joseph F. Hall; she had lived on Baltimore Street Extended in Aberdeen for 52 years and died at home; informant was Miss Roberta Hall, of Aberdeen) [Union U. M. Church Cemetery]

Hall, Mattie November 18, 1871 – June 30, 1923 (no tombstone; death certificate stated she was the married daughter of Philip Stansbury and Elizabeth Smith, all born in Maryland; informant was Joseph Hall, of Aberdeen) [St. James United Cemetery]

Hall, Mildred E. 1905-1989 (small metal funeral home marker) [William C. Rice Memorial Cemetery, St. James U. M. Church]

Hall, Morris Sr. 1910-1986 [Fairview A. M. E. Church Cemetery]

Hall, Oliver 1874 – August 7, 1946, age 72 (no tombstone; death certificate stated he was the son of Isaac Hall and Charelette Brown, all born in Maryland; he married Susie Harris, worked as a farm laborer and died at home in Fallston; informant was Mr. A Hall, of Fallston) [Tabernacle Mount Zion U. M. Church Cemetery]

Hall, Otha Johns April 3, 1862 – May 26, 1943 (no tombstone; death certificate stated he was born in Bel Air, married, and worked as a waiter; his parents were Wesley Hall and Laura Johns, both born in Maryland; informant was Mrs. Mollie Hall, of Bel Air) [Hendon Hill Cemetery]

Hall, Rachael April 2, 1869 – March 19, 1932 (no tombstone; death certificate stated she was the daughter of Lewis Hall, both born in Maryland, but her mother's name and place of birth were not known to informant William Hall, of Hess Corner; she was single, worked as a domestic and died at home at Hess Corner) [West Liberty Church Cemetery]

Hall, Robert died November 15, 1887, age about 80 (no tombstone; his death notice in *The Aegis* on November 25, 1887 stated he had died in Marshall's District; his place of burial was not given [possibly William C. Rice Memorial Cemetery, St. James U. M. Church]

Hall, Rosetta April 11, 1897 – September 24, 1913 (no tombstone; death certificate stated she was the daughter of Lucy Hall, both born in Harford Co., but her father's name was not known to informant, her mother, Lucy Hall, of Bel Air) [Mt. Zion U. M. Church Cemetery]

Hall, Rosie 1847 – April 7, 1912 (no tombstone; death certificate stated she was the daughter of Henry Winder and Harriet Brice, all were born in Maryland; she was a widow and died at Mountain and buried at West Liberty Church; informant was Annie Talbot, of Mountain) [West Liberty Church Cemetery]

Hall, Ruth E. died August 15, 1937, age about 75 (on same obelisk with E. Merryman Hall and Sarah C. Wann; also, R. E. H. on footstone; death certificate stated she was the daughter of Abraham Wann and Elizabeth ---- (blank) and all were born in Maryland; she was the widow of Marriman *(sic)* Hall, died at home in Fallston where she had lived all her life and was buried at "Mountain;" informant was Abbie Hall, of Fallston) [Mt. Zion U. M. Church Cemetery]

Hall, Sarah May 10, 1888 – May 25, 1914 (no tombstone; death certificate stated she was born near Aberdeen, the daughter of John Tildon and Mary Field, both born in Harford Co.; she was married, died at home near Aberdeen and was buried in "Sidney Park Cemetery;" informant was John T. Hall, of Aberdeen) [Union U. M. Church Cemetery]

Hall, Sarah L. 1867-1947 (on same tombstone with husband Joseph E. Hall and son Lee W. Hall; death certificate stated she was born October 8, 1871 in Harford Co., married Josiah Lee Hall, lived at 133 Archer St. in Bel Air and died on July 20, 1947 at Harford Memorial Hospital in Havre de Grace; informant was her husband who stated her father was Josiah Lee, but her mother's name was not known) [Asbury Cemetery]

Hall, Villard 1915-2008 (small metal funeral home marker) [Gravel Hill Cemetery]

Hall, Virginia February 28, 1860 – March 20, 1940 (no tombstone; James Dorsey Card File, African American Obituaries, maintained at the Historical Society of Harford County, has a card with obituary abstracted from the *Bel Air Times* dated March 22, 1940 stating she was the widow of William A. Hall who died about two months ago and she died at her home near Jarrettsville, survived by two sons and two daughters) [Fairview A. M. E. Church Cemetery]

Hall, Walter April 4, 1913 – June 4, 1913 (no tombstone; death certificate stated he was born in Maryland, the son of James Lewis, born in Virginia, and Louisa Hall, born in Maryland, and they lived in Bel Air; informant was his mother) [Hendon Hill Cemetery]

Hall, Walter F. February 8, 1885 – June 9, 1940 (on the same tombstone with Abbie Jane Hall; Kurtz Funeral Home Record Book 1937-1943, p. 145, stated he was born in Madonna, the son of William A. Hall and Alverda -----, both born in Harford Co.; he married Abbie ----, worked as a farm laborer, lived near Fallston and died at University Hospital, Baltimore) [Fairview A. M. E. Church Cemetery]

Hall, Wesley died August 17, 1908, age not given (no tombstone; obituary in *The Aegis* on August 21, 1908 stated he was well known in Bel Air and died at Springfield Asylum where he was sent some months ago; "He was not great as men are called great, but he was deserving according to his light and his opportunities, which is far more than can be said of many a brighter genius;" also see Laura Hall [probably Hendon Hill Cemetery]

Hall, William A. July 3, 1871 – August 15, 1914 (no tombstone; death certificate stated he was the son of Albert Jamerson and Elizabeth Hall, all born in Maryland; he was single, worked as a laborer, and died in Churchville; informant was Elizabeth James, of Belcamp RFD) [Asbury Cemetery]

Hall, William A. Jr. June 10, 1899 – December 21, 1996 (on same tombstone with Elizabeth J. Hall) [Fairview A. M. E. Church Cemetery]

Hall, William A. Sr. March 31, 1858 – February 7, 1940 (on same tombstone with Louisa A. Hall when copied in 1987, but not found in 2018, possibly toppled over; however, his wife's name was Virginia; death certificate stated William Albert Hall was born at Black Horse, Harford Co., the son of Robert Hall and Louisa Berry, both were born in Harford Co.; he married Alverta Gover, was a farmer and lived near Jarrettsville for 70 years; informant was Jake Hall, of Rocks) [Fairview A. M. E. Church Cemetery]

Hall, William Emory (no tombstone; death certificate stated he was born July 18, 1912 and died June 26, 1913, the son of George Hall and Sadie Jamison, and they were all born in Maryland and lived at Rocks RFD #2; informant was his father) [Chestnut Grove A. M. E. Church Cemetery, formerly LaGrange Cemetery at Rocks]

Hall, William Lester (Buster Bowser) March 25, 1915 – January 26, 1975 (no tombstone; obituary in *The Aegis* on January 30, 1975 stated he was the son of John Henry Hall and Bessie Brown, and husband of Daisy Jane Hall, of Havre de Grace; he died in Harford Memorial Hospital, survived by his wife and mother) [Union M. E. Church Cemetery]

Hall, Wilson E. July 4, 1904 – March 24, 1938 (no tombstone; death certificate stated he was the unmarried son of James Hall and Viola Green; informant was Mrs. Florence V. Giles) [Union U. M. Church Cemetery]

Hamilton, Harriet Etta September 2, 1891 – December 23, 1918 (no tombstone; death certificate stated she was the married daughter of John Govens and Georgianna Berry, all born in Harford Co., and she died at home near Monkton; informant was Georgianna Govens, of Monkton) [Union U. M. Church Cemetery]

Hamlet, Ellen R., "Our Beloved Mom" August 31, 1921 – November 26, 2002 [Community Baptist Church Cemetery]

Hamlet, John W. September 22, 1921 – December 8, 1990, U.S. Army, World War II [Community Baptist Church Cemetery]

Hammond, David December 7, 1920 – September 21, 1986, Pvt., U.S. Army [St. James United Cemetery]

Hammond, Margaret Chambers 1875-1958 [Clark's U. M. Church Cemetery]

Hammons(?), James Jr. (owner of a lot in section 13 some time after 1951) [Mt. Calvary U. A. M. E. Church Cemetery]

Hampton, Eleanor B. August 10, 1939 – August 21, 2003 (on same tombstone with Jesse L. Hampton Sr.) [St. James United Cemetery]

Hampton, Jesse L. Sr. December 8, 1938 -   (on same tombstone with Eleanor B. Hampton inscribed "Together Forever") [St. James United Cemetery]

Hanciles, Cleophas M. 1944-2015 (small metal funeral home marker) [St. James United Cemetery]

Hanna, Lawrence 1892 – died between April 22, 1940 at 11:30 p.m. and April 23, 1940 at 12:30 a.m. (no tombstone; death certificate stated he was born in North Carolina, parents unknown, and was a railroad laborer; he died in a house fire on Edmund Street Extended in Aberdeen) [Union U. M. Church Cemetery]

Hanna, Tia December 28, 1984 – October 10, 2007 [Berkley Memorial Cemetery]

Hansome, Emmaline died August 22, 1916, age about 71 (no tombstone; death certificate stated she was born in Virginia, the daughter of Agnes Leftwich, born in Virginia, but informant C. H. Bennett, of Darlington, did not know her father's name; she died single in Darlington) [Berkley Memorial Cemetery]

Harden, Shatoya L. 1987-1987 [Union U. M. Church Cemetery]

Hardin, Willie C. 1904-2003 (small metal funeral home marker) [St. James United Cemetery]

Harding, Nettie C. died April 25, 1922 [Union U. M. Church Cemetery]

Hardy, ---- stillborn female on May 24, 1932 (no tombstone; death certificate stated she was born in Havre de Grace, the daughter of Clifford Johnson, born in Seaford, DE, and Margretha Hardy, born in Aberdeen; she died in the Havre de Grace Hospital; informant was her mother Margretha Hardy, of Aberdeen) [Mt. Calvary U. A. M. E. Church Cemetery]

Hardy, Alice Giles died January 7, 1988, age 77 (no tombstone; obituary in *The Aegis* on January 14, 1988 stated she was born in Aberdeen, the daughter of Samuel Giles and Viola Green, and was the widow of Leonard Clarence Hardy; she lived in Aberdeen and died at Harford Memorial Hospital, survived by one son Clarence Leonard Hardy, one daughter Sophia Peaco, 8 grandchildren, 19 great-grandchildren, 1 great-great-grandchild, and 3 sisters) [Mt. Calvary U. A. M. E. Church Cemetery]

Hardy, Catherine M. August 9, 1923 – October 1, 1923 (no tombstone; death certificate stated she was born in Baltimore, the daughter of Silver Spencer, born in Maryland, and Sadie Hardy, born in New Jersey; informant was Sadie Hardy, of Aberdeen) [Mt. Calvary U. A. M. E. Church Cemetery]

Hardy, Effie M. July 26, 1909 – December 14, 1929 (no tombstone; death certificate stated she was born in Maryland, daughter of Josie Hardy, born in New Jersey, and Gertrude Moulton, born in Maryland; she was single and died at home in Aberdeen; informant was her mother) [Mt. Calvary U. A. M. E. Church Cemetery]

Hardy, Gertrude August 17, 1880 – January 11, 1940 (no tombstone; death certificate stated she was the daughter of James Moulton and Harriet Washington, all born in Aberdeen, married Josiah Hardy, lived in Aberdeen and died a widow at Harford Memorial Hospital in Havre de Grace; informant was Miss Jessie Hardy, of Aberdeen) [Mt. Calvary U. A. M. E. Church Cemetery]

Hardy, Josiah February 14, 1879 – February 27, 1935 (no tombstone; death certificate stated he was born in Camden, NJ, the son of Josiah Hardy and Corelia Davis, both born in Loomsburg, VA; he married Gertrude ----, worked as a day laborer and died at home on Park Ave. in Aberdeen; informant was Gertrude Hardy, of Aberdeen) [Mt. Calvary U. A. M. E. Church Cemetery]

Hardy(?), R----? (owned a lot in section 41 some time after 1951) [Mt. Calvary U. A. M. E. Church Cemetery]

Harlin, Calvin L. February 25, 1919 – July 7, 1961, Indiana, PFC, HQ Co., 366 Infantry, World War II [Mt. Calvary U. A. M. E. Church Cemetery]

Harriday, John H. January 10, 1910 – March 24, 1978, U.S. Army World War II (tombstone; obituary in *The Aegis* on March 30, 1978 stated John Henry Harriday was born in Catonsville, the son of Joseph Harriday and Leona Roford and married Anna Jane ---- who predeceased him; he was a former employee of the Old Fresh Air Camp on Whitaker Mill Road; he lived at 1256 W. Jarrettsville Road, Forest Hill, and died at Loch Raven VA Hospital in Baltimore, survived by 1 daughter, 2 step-daughters and 1 step-son Wilson Lowery, Jr.) [Tabernacle Mount Zion U. M. Church Cemetery]

Harrington(?), William Elijah, son of Harry(?) October 13, 1807 – October 2, 1878 (tombstone partly difficult to read) [Mt. Zion U. M. Church Cemetery]

Harris, ---- (no tombstone, but Kurtz Funeral Home records stated Thomas Harris' child was buried in an "im wallnut" coffin on November 14, 1880 from J. Francis' house) [West Liberty Church Cemetery]

Harris, ---- stillborn male on April 23, 1920 (no tombstone; death certificate stated he was the son of Franklin Harris and Lilly Morris, all were born in Maryland; he died at Abingdon and was buried in the "Colllored *(sic)* Cemetery, Abingdon;" informant was his father) [John Wesley U. M. E. Church Cemetery in Abingdon]

Harris, ---- stillborn male on June 25, 1919, miscarriage at 7 months (no tombstone; death certificate stated he was the son of William F. Harris and Lilly Morris, all were born in Maryland; he died at Abingdon; informant was his mother, Lilly Harris) [John Wesley U. M. E. Church Cemetery in Abingdon]

Harris, A. Louise died September 24, 2006, age 87 (no tombstone; obituary in *The Aegis* on September 27, 2006 stated she was born in Union Bridge, the daughter of Howard Norton and Viola Serina Hollingsworth, and the widow of Lloyd A. "Bill" Harris; she was a homemaker who was affectionately called "Sister" and she was a senior usher and "Mother of the Church" at John Wesley United Methodist Church; she lived in Abingdon and died at Manor Care in Rossville (in Baltimore Co.), survived by 5 sons, 6 daughters, 2 sisters, 34 grandchildren, 86 great-grandchildren and 36 great-great-grandchildren; she was also predeceased by 1 daughter, 7 brothers, and 2 grandsons) [John Wesley U. M. E. Church Cemetery in Abingdon]

Harris, Agnes Elizabeth December – (blank), 1948 – February 11, 1949 (no tombstone; death certificate stated she was the daughter of Norris Marshall Harris and Catherine C. Hooks, of Havre de Grace) [Union U. M. Church Cemetery]

Harris, Albert died September 7, 19--, age 79 (no tombstone; undated obituary at the Historical Society of Harford County stated he was born in Kingsville, son of the late Mr. & Mrs. Abraham Harris, and husband of Caroline Davis Harris, of 2043 Battle St. in Edgewood, and he died in Franklin Square Hospital (Baltimore Co.); he retired from the B&O Railroad in 1960 after serving as a trackman for over 30 years; he was survived by his wife, one son, one daughter and seven grandchildren) [Community Baptist Church Cemetery]

Harris, Alberta March 8, 1868 – May 16, 1941 (no tombstone; death certificate stated she was the daughter of John T. Kennett and Harriett C. R. Hamilton, all born in Harford Co.; she married Jerome Harris and lived near Bel Air all her life; informant was Hazzard Harris) [Asbury Cemetery]

Harris, Amanda R. died June 30, 1980, age 75 (no tombstone; obituary in *The Aegis* on July 3, 1980 stated she was born in Denton and was the widow of William H. Harris; she operated a store in Aberdeen for over 30 years and died at Harford Memorial Hospital in Havre de Grace, survived by a brother Isaac Satterfield, 3 grandchildren and 4 great-grandchildren) [Union U. M. Church Cemetery]

Harris, Annie died on June 27, 1909, age 20 (no tombstone; death certificate stated she was born in Maryland. the daughter of Edward Rice and Charlotte McComas and the wife of Lloyd Harris; she died at home in Michaelsville and informant was her aunt Mary Pitt; place of burial was not indicated, but probably in Old Union Chapel Cemetery at Michaelsville; possibly reinterred later in Union Chapel Cemetery near Aberdeen) [Union U. M. Church Cemetery]

Harris, Annie L., "Mother" May 12, 1916 – October 27, 2002 (tombstone; obituary in *The Aegis* on October 30, 2002 stated she was born in Magnolia, the daughter of James Alexander Gilbert and Ossie Mae Johnson, and was the widow of John Albert Harris; she lived in Joppa, cared for many children around Abingdon and died at Harford Memorial Hospital, survived by 2 sons, 2 daughters, 1 brother, 1 grandchild and 2 god-children) [John Wesley U. M. E. Church Cemetery in Abingdon]

Harris, Ardell (Mrs.) 1922-1965 (copied in 1987, but not found in 2018) [Cedars Chapel Cemetery]

Harris, Baby July 24, 1946 – July 26, 1946 (no tombstone; death certificate stated he was the son of William Harris and Marie Hawkins) [Skinner Cemetery]

Harris, Barbara M. April 27, 1942 – September 16, 1995 (tombstone; obituary in *The Aegis* on September 22, 1999 stated Barbara Marie Harris was born in Street, the daughter of Clarence Edward Walton and the late Mary Alice Camelia Davis, and married William T. Harris in 1963; she worked as a custodian for Stark and Keenan in Bel Air, lived in Abingdon and died at Mariner Health of Bel Air, survived by her husband, two sons, a daughter and three grandchildren) [Chestnut Grove A. M. E. Church Cemetery, formerly LaGrange Cemetery at Rocks]

Harris, Bernice E., "Mother" March 20, 1930 – March 28, 1988 [John Wesley U. M. E. Church Cemetery in Abingdon]

Harris, Bertha O. March 21, 1922 -   (on same tombstone with Eugene R. Harris) [Berkley Memorial Cemetery]

Harris, Bessie M., "Mother" March 15, 1906 – July 8, 1975 (tombstone; she married James H. Harris, Sr. and her obituary in *The Aegis* on July 17, 1975 stated she was a retired cook from Aberdeen Proving Ground and died at Harford Memorial Hospital in Havre de Grace, survived by four sons, a brother, a sister, her mother Mrs. Julia M. Howard, 15 grandchildren and 9 great-grandchildren   [St. James United Cemetery]

Harris, C. Elizabeth "Daughter" 1899-1978 (tombstone; obituary in *The Aegis* stated Charlotte Elizabeth Harris was born in Baltimore, the daughter of Thomas Braxton and Keizal Fountain, and was employed as a cook for many years in private homes in Baltimore; she married William Harris, lived in Abingdon and died a widow in Harford Memorial Hospital, survived by 1 son, 1 daughter, 1 brother, 2 sisters, 16 grandchildren, 32 great-grandchildren and 5 great-great-grandchildren) [John Wesley U. M. E. Church Cemetery in Abingdon]

Harris, Caroline died June 24, 1984, age 89 (no tombstone; obituary in *The Aegis* stated she was born in Loreley, Baltimore Co., the daughter of Andrew and Marguerite Davis, and was the widow of Albert Harris; she lived in Edgewood and died at Mercy Hospital in Baltimore, survived by one son, two daughters, and four grandchildren) [Community Baptist Church Cemetery]

Harris, Carrie Kenly May 19, 1879 – March 22, 1951 (no tombstone; death certificate stated she was born in Maryland, the daughter of William Kenly and Rebecca Paca, and died a widow at home in Perryman; informant was William F. Kenly) [Union U. M. Church Cemetery]

Harris, Casandra died December 26, 1914, age about 68 (no tombstone; death certificate stated she was the daughter of ---- (blank) Clark and Delia Cox, all born in Maryland; she died a widow at Cedars; informant was George Harris, of Street, MD) [Berkley Memorial Cemetery]

Harris, Catherine E. February 1, 1910 – July 10, 1988 [Fairview A. M. E. Church Cemetery]

Harris, Charles 1891 – June 9, 1927 (no tombstone; death certificate stated he was unmarried and died at Darlington; parents not known informant was Liza Gainer, of Washington, D.C.) [St. James United Cemetery]

Harris, Charles Franklyn died July 19, 1942, age 80 (no tombstone; death certificate stated he was unmarried and died in Havre de Grace) [St. James United Cemetery]

Harris, Charlotte 1863 – October 28, 1936 (no tombstone; death certificate stated she was the daughter of Henry Williamson and Lucy Tasker, all born in Calvert Co.; she married Charles Edward Harris who was still living when she died at Kalmia where they had lived for 19 years; informant was Henry Williamson, of Bel Air) [Clark's U. M. Church Cemetery]

Harris, Cornelia (no tombstone, but likely buried next to husband Hazzard Harris) [Asbury Cemetery]

Harris, Cornelius died June 12, 1993, age 68 (no tombstone; obituary in *The Aegis* on June 16, 1993 stated he was a native of Abingdon and son of William Franklin Harris and Lillian Morris; he was an Army veteran of World War II, married Grace Cooper, worked as a bus driver at Edgewood Arsenal and died at the Baltimore VAMC; he was survived by his wife of 40 years, Grace Cooper Harris, and 5 sons, 2 daughters and 11 grandchildren) [John Wesley U. M. E. Church Cemetery in Abingdon]

Harris, Dale M. 16 Aug 1966 -   (on same tombstone with Carol Anne and Gregory Michael Wheeler) [John Wesley U. M. E. Church Cemetery in Abingdon]

Harris, Daniel E. (Rev.) 1846-1932 (on same tombstone with Emma Harris) [St. James United Cemetery]

Harris, Davanna M. April 11, 1974 – July 7, 1997 [St. James United Cemetery]

Harris, Delinia Helen, "Our Daughter" February 15, 1969 – December 21, 1970 (tombstone; obituary in *The Aegis* on December 31, 1970 stated she was daughter of Charles Albert Harris and Linda Lee and died at home in Street, survived by her parents and grandparents William and Helen Lee) [Clark's U. M. Church Cemetery]

Harris, Dennis W. died February 19, 1914, age about 57 (no tombstone; death certificate stated he was the son of Dennis Harris, both born in Prince George's Co., MD, but the name of his mother was not known to informant Sophia Harris, of Bagley; he was married, worked as a laborer and died at Bagley) [Tabernacle Mount Zion U. M. Church Cemetery]

Harris, Dennis W. Jr. 1883-1939 (on same tombstone with Sophia Harris and James H. Harris; his first name was spelled Denis on the tombstone; no death certificate was found in Harford Co.) [Tabernacle Mount Zion U. M. Church Cemetery]

Harris, Don Ulysses September 7, 1950 – April 15, 2012 (tombstone; obituary and photo in *The Aegis* on April 20, 2012 stated he was born in Elkton, the son of Evelyn C. Harris and Ralph Murray, and married Carolyn Nutter; he collected and restored care after retiring from his Aberdeen Proving Ground contracting job; he lived in Aberdeen and died at the University of Maryland Medical Center in Baltimore, survived by his wife, his parents, three sons (Dwayne Hague, Vivien Cargill, Vance Cargill, a grandson (Tyrell Hague), two brothers

(Harold Love, Jr. and Ralph R. Murray), six sisters, and several aunts, uncles, nieces, nephews and cousins); he was predeceased by brothers Maurice Harris and Michael Love, sister Antoinette Harris, grandmother Helen Murray and stepfather Harold Love, Sr.) [Berkley Memorial Cemetery]

Harris, Earl Thomas December 25, 1923 – May 1, 1933 (no tombstone; death certificate stated he was the son of Franklin Harris and Lilly Morris, all born in Maryland; he died at Van Bibber and was buried at "John Wesley;" informant was Franklin Harris, of Edgewood) [John Wesley U. M. E. Church Cemetery in Abingdon]

Harris, Earl Thomas died May 20, 1972, age 65 (no tombstone; obituary in *The Aegis* stated he was born in Abingdon, the son of John Harris and Lillie Washington; he married Edith Cromwell, lived at 2609 Old Philadelphia Road, and retired in July 1971 after 50 years of service to the B&O Railroad as a trackman; he died at home and was survived by his wife, 1 son Frederick Brown *(sic)*, of Chase, 1 step-daughter Mrs. Georgianna Harris, of Abingdon, and 3 brothers, 1 sister and "a host of grandchildren and great-grandchildren") [John Wesley U. M. E. Church Cemetery in Abingdon]

Harris, Edith E. 1900-1976 (tombstone; obituary in *The Aegis* on May 27, 1976 stated Edith Elizabeth Harris was born in Annapolis, the daughter of Abraham and Rebecca Dorsey, and was the widow of Earl Thomas Harris; she lived in Abingdon for many years and died at the Fallston Nursing Center, survived by a daughter, a sister, 13 grandchildren, 40 great-grandchildren and 3 great-great-grandchildren) [John Wesley U. M. E. Church Cemetery in Abingdon]

Harris, Edith E. October 25, 1877 – February 3, 1897 [St. James United Cemetery]

Harris, Edna Louise died June 5, 2018, age 74 (no tombstone; funeral notice in *The Aegis* stated she lived in Bel Air and was buried in the cemetery at John Wesley United Methodist Church) [John Wesley U. M. E. Church Cemetery in Abingdon]

Harris, Eleanor Walton July 21, 1902 – October 19, 1981 (tombstone; obituary in *The Aegis* on November 5, 1981 stated Eleanor Alice Harris was born in Harford Co., the daughter of William Walton and Sarah Smith, married Harry Harris and once resided in Philadelphia; she was a Steward of St. James United Methodist Church and upon her death she was survived by her husband, a son, a daughter, a sister, 4 grandchildren, 6 great-grandchildren, 2 great-great-grandchildren and 1 great-great-great-grandchild) [William C. Rice Memorial Cemetery, St. James U. M. Church]

Harris, Elizabeth March 25, 1916 – May 26, 1916 (no tombstone; death certificate stated she was the daughter of Ezekiel Harris and Etta Snowden, of Darlington; all were born in Maryland) [Cedars Chapel Cemetery]

Harris, Emma 1861-1927 (on same tombstone with Daniel E. Harris; death certificate stated she was daughter of Sydney Butler and Elizabeth Carroll. and died December 8, 1926 age about 61) [St. James United Cemetery]

Harris, Emma Nelson June 21, 1886 – November 1, 1939 (no tombstone; death certificate stated she was born in Harford Co., the daughter of George Ridgeley, born in Maryland, and Mary Garrett, born in Harford Co.; she married John Edward Harris and died at home at 415 Lodge Alley in Havre de Grace; informant was her husband) [Asbury Cemetery]

Harris, Estella V. August 9, 1893 – September 27, 1965 (on same tombstone with Grason Harris, Sr.; her marker was copied in 1987 as "1890-1965" so it was apparently a temporary metal marker at the time) [Fairview A. M. E. Church Cemetery]

Harris, Eugene R. August 1, 1921 – June 27, 1998 (on same tombstone with Bertha O. Harris; obituary in *The Aegis* on July 1, 1998 stated Eugene R. "Buddy" Harris was born in Baltimore County, the son of David Harris and Hanna Rumsey, and married in 1946 to Bertha Olivia Collins, of Kalmia; he served in the Army, worked at Bainbridge Naval Training Center and retired in 1985 from Aberdeen Proving Ground; he died at the Perry Point VA Medical Center and was survived by his wife, a son, a stepdaughter, six grandchildren, four great-grandchildren, seven sisters and a host of nieces, nephews and cousins) [Berkley Memorial Cemetery]

Harris, Ezekiel March 17, 1892 – April 4, 1942 (no tombstone; death certificate stated he was the son of Hazzard Harris and Casandra Harris, all born in Harford Co.; he married Etta Harris, worked as a stone quarry laborer and died at home in Dublin; informant was his wife) [Berkley Memorial Cemetery]

Harris, Freda I. died March 20, 1968, age 44 years, 9 months, 2 days (tombstone; obituary in *The Aegis* on February 29, 1968 stated she was the wife of George E. Harris, of Bel Air; she died at Harford Memorial Hospital in Havre de Grace and was survived by her husband, a daughter Mrs. Freda L. Barnes, seven sisters, one brother and five grandchildren) [Clark's U. M. Church Cemetery]

Harris, George Edward March 5, 1863 – December 26, 1922 (no tombstone; death certificate stated he was the married son of Henry Harris and Eliza Hall, all born in Maryland; informant was Maria Harris, of Havre de Grace) [Union U. M. Church Cemetery]

Harris, George Edward May 15, 1923 – July 19, 1977, PFC, U.S. Army, World War II (tombstone; obituary in *The Aegis* stated he was born in Harford Co., son of Devoid Harris and Hannah Corns, lived in Bel Air and was the husband of the late Freda Gibson Harris; he was "a skilled laborer" and a veteran of World War II; he died at Fallston General Hospital, survived by a brother, a step-daughter, five step-grandchildren, an aunt, a niece, a nephew, four great nieces, a great nephew, and "a host of other relatives") [Clark's U. M. Church Cemetery]

Harris, George Jr. April 4, 1914 – April 17, 1914 (no tombstone; death certificate stated he was the son of George Harris, Sr., born in Virginia, and Adeline Taylor, born in Maryland) [St. James United Cemetery]

Harris, George W. died July 3, 1931, age 54 [Union U. M. Church Cemetery]

Harris, Georgianna February 2, 1872 – January 22, 1940 (no tombstone; death certificate stated she was born in Maryland, but her parents were unknown to informant Albert Stevenson, of Joppa; she was a domestic in Joppa and the widow of Asbury Harris) [Asbury Cemetery]

Harris, Gladys Roberta died October 22, 1989, age 67 (no tombstone; obituary in *The Aegis* on November 1, 1989 stated she was the daughter of David Jackson and Clara Preston, and the widow of Thomas Emual Harris; she worked for many years as a school aide, nurses aide and child care worker, and she was considered the poet laureate of Fairview AME Church; she died at Fallston General Hospital and was survived by 2 sons, 2 daughters, 14 grandchildren, 5 great-grandchildren, 2 brothers, 3 sisters) [Fairview A. M. E. Church Cemetery]

Harris, Grason Sr. September 22, 1883 – February 28, 1956 (on same tombstone with Estella V. Harris) [Fairview A. M. E. Church Cemetery]

Harris, Hannah E. March 4, 1934 – November 18, 1988 [Cedars Chapel Cemetery]

Harris, Harlan March 26, 1926 – February 25, 1965, Maryland, Pfc, U.S. Army, World War II [John Wesley U. M. E. Church Cemetery in Abingdon]

Harris, Harriet Elizabeth, daughter of John and Milcah Harris. May 9, 1848 – September 2, 1903 (tombstone; no death certificate in Harford County) [Old Union Chapel M. E. Church Cemetery]

Harris, Hazzard April 26, 1833 – September 22, 1911 (no tombstone; death certificate stated he was the son of Hazzard Harris and Cornelia Prigg, all born in Harford Co.; he was married, worked as a carpenter and lived near Churchville; informant was Jerome Harris, of Aberdeen; place of burial not given, but stated he was buried near Churchville [probably Asbury Cemetery]

Harris, Hazzard August 29, 1890 – November 2, 1952, Maryland, Wagoner, U.S. Army, World War 1 (tombstone; his military service is not listed in *Maryland in the World War, 1917-1919*) [Asbury Cemetery]

Harris, Hazzard died August 13, 1913, age about 71 (no tombstone; death certificate stated he was born in Maryland, the illegitimate son of Eliza Harris who was also born in Maryland; he was married (name of wife not given), worked as a farmer, lived in Darlington and died accidentally from a boiler explosion; informant was George Harris, of Darlington) [Berkley Memorial Cemetery]

Harris, Henry September 12, 1842 – June 12, 1890 (inscribed "Though lost to sight, to memory dear") [Old Union Chapel M. E. Church Cemetery]

Harris, Henry H. died May 11, 1919, age 48 (no tombstone; death certificate stated he was the son of Mandy Harris, both born in Maryland, but informant Mary Jordon, of Darlington, did not know his father's name; he was a barber in Darlington and was found shot dead) [Berkley Memorial Cemetery]

Harris, James died May 24, 1925, age about 57 (no tombstone; death certificate stated he was born in

Maryland, but informant Georgie Hawkins, of Havre de Grace, did not know the names of his parents; he was a widowed laborer who died at home in Havre de Grace) [Green Spring U. M. Church Cemetery]

Harris, James February 20, 1889 – November 30, 1932 (no tombstone; death certificate stated he was born in Harford Co., the son of Lawson Harris and Susanna Brow (Brown?), both born in Maryland; his wife was Elizabeth ---- and he worked as a laborer in a quarry; he lived at 123 S. Washington Street in Havre de Grace and was divorced by the time of his death in Havre de Grace Hospital; informant was Mrs. George Bond, of Perry Point) [Gravel Hill Cemetery]

Harris, James died March 1, 1955, aged about 70 (no tombstone; Pennington Funeral Home records did not state his birth place and his parents' names, but stated he had lived in Havre de Grace for 10 years; he was buried in St. James Colored Cemetery and they mistakenly stated he was white [St. James United Cemetery]

Harris, James H. 1881-1952 (on same tombstone with Sophia Harris and Dennis W. Harris, Jr.) [Tabernacle Mount Zion U. M. Church Cemetery]

Harris, Jess (no dates recorded in 1987, not listed in 2002, and not found in 2018) [Gravel Hill Cemetery]

Harris, John A. April 21, 1912 – March 20, 1987, SSgt., U.S. Army, World War II (tombstone; obituary in *The Aegis* on March 26, 1987 stated John Albert Harris, Sr. was the son of John C. Harris and Lillie Washington, served in World War II, retired from the B&O Railroad after 44 years service and also served with the McComas Funeral Home in Abingdon for three generations; he lived in Abingdon and died at the Loch Raven VAMC in Baltimore, survived by his wife, Annie L. Gilbert Harris, 3 sons, 2 daughters, and grandchildren) [John Wesley U. M. E. Church Cemetery in Abingdon]

Harris, John C. April 21, 1876 – October 29, 1932 (no tombstone; death certificate stated he was the son of Ayers Harris, both born in Maryland, but his mother was not known to informant, his wife Lillian Harris; he worked as a railroad laborer, died at home in Abingdon and was buried at "John Wesley" Cemetery; James Dorsey Card File, African American Obituaries, maintained at the Historical Society of Harford County, has an obituary abstraction from the *Bel Air Times* on November 4, 1932 stating he was a well known man at Abingdon M. E. Church, survived by his wife and 5 children) [John Wesley U. M. E. Church Cemetery in Abingdon]

Harris, John W. September 30, 1867 – August 24, 1928 (no tombstone; death certificate stated he was the unmarried son of Henry Harris; mother unknown; informant William Bowser) [Union U. M. Church Cemetery]

Harris, Larry Lee February 9, 1949 – April 23, 2002 (inscribed "In Loving Memory") [Fairview A. M. E. Church Cemetery]

Harris, Laura 1888 – August 13, 1950 (no tombstone; death certificate stated she was the widowed daughter of Sidney Butler, but her mother's name was not known to informant Robert Harris) [St. James United Cemetery]

Harris, Laura B. died October 5, 1981, age 86 (no tombstone; obituary in *The Aegis* on October 22, 1981 stated she was born in Maryland, the daughter of James and Henrietta Bright, and died in Philadelphia, the widow of James H. Harris, and was survived by three nieces) [Tabernacle Mount Zion U. M. Church Cemetery]

Harris, Lawson died April 28, 1907, age 80 (no tombstone; death certificate stated he was the son of Hazzard Harris and Mille Prigg, all born in Harford Co.; he worked as a laborer at Havre de Grace and was a widower; informant was his son Malachi Harris; place of burial was not given [probably Asbury Cemetery]

Harris, Lewis Ellsworth October 22, 1919 – November 5, 1979, TEC4, U.S. Army, World War II (tombstone and obituary in *The Aegis* on November 15, 1979; formerly of Peach Bottom, PA, he was the son of Jacob and Mary Harris and worked at Lukens Steel in Coatsville, PA for 24 years; he married Marjorie G. ---- (last name was not given), later moved to Havre de Grace and died at Harford Memorial Hospital, survived by his wife, a daughter, two grandchildren, four sisters and a brother) [Berkley Memorial Cemetery]

Harris, Lillian B. "Daughter" 1903-1958 (on same tombstone with mother Lillie Harris) [John Wesley U. M. E. Church Cemetery in Abingdon]

Harris, Lillie "Mother" 1878-1965 (on same tombstone with Lillian B. Harris; obituary in *The Aegis* on October 21, 1965 stated she was a well-known resident of Abingdon and the widow of John C. Harris; she died at home on October 15, 1965, age 87, survived by 4 sons, 1 daughter, 18 grandchildren, 54 great-grandchildren and 5 great-great-grandchildren) [John Wesley U. M. E. Church Cemetery in Abingdon]

Harris, Lillie Gertrude 1896 – December 24, 1927 (no tombstone; death certificate stated she was the daughter of John Morris and Annie ---- (blank), all born in Maryland; she was married, lived in Van Bibber and "dropped dead while mixing up dough for bread;" informant was William F. Harris, of Edgewood) [John Wesley U. M. E. Church Cemetery in Abingdon]

Harris, Littleton E. R. February 20, 1871 – September 15, 1896 (inscribed "Blessed are the dead that died in the Lord") [Old Union Chapel M. E. Church Cemetery]

Harris, Lloyd A. 1920-1994, U.S. Army, World War II (tombstone; obituary in *The Aegis* on November 9, 1994 stated Lloyd A. "Bill" Harris was born in Baltimore, the son of Andrew Harris and Charlotte Braxton, and married Louise Norton; he served in World War II and was a member of American Legion Post 55 and VFW Post 6054; he was a vice president of the Harford County NAACP and retired in 1967 after 28 years of government service; he had owned and operated Harris Brothers Trash Service, which he started in 1951, and also owned and managed the Bush Valley Landfill; he lived in Abingdon and died at Perry Point VAMC on November 5, 1994, survived by his wife and 5 sons, 8 daughters, 37 grandchildren, 58 great-grandchildren, and he was the father of the late Viola S. Jones; his Howard K. McComas III Funeral Home card states he was born on June 5, 1920) [John Wesley U. M. E. Church Cemetery in Abingdon]

Harris, Louise P. 1902-1973 ("At Rest") [Union U. M. Church Cemetery]

Harris, Lucy died December 10, 1880, age not given (no tombstone; death notice in *The Aegis* on December 17, 1880 stated she was found dead in the public road near Cedarville; an inquest determined she died of natural causes; no place of burial was indicated) [probably Cedars Chapel Cemetery]

Harris, Mariah Marie March 1, 1867 – April 25, 1940 (no tombstone; death certificate stated she was the widow of George Edward Harris and daughter of Isaac Jiles and Ruth ----) [Union U. M. Church Cemetery]

Harris, Marjorie Gladys died May 8, 1994, age 73 (obituary in *The Aegis* on May 25, 1994 stated she was born in Havre de Grace, the daughter of Olivia Skinner and John Newby and the widow of Lewis Ellsworth Harris; she moved to Philadelphia and returned in 1976 to Havre de Grace and died at Harford Memorial Hospital, survived by a daughter (Myrna O. Thompson), a brother (Rudolph Risby), two grandchildren and three great-grandchildren) [Berkley Memorial Cemetery]

Harris, Martha J. March 1, 1866 – July 6, 1936 (no tombstone; death certificate stated she was born in York Co., PA, the daughter of Henry Bond, born in Bel Air, and Sarah Cole, born in Port Deposit; she married Malcolm Harris, lived near Havre de Grace and died a widow; informant was John Bond, of Havre de Grace RFD) [Green Spring U. M. Church Cemetery]

Harris, Mary February 10, 1885 – June 14, 1942 (no tombstone; death certificate stated she was the daughter of James Smith and Mary Hollins, all born in Harford Co.; she married Thomas Harris and died in rural Darlington; informant was Thomas Harris, of Street RFD) [Clark's U. M. Church Cemetery]

Harris, Mary June 21, 1875 – October 23, 1916 (no tombstone; death certificate stated she died in Poole, the daughter of Benjamin Gray and Catherine Williamson, all born in Maryland; she was married and the informant was George Harris, of Street, MD) [Clark's U. M. Church Cemetery]

Harris, Mary Hattie June 18, 1904 – July 20, 1934 (no tombstone; death certificate stated she was born in Baltimore Co., the daughter of Henry Harris and Carosel Tasco) [Union U. M. Church Cemetery]

Harris, Mary Lizy (no dates recorded in 1987, not listed in 2002 and not found in 2018) [Gravel Hill Cemetery]

Harris, Maryetta May 20, 1924 – September 30, 1924 (no tombstone; death certificate stated she was the daughter of Ezekiel Harris, both born in Harford Co., and he lived in Darlington, but her mother was unknown, yet born in Harford County; informant was Ezekiel Harris) [Cedars Chapel Cemetery]

Harris, Mayfield died May 23, 1982, age 77 (obituary in *The Aegis* on May 27, 1982 stated she was the daughter of Isaac and Martha Jackson and the widow of Robert O. Harris; she lived in Havre de Grace and died at Harford Memorial Hospital, survived by a son, two brothers, seven grandchildren and seven great-grandchildren) [Berkley Memorial Cemetery]

Harris, Norris Oliver "Bill" died January 24, 1984, age 60 (no tombstone; obituary in *The Aegis* on February 2, 1984 stated lived in Havre de Grace and died at Harford Memorial Hospital; he owned the Swan Inn in Havre de Grace and was president of the In Crowd Social Club in Aberdeen; he was survived by 4 sons, 4 daughters, 11 grandchildren; his wife was not mentioned) [Berkley Memorial Cemetery]

Harris, Oneshe E. 10-8-95 (handwritten on a flat cement slab) [St. James United Cemetery]

Harris, Paul D. April 6, 1914 – November 26, 1982 (tombstone; obituary in *The Aegis* on December 2, 1982 stated Paul Daniel Harris was a lifelong resident of Abingdon and the son of John Harris and Lillie Washington; he married (wife's name was not mentioned), worked as a trackman for the B & O Railroad, and died at Harford Memorial Hospital in Havre de Grace, survived by 3 sons, 6 daughters, 39 grandchildren and 17 great-grandchildren) [John Wesley U. M. E. Church Cemetery in Abingdon]

Harris, Paul Edward 1935-1978 [John Wesley U. M. E. Church Cemetery in Abingdon]

Harris, Raymond E. July 5, 1933 – August 23, 1895 (two tombstones with one inscribed "U.S. Army" and one inscribed "Loving Husband and Father") [Cedars Chapel Cemetery]

Harris, Robert Jr. March 9, 1933 – August 17, 1933 (no tombstone; death certificate stated he was the son of Robert Harris and Mayfield Jackson, of Havre de Grace) [St. James United Cemetery]

Harris, Robert I. 1875-1935 (tombstone; death certificate stated he was born on February 7, 1875 and died on June 15, 1935, the unmarried son of Philip E. Harris and Francis O. Johnson) [St. James United Cemetery]

Harris, Robert LeRoy November 29, 1868 – April 1, 1936 (no tombstone; death certificate stated he was the son of Robert Harris and Elizabeth Branigen; informant was wife Loretta Harris) [St. James United Cemetery]

Harris, Robert O. died January 26, 1970, age not given (obituary in *The Aegis* stated he was the son of the late Roy and Laura Harris; he lived at 106 St. John Street in Havre de Grace and died at Harford Memorial Hospital, survived by wife Mayfield Harris and son Norris O. Harris) [Berkley Memorial Cemetery]

Harris, Sarah died January 30, 1912, "age 60 years (uncertain);" (no tombstone; death certificate stated she was born in Harford Co., but informant J. Amos Jones, of Berkley, did not know her parents' names and birth places; she was single, worked as a cook and died in Berkley) [Berkley Memorial Cemetery]

Harris, Sarah A. February – (blank), 1857 – August 16, 1919 (no tombstone; death certificate stated she was born in Maryland, the married daughter of Alvin Armstrong and Memory Leucius(?), both born in Virginia; informant was Will Harris, of Havre de Grace [St. James United Cemetery]

Harris, Sarah E. January 5, 1824 – January 9, 1927 (no tombstone; death certificate stated she was born in Maryland, but her parents were unknown to informant King Nickinson, of Perryman, and she died a widow with burial at "Union M. E. Cemetery;" obituary in *The Aegis* on January 14, 1927 stated Sarah Elizabeth Harris died at Perryman on the farm of Parker Mitchell for whom she had been a servant; oldest son John Gould Harris, age 88, came from Philadelphia to attend her funeral at the "African M. E. Church near Swan Creek") [Union U. M. Church Cemetery]

Harris, Silvester Charles November 13, 1914 – May 30, 1934 (no tombstone; death certificate stated he was the son of John Harris and Lillian Washington, all born in Maryland; he was single, worked as a laborer, died at home in Abingdon and was buried at "John Wesley") [John Wesley U. M. E. Church Cemetery in Abingdon]

Harris, Sophia 1846-1918 (on same tombstone with James H. Harris and Dennis W. Harris, Jr.) [Tabernacle Mount Zion U. M. Church Cemetery]

Harris, Sophie 1866 – January 10, 1923 (no tombstone; death certificate stated she was the unmarried daughter of William Harris and Mary Armstrong, of Havre de Grace) [St. James United Cemetery]

Harris, Stephen J. June 20, 1857 – June 23, 1916 (no tombstone; death certificate stated he was born in Harford Co., the married son of John Harris and Milcah Denison, born in Maryland) [Union U. M. Church Cemetery]

Harris, Susan (no dates recorded in 1987, not listed in 2002 and not found in 2018) [Gravel Hill Cemetery]

Harris, Thomas E. 1909-1972 (small metal funeral home marker) [Fairview A. M. E. Church Cemetery]

Harris, Vernon November 17, 1924 – October 30, 1959, Maryland, Cpl, 506 Port Bn, TC, World War II [John Wesley U. M. E. Church Cemetery in Abingdon]

Harris, Walter died February --, 1914, age not given (no tombstone; his death notice in *The Aegis* on February 27, 1914 under "Fallston News" stated he died last week at his home near Fallston; however, no death certificate was found for him in Harford Co.) [Tabernacle Mount Zion U. M. Church Cemetery]

Harris, Walter January 21, 1929 – February 23, 1932 (no tombstone; death certificate stated he was the son of R. O. Harris and Mayfield Jackson, of Havre de Grace) [St. James United Cemetery]

Harris, William (no dates recorded in 1987, not listed in 2002 and not found in 2018) [Gravel Hill Cemetery]

Harris, William August 23, 1853 – September 30, 1942 (no tombstone; death certificate stated he was the unmarried son of Robert Harris, born in Havre de Grace, and Elizabeth Branigan, born in Washington, D.C.; informant was Ovington Harris, of Baltimore) [St. James United Cemetery]

Harris, William June 7, 1905 – October 7, 1918 (no tombstone; death certificate stated he was the son of Roy Harris and Laura Butler, of Havre de Grace) [St. James United Cemetery]

Harris, William Andres (Norton) May 26, 1939 – July 16, 1939 (no tombstone; death certificate stated he was born in Abingdon, the son of Lloyd Harris, born in Baltimore, and Louisa A. Norton, born in Abingdon; informant was his mother) [John Wesley U. M. E. Church Cemetery in Abingdon]

Harris, William F. August 21, 1898 – October 25, 1972 [John Wesley U. M. E. Church Cemetery in Abingdon]

Harris, William Franklin September 18, 1920 – July 21, 1922 (no tombstone; death certificate stated he was the son of William Franklin Harris and Lilian Morris, all born in Maryland; he died at Van Bibber; informant was his father, of Edgewood) [John Wesley U. M. E. Church Cemetery in Abingdon]

Harris, William T., "Mr. Bill" died March 30, 1970, age 78 (no tombstone; obituary in *The Aegis* on April 2, 1970 stated he married Amanda Satterfield, was a retired ammunition handler from Aberdeen Proving Ground and died at home at 535 Edmund Street in Aberdeen; he was survived by his wife and two sisters) [Union U. M. Church Cemetery]

Harrison, Alice 1932-2005 (inscribed "In Loving Memory" and "In Our Hearts Always") [Berkley Memorial Cemetery]

Harrison, Chester A. April 1, 1931 – December 16, 2000, Pvt., U.S. Army, Korea [Berkley Memorial Cemetery]

Harrison, Dorothy E. "Dottie" "Beloved Sister" January 2, 1940 – December 26, 2016 (inscribed "Memory is a golden chain that binds us till we meet again") [Chestnut Grove A. M. E. Church Cemetery, formerly LaGrange Cemetery at Rocks]

Harrison, Mary Elezebeth October 9, 1933 – December 12, 1933 (no tombstone; death certificate stated she was born at Forest Hill, the daughter of William Harrison, born in Martinsburg, WV, and Grace Wilson, born in Maryland; died at home in Pylesville; informant was her mother) [Chestnut Grove A. M. E. Church Cemetery, formerly LaGrange Cemetery at Rocks]

Harrison, Mary Elizabeth August 24, 1909 – July 15, 1911 (no tombstone; death certificate stated she was born in Sussex Co., DE, the daughter of Webster Harrison, born in Jamaica West Indies, and Nancy Pitts, born in Berlin, MD; she died at Creswell; informant was her father) [John Wesley U. M. E. Church Cemetery in Abingdon]

Harrison, Maurice S. Sr. 1964-2006, U.S. Army [Berkley Memorial Cemetery]

Harrison, Minerva died May 24, 1912, age 72 (no tombstone; death certificate stated she was the widowed daughter of W. Butler, of Havre de Grace; name of husband and mother not given) [St. James United Cemetery]

Harrison, Terrill 1986-2015 (small metal funeral home marker) [Berkley Memorial Cemetery]

Hart, Dean B. 1984-2013 (small metal funeral home marker) [Berkley Memorial Cemetery]

Harts, Joseph March 8, 1877 – August 4, 1936 (no tombstone; death certificate stated he was born in Harford Co., the son of Samuel Harts, born in North Carolina, and Mary Dallam, born in Harford Co., and was the husband of Alice Harts who had predeceased him; he died in an auto accident on Route 22 near Carsins Run) [Union U. M. Church Cemetery]

Harts, Mary January 1, 1854 – July 20, 1925 (no tombstone; death certificate stated she was widowed daughter of Sarah Clark, but her mother was unknown to informant Mary Johnson) [Union U. M. Church Cemetery]

Harts, Mary Alice April 12, 1864 – October 20, 1935 (no tombstone; death certificate stated she was the daughter of David Norton and Sarah J. Barnes, all were born in Harford Co.; she married Joseph Harts, lived "outside Bel Air Road" near Aberdeen for 2 years, died there and was buried at "John Wesley Cemetery;" informant was her husband Joseph Harts) [John Wesley U. M. E. Church Cemetery in Abingdon]

Harts, Mary Elizabeth August 15, 1946 – March 14, 1949 (no tombstone; death certificate stated she was the daughter of Robert F. Harts and Eva Harris and died at 837 Erie St. in Havre de Grace) [Union U. M. Church Cemetery]

Harts, Robert Fernandus August 27, 1893 – November 6, 1949 (no tombstone; death certificate stated he was born in Maryland, the son of Henry Harts and Sarah Harvey, married, worked as a truck driver in the grocery business, lived at 837 Erie Street in Havre de Grace and died at Harford Memorial Hospital; informant was Mrs. Eva R. Harts) [Union U. M. Church Cemetery]

Harts, Virginia Annie Keziah died January 5, 1905, age 1 year and 4 months (no tombstone; death certificate stated she was the daughter of Joseph and Jennie Harts and died at Michaelsville; place of burial was not indicated, but probably in Old Union Chapel Cemetery at Michaelsville; possibly reinterred later in Union Chapel Cemetery near Aberdeen) [Union U. M. Church Cemetery]

Harvey, Corey A. August 29, 1984 – February 4, 1990 [Gravel Hill Cemetery]

Harvey, Frank died November 14, 1912, age 56 (on same obelisk with Louisa J. Harvey, William L. Harvey, Walter F. Harvey, Henry A. Hudgins, Hermeon H. Hudgins, Walter F. Harvey II and Robert L. Harvey; Frank Harvey's death certificate stated born November 9, 1858) [St. James United Cemetery]

Harvey, Infant stillborn male on 20 Jun 1911 (no tombstone; death certificate stated he died in Havre de Grace and was the son of Walter Harvey, of Virginia, and Emma Willis, of Delaware) [St. James United Cemetery]

Harvey, Louisa J. died May 15, 1909, age 48 (on same obelisk with Frank Harvey, William L. Harvey, Walter F. Harvey, Henry A. Hudgins, Hermeon H. Hudgins, Walter F. Harvey II and Robert L. Harvey) [St. James United Cemetery]

Harvey, Robert Lee 1925-1984, SSG U.S. Army, World War II (tombstone; also named on same obelisk with Frank Harvey, Louisa J. Harvey, Walter F. Harvey, Henry A. Hudgins, Hermeon H. Hudgins, Walter F. Harvey II and William L. Harvey) [St. James United Cemetery]

Harvey, Walter F. 1881-1929 (on same obelisk with Frank Harvey, Louisa J. Harvey, William L. Harvey, Henry A. Hudgins, Hermeon H. Hudgins, Walter F. Harvey II and Robert L. Harvey; death certificate of Walter Harvey states born January 26, 1883, died February 29, 1929) [St. James United Cemetery]

Harvey, Walter F. II 1923-   (on same obelisk with Frank Harvey, Louisa J. Harvey, Walter F. Harvey, Henry A. Hudgins, Hermeon H. Hudgins, William L. [St. James United Cemetery]

Harvey, William L. 1879-1917 (on same obelisk with Frank Harvey, Louisa J. Harvey, Walter F. Harvey, Henry A. Hudgins, Hermeon H. Hudgins, Walter F. Harvey II and Robert L. Harvey; death certificate stated born September 16, 1878 and died May 30, 1917) [St. James United Cemetery]

Hash, Anthony Easter April 10, 1955 – October 7, 1995 [Berkley Memorial Cemetery]

Hash, Bert Joseph Sr. November 23, 1919 – April 6, 2005, 1st Sgt., U.S. Army (on same tombstone with Stella Jean Hash) [Berkley Memorial Cemetery]

Hash, Stella Jean February 19, 1922 – January 16, 1991 [Berkley Memorial Cemetery]

Hash, William Freeman June 10, 1931 – August 23, 1999 [Berkley Memorial Cemetery]

Haskins, Eliza Louise December 23, 1924 – May 11, 1941 (no tombstone; death certificate stated she was born in Richmond, VA, but her parents' names were not known to informant Mrs. Bettie L. Haskins, of Aberdeen; she was single, had no occupation and lived at Smith Michael's Camp in Aberdeen; she was shot at her home and died in Harford Memorial Hospital) [Mt. Calvary U. A. M. E. Church Cemetery]

Haskins, Junius March 10, 1915 – May 27, 1958 (no tombstone; death certificate and Pennington Funeral Home records state he was born in Virginia, the son of Lee Wesley Haskins and Jane Jones; he served in World War II, worked as a laborer, married, divorced, and lived at 40 Hanover St. in Aberdeen; he died at the Perry Point Veterans Administration Hospital in Cecil Co., MD; the information was taken from hospital records) [Mt. Calvary U. A. M. E. Church Cemetery]

Haskins, Larry – see Clarence E. Banks, Sr. [Mt. Calvary U. A. M. E. Church Cemetery]

Hathaway, Cordelius A. 1918-1985 (on same tombstone with Lucille B. Hathaway and Terry W. Hathaway) [St. James United Cemetery]

Hathaway, Elsner Bennett June 30, 1871 – April 29, 1943 (no tombstone; death certificate stated he was born in Paris, KY, the son of ---- Hathaway ("no record") and Ellen Bennett; he married Pearl A. ----, worked as a clocker in Havre de Grace, and died in Harford Memorial Hospital) [St. James United Cemetery]

Hathaway, Lesa 1981-2015 (small metal funeral home marker) [Mt. Calvary U. A. M. E. Church Cemetery]

Hathaway, Lucille B. 1919-1983 (on same tombstone with Cordelius A. Hathaway and Terry W. Hathaway) [St. James United Cemetery]

Hathaway, Terry W. 1945-1988 (on same tombstone with Lucille B. Hathaway and Cordelius A. Hathaway) [St. James United Cemetery]

Hathaway, Vicki 1957-2006 (small metal funeral home marker) [St. James United Cemetery]

Hawkins, ---- stillborn male died on November 5, 1916, a 7-month pregnancy (no tombstone; death certificate stated he was born at Lapidum, the son of Arthur Hawkins and Helen Webster, and they both were born in Harford Co.; informant was Charles Hawkins, of Havre de Grace RFD #1) [Gravel Hill Cemetery]

Hawkins, Annie died May 18, 1913, age about 100 (no tombstone; death certificate stated she was the daughter of Samuel Hawkins, both born in Harford Co., but mother's name was unknown to informant Alford Stokes, of Havre de Grace; she died a widow at Gravelly Hill) [Gravel Hill Cemetery]

Hawkins, Bernard R. September 17, 1920 – June 21, 2008, Pvt., U.S. Army, World War II (tombstone; obituary and photo in *The Aegis* on June 18, 2008 stated Bernard Russell Hawkins was born in Urbana, the son of John and Janie Hawkins, and was the husband of the late Catherine Cevis Hawkins; he spent most of his life in Delta, PA and was discharged from the Army in 1945; he was employed at the former Miller Chemical Fertilizer Plant until his retirement in 1983; he lived in Edgewood and died at the Lorien Riverside Nursing Home, survived by 2 daughters, a son, a brother, two sisters, 8 grandchildren, 12 great-grandchildren and 1 great-great-grandchild) [Berkley Memorial Cemetery]

Hawkins, Calvin January 27, 1932 – February 15, 1935 (no tombstone; death certificate stated he was the son of James E. Hawkins and Frances Skinner, of Havre de Grace) [Skinner Cemetery]

Hawkins, Calvin July 1, 1933 – March 21, 1985, SP4, U.S. Army, Korea [St. James United Cemetery]

Hawkins, Carolyn Lee May 16, 1951 – June 14, 2013 (no tombstone; obituary and photo in *The Aegis* stated she was born in Havre de Grace, third of ten children of the late George and Mary Wilson, and worked for the Harford County Public Library from 1980 to 2008; she died at Sinai Hospital in Baltimore, survived by 3 children, 1 aunt, 5 sisters, 3 brothers, an adopted sister, a goddaughter, and a host of nieces, nephews, and special friends) [St. James United Cemetery]

Hawkins, Catherine L. January 18, 1923 – March 1, 2005 (tombstone; obituary and photo in *The Aegis* on March 9, 2005 stated Catherine Louise "Weesie" Hawkins was born in Street, the daughter of John and Mary Cevis, and worked at Whiteford Packing Co. for many years and was a sewing machine operator at Fawn Grove

Manufacturing Company and Gleneagles Manufacturing Company in Bel Air; she lived in Havre de Grace and died at Harford Memorial Hospital, survived by her husband of 63 years Bernard Hawkins, 3 children, 8 grandchildren, 13 great-grandchildren, 3 brothers, 1 sister, and a host of nieces, nephews and other relatives) [Berkley Memorial Cemetery]

Hawkins, Clarence Oliver died August 3, 1983, age 50 (no tombstone; obituary in *The Aegis* on August 18, 1983 stated he was formerly of Philadelphia, a son of Ella Mae Hawkins of Havre de Grace and the late Ralph Hawkins, lived in Aberdeen and died at Harford Memorial Hospital, survived by five daughters, three sons, four sisters, and eight brothers) [Berkley Memorial Cemetery]

Hawkins, Earl H. (no dates; on same tombstone with Fred H., George H., John W., Mattie H., Roy H., Sarah H. and Theordore Hawkins) [Gravel Hill Cemetery]

Hawkins, Earnest Levine, "Gram" March 21, 1965 – January 15, 2007 (with his photo) [St. James United Cemetery]

Hawkins, Edward LeRoy November 3, 1941 – November 12, 1941, a premature birth (no tombstone; death certificate stated he was born near Aberdeen, the son of James I. Hawkins, born in St. Mary's Co., and Emily F. Kelley, born near Aberdeen; informant was his father) [Mt. Calvary U. A. M. E. Church Cemetery]

Hawkins, Eliza 1859-1927 (tombstone; death certificate stated she was born on December 25, 1859, married ----, and died on November 2, 1927; she was the daughter of James Floyd, but her mother was not known to informant Sadie Williams, of Havre de Grace RFD) [Gravel Hill Cemetery]

Hawkins, Ella L. died March 14, 1984, age 86 (no tombstone; obituary in *The Aegis* stated she was the daughter of Samuel and Sarah E. Johnson, of Havre de Grace, and she was employed for many years at Carroll's Laundry; she died at Citizens Nursing Home and was survived by three nieces and a nephew) [St. James United Cemetery]

Hawkins, Emily Frances Kelly January 14, 1913 – July 26, 1997 ("Emley Hawkins" owned a lot in section 13 some time after 1951; no tombstone; obituary and photo in *The Aegis* on August 6, 1997 stated she was born at Oakington, daughter of Rev. Samuel B. Kelly and Mary Elizabeth Banks, and they moved to Aberdeen shortly after her birth; she married the late James I. Hawkins at age 16 and had five children; she worked for the Federal Public Housing Authority and then for the Harford County School System until 1963; she was active in the church and was a member of the Willing Workers; she entered the Bel Forest Nursing and Rehabilitation Center in 1990 and died in 1997, survived by two sons, two daughters, 17 grandchildren, 37 great-grandchildren and 19 great-great-grandchildren) [Mt. Calvary U. A. M. E. Church Cemetery]

Hawkins, Estella M. February 28, 1917 – February 11, 1930 (no tombstone; death certificate stated she was the daughter of George Hawkins and Mattie Webster, all born in Maryland, and she died in Havre de Grace Hospital; informant was Mrs. George Hawkins, of Lapidum) [Gravel Hill Cemetery]

Hawkins, Ethel Aikens died October 14, 1968 (no tombstone; obituary in *The Aegis* on October 17, 1968 stated she was the daughter of John Aikens and Mary M. Rumsey, and the wife of Percy J. Hawkins, of Havre de Grace; she died in Harford Memorial Hospital, survived by her parents, husband, 4 sons, 3 daughters, 3 sisters and 1 sister [Berkley Memorial Cemtery]

Hawkins, Frances June 9, 1911 – May 30, 1937 (no tombstone; death certificate stated she was the daughter of Henry Skinner and Minnie Richardson) [Skinner Cemetery]

Hawkins, Fred G. January 5, 1900 – August 23, 1946 (no tombstone; death certificate stated he was the son of George E. Hawkins, Sr. and Mattie H. Webster, all born in Harford Co.; he was single, worked as a laborer, lived near Havre de Grace and died in Harford Memorial Hospital; informant was George Hawkins, of 738 Otsego St., Havre de Grace) [Gravel Hill Cemetery]

Hawkins, Fred H. (no dates; on same tombstone with Earl H., George H., John W., Mattie H., Roy H., Sarah H. and Theordore Hawkins) [Gravel Hill Cemetery]

Hawkins, George E. 1909-1990 (on same tombstone with Hilda P. Hawkins) [St. James United Cemetery]

Hawkins, George H. (no dates; on same tombstone with Earl H., Fred H., John W., Mattie H., Roy H., Sarah H. and Theordore Hawkins) [Gravel Hill Cemetery]

Hawkins, George Owens died November 21, 1979, age 103 (no tombstone; obituary in *The Aegis* stated he was the husband of the late Matty Webster Hawkins, lived at 100 Revolution St. in Havre de Grace and worked for the C. B. Silver & Son Cannery for 30 years; he died at home and was survived by two sons Howard and George, two daughters Cora Webster and Virginia Hannah, 7 grandchildren, 10 great-grandchildren and 25 great-great-grandchildren) [Gravel Hill Cemetery]

Hawkins, Helen B. July 11, 1876 – November 5, 1916 (no tombstone; death certificate stated she was the daughter of M. N. Webster and Sarah Bessicks, all born in Harford Co.; she lived at Lapidum, was married at the time of her death and died in childbirth; informant was Charles Hawkins, of Havre de Grace RFD) [Gravel Hill Cemetery]

Hawkins, Helen Cecelia Skinner "Lunch" died May 27, 1993, age 84 (no tombstone; obituary in *The Aegis* on June 9, 1993 stating she was the daughter of Mr. & Mrs. Henry Skinner and for a time she lived in California, returning to Havre de Grace in the late 1930s; she was survived by a daughter, daughter-in-law, 11 grandchildren, 14 great-grandchildren, and 1 great-great-granddaughter) [St. James United Cemetery]

Hawkins, Henry Allen June 4, 1907 – November 9, 1955, Maryland, BM2, USNR, World War II [St. James United Cemetery]

Hawkins, Hilda P. 1908-2001 (on same tombstone with George E. Hawkins; obituary and photo in *The Aegis* on February 21, 2002 stated she was born in Havre de Grace on November 24, 1908, the daughter of William H. Peaco, Sr. and Alice M. Jones; she worked faithfully for her church for many years and was employed as a domestic worker at the former Bainbridge Naval Training Station, Aberdeen Proving Ground and for private families; she later worked for C. J. Smith Realty and became the first African-American woman to sell real estate in Harford County; affectionately called "Susie" and "Nancy" she died at Harford Memorial Hospital, survived by a sister, 2 grandchildren, 12 great-grandchildren and was preceded in death by her husband George E. Hawkins, Jr. and three siblings) [St. James United Cemetery]

Hawkins, Howard F., "Loving Father" May 30, 1907 – July 4, 1988 (tombstone; obituary in *The Record* on July 20, 1988 stated he was born in Harford County, one of nine children of George and Mattie Hawkins, and was formerly married to Julia Durbin; he retired from Perry Point VAMC in 1956 and died at home in Havre de Grace, survived by his wife of 43 years Grace Waters Hawkins, a daughter Shirley Collins, two sisters, three stepsons, six grandchildren, and nine great-grandchildren; he was also the father of the late Marion Cage) [St. James United Cemetery]

Hawkins, Irene November 14, 1923 – March 1, 1937 (no tombstone; death certificate stated she was the daughter of Ralph Hawkins and Ella Maddox, all born in Maryland, and she died at Harford Memorial Hospital) [Skinner Cemetery]

Hawkins, James I. Sr. died November 11, 1973, age 64 ("James Hawkins" owned a lot in section 13 some time after 1951; no tombstone; obituary in *The Aegis* stated he was born in St. Mary's Co., the son of Douglas and Nellie Hawkins, lived at 411 Oak St. in Aberdeen, worked as a truck driver for Follmer Trucking Co., died at Harford Memorial Hospital in Havre de Grace, and was survived by his wife Emily F. Hawkins, 2 sons, 3 daughters, 16 grandchildren and 11 great-grandchildren) [Mt. Calvary U. A. M. E. Church Cemetery]

Hawkins, James Isaac Jr. April 21, 1934 – January 20, 1999 (no tombstone; obituary and photo in *The Aegis* on January 27, 1999 stated he was born in Aberdeen, the son of James Hawkins, Sr. and Emily Hawkins; he served in the Air Force and later worked at the Perry Point VAMC and the Aberdeen Proving Ground, as well as the Cecil County Department of Social Service; he was active in the church and served as a trustee, usher and organist; he died at Stella Maris Hospice in Towson, survived by a son Vernell Hawkins, an aunt Edith Giles, two sisters, 10 nieces, 6 nephews, and a host of great-nieces, great-nephews and cousins) [Mt. Calvary U. A. M. E. Church Cemetery]

Hawkins, James O. April 14, 1877 – August 31, 1924 (no tombstone; death certificate stated he was the son of Richard Hawkins and Eliza Floyd, all born in Maryland; he was married, worked as a laborer and died at home near Havre de Grace; informant was Richard Hawkins) [Gravel Hill Cemetery]

Hawkins, James Walker "Jimmy" October 2, 1959 – December 22, 1996 (no tombstone; James Dorsey Card File, African American Obituaries, maintained at the Historical Society of Harford County, has a card with an obituary from *The Aegis* on January 8, 1997 stating he was born in Havre de Grace, the son of Josephine Higgins Sally and James Walter Hawkins, Sr., of Philadelphia, PA, and stepson of Elfred Sally, of Baltimore; he died at Joseph Richey Hospice in Baltimore, survived by his father, stepfather, a son, six brothers, three sisters, his 95-year-old maternal grandmother Beulah Higgins, and devoted friend Cora Burnett) [St. James United Cemetery]

Hawkins, John W. (no dates; on same tombstone with Earl H., Fred H., George H., Mattie H., Roy H., Sarah H. and Theordore Hawkins) [Gravel Hill Cemetery]

Hawkins, Julia R., "Loving Mother" February 9, 1912 – February 9, 2005 (tombstone; obituary and photo in *The Aegis* stated Julia Rebecca Hawkins was born in Havre de Grace, the daughter of Harry and Eva Durbin, and was active in the church from an early age; she was a Red Cross volunteer during World War II and worked in the dietetic department at Perry Point VAMC from 1949 to 1979; she lived in Havre de Grace and died at Harford Memorial Hospital, survived by a daughter, eight grandchildren, ten great-grandchildren and six great-great-grandchildren; she was preceded in death by her parents, her husband Howard Hawkins, her daughter Marion A. Cage and her brother Albert Durbin) [St. James United Cemetery]

Hawkins, Mabel V. September 23, 1924 – February 9, 1926 (no tombstone; death certificate stated she was the daughter of Arthur Hawkins and Eva Taylor, all born in Maryland; she died at Lapidum; informant was Arthur Hawkins, of Havre de Grace RFD) [Gravel Hill Cemetery]

Hawkins, Mamie J. 1910-2002 (small metal funeral home marker; obituary and photo in *The Aegis* on July 19, 2002 stated Mamie Joyner Hawkins was born December 26, 1910 in Holly Hill, SC, the daughter of Frank Joyner, the stepdaughter of Mabel Jenkins Joyner, and the wife of Raymond Hawkins who died on November 11, 1980; she lived in Havre de Grace and worked at Carroll's Laundry until it closed and then she was employed at Brevin Nursing Home; she and her husband were guardian to Nolan Bullock; she died at Citizens Care Center on July 11, 2002 and was survived by her younger brother Peter Joyner, her sister Elizabeth Joyner Sawyer (Mrs. Thomas W.), and a host of nieces, nephews and cousins) [St. James United Cemetery]

Hawkins, Marie "Cookie" May 14, 1949 – February 20, 2001 (inscribed "Gone to Dance with the Lord;" obituary and photo in *The Aegis* on March 14, 2001 stated she was born in Murfreesboro, NC, the daughter of the late Arthur Lee Fleetwood and Catherine Fleetwood, lived in Havre de Grace and worked for Harford Memorial Hospital for more than 25 years; she died in that hospital, survived by one son Thomas E. Hawkins, three brothers, four sisters, six grandchildren, six uncles, seven aunts, several nieces and nephews, and a host of cousins) [Gravel Hill Cemetery]

Hawkins, Mary Frances 1947-2016 (small metal funeral home marker) [St. James United Cemetery]

Hawkins, Mary Martha October 17, 1882 – May 21, 1944 (no tombstone; death certificate stated she was born in Harford Co., the daughter of Abram Webster and Mary Prigg, both born in Maryland, and the wife of George E. Hawkins; she lived and died at 515 Alliance St., Havre de Grace; informant was George E. Hawkins, Jr., of Havre de Grace) [Gravel Hill Cemetery]

Hawkins, Mattie H. (no dates; on same tombstone with Earl H., Fred H., George H., John W., Roy H., Sarah H. and Theordore Hawkins) [Gravel Hill Cemetery]

Hawkins, Oscar buried October 6, 2018, age about 70 (information from Charles Warfield, trustee, on the day of the burial) [Mt. Calvary U. A. M. E. Church Cemetery]

Hawkins, Percy James November 21, 1928 – June 19, 1989, U.S. Army, World War II (tombstone; obituary in *The Record* on July 12, 1989 stated he was a bishop in Gospel Tabernacle Church in Havre de Grace and died at Perry Point VAMC, survived by his wife Gertrude Hawkins, three daughters, three sons, a brother Ernest Hawkins, and six grandchildren) [St. James United Cemetery]

Hawkins, Raymond June 10, 1907 – September 11, 1980, PFC, U.S. Army, World War II [St. James United Cemetery]

Hawkins, Richard died January 6, 1931, age about 103 (no tombstone; death certificate stated he was born in Maryland, worked as a laborer and lived in Havre de Grace; informant was George Hawkins, of Lapidum, who did not know the names of Richard's parents) [Gravel Hill Cemetery]

Hawkins, Richard February 8, 1904 – June 18, 1934 (no tombstone; death certificate stated he was born in Harford Co., the son of George Hawkins and Mattie Webster, both born in Maryland; he was single, worked as a laborer, was injured in an automobile accident and died in Havre de Grace Hospital; informant was George Hawkins, Jr., of Havre de Grace) [Gravel Hill Cemetery]

Hawkins, Roy June 5, 1894 – February 1, 1949 (no tombstone; death certificate stated he was born in Maryland, the son of Samuel Preston and Sadie Hawkins, never married, worked as a laborer, lived at 514 Revolution St. in Havre de Grace and died at Harford Memorial Hospital; informant was Howard Hawkins, of Havre de Grace) [Gravel Hill Cemetery]

Hawkins, Roy H. (no dates; on same tombstone with Earl H., Fred H., George H., John W., Mattie H., Sarah H. and Theordore Hawkins) [Gravel Hill Cemetery]

Hawkins, Sarah H. (no dates; on same tombstone with Earl H., Fred H., George H., John W., Mattie H., Roy H. and Theordore Hawkins) [Gravel Hill Cemetery]

Hawkins, Theordore (no dates; on same tombstone with Earl H., Fred H., George H., John W., Mattie H., Roy H. and Sarah H. Hawkins) [Gravel Hill Cemetery]

Hawkins, Thomas Earl November 10, 1965 – August 12, 2004 [Gravel Hill Cemetery]

Haycock, James March 6, 1870 – September 6, 1932 (no tombstone; death certificate stated he was born in Havre de Grace, the son of John Haycock, of Havre de Grace, and Laura Smith, of Port Deposit, MD); he married Laura ---- and died a widower; informant was Carrie Hawkins [St. James United Cemetery]

Haycock, John (no dates on tombstone) [Union U. M. Church Cemetery]

Haycock, Laura E. July 14, 1869 – August 7, 1923 (no tombstone; death certificate stated she was the married daughter of John Smith, but her mother was unknown to informant Cornelia Haycock, of Havre de Grace) [St. James United Cemetery]

Haycock, Thomas "Banty" 1851-1942 (tombstone inscription; also called "Old Faithful;" death certificate stated he was born about June 15, 1863 *(sic)*, the son of Thomas Haycock and Sophia Pinion, all were born in Harford Co.; he lived in Aberdeen for 17 years, was single and died approximately January 12, 1942 when found dead; informant was Charles B. Osborn, Sr. of Aberdeen; obituary in the *Havre de Grace Republican* on January 17, 1942 stated Thomas (Banty) Hacock *(sic)*, age about 85 years, died "from a heart attack or by freezing") [Mt. Calvary U. A. M. E. Church Cemetery]

Hayman, Lottie S. July 25, 1904 – February 5, 1939 (no tombstone; death certificate stated she was the daughter of Albert R. Hayman and Lottie Peakco, all born in Maryland; she married William Hayman, died in Bel Air and buried in "Mountain Cemetery;" informant was her husband) [Mt. Zion U. M. Church Cemetery]

Haymon, George W. May 3, 1908 – November 25, 1947, Maryland, Pfc, Air Corps, World War II (tombstone; no death certificate was found in Harford County) [Fairview A. M. E. Church Cemetery]

Haynes, Charles William March 21, 1865 – January 25, 1941 (no tombstone; death certificate stated he was born in West Virginia, the son of Moses Haynes and Elizabeth Hines; he was married, wife's name not given, and he died in Harford Memorial Hospital in Havre de Grace) [St. James United Cemetery]

Haynes, Ellen December 9, 1921 – December 12, 1924 (no tombstone; death certificate stated she was born in Maryland, the son of David Haynes, born in Kentucky, and Eva Brown, born in Maryland; she died in Joppa and was buried in "Mountian Cemetery;" informant was Eva Haynes, of Joppa) [Mt. Zion U. M. Church Cemetery]

Hayward, Belle August 7, 1876 – May 11, 1912 (no tombstone; death certificate stated she died a widow in Havre de Grace, parents unknown to informant Sarah Fletcher, of Havre de Grace) [St. James United Cemetery]

Head, Marguerite A. November 18, 1925 – April 1, 2005 [Tabernacle Mount Zion U. M. Church Cemetery]

Head, Ollie M. July 22, 1925 – May 22, 2003, TEC 5, U.S. Army, World War II [Tabernacle Mount Zion U. M. Church Cemetery]

Head, William L. March 20, 1945 – March 17, 2006 (tombstone with photo) [Tabernacle Mount Zion U. M.

Church Cemetery]

Helm, Annie Learie February 5, 1904 – December 13, 1946 (no tombstone; death certificate stated she was born in Virginia, the daughter of Henry Green and ---- (mother unknown), married Joseph Bennett Helm and lived in Havre de Grace) [St. James United Cemetery]

Hemore, Beatrice June 15, 1898 – November 25, 1950 (no tombstone; death certificate stated he was born in Harford County, parents not known to informant John Hemore, and was married) [St. James United Cemetery]

Hemore, Frances September 26, 1842 – June 16, 1899 [Green Spring U. M. Church Cemetery]

Hemore, Jarrett 1859-1924 (tombstone; death certificate stated Jarrett T. Hemore was born December 31, 1858, the son of Henry Hemore, both born in Maryland, but his mother's name was not known to informant Alfred Hemore, of Darlington RFD; he was married, worked as a laborer, lived near Darlington and died at home on May 18, 1924) [Green Spring U. M. Church Cemetery]

Hemore, John died January 11, 1944, age 71 (no tombstone; death certificate stated he was the son of Rosa Hemore, both born in Harford Co., but her father's name was not known to the informant Mrs. Matilda Hemore, of Bel Air RFD; he was married, worked as a laborer on a farm, and died at home in rural Bel Air) [Clark's U. M. Church Cemetery]

Hemore, John Henry November 10, 1850 – December 6, 1912 (no tombstone; death certificate stated he was a widower and was born in Maryland, the son of Wesley Hemore and Matilda Rice, but their places of birth were not known to informant Blanch Johnson, his daughter; Pennington Funeral Home stated he died in Havre de Grace and was buried at the Union Chapel Cemetery in Perryman; see comments under Mary Jane Hemore) [Union U. M. Church Cemetery]

Hemore, Mary December 25, 1881 – December 11, 1946 (no tombstone; death certificate stated she was the widow of Jarrett Thomas Hemore, yet it gave her name as Mary Hemore Snowden (Mary Hemore was typed on the certificate and Snowden was handwritten after it); she was born in Virginia, but her parents' names were not known to informant William Albert Hemore, of Havre de Grace RFD #1; her usual residence was in rural Fallston, but she had been living in rural Bel Air for the past 13 months)

Hemore, Mary Elizabeth December 25, 1880 – April 14, 1936 (no tombstone; death certificate stated she was born in Harford Co., the daughter of William Warren and Harriet Bank, both born in Virginia; she did "house duties" for 40 years and died a widow at 217 Freedom Alley in Havre de Grace; informant was John Wesley Hemore, of Havre de Grace) [Asbury Cemetery]

Hemore, Mary Jane died February 20, 1911, age 57 (no tombstone; death certificate stated she was married and the daughter of Philip Monk and Mary Freeman, all born in Maryland; Pennington Funeral Home stated she died in Havre de Grace and was buried in Perryman; name of cemetery was not given, but it was probably Union Chapel Cemetery in Michaelsville; possibly reinterred later in Union Chapel Cemetery near Aberdeen) [Union U. M. Church Cemetery]

Hemore, Matilda E. died April 3, 1978, age 95 (no tombstone; obituary in *The Aegis* on April 6, 1978 stated she was the daughter of Charlie and Lucy Ray and the widow of John Hemore; she lived in Street and died at Fallston General Hospital, survived by a daughter, a granddaughter, a great-grandson, and 4 great-great-grandsons; James Dorsey Card File at the Historical Society of Harford County states "Mother Matilda Ellen Moore" was born June 14, 1882) [Clark's U. M. Church Cemetery]

Hemore, Susie died September 10, 1932, age about 65 (no tombstone; death certificate stated she was born in Maryland, the daughter of Annie Stephenson, but her father was not known to the informant, her husband, John Hemore) [St. James United Cemetery]

Hemore, William died June 25, 1914, age about 41 (no tombstone; death certificate stated he was the unmarried son of Sidney Hemore and Rosie Lee, and died accidentally at Swan Creek; informant was Mrs. John Hemore of Aberdeen) [St. James United Cemetery]

Hemore, William Alfred August 1903 – April 1985 [St. James United Cemetery]

Henderson, Ada G. February 23, 1884 – March 2, 1988 [St. James United Cemetery]

Henderson, Ida Mae 1915-2010 (small metal funeral home marker) [Berkley Memorial Cemetery]

Henderson, Leon G. 1908-1976, Cpl., U.S. Army, World War II [St. James United Cemetery]

Henry, Celia 1916-1983 (tombstone with Sarah E. Thompson inscribed "Sisters") [St. James United Cemetery]

Henry, George (owner of a lot in section 9 some time after 1951) [Mt. Calvary U. A. M. E. Church Cemetery]

Henry, Linda 1953-1983 (copied in 1987, but not found in 2018) [Asbury Cemetery]

Henry, Pearl Croxsell February 2, 1897 – March 20, 1946 (no tombstone; death certificate stated she was the daughter of Edward Croxsell and Annie Brown, and the wife of Joseph A. Henry) [St. James United Cemetery]

Henry, Viola K. 1920-2009 (small metal funeral home marker) [St. James United Cemetery]

Henson ---- stillborn female on August 17, 1927 (no tombstone; death certificate stated she was the daughter of Andrew F. Henson and Marie Briscow, all born in Maryland; she died at home in Joppa and was buried at "Mountain Co. Cem.;" informant was her father) [Mt. Zion U. M. Church Cemetery]

Henson, Andrew F. September 27, 1921 – October 28, 1992, U.S. Army, World War II [Mt. Zion U. M. Church Cemetery]

Henson, Andrew F. Sr. (Rev.), "Father" October 7, 1888 – February 2, 1984 (tombstone; obituary in *The Aegis* stated he was the son of Augustus Henson and Annie Scott and was educated at the McComas Institute in Joppa and the Fallston School; he married Marie Briscoe, was an associate pastor of Mt. Zion U. M. Church and died at Fallston General Hospital; his wife had predeceased him and he was survived by 2 sons, 1 daughter, 1 foster sister, 17 grandchildren, 62 great-grandchildren, 2 great-great-grandchildren) [Mt. Zion U. M. Church Cemetery]

Henson, Annie December 25, 1851 – May 27, 1923 (no tombstone; death certificate stated she was born in Maryland, but her parents' names and places of birth were not known to informant Lou Johnson, of Abingdon; she died a widow at home in Abingdon) [John Wesley U. M. E. Church Cemetery in Abingdon]

Henson, Augustus January 7, 1845 – April 30, 1922 (tombstone copied in 1987, but mostly illegible in 2018; death certificate stated he was born in Harford Co., the son of George Henson and Isabelle Adam, both born in Maryland; he was married, worked as a farmer, died at home at Wilna and was buried in "Mountain Colored Cemetery;" informant was Mrs. B. Harbert, of Wilna) [Mt. Zion U. M. Church Cemetery]

Henson, Bertha October 12, 1896 – January 13, 1912 (no tombstone; death certificate stated she was born in Abingdon, the daughter of George Smith and Louise Henson, birth places not known; she died in Sewell; informant was Laura Beasley, of Abingdon) [John Wesley U. M. E. Church Cemetery in Abingdon]

Henson, Carl R., "Loving Father" February 1953 – October 1, 1988 (tombstone; obituary in *The Aegis* on October 13, 1988 stated Carl Roger Henson was the son of the late Harry and Florence Henson, and the husband of Eve (Brown) Henson, of Havre de Grace; he was employed by American Cyanide Co. in Havre de Grace and was also a barber at "Concepts" in Aberdeen; he died October 1, 1988, age 35, and was survived by his wife, 3 daughters, 1 sister, 4 brothers and step-mother Lynita Henson, of Perryman) [Mt. Zion U. M. Church Cemetery]

Henson, Florence E. 1928-1983 (on same tombstone with Harry R. Henson inscribed "Together Forever;" obituary in *The Aegis* stated she died at Franklin Square Hospital (Baltimore Co.) on February 23, 1983 and was the wife of Harry Roger Henson, of Perryman; she was survived by her husband, 6 sons, 1 daughter, 2 brothers and 1 sister) [Mt. Zion U. M. Church Cemetery]

Henson, Harry R. 1925-1986 (on same tombstone with Florence E. Henson inscribed "Together Forever;" obituary in *The Aegis* on December 25, 1986 stated Harry Henson, of Aberdeen, died on December 11, 1986 at Franklin Square Hospital; he was retired from the civil service and was a member of the Historical Society of Harford County and served on the finance committee and trustee, steward and cemetery committee of Mt. Zion U. M. Church; he was survived by his wife Lynita Henson, 1 daughter, 5 sons, 1 brother, 1 sister, 3 step-sons, 3 step-daughters and "numerous grandchildren and great-grandchildren") [Mt. Zion U. M. Church Cemetery]

Henson, Louiza 1840 – May 12, 1912 (no tombstone; death certificate stated she was the daughter of Louis Turner, both born in Maryland, but the name of her mother was not known to informant Clara Turner, of Abingdon) [John Wesley U. M. E. Church Cemetery in Abingdon]

Henson, Marie B. November 2, 1887 – November 23, 1951 [Mt. Zion U. M. Church Cemetery]

Henson, Mildred Etta Bond September 14, 1923 – July 24, 1967 (tombstone; obituary in *The Aegis* on July 27, 1967 stated Mildred B. Henson was the daughter of Mr. & Mrs. Harry Bond, of Havre de Grace, and the wife of Andrew F. Henson, Jr., of 2113 Battle Street in Edgewood; she was also survived by 4 sons and 3 daughters) [Mt. Zion U. M. Church Cemetery]

Henson, Thomas W. February 8, 1950 – November 26, 1983, Pvt., U.S. Army (tombstone; obituary in *The Aegis* on December 8, 1983 stated Thomas Winfield Henson, of Aberdeen, son of Harry R. Henson and the late Florence E. Henson, died in an automobile accident on I-95 north of White Marsh; survived by his father, step-mother Lynita Henson, 5 brothers, 1 sister, 4 step-brothers and 3 step-sisters) [Mt. Zion U. M. Church Cemetery]

Henson, Wesley died March 1, 1911, age 53 (no dates on tombstone; death certificate stated he was born in Mobile, AL, but informant William H. McCleary, of Berkley, did not know his parents' names, yet stated his father "unknown, must have been white;" he was married (wife's name not given), worked as a "gardner & ostler, care of garden & man servant" and died at his home in Berkley; marriage certificate states Wesley Hinson *(sic)* married Alice Armstrong in 1877 at Dublin) [Berkley Memorial Cemetery]

Heuitt, Elisha March 18, 1844 – December 31, 1921 (on same tombstone with Hannah Heuitt; death certificate stated Elisha "Hewitt" was born at Rocks, married, was a laborer, and died at Pylesville; informant was John Thomas Leonard, of Pylesville, who stated Elisha's mother was Eliza Hewitt, but he did not know his father's name or where they were born; J. C. Taylor Marble Co. records stated "(colored) Elisha and Hannah Heuitt's Granite head stone and posts was put up Aug 1929 Chestnut Grove, ordered by Mary E. Leonard c/o Joseph Whiting, Box 102A, White Plains, NY) [Chestnut Grove A. M. E. Church Cemetery, formerly LaGrange Cemetery at Rocks]

Heuitt, Hannah March 8, 1854 – April 27, 1932 (on same tombstone with Elisha Heuitt) [Chestnut Grove A. M. E. Church Cemetery, formerly LaGrange Cemetery at Rocks]

Heuitt, John Rush, son of Elisha and Hannah Heuitt (no dates; buried beside John Wilson Heuitt) [Chestnut Grove A. M. E. Church Cemetery, formerly LaGrange Cemetery at Rocks]

Heuitt, John Wilson, son of Elisha and Hannah Heuitt (no dates; buried next to John Rush Heuitt) [Chestnut Grove A. M. E. Church Cemetery, formerly LaGrange Cemetery at Rocks]

Heuitt, Oceola September 29, 1911 – May 17, 1997 (no tombstone; James Dorsey Card File, African American Obituaries, that is maintained at the Historical Society of Harford County, has a card with obituary from an unidentified newspaper on May 28, 1997 stating Oceola Hueitt *(sic)* was the daughter of Charles W. Brooks and Ella Butler, and she married on August 26, 1948 to Samuel K. Hueitt, Sr. who predeceased her; she lived in Joppa and died at Fallston General Hospital, survived by a son, a daughter, a sister-in-law, 8 grandchildren and 1 great-great-grandchild) [Chestnut Grove A. M. E. Church Cemetery, formerly LaGrange Cemetery at Rocks]

Hewitt, Clarence E. 1908-1973 (on same tombstone with Ella L. Hewitt inscribed "Together Forever;" obituary in *The Aegis* on January 25, 1973 stated Clarence Edward Hewitt, of 3011 Reckord Road, Fallston, died suddenly at home on January 22, 1973, age 64) [Tabernacle Mount Zion U. M. Church Cemetery]

Hewitt, Edward died January 25, 1928, age about 40 (no tombstone; death certificate stated he was the unmarried son of Clifton Hewitt and Mary Anderson, of Havre de Grace) [St. James United Cemetery]

Hewitt, Ella L. October 20, 1906 – December 25, 2008 (on same tombstone with Clarence E. Hewett and inscribed "Together Forever;" obituary and photo in *The Aegis* on December 31, 2008 stated Ella Louise Hewitt was born in Bel Air, the daughter of David Henry Cox and Eva Blanche Spencer, and was the widow of Clarence E. Hewitt; she died at her home in Fallston, survived by a daughter-in-law Arnetta Hewitt, two grandchildren, several great-grandchildren, several great-great-grandchildren, and one great-great-great-grandson; she was predeceased by her only son Charles T. Hewitt, her sister Blanche E. Cox, and her brother Charles Henry Cox) [Tabernacle Mount Zion U. M. Church Cemetery]

Hewitt, James Edward October 3, 1862 – March 12, 1928 (no tombstone; death certificate stated he was born in Harford Co., the son of George Hewitt and Mary Hackett, both born in Maryland; he was married and died near Fallston; informant was Frances Hewitt) [Tabernacle Mount Zion U. M. Church Cemetery]

Hewitt, John Wesley died November 20, 1934, age about 75 (no tombstone; James Dorsey Card File, African American Obituaries, maintained at the Historical Society of Harford County, has a card with obituary abstracted from the *Bel Air Times* on November 23, 1934 stating he was born at Records Mill and for many years was the trusted driver of Mr. Reckord's teams; he was declared to be the finest coachman in the county; later he moved to Stevenson Archer's place, then for many years was a faithful servant to Bertram Stump and for the past five years he worked for Mr. & Mrs. Charles Shaw in Bel Air; he died at Johns Hopkins Hospital in Baltimore; no family information was given; J. C. Taylor Marble Co. records stated "Wesley Huett's and wife's Marble head stone was put up Dec 26th 1936, Tabernacle Col. near Benson, ordered by Katie Bishop, Bel Air, MD") [Tabernacle Mount Zion U. M. Church Cemetery]

Hewitt, Lisa Elaine died October 24, 1970, age 1 year (no tombstone; obituary in *The Aegis* on November 5, 1970 spelled her name Heuitt and stated she was the daughter of Harvey Turner and Brenda (Ward) Heuitt, of 2064 Battle St. in Edgewood; she was survived by her parents, three brothers and both sets of grandparents) [Tabernacle Mount Zion U. M. Church Cemetery]

Hewitt, May Louisa October 14, 1863 – December 7, 1930 (no tombstone; death certificate stated she was the daughter of Wesley Moore and Jane Stump, all born in Maryland; she was married and died in Bel Air; informant was Wesley Hewitt, of Bel Air) [Tabernacle Mount Zion U. M. Church Cemetery]

Hewitt, Sarah Fanny January 26, 1867 – July 31, 1934 (no tombstone; death certificate stated she was born in Bel Air, the daughter of William Fisher and Louisa Moore, both born in Maryland; she was the widow of James Edward Hewitt and died at "Reckford" in Harford County) [Tabernacle Mount Zion U. M. Church Cemetery]

Hickman, George A., "Grandson" August 15, 1972 (on same tombstone with Myrtle B. Hickman) [Berkley Memorial Cemetery]

Hickman, Myrtle B., "Beloved Wife and Mother" 1921-1967 (on same tombstone with George A. Hickman) [Berkley Memorial Cemetery]

Hickman, Vanessa D. February 25, 1955 – April 4, 2003 [Berkley Memorial Cemetery]

Hicks, Frederick August 6, 1847 – August 29, 1921 (no tombstone; death certificate stated he was born in North Carolina, married, worked as a laborer and died in Bel Air; informant was Tom Hicks, of Bel Air, who did not know Frederick's father's name and his mother was ---- (blank) Banfolk(?) (illegible), both born in North Carolina [Chestnut Grove A. M. E. Church Cemetery, formerly LaGrange Cemetery at Rocks]

Hicks, John June 2, 1902 – January 23, 1928 (no tombstone; death certificate stated he was born in Virginia, unmarried, parents unknown, and died in Darlington) [St. James United Cemetery]

Hicks, Thomas March 24, 1874 – April 17, 1932 (no tombstone; death certificate stated he was born in Harford Co., married, worked as a laborer and was a widower when he died in Havre de Grace Hospital and was buried in Lagrange Cemetery; his father, name unknown, was born in North Carolina and his mother, Ella Blaney, was born in Baltimore; informant was Douglas Hicks, of 825 E. 167th St., New York) [Chestnut Grove A. M. E. Church Cemetery, formerly LaGrange Cemetery at Rocks]

Higgenbotham, Signora R. 1914-1988 [Berkley Memorial Cemetery]

Higgins, Beulah P. October 7, 1901 – April 11, 2003 (on same tombstone with Clark D. Higgins; photo and a lengthy obituary in *The Aegis* stated Beulah Pauline Higgins was the daughter of Floyd Choate and Fannie Lee, and as a young girl she attended school in Allegheny Co., N.C., where her grandparents Jeff and Hulda Choate raised her; she married Clark Dewitt Higgins on December 26, 1920 and they had 14 children, including quadruplets when she was age 34; she was affectionately known as "Mom-Mom" and she called her grandsons "Best Boys" and her granddaughters "Sugar Dills;" she died in Street, survived by 2 sons, 3 daughters, 59 grandchildren and great-grandchildren, but the article also stated she had 68 grandchildren and more than 200 great-grandchildren and great-great-grandchildren) [Fairview A. M. E. Church Cemetery]

Higgins, Charles E. 1931-2016 [William C. Rice Memorial Cemetery, St. James U. M. Church]

Higgins, Clark D. March 22, 1898 – August 6, 1982 (on same tombstone with Beulah P. Huggins; obituary in *The Aegis* on August 12, 1982 stated he was born in North Carolina, the son of Charles and Nancy Higgins, and husband of Beulah P. Higgins; died at home at Street and was survived by his wife, 2 sons, 9 daughters, 65 grandchildren, and 72 great-grandchildren) [Fairview A. M. E. Church Cemetery]

Higgins, Geoffrey J., "Husband and Father" 1961-2001 [Community Baptist Church Cemetery]

Higgins, Harry E. 1957-2015 (small metal funeral home marker) [Community Baptist Church Cemetery]

Higgins, James Robert May 13, 1913 – September 29, 1923 (no tombstone; death certificate stated he was born in Baltimore and died in Churchville, the son of Robert Higgins, born in Virginia, and Luella Dorsey, born in Harford Co.; informant was Lizzie Benns, of Aberdeen RFD) [Asbury Cemetery]

Higgins, Richard C. died March 8, 2008, age 55 (no tombstone; obituary in *The Aegis* on March 12, 2008 stated he died at home in Street, survived by his wife Carolyn D. Higgins, of Abingdon, his mother and father Elsie Mae and Charles Higgins, of Street, five sisters, one brother, two daughters and one grandson) [Clark's U. M. Church Cemetery]

Higgins, Richard Clark February 2, 1953 – March 8, 2008 [William C. Rice Memorial Cemetery, St. James U. M. Church]

Hill, Aquilla, son of James & Milcah Hill, December 18, 1839 – January 17, 1909 (tombstone; death certificate stated he was born in Havre de Grace, the son of James Hill and Milkie Aikens, both of whom were born in Maryland; he was single, worked as a laborer and died in Havre de Grace on January 17, 1909, age 69 years and 1 month; informant was his brother James Hill) [Hill-Johnson Cemetery]

Hill, Constance L. August 20, 1961 – November 1, 1961 (on same tombstone with Samuel W. Hill) [Fairview A. M. E. Church Cemetery]

Hill, Cordelia A. December 10, 1885 – March 15, 1912 (no tombstone; death certificate stated she was married and a housewife in Bel Air, the daughter of Noah Wastcoat and Agusta Prigg of Harford Co.; informant was Carvel Wastcoat, of Bel Air) [Hendon Hill Cemetery]

Hill, David J. died July 19, 1900, age 30 (inscribed "In Memory Of" and death certificate stated David Hill was born in Maryland, the son of Mary Thompson and ---- Hill (name not known); he worked as a laborer, died a widower in Michaelsville and had no children) [Old Union Chapel M. E. Church Cemetery]

Hill, Eben P. 1878-1937 (on same tombstone with Virginia H. Webster; death certificate stated he was born August 8, 1877 in Darlington, the son of Edward Hill, born in Pennsylvania, and Amelia Presberry, born in Harford Co.; he married Harriett ----, worked as a farm laborer and died when struck by a falling tree while cutting wood for himself near Darlington where he had lived for 47 years; informant was Mrs. Harriett Hill, of Darlington) [Berkley Memorial Cemetery]

Hill, Fannie 1872 – November 6, 1929 (no tombstone; death certificate stated he was the daughter of Charles James, but her mother was not known to informant Wilmer James; she died a widow in Havre de Grace) [St. James United Cemetery]

Hill, George R. died December 12, 1926, age about 65 (no tombstone; death certificate stated he was the son of James Hill, but his mother was not known to informant Rufus Galloway; he died a widower in Havre de Grace) [St. James United Cemetery]

Hill, Hattie R. (no tombstone; obituary in *The Aegis* on June 12, 1969 stated she was the daughter of Samuel and Margaret Collin and died on June 5, 1969, age not given; she was survived by 2 brothers, 1 sister, sons Stanford Hill and Robert Kell, and several nieces and nephews [Clark's U. M.. Church Cemetery]

Hill, Ida E. April 24, 1885 – July 26, 1939 (no tombstone; death certificate stated she was the daughter of Isaac Jackson, of Virginia, and Charlett Brown, of Harford Co., and the wife of John Hill; she died at home in Havre de Grace; informant was Carl Jackson) [St. James United Cemetery]

Hill, James died August 13, 1927, age 21 (no tombstone; death certificate stated he was single and worked as a laborer, but informant R. H. Fairservise(?), c/o Stone and Webster Inc., Havre de Grace, did not know where he was born nor who his parents were; he died in Darlington [Berkley Memorial Cemetery]

Hill, James January 8, 1833 – March 4, 1911 (U.S.C.T. grave marker located by James E. Chrismer in 2019;

death certificate stated he was single and the son of Aquilla Hill, but his mother's name was unknown to the undertaker J. C. Pennington) [Skinner Cemetery]

Hill, James "My Father" died September 13, 1860 in his 62nd year [Hill-Johnson Cemetery]

Hill, James L. February 24, 1927 – February 19, 1928 (no tombstone; death certificate stated he was the son of Virginia Hill, both born in Maryland, but informant Harriett Hill, of Castleton, did not know his father's name) [Berkley Memorial Cemetery]

Hill, Jerome, son of Mary Ann Hill, died August 23, 1870, aged 18 years, 3 days [Hill-Johnson Cemetery]

Hill, John 1876-1969 (on same tombstone with Mary A. Hill inscribed "In Memory Of" and also a separate military marker for him inscribed "March 24, 1876 – October 30, 1969, Cpl., Co. A, 24th Regt. Inf., Spanish-American War;" obituary in *The Aegis* on November 6, 1969 stated he was the son of Thomas and Martha Hill and he lived at 618 Edmund St., Aberdeen, and died at Perry Point VAMC, survived by two daughters, two sisters, one brother, and several grandchildren and great-grandchildren) [Berkley Memorial Cemetery]

Hill, Joseph L. March 8, 1945 – October 18, 1999, SP4, U.S. Army, Vietnam [St. James United Cemetery]

Hill, Louis Co. H., 28 U.S. Calvary (no dates on his tombstone; military records stated Lewis H. Hill served as a corporal in Co. G, 30th Regiment Infantry, United States Colored Troops, Maryland Volunteers, from May 28, 1864 to December 10, 1865; death certificate stated Lewis Hill, born in Harford Co., son of James Hill, born in Harford Co., and ---- (blank), was single, worked as a laborer and died at home in Havre de Grace on December 14, 1904, age 69; M. H. Fahey was the coroner; informant was brother James Hill, Jr.) [Hill-Johnson Cemetery]

Hill, Margaret V. died July 22, 1911, age about 44 (no tombstone; death certificate stated she was the married daughter of John H. Christy and Hester Reed, all born in Harford Co.; informant was N. E. Hill, of Perryman) [Union U. M. Church Cemetery]

Hill, Mary A. 1893-1966 (on same tombstone with John Hill inscribed "In Memory Of") [Berkley Memorial Cemetery]

Hill, Mary J., wife of David J. Hill, died January 19, 1899, age 20 (inscribed "Rest beloved one") [Old Union Chapel M. E. Church Cemetery]

Hill, Milton (owner of a lot in section 41 some time after 1951) [Mt. Calvary U. A. M. E. Church Cemetery]

Hill, Pearl E. August 12, 1935 – December 19, 1992 (picture on inscribed "Forever In Our Hearts;" obituary and photo in *The Aegis* on December 23, 1992 stated Pearl Elizabeth Smith Hill was born in Churchville, the daughter of the late Rev. George A. Smith and Pearl Evelyn Jones; after the death of her parents she raised her youngest brother Edward "Big Boy" Smith and her sister Mildred Dennis; she retired from the Harford County Board of Education, lived in Bel Air and died at Fallston General Hospital, survived by her husband of 34 years, Standiford "Bunny" Hill, 3 sons, 2 daughters, 2 brothers, 4 sisters, 7 grandchildren and 2 great-grandchildren) [Asbury Cemetery]

Hill, Phoebe Jane died December 4, 1923, age unknown (no tombstone; death certificate stated she was the daughter of Lundsy Bond and Matilda Daisty, all born in Maryland, she was a widow and died at home near Bel Air; informant was Thomas B. Hill, of Darlington) [Asbury Cemetery]

Hill, Robert Nathan Sr., "Daddy" May 24, 1930 – August 18, 2002 (inscribed "It Is Well With My Soul") [St. James United Cemetery]

Hill, Samuel W. April 18, 1958 – August 25, 1972 [Fairview A. M. E. Church Cemetery]

Hill, Susie Etta Irvin, "Mommy" July 11, 1930 – April 3, 1981 (tombstone; obituary in *The Aegis* on 16 Apr 1981 stated she was the wife of Robert N. Hill, Sr. and she served in the Army from 1949 to 1951) [St. James United Cemetery]

Hill, Thomas B. 1875-1959 (inscribed "Sweetly Resting") [Clark's U. M. Church Cemetery]

Hill, U. Oliver February 11, 1894 – June 13, 1946 (no tombstone; death certificate stated he was the unmarried son of George R. Hill and Rosiana Ellis, and he died at home in Havre de Grace; informant was Mrs. C. Hall)

[St. James United Cemetery]

Hill, Velma M. February 8, 1927 – February 15, 1928 (no tombstone; death certificate stated she was the daughter of Harriett Bond, born in Darlington, who did not know father's name) [Berkley Memorial Cemetery]

Hill, Virginia L. August 1, 1890 – July 16, 1921 (no tombstone; death certificate stated she was the daughter of John Welson *(sic)* and Sara Jane Parrott, all born in Maryland and she was married and lived in Bel Air; informant was Agustus Hill, of Bel Air) [Asbury Cemetery]

Hill, William March 6, 1887 – December 16, 1932 (no tombstone; death certificate stated he born in Perryman, the son of Nathan Hill, born in Washington, DC, and Margaret Christy, born in Perryman, and the husband of Martha Hill) [Union U. M. Church Cemetery]

Hill, William Alfred November 4, 1911 – April 1, 1961, Maryland, PFC, 24 Inf., World War II, BSM [Clark's U. M. Church Cemetery

Hill, Willis D. July 12, 1938 – December 4, 2000, U.S. Army [St. James United Cemetery]

Hilton, Aaron died August 18, 1921 age about 86 (no tombstone; death certificate stated he was the son of Isaaac Hilton, mother unknown, all born in Maryland; he was married and worked as a farmer in Aldino; informant was Alfred B. Hilton, of Street; *The Aegis* on May 29, 1896 reported "Aaron Hinton, of Level" had been granted a government pension) [Green Spring U. M. Church Cemetery]

Hilton, David D. died December 26, 1917, age 51 (no tombstone; death certificate stated he was the son of Edward Hilton and Elizabeth Rigby, all born in Maryland; he was married and worked as a farmer near Level; informant was John Bond, of near Level) [Green Spring U. M. Church Cemetery]

Hilton, Elisha 1869-1954 [Green Spring U. M. Church Cemetery]

Hilton, Eliza S. February 3, 1836 – May 31, 1919 (no tombstone; death certificate stated she was the daughter of Peter Stansbury and Harriet Lisby, all were born in Maryland; she was a widow and died near Havre de Grace; informant was Mrs. Robert Osborne, of Havre de Grace RFD) [Green Spring U. M. Church Cemetery]

Hilton, Francis V. September 5, 1879 – October 24, 1943 [Green Spring U. M. Church Cemetery]

Hilton, Frank October 15, 1869 – April 1, 1935 (no tombstone; death certificate stated he was the son of Lloyd and Alice Hilton, all born in Harford Co.; married Ella O. ---- and was a farm laborer at Level until December 1934; informant was Ella O. Hilton, of Havre de Grace) [Green Spring U. M. Church Cemetery]

Hilton, Harriet August 20, 1795 – September 9, 1897 (no tombstone; obituary in *The Aegis* on September 10, 1897 stated she died "Thursday night" at the home of her son Henry Hilton near Garland; she was born free and her parents in her youth bound her to Mrs. Cassie Stump, the grandmother of Mr. Henry Archer of Stafford; at age 18 she married Isaac Hilton and had 14 children; her place of burial was not mentioned in the obituary; also see the *Harford Democrat* on September 3, 1897) [Green Spring U. M. Church Cemetery]

Hilton, Henry S. February 10, 1830 – January 28, 1908, Maryland, Sgt., CO., H, U.S. Cld Inf, Civil War (tombstone; military records state he served as a sergeant in Co. H, 4th Regt., U.S.C.T.; death certificate of Henry Stump Hilton stated he was the son of Isaac Hilton and Harriet Gorden, and all were born in Maryland; he married Eliza Stansbury and was a farmer at Gravelly Hill; informant was his wife Eliza Hilton) [Green Spring U. M. Church Cemetery]

Hilton, Isaac 1795 – 1881/1887 (no tombstone; information about him was gleaned from the obituary of his wife Harriet in *The Aegis* on September 10, 1897 that stated he died 16 years ago, but another unidentified article stated 10 years go; he is most likely buried beside his wife) [probably Green Spring U. M. Church Cemetery]

Hilton, Josephine Irene 1889-1977 (tombstone; obituary in *The Aegis* on September 23, 1977 stated Josephine Hilton was the daughter of George W. and Amelia Bond and the widow of William Raymond Hilton, Sr.; she lived in Havre de Grace and died at Fallston General Hospital on September 15, 1977, age 87, survived by a son, a brother, and two sisters) [Gravel Hill Cemetery]

Hilton, Levinia, wife of Abraham Hilton, died March 3, 1878 [Green Spring U. M. Church Cemetery]

Hilton, Margaret Virginia (no tombstone; death certificate stated she was born March 25, 1916 and died April 9, 1916, the daughter of Elisha Hilton and Frances Collins, and all were born in Maryland; informant was Frances Hilton, of Aberdeen RFD) [Green Spring U. M. Church Cemetery]

Hilton, Martha July 8, 1870 – August 30, 1948 (no tombstone; death certificate stated she was born in Harford Co., the daughter of Henry Hilton and Elizabeth Stansbury, both born in Maryland; she was single, lived in rural Bel Air and spent the last 2½ years of her life in the Harford County Alms House where she died; informant was Madison R. Hilton, of 2347 N. Canal St., Philadelphia 33, PA) [Green Spring U. M. Church Cemetery]

Hines, Dennis died November 23, 1906, age 73 (no tombstone; death certificate stated he was born in Maryland, died at Deer Creek and his wife was named Mary; the informant, J. R. Ely, J. P., did not know his parents' names; his death notice in *The Aegis* on November 30, 1906 stated "Uncle" Dennis Hines was a familiar figure in the Deer Creek and Kalmia area; place of burial not given [probably Clark's U. M. Church Cemetery]

Hines, Maria August "unknown," 1833 – August 19, 1913 (no tombstone; death certificate stated she was born in Maryland, the daughter of Andrew Bond, but her mother and places of birth of her parents were not known to the informant Elijah White, of Street; she was a widow and a cook who died at home on Deer Creek [Clark's U. M. Church Cemetery]

Hinton, Polly 1918-2003 [St. James United Cemetery]

Hoelly, C. 193- (last number missing on marker) – 1983 (copied in 2018, but not recorded in 1987 and 2002) [Gravel Hill Cemetery]

Hoelly, Dwight 1963-1993 (handwritten on a flat cement slab) [St. James United Cemetery]

Hoes, Hattie 1908-1986 (small metal funeral home marker) [John Wesley U. M. E. Church Cemetery in Abingdon]

Hoke, Bessie V., "Nanny" May 7, 1886 – May 16, 1985 [Union U. M. Church Cemetery]

Hoke, Charles November 15, 1865 – February 15, 1928 (no tombstone; death certificate stated he was the married son of Peter Hoke and Jane Tildon; informant was George Hoke) [Union U. M. Church Cemetery]

Hoke, Charlotte, "Infant Daughter" October 2, 1945 – April 18, 1946 (tombstone; death certificate stated she was the infant daughter of Tevis L. Hoke and Margaret Smith) [Union U. M. Church Cemetery]

Hoke, Donald February 29, 1916 – September 29, 1916 (no tombstone; death certificate stated he was the son of Bert Hoke and Ida Brown, all born in Maryland) [Union U. M. Church Cemetery]

Hoke, Edith B. 1913-   (on same tombstone with Jerome C. Hoke) [Union U. M. Church Cemetery]

Hoke, Ernest A. June 2, 1921 – April 9, 1970, Maryland, 535 Signal HV Const. Co., World War II [Union U. M. Church Cemetery]

Hoke, George W. August 24, 1885 – January 11, 1950 (no tombstone; death certificate stated he was born in Maryland, the son of Charles W. Hoke and Eliza Dennison, and worked as a day laborer; he lived in Aberdeen all his life and died a widower at home on Baltimore Street Extended; informant was Sarah E. Smith) [Union U. M. Church Cemetery]

Hoke, Henry died July 4, 1924, age about 68 (no tombstone; death certificate stated she was the married daughter of William Bowser and Eliza Hall) [St. James United Cemetery]

Hoke, Houston Henry February 20, 1916 – July 27, 1916 (no tombstone; death certificate stated he was the son of Bert Hoke and Ida Brown, all born in Maryland) [Union U. M. Church Cemetery]

Hoke, Ida R. "Mother" May 11, 1879 – June 20, 1944 [Union U. M. Church Cemetery]

Hoke, Jannette July 1, 1850 – December 13, 1924 (no tombstone; death certificate stated she was the married daughter of William Bowser and Eliza Hall, and she died in Aberdeen; informant was Ida Washington) [Union U. M. Church Cemetery]

Hoke, Jerome C. 1911-1965 (on same tombstone with Edith B. Hoke) [Union U. M. Church Cemetery]

Hoke, John I. 1887-1926 (inscribed "At Rest;" death certificate stated he was the married son of Charles W. Hoke and Eliza Dennison, and he was born on April 2, 1887 and died on May 14, 1926; informant was Bessie V. Hoke, of Perryman) [Union U. M. Church Cemetery]

Hoke, Katie November 4, 1897 – June 20, 1920 (no tombstone; death certificate stated she was single and born in Philadelphia, the daughter of Henry Hoke and Lizzie Osborn, both of Maryland; she died at home in Havre de Grace; informant was her father) [St. James United Cemetery]

Hoke, Malvina died October 16, 1937, age about 82 (no tombstone; death certificate stated she was the daughter of Henry Richardson, of Oakington, MD, and Hager Rodes, of Belvedis?, MD); she died a widow in Havre de Grace; informant was Frank Ridgeley) [St. James United Cemetery]

Hoke, Margaret, "Mother" July 9, 1921 – November 11, 2015 (inscribed "In Loving Memory") [Berkley Memorial Cemetery]

Hoke, Mary Olivia September 2, 1888 – February 17, 1916 (no tombstone; death certificate stated she was the married daughter of Robert A. Kell and Mary Rice, all born in Harford Co.) [Union U. M. Church Cemetery]

Hoke, Oliver B. January 29, 1918 – April 13, 1918 (no tombstone; death certificate stated he was the son of Wesley B. Hoke and Ida Brown, all born in Harford Co.) [Union U. M. Church Cemetery]

Hoke, Otelia I. 1918-1991 [Union U. M. Church Cemetery]

Hoke, Phillip (owner of a lot in section 41 some time after 1951) [Mt. Calvary U. A. M. E. Church Cemetery]

Hoke, Phillip Nathaniel died October 30, 1981, age 18 (no tombstone; obituary in *The Aegis* stated he died at Harford Memorial Hospital in Havre de Grace as the result of an automobile accident; he was born in Havre de Grace, the son of Robert Cecil Hoke III and Wahseeola Fax who resided at 1247 Battery Drive; he was survived by his parents, 3 brothers, 3 sisters, grandmother Pearl Fax Hurst, of Aberdeen, and grandparents Robert C. Hoke II, of California, and Rachael Hoke Day, of Washington, D.C.) [Mt. Calvary U. A. M. E. Church Cemetery]

Hoke, Robert Cecil Sr. January 30, 1895 – June 18, 1972, Maryland, Pvt., U.S. Army, World War II (tombstone; military records state he lived in Aberdeen and was inducted into the service on August 23, 1918; he served in Co. K, 811 Pion. Inf., was overseas from October 10, 1918 to June 28, 1919 and was honorably discharged on July 7, 1919) [Union U. M. Church Cemetery]

Hoke, W. Berthket August 9, 1894 – October 14, 1929 (no tombstone; death certificate stated he was the married son of Benjamin Hoke and Samela Stephenson; informant was Mrs. Ida R. Hoke, of Perryman, MD) [Union U. M. Church Cemetery]

Holland, Adrienne V., "Daughter" 1961-   (on same tombstone with Charles H. and Evelyn R. Holland) [Chestnut Grove A. M. E. Church Cemetery, formerly LaGrange Cemetery at Rocks]

Holland, Alvin Sr. January 17, 1944 -   (on same tombstone with Pearl M. Ushering Holland) [St. James United Cemetery]

Holland, Annie O. December 11, 1914 – September 21, 2005 (on same tombstone with William Holland; obituary and photo in *The Aegis* on September 23, 2005 stated Annie Olivia Holland was born in Havre de Grace, daughter of Rev. George Alfred Mitchell and Eleanora Waters; "Miss Annie" lived on the corner of Stokes Street and Pennington Avenue since 1938; she was the widow of William O. Holland, Sr. and died at home, survived by 5 children, 17 grandchildren, 23 great-grandchildren, and 5 great-great-grandchildren) [St. James United Cemetery]

Holland, Benjamin March 24, 1888 – January 9, 1950 (no tombstone; death certificate stated he was the son of Henry Holland and Martha Evans, and lived in rural Jarrettsville; informant was his wife Cora Holland) [St. James United Cemetery]

Holland, Benjamin H. March 24, 1888 – January 9, 1950 (tombstone; death certificate stated Benjamin Harrison Holland was born in Maryland, the son of Henry Holland and Martha Evans; he was an animal tender in medical research and lived and died in rural Jarrettsville near Street; informant was his wife Cora Holland, of Street, MD) [William C. Rice Memorial Cemetery, St. James U. M. Church]

Holland, Beulah May premature birth and death on February 27, 1923 (no tombstone; death certificate stated she was the daughter of Mord *(sic)* S. Holland and Mabel F. Groom, and they all were born in Harford Co.; informant was Charles Denson, of Street, MD) [Fairview A. M. E. Church Cemetery]

Holland, Charles Alfred died November 11, 1979, age 84 (no tombstone; obituary in *The Aegis* on November 15, 1989 stated he was born in Perryman, the son of William T. and Hattie Holland; he lived in Havre de Grace, died at Harford Memorial Hospital, was predeceased by his wife Helen Holland and survived by 2 sons James Edward Holland and Vernon Holland, 13 grandchildren, 14 great-grandchildren, 1 great-great-grandchild, and 2 sisters) [Union U. M. Church Cemetery]

Holland, Charles H. 1927-2013 (on same tombstone with Evelyn R. and Adrienne V. Holland, but his year of death is not inscribed; funeral notice and photo in *The Aegis* on December 18, 2013 stated Charles Henry Holland, of Street, MD, died at Upper Chesapeake Medical Center in Bel Air on December 12, 2013, age 85, but his tombstone stated he was born 1927, thus age 86) [Chestnut Grove A. M. E. Church Cemetery, formerly LaGrange Cemetery at Rocks]

Holland, Charles M. 1964-2011 (small metal funeral home marker) [St. James United Cemetery]

Holland, Charles N. March 18, 1924 – February 7, 1971, Pvt., 435 QM Gas Supply Co., World War II (tombstone; obituary in *The Aegis* stated "Lovey" was born in Perryman, the son of Charles A. and Helen Holland of 387 Wilson St. in Havre de Grace, served in World War II, and died at Perry Point VA Hospital, survived by a son Charles K. Holland, 2 brothers James Edward Holland and Vernon Holland, and 3 sisters) [Union U. M. Church Cemetery]

Holland, Charles Nelson December 15, 1892 – December 22, 1947 (no tombstone; Kurtz Funeral Home Record Book 1944-1949, p. 185, stated he was born at Madonna, the son of Henry Clay Holland and Martha Evans, both born in Baltimore Co.; he was single, worked as a farm laborer and died at home in Federal Hill; informant was Mrs. Clarence Robinson, of Rocks; death certificate gave the same information) [William C. Rice Memorial Cemetery, St. James U. M. Church]

Holland, Charlotte R. May 16, 1863 – August 28, 1928 (on same tombstone with Henry V. Holland; death certificate stated she was born June 1, 1862 and died August 26, 1928; she was married and the daughter of William Stewart, but her mother was unknown to Henry V. Holland) [Union U. M. Church Cemetery]

Holland, Clifford O. December 9, 1910 – November 10, 1982 [Berkley Memorial Cemetery]

Holland, Clinton J. January 2, 1923 – July 23, 1958, West Virginia, Cpl, Btry D, 30 AAA AW Bn. [William C. Rice Memorial Cemetery, St. James U. M. Church]

Holland, Doris M. July 21, 1927 – June 9, 2009 [Chestnut Grove A. M. E. Church Cemetery, formerly LaGrange Cemetery at Rocks]

Holland, Edith Elizabeth, "Mother" March 29, 1928 – Jan 8, 2005 (inscribed "Her children rise up and call her blessed. Isaiah 31:28" and obituary and photo in *The Aegis* on January 14, 2005 stated she was born in Havre de Grace, the fourth of 14 children born to James C. Lee and Susie V. Lee; she worked at Carroll's Laundry and later went to Philadelphia where she was employed as a nanny for several years; upon returning to Harford County she worked at Aberdeen Proving Ground; in 1961 she began working at Perry Point VAMC and retired in 1987; she married Marvin C. Holland in 1953 and became a very active member and office holder in St. Matthew AUMP Church in Havre de Grace; she died at Harford Memorial Hospital, survived by her three daughters and five grandchildren) [St. James United Cemetery]

Holland, Edna M. July 10, 1939 -   (on same tombstone with John E. Holland, Sr.) [Chestnut Grove A. M. E. Church Cemetery, formerly LaGrange Cemetery at Rocks]

Holland, Evelyn R., "Wife" 1928-1986 (on same tombstone with Charles H. and Adrienne Holland; obituary in *The Aegis* on March 13, 1986 stated she was born in Baltimore, daughter of the late Charles and Mabel Akins, and wife of Charles H. Holland; she lived in Street and died at home on March 8, 1986, age 58, survived by four daughters, two brothers, and three sisters) [Chestnut Grove A. M. E. Church Cemetery, formerly LaGrange Cemetery at Rocks]

Holland, Everett R. January 21, 1936 – February 13, 1971, Maryland, A3C, U.S. Air Force [Berkley Memorial Cemetery]

Holland, Frances M. 1892-1958 (on same tombstone with William T. Holland; obituary in *The Democratic Ledger* on March 6, 1958 stated she was born in Perryman, the daughter of the late Wesley S. and Harriett Preston, and married William Thomas Holland; she lived at 201 N. Stokes St. in Havre de Grace and died at Harford Memorial Hospital on March 3, 1958, age 63, survived by her husband, two sons Sligord O. Holland and Oliver Holland, and three brothers George, John and Neal Preston) [Union U. M. Church Cemetery]

Holland, Geneva C. January 1, 1919 – February 27, 1992 (on same tombstone with Clifford O. Holland; obituary in *The Aegis* on April 1, 1992 stated Geneva "Gee Gee" Cromwell Holland was born in Baltimore, the daughter of James and Bertha Cromwell, and moved to Harford County in the early 1940s; she held office in her church, in the Elks and in NAACP; she lived in Havre de Grace and died at Citizens Nursing Home, survived by her sister, 3 step-daughters, 1 aunt, 1 sister-in-law, and 11 nieces and nephews) [Berkley Memorial Cemetery]

Holland, Georgeanna 1852 – December 30, 1917 (no tombstone; death certificate stated she was the daughter of Lewis Turner and Maria Hollis, all born in Harford Co.; she was married and died at Federal Hill; informant was Henry Holland, of Rocks; James Dorsey Card File, African American Obituaries, maintained at the Historical Society of Harford County, has a card with obituary abstraction from the *Bel Air Times* on January 4, 1918 stating she died at home near Federal Hill, but gave no family information; "She was the type of woman of her race that is rapidly becoming extinct. The younger generation would do well to emulate her characteristics of faithfulness, kindness and sterling worth.") [William C. Rice Memorial Cemetery, St. James U. M. Church]

Holland, Hattie February 23, 1870 – December 19, 1919 (no tombstone; death certificate stated she was born in Harford Co. and was the married daughter of Louis Brown, birth place unknown, and Elizabeth Heath, born in Harford Co.; informant was George Holland, of Aberdeen) [Union U. M. Church Cemetery]

Holland, Helen V. died January 13, 1973, age not given (no tombstone; obituary in *The Aegis* stated she was born in Perryman, the daughter of the late John and Mary Christy, married Charles A. Holland, lived at 387 Wilson Street in Havre de Grace, and died at Harford Memorial Hospital, survived by her husband, two sons James E. Holland and Vernon A. Holland, three daughters, two sisters, 11 grandchildren, and 10 great-grandchildren) [Union U. M. Church Cemetery]

Holland, Henry died April 14, 1919, age about 73 (no tombstone; death certificate stated he was the son of Charles Holland and Charlotte Holland, all born in Maryland; he worked as a farm hand and died a widower at "Rocks RD, Federal Hill;" informant was his daughter, Lizzie Johnson, of Rocks RFD) [William C. Rice Memorial Cemetery, St. James U. M. Church]

Holland, Henry V. September 12, 1858 – May 17, 1946 (on same tombstone with Charlotte R. Holland) [Union U. M. Church Cemetery]

Holland, James H. died April 11, 1919, age about 49 (no tombstone; death certificate stated he was the married son of Robert Holland, both born in Harford Co., but his mother was unknown to informant Susie Holland, of Aberdeen) [Union U. M. Church Cemetery]

Holland, James R. September 12, 1897 – August 9, 1964 [Union U. M. Church Cemetery]

Holland, James Thomas "Tommy" died January 26, 1993, age not given (no tombstone; obituary and photo in *The Aegis* on February 3, 1993 stated he was born in Philadelphia, son of the late James Raymond and Lucy Ann Holland, and married Marjorie Marie Galloway of Havre de Grace in 1975; he worked for the railroads, BG&E, and was a licensed practical nurse at the Perry Point VAMC for 35 years; he lived in Havre de Grace and died at Perry Point VAMC, survived by his wife, two step-daughters Ava Lee and Rosalind James, seven grandchildren, one great-grandson, and ten brothers and sisters-in-law) [Union U. M. Church Cemetery]

Holland, John E. Sr. August 1, 1936 – May 28, 1999 (on same tombstone with Edna M. Holland) [Chestnut Grove A. M. E. Church Cemetery, formerly LaGrange Cemetery at Rocks]

Holland, Keith 1958-1966 [Berkley Memorial Cemetery]

Holland, Levinia died January 1, 1930, age about 50 (no tombstone; death certificate stated she was the daughter of Charles Dars and Susan Scott, all born in Maryland; she was a widow and lived and died in Havre de Grace; informant was Mrs. Ella Warfield, of Havre de Grace) [Asbury Cemetery]

Holland, Maranda died December 21, 1882, age not given [Clark's U. M. Church Cemetery]

Holland, Marvin Clifford, "Son" September 12, 1933 – April 26, 1991 (on same tombstone with Elva Nora Johnson) [St. James United Cemetery]

Holland, Mary S. November 21, 1855 – August 21, 1916 (no tombstone; death certificate stated she was the married daughter of Richard Turner, both born in Virginia, but her mother was unknown to informant James A. Holland, of Perryman) [Union U. M. Church Cemetery]

Holland, Milton E. April 19, 1924 – November 26, 2011 [Chestnut Grove A. M. E. Church Cemetery, formerly LaGrange Cemetery at Rocks]

Holland, Norman L. Sr. June 19, 1930 – December 28, 1974 [Fairview A. M. E. Church Cemetery]

Holland, Pearl M. Ushering August 8, 1942 -   (on same tombstone with Alvin Holland, Sr.) [St. James United Cemetery]

Holland, Reuben E. September 17, 1893 – October 20, 1969, Pvt. U.S. Army, World War I (tombstone; military records state Reuben Elsworth Holland was born in Perryman, lived at 550 Alliance St., Havre de Grace, and was inducted into the service on August 2, 1918; he served in SC and then in Co. C, 426 Res Lab Bn on September 7, 1918, and was honorably discharged on March 11, 1919; obituary in *The Aegis* on October 30, 1969 stated he was the son of the late William T. and Harriet Holland, lived at 387 Wilson St. in Havre de Grace, and died at Perry Point VA Hospital, survived by two brothers and several nieces and nephews) [Union U. M. Church Cemetery]

Holland, Robert B. December 3, 1880 – February 12, 1951 (no tombstone; death certificate stated he was born in Maryland, the son of ---- (blank) Tildon and Sarah Holland, worked as a farm day laborer, lived on Edmund St. Ext. in Aberdeen and died at the County Home in Bel Air where he lived about 2 months; he was married and informant was Hester Holland) [Union U. M. Church Cemetery]

Holland, Sarah F. May 2, 1925 – July 16, 1926 (no tombstone; death certificate stated she was the daughter of Charles Holland and Hellen Christy; informant was Thomas Holland) [Union U. M. Church Cemetery]

Holland, Susan V. March 12, 1865 – April 11, 1931 (no tombstone; death certificate stated she was the widowed daughter of William Holland and Mana Lewis; informant was I. W. Wilmore) [Union U. M. Church Cemetery]

Holland, Susie G. March 8, 1867 – June 11, 1924 (no tombstone; death certificate stated she was the widowed daughter of Henry Welsh and ---- Shorts; informant was Hannah Richardson) [Union U. M. Church Cemetery]

Holland, T. J. Jr. 1975-2017 (small white wooden cross grave marker) [Chestnut Grove A. M. E. Church Cemetery, formerly LaGrange Cemetery at Rocks]

Holland, Vivian Ann "1926 daughter 1939" [William C. Rice Memorial Cemetery, St. James U. M. Church]

Holland, William "Skip" March 8, 1912 – October 31, 1985 (on same tombstone with Annie O. Holland; obituary in *The Aegis* on November 7, 1985 stated William O. Holland was among the first to graduate from Havre de Grace Colored High School in 1932, married Annie O. Mitchell, retired from Aberdeen Proving Ground and died at his home in Havre de Grace, survived by his wife, three daughters, two sons, 16 grandchildren and 3 great-grandchildren) [St. James United Cemetery]

Holland, William T. 1889-1970 (on same tombstone with Frances M. Holland; obituary in *The Aegis* stated William Thomas Holland was the son of the late William T. and Harriett Holland, and husband of the late Frances Holland, lived at 201 N. Stokes St., was a mason and active in the church, and died at Harford Memorial Hospital on July 9, 1970, survived by two sons, one brother, 7 grandchildren and 14 great-grandchildren) [Union U. M. Church Cemetery]

Holland, William T. died May 17, 1904, age 56 (no tombstone; death certificate stated he was the husband of Harriet Holland, and the son of William Holland and Maria Lewis, all born in Harford County; he was a farmer and died at Michaelsville; place of burial was not indicated [probably Union U. M. Church Cemetery]

Holley, ---- died May 17, 1948, an 18 month pregnancy, lived only 22 minutes (no tombstone; death certificate stated that he was the son of Allen Stansbury Holley (age 27, government employee) and Vera Marie Korman (age 23, housewife) who lived at 11 Battle Street in Edgewood, the infant died at Harford Memorial Hospital in Havre de Grace) [Fairview A. M. E. Church Cemetery]

Holley, Carrie O. Williams died July 5, 1995, age 77 (no tombstone; James Dorsey Card File, African American Obituaries, maintained at the Historical Society of Harford County, has a card with obituary from *The Aegis* on July 12, 1995 stating she was the wife of the late Isaac Holley and for several years she worked for the post exchange at the Edgewood Arsenal; she was a resident of Bel Forest Nursing and Rehabilitation Center and died at Fallston General Hospital, survived by two sons, two sisters, and several grandchildren) [Tabernacle Mount Zion U. M. Church Cemetery]

Holley, Mary died January 24, 1990, age 85 (no tombstone; obituary in *The Aegis* on January 31, 1990 state she was born in Fallston, the daughter of Isaiah and Amelia Quickley, but the name of her husband was not given; she died at the Ivey Nursing Home in Baltimore, survived by one brother William Quickley and one sister Elsie Brown, and nieces and nephews) [Tabernacle Mount Zion U. M. Church Cemetery]

Holley, Robert September 11, 1888 – December 9, 1954, Pvt., 811 Pion Inf. (tombstone; military records stated he was born in Churchville, lived in Aberdeen, was inducted into the service on August 23, 1918, served in Co. F, 811 Pioneer Inf., was overseas from October 20, 1918 to July 25, 1919 and was honorably discharged on July 29, 1919) [Union U. M. Church Cemetery]

Holliday, Alex (Alexander) died January 8, 1915, age not given (no tombstone; obituary in *The Aegis*, January 15, 1915, stated he died in Baltimore and was for many years a faultless servant at the Homestead in Bel Air, the old Farnandis estate; a testimonial was given by the lady with whom he lived) [Hendon Hill Cemetery]

Holliday, Clarence E., son of G. and M. V. Holliday, died June 26, 1878, age 3 months and 11 days (inscribed "Budded on Earth to Bloom in Heaven") [West Liberty Church Cemetery]

Holliday, Elizabeth died February 4, 1886 in her 105th year (no tombstone; obituary in *The Aegis* on February 12, 1886 stated she had been known for the last 50 years or more as "Aunt Bettie" and died at the home of her grandson near Bel Air; she was a servant to the Amos family and belonged to the late George R. Amos when the emancipation act was passed; she left 7 children, 11 grandchildren and 16 great-grandchildren; her place of burial was not reported [probably Hendon Hill Cemetery]

Holliday, Frederick N. died November 13, 1916, age 23 (tombstone; death certificate stated he was born in Havre de Grace on August 25, 1891, the son of William T. Holliday, of Denton, MD, and Alberta Anderson, of Havre de Grace; he was unmarried and died at home in Havre de Grace) [St. James United Cemetery]

Holliday, Grace died December 18, 1893, age 13 (no tombstone; death notice in *The Aegis* on December 22, 1893 stated she was the daughter of Alexander Holliday and was accidentally shot and killed by Clara Brown, a 15-year-old playmate, at her home near the Bel Air tollgate; burial place not reported, but her father is buried at Hendon Hill so she probably is also; *The Aegis* on January 12, 1894 reported Clara Brown was a cousin of Grace Holliday) [probably Hendon Hill Cemetery]

Holliday, Mary Susan, wife of James Holliday, died April 16, 1885, age 21 years, 10 months and 1 day (tombstone; however, Kurtz Funeral Home records stated James Holaday's wife was buried in a plain cherry coffin on April 18, 1880 from Woodard's tenant house) [West Liberty Church Cemetery]

Hollingsworth, Amanda F. 1907-   (on same tombstone with Walter J. Hollingsworth) [Union U. M. Church Cemetery]

Hollingsworth, Eliza, "Mother" died March 22, 1889, age 66 (inscribed "Gone but not forgotten" and "At Rest") [Old Union Chapel M. E. Church Cemetery]

Hollingsworth, Emily A. January 19, 1874 – March 6, 1927 (no tombstone; death certificate stated she was the daughter of William Parker and Rebecca Prig, all born in Maryland; she was married and died at home in Perryman; informant was Lloyd Hollingsworth) [Mt. Calvary U. A. M. E. Church Cemetery]

Hollingsworth, Eva 1927-2018 (small metal funeral home marker) [St. James United Cemetery]

Hollingsworth, Frank Anna April 9, 1870 – March 30, 1911 (no tombstone; death certificate stated she was single and daughter of Henry Hollingsworth and Eliza Lisby, born Maryland) [Union U. M. Church Cemetery]

Hollingsworth, Hattie March 30, 1861 – October 29, 1918 (inscribed "In Memory Of;" death certificate stated Harriett M. Hollingsworth was born on March 30, 1863, the daughter of Robert Kell and Sarah Thompson, all born in Maryland; informant was William Henry Hollingsworth, of Perryman) [Union U. M. Church Cemetery]

Hollingsworth, Henry H. Jr. November 3, 1850 – May 18, 1934 (no tombstone; death certificate stated he was the son of Henry H. Hollingsworth and Eliza Lisby and the husband of Hattie Kell Hollingsworth who had predeceased him; informant was Emory Ringgold, of Aberdeen) [Union U. M. Church Cemetery]

Hollingsworth, Henry Sr. died February 2, 1892 in his 68th year (no tombstone; obituary in *The Aegis* on February 12, 1892 stated he was giant man who died of pneumonia at his home near Perryman and was buried at Union Chapel near Michaelsville; being a man of muscular power he was much sought after for heavy work and was an excellent wheat stacker and coon hunter; he was industrious, economical, and left a large number of children, most of them boys; possibly reinterred later in the Union Chapel Cemetery near Aberdeen) [Union U. M. Church Cemetery]

Hollingsworth, John W. November 17, 1859 – May 14, 1918, Ardmore, PA (tombstone) [Asbury Cemetery]

Hollingsworth, Lloyd November 19, 1864 – February 21, 1935 (no tombstone; death certificate stated he was born in Perryman, son of Henry Hollingsworth and Eliza Lisby, both born in Maryland; he married Emily Parker, worked as a day laborer for 50 years, lived in Perryman and died at Havre de Grace Hospital; informant was William M. Hollingsworth, of Perryman) [Mt. Calvary U. A. M. E. Church Cemetery]

Hollingsworth, Mary A. June 16, 1914 – March 16, 1920 (no tombstone; death certificate stated she was the daughter of Lloyd J. Hollingsworth and Emily Parker, all were born in Maryland; she was single and died at home in Perryman; informant was her father) [Mt. Calvary U. A. M. E. Church Cemetery]

Hollingsworth, Mason Grafton February 17, 1907 – July 31, 1915 (no tombstone; death certificate stated he was the son of Lloyd Hollingsworth and Emma Parker, all born in Maryland, and they lived at Cole) [Union U. M. Church Cemetery]

Hollingsworth, Norman Sylvester August 24, 1899 – July 22, 1915 (no tombstone; death certificate stated he was the son of Lloyd Hollingsworth and Emily Parker, all born in Maryland, and they lived at Cole) [Union U. M. Church Cemetery]

Hollingsworth, W---(?) (first name illegible) May 27, 1825 – February 2, 1892 (tombstone badly eroded in the upper left portion) [Old Union Chapel M. E. Church Cemetery]

Hollingsworth, Walter J. (Dr.) 1891-1981 (on same tombstone with Amanda F. Hollingsworth) [Union U. M. Church Cemetery]

Hollingsworth, William H. 1851-1934 [Union U. M. Church Cemetery]

Hollingsworth, William M. May 6, 1893 – May 26, 1958, Maryland, Pvt., Co. A, 808 Pioneer Inf., World War I (tombstone; military records state he was born in Perryman, was inducted into service as a private on June 19, 1918, served in 154 Dep. Brig. and in Co. A., 808 Pioneer Inf., was overseas at Meuse Argonne until June 22, 1919, honorably discharged June 27, 1919) [Mt. Calvary U. A. M. E. Church Cemetery]

Hollingsworth, Wilton A. August 12, 1896 – January 20, 1924 (no tombstone; death certificate stated he was the son of Lloyd Hollingsworth and Emily Parker, all born in Maryland; he was shot and died at Havre de Grace Hospital; informant was Lloyd J. Hollingsworth, of Perryman) [Mt. Calvary U. A. M. E. Church Cemetery]

Hollis, --- stillborn premature male died March 16, 1917 (no tombstone; death certificate stated he was the son of Lewis and Elizabeth Hollis, of Bel Air, who were born in Harford County) [Asbury Cemetery]

Hollis, Ann 1810 – December 9, 1896, age 86 years [Tabernacle Mount Zion U. M. Church Cemetery]

Hollis, Grace September 19, 1919 – February 5, 1938 (no tombstone; death certificate stated she was the daughter of Albert Winns and Ella Chris *(sic)*, all born in Harford Co.; she married Oscar Hollis and died at Level; informant was Oscar Hollis, of Aberdeen RFD) [Green Spring U. M. Church Cemetery]

Hollis, Mary J., wife of Elias Hollis and daughter of Lewis and Mary J. Benns, died October 11, 1900, age 29 years, 2 months, 11 days (illegible verse on tombstone) [Asbury Cemetery]

Hollis, Oscar W. June 2, 1915 – February 21, 1992, U.S. Navy (tombstone in section 2) [Mt. Calvary U. A. M. E. Church Cemetery]

Hollis, Sarah died October 1, 1917, age about 54 (no tombstone; death certificate stated she was the daughter of Rosa Hollis, both born in Maryland, but informant William V. Smith, of Street, MD, did not know his father's name or birth place; she died a widow at Poole) [Berkley Memorial Cemetery]

Holly, Isaac Medford Jr. died August 16, 1986, age 78 (no tombstone; obituary in *The Aegis* on September 4, 1986 spelled his name Holley although his wife's obituary spelled the name Holly; he was born on Gunpowder Neck in Edgewood, the son of Isaac and Nellie Holley *(sic)*, and retired from the Patapsco and Back River Railroad of the Bethlehem Steel Corporation at their Sparrows Point Plant in Baltimore County; he died at Fallston General Hospital and was survived by his wife Carrie Olivia Holley *(sic)*, three sons, eight grandchildren, eight great-grandchildren, three sisters, two brothers, and several nieces and nephews) [Mt. Zion U. M. Church Cemetery]

Holly, James Arthur January 8, 1932 – January 9, 1932, premature birth, lived 36 hours (no tombstone; death certificate spelled his name Holley and stated he was the son of James E. Holley *(sic)* and Myrtle L. Hall, all born in Maryland; he died at home in Cooptown and was buried in "Fairview Col. Cem.;" informant was James E. Holley, of Sharon) [Fairview A. M. E. Church Cemetery]

Holly, James E. 1910-1975 (on same tombstone with Myrtle H. Holly) [Fairview A. M. E. Church Cemetery]

Holly, M. T. died 1963 (copied in 2002 and 2018; listed as Mary Taylor Holly in 1987) [Gravel Hill Cemetery]

Holly, Mary Elizabeth died September 24, 1913, aged about 65 (no tombstone; death certificate stated she was the daughter of Hesikah Scott and Elizabeth Webster, all born in Harford Co.; she was married and died at Aldino; informant was John Wesley Scott, of Bel Air RFD; certificate stated she was buried at Churchville [probably Asbury Cemetery]

Holly, Myrtle H. 1915-2002 (on same tombstone with James E. Holly; obituary in *The Aegis* on August 21, 2002 stated Myrtle Louise Holly was born March 11, 1915, the daughter of Walter and Abbie Hall, and was the widow of James Elwood Holly; active in the church, she was called "Bom Mom" by her grandchildren; she died at home in Jarrettsville on March 9, 2002, age 87, and was survived by two daughters, five grandchildren, four sisters, five sisters-in-law, one brother-in-law, nine great-grandchildren, five great-great-grandchildren, three grandsons-in-law, and a host of nieces, nephews and cousins) [Fairview A. M. E. Church Cemetery]

Holly, Nellie Demby died March 14, 1983, age 98 (no tombstone; obituary in *The Aegis* on April 17, 1983 state she was the widow of Isaac M. Holly, lived in Joppa and died at Fallston General Hospital, survived by 3 sons, 3 daughters, 20 grandchildren, 43 great-grandchildren, 19 great-great-grandchildren, "and many other relatives") [Mt. Zion U. M. Church Cemetery]

Holly, Robert J. died November 14, 1912, age 78 (no tombstone; death certificate stated he was born in Virginia, parents' names unknown, married and worked as a laborer at Aberdeen; informant was his wife, name not given; certificate stated he was buried in Churchville, but did not give place of burial [probably Asbury Cemetery]

Holly, Wilton Alexander July 19, 1915 – May 28, 1981, PFC, U.S. Army, World War II (tombstone; obituary in *The Aegis* on June 4, 1981 stated he was born in Magnolia, served in the Army in World War II, and was survived by his mother Nellie Holly, four sisters and four brothers) [Mt. Zion U. M. Church Cemetery]

Holman, Viola 1904 – September 3, 1929 (no tombstone; death certificate stated she was the daughter of Charles Dutton and Jane Hines and all were born in Maryland; she was married and died at Kalmia; informant was Jane Hines, of Bel Air) [Clark's U. M. Church Cemetery]

Holmes, Bernice Norman October 7, 1935 – April 19, 1974 [Fairview A. M. E. Church Cemetery]

Holmes, Bertha M. February 10, 1893 – August 18, 1992 (on same tombstone with Melvin Holmes) [Berkley Memorial Cemetery]

Holmes, Charles March 15, 1872 – March 21, 1933 (no tombstone; death certificate stated he was the son of Sallie Homes *(sic)*, father unknown, and lived in Perryman; he was divorced from Elizabeth Peco, according to informant Walter Stansbury, of Perryman) [Union U. M. Church Cemetery]

Holmes, Eliza 1839 – February 12, 1911 (no tombstone; death certificate stated she was born in Harford Co and was the widowed daughter of Bonaparte Southland, born in Virginia; names of her mother and husband were not given; she died in Havre de Grace) [St. James United Cemetery]

Holmes, Melvin July 5, 1893 – August 14, 1977 (on same tombstone with Bertha M. Holmes) [Berkley Memorial Cemetery]

Holmes, R. Frank August 30, 1896 – May 11, 1923 (no tombstone; death certificate stated he was the married son of John Holmes and Rose Bowser, and he died in Havre de Grace) [St. James United Cemetery]

Holtz, Ellen M. 1913-1987 [Union U. M. Church Cemetery]

Hooks, ---- stillborn female on March 17, 1919 (no tombstone; death certificate stated she was the daughter of William B. Hooks and Leona Monk, all born in Maryland) [Union U. M. Church Cemetery]

Hooks, Alice July 1, 1907 – April 18, 1923 (no tombstone; death certificate stated she was born in Harford Co., the daughter of Joshua Hooks and Mattie Stansbury, both born in Maryland) [Union U. M. Church Cemetery]

Hooks, Catherine R. 1922-2003 (inscribed "In Memory Of Loving Mother") [St. James United Cemetery]

Hooks, Easter March 7, 1929 – May 28, 1995 (on same tombstone with William D. Hooks) [Union U. M. Church Cemetery]

Hooks, Hattie stillborn female on January 9, 1925 (no tombstone; death certificate stated she was the daughter of William D. Hooks and Leona Priscilla Monks) [Union U. M. Church Cemetery]

Hooks, James J. October 3, 1860 – January 3, 1917 (no tombstone; death certificate stated he was the married son of Isaac Hooks, both born in Calvert Co., but his mother was not known to informant Mattie Hooks, of Perryman) [Union U. M. Church Cemetery]

Hooks, Joshua stillborn male on October 13, 1923 (no tombstone; death certificate stated he was the son of William Hooks and Leona Pitt) [Union U. M. Church Cemetery]

Hooks, Samuel F. May 17, 1898 – February 16, 1931 (no tombstone; death certificate stated he was single and the son of James J. Hooks and Martha Stansbury; informant was Mrs. W. D. Hooks) [Union U. M. Church Cemetery]

Hooks, William D. June 23, 1919 – April 5, 2007 (on same tombstone with Easter Hooks) [Union U. M. Church Cemetery]

Hooks, William D. October 20, 1892 – March 3, 1935 (no tombstone; death certificate stated he was the son of Joshua J. Hooks, born in Baltimore, and Martha Stansbury, born in Perryman, and he had been separated from his wife Henrietta for 22 years) [Union U. M. Church Cemetery]

Hooper, John Wesley died April 17, 1909, age 58 (tombstone; death certificate stated he was the son of Steven Hooper and Annie Hall, birth places unknown; he was a farmer at Carsins Run who was injured when a tree fell on him and he died of pneumonia; informant was his wife Eliza) [Mt. Calvary U. A. M. E. Church Cemetery]

Hooper, Sarah died August 26, 1913, age 51 (no tombstone; death certificate stated she was the daughter of Elijah Howard and Mary Dorsey, all born in Harford Co.; she was married, worked as a servant and died in Bel Air; informant was Annie Daugherty, of Bel Air) [Asbury Cemetery]

Hopkins Clara A. March 4, 1870 – February 11, 1921 (no tombstone; death certificate stated she was the daughter of Wesley Washington and Mary Hill, all born in Maryland; she was married and lived and died in Castleton; informant was John W. Hopkins, of Street, MD) [Berkley Memorial Cemetery]

Hopkins Laura G. August 18, 1856 – October 14, 1941 (no tombstone; death certificate stated she was born near Bel Air, the daughter of "Ruth Amenenda G" and ---- [(father unknown), born in Maryland; she married George E. Hopkins and died a widow in Bel Air; informant was Ruth E. Presberry, of Bel Air) [Berkley

Memorial Cemetery]

Hopkins, Anne Moore May 30, 1881 or 1891 – January 4, 1945 (tombstone is inscribed Anne Moore Hopkins, born May 30, 1881, but death certificate in 1945 stated Annie (Moore) Hopkins was born May 30, 1891 and married David Hopkins, now age 65, who stated Annie was born in Maryland and died January 4, 1945, but he did not know her parents' names nor their places of birth; her death notice in the *Havre de Grace Republican* on January 6, 1945 stated Mrs. Annie M. Hopkins died at her home at 113 Strawberry Alley with services held at St. Matthew's Church and interment at "Gravelly Hill," but did not report her age) [Gravel Hill Cemetery]

Hopkins, Annie May 8, 1888 – October 20, 1913 (no tombstone; death certificate stated she was the daughter of William Bond and Mary Barrett, all born in Maryland; she was married and employed doing house work; died at Creswell; informant was Mary Thomas of Belcamp) [Asbury Cemetery]

Hopkins, Delores C., "Our Daughter" November 28, 1950 – April 17, 1968 (inscribed "An Angel Visited The Earth One Morning & Took A Flower Away") [Berkley Memorial Cemetery]

Hopkins, Edith November 29, 1890 – October 4, 1911 (no tombstone; death certificate stated she was the daughter of John Hopkins and Cleo Washington, all born in Maryland; she was single and died at home in Castleton; informant was John Hopkins, of Darlington) [Berkley Memorial Cemetery]

Hopkins, Frances E. March 7, 1899 – August 6, 1924 (death certificate; no tombstone; neé Frances Elizabeth "Lizzie" Foreman, dau. of Albert Hopkins and Frances Andrew) [Gravel Hill Cemetery]

Hopkins, Garnette E. October 18, 1919 – April 19, 1988 (on same tombstone with James E. Hopkins and also inscribed with their marriage date of December 22, 1945) [Berkley Memorial Cemetery]

Hopkins, George Edward March – (blank), 1853 – May 2, 1940 (no tombstone; death certificate stated he was born at Cedars, Harford Co., son of ---- (blank) Hopkins and Catherine Rumsey, both born in Maryland; he married Laura Gough (age 83 in 1940), worked as a laborer and died in Bel Air where they had lived for 10 years; informant was Laura G. Hopkins, of Bel Air) [Berkley Memorial Cemetery]

Hopkins, George W. April 2, 1861 – April 1, 1915 (no tombstone; death certificate stated he was the married son of Sidney Hopkins and Liza Rice, and he died in Havre de Grace) [St. James United Cemetery]

Hopkins, James E. December 23, 1917 – October 24, 1974 (on same tombstone with Garnette E. Hopkins, but without his death date; also inscribed with their marriage date of December 22, 1945; James Dorsey Card File, African American Obituaries, maintained at the Historical Society of Harford County, has a card with obituary from *The Aegis* on November 2, 1994 stating James Eldridge Hopkins was born in Boston, VA, the son of the late Eldridge Hopkins and Emma Perry; he served in the Army from 1941 to 1945, lived in Perryville and worked at the Perry Point VAMC until retiring in 1981; he died a widower at the Perry Point VAMC and was married to Garnette Watkins who predeceased him; he was survived by a son, three brothers, two sisters and one granddaughter) [Berkley Memorial Cemetery]

Hopkins, John B. C. January 19, 1866 – March 1, 1922 (no tombstone; death certificate stated he was the son of John Hopkins, both born in Maryland, but informant Gilbert Hopkins, of Castleton, did not know his mother's name; he worked as a laborer and died a widower in Castleton) [Berkley Memorial Cemetery]

Hopkins, John W. February 2, 1889 – June 4, 1922 (no tombstone; death certificate stated he was the son of John B. Hopkins and Clara Washington, all born in Maryland; he was married, worked as a farmer and died at home at Poole; informant was Ella Aikens, of Berkley) [Berkley Memorial Cemetery]

Hopkins, Lillian May March 21, 1916 – July 14, 1921 (no tombstone; death certificate stated she was the daughter of Austin Nortin and Rachel Hopkins, all born in Maryland; she died at home at Poole; informant was Rachel Webster, of Stree, MD) [Berkley Memorial Cemetery]

Hopkins, Mary June 27, 1874 – May 2, 1925 (no dates on tombstone; death certificate stated Mary A. Hopkins was born in Delaware, the daughter of Solomon and Emma Thompson, birth places unknown to informant George Hopkins, of Darlington; she was married at the time of her death) [Berkley Memorial Cemetery]

Hopper, William died September 20, 1924, age about 43 (no tombstone; death certificate stated he was married and died in Havre de Grace, parents unknown to informant Joseph Durbin) [St. James United Cemetery]

Horsey, Margaret died May 28, 1920, age 7(?) years [Hendon Hill Cemetery]

Houck, Marie J., "Mother" 1878-1967 [West Liberty Church Cemetery]

Howard, ---- stillborn male died October 15, 1923 (no tombstone; death certificate stated he was the son of John R. Howard and Flora May Williams, of Bel Air. And they all were born in Maryland; informant was her father) [Hendon Hill Cemetery]

Howard, Amanda died December 9, 1946 (on same tombstone with James Howard) [John Wesley U. M. E. Church Cemetery in Abingdon]

Howard, Ann died November 23, 1902 in her 84th year (on the same obelisk with Nelson Howard; death certificate stated she was the daughter of Hector and Matilda Bosley and the wife of Nelson Howard; she died at Rutledge on November 23, 1902, age 80, per Dr. Smith) [West Liberty Church Cemetery]

Howard, Annie died August 4, 1921, age 61 (no tombstone; death certificate stated she was a widow and had been employed as a cook in Bel Air; died at home in Bel Air; her parents were not known, but they were born in Maryland; informant was Ora Howard, of Bel Air) [Hendon Hill Cemetery]

Howard, Carrie died June 11, 1908 (on same tombstone with Lula Howard that states she died on June 8, 1918; however, death certificate stated Carrie Virgie Ann Howard was born in Abingdon, the daughter of James B. Howard, born at Furnace, and Amanda Lee, born in Abingdon; she worked as a ladies maid and died on June 11, 1908 at the age of 15 years, 9 months and 20 days; informant was Mrs. J. Howard, her mother) [John Wesley U. M. E. Church Cemetery in Abingdon]

Howard, Elizabeth D. 1917-1969 (copied in 1987, but not found in 2018) [Berkley Memorial Cemetery]

Howard, George Archer June 11, 1899 – February 5, 1947, Maryland, Pvt., Co. B, 301 Stevedore Regt., QMC, World War I (inscribed born in 1899 and his military record also stated born in 1899, but death certificate stated he was born in 1900 in Bel Air; he married Lillian ---- and was unemployed at the time of his death in Bel Air; his parents were Grant Howard and Annie Rice, both born in Maryland; informant was Mrs. Lillian Howard, of 411 W. 128th St., Apt, 30, New York 27, NY) [Hendon Hill Cemetery]

Howard, Grant died January 4, 1918, age unknown (no tombstone; death certificate stated he was a widower and worked as a laborer in Bel Air; his parents were Elijah Dorsey and Eliza Howard and all were born in Harford Co., informant was Hannah Toney, of Bel Air) [Hendon Hill Cemetery]

Howard, James "Father" 1875-1953 (on same tombstone with Julia Howard) [Mt. Calvary U. A. M. E. Church Cemetery]

Howard, James died August 29, 1927, age about 70 (no tombstone; death certificate stated he was the son of Lijah *(sic)* Howard and Hannah Howard, all born in Maryland; he was married, worked as a farm laborer, and died near Bel Air; informant was Ora Howard, of Bel Air) [Clark's U. M. Church Cemetery]

Howard, James died June 8, 1914, age not given (on same tombstone with Amanda Howard; death certificate stated James Abram Howard was born September 15, 1863, the son of Joseph Howard and Cecellia Andoris(?), and all were born in Maryland; he married Amanda ----, worked as a railroad laborer, lived in Abingdon and died on June 8, 1914 in Abingdon) [John Wesley U. M. E. Church Cemetery in Abingdon]

Howard, James W. died October 11, 1900, age 6 months (no tombstone; death certificate stated he was the son of James Foreman and Carrie Howard; he died in Berkley, but place of burial was not given [probably Berkley Memorial Cemetery]

Howard, John R. August 27, 1893 – February 16, 1937, Maryland, Corporal, Battery E, 351 Field Artillery, World War I (tombstone; death certificate stated he was born in Bel Air where he was a general store keeper and his wife was Flora Howard; he was the son of Grant Howard and Annie Rice, both born near Bel Air; informant was Hannah Toney) [Hendon Hill Cemetery]

Howard, Julia "Mother" 1889-1952 (on same tombstone with James Howard) [Mt. Calvary U. A. M. E. Church Cemetery]

Howard, Lula died February 24, 1923 (on same tombstone with Carrie Howard; death certificate stated Lula D.

Howard was born on February 6, 1904, the daughter of James A. Howard and Carrie Amanda Lee, all born in Maryland; she died an unmarried school girl in Sewell; informant was her mother Carrie A. Howard, of Sewell) [John Wesley U. M. E. Church Cemetery in Abingdon]

Howard, Millard Theodore died June 27, 1971, age 70 (no tombstone; obituary in *The Aegis* stated he was born in Abingdon, the son of James Howard and Amanda Lee, and married Emma Giles, worked for the B&O Railroad for many years and was the last survivor of a large well-known family in Abingdon; he lived on B&O Road, died at Harford Memorial Hospital and was survived by his wife, a son, seven grandchildren and three great-grandchildren) [John Wesley U. M. E. Church Cemetery in Abingdon]

Howard, Nelson November 17, 1828 – June 2, 1894 (on same obelisk with wife Ann Nelson) [West Liberty Church Cemetery]

Howard, Samuel died November 13, 1897, age about 35 (no tombstone; reported in *The Aegis* on November 19, 1897 that he was shot to death by Charles Anderson, Jr.) [Hendon Hill Cemetery]

Howard, Tommie January 2, 1907 – April 22, 1961 [Berkley Memorial Cemetery]

Howell, Susie F. Jones, "Beloved Daughter and Mother" December 20, 1957 – January 31, 2010 [Berkley Memorial Cemetery]

Hubbard, Ida May Watters May 20, 1930 – November 21, 1995 [John Wesley U. M. E. Church Cemetery in Abingdon]

Hudgins, Henry A. May 19, 1905 – January 27, 1965 (tombstone; his name also appears on an obelisk with Frank Harvey, Louisa J. Harvey, Walter F. Harvey, William L. Harvey, Hermeon H. Hudgins, Walter F. Harvey II and Robert L. Harvey) [St. James United Cemetery]

Hudgins, Hermeon H. 1906-   (on the same obelisk with Frank Harvey, Louisa J. Harvey, Walter F. Harvey, Henry A. Hudgins, William L. Harvey, Walter F. Harvey II and Robert L. Harvey) [St. James United Cemetery]

Hudson, Reed November 18, 1913 – February 10, 1962, South Carolina, PFC, Co G, 25 INF, World War II [John Wesley U. M. E. Church Cemetery in Abingdon]

Huff, Eugene, "Caring Father" June 20, 1915 – December 4, 2005 [Mt. Calvary U. A. M. E. Church Cemetery]

Huff, Helen L. neé Dickerson, "Loving Mother" August 30, 1925 – March 10, 1977 [Mt. Calvary U. A. M. E. Church Cemetery]

Hughes, Barbara Tryphena Cromwell May 10, 1939 – August 28, 2001 (inscribed "In Loving Memory Of" and "Your Love Lives In Us Forever" with her photo) [St. James United Cemetery]

Hughes, Sarah 1780-1883 (no tombstone; death notice in the *Havre de Grace Republican* on August 10, 1883 stated "Sarah Hughes, colored, a native of Abingdon, this county, died in Wilmington, Del., on Saturday last, at the good old age of 103 years. Her remains were brought to this city for interment;" place of burial was not reported) [probably St. James United Cemetery]

Humber, Charles February 14, 1914 – June 27, 1991 (on same tombstone with Lillie L. Humber) [Community Baptist Church Cemetery]

Humber, Lillie L. August 15, 1915 -   (on same tombstone with Charles Humber) [Community Baptist Church Cemetery]

Hundley, Ada P. 1897 – July 6, 1978 (no tombstone; obituary in *The Aegis* on July 13, 1978 stated she the daughter of Amos and Hanna Presbury and the wife of the late John Hundley, of Havre de Grace; she died at Laurelwood Nursing Center in Elkton and was survived by a step-daughter, a brother, six grandchildren and nine great-grandchildren) [Berkley Memorial Cemetery]

Hunt, Athaniel 1947-1978 (copied in 1987, but not found in 2018) [St. James United Cemetery]

Hunt, Katherine T. 1930-1967 [Community Baptist Church Cemetery]

Hunt, Marcus William December 16, 1986 – August 7, 2005 (inscribed "In Loving Memory" and "Blessed are the pure in heart for they shall see God. Matthew 5:8") [Clark's U. M. Church Cemetery]

Hurley, Baby Girl August 21, 1946 – August 27, 1946 (no tombstone; death certificate stated she was the premature daughter of Lawrence Hurley and Bernadine Williams, of Havre de Grace, and she died in Harford Memorial Hospital) [St. James United Cemetery]

Hurt, Berthenia E. 1905-1992 [Berkley Memorial Cemetery]

Hutton, James A. died January 2, 1924, age about 80 (no tombstone; death certificate stated he was the son of Owen Hutton, both born in North Carolina, but the name of his mother and her place of birth were not known to informant Annie Hutton, of Abingdon; he was married, worked as a laborer and died in Abingdon) [John Wesley U. M. E. Church Cemetery in Abingdon]

Hutton, Sarah died January 27, 1924, age about 80 (no tombstone; death certificate stated she was born in North Carolina, but her parents' names and places of birth were not known to informant C. C. Cronin, of Sewell; she was a widow and died in Abingdon) [John Wesley U. M. E. Church Cemetery in Abingdon]

Ingram, Alberta S., "My Beloved Wife" November 4, 1949 – January 4, 1992 (inscribed "Our father who art in heaven") [Clark's U. M. Church Cemetery]

Ingram, Phillip M. March 4, 1947 – September 3, 1986, U.S. Army, Vietnam [St. James United Cemetery]

Ingram, Rella March 8, 1925 – September 17, 1981 [St. James United Cemetery]

Ingram, Willie Junior March 22, 1948 – March 23, 1948 (no tombstone; death certificate stated he was born in Havre de Grace, the premature son of Willie Miller, of Sumpter, SC, and Ralla Roads, of Greenwood, MS, but his last name is Ingram, not Miller, on the death certificate) [St. James United Cemetery]

Ivin, Loraine O. March 1, 1916 – August 21, 1916 (no tombstone; death certificate stated she was born in Havre de Grace, the daughter of Andrew Ivin, of Newark, DE, and Ossena Allison, of Rowlandsville, MD) [St. James United Cemetery]

Izean, Helena E. died June 6, 1975, age 54 (no tombstone; obituary in *The Aegis* on June 12, 1975 stated she was the daughter of William and Emily Clark, worked as a nurse and lived at 2064 Battle Street in Edgewood; formerly of Fallston, she married Joseph Izean and died at Fallston General Hospital) [Tabernacle Mount Zion U. M. Church Cemetery]

Jackson, ---- born May 13, 1942, lived only 30 minutes (no tombstone; death certificate stated she was born in Bel Air, daughter of George and Mildred Jackson, both born in Harford County; informant was her father George Jackson, of Bel Air) [Fairview A. M. E. Church Cemetery]

Jackson, Albert V. November 26, 1917 – November 28, 2001 (tombstone with his photo) [St. James United Cemetery]

Jackson, Barbara E. 1935-2018 (small metal funeral home marker) [Berkley Memorial Cemetery]

Jackson, Bertha I. July 24, 1925 -   (on same tombstone with Lisa A. Jackson) [Berkley Memorial Cemetery]

Jackson, Bessie Marie March 18, 1908 – March 4, 1911 (no tombstone; death certificate stated she was born in Harford Co., the daughter of Lewis H. Jackson and Margaret Brittian, both were born in Maryland; she died at home at Taylor and informant was her father, of Monkton) [West Liberty Church Cemetery]

Jackson, Burton died January 22, 1931, age about 38 (no tombstone; death certificate stated he was the son of Richard A. Jackson, of Massachusetts, and Sarah Emma Beck, of Maryland; he was divorced and died in Havre de Grace; informant was Naomi Brown) [St. James United Cemetery]

Jackson, Chantel Lorraine August 15, 1987 – August 14, 2002 (inscribed "In Loving Memory" with her image on the tombstone) [Berkley Memorial Cemetery]

Jackson, Charles January – (blank), 1852 – January 9, 1915 (no tombstone; death certificate stated Charles H. Jackson was born in Harford Co., the son of Amos Jackson, birth place unknown, and Martha Whittington, born in Baltimore Co.; he was married, worked as a laborer and died in Bel Air; informant was Martha Turner, of Van

Bibber) [Tabernacle Mount Zion U. M. Church Cemetery]

Jackson, Charles Wilson July 1, 1910 – February 3, 1911 (no tombstone; death certificate stated he was the son of John and Bessie I. Jackson, all born in Harford Co.; he died at Jarrettsville; informant was his father John Jackson, of White Hall) [Fairview A. M. E. Church Cemetery]

Jackson, Charlotte March 3, 1849 – April 9, 1924 (no tombstone; death certificate stated she was the daughter of William Brown, but her mother was not known to informant Lydia Jackson; she died a widow in Havre de Grace) [St. James United Cemetery]

Jackson, Clara P. January 30, 1884 – November 21, 1974 [Clark's U. M. Church Cemetery]

Jackson, Clarence August 25, 1894 – January 8, 1959, Maryland Pvt., Co. D, 811 Pioneer Inf., World War I [Tabernacle Mount Zion U. M. Church Cemetery]

Jackson, Eliza died December 16, 1930, age about 60 (no tombstone; death certificate stated she was a widow, born in Maryland and died in Havre de Grace; her parents' names and places of birth were not known to informant George Dougherty, of Havre de Grace) [Green Spring U. M. Church Cemetery]

Jackson, Ernest September 19, 1900 – September 22, 1947 (no tombstone; death certificate stated he was the son of Joseph Martin and Clara Jackson, of Havre de Grace; he worked a cook, married Pearl V. ---- and died in Harford Memorial Hospital) [St. James United Cemetery]

Jackson, Estella E. August 30, 1907 – August 21, 2000 (tombstone; obituary in *The Aegis* on August 25, 2000 stated Estella Elourie Jackson was the daughter of Crockett and Elizabeth Wolfe; she was a domestic worker, a member of New Hope Baptist Church, and the widow of Clarence Jackson; she died at home in Bel Air, survived by a sister Annie Washington, two nieces Mildred McMillan and Pauline Gentry, and a nephew Nelson Jackson) [Tabernacle Mount Zion U. M. Church Cemetery]

Jackson, Fonda Juanita died March 4, 1998, age 47 (obituary and photo in *The Aegis* on March 25, 1998 stated she was born in Aberdeen, daughter of Pauline M. Jackson and the late Fred D. Jackson, lived in Darlington and died at Harford Memorial Hospital in Havre de Grace, survived by her mother, 2 sisters, 1 brother, 3 aunts, 3 nieces, 6 nephews and several cousins) [Berkley Memorial Cemetery]

Jackson, Frank died June 17, 1930, age 79 (no tombstone; obituary in *The Aegis*, June 20, 1930, stated "for quite a while has been a very unique character around town" and died at home in Bel Air; he was a former slave who had once belonged to Parson Wilson, a Baptist minister who owned the Dr. Robinson farm at Sharon; death certificate stated he died on June 16, 1930, age 75, birth date unknown, but he was born in Harford Co; he was married and worked as a janitor in Bel Air; his parents were Henry Jackson and Adeline James, both born in Maryland; informant was Adeline Taylor, 111 Alice Ann St., Bel Air) [Hendon Hill Cemetery]

Jackson, George July 14, 1869 – February 18, 1939 (no tombstone; death certificate stated he was the son of Andrew Jackson, both born in Harford Co., but his mother's maiden was unknown to informant Miss Carrie Jackson, of 124 Alice Anne St., Bel Air, but her first name was Ida; he worked as a laborer and died a widower at 124 Alice Anne St., Bel Air) [Tabernacle Mount Zion U. M. Church Cemetery]

Jackson, George N. 1918-1971 (on same tombstone with Mildred V. Jackson) [Fairview A. M. E. Church Cemetery]

Jackson, Harry December 26, 1900 – June 19, 1983, Havre de Grace, MD [St. James United Cemetery]

Jackson, Harry (Rev.) 1900-1985 (on same tombstone with Martha Jane Jackson) [Tabernacle Mount Zion U. M. Church Cemetery]

Jackson, Harry G. March 19, 1900 – August 30, 1991 (tombstone; obituary in *The Aegis* on September 4, 1991 stated Harry Grayson Jackson was born in White Hall, son of George E. Jackson and Missauri Cromwell, and married Dora Smith who predeceased him; he was a farmer in Cooptown and died in Fallston General Hospital, survived by two sisters, a brother and nieces and nephews) [Fairview A. M. E. Church Cemetery]

Jackson, Herbert Clifton died June 21, 1944, having lived only 9½ hours (no tombstone; death certificate stated he was born in Bel Air, son of Herbert Jackson, born in Bel Air, and Pearl Forrester, born in Baltimore

Co.; informant was Herbert Jackson) [Hendon Hill Cemetery]

Jackson, Infant (female) January 4, 1924 – January 9, 1924 (no tombstone; death certificate stated she was the daughter of Milton Tucker and Mary Jackson, of Havre de Grace) [St. James United Cemetery]

Jackson, Infant (male) November 11, 1917 – November 15, 1917 (no tombstone; death certificate stated he was the son of Earnest Jackson and Pearl James, of Havre de Grace) [St. James United Cemetery]

Jackson, Isaac January 1, 1838 – August 29, 1926 (no tombstone) [St. James United Cemetery]

Jackson, Isaac B. died August 6, 1925, age about 35 (no tombstone; death certificate stated he was the married son of Isaac Jackson and Charlotte Johnson; informant was Lydia Jackson) [St. James United Cemetery]

Jackson, Isabella April 5, 1835 – April 7, 1931 (no tombstone; death certificate stated she was born in Harford Co., the daughter of William Turner, born in Maryland, but her mother's name was not known to informant David Jackson, of Jarrettsville; she died a widow at home in Jarrettsville [Fairview A. M. E. Church Cemetery]

Jackson, J. Clay August 15, 1884 – October 6, 1963 ("In Memory of") [Clark's U. M. Church Cemetery]

Jackson, James born "about" January 31, 1902, Los Angeles, CA – June 19, 1948, Harford Memorial Hospital (no tombstone; death certificate stated he lived in Havre de Grace, and was a widowed laborer, but his wife and parents were not known to informant Mrs. Helen S. Hawkins, of Havre de Grace, MD) [Skinner Cemetery]

Jackson, John H. 1907-1988 (tombstone; obituary in *The Aegis* stated John Henry Jackson was a farm laborer, lived in Darlington and died on March 8, 1988, age 81, at Citizens Nursing Home in Havre de Grace, survived by a son, one grandson, two brothers and two sisters) [Berkley Memorial Cemetery]

Jackson, John H. February 16, 1913 – August 10, 1968 (tombstone; obituary in *The Aegis* on August 15, 1968 stated John Howard Jackson, husband of Celia A. Gibson Jackson, of Troyer Road, Monkton, died at Greater Baltimore Medical Center, Baltimore, survived by his wife, three sons, one brother and three sisters) [West Liberty Church Cemetery]

Jackson, Laura died March 14, 1981, age 60 (no tombstone; obituary in *The Aegis* on March 19, 1982 stated Laura I. Jackson was born in Havre de Grace, the daughter of the late George and Eleanor Mitchell, and married Howard Jackson; she died at Harford Memorial Hospital and was survived by her husband, 13 children, 3 brothers, and 1 sister) [St. James United Cemetery]

Jackson, Laura F. died January 15, 1941, age about 85 (no tombstone; death certificate stated she was born on August 10, year unknown, in Bel Air, married James Jackson, was widowed and died at home at 111 Alice Ann St.; her parents were John and Caroline Wilson, both of Canada; informant was George Wilson, of Bel Air) [Hendon Hill Cemetery]

Jackson, Leonard 1880 – July 14, 1945 (no tombstone; death certificate stated he was born in North Carolina, parents not known, and his usual residence was in Chester, Delaware Co., PA; he died in Harford Memorial Hospital in Havre de Grace) [St. James United Cemetery]

Jackson, Lisa A. July 16, 1960 -   (on same tombstone with Bertha I. Jackson) [Berkley Memorial Cemetery]

Jackson, Maggie July 15, 1884 – March 16, 1914 (no tombstone; death certificate stated she was born in Bel Air, the daughter of John Hall and Jane Stewart, both born in Harford Co.; she was married and died in Havre de Grace; informant was Richard Jackson, of Havre de Grace) [Asbury Cemetery]

Jackson, Martha Jane 1901-   (on same tombstone with Rev. Harry Jackson) [Tabernacle Mount Zion U. M. Church Cemetery]

Jackson, Martha V. 1912-2007 (small metal funeral home marker; obituary and photo in *The Aegis* on April 25, 2007 stated "Tiny" was born in Bel Air on February 13, 1912, the daughter of Hallie and Laure Jackson, and never married nor had children, but shared many years with her devoted friend James "Joe Ghost" Maxfield who died in October 1983; she lived in Havre de Grace and died at Harford Memorial Hospital, survived by three cousins, and a special friend Walter Hunter, of York, PA) [Asbury Cemetery]

Jackson, Mary 1907-1954 (copied in 1987, but not found in 2018) [St. James United Cemetery]

Jackson, Mary Elizabeth June 17, 1875 – January 28, 1943 (no tombstone; death certificate stated she was born in Harford Co., the daughter of Samuel Dorsey, born in Baltimore, but her mother's name was not known to informant Mrs. Mable Jackson, of Bel Air; she married Alford Jackson and died in Bel Air where she had lived all her life; she was buried in "Mountain Cemetery near Bel Air," but it was actually located on Singer Road near Mountain and ther McComas Institute) [Mt. Zion U. M. Church Cemetery]

Jackson, Maurice L. 1935-2011, U.S. Army [Berkley Memorial Cemetery]

Jackson, Melinda April 14, 1916 – May 23, 1917 (no tombstone; death certificate she was the daughter of Isaac Garrison and Martha Jackson, of Havre de Grace) [St. James United Cemetery]

Jackson, Mildred V. April 26, 1912 – July 18, 2003 (on same tombstone with George N. Jackson) [Fairview A. M. E. Church Cemetery]

Jackson, Nellie R. October 2, 1848 – January 16, 1949 (no tombstone; death certificate stated she was born in Maryland, the daughter of William H. Hollingsworth and Eliza Lisby; she lived on Bush Chapel Road near Aberdeen and died a widow; informant was Thomas H. Hollingsworth) [Asbury Cemetery]

Jackson, Olivia M. 1908-   (on same tombstone with Rev. R. L. Jackson) [Mt. Calvary U. A. M. E. Church Cemetery]

Jackson, Pauline Elaine December 17, 1957 – February 25, 2015 (inscribed "Forever In Our Hearts") [St. James United Cemetery]

Jackson, Phillip A. died January 24, 1996, age 56 (no tombstone; James Dorsey Card File, African American Obituaries, maintained at the Historical Society of Harford County, has a card for him with an obituary from *The Aegis* on February 7, 1996 stating he was born in Baltimore, the son of Herbert Arlington Jackson and Pearl Seritta Foster, and was the husband of Evelyn Alice Dorsey; he was an appliance salesman for Luskin's in Towson and operated Phil's Produce, corner of Route 7 and Joppa Farm Road, in Joppa; he lived in Bradshaw and died at Fallston General Hospital, survived by his wife of 33 years, a son, a daughter, two brothers, four sisters, and one grandchild) [Asbury Cemetery]

Jackson, R. L. (Rev.) 1911-1975 (on same tombstone with Olivia M. Jackson) [Mt. Calvary U. A. M. E. Church Cemetery]

Jackson, Rebecca, wife of Henry Jackson, died 1896 (1891?), age 59 (copied in 1987, but not found in 2018) [Mt. Zion U. M. Church Cemetery]

Jackson, Richard H., "Loving Husband and Father" February 10, 1927 – October 25, 1997 (tombstone with his photo; James Dorsey Card File, African American Obituaries, maintained at the Historical Society of Harford County, has a card for him with an obituary with his photo from *The Aegis* on November 5, 1997 stating he was born in Havre de Grace, worked as a laundry technician for the Perry Point VAMC for 35 years, married Carrie ----- in 1960 and died at Fallston General Hospital, survived by his wife, son, three daughters, 5 grand-children a great-grandchild and "a host of brothers, sisters, other relatives and friends") [St. James United Cemetery]

Jackson, Roland October 27, 1889 – January 30, 1926 (no tombstone; death certificate stated he was the married son of William Jackson and Sarah Boyer; informant was Mrs. Fannie Jackson, of Havre de Grace) [Union U. M. Church Cemetery]

Jackson, Ruth, "Our Beloved Mother" January 13, 1926 – November 30, 1989 [St. James United Cemetery]

Jackson, Samuel I. June 26, 1935 – January 22, 2015, Pvt., U.S. Army [Berkley Memorial Cemetery]

Jackson, Sarah M., wife of William Jackson, died January 8, 1919, age 68 *(sic)* (tombstone inscribed "Darling We Miss Thee" (copied in 1987, but illegible in 2018); death certificate stated she was born in Pennsylvania on March 1, ---- (blank), daughter of David Barze and Rachel Murry, but places of birth unknown to informant Louisa Jackson, of Street, MD; she was aged 70 years, 10 months, 8 months) [Clark's U. M. Church Cemetery]

Jackson, Sharmetta 1958-2012 (small metal funeral home marker) [William C. Rice Memorial Cemetery, St. James U. M. Church]

Jackson, Sheila Shackelford, "Beloved Mother and Grandmother" March 15, 1950 – January 22, 2001 [St.

James United Cemetery]

Jackson, Verlene Wing, "Our Little Mother" October 9, 1951 – April 24, 1979 [St. James United Cemetery]

Jackson, Viola L. July 31, 1930 – November 4, 1942 (no tombstone; death certificate stated she was the daughter of Howard Jackson and Viola Stansbury, of Havre de Grace) [St. James United Cemetery]

Jackson, Warren March 26, 1923 – July 21, 1923 (no tombstone; death certificate stated he was the son of Robert Jackson, of Delaware, and Edith Skinner, of Havre de Grace) [St. James United Cemetery]

Jackson, William 1855-1933 (tombstone inscription but death certificate stated he died on December 16, 1932, age about 80, date of birth unknown to the informant Ben Johnson, of Street P. O., who also stated he was born in Virginia, but he did not know his parents' names or places of birth; he was a widower and had worked as a farmer near Street P. O.) [Clark's U. M. Church Cemetery]

Jackson, William, husband of Nellie Jackson, died January 27, 1923, age 83, "At Rest" (tombstone; death certificate stated he was born April 4, 1840 in Virginia and died in Churchville, age 82 years, 9 months; he was the son of Henry Jackson and worked as a carpenter, but his mother's name was not known to informant, his wife, Nellie Jackson, of Churchville; his death notice in *The Aegis* on February 2, 1923 stated he was a highly esteemed man of the Churchville neighborhood and for 41 years acted as sexton of Trinity Church, serving with fidelity and skill; the vestrymen of that church attended his funeral and acted as pallbearers on Tuesday (January 30, 1923) at Asbury Church as a mark of appreciation of his service) [Asbury Cemetery]

Jacobs, Robert March 4, 1891 – February 18, 1934 (no tombstone; death certificate stated he was born in Virginia, parents unknown, and he died in Havre de Grace Hospital) [St. James United Cemetery]

James, Abram died November 2, 1909, age 75 (no tombstone; death certificate stated he was the son of James James and Alie Jackson; he was born in Harford Co., was single, worked as a laborer and died in Berkley; place of burial not given [probably Berkley Memorial Cemetery]

James, Annie died April 8, 1937, age about 53 (no tombstone; death certificate stated she was the unmarried daughter of Charlie James and Mary Ellen Brooks, of Havre de Grace) [St. James United Cemetery]

James, Anthony Perry "Rocky" July 5, 1961 – December 4, 2014 [Berkley Memorial Cemetery]

James, Beatrice M. November 6, 1919 – December 20, 1987 (on same tombstone with James A. James) [Berkley Memorial Cemetery]

James, Bernard L. Sr. May 17, 1928 -   (on same tombstone with Caroline James) [Berkley Memorial Cemetery]

James, Caroline "Lena" May 31, 1931 – July 25, 1991 (tombstone; obituary and photo in *The Aegis* on July 31, 1991 stated Caroline W. James was a native and lifelong resident of Perryville and daughter of the late Collins S. Williams, Sr. and Frances Dykes; she married Bernard L. James, Sr. and worked as a dietetics supervisor at the Citizens Nursing Home in Havre de Grace; she died at Harford Memorial Hospital and was survived by her husband, 4 sons, 2 daughters, 4 sisters and 5 grandchildren) [Berkley Memorial Cemetery]

James, Cheryl B. 1963-1988 ("Gone But Not Forgotten" handwritten on a flat cement slab) [St. James United Cemetery]

James, Eldon J. May 15, 1947 – March 14, 1999, U.S. Air Force, Vietnam [St. James United Cemetery]

James, Ella May 29, 1873 – March 9, 1926 (no tombstone; death certificate she was the married daughter of Henry Christy and Estelle Tinson; informant was Wilmer James) [St. James United Cemetery]

James, Ellen died January 6, 1903, age 50 (inscribed "We engrave thy name on marble, Thy memory in our heart;" death certificate stated she was the daughter of George Hewitt, married George James and died in Bel Air on January – (blank), 1903, age 49) [Tabernacle Mount Zion U. M. Church Cemetery]

James, Elmira January 14, 1877 – November 10, 1912 (no tombstone; death certificate stated she was the daughter of James W. Parker and Rebecca Taylor, all were born in Maryland; she was married and died at home in Darlington; informant was James H. James, of Darlington) [Berkley Memorial Cemetery]

James, Emma Elizabeth March 25, 1906 – November 17, 1943 (no tombstone; death certificate stated she was the daughter of William Dutton and Osciana Dutton, and the widow of Demas James; she live at 419 Lodge Alley in Havre de Grace and was buried in "Swan Creek Cemetery") [Union U. M. Church Cemetery]

James, Floyd C. August 6, 1946 – May 12, 2000, U.S. Marine Corps [Berkley Memorial Cemetery]

James, Frances 1834 – December 19, 1913 (no tombstone; death certificate stated she was the daughter of Stewart Cox, both born in Harford Co., but informant John Gordon, of Darlington, did not know her mother's name; she was a widow who died in Darlington) [Berkley Memorial Cemetery]

James, Geneva C. April 17, 1909 – November 10, 1950 (no tombstone; death certificate stated she was born in Havre de Grace, the daughter of Norris Meade and Annie Brown; she lived and died at 617 Freedom Street in Havre de Grace; informant was James James at that same address) [Berkley Memorial Cemetery]

James, George T. born about 1863 – January 31, 1934 (no tombstone; death certificate stated he was the widowed son of Alfred Jackson, both born in Bel Air, mother and wife unknown; he died in Havre d Grace; informant was Wilmer James, of Havre de Grace) [St. James United Cemetery]

James, George Willis May 30, 1878 – July 29, 1947 (no tombstone; death certificate stated he was the son of Samuel James and Martha M. Walton, all born in Harford Co.; married Ella Ruff, worked as a farmer and died a widower at 120 Aliceanne St. in Bel Air where he lived for 40 years; informant was Mrs. Bertha J. Westcott, 120 Aliceanne St.; he was buried in "Mountain Cemetery, Wilna, Harford Co.") [Mt. Zion U. M. Church Cemetery]

James, Georgie E. December 17, 1901 – November 21, 1918 (no tombstone; death certificate stated she was the daughter of William James and Aleathia Rice, all born in Harford Co.; she was single and died at home in Wilna; informant was Aleathia James, of Wilna) [Chestnut Grove A. M. E. Church Cemetery, formerly LaGrange Cemetery at Rocks]

James, India Anna Haines June 4, 1870 – June 5, 1967 [Berkley Memorial Cemetery]

James, Infant stillborn female on January 8, 1913 (no tombstone; death certificate stated she was the daughter of Wilmer James and Ella Christy, of Havre de Grace) [St. James United Cemetery]

James, Infant stillborn male on May 23, 1929 (no tombstone; death certificate stated he was the son of James James and Geneva Meads, of Havre de Grace) [St. James United Cemetery]

James, Irvin L. 1971-2015 (small metal funeral home marker) [St. James United Cemetery]

James, James A. April 3, 1905 -   (on same tombstone with Beatrice M. James) [Berkley Memorial Cemetery]

James, James H. 1874-1958 (on same tombstone with Myrtle L. James) [Berkley Memorial Cemetery]

James, James Henry August 6, 1911 – October 9, 1911 (no tombstone; death certificate stated he was the son of Robert James and Stella Christie, of Havre de Grace) [St. James United Cemetery]

James, Mae G. 1923-   (on same tombstone with Medfield C. James) [Union U. M. Church Cemetery]

James, Marguerett December 15, 1921 – May 25, 1922 (no tombstone; death certificate stated she was the daughter of Henry James and Diana Bond, all born in Maryland; she died at home in Berkley; informant was Henry James, of Havre de Grace) [Berkley Memorial Cemetery]

James, Medfield C. 1914-1989 (on same tombstone with Mae G. James; James Dorsey Card File, African American Obituaries, maintained at the Historical Society of Harford County, has a card for Medfield Curtis "Sammy" James, husband of Mae Christy, of Perryman, with death noted in *The Record* on November 29, 1989) [Union U. M. Church Cemetery]

James, Mary Palmer May 20, 1878 – November 25, 1955 (no tombstone; Pennington Funeral Home records state she was born in Frederick, MD, daughter of Charles Palmer and Mary Doyle, and died a widow in Havre de Grace where she lived for 28 years; informant was James R. Jackson, of Baltimore [St. James United Cemetery]

James, Myrtle L. 1893-   (on same tombstone with James H. James) [Berkley Memorial Cemetery]

James, Rachel E. February 3, 1861 – December 3, 1932(no tombstone; death certificate stated she was born in

Churchville, the daughter of Joseph Hall and Rachel A. Garrett, both born in Harford Co.; she was the widow of James James when she died in Berkley where they had lived for 50 years; informant was Annie Webster, of Darlington) [Berkley Memorial Cemetery]

James, Robert Davis died January 24, 1917, age about 26 (no tombstone; death certificate stated he was the unmarried son of John James and Mary Davis, of Havre de Grace) [St. James United Cemetery]

James, Sarah E., "Wife" 1937-1978 [Berkley Memorial Cemetery]

James, Sarah F. October 5, 1941 – October 14, 2003 [Berkley Memorial Cemetery]

James, William E. 1858-1930 [Berkley Memorial Cemetery]

James, Wilmer December 20, 1873 – December 5, 1940 (no tombstone; death certificate stated he was the son of Charles James, of Churchville, and Mary Brookes, of Brooklyn, NY; he married Mary Parker and died in Havre de Grace) [St. James United Cemetery]

James, Zenelia D. August 30, 1954 – May 4, 1983, A1, U.S. Air Force [St. James United Cemetery]

Jamison, Albert June 12, 1849 – June 2, 1942 (no tombstone; death certificate stated Albert Jameson *(sic)* was the son of John Brooks and Sarah J. Jameson, and all born in Maryland; he was single, worked as a laborer and died at home in Darlington; informant was George W. Jameson, of Darlington) [Berkley Memorial Cemetery]

Jamison, Annie died March 16, 1948, age not given (no tombstone; Kurtz Funeral Home Record Book 1944-1949, p. 205, stated she was born in Harford Co. and died at the Havre de Grace Hospital, but gave no other information; her funeral bill was paid by the Welfare Board; death certificate stated she was lived at Rocks and was the daughter of ---- Nolan, but her mother was not known to informant Mrs. Charles Walton, of Rocks) [William C. Rice Memorial Cemetery, St. James U. M. Church]

Jamison, Carrie Berley August 8, 1873 – April 18, 1943 (no tombstone; Kurtz Funeral Home Record Book 1937-1944, p. 270, stated she was born in Baltimore, the daughter of William Berley, but the name of her mother was not given; she married James H. Jamison and died a widow at her home at Rocks; death certificate added that she worked a house servant and informant was Frank Thomas, of Rocks) [William C. Rice Memorial Cemetery, St. James U. M. Church]

Jamison, Celeste A. 1922-2000 (on same tombstone with George A. Jamison) [Fairview A. M. E. Church Cemetery]

Jamison, Charles Allen "Chucky" died August 25, 2004, age 45 (no tombstone; obituary and military photo in *The Aegis* on September 1, 2004, stated he was born in Chester, PA, the son of Celeste Amelia Bishop Jamison and the late George Arthur Jamison; he worked many years at Lock Joint in Aberdeen, detailed cars at Bel Air Auto Auction, and worked at Widener University in Pennsylvania; he joined the Army and was medically discharged after a brief time in the service; he lived in Havre de Grace, died at Joseph Richey Hospice in Baltimore and was survived by a brother, 4 sisters, and a number of aunts, uncles, nieces and nephews) [Gravel Hill Cemetery]

Jamison, Charles H. 1891-1963 (on same tombstone with Hallie T. Jamison) [Fairview A. M. E. Church Cemetery]

Jamison, Frances January 30, 1851 – January 18, 1941 (no tombstone; death certificate stated she was the daughter of George Presberry and Sarah Prigg, all born in Harford Co.; she married Stephenson Jamison and died a widow in Darlington; informant was George W. Jamison, of Darlington) [Berkley Memorial Cemetery]

Jamison, Frances P. 1882-1901 (tombstone; death certificate stated she died at Darlington on June 24, 1901, age 19 years and 4 months) [Berkley Memorial Cemetery]

Jamison, George A. 1919-1971 (on same tombstone with Celeste A. Jamison) [Fairview A. M. E. Church Cemetery]

Jamison, George W. July 6, 1875 – April 9, 1941 (no tombstone; death certificate stated he was born in Darlington, the son of Steven Jamison and Frances Presberry, both born in Harford Co.; he was single, worked as a farm laborer and died from burns sustained in field fire in rural Darlington; informant was Rebecca Shorter, of

Darlington) [Berkley Memorial Cemetery]

Jamison, Hallie T. 1900-   (on same tombstone with Charles H. Jamison) [Fairview A. M. E. Church Cemetery]

Jamison, James H. – see James H. Jimerson [William C. Rice Memorial Cemetery, St. James U. M. Church]

Jamison, John W. 1920-   (on same tombstone with Vorheese D. B. Jamison) [Fairview A. M. E. Church Cemetery]

Jamison, John W. July 4, 1867 – November 25, 1945 (no tombstone; Kurtz Funeral Home Record Book 1944-1949, p. 85, stated he was born at Federal Hill, the son of Kate Jamison, born in Harford Co., but his father was not known to informant Charles Jamison, of Forest Hill; he married ---- (blank), worked as a road laborer and died at Crownsville Sanitarium) [William C. Rice Memorial Cemetery, St. James U. M. Church]

Jamison, Norma Mae Alexander April 30, 1921 – February 1, 1948 (tombstone; Kurtz Funeral Home Record Book 1944-1949, p. 195, stated Norma Jamison was born in Baltimore, daughter of Fred Alexander, born in Cecil Co., and Alice Simson, born in Baltimore; she married James Jamison and lived on Conowingo Road in Mt. Zoar, Cecil Co.; she died in Elkton Hospital and was buried in Fairview Cemetery; informant was Mrs. Charles Jamison, of Forest Hill) [Fairview A. M. E. Church Cemetery]

Jamison, Richard April 2, 1851 – December 29, 1914 (no tombstone; death certificate stated he was the son of Richard Jamison and Elizabeth Thomas, all born in Maryland; he was married, worked as a farm laborer and died in Edgewood; informant was Florence Jamison, of Edgewood; buried in "Magnolia Col. Cemetery" by Howard K. McComas, Undertaker, in Abingdon) [Foster's Hill Cemetery]

Jamison, Stephen November 29, 1842 – October 30, 1919 (no tombstone; death certificate stated Stephen "Jimmison" was the son of George Cooper and Martha Jimmison, all born in Maryland; married, worked as a farmer and died in Darlington; informant was Frances Jimmison, of Darlington) [Berkley Memorial Cemetery]

Jamison, Vorheese D. B. 1921-1991 (on same tombstone with John W. Jamison; married February 11, 1946) [Fairview A. M. E. Church Cemetery]

Jamison, William J. 1871-1913 (tombstone; death certificate stated William Jameson was born May 13, 1871, the son of Albert Jamison and Sarah Haynes, all born in Maryland; he worked as a laborer and died a widower in Darlington on April 18, 1913; informant was James Parker, of Darlington) [Berkley Memorial Cemetery]

Jarrett, Maria died January 6, 1894, age 80 (no tombstone; her death notice in *The Aegis* on January 26, 1894 stated she died at home near Hickory where she had lived for 50 years; her place of burial was not reported, but it was probably at Tabernacle where Romulus or Romulish Jarrett is buried and Maria Brown married Joshua Jarrett who were his parents) [Tabernacle Mount Zion U. M. Church Cemetery]

Jarrett, Romulus or Romulish 1854 or 1859 – September 1, 1912 (no tombstone; death certificate stated he was age 53, thus born in 1859, but 1880 Harford Co. Census stated he was age 26, thus born in 1854; he was born in Baltimore Co., the son of Joshua Jarrett, born in Baltimore Co., and Maria Brown, born in Maryland; he was married, worked as a laborer and died in Bel Air; informant was Mary Jarrett, of Bel Air) [Tabernacle Mount Zion U. M. Church Cemetery]

Jarvis, Thomas E. Jr. July 19, 1975 - March 29, 2017 (inscribed "In Memory Of" and "Forever In Our Hearts") [Berkley Memorial Cemetery]

Jasper, Mary C. August 14, 1855 – December 17, 1921 (no tombstone; death certificate stated she was married and did laundry work in Bel Air; she was the daughter of F. Bond and Ann Bond and they all were born in Maryland; informant was Richard Jasper, of Bel Air) [Hendon Hill Cemetery]

Jasper, Richard March – (blank), 1944 – July 26, 1924 (no tombstone; death certificate stated he worked as a laborer and died a widower in Bel Air; he was born in Maryland and his parents were born in Virginia, but the names were unknown to informant Mary Bond, of Bel Air RFD) [Hendon Hill Cemetery]

Jaynes, John Jr. July 27, 1904 - February 6, 1985, Sgt., U.S. Army, World War II (obituary states John C. Jaynes, Jr. was born in Lawnside, NJ, owned Johnnie's Arena from 1950 to 1968, and was the first black official – Court Bailiff – for the Circuit Court; he died in Camden, NJ) [Berkley Memorial Cemetery]

Jefferson, Harlee September 6, 1926 – September 22, 1995, U.S. Army, World War II, Korea (tombstone; James Dorsey Card File, African American Obituaries, maintained at the Historical Society of Harford County, has a card for him with an obituary from *The Aegis* on October 11, 1995 stating he was born in Waco, TX, served in the Navy as a steward's mate first class in World War II, then in the Army during the Korean War; he continued to work for the federal until his retirement in 1988; he lived in Aberdeen, volunteered at Perry Point VA Medical Center and received an award in 1995) [Union U. M. Church Cemetery]

Jeffery, Johnnyann 1902-1962 (small white ceramic cross with her name on it, but some letters were missing) [Fairview A. M. E. Church Cemetery]

Jenifer, Alice 1913-1978 (copied in 1987, but not found in 2018) [St. James United Cemetery]

Jenifer, Sylvester R., "Beloved Husband, Father, Grandfather, Great-Grandfather" April 20, 1932 - August 31, 2016, PFC, U.S. Army, Korea [Berkley Memorial Cemetery]

Jenkins, ---- (no tombstone, but Kurtz Funeral Home records stated Lewis Jenkins' wife was buried in a walnut coffin on August 21, 1882 from his house on the road from Cooptown to Gross' Mill, 1½ miles from Cooptown, and "buried at Hendin Hill near Bull's Mills") [Hendon Hill Cemetery]

Jenkins, Bessie DeShields died August 4, 1977, age 77 (no tombstone; obituary in *The Aegis* stated she was born at Mardela Spring, Eastern Shore, and was the daughter of Rev. Jacob Franklin DeShields and Louise DeShields, and widow of Gabriel Preston Jenkins; she lived at 132 Alice Anne Street in Bel Air, and died at Fallston General Hospital, survived by a sister Anna Johnson, of Philadelphia, and a brother Charles DeShields, of Baltimore) [Fairview A. M. E. Church Cemetery]

Jenkins, Bessie Elizabeth February 4, 1883 – August 2, 1934 (no tombstone; death certificate stated she was born in Harford Co., daughter of Gabriel Hill and Phoebe Bond, both born in Maryland, and wife of Charles H. Jenkins; she died at home in Forest Hill; informant was her husband) [Fairview A. M. E. Church Cemetery]

Jenkins, Betty Elizabeth July 4, 1873 – October 31, 1948 (no tombstone; death certificate stated she was the daughter of January Banister and Mary Mullgow, all born in South Carolina, and widow of Thomas Jenkins; she died in Havre de Grace) [St. James United Cemetery]

Jenkins, Cecelia Catherine died August 30, 1977, age 81 (no tombstone, obituary in *The Aegis* stated she was born in Harford Co., the daughter of William Benjamin Chase and Mary Dennison; she lived at 438 Washington St. in Aberdeen and died at Harford Memorial Hospital in Havre de Grace, survived by an aunt, a sister-in-law, three nephews and three nieces) [Union U. M. Church Cemetery]

Jenkins, Charles H. May 17, 1862 – February 14, 1940 (no tombstone; death certificate stated he was the son of Lewis Jenkins and Fannie ---- (unknown), all born in Maryland; he married Bessie ----, worked as a laborer in Forest Hill and died a widower; informant was Thomas B. Jenkins, of Forest Hill) [Fairview A. M. E. Church Cemetery]

Jenkins, Dora 1910-1968 (tombstone; obituary in *The Aegis* stated she was the daughter of the late Mr. and Mrs. Moses Minor; she married James W. Jenkins, lived at 553 Alliance St. in Havre de Grace, died at Harford Memorial Hospital and was survived by her husband, two nephews, one stepdaughter, three brothers and one sister) [Berkley Memorial Cemetery]

Jenkins, Ella December 12, 1891 – January 31, 1938 (no tombstone; death certificate stated she was the daughter of P. H. Bradley and Adriana Bradley, all born in South Carolina and wife of John Jenkins; she died in Havre de Grace) [St. James United Cemetery]

Jenkins, Gertrude Louise Green died on December 5, 1993, age 81 (no tombstone; obituary in *The Aegis* on December 15, 1993 stated she was born in Wilmington, NC, lived in Havre de Grace, was the widow of William Jenkins, and died at Harford Memorial Hospital, survived by a sister, a step-daughter, and "three grandchildren, great-grandchildren, and great-great-grandchildren") [St. James United Cemetery]

Jenkins, Golden Moore March 16, 1937 – March 18, 1937 (no tombstone; death certificate stated he was born in Forest Hill, the son of Briley Jenkins, born in Forest Hill, and Henrietta Turner, born in Harford Co.; he died at home in Forest Hill; informant was his father) [Fairview A. M. E. Church Cemetery]

Jenkins, Henrietta 1904-1985 (on same tombstone with T. Briely Jenkins; copied in 1987, but not found in 2018) [Fairview A. M. E. Church Cemetery]

Jenkins, James W. December 12, 1915 – July 30, 1985, Pvt., U.S. Army, World War II (tombstone; obituary in *The Aegis* on August 3, 1985 stated he was born in Holly Hill, SC, the son of John and Ella Jenkins, and was the husband of Margaret P. Jenkins; he was employed by the Pennsylvania Railroad and the Perry Point VAMC; obituary mistakenly stated he was a veteran of World War I; he served in World War II, lived in Havre de Grace and died at the Veterans Center Hospital in Wilmington, DE, survived by his wife, one brother, two daughters, three sons and six grandchildren, and a number of nieces and nephews) [Berkley Memorial Cemetery]

Jenkins, John W. 1889-1970 (tombstone; obituary in *The Aegis* on September 10, 1970 stated John Wesley Jenkins, Sr., son of the late Thomas and Betty Jenkins, lived at 553 Alliance St. in Havre de Grace and died on September 4, 1970 at Harford Memorial Hospital, survived by two sons, one brother, one sister, four grandchildren and twelve great-grandchildren) [Berkley Memorial Cemetery]

Jenkins, John W. March 1, 1933 – May 11, 1999, U.S. Army, Korea (tombstone inscribed 1935, but obituary and photo in *The Aegis* on May 19, 1999 stated John Wesley Jenkins, Jr. was born in 1933, the youngest and the last remaining child of 18 children born to John and Ella Jenkins, and he died at age 66; "Uncle Johnny" served in the Army from 1953 to 1955 and retired from Aberdeen Proving Ground and Edgewood Arsenal in 1986; he lived and died in Havre de Grace, survived by 2 nieces, a nephew, 14 great-nieces and great-nephews, 29 great-great-nieces and great-great-nephews, and a host of cousins) [St. James United Cemetery]

Jenkins, Lula 1909-1979 [St. James United Cemetery]

Jenkins, Margaret Pearl Carter died January 9, 19-- (no tombstone; The James Dorsey Card File, African American Obituaries, maintained at the Historical Society of Harford County, has a card for her with an obituary from *The Aegis* (date was missing, but it was probably in the 1990s) stating she was born in Walterboro, S.C., the daughter of the late John Carter and Emma Evans; she was the widow of both Monroe Johnson and James Jenkins, and moved to Harford County over 50 years ago; she lived in Havre de Grace and died at Harford Memorial Hospital, survived by a daughter, two step-children, three sisters, four nephews, a niece, five grandchildren, and six great-grandchildren) [St. James United Cemetery]

Jenkins, Margaret Pearl died January 9, 1993, age not given (no tombstone; obituary and photo in *The Aegis* on January 2, 1993 did not indicate where she was buried, but it was probably beside her husband; she was born in Walterboro, SC, the daughter of John Carter and Emma Evans, and moved to Harford County more than 50 years ago; she was an active members and officer in Union United Methodist Church and several service organizations; she was the widow of both Monroe Johnson and James Jenkins, lived in Joppa and died at Fallston General Hospital, survived by three sisters, a daughter, two step-children, four nephews, a niece, five grandchildren and six great-grandchildren) [Berkley Memorial Cemetery]

Jenkins, Mercy P. October 31, 1894 – March 16, 1929 (no tombstone; death certificate stated she was the daughter of John Hall and Mary Simms, all born in Maryland; she was married and lived at Pylesville, but informant Mary Hall did not know her husband's name) [Chestnut Grove A. M. E. Church Cemetery, formerly LaGrange Cemetery at Rocks]

Jenkins, Miranda V. December 11, 1883 – February 5, 1914 (no tombstone; death certificate stated she was the daughter of Joseph Ruff, both were born in Harford Co., and Ellen Hewitt, born in Baltimore Co.; she was married and died in Bel Air; informant was Mary Norton) [Tabernacle Mount Zion U. M. Church Cemetery]

Jenkins, Oliver died September 15, 1981, age 88 (no tombstone; obituary in *The Aegis* stated he was the husband of the late Beulah Snow Jenkins, a veteran of World War I and retired from the Pennsylvania Railroad; he lived in Havre de Grace and died at Perry Point VA Hospital, survived by four daughters, a sister, 38 grandchildren, 40 great-grandchildren, and 3 great-great-grandchildren) [St. James United Cemetery]

Jenkins, Otho Lee March 15, 1928 – May 4, 1928 (no tombstone; death certificate initially stated his name was Otho, but someone lined it out and printed Earther above it; he was born in Maryland, the son of John Bradley and Ella Bradley, both of South Carolina, and died in Havre de Grace) [St. James United Cemetery]

Jenkins, Shirley Mae February 9, 1948 – November 20, 1973 (tombstone; obituary in *The Aegis* stated she was born in Havre de Grace, the daughter of John B. and Nina Laurie, and the wife of Sgt. Robert L. Jenkins; she lived at 40 Aberdeen Ave. in Aberdeen and was employed at the Aberdeen Proving Ground commissary; she died at the Philadelphia Naval Station in Pennsylvania and was survived by her husband, her parents, two sons, a brother, three sisters, four nieces and two nephews) [Berkley Memorial Cemetery]

Jenkins, T. Briely 1896-1981 (on same tombstone with Henrietta Jenkins; copied in 1987, but not found in 2018; obituary in *The Aegis* on May 21, 1981 stated Thomas Briley *(sic)* Jenkins was the husband of the late Henrietta Turner and lived in Forest Hill; he worked as a chauffeur and died at home on May 17, 1981, age 84, survived by two daughters, a step-daughter, a sister, 11 grandchildren, and 12 great-grandchildren) [Fairview A. M. E. Church Cemetery]

Jenkins, Thomas December 15, 1873 – July 4, 1931 (no tombstone; death certificate stated he was the son of Paumpey Jenkins and Peggy Jenkins, all born in South Carolina, and husband of Betty Jenkins; he died at home in Havre de Grace) [St. James United Cemetery]

Jiles, Olie died April 7, 1966, age 72 (no tombstone; obituary in *The Aegis* on April 14, 1966 stated she was the widow of Carroll Jiles and a daughter of John Taylor and Martha Rumsey; she lived at Old Bay Farm in Havre de Grace and died at Spring Grove Hospital; she was survived only by a sister Pearl Milburn, of Philadelphia, PA) [Mt. Calvary U. A. M. E. Church Cemetery]

Jimerson, Bernard January 7, 1927 – November 18, 1967, Pennsylvania, Cpl., 2 QM Tng Bn, World War II [Mt. Zion U. M. Church Cemetery]

Jimerson, Florence August 5, 1856 – October 7, 1944 (no tombstone; death certificate stated she was born in St. Mary's Co., the daughter of William Turner and Jane A. Armstrong, both born in Maryland; she lived in Magnolia and died a widow, but her husband's name was not known to informant Mrs. Eda. J. Briley, of Magnolia; Florence was indicated as buried at "John Westley Cemetery, Magnolia" [Foster's Hill Cemetery]

Jimerson, James Henry September 5, 1863 – December 1, 1925 (no tombstone; death certificate stated he was the son of James Amoss *(sic)* and Catherine Smith *(sic)*, all born in Harford Co.; he was married, worked as a day laborer in farming, died at home at Federal Hill and was buried in "Federal Hill Cemetery;" informant was his wife, Carrie Jimerson, of Rocks; marriage records state James Henry Jamison married Carrie Burley on October 27, 1898) [William C. Rice Memorial Cemetery, St. James U. M. Church]

Jimison, ---- (no tombstone, but Kurtz Funeral Home records stated William Jimison's child was buried in an "im rosewood" coffin on January 21, 1882 from John Emerich's) [West Liberty Church Cemetery]

Jimison, Martin June 9, 1861 – February 9, 1927 (inscribed "Faithful Servant to the Jarrett Family;" death certificate stated Martin Jemison *(sic)* was born in Harford Co., but the names and birth places of his parents were not known to informant Ida Taylor, of Jarrettsville; he was single, worked as a farm laborer and died at Havre de Grace Hospital in Havre de Grace) [William C. Rice Memorial Cemetery, St. James U. M. Church]

Jimison, Tobe (not found in 2018, but J. C. Taylor Marble Co. records stated "Tobe Jimison's head stone was put up July 13th 1927 Federal Hill") [William C. Rice Memorial Cemetery, St. James U. M. Church]

Johns, Japheth February 4, 1910 – June 3, 1976, Cpl., U.S. Army, World War II (tombstone; "Mr. Johns" owned a lot in section 14 some time after 1951; obituary in *The Aegis* on June 10, 1976 stated Japheth (J. C.) Johns was born in Livingston, TX, a son of the late Andrew J. and Jennie Johns, married Margaret East, resided at 430 Law Street in Aberdeen, served in the U.S. Army in World War II, retired from Aberdeen Proving Ground, and died at Harford Memorial Hospital in Havre de Grace, age 66, survived by his wife, 5 sons, 4 daughters, 19 grandchildren and 11 great-grandchildren) [Mt. Calvary U. A. M. E. Church Cemetery]

Johns, Margarette East, "Beloved Wife and Mother" May 24, 1907 – November 5, 1989 ("Mrs. Johns" owned a lot in section 14 some time after 1951; tombstone also inscribed "Jesus Mighty Warrior") [Mt. Calvary U. A. M. E. Church Cemetery]

Johnson, ---- (no tombstone, but Kurtz Funeral Home records stated Jarrett Johnson's son was buried in an "im cherry" coffin on September 12, 1880 from Jarrett Johnson's near Good Will) [West Liberty Church Cemetery]

Johnson, ---- (no tombstone, but Kurtz Funeral Home records stated Joshua Johnson's son was buried in an "im cherry" coffin on November 14, 1880 from Jacob Hildt's tenant house) [West Liberty Church Cemetery]

Johnson, ---- (owner of a lot in section 9 some time after 1951) [Mt. Calvary U. A. M. E. Church Cemetery]

Johnson, ---- premature male birth at 7 months, born and died August 6, 1822, lived only 18 hours (no tombstone; death certificate stated he was born in Harford Co., and died at Ady, the son of Benjamin Johnson and Beulah Lee, both born in Maryland; informant was his father) [Clark's U. M. Church Cemetery]

Johnson, ---- stillborn female on October 12, 1949 (no tombstone; Kurtz Funeral Home Record Book 1944-1949, p. 287, stated born and died at Havre de Grace Hospital; parents were David Miller and Janie Johnson; she was buried that same day) [Chestnut Grove A. M. E. Church Cemetery, formerly LaGrange Cemetery at Rocks]

Johnson, ---- stillborn male on January 10, 1922 (no tombstone; death certificate stated he was the son of Joseph N. Johnson and Mary Barnes, all born in Harford Co.) [Union U. M. Church Cemetery]

Johnson, ----m? M. 1919-1994 (marker partly illegible) [John Wesley U. M. E. Church Cemetery in Abingdon]

Johnson, Alfred William Jr. November 10, 1925 – November 30, 2014 (on same tombstone with Blanche Dorothy Gordon Johnson and inscribed "married December 25, 1947;" funeral notice and photo in *The Aegis* stated he lived in Edgewood and died at his residence) [St. James United Cemetery]

Johnson, Alice B. September 25, 1935 – March 26, 2012 (no tombstone; funeral notice appeared in *The Aegis* on April 4, 2012) [Clark's U. M. Church Cemetery]

Johnson, Alice Frances May 31, 1923 – May 31, 1990 [St. James United Cemetery]

Johnson, Allan P. May 6, 1909 – December 18, 1979, TEC5, U.S. Army, World War II (tombstone; obituary in *The Aegis* stated Allen *(sic)* P. Johnson was born in West Virginia, the son of Gold and Odelia Johnson, and was a retired nurse's assistant at Perry Point VAMC; he lived in Havre de Grace, died at Perry Point VAMC, and was survived by a son Monte Johnson, a stepson Marvin Holland, a brother Guy M. Johnson, and eight sisters) [St. James United Cemetery]

Johnson, Alverta O. January 15, 1921 – October 8, 2009 (on same tombstone with James I. Johnson, but her date of death is not inscribed; obituary and photo in *The Aegis* on October 14, 2009 stated she was born in Baltimore, the daughter of Herman Holmes and Addie Osborn, and was the widow of James Johnson, Sr.; she lived in Edgewood; no heirs were named) [Community Baptist Church Cemetery]

Johnson, Amelia, wife of Shadrach Johnson, died June 25, 1891, age 52 (inscribed "In Memory of") [Asbury Cemetery]

Johnson, Amy D. 1903-1965 [Clark's U. M. Church Cemetery]

Johnson, Ann died May 16, 1885, upwards of 90 years (no tombstone; obituary in *The Aegis* on May 22, 1885 stated that although not born a slave she had always lived with and was employed by David Hanway's family; she was buried at Hendon's Hill on May 18, 1885) [Hendon Hill Cemetery]

Johnson, Anthony T. 1966-1994 (on same tombstone with Darlene T. Johnson; James Dorsey Card File, African American Obituaries, maintained at the Historical Society of Harford County, has a card for him with an obituary from *The Aegis* on September 7, 1994 stating he was born in Havre de Grace, the son of Howard T. Johnson, of Edgewood, and Darlene D. Sykes, of Colonial Heights, VA; he was a truck driver for Coale Truck Transport Co. in Joppa for seven years and died while working in Columbus, OH, survived by a close friend, a daughter, a brother, a sister, a stepmother, a step-brother, two step-sisters, his paternal grandmother Jean Johnson and maternal step-grandfather William Warfield) [Berkley Memorial Cemetery]

Johnson, Archibald December 4, 1947 – January 31, 2000, SP5, U.S. Army, Vietnam [Community Baptist Church Cemetery]

Johnson, Arthur F. 1905-1974 (on same tombstone with Birdie V. Johnson; obituary in *The Aegis* on January 17, 1974 stated he was a retired custodian and lived at 2531 Laurel Brook Road, Fallston; he was the husband of Birdie V. (Brown) Johnson and died at Good Samaritan Hospital (in Baltimore) on January 14, 1974, age 68, survived by his wife, two daughters, two brothers, a sister, six grandchildren and five great-grandchildren; obituary of his brother Clarence Johnson on December 19, 1968 stated Arthur's middle name was Franklin)

[Tabernacle Mount Zion U. M. Church Cemetery]

Johnson, Augustus Sr. 1890-1970 [Gravel Hill Cemetery]

Johnson, Avon D. died October 8, 1969, age 18 (no tombstone; obituary in *The Aegis* on October 26, 1969 stated he was the son of Evelyn Johnson and William B. Miller; he lived at 511 Alliance St., Havre de Grace, and was a senior in high school; he died at home and was survived by his parents and maternal grandfather Bishop Alfred W. Johnson, of Wilmington, DE) [Berkley Memorial Cemetery]

Johnson, Azenier December 10, 1890 – June 3, 1911 (no tombstone; death certificate stated she was born in Harford Co., the daughter of George Johnson, born in Georgia, and Sabina Warfield, born in Harford Co.; she was single, worked as a servant and died at home in Darlington; informant was George Johnson, of Darlington) [Berkley Memorial Cemetery]

Johnson, Baby (no dates when copied in 1987, but not found in 2018) [St. James United Cemetery]

Johnson, Ben died February 14, 1930, age about 55 (no tombstone; death certificate stated he died in Havre de Grace, parents and marital status unknown to informant Nasson McVey) [St. James United Cemetery]

Johnson, Benjamin died October 17, 1889, age 80 years, 11 months, 8 days (on same tombstone with wife Charlotte Johnson when copied in 2000, but tombstone has since toppled over) [West Liberty Church Cemetery]

Johnson, Benjamin "Benny" died October 28, 1994, age 86 (no tombstone; obituary in *The Aegis* on November 23, 1994 stated he was the son of Benjamin Johnson and Emma Smith Akins, and father of the late Otho and Theodore Johnson; he lived in Street, married Beulah Lee in 1928, retired from the B&O Railroad in Aberdeen, was a deacon of Hollie Mariah Church in Philadelphia and died at Harford Memorial Hospital in Havre de Grace; he was survived by his wife, a daughter, a sister, 15 grandchildren and 8 great-great-grandchildren) [Clark's U. M. Church Cemetery]

Johnson, Benjamin, beloved husband of Amanda Johnson, died April 6, 1890, age 88 [Hendon Hill Cemetery]

Johnson, Benjamin M. April 20, 1911 – December 24, 1968, TEC5, 1914 Ord Ammo Co., AVN, World War II [Union U. M. Church Cemetery]

Johnson, Benjamin Oscar July 26, 1887 – February 23, 1936 (no tombstone; death certificate stated he was the son of Benjaman Johnson and Levia Stansbury) [Union U. M. Church Cemetery]

Johnson, Bertha (Mrs.) December 18, 1888 – June 2, 1921 (no tombstone;death certificate stated she was born at Sharon, the daughter of Spencer Murray and Georgianna Turner, was married and died at home in Forest Hill; informant was Charles Howard Johnson, of Forest Hill) [Fairview A. M. E. Church Cemetery]

Johnson, Bessie Irene November 2, 1893 – November 8, 1915 (no tombstone; death certificate stated she was the daughter of Henry and Martha Holland, all born in Harford Co.; she was married and lived in Fallston RFD; informant was Howard Johnson, of Fallston RFD) [West Liberty Church Cemetery]

Johnson, Betty J. January 8, 1952 – September 13, 2002 (tombstone; obituary and photo in *The Aegis* on September 20, 2003 stated she was born on January 1, *(sic)* 1952 in Havre de Grace, the daughter of the late Theodore Johnson, Sr. and Shirley Johnson, of Fallston, and worked as a distribution clerk at Upper Chesapeake Medical Center; she lived in Joppa and died at Upper Chesapeake, survived by her mother, her two children Aylsworth Johnson and Chanelle Fisher, two grandchildren Kierra and Keyana Johnson, her grandmother Bullah Johnson, nine brothers and four sisters) [Clark's U. M. Church Cemetery]

Johnson, Beulah B. February 22, 1909 – April 5, 2003 (no tombstone; obituary and photo in *The Aegis* on April 11, 2003 stated she was born in Street, the daughter of Thomas Lee and Susan Williamson, and was the wife of the late Benjamin Johnson for 67 years; three children, the late Otho and Theodore "Buddy" Johnson and Alice Johnson, were born to her and her late husband; she died at Upper Chesapeake Medical Center and was survived by her daughter Alice, 14 grandchildren, 30 great-grandchildren, 9 great-great-grandchildren and a host of other relatives; she was predeceased by three brothers and a granddaughter) [Clark's U. M. Church Cemetery]

Johnson, Birdie V. 1908-1974 (on same tombstone with Arthur F. Johnson; obituary in *The Aegis* on June 6,

1974 stated she died at home on May 29, 1974, age 65, and her maiden name was Brown; she died at home at 2531 Laurel Brook Road, Fallston, and was survived by 2 daughters, 6 grandchildren, 5 great-grandchildren, and 2 brothers) [Tabernacle Mount Zion U. M. Church Cemetery]

Johnson, Blanche Dorothy Gordon January 16, 1929 – May 8, 2009 (on same tombstone with Alfred William Johnson, Jr. and inscribed "married December 25, 1947;" funeral notice and photo in *The Aegis* on May 13, 2009 stated she lived in Havre de Grace and died at Citizens Care Center) [St. James United Cemetery]

Johnson, C. A. 1904(?) – 1985 [Union U. M. Church Cemetery]

Johnson, Caroline, "Our Mother" May 9, 1846 – December 23, 1910 (on same tombstone with Jehu Johnson) [Tabernacle Mount Zion U. M. Church Cemetery]

Johnson, Carrie Regina September 12, 1929 – December 7, 1930 (no tombstone; death certificate stated she was born in Maryland, the daughter of Henry Johnson, born in West Virginia, and Carrie Hurd, born in Maryland, and died at Pleasantville; informant was her father) [Tabernacle Mount Zion U. M. Church Cemetery]

Johnson, Catherine G., "Wife & Mother" 1924-1979 (tombstone; obituary in *The Aegis* stated she was the wife of Henry Johnson, Jr., of Bel Air, and died at Good Samaritan Hospital in Baltimore on November 22, 1979, age 55, survived by husband, 7 daughters, 2 sons, 6 grandchildren and a sister) [Berkley Memorial Cemetery]

Johnson, Charles 1850-1928 (on same tombstone with Jacob H., Joseph I. and Nellie E. Johnson; death certificate stated he was the son of Benjamin and Jane Johnson and died May 3, 1928, age about 85; he was married, worked as a farmer and died in Bel Air; informant was Jacob Johnson, of Fallston) [Tabernacle Mount Zion U. M. Church Cemetery]

Johnson, Charles Jr. November 1, 1852 – December 13, 1913 (no tombstone; death certificate stated he was the son of Charles Johnson, Sr. and Sarah Jones, all born in Harford Co.; he was single, worked as a laborer, died at home near Aberdeen and buried in "Sidney Park Cemetery;" informant was William Johnson, of Aberdeen) [Union U. M. Church Cemetery]

Johnson, Charles H. (Bishop) May 30, 1895 – February 20, 1976, Cpl., U.S. Army, 370th Regiment, World War I (tombstone; obituary in *The Aegis* stated he was born in Boyce, VA, the son of Alfred and Mary Johnson, was a veteran of World War II *(sic)* and the husband of Lelia M. Johnson; he was founder and senior presiding Bishop of the Pentecostal Assembly of Churches of Jesus Christ Inc.; he lived in Havre de Grace and died at Harford Memorial Hospital, survived by his wife, two brothers Bishop Alfred W. Johnson and Clarence Johnson, a sister Edna Johnson, a step-son Fred Lacy, two step-daughters Joan Tucker and Otelia Littleton, and two grandchildren) [St. James United Cemetery]

Johnson, Charles H. January 6, 1919 – January 27, 2002 (inscribed, but without his date of death; obituary in *The Aegis* on January 30, 2002 stated Charles Henry Johnson was born in Churchville, the son of the late Stella Johnson; he lived in Churchville and worked at the Edgewood Arsenal until 1974, then worked as a custodian at Hickory Elementary School until 1986 and after retirement he worked for Ethan Allen Home Interior Furniture Store for many years; he died at Lorien Health Systems in Belcamp, survived by a niece Reatha Outlaw, and nephew Standiford Hill, and a host of cousins) [Asbury Cemetery]

Johnson, Charles H. June 8, 1890 – February 28, 1953, Maryland, PFC, 840th Co. Trans Corps, World War I [Asbury Cemetery]

Johnson, Charles Leon died March 16, 1973, age not given (no tombstone; obituary in *The Aegis* stated he as born in Perryman, the son of the late Benjamin and Olivia Johnson; he lived at 201 North Adams St. in Havre de Grace and died at Harford Memorial Hospital, survived by two daughters, one grandchild and one great-grandchild) [Union U. M. Church Cemetery]

Johnson, Charlotte died September 10, 1896, age 87 years (on same tombstone with wife Charlotte Johnson, as copied in 2000, but tombstone has since toppled over) [West Liberty Church Cemetery]

Johnson, Cheryl Lynn April 21, 1964 – January 2, 2005 (no tombstone; obituary and photo in *The Aegis* on January 5, 2005 stated she was born in Havre de Grace, lived in Aberdeen and died at Harford Memorial Hospital in Havre de Grace; no family information was given; viewing was at Union United Methodist Church, interment was private [Union U. M. Church Cemetery]

Johnson, Clarence November 29, 1880 – May 3, 1969 (on same tombstone with wife Janie O. Johnson) [West Liberty Church Cemetery]

Johnson, Clarence October 17, 1902 – December 16, 1968, Maryland, PFC, Infantry, World War II (tombstone; obituary in *The Aegis* on December 19, 1968 stated Clarence Edward "Happy" Johnson died on December 16, 1968, but it did not give his age nor mention his service; he was the son of Jacob and Nellie Johnson and husband of Lucy G. Johnson, formerly of Fallston; he died at the home of his brother George Johnson, of Bradshaw) [Tabernacle Mount Zion U. M. Church Cemetery]

Johnson, Claudia P. November 16, 1897 – January 23, 1968 (on same tombstone with J. Howard Johnson) [West Liberty Church Cemetery]

Johnson, Cora Albert died September 16, 1905, age 17 years, 7 months, 7 days (no tombstone; death certificate stated she was the daughter of Jacob L. Johnson and Kate Brown, all born in Maryland, and she died at Boothby Hill; place of burial not given [probably Old Union Chapel Cemetery at Michaelsville [possibly reinterred in Union U. M. Church Cemetery nearAberdeen]

Johnson, Curtis Garfield September 26, 1931 – January 5, 1986 (no tombstone; obituary in *The Aegis* stated he was the son of Riley and Jamie Johnson, lived at Rocks and worked as a handyman; he was buried at "Rocks AME Church" and survived by his parents, 4 sisters and 4 brothers) [Chestnut Grove A. M. E. Church Cemetery, formerly LaGrange Cemetery at Rocks]

Johnson, Daniel August 20, 1875 – October 1, 1914 (no tombstone; death certificate stated he was born in Harford Co., the son of Shadrach Johnson and Amelia Dorsey, both born in Maryland; he worked as a farmer, was married, lived and died in Churchville; informant was Mary E. Johnson, of Bel Air) [Asbury Cemetery]

Johnson, Daniel died August 2, 1990, age 68 (no tombstone; obituary in *The Aegis* on August 22, 1990 stated he was born in Mississippi, the son of Jesse and Millie Johnson, and retired after 37 years as a master barber at Aberdeen Proving Ground; he lived in Aberdeen and died at Harford Memorial Hospital in Havre de Grace, survived by his wife Blanche Hawkins Johnson, two sons, a daughter, six grandchildren and five great-grandchildren) [Berkley Memorial Cemetery]

Johnson, Daniel A. November – (blank), 1887 – April 12, 1943 (no tombstone; death certificate stated he was the son of John Priggs and Laura Johnson, and husband of Sarah E. Johnson) [Union U. M. Church Cemetery]

Johnson, Daniel C. 1913-1966 (on same tombstone with Emma Hall Johnson) [Asbury Cemetery]

Johnson, Darlene D. 1947-   (on same tombstone with Anthony T. Johnson) [Berkley Memorial Cemetery]

Johnson, Deon 1917-1988 [Tabernacle Mount Zion U. M. Church Cemetery]

Johnson, Dorothy January 21, 1914 – October 31, 1923 (no tombstone; death certificate stated she was the daughter of Daniel Johnson and Mary E. Johnson, all born in Churchville; informant was Mary Johnson, of Churchville) [Asbury Cemetery]

Johnson, Dorothy Ella May June 2, 1920 – March 13, 1921 (no tombstone; death certificate stated she was the daughter of Riley Johnson and Jannie Jones, of near High Point, all born in Harford Co.) [Chestnut Grove A. M. E. Church Cemetery, formerly LaGrange Cemetery at Rocks]

Johnson, Earline H. died February 15, 1885, age 68 [Green Spring U. M. Church Cemetery]

Johnson, Edith A. October 12, 1899 – May 7, 1911 (no tombstone; death certificate she was the daughter of Jacob Johnson, both born in Harford Co., and Alice Hewitt, born in Baltimore Co.; she died at home in Bel Air; informant was her father) [Tabernacle Mount Zion U. M. Church Cemetery]

Johnson, Edward March 20, 1876 – January 24, 1950 (no tombstone; death certificate stated he was born in Harford Co., the son of Cedric Johnson and Millie ---- (blank); he worked on a farm, married, and died in rural Bel Air; informant was Mrs. Mary Alice Johnson) [Asbury Cemetery]

Johnson, Edward Michael January 20, 1950 – March 8, 1978, Pvt., U.S. Marine Corps (tombstone; obituary in

The Aegis stated he was born in New York City, the son of Edward Johnson, of Brooklyn, NY and Leenora Johnson, of Harrisburg, PA; he lived in Aberdeen, was employed by the City of Havre de Grace, was injured in an automobile accident and died at Harford Memorial Hospital; he was survived by his parents, three brothers, three sisters, and a grandmother Hattie Johnson, of Brooklyn NY) [St. James United Cemetery]

Johnson, Edward Randolph November 11, 1901 – June 6, 1915 (no tombstone; death certificate stated he was born in Baltimore, the son of Richard W. Johnson, born in Mississippi, and Sarah Rollins, born in Baltimore; he accidentally drowned in Bel Air; informant was his mother Sarah Dorsey) [Fairview A. M. E. Church Cemetery]

Johnson, Elizabeth, "Our Mother" died May 21, 1938 – see Mary Elizabeth Johnson [Asbury Cemetery]

Johnson, Elizabeth I. Berry March 2, 1913 – October 11, 1995 [William C. Rice Memorial Cemetery, St. James U. M. Church]

Johnson, Ellen Bond 1947-2016 (small metal funeral home marker) [St. James United Cemetery]

Johnson, Ellen M. March 10, 1898 – January 20, 1914 (no tombstone; death certificate stated she was the daughter of Jacob Johnson and Alice Hewitt, all born in Harford Co. she was single, worked as a nurse and died in Bel Air; informant was Mary Norton, of Bel Air) [Tabernacle Mount Zion U. M. Church Cemetery]

Johnson, Elsworth S. January 4, 1898 – October 4, 1912 (no tombstone; death certificate stated he was the son of Arthur and Alberta Johnson, all born in Harford Co., and they lived in Bel Air) [Hendon Hill Cemetery]

Johnson, Elva Nora, "Mother" October 20, 1913 – January 28, 1977 (on same tombstone with Marvin Clifford Holland; obituary in *The Aegis* on February 3, 1977 stated she was born in Havre de Grace, the daughter of the late Noah and Julia A. Ridgeley, and married Allen P. Johnson; she lived at 730 Otsego St., Havre de Grace, and died at Harford Memorial Hospital, survived by her husband, two sons, a brother, a sister, 6 grandchildren, a nephew and a great-nephew) [St. James United Cemetery]

Johnson, Emma Hall 1917-1967 (on same tombstone with Daniel C. Johnson) [Asbury Cemetery]

Johnson, Emma J. October 9, 1875 – July 23, 1914 (no tombstone; death certificate stated she was the daughter of Nathan Johnson and Eliza Chambers, all born in Harford Co.; she performed general work and died in Churchville; informant was William N. Johnson of Churchville) [Asbury Cemetery]

Johnson, Estelle V. September 5, 1899 – July 18, 1947 (no tombstone; death certificate stated she was the wife of William Johnson and the daughter of George Stansbury and Hattie Christy) [Union U. M. Church Cemetery]

Johnson, Etta V. February 17, 1898 – December 19, 1980 [Clark's U. M. Church Cemetery]

Johnson, Evelyn Taylor died May 13, 1940, age 30 (no tombstone; her death notice in the *Havre de Grace Republican* on May 18, 1940 stated she was the daughter of William and Georgianna Johnson and the wife of Leon Johnson of Gravelly Hill; funeral services were at Gravelly Hill Church with burial in the adjoining cemetery; death certificate stated Evelyn Bradford Johnson was born April 17, 1910 in Harford Co., the daughter of William H. Taylor and Georgiana ---- (blank), both born in Maryland; also stated her usual residence was at 1103 Montgomery Street in Harrisburg, PA, but she had been back home for 12 months; informant was her husband Leon Johnson, of Havre de Grace RFD#1) [Gravel Hill Cemetery]

Johnson, Fannie Marie, "Beloved Mother, Grandmother" 1924-1990 [Tabernacle Mount Zion U. M. Church Cemetery]

Johnson, Fred William Jr. November 10, 1925 – November 30, 2014, PFC, U.S. Marine Corps, World War II [St. James United Cemetery]

Johnson, Frederick Douglas died on November 8, 1997, age 64 (no tombstone; The James Dorsey Card File, African American Obituaries, maintained at the Historical Society of Harford County, has a card for him with an obituary from *The Aegis* on November 12, 1997 stating "Fred" was born in Maryland, the son of Henry Johnson, Sr. and Carrie Elizabeth Hurd, and the husband of the late Margaret Elizabeth Johnson; he worked as a truck driver for Fleet Transit and played guitar in a quartet for local churches; he lived in Fallston and died at the home of his sister Charlotte Chase in Joppa, survived by three sons, a daughter, a brother, a sister and six grandchildren) [Tabernacle Mount Zion U. M. Church Cemetery]

Johnson, G. A. 1864-1935 (tombstone; death certificate stated Georgeanna Johnson was born on November 25, 1864, the daughter of John Pitt and Frances Harris, and died on January 26, 1935, the widow of Joseph Johnson) [Union U. M. Church Cemetery]

Johnson, Garfield Henry March 23, 1932 – February 21, 1975 (no tombstone; obituary in *The Aegis* stated he was born in Perryman, the son of James Arthur Johnson and Mayfield Peaco, and was the husband of Roberta M. Johnson; he lived at 102 Spesutia Road in Perryman, retired from the federal government and died at Franklin Square Hospital in Baltimore County, survived by his wife, mother, brother Benjamin S. Johnson and sister Olivia A. Forney) [Union U. M. Church Cemetery]

Johnson, George died July 1, 1922, age about 75 (no tombstone; death certificate stated he was born in Virginia, but his parents were not known to informant May Dorsey, 919 Daren St., Philadelphia, PA; he worked as a laborer and died a widower at home in Darlington) [Berkley Memorial Cemetery]

Johnson, George, "Our Father" died October 1, 1907, age 58 years and 2 months (tombstone; death certificate stated he was age 58 years, 2 months and 12 days at the time of his death in Churchville where he was a farm laborer; he was born in Baltimore, as were his parents, but informant Mary E. Johnson, his daughter, did not know his father's name, but his mother was Mary) [Asbury Cemetery]

Johnson, George Emory, beloved son of John and Caroline Johnson, died June 20, 1898, age 21 years, -- (4?) months, 27 days [Tabernacle Mount Zion U. M. Church Cemetery]

Johnson, George H. 1901-1965 (on same tombstone with Mildred G. Johnson) [Asbury Cemetery]

Johnson, George Matthew died July 21, 1978, age 57 (no tombstone; obituary in *The Aegis* on July 27, 1978 stated he lived at 1048 Pfeffer Road in Bradshaw, Baltimore Co., and was the husband of Isabelle Webster; he worked at Aberdeen Proving Ground for 30 years and died at Fallston General Hospital) [Tabernacle Mount Zion U. M. Church Cemetery]

Johnson, George W. (no dates; his wife Mary Anne Johnson may be buried here so he may also be here) [Mt. Zion U. M. Church Cemetery]

Johnson, George W. November 5, 1891 – September 25, 1956 Maryland, PFC, 16 CO, 152 Depot Brigade, World War I (tombstone; Pennington Funeral Home records stated he was born on November 5, 1892 *(sic)* in Pennsylvania, the son of George Johnson and Julia Young; he was married, worked as a laborer, lived at Street, served in World War I, died at Perry Point Veterans Administration Hospital and was buried in Chestnut Grove Cemetery at Rocks) [Chestnut Grove A. M. E. Church Cemetery, formerly LaGrange Cemetery at Rocks]

Johnson, Georgeanna – see G. A. Johnson [Union U. M. Church Cemetery]

Johnson, Gloria O., "Sister" 1927-1995 (handwritten on flat cement slab) [St. James United Cemetery]

Johnson, Hannah E. January 1, 1903 – April 9, 1982 (on same tombstone with Susie A. Daugherty; obituary in *The Aegis* on April 22, 1982 stated Hannah E. Banks Johnson was born in Harford Co., lived at Churchville, was a practical nurse in Maryland and Pennsylvania; was the widow of Grason Johnson and died at Citizens Nursing Home in Havre de Grace, survived by 3 sisters, 2 brothers, and several nieces, nephews, cousins and foster children) [Asbury Cemetery]

Johnson, Harriett died on June 14, 1929 age about 90 (no tombstone; death certificate stated she was the daughter of Thomas Hall and Betsy Hall, all born in Maryland; she was a widow and died at home at Kalmia; informant was Maggie Rumsey, of Bel Air RFD #3) [Clark's U. M. Church Cemetery]

Johnson, Harriett February 4, 1910 – September 9, 1911 (no tombstone; death certificate stated she was born in Maryland, the daughter of Ben Johnson, born in Pennsylvania, and Emma Smith, born in Maryland; they lived at Ady; informant's name was not given on the death certificate) [Clark's U. M. Church Cemetery]

Johnson, Harry D. September 17, 1926 – May 9, 2011 (on the same tombstone with Sarah G. Johnson and inscribed "The Lord is my Shepherd, I shall not want;" obituary and photo in *The Aegis* on May 13, 2011 stated Harry Denwood Johnson graduated from Havre de Grace High School and enlisted in the U. S. Army, after which he was employed as an electrician at Edgewood Arsenal and Aberdeen Proving Ground for over 30 years; he was preceded in death by his wife of 59 years Sarah G. Johnson, and was survived by 3 sons, a daughter, 9 grandchildren, a brother, a brother-in-law and a sister-in-law) [Clark's U. M. Church Cemetery]

Johnson, Harry Theodore August 16, 1907 – September 13, 1973 (no tombstone; obituary in *The Aegis* stated he was born in Mt. Pleasant, WV and moved to Havre de Grace in 1909; he was the foster son of John and Eva Richardson; he lived at 221 N. Ohio St., retired as a truck driver for Edgewood Arsenal and died at Harford Memorial Hospital, survived by three sons, a daughter, a brother and 15 grandchildren; his wife was not mentioned in the obituary) [Berkley Memorial Cemetery]

Johnson, Havlain 1902-1972 [Berkley Memorial Cemetery]

Johnson, Hazel 1936-1984 (copied in 1987, but not found in 2018; James Dorsey Card File, African American Obituaries, maintained at the Historical Society of Harford County, has two cards, one stating Hazel Marie Johnson, neé Peaker, was born on November 11, 1936 and died on March 23, 1984, and the other one stating she was the daughter of Laura A. Cooper and Harold Norton) [John Wesley U. M. E. Church Cemetery in Abingdon]

Johnson, Henry 1866-1937 *(sic)* (his last name was not inscribed on the tombstone; death certificate stated he was born March 12, 1866 in Baltimore Co. and died April 6, 1939 near Havre de Grace; his parents were Richard Johnson and Julia Gray, both born in Maryland; he married Rebecca J. ----, was a farmer and a widower; informant was Augustus Johnson) [Gravel Hill Cemetery]

Johnson, Henry November 10, 1906 – March 6, 1964 [Tabernacle Mount Zion U. M. Church Cemetery]

Johnson, Henry April 12, 1925 – April 25, 1925 (no tombstone; death certificate stated he was born in Maryland, the son of Henry Johnson, born in West Virginia, and Carrie Herd, born in Maryland, and they lived in Fallston; informant was his father) [Tabernacle Mount Zion U. M. Church Cemetery]

Johnson, Henry died April 22, 1924, age 2 months (no tombstone; death certificate stated he was the son of Henry Johnson, of Fallston, both born in Maryland; his mother's name was not given, but she was born in Maryland according to informant Henry Johnson) [Tabernacle Mount Zion U. M. Church Cemetery]

Johnson, Henry died September 25, 1927, age 35 (no tombstone; death certificate stated he died in Darlington, parents unknown to the Stone & Webster Co.) [St. James United Cemetery]

Johnson, Henry Jr. died June 4, 2017, age 84 (no tombstone; obituary in *The Aegis* stated he lived in Aberdeen and died at Belcamp, survived by sister Charlotte Chase) [John Wesley U. M. E. Church Cemetery in Abingdon]

Johnson, Henry Clinton December 24, 1924 – April 20, 1925 (no tombstone; death certificate stated he was the son of John Howard Johnson and Claudia Jones, all born in Harford Co.; he died at home at Good Will near Rutledge; informant was his father, of Fallston) [West Liberty Church Cemetery]

Johnson, Hester died June 5, 1905, age 88, "mother of Caroline Johnson" (tombstone; death certificate stated she died a widow at Laurel Brook, age 88, but the names of her parents were not known to informant, her daughter Caroline Johnson; obituary in *The Aegis* on June 15, 1905 stated she was 87 and survived by 18 grandchildren and 35 great-grandchildren) [Tabernacle Mount Zion U. M. Church Cemetery]

Johnson, Hilda Marie July 2, 1914 – February 16, 1915 (no tombstone; death certificate stated she was the daughter of J. Ed Johnson and Naomi Brown, of Havre de Grace) [St. James United Cemetery]

Johnson, Hilda W. died -- July 1966 (small metal funeral home marker with letters and numbers missing) [William C. Rice Memorial Cemetery, St. James U. M. Church]

Johnson, Hillen Augustus died October 21, 1969, age not given (no tombstone; obituary in *The Aegis* in October 3, 1969 stated he was the son of Henry and Rebecca Johnson, and husband of Mrs. Frank Lee Johnson and lived at 612 Concord St. in Havre de Grace; he owned Johnson's Hotel and also worked for Pitcock's Hardware Store; he died at Harford Memorial Hospital, survived by his wife, 4 sons, 3 daughters, 19 grandchildren and 3 great-grandchildren) [Gravel Hill Cemetery]

Johnson, Hoffman R. October 1, 1894 – October 14, 1913 (no tombstone; death certificate stated he was the son of Jacob L. Johnson and Katie Brown, all born in Harford Co.) [Union U. M. Church Cemetery]

Johnson, Isabelle V. died January 2, 1998, age 78 (no tombstone; James Dorsey Card File, African American Obituaries, maintained at the Historical Society of Harford County, has a card for her with an obituary from *The*

Aegis on January 7, 1998 stating she was born in Street, the daughter of Edward Dutton and Emily Jaynes, and widow of Willis R. Johnson; she lived in Jarrettsville, was a domestic worked for more than 60 years and was a member of the Isiah Baptist Church in Monkton; she died at Fallston General Hospital, survived by two sons, two daughters, three sisters, ten grandchildren and five great-grandchildren) [Clark's U. M. Church Cemetery]

Johnson, Isiah died May 27, 1914, age about 75 (no tombstone; death certificate stated he was the son of George Johnson and Mary Ann Green, all born in Harford Co.; he died in Bel Air and was buried in "Mountian Colored Cemetery;" informant was Josephine Johnson, of Bel Air) [Mt. Zion U. M. Church Cemetery]

Johnson, J. Howard January 29, 1892 – October 17, 1972 (no same tombstone with Claudia P. Johnson) [West Liberty Church Cemetery]

Johnson, Jacob died January 25, 1934, age 60 (tombstone; death certificate stated he was born in Harford Co. in 1874, worked as a laborer and was the widower of Alice Hughes; his parents were Isaiah Johnson, born at Long Green, and Emmalunge(?) Johnson, born at Reckordville; informant was Louisa Johnson, of 1616 Argyle Avenue in Baltimore; J. C. Taylor Marble Co. records stated "Jacob Johnson's Marble head stone was put up July 10th 1934 Hendon Hill, ordered by Wylie W. Hopkins, Bel Air; James Dorsey Card File, African American Obituaries, maintained at the Historical Society of Harford County, has a card for him stating "Jacob Johnson lived on Lee St., old cook, drank whiskey, buried by H. Hopkins' father") [Hendon Hill Cemetery]

Johnson, Jacob H. 1875-1933 (on same tombstone with Charles Johnson and Nellie E. Johnson) [Tabernacle Mount Zion U. M. Church Cemetery]

Johnson, Jacob Lewis May 18, 1855 – March 9, 1916 (no tombstone; death certificate stated he was married and the son of William Johnson and Susan Tilden, all born in Maryland) [Union U. M. Church Cemetery]

Johnson, Jacob S. May 20, 1859 – July 10, 1925 (no tombstone; death certificate stated he was born in Maryland, but the names of his parents, who were born in Maryland, were not known to informant Louisa Johnson, of Aberdeen; he was married and worked as a day laborer) [Mt. Calvary U. A. M. E. Church Cemetery]

Johnson, Jacqueline J. 1956-2000 [Gravel Hill Cemetery]

Johnson, James A. Jr. April 9, 1925 – July 1, 1947, Maryland, Pvt., 888 Ambulance Co., World War II (tombstone; death certificate stated he was the son of James A. Johnson, Sr. and Mayfield Peaco, of Perryman, and he died at Harford Memorial Hospital in Havre de Grave after being injured in an auto accident on Route 40 near Aberdeen) [Union U. M. Church Cemetery]

Johnson, James A. Sr., "Father" 1885-1962 (on same tombstone with Otelia L. Johnson) [Union U. M. Church Cemetery]

Johnson, James Benton 1934-1975, SP3, U.S. Army, Korea [Community Baptist Church Cemetery]

Johnson, James E. April 14, 1950 – February 20, 1999, U. S. Army, Vietnam (tombstone; obituary in *The Aegis* on February 26, 1999 stated James Edward Johnson was born in Havre de Grace, the son of Dorothy M. Johnson, of Street, MD, and Edward Fisher, and was a truck driver for Perry Point VAMC and a U. S. Army veteran of Vietnam; he lived in Aberdeen, died at Harford Memorial Hospital and was survived by his wife of 11 years Francine A. S. Crockson Johnson, one son Derrick L. Sneed, two stepsons Kevin L. Jordan and Wesley B. Slater, one daughter Tammy Renee Johnson, three brothers Gary O. Johnson, Edward Murry and Clifton E. Johnson, and three grandchildren) [Clark's U. M. Church Cemetery]

Johnson, James Edward July 8, 1926 – January 4, 1933 (no tombstone; death certificate stated he was son of Robert Johnson and Florence Williams and died in a house fire near Perryman) [Union U. M. Church Cemetery]

Johnson, James Edward June 23, 1892 – December 29, 1958 (no tombstone; death certificate stated he was the son of James W. Johnson and Jerroleen Brown and he was born in Fallston and died at home on Record Road; he was divorced; informant was Clorenda Burns, of Fallston) [Tabernacle Mount Zion U. M. Church Cemetery]

Johnson, James H. 1891 – October 4, 1946 (no tombstone; death certificate stated he was born in St. Paul, MN, married, worked as a cook, died near Bel Air where he had lived for 40 years; his parents were unknown to informant, his wife, Alberta Westcott Johnson, of Bel Air) [Hendon Hill Cemetery]

Johnson, James Henry October – (blank), 1844 – August 18, 1940 (no tombstone; Kurtz Funeral Home Record Book 1937-1943, p. 154, stated he was born in Harford Co., married Martha ---- and died a widower at Provident Hospital in Baltimore; funeral ordered by and charged to Howard and William Johnson) [West Liberty Church Cemetery]

Johnson, James I. (Deacon) October 3, 1911 - (on same tombstone with Alverta O. Johnson) [Community Baptist Church Cemetery]

Johnson, James S. June 23, 1940 – February 24, 1941 (no tombstone; death certificate stated he was the son of Spencer Johnson, of Havre de Grace, and Louise Taylor, of Davenville, IL) [St. James United Cemetery]

Johnson, James Thomas September 5, 1915 – December 25, 1922 (no tombstone; death certificate stated he was the son of Donald Johnson and Angeline R. Rice, all born in Harford Co.; he died near Madonna; informant was his father Donald Johnson, of Rocks RFD) [Chestnut Grove A. M. E. Church Cemetery, formerly LaGrange Cemetery at Rocks]

Johnson, James W. Jr., "Sonny" December 17, 1927 – December 21, 2007, PFC, U.S. Army [Union U. M. Church Cemetery]

Johnson, James W. October 6, 1895 – March 12, 1917 (no tombstone; death certificate stated he was married and worked as a waiter in Bel Air; his parents were Arthur Johnson and Alverta Westcoat and they were all born in Harford Co.; informant was Alverta Johnson, of Bel Air) [Hendon Hill Cemetery]

Johnson, James W., husband of Jeeroleen Johnson, died June 4, 1918, age 47 (tombstone; death certificate stated James Wesley Johnson, son of Jehu and Caroline Johnson, all born in Harford Co., was born on January 2, 1871 and married, worked as a laborer and died in Fallston; informant was his wife "Jeraline") [Tabernacle Mount Zion U. M. Church Cemetery]

Johnson, James Walter January 9, 1895 – September 7, 1972, Pvt., U.S. Army, World War I (tombstone; military records stated he was born in Baltimore, inducted into service in Aberdeen on August 23, 1918, served in the 153 Depot Brigade and honorably discharged on December 10, 1918) [Union U. M. Church Cemetery]

Johnson, Janie O. December 23, 1883 – September 12, 1965 (on same tombstone with Clarence Johnson) [West Liberty Church Cemetery]

Johnson, Jean Giles 1922-2005 (small metal funeral home marker) [Clark's U. M. Church Cemetery]

Johnson, Jehu, "Our Father" February 11, 1841 – August 25, 1911 (on same tombstone with Caroline Johnson) [Tabernacle Mount Zion U. M. Church Cemetery]

Johnson, Jehu died July 25, 1940, no age given (no tombstone; a notice in *The Aegis* on August 2, 1940 stated he lived on the W. A. Harlan farm in Fallston for several years and for the past 21 years was employed at the Friends School in Baltimore; he died at home in Baltimore) [Tabernacle Mount Zion U. M. Church Cemetery]

Johnson, Jessica Mae died January 5, 1967, age not given (no tombstone; obituary in *The Aegis* on January 12, 1967 stated she was the daughter of Jessie J. Johnson and Margaret Johnson of Box 267 Westwood Manor Farm, Old Level Road, Churchville; survived by her parents, 3 sisters and 2 brothers) [Berkley Memorial Cemetery]

Johnson, John V. Sr. February 17, 1930 – October 8, 2007, U.S. Army (tombstone; obituary in *The Aegis* on October 12, 2007 stated John Vernon Johnson, Sr. was the son of Augustus and Mary L. Johnson and he served in the Army from February 15, 1951 to March 25, 1953; he married the late Alice Frances Johnson on July 1, 1960 and was a maintenance manager for more than 35 years for the late Dr. Foley of Havre de Grace; he was known as "Mr. Fix It" and would fix anything for anyone; he lived in Havre de Grace and died at St. Frances Hospital in Wilmington, DE, survived by two sons, eight daughters, one sister, two brothers, and "several grandchildren and great-grandchildren") [Gravel Hill Cemetery]

Johnson, Joseph January 4, 1861 – February 6, 1937 (no tombstone; death certificate stated he was born in Harford Co., did farm work, and was the widower of Sarah Johnson; he lived near Forest Hill and died at Harford Memorial Hospital in Havre de Grace; his parents were Isaiah Johnson and Emily Johnson, both born in Maryland; informant was Louisa Carter, of 1616 Argyle Ave. in Baltimore; *The Havre de Grace Republican*, February 13, 1937, in "Hospital News," reported Joseph Johnson, of Forest Hill, was among those receiving medical treatment, yet he had died a week earlier and was buried February 9, 1937) [Hendon Hill Cemetery]

Johnson, Joseph F. September 24, 1859 – February 27, 1915 (no tombstone; death certificate stated he was the married son of William Johnson and Susan Tilden, all born in Maryland) [Union U. M. Church Cemetery]

Johnson, Joseph I. 1904-1964 (on same tombstone with Charles, Jacob H. and Nellie E. Johnson) [Tabernacle Mount Zion U. M. Church Cemetery]

Johnson, Joseph Norman died August 4, 1977, age 79 (no tombstone; obituary in *The Aegis* stated he was born in Perryman, the son of Jacob and Katie Johnson, lived in Havre de Grace, was a retired track man for the Pennsylvania Railroad and died at Harford Memorial Hospital, survived by his wife Bertha M. Johnson, a son John L. Johnson, and a brother William R. Johnson) [Union U. M. Church Cemetery]

Johnson, Josua *(sic)* died November 27, 1917, age 34 (no tombstone; death certificate stated he was born in Harford Co., the son of Issak Johnson and Emeline Jackson, both born in Maryland; he was married, worked as a laborer and died in Bel Air; informant was Hannah Johnson) [Asbury Cemetery]

Johnson, Katie F. August 20, 1862 – January 8, 1925 (no tombstone; death certificate stated she was the widowed daughter of Robert Brown and Eliza Tilden; informant was Robert B. Johnson, of Perryman, MD) [Union U. M. Church Cemetery]

Johnson, Kenneth L. 1945-2016 (small metal funeral home marker) [Berkley Memorial Cemetery]

Johnson, Lena Mae 1927-2010 (small metal funeral home marker; funeral notice and photo in *The Aegis* on April 30, 2010 stated she died at her home in Darlington on April 27, 2010, age 82) [Cedars Chapel Cemetery]

Johnson, LeRoy October 12, 1912 – February 4, 1935 (no tombstone; death certificate stated he was the son of Leon Johnson and Rebie Bowser) [Union U. M. Church Cemetery]

Johnson, Lewis A. August 21, 1871 – April 18, 1950 (no tombstone; death certificate stated he was a retired State Roads laborer, born in Harford Co. and died a widower near Darlington; parents were unknown to informant Rufford Johnson, 1922 West Diamond St., Philadelphia, PA) [Berkley Memorial Cemetery]

Johnson, Lewis March 24, 1896 – November 9, 1950 [Hendon Hill Cemetery]

Johnson, Lillian (Lillian Jordan) *(sic)* died April 2, 1944, age about 52 (no tombstone; death certificate stated she was unmarried and born in Virginia, parents unknown to Sheriff Charles Stephens; she lived on Greenway's farm near Havre de Grace and died in an auto accident) [St. James United Cemetery]

Johnson, Louise January 30, 1931 – September 22, 1931 (no tombstone; death certificate stated he was born in Maryland, son of Arthur Johnson, birth place unknown, and Laura Washington, born in Maryland; he died at home in Abingdon of "whooping cough as pronounced by Dr. Polk at John Hopkins Hospital, September 18, 1931" and was buried in "John Wesley Cemetery;" informant was Viola Preston, of Abingdon) [John Wesley U. M. E. Church Cemetery in Abingdon]

Johnson, Lucy, daughter of Shadrach and Jane Johnson, died October 21, 1903, age 30 years, 9 months, 1(?) day (illegible verse on tombstone) [Asbury Cemetery]

Johnson, Margaret Elizabeth died May 15, 1995, age 61 (no tombstone; obituary in *The Aegis* on May 17, 1995 stated she was born in Prince George's Co., the daughter of George Thomas Hill and Margaret Estelle Williams; she lived in Fallston and died at St. Joseph Hospital, survived by her husband Frederick Douglas Johnson, a son, two brothers and two sisters) [Tabernacle Mount Zion U. M. Church Cemetery]

Johnson, Margaret Lucile November 6, 1944 – December 26, 1944 (no tombstone; death certificate stated she was born at Rocks, the daughter of Riley Johnson, born at Peach Bottom, PA, and Janie Jones, born at Jarrettsville; informant was Janie Jones, of Rocks) [Chestnut Grove A. M. E. Church Cemetery, formerly LaGrange Cemetery at Rocks]

Johnson, Margery M. "Love All ----" (illegibly handwritten on a flat cement slab, badly weathered) [St. James United Cemetery]

Johnson, Marshal Herold July 15, 1938 – April 5, 1939 (no tombstone; death certificate stated he was born at

Rocks, the son of Riley Johnson, born in Peach Bottom, York Co., PA, and Janie Jones, born in Jarrettsville, and died at home at Rocks; informant was his father; Kurtz Funeral Home Record Book 1937-1943, p. 104, stated the same information) [Chestnut Grove A. M. E. Church Cemetery, formerly LaGrange Cemetery at Rocks]

Johnson, Martha died August 2, 1915, age 2 years and 2 months (no tombstone; death certificate stated she was the daughter of Walter Johnson and Lizzie Holland, all born in Harford Co.; she died at Rutledge; informant was her father, of Fallston RFD) [West Liberty Church Cemetery]

Johnson, Martha died January 17, 1919, age about 56 (no tombstone; death certificate stated she was the daughter of Jarrett Johnson, both born in Maryland, but the name of her mother was not known to informant, her husband, J. Henry Johnson, of Jarrettsville; she was married and died at home near Rutledge) [West Liberty Church Cemetery]

Johnson, Mary (copied in 1987, not listed in 2002 and not found in 2018) [Gravel Hill Cemetery]

Johnson, Mary aged 35 years (no dates on tombstone) [Hendon Hill Cemetery]

Johnson, Mary October 15, 1899 – March 5, 1990 [Berkley Memorial Cemetery]

Johnson, Mary Alice August 3, 1874 – March 5, 1941 (no tombstone; death certificate stated she was born in Baltimore and was the daughter of Robert Thomas, born in Petersburg, VA, and Susan Dunmore, born in Port Deposit, MD; she married Franklin Johnson (age 80 in 1941) and lived and died in Havre de Grace RFD; informant was her husband) [Asbury Cemetery]

Johnson, Mary Ann, wife of George A. Johnson, died January 14, 1871 in 52nd year [Hill-Johnson Cemetery]

Johnson, Mary Anne died November 19, 1891 at an advanced age (no tombstone; death notice in *The Aegis* on November 27, 1891 stated she was the wife of George W. Johnson, of the Mountain; her maiden name was Green and she was brought up on Deer Creek by Elisha Cook; place of burial was not given, but it was probably at Mt. Zion Church) [Mt. Zion U. M. Church Cemetery]

Johnson, Mary Elizabeth June 4, 1863 – May 21, 1938 (tombstone copied in 1987 stated she died May 21, 1938, age 87, which is incorrect; death certificate stated Mary Elizabeth Johnson was born in Michaelsville on June 4, 1863 and died on May 21, 1938, age 74 years, 11 months and 17 days, and she was the daughter of Henry Hollinworth, born in Michaelsville, and Eliza Lisby, birth place unknown; she lived near Churchville and was the widow of George Johnson; informant was Mrs. Carrie Thompson, of Churchville) [Asbury Cemetery]

Johnson, Mary Jane March 24, 1855 – October 4, 1940 (no tombstone; Kurtz Funeral Home Record Book 1937-1944, p. 159, stated born in Harford Co., daughter of Daniel Cork; birth place and name of mother were not known; she died a widow at Federal Hill) [William C. Rice Memorial Cemetery, St. James U. M. Church]

Johnson, Mary Mildred died August 3, 1926, age 4 months (no tombstone; death certificate stated she was the daughter of Henry Johnson and Carrie Hurd, of Fallston, and all were born in Maryland) [Tabernacle Mount Zion U. M. Church Cemetery]

Johnson, Mary S. died February 28, 1934, age about 72 (no tombstone; death certificate stated she was born in Pennsylvania, the daughter of Henry Bond and Sarah Cole, both born in Maryland; she lived in Havre de Grace RFD, died in Havre de Grace Hospital and was the widow of John Johnson; informant was John Bond, of Havre de Grace RFD #1) [Green Spring U. M. Church Cemetery]

Johnson, Mary Susan born about June 1879 – November 12, 1941 (no tombstone; death certificate stated she was born in Byce, VA, the daughter of Phil Johnston, mother not known to informant Rev. Charles H. Johnson, of Havre de Grace; she was the widow of Alfred W. Johnson) [St. James United Cemetery]

Johnson, Mary White died June 6, 1968, age 62 (no tombstone; obituary in *The Aegis* stated she was the wife of Harry T. Johnson, Sr., of 860 Erie St., Havre de Grace, and died at Brevin Nursing Home, survived by her husband, two sons, and a large number of foster sons and daughters) [Berkley Memorial Cemetery]

Johnson, Mayfield Peaco died April 8, 1984, age 81 (no tombstone; obituary in *The Aegis* stated she was born in Havre de Grace, the daughter of James and Annie Peaco, and was the widow of James Arthur Johnson; she lived in Havre de Grace and died from injuries sustained from a fire in her home; she was survived by a daughter

Olivia Fornery, a son Benjamin Johnson, six grandchildren, ten great-grandchildren, and two great-great-grandchildren) [Union U. M. Church Cemetery]

Johnson, Mildred July 10, 1912 – October 8, 1912 (no tombstone; death certificate stated she was born in Harford Co. and her mother was Lily Johnson, born in Baltimore, but the name of her father and his place of birth were unknown to informant Charles Dorsey, of Bel Air) [Hendon Hill Cemetery]

Johnson, Mildred G. 1905-2001 (on same tombstone with George H. Johnson, but her year of death was not inscribed; obituary and photo in *The Aegis* on August 1, 2001 stated Mildred Greene Johnson was born in Baltimore, the daughter of William Henry Greene and Mary Delaphine Fletcher, and was the wife of the late George Henry Johnson for 29 years; she worked as a domestic housekeeper and in 1950 moved to Churchville; she died at Citizens Care Center in Havre de Grace, survived by a nephew, four grandchildren, eight great-grandchildren, and ten great-great-grandchildren; she was preceded in death by a daughter Geraldine M. Gladden and a sister Edna Greene) [Asbury Cemetery]

Johnson, Monte Alan December 21, 1953 [St. James United Cemetery]

Johnson, Moses died March 26, 1888, age 75 (no tombstone; death notice in *The Aegis* on March 30, 1888 stated he died near Pleasantville; burial place was not given, but J. C. Taylor Marble Co. records state "Moses Johnson's tombstone was put up Nov 10th 1888 Col. Church near the X Roads" (Upper Cross Roads) [West Liberty Church Cemetery]

Johnson, Myrtle J. June 16, 1901 – February 11, 1989 [St. James United Cemetery]

Johnson, Myrtle M., "Mother" August 16, 1925 – November 10, 2000 (tombstone; obituary and photo in *The Aegis* on November 22, 2000 stated she was the daughter of Hilda Peaco Hawkins and the late George E. Hawkins and in the early 1950s she moved to Long Island, NY with her two children M. Sandra and Richard L. Wallace, was employed many years as a ward clerk for the Long Island Jewish Hospital and in 1982 returned to Havre de Grace; she died at Harford Memorial Hospital, survived by her mother, a daughter M. Sandra Mosley, a son Richard L. Wallace, an aunt Marie Brown, 18 grandchildren, and 24 great-grandchildren) [St. James United Cemetery]

Johnson, Nathaniel November 17, 1836 – January 27, 1917 (no tombstone; death certificate stated he was born in Maryland, son of Shadrach Johnson and Emeline Cooper, birth places unknown to informant William Johnson, of Churchville; he was married and worked as a farmer near Churchville; his funeral notice in the *Bel Air Times* on February 2, 1918 stated "Nathan" died at age 81 at his home near Churchville and was survived by his wife and one son; he was a trustee and active member of Asbury Church and was connected with its Temperance organization for 62 years) [Asbury Cemetery]

Johnson, Nattie Belle October 2, 1853 – Septeber16, 1935 (no tombstone; death certificate stated she was born in Virginia, the daughter of John Fields, birth place unknown, and Mahalia Alexander, born in Virginia; she was married and died at home near Jarrettsville; informant was her husband Nicholas Johnson, of Rocks RFD) [William C. Rice Memorial Cemetery, St. James U. M. Church]

Johnson, Neimiah D., "Son – Father" September 10, 1977 – May 12, 2001 (inscribed "Forever in our Hearts") [Clark's U. M. Church Cemetery]

Johnson, Nellie E. 1880-1921 (on same tombstone with Charles, Jacob H. and Joseph I. Johnson; death certificate stated she was the daughter of Henry Matthews and Malinda Fountain, all born in Howard Co., MD; she was born in June "unknown" 1879, married, and died March 14, 1921, age 48 years and 9 months; informant was Jacob Johnson, of Fallston) [Tabernacle Mount Zion U. M. Church Cemetery]

Johnson, Nicholas Leon died January 17, 1988, age 70 (no tombstone; obituary in *The Aegis* on January 21, 1988 stated he was born in Jarrettsville, the son of Nicholas Johnson and Nettie Fields, and was a retired cement finisher; he lived in Bel Air, died at Fallston General Hospital and was survived by one niece Earnesone Bryan Beasley, of Aberdeen) [Tabernacle Mount Zion U. M. Church Cemetery]

Johnson, Nicholas McKinley March 19, 1894 – January 31, 1943 (no tombstone; Kurtz Funeral Home Record Book 1937-1944, p. 263, stated he was born in Jarrettsville, the son of Joshua Johnson, birth place not known, and Mary Jane Cork, born in Harford Co.; he married Nettie Belle Fields, worked as a farm laborer and died at home at Federal Hill; funeral arrangements were made by his daughter Margaret Irene Bryan; death certificate added that he died a widower in rural Jarrettsville and his daughter Margaret lived in Bel Air) [William C. Rice Memorial Cemetery, St. James U. M. Church]

Johnson, Otelia L."Wife" August 23, 1897 – April 29, 1939 (on same tombstone with James A. Johnson Sr.) [Union U. M. Church Cemetery]

Johnson, Otho E. June 7, 1928 – August 6, 1955, Maryland, PFC, 85 CML Smoke Generator Co. [Clark's U. M. Church Cemetery]

Johnson, Pamela October 28, 1958 – January 8, 1998 (tombstone; James Dorsey Card File, African American Obituaries, maintained at the Historical Society of Harford County, has a card with obituary and photo from an unidentified newspaper on January 21, 1998 stating Pamela Williams-Johnson was born October 29, 1958 in Havre de Grace, the daughter of Evelyn and Frank "Pam" Johnson, of Aberdeen, and worked as a cook, receiving several awards; she died at the home of her parents and was also survived by three children, twins Annie and Antoinette Johnson and Chanelle Owens, three sisters, three brothers Frank Roscoe, Keith Malloy and Frank Williams, Jr., a grandson Jermaine L. Wilson, Jr., a devoted great aunt Evelyn E. Brown, and other relatives) [Berkley Memorial Cemetery]

Johnson, Pansy M. October 30, 1914 – December 29, 1914 (no tombstone; death certificate stated she was the daughter of James Johnson and Lillian Osborn and they were all born in Bel Air) [Hendon Hill Cemetery]

Johnson, Pauline E. October 11, 1923 – February 3, 2003 (no tombstone; obituary and photo in *The Aegis* on February 12, 2003 stated she was born in Harford County, daughter of Corbin Johnson and Anna Miller, and was married to the late Charles Govans; she lived in Philadelphia for many years and returned to Maryland in 1986 to live with her sisters Florence R. Smothers; her godchild in Philadelphia was Linda Jenkins who was more like a daughter and Mary Stewart of Darlington was her "road buddy" and they were inseparable; she was preceded in death by a sister Marine Johnson and two brothers Charles V. and John A. Johnson; she worked many years as a domestic and died (place was not stated) and was survived by four brothers, six sisters, three sisters-in-law and three godchildren) [Clark's U. M. Church Cemetery]

Johnson, Pearl died October 30, 1918, age about 17 (no tombstone; death certificate stated she was the daughter of Thomas Johnson and Anna Meek, all of Havre de Grace, all born in Virginia) [St. James United Cemetery]

Johnson, Phoeba died October 2, 1918, age about 80 (no tombstone; death certificate stated she was born in Maryland, the daughter of Nero Hollis, but her mother's name was not known to informant Elias Hollis, of Aberdeen; she was a widow and died at Kalmia) [Asbury Cemetery]

Johnson, Priscilla died July 9, 1941, age about 77 (no tombstone; death certificate stated she born in Maryland, the daughter of Mollie Johnson, born in Maryland, but her father's name was not known to informant Mrs. Della Moore, of Bel Air; she was single and died at home in Bel Air where she had lived for 9 years) [Berkley Memorial Cemetery]

Johnson, Rebecca 1868-1924 (copied in 1987, not listed in 2002, not found in 2018) [Gravel Hill Cemetery]

Johnson, Richard March 18, 1874 – February 1, 1933 (no tombstone; death certificate stated he was born in Towson, MD, the son of William Johnson, born in Maryland, and Carroll Smith, born in Bel Air; he married Maggie ----, worked as a day laborer in Bel Air and died at home at 109 Alice Ann Street; informant was his wife Mrs. Maggie Johnson, of Bel Air) [Tabernacle Mount Zion U. M. Church Cemetery]

Johnson, Richard Wellington May 23, 1904 – June 6, 1915 (no tombstone; death certificate stated he was born in Baltimore, the son of Richard W. Johnson, born in Mississippi, and Sarah Rollins, born in Baltimore; he accidentally drowned in Bel Air; informant was his mother Sarah Dorsey) [Fairview A. M. E. Church Cemetery]

Johnson, Riley died August 29, 1977, age 77 (no tombstone; obituary in *The Aegis* state he was a veteran of World War I, worked as a farmer, lived on Coen Road in Rocks and was the husband of the late Janie S. Johnson; he died at Perry Point VAMC, survived by three sons, four daughters, a brother, a sister, 24 grandchildren and four great-grandchildren; military records stated he was born at Slate Hill, PA on April 5, 1896 and was inducted into the service at "Maryland St., Dublin, Harford Co." on September 1, 1918, served in Co. D., 811 Pioneer Inf., was overseas from October 20, 1918 to July 4, 1919 and honorably discharged on July 10, 1919) [Chestnut

Grove A. M. E. Church Cemetery, formerly LaGrange Cemetery at Rocks]

Johnson, Rita Odessa – see Ruth O. Johnson [Gravel Hill Cemetery]

Johnson, Robert March 6, 1926 – September 26, 1986, STM1, U.S. Navy, World War II (tombstone; obituary in *The Aegis* on October 2, 1986 stated Robert Spencer Johnson served two years in the Navy, was the husband of Lena M. Johnson, of Darlington, and died at the Perry Point VAMC, survived by his wife, one son Robert L. Murray, three sisters Agnes White, Alice L. Murray and Esther Ann Dorsey, and one brother Clarence Johnson, Sr.) [Cedars Chapel Cemetery]

Johnson, Roberta Jane died December 21, 1967, age 86 (no tombstone; obituary in *The Aegis* on January 4, 1968 stated she was the widow of George W. Johnson, of Rock Ridge Road in Rocks, and died at Citizens Nursing Home in Havre de Grace; no surviving family members were named) [Chestnut Grove A. M. E. Church Cemetery, formerly LaGrange Cemetery at Rocks]

Johnson, Ruth O. died July 14, 1993, age not given (copied in 1987, but not found in 2018; obituary and photo in *The Aegis* stated Ruth Odessa Johnson was a retired school teacher who married Augustus H. Johnson in 1969 and was a member of NAACP, the Johnson Singers, and the Willing Workers; she died at Harford Memorial Hospital, survived by husband, mother Frances Dorsey, aunts and uncles; obituary without the photo appeared in *The Aegis* on August 18, 1993 and gave the same information for a Rita Odessa Johnson) [Gravel Hill Cemetery]

Johnson, Sabina August 20, 1854 – July 23, 1915 (no tombstone; death certificate stated she was the daughter of William Archer and Casanda *(sic)* Archer, all born in Maryland; she married and died at home in Darlington; informant was Georgeanna Johnson, of Darlington) [Berkley Memorial Cemetery]

Johnson, Samuel James died June 29, 1993, age 70 (no tombstone; obituary in *The Aegis* on July 7, 1993 stated he was born in Wilmington, DE, the son of Charles Johnson and Mary Hayward, and served in the Army in World War II; he lived in Aberdeen, was a chef for various restaurants and died at the Perry Point VAMC, survived by his wife Mildred Ringgold, a brother George Johnson, and sisters Elizabeth Coston and Barbara Johnson, both of Delaware) [Mt. Calvary U. A. M. E. Church Cemetery]

Johnson, Sandra Jean, "Beloved Mother" and "Mom Mom Sam" April 2, 1947 – March 17, 2013 (tombstone inscription; funeral notice and photo in *The Aegis* on March 22, 2013 stated she died at home in Bel Air) [Berkley Memorial Cemetery]

Johnson, Sarah, "Mother" 1865-1933 (on same tombstone with William Johnson; death certificate stated she was born in Virginia on December 31, 1867, the daughter of William Braxton and Betsy Woods, and she died on April 26, 1933, the widow of William Johnson) [Union U. M. Church Cemetery]

Johnson, Sarah C., "Loving Wife, Mother and Grandmother" February 3, 1957 – July 24, 2017 [Berkley Memorial Cemetery]

Johnson, Sarah E. March 12, 1867 – December 16, 1931 (no tombstone; death certificate stated she was the daughter of William Beals and Emma Sears, and the widow of Richard Johnson) [St. James United Cemetery]

Johnson, Sarah E. November 29, 1883 – October 5, 1946 (no tombstone; death certificate stated she was the daughter of Samuel Harts and Mary Dallam, and widow of Daniel A. Johnson) [Union U. M. Church Cemetery]

Johnson, Sarah G. October 30, 1929 – January 27, 2011 (on the same tombstone with Harry D. Johnson and inscribed "The Lord is my Shepherd, I shall not want;" obituary and photo in *The Aegis* on February 2, 2011 stated Sarah Gladys Rice Johnson was one of five children born to Vallee and Helen Rice, of Bel Air, and she was employed by the Perry Point VAMC for 40 years; she was survived by her husband Harry F. Johnson, four children and a brother McKinley Rice; she was preceded in death by three siblings, Creola, Edna, and Vallee) [Clark's U. M. Church Cemetery]

Johnson, Sarah J. Mrs. died December 28, 1916, age 59 (no tombstone; death certificate stated she was born in Annapolis, the daughter of George Reed, but her mother's name and place of birth were not known to informant J. S. Johnson, of Aberdeen) [Mt. Calvary U. A. M. E. Church Cemetery]

Johnson, Sarah Louisa April 4, 1931 – July 28, 1931 (no tombstone; death certificate stated she was the daughter of Benjamin Johnson and Beulah Lee, all born in Maryland; they lived at Ady; informant was Benjamin

Johnson, of Street RFD) [Clark's U. M. Church Cemetery]

Johnson, Sarah W. March 6, 1874 – February 28, 1935 (no tombstone; death certificate stated she was the daughter of Stephen H. Wilson and Hannah Presberry, all born in Harford Co., married Lewis W. Johnson and died in Darlington where they lived for 25 years; informant was her husband) [Berkley Memorial Cemetery]

Johnson, Shadrach, husband of Amelia Johnson, died December 12, 1903 (1908?), age 72 years, 9 months and 1 day (inscribed "In Memory of" and included a verse that was weathered and illegible) [Asbury Cemetery]

Johnson, Shadrach, son of Shadrach and Amelia Johnson, died December 1, 1901, age 23 years, 2 months and 24 days (inscribed with an illegible verse) [Asbury Cemetery]

Johnson, Sheldon 1951-2005 (small metal funeral home marker; obituary and photo in *The Aegis* on March 23, 2005 stated Sheldon L. "Shellie" Johnson was born February 26, 1951 in Havre de Grace and worked 23 years at Hazelton Systems; during his early life he lived with his aunt and uncle Delores and Isaac "Bug" Cole in Rockville; he later returned to Havre de Grace and spent time with his siblings, mother and grandmother the late Ella Bordley in Aberdeen; he died at Lorien Nursing and Rehabilitation Center in Belcamp on March 12, 2005, survived by two sons, a daughter, his mother Ella Mae Patten, three sisters, two brothers, an uncle, and nieces and nephews; he was predeceased by his grandmother, a brother, an uncle, an aunt, and his grandfather Isaac Cole) [St. James United Cemetery]

Johnson, Stanley Otis April 25, 1951 – March 20, 1991 [Union U. M. Church Cemetery]

Johnson, Steve W. Jr. September 20, 1964 – October 3, 2008, U.S. Army (tombstone; funeral notice and photo in *The Aegis* on October 8, 2008 stated he lived in Havre de Grace) [St. James United Cemetery]

Johnson, Theodore R. 1900-1976 (small metal funeral home marker; obituary in *The Aegis* stated "Ted" was born in Kalmia, the son of George and Lettie Johnson, married Joan Giles, lived on David Road in Street, and was a custodian at Highland Elementary School for 24 years prior to his retirement in 1965; he was survived by his wife, 3 sons, 5 daughters, a step-daughter and 12 grandchildren) [Clark's U. M. Church Cemetery]

Johnson, Veronica D., "Monie" April 7, 1961 – February 17, 2003 (tombstone inscription with her photo) [St. James United Cemetery]

Johnson, Walter H. March 4, 1883 – April 2, 1927 (no tombstone; death certificate stated he was the son of Henry and Martha Johnson, all born in Maryland; he was married, worked as a farm hand and died at home near Monkton; informant was his wife Elizabeth Johnson) [West Liberty Church Cemetery]

Johnson, William, "Father" 1845-1933 (on same tombstone with Sarah Johnson; death certificate stated he was born in West Virginia on March 1, 1857 and his wife Sarah did not know his parents; he died on April 7, 1933 in Aberdeen) [Union U. M. Church Cemetery]

Johnson, William C. July 4, 1888 – August 10, 1963 [West Liberty Church Cemetery]

Johnson, William Carroll September 12, 1884 – November 22, 1911 (no tombstone; death certificate stated he was born in Harford Co., the son of George Johnson and Lizzie Hollingsworth, both born in Maryland, and worked as a laborer near Churchville; informant's name was not given) [Asbury Cemetery]

Johnson, William E. August 25, 1887 – March 18, 1918 (no tombstone; death certificate stated he was married, worked as a machinist and lived in Emmorton; his parents were Charles H. Johnson and Alice R. Collins and they were all born in Harford Co.; informant was Alice R. Collins, of Emmorton) [Hendon Hill Cemetery]

Johnson, William E. November 20, 1896 – December 1, 1977, PFC, U.S. Army, World War I (tombstone; military record stated he was born at Churchville on November 20, 1897 *(sic)*, resided at Bel Air RFD #1 when inducted on September 1, 1918, served in Co. D., 811 Pioneer Inf. and then in Co. C, 63 Pioneer Inf., and was honorably discharged on December 18, 1918; obituary in *The Aegis* on December 8, 1977 stated William Elwood Johnson, son of Daniel and Mary E. Johnson, of Churchville, was a retired dietetic supervisor at the Perry Point VA Hospital and died at age 81 in Harford Memorial Hospital) [Asbury Cemetery]

Johnson, William E. December 29, 1933 – March 5, 1934 (no tombstone; death certificate stated he was the son of LeRoy Johnson and Vivian Brown) [Union U. M. Church Cemetery]

Johnson, William H. died July 10, 1908, age 3 years, 6 months (no tombstone; death certificate stated he was the son of Joshua Johnson and Hannah -----de (illegible), of Thomas Run; written on the back of the certificate is "Asbury") [Asbury Cemetery]

Johnson, William H. June 5, 1915 – June 17 1915, was a premature birth at 7½ months (no tombstone; death certificate stated he was the son of Howard Johnson and Bessie Holland, all were born in Maryland; informant was his father, of Fallston RFD) [West Liberty Church Cemetery]

Johnson, William Henry, "Son" 1939-1947 [Mt. Zion U. M. Church Cemetery]

Johnson, William Nelson March 5, 1874 – March 25, 1936 (no tombstone; death certificate stated he was the son of Nathaniel Johnson and Eliza Chambers, all born in Churchville; he was single and was a farmer at Havre de Grace RFD #1; informant was Franklin Johnson, also of RFD #1) [Asbury Cemetery]

Johnston, Amanda February 10, 1846 – January 25, 1919 (no tombstone; death certificate stated she was born in Maryland, was a single maid and died at Pylesville; names and places of birth of her parents were not known to informant John T. Krmka *(sic)*, of Pyleville) [William C. Rice Memorial Cemetery, St. James U. M. Church]

Jolly, Julia 1877 – March 9, 1912 (no tombstone; death certificate stated she was the daughter of James Bond and Julia Bond, all born in Maryland; she was married and died at gome near Dublin; informant was Samuel Jolly, of Street, MD) [Clark's U. M. Church Cemetery]

Jones, --- May 29, 1925 – June 1, 1925 (no tombstone; death certificate stated he was the son of James Joshua Jones and Ennara(?) Oleita Gilbert, all born in Maryland [William C. Rice Memorial Cemetery, St. James U. M. Church]

Jones, Addison January 28, 1878 – March 2, 1945 (no tombstone; death certificate stated he was the son of Sylvester Jones and Mary Washington, all born in Maryland; he was a farmer near Aberdeen and died at Harford Memorial Hospital; informant was his wife Mary Jones) [Green Spring U. M. Church Cemetery]

Jones, Agnes R. (Mrs.) December 10, 1889 – August 21, 1937 (no tombstone; death certificate stated she was the daughter of Welmore James and Ella Christy, and the wife of Edmond Jones) [St. James United Cemetery]

Jones, Alfred died December 20, 1915, age 53 (no tombstone; death certificate stated he was the son of Alfred Jones, both born in Virginia, but the name of his mother was not known to informant George T. Pennington, Undertaker, of Havre de Grace) [Union U. M. Church Cemetery]

Jones, Alice 1848-1933 (on same tombstone with Eller D. Jones and William Jones; death certificate of Alice Jones states born March 15, 1866 and died April 21, 1933, widow of Austin) [St. James United Cemetery]

Jones, Alpheus, "Husband" 1914-2001 (on same tombstone with wife Lila M. Jones) [Community Baptist Church Cemetery]

Jones, Alvin L. March 7, 1952 – April 20, 2009, Sgt., U.S. Army [St. James United Cemetery]

Jones, Anny April 12, 1843 – April 14, 1911 (no tombstone; death certificate stated she was the daughter of Benjamin Carr and Rachel Harris, all born in Somerset Co., MD; she worked as a servant and died a widow in Bel Air; informant was Emily Ruff, of Bel Air) [Mt. Zion U. M. Church Cemetery]

Jones, Arthur M. 1897-1983 [Berkley Memorial Cemetery]

Jones, Austin died December 22, 1912, age about 60 (no tombstone; death certificate stated he was born in Virginia, parents unknown, and was married, wife unknown; informant William Jones, of Havre de Grace) [St. James United Cemetery]

Jones, Baby stillborn female on April 11, 1916 (no tombstone; death certificate stated she was born and died in Pylesville, the daughter of James Jones and Oleta Amoss, both of Maryland) [William C. Rice Memorial Cemetery, St. James U. M. Church]

Jones, Baby stillborn male on May 27, 1926 (no tombstone; death certificate stated he was the son of Leonard Jones and Hazel Stansbury; informant James Stansbury, of Havre de Grace) [Union U. M. Church Cemetery]

Jones, C. 1994 (handwritten on a flat cement slab) [St. James United Cemetery]

Jones, Celesta E. July 4, 1871 – November 26, 1942 (no tombstone; death certificate stated she was the daughter of Robert Brown and the widow of William Jones; mother unknown to informant Leo Jones, of Havre de Grace) [St. James United Cemetery]

Jones, Charles Clifton October 21, 1913 – December 22, 1913 (no tombstone; death certificate stated he was born in Havre de Grace, the son of Charles Alfred Jones, born in Delaware, and Lucy Johnson, born in Maryland; informant was Charles A. Jones, of Havre de Grace) [Gravel Hill Cemetery]

Jones, Charles E. October 22, 1920 – January 12, 1989 [Fairview A. M. E. Church Cemetery]

Jones, Charles H. died March 4, 1988, age 90 (no tombstone; obituary in the *Delta Star* on March 10, 1988 stated "Merryman" was born in Harford County and was the husband of the late Frances Whye Smith; formerly of Delta RFD #1, he died at the Heatherbank Nursing Center in Columbia, survived by two step-children and nieces and nephews) [William C. Rice Memorial Cemetery, St. James U. M. Church]

Jones, Charles Wesley May 13, 1898 – December 3, 1932 (no tombstone; death certificate stated he was the son of Lloyd Taylor and Ida Preston, all were born in Harford Co.; he married Margaret Hemore, worked as a laborer for a contractor, lived at 123 S. Washington St. and died in Havre de Grace Hospital; informant was Will Taylor, of Havre de Grace) [Gravel Hill Cemetery]

Jones, Charlie 1874-1925 (no dates on tombstone; death certificate of Charles W. Jones stated he died on January 6, 1925, age about 51, worked as a farmer and died a widower in Havre de Grace; his parents were not known to informant Miss Ida Preston, of Havre de Grace) [Gravel Hill Cemetery]

Jones, Clifford E. 1918-1928 (tombstone; death certificate stated he was born September 19, 1918 and died February 21, 1928; see Florence E. Jones) [St. James United Cemetery]

Jones, Cornelia E. July 1, 1923 -   [Berkley Memorial Cemetery]

Jones, Cornelius Jr. August 26, 1926 – October 17, 1971, Maryland, PFC, Co. B., 229 Engineer Bn, World War II [Berkley Memorial Cemetery]

Jones, Cornelius Jr. died October 17, 1971, age not given (no tombstone; obituary in *The Aegis* stated he was the son of Mrs. Margaret Jones and the late Cornelius Jones, Sr., of 330 Wilson Street in Havre de Grace; he was a veteran of World War II and died at the Perry Point Veterans Administration Hospital, survived by his mother, 1 daughter, 2 brothers, 4 sisters, and 1 granddaughter) [Tabernacle Mount Zion U. M. Church Cemetery]

Jones, Curtis E. February 12, 1923 – May 22, 1981 (tombstone copied in 1987 as Curtis Eugene Jones, yet when viewed in 2018 there was no middle name, only a middle initial E.) [Fairview A. M. E. Church Cemetery]

Jones, Derrick Allan December 12, 1981 – March 15, 2005 (inscribed "Our Beloved. His courage, his smile, his grace, gladdened the heart" and included his photo) [St. James United Cemetery]

Jones, Doretha B. 1915-1982 [Berkley Memorial Cemetery]

Jones, E. Oleater 1892-1950 (on same tombstone with James J. Jones; death certificate stated Emma Oleater Jones was born in Jarrettsville on December 19, 1892, the daughter of James Amoss and Mary Elizabeth Kell; she was married and died at home on June 25, 1950 at Upper Cross Roads, Fallston RFD, where she had lived for five years; informant was James J. Jones, of Fallston) [Fairview A. M. E. Church Cemetery]

Jones, Edith Eliza May 14, 1932 – June 1, 1932 (no tombstone; death certificate stated she was the daughter of Charles Jones and Margaret Hemore; informant was Margaret Jones, of Churchville) [Asbury Cemetery]

Jones, Eliza, wife of Joshua Jones, August 18, 1823 – February 10, 1910 [Chestnut Grove A. M. E. Church Cemetery, formerly LaGrange Cemetery at Rocks]

Jones, Elizabeth C. June 2, 1905 – September 2, 1964 (inscribed "Asleep in Jesus") [Asbury Cemetery]

Jones, Ella December 24, 1892 – August 28, 1927 (no tombstone; death certificate stated she was the daughter of Cornillus Byrd and Emlie Doughswell, all born in Virginia, and she was a widow in Havre de Grace; informant was Edward Hilton, of Havre de Grace RFD) [Green Spring U. M. Church Cemetery]

Jones, Ella May October 28, 1879 – November 12, 1918 (no tombstone; death certificate stated she was the daughter of March Evans and Susan Taylor, all born in Maryland; she was married and died at home at Rocks; informant was Bessie Buchanan, of Jarrettsville) [Chestnut Grove A. M. E. Church Cemetery, formerly LaGrange Cemetery at Rocks]

Jones, Eller D. 1841-1942 (on same tombstone with Alice and William Jones) [St. James United Cemetery]

Jones, Emma August 20, 1912 – August 28, 1934 (no tombstone; death certificate stated she was the daughter of Levon Freeman and Mary Brown, all born in North Carolina, and wife of the informant James Jones, of Havre de Grace) [St. James United Cemetery]

Jones, Emma C. August 19, 1926 – October 15, 1925 (no tombstone; death certificate stated she was the daughter of Arthur M. Jones, of Delaware, and Forezelia Lehman, of Maryland) [St. James United Cemetery]

Jones, Eric Christopher, "Father, Son, Brother, Friend" October 22, 1981 – January 28, 2015 [Clark's U. M. Church Cemetery

Jones, Ernest O. October 7, 1923 – May 26, 2001, Cpl., U.S. Army, World War II [Berkley Memorial Cemetery]

Jones, Ernest, "Beloved Husband, Father, Grandfather, Brother and Friend" April 1, 1948 – October 22, 2015 (tombstone with his photo) [St. James United Cemetery]

Jones, Estella C. August 16, 1896 – November 3, 1983 (tombstone; obituary in *The Aegis* on November 9, 1983 stated Estella C. Jones was born on Gravel Hill, the daughter of George Bond and Amelia Harris, and was the widow of James R. Jones; she lived in Aberdeen and died at Harford Memorial Hospital in Havre de Grace) [Gravel Hill Cemetery]

Jones, Estella M. 1904-1985 (copied in 1987, but not found in 2018; obituary in *The Aegis* stated Estella Miller Jones was born in Harford County, the daughter of William Hubert Jones and Margaret Miller, married William J. Jones, lived in Havre de Grace, died on February 23, 1985 at the Laurelwood Nursing Home in Elkton and was survived by her husband, a son Leslie Long, and a brother Robert Warren) [Berkley Memorial Cemetery]

Jones, Fannie Lee June 11, 1927 - January 13, 1995 (tombstone; James Dorsey Card File, African American Obituaries, maintained at the Historical Society of Harford County, has a card for her with an obituary from *The Aegis* stating she was born in Flemingsbury, KY and died at Fallston General Hospital; she was the mother of the late William Jones and was survived by her husband of 47 years Perry Thomas Jones, four daughters, two sons, three sisters, two brothers, 13 grandchildren and 3 great-grandchildren) [St. James United Cemetery]

Jones, Florence (no dates recorded in 1987, not listed in 2002, and not found in 2018) [Gravel Hill Cemetery]

Jones, Florence E. 1921-2001 (small metal funeral home marker next to tombstone of Clifford E. Jones) [St. James United Cemetery]

Jones, Franklin D. "Stump" March 19, 1939 – January 20, 1992 [Berkley Memorial Cemetery]

Jones, Genevieve W. 1917-2010 (on same tombstone with Ishmael C. Jones; obituary and photo in *The Aegis* on November 3, 2010 stated Genevieve Webster Presberry Jones was born on May 9, 1917, the daughter of Carroll James and Annie Webster, and died on October 11, 2010 at the Hart Heritage Estate Assisted Living in Street; she was known to many as "Aunt Genny" and was preceded in death by first husband Wilson Presberry and second husband Ishmael Jones; she was survived by a daughter Christine Presberry Tolbert, a sister Nina Dorsey, a grandson, two great-granddaughters, a foster great-grandson, and many other relatives; she is also presented in *A Journey Through Berkley*, p. 73) [Berkley Memorial Cemetery]

Jones, George Franklin January 3, 1911 – April 23, 1911 (no tombstone; death certificate stated he was born in Harford Co., the son of George R. Jones, born in Harford Co., and Mamie E. Hacket, born in Wilmington, DE; he was buried at Mountain Colored Church; informant was his father George R. Jones of Wheel) [Mt. Zion U. M. Church Cemetery]

Jones, George R. November 23, 1888 – December 11, 1955 (on same tombstone with Mary E. Jones) [Mt. Zion U. M. Church Cemetery]

Jones, Gertrude Joyner died on September 14, 1993, age 56 (no tombstone; James Dorsey Card File, African

American Obituaries, maintained at the Historical Society of Harford County, has a card for her with an obituary from *The Aegis* on September 29, 1993 stating she was born in Sampson Co., NC, moved to Havre de Grace as a child, then moved to Elizabeth, NJ, returned to Maryland and worked at the Perry Point VAMC; she enjoyed collecting photos and mementos of family and friends; she had been married to John T. Jones, of Chicago, and died at Harford Memorial Hospital, survived by a daughter, four brothers and two granddaughters) [St. James United Cemetery]

Jones, Glenn L. July 15, 1969 – January 8, 1995 (inscribed "Your Loving Wife" and "In Memory Of" on a heart-shaped tombstone) [St. James United Cemetery]

Jones, H. P. (no dates when copied in 1987, but not found on 2018) [St. James United Cemetery]

Jones, Harriett A. died September 26, 1922, age about 59 (no tombstone; death certificate stated she was the daughter of Stephen Preston, both born in Maryland, but the name and birth place of her mother was not known to informant Charles Jones, of Gravelly, Havre de Grace RFD; she was married, died at Earlton and was buried at Gravelly Hill) [Gravel Hill Cemetery]

Jones, Harriett February 1, 1860 – August 18, 1918 (no tombstone; death certificate stated she was born in Maryland, married and died at Rocks; the names and birth places of her parents were not known to informant Preston Clark, of Rocks) [William C. Rice Memorial Cemetery, St. James U. M. Church]

Jones, Hazel E. July 4, 1920 -   (on same tombstone with Michael D. Gunter and B. Rosetta Gunter) [St. James United Cemetery]

Jones, Hazel V. August 11, 1907 – April 4, 1983 [Union U. M. Church Cemetery]

Jones, Infant (female) July 12, 1916 – July 13, 1916 (no tombstone; death certificate stated she was the premature daughter of William Jones and Irene Hawkins, of Havre de Grace) [St. James United Cemetery]

Jones, Infant (female) stillborn on July 18, 1916 (no tombstone; death certificate stated she was the daughter of Charles Jones, of Newark, DE, and Susie Johnson, of Havre de Grace) [St. James United Cemetery]

Jones, Iola May 23, 1873 – January 6, 1890 (on same obelisk with Sylvester Jones and Virgie Jones) [Green Spring U. M. Church Cemetery]

Jones, Isaac O. April 12, 1876 – February 25, 1941 (no tombstone; death certificate stated he was the son of Sylvester Jones and Mary E. Washington, all born in Harford County; he was a crop farmer at Aldino and was married to Lillian ---- at the time of his death; informant was Addison Jones, of Aberdeen RFD) [Green Spring U. M. Church Cemetery]

Jones, Ishmael C. 1918-   (on same tombstone with Genevieve W. Jones) [Berkley Memorial Cemetery]

Jones, James died May 5, 1909, age about 75 (no tombstone; death notice in *The Aegis* on May 7, 1909 stated he was in the Jarrett family for nearly 40 years and died in the employ of Charles H. Amoss of Jarrettsville; place of burial was not given, but possibly at St. James Church) [William C. Rice Memorial Cemetery, St. James U. M. Church]

Jones, James September 29, 1926 – October 26, 1926 (no dates on the tombstone; death certificate stated James W. Jones was the son of Charlie Jones and Margaret Hemore, all were born in Maryland, and lived in Havre de Grace; informant was his father Charlie Jones) [Gravel Hill Cemetery]

Jones, James E. 1914-1982 (on same tombstone with Marjorie B. Jones; James Dorsey Card File, African American Obituaries, maintained at the Historical Society of Harford County, has a card for him stating James Ellwood Jones, born April 1, 1914, died September 15, 1982) [Fairview A. M. E. Church Cemetery]

Jones, James E. died April 14, 1887, age 55 ("In Memory of" with an illegible verse) [Asbury Cemetery]

Jones, James J. 1889-1985 (on same tombstone with E. Oleater Jones; obituary in *The Aegis* on April 25, 1985 stated James Joshua Jones, of Cooptown, formerly of Fallston, died on April 21, 1985 at Eastpoint Nursing Home; his wife Oleater Amos Jones predeceased him; he was survived by 3 daughters, 5 sons, 12 grandchildren, 6 great-grandchildren, and a brother) [Fairview A. M. E. Church Cemetery]

Jones, John May 12, 1852 – November 18, 1917 (no tombstone; death certificate stated he was born in Virginia, but the names and birth places of his parents were not known to informant Ella Jones, of Aberdeen RFD; he was married, worked as a day laborer and died at Aldino) [Green Spring U. M. Church Cemetery]

Jones, John H. April 4, 1871 – October 20, 1933 (no tombstone; death certificate stated he was born in Baltimore, the son of Susie Jones, but his father's name was not known to informant George Jones, of Bel Air; he married Sarah ----, worked as a day laborer in Bel Air and died widow at home at 111 N. Bond Street) [Tabernacle Mount Zion U. M. Church Cemetery]

Jones, John Rush July 12, 1877 – April 18, 1932 (no tombstone; death certificate stated he was born in Harford Co., worked as a farm laborer at Rocks and died a widower; his parents were Joshua Jones, born in Harford Co., and "Sarah Louise ?" *(sic)* whose place of birth was not known to informant Jane Johnson, of Rocks) [Chestnut Grove A. M. E. Church Cemetery, formerly LaGrange Cemetery at Rocks]

Jones, John Rush Jr. August 17, 1908 – February 22, 1911 (no tombstone; death certificate stated he was born in Jarrettsville, the son of John Rush Jones and Ella May Evans; informant was his father) [Fairview A. M. E. Church Cemetery]

Jones, John W. January 22, 1891 – September 9, 1928 (no tombstone; death certificate stated he was born at "Rocks, Deer Creek, MD," the son of John W. Jones and Sarah James, both born in Maryland; he was married and a mechanic and accidentally fell from the third story porch of Havre de Grace Hospital and died; informant was Mrs. John W. Jones, of Rocks) [Tabernacle Mount Zion U. M. Church Cemetery]

Jones, Johnnie Lee died March 13, 1991, age 82 (no tombstone; James Dorsey Card File, African American Obituaries, maintained at the Historical Society of Harford County, has a card for him with an obituary from *The Aegis* on March 20, 1991 stating he was born Grogetown, GA, the son of Johnnie L. and Mary Lou Jones, married Nettie M. ----, served in the Army in World War II and was discharged in October, 1945; he worked as a general contractor at Aberdeen Proving Ground, lived in Aberdeen and died at Harford Memorial Hospital, survived by his wife, a son Jimmie Lee Jones, and a brother and a sister) [Mt. Calvary U. A. M. E. Church Cemetery]

Jones, Joseph Henry born about 1898 – November 3, 1947 (no tombstone; death certificate stated he was the son of George Jones and Emma Jones, and died a widower at 520 Young St. in Havre de Grace) [Union U. M. Church Cemetery]

Jones, Josephine died May 28, 1938, age about 50 (no tombstone; death certificate stated she was the wife of Alfred Jones and the daughter of William Jackson, mother unknown) [Union U. M. Church Cemetery]

Jones, Joshua J. (no tombstone; death certificate stated he was born July 29, 1827 in Harford Co., the son of ---- Jones and ---- (mother's name and birth place unknown), worked as a laborer and was a widower at the time of his death in Jarrettsville on April 29, 1914; informant was Florence Thomas, of Jarrettsville) [Chestnut Grove A. M. E. Church Cemetery, formerly LaGrange Cemetery at Rocks]

Jones, Laura R. March 1, 1902 – August 28, 1919 (no tombstone; death certificate she was the daughter of Sam A. Jones, of Virginia, and Delia Waters, of Havre de Grace) [St. James United Cemetery]

Jones, Leonard Austin Sr. died July 16, 1990, age 87 (no tombstone; James Dorsey Card File, African American Obituaries, maintained at the Historical Society of Harford County, has a card for him with an obituary from *The Aegis* on July 25, 1990 stating he was born in Nashville, TN and was the husband of the late Hazel V. Stansbury; from the age of 11 and for the next 64 years he worked with horses, as an exercise boy, walker and then jockey; formerly of Havre de Grace, he died in Washington, D.C., survived by a son Leonard A. Jr., two grandchildren and two great-grandchildren) [Union U. M. Church Cemetery]

Jones, Levenia March 28, 1880 – October 15, 1925 (no tombstone; death certificate stated she was the daughter of Samuel Gibson and Elizabeth Banks, and all were born in Maryland; she was married at the time of her death in Havre de Grace Hospital; informant was William Gibson, of Vale) [Asbury Cemetery]

Jones, Lila M., "Wife" 1917-1969 (on same tombstone with husband Alpheus Jones; obituary in *The Aegis* on June 12, 1969 stated she was the wife of Althens (actually Alpheus) Jones, of Joppa, and she died at the Johns Hopkins Hospital on June 4, 1969, survived by her husband, two sons, five sisters, two brothers, and three grandchildren) [Community Baptist Church Cemetery]

Jones, Lillie A. January 2, 1871 – January 15, 1967 [Union U. M. Church Cemetery]

Jones, Louisa died April 9, 1905, age 75 (no tombstone; death notice in *The Aegis* on April 14, 1905 stated she died at the home of her daughter Polly Amos near Jarrettsville; she was a servant to the Miller family during slavery times and for some years past she had been employed by William Hope; place of burial not given [possibly William C. Rice Memorial Cemetery, St. James U. M. Church]

Jones, Margaret March 28, 1907 – October 5, 1936 (no tombstone; death certificate stated she was the daughter of Jarrett Jones and Mary Bordley, all born in Maryland; she was single, lived in Bel Air, was a cook at the Harford County jail and died in an auto accident on Bel Air Road, one mile south of Bel Air; informant was Mary Bordley, of Bel Air) [Green Spring U. M. Church Cemetery]

Jones, Marie B. April 29, 1926 – October 6, 2007 (inscribed "In Loving Memory" with her photo) [Community Baptist Church Cemetery]

Jones, Marion B. 1910-1986 [Berkley Memorial Cemetery]

Jones, Marjorie 1919-   (on same tombstone with James E. Jones) [Fairview A. M. E. Church Cemetery]

Jones, Mary B. April 9, 1881 – March 17, 1951 (no tombstone; death certificate stated she was born in Darlington, the daughter of Richard Bowser and Ellen Parson; she was a widow and lived in rural Bel Air; informant was Pearl Smith who also lived in rural Bel Air) [Green Spring U. M. Church Cemetery]

Jones, Mary E. June 27, 1888 – June 20, 1958 (on same tombstone with George R. Jones) [Mt. Zion U. M. Church Cemetery]

Jones, Mary E. March 27, 1854 – January 26, 1931 (no tombstone; death certificate stated she was the daughter of Isaac Washington and Maria Hopkins, all born in Maryland; she lived at Level and died a widow; informant was Isaac Jones, of Havre de Grace) [Green Spring U. M. Church Cemetery]

Jones, Mary Elizabeth July 12, 1915 – October 19, 1915 (no tombstone; death certificate stated she was born at Rocks, the daughter of John Rush Jones, born in Harford Co., and Ella M. Evans, born in Maryland; informant was J. Rush Jones, of Rocks) [West Liberty Church Cemetery]

Jones, Mary Hazel February 23, 1917 – July 27, 1918 (no tombstone; death certificate stated she was the daughter of James J. Jones and E. Oleater Amos, all born in Maryland; she died at home in Pylesville; her father was informant) [William C. Rice Memorial Cemetery, St. James U. M. Church]

Jones, Mary L. died April 8, 1901 (1904?) (illegible), age 75 years, 2 months and 15 days [West Liberty Church Cemetery]

Jones, Mary Louise – see Mary Louise Pringle [Chestnut Grove A. M. E. Church Cemetery]

Jones, Melvin L. Sr. November 26, 1928 – October 9, 1998 [Fairview A. M. E. Church Cemetery]

Jones, Michelle Daily Sunrise December 16, 1969 – Sunset July 22, 2010 (inscribed "Loving Memories" and "Mom and the Family" with a long poem and her photo) [Berkley Memorial Cemetery]

Jones, Nettie M. November 11, 1911 – June 16, 1998 (no tombstone; James Dorsey Card File, African American Obituaries, that is maintained at the Historical Society of Harford County, has a card with obituary from an unidentified newspaper on July 2, 1997 stated she was born in Jefferson, GA, the daughter of Preston and Lizzie Marion, and in 1942 she moved to Maryland and married Johnnie Lee Jones who preceded her in death; she lived in Aberdeen and died at Harford Memorial Hospital in Havre de Grace, survived by a son, four sisters and a host of nieces and nephews) [Mt. Calvary U. A. M. E. Church Cemetery]

Jones, Ocellous February 18, 1930 – February 14, 1971, Maryland, PFC, U.S. Marine Corps, Korea [Berkley Memorial Cemetery]

Jones, Oliver Angelo September 9, 1958 – May 27, 1979, AGHAA, U.S. Navy [St. James United Cemetery]

Jones, Oscar died November 17, 1914, age unknown (no tombstone; death certificate stated he was single and died in Havre de Grace Hospital, nothing further known) [St. James United Cemetery]

Jones, Perry Thomas June 10, 1921 – December 24, 2001, SFC, U.S. Army, World War II, Korea [St. James United Cemetery]

Jones, Rachel Ann died March 6, 1905, age 51 (no tombstone; death certificate stated she was the wife of Henry Jones and her father was John Smith; she was born in Harford Co. and died at Federal Hill; place of burial was not given [possibly William C. Rice Memorial Cemetery, St. James U. M. Church]

Jones, Randal O., "Our Darling" 1955-1957 (tombstone with image of a lamb) [Berkley Memorial Cemetery]

Jones, Rosie (no dates when copied in 1987, not listed in 2002 and not found in 2018) [Gravel Hill Cemetery]

Jones, Ruth M. January 22, 1946 – January 29, 1991 [Berkley Memorial Cemetery]

Jones, Sallie died December 3, 1928, age 59 (no tombstone; death certificate stated she was the daughter of Martha Smothers, both born in Maryland, but informant John H. Jones, of Bel Air, did not know her father's name; she was married and died in Bel Air) [Tabernacle Mount Zion U. M. Church Cemetery]

Jones, Sarah J. September 24, 1857 – August 3, 1926 (no tombstone; death certificate stated she was the widowed daughter of James R. Thomas and Elinor Mathews, of Havre de Grace) [St. James United Cemetery]

Jones, Sheila D. "Beloved Younger Sister" August 1967 – March 1968 (broken tombstone) [Berkley Memorial Cemetery]

Jones, Stella Miller (no dates copied in 1987, not listed in 2002 and not found in 2018) [Gravel Hill Cemetery]

Jones, Sylvester January 27, 1848 – February 4, 1915 (no tombstone; death certificate stated he was the son of John Jones and Margaret Bond, all born in Harford Co.; he worked as a laborer near Level and was married at the time of his death; informant was Annie Jones) [Green Spring U. M. Church Cemetery]

Jones, Sylvester June 2, 1888 – September 6, 1909 (on same obelisk with Virgie Jones and Iola Jones) [Green Spring U. M. Church Cemetery]

Jones, Terry Yom October 7, 1954 – August 27, 2001, SP4, U.S. Army [St. James United Cemetery]

Jones, Viola 1952-1982 (copied in 1987, but not found in 2018; obituary in *The Aegis* on January 14, 1982 stated Viola Serina Jones was born in Havre de Grace, the daughter of Lloyd Harris and Louise Norton, of Abingdon, and married Worthington W. Jones; they lived in Edgewood and she died at Johns Hopkins Hospital in Baltimore on January 4, 1982, age 29; she was survived by her husband, her parents, and a son Vandelle Harris; James Dorsey Card File, African American Obituaries, maintained at the Historical Society of Harford County, has a card for her stating Viola Serina Jones (neé Harris) was born on March 7, 1952 and died on January 4, 1982) [John Wesley U. M. E. Church Cemetery in Abingdon]

Jones, Virgie December 11, 1879 – January 14, 1906 (on same obelisk with Sylvester and Iola Jones) [Green Spring U. M. Church Cemetery]

Jones, Walter August 9, 1941 – August 4, 1946 (no tombstone; death certificate stated he was the son of Melvin Jones, of Terre Haute, IN, and Hazel Pinion, of Perryman, MD) [St. James United Cemetery]

Jones, Warren S. June 13, 1923 – October 4, 1981, U.S. Army, World War II [Union U. M. Church Cemetery]

Jones, William 1870-1922 (on same tombstone with Eller D. and Alice Jones; death certificate stated he was born on August 29, 1870 and died on October 14, 1922, the married son of Austin Jones, of Virginia, and Alice Berry, of Cecil Co., MD; informant was Mrs. William Jones, of Havre de Grace) [St. James United Cemetery]

Jones, William A., "Beloved Son" April 7, 1952 – October 27, 1987 [St. James United Cemetery]

Jones, William Francis June 27, 1819 – February 2, 1920 (no tombstone; death certificate stated he was the son of James Jones and Oleter Amos, all were born in Maryland; he died at Clermont Mills; informant was his father) [William C. Rice Memorial Cemetery, St. James U. M. Church]

Jones, William H. January 7, 1912 – June 29, 1938 (no tombstone; death certificate stated he was the son of Howard E. Jones and Mary E. Turner, and the husband of Fairybelle Joyner; he was swimming in a public place on the Susquehanna River and accidentally drowned) [Union U. M. Church Cemetery]

Jones, William McKinley died September 30, 1984, age 80 (no tombstone; obituary in *The Aegis* stated he was born in Bradshaw, the son of Jerimiah Jones and Laura Brown and the husband of Lucille Stiles Jones; he lived in Joppa, retired as a foreman from the B&O Railroad after more than 30 years of service and died at Franklin Square Hospital in Baltimore County) [Asbury Cemetery]

Jordan, Alberta F. 1905-1987 (tombstone; obituary in *The Aegis* on January 7, 1988 stated Alberta Frances Jordan, of Bel Air, died December 31, 1987 at Great Baltimore Medical Center; she was born near Darlington, the daughter of Lewis Gwynn and Carrie Bell, and was a former communion steward and a past president and chaplain of the Usher's Board at Clark's U. M. Church; she was employed by Mr. & Mrs. Thomas Schluderberg in Baltimore for nearly 20 years before joining the household of Brodnax Cameron, Sr., of Bel Air, and then for Mr. & Mrs. Talbot J. Albert, of Fallston; she was survived by a son, 3 sisters, 2 brothers, 4 grandchildren, and 2 great-grandchildren) [Clark's U. M. Church Cemetery]

Jordan, Anna M. May 8, 1868 – June 8, 1938 (no tombstone; death certificate stated she was the widow of Robert Jordan and the daughter of Ned Tilden and Sarah Harris; born on Spesutia Island) [Union U. M. Church Cemetery]

Jordan, Douglas Lewis November 17, 1954 – October 21, 1988 [Union U. M. Church Cemetery]

Jordan, Edward R. 1902-1970 (tombstone; obituary in *The Aegis* stated Edward Ross Jordan, husband of Alverta (Alberta) Jordan, of 1312 Prospect Mill Road, Bel Air, died on August 4, 1970 at Harford Memorial Hospital in Havre de Grace; son of Julius and Bertha Jordan; retired from Gulf Oil Corporation; he was survived by his wife, 1 son, 2 brothers, 3 sisters, and 2 grandchildren) [Clark's U. M. Church Cemetery]

Jordan, Lillian – see Lillian Johnson [St. James United Cemetery]

Jordan, Richard H. April 24, 1932 – March 16, 1993, U.S. Army, World War II, Korea [St. James United Cemetery]

Jordan, Robert August 22, 1848 – October 30, 1926 (no tombstone; death certificate stated he was the married son of Charlie Jordan and Mary Jordan; informant was Annie Mary Jordan) [Union U. M. Church Cemetery]

Jordan, Samuel Irving died January 22, 2015, age 79 (funeral notice and photo in *The Aegis* stated he lived in Aberdeen and died at Harford Memorial Hospital in Havre de Grace) [Berkley Memorial Cemetery]

Jordan, Silas died March 12, 1949, age about 50 (no tombstone; death certificate stated he was killed by a car on Route 7 in Aberdeen; no further information given) [St. James United Cemetery]

Joyner, Annie Amelia Swann 1918-1984 [St. James United Cemetery]

Joyner, Arlene C. 1930-1993 (names and dates handwritten on a flat cement slab; James Dorsey Card File, African American Obituaries, maintained at the Historical Society of Harford County, has a card for her with an obituary and photo from an unidentified newspaper dated June 2, 1993 stating Arlene Catherine Joyner, of Havre de Grace, the first black female barber in Harford County, was born in Havre de Grace, the daughter of Catherine Barnes and the late Charles Bond, and her husband was the late Norman Joyner; she attended the Apex Barbering School in Baltimore and for many years worked at the Perry Point VAMC; she was survived by her mother and brother, four sons, one daughter, 14 grandchildren, four sisters, five half-sisters, one half-brother and many other relatives) [St. James United Cemetery]

Joyner, Delores Frances died June 8, 1977, age 46 (no tombstone; obituary in *The Aegis* on June 16, 1977 stated she was the daughter of Mildred Trotter, of Brooklyn, NY, and the late Joseph Grant, and the wife of Peter Joyner; she lived at 550 Alliance St., Havre de Grace, and died at Johns Hopkins Hospital, survived by her husband, her mother, a son, a daughter, and a sister) [St. James United Cemetery]

Joyner, Frank September 25, 1888 – April 30, 1933 (no tombstone; death certificate stated he was the son of Henry Joyner, mother unknown, all born in South Carolina; he married Mable ---- and died in Havre de Grace; informant was Morris Joyner) [St. James United Cemetery]

Joyner, Gwendolyn 1953-2003 (handwritten on a flat cement slab) [St. James United Cemetery]

Joyner, James L. 1934-2002 (small metal funeral home marker) [St. James United Cemetery]

Joyner, Mable J. March 15, 1899 – February 2, 1961 (inscribed "Jesus Loves Me This I Know") [St. James United Cemetery]

Joyner, Morris 1907-1976, SSgt., U.S. Army, World War II [Berkley Memorial Cemetery]

Joyner, Norman F. March 23, 1918 – November 23, 1974, Sgt., U.S. Army, World War II [St. James United Cemetery]

Juricks, Ellen Smith December – (blank), 1905 – January 28 1947 (no tombstone; death certificate stated she was born in Baltimore, the daughter of Joseph McKinney, of the British Isles, and Frances Dutton, of Havre de Grace; she was married, husband's name not given, and died in Harford Memorial Hospital; informant was Mrs. Sarah Moubray, of Baltimore) [St. James United Cemetery]

Kane, Ellen Nora June 19, 1871 – May 25, 1942 (no tombstone; death certificate stated she was the daughter of Helen Kane, but her father was unknown to informant Alex Freeman) [Union U. M. Church Cemetery]

Kane, Rose died December 2, 1918, age about 72 (no tombstone; death certificate stated she was the daughter of Henry Giles and Mary Keithley, all born in Maryland, and died a widow in Havre de Grace; informant was Mrs. Lloyd Richardson, of Havre de Grace) [Asbury Cemetery]

Kean, Agatha December 29, 1906 – date of death blank (on same tombstone with Marvin Kean) [West Liberty Church Cemetery]

Kean, Marvin December 19, 1898 – May 10, 1965 (on same tombstone with wife Agatha Kean) [West Liberty Church Cemetery]

Keith, Jonathan A., "My Beloved Son" August 7, 1964 – August 14, 1995 [Berkley Memorial Cemetery]

Kell, Amanda February 15, 1884 –   (on same tombstone with husband Benjamin Franklin Kell) [Fairview A. M. E. Church Cemetery]

Kell, Benjamin Franklin December 25, 1841 – November 13, 1934 (on same tombstone with wife Amanda Kell; death certificate stated he was born at Forest Hill, the son of Basil and Maria Kell, both born in Harford Co., he married Amanda ----, worked as a farm laborer and died at home in High Point where he had lived all his life; informant was his wife Amanda Kell; Kurtz Funeral Home Records stated the same and that he died at home near High Point) [Fairview A. M. E. Church Cemetery]

Kell, Bertha February 22, 1874 – September 28, 1915 (no tombstone; death certificate stated she was the daughter of Robert Kell and Mary Rice, all born in Harford Co.) [Union U. M. Church Cemetery]

Kell, Effie E. Louise, "Beloved Mother and Grandmother" June 25, 1930 – April 25, 1998 (inscribed "Jesus Mercy" and "A Tribute to Grandma") [St. James United Cemetery]

Kell, Eliza died February 25, 1923, age about 51 (no tombstone; death certificate stated she was the unmarried daughter of Robet Kell, both born in Maryland, but mother unknown to informant Alverta Holliday, of Havre de Grace) [St. James United Cemetery]

Kell, Emily L. 1883-1960 (on same tombstone with Robert A. Kell) [Union U. M. Church Cemetery]

Kell, Gabriel Jackson October 16, 1903 – May 4, 1935 (no tombstone; death certificate stated he was the son of Edward Kell and Josephine Hill, all born in Harford Co.; married Nellie ----, worked as a farm laborer, and died at home near Mountain Church; informant was Mrs. Nellie Kell, of Bel Air) [Clark's U. M. Church Cemetery]

Kell, George E. 1861-1921 [Union U. M. Church Cemetery]

Kell, Hannah M. February 5, 1897 – October 1, 1945 (no tombstone; death certificate stated she was born at "Clark's Chapel, MD" *(sic)*, the daughter of John T. Williams and Rachel Collins, both born in Maryland; she married Nathan A. Kell and died at home at 127 Alice Ann Street, Bel Air; informant was Nathaniel Kell, of 127 Alice Ann Street, Bel Air) [Clark's U. M. Church Cemetery]

Kell, Henry died August 18, 1906, age 66 (no tombstone; death certificate stated he was the son of Bazil Kell and Maria Bond, all born in Maryland; he was single, worked as a laborer and died in Bel Air; "Hendon Hill" was written on the back of death certificate) [Hendon Hill Cemetery]

Kell, Ida M. September 18, 1903 – May 1, 1917 (no tombstone; death certificate stated she was the daughter of Harry Kell and Mary Hart and died at home near Cole) [Old Union Chapel M. E. Church Cemetery]

Kell, Ida M. September 18, 1903 – May 1, 1917 (no tombstone; death certificate stated she was the daughter of Harry Kell and Mary Hart and died at home near Cole) [Union U. M. Church Cemetery]

Kell, John Edward February 17, 1875 – September 2, 1917 (no tombstone; death certificate stated he was the son of B. Franklin Kell and Darcus Ann Johnson, all born in Harford Co.; he worked as a cook and waiter and died a widower in Forest Hill; informant was Benjamin Green) [Fairview A. M. E. Church Cemetery]

Kell, Johnny Jay stillborn "prematurity" on September 27, 1948 (no tombstone; death certificate stated he was the son of Morgan Tildon and Effie Ethel Louise Kell of rural Aberdeen) [Union U. M. Church Cemetery]

Kell, Josephine died August 8, 1906, age not given (no tombstone; death certificate stated she was the wife of Edward Kell and the daughter of Gabriel Hill and Phoebe Bond, all born in Maryland; she died in Highland and on the back of her certificate it is written "Asbury") [Asbury Cemetery]

Kell, Lillie Howard April 22, 1903 – April 26, 2003 (on same tombstone with Walter F. Kell that is inscribed "married August 20, 1942," but her name and year of birth and death are on a small metal funeral home marker; obituary in *The Aegis* in April 23, 2003 stated Lillie Mae Howard Kell was born in Durham, N.C., the daughter of James and Julia Howard; she worked from 1941 to 1964 at the former Bainbridge Naval Training Center in Port Deposit and from 1964 to 1985 at Perry Point VAMC where she retired; Lillie was married to Walter Kell for 55 years and lived in Aberdeen; she was cared for by Alcure Walker and died at Citizens Care Center in Havre de Grace on April 16, 2003, survived by one daughter, one son, 9 grandchildren, 20 great-grandchildren, 3 great-great-grandchildren, and 5 cousins) [Mt. Calvary U. A. M. E. Church Cemetery]

Kell, Mary E January 14, 1860 – April 23, 1932 (no tombstone; death certificate stated she was the widow of Robert Kell, Sr. and daughter of Freeborn Rice, mother's name unknown) [Union U. M. Church Cemetery]

Kell, Nathan A. February 22, 1892 – June 15, 1960, Maryland, Pfc, Sup Co, 811 Pion Inf, World War I (tombstone; military records state he was born in Forest Hill and was inducted into the service on August 23, 1918, served overseas from October 20, 1918 to July 23, 1919 and was honorably discharged on July 29, 1919) [Fairview A. M. E. Church Cemetery]

Kell, Nellie Elizabeth December 28, 1903 – March 31, 1999 (no tombstone; obituary in *The Aegis* on April 7, 1999 stated she was born in Hickory, the daughter of John and Matilda Hemore, and married John Kell in 1926 who predeceased her as did a daughter Silva James; she lived in Street, died at Harford Memorial Hospital in Havre de Grace and was survived by a grandson, 4 great-grandsons, a great-granddaughter, and 8 great-great-grandchildren) [Clark's U. M. Church Cemetery]

Kell, Robert A. 1890-1970 (on same tombstone with Emily L. Kell) [Union U. M. Church Cemetery]

Kell, Robert A. died November 8, 1919, age about 55 (no tombstone; death certificate stated he was the married son of Robert Kell, both born in Maryland, but his mother was unknown to informant George Kell, of Aberdeen) [Union U. M. Church Cemetery]

Kell, Robert J. October 1, 1911 – December 20, 1971, TEC4, H. & S. Co., 356 Engrs, World War II [Clark's U. M. Church Cemetery]

Kell, Sarah, wife of Robert Kell, died February 7, 1881 in her 49th year [Union U. M. Church Cemetery]

Kell, Susie E. 1866-   (sunken stone, dates not readable) [Union U. M. Church Cemetery]

Kell, Walter A. Jr. December 15, 1932 – June 14, 1948 (no tombstone; death certificate stated he was the son of Walter F. *(sic)* Kell, Sr. and Lidia B. Williams, lived on Edmund St. in Aberdeen and drowned at the yacht basin in Havre de Grace) [Union U. M. Church Cemetery]

Kelley, Roshell December 12, 1916 – December 13, 1916 (no tombstone; death certificate stated she was the daughter of Samuel Kelley, born in Weschester, PA, and Mary E. Banks, born in Oakington, MD, and died at home in Havre de Grace RFD) [St. James United Cemetery]

Kelly, ---- stillborn male on November 7, 1918, premature birth at 3½ months (no tombstone; death certificate stated he was the son of Frank Kelly, born in Maryland, and Martha Maud Barringer, born in North Carolina) [Union U. M. Church Cemetery]

Kelly, Barbara J., "BJ" 1955-1996 (no tombstone; name and dates inscribed on a large white wooden cross) [St. James United Cemetery]

Kelly, Clara (owned a lot in section 7 some time after 1951) [Mt. Calvary U. A. M. E. Church Cemetery]

Kelly, D. (owned a lot in section 7 some time after 1951) [Mt. Calvary U. A. M. E. Church Cemetery]

Kelly, Harrison W. Jr. August 12, 1948 – August 12, 1989 (inscribed "The Lord Is My Shepherd") [St. James United Cemetery]

Kelly, Harrison W. Sr. 1928-1981 (copied in 1987, but not found in 2018; obituary in *The Aegis* on November 12, 1981 stated he was born in Aberdeen, son of Edith Kelly Giles and the late Leonard Hardy, worked as an exercise boy, married Hazel Branch, lived at 645 Hickory Circle in Aberdeen, died at Franklin Hospital in Long Island, NY on November 8, 1981 and was survived by his wife, mother, 5 sons, 2 daughters, 2 sisters, and 5 grandchildren) [Mt. Calvary U. A. M. E. Church Cemetery]

Kelly, Hazel Mae 1930-2000 (small metal funeral home marker) [Mt. Calvary U. A. M. E. Church Cemetery]

Kelly, Irene I. 1910-   (on same tombstone with Oscar M. Jackson) [Mt. Calvary U. A. M. E. Church Cemetery]

Kelly, Jesse J. August 10, 1894 – October 26, 1959, Maryland, Pvt., 16 Co. 154 Depot Brig., World War I (tombstone; military records state Jesse James B. Kelly was born in Oakington on August 10, 1895 and lived in Aberdeen; he was inducted into the service on September 1, 1918, served in the 153 Dep Brig. and was honorably discharged on December 13, 1918) [Union U. M. Church Cemetery]

Kelly, Marie E. died September 17, 1972, age 65 (no tombstone; obituary in *The Aegis* on September 21, 1972 stated she was born in Charleston, SC, daughter of the late Mr. & Mrs. John Albert Clark, married Aubrey Kelly, of Bush Road, Aberdeen, and died at Harford Memorial Hospital in Havre de Grace) [Mt. Calvary U. A. M. E. Church Cemetery]

Kelly, Martha Maud May 14, 1899 – November 7, 1918 (no tombstone; death certificate stated she was the married daughter of John F. and Cora L. Barringer, all born in North Carolina) [Union U. M. Church Cemetery]

Kelly, Mary (owned a lot in section 7 some time after 1951) [Mt. Calvary U. A. M. E. Church Cemetery]

Kelly, Oscar M. 1905-1970 [Mt. Calvary U. A. M. E. Church Cemetery]

Kelly, Shirley C. 1956-1957 (copied in 1987, not found in 2018) [Mt. Calvary U. A. M. E. Church Cemetery]

Kelly, Walter F. September 17, 1906 – June 24, 1992 (on same tombstone with Lillie Howard Kell that is inscribed "married August 2, 1942") [Mt. Calvary U. A. M. E. Church Cemetery]

Kemp, Thomas William December 9, 1880 – October 15, 1931 (no tombstone; death certificate sated he was born in Bahama Islands, son of Zacarah Kemp, of same place, and Ferender ----, of Florida; he married Edna Page and died at home in Havre de Grace) [St. James United Cemetery]

Kenly, Annie died August 18, 1901, age 81 (no tombstone; death certificate stated she was the wife of John Kenly and the daughter of Frank and Nettie Hollingsworth; she was born in Harford County, had worked as a servant and died at Cole, survived by her husband and four children; place of burial not given [probably Union U. M. Church Cemetery]

Kenly, Annie Eliza April 11, 1854 – December 11, 1950 (no tombstone; death certificate stated she was born in Perryman, the daughter of John Carvel Williams and Margaret Reed, and died a widow at home at 825 Juniata St. in Havre de Grace where she had lived for 4 years; informant was Ida Stansbury, of Havre de Grace) [Union U. M. Church Cemetery]

Kenly, Annie May November 20, 1927 – January 3, 1929 (no tombstone; death certificate stated she was the daughter of George W. Kenly and Hattie J. Hollingsworth) [Union U. M. Church Cemetery]

Kenly, Buttons – see Walter Buttons Kenly [Mt. Calvary U. A. M. E. Church Cemetery]

Kenly, Carrie Elizabeth October 11, 1946 – February 21, 1947 (no tombstone; death certificate stated she was the daughter of Walter Sconion and Flossie Kenly, of Perryman. MD) [Union U. M. Church Cemetery]

Kenly, Charles W. January 9, 1922 – February 11, 1999, U.S. Army, World War II [Berkley Memorial Cemetery]

Kenly, Christina Rebecca March 17, 1843 – April 18, 1915 (no tombstone; death certificate stated she was the married daughter of William Paca and Hester Williams, all born in Maryland; informant was of William Kenly, of Perryman) [Union U. M. Church Cemetery]

Kenly, David B. January 30, 1900 – December 9, 1945 (no tombstone; death certificate stated he was the son of Richard Kenly and Margaret Hopkins, all were born in Harford Co.; he was single, served in World War II, worked as a laborer in plumbing and died at home in Darlington; informant was Mrs. Margaret Kenly, of Darlington) [Berkley Memorial Cemetery]

Kenly, Dorothy Elizabeth July 2, 1934 – July 5, 1934, premature birth (no tombstone; death certificate stated she was born in Harford Co., the daughter of Ralph Wallace, born in Harford Co., and Rosa LaRue, born in Cecil Co.; informant was Rosa Kenly, of Darlington) [Berkley Memorial Cemetery]

Kenly, Ethel R. July 14, 1931 – September 20, 1931 (no tombstone; death certificate stated she was the daughter of Mary Kenly and Prince Stansbury) [Union U. M. Church Cemetery]

Kenly, Etta June 19, 1909 – July 13, 1997 (no tombstone; owner of a lot in section 12 some time after 1951; obituary in *The Aegis* on July 30, 1997 stated Etta J. Kenly was born in LaPlata, the daughter of Spencer and Leslie Shivers, and was the widow of Walter Kenly; at a young age her family moved to Stepney and later she became active in the church; she lived in Havre de Grace and died at Harford Memorial Hospital, survived by a son Winfield Parker, Sr., a daughter Mable O. Brown, a son-in-law William Christy, Sr., four brothers, 25 grandchildren, 64 great-grandchildren, 40 great-great-grandchildren and 2 great-great-great-grandchildren) [Mt. Calvary U. A. M. E. Church Cemetery]

Kenly, Evalyn F. May 27, 1911 – February 17, 1918 (no tombstone; death certificate stated she was the daughter of George Kenly and Rose Rice, all born in Maryland, and she burned to death in a house fire in Stafford; informant was George Kenly, of Darlington) [Berkley Memorial Cemetery]

Kenly, Flossie June 16, 1929 – January 29, 1948 (no tombstone; death certificate stated she was the daughter of George W. Kenly and Hattie J. Hollingsworth, of Perryman) [Union U. M. Church Cemetery]

Kenly, George April 27, 1914 – February 17, 1918 (no tombstone; death certificate stated he was the son of George Kenly and Rose Rue, all born in Maryland, and he burned to death in a house fire in Stafford; informant was George Kenly, of Darlington) [Berkley Memorial Cemetery]

Kenly, George H. 1911-1984 (tombstone; he actually died on January 6, 1985 as reported in obituary in *The Aegis* on January 17, 1985; he was born on Spesutia Island, the son of Hattie Kenly, of Aberdeen, and the late George Kenly, lived in Aberdeen, married ---- (wife's name not mentioned) and died at Harford Memorial Hospital, survived by his mother, three step-sons Lewis Monk, William Hooks and James Hooks, three step-daughters Catherine Hooks, Sarah Kenly and Anita Christy, four brothers, one sister, and 24 grandchildren) [Union U. M. Church Cemetery]

Kenly, George W. May 22, 1883 – December 29, 1946 (no tombstone; death certificate stated he was the son of William Kenly and Sadie ---- (blank), and the husband of Hattie Hollingsworth) [Union U. M. Church Cemetery]

Kenly, Harriet died March 10, 1905, age 75 (no tombstone; death certificate stated she died at Kalmia and was the widow of Lewis Kenly; her father's name was unknown, but her mother was named Gover; the informant was John Johnson, a non-relative; her death notice in *The Aegis* on March 17, 1905 stated she lived in the Clark's Chapel neighborhood and was a cook and servant for many years in the home of James Lee; on the back of the certificate it was written she was buried at Clark's Chapel on March 12, 1905) [Clark's U. M. Church Cemetery]]

Kenly, Hattie J. January 29, 1889 – November 6, 1986 (tombstone; obituary in *The Aegis* on November 13, 1986 stated she was the widow of George Kenly, lived in Aberdeen, died at Francis Scott Key Medical Center (in Baltimore), was the oldest living member of Union United Methodist Church, and was survived by four sons Charles, William, Isaac and Mattson Kenly, one daughter Hazel Murphy, 42 grandchildren, and 17 great-grandchildren) [Union U. M. Church Cemetery]

Kenly, Isiah November 28, 1919 – August 25, 2000 (no tombstone; owner of a lot in section 7 some time after 1951; obituary in *The Aegis* on September 6, 2000 stated Isiah H. Kenly was born in Perryman, the son of George Kenly and Hattie Hollingsworth, and he joined the Army in 1942 and was honorably discharged in 1946; he lived in Aberdeen, was the service officer for VFW Post 6054 in Perryman and died at Harford Memorial Hospital in Havre de Grace, survived by a daughter Wanda Burrell, a sister Hazel Kenly Murphy, a brother Madison Hollingsworth Kenly, 9 sisters-in-law, 1 brother-in-law, 6 grandchildren and 8 great-grandchildren, and a host of other relatives and friends) [Mt. Calvary U. A. M. E. Church Cemetery]

Kenly, James E. February 18, 1925 -   ("The Lord Is My Shepherd") [Union U. M. Church Cemetery]

Kenly, John died June 17, 1904, age 28 (no tombstone; death certificate stated he was born at Cedars, the son of Henry Lee and Mary Jane Kenly, all born in Harford Co.; informant was John E. Presbury, a non-relative; he died at Cedars or Poole P. O., but place of burial not given [probably Cedars Chapel Cemetery]

Kenly, John H. November 4, 1896 – December 5, 1919 (no tombstone; death certificate stated he was the unmarried son of John H. Kenly and Ann Williams, all born in Harford County) [Union U. M. Church Cemetery]

Kenly, John H. stillborn male on March 15, 1924 (no tombstone; death certificate stated he was the son of George W. Kenly and Hattie Hollingsworth) [Union U. M. Church Cemetery]

Kenly, Julia died September 26, 1912, age about 90 (death certificate stated she was a servant, lived at Castleton and died a widow, but her parents were not known to informant Henry Bond) [Cedars Chapel Cemetery]

Kenly, Leona P. February 8, 1896 – June 25, 1969 (tombstone; obituary in *The Aegis* stated she was the daughter of Louis Monk and Harriett Rice, and the wife of George Herman Kenly; she lived at 602 Pinehurst Street in Aberdeen and died at her home, survived by her husband, 3 sons, 3 daughters, 4 brothers, 3 sisters, 22 grandchildren and 8 great-grandchildren) [Union U. M. Church Cemetery]

Kenly, Lewis died October 6, 1889, age about 70 (no tombstone; death notice in *The Aegis* on October 11, 1889 stated he was noted for his efforts to benefit his race and a few years ago he gave $130 in work and land to build a school house on his place for colored children; he was buried at Cedarville on October 8, 1889 [probably Cedars Chapel Cemetery]

Kenly, Margaret (owner of a lot in section 8 some time after 1951) [Mt. Calvary U. A. M. E. Church Cemetery]

Kenly, Margaret L. July 16, 1888 – May 19, 1966 [Union U. M. Church Cemetery]

Kenly, Mary E. October 14, 1913 – July 25, 1931 (no tombstone; death certificate stated she was the daughter of George W. Kenly and Hattie Hollingsworth) [Union U. M. Church Cemetery]

Kenly, Rebecca March 17, 1843 – April 18, 1915 (no tombstone; death certificate stated Christena Rebecca Kenly was the married daughter of William Paca and Hester Williams, all born in Maryland; informant was William Kenly; *The Aegis* on April 23, 1915 reported Rebecca "Teny" Kenly died at home near Michaelsville and was buried at Union Chapel near Michaelsville; she was a faithful servant to the late George A. Courtney) [Old Union Chapel M. E. Church Cemetery; probably reinterred in Union U.. M. Church Cemetery]

Kenly, Richard February 2, 1849 – September 29, 1916 (no tombstone; death certificate stated he was born in Maryland, son of William Kenly and Pheme Aikens, but places of birth unknown to informant Margaret Kenly, of Darlington; he married, worked as a laborer and died at home in Stafford) [Berkley Memorial Cemetery]

Kenly, Walter September 9, 1945 – October 6, 1945 (no tombstone; death certificate stated he was the son of Flossie Kenly and Walter Edward Sconion) [Union U. M. Church Cemetery]

Kenly, Walter Buttons died July 19, 1975, age not given (no tombstone; Buttons Kenly owned a lot in section 12 some time after 1951; obituary in *The Aegis* stated he was the son of Hattie J. Kenly and George Wesley

Kenly; he had been employed at Aberdeen Proving Ground and the B&O Railroad and retired from the National Guard in Havre de Grace in 1974; he lived in Aberdeen and died at home, survived by his wife Etta J. Kenly, 3 daughters, 3 sons, 5 brothers, 2 sisters, and 45 grandchildren) [Mt. Calvary U. A. M. E. Church Cemetery]

Kenly, William October 1, 1916 – February 17, 1918 (no tombstone; death certificate stated he was the son of George Kenly and Rose Rue, all born in Maryland, and he burned to death in a house fire in Stafford; informant was George Kenly, of Darlington) [Berkley Memorial Cemetery]

Kenly, William F. July 15, 1843 – September 29, 1925 (no tombstone; death certificate stated he was the widowed son of Frank Kenly and Annie Hollingsworth; informant was George W. Kenly) [Union U. M. Church Cemetery]

Kenly, William F. July 31, 1917 – November 10, 1999, TEC5, U.S. Army, World War II (tombstone; obituary and photo in *The Aegis* on December 8, 1999 stated he was born in Perryman, the son of George and Hattie Hollingsworth, served in the Army from October 23, 1942 to January 15, 1946 when honorably discharged; he lived in Aberdeen, retired with 44 years of government service and died at home, survived by his wife Sarah Hooks Kenly, two sons, two daughters, 15 grandchildren, 25 great-grandchildren, and other relatives) [Berkley Memorial Cemetery]

Kennard, ---- stillborn female died January 27, 1919, "due to difficult birth" (no tombstone; death certificate stated she was born in Harford Co., the daughter of Clarence Scott, born in Washington, DC, and Rosa Kennard, born in Harford Co., and died at Fulford; informant was Dr. A. F. VanBibber, of Bel Air) [Asbury Cemetery]

Kennard, Affie died June 8, 1893 in her 75th year (inscribed "In Memory Of" when copied in 1987, but inexplicably not found in 2018; prior to her death *The Aegis* on April 21, 1893 reported "Effie Kennard," an old colored woman, living near Joppa, was seized with a convulsion followed by a coma that was so death-like on Friday that her small granddaughter told her neighbors she had died; her coffin was made, her grave was ordered to be dug and her funeral was announced for Sunday; however, on the morning of her burial she awoke, felt faint from her long fast and indulged in a substantial meal) [John Wesley U. M. E. Church Cemetery in Abingdon]

Kennard, Corrina D. February 25, 1918 (date was centered under her name on a small tombstone; no death certificate found in Harford County) [Clark's U. M. Church Cemetery]

Kennard, David M. September 6, 1903 – November 17, 1925 (no tombstone; death certificate stated he was the son of David R. Kennard and Mamie Butler, all born in Maryland; he was single and worked as a laborer on State Roads; informant was Mamie B. Kennard, of Bel Air) [Asbury Cemetery]

Kennard, David Richard July 9, 1867 – March 27, 1943 (no tombstone; death certificate stated he was born in Harford Co., the son of John Kennard and Hannah Jones, married Mamie ----, lived at Bel Air RFD #2, and died at Harford Memorial Hospital in Havre de Grace; information on the certificate was compiled from hospital records) [Asbury Cemetery]

Kennard, Elmore R. December 19, 1913 – June 21, 1973, Maryland, Sgt, U.S. Army, World War II [Clark's U. M. Church Cemetery]

Kennard, Harriett – see Harriett C. R. Kennett [Asbury Cemetery]

Kennard, John Thomas June – (blank), 1841 – January 26, 1914 (no tombstone; death certificate stated he was the son of Peter Kennard and Isabella Derbin, all were born in Maryland; he worked as a laborer, was married, and lived in Churchville; informant was Harriett Kennard) [Asbury Cemetery]

Kennard, Mabel (Mable) died August 1, 1982, age 88 (no tombstone; death certificate in *The Aegis* on August 5, 1982 stated Mabel Kennard was born in Abingdon, the daughter of David and Mammie (Mamie) Kennard, and died at the home of her niece, Hattie Smith; *The Aegis* on August 12, 1982 reported Mable Kennard died at home on Asbury Road) [Asbury Cemetery]

Kennard, Mamie March 20, 1870 – March 23, 1944 (no tombstone; death certificate stated she was the daughter of Samuel Butler and Annie Harris, all born in Abingdon, Harford Co., and she was married to David R. Kennard and lived and died a widow near Bel Air; informant was Mamie Brown, of 464 Alliance St., Havre de Grace) [Asbury Cemetery]

Kennard, Remus June 23, 1916 – October 2, 1916 (no tombstone; death certificate stated he was the son of David R. Kennard and Mamie B. Butler, and they all were born in Harford Co.; Remus died at Churchville; informant was David Kennard, of Bel Air) [Asbury Cemetery]

Kennard, Rosalie – see Rosalie Kennett [Asbury Cemetery]

Kennard, Roy Alexander February 2, 1899 – March 17, 1924 (no tombstone; death certificate stated he was born in Abingdon, the son of David R. Kennard, born in Churchville, and May B. *(sic)* (in all likelihood it would have been Mamie Butler), born in Abingdon; he was single, worked for the Sate Roads and lived near Bel Air; informant was his father) [Asbury Cemetery]

Kennard, Sarah J., "Beloved Mom and Grandma" November 16, 1917 – September 22, 2002 [Clark's U. M. Church Cemetery]

Kennett, Harriett C. R. September 1, 1847 – March 3, 1940 (no tombstone; her tombstone stated she was the daughter of David Hamilton, born in Baltimore, and Julia A. Johnson, born in Harford Co.; she was born in Harford Co., married John Kennett, lived near Bel Air and was a widow at the time of her death; informant was Mr. Hazzard Harris, of Aberdeen, but it appears from others buried here that her name was probably Kennard and not Kennett) [Asbury Cemetery]

Kennett, Rosalie April 11, 1895 – February 12, 1919 (no tombstone; death certificate stated she was the daughter of David Kennett and Mamie Butler, all born in Harford Co.; she was single, worked as a housemaid and died near Fulford; informant was David Kennard, of Churchville, so it appears her name was probably Kennard and not Kennett) [Asbury Cemetery]

Kesterson, James R. died December 8, 1926, age about 57 (no tombstone; death certificate stated he was the married son of Humphrey Kesterson and Harried Redmond, all born in Virginia) [Union U. M. Church Cemetery]

Killibrew, Othar April 6, 1919 – September 8, 1980, PFC, U.S. Army, World War II [St. James United Cemetery]

Kimbrough, Thomas L. February 17, 1911 – November 8, 1914 (no tombstone; death certificate stated he was the son of Walter Kimbrough, born in Virginia, and Eliza R. Tildon, born in Maryland, and he died at Michaelsville) [Union U. M. Church Cemetery]

King, Charles January 17, 1937 -   (same tombstone with Gladys V. King inscribed "Together Forever") [St. James United Cemetery]

King, Edna Mary died January 28, 1903, age 2 years, 4 months, 27 days (no tombstone; death certificate stated she was born in Pennsylvania, the daughter of John King and Susan Murry, and she died in Berkley; place of burial not given [probably Berkley Memorial Cemetery]

King, Gladys V. November 5, 1952 – May 9, 2007 (on same tombstone with Charles King) [St. James United Cemetery]

Kinly, John died November 8, 1921, age unknown (no tombstone; death certificate stated he was single and worked as a laborer in Bel Air; he died in Havre de Grace Hospital and his age and parents were unknown to the hospital) [Hendon Hill Cemetery]

Kirksey, Charles Leon December 17, 1961 – August 27, 2007 (inscribed "Always In Our Hearts;" obituary in *The Aegis* on August 31, 2007 stated Charles Leroy *(sic)* Kirksey was the son of the late Marlene V. Ringgold Kirksey and Benjamin F. Kirksey, of Saraland, AL; he was known as "Beaver" and was a licensed barber among other things; he was formerly of Churchville and was survived by his father, his stepmother Donna Kirksey, 3 brothers, 6 sisters, 1 uncle, 3 aunts, 15 nephews, 11 nieces and 14 great-nephews and great-nieces) [John Wesley U. M. E. Church Cemetery in Abingdon]

Kirksey, Marlene 1935-1982 (tombstone; obituary in *The Aegis* on April 1, 1982 stated Marlene Valarie Kirksey was born in Churchville, the daughter of Ollie Ringgold and Lillian Smith, and died at Mercy Hospital in Baltimore on March 26, 1982, age 47; she was survived by her parents, and four sons (Kenneth Ringgold and Charles, Gary and Michael Kirksey), five daughters, two brothers, three sisters, and eight grandchildren) [John

Wesley U. M. E. Church Cemetery in Abingdon]

Kuhn, Paula Rose 1961-2005 (small metal funeral home marker) [Berkley Memorial Cemetery]

Kyler, Marilyn L., "Loving Wife and Mother" December 15, 1929 – January 5, 2008 [Berkley Memorial Cemetery]

Kyler, Ralph R. Jr., "Beloved Son" June 17, 1952 – May 26, 1972 (inscribed "In Memory") [Berkley Memorial Cemetery]

Lacy, Mildred E. 1889-1972 (on same tombstone with William R. Lacy; obituary in *The Aegis* on October 12, 1972 stated Mildred John Lacy was born in Virginia, the daughter of Warner Johnson and Fannie Lewis, and wife of the late William Roger Lacy; she moved to this area in 1936 and worked for Donaldson Brown in Port Deposit; she joined Mt. Zion Baptist Church and served as the Superintendent of Sunday School for 25 years; she lived at 567 Girard St. in Havre de Grace and died on October 6, 1972 in Harford Memorial Hospital, survived by a sister, Mrs. Flossie Jackson, of Wheeling, WV) [Union U. M. Church Cemetery]

Lacy, William R. 1889-1952 (on same tombstone with Mildred E. Lacy) [Union U. M. Church Cemetery]

Lampkin, Ida Belle, "Grandma Ida" August 11, 1926 – December 4, 2001 [Mt. Zion U. M. Church Cemetery]

Lampkin, Joseph R. "Rickey" December 10, 1951 – March 23, 1985 (tombstone; James Dorsey Card File, African American Obituaries, maintained at the Historical Society of Harford County, has a card for him with an obituary from *The Aegis* on March 28, 1985 stating Joseph Ricardo Lampkin was born in Philadelphia, the son of the late Ida Peaker, of Bel Air, and Joseph Lampkin, of Philadelphia; he was manager of the Reconditioning Department of Village Dodge and Volvo in Bel Air and was a member of American Legion Post 55; he died at Fallston General Hospital as a result of injuries sustained in an auto accident on Route 1 in Bel Air; he was survived by his parents, son Joseph Jr., two brothers, and other relatives) [Mt. Zion U. M. Church Cemetery]

Lane, Caroline Jiles October 20, 1844 – February 22, 1932 (no tombstone; death certificate stated she was the daughter of Henry Jiles and Rachel Dowden, and widow of John F. Lane) [St. James United Cemetery]

Lane, Vivian J. 1913-1956 [St. James United Cemetery]

Langford, Jorden 2007-2007 (small metal funeral home marker) [St. James United Cemetery]

LaPrade, Helen May Moore February 22, 1921 – April 21, 1944 (no tombstone; death certificate stated she was born at Asbury, Bel Air, the daughter of Elsworth Wesley Moore, born in Baltimore, and Grace Johnson, born in Bel Air; she was married (husband's name not given), worked as a munitions worker, lived at 7 Howard St. in Bel Air, committed suicide by drinking lysol and died at Harford Memorial Hospital in Havre de Grace; informant was her father Elsworth Moore, of Bel Air) [Tabernacle Mount Zion U. M. Church Cemetery]

LaRue, Earl W. Jr. December 28, 1940 -   (on same tombstone with Joan E. LaRue inscribed "In Loving Memory" and "married 55 years") [Berkley Memorial Cemetery]

LaRue, Joan E. December 28, 1943 – December 17, 2017 (on same tombstone with Earl W. LaRue, Jr. inscribed "In Loving Memory" and "married 55 years") [Berkley Memorial Cemetery]

LaRue, Lillian V., "Mother and Grandmom" January 13, 1919 – January 12, 2000 (inscribed "In Loving Memory") [Berkley Memorial Cemetery]

LaRue, Rachel A. April 6, 1896 – April 11, 1928 (no tombstone; death certificate stated she was the married daughter of Edward Allison, but her mother was unknown to informant Silver Spencer) [Union U. M. Church Cemetery]

Laurie, Ellen L. 1944-1971 (on same tombstone with John W. Laurie) [Berkley Memorial Cemetery]

Laurie, John B. 1910-1974 [St. James United Cemetery]

Laurie, John W. 1943-   (on same tombstone with Ellen L. Laurie) [Berkley Memorial Cemetery]

Laurie, Juanita Christine October 6, 1940 – March 16, 1947 (no tombstone; death certificate stated she was the daughter of John B. Laurie, of Georgia, and Nina Freeman, of Maryland) [Union U. M. Church Cemetery]

Laurie, Nina Rosenna September 1, 1912 – June 20, 2011 (tombstone with photo of her and husband John B. Laurie; funeral notice and photo in *The Aegis* on June 24, 2011 stated she lived in Havre de Grace and died at the Citizens Care Center) [St. James United Cemetery]

Lawrence, A. J., Baby Boy of Mr. & Mrs. Alando C. Lawrence, Sr., June 17, 2001 (heart-shaped tombstone) [St. James United Cemetery]

Lawrence, Matthew 1925-2005 (small metal funeral home marker) [Berkley Memorial Cemetery]

Lawson, Arthur died August 4, 1928, age about 35 (no tombstone; death certificate stated he was born in Georgia and was single; his parents were unknown to informant Parker Mitchell) [Union U. M. Church Cemetery]

Lawson, Charles L., "His Son" 1909-1934 (on same tombstone with Robert I. Lawson and Della R. Lawson) [Berkley Memorial Cemetery]

Lawson, Della R., "His Wife" 1891-1957 (on same tombstone with Robert I. Lawson and Charles L. Lawson) [Berkley Memorial Cemetery]

Lawson, Mary E. December 29, 1888 – September 28, 1966 [Mt. Calvary U. A. M. E. Church Cemetery]

Lawson, Robert I. 1882-1946 (on same tombstone with Della R. Lawson and Charles L. Lawson; death certificate stated he was born December 1, 1884 and died May 29, 1946, the son of Anna Lawson, both born in Harford Co.; his father's name was unknown to informant Mrs. Della Lawson, of Darlington; he married, worked as a laborer and died in Darlington) [Berkley Memorial Cemetery]

Lawson, Sarah Annie died January 26, 1933, age 64 (no tombstone; death certificate stated she was born in Lancaster, PA, but her parents were unknown to informant Mary E. Cain, 212 Rose St., Reading, PA; she married Edward Lawson and died a widow at Berkley) [Berkley Memorial Cemetery]

Lawson, Tate 1841-1920 [St. James United Cemetery]

Lawyer, Mary Ann 1943-2018 (small metal funeral home marker) [St. James United Cemetery]

Leager, Hannah Jane died January 27, 1915, age about 65 (no tombstone; death certificate stated she was born in Harford Co., daughter of Daniel Leager, born in Maryland, but the name of her mother was not known to informant Emma Skinner, of Havre de Grace; she was not married) [Skinner Cemetery]

Leak, Robert Edward December 15, 1934 – February 3, 1936 (no tombstone; death certificate stated he was the son of Ulysses Leak, of South Carolina, and Vivian Brown, of Perryman, MD) [Union U. M. Church Cemetery]

Leak, Viola December 10, 1921 – February 9, 1935 (no tombstone; death certificate stated she was born in Spartanburg, SC, the daughter of James Austian and Hester Leak, born of SC) [Union U. M. Church Cemetery]

Lee-Davis, Margaret M., "Beloved Sister" April 7, 1923 – February 17, 1991 (inscribed "23 Psalm") [St. James United Cemetery]

Lee, ---- stillborn male on April 8, 1933, premature 6 month birth (no tombstone; death certificate stated he was the son of Walter Lee, both born in Maryland, and Anna McMillian, born in Virginia; died at McCann's Corner; informant was his father Walter, of Darlington) [Clark's U. M. Church Cemetery]

Lee, ---ube(?) October 3, 1864 – October 11, 1898 (tombstone noted as toppled in 1987, but not found in 2018) [Chestnut Grove A. M. E. Church Cemetery, formerly LaGrange Cemetery at Rocks]

Lee, Alice M., "Beloved Daughter" August 9, 1909 – May 17, 1985 (tombstone; obituary in *The Aegis* on May 23, 1985 stated Alice Mae Lee was born in Perryman, the daughter of Elizabeth O. Lee of Havre de Grace; she retired from the Dietetic Department of the Perry Point VA Medical Center and died at Good Samaritan Hospital in Baltimore, survived by her mother, an adopted daughter Mary Catherine Barnes, 3 grandchildren and 7 great-grandchildren) [Union U. M. Church Cemetery]

Lee, Anna died February 16, 1989, age 88 (no tombstone; obituary in *The Aegis* on February 23, 1989 stated she was born in Grayson, Co., VA, the daughter of Lee McMillan and Dora Mintenal; she married Earnest Walter Lee, lived in Street and died at Harford Memorial Hospital; she was survived by 5 sons, 2 daughters, 32 grandchildren, 34 great-grandchildren and 4great-great-grandchildren) [Clark's U. M. Church Cemetery]

Lee, Annie died January 1, 1924, age 51 (no tombstone; death certificate stated she was the daughter of William Lee and Jane Dorsey, all born in Maryland; she was single, did housework and died in Havre de Grace ; informant was W. Sidney Lee, of Darlington) [Green Spring U. M. Church Cemetery]

Lee, Belle, wife of James Lee, died October 3, 1904, age 35 (tombstone; death certificate stated she was 40, born in North Carolina, married James Lee and did washing and ironing work in Bel Air; the names of her parents were not known to the informant, her husband) [Hendon Hill Cemetery]

Lee, Bertie Curtis died June 7, 1906, age 20, at Kalmia (no tombstone; death certificate stated she was born in Harford Co., wife of George H. Lee and daughter of Isaac and Caroline Curtis, but it did not give her place of burial; probably buried at Clark's Chapel since her parents are buried here) [Clark's U. M. Church Cemetery]

Lee, Betty (no tombstone; death certificate stated she was born on January 17, 1835, the daughter of John Clark and Katie Harris, all born in Maryland; she lived and worked as a servant at Federal Hill and was married at the time of her death on December 15, 1916; informant was her son James Lee, of Rocks) [Chestnut Grove A. M. E. Church Cemetery, formerly LaGrange Cemetery at Rocks]

Lee, Carol Lolita died February 9, 1996, age 74 (no tombstone; James Dorsey Card File, African American Obituaries, maintained at the Historical Society of Harford County, has a card for her with an obituary from an unidentified newspaper on February 21, 1996 stating she was born in Havre de Grace, the daughter of William H. and Beatrice Ida Merchant, and the wife of the late George Lee to whom she had been married for more than 35 years; she died at Harford Memorial Hospital, survived by a brother Colston and a sister Amelia) [St. James United Cemetery]

Lee, Charles W. died August 18, 1977, age 68 (no tombstone; obituary in *The Aegis* on August 25, 1977 stated he was born in Perryman, served in World War II and retired as a foreman from the Edgewood Arsenal; he lived in Havre de Grace and died at University Hospital in Baltimore, survived by his wife Freida Lee, his mother Elizabeth Lee, a sister Alice M. Lee, 2 step-daughters, 13 grandchildren and 9 great-grandchildren) [Union U. M. Church Cemetery]

Lee, Cheyenne 1958-2014 (small metal funeral home marker) [Berkley Memorial Cemetery]

Lee, Dante died May 20, 1988, age not stated (no tombstone; obituary in *The Aegis* on May 26, 1988 stated he was the infant son of William H. and Jacqulyn *(sic)* Lee, of Alexandria, VA, and died at Fairfax General Hospital in Fairfax, VA; he was survived by his parents and grandparents Mr. & Mrs. William H. Lee, of Bel Air) [Clark's U. M. Church Cemetery]

Lee, David "Bim" April 26, 1952 – December 23, 2007 (inscribed "I have fought a good fight, I have finished my course, I have kept the faith") [Clark's U. M. Church Cemetery]

Lee, E. Louisa 1856-1929 (on same tombstone with Jacob F., Mary H., Hezekiah, Loucinder, and Edward; death certificate stated "Lousia E. Lee" was born September 15, 1861, the daughter of James Smith and Mary Lee, all born in Maryland; she lived in Darlington and died a widow on September 23, 1929; informant was Rachel R. Smith, 1621 Parrish St., Philadelphia, PA) [Berkley Memorial Cemetery]

Lee, Edward 1890-1890 (on same tombstone with Jacob F., Mary H., Hezekiah, Loucinder, and E. Louisa Lee) [Berkley Memorial Cemetery]

Lee, Edward Emmanuel August 11, 1910 – April 27, 1912 (no tombstone; death certificate stated the son of Edward E. Lee, both born in Harford Co., and Bertha Butler, born in Baltimore Co.; he died in Abingdon; informant was his father) [John Wesley U. M. E. Church Cemetery in Abingdon]

Lee, Eliza Elizabeth August 12, 1875 – June 1, 1928 (no tombstone; death certificate stated she was born in Harford Co., the daughter of John Smith, birth place unknown, and Kate Jamison, born in Harford Co.; she was married, died at home at Federal Hill and was buried in "Federal Hill Cemetery;" informant was James Lee, of Rocks) [William C. Rice Memorial Cemetery, St. James U. M. Church]

Lee, Elizabeth Olivia died July 31, 1990, age 100 (no tombstone; obituary in *The Aegis* on August 15, 1990 stated she was born in Perryman, the daughter of James and Rachel Lee, and died at home in Havre de Grace;

she formerly worked at the old Colonial Hotel (later became the Brevin Nursing Home) and owned and operated a restaurant next to her home; she was survived by a granddaughter, one great-granddaughter, two great-grandsons, and Vincent Barnes with whom she lived; her photo appeared in *The Record* on May 16, 1990) [Union U. M. Church Cemetery]

Lee, Ellsworth L. Sr. February 26, 1916 – August 11, 1986, TEC4, U.S. Army, World War II [John Wesley U. M. E. Church Cemetery in Abingdon]

Lee, Emily died July 31, 1920, age about 50 (no tombstone; death certificate stated she was a widow and the daughter of Israel Robinson, both born in Maryland, but her mother was unknown to informant Mrs. Frank Martin, of Havre de Grace) [Union U. M. Church Cemetery]

Lee, Emma Luisa August 7, 1885 – November 29, 1929 (no tombstone; death certificate stated she was married and born in Maryland, died in Dublin, the daughter of William Jackson, born in Virginia, and Sarah Reed, born in Pennsylvania; informant was Thomas Lee, of Street, MD) [Clark's U. M. Church Cemetery]

Lee, Ernest T. Sr. March 17, 1924 – April 11, 1992, Cpl., U.S. Army (tombstone; obituary in *The Aegis* on April 17, 1992 stated Ernest Thomas Lee, Sr. was born in Forest Hill, the son of Ernest Walter Lee and Anna McMillan; he married, served in the Army during the Korean War, lived in Street, was an active members of John Wesley UME Church in Abingdon and retired from Loch Joint in Perryman; he died at Fallston General Hospital, survived by his wife Rosa E. Lewis, 5 sons, 2 daughters, 4 brothers, 2 sisters and 4 grandchildren) [John Wesley U. M. E. Church Cemetery in Abingdon]

Lee, Genieve Minor died June 13, 1966 [St. James United Cemetery]

Lee, George died 11 Sep 1921, age 70 (no tombstone; death certificate stated he was the son of Bruce Bond and "Georanna" (Georganna) Lee, all born in Maryland; he was a cook and died a widow in Bel Air; informant was Oliver Brown, of Bel Air) [Tabernacle Mount Zion U. M. Church Cemetery]

Lee, George E. 1910-1982 (on same tombstone with Lolita M. Lee amd also another marker inscribed George Lee, January 21, 1910 – February 17, 1982, TEC5, U.S. Army, World War II) [St. James United Cemetery]

Lee, George Franklin January 17, 1946 – February 28, 1946 (no tombstone; death certificate stated he was born in Harford Co., the son of Ernest W. Lee, born in Harford Co., and Anna McMullen, born in Grayson Co., VA; he died at home at Poplar Grove in rural Street near Dublin and the informant was his father, of Street RFD) [Clark's U. M. Church Cemetery]

Lee, Hannah September 24, 1883 – January 1, 1951 (no tombstone; death certificate stated she was born at Rock Run, Harford Co., the daughter of Sidney Lee and Mary Peaco; she was single, worked as a housemaid, lived at 136 Baltimore St. in Aberdeen all her life and died there; informant was Mrs. Laura Dorsey who lived at the same address) [Green Spring U. M. Church Cemetery]

Lee, Harrison C. April 2, 1890 – January 7, 1978 (no tombstone; Pennington Funeral Home records stated he was born in Maryland, the son of Sidney Lee and Ellen Pekoe, both of Delaware, and he died at Perry Point Veterans Hospital in Cecil Co., MD; informant was his step-daughter Ida Brown, of Aberdeen; military records stated he was age 29 years *(sic)* and 4 months when he was inducted as a private on August 23, 1918 and served in ther153 Dep. Brig. until honorably discharged on January 20, 1919) [St. James United Cemetery]

Lee, Harry G. (tombstone not found in 2018, but J. C. Taylor Marble Co. records stated "Harry G. Lee (col) tomb(stone) was put up Dec 7th 1888 Lagrange near Rocks") [Chestnut Grove A. M. E. Church Cemetery, formerly LaGrange Cemetery at Rocks]

Lee, Hattie November 29, 1910 – November 6, 1911 (no tombstone; death certificate stated she was born in Harford Co., the daughter of Samuel Lee and Eva Jones, both born in Maryland; she died at home in Bel Air; the informant was her father Samuel Lee, of Bel Air) [Clark's U. M. Church Cemetery]

Lee, Helen L. July 5, 1899 – April 19, 1927 (no tombstone; death certificate stated she was the daughter of George Thomas and Margaret Jones, all born in Maryland; she was married and died in Havre de Grace; informant was Julia J. Swann, of Jarrettsville) [Clark's U. M. Church Cemetery]

Lee, Henrietta died October 23, 1889, very old (no tombstone; her death notice in *The Aegis* on October 25,

1889 stated she died suddenly at the house of Letitia Dorsey on the Bel Air turnpike near Archer & Howard's Mill; place of burial was not stated [probably Tabernacle Mount Zion U. M. Church Cemetery]

Lee, Hezekiah 1884-1910 (on same tombstone with Jacob F., Mary H., Loucinder, Edward, and E. Louisa Lee) [Berkley Memorial Cemetery]

Lee, Howard E. March 18, 1929 – March 14, 2009, U.S. Army, Korea [St. James United Cemetery]

Lee, J. Frank April – (blank), 1880 – June 27, 1954 (no tombstone; Pennington Funeral Home records stated he was born in Havre de Grace, the son of William Sidney Lee and Mary Ellen Peaco; he married ---- (blank), worked as a farm laborer and died at home on Ontario St. Extended in Havre de Grace; informant was Mrs. George Daugherty, of Revolution St.) [Green Spring U. M. Church Cemetery]

Lee, Jacob F. 1851-1928 (on the same tombstone with E. Louisa, Mary H., Hezekiah, Loucinder, and Edward Lee; death certificate stated Jacob Frank Lee was born September 8, 1851, the son of Frank Lee and Jane Dorsey, all born in Maryland; he was married, worked as a farmer and died July 30, 1928 at home in Darlington; informant was John Lee, of Darlington) [Berkley Memorial Cemetery]

Lee, James April 1, 1873 – November 12, 1928 (no tombstone; death certificate stated he was the son of Jube Lee and Betty Clark, all born in Harford Co.; he married Mable ----, worked as a farm laborer until July 1928, lived at Federal Hill and committed suicide at his home; informant was Nicholas Lee, of Pylesville) [William C. Rice Memorial Cemetery, St. James U. M. Church]

Lee, James died May 16, 1914, age not known (no tombstone; death certificate stated he was a widower, worked as a laborer and died in Bel Air and was the son of George Lee and Susan Hall; their birth places were not known to informant Margaret Taylor, of Bel Air) [Hendon Hill Cemetery]

Lee, James C. July 5, 1890 – October 7, 1968 (tombstone; obituary in *The Aegis* on October 10, 1968 stated James Carroll Lee was born in Perryman and lived in Havre de Grace over 50 years; he was survived by his wife Susie V. Lee, 5 sons, 5 daughters, 18 grandchildren, and sister Elizabeth Lee [Union U. M. Church Cemetery]

Lee, James E. August 2, 1925 – July 4, 2002, S1, U.S. Navy, World War II [St. James United Cemetery]

Lee, James Elloise December 23, 1919 – August 7, 1947 (no tombstone; death certificate stated he was the son of Edward Lee and Bertha E. Butler, all born in Abingdon; he married Mary Ruth ---, lived at Van Bibber and worked as a trackman for the Pennsylvania Railroad; he was struck and killed by a train in Edgewood; informant was Edward Lee, of Abingdon) [John Wesley U. M. E. Church Cemetery in Abingdon]

Lee, James Robert August 1, 1930 – September 25, 1930 (no tombstone; death certificate stated he was born in Harford Co., the son of Walter Lee, born in Maryland, and Anna McMillan, born in Virginia; he died at McCann's Corner and the informant was Anna Lee, of Street, MD) [Clark's U. M. Church Cemetery]

Lee, John S. April 17, 1882 – August 7, 1964 (on same tombstone with Lillie Lee) [Cedars Chapel Cemetery]

Lee, Josiah died November 12, 1908, age 56 [Tabernacle Mount Zion U. M. Church Cemetery]

Lee, Jupiter June 10, 1837 – May 9, 1919 (no tombstone; death certificate stated he was a farm hand and widower a Federal Hill; the names of his parents and their places of birth were not known to informant, his son James Lee, of Rocks RFD) [Chestnut Grove A. M. E. Church Cemetery, formerly LaGrange Cemetery at Rocks]

Lee, Larry LeRoy died at birth on May 13, 1949 (no tombstone; death certificate stated he was the son of Melvin Lee and Sarah Louise Hall who lived at 133 Archer St. in Bel Air) [Asbury Cemetery]

Lee, Leon M. August 13, 1936 – April 17, 1958 [Union U. M. Church Cemetery]

Lee, LeRoy E. June 16, 1900 – July 16, 1949 (no tombstone; death certificate stated he was born in Abingdon, the son of Clarence Peaker and Edith Lee, both born in Maryland; he married Edna Felton (age 38 in 1949), worked as a Senior Laborer for the U.S. Government and was divorced at the time of his death in Abingdon where he lived for 7 years; informant was Alease Lee, 863 Harlem Ave., Baltimore) [John Wesley U. M. E. Church Cemetery in Abingdon]

Lee, Lillie October 16, 1884 – April 30, 1986 (on same tombstone with John S. Lee) [Cedars Chapel Cemetery]

Lee, Lolita M. 1921-1996 (on same tombstone with George E. Lee) [St. James United Cemetery]

Lee, Loucinder 1889-1890 (on same tombstone with Jacob F., Mary H., Hezekiah, E. Louisa, and Edward Lee) [Berkley Memorial Cemetery]

Lee, Louisa E. – see E. Louisa Lee [Berkley Memorial Cemetery]

Lee, Lucy C. September 21, 1872 – September 5, 1930 (no tombstone; death certificate stated she was the widowed daughter of John Ringgold and Susie Parson and all were born in Maryland) [Union U. M. Church Cemetery]

Lee, Mary Ellen July 7, 1863 – June 15, 1938 (tombstone; death certificate stated she was the daughter of John H. Peaco and Harriet Foreman, all born in Harford Co., and married William Sidney Lee who was living at the time of her death near Havre de Grace; informant was Mrs. Jannie Daugherty, of Havre de Grace) [Green Spring U. M. Church Cemetery]

Lee, Mary H. 1859-1890 (on same tombstone with Jacob F., E. Louisa, Hezekiah, Loucinder, and Edward Lee) [Berkley Memorial Cemetery]

Lee, Mary J. (no dates; inscribed "and Family" on same tombstone with Albert Dutton and Family) [Mt. Calvary U. A. M. E. Church Cemetery]

Lee, Mary Liza May 14, 1878 – December 27, 1931 (no tombstone; death certificate stated she was born in Hopewell, daughter of George Murphy, born in North Carolina, and Frances Bosley, born in Georgia; she married William Lee, worked as a laundress in Aberdeen and died at Havre de Grace Hospital; informant was William Lee, of Aberdeen RFD) [Mt. Calvary U. A. M. E. Church Cemetery]

Lee, Melvin May 5, 1914 – October 14, 1914 (no tombstone; death certificate stated he was the son of Thomas Lee and Susan Williamson, all born in Maryland; informant was his father Thomas Lee, of Street RFD) [Clark's U. M. Church Cemetery]

Lee, Michael Anthony died August 4, 1990, age 4 months (no tombstone; obituary in *The Aegis* on August 8, 1990 stated he was born in Rossville, the son of Michael E. Lee, of Havre de Grace, and Jill R. Jarvis, of Joppa, and died at Fallston General Hospital, survived by his parents, a sister Jennifer R. Presbury, and his grandparents Mr. & Mrs. David W. Jarvis of Joppa, and Rosetta Byrd and Harrison Byrd, of Havre de Grace) [Community Baptist Church Cemetery]

Lee, Myrtle March 26, 1905 – August 9, 1935 (no tombstone; death certificate stated she was born in Harford Co., the daughter of Frank Lee and Della Smith, both born in Maryland; she was single, lived in Havre de Grace, was shot and died at Havre de Grace Hospital; informant was Mrs. Jennie Dougherty, of Havre de Grace) [Green Spring U. M. Church Cemetery]

Lee, Nellie E. died June 25, 1979, age 106 (obituary in *The Aegis* on July 5, 1979 stated she was the wife of the late Harrison Lee and was the oldest resident of Harford County; she was born in Churchville and died at the Citizens Nursing Home in Havre de Grace where she had resided since 1975; survived by 2 daughters, a son and numerous grandchildren, great-grandchildren and great-great-grandchildren) [Berkley Memorial Cemetery]

Lee, Pauline W. 1891-1964 [Asbury Cemetery]

Lee, Percy Leon May 29, 1931 – November 13, 1931 (no tombstone; death certificate stated he was the son of Percy C. Lee, of Pennsylvania, and Susie Cole, of Havre de Grace) [St. James United Cemetery]

Lee, Sharon Yvette, "Loving Wife, Daughter & Mother" August 9, 1965 – June 9, 2017 [John Wesley U. M. E. Church Cemetery in Abingdon]

Lee, Susie V., "Beloved Mother" October 24, 1906 – March 13, 1984 (tombstone also inscribed with the words "23 Psalm" and "IF by Rudyard Kipling") [St. James United Cemetery]

Lee, Thomas W. died March 16, 1973, age 90 (no tombstone; obituary in *The Aegis* stated he "was the son of the late George and Amelia White" and lived in Street; died at the Bel Air Nursing and Convalescent Center and was survived by 1 daughter, 2 sons, 14 grandchildren, 55 great-grandchildren and 6 great-great-grandchildren) [Clark's U. M. Church Cemetery]

Lee, Vernon Wilbur May 1, 1926 – December 3, 1947 (no tombstone) [St. James United Cemetery]

Lee, Willa Virginia November 21, 1925 – September 28, 1926 (no tombstone; death certificate stated she was born and died in Harford Co., the daughter of Walter Lee, born in Harford Co., and Anna McMullen, born in Virginia; informant was Walter Lee, of Street RFD) [Clark's U. M. Church Cemetery]

Lee, William June 23, 1869 – July 30, 1933 (no tombstone; death certificate stated he was born in Harford Co., the son of Charles Lee, born in Harford Co., and Mary J. Worthington, born in Philadelphia; he married Mary ----, worked as a day laborer for 40 years and died a widower at home in Aberdeen; informant was Mrs. Emma Warfield, of Aberdeen) [Mt. Calvary U. A. M. E. Church Cemetery]

Lee, William died September 30, 1884, about age 80 (no tombstone; death notice in *The Aegis* on October 3, 1884 stated he lived alone in a cabin near the homee of Maj. A. M. Hancock, several miles northeast of Bel Air (actually east of Bel Air and south of Churchville), and was found dead in bed; his place of burial was not given, but possibly at Asbury Church) [Asbury Cemetery]

Lee, William E. May 16, 1916 – October 9, 1934 (no tombstone; death certificate stated he was born in Baltimore, the son of Edgar Lee and Bessie DeShields, both born in Maryland; he was single, worked as a laborer in Bel Air and died in Havre de Grace Hospital; informant was Elizabeth Brown, of Havre de Grace]

Lee, William H. Jr. August 12, 1952 – August 9, 2015, U.S. Army (tombstone; funeral notice in *The Aegis* stated he lived in Temple Hills, MD and died at Mandrin Hospice House, Harwood, MD) [Clark's U. M. Church Cemetery]

Lee, William Henry Sr. April 6, 1927 – April 7, 2006 (inscribed "Our Beloved Hat Rack" and U. S. Army, U. S. Air Force; obituary in *The Aegis* on April 12, 2006 stated "Hat Rack" was born in Street, the son of Walter Earnest Lee and Anna McMillian; he served in World War II, married Helen Viola Waters in 1953 and retired from Edgewood Arsenal as a post engineer in 1975; died at Johns Hopkins Bayview Medical Center in Baltimore, survived by his wife, 2 sons, 5 daughters, 8 grandchildren and "a host of great-grandchildren") [Clark's U. M. Church Cemetery]

Lee, William Sidney June 2, 1853 – December 8, 1940 (no tombstone; death certificate stated he was born in Harford Co., the son of Isaac Lee, born in Baltimore, and Jane Dorsey, born in Harford Co.; he married Ella ----, worked as a farm laborer, and died a widower near Havre de Grace; informant was Mrs. Jannie Daugherty, of Havre de Grace) [Green Spring U. M. Church Cemetery]

Lee, Willis Otho November 21, 1925 – October 16, 1926 (no tombstone; death certificate stated he was born and died at Poole, the son of E. Walter Lee, born in Maryland, and Anna McMullen, born in Virginia; informant was E. Walter Lee, of Street, MD) [Clark's U. M. Church Cemetery]

Leeth, Alma E. Sunrise January 27, 1925 – Sunset March 19, 2013 (inscribed "Forever In Our Hearts") [Berkley Memorial Cemetery]

Leggar, Thomas Edward died September 9, 1915, age about 78 (no tombstone; death certificate stated he was the married son of Nathan Leggar and Milkie Henson, all born in Harford County; informant was Thomas Leggar, of Havre de Grace) [St. James United Cemetery]

Lehman, Emma J. July 1881 – January 1978 (tombstone; obituary in *The Aegis* on February 2, 1978 stated Emma Jane Lehman was the daughter of Zechariah and Cassie Brown, but her husband was not named; she lived in Havre de Grace and died January 28, 1978 at Harford Memorial Hospital, survived by 4 sons, 3 daughters, 25 grandchildren, 28 great-grandchildren, and 5 great-great-grandchildren) [Berkley Memorial Cemetery]

Lehman, George 1916-1990, U.S. Army, World War II [Berkley Memorial Cemetery]

Lehman, Junes 1882-1929 (copied in 1987, but not found in 2018) [St. James United Cemetery]

Lehman, Raymond W. December 9, 1924 – March 4, 1992, Sgt., U.S. Army, World War II (tombstone; James Dorsey Card File, African American Obituaries, maintained at the Historical Society of Harford County, has a card for him with an obituary from *The Aegis* on March 11, 1992 stating he was born in Havre de Grace, son of the late James Lehman and Emma Brown; he lived in Aberdeen, was a sergeant in the Army during World War II, worked as an aeronautical engineering technician at Aberdeen Proving Ground, retired in 1985 after 35 years of service, was a Little League baseball and football coach and managed a local rock band called the Ecuadors; he died at Harford Memorial Hospital, survived by his wife Marlene Gregg Lehman, three sons, a sister, two brothers, four grandchildren and a great-granddaughter) [Berkley Memorial Cemetery]

Leman, Harry W. January 26, 1915 – February 20, 1915 (no tombstone; death certificate stated he was the son of P. A. Leman, of Virginia, and Emma Brown, of Havre de Grace) [St. James United Cemetery]

Lenoir, Andrew died February 9, 1922, age 54 (no tombstone; death certificate stated he was born in Ohio, but his parents' names and their places of birth were not to informant Carrie Lewis, of Bel Air; he was a laborer, died in Bel Air and was buried in "Mountain Cemetery") [Mt. Zion U. M. Church Cemetery]

Lenoir, Florence March 9, 1877 – April 16, 1940 (no tombstone; death certificate stated she was the daughter of Stephen Peakar and Eliza Bishop, all born in Maryland; she married Andrew Lenoir and died a widow in Bel Air where she lived for 27 years; informant was Samuel Peakar, of Abingdon) [Mt. Zion U. M. Church Cemetery]

Lenord, William died April 24, 1935, age 80 (no tombstone; death certificate stated he was born in 1855 in Maryland, married Florence ----, worked as a farm laborer until 1927 and died at Pylesville; his parents were William Lenord and Lucinda Hays, both born in Maryland; informant was Thomas Lenord, of Pylesville) [Chestnut Grove A. M. E. Church Cemetery, formerly LaGrange Cemetery at Rocks]

Leonard, Edith Rosella July 11, 1917 – August 11, 2009 (tombstone; obituary and photo in *The Star* on August 20, 2009 stated Edith Roselle Leonard was born in the Rocks area and was the daughter of James Douglas and Pauline Miller; she married Lewis V. Leonard and they had 18 children; she was once employed at the Bainbridge Naval Center and the former Whiteford Packing Company; she lived in Havre de Grace and died a widow at Citizens Care and Rehabilitation Center, survived by 10 children (two surnamed Carter and eight surnamed Leonard), 29 grandchildren, 40 great-grandchildren, and 10 great-great-grand-children), and she was preceded in death by 8 children and a sister Sarah Hawkins) [Tabernacle Mount Zion U. M. Church Cemetery]

Leonard, Florence V. May 22, 1895 – December 27, 1948 (no tombstone; Kurtz Funeral Home Record Book 1944-1949, p. 252, stated she was born in Bel Air, but her parents were not known to informant Mary E. Jones, of White Hall; she married Bud Leonard, worked as a house maid in private homes and died a widow at home in White Hall RD; death certificate added that her husband was William R. Leonard, her usual residence was Pylesville, but she died at White Hall RD where she had lived for 9 months; same informant was named) [Fairview A. M. E. Church Cemetery]

Lesley, Bessie March 2, 1892 – May 15, 1926 (no tombstone; death certificate stated she was the daughter of Jacob Johnson and Sarah Reed, all born in Maryland; she was married and died at home in Havre de Grace; informant was Edward Lesley, 412 Freedom Alley) [Mt. Calvary U. A. M. E. Church Cemetery]

Leslie, Earlene April 13, 1890 – December 1, 1947 (no tombstone; death certificate stated she was born in Pennsylvania, the daughter of ---- Scott, mother unknown), and married Edward Leslie; they lived in Havre de Grace and she died in Harford Memorial Hospital [St. James United Cemetery]

Lester, Athalene Martha November 18, 1933 – November 9, 2002 [St. James United Cemetery]

Lester, Clifford born and died October 15, 1927 (no tombstone; death certificate stated he was the son of Paul Lester, of Alabama, and Olivia Richardson, of Havre de Grace) [St. James United Cemetery]

Lester, Edward premature birth on December 7, 1924 (no tombstone; death certificate stated he was the son of Paul Lester, of Alabama, and Olivia Richardson, of Havre de Grace)) [St. James United Cemetery]

Lester, Infant March 4, 1924 – March 5, 1924 (no tombstone; death certificate stated she was the daughter of Paul Lester, of Alabama, and Olivia Richardson, of Havre de Grace)) [St. James United Cemetery]

Lester, Mr. (owner of a lot in section 31 some time after 1951) [Mt. Calvary U. A. M. E. Church Cemetery]

Lester, Mrs. (owner of a lot in section 39 some time after 1951) [Mt. Calvary U. A. M. E. Church Cemetery]

Lester, Paul J. 1897-1968 [Berkley Memorial Cemetery]

Lester, Paul Jr. September 13, 1928 – July 3, 1983, PFC, U.S. Army, Korea (tombstone; obituary in *The Aegis* on July 7, 1983 stated he was born in Havre de Grace, the son of Paul Lester, Sr. and Olivia Richardson, had been employed by BG&E and was a member of American Legion Post 55; he lived in Bel Air and died at Fallston General Hospital, survived by his wife Athaline Martha Lester, five sons, three daughters, one brother and one sister) [St. James United Cemetery]

Lester, Victoria May 20, 1932 – May 24, 1932 (no tombstone; death certificate stated she was the daughter of Paul Lester, of Alabama, and Olivia Richardson, of Havre de Grace) [St. James United Cemetery]

Lewis, ---- December 19, 1919 – January 5, 1920 (no tombstone; death certificate stated he died at Kalmia and was an unnamed son of Irvin Lewis and Agnes C. Green, all born in Harford Co.; informant was Irvin Lewis, of Bel Air) [Clark's U. M. Church Cemetery]

Lewis, ---- died October 26, 1893 (no tombstone; death notice in *The Aegis* on November 10, 1893 stated a boy of John Lewis, aged between 4 and 5 years, was fatally burned at home near Kalmia while playing with the fire in a stove; place of burial was not reported [probably Clark's U. M. Church Cemetery]

Lewis, Albert C. 1911-1989 (on same tombstone with Hattie E. Lewis) [Asbury Cemetery]

Lewis, Amelia died November 14, 1925, age 42 (no tombstone; death certificate stated she was married and employed as a cook in Bel Air; her father was Isaac Dorsey, but her mother was not known to informant Robert Lewis, of Bel Air; Amelia and Isaac were born in Maryland) [Hendon Hill Cemetery]

Lewis, Catherine Louise April 27, 1934 – December 7, 1935 (no tombstone; death certificate stated she was born near Schucks Corner, the daughter of Albert Lewis, born in Bel Air, and Hattie Kennard, born in Harford Co.; informant was Albert Lewis, of Bel Air) [Asbury Cemetery]

Lewis, Charles Kenneth July 2, 1949 – January 22, 1950 (no tombstone; death certificate stated he was born in Harford Co., the son of Ernest Lee and Rosie E. Lewis who lived in rural Bel Air; informant was John N. Lewis) [Clark's U. M. Church Cemetery]

Lewis, Charlie born about April 16, 1849 – May 25, 1928 (no tombstone; death certificate stated he was the son of Julia Lewis, both born in Maryland, but the name of his father was not known to informant Robert A. Lewis, of Bel Air; he was a preacher, married and divorced, and died in Havre de Grace Hospital) [Mt. Calvary U. A. M. E. Church Cemetery]

Lewis, Clifton 1900-1969 (on same tombstone with Myrtle Lewis) [William C. Rice Memorial Cemetery, St. James U. M. Church]

Lewis, Hattie E. 1917-1987 (on same tombstone with Albert C. Lewis; her name was listed as Hattie Ellen Lewis when copied in 1987 and Albert was not listed, but in 2018 both names are shown on the tombstone and her name is inscribed as Hattie E. Lewis, not Hattie Ellen Lewis) [Asbury Cemetery]

Lewis, Henrietta M. May 31, 1881 – February 14, 1913 (no tombstone; death certificate stated she was born in Harford Co., the daughter of William Cohen, born in Harford Co., and Mary A. Price, born in Boston, MA; she was married and died at Kalmia; informant was Robert Lewis, of Bel Air) [Asbury Cemetery]

Lewis, Infant stillborn female on March 1, 1929 (no tombstone; death certificate stated she was the daughter of Becuhard(?) Lewis and Marie Williams, of Havre de Grace) [St. James United Cemetery]

Lewis, Myrtle 1901-   (on same tombstone with Clifton Lewis) [William C. Rice Memorial Cemetery, St. James U. M. Church]

Lewis, Narvel Colburn September 8, 1946 – June 17, 1951 (no tombstone; death certificate stated he was the son of James Rumsey and Rosa E. Lewis, of Bel Air; died at Harford Memorial Hospital in Havre de Grace; information gleaned by an unidentified person from the hospital records) [Clark's U. M. Church Cemetery]

Lewis, Pearl O. December 17, 1913 – April 21, 1914 (no tombstone; death certificate stated she was the daughter of Albert Lewis and Hattie James, all born in Harford Co.; informant was Albert Lewis, of Bel Air) [Clark's U. M. Church Cemetery]

Lewis, Ralph March 7, 1905 – March 8, 1912 (no tombstone; death certificate stated he was the son of Robert A. Lewis and Mary Coen, all born in Maryland; he died at Kalmia; informant was Robert Lewis, of Bel Air) [Asbury Cemetery]

Lewis, Rossetta died September 25, 1920, age 52 (no tombstone; death certificate stated she was the daughter of George H. Douglas and Mary J. Preston, all were born in Maryland; she was married, and died at Kalmia; informant was John H. Lewis, of Bel Air) [Clark's U. M. Church Cemetery]

Lingham, Amanda Jane June 28, 1854 – October 12, 1909 (no tombstone; death certificate stated she died October 12, 1909, age 55 years, 3 months, 15 days, but the 1900 census stated she was born in September 1848; death certificate stated she was born at Stepney, the daughter of ---- and Amanda Cole; she was the widow of Robert Lingham and died at her home in Abingdon; place of burial was not stated; informant was her daughter Pinkey Carrington) [John Wesley U. M. E. Church Cemetery in Abingdon]

Lingham, Jennie 1874-1961 (on same tombstone with Robert W. Lingham; family states Jennie C. Lingham (neé Berry) was the wife of Robert Wesley Lingham) [John Wesley U. M. E. Church Cemetery in Abingdon]

Lingham, Lillian R. 1886-1962 (on same tombstone with T. Edward Lingham) [John Wesley U. M. E. Church Cemetery in Abingdon]

Lingham, Marie N. died March 6, 1997, age 84 (no tombstone; obituary in *The Aegis* on March 12, 1997 stated she was born in Joppa, daughter of Frank and Alice Brown and widow of Robert Lingham, lived in Joppa and died at Laurelwood Nursing Home in Elkton, survived by two daughters Geraldine Daniels and Genevieve Gregg, one grandson Anthony Malloy and six step-grandchildren; obituary stated her burial was in the St. James Cemetery in Havre de Grace and not at the John Wesley Church in Abingdon with her husband) [St. James United Cemetery]

Lingham, Robert born between 1786 and 1792 – died between 1850 and 1860 (no tombstone; no record of his death has been found nor his place of burial [probably John Wesley U. M. E. Church Cemetery in Abingdon]

Lingham, Robert drowned on May 25, 1890 (no tombstone; death notice in *The Aegis* on May 30, 1890 and June 6, 1890 stated he drowned in the Chesapeake Bay near Havre de Grave on May 25, 1890 when the sailboat he was riding in with three others upset; his body was found on May 31, 1890 about 12 miles up the Sassafras River in Cecil Co.; since he was unknown to the residents he was buried in the sand on the shore; some of his family later recovered his body and returned it to Havre de Grace for burial in the "Gravelly Hill Cemetery") [Gravel Hill Cemetery]

Lingham, Robert Jr. born circa 1813-1817 – died March 5, 1887 (no tombstone; obituary in *The Aegis* on March 11, 1887 stated he worked many years for Thomas W. Hall and died at his home near Abingdon; place of burial was not reported [probably John Wesley U. M. E. Church Cemetery in Abingdon]

Lingham, Robert W. 1870-1946 (on same tombstone with Jennie C. Lingham; family records state Robert Wesley Lingham was possibly a son of Robert Lingham and 2nd wife Amanda Norton) [John Wesley U. M. E. Church Cemetery in Abingdon]

Lingham, Robert Wesley Jr. 1904 – May 23, 1974 (no tombstone; obituary in *The Aegis* stated he was born at Loreley in Baltimore Co., the son of Robert Lingham and Jennie Berry, and formerly worked for the Bethlehem Steel Company; he married Marie N. Brown and died at his home at 808 Philadelphia Road in Joppa, survived by his wife, daughter 5 grandchildren) [John Wesley U. M. E. Church Cemetery in Abingdon]

Lingham, Sharlotte born circa 1792 and died between 1840 and 1850 (no tombstone, no record of her death has been found, and no place of burial, but in all likelihood she is buried in an unmarked grave beside her husband Robert Lingham) [John Wesley U. M. E. Church Cemetery in Abingdon]

Lingham, T. Edward 1879-1960 (on same tombstone with Lillian R. Lingham; family records state Thomas Edward Lingham was a son of Robert Lingham and his second wife Amanda Norton) [John Wesley U. M. E. Church Cemetery in Abingdon]

Lingham, William July 19, 1877 – July 13, 1944 (no tombstone; death certificate stated he was born in Abingdon, the son of Robert Lingham and Amanda Norton whose birth places were not known to informant, his wife, Carrie Lingham, of Abingdon; he worked as a laborer and died in Abingdon where he lived all his life) [John Wesley U. M. E. Church Cemetery in Abingdon]

Lipscomb, John 1882 – October 22, 1943 (no tombstone; death certificate stated he was the son of John

Lipscomb and Mary Moore, all born in Virginia; he was a day laborer and lived in Aberdeen, but died in the Harford County Home near Bel Air where he had lived for two days; informant was Mrs. Bessie Blaine, of Havre de Grace RFD#1) [Green Spring U. M. Church Cemetery]

Lisbon, Adam died September 22, 1912, age about 75 (no tombstone; death certificate stated he was a single farm hand who died at Cooptown; his place of birth and the names and places of birth of his parents were not known to informant James Amoss, Sr., of Jarrettsville) [Fairview A. M. E. Church Cemetery]

Lisby, ---- stillborn male died April 26, 1918 (no tombstone; death certificate stated he died in Bel Air and was the son of James Lisby and Henrietta Westcott; all were born in Maryland) [Hendon Hill Cemetery]

Lisby, Adella C. (Mrs.) died on September 3, 1961, age not given (no tombstone; obituary in *The Record* on September 7, 1961 stated she was the daughter of the late Wilkerson and Ella Carney and died suddenly at Harford Memorial Hospital as the result of an accidental fall at her home at 550 Revolution Street; she was survived by a son, 2 daughters, 2 brothers, and several grandchildren and great-grandchildren) [Berkley Memorial Cemetery]

Lisby, Annie died June 20, 1914, age about 56 (no tombstone; death certificate stated she was the daughter of Charles Jones and Harriet Richardson, all born in Harford Co.; she lived near Havre de Grace and was married at the time of her death; informant was John Lisby; her death notice in *The Aegis* on June 26, 1914 stated "a colored woman named Lisby from Gravelly Hill became ill while in her carriage in front of a store here last Saturday and was taken at once to the hospital but died before reaching it") [Gravel Hill Cemetery]

Lisby, Annie M. died July 8, 1988, age 99 (no tombstone; obituary in *The Aegis* on July 21, 1988 stated she was born in Harford County, the daughter of Nelson and Eliza Presberry, and was the widow of George D. Lisby; she was active in the church and died at the Francis Scott Key Medical Center in Baltimore, survived by two nephews and two nieces) [Union U. M. Church Cemetery]

Lisby, Charles Westcott July 1, 1919 – July 17, 1919 (no tombstone; death certificate stated he was born in Bel Air, the son of James Lisby and Henrietta Westcott who were both born in Maryland) [Hendon Hill Cemetery]

Lisby, Charlie H. January 25, 1854 – November 10, 1925 (no tombstone; death certificate stated he was the son of John Lisby and Ellen Hollingsworth, all born in Maryland; he was married, worked as a laborer and died a widower at Level; informant was Mrs. Elizabeth Garrett, of Havre de Grace) [Gravel Hill Cemetery]

Lisby, Dorothy M. 1923-1999 (on same handwritten flat cement slab with John Lisby; obituary and photo in *The Aegis* on June 16, 1999 stated Dorothy Mayfield Presbury Lisby was born February 28, 1923 in Havre de Grace, the daughter of Jeremiah and Edna Presbury, and the widow of John Lisby whom she married in 1947; she was employed at Elsner's Canning Co. in Havre de Grace and later worked at Aberdeen Proving Ground and Perry Point VAMC; she died at home in Havre de Grace on October 4, 1999, survived by a son James Albert Lee, three granddaughters, nine great-grandchildren, a grandson-in-law, a great-great-granddaughter, three brothers, one sister, three sisters-in-law, and was predeceased by a great-grandson, a sister and a brother) [St. James United Cemetery]

Lisby, Florence M. February 4, 1869 – April 2, 1924 (no tombstone; death certificate stated she was born in Maryland, the daughter of Robert Russ, born in Delaware, but her mother's name was not known to informant George Lisby, of "Gravelly Hill near Havre de Grace;" she was married and died near Havre de Grace) [Gravel Hill Cemetery]

Lisby, George D. died March 8, 1984, age 92 (no tombstone; obituary in *The Aegis* stated he was born in Perryman, the son of Joseph and Jane Lisby, and was the husband of Annie M. Lisby; he was active in the church, serving as trustee and church treasurer for 34 years, and lived in Aberdeen and died at home, survived by his wife and a sister Mary J. Hall) [Union U. M. Church Cemetery]

Lisby, George D. died May 18, 1997, age 62 (no tombstone; obituary and photo in *The (*Baltimore) *Sun* on May 24, 1997 stated he was a lifelong resident of Aberdeen and a longtime Harford County school teacher, administrator and school board member, worked at the State Department of Education from 1971 until his retirement in 1984, and died at Harford Memorial Hospital, survived by his wife Victoria Parsons Lisby, whom he married in 1964, three sons, two daughters, a sister, six grandchildren and one great-grandchild) [Berkley

Memorial Cemetery]

Lisby, George died May 15, 1931, age about 74, date of birth unknown (no tombstone; death certificate stated he was the son of John Lisby and Ellen Hollingsworth, all were born in Maryland; he was married, worked as a farmer and died in Havre de Grace Hospital; the information was gleaned from the records by someone in the Havre de Grace Hospital) [Gravel Hill Cemetery]

Lisby, Henrietta August 7, 1881 – November 2, 1928 (no tombstone; death certificate stated she was born in Maryland, married and died in Bel Air; her parents were Noah Wescott, born in North Carolina, and Augusta Spriggs, born in Maryland, and informant was James S. Lisby) [Hendon Hill Cemetery]

Lisby, Hilda September 24, 1990 – September 27, 1915 (no tombstone; death certificate stated she was the daughter of George Cox and Georgie Hawkins, all born in Harford Co.; she lived near Havre de Grace and was married at the time of her death; informant was Georgie Cox, of Havre de Grace RFD) [Gravel Hill Cemetery]

Lisby, Hilton Leroy August 28, 1911 – December 4, 1911 (no tombstone; death certificate stated he was the son of Robert Bowser and Jane Christy, all born in Maryland) [Union U. M. Church Cemetery]

Lisby, James Wiley April 6, 1915 – September 21, 1916 (no tombstone; death certificate stated he was born and died in Bel Air and was the son of James Lisby and Henrietta Westcoat, both born in Maryland; informant was James Frisby, of Bel Air) [Hendon Hill Cemetery]

Lisby, Jane Nettie May 30, 1872 – October 5, 1913 (no tombstone; death certificate stated she was a widow and the daughter of Isaac Williams and Rachael Christy, all born in Maryland) [Union U. M. Church Cemetery]

Lisby, John 1912-1997 (on same handwritten flat cement slab with Dorothy M. Lisby; James Dorsey Card File, African American Obituaries, maintained at the Historical Society of Harford County, has a card with obituary from an unidentified newspaper on September 24, 1997 stating John Fieldon Lisby was born November 10, 1912 in Philadelphia, the son of Evelyn Fripp, and married Dorothy Presbury in 1943; he lived in Aberdeen, worked for the Veterans Administration hospital for 38 years and died at Harford Memorial Hospital in Havre de Grace on September 12, 1997; he was survived by his wife, a son, three granddaughters and nine great-grandchildren, among other relatives) [St. James United Cemetery]

Lisby, John Wesley 1847-1939 (no tombstone; death certificate stated he was born April 11, 1847, the son of Henry and Cassandra Lisby, all born in Maryland; he married Eva ----, worked as a laborer until 1921 and died a widower at his home near Gover's Hill in Havre de Grace on January 29, 1939; informant was Mrs. Rachel Scott, of Havre de Grace) [Gravel Hill Cemetery]

Lisby, Joseph Henry March 16, 1837 – July 5, 1931 (no tombstone; death certificate stated he was the son of Henry Lisby and Cassandra Pearson, all born in Maryland; he was a widower, wife named Phoebe, and he was a farmer all his life until he retired in February 1930; he died in Havre de Grace; informant was Mrs. Rachel Scott, of Havre de Grace; James Dorsey Card File, African American Obituaries, maintained at the Historical Society of Harford County, has a card for him with an obituary abstraction from the *Bel Air Times* on July 10, 1931 stating Joseph Lisby, aged 93, one of the oldest colored residents of Havre de Grace, died July 6, 1931, leaving a brother John and a sister in Pennsylvania) [Gravel Hill Cemetery]

Lisby, Margaret I. 1900-1984 (inscribed "Living In Our Hearts;" obituary in *The Aegis* stated she was born in Darlington, the daughter of Thomas and Georgianna Cain, and the widow of Otho Lisby; she was active in the church and was president of Willing Workers; she lived in Aberdeen and died at the John L. Deacon Medical Center in Baltimore, survived by two sons Otho and George Lisby, a daughter Cora Fleming, two brothers Edward H. Cain and Edward Presberry, a sister Agnes Presberry, 9 grandchildren, 6 great-grandchildren) [Union U. M. Church Cemetery]

Lisby, Mary 1844-1925 (tombstone; death certificate stated she was born in June 1844 and died on September 12, 1925; she was the widowed daughter of Peter Stansbury, but her mother was not known to informant William T. Hollands, of Havre de Grace) [Union U. M. Church Cemetery]

Lisby, Otho M. 1900-1944 (inscribed "In Loving Memory;" death certificate stated he was the son of Joseph T. Lisby and Jane Christy, and the husband of Margaret Cain Lisby) [Union U. M. Church Cemetery]

Lisby, Phoebe Hollis 1854-1928 (no tombstone; death certificate stated she was born December 24, 1854 and died September 6, 1928 in Havre de Grace; informant Rachel L. Scott stated Phoebe was married and born in Maryland, but she did not know the names of her parents) [Gravel Hill Cemetery]

Lisby, Solomon J. April 29, 1848 – April 29, 1911 (no tombstone; death certificate stated he was married and the son of William Lisby and Annie Smith, all born in Maryland) [Union U. M. Church Cemetery]

Little, Barry L. 1960-2000 (small metal funeral home marker) [St. James United Cemetery]

Little, Charmayne 1959-2011 (small metal funeral home marker) [St. James United Cemetery]

Littleton, Alberta Rumsey 1937-1978 [Clark's U. M. Church Cemetery]

Litton, Charles, Co. G, 8 U.S. Vol. Inf., Spanish American War (no dates on tombstone; death certificate stated he was born in Tennessee, the son of Charles Litton, born in Virginia, but the name of his mother was not known to informant Lucy Litton, of Benson; he worked as a laborer, married Lucy ---- (age 69 in 1941) and was a pensioned veteran of the Spanish American War; he lived at Benson about 20 years and died January 1, 1940, age about 65) [Tabernacle Mount Zion U. M. Church Cemetery]

Logan, Charles William May 17, 1868 – February 6, 1930 (no tombstone; death certificate stated he was married and worked as a laborer; died in Havre de Grace Hospital; his parents' names were unknown to informant, Mrs. Susan Logan, of Bel Air, but she stated he was born in Virginia) [Hendon Hill Cemetery]

Long, Emma Miller 1906-1923 (no dates on tombstone, but death certificate stated Emma L. Long was born July 3, 1906 in Maryland, the daughter of Robert Warren, born in Pennsylvania, and Maggie Miller, born in Maryland; she was married, lived in Havre de Grace and died in Havre de Grace Hospital on July 14, 1923; informant was ---- Long, of Havre de Grace) [Gravel Hill Cemetery]

Long, Norris February 22, 1922 – December 3, 1973 [Berkley Memorial Cemetery]

Long, William June 16, 1908 – February 24, 1952 (no tombstone; Pennington Funeral Home records stated he was born at Aldino, the son of Wilson Long and Mary Bond, married ---- (blank), worked as a laborer and lived on Warren Street in Havre de Grace; informant was Lawrence Long, of Muirkirk, MD) [Green Spring U. M. Church Cemetery]

Loveday, Harriet, "Our Mother" died April 26, 1886, age 70 (inscribed "By her children" and "Gone but not forgotten" and "The lonely stars are beaming upon a silent grave, Where sleepeth without dreaming the one we could not save") [Old Union Chapel M. E. Church Cemetery]

Lowery, Bessie Mae died October 10, 1995, age 92 (no tombstone; obituary in *The Aegis* on November 8, 1995 stated she was the daughter of Annie Osborne and Benjamin Cox, lived in Bel Air and died at Fallston General Hospital, survived by a son, 5 daughters, 16 grandchildren, 25 great-grandchildren, 7 great-great-grandchildren) [Asbury Cemetery]

Lowery, Ella Mae died May 26, 1957, no age given (no tombstone; obituary in *The Aegis* on June 6, 1957 stated she was a grandmother and the wife of James Edward Lowery) [Tabernacle Mount Zion U. M. Church Cemetery]

Lowery, James P. September 17, 1931 – October 24, 1977, PFC, U.S. Army, Korea (tombstone; obituary in *The Aegis* on October 27, 1977 stated he was the son of Wilson L. Lowery, Sr., of Joppa, Dembytown Road, and the late Anna Brown Harriday; he was born in Maryland, married Harrietta Lester, served in the Korean War, worked as a supervisor at St. Elizabeth Hospital in Washington, DC, and died at Community Memorial Hospital in Washington) [Tabernacle Mount Zion U. M. Church Cemetery]

Lowery, Wilson Leon Sr. died January 15, 1979, age 70 (no tombstone; obituary in *The Aegis* on January 28, 1979 stated his wife Jane Lowry had predeceased him) [Tabernacle Mount Zion U. M. Church Cemetery]

Lowry, Ellen October 8, 1846 – January 19, 1930 (no tombstone; death certificate stated she was born in Maryland, the son of Annie M. Shivart, born in Maryland, but her father's name was not known to informant Albert Lowery *(sic)*, of Joppa; she died a widow at Joppa and was buried in "Mountain Cemetery") [Mt. Zion U. M. Church Cemetery]

Lowry, Grace Meldon April 23, 1921 – June 23, 1921 (no tombstone; death certificate stated she was born in Joppa, the daughter of Adolph Lowry, born in Joppa, and Eliza Pekar (Peaker), born in Emmorton, and she was buried in "The Mountain Colored Cemetery") [Mt. Zion U. M. Church Cemetery]

Lowry, Lewis died June 28, 1903, age 51 years, 2 months and 10 days (no tombstone; death certificate stated he was born in Talbot Co., MD, the son of Horace and Rachel Lowry; he married Ellen ----, worked as a farmer and died at Singer; informant was William Peaco, a non-relative; his place of burial was not indicated [probably Mt. Zion U. M. Church Cemetery]

Lowry, Mary C. died January 1, 1905, age 4 years, 2 months and 28 days (no tombstone; death certificate stated she was the daughter of Elbert Lawry (Albert Lowry) and Lottie Peeker (Peaker), all born in Maryland; she was burned and died at Mountain; her place of burial was not indicated) [probably Mt. Zion U. M. Church Cemetery]

Lucas, T. T. May 25, 1846 – January 24, 1918 (no tombstone; death certificate stated he was the son of J. L. Lucas and Sarah Hedgmon, all born in Virginia; he was a widower and a minister who died at Level; informant was William Turner, of Aberdeen) [Green Spring U. M. Church Cemetery]

Lucus, Mary M. 1907 – August 2, 1946 (no tombstone; death certificate stated she was born in Elorie, SC, married, and died near Bel Air; her father was Henry Palmer, born in South Carolina, but her mother was unknown to informant Waymon Lucus, of Bel Air) [Hendon Hill Cemetery]

Lunsford, Richard Dean May 1, 1907 – October 17, 1974, PFC, U.S. Army, World War II (Pennington Funeral Home records stated he was born in Roxboro, NC, the son of Samuel Lunsford and Anna Mae Raney; he married Virginia ----, who was the informant, and they lived in Havre de Grace) [St. James United Cemetery]

Lunsford, Richard D. Jr., "Beloved Husband, Brother, Father and Friend" March 10, 1937 – September 13, 2000 (inscribed "The Wind Beneath Our Wing" with his photo) [St. James United Cemetery]

Lunsford, Samuel "Sept ? 1885" *(sic)* – April 5, 1959 (no tombstone; Pennington Funeral Home records stated he was born in North Carolina and died at age 73; he was the son of Louis Lunsford and "unknown" and had been a carpenter in Havre de Grace for 9 months; informant was Richard Lunsford [St. James United Cemetery]

Luster, Levy died January 10, 1931, age about 50 (no tombstone; death certificate stated he was born in Maryland, worked as a laborer and was married at the time of his death in Havre de Grace; the names of his parents were not known to informant Maria Luster) [Green Spring U. M. Church Cemetery]

Lyle, Arthur, son of George M. and Margaret Lyle, died July 1, 1890, age 17 (tombstone; J. C. Taylor Marble Co. records state "George Lyle's son's headstone was put up Nov 28th 1893") [Hendon Hill Cemetery]

Lyle, George M. died May 2, 1908, age 65 (no tombstone; death certificate stated he was a restaurant proprietor in Bel Air, born in Maryland, wife named Margaret, but the names of his parents were unknown to informant, son Robert Lyle; obituary in *The Aegis* on May 8, 1908 stated he was raised a slave in the Smithson family of Cecil County and afterwards came to Bel Air and had a restaurant for 40 years); place of burial not indicated [probably Hendon Hill Cemetery]

Lyle, Margaret L. died April 9, 1906, age 56 (no tombstone, but on the back of death certificate is written "Hendon Hill;" she was born in Maryland, married George M. Lyle and lived in Bel Air; her parents were Jarrett and Caroline Wilson; informant was her son Robert Lyle) [Hendon Hill Cemetery]

Lyle, William H., son of George M. and Margaret Lyle, December 31, 1867 – December 30, 1903 [Hendon Hill Cemetery]

Lyles, Catherine Marguerite Fauntleroy died July 10, 1996, age 90 (no tombstone; obituary in *The Aegis* on July 24, 1996 stated she was born in Essex Co., CT, the daughter of William H. and Margaret T. Fauntleroy, and widow of Rev. William T. Lyles; she taught in Anne Arundel County schools and for 34 years in Baltimore City Public Schools; she was active member of Sharon Baptist Church for 76 years; formerly of Fallston, she died in Baltimore, survived by a son, a daughter, a brother, a sister, five grandchildren, four great-grandchildren and a special companion Phyllis G. Baker) [William C. Rice Memorial Cemetery, St. James U. M. Church]

Lyles, William T. (Rev.) July 20, 1904 – May 6, 1987 [William C. Rice Memorial Cemetery, St. James U. M. Church]

M---- (Moore?), J. M. (tombstone is fragmented and a large piece of it was mounted sideways on the old base) [Tabernacle Mount Zion U. M. Church Cemetery]

Mabray, Edith Thomas "Daughter," "Granddaughter" 1910-1972 [William C. Rice Memorial Cemetery, St. James U. M. Church]

Mack, Curtis Lee 1953-2006 (small metal funeral home marker) [Berkley Memorial Cemetery]

Mack, Flossie, "Mother – Grandmother" September 5, 1929 – January 15, 2002 (inscribed "In Loving Memory") [Berkley Memorial Cemetery]

Mack, John Ann 1870-1941 (inscribed "Gone but not forgotten") [Gravel Hill Cemetery]

Mack, Katherine L. Moore March 7, 1910 – July 30, 1941 (no tombstone; death certificate stated she was born in Bel Air, married, and died at home on Bond Street; her parents were Steven Moore and Hannah Smith, both born in Bel Air; informant was Mrs. Hannah Moore, of Bel Air) [Hendon Hill Cemetery]

Mack, Rickey Herschel Jr. Sunrise February 2, 1980 – Sunset August 13, 1907 (small metal funeral home marker) [Clark's U. M. Church Cemetery]

Mack, Veryl Terrance "Donkey" died September 24, 1973, age 16 (no tombstone; obituary in *The Aegis* on October 4, 1973 stated he died at 2064 Battle Street, Edgewood Heights, Edgewood; he was born in Havre de Grace, the son of John Mack, Sr. and Flossie M. Mack, of Edgewood, and was survived by his parents, five brothers and four sisters) [Berkley Memorial Cemetery]

Macon, Alonzo L. "Loved One and Father" 1.30.19 3-15-79 (actual inscription) [St. James United Cemetery]

Macon, Baby (male) November 9, 1947 – November 10, 1947 (no tombstone; death certificate stated he was born premature at eight months and died in Harford Memorial Hospital, the son of Stroman Macon, of North Carolina, and Ada Grimes, of Havre de Grace) [St. James United Cemetery]

Madden, Bertha C. March 3, 1898 – November 30, 1986 [Union U. M. Church Cemetery]

Maddicks, Hattie June 25, 1914 – June 12, 1917 (no tombstone; death certificate stated she was born in Harford Co. and died in Bel Air, daughter of Henry Maddicks, birth place not known, and Stella Waters, born in Harford Co.; informant was William Anderson, of Bel Air) [Hendon Hill Cemetery]

Maddox, Abigail February 5, 1881 – November 21, 1939 (no tombstone; death certificate stated she was the daughter of George Smith and Eliza Green, all born in Lancaster Co., PA, and died a widow in Bel Air where she had lived for 40 years; her husband was Murray Maddox; informant was Mrs. Nettie Durbin, of Bel Air) [Tabernacle Mount Zion U. M. Church Cemetery]

Maddox, Graham Albert May 1, 1891 – September 6, 1901 (tombstone; death certificate stated Graham Albert "Maddux" was a native of U.S.A., but Dr. W. S. Archer did not know his parents' names) [Tabernacle Mount Zion U. M. Church Cemetery]

Maddox, John S. August 16, 1897 – August 26, 1919 (no tombstone; death certificate stated he was the son of J. Massey Maddox and Sophia Ruff, all born in Maryland; he was single, worked as a waiter and died in Bel Air; informant was Massey Maddox, of Bel Air) [Tabernacle Mount Zion U. M. Church Cemetery]

Maddox, Ruth March 29, 1922 – February 15, 1923 (no tombstone; death certificate stated she was the daughter of John H. Maddox and Stella Waters, all born in Maryland, and they lived at Watervale; informant was her father) [Hendon Hill Cemetery]

Maddox, Sadie March 12, 1921 – May 22, 1921 (no tombstone; death certificate stated she was the daughter of John Maddox and Stella Watters, all born in Maryland and they lived at Vale) [Hendon Hill Cemetery]

Maddox, Sophia died June 15, 1915, age 61 (no tombstone; death certificate stated she was the daughter of Philip Ruff and Rachel J. Bond, all born in Harford Co.; she was married and died in Bel Air; informant was J. M. Maddox, of Bel Air) [Tabernacle Mount Zion U. M. Church Cemetery]

Madric, Luvenia L. April 22, 1989 – July 11, 2013 (small metal handmade marker) [Berkley Memorial Cemetery]

Mahanes, James A. January 23, 1905 – November 5, 1987 (on same tombstone with Mattie M. Mahanes, but his date of death is not inscribed on their tombstone; a separate military marker indicates he served in the U.S. Army in World War II and gives his date of death) [Berkley Memorial Cemetery]

Mahanes, Mattie M. January 10, 1910 – March 1, 1986 (on same tombstone with James A. Mahanes) [Berkley Memorial Cemetery]

Mallary, Baby stillborn male on October 29, 1941 (no tombstone; death certificate stated he was the son of George Giles, of Aberdeen, and Rosalie Mary Mallary, of Havre de Grace) [St. James United Cemetery]

Maller, Kimberly Renee August 24, 1968 – April 14, 2007 (with photo) [Berkley Memorial Cemetery]

Malloy, Barbara C. January 11, 1953 – September 2, 1998 [Berkley Memorial Cemetery]

Malloy, Eugene 1902-1966 (on same tombstone with Eva Malloy) [Berkley Memorial Cemetery]

Malloy, Eugene T. 1939-2017 (small metal funeral home marker) [Berkley Memorial Cemetery]

Malloy, Eva 1900-1968 (on same tombstone with Eugene Malloy) [Berkley Memorial Cemetery]

Mann, Katharine F. October 9, 1918 – July 10, 1972 [Berkley Memorial Cemetery]

Mann, Samantha 1991-1991 (on same tombstone with Shanika Day) [Berkley Memorial Cemetery]

Manns, Julia A., daughter of Ancle and S. Manns, March 17, 1917 – August 20, 1917 (tombstone; death certificate stated she was the daughter of "Ansel Mans" and Sivilla Jordan, all born in Maryland; informant was her father, of Street, MD) [Chestnut Grove A. M. E. Church Cemetery, formerly LaGrange Cemetery at Rocks]

Manuel, Gladys August 20, 1912 – August 24, 1912 (no tombstone; death certificate stated she was the daughter of William Manuel and Eliza Pitts, all were born in Maryland; her name was misspelled Glayds and she died at Creswell; informant was her father) [Mt. Calvary U. A. M. E. Church Cemetery]

Marshall, Annie December 25, 1894 – March 24, 1911 (no tombstone; death certificate stated she was the daughter of Dennis Marshall and Annie Hollis, all born in Maryland; she was single, a house maid, and died in Darlington; informant was Catharine Marshall, of Darlington) [Clark's U. M. Church Cemetery]

Marshall, Annie October 15, 1872 – April 29, 1927 (no tombstone; death certificate stated she died a widow in Darlington, the daughter of Phebe Johnson, both born in Maryland, but her father's name was not known to the informant Virginia Marshall, of Darlington) [Clark's U. M. Church Cemetery]

Marshall, Catherine died October 27, 1914, age about 65 (no tombstone; death certificate stated she was the daughter of William Marshall and Mary Jackson, all born in Virginia, and she died a widow in Havre de Grace; informant was Charles Coleman, of Havre de Grace) [St. James United Cemetery]

Marshall, J. Henry March 3, 1846 – June 12, 1934 (inscribed "At Rest" with those dates, but death certificate stated he was born on March 5, 1843 and died on June 11, 1934) [St. James United Cemetery]

Marshall, Kathryn August 9, 1897 – July 10, 1962 (no tombstone; Harkins Funeral Home Records stated she was born in Harford Co., the daughter of Benjamin Marshall and Anna Johnson; she was single, lived in Darlington, died at Crownsville State Hospital and her funeral was authorized by William Scott, of Darlington) [Clark's U. M. Church Cemetery]

Martin, Della V. 1920-2001 (inscribed "Forever In Our Hearts") [St. James United Cemetery]

Martin, E. A., "Mother" Rosie Warfield 1857-1928 (as copied in 1992, but not found in 2018) [Union U. M. Church Cemetery]

Martin, Esther August 4, 1931 – January 31, 2014 (inscribed "Always In Our Hearts") [Berkley Memorial Cemetery]

Martin, Jerry Lee January 11, 1940 – September 5, 2009, SFC, U.S. Army (on same tombstone with Mildred V. Martin) [Berkley Memorial Cemetery]

Martin, Mary June 1, 1863 – June 23, 1911 (no tombstone; death certificate stated she was the daughter of John Rumsey and Harriet Kane, and they were all born in Harford Co., informant was Alfred Durbin, of Havre de

Grace) [Skinner Cemetery]

Martin, Mildred V. February 22, 1947 -   (on same tombstone with Jerry Lee Martin) [Berkley Memorial Cemetery]

Martin, Moses V. November 12, 1855 – July 14, 1917 (no tombstone; death certificate stated he was the son of Lewis Martin and Annie Fox, all born in Harford Co.; he was a married preacher and died in Havre de Grace; informant was Mrs. Frankanna Martin, of Havre de Grace) [Skinner Cemetery]

Mason, Ada Lee May 26, 1936 – February 16, 2000 (inscribed "We Love You Mom" with her photo) [Fairview A. M. E. Church Cemetery]

Mason, Derek C. II June 24, 1977 – May 25, 2000 (buried in section 19; inscribed "Namdi" and "Big Nu") [Mt. Calvary U. A. M. E. Church Cemetery]

Mason, Madeline Hilton, "Loving Mother, Grandmother and Great-Grandmother" April 20, 1902 – September 20, 2007 (inscribed on the back of her tombstone: "Always Be Thankful, Treat Others As You Would Like To Be Treated") [Green Spring U. M. Church Cemetery]

Mason, Parrish Morris died May 14, 1992, age 83 (no tombstone; James Dorsey Card File, African American Obituaries, maintained at the Historical Society of Harford County, has a card for him with an obituary and photo from an unidentified, undated newspaper stating he was born in Baltimore, the son of William and Melinda Mason, and worked as a farmer; he lived in the Brevin Nursing Home, died at Harford Memorial Hospital in Havre de Grace and was survived by a brother Thaddeus L. Mason, Sr., and a niece and four nephews) [Asbury Cemetery]

Massey, Tonya Rae March 8, 1963 – September 22, 2002 (inscribed "Tyler I Will Always Love You") [St. James United Cemetery]

Matthews, Charles H. February 28, 1844 – May 5, 1919 (no tombstone; death certificate stated he was a widower and was employed as a "cachman" in Bel Air; Charles and his father Robert Matthews were born in Maryland, but his mother's name was not known by informant Tillie Matthews, of Bel Air; *The Aegis* on May 9, 1919 stated he lived with the late Col. Herman Stump for many years) [Hendon Hill Cemetery]

Matthews, Chyna L. 2000-2000 (metal funeral home marker) [Chestnut Grove A. M. E. Church Cemetery, formerly LaGrange Cemetery at Rocks]

Matthews, Delores A. 1929 – (no death date inscribed, but she died after 1994, and on same tombstone with Robert Matthews) [Tabernacle Mount Zion U. M. Church Cemetery]

Matthews, Gertrude J. 1898-1980 [St. James United Cemetery]

Matthews, Harriet Matilda November 25, 1879 – November 17, 1935 (no tombstone; death certificate stated she was born in Bel Air, the daughter of Charles H. Matthews, born in Maryland, and Bettie Turner, born in Upper Cross Roads; she was single and died at home in Bel Air; informant was Bessie F. Matthews, of Bel Air) [West Liberty Church Cemetery]

Matthews, Louisa died January 1, 1915, age 18 years, 7 months (no tombstone; death certificate stated she was born in Baltimore, the daughter of Charles Matthews, birth place unknown, and Eliza A. Barrett, born in Baltimore; she was single and died in Fulford; informant was Annie Barrett, of Bel Air) [Asbury Cemetery]

Matthews, Mary L., "Mother" wife of Jeremiah Matthews, daughter of John and Caroline Johnson, February 12, 1868 – March 27, 1931 (tombstone; J. C. Taylor Marble Co. records stated "Mary L. Matthews' Marble head stone was put up May 16th 1931 Tabernacle Cemetery, Benson, ordered by J.S.?? Johnson, 2514 Oak St., Baltimore, MD) [Tabernacle Mount Zion U. M. Church Cemetery]

Matthews, Robert 1923-1994 (on same tombstone with Delores A. Matthews; obituary in *The Aegis* on May 18, 1994 stated he died on May 13, 1994, age 70, a World War II Army veteran; he was born in Waynesboro, GA, the son of Linzy and Jessie Matthews, lived in Kingville and retired after 42 years as a medical research technician at Edgewood Area of Aberdeen Proving Ground; he died at Fallston General Hospital, survived by his wife Delores Robinson Matthews, son, daughter, 3 brothers, 4 grandchildren, 6 great-grandchildren) [Tabernacle

Mount Zion U. M. Church Cemetery]

Matthews, Robert R. March 30, 1898 – February 20, 1941 (no tombstone; death certificate stated he was born in Detroit, MI, served in World War I, married Mary Wilson (age 39 in 1941), worked as a laborer, and died at Forest Hill; his parents were Jeff Matthews and Paddy Cox; their places of birth were unknown to informant, Mrs. Mary W. Matthews, of Bel Air) [Hendon Hill Cemetery]

Matthews, Samuel 6th month 8th day 1842 – 2nd month 26th day 1895 [Mt. Zion U. M. Church Cemetery]

Matthews, Thomas "Eggie" August 10, 1946 – July 24, 1994 (no tombstone; James Dorsey Card File, African American Obituaries, maintained at the Historical Society of Harford County, has a card with obituary from an unidentified newspaper on August 3, 1994 stating he was the son of Delores Matthews and the late Robert Matthews, served in the Army in Vietnam and was a machinist for United Container Machinery for 26 years; he belonged to the Satan's Triangle Motorcycle Club in Abingdon and the Zig Zag and Boone's Farm softball teams; he was a native of Joppa and died at St. Joseph Hospital (in Towson), survived by his wife Janice Fisher Matthews, two sons, a sister, and four grandchildren) [Tabernacle Mount Zion U. M. Church Cemetery]

Mattison, Irene 1900-1982 (copied in 1987, but was not found in 2018; obituary in *The Aegis* on September 9, 1982 stated Irene Blackmon Mattison was born in Anderson, SC, the daughter of David Blackmon and Missouri Golikely, and the widow of Alonzo Mattison; she was formerly employed by the R. J. Reynolds Tobacco Co. in Winston-Salem, NC, died at home in Edgewood on September 6, 1982, age 82, and was survived by 1 brother, 2 sisters, 2 grandchildren and 14 great-grandchildren) [John Wesley U. M. E. Church Cemetery in Abingdon]

Maxfield, Father (no tombstone; probably died in early 1850s) [Old Union Chapel M. E. Church Cemetery]

Maxfield, Hazel Marie (no tombstone; death certificate stated she was born on August 3, 1916 at Vale and died on August 14, 1917, the daughter of Raymond Maxfield and Ruth Rice, both born in Harford Co.; informant was Raymond Maxfield, of Rocks) [Chestnut Grove A. M. E. Church Cemetery, formerly LaGrange Cemetery at Rocks]

Maxfield, James died July 27, 1936, age 53 (no tombstone; death certificate stated he was born at Preston Mill, the son of Thomas Maxfield, born at Clermont Mill, and James *(sic)* Hall, born in Harford Co.; he was single and died at Fallston; informant was William Rice, of Rocks) [Chestnut Grove A. M. E. Church Cemetery, formerly LaGrange Cemetery at Rocks]

Maxfield, James E. 1911 – October 24, 1985 (no tombstone; obituary in *The Aegis* on October 27, 1985 stated James Emmanuel "Jo Ghost" Maxfield, of Edgewood, a lifelong resident of Harford County, was the son of Dora Lee and M. Maxfield and died at Fallston General Hospital; he was survived by Martha Jackson, 2 daughters, 1 son, and 7 grandchildren; James Dorsey Card File, African American Obituaries, at the Historical Society of Harford County, has a funeral card stating he was born on December 21, 1911 [Asbury Cemetery]

Maxfield, L. Mary died June 19, 1904, age 33 (no tombstone; death certificate stated she was the wife of Samuel Maxfield, of Street, MD, and died in child birth; her parents' names were not given) [Chestnut Grove A. M. E. Church Cemetery, formerly LaGrange Cemetery at Rocks]

Maxfield, Mary J. (no tombstone; death certificate stated she was a mulatto, born in Harford Co., the daughter of Samuel Hall and ---- Preston, and was a widow at the time of her death in Pylesville in April 1916, age 103 (exact date not given, but last seen alive by the doctor on April 20 and buried on April 27); informant was Cory Maxfield, of Pylesville) [Chestnut Grove A. M. E. Church Cemetery, formerly LaGrange Cemetery at Rocks]

Maxfield, Thomas died June 19, 1884, believed to be age 97 (no tombstone; death notice in *The Aegis* on June 27, 1884 stated he died near the Rocks and was buried at La Grange Cemetery; he was able to work for his neighbors up to within two years before his death) [Chestnut Grove A. M. E. Church Cemetery, formerly LaGrange Cemetery at Rocks]

Mayan, Henry September – 1853 – November 15, 1918 (no tombstone; death certificate stated he was a widowed laborer, son of Ned Mayan, mother not known, and he lived at Street where he committed suicide by hanging) [Chestnut Grove A. M. E. Church Cemetery, formerly LaGrange Cemetery at Rocks]

Maye, Joe "Loving Husband, Father and Pop-Pop" August 2, 1942 – December 5, 2010 [Berkley Memorial

Cemetery]

Mayhew, Addie Estella February 7, 1901 – November 4, 1974 ("Mrs. Mayew" owned a lot in section 19 some time after 1951; her name on the same tombstone with Rev. Lewis E. Mayhew, inscribed Addie E. Mayhew, 1901-1974; obituary in *The Aegis* on November 7, 1974 stated Addie Estella Mayhew was born in Virginia, the daughter of William and Estella Mayo, and married Rev. Lewis E. Mayhew; they lived at 210 Spesutia Road in Perryman and she died at Harbor View Nursing and Convalescent Home in Baltimore, survived by her husband, 2 daughters, 2 brothers, 2 sisters, 5 grandchildren, 21 great-grandchildren and 1 great-great-grandchild) [Mt. Calvary U. A. M. E. Church Cemetery]

Mayhew, Lewis E. (Rev.) 1903-1983 ("Mr. Mayew" owned a lot in section 19 some time after 1951; Rev. Lewis E. Mayhew is on the same tombstone with Addie E. Mayhew) [Mt. Calvary U. A. M. E. Church Cemetery]

Mayo, Annabelle V., "Beloved Wife and Mother" 1935-1982 [St. James United Cemetery]

Mayo, Frank "Billy" Jr., "Beloved Son and Brother" 1952-1995 [St. James United Cemetery]

Mayo, Fred December 16, 1931 – January 12, 2006, SFC, U.S. Army (on another tombstone is Fred Mayo, 1931-2006, Husband, with Naomi Mayo, Wife, and inscribed "Love Everlasting") [St. James United Cemetery]

Mayo, Naomi 1936-   (on same tombstone with Fred Mayo) [St. James United Cemetery]

McCall, Rachael J. December 25, 1856 – February 3, 1922 (no tombstone; death certificate stated she was the daughter of Henry Williamson and Lucy Tasker, all born in Maryland; she was married, a cook, and died at Kalmia; the informant was Henry Williamson, of Bel Air) [Clark's U. M. Church Cemetery]

McClain, Lewis October 30, 1913 – November 21, 1913 (no tombstone; death certificate stated Lewis McClain died at Poole and he was the son of Charles McClain and Olivia Webster, all born in Harford Co.; informant was Charles McClain, of Darlington) [Cedars Chapel Cemetery]

McClease, Mardren Taylor December 7, 1916 – July 3, 2009 [Berkley Memorial Cemetery]

McComas, Caleb J. February 27, 1849 – December 7, 1943 (no tombstone; death certificate misspelled his first name Calleb and stated he was the husband of Ida K. McComas who predeceased him; his parents' names were unknown) [Union U. M. Church Cemetery]

McComas, Harriet July 1, 1855 – July 27, 1914 (no tombstone; death certificate stated she was married and the daughter of John W. Brown and Sallie Rice, all born in Harford Co.) [Union U. M. Church Cemetery]

McComas, Ida K. October 10, 1870 – October 16, 1937 (no tombstone; death certificate stated she was the wife of Caleb McComas and the daughter of William Kenly and Tenie Paco) [Union U. M. Church Cemetery]

McCray, Nellie S., "Loving Mother, Loving Devoted Wife" February 21, 1945 – October 23, 1995 [St. James United Cemetery]

McCreary, Minnie M., "Aunt" February 19, 1911 – May 28, 1993 (inscribed "In Loving Memory;" James Dorsey Card File, African American Obituaries, maintained at the Historical Society of Harford County, has a card for her with an obituary and photo from *The Aegis* on June 9, 1993 stating she was born in Red Springs, NC and was raised in Lumberton, NC; one of 14 children, she stayed on the family farm and helped care for the family until she married Eugene McCreary; they lived in Havre de Grace where they raised their son Stanley who was killed in Vietnam; she was also known as "Ma Minnie" by the children she loved and died at Harford Memorial Hospital, survived by nieces, nephews, a goddaughter, and a lifelong friend Willie Walton) [Berkley Memorial Cemetery]

McCreary, Stanley E. April 21, 1948 – April 7, 1969, Maryland, PFC, U.S. Army, 5th Infantry, 25th Infantry Division, Vietnam, BSM & OLC-PH [Berkley Memorial Cemetery]

McDaniel, Clarence September 17, 1919 – October 11, 1995 (on same tombstone with Galdys H. McDaniel) [Foster's Hill Cemetery]

McDaniel, Gladys H. July 1, 1923 – November 14, 1987 (on same tombstone with Clarence McDaniel) [Foster's Hill Cemetery]

McDaniel, Herbert died May 4, 1926, age 43? *(sic)* (no tombstone; death certificate stated he was born in Virginia, as were his parents, but their names were not known to informant Irene Rogers; he was married, worked in a quarry, lived in Havre de Grace and died in a train accident) [Green Spring U. M. Church Cemetery]

McDaniel, James died February 26, 1927, age 32 (no tombstone; death certificate stated he was born in North Carolina, but his parents were not known to informant Stone & Webster (Co.) in Darlington; he was single, worked as a contracting laborer and died in Darlington) [Berkley Memorial Cemetery]

McDaniel, William died between January 18 and 22, 1940, age 75 (no tombstone; death certificate stated he was a laborer who lived in Van Bibber and died near Edgewood where he had lived for 10 years; informant, Eason Starr, of Edgewood, knew nothing else about him) [John Wesley U. M. E. Church Cemetery in Abingdon]

McDaniels, Georganna October 20, 1877 – July 20, 1930 (no tombstone; death certificate stated she was the daughter of Shirley Waters and Mary Dallam, all born in Maryland; she was a widow and died in Havre de Grace; informant was Ida Giddings, of Havre de Grace) [Green Spring U. M. Church Cemetery]

McDiarmid, Scott 1877-1956 [Community Baptist Church Cemetery]

McFarland, Charles Henry December 9, 1853 – June 5, 1932 (no tombstone; death certificate stated he was born in Pennsylvania, the son of John McFarland, birth place unknown, and Agnes Goodling, born in Ohio; he married Alice M. ----, worked as a farmer for 50 years until November 1926, retired, and died at home in Havre de Grace; informant was Mrs. Elizabeth A. Osborne) [Mt. Calvary U. A. M. E. Church Cemetery]

McGaw, Aquilla died May 9, 1918, age about 70 (no tombstone; death certificate stated he was a widower and the son of William McGaw, both born in Maryland, but his mother was unknown to informant Annie Giles, of Havre de Grace) [Union U. M. Church Cemetery]

McGaw, Frances June 3, 1880 – June 8, 1931 (no tombstone; death certificate stated she was the daughter of Daniel Harris and Martha Brown; she died a widow in Havre de Grace) [St. James United Cemetery]

McGaw, Sarah died February 5, 1917, age about 67 (no tombstone; death certificate stated she was born in Darlington, the daughter of John E. Seers and Mary J. Ringgold; she married and died in Havre de Grace; informant was Aquilla McGaw) [St. James United Cemetery]

McKenzie, Barbara Joyner died on February 14, 1992, age 53 (no tombstone; The James Dorsey Card File, African American Obituaries, maintained at the Historical Society of Harford County, has a card for her with an obituary from *The Aegis* on February 26, 1992 stating she was born in Hamlet Co., NC, the daughter of the late Morgan and Amelia Joyner, and worked as a nursing assistant at the Citizens Nursing Home and for 15 years at Harford Memorial Hospital; she later died at that hospital and was survived by 2 sons Harry L. Joyner and Ronald L. McFarland, 4 daughters, 4 brothers, a sister, and 8 grandchildren; anotobituary with her photo appeared in *The Aegis* on March 4, 1992]

McKinney, Angela V. November 23, 1965 -   (on same tombstone with Samuel L. McKinney, Jr.) [St. James United Cemetery]

McKinney, James S. 1917-1974 (small metal funeral home marker) [Fairview A. M. E. Church Cemetery]

McKinney, Johnett January 23, 1928 – April 2, 1984, PFC, U.S. Army, Korea [St. James United Cemetery]

McKinney, Maggie B. March 25, 1913 – June 20, 1995 [Fairview A. M. E. Church Cemetery]

McKinney, Samuel L. Jr. November 28, 1963 – July 25, 2015 (on same tombstone with Angela V. McKinney) [St. James United Cemetery]

McKnight, Julie 1901 – December 17, 1948 (no tombstone; death certificate stated she was born in Jackson Co., Arkansas, the daughter of Isaac Hobbs, born in Alabama, and Mary Jane Lofton, born in Arkansas, and the wife of Adam McKnight; she died at home in rural Joppa where she had lived for 14 months and was buried in Mandyville Baptist Cemetery in Joppa RFD; informant was her husband Adam McKnight, of Joppa RFD) [Community Baptist Church Cemetery]

McLain, ---- stillborn female died January 1, 1915 at Cedars (no tombstone; death certificate stated she was the daughter of Charles McClain *(sic)* and Olivia ----, all born in Maryland; informant was her father, of Darlington

RFD) [Cedars Chapel Cemetery]

McLain, ---- stillborn female died October 24, 1918 (no tombstone; death certificate stated she died at Poole and was the daughter of Charles E. McLain and Olivia Webster, all born in Maryland; informant was Charles E. McLain, of Street, MD) [Cedars Chapel Cemetery]

McLain, Charles February 2, 1890 – May 14, 1935 (no tombstone; death certificate stated he was born in Darlington, the son of Walter Walters and Nellie McLain, both born in Maryland; he was married to Olivia ----, worked as a laborer, lived in Street, was struck by falling timber and died at Havre de Grace Hospital; the informant was Olivia McLain, of Darlington) [Clark's U. M. Church Cemetery]

McLain, Charles E. August 8, 1952 – September 17, 2004 (on same tombstone with Gloria M. McLain with an image of a flying goose in each corner and a verse inscribed down the middle) [Berkley Memorial Cemetery]

McLain, Cornelius William Sr. died September 25, 1995, age 71 (no tombstone; James Dorsey Card File, African American Obituaries, maintained at the Historical Society of Harford County, has a card for him with an obituary from *The Aegis* on September 27, 1995 stating he was a World War II Army veteran and a heavy equipment operator at Edgewood Arsenal; he died in Street, survived by his wife Ernestine Divers McLain, two sons, three daughters, a sister, 5 grandchildren and 3 great-grandchildren) [Cedars Chapel Cemetery]

McLain, Darlene Denise 1954-1994 (on same tombstone with Jerry G. McLain) [Berkley Memorial Cemetery]

McLain, Elsie M. August 12, 1925 – July 16, 2010 (inscribed "We Still Love You And Miss You Dearly") [Berkley Memorial Cemetery]

McLain, George died March 4, 1947, age about 46 (no tombstone; death certificate stated he was single and died in Harford Memorial Hospital; parents unknown to informant George McLain, of Havre de Grace) [St. James United Cemetery]

McLain, Georgia Anna died February 2, 1927, age unknown (no tombstone; death certificate stated she died a widow in Poole, but her parents' names and their places of birth were not known to the informant Charles E. McLain, of Street, MD) [Clark's U. M. Church Cemetery]

McLain, Gloria M. November 18, 1951 -   (on same tombstone with Charles E. McLain with an image of a flying goose in each corner and a long verse inscribed down the middle) [Berkley Memorial Cemetery]

McLain, Jerry G. 1953-1994 (on same tombstone with Darlene Denise McLain) [Berkley Memorial Cemetery]

McLain, Marvin Edward October 5, 1919 – September 4, 1987, PFC, U.S. Army, World War II [Berkley Memorial Cemetery]

McLain, William O'Neal June 15, 1942 – July 29, 2003, SP4, U.S. Army, Vietnam (tombstone; obituary in *The Aegis* on August 6, 2003 stated he was the son of Alice C. Starks and the late Cornelius McLain an after graduation from high school he move to New Haven, CT; a year later he was drafted into the Army, served several years, was honorably discharged, returned to New Haven and worked 12 years as an automobile mechanic; in 1982 he returned to Maryland and worked in building management at Perry Point VAMC for 20 years; he died there and was survived by his mother and stepfather Alice and Gerald Starks, of Street, MD, stepmother Ernestine McLain, of Street, MD, brother Cornelius McLain, of Darlington, three sisters, five aunts, one uncle, and special friend Vernell White, of Hamlet, NC) [Berkley Memorial Cemetery]

McLeod, Tonya L. 1966-2000 (heart-shaped tombstone) [St. James United Cemetery]

McMillan, Barbara A. February 19, 1950 - December 22, 2006 (inscribed with image of a cabin and mountain scene) [Berkley Memorial Cemetery]

McMillan, Edna R. November 25, 1940 – July 12, 1987 (on same tombstone with Louis M. McMillan) [Fairview A. M. E. Church Cemetery]

McMillan, Howard F. April 28, 1916 – April 7, 2008 (on same tombstone with Reba M. McMillan) [Fairview A. M. E. Church Cemetery]

McMillan, Louis M. January 25, 1934 – April 18, 1999 (on same tombstone with Edna R. McMillan) [Fairview

A. M. E. Church Cemetery]

McMillan, Reba M. August 15, 1920 – February 11, 2016 (on same tombstone with Howard F. McMillan) [Fairview A. M. E. Church Cemetery]

McMillin, William stillborn on January 9, 1921 (no tombstone; death certificate stated he was born at Street, the son of Annie McMillin, born in Virginia, and William Akins, born in Maryland; informant was Annie McMillin, of Street P. O.) [Clark's U. M. Church Cemetery]

McMullen, Cynthia C. 1957-2015 (on same tombstone with Gertrude E. McMullen) [St. James United Cemetery]

McMullen, Gertrude E. 1922-1994 (on same tombstone with Cynthia C. McMullen; there is also a handwritten flat cement slab with her name and dates as well as a large white wooden cross with her name and dates with this inscription: "Just A Closser *(sic)* Walk With Thee") [St. James United Cemetery]

McQuay, James died March 24, 1927, age 70 (no tombstone; death certificate stated he was the son of E. McQuay and Rachael Clastury(?), all born in Maryland; he was single, worked as a farm laborer and died in Magnolia; informant was William Demby, of Magnolia) [Foster's Hill Cemetery]

McWhite, ---- (owner of lots in section 26 some time after 1951 and marked as paid in full) [Mt. Calvary U. A. M. E. Church Cemetery]

McWhite, David Lee Dec 30, 1948 – March 6, 1999 (inscribed "In Loving Memory Son Brother") [Mt. Calvary U. A. M. E. Church Cemetery]

McWhite, Jimmie August 14, 1942 - September 18, 2013 (inscribed "The Lord is my Shepherd") [Mt. Calvary U. A. M. E. Church Cemetery]

McWhite, Ola D. May 1, 1915 – January 2, 2005 (inscribed "In Loving Memory of Mother" and "The Lord is my Shepherd") [Mt. Calvary U. A. M. E. Church Cemetery]

McWhite, Raymond B. 1915-1980 [Mt. Calvary U. A. M. E. Church Cemetery]

Meadows, Grace A. December 25, 1914 – November 2, 1970 [William C. Rice Memorial Cemetery, St. James U. M. Church]

Meadows, Irene E. 1913-1966 (on same tombstone with James Meadows and Hattie Wallace) [Chestnut Grove A. M. E. Church Cemetery, formerly LaGrange Cemetery at Rocks]

Meadows, James T. 1906-1983 (on same tombstone with Irene Meadows and Hattie Wallace) [Chestnut Grove A. M. E. Church Cemetery, formerly LaGrange Cemetery at Rocks]

Meads, Annioris V. November 19, 1904 – July 25, 1927 (no tombstone; death certificate stated he was married and the son of A. V. Meads and Annie Meads; informant was Sarah E. Meads) [Union U. M. Church Cemetery]

Mears, Ruth E. (Rev.) July 24, 1923 – February 24, 1994 (Rev. Mears owned a lot in section 19 some time after 1951; inscribed "Beloved") [Mt. Calvary U. A. M. E. Church Cemetery]

Merchant, Edna B. 1919-1951 (on same tombstone with I. Beatrice, Joyce, William J., and William H. Merchant) [St. James United Cemetery]

Merchant, I. Beatrice January 10, 1896 – January 29, 1972 (on same tombstone with William J., Joyce, Edna B., and William H. Merchant) [St. James United Cemetery]

Merchant, Joyce "Patsy" 1934-1946 (on same tombstone with I. Beatrice, William J., Edna B., and William H. Merchant; death certificate stated born March 16, 1934 and died August 29, 1946) [St. James United Cemetery]

Merchant, William H. 1917-1974 (on same tombstone with I. Beatrice, Joyce, Edna B, and William J. Merchant) [St. James United Cemetery]

Merchant, William J. September 9, 1887 – July 29, 1949 (on same tombstone with I. Beatrice, Joyce, Edna B., and William H. Merchant) [St. James United Cemetery]

Meyers, Jeanette Holley December 6, 1932 – February 17, 2009 (two grave markers: one stated Jeanette Holley

Meyers and the other stated Jeanette H. Meyers) [Fairview A. M. E. Church Cemetery]

Michael, John Henry September 9, 1945 – November 13, 1945 (no tombstone; death certificate stated he was born in Aberdeen, MD, the son of John Henry Michael, born in Jacksonville, MS, and Jessie Dryvell(?), born in South Carolina) [Union U. M. Church Cemetery]

Milburn – small stone marker about 5 inches square and lying flat in the ground [Berkley Memorial Cemetery]

Milburn, Henrietta died April 24, 1893, age not given (no tombstone; death notice in *The Aegis* on April 28, 1893 stated she was the wife of Joseph Milburn and was buried "at the Tabernacle") [Tabernacle Mount Zion U. M. Church Cemetery]

Milburn, Joseph (no tombstone, but his wife Henrietta is buried here so he probably is also) [Tabernacle Mount Zion U. M. Church Cemetery]

Miller, Agnes October – (blank), 1899 – March 6, 1946 (no tombstone; death certificate stated she was born in Union, SC, the daughter of Charles Buggs, mother unknown; she married James Miller and died in Harford Memorial Hospital; informant was Willie Hodge, of Philadelphia, PA) [St. James United Cemetery]

Miller, Bertie C. 1914-1983 [St. James United Cemetery]

Miller, Betty Lou February 17, 1938 – March 13, 2007 (inscribed "In Loving Memory") [John Wesley U. M. E. Church Cemetery in Abingdon]

Miller, Carolyn V. February 12, 1970 – June 4, 2007 (on the same tombstone with Kevin R. Miller inscribed "In Living Memory" with photos and "Psalm 91" inscribed under her name) [Berkley Memorial Cemetery]

Miller, Clyde R. July 29, 1931 – November 30, 1936 (no tombstone; death certificate stated he was born in Aberdeen, the son of Solomon Miller and Jessie A. Dupree, both born in South Carolina, and he died in house fire) [Union U. M. Church Cemetery]

Miller, Coroline died September 27, 1920 (inscribed "In Memory Of") [Berkley Memorial Cemetery]

Miller, Daisy P. May 31, 1935 – December 1, 2009 [John Wesley U. M. E. Church Cemetery in Abingdon]

Miller, Frances Rebecca September 24, 1854 – September 26, 1927 (no tombstone; death certificate stated she was born in Maryland, the daughter of Sarah Burch, but her father's name was not known to informant Jermira *(sic)* Miller (probably her husband), of Havre de Grace RFD #1) [Gravel Hill Cemetery]

Miller, George Franklin January 9, 1857 – April 19, 1911 (no tombstone; death certificate stated he was the son of George F. Miller and Hester Chum, all born in Maryland; he was married, worked as a farm laborer, and died at Poole; informant was Thomas H. Snowden, of Street RFD) [Clark's U. M. Church Cemetery]

Miller, George H. died July 14, 1922, age about 50 (no tombstone; death certificate stated he was married and born in Maryland, but parents were unknown to informant George Ringgold) [Union U. M. Church Cemetery]

Miller, James 1877-1960 (inscribed "Rest In Peace") [Berkley Memorial Cemetery]

Miller, Jermiah December 25, 1843 – August 18, 1940 (no tombstone; death certificate stated he was born in Harford Co., the son of Jane Dorsey, born in Maryland, but his father's name was not known to informant Mrs. Stella M. Jones, of Havre de Grace; he married Frances ----, was a retired farmer and a widower when he died in Havre de Grace) [Gravel Hill Cemetery]

Miller, Jessie B. September 15, 1915 – January 17, 1946 (no tombstone; death certificate stated she was the daughter of Sul(?) Prince and Annie Dupree, all born in South Carolina, and she was the widow of King S. Miller) [Union U. M. Church Cemetery]

Miller, Kevin R. October 8, 1967 -   (on the same tombstone with Carolyn R. Miller inscribed "In Living Memory" with photos and "Psalm 34" inscribed under his name) [Berkley Memorial Cemetery]

Miller, Laura died April 29, 1913, age about 54 (no tombstone; death certificate stated she was the daughter of Charles Preston and Fannie Cooper, and all were born in Harford Co.; she did housework and died a widow at Cedars; informant was Laura Anderson, of Street, MD) [Clark's U. M. Church Cemetery]

Miller, Lewis August 15, 1877 – January 19(?), 1922 (no tombstone; death certificate stated he was born in Harford Co., parents' names and birth places unknown to informant John Miller, of Cardiff; he was single, worked as a laborer and died in Whiteford) [William C. Rice Memorial Cemetery, St. James U. M. Church]

Miller, Samuel Jr. 1960-1980 [St. James United Cemetery]

Miller, Sarah E. May 3, 1930 - (tombstone with small brass plate inscribed "Presberry Memorials" attached) [Community Baptist Church Cemetery]

Miller, Sidney H. November 5, 1840 – September 29, 1936 (no tombstone; death certificate stated he was the son of Richard Miller and Priscilla Aikens, and all were born in Harford Co.; he married Caroline ----, worked as a farm laborer and died a widower in Darlington where he had lived for 6 years; informant was Harriett Wilson, of Darlington) [Berkley Memorial Cemetery]

Miller, Willie October 15, 1921 – February 3, 2013, U.S. Army [St. James United Cemetery]

Mills, Annie L. 1880-1971 (tombstone; obituary in *The Aegis* stated she was born in Towson, daughter of Samuel Williams and Margaret Myers, and was the widow of Rev. Samuel Mills; she died at home at 559 Lewis St., Havre de Grace, survived by one son Samuel I. Mills, three daughters Laura M. Dennison, Matilda A. Wainwright and Hattie V. Mills, one brother, three sisters, and sixteen grandchildren) [St. James United Cemetery]

Mills, Hattie Virginia died June 19, 1998, age 69 (no tombstone; James Dorsey Card File, African American Obituaries, maintained at the Historical Society of Harford County, has a card with her funeral service announcement in an unidentified newspaper on June 24, 1998 stating she lived in Havre de Grace and died at Harford Memorial Hospital) [St. James United Cemetery]

Mills, Samuel I. 1865-1936 (tombstone; death certificate stated born December 10, 1865 in Somerset Co., MD and died February 22, 1937 in Havre de Grace) [St. James United Cemetery]

Mills, Virginia May born and died December 14, 1941 (no tombstone; death certificate stated she was born premature, the daughter of Clifton Phillips and Hattie Virginia Mills) [St. James United Cemetery]

Mills, William G. November 17, 1918 – July 3, 1970, Maryland, CK2, U.S. Navy, World War II [St. James United Cemetery]

Mingo, Sarah I. March 6, 1940 – August 29, 2003 (small metal funeral home marker) [Foster's Hill Cemetery]

Minor, Dennis N. 1915-2011 (small metal funeral home marker) [St. James United Cemetery]

Minor, George August 20, 1888 – January 18, 1938 (no tombstone; death certificate stated he was born in Warrenton, VA, the son of Joshua Minor an Susan Morgan; he married Mable ---- (Richardson) and died in Havre de Grace; informant was Mable Minor, of Wilmington, DE) [St. James United Cemetery]

Minor, Mable, "Mother" died November 22, 1954 [St. James United Cemetery]

Minor, Mary E. December 27, 1922 – March 27, 1923 (no tombstone; death certificate stated she was the daugte of George Minor and Mable Richardson, of Havre de Grace) [St. James United Cemetery]

Misiak, Gertrud Lehmann Tandek 1909-1991 [Foster's Hill Cemetery]

Mitchell, Arthur A. (Rev.) December 2, 1902 – April 26, 1988 (on same tombstone with Susie J. Mitchell) [St. James United Cemetery]

Mitchell, Arthur A. Jr. October 2, 1959 – January 31, 1992, SFC, U.S. Army [St. James United Cemetery]

Mitchell, Baby (female) September 26, 1926 – September 27, 1926 (no tombstone; death certificate stated she was the daughter of G. A. Mitchell and Elleanor Waters, of Havre de Grace) [St. James United Cemetery]

Mitchell, Charles E. 1937-1979 [William C. Rice Memorial Cemetery, St. James U. M. Church]

Mitchell, Eleanora 1882-1957 (on same tombstone with Rev. George A. Mitchell; copied in 1987 and by 2018 tombstone had been toppled over) [St. James United Cemetery]

Mitchell, George A. (Rev.) 1882-1969 (on same tombstone with Eleanora Mitchell; copied in 1987 and by 2018 the tombstone had been toppled over) [St. James United Cemetery]

Mitchell, Infant stillborn male on February 26, 1923 (no tombstone; death certificate stated she was the daughter of George Mitchell and Eleanora Waters, of Havre de Grace) [St. James United Cemetery]

Mitchell, James R. February 11, 1874 – August 13, 1946 (no tombstone; death certificate stated he was born at Paradise, Harford Co., the son of Lewis Mitchell and Easter Robinson, both born in Virginia; he married Laura C. B. ---- and died in Havre de Grace) [St. James United Cemetery]

Mitchell, Lamont J. 1968-1987 (inscribed "Gone But Not Forgotten" when copied in 1987, but not found in 2018) [Gravel Hill Cemetery]

Mitchell, Lillie Ida Taylor "BaWeedy" July 16, 1921 – April 6, 1998 (no tombstone; James Dorsey Card File, African American Obituaries, maintained at the Historical Society of Harford County, has a card for her with an obituary from *The Aegis* on April 15, 1998 stating she was born in Bel Air, the daughter of Joseph Johnson and Jamie Taylor, and wife of the late Ervin Lewis "Bussie" Mitchell; she died in Bel Air and was survived by two sisters, a brother, 3 grandchildren, 2 great-grandchildren and a great-great-grandchild, and she was also mother of the late Charles "Chappie" Mitchell) [St. James United Cemetery]

Mitchell, Mervin 1919-1992 (small metal funeral home marker) [William C. Rice Memorial Cemetery, St. James U. M. Church]

Mitchell, Susie J. May 14, 1919 – October 12, 1999 (on same tombstone with Rev. Arthur A. Mitchell) [St. James United Cemetery]

Mitchell, William June 25, 1858 – June 2, 1922 (no tombstone; death certificate stated he was born in Maryland, but names of his parents and birth places were not known to informant Annie Mitchell, of Aberdeen; he was married, worked as a day laborer and died near Aberdeen) [Mt. Calvary U. A. M. E. Church Cemetery]

Mitchum, James L., "Loving Husband, Father and Friend" October 26, 1956 – July 3, 2016 (tombstone with photo, and Comcast Truck 51332 image inscribed on it) [St. James United Cemetery]

Monk, Alfred August 10, 1874 – December 5, 1943 (no tombstone; death certificate stated he was the son of Lewis Henry Monk and Catherine Rice) [Union U. M. Church Cemetery]

Monk, Bertha S. January – (blank), 1889 – May 18, 1919 (no tombstone; death certificate stated she was the married daughter of William J. Christy and Martha Johnson, all born in Harford Co.; informant was Thadious Monk, of Perryman) [Union U. M. Church Cemetery]

Monk, Elsie Jane December 14, 1856 – April 19, 1931 (no tombstone; death certificate stated she was born in Florida, parents unknown, died a widow; informant was Mrs. Caroline Bowser) [Union U. M. Church Cemetery]

Monk, Frances E. March 15, 1910 – June 10, 1925 (no tombstone; death certificate stated she was the daughter of Richard Ward and Mary Monk) [Union U. M. Church Cemetery]

Monk, Harriet R. September 12, 1866 – December 10, 1936 (no tombstone; death certificate stated she was born in Aberdeen, but her parents were not known to informant Mrs. Sadie Smith, of Aberdeen; she married Philip Monk and died a widow at home at Baltimore Park in Aberdeen where she had lived all her life) [Mt. Calvary U. A. M. E. Church Cemetery]

Monk, Hattie C. April 7, 1878 – July 23, 1923 (no tombstone; death certificate stated she was the daughter of Edward Rice and Charlotte Rice, all born in Harford Co.; informant was Louis Monk) [Union U. M. Church Cemetery]

Monk, Herbert L. S. February 19, 1916 – August 28, 1916 (no tombstone; death certificate stated he was the son of Richard Ward and Mary Monk, of Havre de Grace) [St. James United Cemetery]

Monk, James, son of Jacob and Maria Monk, 1848-1917 (tombstone; death certificate stated James Henry Monk was born March 4, 1848 and died a widower on April 24, 1917; he was the son of Jacob Monk and Maria Fleetwood, all born in Maryland; informant was Peter Monk, of Perryman) [Union U. M. Church Cemetery]

Monk, John D. died 1938 (tombstone; death certificate stated he was born January 23, 1868 and died July 30,

1938, the husband of Isabelle Monk and the son of Philip Monk, but his mother was unknown; he was buried in "Swan Creek Cemetery") [Union U. M. Church Cemetery]

Monk, Lidie died July 21, 1943, age about 55 (no tombstone; death certificate stated she was the wife of Well Monk, and the daughter of Snapp Whims and Mary McGaw) [Union U. M. Church Cemetery]

Monk, Louis Henry died March 20, 1994, age 90 (no tombstone; obituary in *The Aegis* on March 30, 1994 stated he was born in Perryman, the son of Louis Monk and Hattie Rice; he worked for the Pennsylvania Railroad and "Daddy Rough," "Precious Hearts" and "Pop Pop" were some of his nicknames; at times he was a lay minister, an assistant pastor, was ordained in Baltimore in 1955, held many offices, and also with the Council Brotherhood; he died in Baltimore, survived by a daughter Ruth Holmes, an adopted daughter Naomi Petway, 8 grandchildren, 20 great-grandchildren, 15 great-great-grandchildren) [Green Spring U. M. Church Cemetery]

Monk, Martha Louise died October 1, 1972, age not given (no tombstone; obituary in *The Aegis* stated she was the daughter of the late Isaac and Charlotte Jackson, and she died at home at 914 Warren St. in Havre de Grace, survived by two sons, Howard Jackson and Albert S. Jackson, and two daughters, Mrs. Mayfield Harris and Mrs. Alice Jennifer, all of Havre de Grace) [Berkley Memorial Cemetery]

Monk, Mary April 26, 1881 – September 22, 1946 (no tombstone; death certificate stated she was the daughter of George Cox and Mary Frances Cox, and the widow of Isaac Monk, and she was buried in "Swan Creek Cemetery") [Union U. M. Church Cemetery]

Monk, Mattie R. February 25, 1895 – April 2, 1937 (no tombstone; death certificate stated she was the daughter of Henry Smith and Maggie Giddings, of Havre de Grace; she married Joshua Monk and died in Havre de Grace Hospital; informant was Eugene Giddings, of Havre de Grace) [St. James United Cemetery]

Monk, Peter G. died January 3, 1923, age 67 (no tombstone; death certificate stated he was born in Harford Co., the son of Jacob Monk, born in Harford Co., and Marian Fleetwood, born in Maryland; informant was Mrs. Peter Monk, of Perryman) [Union U. M. Church Cemetery]

Monk, Ralph April 27, 1917 – July 20, 1933 (no tombstone; death certificate stated he was the son of William D. Monk and Leona Monk) [Union U. M. Church Cemetery]

Monk, Roy September 5, 1893 – July 15, 1920 (no tombstone; death certificate stated he was born in Perryman and was the married son of Jacob Monk and Ella Frisby, all born in Harford Co.; informant was Ella Monk, of Havre de Grace) [Union U. M. Church Cemetery]

Monk, Sarah E. died December 30, 1970, age not given (no tombstone; obituary in *The Aegis* stated she was the wife of the late Garfield Monk, lived at 916 Elizabeth St. in Havre de Grace and died at Harford Memorial Hospital, survived by three sons and one daughter) [Union U. M. Church Cemetery]

Monk, Smaley C. died March 6, 1917, age about 38 (no tombstone; death certificate stated she was the daughter of John Monk, both born in Harford Co., but her mother was not known to the staff at the Havre de Grace Hospital) [Union U. M. Church Cemetery]

Monk, Susie, wife of Thad Monk, 1887-1918 ("At Rest") [Union U. M. Church Cemetery]

Monk, Thasseus *(sic)* July 18, 1873 – August 17, 1932 (no tombstone; death certificate stated he was the son of Louis H. Monk and Catherine Rice, and husband of Susie Monk who predeceased him; her tombstone stated "wife of Thad," so his first name might actually have been Thaddeus) [Union U. M. Church Cemetery]

Monk, Virgie Virginia June 3, 1896 – March 1, 1977 (no tombstone; obituary in *The Aegis* stated she was born in Darlington, the daughter of Vincent Smith and Mary Hemore, and she married Louis Monk; she lived in Havre de Grace and died at Harford Memorial Hospital, survived by her husband, a daughter Ruth Holmes, a sister Ruth Graves, 8 grandchildren, and 11 great-grandchildren, and nieces and nephews) [Green Spring U. M. Church Cemetery]

Monk, William 1909-1975 (copied in 1987, but not found in 2018; obituary in *The Aegis* stated William Henry Monk was born in Perryman, the son of Louis and Hattie Monk, and the husband of Hilda Monk, of 213 S. Union Avenue, Havre de Grace; he died at Harford Memorial Hospital, survived by his wife, two sons William H. Monk, Jr. and Lewis C. Monk, three brothers, three sisters, 18 grandchildren and 3 great-grandchildren) [St.

James United Cemetery]

Monk, William S. August 16, 1882 – February 4, 1945 (no tombstone; death certificate stated he was the son of Robert Monk, born in Maryland, and Elsie Williams, born in Florida) [Union U. M. Church Cemetery]

Montague, Virginia 1944-1979 [St. James United Cemetery]

Moore, ---- October 11, 1915 – October 13, 1915 (no tombstone; death certificate stated he was a premature birth at five months and lived only 2 days; his parents were Steve Moore and Hannah Smith, both born in Maryland; informant was Robert S. Page, of Bel Air) [Hendon Hill Cemetery]

Moore, Benjamin N. Co. B, 23rd U. S. C. I. (tombstone, but no dates; Civil War veteran; death certificate stated Benjamin Moore was born in Baltimore Co., the son of John Moore, born in Harford Co., but informant Jane Fairfax, of Fallston, did not know his mother's name; he worked as a laborer and died a widower near Reckord on November 4, 1914, age about 75; his death notice in *The Aegis* on November 6, 1914 stated Benjamin M. Moore was in the employ of Mrs. William T. Watson, near Fallston, and died there a few days ago; he was the brother of Wesley Moore and had served in the Army during the Civil War, 1861-1865; after serving in the war he was employed by Mrs. Oliver H. Amoss and upon her death went to her near kinswoman Mrs. Watson; he was a highly respectable man) [Tabernacle Mount Zion U. M. Church Cemetery]

Moore, Delores W., "My Loving Wife" January 20, 1939 – August 5, 1981 [John Wesley U. M. E. Church Cemetery in Abingdon]

Moore, Elpertis June 6, 1944 – July 22, 1961 (inscribed "In Loving Memory of a Son, Brother & Uncle") [Berkley Memorial Cemetery]

Moore, George M., husband of Cecelia E. Moore, December 24, 1869 – March 2, 1932 (inscribed "Though Lost to Sight, To Memory Dear;" death certificate stated George Michael Moore was the married son of Lloyd A. Moore and Mary Jane Paca, all born in Harford Co.; his wife was Cecelia E. Tildon, of Bel Air RFD #2) [Union U. M. Church Cemetery]

Moore, George Sr. 1939-1989 (temporary marker recorded in 1987 and 2002, but not found in 2018) [Gravel Hill Cemetery]

Moore, Isabelle died March 31, 1928, age about 65 (no tombstone; death certificate stated she was born in Maryland, worked as a storekeeper in Bel Air, married and divorced; informant was Carrie Armstrong, of Bel Air, who mistakenly stated Isabelle's father was a Moore and she did not know her mother's name; Harford Co. Equity Court records indicate Mark Moore married Belle Cox in 1874 and they separated in 1903 and were divorced in 1904) [Tabernacle Mount Zion U. M. Church Cemetery]

Moore, Josephine January 17, 1885 – June 18, 1936 (no tombstone; death certificate stated she was the daughter of James Gilbert, born in Harford Co., and Sarah Robinson born in Cecil Co., and the widow of Jacob Moore; informant was her "daughter," name not given, of Havre de Grace) [St. James United Cemetery]

Moore, Louisa September 25, 1864 – September 9, 1933 (no tombstone; death certificate stated she was the widow of Mark Moore; she was born at Bush, Harford Co., and died at home in Bel Air; informant was Mrs. Hannah Moore, of Bel Air; James Dorsey Card File, African American Obituaries, maintained at the Historical Society of Harford County, has a card for her with an obituary from the *Bel Air Times* on September 15, 1933 stating she was "one of the highest types of colored women in the county" and for 18 years she was employed by the family of Mr. J. Woodley Richardson) [Hendon Hill Cemetery]

Moore, Loutonia August 15, 1900 – May 31, 1945 (tombstone mistakenly stated she died May 4, 1945; death certificate stated Letonia Moore was born in Baltimore, the daughter of George Moore and Annie Map, lived in Havre de Grace, never married and died at home at 329 Strawberry Alley on May 31, 1945; informant was Susannah Christy, of Havre de Grace; death notice in the *Havre de Grace Republican* on June 2, 1945 stated she was age 44) [Gravel Hill Cemetery]

Moore, Malissie May 25, 1871 – December 15, 1943 (no tombstone; death certificate stated she was the daughter of Henry and Grace Aikens, all born in Harford Co.; she lived in Darlington and was the widow of William Moore; informant was H. Taft Aikens, of Darlington; death certificate mistakenly stated she was a white woman) [Green Spring U. M. Church Cemetery]

Moore, Mark died April 29, 1929, age 74 (no tombstone; death certificate stated he was the son of Mark Moore and Jane Prigg, all born in Maryland; he married, worked as a laborer and died in Bel Air; informant was John Moore, of Bel Air) [Tabernacle Mount Zion U. M. Church Cemetery]

Moore, Martha E. January 28, 1912 – July 9, 1918 (no tombstone; death certificate stated she was the daughter of Stephen P. Moore and Hannah E. Smith, all born in Maryland, and she lived and died in Bel Air; informant was her mother Hannah E. Moore, of Bel Air) [Hendon Hill Cemetery]

Moore, Mary Elizabeth December 16,1905 – June 30, 1959 (no tombstone; Pennington Funeral Home records stated she was born at Magnolia, the unmarried daughter of Jake Moore and Josephine Gilbert, and died in Havre de Grace; informant was Helen Moore Roberts [St. James United Cemetery]

Moore, Nathaniel March 4, 1880 – May 24, 1945 (no tombstone; death certificate stated he was born in Harford Co., the son of Robert and Rachel Moore, both born in Maryland; he married Ella ----, worked as a laborer and died in Harford Memorial Hospital in Havre de Grace; he had lived in Havre de Grace all of his life; informant was his wife Ella Moore, 2 Harthorn Place, Summit, NJ) [Berkley Memorial Cemetery]

Moore, Stephen P. "Steve" died April 1, 1954, age not stated (no tombstone; obituary in *The Aegis*, April 8, 1954, stated he died in Mercy Hospital in Baltimore and was a former store operator and race horse owner in Bel Air; among his survivors was his wife Hannah Moore) [Hendon Hill Cemetery]

Moore, Wesley (William Wesley Moore) died January 7, 1908, age 88 (no tombstone; death certificate stated he was born in Harford Co., the son of John Q. and Fannie Moore, and was a laborer in Bel Air who died at age 84 or 88, but obituary in *The Aegis* on January 17, 1908 stated "Uncle Wess" died at age 88 and was a skillful mechanic especially in rough carpentering and as a shoemaker; he was a former slave and for many years a servant in the Archer family) [Tabernacle Mount Zion U. M. Church Cemetery]

Moore, William Osborne 1887-1934 (tombstone; death certificate stated he was born August 17, 1887 in Bel Air and died June 10, 1934 at 19 W. Pennsylvania Ave.; he was the son of Mark Moore and Isabella Moore, both were born in Maryland; he was married to Mary Adele ---- and worked as a cleaner and presser; informant was his wife; J. C. Taylor Marble Co. records stated "Wm. Osborne Moore's Granite Monument was put up Oct 9th 1934, Tabernacle (Colored) Benson, ordered by his wife Mrs. Wm. Osborne Moore, Bel Air") [Tabernacle Mount Zion U. M. Church Cemetery]

Moore, William Thomas died December 10, 1939, age about 80 (no tombstone; death certificate stated he was the son of Joseph Moore and Eliza ----, and all were born in Harford Co.; he married Malisha ---- and worked as a crop farm laborer near Darlington; informant was Mrs. William T. Moore, of Darlington) [Green Spring U. M. Church Cemetery]

Morgan, Annie died August 5, 1922, age about 35 (no tombstone; death certificate stated she was married, worked as a domestic, and died at Havre de Grace Hospital, but informant William Morgan, of Street, MD, did not know her parents' names nor their places of birth) [Chestnut Grove A. M. E. Church Cemetery, formerly LaGrange Cemetery at Rocks]

Morgan, Annie, wife of Jarrett Morgan, died July 18, 1922, age 77 (tombstone date, but death certificate stated she died July 27, 1922 at home at Level; informant was Jarrett Morgan who stated she was the daughter of Jacob Haines and Sarah Waxwood and they all were born in Maryland) [Green Spring U. M. Church Cemetery]

Morgan, Charlotte November 18, 1800 – May 20, 1876 [John Wesley U. M. E. Church Cemetery in Abingdon]

Morgan, Classie M. May 1927 – December 2015 ("In Loving Memory") [Berkley Memorial Cemetery]

Morgan, Henry September --, 1883 – November 15, 1918 (no tombstone; death certificate stated he was the son of Ned Morgan, both born in Maryland, but informant Charles Famous, of Street, MD, did not know his mother's name; he was a laborer and died at Street) [Chestnut Grove A. M. E. Church Cemetery, formerly LaGrange Cemetery at Rocks]

Morgan, Jarrett December 20, 1840 – November 23, 1934, Maryland, Pvt., Co. F, 4th Regt, U.S. Inf., Civil War (tombstone; military records stated he served as a private in Co. F, 4th Regt., U. S. C. T.; death certificate stated he was born in Darlington, but his parents were not known to informant Emily Miller, of Mt. Airy, PA; he married Annie ----, lived at Level for 50 years and worked as a farm laborer until 1930 when he was almost age 90) [Green Spring U. M. Church Cemetery]

Morgan, John W. July 23, 1876 – May 20, 1933 (no tombstone; death certificate stated he was the son of William Morgan and Amelia Leonard, all born in Harford Co.; he married Sarah ----, worked as farm laborer and died at home in Dublin where he had lived for 25 years; informant was Sarah Morgan, of Street, MD) [Berkley Memorial Cemetery]

Morgan, Mary E. H. 1890-1957 (on same tombstone with "Sister" Georgia A. H. Bason; Harkins Funeral Home Records stated she was born November 10, 1890, the daughter of Elisha Hewitt and Hannah Smith, and she lived at Delta R. D. and died a widow on September 26, 1957 at York Hospital; informant was her sister Mrs. Georgie Bason of 111 Lincoln St., Apt C., York, PA) [Chestnut Grove A. M. E. Church Cemetery, formerly LaGrange Cemetery at Rocks]

Morgan, Melvin March 6(?), 1907 – January 27, 1914 (no tombstone; death certificate stated he was born in Harford Co., the son of John Morgan and Sallie Johnson, both born in Maryland; he died at home in Poole; informant was John Morgan, of Street, MD) [Berkley Memorial Cemetery]

Morgan, Odie died October 26, 1923, age 51, "At Rest" (tombstone; death certificate stated "Oddie" was born on April 20, 1870, the son of Jarrett Morgan and Caroline Billingsley, all born in Maryland; he was married, worked as a laborer and died in Havre de Grace on October 20, 1923; informant was Jarrett Morgan, of Havre de Grace RFD) [Green Spring U. M. Church Cemetery]

Morgan, Rosella March 21, 1895 – May 17, 1918 (no tombstone; death certificate stated she was the daughter of William Thompson and Martha Howard, and all were born in Maryland; she was married and died at home in Poole; informant was Edward Morgan, of Street, MD) [Berkley Memorial Cemetery]

Morgan, William died February 11, 1909, age 74 (inscribed "In Memory Of" and "Asleep In Jesus;" obituary in *The Aegis* on February 19, 1909 stated he died at home in Bel Air and for more than a half century was carriage driver for Henry D. Farnandis at *Stockdale* and after his death he remained in the employ of Miss Bessie Farnandis; "few of the dead are followed to their resting place by so large and so respectful a cortege as that which attended William's remains to Abingdon;" death certificate stated he was born in Bel Air, the son of Edward Hall and Charlotte Hall, married Mary E Nugent, worked as a laborer, and died in Bel Air on February 11, 1909, age 74; informant was his niece Carrie Lingan) [John Wesley U. M. E. Church Cemetery in Abingdon]

Morgan, William B. July 29, 1835 – January 5, 1916 (no tombstone; death certificate stated he was the son of Robert Morgan, both born in Maryland, but his mother was not known to informant John Morgan, of Street, MD; he worked as a laborer and died a widower in Poole) [Berkley Memorial Cemetery]

Morlock, ---- stillborn male died June 19, 1921 (no tombstone; death certificate stated he was the son of John T. Morlock and Ella Butler, of Pylesville, and they were all born in Maryland) [Chestnut Grove A. M. E. Church Cemetery, formerly LaGrange Cemetery at Rocks]

Morlock, ---- stillborn male on July 30, 1919 (no tombstone; death certificate stated he was the son of John T. Morlock and Ellen Butler, of Rocks, and they were all born in Maryland) [Chestnut Grove A. M. E. Church Cemetery, formerly LaGrange Cemetery at Rocks]

Morrison, James H. March 1, 1905 – June 16, 1946, Maryland, STM1, USNR, World War II (tombstone; death certificate stated he was born in "March 1906" in Louisville, KY and was shot in Havre de Grace on June 15, 1946 and died on June 16, 1946, age about 40) [St. James United Cemetery]

Morsey, Easley Eva 1888-1973 (copied in 1987, but not found in 2018) [St. James United Cemetery]

Morton, Grace L. March 19, 1920 – August 31, 2015 (on same tombstone with Joseph Morton, Jr.) [St. James United Cemetery]

Morton, Joseph Jr. June 17, 1930 – September 12, 2000 (on same tombstone with Grace L. Morton) [St. James United Cemetery]

Moses, Gloria M. October 7, 1950 – February 7, 2002 [Tabernacle Mount Zion U. M. Church Cemetery]

Moses, Julia A. "Mother" 1855-1930 (tombstone; death certificate stated Julia Ann Moses died on July 9, 1930, age about 72, the daughter of Lewis Pinion and Henrietta Maxwell, all born in Maryland; she was a widow in Havre de Grace; informant was Mrs. Mary Durbin, of Havre de Grace) [Gravel Hill Cemetery]

Moses, Peter May 16, 1847 – July 11, 1890, Company A, 10th U.S. Colored Infantry; an unidentified newspaper in the vertical files of the Historical Society of Harford County stated he was one of four Union soldiers who served in the Civil War who was buried in this cemetery) [Gravel Hill Cemetery]

Moses, Theresa Lorretta died April 27, 1993, age 52 (no tombstone; obituary in *The Aegis* on April 5, 1993 stated she was born in York, PA, the daughter of Clarence W. Govans, of Havre de Grace, and Jessie Giles Govans, of Forest Hill; she lived in Baltimore and died at Sinai Hospital, survived by 2 sons, 2 daughters, a sister and a grandchild) [William C. Rice Memorial Cemetery, St. James U. M. Church]

Motts, William 1928-1978 [St. James United Cemetery]

Moulton, Alba August 6, 1867 – September 12, 1950 (no tombstone; death certificate stated he was born in Maryland, the son of Alba Moulton and Harriet Washington, worked as a day laborer on a farm, lived on Paradise Road in Aberdeen and died a widower at the County Home in Bel Air where he had lived about 17 years; information from the county home records) [Union U. M. Church Cemetery]

Moulton, Cora A. 1867-1939 ("At Rest") [Union U. M. Church Cemetery]

Moulton, Harriet A. June 2, 1847 – July 2, 1925 (no tombstone; death certificate stated she was born in Harford Co., daughter of Hamp Washington and Sidney Bower, both born in Maryland; informant was James Moulton, of Aberdeen) [Mt. Calvary U. A. M. E. Church Cemetery]

Moulton, James February 2, 1857 – June 15, 1932 (no tombstone; death certificate misspelled his name as Maullon and his father's name as Malton; he was born in Spotsylvania, VA, the son of Elija Malton *(sic)* and Delfie Smith, both born in Virginia; he married Harrett ----, worked as a laborer and died a widower in Aberdeen; informant was Addie V. Young, of Woodbery, NJ) [Mt. Calvary U. A. M. E. Church Cemetery]

Moulton, Richard Anderson died June 20, 1913, age about 57 (no tombstone; death certificate stated he was the son of Elijah and Delphia Moulton, all born in Virginia; he was single and worked as a laborer and teamster in Aberdeen; informant was James Moulton, of Aberdeen) [Mt. Calvary U. A. M. E. Church Cemetery]

Muckelvaney, Dorothy L. August 29, 1928 – August 13, 2014 [Berkley Memorial Cemetery]

Muckelvaney, John C. December 8, 1923 – November 4, 1985, U.S. Navy, World War II, Korea [Berkley Memorial Cemetery]

Muela, Zeta Chanel 2001-2003 (inscribed "In Memory Of" and "We Love You") [St. James United Cemetery]

Munday, Marie Olean April 5, 1917 – August 9, 1933 (no tombstone; death certificate stated she was the daughter of John Washington and Beulah Briley, all born in Maryland; she married John Munday and died at Van Bibber; informant was John Washington, of Edgewood) [John Wesley U. M. E. Church Cemetery in Abingdon]

Murphy, Effie M. May 15, 1876 – October 14, 1933 (no tombstone; death certificate stated she was born in Aberdeen, the daughter of James Moulton and Harrett Washington, both born in Virginia; she was married to James H. Murphy for 28 years and died at home at Back St. Ext. in Aberdeen; informant was mistakenly written on the certificate as Mrs. James H. Murphy) [Mt. Calvary U. A. M. E. Church Cemetery]

Murphy, Hazel B. July 25, 1925 – July 1, 2010 (inscribed "Forever In Our Hearts") [Mt. Calvary U. A. M. E. Church Cemetery]

Murphy, Ida Viola 1895-1967 (on same tombstone with Joseph Lee Bowser; obituary in *The Aegis* on August 3, 1967 stated she was a daughter of David Richard Kennard and Mamie Rebecca Butler, and widow of Allen Eugene Murphy; she resided at 49 Monroe St. in Aberdeen, died at Harford Memorial Hospital in Havre de Grace on July 26, 1967 and was survived by 5 sons, 8 daughters, 41 grandchildren, and 8 great-grandchildren) [Mt. Calvary U. A. M. E. Church Cemetery]

Murphy, James (owner of a lot in section 31 some time after 1951) [Mt. Calvary U. A. M. E. Church Cemetery]

Murphy, Mary Annet June 20, 1942 – October 11, 1942 (no tombstone; death certificate stated she was born in Havre de Grace, daughter of Herold Brown, born in Perryman, and Nancy Murphy, born in Harford Co.; informant was Miss Nancy Murphy, 507 Lawrence St., Havre de Grace) [Green Spring U. M. Church Cemetery]

Murphy, Mazie April 16, 1895 – January 25, 1928 (no tombstone; death certificate stated she was the married daughter of Robert J. Bowser and Harriett Christy, and died at home in Havre de Grace; informant was Hollis Bowser, of Perryman, MD) [Union U. M. Church Cemetery]

Murphy, Melvin E. 1921-1983 (copied in 1987, but not found in 2018; obituary in *The Aegis* on June 16, 1983 stated Melvin Eugene Murphy was born in Bel Air, the son of Allen and Ida Murphy, and married Mildred Presbury, lived in Bel Air, worked for Baltimore Gas & Electric and died at Harford Memorial Hospital in Havre de Grace on June 13, 1983; he was survived by his wife, 2 god-daughters, 2 brothers and 8 sisters) [Mt. Calvary U. A. M. E. Church Cemetery]

Murphy, Mildred V. May 9, 1921 – August 10, 2012 [Mt. Calvary U. A. M. E. Church Cemetery]

Murphy, Mildred Virginia died August 5, 1990, age 64 (no tombstone; James Dorsey Card File, African American Obituaries, maintained at the Historical Society of Harford County, has a card for her with an obituary from *The Aegis* stating she was born in Harford County, the daughter of the late William Presberry and Clara Parker, and her husband Melvin Murphy died in 1983; she worked in finance and accounting at the Aberdeen Proving Ground and died at home in Aberdeen, leaving no immediate survivors) [Mt. Calvary U. A. M. E. Church Cemetery]

Murphy, Raymond Allen February 6, 1932 – May 30, 1986, TN, U.S. Navy, Korea (tombstone; "Raymond Allen" owned a lot in section 8 some time after 1951) [Mt. Calvary U. A. M. E. Church Cemetery]

Murphy, Shirley (owned a lot in section 31 some time after 1951) [Mt. Calvary U. A. M. E. Church Cemetery]

Murray, Blanche E. 1914-1955 (on same tombstone with Earl G. Murray) [Clark's U. M. Church Cemetery]

Murray, Earl G. 1908-1981 (Masonic symbol) (on same tombstone with Blanche E. Murray) [Clark's U. M. Church Cemetery]

Murray, Edna C. July 18, 1927 – April 6, 1995 [Clark's U. M. Church Cemetery]

Murray, Jessie died November 1, 1926, age 64 (no tombstone; death certificate stated he was the son of George Murray, born in Georgia; he worked as a laborer, died a widower in Edgewood and was buried in "Abingdon Co. Cemetery;" his place of birth and name of his mother were not known to informant Thomas J. Murray, 630 W. Manter(?) St., Philadelphia) [John Wesley U. M. E. Church Cemetery in Abingdon]

Murray, Joseph J. 1927-2015 (small metal funeral home marker) [Fairview A. M. E. Church Cemetery]

Murray, Katie August 11, 1872 – December 4, 1932 (no tombstone) [St. James United Cemetery]

Murray, Mildred O., "Beloved Mother" June 8, 1922 – April 23, 2005 (inscribed "Forever In Our Hearts") [Berkley Memorial Cemetery]

Murray, Pearl M. "Daughter" 1950-1988 [Foster's Hill Cemetery]

Murray, Samuel J. June 10, 1858 – June 8, 1932 (no tombstone; death certificate stated he was born in Chestertown, MD, worked as a chef and died in Havre de Grace; parents unknown to informant, his wife Kate Murray) [St. James United Cemetery]

Murray, Willie July 1, 1896 – June 1, 1943 (no tombstone; death certificate and Kurtz Funeral Home Record Book 1937-1943, p. 276, stated he was born in Forest Hill, the son of Spencer Murray who was born in Maryland, but the name of his mother was not given; he was single, worked as a laborer, and died at the County Home near Bel Air; informant was Ellswoeth Tate, of Forest Hill [Fairview A. M. E. Church Cemetery]

Murry, Ellis died May 14, 1928, age 38 (no tombstone; death certificate stated he was born in Harford Co., the son of Spencer Murry and Georgann Turner, both born in Maryland; he was single and died at home at Federal Hill; informant was Henry Robinson, of Rocks) [William C. Rice Memorial Cemetery, St. James U. M. Church]

Murry, Mr. (owned a lot in section 7 some time after 1951) [Mt. Calvary U. A. M. E. Church Cemetery]

Murry, Mrs. (owned a lot in section 7 some time after 1951) [Mt. Calvary U. A. M. E. Church Cemetery]

Neckenson, King D. April 12, 1874 – December 2, 1934 (no tombstone; death certificate stated he was the son of King D. Neckenson and Sarah Stansberry, and a widower, wife unknown) [Union U. M. Church Cemetery]

Nelms, Alma Dorsey February 26, 1916 – January 25, 2004 [Union U. M. Church Cemetery]

Nelms, Garrett H. September 23, 1918 – January 22, 1996, U.S. Army, World War II (tombstone; James Dorsey Card File, African American Obituaries, maintained at the Historical Society of Harford County, has a card for him with an obituary from *The Aegis* on January 31, 1996 stating he was a native of Memphis, graduated from Tuskegee Institute in Alabama and moved to Detroit; he served in the Army as a military policeman and was stationed at Aberdeen Proving Ground and then Fort Meade; he returned to Detroit where he worked for Bohn Aluminum Corp. and then for General Motors where he was a supervisor; upon retirement he moved to Maryland, lived in Aberdeen and died at Harford Memorial Hospital in Havre de Grace, survived by his wife Alma Mae Dorsey Green Nelms and an adopted son Charles Gregg) [Union U. M. Church Cemetery]

Nelson, Mrs. (owner of a lot in section 19 some time after 1951) [Mt. Calvary U. A. M. E. Church Cemetery]

Newkirk, Hattie July 10, 1912 – February 11, 1912 (no tombstone; death certificate stated she was born in Harford Co. and was the daughter of Thomas Newkirk, born in North Carolina, and Hattie Delarge, born in South Carolina, and they lived in Bel Air) [Hendon Hill Cemetery]

Newton, Barbara D. 1926-1995 (small metal funeral home marker) [Union U. M. Church Cemetery]

Nexon, David (owner of a lot in section 18 some time after 1951) [Mt. Calvary U. A. M. E. Church Cemetery]

Nicholas, Helen E. 1923-1964 [St. James United Cemetery]

Nichols, Emory died February 13, 1929, age about 75 (no tombstone; death certificate spelled his name Nicholes, but spelled his father's name Nichols; he was the son of Lymas Nichols, both born in Maryland, but the name of his mother was not known to informant Carrey Lingham, of Abingdon; he married, worked as a laborer and died in Abingdon) [John Wesley U. M. E. Church Cemetery in Abingdon]

Nichols, Susan 1861 – April 3, 1930 (no tombstone; death certificate stated she was the daughter of Lewis Peaker and Annie Hops, all born in Maryland; she died a widow in Van Bibber and was buried in John Wesley Cemetery; informant was Carrie Lingham, of Abingdon) [John Wesley U. M. E. Church Cemetery in Abingdon]

Nicholson, Daisy B. 1910-2008 (small metal funeral home marker) [St. James United Cemetery]

Nickinson, King David – see King D. Neckenson, Ada Nickison, and Lottie Carry [Union U. M. Church Cemetery]

Nickison, Ada June 9, 1883 – June 3, 1919 (no tombstone; death certificate stated she was the married daughter of Harrison Williams and Annie S. Sims, all born in Harford Co.; informant was King David Nickson *(sic)*, of Aberdeen RFD) [Union U. M. Church Cemetery]

Nickles, Melvin died June 25, 1931, age about 30 (no tombstone; death certificate stated he was born in North Carolina, but his parents were not known to informant Leonard Wallace of 766 Hobart Place, Washington, D.C.; he was single, was killed in an automobile accident on Philadelphia Road near Belcamp cross roads, and buried in "John Wesley Cemetery") [John Wesley U. M. E. Church Cemetery in Abingdon]

Niles, Conan (no marker, but a bouquet with his name on it) [St. James United Cemetery]

Nixon, Bessie (owner of a lot in section 18 some time after 1951) [Mt. Calvary U. A. M. E. Church Cemetery]

Nocho-Lee, Ruth Ann March 3, 1942 – October 6, 2014 [Berkley Memorial Cemetery]

Nolan, Daphne Laverne October 30, 1967 – June 9, 2008 (her name and dates are on a small 5" x 8" x 2" black box attached to the left side of the tombstone of Bernice E. Harris and it is inscribed "In Memory Of" and is also inscribed "A Loving Mother & Sister. If love alone could have saved you, you would have lived forever.") [John Wesley U. M. E. Church Cemetery in Abingdon]

Norman, Clyde February 10, 1895 – September 17, 1968 (no tombstone; Pennington Funeral Home records stated he was born in Rover City, N.C., the son of Abraham Norman, but his mother was unknown; he was single, served in World War I, worked as a laborer, lived at 231 Poplar St. in Baltimore and died at Perry Point VA Hospital in Cecil Co.) [Berkley Memorial Cemetery]

Norman, Ellis Donald 1893-1962 (on same tombstone with Grace E. Norman) [Fairview A. M. E. Church Cemetery]

Norman, Grace E. 1899-1960 (on same tombstone with Ellis Donald Norman) [Fairview A. M. E. Church Cemetery]

Norman-Jones, Edith Doretta December 12, 1932 – June 6, 1997 (no tombstone; James Dorsey Card File, African American Obituaries, maintained at the Historical Society of Harford County, has a card for her with an obituary from *The Record* on June 20, 1997 stating she was born in Bel Air, the ninth child of the late Ellis D. Norman and Grace Choates, and she worked for Aberdeen Proving Ground for 35 years; she lived in Aberdeen and died from injuries sustained in an automobile accident on I-95; she was survived by a son, four sisters, six nephews and seven nieces; one brother and four sisters predeceased her; a memorial service in a subsequent newspaper gave her name as Edith Doreatha Jones) [Fairview A. M. E. Church Cemetery]

Norris, ---- (no tombstone, but Kurtz Funeral Home records stated Harry Norris' child was buried in an "im cherry" coffin on March 13, 1880 "from near the Baptist") [West Liberty Church Cemetery]

Norris, Arianna (illegible dates on badly weathered obelisk with Caroline, Emma Isabel, Florence A. and J. Henry Norris, Sr.) [West Liberty Church Cemetery]

Norris, Arthur Leroy "Blockie" died August 23, 1992, age 75 (no tombstone; James Dorsey Card File, African American Obituaries, maintained at the Historical Society of Harford County, has a card for him with an obituary from *The Aegis* on August 26, 1992 stating he lived in Aberdeen, worked for the maintenance department for the Town of Bel Air and died at Harford Memorial Hospital in Havre de Grace, survived by his wife Nellie D. Norris, 3 sons, 7 daughters, 73 grandchildren, 113 great-grandchildren and 5 great-great-grandchildren) [Union U. M. Church Cemetery]

Norris, Caroline (illegible dates on badly weathered obelisk inscribed with Arianna, Emma Isabel, Florence A. and J. Henry Norris, Sr.) [West Liberty Church Cemetery]

Norris, Caroline E. died January 16, 1913, age 100 (no tombstone; death certificate stated she was the daughter of Joshua Hicks and Lucy Jordan, all born in Maryland; she had worked as a domestic servant and was a widow when she died at Upper Cross Roads; informant was George W. Norris, of Upper Cross Roads) [West Liberty Church Cemetery]

Norris, Elizabeth May – (blank), 1907 – October 2, 1928, age 21 years, 5 mos. (no tombstone; death certificate stated she was married and died in Bel Air; her father was Walter Bond, but her mother was not known to informant Louis Norris, of Bel Air; they were all born in Maryland) [Hendon Hill Cemetery]

Norris, Emma Isabel (illegible dates on badly weathered obelisk inscribed with Arianna, Caroline, Florence A. and J. Henry Norris, Sr.) [West Liberty Church Cemetery]

Norris, Florence A. (illegible dates on badly weathered obelisk inscribed with Arianna, Caroline, Emma Isabel, and J. Henry Norris, Sr.) [West Liberty Church Cemetery]

Norris, George Washington "1839-?" *(sic)* – August 30, 1934, age about 95 (no tombstone; death certificate stated he was born in Harford Co., the son of Henry Norris, born in Maryland, and Caroline Hicks, born in Harford Co.; he was single, worked as a farm laborer until 1910 and died at home at Upper Cross Roads; informant was Carlos Norris, of Fallston; Kurtz Funeral Home Records stated the same and Carlos and Marie Norris authorized the funeral) [West Liberty Church Cemetery]

Norris, George Washington October – (blank), 1893 – May 17, 1914 (no tombstone; death certificate stated he was the son of Emma Isabelle Norris, both born in Maryland, but his father was unknown to informant, his uncle, George W. Norris, of Upper Cross Roads; he was single, worked as a laborer and died at Upper Cross Roads) [West Liberty Church Cemetery]

Norris, Henrietta Ora died January 5, 1967, age not given (no tombstone; obituary in *The Aegis* on January 19,

1967 stated she died at home in Towson, survived by her husband Ralph C. Norris and brother James Gray [Clark's U. M. Church Cemetery]

Norris, J. Henry Sr., born 1894(?,) died ----(illegible dates on badly weathered obelisk inscribed with Arianna, Caroline, Emma Isabel, and Florence A. Norris) [West Liberty Church Cemetery]

Norris, Jesse died April 18, 1910, age 90 (on same tombstone with wife Mary Norris; tombstone was found laying flat on the ground in a wooded area on the south side edge of the cemetery; death certificate stated he was born in Harford Co., worked as a laborer in Bel Air and was married to Mary ----; his mother was Sarah Turner, but informant Mary Norris, his wife, did not know his father's name; she also said Jesse died April 18, 1910, age 83) [West Liberty Church Cemetery]

Norris, Marie March 24, 1888 – April 8, 1947 (no tombstone; Kurtz Funeral Home Record Book 1944-1949, p. 149, stated she was born near Abingdon, the daughter of Neel Curtis, born in St. Mary's Co., and Harriet Hooper, born in Maryland, and married Carlos Norris; they lived near Upper Cross Roads for 10 years before she died in the Havre de Grace Hospital; death certificate stated informant was Elizabeth Pender, 722 W. Franklin St., Baltimore) [Fairview A. M. E. Church Cemetery]

Norris, Mary July 5, 1822 – death date blank (on same tombstone with husband Jesse Norris; death certificate state Mary E. Norris was born July 4, 1819 and died October 7, 1925, age 106; she was a widow who lived in Bel Air and was the daughter of Joshua Jarrett and M. Brown, all born in Maryland; informant was Mary E. Jarrett, of Bel Air) [West Liberty Church Cemetery]

Norris, Nellie D. 1925-2006 (small metal funeral home marker) [Mt. Calvary U. A. M. E. Church Cemetery]

Norton, ---- stillborn male on November 12, 1917 (no tombstone; death certificate stated he was the son of Howard Norton and Viola Hollingsworth, all born in Maryland; informant was his father, of Abingdon) [John Wesley U. M. E. Church Cemetery in Abingdon]

Norton, Arnold A., "Loving Father" February 10, 1964 – March 28, 1998 (tombstone; obituary and photo in *The Aegis* on April 1, 1998 stated Arnold Austin Norton was born in Baltimore, the son of Robert James Norton, Sr. and Doris Frances Clark; he was a production worker, lived in Aberdeen, died at Harford Memorial Hospital in Havre de Grace, and was survived by his parents, a daughter Shakena A. Norton, six brothers, and seven sisters) [John Wesley U. M. E. Church Cemetery in Abingdon]

Norton, Charles H. April 2, 1921 – April 10, 1980, Pvt., U.S. Army, World War II (tombstone; obituary in *The Aegis* on April 24, 1980 stated Charles Henry Norton was born in Abingdon, the son of the late Howard Norton and Viola Hollingsworth; he served in the Army in World War II, lived in Baltimore and died at City Hospital, survived by 5 brothers aand 3 sisters) [John Wesley U. M. E. Church Cemetery in Abingdon]

Norton, Constance H. 1904-1963 (on same tombstone with Malcolm S. Norton inscribed "In Memory Of") [Berkley Memorial Cemetery]

Norton, David May 9, 1846 – December 21, 1912 (no tombstone; death certificate stated he was the son of Albert and Sarah Norton, all born in Harford Co.; he was married, worked as a laborer and died in Bel Air; informant was Lizzie Ruff, of Bel Air; military records state he was a private, Co. A, 30th Regt. Inf., U.S.C.T., January 23, 1864 to December 10, 1865) [John Wesley U. M. E. Church Cemetery in Abingdon]

Norton, George Samuel died January 18, 1991, age 69 (no tombstone; obituary in *The Aegis* on January 23, 1991 stated he was born in Abingdon, the son of Howard A. Norton and Viola Hollingsworth, and his wife was the late Myra Demby Norton; he was a retired warehouseman from Aberdeen Proving Ground, lived in Joppa and died at Franklin Square Hospital, survived by three brothers and three sisters) [Foster's Hill Cemetery]

Norton, George W. April 9, 1910 – February 9, 1972, CPL, Army Air Force, World War II (tombstone; obituary in *The Aegis* on February 17, 1972 stated George William Norton, age 61, son of the late Jacob Henry Norton and Martha Watters, and husband of Charlotte A. V. Porter, of 8300 Bradshaw Road, Bradshaw, died at Franklin Square Hospital; he was a custodian for the Board of Education of Baltimore County; services were conducted at Ebenezer Baptist Church in Magnolia with burial in the adjoining cemetery) [Foster's Hill Cemetery]

Norton, Harold Albert August 30, 1916 – June 18, 1997, U.S. Navy, World War II (tombstone; obituary in *The*

Aegis on June 25, 1997 stated Harold Albert Norton, Sr. was born in Abingdon, the son of Howard Arthur Norton and Viola Serena Hollingsworth, and husband of the late Alice James Brown Norton; he lived in Baltimore, worked as a chauffeur and died at Charlotte Hall Veterans Home in Charlotte Hall, MD, survived by a son, two daughters, two brothers, three sisters, 16 grandchildren and 14 great-grandchildren) [John Wesley U. M. E. Church Cemetery in Abingdon]

Norton, Howard 1890-1963 [John Wesley U. M. E. Church Cemetery in Abingdon]

Norton, James Isaac April 15, 1882 – March 28, 1943 (no tombstone; death certificate stated he was born in Abingdon, the son of David Norton, born in Darlington, and Sallie Bond, born in Benson; he married Anna Norton (age 68 in 1949), worked as a laborer in industry and died at home in Abingdon where he lived for 18 years; informant was Annie Norton) [John Wesley U. M. E. Church Cemetery in Abingdon]

Norton, Jeroleena, neé Presberry, May 7, 1909 – February 10, 1993 [Tabernacle Mount Zion U. M. Church Cemetery]

Norton, Kenneth E. Sr. 1931-2004 (tombstone; obituary and photo in *The Aegis* on January 21, 2004 stated he was born in Havre de Grace and was the son of Howard Arthur Norton and Viola Serena Hollingsworth; he lived in Abingdon, retired from Harford County government after 25 years as a meter reader and a mechanic, and died at Upper Chesapeake Medical Center in Bel Air, survived by his wife of 38 years Mildred R. Harris Norton, 2 sons, 5 daughters, three sisters, 8 grandchildren and 10 great-grandchildren) [John Wesley U. M. E. Church Cemetery in Abingdon]

Norton, Malcolm S. 1902-1979 (on same tombstone with Constance M. Norton inscribed "In Memory Of") [Berkley Memorial Cemetery]

Norton, Mary died February 3, 1901 (no tombstone; death notice in *The Aegis* on February 15, 1901 stated she was a cook for the San Domingo Ducking Club for a number of years and was buried at Abingdon, "an aged and respectable colored woman;" death certificate stated she was aged 80 and died at Magnolia) [John Wesley U. M. E. Church Cemetery in Abingdon]

Norton, Mary R. May 3, 1924 – August 27, 2000 (on same tombstone with William A. Norton, Sr. inscribed "Together Forever") [John Wesley U. M. E. Church Cemetery in Abingdon]

Norton, Miriam A., "His Wife" March 11, 1863 – November 15, 1919 (inscribed "She was a Devoted Wife and a Loving Mother;" death certificate stated she was the daughter of William Parker and Rebecca Foreman, all born in Maryland, married and died at home in Darlington; informant was Thomas N. Norton, of Darlington) [Berkley Memorial Cemetery]

Norton, Myra 1924-1984 (tombstone; obituary in *The Aegis* on July 12, 1984 stated Myra Shrove Norton was born in Magnolia, the daughter of Alexander Demby and Blanche Franklin, and the wife of George S. Norton; she lived in Magnolia and died at Fallston General Hospital, survived by her husband, two sisters, and many other relatives) [Foster's Hill Cemetery]

Norton, Rachel S. died October 2, 1915, age 76 (no tombstone; death certificate stated she was the daughter of Robert Evans, both born in New Jersey, but her mother was unknown to informant T. M. Norton, of Darlington; she was a widow and a cook who did general house work) [Cedars Chapel Cemetery]

Norton, Sarah J. August 27, 1841 – May 8, 1914 (no tombstone; death certificate stated she was the daughter of Colvin (Calvin?) Bond, both born in Harford Co., but her mother was not known to informant Lizzie Ruff, of Bel Air; she died a widow in Bel Air) [John Wesley U. M. E. Church Cemetery in Abingdon]

Norton, Theodore F. January 19, 1844 – June 11, 1912 (no tombstone; death certificate stated he was born in Harford Co., the son of Thomas Norton, born in Virginia, but his mother was not known to informant Thomas Norton, of Darlington; he was married and a laborer in Darlington) [Cedars Chapel Cemetery]

Norton, Thomas N. November 15, 1861 – May 15, 1948 (on same tombstone with Miriam A. Norton) [Berkley Memorial Cemetery]

Norton, Viola 1892-1955 [John Wesley U. M. E. Church Cemetery in Abingdon]

Norton, Viola R. December 5, 1893 – April 8, 1920 (no tombstone; death certificate stated she was the daughter of T. N. Morton and Mariam Parker, all born in Maryland; she was single, worked as a school teacher and died at home in Darlington; informant was her father) [Berkley Memorial Cemetery]

Norton, William A. Sr. April 22, 1923 – November 13, 1986 (on same tombstone with Mary R. Norton that is inscribed "Together Forever;" there is also a military marker that gives his name without the Sr., his dates of birth and death, and TEC5, U.S. Army, World War II; obituary in *The Aegis* on November 22, 1984 stated William Arthur Norton was born in Abingdon, the son of Howard A. Norton and Viola Hollingsworth, and married Mary Ruth Watters; he served in the U.S. Army during World War and retired from Edgewood Arsenal in 1982 as a warehouseman after more than 30 years service; he died at Harford Memorial Hospital and was survived by his wife, four sons, four daughters, four brothers, three sisters, "and numerous grandchildren") [John Wesley U. M. E. Church Cemetery in Abingdon]

Norwood, Lizzie died May 4, 1922, age about 61 (no tombstone; death certificate stated she was born in Virginia, parents unknown, and she died a widow in Havre de Grace) [St. James United Cemetery]

Norwood, Pruedence J. February 13, 1950 – February 15, 1950 (no tombstone; death certificate stated she was the daughter of Kennath Norwood and Rosetta P. Ardell, of Havre de Grace) [St. James United Cemetery]

Nottage, Bertram M. 1961-2008 (small metal funeral home marker) [Berkley Memorial Cemetery]

Nottage, Thomas E. Jr. 1929-1975, Cpl., U.S. Army, Korea [Berkley Memorial Cemetery]

Nunley, Lisa L. January 1, 1983 – March 30, 1983 (on same tombstone with Darnell M. Warfield; obituary in *The Aegis* on April 7, 1983 twice reported Lisa Lynnee Nunley, the first baby born in Harford County in 1983, suddenly died at her mother Barbara Warfield's home on Liberty St., Swan Meadows, in Aberdeen and she was pronounced dead at Harford Memorial Hospital, Havre de Grace; cause of death was Sudden Infant Death Syndrome; she was survived by her parents, Ms. Warfield and Kevin D. Nunley, her grandparents, and a sister Lynnell Warfield) [Mt. Calvary U. A. M. E. Church Cemetery]

Nutter, Irene J. Barclay March 27, 1925 – August 7, 1998 "In Loving Memory" [Berkley Memorial Cemetery]

Nye, Sarah died September 18, 1891, age 65, "A faithful servant" [Hendon Hill Cemetery]

Oliver, Edward A. October 15, 1891 – April 20, 1940, Maryland, Pvt., 521 Service Bttn., Engineering Corps, World War I (tombstone; death certificate stated he was born at Swan Creek, Harford Co., worked as a farmer, was married, lived near Bel Air and died at Harford Memorial Hospital, Havre de Grace; his parents were Charles Bowser and Mary Bowser, but their places of birth were not known to informant Lewis Taylor, of Bel Air) [Hendon Hill Cemetery]

Oliver, Georganna died April 30, 1947, age 70 (no tombstone; death certificate stated she was born in Washington, DC, the daughter of William Warren, birth place unknown, and Lizzie ----, born in Maryland; she married William Oliver, lived at 201 Freedom Alley in Havre de Grace and died a widow; informant was John Talbot, of Havre de Grace) [Asbury Cemetery]

Oliver, Mary M. 1875-1928 (last name not inscribed on tombstone; death certificate stated she was born February – (blank), 1875, married, and died July 10, 1928 near Fountain Green; her mother was Laura Gough, but her father was unknown to informant Robert E. Oliver, of Bel Air) [Hendon Hill Cemetery]

Oliver, Robert E. November 16, 1865 – May 28, 1937 (no tombstone; obituary in *The Aegis*, June 4, 1937, stated he had been employed on the farm of Harry W. Whistler for 29 years and at Prospect Hill Stud Farm for the past 2 years; death certificate stated he was born in Bel Air, lived at Shuck's Corner, his wife was Laura V. Oliver, and his parents were Samuel Oliver and Catherine Hall, both born in Bel Air; informant was his wife Mrs. Laura V. Oliver) [Hendon Hill Cemetery]

Onely, Bessie A. August 1, 1897 – May 28, 1971 (tombstone; obituary in *The Aegis* on June 3, 1971 reported she was of near Delta, PA, neé Peaco, and died in York Hospital; her husband's name was not mentioned, but it stated she was the sister of Thomas Peaco, of Delta, PA) [Chestnut Grove A. M. E. Church Cemetery, formerly LaGrange Cemetery at Rocks]

Onely, Lawrence March 18, 1931 – December 11, 1991 (tombstone; obituary of Bessie A. Onely in 1971 indicated she was the mother of Lawrence A. Onely, of Harrisburg, PA) [Chestnut Grove A. M. E. Church Cemetery, formerly LaGrange Cemetery at Rocks]

Only, Penelopy May 5, 1801 – December 31, 1872 [Barn Hill Cemetery]

Opher, Mary Cathrine March 11, 1908 – December 4, 1920 (no tombstone; death certificate stated she was born in Frederick Co., the daughter of Mosses *(sic)* Opher, born in Dorchester Co., and Esther Carr, born in Frederick Co., MD; informant was her mother, Esther Opher, of Rocks) [William C. Rice Memorial Cemetery, St. James U. M. Church]

Opher, Moses Co. B, 13 U.S. Cld. Inf. (tombstone; death certificate stated he was born May 16, 1845 in Dorchester Co., MD and died September 16, 1915 at Rocks; he was the son of Moses Opher, of Dorchester Co., but his mother was not known to informant Ester R. Opher, of Rocks; he was a minister; military records state "Moses Ophir" served as a private in Co. A, 19th Regt. Inf., U. S. C. T., from May 11, 1864 to January 13, 1867) [William C. Rice Memorial Cemetery, St. James U. M. Church]

Orsborne, Cherry December 6, 1916 – December 10, 1916 (no tombstone; death certificate stated he was born in Darlington, the son of Edward Monroe Orsborne, born in Bel Air, and Cordelia Smith, born in Darlington; he died at home in Darlington; informant was William Smith) [Berkley Memorial Cemetery]

Orsborne, Damarreo Olando died May 16, 1982, age 8 months (no tombstone; obituary in *The Aegis* stated he was born in Baltimore, the son of Clarence E. Orsborne and Lisa R. Christy, of Aberdeen, and died at Johns Hopkins Hospital, survived by his parents, grandmother Rose Christy, of Aberdeen, and great-grandmother Mrs. Allender, of Havre de Grace) [Union U. M. Church Cemetery]

Osborn, Benjamin H. July 28, 1868 – January 5, 1950 (no tombstone; death certificate stated he was born in Harford Co., the son of George Henry Osborn and Julia Ann Cooper; he was a retired janitor, a widower, and had lived in rural Bel Air for 18 years; informant was Mary A. Osborn, of Bel Air) [Asbury Cemetery]

Osborn, Delia Matthews January 16, 1853 – July 28, 1932 (no tombstone; death certificate stated she was the daughter of Valentine and Millie Spencer, all born in Bel Air; she was the widow of Thomas Osborn and died in Bel Air; informant was Pauline Lee, of Bel Air) [Asbury Cemetery]

Osborn, George H. died February 15, 1908, age -- (copied in 1987, but not found in 2018) [Asbury Cemetery]

Osborn, Julia Ann February 8, 1848 – December 30, 1935 (no tombstone; death certificate stated she was the daughter of Emily Jane Cooper, both born in Churchville, but her father's name was not known to informant Benjamin H. Osborn, of Bel Air RFD #1; she was the widow of George Henry Osborn) [Asbury Cemetery]

Osborn, Mary Jane July 25, 1907 – August 13, 1923 (no tombstone; death certificate stated she was the daughter of William Osborn and Mabel Washington, all born in Maryland, and she died in Sewell; informant was Mabel Osborn, of Sewell) [Asbury Cemetery]

Osborn, Phoebe died September 14, 1911, age about 80 (no tombstone; death certificate states she was the married daughter of Daniel Legar, of Harford Co., and Margaret Decoursey, of Virginia; informant was Wesley Osborn, of Havre de Grace) [St. James United Cemetery]

Osborn, Thomas August – (blank), 1848 – March 23, 1926 (no tombstone; death certificate stated he was the son of Samuel Osborn, both born in Maryland, but his mother's name was not known to informant Mrs. Thomas Osborn, of Bel Air; he was married and a laborer) [Asbury Cemetery]

Osborn, William died June 25, 1912, age 49 (no tombstone; death certificate stated he was born in Maryland, the son of Samuel and Maria Osborn, birth places unknown; he was married and worked as a farmer at Belcamp; informant was Mabel Osborn, of Belcamp) [Asbury Cemetery]

Osborne, ---- stillborn female on April 16, 1928 (no tombstone; death certificate stated she was the daughter of Clarence Osborne and Cecelia Dorsey, of Bel Air) [Asbury Cemetery]

Osborne, ---- stillborn female on November 29, 1924 (no tombstone; death certificate stated she was the daughter of Clarence M. Osborne and Cecilia Dorsey, and all were born in Maryland; informant was Clarence Osborne, of Bel Air) [Clark's U. M. Church Cemetery]

Osborne, ---- stillborn male on October 16, 1925 (no tombstone; death certificate stated he was the son of Clarence M. Osborne and Cecelia Dorsey, of Bel Air) [Asbury Cemetery]

Osborne, Charles F. May 10, 1943 – November 1, 1984, SP4, U.S. Army, Vietnam [Union U. M. Church Cemetery]

Osborne, Charles Franklin April 8, 1864 – February 22, 1931 (no tombstone; death certificate stated he was the son of William H. Osborne and Mary J. Warfield; informant was Mrs. C. F. Osborne) [Union U. M. Church Cemetery]

Osborne, Charles Henry (aka Harry Osborn) December 19, 1872 – June 22, 1940 (no tombstone; obituary in *The Aegis*, July 5, 1940, stated he was the son of Thomas Osborne and a life-long resident of Bel Air; associated with horses throughout his early life, he was one of the most expert hostlers in the community; death certificate stated "Charles Henry Osborn (by name of Harry Osborn)" was born at Churchville, worked as a laborer, married Elizabeth C. Rice (age 65 in 1940) and died at home on Bond St. in Bel Air; his parents were Thomas Osborn and Elizabeth Legal, both born in Maryland; informant was Mrs. Elizabeth R. Osborn, of Bel Air) [Hendon Hill Cemetery]

Osborne, Clarence "Scrap" died July 28, 1967, age not given (no tombstone; obituary in *The Aegis* on August 3, 1967 stated he resided in Magnolia and died at the Loch Raven Veterans Hospital in Baltimore; he was survived by 5 children, 3 sisters and 2 brothers; wife not mentioned) [Foster's Hill Cemetery]

Osborne, Clarence E. 1937-2001 (small metal funeral home marker) [St. James United Cemetery]

Osborne, Cordelia E., "Father" *(sic)* 1896-1950 [Berkley Memorial Cemetery]

Osborne, Daniel died January 6, 1947, age about 65 (no tombstone; death certificate stated he was born in Harford County, the son of Henry Osborne and Mary Murphy, birth places unknown to informant, his wife, Mrs. Elizabeth A. Osborne, 727 Lodge St., Havre de Grace; he worked as a laborer and died at home in Havre de Grace) [Mt. Calvary U. A. M. E. Church Cemetery]

Osborne, David A. September 9, 1941 -   (on same tombstone with Ruth Ann Sills Osborne) [St. James United Cemetery]

Osborne, Elizabeth McFarland January 8, 1886 – October 13, 1955 (no tombstone; Pennington Funeral Home records stated she was born in Carlisle, PA, the daughter of Henry McFarland and "?" *(sic)*, lived in Havre de Grace and died a widow at Harford Memorial Hospital; informant was Mrs. Philip Fickins, 397 Wilson St., Havre de Grace; Richard and June Lunsford paid the funeral bill) [Mt. Calvary U. A. M. E. Church Cemetery]

Osborne, Ethel 1896-1981 [Green Spring U. M. Church Cemetery]

Osborne, Harriet A. 1858-1924 (tombstone; death certificate stated "Harriett" was born December 14, 1858, the daughter of Henry Hilton and Eliza Stansbury, and they were all born in Maryland; she was married at the time of her death at home near Havre de Grace on February 29, 1924; informant was Robert Osborne, of Havre de Grace RFD) [Green Spring U. M. Church Cemetery]

Osborne, Mary J. died September 5, 1909, age 82 [St. James United Cemetery]

Osborne, Nora November 4, 1914 – January 19, 1924 (no tombstone; death certificate stated she was the son of William Osborne and Mable Washington, all born in Maryland and they lived at Sewell; informant was her mother Mable Osborne) [John Wesley U. M. E. Church Cemetery in Abingdon]

Osborne, Robert L. 1866-1939 [Green Spring U. M. Church Cemetery]

Osborne, Ruth Ann Sills October 8, 1950 – May 24, 2016 (on same tombstone with David A. Osborne) [St. James United Cemetery]

Osborne, Samuel Pearl June 30, 1897 – January 3, 1953, Maryland, Corporal, Co. D, 811 Pioneer Inf., World War I [Hendon Hill Cemetery]

Overton, Brenda November 6, 1952 – September 3, 1973 [Union U. M. Church Cemetery]

Overton, Etha Mae 1924-2016 [Union U. M. Church Cemetery]

Overton, Italy 1974-2017 (small metal funeral home marker; funeral notice and photo in *The Aegis* stated he was formerly of Aberdeen, lived in Laurel and died on April 22, 2017, age 92, at Laurel Regional Hospital) [Union U. M. Church Cemetery]

Owens, Amari Joneil and **Owens, Jamari Ameil** July 8, 2005 [St. James United Cemetery]

Owens, Jamari Ameil and **Owens, Amari Joneil** July 8, 2005 [St. James United Cemetery]

Owens, Jerusha A. 1908-1974 [Berkley Memorial Cemetery]

Owens, Malcolm W. September 3, 1908 – October 26, 1990 [Berkley Memorial Cemetery]

Oxford, William December 22, 1865 – June 16, 1940 (no tombstone; death certificate stated he was single and the son of Charles Oxford, of Baltimore Co., and mother's name unknown) [St. James United Cemetery]

P-illi(?) (flat cement marker with large silver letters and second letter is missing) [St. James United Cemetery]

Paca, Anna E April 15, 1874 – December 11, 1940 (no tombstone; death certificate stated she was wife of John H. Paca and the daughter of William Kenley, but her mother was unknown) [Union U. M. Church Cemetery]

Paca, James Wesley, "Beloved Husband of Martha C. Paca" December 29, 1837 – July 4, 1916 (inscribed "Gone But Not Forgotten, Asleep But Not Dead;" death certificate stated he was the married son of William Paca and Hester Sims, all born in Maryland; informant was Martha Paca, of Perryman) [Union U. M. Church Cemetery]

Paca, John W. April 16, 1864 – March 17, 1941 (no tombstone; death certificate stated he was the son of John W. Paca and Martha Simms, and the husband of the deceased Anna E. Paca) [Union U. M. Church Cemetery]

Paca, Martha C., "Beloved Wife of James W. Paca" April 1, 1842 – January 10, 1931 (inscribed without her date of death; death certificate spelled her name "Paco" and stated she died a widow and was the daughter of Jacob H. Simms and Henrietta Johnson; informant was John "Paco" of rural Aberdeen) [Union U. M. Church Cemetery]

Paca, Sarah A. 1868-1927 (tombstone; death certificate spelled her name "Paco" and stated she was born on August 18, 1867, the daughter of Louis Giles and Annie Thomas; she was married and died March 2, 1927; informant was Charles W. "Paco" of Aberdeen) [Union U. M. Church Cemetery]

Paca, Susie A., "Beloved Wife of John H. Paca" December 3, 1867 – March 9, 1910 (tombstone; death certificate stated she was the daughter of Thomas Meadow and Lucy Janger, all born in Virginia; she married John H. Paca and died at home in Perryman; informant was sister Lucy Rice) [Union U. M. Church Cemetery]

Pace, Chevron Tirell, "Architect / Musician" June 7, 1977 – September 7, 2003 (inscribed "I can do all things through Christ which strengthen me. Philippians 4:13") [Clark's U. M. Church Cemetery]

Parker, Alice R., daughter of J. W. and R. J. Parker, died May 13, 1891, aged 23 years, 10 months and 22 days [Berkley Memorial Cemetery]

Parker, Baby stillborn female on December 18, 1928 (no tombstone; death certificate stated she was the daughter of William H. Presbury and Clara Parker, all born in Maryland; she died at home in Aberdeen and informant was her father) [Mt. Calvary U. A. M. E. Church Cemetery]

Parker, Dorothy Virginia September 23, 1914 – April 8, 1995 (tombstone; James Dorsey Card File, African American Obituaries, that is maintained at the Historical Society of Harford County, has a card for her with an obituary from *The Aegis* on September 20, 1995 stating she was the daughter of Ada Idella Brown and Raymond Buchanan, and after she moved to New York in pursuit of a nursing career she moved back to Aberdeen and worked with Curtis C. Morgan and family for 30 years; she died at home in Perryman, survived by her husband William Taft Parker, a son, a sister, and three grandchildren) [Mt. Calvary U. A. M. E. Church Cemetery]

Parker, Earlyne Rhoads, "Loving Mother and Wife" September 8, 1932 – March 2, 1988, Pvt. *(sic)*, U.S. Air Force (tombstone; buried in section 41; obituary in *The Havre de Grace Record* on March 9, 1988 stated she was born in Jersey City, NJ, the daughter of Arletha Twitty of Jersey City and the late Earl Randolph, and the wife of Robert Parker; she resided in Aberdeen and was struck and killed by an automobile at the intersection of Routes

40 and 22; she was survived by her husband, her mother, 3 sons, 3 daughters, and 5 grandchildren) [Mt. Calvary U. A. M. E. Church Cemetery]

Parker, James November 22, 1894 – March 1, 1974 (on same tombstone with Verna Jane Parker) [Clark's U. M. Church Cemetery]

Parker, James T. January 2, 1873 – May 25, 1926 (no tombstone; death certificate stated he was the son of James W. Parker and Rebecca Taylor, and they all were born in Maryland; he married Janie ----, worked as a laborer for a cemetery sexton and died at home in Darlington; informant was Mrs. Janie Parker, of Darlington) [Berkley Memorial Cemetery]

Parker, James William October 3, 1830 – September 21, 1913 (on same obelisk with Rebecca J. Parker inscribed "At Rest" and it only gave his name as J. W. Parker and his date of birth; death certificate gave complete dates of birth and death and stated he was the son of Adam Parker and Kitty ---- "unknown" and all were born in Maryland; he worked as a laborer and died a widower at Shure's Landing; informant was James Parker, also of Shure's Landing) [Berkley Memorial Cemetery]

Parker, Lloyd 1853-1954 [Mt. Calvary U. A. M. E. Church Cemetery]

Parker, Loyd December 25, 1902 – September 21, 1914 (no tombstone; death certificate stated he was the son of Loyd G. Parker and Rose Green, al born in Harford Co.; he died at home near Aberdeen; informant was his father) [Mt. Calvary U. A. M. E. Church Cemetery]

Parker, Lucile died March 7, 1923, age about 52 (no tombstone; death certificate stated she was the daughter of Hiram Parker, both born in Virginia, but mother's name unknown) [St. James United Cemetery]

Parker, Margaret T. December 10, 1895 – August 16, 1896 [Berkley Memorial Cemetery]

Parker, Mary Elizabeth Hall died January 14, 19-- (year missing), age 94 (no tombstone; James Dorsey Card File, African American Obituaries, maintained at the Historical Society of Harford County, has a card for her with an undated obituary stating she was born on Pleasantville, near Fallston, daughter of Charles Hall and Amanda Cromwell, and wife of the late William T. Parker; she died at home in Phoenix, survived by a sister, two nephews and a niece) [West Liberty Church Cemetery]

Parker, Patty died on February 20, 1880, age 80, at Gravelly Hill (no marker; funeral notice of Mrs. Patty Parker was published in the *Havre de Grace Republican* on February 27, 1880) [Gravel Hill Cemetery]

Parker, Rebecca J. March 4, 1845 – February 25, 1913 (on same obelisk with J. W. Parker and inscribed "At Rest;" death certificate stated Rebecca Parker was born March 4, 1844, the daughter of Abraham Prigg and Charity Taylor, all born in Maryland; she was married and died at home in Bel Air; informant was James T. Parker, of Darlington) [Berkley Memorial Cemetery]

Parker, Robert August 3, 1915 – February 11, 1919 (no tombstone; death certificate stated he was the son of Loyd Parker and Rosa Green, all were born in Maryland; he died at home near Aberdeen; informant was his father) [Mt. Calvary U. A. M. E. Church Cemetery]

Parker, Rose E. 1874-1968 (on same tombstone with Lloyd Parker; obituary in *The Aegis* on February 8, 1968 stated Rose Etta Parker was the daughter of Ambrose Curtis and Margaret Green, and the widow of Lloyd Parker; she lived at Route 1, Aberdeen, and died in Harford Memorial Hospital in Havre de Grace on February 2, 1968, age 93, survived by 2 sons, 5 daughters, 11 grandchildren, 20 great-grandchildren and 8 great-great-grandchildren) [Mt. Calvary U. A. M. E. Church Cemetery]

Parker, Samuel O. January 15, 1873 – February 19, 1918 (copied in 1987, but not found in 2018; death certificate stated Samuel Parker was born in August, 1873 in Harford Co., son of William Parker, birth place unknown, and died February 9, 1918, age 45, in Havre de Grace; he was married and worked as a day laborer; the name of his mother and her birth place were not known to informant Sarah Parker, of Aberdeen) [Mt. Calvary U. A. M. E. Church Cemetery]

Parker, Sarah Jane June 25, 1860 – March 11, 1936 (no tombstone; death certificate stated she was the daughter of Stephen Jamison and Frances Presberry, all born in Harford Co.; she married James T. Parker and died a widow at home in Darlington where she lived for 60 years; informant was Rebecca Shortter, of

Darlington) [Berkley Memorial Cemetery]

Parker, Verna Jane August 23, 1903- February 22, 1973 (on same tombstone with James Parker) [Clark's U. M. Church Cemetery]

Parker, William H. April 1, 1843 – August 4, 1919 (no tombstone; death certificate stated he was a widower and the son of William Parker, both born in Maryland, but his mother was unknown to informant Mrs. Frankanna Martin, of Havre de Grace) [Union U. M. Church Cemetery]

Parker, William T. October 22, 1907 – August 27, 1999 [Mt. Calvary U. A. M. E. Church Cemetery]

Parker, Winfield E. 1910-1985 [Mt. Calvary U. A. M. E. Church Cemetery]

Parker, Winfield E. October 18, 1934 – October 4, 2006, U.S. Navy [Mt. Calvary U. A. M. E. Church Cemetery]

Parks, Michael Theodore died February 6, 1983, age 27 (no tombstone; obituary in *The Aegis* on February 17, 1983 stated he lived in Aberdeen and was a student at Airco Technical Institute in Baltimore; he was survived by his mother Alice Parks, of Aberdeen, his father Donald T. Parks, of Virginia, and 5 brothers and 3 sisters) [Mt. Calvary U. A. M. E. Church Cemetery]

Parrish, Cora L. 1906-1971 (on same tombstone with William D. Parrish; obituary in *The Aegis* stated Cora Lee Parrish was born at North Point, Baltimore Co., the daughter of James Lewis and Eleanor Bundy, and married William Davis Parrish, now of 131 Mandyville Road in Joppa; she died at Baltimore City Hospital on March 23, 1971, survived by her husband, 4 sons, 3 daughters, 1 brother, 3 sisters, 19 grandchildren, and 52 great-grandchildren) [Community Baptist Church Cemetery]

Parrish, Evelyn L. 1904-   (OES Star symbol engraved on same tombstone with Walter L. Parrish) [Berkley Memorial Cemetery]

Parrish, Walter L. 1899-1970 (Masonic symbol engraved on same tombstone with Evelyn L. Parrish; obituary in *The Aegis* stated he was a carpenter who died April 28, 1970, age 70, at his home on Spesutia Road in Perryman and was survived by his wife, 3 sons, 2 daughters, 40 grandchildren and 22 great-grandchildren) [Berkley Memorial Cemetery]

Parrish, William D. 1889-1985 (on the same tombstone with Cora L. Parrish; obituary in *The Aegis* on March 7, 1985 stated he was born in Cumberland Co., VA, the son of Dolly Lewis and Jacob Parrish, and was the husband of Cora Lee Parrish; "was a labor at a sawmill, farm and carpenter; he also worked at the Sparrows Point Steel Mill and the Edgewood Arsenal;" died at Valley View Nursing Home in Towson on February 27, 1985, survived by 7 children, 18 grandchildren, 51 great-grandchildren) [Community Baptist Church Cemetery]

Parrott, Bertha (no dates) [Clark's U. M. Church Cemetery]

Parrott, Carroll S. May 12, 1887 – January 25, 1925 (no tombstone; death certificate stated he was the son of Sarah Parrott, but his father's name was unknown to informant Walter Parrott, of Bel Air RFD #1; he was single and worked as a laborer in Bel Air) [Asbury Cemetery]

Parrott, Eli December 15, 1842 – March 26, 1912 (no tombstone; death certificate stated he was born in Virginia, parents' names unknown; he was married, worked as a farm laborer and died at Thomas Run; informant was James A. Parrott, of Bel Air) [Asbury Cemetery]

Parrott, Elizabeth Banks, wife of James Parrott, died May 31, 1910, age 23 (tombstone partly inscribed "The Lord is my light") [Asbury Cemetery]

Parrott, Estella September 3, 1884 – November 11, 1933 (on same tombstone with Sara, William and Bertha Parrott; the tombstone only gave her date of death; death certificate stated she was born in Maryland, her father was unknown, her mother was a Highland, and their birth places were unknown to the informant, her husband William Parrott, of Bel Air RFD #10) [Clark's U. M. Church Cemetery]

Parrott, James A. May 12, 1881 – March 1, 1933 (no tombstone; death certificate stated he was the son of Ely Parrott, born in Virginia, and Hannah Chambers, born in Maryland; he was born in Maryland, worked as a sawyer, married Elizabeth Banks and was a widower when he died in Bel Air RFD; informant was Walter

Parrott) [Asbury Cemetery]

Parrott, Joseph H. died on 10 or 11 March 1939, age about 70 (no tombstone; death certificate stated he was the son of Eli Parrott and Hannah Chambers, all born in Maryland; he married Flicha ---- and lived, worked and died near Churchville; informant was Elsworth Cooper, of Bel Air RFD, who did not know Joseph's date of birth; the day of his death in March 1939 was missing from the death certificate, but he was buried on March 13, 1939) [Asbury Cemetery]

Parrott, Millie, "Mother" 1853-1935 [Union U. M. Church Cemetery]

Parrott, Sara died October 20, 1934 (no birth date nor age were inscribed; on same tombstone with Estella, William and Bertha Parrott; no death certificate found in Harford County) [Clark's U. M. Church Cemetery]

Parrott, Telitha died December 24, 1952, age 68 (no tombstone, death notice in *The Aegis* on January 2, 1953 stated she was found dead in bed at her home at Schuck's Corner on Christmas morning and "apparently had succumbed 24 hours earlier") [Asbury Cemetery]

Parrott, William H. April 22, 1885 – March 14, 1948 (tombstone only gave his date of death and no middle initial; on same tombstone with Estella, Sara and Bertha Parrott; death certificate stated he was the son of Elye Parrott and Sarah Parrott, all born in Harford Co.; married to Bertha C. Snowden, worked as a day laborer for private families, and died at Schucks Corner in rural Bel Air where he had lived for 62 years; informant was Mrs. William H. Parrott, of Bel Air RFD) [Clark's U. M. Church Cemetery]

Parson, Calvin 1870 – March 13, 1948 (no tombstone; death certificate stated he died a widower in Havre de Grace, parents unknown; his wife was Ella ----; informant was Calvin Parson, Jr.) [St. James United Cemetery]

Parson, Ella died September 3, 1918, age about 47 (no tombstone) [St. James United Cemetery]

Parson, Norma 1898-1983 [St. James United Cemetery]

Pascall, Lillie (owned a lot in section 16 some time after 1951) [Mt. Calvary U. A. M. E. Church Cemetery]

Patten, Ella Mae 1930-2014 (small metal funeral home marker) [St. James United Cemetery]

Paul, Pauelie died March 6, 1918, age 34 (no tombstone; death certificate stated he was born in South Carolina, the son of Joshia Paul, but his mother was unknown to informant Sgt. DeGroat on Aberdeen Proving Ground where Paul worked as a laborer for a contractor) [Union U. M. Church Cemetery]

Payne, Iva February 22, 1887 – February 26, 1932 (no tombstone; death certificate stated she was the wife of Lee Payne, of Swan Creek, and the daughter of Robert Crockett and Eliza Williams who were born Virginia as was Iva) [Union U. M. Church Cemetery]

Payne, William Parvine March 8, 1890 – April 17, 1941 (no tombstone; death certificate stated he was born in Maryland, but parents not known to informant Minty Payne, of Edgewood; he married Minty Gilbert (age 49 in 1941), worked as a laborer and died in Abingdon where they had lived for 10 years) [Foster's Hill Cemetery]

Peaco, ---- stillborn female on April 2, 1916, premature birth about 7 months (no tombstone; death certificate stated she was born in Abingdon, the daughter of Samuel Peaco and Geraldine Beasley, both born in Maryland; informant was Laura Beasley, of Abingdon) [John Wesley U. M. E. Church Cemetery in Abingdon]

Peaco, Abraham Henry November 30, 1868 – December 3, 1937 (no tombstone; death certificate stated he was born in Harford Co., the son of Alfred Peaco, of Cecil Co., and Lizzie Dorsey, of Pennsylvania; he married Sarah French, was a barber, and died in Havre de Grace; informant was Sarah Peaco) [St. James United Cemetery]

Peaco, Alice M., wife of William H. Peaco, 1892-1954 (on same tombstone with her husband, inscribed "May She Rest In Peace") [St. James United Cemetery]

Peaco, Catherine -- 20(?) (her name and dates illegible on the same badly weathered flat tombstone with William Peaco; she was actually the wife of Wesley William Peaco) [Berkley Memorial Cemetery]

Peaco, Daniel W. Sr. January 23, 1926 – December 26, 1981, TEC5, U.S. Army, World War II [Mt. Calvary U. A. M. E. Church Cemetery]

Peaco, Eleanora, "Daughter" 1910-2003 (on same tombstone with Lonnie W. Peaco and Mary B. Peaco) [Fairview A. M. E. Church Cemetery]

Peaco, Elizabeth A. February 27, 1828 – September 14, 1908 (inscribed with a verse that is partly illegible) [St. James United Cemetery]

Peaco, Elizabeth A. July 14, 1892 – June 27, 1989 (tombstone; obituary in *The Record* on July 12, 1989 stated she was known as "Aunt Lizzie" to many in Harford County where she was born; she worked many years in Ocean City, MD and Pleasantville, NJ, returned to Havre de Grace, was active in the church and died at Church Home Hospital in Baltimore, survived by three nieces and many great nieces and great nephews) [St. James United Cemetery]

Peaco, Ernestine O. June 15, 1922 – December 18, 2000 (inscribed "In Loving Memory of Mother") [St. James United Cemetery]

Peaco, George May 21, 1886 – June 24, 1934 (no tombstone; death certificate stated he was the unmarried son of A. H. Peaco and Sarah French, worked as a laborer and died in Havre de Grace) [St. James United Cemetery]

Peaco, Harriet December 20, 1858 – January 21, 1918 (no tombstone; death certificate stated she was the daughter of Timothy Shields and Mary Hilton, all born in Maryland; she was married and died at Lapidum; informant was Jacob Peaco, of Havre de Grace RFD) [Green Spring U. M. Church Cemetery]

Peaco, Hezekiah (no tombstone; death certificates stated he was born on May 22, 1861 in Harford Co., the son of John Peaco and Mary Boyins, both born in Maryland; he worked as a laborer at Pylesville and was married at the time of his death on May 27, 1914; informant was Dr. W. E. Arthur, of Cardiff) [Chestnut Grove A. M. E. Church Cemetery, formerly LaGrange Cemetery at Rocks]

Peaco, Howard February 17, 1889 – July 3, 1932 (no tombstone; death certificate stated he was the unmarried son of Abraham H. Peaco and Sarah French, worked as a laborer and died in Havre de Grace) [St. James United Cemetery]

Peaco, Howard I. September 17, 1901 – August 8, 1932 (no tombstone; death certificate stated he was the son of Isaiah Peaco and Mary S. Kenly) [Union U. M. Church Cemetery]

Peaco, Infant (male) January 19, 1928 – January 21, 1928 (no tombstone; death certificate stated he was the premature son of William Davis and Hilda Peaco) [St. James United Cemetery]

Peaco, Isaiah July 9, 1876 – September 16, 1937 (no tombstone; death certificate stated he was the son of James Peaco and Martha Simmons(?), and the husband of the deceased Mary Peaco) [Union U. M. Church Cemetery]

Peaco, Jacob died July 19, 1943, age 71 (no tombstone; death certificate stated he was born in Harford Co., but the names of his parents were not known to informant Mrs. Elizabeth Peaco, of Havre de Grace; he married Elizabeth ---- (born 1887), worked as a laborer, and lived and died at home at Juniata & Erie Streets in Havre de Grace) [Green Spring U. M. Church Cemetery]

Peaco, James Morris October 24, 1917 – October 30, 1917 (no tombstone; death certificate stated he was born in Maryland and died in Abingdon, the son of Ida Peaco, born in Maryland, but the name of his father was not known to informant, his mother, Ida Peaco, of Abingdon) [John Wesley U. M. E. Church Cemetery in Abingdon]

Peaco, John Edrus December 22, 1923 – October 15, 1972, Pennsylvania, TEC4, 393 QM Truck Co., World War II (tombstone; obituary in *The Aegis* on October 26, 1972 stated he was born in Delta, PA, son of Mrs. Erma Robinson, of Aberdeen, and Thomas Peaco, of PA, served in the Army, lived at 615 Edmund St. in Aberdeen, died at Fort Howard VA Hospital and was survived by his wife Mary F. Peaco, of Paterson, NJ, two sons, three brothers, one sister, his step-father George Robinson, of Aberdeen, and one grandson) [Mt. Calvary U. A. M. E. Church Cemetery]

Peaco, Lewis died January 17, 1889, age about 80 (no tombstone; his death notice in *The Aegis* in January 25, 1889 stated he died in Abingdon, upwards of 80 years of age, and had formerly belonged to the late George William Hall, of Abingdon District; his place of burial was not given [probably John Wesley U. M. E. Church Cemetery in Abingdon]

Peaco, Lloyd L. November 6, 1893 – May 3, 1985, Pvt. U.S. Army, World War I (tombstone; obituary in *The Aegis* on May 12, 1985 stated he was born in Harford County, worked for Maryland National Bank for 30 years and afterwards for Lyons Pharmacy; he died at Perry Point VAMC and was survived by a sister Elizabeth Peaco and four nieces; military records stated Lloyd Lowndes Peaco was born in Havre de Grace on January 6, 1896 *(sic)* and he was inducted into the service on June 19, 1918, served in the 154 Depot Brigade and was honorably discharged on February 4, 1919) [St. James United Cemetery]

Peaco, Lonnie W., "Father" 1877-1952 (on same tombstone with Mary B. Peaco and Eleanora Peaco) [Fairview A. M. E. Church Cemetery]

Peaco, Lydia A. October 14, 1840 – March 9, 1920 (no tombstone; death certificate stated she was born in Harford Co., the daughter of Samuel Dorsey, born in Harford Co., and Violet Howard, born in Baltimore Co.; she worked as a domestic, died a widow near Bel Air and was buried at "Mountain Colored Cemetery;" informant was Mary Watters, of Bel Air) [Mt. Zion U. M. Church Cemetery]

Peaco, Mary September 6, 1835 – May 20, 1919 (no tombstone; death certificate stated she was the daughter of James Peaco and Ellen Foreman, all born in Maryland; she was a widow and died at home at Garland; informant was Ella Lee, of Havre de Grace RFD) [Green Spring U. M. Church Cemetery]

Peaco, Mary B., "Mother" 1880-1947 (on same tombstone with Lonnie W. Peaco and Eleanora Peaco) [Fairview A. M. E. Church Cemetery]

Peaco, Mary Jane June 29, 1903 – September 26, 1917 (no tombstone; death certificate stated she was the daughter of Malachi Harris and Sarah E. Peaco, and they were all born in Maryland; she died in Havre de Grace; informant was Elsie Peaco, of Havre de Grace) [Skinner Cemetery]

Peaco, Mary L. died April 18, 1939, age about 53 (no tombstone; death certificate stated she was born in Havre de Grace, the daughter of Jacob Peaco and Mary Liza ----, both were born in Harford Co.; she never married, worked as a domestic until 1934 and died at Harford Memorial Hospital; informant was Edith Turner, of Havre de Grace RFD) [Green Spring U. M. Church Cemetery]

Peaco, Mary S. January 22, 1875 – February 20, 1937 (no tombstone; death certificate stated she was the wife of I. S. Peaco and the daughter of William Kenley and Rebecca Peaco) [Union U. M. Church Cemetery]

Peaco, Morgan M. (no tombstone; death certificate stated he was born October 22, 1887 in Pennsylvania, the son of Hezekiah Peaco and Venie Howard, both born in Maryland; he worked as a laborer at Pylesville and was married at the time of his death on February 6, 1914; informant was Hezekiah Peaco, of Pylesville) [Chestnut Grove A. M. E. Church Cemetery, formerly LaGrange Cemetery at Rocks]

Peaco, Olivia September 1, 1910 – April 27, 1989 (tombstone; obituary in *The Record* on May 3, 1989 stating "Levy" was the daughter of Alice M. and William H. Peaco, Sr. and she worked at the Bainbridge Naval Base and at Aberdeen Proving Ground; she played the piano and guitar and often entertained at church; she died at Harford Memorial Hospital and was survived by two sisters, a brother-in-law, one sister-in-law, and one god-daughter) [St. James United Cemetery]

Peaco, Russell LeRoy Jr. died November 7, 1972, age 18 (no tombstone; obituary in *The Aegis* stated he lived at 615 Edmund St. in Aberdeen, was a student at Harford Community College near Bel Air and died at Harford Memorial Hospital in Havre de Grace, survived by his grandmother Mrs. Erma Robinson, his father Russell L. Peaco, Sr., of Baltimore, his mother Mrs. Edith T. Shelley, of Edgewood, his grandfather Thomas Peaco, of Pennsylvania, his step-grandfather George Robinson, of Aberdeen, three brothers Royce Peaco, of Boston, MA, Ronald Shelley and Horace G. Shelley, both of Edgewood, and five sisters Mrs. Janet F. Boyd, of Pensacola, FL, Susan Peaco, of Boston, and Denise E. Peaco, Mrs. Diana Williams and Lynette M. Shelley, all of Edgewood) [Mt. Calvary U. A. M. E. Church Cemetery]

Peaco, Sarah E. January 5, 1866 – January 6, 1913 (no tombstone; death certificate stated she was the widowed daughter of Charles Coleman and Mary J. Skinner; informant was John Peaco) [St. James United Cemetery]

Peaco, Sarah Elizabeth died January 25, 1959, age 84 (no tombstone; obituary in The Democratic Ledger on January 29, 1959 stated she was born in Aberdeen and died at her home in the 400 block of Freedom Lane in Havre de Grace, and was the widow of Abraham Peaco; she was survived by 3 sons, William, Lloyd and Charles

Peaco, and a daughter Elizabeth Peaco) [St. James United Cemetery]

Peaco, Sarah Elizabeth died July 26, 1970, age not given (no tombstone; obituary in *The Aegis* stated she died at home at 560 Girard St., Havre de Grace, and was survived by her husband Lloyd Peaco and several nieces and nephews) [St. James United Cemetery]

Peaco, Thomas H. died December 24, 1980, age 76 (no tombstone; obituary in *The Aegis* on January 1, 1981 stated he was a former employee of Aberdeen Proving Ground and a former resident of Fawn Grove and Delta; he lived at Dover RFD #3, PA, and was the husband of the late Emma Boanes Peaco; he died at York Hospital and was survived by sons Daniel, William and Lewis Peaco, daughters Betty Stokes, Bessie Peaco, Della Haines and Helen Peaco, 19 grandchildren, and 17 great-grandchildren) [Mt. Calvary U. A. M. E. Church Cemetery]

Peaco, Wesley William February --, 1898 – December 10, 1969 (name inscribed as William Peaco on the same badly weathered flat tombstone with Catherine Peaco; obituary in *The Aegis* stated Wesley W. Peaco was the son of Isaiah and Mary Peaco and a retired employee of the Perry Point VAMC; he lived at 916 Warren Street in Havre de Grace and died at home on December 10, 1969, age 71, survived by his wife Catherine A. Peaco and two daughters) [Berkley Memorial Cemetery]

Peaco, William H. 1887-1959 (on same tombstone with Alice M. Peaco) [St. James United Cemetery]

Peaco, William H. August 13, 1912 – May 26, 1972, SSgt., 371 Inf., World War II (tombstone; obituary in *The Aegis* stated he was born in Havre de Grace, the son of the late William H. Sr. and Alice Mae Peaco, and was a nursing assistant at the Perry Point VAMC; he lived at 922 Elizabeth St. in Havre de Grace and died at Harford Memorial Hospital, survived by his wife Ernestine Peaco, 2 sons Joseph O. Burke and William G. Burke, 1 daughter Cynthia F. Burke, and 3 sisters Mrs. Hilda Hawkins, Miss Olivia Peaco and Mrs. Marie Brown) [St. James United Cemetery]

Peaco, William T. died on August 28, 1936, age about 70 (no tombstone; death certificate stated he was not married and the son of James W. Peaco and Martha Simms) [Union U. M. Church Cemetery]

Peaker, ---- stillborn male on May 23, 1933 (no tombstone; death certificate stated he was the son of John H. Peaker and Cornelia Green, all born in Maryland; he died at home in Cooptown; informant was Mrs. Ida Green) [Fairview A. M. E. Church Cemetery]

Peaker, ---- stillborn male, premature birth on April 19, 1930 (no tombstone; death certificate stated he was the son of Samuel Peaker and Geraldine Beasley, all born in Maryland; buried in "John Wesley Cemetery;" informant was Geraldine Peaker, of Abingdon) [John Wesley U. M. E. Church Cemetery in Abingdon]

Peaker, ---n-e (?) 1911-1990 (small metal funeral home marker with some of the letters missing) [Mt. Zion U. M. Church Cemetery]

Peaker, Alline F., "Memom" 1915-1995 (tombstone; obituary in *The Aegis* on October 18, 1995 stated Alline Frances Peaker was born in Pylesville, the daughter of Mora Holland and Mabel Gover, and was a food server at the Edgewood Arsenal Post Exchange; she was the widow of Henry Peaker and died at home in Street on October 14, 1995, age 80, survived by a stepdaughter, four brothers, three grandchildren, and five great-grandchildren) [Fairview A. M. E. Church Cemetery]

Peaker, Anna Maria January 15, 1843 – November 16, 1919 (no tombstone; death certificate stated she was the daughter of Peggy Barton, both were born in Maryland, and she died in Abingdon; her name was spelled Peco on the certificate, yet the name of her father was not known to informant Virginia Peaker, of Abingdon) [John Wesley U. M. E. Church Cemetery in Abingdon]

Peaker, Carrie December 31, 1892 – January 26, 1958 (no tombstone; death certificate stated she was born in Harford Co., the daughter of Stephen Peaker and Sarah F. White, both born in Maryland; she lived in Bel Air, married and later separated, died at Harford Memorial Hospital and was buried in "Mountain Methodist Cemetery, Joppa;" informant was W. T. Peaker, of RFD Edgewood) [Mt. Zion U. M. Church Cemetery]

Peaker, Carroll L. 1920-1977 (on same tombstone with Cecilia J. Peaker) [John Wesley U. M. E. Church Cemetery in Abingdon]

Peaker, Cecilia J. 1932-2013 (on the same tombstone with Carroll L. Peaker, but her year of death had not been inscribed; funeral notice and photo in *The Aegis* on December 11, 2013 stated she died at her home in Abingdon on October 8, 2013, age 81) [John Wesley U. M. E. Church Cemetery in Abingdon]

Peaker, Charles May 30, 1873 – May 13, 1949 (no tombstone; death certificate stated he was born in Maryland, the son of James W. Peaker and Martha Simms; he married, worked as a day laborer and died at Thomas Run in rural Bel Air where he lived for 5 years; informant was Mrs. Charles Peaker) [Union U. M. Church Cemetery]

Peaker, Charles H. died April 15, 1972, age 55 (no tombstone; obituary in *The Aegis* stated he was a son of Samuel and Geraldine Peaker of Rhode Island, and the husband of Ada Peaker of 505 Dembytown Road in Joppa; he was a trackman on the railroad for 38 years and died at Franklin Square Hospital, survived by his wife, daughter, three sisters, and four brothers) [Foster's Hill Cemetery]

Peaker, Clarence A. 1914-1965 [Mt. Zion U. M. Church Cemetery]

Peaker, Eliza E. 1849 – February 4, 1927 (no tombstone; death certificate stated she was the daughter of Peter Peaker and Rachel Hilton, all born in Maryland; she died a widow at Emmorton and was buried in "Mt. M. E. Cem.;" informant was Stephen Peaker, of Emmorton) [Mt. Zion U. M. Church Cemetery]

Peaker, Evelyn B. March 17, 1909 – October 26, 1978 (tombstone; obituary in *The Aegis* on November 2, 1978 stated Evelyn (Patty) Braxton Peaker was born in Baltimore, daughter of Thomas Braxton and Keziah Fountaine, and lived in Abingdon; she was employed as a nursing assistant with private families and nursing homes and died in Harford Memorial Hospital, survived by a son Samuel Redd, a brother Allen Braxton, a sister Eleanor Vessels, 5 grandchildren and 3 great-grandchildren) [John Wesley U. M. E. Church Cemetery in Abingdon]

Peaker, Genevieve W. 1917-1983 (tombstone; obituary in *The Aegis* on January 6, 1983 stated Genevieve "Gen" Elizabeth Peaker was born October 24, 1917, the daughter of Robert Lawrence and Sarah Elizabeth Whittington; she died at home in Bel Air and was survived by her step-mother Addie Whittington, two daughters, a son, 12 grandchildren and 6 great-grandchildren) [Mt. Zion U. M. Church Cemetery]

Peaker, George A., "Uncle" August 6, 1903 – September 13, 1989 [Mt. Zion U. M. Church Cemetery]

Peaker, Georgianna Harris, "Mother" 1919-1989 [John Wesley U. M. E. Church Cemetery in Abingdon]

Peaker, Gladys October 8, 1932 – December 24, 1932 (no tombstone; death certificate stated she was born in Harford Co., the daughter of Samuel H. Peaker and Geraldine Beasley, both born in Maryland; buried at "John Wesley;" informant was Samuel Peaker, of Abingdon) [John Wesley U. M. E. Church Cemetery in Abingdon]

Peaker, Henry Clay May 22, 1915 – February 13, 1983, TEC 5, U.S. Army, World War II, Korea (tombstone and military marker; obituary in *The Aegis* on February 17, 1983 stated he was born in Harford County, served in the U.S. Army, married Alline ----, and was a retired dog groomer from "Handful" in Kingsville; he lived in Joppa and died at Perry Point Veterans Administration Center, survived by his wife, 3 sisters and numerous nieces and nephews) [Mt. Zion U. M. Church Cemetery]

Peaker, Joe Louis died August 18, 1980, age 30 (no tombstone; obituary in *The Aegis* on August 28, 1980 stated he was born in Havre de Grace, the son of William Wesley Peaker, Sr., of Aberdeen, and Irene Thomas Gilbert, of Edgewood; he married Joyce Hollis, lived at 56 Liberty St. in Aberdeen and died at Lutheran Hospital in Baltimore, survived by his wife, his parents, three children Joe Jr., Devale and Andre Peaker, two brothers, and a sister) [Tabernacle Mount Zion U. M. Church Cemetery]

Peaker, John Clayton September 6, 1875 – December 27, 1937 (no tombstone; death certificate stated he was born in Harford Co., son of Stevenson Peaker and Eliza Bishop, both born in Maryland; he married Rachel S. ----, worked as a railroad trackman for 25 years and lived near Abingdon; he was struck by an automobile on Route 40 in Abingdon, died at Havre de Grace Hospital and was buried at "John Wesley, Abingdon;" informant was Stephen N. Peaker, of Edgewood RFD) [John Wesley U. M. E. Church Cemetery in Abingdon]

Peaker, John Henry died October 24, 1987, age 76 (no tombstone; obituary in *The Aegis* on October 29, 1987 stated he was born in Abingdon, the son of John C. Peaker and Laura Peaco, and retired as chief custodian with the Baltimore County Board of Education after 17 years service and was a member of the Board of Education, Teachers Association; he died at the Belair Convalesarium in Baltimore, survived by his wife Georgeanna Cromwell Peaker, a son Calvin D. Harris of Abingdon, a daughter Alice Bettors of Baltimore, 11 step-children,

11 grandchildren "and many great-grandchildren") [John Wesley U. M. E. Church Cemetery in Abingdon]

Peaker, Jonathan Eugene January 24, 1952 – December 17, 2000 (no tombstone; his brief obituary in *The Aegis* on December 20, 2000 stated he lived in Aberdeen and died at Johns Hopkins Bayview Medical Center in Baltimore) [John Wesley U. M. E. Church Cemetery in Abingdon]

Peaker, Joseph May 22, 1915 – May 27, 1915 (no tombstone; death certificate stated he was the son of Lloyd Peaker, born in Harford Co., and Julia Dorsey, born in Baltimore, and died at home at Mountain; informant was his mother Julia Peaker) [Mt. Zion U. M. Church Cemetery]

Peaker, Julia L. January 6, 1885 – September 16, 1927 (no same tombstone with Lloyd T. Peaker; death certificate stated she was born in 1883 in Baltimore, the daughter of Joseph Dorsey and Sarah Dorsey, both born in Howard Co.; she was married, died in Havre de Grace Hospital and was buried in "The Mountain Cemetery;" informant was Lloyd Peaker, of Joppa) [Mt. Zion U. M. Church Cemetery]

Peaker, Lillian December 29, 1886 – October 24, 1918 (no tombstone; death certificate stated she was the daughter of Stephen Peaker and Eliza Bishop, all born in Harford Co., and she died at "The Mountain;" informant was Stephen Peaker, Jr., of Emmorton; her surname had been misinterpreted as Teaker instead of Peaker and was therefore misfiled) [Mt. Zion U. M. Church Cemetery]

Peaker, Lloyd T. October 16, 1869 – June 9, 1951 (on same tombstone with Julia L. Peaker) [Mt. Zion U. M. Church Cemetery]

Peaker, Lottie Cecelia died August 7, 1996, age 74 (no tombstone; obituary in *The Aegis* on August 14, 1996 stating she was born in Abingdon, the daughter of Samuel Peaker and Geraldine Beasley; she lived in Bel Air, retired as a custodian from the public school system and died at Fallston General Hospital, survived by two brothers, a sister, and three godchildren) [John Wesley U. M. E. Church Cemetery in Abingdon]

Peaker, Mattie V. February 1, 1908 – November 14, 1986 (on the same tombstone with Patti J. Watson; obituary and photo in *The Aegis* on November 20, 1996 stated she was born in Long Green, the daughter of Israel Nolan and Sally Custus, and was the widow of Walter T. Peaker; she lived in Joppa and died at Bel Forest Nursing and Rehabilitation Center, survived by two sons, two daughters, a stepdaughter, a sister, 15 grandchildren, 18 great-grandchildren and 7 great-great-grandchildren) [Mt. Zion U. M. Church Cemetery]

Peaker, Mazie 1902-1925 (on same tombstone with Walter T. Peaker; death certificate stated she was born on April 20, 1902 in Harford Co., the daughter of John Henry Gibson, born at Thomas Run, and Sarah E; Gibson, born in Harford Co.; she was married, worked as a domestic, died on February 15, 1925 at Emmorton and was buried in "Mountain Cemetery;" informant was Walter T. Peaker, of Joppa) [Mt. Zion U. M. Church Cemetery]

Peaker, Pauline January 12, 1928 – September 11, 1928 (no tombstone; death certificate stated she was the daughter of Samuel Peaker and Geraldine Blasby, all born in Maryland; she died in Abingdon and informant was her mother Geraldine Peaker) [John Wesley U. M. E. Church Cemetery in Abingdon]

Peaker, Rachel Ann 1885 – December 1, 1943 (no tombstone; death certificate stated she was born at Bush, the daughter of William Cohen and Mary Cohen, both born in Maryland; she married John Peaker and died a widow on Bond St. in Bel Air where she had lived for 30 years; informant was Mrs. Della Moore, also of Bond St., Bel Air) [Berkley Memorial Cemetery]

Peaker, Sarah Frances September 3, 1874 – October 5, 1942 (no tombstone; death certificate stated she was the daughter of James Bond and Laura White, all born in Harford Co.; she married Stephen Peaker (age 67 in 1942) and died at home in rural Bel Air; she was buried at "Mountain Cemetery, Mountain, Md.;" informant was Stephen Peaker, of Edgewood RFD) [Mt. Zion U. M. Church Cemetery]

Peaker, Solomon "Saul" February 2, 1892 – November 22, 1948 (no tombstone; death certificate stated he was born in Maryland, the son of Susan Peaker, but his father was not known to informant Carrie Lingham, of Abingdon; he lived in Abingdon, was struck by a car on Route 7 and died in Harford Memorial Hospital in Havre de Grace after a 44 hour and 20 minute stay) [John Wesley U. M. E. Church Cemetery in Abingdon]

Peaker, Stephen April 4, 1867 – November 22, 1943 (no tombstone; death certificate stated he was born in Harford Co., the son of Stephen and Elizah Peaker, birth places unknown; he married Sarah F. ---- (blank), worked as a farm hand and died a widower in rural Bel Air; he was buried at Joppa and the cemetery was not indicated, but it was most likely at Mountain; informant was George A. Peaker, 200 Archer St., Bel Air) [Mt. Zion U. M. Church Cemetery]

Peaker, Stephen March 22, 1944 – April 23, 1919 (no tombstone; death certificate stated he was the son of Edward Peaker and Sarah Hill, all born in Maryland; he was married, worked as a laborer and died the Havre de Grace Hospital; informant was Eliza Peaker, of Jopps RFD) [Mt. Zion U. M. Church Cemetery]

Peaker, Walter T. 1893-1961 (on same tombstone with Mazie Peaker) [Mt. Zion U. M. Church Cemetery Pierson, Anita Beatrice April 14, 1919 – May 9, 1920 (no tombstone; death certificate stated she was born in Camden, NJ, the daughter of John Pierson, born in Baltimore, and Anna White, born in Harford Co,; she died at The Mountain and was buried in "Mountain Colored Cemetery;" informant was her father, John Peirson *(sic)* of The Mountain, who signed the death certificate) [Mt. Zion U. M. Church Cemetery]

Peck, Matilda – see Matilda Webster [Clark's U. M. Church Cemetery]

Peco, Anna Maria – see Anna Maria Peaker [John Wesley U. M. E. Church Cemetery in Abingdon]

Peco, Infant (female) June 26, 1914 – June 27, 1914 (no tombstone; death certificate stated she was daughter of Lizzie Peco, father unknown; informant was Abraham Peco, of Havre de Grace [St. James United Cemetery]

Pecoe, Thelma Lorain October 27, 1919 – August 21, 1920 (no tombstone; death certificate stated she was the daughter of Lonie W. Pecoe and Mary B. Johnson, all born in Harford Co.; she died at home near Cooptown; informant was her mother Mary B. Pecoe, of Forest Hill RFD) [Fairview A. M. E. Church Cemetery]

Peevy, Frances R. May 14, 1889 – April 25, 1967 (on same tombstone with John C. Peevy) [Union U. M. Church Cemetery]

Peevy, John C. April 25, 1894 -   (on same tombstone with Frances R. Peevy) [Union U. M. Church Cemetery]

Pena, Jonathan 2002-2003 [St. James United Cemetery]

Penny, Harriett Ann born about 1844 – July 24, 1929 (no tombstone; death certificate stated she was the daughter of "Un Orange Wagge" and "Charity Wage" and were all born in Maryland; she was married and died in Bel Air; informant was Ora Howard, of Bel Air) [Hendon Hill Cemetery]

Perez, Renee D. 1979-2006 (small metal funeral home marker) [St. James United Cemetery]

Perkins, Melvin C. December 14, 1927 – September 4, 1953, Maryland, PFC, QM Service Co. [St. James United Cemetery]

Perry, Benton 1893-1978 (copied in 1987, but not found in 2018; obituary in *The Aegis* on October 5, 1978 stated Benton L. Perry, of Havre de Grace, died on October 2, 1978 at Harford Memorial Hospital; he was born in Virginia, married Sarah Giles and was survived by his wife and a daughter) [Berkley Memorial Cemetery]

Perry, George W. April 12, 1933 – July 4, 1995, SFC, U.S. Army, Korea, Vietnam (tombstone in section 24) [Mt. Calvary U. A. M. E. Church Cemetery]

Perry, Rosa L. February 22, 1917 – October 6, 1999 (inscribed "In Loving Memory") [St. James United Cemetery]

Peters, Hannah 1890-1963 [Foster's Hill Cemetery]

Peters, Nathan died January 20, 1929, age about 60 (no tombstone; death certificate stated he was the widowed son of Joseph Peters and Rachael Giles; informant was Theodore Peters) [Union U. M. Church Cemetery]

Peters, Susan A. died December 26, 1922, age about 50 (no tombstone; death certificate stated she was the married daughter of Louis Winchester and Sarah Ringgold, all born in Maryland; informant was Nathan Peters, of Havre de Grace) [Union U. M. Church Cemetery]

Peters, Theodore Jr. 1914-1987 [Foster's Hill Cemetery]

Peters, William Alexander died December 11, 1937, age about 78 (no tombstone; death certificate stated he was the son of James Peters and Rachael Jales(?), all born in Maryland; he worked as a laborer until 1930 and died a widower in Magnolia; informant was Theo. Peters, of Magnolia) [Foster's Hill Cemetery]

Peterson, Charles H. died August 26, 1912, age about 60 (no tombstone; death certificate stated he was the married son of John Peterson, but mother unknown to informant Susie Peterson) [St. James United Cemetery]

Pevey, Mary E. June 12, 1923 – August 2, 1923 (no tombstone; death certificate stated she was the daughter of Garfield Pevey, born in Maryland, and Rose Gant, born in Charles Co., MD; she died at Calvary; informant was Garfield Pevey, of Aberdeen) [Asbury Cemetery]

Phillips, Delia died August 23, 1918, age about 51 (no tombstone; death certificate stated she was the married daughter of Robert Brown and Dinah Christy; informant was James Brown) [Union U. M. Church Cemetery]

Phillips, Easter P. died January 11, 1925, age about 62 (no tombstone; death certificate – the name Giddinger was written in first, then lined out, and Phillips was written above it) [St. James United Cemetery]

Pierce, Altamese "Meese" August 18, 1942 – September 12, 1992 [Berkley Memorial Cemetery]

Pierce, Josephine April 5, 1892 – December 1, 1935 (no tombstone; death certificate stated she was the daughter of George Hill and Rose Ellis, and the wife of James Pierce; informant was Rufus Wing, of Havre de Grace) [St. James United Cemetery]

Pinion, Amanda died November 28, 1927, age about 62 (no tombstone; death certificate stated S. Amanda Pinion was the married daughter of Isaac Lee and Harriet A. Hollingsworth; informant was Annabelle Fletcher, of Havre de Grace) [St. James United Cemetery]

Pinion, Carrie J. 1865-   (on same tombstone with John L. Pinion) [Union U. M. Church Cemetery]

Pinion, Edna died December 30, 1902, age 6 months (no tombstone; death certificate stated she was the daughter of Frances Rumsey, father's name not given, and she was burned and died at home near Cole; place of burial was not indicated [probably Union U. M. Church Cemetery]

Pinion, Ellen died January 23, 1903, age 106 (no tombstone; obituary in the *Havre de Grace Republican* on January 31, 1903 stated she was the oldest person in Havre de Grace and retained her faculties until near the end; her first child was born in 1813 and she recalled the date because it was the year the British burned Havre de Grace; Laura Haycock is a granddaughter and Ellen was survived by great-great-grandchildren; her place of burial was not reported [probably Union U. M. Church Cemetery]

Pinion, Hannah March 18, 1843 – March 18, 1912 (no tombstone; death certificate stated she was the widowed daughter of Steven Stansbury and Maria Izer, all born in Maryland) [Union U. M. Church Cemetery]

Pinion, Helen Irene October 18, 1923 – October 3, 1942 (no tombstone; death certificate stated she was the daughter of George A. Pinion and Lillie E. Dorsey, of Perryman) [Union U. M. Church Cemetery]

Pinion, Infant stillborn female on July 28, 1911 (no tombstone; death certificate stated she was the daughter of William Pinion and Annie Bishop, of Havre de Grace) [St. James United Cemetery]

Pinion, Infant stillborn male on September 12, 1915 (no tombstone; death certificate stated he was the son of George Pinion and Edna Richardson, of Havre de Grace) [St. James United Cemetery]

Pinion, John L. 1857-1958 (on same tombstone with Carrie J. Pinion) [Union U. M. Church Cemetery]

Pinion, Lillie Bowser December 5, 1886 – January 21, 1922 (no tombstone; death certificate stated she was the married daughter of Robert J. Pinion and Harriett Christy, all were born in Maryland; informant was Raymond Pinion, of Perryman) [Union U. M. Church Cemetery]

Pinion, Lucinda June 12, 1910 – May 2, 1929 (no tombstone; death certificate stated she was unmarried and the daughter of Annie Pinion and Andrew Rice; informant was Robert Dennison) [Union U. M. Church Cemetery]

Pinion, Mary E. April 11, 1888 – October 6, 1949 (no tombstone; death certificate stated she was the widowed daughter of Maggie Giddings, father unknown to informant, son George Pinion) [St. James United Cemetery]

Pinion, Phillip S. 1861-1932 [Union U. M. Church Cemetery]

Pinion, Raymond September 20, 1915 – December 16, 1915 (no tombstone; death certificate stated he was the son of Robert Denison and Mabel Pinion, all born in Maryland) [Union U. M. Church Cemetery]

Pinion, Raymond A. 1884-1987 [Union U. M. Church Cemetery]

Pinion, Raymond O. 1927-2011 (small metal funeral home marker) [Berkley Memorial Cemetery]

Pinion, Robert May 2, 1929 – May 12, 1929 (no tombstone; death certificate stated he was son of Philip Ricks and Lucinda Pinion, and died from "injuries at birth" and lived "11 days") [Union U. M. Church Cemetery]

Pinion, Ward O. August 19, 1914 – October 20, 1927 (no tombstone; death certificate stated he was the son of Raymond A. Pinion and Lilly Bowser, of Perryman) [Union U. M. Church Cemetery]

Pinion, William H. February – (blank), 1884 – August 4, 1946 (no tombstone; death certificate stated he was the son of Lewis Pinion and Heneratia Pinion; he married Mary E. ---- and died in an auto accident near Perryman; informant was Mrs. Hazel Jones, of Havre de Grace) [St. James United Cemetery]

Pinkney, George M. N. 1901-1941 [Asbury Cemetery]

Pinkney, Hattie died January 16, 1932, age unknown (no tombstone; death certificate stated she was born in Harford Co., the daughter of George Chambers and Jane Wells, both born in Maryland, married and died at home at Bel Air RFD; informant was Nathan Pinkney) [Asbury Cemetery]

Pinkney, Hester J. (no tombstone; death notice in *The Aegis* on August 23, 1907 stated she was "a highly regarded young person of near Benson who died a few days ago" and was buried at the "Mountain colored church") [Mt. Zion U. M. Church Cemetery]

Pinkney, James died June 8, 1918, age about 86 (no tombstone; death certificate stated he was born in Harford Co., the son of James Pinkney and Henrietta Richardson, both born in Maryland; he was married, worked as a farm laborer and died at Benson; informant was James W. Pinkney, of 628 Gold St. in Baltimore; buried in the "Mountain Colored Cemetery") [Mt. Zion U. M. Church Cemetery]

Pinkney, Sarah Ann Cornelia died November 6, 1919, age 75 years and 4 months (no tombstone; death certificate stated she was the daughter of Thomas Giles, both born in Harford Co., but the name of her mother was not known to informant Annie Tasker, of Benson; Sarah was a widow and died in Benson) [Mt. Zion U. M. Church Cemetery]

Pitt, Ada M. February 2, 1901 – December 14, 1925 (no tombstone; death certificate stated she was the unmarried daughter of William A. Pitt and Emma Jones; informant was Frances Pitt) [Union U. M. Church Cemetery]

Pitt, Bertha I. June 16, 1889 – August 30, 1937 (no tombstone; death certificate stated she was the wife of Charles W. Pitt and the daughter of Robert Christy and Ellin Allen) [Union U. M. Church Cemetery]

Pitt, Birdie Angelina April 25, 1913 – December 3, 1915 (no tombstone; death certificate stated she was the daughter of R. Lay and Lilly Pitt, all born in Maryland) [Union U. M. Church Cemetery]

Pitt, Carrie V. March 25, 1899 – November 9, 1933 (no tombstone; death certificate stated she was the wife of John S. Pitt and the daughter of Joe S. Hardy, born in New Jersey, and Gertrude Moulton, born in Harford County) [Union U. M. Church Cemetery]

Pitt, Cecelia Odessa March 29, 1937 – October 19, 1937 (no tombstone; death certificate stated she was the daughter of Walter James Pitt and Eva Geneva Giles) [Union U. M. Church Cemetery]

Pitt, Daniel T. November 25, 1935 – April 2, 1936 (no tombstone; death certificate stated he was born in Aberdeen, the son of Andrew Chase and Jessie Pitt, both born in Maryland) [Union U. M. Church Cemetery]

Pitt, Dorothy M. July 8, 1917 – April 14, 1918 (no tombstone; death certificate stated se was the daughter of John M. Pitts and Carrie V. Hardy, all born in Harford Co.) [Union U. M. Church Cemetery]

Pitt, Ella (owner of a lot in section 47 some time after 1951) [Mt. Calvary U. A. M. E. Church Cemetery]

Pitt, Ella April 1, 1872 – September 7, 1946 (no tombstone; death certificate stated she was the daughter of Trilus Whymms and ---- (blank); she died a widow, husband was not named) [Union U. M. Church Cemetery]

Pitt, Emma G. March 10, 1900 – December 5, 1915 (no tombstone; death certificate stated she was the daughter of William A. Pitt and Emma Jones, all born in Harford Co.) [Union U. M. Church Cemetery]

Pitt, Frances stillborn on June 29, 1927 (no tombstone; death certificate stated she was the daughter of Willie Whims, born in Virginia, and Jessie Pitt, born in Aberdeen) [Union U. M. Church Cemetery]

Pitt, Frances E. February 7, 1879 – February 28, 1926 (no tombstone; death certificate stated she was the married daughter of John W. Pitt and Frances Harris, but she later divorced) [Union U. M. Church Cemetery]

Pitt, Frances M. 1848-1926 (on same tombstone with John W. Pitt, but inscribed dates 1843-1938 are incorrect; death certificate stated Mary F. Pitt was born on March 10, 1848 and died on February 18, 1926, the daughter of John Harris and Milky Giles, and she was the wife of John W. Pitt, of 551 Lafayette Ave., Havre de Grace) [Union U. M. Church Cemetery]

Pitt, George A. died March 18, 1920, age about 50 (no tombstone; death certificate stated he was the unmarried son of John A. Pitt and Grace Reid, all born in Harford Co.) [Union U. M. Church Cemetery]

Pitt, Hazel L. January 17, 1926 – September 16, 1941 (no tombstone; death certificate stated she was the daughter of John Pitt and Carrie Hardy) [Union U. M. Church Cemetery]

Pitt, Ida Mae, "Sister" October 24, 1911 – August 4, 1980 [Berkley Memorial Cemetery]

Pitt, James Albert February 2, 1882 – July 19, 1945 (no tombstone; death certificate stated he was the son of Albert James Pitt and Mary C. Stansbury, and the husband of Ella Whims Pitt) [Union U. M. Church Cemetery]

Pitt, John Stanley 1894-1977 (copied in 1987, not found in 2018) [Mt. Calvary U. A. M. E. Church Cemetery]

Pitt, John W. 1843-1939 (on same tombstone with Frances M. Pitt, but inscribed dates 1853-1926 are incorrect; death certificate stated he was born on May 10, 1843 and died on April 4, 1939, son of John Pitt, Sr. and Julia Ann Johnson, and the husband of Mary Frances Pitt) [Union U. M. Church Cemetery]

Pitt, Josiah E., "Brother" May 27, 1880 – December 20, 1964 [Union U. M. Church Cemetery]

Pitt, Margaret S. 1867-1944 [Union U. M. Church Cemetery]

Pitt, Martha C., "Mother" December 2, 1876 – March 14, 1967 [Union U. M. Church Cemetery]

Pitt, Mary Frances – see Frances M. Pitt [Union U. M. Church Cemetery]

Pitt, Mary O. March 4, 1894 – May 21, 1912 (no tombstone; death certificate stated she was single, born in Harford Co., and the daughter of William A. Pitt, born in Harford Co., and Emma Jones, born in Baltimore Co.) [Union U. M. Church Cemetery]

Pitt, Roselea stillborn on June 29, 1937 (no tombstone; death certificate stated she was the daughter of Willie Whims, born in Virginia, and Jessie Pitt, born in Aberdeen) [Union U. M. Church Cemetery]

Pitt, Thomas died February 15, 1901, age 25 (no tombstone; death certificate stated he was born in Maryland, the son of Cassie Pitt and Isaac Brown; he was single, worked as a farm hand and died at Cole; place of burial was not indicated [probably Union U. M. Church Cemetery]

Pitt, Virginia January 1, 1873 – October 13, 1935 (no tombstone; death certificate stated she was the wife of Alford E. Pitt and daughter of Howard Dause, but her mother was unknown) [Union U. M. Church Cemetery]

Pitt, Walter R. 1906-1966 [Union U. M. Church Cemetery]

Pitt, William died March 4, 1918, age about 67 (no tombstone; death certificate stated he had died a widower and was the son of Isaac Pitt, both born in Harford Co., but his mother was not known to informant Mr. E. J. Hoke, of Perryman RFD) [Union U. M. Church Cemetery]

Pitt, William A. died February 24, 1923, age about 56 (no tombstone; death certificate stated he was the son of John Pitt and Gracie Reed, all born in Maryland, and he died a widower) [Union U. M. Church Cemetery]

Pitts, Cornelius "1956-1889 (way it was)" (as copied in 1987, but not found in 2018) [Mt. Calvary U. A. M. E. Church Cemetery]

Poe, John C. September 18, 1941 – October 6, 1998 [St. James United Cemetery]

Porcher, Willie November 14, 1914 – May 4, 1967, Maryland, ST3, USNR, World War II (tombstone; obituary in *The Aegis* on May 11, 1967 stated he was the son of the late William Porcher and Janie Jackson, and husband of Mary Peters Porcher, of 512 Dembytown Road, Magnolia; he died suddenly at Harford Memorial Hospital; services were conducted at Ebenezer Baptist Church with burial in adjoining cemetery) [Foster's Hill Cemetery]

Porter, Robert (owner of a lot in section 17 some time after 1951) [Mt. Calvary U. A. M. E. Church Cemetery]

Potter, Ella H., "Mother" 1905-1980 [Berkley Memorial Cemetery]

Potts, Cammille L. 2002-2002 (small metal funeral home marker) [St. James United Cemetery]

Poulson, John died February 10, 1897, age 57 (no tombstone; death notice in *The Aegis* on February 12, 1897 stated he was buried at Tabernacle Church near Benson, but no further information) [Tabernacle Mount Zion U. M. Church Cemetery]

Pounds, Albert B. July 14, 1934 – May 22, 2007, U.S. Air Force, Korea (tombstone; obituary and photo in *The Aegis* on May 30, 2007 stated he was born in Churchville, the son of the late James and Rebecca Pounds, and entered the Air Force in 1952; he was a butcher at Fountain Green Food Market, a UPS driver, and a cement finisher; he also coached baseball for the Boons Farm Playboys and Troubleshooters, and sang in the church choir; among his nicknames were "Silver Fox," "Arab Addie," "Al," and "Weaver;" he died at his home in Churchville, survived by an adopted son and daughter, two brothers, three sisters, three adopted brothers, six sisters-in-law, and a special friend Bernard Erby, of Perryville) [Asbury Cemetery]

Pounds, Charles M. April 7, 1947 – December 25, 1980 (inscribed "Love, Daddy's Little Girls, Charlyne, Really & Theressa;" obituary in *The Aegis* on January 1, 1981 stated Charles McKinely Pounds was born in Baltimore, the son of the late James Pounds and Ellen Smith, lived in Churchville and was employed by the Town of Bel Air; he died in an automobile accident on Wheel Road near Bel Air and was survived by three daughters, six brothers and three sisters; Mr. Pounds' wife was not mentioned) [Asbury Cemetery]

Pounds, Ellen Rebecca September 30, 1906 – February 14, 1976 (no tombstone; obituary in *The Aegis* stated she was born in Churchville, the daughter of John Smith and Carrie Cooper, and was the wife of James Pounds; she died at Harford Memorial Hospital in Havre de Grace, survived by her husband, three daughters, eight sons, and 27 grandchildren) [Asbury Cemetery]

Pounds, James August 12, 1900 – August 28, 1977 (on the same tombstone with Rebecca Pounds; obituary in *The Aegis* on September 1, 1977 stated he was born in Jacksonville, FL, was the husband of the late Ellen Rebecca Pounds and worked at Aberdeen Concrete Company many years; died at the Citizens Nursing Home in Havre de Grace, survived by 3 daughters, 8 sons, 1 sister, 1 brother, 27 grandchildren) [Asbury Cemetery]

Pounds, Marshall Leon Sr. died August 3, 1979, age 38 (no tombstone; obituary in *The Aegis* on August 9, 1979 stated he was born in Bel Air, the son of the late James Pounds and Rebecca Smith; he worked for Bel Air Memorial Gardens and was formerly employed by Harford County Department of Public Works; he also organized his own softball team called the D. J. Gents of Edgewood; he was the husband of Ruth Preston Pounds, of Churchville, and died at Fallston General Hospital, survived by his wife, 2 sons, 7 brothers and 3 sisters) [Asbury Cemetery]

Pounds, Rebecca September 30, 1906 – February 14, 1976 (on same tombstone with James Pounds; obituary in *The Aegis* on February 19, 1976 stated Ellen Rebecca Pounds was born in Churchville, the daughter of John Smith and Carrie Cooper and wife of James Pounds; she died at Harford Memorial Hospital in Havre de Grace, survived by 3 daughters, 8 sons and 27 grandchildren) [Asbury Cemetery]

Pounds, Ruth M. May 14, 1942 – October 4, 1983 (tombstone; obituary in *The Aegis* on October 13, 1983 stated she lived in Churchville, was the widow of Marshall Leon Pounds and operated a beauty salon in Bel Air; she died in Harford Memorial Hospital and was survived by her parents Leroy A. Preston and Dorothy Moals, of Baltimore, grandmother Mary Thomas, and 2 sons,1 brother and 4 sisters) [Asbury Cemetery]

Pounds, Samuel T. "Sam" October 3, 1938 – August 18, 2004 (tombstone; obituaries in *The Aegis* on August 20 and August 26, 2004 with his photo, stated he was born in Churchville, the son of James Pounds and Rebecca

Smith, and lived in Bel Air, worked in cement construction and was a founder of Clark's Chapel's first baseball team called the "Troubleshooters" and was the team's star pitcher; he acquired many nicknames including "Gooese," "Gooseneck," "Uncle Sam," Junior," "Junee," "Pounds," "Poundcake" and "Samuels;" he died at Upper Chesapeake Medical Center, survived by his wife of 41 years Mary N. Pounds, five daughters, three brothers, three sisters, two adopted brothers, his mother-in-law Essie L. Smith, 6 brothers-in-law, 13 sisters-in-law, 10 grandchildren and 3 great-grandchildren) [Asbury Cemetery]

Powell, Catherine M. 1924-1979 [St. James United Cemetery]

Powell, George E. August 29, 1912 – December 16, 1912 (no tombstone; death certificate stated he was born in Harford Co., the son of John W. Powell, born in Baltimore Co., and Anna R. Ford, born in York, PA; he died at Reckord, informant was "mother, Hyde R.D.") [Tabernacle Mount Zion U. M. Church Cemetery]

Powell, Jeanne, "Mother" 1895-1982 [St. James United Cemetery]

Powell, John died April 26, 1919, age unknown (no tombstone; death certificate stated he was married and a farm laborer when he died in Reckord; his birth place and his parents' names and their places of birth were not known to informant Charles E. Hornberger, Undertaker) [Tabernacle Mount Zion U. M. Church Cemetery]

Presberry, ---- March 1, 1924 – March 9, 1924 (no tombstone; death certificate stated he was the illegitimate son of Kasirah Presbery *(sic)*, of Darlington, both born in Maryland) [Berkley Memorial Cemetery]

Presberry, Agnes Elizabeth February 17, 1922 – November 23, 2012 (no tombstone; obituary and photo in *The Aegis* on November 28, 2012 stated she was born in Darlington, the daughter of Thomas Cain and Kizah Presberry, and died at the Citizens Care and Rehabilitation Center in Havre de Grace, survived by several nieces, nephews, great-nieces, great-nephews, great-great-nieces, great-great-nephews, and a host of cousins and friends) [Berkley Memorial Cemetery]

Presberry, Alice Olivia 1911-1977 (inscribed "Church Organist and Sunday School Superintendent") [Berkley Memorial Cemetery]

Presberry, Allen March 10, 1896 – March 29, 1946 (no tombstone; death certificate stated he was the son of Rachel Presberry, both born in Harford Co., but his father's name was not known to informant Mrs. Edna Presberry, 18 Center St. Port Deposit; he married Daisy ----, worked as a laborer and died at home in Darlington where he had lived all of his life) [Berkley Memorial Cemetery]

Presberry, Anne V. April 212, 1920 – March 20, 1998 [Berkley Memorial Cemetery]

Presberry, Annie died February 17, 1940, age about 68 (no tombstone; death certificate stated she was the daughter of William Webster and Annie Webster, all born in Harford Co.; she married John E. Presberry and died a widow in Darlington; informant was Robert Presberry) [Berkley Memorial Cemetery]

Presberry, Anthony J. February 28, 1961 -   (on same tombstone with James L. Braxton, Isabell Braxton and Ruth Ann Presberry) [Berkley Memorial Cemetery]

Presberry, Berdell Jr. born and died on July 18, 1948, lived only 9 hours and 18 minutes (no tombstone; death certificate stated he was born and died at Harford Memorial Hospital in Havre de Grace; he was the son of Berdell Presberry and Margaret Preston, both born in Maryland, and their usual residence was Darlington RFD #2) [Berkley Memorial Cemetery]

Presberry, Carrol August 5, 1893 – September 22, 1913 (no tombstone; death certificate stated he was the son of George Presbary *(sic)* and Sarah Wilson, all born in Harford Co.; he was single, worked as a laborer and died at home in Darlington; informant was his father) [Berkley Memorial Cemetery]

Presberry, Donald, "Our Baby" January 28, 1961 – February 9, 1961 [Berkley Memorial Cemetery]

Presberry, Earl O. October 13, 1918 – September 12, 2004, Cpl., U.S. Army, World War II [Berkley Memorial Cemetery]

Presberry, Eddie Jr. January 1, 1910 – May 23, 1911 (no tombstone; death certificate stated he was born in Harford Co., son of John Eddie Presberry and Debrrh *(sic)* Webster, born in Maryland; he died at home at Shure's Landing; informant was J. Eddie Presberry, of Darlington) [Berkley Memorial Cemetery]

Presberry, Edith A. June 2, 1923 – October 12, 2002 (on same tombstone with Edward J. Presberry) [Berkley Memorial Cemetery]

Presberry, Edward J. March 18, 1920 – July 7, 2005 (on same tombstone with Edith A. Presberry) [Berkley Memorial Cemetery]

Presberry, Emma "died about January 1, 1928, age about 12, death was caused by exposure, frozen to death" (no tombstone; death certificate stated she was the daughter of Daisy Presberry, both born in Maryland, but her father's name was not known by her mother who was informant; she was a school girl who died in Castleton) [Berkley Memorial Cemetery]

Presberry, Estella 1915-1990 (on same tombstone with Leroy Presberry; James Dorsey Card File, African American Obituaries, maintained at the Historical Society of Harford County, has a card with obituary from an unidentified newspaper dated September 19, 1990 stating that she was a retired domestic worker who died at home in Darlington on September 3, 1990, survived by two daughters, two sisters, two brothers surnamed Gray, seven grandchildren and two great-grandchildren) [Berkley Memorial Cemetery]

Presberry, Frank October 25, 1911 – November 20, 1911 (no tombstone; death certificate stated he was the son of John Eddie Presbery *(sic)* and W. Annie Webster, all born in Maryland; he died in Darlington; informant was Herbert S. Bailey of the John B. Bailey & Son Funeral Home) [Berkley Memorial Cemetery]

Presberry, George November 7, 1872 – February 5, 1948 (no tombstone; death certificate stated he was the son of Henry Presberry and Kizah Prigg, all born in Harford Co.; he was single, worked as a farm laborer, died at home in rural Darlington; informant was James H. Presberry) [Berkley Memorial Cemetery]

Presberry, George Robert October 1, 1924 – February 15, 1925 (no tombstone; death certificate stated George Robert Presbery *(sic)* was born in Harford Co., son of Robert Presbury *(sic)* and Margaret Green, both born in Maryland; he lived and died in Forest Hill; his father Robert Presberry *(sic)* was the informant [Fairview A. M. E. Church Cemetery]

Presberry, George W. June 15, 1852 – May 6, 1918 (no tombstone; death certificate stated he was the son of George Presberry, both born in Harford Co., but his mother's name was not known to informant Oliver Presberry, of Darlington, but she was born in Harford Co.; he was married, worked as a laborer and died at home in Darlington) [Berkley Memorial Cemetery]

Presberry, Grace M. January 26, 1922 – July 31, 1937 (no tombstone; Kurtz Funeral Home Record Book 1937-1943, p. 30, stated she was a school girl and the daughter of Robert Presberry and Margaret M. Green, all born at Forest Hill; she died at Provident Hospital in Baltimore) [Fairview A. M. E. Church Cemetery]

Presberry, Harriett K. March 1, 1848 – February 4, 1922 (no tombstone; death certificate stated she was the daughter of Henry Prigg and Harriett Haines, all born in Maryland; she married and died a widow in Berkley; informant was Edward W. Presberry, of Darlington) [Berkley Memorial Cemetery]

Presberry, Harrison died September 11, 1942, age 49 (no tombstone; death certificate stated he was the son of Henry Presberry and Casia Prigg, all born in Harford Co.; he was single, worked as a farm laborer and died at home in rural Darlington; informant was Estella V. Presberry) [Berkley Memorial Cemetery]

Presberry, Hazzard 1856-1929 (on same tombstone with Sarah E. Presberry) [Berkley Memorial Cemetery]

Presberry, Henry J. Jr. February 24, 1875 – March 12, 1946 (no tombstone; death certificate stated he was born in Castleton, the son of Henry J. Presberry, Sr. and Kiszar Prigg, both born in Maryland; he married Susian *(sic)* A. ----, worked as a laborer and died a widower at home in rural Darlington where he had lived all his life; informant was Miss Alice Presberry) [Berkley Memorial Cemetery]

Presberry, Herbert S. August 11, 1902 – November 11, 1966 [Tabernacle Mount Zion U. M. Church Cemetery]

Presberry, Hollis P., "Beloved Husband of Marjorie" March 26, 1912 – May 27, 1975 [Fairview A. M. E. Church Cemetery]

Presberry, Howard C. Sr. March 21, 1930 – May 17, 2007, PFC, U.S. Army, Korea [Berkley Memorial Cemetery]

Presberry, Ida E. 1888-   [Berkley Memorial Cemetery]

Presberry, James H. 1904-1978 (on same tombstone with Leolia W. Presberry inscribed "Together Forever") [Berkley Memorial Cemetery]

Presberry, Jane "unknown 1844 – died February 20, 1938, age about 93" (no tombstone; death certificate stated she was the daughter of Henry Howard and Louisa Foreman, all born in Harford Co.; she married Robert Presberry and died a widow at him in Berkley where she had lived all her life; informant was James Presberry, of Darlington) [Berkley Memorial Cemetery]

Presberry, John E. died November 20, 1933, age 60 (no tombstone; death certificate stated he was the son of Robert Presberry and Jane Foreman, all born in Darlington; he married Annie ----, worked as a farm laborer and died in Darlington; informant was Robert Presberry) [Berkley Memorial Cemetery]

Presberry, John M. January 29, 1881 – April 2, 1933 (no tombstone; death certificate stated he was the son of Henry Presberry and Kaizziah Prigg, all born in Castleton; he married Daisy ----, worked as a farmer and died at home in Castleton; informant was his wife Daisy Presberry) [Berkley Memorial Cemetery]

Presberry, John W. 1959-2003 (small metal funeral home marker) [Berkley Memorial Cemetery]

Presberry, Justin R. January 1, 1992 (image of a boy with a baseball bat bending over and holding a frog) [Berkley Memorial Cemetery]

Presberry, Katie August 14, 1917 – October 4, 1917 (no tombstone; death certificate stated she was the daughter of John E. Presberry and Deborah Webster, all born in Maryland; she died at home in Darlington; informant was her father) [Berkley Memorial Cemetery]

Presberry, Kiziah E., "Mother" September 6, 1887 – June 15, 1952 (inscribed "Born in Castleton" and "By Her Children Edward – Agnes – Isabell") [Berkley Memorial Cemetery]

Presberry, Leolia W. 1913-   (on same tombstone with James H. Presberry inscribed "Together Forever") [Berkley Memorial Cemetery]

Presberry, Leon April 16, 1923 – October 20, 1923 (no tombstone; death certificate stated he was the son of Howard Gray and Martha Presbery *(sic)*, and they all were born in Maryland; he died at home in Darlington; informant was Howard Gray, of Darlington) [Berkley Memorial Cemetery]

Presberry, Leonard 1944-2011 (small metal funeral home marker) [Clark's U. M. Church Cemetery]

Presberry, Leroy 1910-1986 (on same tombstone with Estella Presberry) [Berkley Memorial Cemetery]

Presberry, Marcus January 3, 1907 – April 15, 1976, S2, U.S. Navy, World War II [Berkley Memorial Cemetery]

Presberry, Margaret M. September 25, 1904 – January 22, 1968 (on same tombstone with Robert C. Presberry) [Fairview A. M. E. Church Cemetery]

Presberry, Martha E. April 3, 1919 – March 15, 1930 (no tombstone; death certificate stated she was the daughter of Allen Presberry and Daisy Dorsey, all born in Maryland; she was a school girl and died at home in Castleton; informant was her father) [Berkley Memorial Cemetery]

Presberry, Mary E. October 12, 1915 – August 26, 1992 (tombstone; The James Dorsey Card File, African American Obituaries, maintained at the Historical Society of Harford County, has a card with obituary from an unidentified newspaper dated September 2, 1992 stating she was born in Portbridge, Cecil Co., daughter of Levi and Myrtle Cora Boddy, and was the widow of Thomas Presberry; she lived in Bel Air and died at Harford Memorial Hospital, survived by two sons, two brothers, two sisters, 10 grandchildren, 2 great-grandchildren) [Berkley Memorial Cemetery]

Presberry, Mary Frances February 15, 1916 – August 4, 1922 (no tombstone; death certificate stated she was the daughter of John E. Presberry and Deborah A. Webster, all born in Maryland; she died at home in Berkley; informant was Robert Presberry, of Berkley) [Berkley Memorial Cemetery]

Presberry, Noble William August 6, 1896 – May 1, 1929, Maryland, Pvt, 354 Fld Rmt Sq QMC, World War I (tombstone; military records state he was born in Forest Hill, was inducted into service on September 26, 1918, last served at Camp Meade, and was honorably discharged on May 17, 1919; no death certificate was found in Harford County) [Fairview A. M. E. Church Cemetery]

Presberry, Priscilla Annie died September 17, 2001, age 92 (no tombstone; obituary and photo in *The Aegis* on September 26, 2001 stated she was born in Darlington, the daughter of George and Annie Dorsey, and was the widow of Marcus Presberry; she was a domestic worker for Ann McGee for twenty years and was president of the Stewardess Board of Hosanna AME Church; she lived in Darlington and died at Gardens Assisted Living Facility, survived by a brother Charles Dorsey, four sisters Helen Buchanan, Mildred Murray, Ella Mae Amos and Carrie Stump, and many nieces and nephews) [Berkley Memorial Cemetery]

Presberry, Robert April 7, 1846 – March 24, 1928 (no tombstone; death certificate stated he was the son of George Presberry and Sarah Prigg, all born in Maryland; he married, worked as a farmer and died at home in Berkley; informant was James O. Presberry, of Berkley) [Berkley Memorial Cemetery]

Presberry, Robert L. April 10, 1900 – November 28, 1982 (on same tombstone with Margaret M. Presberry; obituary in *The Aegis* on December 2, 1982 stated Robert Lee Presbury, husband of the late Margaret Greene Presbury, was employed at Bainbridge and Aberdeen Proving Ground and died at Harford Memorial Hospital; he was survived by five daughters, four sons, seventeen grandchildren, four great-grandchildren, and one sister) [Fairview A. M. E. Church Cemetery]

Presberry, Ruth Ann April 24, 1941 – September 30, 1985 (on same tombstone with James L. Braxton, Isabell Braxton and Anthony J. Presberry) [Berkley Memorial Cemetery]

Presberry, Sarah E., "His Wife" 1863-1928 (on same tombstone with Hazzard Presberry; death certificate stated she was born on September 6, 1864 *(sic)*, the daughter of Lewis Spriggs, both born in Maryland, but her mother's name was not known to informant Hazzard Presberry, of Darlington; she died on May 10, 1928 at home in Darlington) [Berkley Memorial Cemetery]

Presberry, Susan February 17, 1875 – January 15, 1939 (no tombstone; death certificate stated Susan Presbury *(sic)* was the daughter of Sylvester Washington and Mary E. Hill, all born in Harford Co.; she married Henry Presberry *(sic)* and died at home in Darlington; informant was her husband) [Berkley Memorial Cemetery]

Presberry, Susan V. May 6, 1864 – February 6, 1939 (no tombstone; death certificate stated she was the daughter of Edward Wilson and Mary A. Turner, all born in Harford Co.; she married George Presbury and died a widow at home in Berkley; informant was her husband) [Berkley Memorial Cemetery]

Presberry, Thomas April 12, 1907 – June 13, 1990, U.S. Army Air Corps, World War II [Berkley Memorial Cemetery]

Presberry, William D. 1907-1968 [Berkley Memorial Cemetery]

Presberry, William Edward October 3, 1869 – September 23, 1940 (no tombstone; death certificate stated William Edward Presbury *(sic)* was the son of Henry Presberry *(sic)* and Kasia Prigg, all born in Harford Co.; he married Eliza ----, worked as a farm laborer and died a widower in Darlington; informant was Henry Presberry, of Darlington) [Berkley Memorial Cemetery]

Presberry, William M. Sr. 1906-1958 (Masonic symbol on tombstone) [Berkley Memorial Cemetery]

Presbury, ---- premature male born on January 23, 1918, lived 5 minutes (no tombstone; death certificate stated he was the son of Howard Gray and Martha Presbury, all born in Harford Co., and he died at Thomas Run; informant was Martha Presbury, of Bel Air RFD) [Berkley Memorial Cemetery]

Presbury, ---- stillborn female born on November 23, 1951 and buried on November 26, 1951 (no tombstone; Pennington Funeral Home records stated "Baby Girl Presbury" was the daughter of Mason Dorsey and Mary F. Presbury; died at Harford Memorial Hospital; informant was Mason Dorsey, of Bel Air) [Hendon Hill Cemetery]

Presbury, ---- stillborn male born on January 27, 1931 (no tombstone; death certificate stated he was the son of William Marshall Presbury and Sarah A. Chase, all born in Maryland; informant was Marshall Presbury, of Berkley) [Berkley Memorial Cemetery]

Presbury, Albert November 8, 1876 – April 27, 1941 (no tombstone; death certificate stated he was the son of Henry Presbury and Kzar *(sic)* Prigg, all born in Castleton; he was single, lived in Castleton and died at Harford Memorial Hospital in Havre de Grace; it was noted that the information on death certificate was taken from hospital records) [Berkley Memorial Cemetery]

Presbury, Amous March 4, 1845 – June 11, 1925 (no tombstone; death certificate stated he was born in Harford Co., the son of Roger Presbury, born in Maryland, but his mother's name was not known to informant Grant Presbury, of Aberdeen; he worked as a farmer and was a widower at the time of his death in Aberdeen) [Green Spring U. M. Church Cemetery]

Presbury, Annie B. died February 7, 1986, age 91 (no tombstone; obituary in *The Aegis* on February 13, 1986 stated she lived in Bel Air and was the widow of Edward Presbury; she died at the Brevin Nursing Home in Havre de Grace, survived by 12 grandchildren, 40 great-grandchildren, and 15 great-great-grandchildren) [Clark's U. M. Church Cemetery]

Presbury, Benjamin P. 1842 – January 20, 1912 (no tombstone; death certificate stated he was born in Harford Co., married, worked as a farm laborer, and died at Gravel Hill; his son, George Presbury, was informant, but he did not know the names of Benjamin's parents) [Gravel Hill Cemetery]

Presbury, Bertha L. died October 31, 1907, age 31 (no tombstone; death certificate stated she was born in Port Deposit, the daughter of ---- Wilson and Annie ----, both born in Port Deposit, and the wife of John M. Presbury who was informant; she died in Berkley, but place of burial not given [probably Berkley Memorial Cemetery]

Presbury, Catherine April 8, 1934 – September 3, 2011 [Fairview A. M. E. Church Cemetery]

Presbury, Charles S. 1923-2003 [Chestnut Grove A. M. E. Church Cemetery, formerly LaGrange Cemetery at Rocks]

Presbury, Clarence L. August 31, 1915 – August 18, 1965, Maryland, Co. B, 779 Military Police, World War II [Gravel Hill Cemetery]

Presbury, Cleveland stillborn male on September 12, 1931, "premature birth - 7 months" (no tombstone; death certificate stated he was born near Aberdeen, the son of William Prespbury *(sic)*, born in Harford Co., and Clara Parker, born in Aberdeen; informant was Clara Prespbury *(sic)*) [Mt. Calvary U. A. M. E. Church Cemetery]

Presbury, Clyde L. 1955-1973 [Berkley Memorial Cemetery]

Presbury, Curtis March 1, 1923 – March 4, 1923 (no tombstone; death certificate stated he was the son of Kenton Presbury and Dora Bond, of the Berkley-Darlington area, all born in Maryland) [Berkley Memorial Cemetery]

Presbury, Dolores H. 1938-2018 (small metal funeral home marker) [Berkley Memorial Cemetery]

Presbury, Dorothy A. 1931-1983 (tombstone; the obituary of Earnest J. Rice in *The Aegis*, November 7, 1974, stated Mrs. Dorothy Presbury, of Street, MD, was one of his seven children) [Chestnut Grove A. M. E. Church Cemetery, formerly LaGrange Cemetery at Rocks]

Presbury, Edna (no dates when copied in 1987, not listed in 2002, not found in 2018) [Gravel Hill Cemetery]

Presbury, Edward November 6, 1918 – September 20, 1919 (no tombstone; death certificate stated he was the son of Joshua Presbury and Edna Stansbury, all born in Maryland; informant was Joshua Presbury, of Havre de Grace RFD) [Gravel Hill Cemetery]

Presbury, Eliza H. November 15, 1867 – August 21, 1941 (no tombstone; death certificate stated she was the daughter of George Brooks, both born in Maryland, but her mother's name was not known to informant, Mrs. Annie May Lisby, of Aberdeen RFD; she was the widow of Nelson F. Presbury and died at home near Aberdeen where she had lived for 65 years) [Mt. Calvary U. A. M. E. Church Cemetery]

Presbury, Emma C. February 8, 1876 – November 6, 1925 (no tombstone; death certificate stated she was the daughter of Prince Stansbury and Mary Harris, all born in Maryland; she was married at the time of her death and informant was John Presbury, of Havre de Grace) [Gravel Hill Cemetery]

Presbury, Florence C. 1896-1972 (copied in 1987, but not found in 2018; obituary in *The Aegis* on January 20, 1972 stated Florence Christy Presbury was the daughter of the late Jacob Christy and Susie Warfield, and the widow of Warren Presbury; she lived on Mt. Calvary Road in Aberdeen and died at Harford Memorial Hospital on January 11, 1972; she was a lifetime member of Sidney Park Methodist Church and Union United Methodist Church; she was survived by one brother, two sisters, one godchild) [Mt. Calvary U.A. M. E. Church Cemetery]

Presbury, George W. (no tombstone; death certificate stated he was born May 22, 1884, the son of Benjamin Presbury and Ella Christy, and all were born in Harford Co.; he worked as a laborer near Havre de Grace and was married at the time of his death on October 10, 1915; informant was Mrs. G. W. Presbury, of Havre de Grace RFD) [Green Spring U. M. Church Cemetery]

Presbury, Hattie November 22, 1891 – August 2, 1918 (no tombstone; death certificate stated Hattie Prespbury *(sic)* was born in Harford Co., the daughter of L. J. Hollingsworth and Emily Parker, both born in Maryland; she was married and died at Perryman; informant was Lawrence Prespbury *(sic)*, of Perryman) [Mt. Calvary U. A. M. E. Church Cemetery]

Presbury, Helen L. October 5, 1917 – November 19, 1917 (no tombstone; death certificate stated she was born and died in Havre de Grace, the daughter of Jere *(sic)* Presbury, born in Harford Co., and Edna Stansbury, born in Havre de Grace; informant was his father) [Gravel Hill Cemetery]

Presbury, Helen Marie stillborn on May 13, 1928 (no tombstone; death certificate stated she died at Bel Air RFD, the daughter of Benjamin F. Tyler, born in South Carolina, and Dora Ella Presbury, born in Maryland; the informant was Edward Presbury, of Bel Air) [Clark's U. M. Church Cemetery]

Presbury, Helen May September 25, 1914 – September 29, 1914 (no tombstone; death certificate stated she was the daughter of Winfield Presbury and Lillie Galloway, of Havre de Grace) [St. James United Cemetery]

Presbury, Jerimiah (no dates on tombstone; death certificate stated Jeremiah Presbury was born in Harford Co., the son of Robert Presbury and Catherine Berch, worked as a farm laborer in rural Havre de Grace, and married Edna M. ---- who was age 48 at the time of his death on January 5, 1942, age 50; informant was Mrs. Edna M. Presbury) [Gravel Hill Cemetery]

Presbury, Lloyd (no dates when copied in 1987, not listed in 2002, not found in 2018) [Gravel Hill Cemetery]

Presbury, Mary F. March 3, 1868 – September 16, 1934 (no tombstone; death certificate spelled her name Presbery and stated she was the daughter of George Jackson and Isabelle Turner, all born in Harford Co.; she married William Presbery *(sic)* and died at Forest Hill where she had lived all her life; informant was Stephen H. Presbery *(sic)*, 1906 N. 11th St., Philadelphia) [Fairview A. M. E. Church Cemetery]

Presbury, Nelson F. November 26, 1859 – March 17, 1936 (no tombstone; death certificate stated he was born in Camden, NJ, son of Benjamin Presbury, birth place unknown, and his mother was not known to informant Warren W. Presbury, of Aberdeen; he married Eliza H. ----, worked as a farmer and died at Mt. Calvary near Aberdeen RFD where he had lived for 45 years) [Mt. Calvary U. A. M. E. Church Cemetery]

Presbury, Robert (no dates when copied in 1987, not listed in 2002, not found in 2018) [Gravel Hill Cemetery]

Presbury, Sarah E. September 7, 1884 – October 28, 1918 (no tombstone; death certificate stated she was the daughter of Lloyd Green and Elizabeth Harris, all born in Maryland; she died a widow at home near Havre de Grace; informant was Mrs. Elizabeth Green, of Havre de Grace) [Green Spring U. M. Church Cemetery]

Presbury, Sarah E. "Sadie" died October 29, 1938, age 53 (no tombstone; death certificate stated she was born in Anne Arundel Co., but her parents were unknown to the Bullock Funeral Home in Havre de Grace; she married Lloyd Presbury and died at home in Havre de Grace RFD #1) [Gravel Hill Cemetery]

Presbury, Stephen Henry died June 9, 1910, age 74 or 82 (no tombstone; death notice in *The Aegis* on June 17, 1910 stated he lived near Bagley, died at age 82 and was buried at the "Mountain colored church;" death certificate stated Stephen Henry Presbury was born in Harford Co., lived and died at Bagley, and had worked as a well digger; informant was E. J. F. Presbury, his wife; she did not know the names and places of birth of Stephen's parents) [Mt. Zion U. M. Church Cemetery]

Presbury, W. Walter December 3, 1901 – November 26, 1915 (no tombstone; death certificate gave the wrong birth date and stated he was the son of William Presbury and Mary F. Jackson, all born in Harford Co.; he died in Bel Air; informant was William Presbury, of Forest Hill) [Fairview A. M. E. Church Cemetery]

Presbury, Warren Winfield June 5, 1898 – December 28, 1947 (no tombstone; death certificate stated he was born in Aberdeen, the son of Nelson Presbury, born in Aberdeen, and Liza Brooks, birth place not stated; he worked as a day laborer for Aberdeen Proving Ground, married Florence Christy and died at home on Bush Chapel Road near Aberdeen where he had lived all his life; informant was his wife Florence Presbury) [Mt. Calvary U. A. M. E. Church Cemetery]

Presbury, Wilford H. 1891-1929 (tombstone; military records state he was born in Aberdeen on January 12, 1891, was inducted into service on June 19, 1918, served in 154 Dep Brig and in Co. A and Co. C, 371 Infantry, was overseas at Meuse-Argonne and Bonhomme Sector from August 26, 1918 until February 11, 1919 and was honorably discharged on February 7, 1919; death certificate stated he was born in Harford Co., son of Nelson Presbury, born in New Jersey, and Eliza Brooks, born in "Allvert Co." (Calvert Co., MD); he was single, worked as a laborer for the U.S. Army and drowned in a boating accident on August 15, 1929 at Aberdeen Proving Ground; informant was Warren Presbury, of Aberdeen) [Mt. Calvary U. A. M. E. Church Cemetery]

Presbury, William died April 15, 1948, age not given (no tombstone; James Dorsey Card File, African American Obituaries, maintained at the Historical Society of Harford County, has a card with his death notice abstraction from an unidentified newspaper stating he was found dead at his home in Aberdeen) [Mt. Calvary U. A. M. E. Church Cemetery]

Presbury, William H. April 22, 1869 – July 22, 1946 (no tombstone; death certificate stated he was the son of William H. Presbury, both born in Harford Co., but his mother's name was not known to informant Marshall Presbury, of Forest Hill; he married Mary F. Jackson, worked as a cemetery care taker and died at his home in Forest Hill where he had lived for 36 years) [Fairview A. M. E. Church Cemetery]

Presbury, William Henry June 14, 1870 – November 29, 1935 (no tombstone; death certificate stated he was born in Baltimore, but his parents were not known to informant Mrs. Hannah Hardy, of Aberdeen RFD #3; he worked as a day laborer, lived outside Stepney for 21 years and was found dead in a ditch on the public road near Stepney) [Mt. Calvary U. A. M. E. Church Cemetery]

Presby, Betty died October 10, 1891 in her 12th year [Hendon Hill Cemetery]

Preston, ---- stillborn child (sex not stated) on March 10, 1923 (no tombstone; death certificate stated the child was born of Joseph Preston and Viola Osborn, of Sewell, all born in Maryland) [John Wesley U. M. E. Church Cemetery in Abingdon]

Preston, Alice August 10, 1890 – December 31, 1918 (no tombstone; death certificate stated she was the daughter of Isaac Wilmer and Ida Jones, all born in Maryland; she was married and died at Sewell; informant was Jos.(?) R. Preston, of Sewell) [John Wesley U. M. E. Church Cemetery in Abingdon]

Preston, Anne E., widow of Joshua Preston, died July 4, 1904, age 70 [Hendon Hill Cemetery]

Preston, Annie Servilla Bishop February 19, 1918 – March 13, 2004 [John Wesley U. M. E. Church Cemetery in Abingdon]

Preston, Arthur died January 19, 1883, age about 20 (no tombstone; *The Aegis*, January 26, 1883, reported he was hanged in the Bel Air jail yard for murdering Mary Dorsey on April 12, 1882) [Hendon Hill Cemetery]

Preston, Augusta died August 15, 1916, age about 52 (no dates on tombstone; death certificate stated she was born in Aberdeen, daughter of Lawson Harris, born in Harford Co., and Margaret Dutton, birth place unknown; she lived near Gravelly Hill and was married at the time of her death; informant was Steve Preston, of Havre de Grace RFD) [Gravel Hill Cemetery]

Preston, Blanch I. 1914-1991 (on same tombstone with Joseph A. Preston; obituary in *The Aegis* on March 20, 1991 stated Blanche Irene Preston was born in Edgewood, the daughter of Jerry A. Gilbert and Ossie Johnson, and her husband Joseph A. Preston predeceased her; she lived in Baltimore City, worked as a domestic employee and died on March 13, 1991 at Union Memorial Hospital, survived by two brothers and a sister) [Foster's Hill Cemetery]

Preston, Blanche Irene died March 13, 1991, age 76 (no tombstone; James Dorsey Card File, African American Obituaries, maintained at the Historical Society of Harford County, has a card with obituary from an unidentified newspaper dated March 20, 1991 stating she was born in Edgewood, the daughter of Jerry A. Gilbert and Ossie Johnson, and the widow of Joseph A. Preston; she lived in Baltimore, worked as a domestic employee the Baltimore area, died at Union Memorial Hospital, survived by two brothers and a sister, and was buried in the "John Wesley United Methodist Church cemetery in Joppa") [Mt. Zion U. M. Church Cemetery]

Preston, Clarence J. January 12, 1924 – February 11, 1969, Pennsylvania, Sgt., Co. B. 948 ABN Sig. Bn., World War II [Berkley Memorial Cemetery]

Preston, Cora C. August 5, 1869 – March 23, 1925 (no tombstone; death certificate stated she was the married daughter of Isaac Stansbury and Hanna Curtis; informant was Geo. W. Preston) [Union U. M. Church Cemetery]

Preston, Cornelius C. July 4, 1894 – October 9, 1972 (obituary in *The Aegis* on October 19, 1972 stated Cornelius C. Preston (Neal) was born in Michaelsville, the son of Wesley and Harriet Preston; he lived at 1609 Pulaski Highway in Perryman, retired from Aberdeen Proving Ground and died on October 9, 1972 survived by two brothers, George and John Preston, four nephews, one niece and a devoted friend, Mrs. Bessie Hoke, of Perryman) [Union U. M. Church Cemetery]

Preston, Eliza J. August 28, 1858 – January 9, 1926 (no tombstone; death certificate stated she was the daughter of Alfred and Avarilla Hill, all born in Maryland; she was a widow and died in Aberdeen; informant was Avarilla Byrd, of 1537 Stiles St., Philadelphia, PA) [Gravel Hill Cemetery]

Preston, Elizabeth March 14, 1892 – May 2, 1926 (no tombstone; death certificate stated she was the daughter of Madison Moulton, both born in Virginia, but her mother's name and place of birth were not known to informant Stephen Preston, of Havre de Grace RFD; she was married and lived at Gravelly Hill) [Gravel Hill Cemetery]

Preston, Ephraim A. May 12, 1883 – June 11, 1938 (no tombstone; death certificate stated he was the son of Wesley Preston and Hattie Brown, and husband of Frances Preston who predeceased him) [Union U. M. Church Cemetery]

Preston, F. Dicty October 17, 1873 – February 25, 1949 (no tombstone; death certificate stated he was born and died at Kalmia, the son of Harrison Preston and Mary Gordon, and he was a widower; informant was Mrs. Mary Smith) [Clark's U. M. Church Cemetery]

Preston, Geo. F., "In Memory of My Husband" died July 17, 1884 (inscribed "I stood beside his dying bed, And heard his latest sigh, I was present when his spirit fled, To realms of bliss on high. Harriet") [Clark's U. M. Church Cemetery]

Preston, George P. 1958-1961 (on same tombstone with George P. Bishop) [John Wesley U. M. E. Church Cemetery in Abingdon]

Preston, George Washington August 15, 1879 – December 30, 1974 (no tombstone; obituary in *The Aegis* stated he was born in Perryman, the son of John W. and Harriett Preston, and lived 844 Erie St. in Havre de Grace and retired as a railroad foreman at Aberdeen Proving Ground; he died at Harford Memorial Hospital and was survived by a brother, three nephews and a niece) [Union U. M. Church Cemetery]

Preston, Harriett H. died June 27, 1916, age unknown (no tombstone; death certificate stated she was a widow when she died at Glenville; her parents' names and places of birth were not known to the informant Henry Dutton, of Darlington) [Clark's U. M. Church Cemetery]

Preston, Harrison May 2, 1851 – April 1, 1920 (no tombstone; death certificate stated he was the son of George Preston, both born in Harford Co., but his mother's name was not known to the informant Sidney Smith, of Bel Air; he was a day laborer and died a widower at Kalmia) [Clark's U. M. Church Cemetery]

Preston, Howard Jerome died February 24, 1982, age 73 (no tombstone; obituary in *The Aegis* on February 25, 1982 stated he was the son of Ernest H. Preston and Bertha S. Jarrett and he worked for the Baltimore & Ohio Railroad, the United Clay Mines, and retired as a farm laborer for the Bawer Farms; he was the husband of the late Florene Preston and died at Harford Memorial Hospital in Havre de Grace, survived by four stepchildren and three brothers) [Asbury Cemetery]

Preston, Ida April 3, 1883 – January 21, 1932 (no tombstone; death certificate stated she was the daughter of Charles Jones and Harriet Preston, all born in Maryland; she was single, did "house duties" for 30 years until November 1931, lived in Havre de Grace and died at Havre de Grace Hospital; certificate stated the information was gleaned from hospital records) [Gravel Hill Cemetery]

Preston, J. Ann March 20, 1799 – January 17, 1911 (no tombstone; death certificate stated she was a widow and servant in Bel Air; she was born in Harford Co.; her father was a slave, name not known, and her mother Hannah Tally was born in Harford Co.; informant was Mary C. Hawkins) [Hendon Hill Cemetery]

Preston, James A. April 1, 1850 – April 20, 1916 (no tombstone; death certificate stated he was the son of George Preston and Appy N. Harris, all born in Harford Co.; he was married and a farmer at Kalmia; informant was Mary P. Preston, of Bel Air) [Clark's U. M. Church Cemetery]

Preston, Jarrett Henry May 12, 1887 – September 21, 1934 (no tombstone; death certificate stated he was the son of Wesley S. Preston and Hattie Brown) [Union U. M. Church Cemetery]

Preston, John G. September 22, 1875 – July 10, 1925 (no tombstone; death certificate stated he was the son of William H. Preston and Maranda Barnes, all born in Maryland; he was married and a laborer at Cedars; informant was Mrs. Lena F. Preston, of Street RFD) [Clark's U. M. Church Cemetery]

Preston, John T. 1889 – December 23, 1934 (no tombstone; death certificate stated he was born in Bel Air, but his parents were not known to informant Irine Watters, of Edgewood RFD; he married Viola ----, lived in Abingdon, worked as a laborer, was struck by a B&O train at Van Bibber and was buried in "John Wesley Cem.") [John Wesley U. M. E. Church Cemetery in Abingdon]

Preston, John W. 1899-1984 (tombstone; obituary in *The Aegis* stated John Wesley Preston was born in Perryman, married Annie S. ---- and worked for the railroad and the Board of Education; he lived in Havre de Grace and died at Harford Memorial Hospital on March 1, 1984, survived by his wife, a daughter Rodella A. Stansbury and three grandchildren) [St. James United Cemetery]

Preston, John W. 1924-1985 [St. James United Cemetery]

Preston, Joseph A. 1909-1980 (on same tombstone with Blanch I. Preston) [Foster's Hill Cemetery]

Preston, Joshua died October 3, 1891, age 52 [Hendon Hill Cemetery]

Preston, Loretta September 28, 1934 – February 2, 1935 (no tombstone; death certificate stated she was born in Johns Hopkins Hospital in Baltimore, the daughter of Arthur Johnson, born in Virginia, and Viola Osborn Preston, born in Maryland; she died at home in Abingdon and was buried at "John Wesley;" informant was Viola Preston, of Abingdon) [John Wesley U. M. E. Church Cemetery in Abingdon]

Preston, Lulu May December 12, 1913 – March 4, 1914 (no tombstone; death certificate stated she was the daughter of Hewett O. Preston, both born in Harford Co., and Mary Matilda Wilson, born in Baltimore; she died at home near Aberdeen; informant was Mary Matilda Wilson) [Mt. Calvary U. A. M. E. Church Cemetery]

Preston, Martha died November 21, 1872, age 25 [Hendon Hill Cemetery]

Preston, Mary B. June 26, 1937 – February 6, 1992 (inscribed "Forever In Our Hearts" with her picture; obituary and photo in *The Aegis* on February 19, 1992 stated Mary Bertha "Mary Bert" Smith Preston was born in Churchville, the daughter of the late George Allen and Pearl Evelyn Smith; she lived in Churchville and died at Harford Memorial Hospital in Havre de Grace, survived by her husband Elmer Preston, four sons, two daughters, ten grandchildren, two brothers and five sisters) [Asbury Cemetery]

Preston, Mary Elizabeth December 19, 1908 – March 11, 1933 (no tombstone; death certificate stated she was the daughter of Joseph Preston and Alice Wilmer, all born in Maryland; she was single and lived and died at home in Abingdon; informant was her father) [John Wesley U. M. E. Church Cemetery in Abingdon]

Preston, Mary L. May 11, 1913 – November 30, 1914 (no tombstone; death certificate stated she was the daughter of Ernest J. R. Preston and Bertha S. Jarrett, and they all were born in Harford Co. and lived in Bel Air; informant was her father) [Tabernacle Mount Zion U. M. Church Cemetery]

Preston, Mary Lizy (no dates copied in 1987, not listed in 2002, not found in 2018) [Gravel Hill Cemetery]

Preston, Noah died July 14, 1913, age about 58 (no tombstone; death certificate stated he was the son of Stephen Preston and Mary Fox, all were born in Harford Co.; he was a laborer at Aberdeen and was married at the time of his death; informant was Edward Preston) [Gravel Hill Cemetery]

Preston, Nori (no dates when copied in 1987, not listed in 2002, not found in 2018) [Gravel Hill Cemetery]

Preston, Norman Conthanial April 17, 1912 – October 3, 1912 (no tombstone; death certificate stated he was the son of Joseph Preston and Alice Wilmer, all born in Harford Co., and lived in Abingdon) [John Wesley U. M. E. Church Cemetery in Abingdon]

Preston, Ora died May 5, 1907, age 26 (no tombstone; death certificate stated she was the daughter of Jennie Macall (father's name was not given) and the wife of James Preston; she died in Berkley, but place of burial not given [probably [Berkley Memorial Cemetery]

Preston, Oscar W. October 22, 1891 – July 26, 1914 (no tombstone; death certificate stated he was the son of John Preston and Sarah A. Hall, all born in Harford Co.; he was married, worked as a laborer, died in Bel Air and was buried at Mountain Colored Church; informant was Florence Preston) [Mt. Zion U. M. Church Cemetery]

Preston, Patrisa A. 1952-2006 (small metal funeral home marker) [Berkley Memorial Cemetery]

Preston, Rebecca, "Mother" died March 7, 1916? (illegible) [Clark's U. M. Church Cemetery]

Preston, Stephen August 2, 1860 – March 1, 1935 (no dates on tombstone; death certificate stated he was the son of Stephen Preston and Mary Wheeler, all born in Harford County, and he was a resident of Havre de Grace except for two months at the County Alms House near Bel Air where he died a widower; informant was Maggie Turner, of Havre de Grace) [Gravel Hill Cemetery]

Preston, Stephen died January 8, 1916, age about 32 (no tombstone; death certificate stated he was born near Aberdeen, the son of Noah Preston, born near Level, and Elizabeth Wheems, born in Churchville; he was a laborer, not married, and died at his home near Aberdeen) [Gravel Hill Cemetery]

Preston, Sudie Ames July 26, 1931 – September 8, 2007 (no tombstone; obituary and photo in *The Aegis* on September 14, 2007 stated she was born in Orancock, VA, the daughter of Samuel Ames and Elsie Willis; she worked at Harford Memorial Hospital, Perry Point VAMC, and later retired from Leeds VAMC in Massachusetts; she lived in Aberdeen and died at Harford Memorial Hospital, survived by 3 sons, 1 daughter, 26 grandchildren, 56 great-grand-children, 2 brothers, 5 sisters, 2 daughters-in-law, 3 brothers-in-law, and 4 sisters-in-law) [Berkley Memorial Cemetery]

Preston, Viola Mabel March 19, 1902 – November 30, 1949 (no tombstone; death certificate stated she was born in Harford Co., the daughter of Will Osborne and Mabel Washington; she worked in a restaurant, lived in Bel Air and was a widow when she died in the Harford Memorial Hospital in Havre de Grace; informant was Mabel Osborne, of Abingdon) [Asbury Cemetery]

Preston, Virginia 1938-1980 (name and years on a small metal funeral home marker; James Dorsey Card File, African American Obituaries, that is maintained at the Historical Society of Harford County, has a funeral card stating Virginia Blanche Preston was born on June 25, 1938 and died on February 23, 1980) [John Wesley U. M. E. Church Cemetery in Abingdon]

Preston, William died June 1, 1900, age over 70 (no tombstone; obituary in *The Aegis*, June 1, 1900, stated he died "on Friday" when he fell from a barn on the farm of William H. Tucker, near Hickory; death certificate stated he was a laborer, was married, and died June 1, 1900, but it did not give his age, place of burial, nor names of his wife and parents) [Hendon Hill Cemetery]

Preston, William Frederick February 10, 1936 – October 6, 1936 (no tombstone; death certificate stated he was born in Abingdon, son of Arthur Johnson, born in Virginia, and Viola Osborne, born at Creswell; buried at "John Wesley;" informant was Viola Preston, of Abingdon) [John Wesley U. M. E. Church Cemetery in Abingdon]

Preston, William Henry April 13, 1913 – November 22, 1914 (no tombstone; death certificate stated he was the son of James Preston and Anna Rose and they were all born in Maryland and lived in Bel Air; informant was

Martha Anderson, of Bel Air) [Hendon Hill Cemetery]

Price, ---- (owned a lot in section 7 some time after 1951) [Mt. Calvary U. A. M. E. Church Cemetery]

Price, Annie E. November 23, 1887 – December 13, 1938 (no tombstone; death certificate stated she was the wife of Charlie Price and the daughter of John Brown and Sarah Richardson; she was buried in "U. M.E. Swan Creek Cemetery") [Union U. M. Church Cemetery]

Price, Helen M. May 18, 1915 – July 21, 1919 (no tombstone; death certificate stated she was the daughter of Raford Johnson and Carrie E. Price, all born in Maryland; she died at Kalmia and was buried in "Clarks Chapel Cemetery;" informant was Marie P. Lee, of Bel Air) [Clark's U. M. Church Cemetery]

Prigg, ---- January 19, 1911 – February 25, 1911 (no tombstone; death certificate stated he was the infant unnamed son of Thomas Prigg and Rosetta White, all born in Harford Co.; he died in Berkley and informant was Samuel White, of Berkley) [Berkley Memorial Cemetery]

Prigg, Abraham 1821-1879 (on same toppled over obelisk with Jane, John, Edward and Bertha Prigg) [Green Spring U. M. Church Cemetery]

Prigg, Bertha 1866-1897 (on same toppled over obelisk with Jane, John, Edward and Abraham Prigg) [Green Spring U. M. Church Cemetery]

Prigg, Charles H. February 23, 1861 – February 23, 1911 (no tombstone; death certificate stated he was born in Harford Co., the son of Charles Prigg, born in West India (West Indies), and Mary Warfield, born in Harford Co.; he was married, worked as a laborer, died at home in Havre de Grace and was buried in "Sidney Park Cemetery;" informant was G. T. Pennington, Undertaker, Havre de Grace) [Union U. M. Church Cemetery]

Prigg, Daniel died July 1, 1935, age about 60 (no tombstone; death certificate stated he was the son of Abraham and Jane Prigg, all born in Harford Co.; he was a farm laborer who lived near Churchville and died a widower in Havre de Grace Hospital; informant was James A. Carne, of Bel Air) [Green Spring U. M. Church Cemetery]

Prigg, Della (no dates on tombstone; obituary in *The Aegis* on March 11, 1976 stated Della Jane Prigg, of Abingdon, widow of Jarrett Prigg, died on March 8, 1976, age 94, at the Brevin Nursing Home in Havre de Grace; she was born in Harford County, the daughter of William and Rachel Smith, and spent her entire life in this county; she was survived by two grandchildren, three great-grandchildren, and four great-great-grandchildren) [Green Spring U. M. Church Cemetery]

Prigg, Edna V. November 11, 1921 – August 18, 2005 (tombstone; obituary and photo in *The Aegis* on August 24, 2005 stated Edna Virginia Prigg was born in Darlington, daughter of Allen Presberry and Daisy Dorsey, married Lawrence Prigg and worked for Dr. Dudley Phillips for 49 years and assisted in raising his children; she lived at Forest Hill and died at the Mariner Health Nursing Home, survived by a daughter, five step-children, one grandson, 14 great-grandchildren and a host of other relatives; she was predeceased by her husband, a sister-in-law, a son-in-law, two brothers-in-law, three grandchildren) [Berkley Memorial Cemetery]

Prigg, Edward 1861-1892 (on same toppled over obelisk with Jane, John, Abraham and Bertha Prigg) [Green Spring U. M. Church Cemetery]

Prigg, H. Ellsworth 1927-1985 (tombstone; obituary in *The Aegis* on September 26, 1985 stated Harry Ellsworth Prigg died on September 19, 1985, age 57, and was a son of the late Lawrence and Martha Jane Prigg; he was employed as a truck driver for Richard Watters of Forest Hill for 25 years and died at home in Darlington, survived by one brother Gover Bond, one sister, two sisters-in-law and a host of other relatives) [Berkley Memorial Cemetery]

Prigg, Horace May 19, 1854 – May 3, 1919 (tombstone; death certificate stated he was the son of Henry Prigg and Harriett Haines, all born in Maryland; he married, worked as a farmer and died a widower in Castleton; informant was Lewis J. Prigg, of Castleton) [Berkley Memorial Cemetery]

Prigg, Ida died November 4, 1887, age 15 (no tombstone; an article in *The Aegis* on November 11, 1887 reported she died "a few days ago;" she was the daughter of Abraham Prigg and was injured while playing in Christian Walker's canning factory, near Level, where she was employed; her foot slipped between two tomato boxes and she injured her foot and her side; she initially stated she had broken her ankle, but a minute later stated

"No, it is not my ankle, something gave way in my side;" her condition worsened and she died about a week after the accident; burial was November 6, 1887) [Green Spring U. M. Church Cemetery]

Prigg, James March 8, 1902 – May 13, 1918 (no tombstone; death certificate stated he was the son of Daniel Prigg and Olivia Washington, all were born in Harford Co.; he was single, a day laborer and died near Havre de Grace; informant was Henry Prigg, of Aberdeen) [Green Spring U. M. Church Cemetery]

Prigg, Jane 1829-1912 (on same toppled over obelisk with Abraham, John, Edward and Bertha Prigg; death certificate stated she died on August 25, 1912, age 82 years and 10 months, at Level, the widow of Abraham Prigg, and the daughter of Roger and Jane Presbury; they all were born in Harford Co.; informant was her son Henry Prigg) [Green Spring U. M. Church Cemetery]

Prigg, Janie 1891-1963 (on same tombstone with Lawrence S. Prigg) [Berkley Memorial Cemetery]

Prigg, Jarrett (no dates on tombstone; obituary in *The Aegis* on April 24, 1969 stated he was the husband of Della Prigg, of 733 Schofield Road, Aberdeen, and died on April 19, 1969, age 87, at Brevin Nursing Home in Havre de Grace, survived by his wife and 2 grandchildren) [Green Spring U. M. Church Cemetery]

Prigg, John 1854-1917 (on the same toppled over obelisk with Jane, Abraham, Edward and Bertha Prigg; death certificate stated he was born on October 15, 1854, the son of Abe Prigg and Jane Presbury, and they all were born in Maryland; he was single, worked as a laborer at Level, and died on August 6, 1917; informant was Henry Prigg, of Aberdeen RFD) [Green Spring U. M. Church Cemetery]

Prigg, Lawrence September 10, 1918 – August 22, 1968, Maryland, Cpl., 1377 Base Unit, AAF, World War II [Berkley Memorial Cemetery]

Prigg, Lawrence S. 1889-1939 (on same tombstone with Janie Prigg; death certificate stated Lawrence Prigg was born on August 10, 1889 and was the son of Horace Prigg and Louisa Spriggs, all born in Harford Co; he married Jannie ----, worked as a telegraph line laborer and died at home in Berkley on July 15, 1939; informant was Mrs. Jannie Prigg, of Darlington) [Berkley Memorial Cemetery]

Prigg, Louisa died March 21, 1908, age 13 years, 3 months and 12 days (no tombstone; death certificate stated she was the daughter of Horace Prigg and Louisa Sprigg, all born in Harford Co.; she was a school girl who died at home in Castleton and the place of her burial was not indicated, but it was in all likelihood in this cemetery since her family is buried here) [Berkley Memorial Cemetery]

Prigg, Louisa May 20, 1860 – March 23, 1911 (tombstone; death certificate stated she was the daughter of Louis Sprigg, both born in Baltimore Co., but her mother's name was not known to informant Nelson Prigg, of Castleton; she was married and died at home in Castleton) [Berkley Memorial Cemetery]

Prigg, Oscar December 28, 1882 – April 6, 1930 (no tombstone; death certificate stated he was the son of Horace Prigg and Louisa Spriggs, all born in Maryland; he was married, worked as a laborer in a coal yard and died at home in Castleton; informant was Lewis J. Prigg, of 235 Chestnut Ave., Ardmore, PA) [Berkley Memorial Cemetery]

Prigg, S. R. "D 2 1879" (as copied in 1987, noting stone was leaning against the Hosanna Freedman's School and the copyist also stated "I've heard the farmer moved them from his field.") [Berkley Memorial Cemetery]

Prigg, Sarah March 22, 1870 – March 23, 1948 (no tombstone; death certificate stated she was the daughter of William Holland and Maria Lewis, and the widow of George Warfield *(sic)*) [Union U. M. Church Cemetery]

Prigg, William April 15, 1884 – November 8, 1913 (no tombstone; death certificate stated he was the son of Charles Prigg and Mary Holland, all born in Harford Co.; he was single, worked as a laborer and died in Perryman; informant was Sarah Prigg, of Perryman) [Mt. Calvary U. A. M. E. Church Cemetery]

Priggs, Mary F. June 17, 1859 – November 7, 1922 (no tombstone; death certificate stated she was born in Maryland, the daughter of Charles Lee, born in Maryland, and Mary Worthington, born in Pennsylvania; she died near Aberdeen; informant was Emma Dutton, of Aberdeen) [Mt. Calvary U. A. M. E. Church Cemetery]

Prince, Harmer L. Sr. May 13, 1926 – February 16, 2007, MSG, U.S. Army, World War II, Korea, Vietnam (on same tombstone with Helen L. Prince) [St. James United Cemetery]

Prince, Helen L., "Beloved Wife and Mother" February 20, 1932 – February 7, 2004 [St. James United Cemetery]

Pringle, Annie F. January 12, 1940 – October 22, 1940 (no tombstone; death certificate stated he was born in Harford Co., the daughter of William Pringle, born in South Carolina, and Mary Leonard, born in Harford Co.; they lived in Pylesville; informant was her father) [Chestnut Grove A. M. E. Church Cemetery, formerly LaGrange Cemetery at Rocks]

Pringle, Clarence B. August 24, 1957 – November 12, 1983 [William C. Rice Memorial Cemetery, St. James U. M. Church]

Pringle, John W. March 23, 1941 – September 8, 1941 (no tombstone; death certificate stated he was born in Harford Co.; his mother was Mary Leonard, born in Harford Co., but his father's name was not known to informant, Mary Pringle, of Pylesville) [Chestnut Grove A. M. E. Church Cemetery, formerly LaGrange Cemetery at Rocks]

Pringle, Mary Louise April 16, 1942 – September 16, 1942 (no tombstone; death certificate stated she died at Pylesville and her parents were Howard Jones and Mary Leonard (an apparent error by the registrar since her last name should have been Jones), all were born in Harford Co.; informant was Mary Pringle, of Pylesville) [Chestnut Grove A. M. E. Church Cemetery, formerly LaGrange Cemetery at Rocks]

Pruitt, Cynthia D., "Loving Wife and Mother" October 25, 1953 – October 16, 1992 [St. James United Cemetery]

Pruitt, James Auther August 2, 1949 – March 9, 2018, SFC, U.S. Army (new tombstone, soon to be erected, was laying on the ground) [St. James United Cemetery]

Pugh, George Edward died April 3, 1934, age about 54 (no tombstone; death certificate stated he was the son of Henry Pugh and Julia Spencer, all born in Maryland; he married Mary ---- and lived and worked as a laborer near Fallston; informant was Elizabeth Spencer) [Tabernacle Mount Zion U. M. Church Cemetery]

Purnell, Ellen 1858-1911 (on same tombstone with Stephen and Martha J. Purnell) [St. James United Cemetery]

Purnell, Martha J. 18-- - 1911 (on same tombstone with Ellen and Stephen Purnell, but her name was at the bottom of a toppled tombstone and her birth year was partially covered in cement) [St. James United Cemetery]

Purnell, Stephen 1845-1902 (on same tombstone with Ellen and Martha J. Purnell) [St. James United Cemetery]

Quarles, Alice H. 1879-19__ (on same tombstone with George H. Quarles) [Berkley Memorial Cemetery]

Quarles, George H. 1860-1940 (on same tombstone with Alice H. Quarles) [Berkley Memorial Cemetery]

Quickley, ---- premature female birth on November 22, 1918, lived 9 hours (no tombstone; death certificate stated she died at Watervale, the daughter of Raymond Maxfield, birth place unknown, and Mary Quickley, born in Maryland; informant was Isaac Quickley, of Vale) [Tabernacle Mount Zion U. M. Church Cemetery]

Quickley, ---- premature female born on November 22, 1917 and lived 9 hours (no tombstone; death certificate stated she was the daughter of Raymond Maxfield, birth place unknown, and Mary Quickley, of Watervale, born in Maryland; informant was Isaac Quickley, of Vale) [Tabernacle Mount Zion U. M. Church Cemetery]

Quickley, Amelia November 2, 1879 – October 14, 1961 (no tombstone; information is from Quickley family records) [Tabernacle Mount Zion U. M. Church Cemetery]

Quickley, Beverly Agatha March 11, 1936 – August 25, 1957 (no tombstone; Pennington Funeral Home records stated she was born in Perryman, daughter of Charles T. Sconion and Beatrice Banks, married (husband's name not given), lived on Osborne Lane near Aberdeen, died a widow and was buried in Swan Creek Cemetery; informant was Mrs. Charles T. Sconion; funeral bill was rendered to Charles Sconion and paid by Joshua A. Quickley, Sr.) [Union U. M. Church Cemetery]

Quickley, Gladys Brown died July 25, 1991, age 74 (no tombstone; obituary in *The Aegis* on August 7, 1991 stated she was born in York, PA, the daughter of Bessie Brown, lived in Bel Air and died at Washington Hospital Medical Center, survived by her husband William Quickley and children in Connecticut) [Tabernacle Mount

Zion U. M. Church Cemetery]

Quickley, Isaac February 2, 1871 – January 4, 1955 (no tombstone; information is from Quickley family records) [Tabernacle Mount Zion U. M. Church Cemetery]

Quickley, Isaiah Sr. died September 6, 1971, age 65 (no tombstone; obituary in *The Aegis* on September 9, 1971 spelled his first name "Isaish" and stated he was the husband of the late Lottie Snowden Quickley and father of the late Isaiah Quickley, Jr.; he was formerly of Lake Fanny Road in Bel Air, retired from the Reckordville Mills and died at Mt. Wilson State Hospital, survived by a daughter, three sisters and two brothers) [Tabernacle Mount Zion U. M. Church Cemetery]

Quickley, Pauline (owned a lot in section 42 some time after 1951) [Mt. Calvary U. A. M. E. Church Cemetery]

Quickley, William Henry February 13, 1925 – August 5, 1998 (no tombstone; obituary in *The Aegis* on August 12, 1998 stated he was born in Fallston, the son of Isiah and Melia Quickley, and served in the Army from November 1943 to November 1946, attained the rank of corporal, and received Bronze Stars in 1944 and in 1945; he worked at Aberdeen Proving Ground and died at Fallston General Hospital, survived by many nieces, nephews and friends) [Tabernacle Mount Zion U. M. Church Cemetery]

Quomony, Etta Marie 1923-2007 (small metal funeral home marker) [Berkley Memorial Cemetery]

Quomony, Martha E. 1910-2000 (small metal funeral home marker) [St. James United Cemetery]

Rain, Areese January 1, 1871, Mobile, Ala. – November 21, 196_, Havre de Grace (flat marker with numbers and letters embossed on it and a number was missing from her year of death) [Berkley Memorial Cemetery]

Rainbow, Louis 1855-1933 (on same tombstone with Phoebe Leah Rainbow; death certificate stated he was born in Maryland, worked as a well digger until December 1932 and died on August 2, 1933, age 78, at Rocks, at which time his wife was Clara Rainbow; informant was Mary Wilson, of Rocks, who stated Louis' father was Iza Rainbow, born in Maryland, but did not know Louis' mother's name; Kurtz Funeral Home Records stated the same) [Chestnut Grove A. M. E. Church Cemetery, formerly LaGrange Cemetery at Rocks]

Rainbow, Maria, mother of John Johnson, died February 6, 1880, age 62 [West Liberty Church Cemetery]

Rainbow, Phoebe Leah 1861-1958 (on same tombstone with Louis Rainbow) [Chestnut Grove A. M. E. Church Cemetery, formerly LaGrange Cemetery at Rocks]

Raisin, Annie April 15, 1882 – November 16, 1950 (no tombstone; death certificate stated she was born in Harford Co., daughter of William Gilbert and Martha Scott; she worked as a domestic, died a widow in Abingdon and buried in "Magnolia Baptist Cemetery" in Magnolia; informant was W. O. Raisin, of Abingdon) [Foster's Hill Cemetery]

Raisin, Annie April 15, 1882 – November 16, 1950 (no tombstone; death certificate stated she was the daughter of William Gilbert and Martha Scott, worked as a domestic, died a widow in and buried in Magnolia Baptist Cemetery; informant was W. O. Raisin, of Abingdon) [Community Baptist Church Cemetery]

Raisin, Raymond September 23, 1893 – June 2, 1952 [Foster's Hill Cemetery]

Raisin, William Edward stillborn on July 20, 1943 (no tombstone; death certificate stated he was the son of William O. Raisin and Gladys Warfield, all born in Maryland, and they lived in Abingdon; he was buried in "Magnolia Cemetery, Magnolia" and informant was his father) [Foster's Hill Cemetery]

Ramsay, Elizabeth A., wife of George, died July 13, 1890, age 27 years, 9 months (copied in 1987, but not found in 2018) [Gravel Hill Cemetery]

Ramsay, Florence died October 28, 1918, age 56 (no tombstone; death certificate stated she was the single daughter of George Snowden and Mary Cook, yet her last name was Ramsay; informant was Mary Snowden, of Havre de Grace) [St. James United Cemetery]

Ramsay, Lloyd A. October 10, 1858 – on or about May 18, 1924 (no tombstone; death certificate stated he was found dead in bed 4 or 5 days after death and was buried on May 24, 1924) [St. James United Cemetery]

Ramsay, William died December 6, 1918, age about 38 (no tombstone; death certificate stated he was the unmarried son of William Ramsay and Mary Giles; informant was Lloyd Ramsay) [St. James United Cemetery]

Ramsey, Robert, "Brother" 1851-1929 (tombstone; death certificate stated Robert L. Ramsey was born on March 3, 1851 and accidentally burned to death on December 4, 1929) [St. James United Cemetery]

Ramsey, Samuel died June 29, 1912, age unknown (no tombstone; death certificate stated he was born in Maryland, parents unknown, worked as a farmer, died of old age and was a widower who lived at Havre de Grace RFD #1; informant's name was missing from the death certificate) [Gravel Hill Cemetery]

Randolph, Hazel W. April 30, 1918 – December 28, 1918 (no tombstone; death certificate stated she was the daughter of William Randolph and Bertha Christy, all born in Maryland) [Union U. M. Church Cemetery]

Randolph, Richard D. 1917-1946 ("At Rest") [Mt. Calvary U. A. M. E. Church Cemetery]

Ray, George D. died 9 Jul 1901, age 14 years, 10 months, 21 days (no tombstone; death certificate stated he was the son of Charles Ray and Sarah E. Williamson, all born in Maryland; he died at home at Kalmia and the informant was his mother Sarah E. Ray; on the back of the certificate was written "Clarks Chapel") [Clark's U. M. Church Cemetery]

Ray, Sarah E. February 5, 1859 – January 16, 1945 (no tombstone; death certificate stated she was the daughter of Henry Williamson and Lucy Tasker, all born in Maryland; Sarah married Charles Ray and died a widow at Gibson; informant was Matilda Hemore, of Bel Air) [Clark's U. M. Church Cemetery]

Reasin, John N. July – (blank), 1877 – January 5, 1920 (no tombstone; death certificate stated he was the son of Peise(?) Reasin and Hester Bassie, all born in Maryland; he was married, worked as a laborer and died at Van Bibber; informant was Annie Reason, of Van Bibber) [Foster's Hill Cemetery]

Reason, Hester April ? *(sic)*, 1840 – January 13, 1919 (no tombstone; death certificate stated she was the daughter of Jerry Bessex, both born in Maryland, but her mother's name was not known to informant John Reason, of Van Bibber; she lived and died a widow at Van Bibber) [Foster's Hill Cemetery]

Redd, Peggy Ann June 4, 1937 – July 8, 2011 (inscribed "See you later alligator") [John Wesley U. M. E. Church Cemetery in Abingdon]

Redd, Samuel B. Sr. December 12, 1926 – April 28, 1998 (tombstone inscribed "We Must Accept Life On Life's Terms" and a military marker with these same dates stated Samuel Bernard Redd, Sr., U.S. Army, World War II) [John Wesley U. M. E. Church Cemetery in Abingdon]

Redd, Samuel Bernard Jr. died 1996, age 40 (no tombstone; James Dorsey Card File, African American Obituaries, maintained at the Historical Society of Harford County, has a card with obituary and Army photo from an unidentified newspaper on March 6, 1996 stating he died Friday at Johns Hopkins Hospital; he was born in Havre de Grace, the son of Samuel Bernard Redd, Sr., of Edgewood, and Peggy Ann Thomas Redd, of Abingdon, and he worked as a railroad lineman; he was survived by his parents, a brother, and three sisters) [John Wesley U. M. E. Church Cemetery in Abingdon]

Reed, Andrew January 1, 1844 – March 5, 1915 (no tombstone; death certificate stated he was born in Harford Co., died a widower and was the son of John Reed, born in Perryman, but his mother was not known to informant William Williams, of Perryman) [Union U. M. Church Cemetery]

Reed, Annie M. died December 12, 1915, age about 61 (no tombstone; death certificate stated she was born near Perryman, died a widow and was the daughter of Edward Gibson, also born in Harford Co., but her mother was not known to informant Edward Reed, of Perryman) [Union U. M. Church Cemetery]

Reed, Daniel E. August 16, 1882 – April 6, 1939 (no tombstone; death certificate stated he was the son of Isaac H. Reed and Annie Gibson) [Union U. M. Church Cemetery]

Reed, Eliza A. 1869 – 19___ (death date blank; inscribed "At Rest") [Union U. M. Church Cemetery]

Reed, Ida M. October 3, 1888 – May 5, 1912 (no tombstone; death certificate stated she was married and the daughter of James E. Christy and Lizzie Timbers, all born in Harford Co.) [Union U. M. Church Cemetery]

Reed, Isaac H. July 1, 1848 – July 6, 1912 (no tombstone; death certificate stated he was the married son of

William Reed, both born in Harford Co.; mother unknown to the undertaker) [Union U. M. Church Cemetery]

Reed, Juanita 1925-2011 (small metal funeral home marker) [Union U. M. Church Cemetery]

Reed, Kaleb died April 7, 1922, age 63 (no tombstone; death certificate stated he was born in Maryland and a widower, but his parents were unknown to informant Isaac Brown) [Union U. M. Church Cemetery]

Reed, Lillie Eliza Jane died February 25, 1904, age 21 years, 2 months & 23 days (inscribed "Nearer my God to Thee;" death certificate stated Lilly E. J. Reed died at Hightimber on February 25, 1904, age 24; she was single, did general house work, was the daughter of Isaac H. Reed and Milcah Gibson, and they all were born in Harford County; informant was George Ringgold, a non-relative) [Old Union Chapel M. E. Church Cemetery]

Reed, M. E. Brown 1886-1924 (on same tombstone with E. O. Brown and C. W. E. Brown) [Union U. M. Church Cemetery]

Reed, Morgan stillborn on September 4, 1923 (no tombstone; death certificate stated he was born in Harford Co., the son of Morgan Reed and Thresea Pratt, both born in Maryland; informant was his father, of Aberdeen RFD) [Mt. Calvary U. A. M. E. Church Cemetery]

Reese, Jesse B. Jr. January 18, 1913 – November 22, 1976, SFC, U.S. Army, World War II, Korea, Vietnam (on same tombstone with Louise W. Reese) [St. James United Cemetery]

Reese, Louise W. 1930-   (on same tombstone with Jesse B. Reese Jr.) [St. James United Cemetery]

Reeves, Callie M., wife of Edward E. Reeves, 1888-1942 (on same tombstone with Edward E. Reeves; the obituary of her son Warren Z. Reeves in 2014 mentioned she was a founding member of Clark's U. M. Church) [Clark's U. M. Church Cemetery]

Reeves, Chauncey A. December 29, 1945 – October 23, 1988 (tombstone; obituary in *The Aegis* on October 27, 1988 stated Chauncey Alonza Reeves, age 42, of Bel Air, died at Harford Memorial Hospital in Havre de Grace and was a cook and member of Clark's Chapel; he was survived by his mother Edna R. Murray and grandmother Helen Rice, among others) [Clark's U. M. Church Cemetery]

Reeves, Chauncey R. died February 25, 1984, age 70 (no tombstone; obituary in *The Aegis* in 1984 stated he was born in Richmond, VA, the son of Edward and Callie Reeves, lived in Harford Co. over 30 years, married (wife not named) and died at Harford Memorial Hospital in Havre de Grace; among his survivors was a son Chauncey A. Reeves who is listed above; James Dorsey Card File, African American Obituaries, maintained at the Historical Society of Harford County, has a card with an obituary abstraction from an unidentified newspaper stating Chauncey Rudolph Reeves was born on September 18, 1913) [Clark's U. M. Church Cemetery]

Reeves, Edward E. "Father" 1878-1928 (on same tombstone with Callie M. Reeves; the obituary of his son Warren Z. Reeves in 2014 mentioned that Edward was a founding member of Clark's U. M. Church) [Clark's U. M. Church Cemetery]

Reeves, Martha V. 1922-2010 (on same tombstone with Warren Z. Reeves; brief obituary in *The Aegis* on August 18, 2010 stated she died August 14, 2010, age 88, at home in Bel Air) [Clark's U. M. Church Cemetery]

Reeves, May stillborn on November 12, 1924 (no tombstone; death certificate stated she was born in Harford Co., the daughter of E. E. Reeves, born in North Carolina, and Callie Choate, born in Virginia; he died at home in Darlington; informant was her father) [Berkley Memorial Cemetery]

Reeves, Mildred W., "Mother" January 5, 1916 – July 16, 1973 (tombstone; obituary in *The Aegis* stated Mildred Wilson Reeves, daughter of John J. Wilson, Sr. and the late Annabell Wilson, lived at 716 E. 43rd Street in Baltimore, died at St. Joseph's Hospital in Baltimore and was survived by her father, 2 daughters, 3 brothers, 3 sisters and 8 grandchildren; her husband was not named) [Berkley Memorial Cemetery]

Reeves, Paul W. June 13, 1947 – March 1, 1980, Cpl., U. S. Marine Corps, Vietnam (tombstone; obituary in *The Aegis* on March 4, 1980 stated W. Paul Reeves, age 32, of Whiteford, died in an automobile accident in Kingsville; born in Harford County, he was the son of Mr. & Mrs. Z. Warren Reeves and received the Purple Heart with two clusters while serving in the U. S. Marines; he was single and survived by his parents, 3 siblings and a maternal grandmother Martha Brodie, of Newark, NJ) [Clark's U. M. Church Cemetery]

Reeves, Warren Z. 1922-2014 (on same tombstone with Martha V. Reeves; obituary in *The Aegis* stated Z. Warren Reeves, of Bel Air, died on August 20, 2014 at Gilchrist Hospice in Towson; he was born in Hillsville, VA, the son of Edward E. Reeves and Callie Choate, and was the husband of the late Martha Virginia Reeves; he was also a veteran of World War II; the 1973 obituary of his sister Verna Jane Smothers indicated the "Z" stood for "Zelmar") [Clark's U. M. Church Cemetery]

Reid, Beulah October 8, 1907 – September 16, 1933 (no tombstone; death certificate stated she was born in Aberdeen, the daughter of Alonzo Cotton, of Salisbury, MD, and Estelle Jones, of Havre de Grace; she married Edward Reid, lived in Perryman and died in Havre de Grace Hospital from severe burns while canning; informant was her husband) [Green Spring U. M. Church Cemetery]

Reid, Essa Pratt 1893-1958 (copied in 1987, not found in 2018) [Mt. Calvary U. A. M. E. Church Cemetery]

Reid, Estelle Christy – see Estelle Christy Reid Schroder [Berkley Memorial Cemetery]

Reid, Matthews E. September 5, 1920 – February 3, 1991, PFC, U.S. Army, WW II [Cedars Chapel Cemetery]

Reid, Maydellia E. Reid, "Beloved Sister" 1923-1975 [St. James United Cemetery]

Reid, Morgan 1893-1958 (copied in 1987, not found in 2018) [Mt. Calvary U. A. M. E. Church Cemetery]

Reid, Sadie A., "Our Beloved Mom" May 10, 1922 – November 8, 1995 (inscribed "Rest in Peace") [Cedars Chapel Cemetery]

Reid, Troy E. 1971-2002 (inscribed "O.K. Bye Bye") [Community Baptist Church Cemetery]

Reliford, Garnie (owner of a lot in section 14 some time after 1951) [Mt. Calvary U. A. M. E. Church Cemetery]

Reliford, Garnie Sr. (owner of a lot in section 14 some time after 1951) [Mt. Calvary U. A. M. E. Church Cemetery]

Reliford, Marguerite Carol October 28, 1934 – June 16, 1991 (buried in section 14) [Mt. Calvary U. A. M. E. Church Cemetery]

Repass, Willie 1920-1983 (no tombstone; James Dorsey Card File, African American Obituaries, maintained at the Historical Society of Harford County, has a card with an obituary abstraction stating funeral services were conducted at Clark's U. M. Church and he was survived by the family of his daughter Mrs. Shirley Smothers) [Clark's U. M. Church Cemetery]

Revell, Albert H. 1914-1925 (on same tombstone with Alice R., Eliza J. and James H. Revell inscribed "With Saints Enthroned On High") [Tabernacle Mount Zion U. M. Church Cemetery]

Revell, Alice E. 1917-1941 (on same tombstone with Albert H., Eliza J. and James H. Revell inscribed "With Saints Enthroned On High") [Tabernacle Mount Zion U. M. Church Cemetery]

Revell, Eliza J. 1879-1941 (on same tombstone with Alice R., Albert H. and James H. Revell inscribed "With Saints Enthroned On High") [Tabernacle Mount Zion U. M. Church Cemetery]

Revell, James H. 1866-1922 (on same tombstone with Alice R., Albert H. and Eliza J. Revell inscribed "With Saints Enthroned On High") [Tabernacle Mount Zion U. M. Church Cemetery]

Rex, Marjorie T. 1927-1991 (on same tombstone with Sterling L. Rex) [Mt. Calvary U. A. M. E. Church Cemetery]

Rex, Sterling L. 1931-1993 (on same tombstone with Marjorie T. Rex) [Mt. Calvary U. A. M. E. Church Cemetery]

Rice, Agnes V. February 22, 1897 – June 29, 1958 (on same tombstone with Charles L. Rice) [Union U. M. Church Cemetery]

Rice, Albert McKinley March 28, 1900 – June 20, 1942 (no tombstone; Kurtz Funeral Home Record Book 1937-1943, p. 232, stated he was the son of William Rice and Laura Sands, all born at Rocks; he married, worked as a laborer, divorced and died at Crownsville State Hospital) [Chestnut Grove A. M. E. Church

Cemetery, formerly LaGrange Cemetery at Rocks]

Rice, Alexander died November 18, 1894, age 67 (no tombstone; death notice in *The Aegis* on November 23, 1894 stated "Alick" died at his home near Rocks of Deer Creek and had been drawing a pension for his Civil War service; burial place not stated, but probably Chestnut Grove) [Chestnut Grove A. M. E. Church Cemetery, formerly LaGrange Cemetery at Rocks]

Rice, Alice February 22, 1852 – May 1, 1928 (no tombstone; death certificate stated she was a widow and the daughter of Samuel Chancey and Rachael Spencer; they were all born in Maryland and were residents of Bel Air; informant was Hannah Toney, of Bel Air) [Hendon Hill Cemetery]

Rice, Alice L. 1931-1992 (metal funeral home marker; obituary and photo in *The Aegis* on September 9, 1992 stated Alice Louise Rice, of Wichita Falls, TX, formerly of Harford County, the daughter of Charles Rice Sr. and Mabel Lewis Akins, married William Henry Rice (who predeceased her) and died on September 2, 1992 at Zale-Lipshy University Hospital in Dallas, survived by 2 sons, 2 daughters, 2 brothers, 2 sisters, 7 grandchildren, and 2 great-grandchildren) [Chestnut Grove A. M. E. Church Cemetery, formerly LaGrange Cemetery at Rocks]

Rice, Annie E. March 16, 1848 – September 13, 1920 (no tombstone; death certificate stated she was the daughter of Isaac Preston and Elizabeth Pinkney, all born in Maryland; she died a widow in Pylesville; informant was Ida Rice, of Pylesville) [Chestnut Grove A. M. E. Church Cemetery, formerly LaGrange Cemetery at Rocks]

Rice, Arthur M. December 5, 1884 – July 17, 1946 [Union U. M. Church Cemetery]

Rice, Charles L. May 22, 1890 – November 6, 1952 (on same tombstone with Agnes V. Rice) [Union U. M. Church Cemetery]

Rice, Charlie Mae May 6, 1929 – November 8, 2002 ("In Loving Memory") [Berkley Memorial Cemetery]

Rice, Charlotte died January 1, 1903, age 47 (no tombstone; death certificate stated she was the daughter of Bill Rice and Sallie McComas, and the wife of Edward Rice; she was born in Harford County, died at Michaelsville and was survived by her husband and six children; place of burial was not indicated, but probably in Old Union Chapel Cemetery at Michaelsville; possibly reinterred later in Union Chapel Cemetery near Aberdeen) [Union U. M. Church Cemetery]

Rice, Creola W. April 16, 1898 – February 21, 2003 (on same tombstone with husband Stillie C. Rice, and William C. Rice and his wife Edith C. Rice; obituary and photo in *The Aegis* on February 26, 2003 stated Rev. Creola Walton Rice was born in Harford Co., the daughter of William U. Walton and Sarah Rice, and served as assistant pastor and trustee of St. James United Methodist Church, as pastor of the Harford Charge for eight years and president of the Local Preachers Association; she married Stillie C.Rice and lived and died in Jarrettsville, survived by son William C. Rice, 2 grandchildren, 3 great-grandchildren, 2 godchildren, and five generations of nieces and nephews; *The Aegis* on May 27, 1998 reported she was the first woman to retire from the Baltimore-Washington Conference in 1978) [William C. Rice Memorial Cemetery, St. James U. M. Church]

Rice, Douglas died September 4, 1904, age 11 years (no tombstone; death certificate stated he was born in Harford Co. and died at Clermont Mills, but his parents' names were not given) [Chestnut Grove A. M. E. Church Cemetery, formerly LaGrange Cemetery at Rocks]

Rice, Earnest J. 1903-1974 (on the same tombstone with wife Edith M. Rice which is engulfed in a large bush near the middle of the cemetery; obituary in *The Aegis* on November 7, 1974, reported Earnest Jerome Rice was the husband of Edith M. Rice, of Street, MD, and died at home on October 31, 1974, age 71) [Chestnut Grove A. M. E. Church Cemetery, formerly LaGrange Cemetery at Rocks]

Rice, Edith C. July 25, 1918 – January 31, 1994 (on same tombstone with husband William C. Rice, and Stillie C. Rice and his wife Creola W. Rice; James Dorsey Card File, African American Obituaries, maintained at the Historical Society of Harford County, has a card with obituary and photo from an unidentified newspaper dated February 9, 1994 stating Edith Cecelia Greene Rice was born in Rocks, the daughter of David Greene and Ida Harris and she worked for Kefauver Lumber Co. and Scott's Hardware, now Frank's; she lived in Jarrettsville and died at Johns Hopkins Hospital, survived by her husband William C. Rice, a sister and two brothers) [William C. Rice Memorial Cemetery, St. James U. M. Church]

Rice, Edith M. 1913 – death date not inscribed (on the same tombstone with husband Earnest J. Rice; obituary in *The Aegis* on October 13, 2000 stated Edith Muriel Rice, of Street, MD, was born on December 6, 1913 in Mineral, VA, relocated with her family to Oxford, PA, married Earnest Jerome Rice, and died at the Gilchrist Center in Baltimore on October 8, 2000) [Chestnut Grove A. M. E. Church Cemetery, formerly LaGrange Cemetery at Rocks]

Rice, Emerson W. July 10, 1900 – August 15, 1987 (on same tombstone with wife Mary L. Rice and sister Gladys M. Rice; obituary in *The Aegis* on August 20, 1987 stated he was of Philadelphia, formerly of Forest Hill, and died at Presbyterian Hospital, Philadelphia; he was husband of the late Mary Greene Rice, brother of Gladys Rice, of Jarrettsville, and survived by a sister, 4 grandchildren, 7 sisters-in-law, 2 brothers-in-law, and many nieces and nephews) [Chestnut Grove A. M. E. Church Cemetery, formerly LaGrange Cemetery at Rocks]

Rice, Francis died 1889 (copied in 1987 and 2002, but not found in 2018) [Gravel Hill Cemetery]

Rice, George died November 29, 1912, age about 80 (no tombstone; death certificate stated he worked as a laborer and died a widower at Castleton; his place of birth and the names of his parents were not known to informant William Rice, of Castleton) [Berkley Memorial Cemetery]

Rice, George Anna 1869-1926 (tombstone; death certificate stated Georgianna Rice was born on February 21, 1867 and died a widow on August 16, 1926; she was the daughter of Charles Tinson, but her mother was unknown to informant Andrew Rice, of Perryman) [Union U. M. Church Cemetery]

Rice, Gladys M. September 13, 1906 – August 9, 1988 (on same tombstone with brother Emerson W. Rice and wife Mary L. Rice; obituary in *The Aegis* on August 11, 1988 stated she was the daughter of William and Laura Rice, lived at Jarrettsville and died at Harford Memorial Hospital, survived by two sisters-in-law and nieces and nephews) [Chestnut Grove A. M. E. Church Cemetery, formerly LaGrange Cemetery at Rocks]

Rice, Harriet J. February 15, 1863 – June 15, 1931 (no tombstone; death certificate stated she was the daughter of Steven Stansbury and Anne W. Iser, and she died a widow) [Union U. M. Church Cemetery]

Rice, Harry V. May 27, 1893 – April 4, 1968 [Union U. M. Church Cemetery]

Rice, Hattie Fields February 27, 1889 – July 31, 1950 (no tombstone; death certificate stated she was born in Lynchburg, VA, married, and lived at Rocks for 39 years; her parents were not known to informant John T. Rice, of Rocks) [Chestnut Grove A. M. E. Church Cemetery, formerly LaGrange Cemetery at Rocks]

Rice, Hattie V. 1852-1931 [Union U. M. Church Cemetery]

Rice, Helen E. 1910-2000 (tombstone inscribed with the year of birth only; obituary in *The Aegis* on April 19, 2000 stated Helen Elizabeth Rice, of Bel Air, died on April 15, 2000, age 90, at Harford Memorial Hospital in Havre de Grace; she was born in Bel Air, the daughter of Augustus Hill and Laura Virginia Wilson, and was the widow of Vallee Rice; she was survived by 1 son, 2 daughters, 10 grandchildren, 20 great-grandchildren, 5 great-great-grandchildren, and she was predeceased by 1 son, 1 daughter, 3 brothers, and 1 sister) [Clark's U. M. Church Cemetery]

Rice, Hester September 20, 1860 – September 24, 1912 (no tombstone; death certificate stated she was the daughter of Henry Rice and ----, but mother unknown to informant Henry Rice) [St. James United Cemetery]

Rice, James Archer 1921-1922 (tombstone; death certificate stated he was born December 22, 1921, the son of Andrew A. Rice and Viola Johnson, all born in Maryland, and he died March 8, 1922) [Union U. M. Church Cemetery]

Rice, James Frank March 1, 1889 – March 17, 1928, Maryland, Pvt., Co. A, 371 Inf., World War I (tombstone; death certificate mistakenly stated J. Frank Rice was born March 1, 1888; military record stated James Frank Rice was born March 1, 1889; he was divorced at the time of his death in Bel Air; his parents were Enos Rice and Alice A. Chancey; all born in Maryland; informant was Hannah Toney, of Bel Air) [Hendon Hill Cemetery]

Rice, James Howard March 17, 1895 – October 1, 1972 [Union U. M. Church Cemetery]

Rice, Jane R. March 17, 1855 – November 25, 1906 (no tombstone; death certificate stated she was born in Maryland, married Moses Rice and died at Rocks; her parents were Benjamin and Jane Willis, both born in

Maryland; informant was her son Preston Rice) [Chestnut Grove A. M. E. Church Cemetery, formerly LaGrange Cemetery at Rocks]

Rice, John Ernest died April 29, 1903, age 22 (no tombstone; death certificate stated he was single, worked as a laborer and died at Rocks; his parents were George Rice and Annie Simms, all born in Harford Co.; informant was John Ramsay) [Chestnut Grove A. M. E. Church Cemetery, formerly LaGrange Cemetery at Rocks]

Rice, John Henry "Tony" died July 19, 1912, age about 90 (no tombstone; death certificate stated he was married, worked as a laborer and died at home in Darlington; his place of birth and the names of his parents were not known to informant Nathan Moore; death notice in *The Aegis* on July 26, 1912 stated "Tony Rice" was formerly a slave belonging to Abraham Streett, of Rocks, and was a familiar figure on the streets of Darlington; his extract age was not known, but he was supposed to be about 90 years old) [Berkley Memorial Cemetery]

Rice, John Henry died August 25, 1936, age about 85 (no tombstone; death certificate stated he died a widower in Havre de Grace, but his parents were unknown to informant John Presbury) [Union U. M. Church Cemetery]

Rice, John Paca May 20, 1869 – October 21, 1912 (no tombstone; death certificate stated he was single and the son of John Paca Rice and Mary Stansbury, all born in Maryland) [Union U. M. Church Cemetery]

Rice, Josie L. died May 6, 1905, age 16 years (no tombstone; death certificate stated she was born at Pylesville, daughter of George Rice, born at Rocks, and Annie Barton, born in Harford Co.; informant was James Hall, who was not related) [Chestnut Grove A. M. E. Church Cemetery, formerly LaGrange Cemetery at Rocks]

Rice, Laura Louisa August 2, 1903 – October 7, 1905 (no tombstone; death certificate stated she was born at Rocks and died of extensive burns at home; she was the daughter of William Rice, born at Cooptown, and Laura Sands, born at Clermont Mills; informant was her father) [Chestnut Grove A. M. E. Church Cemetery, formerly LaGrange Cemetery at Rocks]

Rice, Laura R. 1872-1951 (on the same tombstone with William E. Rice; obituary in *The Aegis* on November 30, 1951 stated Laura Rebecca Rice, of Rocks, died on November 21, 1951, leaving seven sons, two daughters, several grandchildren and several great grandchildren) [Chestnut Grove A. M. E. Church Cemetery, formerly LaGrange Cemetery at Rocks]

Rice, Lloyd April 14, 1869 – May 2, 1929 (no tombstone; death certificate stated he was the married son of Lloyd Rice and Cassie Rice; informant was Cassie Monk, of Perryman) [Union U. M. Church Cemetery]

Rice, Maria died February 16, 1912, age 70 (no tombstone; death certificate stated she was born in Maryland and died a widow at Cherry Hill; her parents were not known to informant James Maxfield, of Street, MD) [Chestnut Grove A. M. E. Church Cemetery, formerly LaGrange Cemetery at Rocks]

Rice, Mary Greene 1911-1986 (tombstone; obituary in *The Aegis* on June 26, 1986 stated Mary Elizabeth (Greene) Rice, of Philadelphia, formerly of Forest Hill, died at Misericordia Hospital in Philadelphia on May 25, 1986, age 75, and was the wife of Emerson Rice) [Chestnut Grove A. M. E. Church Cemetery, formerly LaGrange Cemetery at Rocks]

Rice, Mary L. February 8, 1911 – May 25, 1986 (on same tombstone with husband Emerson W. Rice and his sister Gladys M. Rice) [Chestnut Grove A. M. E. Church Cemetery, formerly LaGrange Cemetery at Rocks]

Rice, Mary V. died May 5, 1906, age 49 (no tombstone; death certificate stated she was born in Maryland, married J. R. Rice and lived at Street; her parents were Ned Nye and Sarah Gover, born in Maryland; the place of burial was not indicated, but it was most likely at Chestnut Grove; informant was her husband) [Chestnut Grove A. M. E. Church Cemetery, formerly LaGrange Cemetery at Rocks]

Rice, Moses June 11, 1834 – January 11, 1907 (no tombstone; death certificate stated he was born in Maryland, married Jane ----, worked as a farmer, lived at Chrome Hill, and died a widower; his father was William Rice, born in Madagascar O. *(sic)* and his mother was not known to the informant, his daughter Sarah Walton, but his place of burial was not stated [probably Chestnut Grove A. M. E. Church Cemetery, formerly LaGrange Cemetery at Rocks]

Rice, Paul Kinsey September 9, 1900 – July 16, 1968 (no tombstone; Harkins Funeral Home Records stated he was born in Pylesville, the son of Rigley Rice and Mary Wye; he was single, worked as a janitor and died at the

Calvert Nursing Home in Rising Sun, MD; informant was Herbert Walton, a friend, of Street, MD) [Chestnut Grove A. M. E. Church Cemetery, formerly LaGrange Cemetery at Rocks]

Rice, Rachael died September 16, 1919, age about 50 (no tombstone; death certificate stated she was the daughter of Nathan Ward, both born in Maryland, but her mother's name and place of birth were not known to informant Henry Moore, of Havre de Grace; she died a widow in the Havre de Grace Hospital) [Berkley Memorial Cemetery]

Rice, Ralph Leroy Sr. October 2, 1935 – May 17, 1971 [Cedars Chapel Cemetery]

Rice, Stewart A. July 18, 1927 – January 17, 2002, U.S. Army (tombstone; obituary in *The Aegis* on January 30, 2002 stated he was born in Delta, PA, son of Alice B. Rice, of Darlington, and was the husband of Charley Mae Rice; he served in the Army from 1952 to 1954 and retired from Aberdeen Proving Ground after 28 years service in the property disposal section; he was survived by his wife and mother, two sons, a daughter, a brother, a stepson, a foster daughter, several grandchildren, great-grandchildren, nieces, nephews and a host of family and friends) [Berkley Memorial Cemetery]

Rice, Stillie C. May 26, 1880 – March 23, 1962 (on same tombstone with wife Creola W. Rice, and William C. Rice and his wife Edith C. Rice) [William C. Rice Memorial Cemetery, St. James U. M. Church]

Rice, Vallee 1887-1983 [Clark's U. M. Church Cemetery]

Rice, Valley Coleman August 26, 1928 – September 27, 1977, 1st Lt., U. S. Army, World War II (tombstone inscription, but his obituary in *The Aegis* stated he died October 28, 1977 and lived in Newark, DE; he taught at Bancroft Middle School for 24 years, died at a Veterans Hospital, and was the husband of Lillian Johnson Rice) [Clark's U. M. Church Cemetery]

Rice, Viola died May 5, 1973, age not given (no tombstone; obituary in *The Aegis* stated she was the daughter of the late William and Sarah Johnson, and wife of the late Andrew Rice; she lived and died at 508 Revolution Street in Havre de Grace and was survived by three sons, six grandchildren, three great-grandchildren, and two nephews) [Union U. M. Church Cemetery]

Rice, W. Edward died February 12, 1918, age about 66 (no tombstone; death certificate stated he was the married son of John P. Rice and Emily Lewis, all born in Maryland; informant was Mrs. W. E. Rice, of Havre de Grace) [Union U. M. Church Cemetery]

Rice, Walter L. September 9, 1948 – April 7, 2005, PV2, U.S. Army, Vietnam (tombstone; obituary in *The Aegis* on April 13, 2005 stated Walter Linwood Rice, of Delta, PA, died at Upper Chesapeake Medical Center in Bel Air; he was born in Rocks area of Street, the son of Ernest Jerome Rice and Edith Jackson; he was a carpenter and enjoyed raising and caring for horses; he was survived by 2 brothers, 2 sisters, and several nephews and nieces) [Chestnut Grove A. M. E. Church Cemetery, formerly LaGrange Cemetery at Rocks]

Rice, William B. July 31, 1886 – February 8, 1911 (inscribed "Gone But Not Forgotten;" death certificate stated William Rice was the son of Levin Rice, both born in Perryman, but his mother was not known to informant Dr. R. H. Johnson, of 415 W. Biddle St., Baltimore) [Union U. M. Church Cemetery]

Rice, William C. May 21, 1915 – February 26, 2008 (on same tombstone with wife Edith C., and Stillie C. and Creola W. Rice; cemetery named in his honor) [William C. Rice Memorial Cemetery, St. James U. M. Church]

Rice, William E. 1867-1946 (on the same tombstone with Laura R. Rice; death certificate stated William Emerson Rice was born February 22, 1867 at Cooptown, married Laura ----, worked as a farmer and died near Rocks; his parents were William Rice and Maria Bell, both born in Harford Co.; informant was Gladys Rice, of Rocks; Kurtz Funeral Home Record Book 1944-1949, p. 102, stated his mother was Maria Hill; informant was his son Stillie Rice) [Chestnut Grove A. M. E. Church Cemetery, formerly LaGrange Cemetery at Rocks]

Rich, Elma April 6, 1925 – September 18, 1925 (no tombstone; death certificate stated she was the daughter of Howard Rich and Bertha Johnson, all born in Maryland; she died at Bush; informant was Bertha Johnson, of 1318 Mount Street, Baltimore) [John Wesley U. M. E. Church Cemetery in Abingdon]

Richardson, Agnes W. July 17, 1889 – June 18, 1978 (on same tombstone with Fred F. Richardson) [Gravel Hill Cemetery]

Richardson, Alfred Raymond February 22, 1886 – June 2, 1956 (no tombstone; Pennington Funeral Home records stated he was born in Havre de Grace, the son of James Richardson and Luvenia Richardson, and was divorced at the time of his death in Henryton State Hospital in Carroll Co., MD; informant was Alfred R. Richardson and the funeral bill was rendered to Mrs Olivia Barrett in Bel Air [St. James United Cemetery]

Richardson, Amy died July 6, 1959, age 71 (no tombstone; obituary in *The Democratic Ledger* on July 16, 1959 stated she was the widow of Howard Robinson and she died at Harford Memorial Hospital, survived by three sons) [Berkley Memorial Cemetery]

Richardson, Bernice E. Scott 1937-1997 [St. James United Cemetery]

Richardson, Charles Augustus died October 9, 1937, age about 59 (no tombstone; death certificate stated he was the son of Charles Richardson, mother was unknown, and the husband of Annie M. Richardson) [Union U. M. Church Cemetery]

Richardson, Dorothy M. February 2, 1923 – January 13, 2004 (tombstone inscription; funeral notice in *The Aegis* on January 16, 2004 stated she was born at Turkey Point and died at St. Joseph Hospital in Towson; obituary and photo in *The Aegis* on January 21, 2004 stated Dorothy Maria Richardson was the second youngest child of Henrietta and Collin S. Williams and she married Eugene Robinson on October 8, 1948; she was survived by her husband, a daughter, 3 sons, a sister, a sister-in-law, 4 brothers-in-law, 5 grandchildren, 4 great-grandchildren) [St. James United Cemetery]

Richardson, Edna November 27, 1899 – November 26, 1915 (no tombstone; death certificate stated she was the daughter of Jack Richardson, of Virginia, and Emma Cole, of Havre de Grace) [St. James United Cemetery]

Richardson, Ellen J., wife of Louis, died November 8, 1913, age 68 (tombstone inscription; death certificate stated she was born on November 19, 1854 and died on November 13, 1913) [St. James United Cemetery]

Richardson, Emma J. September 26, 1880 – May 1, 1945 (no tombstone; death certificate stated she was the daughter of George W. Richardson and Martha Tower; informant was Charles Raymond Cooper, of Havre de Grace) [St. James United Cemetery]

Richardson, Eva Virginia March 31, 1878 – November 10, 1929 (no tombstone; death certificate stated she was the married daughter of Lucy Parker, both born in West Virginia, but father unknown to informant John Richardson, of Havre de Grace) [St. James United Cemetery]

Richardson, Evelyn V. February 1, 1924 – March 4, 1994 (picture on same tombstone with Harold Richardson; obituary and photo in *The Aegis* on March 9, 1994 stated Evelyn Virginia Richardson was a native of Havre de Grace and the daughter of George A. Smith and Pearl Jones; she married Harold Richardson who died in 1986 and she was a Gold Star Mother; a son, George Allen Demby, was killed in Vietnam in 1968; she was also the mother of Alexander Demby who died in 1972; she lived in Edgewood, retired as a cook from Aberdeen Proving Ground and died at Francis Scott Key Medical Center in Baltimore, survived by six daughters, two brothers, 19 grandchildren and 17 great-grandchildren) [Asbury Cemetery]

Richardson, Frances died March 22, 1904, age 65 [St. James United Cemetery]

Richardson, Frances September 30, 1866 – February 28, 1945 (no tombstone; death certificate stated she was the daughter of Daniel Sheridan and Sarah ----, and the widow of Robert Richardson; informant was her son Clarence Richardson, of Havre de Grace) [St. James United Cemetery]

Richardson, Fred F. died October 6, 1974, age not given (no tombstone; obituary in *The Aegis* stated he was born in Havre de Grace, the son of the late John H. and Hanna Richardson, and husband of Agnes W. Richardson; he lived at 729 S. Union Ave. in Havre de Grace and retired as a warehouseman from Aberdeen Proving Ground; he died at Harford Memorial Hospital, survived by his wife, a son, a brother, a sister, 4 grandchildren and 4 great-grandchildren) [St. James United Cemetery]

Richardson, Fred F. October 21, 1897 – October 6, 1974 (on same tombstone with Agnes W. Richardson) [Gravel Hill Cemetery]

Richardson, George A. April 10, 1956 -   (death date below ground) [Mt. Zion U. M. Church Cemetery]

Richardson, George Washington April 5, 1865 – January 21, 1946 (no tombstone; death certificate stated he was the son of George Washington Richardson and Margaret Tower, and a retired railroad porter; informant was his wife Hattie Richardson, of Havre de Grace) [St. James United Cemetery]

Richardson, Hannah H. 1875-1949 (on same tombstone with John H. Richardson; death certificate stated she was born at Oakington on April 2, 1865, the daughter of Haggai *(sic)* Richardson, but her father was not known to informant John H. Richardson; she lived in Havre de Grace all her life and was married when she died on January 29, 1949 at 129 S. Union Ave.) [Gravel Hill Cemetery]

Richardson, Harold July 25, 1925 – March 18, 1986 (picture on same tombstone with Evelyn V. Richardson; obituary in *The Aegis* stated Harold Richardson, Jr. was born in Wayne Co., NC, the son of Harold Richardson, Sr. and Lina Ford, and was the husband of Evelyn Richardson; in early childhood he moved to Baltimore and served in the Navy during World War II; he was survived by his wife and mother, 8 daughters, 9 grandsons and 11 granddaughters) [Asbury Cemetery]

Richardson, Harriett Ann November 27, 1861 – August 19, 1946 (no tombstone; death certificate stated she was born in Churchville, the daughter of Henry Welsh and Mary Keetley, and widow of Lloyd Richardson; informant was Mrs. Rosa Green, of Havre de Grace) [St. James United Cemetery]

Richardson, Harriett E. died March 31, 1941, age about 56 (no tombstone; death certificate stated she was the daughter of Ned Leggar and Mary Allen, and the widow of John F. Richardson; she died at home in Havre de Grace; informant was Mrs. Olivia Barrett, of Bel Air) [St. James United Cemetery]

Richardson, Hattie E. 1864 – May 16, 1951 (no tombstone; Pennington Funeral Home records stated she was the widow of George W. Richardson; death certificate stated she died a widow in Havre de Grace; parents unknown to informant Alfred Richardson) [St. James United Cemetery]

Richardson, Hattie O. 1895-1980 (tombstone; obituary in *The Aegis* stated Hattie Oleiva Richardson was born in Harford County, daughter of Ephren and Eliza Stansbury, and widow of Ernest Richardson; she lived at 817 Juniata Street in Havre de Grace and died at Harford Memorial Hospital, survived by son Russell J. Richardson, daughter Barbara Mitchell, a granddaughter, and a sister Bertha Madden) [Union U. M. Church Cemetery]

Richardson, Henry died March 16, 1924, age about 70 (no tombstone; death certificate stated he was the son of Maria Brown, both born in Maryland, but his father was unknown to informant Miss Alverta Donahoo, of Aberdeen; he was single and was a day laborer near Aberdeen) [Gravel Hill Cemetery]

Richardson, Howard February 10, 1912 – March 30, 1992, U.S. Army, World War II (tombstone; obituary in *The Aegis* on April 8, 1992 stating Howard "Buddy" Richardson was born in Havre de Grace, the son of Howard and Amy Richardson, and prior to entering the Army in 1941 he was a cook at the old Lafayette Hotel in Perryville; after the war he was a mechanic with the Yellow Cab Co. in Philadelphia and soon returned to Havre de Grace to care for his mother; he joined the American Cyanamid Co. as a carpenter and also worked at St. John's Towers in Havre de Grace; he died at home and was survived by his wife Bernice Scott Mabrey Richardson whom he married in 1979, two stepsons, and a brother) [St. James United Cemetery]

Richardson, Howard February 28, 1889 – February 24, 1934 (no tombstone; death certificate stated he was the son of Robert Richardson and Frances Sherdon (Sheridan), all born in Havre de Grace; he married Amy ---- and died at home in Havre de Grace; informant was Mrs. Frances Richardson) [St. James United Cemetery]

Richardson, James died December 15, 1955, age about 70 (no tombstone; Pennington Funeral Home records state he was born in Havre de Grace, the son of Robert Richardson and Frances Sheridan; he died a widower; informant was Clarence Richardson [St. James United Cemetery]

Richardson, John F. February 4, 1875 – June 21, 1934 (no tombstone; death certificate stated he was the son of Lloyd Richardson and Elizabeth Bodser (Bowser), all born in Havre de Grace; he married Harriet ---- and died at home in Havre de Grace; informant was Mrs. John F. Richardson [St. James United Cemetery]

Richardson, John H. 1863-1957 (on same tombstone with Hannah H. Richardson; Pennington Funeral Home records stated he was born March 2, 1865 *(sic)* in Richmond, VA and died a widower on March 17, 1957, age about 92, at 729 S. Union Ave. in Havre de Grace where he had lived about 77 years; informant was Agnes Richardson, of 729 S. Union Avenue and the bill was rendered to Fred Richardson; burial at "Gravely Hill" near

Havre de Grace; informant Agnes Richardson did not know his parents' names) [Gravel Hill Cemetery]

Richardson, John S. died August 3, 1887, age about 58 (no tombstone; article in *The Aegis* on August 5, 1887 stated he was a well-known barber, grocer and mayoral candidate in Havre de Grace; he was found dead in Hoke's Run about 2 miles south of town, supposedly on he was on his way to a camp meeting at Oakington; an inquest stated he died from apoplexy and may have survived if he had not fallen into the stream; place of burial was not stated [probably Skinner Cemetery or possibly St. James United Cemetery]

Richardson, Johny (no dates when copied in 1987, but not found in 2018) [St. James United Cemetery]

Richardson, Katherine April 1, 1877 – September 16, 1912 (no tombstone; death certificate stated she was the married daughter of Daniel Holmes, but her mother was unknown to the informant John Richardson, of Havre de Grace) [St. James United Cemetery]

Richardson, Lewis E. April 18, 1901 – July 7, 1961 (on same tombstone with Virgie V. Richardson) [Berkley Memorial Cemetery]

Richardson, Lewis H. September 16, 1950 – June 7, 2004, Sgt., USAF, Vietnam [Berkley Memorial Cemetery]

Richardson, Lloyd N. December 31, 1856 – May 25, 1912 (no tombstone; death certificate stated he was the married son of Philip Richardson, both born in Harford Co., but his mother was unknown to informant G. T. Pennington, undertaker, of Havre de Grace) [St. James United Cemetery]

Richardson, Louis died January 16, 1914, age 67 (tombstone inscription, but death certificate stated "Lewis" died on January 17, 1914, age about 59) [St. James United Cemetery]

Richardson, Martha E., "Mother" 1839 – January 27, 1906, age 66 [St. James United Cemetery]

Richardson, Phebe died December 7, 1889, age 80 [Mt. Zion U. M. Church Cemetery]

Richardson, Robert H. June 2, 1862 – July 3, 1916 (no tombstone; death certificate stated he was the married son of George W. Richardson and Margaret Tower, both born in Kent Co., MD; he was born in Baltimore and died in Havre de Grace; informant was George Richardson) [St. James United Cemetery]

Richardson, Russell J. April 4, 1927 – January 31, 2004, PFC, U.S. Army (tombstone; obituary and photo in *The Aegis* stated he was born in Philadelphia, one of three children born to Ernestine Richardson and Hattie Christy, and served during and after World War II from 1945 to 1947 in France and Germany; he retired in 1984 after 31 years of federal service that included work as an air-conditioning equipment operator at Aberdeen Proving Ground; he was a devoted member of St. Matthew AUMP Church and a trustee and sexton of the United Methodist Men; he lived in Havre de Grace, died at Harford Memorial Hospital and was survived by a sister Barbara Mitchell, two nieces and two great-nieces) [Union U. M. Church Cemetery]

Richardson, Susie died March 31, 1912, age 36 (no tombstone; death certificate stated she was born in Havre de Grace, but her birth date and the names of her parents were unknown to the informant Charles Richardson, of Havre de Grace) [St. James United Cemetery]

Richardson, Virgie V. March 27, 1903 – September 27, 1986 (on same tombstone with Lewis E. Richardson) [Berkley Memorial Cemetery]

Richardson, William Edward January 22, 1911 – February 15, 1912 (no tombstone; death certificate he was the son of Jesse Richardson and Clara Giles, of Havre de Grace) [St. James United Cemetery]

Ricks, George H. 1894-1982, Pvt., U.S. Army, World War I (tombstone; "Mr. Ricks" owned a lot in section 41 some time after 1951) [Mt. Calvary U. A. M. E. Church Cemetery]

Ridgeley, Sarah E. 1883-1950 (tombstone; death certificate stated Sarah Ridgley was the daughter of William H. Faison and ----; she was born on May 20, 1880 and died on April 29, 1950) [St. James United Cemetery]

Ridgely, Carl S. March 13, 1919 – September 24, 2000 (on same tombstone with Lucie B. Ridgely) [Berkley Memorial Cemetery]

Ridgely, George Edward III "Eddie" February 8, 1969 – May 31, 1987 [Union U. M. Church Cemetery]

Ridgely, Gilbert May 18, 1911 – June 28, 1990, PFC, U.S. Army, World War II [Union U. M. Church Cemetery]

Ridgely, Lucie B. September 22, 1914 – August 4, 1969 (on same tombstone with Carl S. Ridgely) [Berkley Memorial Cemetery]

Ridgley, Audry June 20, 1907 – November 14, 1940 (no tombstone; death certificate stated he was born in Havre de Grace, the son of Noah Ridgley and Julia Collins, both born in Harford Co.; he married Elva Ridley *(sic)* and was a laborer who lived at 721 Linden Lane in Havre de Grace; informant was Mrs. Julia Ridgley who also lived at 721 Linden Lane) [Green Spring U. M. Church Cemetery]

Ridgley, Cassie October 19, 1905 – February 21, 1937 (no tombstone; death certificate stated she was the wife of George Ridgley and the daughter of James Warfield and Garrow Shepherd) [Union U. M. Church Cemetery]

Ridgley, Clarence I. February 25, 1908 – February 7, 1987 (on same tombstone with Daisy B. Ridgley and inscribed "married September 10, 1934") [Union U. M. Church Cemetery]

Ridgley, Daisy B. February 22, 1915 – October 23, 2002 (on same tombstone with Clarence I, Ridgley and inscribed "married September 10, 1934") [Union U. M. Church Cemetery]

Ridgley, Elva E. October 18, 1903 – January 8, 1990 [St. James United Cemetery]

Ridgley, George E. Jr. May 13, 1928 – December 10, 1993, Cpl., U.S. Army, Korea (tombstone; James Dorsey Card File, African American Obituaries, maintained at the Historical Society of Harford County, has a card with obituary from an unidentified newspaper dated December 15, 1993 stating George Edward Ridgley, Jr. was a native of Perryman, the son of the late George E. Ridgley, Sr. and Cassie Warfield; he served in Korea and was a member of the VFW, The American Legion, and Disabled American Veterans; he was a retired civilian employee at Aberdeen Proving Ground, lived in Forest Hill and died in Fallston General Hospital, survived by his wife of 40 years Idella Toliver Ridgley, four children, a brother, three sisters, eight grandchildren and four great-grandchildren) [Berkley Memorial Cemetery]

Ridgley, James H. December 13, 1936 – January 22, 1937 (no tombstone; death certificate stated he was the son of Virginia Ridgley and William Kenley) [Union U. M. Church Cemetery]

Ridgley, Julius Calvin died January 14, 1994, age 52 (no tombstone; James Dorsey Card File, African American Obituaries, maintained at the Historical Society of Harford County, has a card with obituary from an unidentified newspaper dated January 26, 1994 stating he was a native of Havre de Grace, the son of Albert S. Garland and Elva Ennis Ridgley; he worked in custodial services at Aberdeen Proving Ground for about 25 years and died at home in Aberdeen, survived by a son, 3 nephews, 4 nieces and 6 great-nephews and nieces) [St. James United Cemetery]

Ridgley, Mary R. September 10, 1858 – September 20, 1935 (no tombstone; death certificate stated she was the daughter of Charles Garrett, both born near Darlington, but her mother's name was not known to informant Emma Harris, of Havre de Grace; she was the widow of James Ridgley and had lived in Havre de Grace for the past 20 years) [Green Spring U. M. Church Cemetery]

Ridgley, Maud M. February 23, 1900 – June 18, 1901 [Green Spring U. M. Church Cemetery]

Ridgley, Noah June 15, 1879 – February 24, 1951 (no tombstone; death certificate stated he was born in Harford Co., the son of Charles Ridgley and Harriett ---- (blank); he was a laborer for Havre de Grace Street Department, married, and lived at 730 Otsego Street for about 50 years; informant was Mrs. Julia Ridgley who lived at the same address) [Green Spring U. M. Church Cemetery]

Ridgley, William October 23, 1938 – December 23, 1944 (no tombstone; death certificate stated he was the son of William F. Kenly and Dorothy V. Ridgley, and died in a house fire) [Union U. M. Church Cemetery]

Rigby, Charles and Martha 12 – 16 – 1854 (copied in 1987, but not found in 2018; the copyist noted the stone was leaning against the Hosanna Freedman's School and stated "I've heard the farmer moved them from his field.") [Berkley Memorial Cemetery]

Rigney, Charles 1846-1934 (on same tombstone with Delia Rigney; James Dorsey Card File, African American

Obituaries, maintained at the Historical Society of Harford County, has a card with obituary abstraction from the *Bel Air Times* on September 14, 1934 stating Charles H. Rigney, a nonagenarian, of the 2nd District, was born in slavery and died last Friday after a short illness from the infirmities of age; death certificate stated Charles H. Rigney was born in Virginia, but his parents were unknown to the staff at Havre de Grace Hospital; he was the husband of Delia Rigney who had predeceased him and it also stated he died on September 7, 1934, age about 77, so apparently he was not a nonagenarian) [Union U. M. Church Cemetery]

Rigney, Cordelia born about November 27, 1826 – died on November 20, 1924 (no tombstone; death certificate stated she was married, aged about 98 years and 11 months; she was born in Harford Co., but her parents were not known to informant Charles Rigney, of Perryman) [Union U. M. Church Cemetery]

Rigney, Delia 1850-1926 (on same tombstone with Charles Rigney) [Union U. M. Church Cemetery]

Rigney, Edward February 16, 1874 – April 13, 1926 (no tombstone; death certificate stated he was the married son of Cordelia Rice, but his father was unknown to informant Charles Rigney) [Union U. M. Church Cemetery]

Ringgold, Bertha E. November 15, 1922 – February 18, 2006 (no tombstone; obituary in *The Aegis* on February 22, 2006 stated she was born in Harford Co., the daughter of Clarence and Margaret Dorsey; she married Daniel E. Ringgold, Sr. and operated her own beauty shop in Aberdeen for many years; she served as a Benevolent Steward and Church Clerk at Mt. Calvary UAME Church and sang in No. 2 Choir and also with Harford County's United Choral Ensemble's Gospel Chorus; she died at home in Havre de Grace, survived by a brother Herbert Parker, a sister Clara Ross, 7 grandchildren, and 18 great-grandchildren) [Mt. Calvary U. A. M. E. Church Cemetery]

Ringgold, Clarence 1963-1964 (copied in 1987, not found in 2018) [Mt. Calvary U. A. M. E. Church Cemetery]

Ringgold, Claude Leroy died September 5, 1989, age 50 (obituary in *The Aegis* on September 13, 1989 stated he was born in Harford Co., the son of Lillian M. (Smith) Ringgold of Churchville and the late Ollie William Ringgold, Sr.; he was the husband of Phyllis Ringgold and lived in Catonsville; he died at St. Agnes Hospital in Baltimore and was survived by his wife, his mother, 2 sons and 4 grandchildren) [John Wesley U. M. E. Church Cemetery in Abingdon]

Ringgold, Daniel (owned a lot in section 1 some time after 1951) [Mt. Calvary U. A. M. E. Church Cemetery]

Ringgold, Ethel B. March 23, 1939 – October 3, 1998 (no tombstone; buried in section 1; obituary in *The Aegis* stated she was born in Nottoway Co., VA, daughter of the late William and Mary Booker, and married Daniel E. Ringgold, Jr.; she retired from Aberdeen Proving Ground and served as clerk, recording steward and a finance committee member of Mt. Calvary; died at home in Havre de Grace, survived by her husband, 3 children and their families) [Mt. Calvary U. A. M. E. Church Cemetery]

Ringgold, Eugene D. 1917-1997 (small metal funeral home marker and a white wooden cross, about 3 feet in height, inscribed "Rest in Peace;" James Dorsey Card File, African American Obituaries, maintained at the Historical Society of Harford County, has a card with obituary from an unidentified newspaper dated September 24, 1997 stating Eugene Douglas Einggold was born January 8, 1917 "in Spesutia Island in Aberdeen," the son of Crawford Giles and Rebecca Ringgold; he "attended Swan Creek Methodist Church, now known as Union United Methodist Church;" he worked for the Race Track Commission in Havre de Grace and served as a cook at Rochester College; he died at Rochester General Hospital in Rochester, NY on September 15, 1997, age 80, survived by two adopted sons, a brother, two sisters-in-law, six nieces, nine nephews and other relatives) [Union U. M. Church Cemetery]

Ringgold, Flossie Q. December 16, 1923 – March 1, 1969 ("At Rest") [Union U. M. Church Cemetery]

Ringgold, George died April 8, 1924, age about 60 (no tombstone; death certificate stated he was widowed and born in Maryland, but his parents were not known to informant Annie Giles) [Union U. M. Church Cemetery]

Ringgold, Gladys O. August 18, 1897 – March 1, 1996 ("At Rest") [Union U. M. Church Cemetery]

Ringgold, Janice P. 1940-2011 (small metal funeral home marker) [St. James United Cemetery]

Ringgold, John June 20, 1863 – August 23, 1917 (no tombstone; death certificate stated he was born in Harford, worked as a farm laborer and was widower when he died in Joppa; informant was Eugene Ringgold, of Joppa, and he did not know the names of John's parents) [Mt. Zion U. M. Church Cemetery]

Ringgold, John H. died February 15, 1885 in his 72nd year [Old Union Chapel M. E. Church Cemetery]

Ringgold, Johna Delores July 7, 1946 – October 11, 1947 (no tombstone; death certificate stated she was the daughter of Lawrence Rinngold, of Oxford, PA, and Geneva Brown, of Perryman, MD) [Union U. M. Church Cemetery]

Ringgold, Lawrence L. Jr. July 17, 1944 – May 17, 1966, PFC, Co. B, 8th Cav., 1st Calvary Div., Vietnam, PH (tombstone; obituary in *The Aegis* on May 26, 1966 stated Lawrence LeRoy "Butch" Ringgold, Jr., of 464 Alliance Street, Havre de Grace, son of Lawrence L. Ringgold, Sr., of Coatesville, PA, and Mrs. Geneva B. Williams, of Aberdeen, died in Vietnam on May 17, 1966; he had served on the Havre de Grace Police Force for 6 months before entering the Army on July 1, 1965 and was sent to Vietnam in December 1965; besides his parents he was survived by his grandfather Walter F. Brown and a sister Deborah Ringgold; another report in *The Aegis* (undated) stated he was the first black officer on the Havre de Grace police force and he died in Vietnam at a place called Happy Valley; the article includes a picture of him) [Union U. M. Church Cemetery]

Ringgold, Lillian M. "Lill" June 14, 1916 – May 27, 2005 (on same tombstone with Ollie W. Ringgold, Sr.; obituary in *The Aegis* on June 1, 2005 stated she was born in Long Island, NY, the daughter of Herbert Bond and Ettie Smith, and moved to Churchville at an early age; she married in December 1941 to Ollie W. Ringgold, Jr. who predeceased her; she was a member of Asbury United Methodist Church until 1989 when the church closed and she then joined John Wesley United Methodist Church in Abingdon; she performed domestic work for various families in Harford Co. and was a member of the Aberdeen Golden Age Club; she was survived by 4 children, 13 grandchildren, 32 great-grandchildren and 12 great-great-grandchildren) [John Wesley U. M. E. Church Cemetery in Abingdon]

Ringgold, Lloyd James "Crick" died February 6, 1996, age 78 (buried in section 39; no tombstone; obituary in *The Aegis* on February 7, 1996 stated he was a native of Aberdeen, the son of the late Annie Syckels (father was not named); he served in the Army in World War II, retired from Baldwin Manor as a groundskeeper and died at home in Aberdeen, survived by 2 half-brothers, William and Julius Ringgold) [Mt. Calvary U. A. M. E. Church Cemetery]

Ringgold, Martha J. "Mother" 1898-1942 (on same tombstone with Thomas S. and Zanetta Ringgold) [Mt. Calvary U. A. M. E. Church Cemetery]

Ringgold, Ollie O. died December 1, 1978, age 84 (no tombstone; obituary in *The Aegis* on December 7, 1978 state he was the son of Emory and Susan Ringgold and was a retired cement finisher at Aberdeen Proving Ground (member of the 25 Year Club); he lived on Gilbert Road near Aberdeen and died at Harford Memorial Hospital in Havre de Grace, survived by 2 sons, 2 daughters, 2 sisters, 9 grandchildren and 15 great-grandchildren) [Union U. M. Church Cemetery]

Ringgold, Ollie W. Jr. March 31, 1915 – January 16, 1987 (on same tombstone with Lillian M. Ringgold; obituary in *The Aegis* on January 21, 1987 stated Ollie William Ringgold, of Churchville, died on January 16, 1987, age 71, at University Hospital in Baltimore; he was born in Aberdeen, the son of Gladys Ringgold of Baltimore and the late Ollie Ringgold; he retired from Aberdeen Proving Ground, Edgewood Area, after 35 years as a cement finisher; he was survived by his mother, wife Lillian M. Ringgold, 2 sons, 3 daughters, 2 brothers, 3 sisters, 13 grandchildren and 15 great-grandchildren) [John Wesley U. M. E. Church Cemetery in Abingdon]

Ringgold, Sarah J. died March 15, 1922, age about 55 (no tombstone; death certificate stated she was the married daughter of James Rumsey and Ellen McGaw, all born in Maryland; informant was George Ringgold, of Havre de Grace) [Union U. M. Church Cemetery]

Ringgold, Shirley Cromwell December 17, 1931 – April 8, 1940 (no tombstone; death certificate stated he was the son of Horace Cromwell and Florence Ringgold, and he fell from a bridge and drowned) [Union U. M. Church Cemetery]

Ringgold, Susan H. 1962-1943 (on same tombstone with William E. Ringgold) [Mt. Calvary U. A. M. E. Church Cemetery]

Ringgold, Thomas S. "Father" 1898-1950 (on same tombstone with Martha J. and Zannetta Ringgold) [Mt.

Calvary U. A. M. E. Church Cemetery]

Ringgold, Tracey S. "1968 (not sure)" *(sic)* (copied in 1987, but not found in 2018) [Mt. Calvary U. A. M. E. Church Cemetery]

Ringgold, William Crawford, son of Susan and Emory Ringgold, 1891-1918 (tombstone; death certificate stated William C. Ringgold was born March 22, 1892, the son of Emmory Ringgold and Susin Hollingsworth, all born in Harford Co.; he was married, worked as a day laborer and died of influenze near Aberdeen on October 31, 1918; informant was his father, of Aberdeen RFD #1; military records state William C. Ringgold was born in Perryman and inducted into World War I as a private at Level on October 27, 1917, age 25 years, 7 months; he was promoted to corporal on December 1, 1917, served in Btry E, 351 FA, and was honorably discharged due to physical disability on January 3, 1918) [Mt. Calvary U. A. M. E. Church Cemetery]

Ringgold, William E. 1864-1959 (on same tombstone with Susan H. Ringgold) [Mt. Calvary U. A. M. E. Church Cemetery]

Ringgold, William R. November 18, 1939 – August 9, 2015 (tombstone inscribed "Always Remembered Never Forgotten" and also a small metal funeral home marker for William Robert Ringgold, with his photo) [Mt. Calvary U. A. M. E. Church Cemetery]

Ringgold, Zannetta, "Daughter" 1921-1947 (on same tombstone with Thomas S. and Martha J. Ringgold) [Mt. Calvary U. A. M. E. Church Cemetery]

Rinn, Herman H. 1936-   (copied in 1987 and 2002, but not found in 2018) [Gravel Hill Cemetery]

Roachelle, Dorothy Walker 1909-1989 [Community Baptist Church Cemetery]

Robert, John H. 1882-1951 (on same tombstone with Ruth W. Robert; when copied in 1987 the birth year was mistakenly inscribed as 1822) [Berkley Memorial Cemetery]

Robert, Ruth W., "His Wife" 1886-19__ (death year blank; on same tombstone with John H. Robert) [Berkley Memorial Cemetery]

Roberts, A. Alcade 1873-1951 (on same tombstone with Minnie P. Roberts) [Berkley Memorial Cemetery]

Roberts, Alberta Barclay June 27, 1920 – July 8, 1997 [Berkley Memorial Cemetery]

Roberts, Emory 1866 – March 31, 1915 (no tombstone; death certificate stated he was born in Maryland, worked as a laborer and died a widower in Fallston; the names and birth places of his parents were not known to informant Daniel Hall, of Fallston RFD) [William C. Rice Memorial Cemetery, St. James U. M. Church]

Roberts, Minnie P. 1873-   (on same tombstone with A. Alcade Roberts) [Berkley Memorial Cemetery]

Robertson, Harold L. February 12, 1934 – February 15, 2002 [Berkley Memorial Cemetery]

Robertson, Norma Jean 1945-2018 (small metal funeral home marker) [Berkley Memorial Cemetery]

Robinson (no dates on two Robinson lot markers) [Mt. Zion U. M. Church Cemetery]

Robinson, ---- (no tombstone, but Kurtz Funeral Home records stated Byron Robinson's daughter was buried in a walnut coffin on June 28, 1883 from J. R. Rutledge's tenant house) [Hendon Hill Cemetery]

Robinson, ---- March 19, 1921 – March 21, 1921, premature male birth, lived 2 days (no tombstone; death certificate stated he was the son of Henry Robinson and Lillie Bradford, all born in Maryland, and he died at High Point; informant was Henry Robinson, of Forest Hill; the undertaker H. G. Walker, of Pleasantville, indicated burial was at "Hickory Cem., Md." but there is no such place [probably Fairview A. M. E. Church Cemetery]

Robinson, ---- stillborn male on September 5, 1936, an eight month pregnancy (no tombstone; death certificate stated he was born in Harford Co., son of Henry Robinson and Lilly Bradford, both born in Maryland; he died at home near Cooptown; informant was his father) [Fairview A. M. E. Church Cemetery]

Robinson, ---- stillborn male, an eight-month pregnancy, died "April 27(?)" *(sic)* 1931 and was buried April 28, 1931 (no tombstone; death certificate stated he died in Bel Air, the son of Henry Robinson, born in Baltimore, and Oceola Brooks, born in Bel Air) [Hendon Hill Cemetery]

Robinson, Agnes Viola June 23, 1921 – April 30, 2002 (no tombstone; obituary and photo in *The Aegis* on May 8, 2002 stated she was born in Forest Hill, the daughter of Howard Stewart and Mary Rebecca Kell, and was the widow of James William Robinson; she worked at Bata Shoe Company and was a faithful member of Fairview AME Church; she died at home and was survived by three sons, two daughters, 13 grandchildren, and 15 great-grandchildren) [Fairview A. M. E. Church Cemetery]

Robinson, Annie Cathrine August 25, 1881 – July 3, 1928 (no tombstone; death certificate stated she was the widowed daughter of Alfred Coates, both born in Frederick Co., MD, but her mother's name was not known to informant Isabel Robinson, of Fallston) [Tabernacle Mount Zion U. M. Church Cemetery]

Robinson, Barnes June 20, 1844 – April 1, 1918 (on the same tombstone with wife Josephine Robinson inscribed "At Rest" and "By Their Children") [West Liberty Church Cemetery]

Robinson, Bobbie November 28, 1952 – January 14, 1953 (no tombstone; Pennington Funeral Home records stated he was the son of Robert E. Lee and Pauline Richardson, of Havre de Grace, and died in Harford Memorial Hospital [St. James United Cemetery]

Robinson, Brinton Sr. 1899-1978 (on same tombstone with Isabella Robinson; obituary in *The Aegis* on January 26, 1978 stated Brinton D. Robinson, Sr., of Whitt Road in Kingsville, died January 24, 1978, age 78, at Fallston General Hospital; he was born in Frederick, the son of the late James and Annie Robinson, and moved to Harford County as a child; he was a farmer and the husband of the late Isabelle Brown and was survived by 2 sons, a foster son, a daughter, a brother, a sister, 3 grandchildren and 5 great-grandchildren) [Tabernacle Mount Zion U. M. Church Cemetery]

Robinson, Brinton D. August 10, 1927 – December 20, 1983 (tombstone; obituary in *The Aegis* on December 22, 1983 stated Brinton Dennis Robinson, Jr. was born in Fallston, the son of Brinton Robinson and Isabella Brown, married Mary Elizabeth Turner, served in the Army during World War II and retired in 1982 as a chemical plant operator after more than 30 years of service; he lived in Joppa and died at Union Memorial Hospital in Baltimore, survived by his wife, two sons, a sister, and three grandchildren) [Tabernacle Mount Zion U. M. Church Cemetery]

Robinson, Caroline died October 10, 1918, age about 70 [St. James United Cemetery]

Robinson, Carrie E. (Mrs.) July 11, 1902 – December 14, 1969 ("Here Lies") [Berkley Memorial Cemetery]

Robinson, Charles Barnes died August 4, 1943, age about 72 (no tombstone; Kurtz Funeral Home Record Book 1937-1943, p. 278, stated he was the son of Barnes Robinson and Mary Holland, all born in Harford Co.; he was single, worked as a laborer and died at home in Forest Hill; death certificate added he had lived at Forest Hill for 1½ years; informant was Henry Robinson, of Forest Hill) [Fairview A. M. E. Church Cemetery]

Robinson, Creola V. 1926-2008 (small metal funeral home marker; obituary and photo in *The Aegis* stated Creola Virginia Robinson was born on March 23, 1926, a daughter of the late Vallee and Helen Rice, married James B. Robinson on February 26, 1949 and had no children; she lived in Bel Air and was an active member of American Legion Post 55 for more than 40 years; she died on March 3, 2008 at Lorien Rehabilitation Nursing Home in Riverside, survived by a sister and a brother and she was predeceased by a sister and a brother) [Clark's U. M. Church Cemetery]

Robinson, Edward L. 1887-1956 (on same tombstone with Laura B. Robinson) [St. James United Cemetery]

Robinson, Erma Olivia October 2, 1910 – December 8, 1972 (inscribed "She was the sunshine of our home") [Mt. Calvary U. A. M. E. Church Cemetery]

Robinson, Ethel E. July 15, 1927 – April 25, 1975 [Berkley Memorial Cemetery]

Robinson, George November 20, 1909 – May 19, 1973, Maryland, SSgt, U.S. Army, World War II (tombstone; obituary in *The Aegis* stated he was born in Carlsbad, NM, and had been employed as a cook at the Maryland House; he lived in Havre de Grace, married Erma ----, and died at Perry Point VAMC, survived three 3 step-sons, a step-daughter, 16 grandchildren and 7 great-grandchildren) [Mt. Calvary U. A. M. E. Church Cemetery]

Robinson, Harry Pearl (no tombstone; death certificate stated he was born on September 1, 1890, the son of Daniel Robinson and Sadie Jimerson, all born in Maryland; he was a farmer at Rocks and was married at the time of his death on March 16, 1914; informant was J. C. Wilson) [Chestnut Grove A. M. E. Church Cemetery, formerly LaGrange Cemetery at Rocks]

Robinson, Henry S. February 7, 1914 – September 9, 1985 (copied in 1987 as simply 1914-1985, but a new tombstone had been erected circa 1996 with the complete dates and his wife Rosella was inscribed also; obituary in *The Aegis* on September 12, 1985 stated Henry Scott Robinson, Jr., husband of Mary R. Robinson, worked as a carpenter and plumber, and died at Fallston General Hospital, survived by his wife, two daughters, one son, five brothers, one sister, 7 grandchildren and 2 great-great-grandchildren) [Fairview A. M. E. Church Cemetery]

Robinson, Henry S. October 29, 1893 – November 22, 1965 (on same tombstone with Lillie V. Robinson) [Fairview A. M. E. Church Cemetery]

Robinson, Ida Glenn, wife of J. Clarence Robinson, 1887-1957 [William C. Rice Memorial Cemetery, St. James U. M. Church]

Robinson, Isabella 1903-1953 (on same tombstone with Brinton Robinson, Sr.) [Tabernacle Mount Zion U. M. Church Cemetery]

Robinson, J. Clarence 1887-1966 (small metal funeral home marker) [William C. Rice Memorial Cemetery, St. James U. M. Church]

Robinson, James died August 2, 1986, age 89 (no tombstone; obituary in *The Aegis* on August 14, 1986 state he was born in Frederick, the son of James and Annie Robinson, and was the husband of the late Elizabeth Taylor Robinson; he spent most of his life in Harford Co., lived in Bel Air, retired from the Mutual Fire Insurance Co., and died at Fallston General Hospital, survived by two daughters, 16 grandchildren and 8 great-grandchildren) [Tabernacle Mount Zion U. M. Church Cemetery]

Robinson, James B. July 6, 1924 – April 3, 1983 (tombstone; obituary in *The Aegis* on April 7, 1983 stated James Robinson, son of Brinton and Isabelle Robinson, and husband of Creola Robinson, of Bel Air, died at Perry Point VA Medical Center; he served in the Army from 1943 to 1946 and was a retired chemist from Edgewood Arsenal; he was survived by his wife, a brother Brinton D. Robinson, of Joppa, and a sister Delores A. Matthews, of Kingsville) [Clark's U. M. Church Cemetery]

Robinson, James E. April 29, 1906 – March 3, 1972, Maryland, Pvt, 3907 QM Truck Co, World War II; obituary in *The Aegis* on March 10, 1972 stated James Edward Robnson was the son of J. Clarence Robinson and Ida Holland, worked as a laborer, served in World War II, lived in Jarrettsville and died at home, survived by a brother and several nieces and nephews) [William C. Rice Memorial Cemetery, St. James U. M. Church]

Robinson, James Stirling March 15, 1942 – March 16, 1942 (no tombstone; Kurtz Funeral Home Record Book 1937-1943, p. 223, stated he died near Madonna, the son of Henry S. Robinson, born in Forest Hill, and Rosella Cromwell, born in White Hall, Baltimore County; death certificate stated the same, but spelled his middle name Sterling and added he was a 6½ month birth and lived only six hours; informant was James S. Robinson, of White Hall) [Fairview A. M. E. Church Cemetery]

Robinson, James William Jr. died September 7, 2003, age 64 (no tombstone; obituary and photo in *The Aegis* on September 10, 2003 stated he was born in Harford County, the son of James W. Robinson, Sr. and Agnes Stewart; he lived in Forest Hill, worked as a cement mason and died at the Upper Chesapeake Medical Center, survived by 3 sons, 2 daughters, 7 grandchildren, 2 great-grandchildren, 2 brothers and 2 sisters) [Fairview A. M. E. Church Cemetery]

Robinson, Jerry R. died May 27, 1922, age about 78 (no tombstone; death certificate stated he was born in Virginia, but his parents were unknown to the informant Mrs. Jerry R. Robinson) [St. James United Cemetery]

Robinson, John L. 1905-1974 [Community Baptist Church Cemetery]

Robinson, Josephine December 17, 1859 – February 3, 1926 (on the same tombstone with Barnes Robinson inscribed "At Rest" and "By Their Children") [West Liberty Church Cemetery]

Robinson, Laura B. 1884-1962 (on same tombstone with Edward L. Robinson) [St. James United Cemetery]

Robinson, Lawrence Norris, "Chick-a-boo" February 19, 1955 – June 12, 1983 (tombstone; obituary in The Aegis on June 23, 1983 stated he was born in Havre de Grace and died at Deaton Medical Center in Baltimore, survived by his wife Tina Robinson, mother Frances Ellis, grandmother Ruth Clush, a son, three daughters, three sisters, and a brother [St. James United Cemetery]

Robinson, Lillie V. July 8, 1895 – July 19, 1970 (on same tombstone with Henry S. Ruff; obituary in *The Aegis* on July 23, 1970 stated Lillian Robinson, wife of the late Henry Robinson, lived most of her life in the Forest Hill area and was survived by 2 daughters, 6 sons, 1 great aunt, 23 grandchildren and 21 great-grandchildren) [Fairview A. M. E. Church Cemetery]

Robinson, M. Katharine 1872-1942 (on same tombstone with Robert Robinson; death certificate stated Katherine Robinson died December 28, 1942, age about 73; she was born in Havre de Grace, the daughter of George Wright and Rachael Harvey, both born in Virginia, and the widow of Robert Robinson; informant was Laura Towles, of Pittsburgh, PA) [St. James United Cemetery]

Robinson, M. Rosella December 23, 1920 – October 12, 1996 (on same tombstone with Henry S. Robinson and a small metal funeral home marker next to it gives her name as Mary R. Robinson; James Dorsey Card File, African American Obituaries, maintained at the Historical Society of Harford County, has a funeral home card for Mary Rosella Robinson) [Fairview A. M. E. Church Cemetery]

Robinson, Mary E. 1928-2010 (small metal funeral home marker; obituary and photo in *The Aegis* on December 24, 2010 stated she was born in Jarrettsville, the daughter of Ruth Viola Hall Turner of Forest Hill and the late Raymond Austin Tuner; she lived in Joppa, worked for 10 years for the Board of Education, and died on December 22, 2010, the widow of Brinton Dennis Robinson, Jr., and was survived by sons Brinton D. III and Harvey R. Robinson, five grandchildren, 14 great-grandchildren, and one great-great-grandson) [Tabernacle Mount Zion U. M. Church Cemetery]

Robinson, Mary J. May 17, 1874 – February 24, 1935 (no tombstone; death certificate stated she was the daughter of Henry Anderson and Caroline Pinion, and the widow of Jerry Robinson; informant was Caroline Robinson, of Havre de Grace) [St. James United Cemetery]

Robinson, Mary Martha died June 5, 1989, age 73 (no tombstone; obituary in *The Aegis* on June 15, 1989 stated she was born in King & Queen Co., VA, the daughter of Alexander Epps and Lottie Smith, and moved to Maryland with her first husband Robert E. Putney; they were the parents of six children; after Robert's death she married John Robinson in 1951 and he also predeceased her; Mary was one of the founding members of the Community Baptist Church and served on the missionary board, in the choir, and on auxiliary committees; she died at Franklin Square Hospital, survived by two sons, four daughters, four brothers, three sisters, 28 grandchildren, 47 great-grandchildren, and 3 great-great-grandchildren) [Community Baptist Church Cemetery]

Robinson, Renay D. died February 28, 2003, age 52 (no tombstone; obituary in *The Aegis* on March 5, 2003 stated she was the daughter of the late Clarence and Gladys McDaniel and she married Warren Holiday Robinson who predeceased her; she lived in Edgewood and died in Clinton, survived by four sisters and a goddaughter) [Foster's Hill Cemetery]

Robinson, Robert, husband of M. Katharine Robinson, May 15, 1878 – January 9, 1939 (on same tombstone with M. Katharine Robinson) [St. James United Cemetery]]

Robinson, Roosevelt Albert August 29, 1943 – February 2, 2006 (no tombstone; obituary in *The Aegis* on February 8, 2006 stated he was born in Coatesville, PA, son of Roosevelt A. Bradshaw and Marjorie A. Robinson-Body, and lived in North East; he worked as a welder for the former Wiley Manufacturing Company in Port Deposit and retired in 1984; he died at Union Hospital in Elkton, survived by two sons, two daughters, five grandchildren, two brothers, three sisters, one aunt, and a host of nieces, nephews and cousins; his wife was not mentioned) [Berkley Memorial Cemetery]

Robinson, Ruth February 20, 1931 – July 24, 1931 (no tombstone; death certificate stated she was the daughter of Henry Scott Robinson and Lillie Bradford, all born in Harford Co.; she died at home in Black Horse; informant was Henry S. Robinson, of White Hall) [Fairview A. M. E. Church Cemetery]

Robinson, Vivian (owned a lot in section 16 some time after 1951) [Mt. Calvary U. A. M. E. Church Cemetery]

Robinson, William C. 1938-2017 (small metal funeral home marker) [Berkley Memorial Cemetery]

Rochester, Wilford F. July 19, 1927 – July 14, 2018, Pvt., U.S. Army, World War II (inscribed "Money We Miss You;" his new military tombstone, soon to be erected, was laying on the ground) [St. James United Cemetery]

Rock, John Nathan 1908 – April 5, 1937 (no tombstone; death certificate stated he was born in Penn Brook, NJ and was the unmarried son of Charles Rock and Viola Brown) [St. James United Cemetery]

Rose, Francis Cabel August 18, 1921 – February 4, 1984, Sgt, U.S. Army, World War II (Memorial information, in part: born in Hilltop, WV, son of Harry B. Rose and Martha Bryant; after the death of his father he was raised by his mother and step-father Rev. Eugene H. Boone, of Paden City, WV; was active in the NAACP; died at Perry Point VA Hospital, Perryville, MD, survived by wife Shirley J. Rose and six siblings. – Information provided by Mrs. Joan E. Wiggins in March, 2020) [John Wesley U. M. E. Church Cemetery in Abingdon]

Rose, George Whittier 1914-1979, STDA 1, U.S. Marine Corps, World War II [John Wesley U. M. E. Church Cemetery in Abingdon]

Rose, George Whittier January 31, 1914 – October 16, 1979 (Memorial information, in part:bBorn in Hilltop, WV, son of Harry B. Rose and Martha Bryant; after the death of his father he was raised by his mother and step-father Rev, Eugene H. Boone, of Paden City, WV; dedicated member of Ames United Methodist Church in Bel Air and American Legion Post 55, serving as the first vice commander and adjutant; World War II veteran (Marine Corps); died in Bel Air, survived by two daughters, a son-in-law, four brothers, three sisters, and other relatives. – Information provided by Joan E. Wiggins, March, 2020) [Clark's U. M. Church Cemetery]

Rose, Harry V. September 11, 1912 – April 1, 1959, West Va., TEC5 Hq Co., 317 Engr Bn, World War II [Clark's U. M. Church Cemetery]

Rose, Harry Vincent August 11, 1947 – February 17, 2000, Sgt., USAF (on same tombstone with Judith Rose) [Fairview A. M. E. Church Cemetery]

Rose, James R. April 16, 1891 – August 7, 1936 (no tombstone; death certificate stated he was the son of Robert and Bettie J. Rose, all born in Virginia; he lived on Main Street Extended in Bel Air for 32 years and worked as a day laborer in a lumber yard for 28 years; his wife Rosie Rose was informant) [Hendon Hill Cemetery]

Rose, Judith Ann October 6, 1955 – October 19, 1994 (on same tombstone with Harry V. Rose; James Dorsey Card File, African American Obituaries, maintained at the Historical Society of Harford County, has a card with obituary from an unidentified newspaper dated October 26, 1992 stating Judith Ann Presbury Rose was born in Havre de Grace, the daughter of Catherine D. Presbury, of Forest Hill, and Harold E. Jefferson, of Fallston; she lived in Bel Air, married Harry V. Rose and died at Fallston General Hospital, survived by a son, a brother and a nephew) [Fairview A. M. E. Church Cemetery]

Rose, Samuel Lee III July 15, 1974 – January 1, 2010, U.S. Marine Corps [Berkley Memorial Cemetery]

Rose, Samuel Lee Jr. February 15, 1948 – January 6, 2005, SFC, U.S. Army [Berkley Memorial Cemetery]

Ross, Clara N. May 4, 1920 – Oct 20, 2007 (inscribed "In Loving Memory of Our Mother") [Mt. Calvary U. A. M. E. Church Cemetery]

Ross, John H. March 23, 1885 – May 10, 1973 (on same tombstone with Mary V. Ross) [Mt. Zion U. M. Church Cemetery]

Ross, Lawrence D. December 8, 1913 – January 19, 1971, Kentucky, TEC4, 607 Ord. Ammo. Co., World War II [Mt. Calvary U. A. M. E. Church Cemetery]

Ross, Mary V. May 24, 1891 – August 7, 19598 (on same tombstone with John H. Ross) [Mt. Zion U. M. Church Cemetery]

Royster, Emma Taylor April 23, 1901 – August 11, 1954 [Gravel Hill Cemetery]

Royster, James (copied in 1987, not listed in 2002 and not found in 2018) [Gravel Hill Cemetery]

Ruff, ---- (male) September 21, 1922 – September 29, 1922 (no tombstone; misfiled death certificate stated he was the son of David Ruff and Mary Hynson, all born in Joppa; he was buried in "Mountain Colored Church" and informant was his father) [Mt. Zion U. M. Church Cemetery]

Ruff, ---- (owner of a lot in section 21 some time after 1951) [Mt. Calvary U. A. M. E. Church Cemetery]

Ruff, Anita March 10, 1930 – August 8, 1930, premature birth at 7 months, lived 4 months, 28 days (no tombstone; death certificate stated she was the daughter of David Ruff and Mary C. Henson, all born in Maryland; informant was David Ruff, of Joppa) [Tabernacle Mount Zion U. M. Church Cemetery]

Ruff, Asbury died June 30, 1892 (no tombstone; a notice in *The Aegis* stated he committed suicide near Fallston by shooting himself; place of burial was not reported [possibly Hendon Hill Cemetery]

Ruff, Christian died April 26, 1916, age 47 (no tombstone; death certificate stated she was the daughter of Kitty Hackett, both born in Harford Co., but informant Emily Ruff, of Bel Air, did not know her father's name; she was a widow who did laundry work in Bel Air) [Tabernacle Mount Zion U. M. Church Cemetery]

Ruff, Cornelia F. April 9, 1893 – September 21, 1981 (on same tombstone with M. Elise Ruff; obituary in The Aegis stated she was the daughter of Stephen and Emily Ruff, lived in Bel Air and died at Manor Care Ruxton, survived by a brother Charles P. Ruff and (sister) Minnie Williams; she was buried at "Mountain Cemetery, Singer Road;" an article about Cornelia Franklin Ruff was written by James R. Dorsey, Sr. and published in *Harford Historic Bulletin No. 35*, Winter, 1988, pp. 1-2 (photo on cover); she was a teacher in the Harford County Public Schools and after her retirement she was organist, teacher and superintendent of the Ames Methodist Episcopal Church School in Bel Air; she was also a founder of the Ross Ruff Educational Fund) [Mt. Zion U. M. Church Cemetery]

Ruff, D. (no dates on tombstone and the top is inscribed "This Band") [Mt. Zion U. M. Church Cemetery]

Ruff, David 1887-1956 [Mt. Zion U. M. Church Cemetery]

Ruff, Dorathy February 18, 1912 – January 17, 1918 (no tombstone; death certificate stated she died at Joppa and was the daughter of David Ruff and Mary Hinson, all were born in Maryland; informant was David H. Ruff, of Joppa; she was buried in "Mountain Col. Church") [Mt. Zion U. M. Church Cemetery]

Ruff, Earl Cecil Sr. February 27, 1926 – September 28, 1987, Cpl., U.S. Army, World War II (tombstone; obituary in *The Aegis* on October 1, 1987 stated he was the husband of Edna A. (Gover) Ruff and was survived by his wife, a brother, a sister, 5 children and 5 grandchildren) [Mt. Zion U. M. Church Cemetery]

Ruff, Emily E., "Mother" 1869-1934 (on same tombstone with Stephen B. Ruff; death certificate stated she was the daughter of Benjaman Cottman and Amy Carr, all born in Maryland; she married Stephen Ruff, died at 234 W. Baltimore Ave. in Bel Air where she had lived for 54 years and was buried in "Mountain Cemetery;" informant was Miss Cornelia F. Ruff, of Bel Air) [Mt. Zion U. M. Church Cemetery]

Ruff, Evelyn died on September 3, 1999, age 97 (no tombstone; obituary and photo in *The Aegis* on September 8, 1999 stated she was born in Bel Air, the daughter of George Robert Jones and Mary Elizabeth Hackett, and was the widow of John H. Ruff; she died at home in Bel Air and was survived by one son Thomas G. Dorsey, Jr., of Edgewood, one sister Waseka Willis, of East Orange, N.J., 10 grandchildren, 23 great-grandchildren and 7 great-great-grandchildren; she was predeceased by a daughter Pearl V. Reeder) [Mt. Zion U. M. Church Cemetery]

Ruff, Floyd A. died September 24, 1994, age 69 (no tombstone; obituary in *The Aegis* on October 5, 1994 stated he was the son of David and Mary Ruff and he served in the Army during the Korean War; he later worked at the Bainbridge Naval Training Center and after it closed he went to work at Aberdeen Proving Ground, retiring after 35 years of federal service; he lived in Harford County all of his life and was survived by a sister Anna Ruff, a cousin Mary Demby, and many other relatives) [Mt. Zion U. M. Church Cemetery]

Ruff, Helen died in 1924, age not given (no tombstone; reported in *The Aegis* on May 2, 1924 that she was a resident of Bel Air until about 10 years ago when she moved to Baltimore and lived with her common law husband "Big Boy" who killed her "about midnight Thursday;" newspaper article also mentioned her brother Leon Hall and her mother Hannah Stewart) [Hendon Hill Cemetery]

Ruff, Isabelle, "Mother" 1919-1976 (on same tombstone with John H. Ruff; obituary in *The Aegis* on April 1, 1976 stated Isabelle Stewart Ruff, of 1254 W. Jarrettsville Road in Forest Hill, was an employee of Bata Shoe

Co. and died on March 29, 1986, age 36, at Fallston General Hospital, survived by a son John Ruff, Jr., her mother Mrs. Mary Stewart, four sisters, a brother, and many nieces and nephews; Mrs. Ruff's husband was not mentioned) [Fairview A. M. E. Church Cemetery]

Ruff, J. (no dates on marker) [Mt. Zion U. M. Church Cemetery]

Ruff, Jeremiah November 29, 1916 – May 23, 1917 (no tombstone; death certificate stated he was the son of David Ruff and Mary E. Hynson, all born at Mountain, and he was buried at "Mountain Colored Cemetery;" informant was his father David Ruff, of Mountain) [Mt. Zion U. M. Church Cemetery]

Ruff, Jesse 1857-1941 (on same obelisk with Jacob Britton, Joshua E. Britton, Rosa H. Britton, David Ruff and Martha Ruff; death certificate stated Jesses Harold Ruff was born "November 31, 1953" and died December 24, 1941; he married Martha Watters, worked as a laborer, died a widower at home on Mountain Road in rural Joppa where he had lived for 83 years and was buried in "Mountain A. M. E. Cemetery;" informant was David Ruff, of Joppa) [Mt. Zion U. M. Church Cemetery]

Ruff, John Finney died June 20, 1963, age not given (no tombstone; obituary in *The Aegis* on June 27, 1963 stated he was a lifelong resident of Bel Air, was employed by Joseph T. Foster for many years and was survived by his daughter Eula; his wife May H. Ruff died sometime ago) [Mt. Calvary U. A. M. E. Church Cemetery]

Ruff, John H., "Son" 1935-1994 (on same tombstone with Isabelle Ruff, but year of his death is not inscribed; obituary in *The Aegis* on September 21, 1994 stated John Henry Ruff, Jr. was born in Forest Hill, the son of the late John Ruff and Isabelle Stewart; he lived in Cooptown, worked as a security guard at the Hillendale Country Club and died at Fallston General Hospital on September 17, 1994, survived by two aunts and cousins) [Fairview A. M. E. Church Cemetery]

Ruff, John Henry July 6, 1907 – December 16, 1963, Maryland, PFC, 464 Aviation, AAF, World War II [Mt. Zion U. M. Church Cemetery]

Ruff, John J. died May 8, 1917, age 22 years and 8 months (no tombstone; death certificate stated he was married, worked as a "schuffer" (chauffeur) and lived and died in Forest Hill; his parents were William E. Ruff and Jennie Williams and they were all born in Harford Co.; informant was William E. Ruff, of Bel Air; James Dorsey Card File, African American Obituaries, maintained at the Historical Society of Harford County, has a card with obituary abstraction from the *Bel Air Times* on May 11, 1917 stating John Ruff, age about 21, died at Forest Hill; he was employed in the home of several of our best citizens and was always faithful and courteous; "Jack" was a nephew of "Ham" Ruff) [Hendon Hill Cemetery]

Ruff, John W. 1916-   (on same tombstone with Mary M. Ruff and Lucille W. Ruff) [Fairview A. M. E. Church Cemetery]

Ruff, Lucille W. 1910-1978 (on same tombstone with John W. Ruff and Mary M. Ruff) [Fairview A. M. E. Church Cemetery]

Ruff, M. Elise February 2, 1890 – December 20, 1980 (on the same tombstone with Cornelia F. Ruff; obituary in *The Aegis* on December 25, 1980 stated Mary Elise Ruff was born in Bel Air, daughter of Stephen B. and Emily Ruff, and died at Fallston General Hospital, survived by a brother Charles P. Ruff and two sisters Cornelia Ruff and Minnie Williams) [Mt. Zion U. M. Church Cemetery]

Ruff, Martha R., wife of Jesse H. Ruff died August 6, 1905, age 45 (illegible tombstone, but death certificate stated she died at Mountain on August 6, 1905, age 45, the wife of Jesse Ruff, and daughter of Abraham and Mary Watters, all born in Maryland; informant was her husband) [Mt. Zion U. M. Church Cemetery]

Ruff, Mary Catherine died February 12, 1906, age 72 (no tombstone; death certificate stated she was the daughter of Joshua and Betsy Barnes, all born in Maryland; she was the wife of William Asbury Ruff and died in Bel Air; informant was her son Richard Ruff; on the back of the death certificate Dr. Purnell Sappington wrote "Hendon Hill, Burial") [Hendon Hill Cemetery]

Ruff, Mary E. 1911-1976 (on same tombstone with William H. Ruff) [Mt. Zion U. M. Church Cemetery]

Ruff, Mary M. 1898-1959 (on same tombstone with John W. Ruff and Lucille W. Ruff) [Fairview A. M. E. Church Cemetery]

Ruff, Mildred L. August 27, 1915 – February 8, 1918 (no tombstone; death certificate stated she was the daughter of David Ruff and Mary Hinson, all born in Maryland; she died at Mountain and was buried at the "Mountain Col. Church;" informant was Mary Ruff, of Mountain) [Mt. Zion U. M. Church Cemetery]

Ruff, Raymond Webster died October 22, 1968, age not given (no tombstone; obituary in *The Aegis* stated he was the husband of Corine B. Ruff of 119 Alice Anne Street, Bel Air, and he died at Harford Memorial Hospital in Havre de Grace, survived by his wife, two sons, two daughters, one brother, one sister, nine grandchildren and three great-grandchildren) [Hendon Hill Cemetery]

Ruff, Richard A. "Ham" July 20, 1862 – January 7, 1912 (tombstone; death certificate stated he was born in Harford Co., married, worked as a laborer in Bel Air, and was the son of William A. Ruff, born in Harford Co., and Mary Barnes, born in St. Mary's Co., MD; informant was Lizzie Ruff; obituary stated "Ham Ruff" died in Bel Air on January 7, 1912, age about 50; he spent his life serving the J. Baldwin Webster family, "an example to his race;" his funeral "was attended by a vast concourse of both white and colored") [Hendon Hill Cemetery]

Ruff, Roberta Evelyn September 1, 1902 – September 3, 1999 [Mt. Zion U. M. Church Cemetery]

Ruff, Roger H. November 29, 1913 – May 31, 1917 (no tombstone; death certificate stated he was the son of David Ruff and Martha Watters, all born in Harford Co.; he died at The Mountain and was buried at Mountain Colored Cemetery; informant was David Ruff, of Joppa) [Mt. Zion U. M. Church Cemetery]

Ruff, Sadie G. November 11, 1911 – November 29, 1914 (no tombstone; death certificate stated she was the daughter of James E. Ruff and Lena M. Maddox, all born in Harford Co. and lived in Bel Air; informant was Massey Maddox, of Bel Air) [Tabernacle Mount Zion U. M. Church Cemetery]

Ruff, Sarah Elizabeth, wife of Richard A. Ruff, October 8, 1867 – December 17, 1929 (tombstone did not include her first name; death certificate stated she was a widow and cook who died in Bel Air; her parents were David Norton and S. Jane Bond and they were all born in Maryland; informant was J. Finney Ruff; J. C. Taylor Marble Co. records stated "(col) Richard A. Ruff and wife's head stone was put up Sept 25th 1930 Hendon Hill, Bel Air, ordered by their daughter Mrs. Clara Sherod, Scarborough, NY) [Hendon Hill Cemetery]

Ruff, Sarah October 4, 1922 – October 20, 1923 (no tombstone; death certificate stated she was the daughter of David Harold Ruff and Mary Hynson, all born in Joppa; she died in Joppa and was buried in "Mountain Cemetery;" informant was Jessie Ruff, of Joppa) [Mt. Zion U. M. Church Cemetery]

Ruff, Stephen B., "Father" 1966-1934 (on same tombstone with Emily E. Ruff) [Mt. Zion U. M. Church Cemetery]

Ruff, Sulena M. Maddox February 14, 1887 – November 15, 1911 (top part of tombstone has been remounted on a base with the bottom part of the tombstone missing the date of death; death certificate stated she was born in Harford Co., the daughter of Joshua M. Maddox, born in Somerset Co., and Sophia Ruff, born in Harford Co.; she was married, worked as a maid, and died in Bel Air; informant was her father Joshua M. Maddox, of Bel Air) [Tabernacle Mount Zion U. M. Church Cemetery]

Ruff, William H. 1911-1983 (on same tombstone with Mary E. Ruff; obituary in *The Aegis* on October 13, 1983 stated William Harold "Pete" Ruff was a son of David H. and Mary Lavinia Ruff, and the husband of the late Mary Ellen Gilbert; he was educated at McComas Institute and was employed by the McComas family and later by G. L. Stancill and Sons Co., retiring after 40 years of service; he lived in Joppa and died on October 4, 1983 at Johns Hospital Hospital, survived by a sister Anna Ruff and brothers Floyd and Earl Ruff) [Mt. Zion U. M. Church Cemetery]

Rumsey, ---- stillborn female died May 6, 1931 (no tombstone; death certificate stated she was the daughter of George Willard Rumsey and Dora Miles, all born in Maryland; informant was Maggie Rumsey, of Kalmia) [Clark's U. M. Church Cemetery]

Rumsey, Bryan Presberry January 13, 1951 – February 13, 1951 (no tombstone; death certificate stated he was born in Harford Co., the son of James T. Rumsey and Irene Presberry, and he died at home in rural Darlingtin; informant was his mother) [Berkley Memorial Cemetery]

Rumsey, Charles S. August 9, 1910 – May 30, 1952 [Clark's U. M. Church Cemetery]

Rumsey, Earl R. 1949-2017 (small metal funeral home marker) [Clark's U. M. Church Cemetery]

Rumsey, Edith May 13, 1931 – May 22, 1932 (no tombstone; death certificate stated she was the daughter of Harvey and Estella Rumsey, of Havre de Grace) [St. James United Cemetery]

Rumsey, Edward O'Neil April 10, 1941 – July 19, 2004 (tombstone inscribed with a toolbox and tools) [St. James United Cemetery]

Rumsey, Emma M. March 31, 1915 – September 6, 1998 [Clark's U. M. Church Cemetery]

Rumsey, Erma E. March 23, 1923 – April 13, 2016 (on same tombstone with Henry B. Rumsey) [Clark's U. M. Church Cemetery]

Rumsey, George died March 6, 1913, age not known (no tombstone; death certificate stated he was a day laborer, parents were unknown, and he died of senile debility in Bel Air; informant was William Kirsling, of Bel Air; Harford County Alms House Book 1, 1909-1949, states George Rumsey, age 70, was received on 12 February 1913 and he was buried on 7 March 1913 at Hendon Hill; William Kirsling was superintendent of the Alms House at that time.) [Hendon Hill Cemetery]

Rumsey, George E. "born about October 19, 1875, died April 7, 1939, age 63 years, 5 months, 17 days" (no tombstone; death certificate stated he was born at Thomas Run, the son of George H. Rumsey and Hannah Preston, places of birth unknown to the informant, his widow, Mrs. Margaret Rumsey, of Kalmia; George worked as a laborer and died at Clark's Chapel) [Clark's U. M. Church Cemetery]

Rumsey, George Willard May 17, 1898 – December 17, 1942 (no tombstone; death certificate stated he was born in Kalmia, the son of George E. Rumsey and Margaret Collins, both born in Harford Co.; he married Dora ----- (age 42 in 1942), worked as a farm laborer and lived in the "Kalmia section" all his life; informant was Dora Rumsey, of Bel Air [actually of near Kalmia]) [Clark's U. M. Church Cemetery]

Rumsey, Gladys March 22, 1936 – September 25, 1936 (no tombstone; death certificate stated she was born and died at Kalmia, the daughter of Willard Rumsey, born in Harford Co., and Dora Miles, born in Chase (Baltimore Co.); informant was her father) [Clark's U. M. Church Cemetery]

Rumsey, H. Leroy June 19, 1942 – February 24, 2005 [Clark's U. M. Church Cemetery]

Rumsey, Hannah Juanita died October 7, 1991, age 59 (no tombstone; James Dorsey Card File, African American Obituaries, maintained at the Historical Society of Harford County, has a card with her obituary from an unidentified newspaper dated October 9, 1991 stating she was born in Harford County, the daughter of the late George W. Rumsey and Dora Miles; she lived in Bel Air and died at Fallston General Hospital, survived by a daughter, two brothers, three sisters and one grandchild) [Clark's U. M. Church Cemetery]

Rumsey, Henry B. May 4, 1921 – January 28, 1995 (on same tombstone with Erma E. Rumsey; James Dorsey Card File, African American Obituaries, maintained at the Historical Society of Harford County, has a card with his obituary from an unidentified newspaper stating Henry Benjamin Rumsey was one of 14 children born to George Willard Rumsey and Dora Annie Rumsey; he served in the Army from 1942 to 1945 and retired in 1974 from Edgewood Arsenal after 30 years of civil service; he died at the Perry Point VA Medical Center, survived by his wife of 49 years Erma Elizabeth Rumsey, three sons, seven daughters, one brother, three sisters, 15 grandchildren and 8 great-grandchildren) [Clark's U. M. Church Cemetery]

Rumsey, Ida B. April 7, 1897 – January 20, 1918 (no tombstone; death certificate stated she was the daughter of Thomas Rumsey, both born in Pennsylvania, and Jennie Peco, born in Maryland; she was single, unemployed and died at Abingdon; informant was Jennie Peco, of Abingdon) [John Wesley U. M. E. Church Cemetery in Abingdon]

Rumsey, Irene V., "Loving Wife" November 27, 1932 – May 26, 1999 [Berkley Memorial Cemetery]

Rumsey, James died March 28, 1940, Maryland, Pvt., 154 Depot Brig. (tombstone ; death certificate stated James Rumsey, Jr. was born March 15, 1894 and died March 31, 1940; military records state he was born on March 15, 1894 in Havre de Grace, was inducted in Prince George Co., VA on July 30, 1918 and was honorably discharged on December 2, 1918) [St. James United Cemetery]

Rumsey, Margaret April 15, 1869 – April 23, 1951 (no tombstone; death certificate stated she was born at "Oldfield, Md.," lived at "(Thomas Run) Oldfield" and died a widow at "Thomas Run;" she was the daughter of Seymore Collins and Harriett ----; informant was Mrs. Hanna Corn, of Bel Air) [Clark's U. M. Church Cemetery]

Rumsey, Patricia A. 1951-2007 [Clark's U. M. Church Cemetery]

Rumsey, Paul L., "Our Brother" March 3, 1949 – April 9, 1975 (tombstone; brief obituary in *The Aegis* in April 17, 1975 stated he was employed at Bel Air Memorial Gardens at the time of his sudden death and mentioned no relatives) [Clark's U. M. Church Cemetery]

Rumsey, Rose May 25, 1903 – December 8, 1947 (no tombstone; death certificate stated she was born in Alabama and died a widow in Havre de Grace; parents and husband were unknown to informant Louis Clark) [St. James United Cemetery]

Rumsey, Sarah 1934-1983 [St. James United Cemetery]

Rumsey, Seymore 1915 – May 30, 1952 (no tombstone; accident report in *The Aegis* on June 6, 1952 stated he had been fishing on a bank of Deer Creek when it crumbled and he fell into the water and drowned; he left a wife and seven children, but no names were given) [Clark's U. M. Church Cemetery]

Rumsey, Terence A. December 27, 1968 – May 21, 2003 (inscribed "Always In Our Hearts") [Clark's U. M. Church Cemetery]

Sallie, Joseph J. March 3, 1934 – December 26, 1993 (tombstone, photo) [Fairview A. M. E. Church Cemetery]

Samples, Frank F. July 13, 1894 – August 2, 1982 (tombstone; obituary in *The Aegis* on August 5, 1982 stated Frank Falsom Samples, son of Walter Samples and Lucinda Banks, was formerly of Springfield, MA and New York, and was the husband of the late Ruth Samples; he lived with his nephew, Walter Banks, of Churchville, for the past 2 years, and *The Aegis* on August 12, 1982 reported he died at Harford Memorial Hospital in Havre de Grace) [Asbury Cemetery]

Samples, Lucinda B., "Wife" died March 26, 1919, age 48 *(sic)*, years, 1 month and 6 days (inscribed "At Rest;" death certificate stated Lucinda Banks Samples was born in Churchville on February 20, 1872, the daughter of George Banks and Julia Cooper, both born in Harford Co.; she was married and died at home in Churchville, age 47 years, 1 month and 6 days; informant was Walter W. Samples, of City Hall, Springfield, MA) [Asbury Cemetery]

Samuels, Louise September 5, 1923 – September 17, 1923 (no tombstone; death certificate stated she was the daughter of Arthur Samuels and Olivia Skinner and they all were born in Maryland; informant was J. A. Skinner, of Havre de Grace) [Skinner Cemetery]

Sanders, Aileen August 24, 1917 – September 3, 1917 (no tombstone; death certificate stated she was the daughter of Ernest Sanders, of South Carolina, and Louise Brooth, of Virginia) [St. James United Cemetery]

Sanders, Sharon Ann 1955-2009 (small metal funeral home marker) [St. James United Cemetery]

Saunders, Eliza M. born about August 15, 1871 – died August 20, 1923 (no tombstone; death certificate stated she was the daughter of James Taylor and Rachel Stewart, all born in Maryland; she was married, lived in Aberdeen and died in Havre de Grace Hospital; informant was Stanley N. Saunders, of Aberdeen) [Mt. Calvary U. A. M. E. Church Cemetery]

Saunders, Samuel N. February 22, 1865 – June 2, 1928 (no tombstone; death certificate stated he was the son of Henry Saunders, both born in Maryland, but the name of his mother and her place of birth were not known to informant Mrs. Mary E. Saunders, of Aberdeen; he was a married preacher and lived in Aberdeen RFD) [Mt. Calvary U. A. M. E. Church Cemetery]

Saxton, Samuel 1896 – February 5, 1950 (no tombstone; death certificate stated he was born in Rome, GA and was the unmarried son of Joseph and Theresa Saxton, of Havre de Grace) [St. James United Cemetery]

Schivers, Lloyd William died March 6, 1981, age 45 (no tombstone; obituary in *The Aegis* on March 19, 1981 stated he was born in Aberdeen, the son of Joseph Schivers, of Havre de Grace, and the late Mabel Parker; he was a SP4 in the Army and retired from the federal government in Washington, DC as a clerk-accountant; he died at his home in Frederick, survived by his father, a son Thomas Lloyd Scott of Bel Air, and 4 brothers, Herbert Parker, and Charles, Frank and Thomas E. Schivers) [Mt. Calvary U. A. M. E. Church Cemetery]

Schoate, Gladys Mary November 6, 1917 – September 11, 1945 (no tombstone; Kurtz Funeral Home Record Book 1944-1949, p. 77, stated she was the daughter of Henry Robinson and Lillie Bradford, all born in Harford Co., and died at Rocks, but she actually died at Henryton Sanitarium; she was married, but her husband's name was not given) [Fairview A. M. E. Church Cemetery]

Schroder, Estelle Christy Reid October 8, 1906 – February 15, 1963 (tombstone; Pennington Funeral Home Records stated she was born in Havre de Grace, the daughter of John Christy and Emma Sorrell; she lived at Frenchtown, Cecil Co., MD, for 15 years and died a widow (husband not named); informant was William Schroder, of Frenchtown) [Berkley Memorial Cemetery]

Schroeder, Isadore B. August 5, 1928 – January 11, 2013 (inscribed "Forever In Our Hearts") [St. James United Cemetery]

Schroeder, William H. Jr. January 26, 1922 – February 10, 1985, TEC 5, U.S. Army, World War II [St. James United Cemetery]

Scoggins, Luther M. Jr. August 7, 1951 – April 2, 1993, U.S. Army, Vietnam [St. James United Cemetery]

Sconion, Beatrice A. 1908-1962 [Union U. M. Church Cemetery]

Sconion, Charles T. Jr., "Son" December 2, 1948 – April 18, 1984 [St. James United Cemetery]

Sconion, Charles T. Sr. August 2, 1924 – March 29, 2003, U.S. Navy, World War II [St. James United Cemetery]

Sconion, Edna 1930-   (on tombstone with Samuel Sconion, Jr. inscribed "married March 27, 1949") [St. James United Cemetery]

Sconion, Ella, "Mother" August 21, 1908 – March 15, 1986 [St. James United Cemetery]

Sconion, Eloise Elizabeth September 8, 1944 – January 5, 1945 (no tombstone; death certificate stated she was the daughter of Charles Sconion and Hazel Kenly) [Union U. M. Church Cemetery]

Sconion, James Maurice January 22, 1967 – November 12, 1988 (football image with "48" inscribed inside it; James Dorsey Card File, African American Obituaries, maintained at the Historical Society of Harford County, has a card stating obituary is in the *Record* 11-30-1988]

Sconion, Joanette C. died January 11, 2009, age 68 (death notice in *The Aegis* stated she lived in Edgewood, died in Perry Point and was buried in Aberdeen) [Union U. M. Church Cemetery]

Sconion, Lloyd Sunrise November 28, 1964 – Sunset July 26, 2002 [St. James United Cemetery]

Sconion, Mary A., "Daughter" December 3, 1932 – April 19, 1989 [St. James United Cemetery]

Sconion, Michael Edward June 3, 1953 – May 27, 2000 (basketball image and football image with "42" inscribed inside them and also an image of a fishing rod and reel) [St. James United Cemetery]

Sconion, Ronald E. 1952-1995 (small metal funeral home marker) [Berkley Memorial Cemetery]

Sconion, Russell Percy Sr. September 13, 1930 – April 30, 1001 (no tombstone; obituary in *The Aegis* on May 4, 2001 stated he was the youngest son of Samuel E. Sconion, Sr. and Ella Z. Christy; he served in the Army from October 12, 1951 to October 11, 1959 (a second obituary in *The Aegis* on June 4, 2001 stated he served until July 11, 1953), married Stella Hawkins in 1952 (married 49 years in 2001), worked at Perry Point VA Hospital and for the City of Aberdeen for 20 years until he retired in 1995; he was survived by his wife, 6 daughters, 1 son, 13 grandchildren, 15 great-grandchildren and a host of relatives and friends; "Rus Sconion" was the owner of a lot in section 13 asome time after 1951) [Mt. Calvary U. A. M. E. Church Cemetery]

Sconion, Samuel E., "Husband" February 8, 1900 – February 13, 1973 (tombstone; buried in section 23; obituary in *The Aegis* on February 22, 1973 stated Samuel Evans Sconion, Sr. was born in Loreley, MD, son of the late Lloyd and Harriet Sconion, and resided at 736 Otsego St. in Havre de Grace; he died at Harford

Memorial Hospital and was survived by his wife Ella, 4 sons, 1 daughter, 1 sister, 24 grandchildren and 17 great-grandchildren) [Mt. Calvary U. A. M. E. Church Cemetery]

Sconion, Samuel Jr. 1928-2006 (on same tombstone with Edna Sconion inscribed "married March 27, 1949") [St. James United Cemetery]

Sconion, Stelle E. died November 24, 2016, age not given (no tombstone; death notice in *The Aegis* stated she was survived by 6 children, 14 grandchildren, 30 great-grandchildren, 5 great-great-grandchildren, 1 brother and a host of relatives and friends) [Mt. Calvary U. A. M. E. Church Cemetery]

Scott, Bess (owner of a lot in section 39 some time after 1951) [Mt. Calvary U. A. M. E. Church Cemetery]

Scott, Bessie November 19, 1900 – October 27, 1987 (on same tombstone with Henry Scott) [Gravel Hill Cemetery]

Scott, Cora H. June 18, 1895 – August 7, 1971 (on same tombstone with Rev. Elisha E. Scott inscribed "Together Forever") [Community Baptist Church Cemete

Scott, Dora V. April 21, 1900 – August 20, 1983 [Mt. Zion U. M. Church Cemetery]

Scott, Elija July 15, 1860 – December 29, 1925 (no tombstone; death certificate stated he was the son of James Scott and Cassie Pinkney, all born in Harford Co.; he was married, worked as a laborer and died at Wheel; informant was Mrs. Harriet A.Scott, of Joppa) [Mt. Zion U. M. Church Cemetery]

Scott, Elisha E. (Rev.) November 15, 1985 – February 10, 1978 (on the same tombstone with Cora H. Scott inscribed "Together Forever") [Community Baptist Church Cemetery]

Scott, Eliza died February 14, 1903 (copied in 1987, but not found in 2018) [Mt. Zion U. M. Church Cemetery]

Scott, Ella M. 1889 – November 8, 1983 (no tombstone; obituary in *The Aegis* on November 17, 1983 stated she was born in Harford Co., the daughter of John Scott and Ella Bond, and was a domestic worker in Bel Air; she died on November 8, 1983, age 94, at Harford Memorial Hospital in Havre de Grace and was survived by nieces and nephews) [Asbury Cemetery]

Scott, Ethel Irene May 2, 1901 – December 18, 1944 (no tombstone; death certificate stated she was the unmarried daughter of William S. Scott and Rachel Lisby, of Havre de Grace) [St. James United Cemetery]

Scott, F. M. 1905-1943 [Berkley Memorial Cemetery]

Scott, Harriett Anne died January 27, 1935, age about 88 (no tombstone; death certificate stated she was born in Harford Co., the daughter of Joshua Waters and Letta Peters, both born in Maryland; she had lived in Joppa for 40 years and was the widow of Elija Scott; she was buried in "Mt. A.M.E. Cem.;" informant was Letta Gray, of Joppa) [Mt. Zion U. M. Church Cemetery]

Scott, Hattie S. July 29, 1921 – March 24, 1976 (tombstone; buried in section 39; obituary in *The Aegis* on April 1, 1976 stated she was born in Harford Co., the daughter of the late James E. Anderson and Sarah McComas, and married Joseph U. Scott; she served as clerk for Mt. Calvary, lived at 2403 Old Post Road in Havre de Grace and died at Harford Memorial Hospital, survived by her husband, 3 sons, 4 daughters, 29 grandchildren, 1 great-grandchild, and 1 sister) [Mt. Calvary U. A. M. E. Church Cemetery]

Scott, Henry September 3, 1901 – September 9, 1995 (on same tombstone with Bessie Scott) [Gravel Hill Cemetery]

Scott, Howard L. III August 4, 1946 – July 12, 1999, PFC, U.S. Army, Vietnam (buried in section 19; inscribed "Lovingly Known as Butch" and "Forever In Our Hearts") [Mt. Calvary U. A. M. E. Church Cemetery]

Scott, Howard L. Jr. September 30, 1925 – August 27, 2001, STM1, U.S. Navy, World War II, Purple Heart [Mt. Calvary U. A. M. E. Church Cemetery]

Scott, James died December 20, 1914, age about 80 (no tombstone; death certificate stated he was the son of Scarff Scott, both born in Harford Co., but mother's name was unknown to informant James Scott, of Bel Air; he was married, had worked as a laborer and died at the Alms House in Bel Air) [Clark's U. M. Church Cemetery]

Scott, James died on September 8, 1894, age not given (no tombstone; death notice in *The Aegis* on September 14, 1894 stated he died near Level by cooking and eating toadstools that he thought were mushrooms; burial place not reported) [possibly Green Spring Church Cemetery]

Scott, Jane March 31, 1942 – October 1, 1918 (no tombstone; death certificate stated she was the daughter of Samuel Orsborn (Osborn) and Rachel Daugerty (Daugherty), all born in Harford Co.; she was a widow who did washing and ironing and died at Carsin Run; informant was Thomas Orsburn (Osborn), of Bel Air) [Asbury Cemetery]

Scott, Jennie V., "Sister" August 31, 1875 – April 18, 1908 [Tabernacle Mount Zion U. M. Church Cemetery]

Scott, Jimmie Lee 1914-1978, U.S. Army, World War II (tombstone; Pennington Funeral Home records stated he was born in Birmingham, AL, but his parents were not known; he lived in Havre de Grace and died on December 12, 1978 at Harford Memorial Hospital [St. James United Cemetery]

Scott, John W. H. June 18, 1868 – October 10, 1942 (no tombstone; death certificate stated he was born in Harford Co., but his parents were not known to informant Mrs. Ella Scott, of 137 Alice Ann St., Bel Air; he was a laborer in Bel Air and lived at the same address) [Asbury Cemetery]

Scott, Joseph U. died September 28, 1981, age 67 (no tombstone; obituary in *The Aegis* on October 1, 1981 stated he was born in Maryland, the son of the late Henry and Sophie Scott; he served in the Navy in World War II, retired from Aberdeen Proving Ground as a forklift operator and died at Harford Memorial Hospital in Havre de Grace; he was married (wife not named) and survived by 3 sons, 4 daughters, 30 grandchildren, and 6 great-grandchildren) [Mt. Calvary U. A. M. E. Church Cemetery]

Scott, Lessie Irene September 6, 1911 – October 30, 1912 (no tombstone; death certificate stated she died at Castleton, the daughter of James Scott and Martha Williamson, all born in Maryland; informant was her father, James Scott, of Castleton) [Clark's U. M. Church Cemetery]

Scott, Lucretia died December 16, 1950, age about 75 (no tombstone; death certificate stated she was born in Fallston, married, and died at home near Bel Air; she was the daughter of Josiah and Jane Lee; informant was John B. Munnikhuysen, of 5526 38th St., Baltimore 18, MD) [Hendon Hill Cemetery]

Scott, Margaret died October 2, 1889, age not stated (inscribed "Faithful Member of the First Presbyterian Church of Bel Air" and "She hath done what she could.") [Tabernacle Mount Zion U. M. Church Cemetery]

Scott, Maria E. January 10, 1828 – May 10, 1911 (no tombstone; death certificate stated she was born in Rockbridge, VA, the daughter of Robert Rose and Betsy Phillips both born in Virginia; she was a widow and worked as a laundress; informant was Sarah Goins, of Bel Air) [Hendon Hill Cemetery]

Scott, Mary died July 9, 1911, age 100, birth date unknown (no tombstone; death certificate stated she was born in Baltimore Co., the daughter of Samuel Wilson, but her parents' birth places and mother's name were unknown to informant Olevia Elias, of Street, MD; she died a widow at Dublin) [Clark's U. M. Church Cemetery]

Scott, Mary V. (name inscribed on a small wooden marker) [St. James United Cemetery]

Scott, Raymond April 13, 1944 – June 30, 1982 (copied in 1987, but not found in 2018; buried in section 39) [Mt. Calvary U. A. M. E. Church Cemetery]

Scott, Robert C. 1946-1977 (tombstone; obituary in *The Aegis* on October 13, 1977 stated he was born in Havre de Grace, the son of Ernestine M. Christy and the late Robert C. Scott, and died in Baltimore on October 5, 1977, survived by his mother, step-father Leroy Christy, a daughter Tia Scott, six brothers Elroy Christy, Leroy Christy, Lineer Christy, Gregory Christy and Duane Christy, and five sisters Susan Smith, Deanna Christy, Delialah Christy, Desiree Christy and Darvina Christy) [St. James United Cemetery]

Scott, Virginia M., "Our Mother, Our Best Friend" February 14, 1927 – December 2, 2012 [Mt. Calvary U. A. M. E. Church Cemetery]

Scott, William Franklyn July 6, 1879 – May 26, 1932 (no tombstone; death certificate stated he was born in Virginia and reportedly committed suicide by drowning in the Susquehanna River at Havre de Grace; his parents were unknown to his wife Rachel L. Scott, of Havre de Grace) [St. James United Cemetery]

Scott, Yvonne K. December 20, 1951 – December 15, 2009 [St. James United Cemetery]

Scroggins, Luther M. 1918-2006, U.S. Army, World War II [St. James United Cemetery]

Scroggins, Luther McClinton died April 2, 1993, age 41 (no tombstone; James Dorsey Card File, African American Obituaries, maintained at the Historical Society of Harford County, has a card with obituary from an unidentified newspaper dated April 9, 1998 stating he was a native of Harford County, the son of Luther M. Scroggins, Sr. and Willie Guary, and a longtime member of Flat Rock Baptist Church in Tallahassee, VA; he lived in Aberdeen, was a meat cutter and died at the Baltimore VAMC, but no mention of his military service; he was survived by five children, five grandchildren, two sisters and a brother) [Union U. M. Church Cemetery]

Scroggins, Willie R. 1927-2017 (small metal funeral home marker) [St. James United Cemetery]

Selby, Mary L. 1925-1978 [Mt. Calvary U. A. M. E. Church Cemetery]

Sewell, Mattie J. July 31, 1900 – November 22, 1984 (on same tombstone with Rev. W. Vernon Sewell) [Fairview A. M. E. Church Cemetery]

Sewell, Rosa died September 4, 1920, age 48 (no tombstone; death certificate stated she was single and worked as a domestic; her parents were John Sewell and ---- (blank) Thompson and they were all born in Maryland and lived in Bel Air; informant was Tom Hicks, of Bel Air)

Sewell, W. Vernon (Rev.) May 29, 1900 – February 24, 1976 (on same tombstone with Mattie J. Sewell) [Fairview A. M. E. Church Cemetery]

Shaw, Earnest J. 1920-   (on same tombstone with Genesta C. Shaw) [Berkley Memorial Cemetery]

Shaw, Genesta C. 1903-1978 (on same tombstone with Earnest J. Shaw) [Berkley Memorial Cemetery]

Shaw, Vetra Lurena, "Mother" May 1, 1951 – February 24, 2003 [Fairview A. M. E. Church Cemetery]

Shepherd, Sterling D. June 11, 1942 – November 11, 1967 [Union U. M. Church Cemetery]

Shepherd, William L. April 21, 1926 – February 27, 1995, U.S. Navy [St. James United Cemetery]

Sheppard, Josie Mildred 1933-2005 (small metal funeral home marker) [St. James United Cemetery]

Sheppard, Sarah 1896-1968 (on same tombstone with Wendell P. Sheppard) [Berkley Memorial Cemetery]

Sheppard, Shirley M., "Loving Mom and Grandmom" 1940-2012 [Berkley Memorial Cemetery]

Sheppard, Wendell P. 1906-1997 (on same tombstone with Sarah Sheppard; obituary in *The Aegis* on July 9, 1997 stated Wendell Paul Sheppard was born in Perryman, the son of John Sheppard and Ida Rebecca Brown, and was the husband of the late Jane Sconion Sheppard; he lived in Aberdeen, retired as a B&O Railroad trackman and died at the Lorien Nursing and Rehabilitation Center in Belcamp on July 3, 1997, age 90, survived by a brother Tevis L. Hoke, a sister Hazel V. Frisby, nine grandchildren, ten great-grandchildren and four great-great-grandchildren; he was the father of William Sheppard who died in 1995) [Berkley Memorial Cemetery]

Sherdan (Sheridan), Samuel February 2, 1849 – March 4, 1925 (no tombstone; death certificate stated he was the widowed son of Daniel Sherdan (Sheridan), but his mother's name was unknown to informant Mrs. Frances Richardson, of Havre de Grace) [St. James United Cemetery]

Sherwood, Sarrah April 2, 1868 – March 30, 1942 (no tombstone; death certificate stated she was born in Harford Co., the daughter of Ann Christy, born in Maryland, but informant, Mrs. Marietta Gordon, of 824 Walnut St., Wilmington, DE, did not know the name of her father; the widow of Augustus Sherwood, she lived at 519 Alliance St., Havre de Grace) [Gravel Hill Cemetery]

Shinn, Mary E. March – (blank), 1882 – July 10, 1924 (no tombstone; death certificate stated she was married and lived and died in Bel Air; her parents were Joseph Dorsey and Mary Daugherty and they were all born in Maryland; informant was Mary Dorsey, of Bel Air) [Hendon Hill Cemetery]

Shivers, Edna May stillborn on November 5, 1937 (no tombstone; death certificate stated she was the daughter of Joseph Shivers, born in Charles Co., and Mildred Murphy, born in Harford Co.; she died at home on Short Lane in Aberdeen RFD; informant was her father) [Mt. Calvary U. A. M. E. Church Cemetery]

Shivers, Ernest (owner of a lot in section 18 some time after 1951) [Mt. Calvary U. A. M. E. Church Cemetery]

Shivers, Jack (owner of a lot in section 12 some time after 1951) [Mt. Calvary U. A. M. E. Church Cemetery]

Shivers, Joseph October 16, 1940 – May 29, 1941 (no tombstone; death certificate stated he was the son of Joseph Shivers and Mildred Murphy, all born in Maryland and lived in Aberdeen; he died in Harford Memorial Hospital in Havre de Grace; information from hospital records) [Mt. Calvary U. A. M. E. Church Cemetery]

Shivers, Kristie Lynn 1959-1959 (on same tombstone with Mabel E. Shivers) [Mt. Calvary U. A. M. E. Church Cemetery]

Shivers, Mabel E. 1914-1940 (on same tombstone with Kristie Lynn Shivers) [Mt. Calvary U. A. M. E. Church Cemetery]

Shivers, Mary Wilson died December 24, 1978, age 54 (no tombstone; obituary in *The Aegis* on January 4, 1979 stated she was the wife of Joseph M. Shivers, lived in Havre de Grace and died at Harford Memorial Hospital, survived by her husband, a step-brother and 5 step-sons) [Mt. Calvary U. A. M. E. Church Cemetery]

Short, Lacy 1910-1984 [St. James United Cemetery]

Showell, Mary 1871-1922 (copied in 2018, but was not listed in 1987 and 2002) [Gravel Hill Cemetery]

Sibert, Alphonso E. 1958-2008 (small metal funeral home marker) [Berkley Memorial Cemetery]

Simmons, Casbury 1909-1927 (tombstone inscription, but death certificate stated Casberry Simmons was born August 3, 1908 in South Carolina and died October 16, 1926 in Havre de Grace) [St. James United Cemetery]

Simmons, Clifton December 25, 1937 – May 29, 1982, SP4, U.S. Army [St. James United Cemetery]

Simmons, Ellen October 1, 1852 – October 22, 1911 (no tombstone; death certificate stated she was the married daughter of Aquilla McGaw, both born in Harford Co., but her mother was unknown to informant George T. Pennington, undertaker, of Havre de Grace) [St. James United Cemetery]

Simmons, Essie 1890-1955 [St. James United Cemetery]

Simmons, Faith December 6, 1916 – June 4, 1995 (on same tombstone with Joseph A. Simmons) [St. James United Cemetery]]

Simmons, Gary 1950-1982 (inscribed "In God's Care") [Mt. Calvary U. A. M. E. Church Cemetery]

Simmons, Infant stillborn male on April 27, 1925 (no tombstone; death certificate stated she was the daughter of Casbery Simmons and Annie Croxsen, of Havre de Grace) [St. James United Cemetery

Simmons, James L. Jr. June 21, 1927 – February 13, 2004, ST3, U.S. Navy, World War II (tombstone; "Mr. Simmons" owned a lot in section 6 some time after 1951) [Mt. Calvary U. A. M. E. Church Cemetery]

Simmons, Joseph A. January 3, 1911 – November 18, 2005 (on same tombstone with Faith Simmons) [St. James United Cemetery]

Simmons, Pearl L., "Beloved Wife and Mother" November 29, 1929 – August 6, 2004 (tombstone; "Mrs. Simmons" owned a lot in section 6 some time after 1951) [Mt. Calvary U. A. M. E. Church Cemetery]

Simms, Charles W. died November 2, 1914, age about 60 (no tombstone; obituary in *The Aegis* on November 6, 1914 stated he was formerly of Michaelsville and died in Baltimore where he held until recently a position in the Custom House; he was recognized as one of the leaders of his people and was buried in Michaelsville; he was buried in the Old Union Chapel Cemetery at Michaelsville; possibly interred later in Union Chapel Cemetery near Aberdeen) [Union U. M. Church Cemetery]

Simms, Henrietta, wife of Jacob Simms Sr., died March 1901, age 82 (tombstone copied in 1992, not found in 2018; death certificate stated she was born in Michaelsville, the daughter of Jesse and Melissa Johnson, and she died a widow on March 14, 1901, age 82 years, 9 months, and 11 days, survived by 6 children) [Union U. M. Church Cemetery]

Simms, Jacob March 15, 1840 – April 11, 1899 (inscribed with this verse: "Dear is the spot where a Christian sleep / And sweet the strains that angels pour. / O! Why should we in anguish weep / He's not lost but gone before.") [Union U. M. Church Cemetery]

Simms, Louisa died April 12, 1903, age 27 years, 1 month, 14 days (inscribed with this verse: "So bright and beautiful was the morning / That our sister passed away / She seemed to hear a voice calling / Leave thy afflicted bed today.") [Asbury Cemetery]

Simms, Margaret died November 16, 1932, age about 80, birth date unknown (no tombstone; death certificate stated she was born in Frederick Co., MD, but her parents' names were not known to informant Charles Hall, of Pylesville; Margaret was a cook and the widow of Samuel Simms; she lived and died at Whiteford P. O. and was buried at Rocks) [Chestnut Grove A. M. E. Church Cemetery, formerly LaGrange Cemetery at Rocks]

Simms, Robert H. April 24, 1873 – March 31, 1929 (no tombstone; death certificate stated he was single and worked as a day laborer, but his place of birth and his parents names and their places of birth were unknown to informant Mr. B. B. Middleton, of Aberdeen) [Mt. Calvary U. A. M. E. Church Cemetery]

Simms, Samuel 1842-1919 (tombstone inscription, but death certificate stated he was born in Harford Co. on August 15, 1843, married, worked as a laborer, lived at Pylesville and died October 27, 1919; his parents were Samuel Simms, Sr. and Dolly ----, both born in Harford Co.; informant was Samuel Wilson, Sr., of Pylesville) [Chestnut Grove A. M. E. Church Cemetery, formerly LaGrange Cemetery at Rocks]

Simon, James T., "Beloved Son and Father" September 22, 1981 – January 12, 2015 (with his photo) [St. James United Cemetery]

Simpson, Eva R. 1926-2003 (white wooden cross, about 3 feet in height, inscribed "At the Cross") [Union U. M. Church Cemetery]

Simpson, Harry Lee 1924-1994 (white wooden cross, about 3 feet in height, inscribed "Peace Be Still") [Union U. M. Church Cemetery]

Simpson, John O. 1900-1958 (small metal funeral home marker) [Mt. Calvary U. A. M. E. Church Cemetery]

Simpson, John William 1922-1986, Sgt., U.S. Army, World War II [Berkley Memorial Cemetery]

Singleton, Edward died October 3, 1928, age about 47 (no tombstone; death certificate stated he was born in South Carolina and was single; parents wunknown to informant Bertha Bibbs) [Union U. M. Church Cemetery]

Skaggs, John A. July 23, 1919 – August 18, 1986, SGM, U.S. Army, World War II, Korea, Vietnam (copied in 1987, but not found in 2018) [Mt. Calvary U. A. M. E. Church Cemetery]

Skinner, Beulah September 12, 1897 – September 17, 1914 (tombstone; death certificate stated she was born in Havre de Grace, daughter of Horace Skinner, of Havre de Grace, and Rose German, of Virginia) [Skinner Cemetery]

Skinner, Elizabeth died February 16, 1920, age about 45 (no tombstone; death certificate stated she was the daughter of James Sorrell and Rachel Armistead, all born in Maryland; she was married and died in Havre de Grace; informant was J. T. Skinner, of Havre de Grace) [Skinner Cemetery]

Skinner, Emma W. 1883-1973 (on same tombstone with William B. Skinner; obituary in *The Aegis* on October 18, 1973 stated Emma Francis Skinner, of 651 Pennington Ave., Havre de Grace, died October 10, 1973 at Harford Memorial Hospital; she was born on September 2, 1883 in Centreville, MD, the daughter William and Emma Frances Willis, and resided in Havre de Grace for the past 64 years; she was survived by a daughter, Mrs. Hudgins, with whom she lived, and 11 grandchildren and 40 great-grandchildren) [St. James United Cemetery]

Skinner, Frances J. about 1842 – December 24, 1920 (tombstone; death certificate stated she was about age 75 and the widowed daughter of James Legar and Mary Scott, all were born in Maryland, and informant was Horace Skinner, of Havre de Grace; but her tombstone stated she was 78) [Skinner Cemetery]

Skinner, Henry died November 5, 1918, age about 68 (tombstone; death certificate stated he was the son of Horace Skinner and Hattie Martin, all born in Maryland; he was married, worked as a laborer and died in Havre de Grace; informant was John T. Skinner, of Havre de Grace) [Skinner Cemetery]

Skinner, Henry, "Father" 1895-1954 [St. James United Cemetery]

Skinner, Horace S. January 1, 1867 – June 30, 1934 (death certificate stated he was buried in Skinner Cemetery, but marker for him and wife Rosa G. Skinner is in St. James United Cemetery) [St. James United Cemetery]

Skinner, Infant stillborn female on May 15, 1944 (no tombstone; death certificate stated she was the daughter of John Wagner Skinner and Rosetta Elizabeth Johnson, of Havre de Grace) [St. James United Cemetery]

Skinner, J. Henry, "Father" 1902-1981 [St. James United Cemetery]

Skinner, J. T. died September 29(?), 1904, under 4 weeks old (no tombstone; death certificate did not state place of burial in Havre de Grace; he was the son of J. T. Skinner and Lizzie Sorrell) [probably Skinner Cemetery]

Skinner, John Henry Jr. July 5, 1913 – September 5, 1872 (copied in 1987; tombstone had toppled over by 2018) [St. James United Cemetery]

Skinner, John T. died May 20, 1930, age about 63 (no tombstone; death certificate stated he was born in Maryland, worked as a laborer in Havre de Grace, was a widower and the son of Jacob Skinner, born in Maryland, but his mother was unknown to informant Henry Skinner; James Dorsey Card File, African-American Obituaries, maintained at the Historical Society of Harford County, has a card for an obituary from the *Bel Air Times* on May 23, 1930 stating Tobe Skinnner died at his home and for many years he brought fish from Havre de Grace to sell to citizens in Bel Air; he was popular and well liked) [probably Skinner Cemetery]

Skinner, Joseph H. – see Henry Skinner [Skinner Cemetery]

Skinner, Juanita March 5, 1916 – August 14, 1916 (no tombstone; death certificate stated she was the daughter of Teavre or Teavie(?) Tildon, born in Harford Co., and Emma Skinner, born in Havre de Grace; informant was "Miss Emma Skinner" of Havre de Grace) [Skinner Cemetery]

Skinner, Lewis died July 5, 1904, age 45 (no tombstone; death certificate stated he was single and the son of John Skinner, mother unknown) [Skinner Cemetery]

Skinner, Marie May 5, 1915 – October 12, 1918 (no tombstone; death certificate stated she was the daughter of Harry Thompson and Annie Skinner, all born in Maryland, and died in Havre de Grace) [Skinner Cemetery]

Skinner, Minnie November 1, 1892 – September 22, 1927 (no tombstone; death certificate stated she was wife of Henry Skinner and the daughter of John Richardson, mother unknown) [Skinner Cemetery]

Skinner, Olivia, "Mother" October 31, 1901 – February 6, 1965 (inscribed "Rock of Ages") [Berkley Memorial Cemetery]

Skinner, Phillis May 25, 1907 – October 4, 1936 (no tombstone; death certificate stated she was born at Conowingo, MD, the daughter of Jacob and Anna Smith, and married John T. Skinner, of Havre de Grace) [St. James United Cemetery]

Skinner, Rosa G. July 15, 1871 – May 3, 1936 (tombstone; death certificate stated Rosie G. Skinner was born July 15, 1872 and died May 3, 1936) [St. James United Cemetery]

Skinner, Sadie October 1, 1882(?) – February 28, 1901 [Skinner Cemetery]

Skinner, Sid(?) illegible dates (Reggie Bishop in 1987 stated the tombstone was illegible and needed rubbing, but it was not found in 2018) [Skinner Cemetery]

Skinner, Thomas G. December 3, 1874 – October 19, 1912 (no tombstone; death certificate stated he was the unmarried son of Sidney H. Skinner, of Havre de Grace, and Frances Leger, of Baltimore) [St. James United Cemetery]

Skinner, Thomas G. died October 18, 1912, age 40 (tombstone; death certificate stated he was born December 3, 1874, the unmarried son of Sidney H. Skinner and Frances Leger; it also stated he was buried in St. James Cemetery) [actually Skinner Cemetery]

Skinner, Victoria died August 5, 1887, age 2 years and 20 days [Skinner Cemetery]

Skinner, Walter died October 17, 1912, age 16 (tombstone; death certificate stated he was born June 21, 1896, son of Horace Skinner, of Havre de Grace, and Rosa German, of Virginia, and was buried in St. James

Cemetery) [actually Skinner Cemetery]

Skinner, William B. 1892-1963 (on same tombstone with Emma H. Skinner) [St. James United Cemetery]

Skinner, William T. or E. died 15 August 1887, age 2 months and 15 days [Skinner Cemetery]

Skinner, Willie 1884 – July 18, 1907 (tombstone; death certificate stated William Skinner, son of J. T. Skinner and Lizzie Sorrell, was single and died at age 20 years, 6 months and 23 days, which would make his birth date December 26, 1886, not 1884) [Skinner Cemetery]

Smallwood, Esther 1901-1957 (copied in 1987, but not found in 2018; same dates as Jessie Smallwood) [St. James United Cemetery]

Smallwood, Jessie 1901-1957 (copied in 1987, but not found in 2018; same dates as Esther Smallwood) [St. James United Cemetery]

Smart, Ann Mariah November – (blank), 1853 – February 9, 1917 (no tombstone; death certificate stated she was the daughter of Jacob Bradford and Caroline James, and all were born in Maryland; she was married and died in Joppa; informant was Joseph Smart, of Joppa) [Mt. Zion U. M. Church Cemetery]

Smart, Joseph September 14, 1846 – January 21, 1933 (no tombstone; death certificate stated he was born in Baltimore Co., the son of Annie Smart, born in Maryland, but his father was not known to informant Emma Smart, of Fallston; he married Maria Bradford and died a widower in Bel Air where he had lived for 2 days in the County Home) [Mt. Zion U. M. Church Cemetery]

Smart, Walter Howard August 8, 1887 – August 11, 1913 (no tombstone; death certificate stated he was born in Harford Co., the son of Joseph Smart, born in Baltimore Co., and Mariah Bradford, born in Harford Co.; he was single, worked as a laborer and died at The Mountain; informant was his father Joseph Smart, of Joppa RFD) [Mt. Zion U. M. Church Cemetery]

Smith, ---- (no tombstone, but Kurtz Funeral Home records stated John Smith's child was buried in a walnut coffin on September 28, 1882 from G. Smithen's tenant house) [West Liberty Church Cemetery]

Smith, ---- February 2, 1921 – February 3, 1921, premature birth, lived 12 hours (no tombstone; death certificate stated "Not Named Baby Smith" was the daughter of Ralph Smith and Carrie Elsie Price, all born in Maryland, she died at home near Poole; informant was Marie Price, of Street, MD) [Berkley Memorial Cemetery]

Smith, ---- February 6, 1916 – February 8, 1916 (no tombstone; death certificate stated "Baby Smith" was the daughter of Harrison Lewis and Martha Smith, all born in Maryland, and she died at home in Poole; informant was William V. Smith, of Darlington) [Berkley Memorial Cemetery]

Smith, ---- stillborn female on August 5, 1927 and "twins mate born alive" (no tombstone; death certificate stated "Unnamed Smith" was the daughter of Ralph Smith and Elsie Price, all born in Maryland; she died at home at Cedars near Darlington; informant was her father) [Berkley Memorial Cemetery]

Smith, ---- stillborn female on June 14, 1913 (no tombstone; death certificate stated she was the daughter of Bryon Smith and Georgie Follan, all born in Harford Co.) [Union U. M. Church Cemetery]

Smith, ---lia(?) J. died ---- (illegible tombstone) [Hendon Hill Cemetery]

Smith, Addison E. January 22, 1920 – November 20, 1980, TEC5, U.S. Army, World War II (tombstone; obituary in *The Aegis* on December 4, 1980 stated Addison Earnest "Smitty" Smith was born and raised in Churchville, the son of the late George Allen Smith and Pearl Jones; he served in the Philippines and Southeast Asia during World War II and the 897th Q. M. Laundry Co. at Fort George Meade and discharged as a sergeant; married to Yvonne ---- and died at the Veterans Administration Hospital in Philadelphia) [Asbury Cemetery]

Smith, Agnes Austin died December 27, 1983, age 63 (no tombstone; obituary in *The Aegis* on January 6, 1983 stated she was born in Millersville, GA and was the wife of Blanton Smith; she lived in Aberdeen and died at Harford Memorial Hospital in Havre de Grace, survived by her husband and a brother Chasecy Austin) [Berkley Memorial Cemetery]

Smith, Albert 1885-1972 (copied in 1987, but not found in 2018) [St. James United Cemetery]

Smith, Alfred C. Jr. died March 16, 1984, age not given (no tombstone; obituary in *The Aegis* stated he was born in Aberdeen, son of the late Alfred C. Smith, Sr. and Florence Smith, and died at Bon Secours Hospital in Baltimore; he was survived by 2 daughters (his wife's name was not mentioned), 2 brothers, 4 sisters and 2 grandchildren) [Union U. M. Church Cemetery]

Smith, Allen S. February 25, 1941, Pennsylvania, Pvt., 549 Eng. Serv. Bn. [Berkley Memorial Cemetery]

Smith, Alma Ruth 1915-2013 (small metal funeral home marker) [John Wesley U. M. E. Church Cemetery in Abingdon]

Smith, Amelia July 10, 1859 – November 25, 1935 (no tombstone; death certificate stated she was the widow of Barney Smith and the daughter of Alek Pennington and Sarah McComas) [Union U. M. Church Cemetery]

Smith, Annie M. January 27, 1892 – January 20, 1965 (on same tombstone with Clarence B. Smith) [Fairview A. M. E. Church Cemetery]

Smith, Annie Priscilla died September 10, 1998, age 77 (obituary and photo in *The Aegis* on November 4, 1998 stated she was born in Darlington, daughter of the late Paul Lester and Dorothy Smith; she lived in Aberdeen, worked as a beautician from 1941 to 1973, lived in New York for more than 20 years and died at Brooklyn Medical Center; she was survived by an aunt in Darlington, an aunt and uncle in Bel Air, and predeceased by a brother, Daniel L. Smith) [Berkley Memorial Cemetery]

Smith, Arthur Richard Jr., "Beloved Father and Grandfather" July 27, 1966 – February 15, 2018, SP4, U.S. Army [Clark's U. M. Church Cemetery]

Smith, Benjamin, Co. A, 30th U. S. C. T. (no dates; military records stated Benjamin Smith entered the service as a private, United States Colored Troops, on June 13, 1864, served under Capt. LeRoy E. Baldwin and was "absent sick, when mustered out" on December 10, 1865) [St. James United Cemetery]

Smith, Benjamin W. September 20, 1896 – June 3, 1964, Maryland, Cpl., Co. D, 811 Pioneer Infantry, World War I (tombstone; military records stated he lived at Aberdeen RFD #2 and was inducted into the service on September 1, 1918, served overseas from October 20, 1918 to July 4, 1919 and was honorably discharged on July 10, 1919) [Berkley Memorial Cemetery]

Smith, Bernard May 2, 1910 – January 24, 1982 (obituary in *The Harford Democrat* on January 27, 1982 (and similarly in *The Aegis* on January 28, 1982) stated he was the son of the late Stewart Smith and Lillian Presberry and a lifelong resident of Darlington; he worked there as a laborer in a garage and died at Harford Memorial Hospital in Havre de Grace, survived by two brothers, Samuel Smith and Lester Smith, and a sister, Esther S. Fennell) [Berkley Memorial Cemetery]

Smith, Bertha Hawkins 1922-1980 [St. James United Cemetery]

Smith, Beulah Mae December 14, 1930 – July 28, 2005 (photo and inscription "I fought a good fight, I have finished my course, I have kept my faith") [Berkley Memorial Cemetery]

Smith, C. L. 1927-1964 [Clark's U. M. Church Cemetery]

Smith, Carole J. May 15, 1942 – January 31, 1985 [Asbury Cemetery]

Smith, Caroline May 14, 1838 – January 2, 1919 (no tombstone; death certificate stated she was a widow and the daughter of Peter Stansbury and Harriett Lisby, all born in Maryland) [Union U. M. Church Cemetery]

Smith, Carrie E. 1899-1974 (on same tombstone with Ralph T. Smith; obituary in *The Aegis* stated Carrie Elsie Smith was the widow of Ralph T. Smith, lived on Cedar Church Road and died at Harford Memorial Hospital on November 12, 1974, age not given; survived by 5 sons, 4 daughters, 14 grandchildren, 3 great-grandchildren) [Cedars Chapel Cemetery]

Smith, Carrie January 15, 1874 – September 25, 1930 (no tombstone; death certificate stated she was George W. Hooper and Rebecca Cooper, all born in Maryland; she was married and lived at Bel Air RFD #1; informant was Mrs. Hester C. Banks, also of Bel Air RFD #1) [Asbury Cemetery]

Smith, Charles I. April 13, 1922 – November 24, 1981 (on same tombstone with Myrtle E. Smith) [Fairview A.

M. E. Church Cemetery]

Smith, Charles W. March 7, 1874 – February 5, 1944 (no tombstone; death certificate stated he was the son of Daniel Smith and Caroline Stansbury, and he was divorced at the time of death) [Union U. M. Church Cemetery]

Smith, Charlotte A. 1870-1946 (tombstone inscription, but; death certificate stated Charlotte Ann Smith was born in September 1872, the daughter of Stephen H. Wilson and Hannah Presbury, all born in Darlington; she married William Vincent Smith and died a widow on October 1, 1946 in Darlington RFD #1; informant was Mrs. Hannah Taylor, address not given) [Berkley Memorial Cemetery]

Smith, Clara V. March 15, 1913 – April 15, 1915 (no tombstone; death certificate stated she was the daughter of John Smith and Annie Haycock, of Havre de Grace) [St. James United Cemetery]

Smith, Clarence B. September 14, 1887 – August 14, 1963 (on same tombstone with Annie W. Smith) [Fairview A. M. E. Church Cemetery]

Smith, Claude G., "My Beloved Husband" 1941-1969 [Berkley Memorial Cemetery]

Smith, Cora E. 1910-2003 (small metal funeral home marker) [Berkley Memorial Cemetery]

Smith, Cornelia March 15, 1862 – September 1, 1926 (no tombstone; death certificate stated she was born in South Carolina and was the widowed daughter of William Copper, also born in South Carolina, but her mother was unknown to informant Mary Taswell, of Aberdeen) [Union U. M. Church Cemetery]

Smith, Cornelius J. November 22, 1918 – January 7, 2003, Sgt., U.S. Army, World War II (tombstone; obituary in *The Aegis* on January 10, 2003 stated he was born in Laurel, MS, the oldest of five children born to George Smith and Annie Barnett; he entered the Army in 1940, served overseas and was a veteran of World War II, retiring after 20 years of service; he entered the real estate field in 1957 and became a builder and broker; he also operated a grocery store and managed a dry cleaning business; he was a Justice of the Peace in 1969 and was designated a committing magistrate in 1971, serving until 1986; he also held offices in the Union United Methodist Church, the VFW, the Masons, and the 8th Support Battalion of the Maryland Defense Force; he died at Upper Chesapeake Medical Center in Bel Air and was survived by 3 children (his wife Helen had predeceased him), 9 grandchildren, 7 great-grandchildren, 1 sister and 1 aunt; his nickname was "Smitty") [Union U. M. Church Cemetery]

Smith, Daniel died November 18, 1906, age 73 (tombstone was inscribed "In Memory Of" and no death certificate was found for him in Harford County) [Old Union Chapel M. E. Church Cemetery]

Smith, Daniel Hollis (no tombstone, but probably buried here because his wife Lydia is buried here) [probably Green Spring U. M. Church Cemetery]

Smith, Daniel L. March 7, 1920 – January 8, 1958, TEC5, U.S. Army, World War II [Berkley Memorial Cemetery]

Smith, Daryl Lamont 1973-2009 (small metal funeral home marker; *The Aegis* on February 11, 2009 stated he lived at Street and died in an auto accident on February 4, 2009, age 35) [Berkley Memorial Cemetery]

Smith, Denise C. February 27, 1951 – July 2, 1982 [Berkley Memorial Cemetery]

Smith, Donald L. 1952-2005, U S. Army [Clark's U. M. Church Cemetery]

Smith, Dora Elizabeth September 20, 1910 – March 28, 2003 (obituary and photo in *The Aegis* in April 2, 2003 stated she was born in Baltimore County, the daughter of Zora Elizabeth Cromwell and George Jackson; she married Elwood H. Smith and died at her home in Joppa, survived by 2 children, 3 grandchildren, many great-grandchildren, a great-great-granddaughter, nieces, nephews, cousins and friends) [Berkley Memorial Cemetery]

Smith, Earl E. December 13, 1929 – August 5, 2000, CPL, U.S. Army, Korea (tombstone; obituary in *The Aegis* on August 11, 2000 stated Earl Eugene Smith was born in Darlington, a son of Ralph T. Smith and Carrie Price; served two years in the U.S. Army, married Mary Catherine ---- on August 12, 1956 and worked for and retired from Bob Bell Chevrolet in Bel Air; he died at Harford Memorial Hospital in Havre de Grace, survived by his wife, a daughter, 2 grandchildren, 2 great-grandchildren, 3 sisters, and 3 brothers) [Cedars Chapel Cemetery]

Smith, Edith A. 1874-1909 (on same tombstone with William T. Smith) [Berkley Memorial Cemetery]

Smith, Eliza died April 14, 1903, age 65 (no tombstone; death certificate stated she was the daughter of Carvil Wells, but her mother's name was unknown; she married Aaron Smith, worked as a cook and died at Michaelsville; place of burial was not indicated, probably in the Old Union Chapel Cemetery at Michaelsville; possibly reinterred later in Union Chapel Cemetery near Aberdeen) [Union U. M. Church Cemetery]

Smith, Elizah 1881-1968 (on same tombstone with Lillie P. Smith) [Berkley Memorial Cemetery]

Smith, Ellen R. June 3, 1927 – April 26, 1993, "In Loving Memory" (tombstone; obituary in *The Aegis* on May 5, 1993 stated Ellen Rebecca "Becky" Smith was the daughter of Rev. George A. Smith and Pearl Jones, of Churchville, her first husband was James H. Demby and she was survived by her second husband of 10 years, Charles H. "Reds" Smith, 5 children, 12 grandchildren, 2 great-grandchildren, 3 sisters, 2 brothers, and 6 adopted daughters) [Asbury Cemetery]

Smith, Emily died November 5, 1912, age 58 (no tombstone; death certificate stated she was born in Harford Co., but the names of her parents and their places of birth were not known to informant Otis Smith, of Bel Air; she was a servant, a widow, died in Be Air and buried in Mountain (aka Mt. Zion) Cemetery; probably the wife of Joseph Smith) [Mt. Zion U. M. Church Cemetery]

Smith, Emma died April 6, 1910, age 4 months (no tombstone; death certificate stated she was born at Carsins Run, the daughter of John Smith and Carrie Cooper, both born in Churchville, and she died at Carsins Run; informant was her father) [Asbury Cemetery]

Smith, Emory April 9, 1900 – June 18, 1939 (no tombstone; death certificate stated he was born in Clinton, MD, the son of Roger Smith and Mary Washington, both born in Maryland; he was single, worked as a day laborer and died at his home on Baltimore St. in Aberdeen where he had lived for 2½ years; informant was Mrs. Sarah Cunningham, of Aberdeen) [Mt. Calvary U. A. M. E. Church Cemetery]

Smith, Essie Lynn 1911-2017 (tombstone; an article in the *Baltimore Sun* on May 13, 2015 and her funeral notice and photo in *The Aegis* on November 3, 2017 stated she was born April 30, 1911 in Glade Valley, NC, moved with her family to Harford Co. in 1919 and married Preston Nicholas Smith in 1932; she died at home in Bel Air on October 29, 2017, age 106) [Clark's U. M. Church Cemetery]

Smith, Eugene March 13, 1928 – July 8, 2001 [Berkley Memorial Cemetery]

Smith, Eva January 29, 1869 – July 9, 1939 (no tombstone; death certificate stated she was the daughter of Thomas and Eva Norton, all born in Harford Co.; she married George W. Smith and died a widow in Darlington; informant was Rudolph Smith, of Darlington) [Berkley Memorial Cemetery]

Smith, Eva Marie January 1, 1927 – May 3, 1976 [Berkley Memorial Cemetery]

Smith, Fannie Bell February 14, 1865 – July 1, 1950 (no tombstone; death certificate stated she was born in Baltimore, married, widowed, and died at 4 Bond St. in Bel Air where she had lived for two years; her father was John Bell, but her mother was not known to informant, Mrs. Hannah Moore, of Bel Air) [Hendon Hill Cemetery]

Smith, Frank August 21, 1892 – November 29, 1923 (no tombstone; death certificate stated he was the son of Benjamin Smith and Eliza Taylor, all born in Maryland; he was married, worked as a laborer and died in Havre de Grace Hospital; informant was Mrs. Myrtle Smith, of Aberdeen) [Mt. Calvary U. A. M. E. Church Cemetery]

Smith, Frank June 4, 1872 – November 10, 1942 (no tombstone; death certificate stated he was the unmarried son of Edward Smith and ---- (unknown), all born in Massachusetts; he worked as farm laborer and died in Harford Memorial Hospital in Havre de Grace) [St. James United Cemetery]

Smith, G. Milton 1880-1937, Spanish-American War veteran [Berkley Memorial Cemetery]

Smith, George 1876-1914 [St. James United Cemetery]

Smith, George died August 7, 1912, age 2 months (no tombstone; death certificate stated he was the son of George E. Green and Vergie Smith, all were born in Harford Co. and they lived near Aberdeen; informant was Vincent Smith, of Aberdeen) [Green Spring U. M. Church Cemetery]

Smith, George A. May 1, 1900 – February 24, 1954 (on same tombstone with Pearl E. and John W. Smith) [Asbury Cemetery]

Smith, George C. April 7, 1912 – August 14, 1918 (no tombstone; death certificate stated he was the son of Walter Hollingsworth and May Smith, all born in Harford Co.; informant was May Smith, of Perryman) [Union U. M. Church Cemetery]

Smith, George Henry February 22, 1896 – September 14, 1911 (no tombstone; death certificate stated he was the son of Joseph Henry Smith and Emma Jane Osborne, and all were born in Bel Air; he was a farm laborer employed by C. Courtney and died in an accident involving runaway horses; informant was his mother Emma J. Smith, of Aberdeen RFD #2; death certificate also stated he was buried at he "Collored Cemetery near Churchville") [Asbury Cemetery]

Smith, George M. died April 1, 1989, age 67 (no tombstone; obituary in *The Aegis* on April 13, 1989 stated he was born in Harford Co., the son of Rev. George Allen Smith and Pearl Evelyn Jones, served in the U.S. Army in World War II, was stationed in France and was also a merchant seaman; he died at the Perry Point Veterans Administration Medical Center and was survived by 8 children, 18 grandchildren, 12 great-grandchildren and other relatives) [Asbury Cemetery]

Smith, George W. died June 7, 1931, age about 70 (no tombstone; death certificate stated he was the son of James J. Smith and Jane Lee, all born in Maryland; he married, worked as a farmer and died at home in Darlington; informant was Eva Smith, of Darlington) [Berkley Memorial Cemetery]

Smith, Georgia A. 1890-1954 [Union U. M. Church Cemetery]

Smith, Griffin Milton April 13, 1880 – December 13, 1937 (no tombstone; death certificate stated he was the son of Henry Smith and Mary Spriggs, all born in Harford Co.; he married Louise ----, worked as a farm laborer and died at home near the Glenville and Darlington area; informant was Mrs. Milton Smith, of Darlington) [Berkley Memorial Cemetery]

Smith, Harvey December 23, 1922 – October 18, 1971, North Carolina, SSgt., U.S. Army, World War II [Berkley Memorial Cemetery]

Smith, Hattie D. April 29, 1915 – December 30, 1985 (on same tombstone with William Smith inscribed "Always In Our Hearts") [Asbury Cemetery]

Smith, Helen C., "Loving Wife and Mother" November 17, 1918 – October 31, 1988 (tombstone; obituary in *The Aegis* on November 3, 1988 stated she was the daughter of Annie M. Dennison, of Aberdeen, and the late Robert Dennison, and wife of Sgt. Cornelius J. Smith; she lived in Havre de Grace and died at Walter Reed Medical Center in Washington, D.C., survived by her husband and mother, 1 son, 2 daughters, 5 grandchildren. 2 great-grandchildren, 2 brothers, and 4 sisters) [Union U. M. Church Cemetery]

Smith, Henry born and died December 26, 1937 (no tombstone; death certificate stated he was born near Havre de Grace, the premature son of Herman Smith, born in North Carolina, and Mary Harvey, born in Delaware) [St. James United Cemetery]

Smith, Henry March – (blank), 1845 – January 31, 1924 (no tombstone; death certificate stated he was the widowed son of Henson Smith, but his wife was not mentioned and his mother was unknown to informant John C. Smith) [Union U. M. Church Cemetery]

Smith, Henry October 15, 1853 – February 16, 1917 (no tombstone; death certificate stated he was the son of Henry Smith and Margaret Shields, all born in Maryland; he was married, worked as a violinist and died at home in Darlington; informant was William Smith) [Berkley Memorial Cemetery]

Smith, Henry stillborn on April 5, 1943 (no tombstone; death certificate stated he was the son of Alfred C. Smith and Florence R. Quomony) [Union U. M. Church Cemetery]

Smith, Henson June 10, 1874 – November 3, 1937 (no tombstone; death certificate stated he was the son of Henry Smith and Martha Williams, and the husband of Mary Smith) [Union U. M. Church Cemetery]

Smith, Herman C. 1906-1990 (on same tombstone with Ruth P. Smith inscribed "Together Forever;" James

Dorsey Card File, African American Obituaries, maintained at the Historical Society of Harford County, has a card with obituary from an unidentified newspaper dated December 26, 1990 stating Herman Conrad Smith was born in Enfield, NC, son of Lillie Hunter and Elijah Smith, and married first to Mary Harvey and had nine children and married second to Ruth Randall in 1973; he moved to Havre de Grace at an early age and for 20 years he was employed at the John Smith Food Co. and then worked for Hinder Ford in Aberdeen until retiring in 1975; he died at Harford Memorial Hospital and was survived by 5 daughters, a sister, a brother, 22 grandchildren, 45 great-grandchildren and 7 great-great-grandchildren) [Berkley Memorial Cemetery]

Smith, Horace died December 6, 1945, age 90 (no tombstone; death certificate stated he was born in Fallston and died at the Harford County Home in rural Bel Air where he had lived for 5 years; the names of his parents were not known to informant Edmund R. Scarborough) [Tabernacle Mount Zion U. M. Church Cemetery]

Smith, Infant (male) March 18, 1925 – March 19, 1925 (no tombstone; death certificate stated he was the son of Jacob Smith and Minnie Rice, of Aberdeen) [St. James United Cemetery]

Smith, Ira Philip April 3, 1903 – May 8, 1927 (no tombstone; death certificate stated he was the son of George Smith and Eva W. Norton, all born in Maryland; he was single, worked as a laborer and died at home in Darlington; informant was his father) [Berkley Memorial Cemetery]

Smith, Irene T. July 28, 1924 – May 29, 1977 (obituary in *The Aegis* stated Irene Taylor Smith was born in Havre de Grace, the daughter of Harriett Taylor and the late Jeremiah Presbury; she lived in Edgewood, was the widow of Harvey Smith and died at Johns Hopkins Hospital in Baltimore, survived by her mother, two sons, four daughters and three grandchildren) [Berkley Memorial Cemetery]

Smith, Jacob Henry Jr. April 9, 1919 – December 17, 1939 (no tombstone; death certificate stated he was the son of Jacob Henry Smith, Sr. and Minnie Rice, of Aberdeen) [Union U. M. Church Cemetery]

Smith, James Robert June 28, 1918 – April 19, 1919 (no tombstone; death certificate stated he was the son of Robert Green, both born in Harford Co., but the name of his mother was not known to informant Willis Smith, of Aberdeen; he died near Aberdeen; informant was his father) [Mt. Calvary U. A. M. E. Church Cemetery]

Smith, James W. August 30, 1918 – July 10, 1919 (no tombstone; death certificate stated he was the son of John Smith and Carrie Cooper, all born in Maryland, and he died at Churchville; informant was John Smith, of Aberdeen RFD) [Asbury Cemetery]

Smith, James Walter June 5, 1924 – July 7, 1988, U.S. Army, U.S. Air Force (tombstone; obituary in *The Aegis* on July 14, 1988 stated he was born in Churchville, the son of James Smith and Rebecca Pounds, married Justina Gregg, served in Army and Coast Guard during World War II, retired from Aberdeen Proving Ground in 1983, died at Fallston General Hospital and was survived by his wife, son, 6 brothers, 6 sisters, 2 stepdaughters, 9 grandchildren) [Asbury Cemetery]

Smith, Jane E. died January 31, 1914, age 73 (no tombstone; death certificate stated she was born in Churchville, the daughter of Shadrach Johnson and Emily Cooper, birth places unknown to informant Charles H. Magness, Jr., of Belcamp; she died a widow in Churchville) [Asbury Cemetery]

Smith, Jane Pearl 1932-2011 (small metal funeral home marker next to Milton O. Smith's metal marker) [Asbury Cemetery]

Smith, Jerome L. December 18, 1940 – January 22, 1941 (no tombstone; death certificate stated he was the son of Preston Smith, born in Harford Co., and Essie Lee, born in Alleghany Co., MD; he died at home in rural Bel Air; the informant was his father) [Clark's U. M. Church Cemetery]

Smith, John C. April 15, 1886 – March 29, 1935 (no tombstone; death certificate stated he was the son of Henry Smith and Martha Williams) [Union U. M. Church Cemetery]

Smith, John E. 1948-2001 (small metal funeral home marker) [St. James United Cemetery]

Smith, John Henry died April 5, 1913, age 30 (no tombstone; death certificate stated born in Pennsylvania, the son of Cope(?) Smith, but his mother was not known to informant James Lee, of Rocks; he was married, worked as a day laborer and died at Jarrettsville) [William C. Rice Memorial Cemetery, St. James U. M. Church]

Smith, John W. "Killed in Action in Korea, June 14, 1953" (on same tombstone with George A. Smith and Pearl E. Smith; death notice in *The Aegis* on June 10, 1954 reported remains returned on June 9, 1954 to Harford County; was the son of Pearl Smith and the late George A. Smith who lived in Churchville) [Asbury Cemetery]

Smith, John W. August 30, 1914 – February 24, 1928 (no tombstone; death certificate stated he was born in Harford Co., son of John W. Smith and Carrie Cooper, both born in Maryland, and died in Churchville; informant was Hester C. Banks, of Bel Air RFD #1) [Asbury Cemetery]

Smith, John W., "Beloved Husband and Father" 1937-2003 [St. James United Cemetery]

Smith, John Walter January 15, 1934 – December 28, 1989, PFC, U.S. Army [Cedars Chapel Cemetery]

Smith, John Wesley died December 3, 1905, age 31 years and 24 days (no tombstone; death certificate stated he was born at Mountain, the son of Jacob Smith and Marie Smart, both born in Harford Co.; he was single, worked as a farm laborer and died at Mountain; informant was his mother; place of burial not given [probably Mt. Zion U. M. Church Cemetery]

Smith, John Westley January 16, 1890 – February 18, 1941 (no tombstone; death certificate stated he was the son of James Smith and Ella Black, all born in Maryland; he was a laborer and a widower in Churchville; informant was Mary Young, of Aberdeen RFD) [Asbury Cemetery]

Smith, Joseph, Co. E, 30 U.S. C. I. (tombstone; Civil War records indicated Joseph Smith, Co. E, 30th Regt. U.. S. C. T., age 25, 5' 6" tall, black eyes, black hair, black complexion, enlisted February 29, 1864 at "Howard" (actually Harford) and mustered at Baltimore, MD on March 4, 1864 by Col. Bowman for 3 years and "Joseph Mallyden mustered out December 10, 1865 at Roanoke Island, N. C.") *Ed. Note:* No idea why he was called Mallyden, not Smith, and a search by James Chrismer, Civil War and African American family expert in Harford County, revealed no such name in USCT records or in 1860-1900 censuses. This is probably the Joseph Smith who died in Bel Air on April 2, 1909, age 75 and his wife was named Emily. She is also buried in Mt. Zion (or Mountain) Cemetery. [Mt. Zion U. M. Church Cemetery]

Smith, Joseph Henry June 13, 1872 – February 13, 1925 (no tombstone; death certificate stated he was the son of Joseph Smith and Emily James, all born in Maryland; he was married and worked as a laborer in Churchville; informant was Emma J. Smith, of Bel Air RFD #1) [Asbury Cemetery]

Smith, Joshua 1856 – January 31, 1921 (no tombstone; death certificate stated he was born in Maryland, married, worked as a laborer and died at Pylesville; parents' name were not known to informant Tom Leonard(?), of Pylesville) [Chestnut Grove A. M. E. Church Cemetery, formerly LaGrange Cemetery at Rocks]

Smith, Lillie P. 1885-1967 (on same tombstone with Elizah Smith) [Berkley Memorial Cemetery]

Smith, Lily Presbury, "His Wife" 1889-1913 (on same tombstone with Stewart Donald Smith; death certificate stated Lily Smith was born October 20, 1889, the daughter of George Presberry *(sic)* and Susan Wilson, all born in Maryland; she married and died at home in Darlington on April 14, 1913; informant was Stewart Smith, of Darlington) [Berkley Memorial Cemetery]

Smith, Lloyd A. died January 21, 1922, age about 63 (no tombstone; death certificate stated he was the son of Benjamin Smith and Mary Johnson; informant was Mrs. Lloyd Smith [St. James United Cemetery]

Smith, Lola E. August 17, 1940 – February 18, 1995, "Beloved Mother and Friend" (tombstone; obituary with photo in *The Aegis* on February 22, 1995 stated Lola Ernestine Smith, of Churchville, was the daughter of William and Hattie Smith, married [husband's name was not given) and died at Riverside Regional Medical Center, Newport News, VA, survived by two sons, two daughters, six sisters, two brothers, five grandchildren and one step-grandson; she was mentioned as a predeceased sister in the obituary of Milton O. Smith in 2007) [Asbury Cemetery]

Smith, Louise Thompson August 12, 2007 – April 19, 2003 (inscribed "In Loving Memory") [Berkley Memorial Cemetery]

Smith, Lucille March 13, 1928 – July 8, 2001 (obituary in *The Aegis* on July 13, 2001 stated she was born in South Carolina, the daughter of the late Oscar Smith and Ellie Goldson, lived in Port Deposit and died at Laurelwood Nursing Center, survived by five sisters and a host of nieces and nephews, and predeceased by two sisters Lottie Lyles and Elvina Bugg) [Berkley Memorial Cemetery]

Smith, Lydia Edith died April 9, 1977, age 64 (no tombstone; obituary in *The Aegis* on April 14, 1977 stated she was born in Harford Co., the daughter of Jarrett Hemore and Mary Bodley, and married Daniel Hollis Smith, who predeceased her; she was a housekeeper at St. Patrick Parish in Havre de Grace for many years and lived at 654 Congress Ave.; she died at Harford Memorial Hospital and was survived by a brother Alfred Hemore of Havre da Grace, and a nephew, of Bel Air, name not given) [Green Spring U. M. Church Cemetery]

Smith, Mabel W. July 11, 1928 – December 26, 2008 (on same tombstone with Milton V. Smith) [Berkley Memorial Cemetery]

Smith, Maggie April 1, 1868 – February 17, 1943 (no tombstone; death certificate stated she was the widow of Henry Smith, but parents unknown to informant Mary Pinion, of Havre de Grace) [St. James United Cemetery]

Smith, Malinda V., "Sister" 1914-1955 [Asbury Cemetery]

Smith, Mamie April 21, 1933 – March 19, 1934 (no tombstone; death certificate stated she was born and died at Dublin, the daughter of Lee Smith, born in Virginia, and Naomi Morgan, born in Maryland; the informant was Lee Smith, of Darlington) [Clark's U. M. Church Cemetery]

Smith, Martha died April 22, 1914, age about 58 (no tombstone; death certificate stated she was the daughter of Joseph Smith and Mary Brown, all born in Perryman; she was single, died at home in Perryman and was buried in "Sidney Park Cemetery;" informant was James Hall, of Perryman RFD) [Union U. M. Church Cemetery]

Smith, Martha J. died March 13, 1922, age about 68 (no tombstone; death certificate stated she was the married daughter of John Williams and Margaret Reed, born in Harford Co.; informant was J. C. Smith, of Perryman) [Union U. M. Church Cemetery]

Smith, Mary (neé Spriggs, wife of Henry Smith, 1853-1917; no marker) [Berkley Memorial Cemetery]

Smith, Mary died January 19, 1938, age about 80 (no tombstone; death certificate stated she was the widowed daughter of William Jones and Sarah Taylor, all born in Maryland, and she was a missionary; she died in Harford Memorial Hospital; informant was Alice Smith, of Havre de Grace) [St. James United Cemetery]

Smith, Mary April 25, 1870 – August 8, 1949 (no tombstone; death certificate stated she was the daughter of John Z. Stansbury and Eliza Lisby, and died a widow on Bush Chapel Road) [Union U. M. Church Cemetery]

Smith, Mary born about June 15, 1862 – January 11, 1925 (no tombstone; death certificate stated she was the daughter of Rose Crockson, both born in Maryland, but the name of her father was not known to informant Vincent Smith, of Aberdeen; she was married and died near Aberdeen) [Green Spring U. M. Church Cemetery]

Smith, Mary C. 1927-2003 (small metal funeral home marker; obituary in *The Aegis* on May 2, 2003 stated Mary Catherine Johnson Smith was born August 11, 1927 in rural Harford Co., the daughter of Calvin Johnson and Anna Miller; she married Earl Eugene Smith on August 12, 1956 and they lived in Street; she died at the Lorien Riverside Nursing and Rehabilitation Center in Belcamp, survived by a daughter, 2 grandchildren, 2 great-grandchildren, 4 brothers, 5 sisters, and she was preceded in death by her husband, 2 sisters and 2 brothers) [Clark's U. M. Church Cemetery]

Smith, Mary E. October 1, 1842 – October 2, 1912 (no tombstone; death certificate stated she was the widowed daughter of William Johnson, but mother unknown to informant Lloyd A. Smith) [St. James United Cemetery]

Smith, Mary H. 1908-1943 (tombstone inscription; death certificate stated Mary Olivia Harvey Smith was born on September 16, 1908 and died on October 1, 1943, the daughter of Walter F. Harvey and Emma F. Willis, and the wife of Herman Smith, of Havre de Grace) [St. James United Cemetery]

Smith, Mary Jane died November 15, 1911, age 84 (no tombstone; death certificate stated she was the daughter of Robert Lee, both born in Maryland, but her mother was not known to informant George W. Smith, of Darlington; Mary was a widow who lived in Darlington) [Cedars Chapel Cemetery]

Smith, Michael E. Jr. died September 16, 1974, age not given (no tombstone; obituary in *The Aegis* stated he was the infant son of Geraldine R. and Michael E. Smith, Sr., of Aberdeen, and the grandson of Mr. & Mrs. John W. Smith, of Port Deposit, and Mr. & Mrs. Freeman Royal, of Aberdeen; he died at Johns Hopkins Hospital in

Baltimore) [Asbury Cemetery]

Smith, Mildred Elenore February 27, 1922 – October 9, 1922 (no tombstone; death certificate stated she was the daughter of David Daugherty and Ellen Rebecca Smith, all born in Maryland, and lived in Churchville; informant was Ellen Rebecca Smith, Route 1, Box 140, Bel Air) [Asbury Cemetery]

Smith, Mildred October 21, 1921 – October 2, 1934 (no tombstone; death certificate stated she was born in Aberdeen, the daughter of Annie Dupree, born in Maryland, but her father was not known to informant Mrs. Saddie Smith, of Aberdeen; she died at home on Broadway) [Mt. Calvary U. A. M. E. Church Cemetery]

Smith, Milton O. 1942-2007 (small metal funeral home marker next to Jane Pearl Smith's small metal marker; obituary in *The Aegis* on May 30, 2007 stated Milton O. Smith, Sr. was born on March 5, 1942 in Churchville, the son of William and Hattie Smith, and married Jane Stokes, of Edgewood, on December 24, 1987; he died on May 23, 2007, survived by 4 sons, 4 daughters, 16 grandchildren, 6 great-grandchildren) [Asbury Cemetery]

Smith, Milton V. June 13, 1915 – December 9, 2007 (on same tombstone with Mabel W. Smith inscribed "Psalm 130 5;" obituary and photo in *The Aegis* on December 12, 2007 stated he was born in Darlington, son of William Vincent Smith and Charlotte Wilson; he was a cook at the Old Blue Bell Restaurant and at Aberdeen Proving Ground; he lived in Bel Air and died at the Bel Air Health and Rehabilitation Center, survived by his wife of 58 years, Mabel W. Smith, two grand-nephews and two great-nieces; in addition to his parents he was predeceased by nine siblings, a niece, a nephew and a great-nephew) [Berkley Memorial Cemetery]

Smith, Minnie June 10, 1896 – February 8, 1941 (no tombstone; death certificate stated she was the wife of Jacob H. Smith and the daughter of Edward Rice and Lottie McComas) [Union U. M. Church Cemetery]

Smith, Minnie E. June 14, 1901 – January 27, 1922 (no tombstone; death certificate stated she was the daughter of George W. Smith and Eva Norton, all born in Maryland; she was single and died at home in Darlington; informant was her father) [Berkley Memorial Cemetery]

Smith, Myrtle E. August 1, 1926 – June 22, 2005 (on same tombstone with Charles I. Smith; obituary in *The Aegis* on June 29, 2005 stated she was born in Jarrettsville, the daughter of James Joshua and Emma Oleita Jones; she married the late Charles Nace Smith on July 27, 1946 and worked for Kroh's Cleaners in Bel Air until her retirement in 1981; she was a very active member Fairview AME Church and served as a trustee; she died at the University of Maryland Hospital in Baltimore and was survived by a son and three brothers) [Fairview A. M. E. Church Cemetery]

Smith, Myrtle E. October 23, 1893 – December 5, 1961 [Asbury Cemetery]

Smith, Nicholas Ralph January 1, 1933 – April 17, 1982, Cpl., U.S. Army, Korea (tombstone; obituary in *The Aegis* on April 29, 1982 stated he was born in Kalmia, the son of Elsie Edwards and the late Preston Nicholas Smith; he served in the Korean War from 1953 to 1955 and was honorably discharged from the Army Reserves in 1961; he worked as a truck driver for Suburban Propane and part-time for BTR Realty; he was very active in Hosanna A. M. E. Church, serving as trustee and usher; he lived in Darlington and died at home, survived by his mother, 2 sons, 2 daughters, 3 brothers, 5 sisters and 6 grandchildren) [Berkley Memorial Cemetery]

Smith, Norris N. August 28, 1893 – July 25, 1918 (no tombstone; death certificate stated he was the son of George W. Smith and Eva Norton, all born in Maryland; he was single, worked as a laborer and died at home at Cedars near Darlington; informant was his father) [Berkley Memorial Cemetery]

Smith, Oliver W. January 31, 1903 – September 23, 1934 (no tombstone; death certificate stated he was born in Churchville, the son of Joseph H. Smith, born in Maryland, and Emma Osborne, born in Churchville, married Anna Turner, worked as a laborer in Abingdon and died in an auto accident on Philadelphia Road; informant was Emma Parrott, of Bel Air RFD) [Asbury Cemetery]

Smith, Oscar O. Sr. May 23, 1926 – January 16, 1980 U.S. Navy, World War II (tombstone; obituary in *The Aegis* on January 24, 1980 stated Oscar Oniel "Popeye" Smith was born in Churchville, the son of the late George and Pearl Smith, served in the U.S. Navy for 2 years, married Marcella ----, and died at the Perry Point Veterans Administration Medical Center; he was survived by his wife, 10 children, 7 grandchildren, 6 sisters and 2 brothers) [Asbury Cemetery]

Smith, Pearl E. September 23, 1901 – October 14, 1956 (on same tombstone with George A. Smith and John W. Smith) [Asbury Cemetery]

Smith, Percy W., "Dedicated Husband, Father and Friend" July 31, 1951 – March 11, 1995 [St. James United Cemetery]

Smith, Preston N. Jr. 1945-2010 (small metal funeral home marker) [John Wesley U. M. E. Church Cemetery in Abingdon]

Smith, Rachael & William (no dates on tombstone; inscribed "In Memory Of" and "By Her Son Harry and Granddaughter Viola") [Berkley Memorial Cemetery]

Smith, Rachael A. 1877-1979 [Berkley Memorial Cemetery]

Smith, Ralph T. 1899-1969 (on same tombstone with Carrie E. Smith; obituary in *The Aegis* stated Ralph Tucker Smith, husband of Carrie Elsie Smith, of Cedar Church Road, Darlington, died June 21, 1969, age not given, at the Pleasant Manor Nursing Home in Baltimore; he was survived by his wife, 4 daughters, 5 sons, 2 grandchildren and 2 great-grandchildren) [Cedars Chapel Cemetery]

Smith, Ralph T., Jr. 1925-1945, PVT, Quartermaster Corps, died in Holland, World War II [Cedars Chapel Cemetery]

Smith, Raymond, "Beloved Husband" June 9, 1908 – January 28, 1985 [Berkley Memorial Cemetery]

Smith, Richard Edward died January 12, 1998, age 52 (no tombstone; James Dorsey Card File, African American Obituaries, maintained at the Historical Society of Harford County, has a card with his funeral announcement in an unidentified newspaper on January 21, 1998 stating he died at home in Abingdon with graveside services held at John Wesley UM Church) [John Wesley U. M. E. Church Cemetery in Abingdon]

Smith, Robert C. August 20, 1918 – October 10, 1919 (no tombstone; death certificate stated he was born in Philadelphia, the son of George Smith, of Philadelphia, and Laura Curtis, of Havre de Grace; informant was his mother Laura Smith, of Havre de Grace) [St. James United Cemetery]

Smith, Robert E. November 30, 1882 – March 4, 1931 (no tombstone; death certificate stated he was the son of J. Henry Smith and Martha J. Williams, and was married, but wife not named) [Union U. M. Church Cemetery]

Smith, Robert James Washington died July 20, 1906, age 6 months, 20 days (no tombstone, death certificate stated he was Fred Brown and Sarah R. Smith and was born and died in Michaelsville; informant was his grandmother Caroline Smith; his place of burial was not indicated, but it was probably in Old Union Chapel Cemetery at Michaelsville; possibly reinterred later in Union Chapel Cemetery near Aberdeen [Union U. M. Church Cemetery]

Smith, Robert T. October 3, 1856 – June 6, 1929 (no tombstone; death certificate stated he was the son of Daniel Smith and Caroline Stansbury, and died a widower in Aberdeen; informant was Miss Hattie C. Smith, of Aberdeen) [Union U. M. Church Cemetery]

Smith, Ruth (owner of a lot in section 2 some time after 1951) [Mt. Calvary U. A. M. E. Church Cemetery]

Smith, Ruth P. 1913-1986 (on same tombstone with Herman C. Smith inscribed "Together Forever;" obituary in *The Aegis* on October 23, 1986 stated Ruth Pauline Smith was born in New York City, daughter of Peyton Ford, of Philadelphia, and the late Charlotte Ford; she lived in Havre de Grace, died at Harford Memorial Hospital, and was survived by her father, her husband Herman C. Smith, a daughter, 5 step-daughters, 2 brothers, 5 sisters, 2 grandchildren and 2 great-grandchildren) [Berkley Memorial Cemetery]

Smith, Sadie July 15, 1886 – July 19, 1946 (no tombstone; death certificate stated she was the daughter of George Frisby and Harriet Green, and the widow of Willis Smith; she died in Harford Memorial Hospital in Havre de Grace; informant was Kate Williams, of Abetrdeen) [Union U. M. Church Cemetery]

Smith, Samuel Durbin died September 25, 1922, age about 38 (no tombstone; death certificate state he was the married son of Samuel Smith and Mary Durbin, and he died in Havre de Grace Hospital; informant was Mrs. Samuel D. Smith, of Havre de Grace) [St. James United Cemetery]

Smith, Sarah died March 15, 1878, age 60 (broken tombstone) [Hendon Hill Cemetery]

Smith, Sarah J. died May 11, 1923, age about 55 (no tombstone; death certificate stated she was the married daughter of James Moulton and Margaret Smith; informant was Nelson Durbin) [St. James United Cemetery]

Smith, Sarah Jane February 28, 1874 – January 26, 1949 (no tombstone; death certificate stated she was born at Rocks and was the widowed daughter of Moses Rice and Jane Willis; informant was Mrs. Stillie Rice, of Rocks; Kurtz Funeral Home Record Book 1944-1949, p. 261, listed her name as Sarah Jane Walton Smith) [William C. Rice Memorial Cemetery, St. James U. M. Church]

Smith, Sarah Jane July 16, 1914 – July 21, 1914 (no tombstone; death certificate stated she was the daughter of William J. Smith and Georgianna Holland, all born in Maryland) [Union U. M. Church Cemetery]

Smith, Shalon-Tai Monique June 18, 1978 – November 28, 2004 (photo image on her tombstone and inscribed "In Loving Memory" and at the bottom "Desiree" and "Little Ricky;" obituary and photo in *The Aegis* on December 8, 2004 gave a very detailed accounting of her life, stating she was born in Havre de Grace, the daughter of James Edward Sumpter, Jr. and Carole Smith, of Aberdeen; she lived in Edgewood and died at the Upper Chesapeake Medical Center in Bel Air, survived by her daughters Desiree Joneice Smith and Ricky Sytoria McCall (born October 13), fiancé Ricky McCall, sisters Toniette Renee Sumpter and Rajyne Nesita Andrea Walton, brothers Michael Laquint Watters and Nicholas Lamar Delante Brown, grandfather James E. Sumpter , Sr. and wife Jean, grandmother Zilpha P. Smith and husband Cornelius, grandmother Lois Young, great-grandmothers Hattie R. Galloway, Thelma Blake and Essie L. Smith, great-great-grandmother Helen Stansbury, aunts Julia Edwards and Tony Smith, uncles Ralph D. Smith, Staffen D. Smith, Glenn Sumpter, Kenneth Sumpter, Anthony Sumpter and Trevor Smith, and other relatives) [Berkley Memorial Cemetery]

Smith, Solomon J. May 26, 1871 – July 12, 1922 (no tombstone; death certificate stated he was the widowed son of Daniel Smith and Caroline Stansbury, all born in Maryland; informant was Robert T. Smith, of Aberdeen) [Union U. M. Church Cemetery]

Smith, Stephen W. January 23, 1897 – January 17, 1947 (inscribed "S. W. Smith, 1893-1947" but death certificate stated he was born in 1897, not 1893, in Darlington, the son of William D. Smith and Charlotte Ann Wilson, and they both were born in Maryland; he married Pearl B. ----, worked as a laborer and died at home in Aberdeen; informant was Mrs. Hannah Taylor, 224 N. Main St., Port Deposit, MD) [Berkley Memorial Cemetery]

Smith, Stewart Donald September 30, 1890 – April 7, 1925 (on same tombstone with Lily Presbury Smith, but his dates were mistakenly inscribed as 1890-1924; death certificate stated he was born in 1890, not 1889, and he died in 1925, not 1924; he was the son of Henry Smith and Mary E. Spriggs, all born in Maryland, he married, worked as a laborer and died at home in the Glenville-Darlington area; informant was Mrs. Mary E. Smith, of Darlington) [Berkley Memorial Cemetery]

Smith, Thomas died October 8, 1896, age not given (no tombstone; death notice in *The Aegis* on October 16, 1896 stated he was the son of Henry Smith, Jr., of Darlington, and was accidentally shot while gunning a short time ago and died last Thursday; his place of burial was not reported, but it was possibly in Cedars Cemetery at St. James UAME Church) [Cedars Chapel Cemetery]

Smith, Thomas R., son of Henry & Mary Smith, (inscribed "Our Son" and dates illegible on a very weathered tombstone) [Berkley Memorial Cemetery]

Smith, Vincent H. May 10, 1870 – October 15, 1927 (no tombstone; death certificate stated he was the son of Isaac Smith, both born in Maryland, but his mother's name was not known to informant Virgie Monk, of Aberdeen; he was a widower and day laborer in Aberdeen) [Green Spring U. M. Church Cemetery]

Smith, Viola M. July 28, 1910 – May 3, 1925 (no tombstone; death certificate stated she was the daughter of Daniel Smith and Elizabeth Stansbury) [Union U. M. Church Cemetery]

Smith, W. F. 1869-1943 [Berkley Memorial Cemetery]

Smith, Warren E. 1958-2014 (small metal funeral home marker) [Asbury Cemetery]

Smith, Willhelmina June 29, 1911 – October 15, 1911 (no tombstone; death certificate stated she was born in

Darlington, the daughter of William V. Smith and Charlotte Wilson, both born in Harford Co.; she died at home in Darlington RFD #1; informant was her father) [Berkley Memorial Cemetery]

Smith, William & Rachael (no dates; tombstone inscribed "In Memory Of" and "By Her Son Harry and Granddaughter Viola") [Berkley Memorial Cemetery]

Smith, William April 9, 1912 – March 8, 1969, "Always In Our Hearts" (on same tombstone with Hattie D. Smith; obituary in *The Aegis* on March 13, 1969 stated he was the son of the late John and Carrie Smith and the husband of Hattie V. Smith of Asbury Road in Churchville; he worked as a truck driver for the Army Chemical Center at Edgewood and died at Harford Memorial Hospital in Havre de Grace; he was survived by his wife, 2 sons, 7 daughters, 3 sisters, 20 grandchildren, 10 nieces and 13 nephews) [Asbury Cemetery]

Smith, William died February 26, 1932, age 52 (no tombstone; death certificate stated he was born in New Jersey, but his parents were not known to informant Thomas Green, of Abingdon; he worked as a laborer, died at Havre de Grace Hospital and was buried in "Abingdon") [John Wesley U. M. E. Church Cemetery in Abingdon]

Smith, William died January 30, 1927, age about 33 (no tombstone; death certificate stated he was born in New York, worked as a cook in Darlington and was shot to death; the undertaker, H. S. Bailey, of Darlington, did not know the names of his parents nor their places of birth; *The Aegis* on February 4, 1927 (and April 22, 1927) reported William Smith and James Davis were shot by William Jones after a dispute over a pistol near the dance hall at Shure's Landing. They were workers at the Stone & Webster Camp at the Conowingo Dam site.) [Berkley Memorial Cemetery]

Smith, William October 16, 1839 – January 9, 1919 (no tombstone; death certificate stated he was born in Maryland, the son of Henry Smith, but his mother's name and birth place was not known to informant Mrs. William Smith, of Darlington; he married, worked as a laborer and died at home in Darlington) [Berkley Memorial Cemetery]

Smith, William E. May 7, 1930 – June 16, 2000, SSgt., U.S. Air Force, Vietnam [Asbury Cemetery]

Smith, William Edward March 9, 1920 – January 17, 1973, Maryland, Pvt., U.S. Army, World War II [John Wesley U. M. E. Church Cemetery in Abingdon]

Smith, William K. Sr. August 18, 1936 – May 14, 2000, Sgt., U.S. Air Force, Korea (tombstone; obituary in *The Aegis* stated William Kennard Smith, Sr. was the son of William and Hattie Smith and everyone who knew him called him Boy or Boyd; he served in the U.S. Air Force from 1955 to 1959 and died at Fallston General Hospital; he was married ---- (wife's name was not mentioned) and was survived by 1 daughter, 4 sons, 9 grandchildren, 1 brother, 6 sisters, and other relatives, and was predeceased by a son Brian and a sister Lola Smith) [Asbury Cemetery]

Smith, William T. 1873-1942 (on same tombstone with Edith A. Smith; death certificate stated he was born November 12, 1874, not 1873, and was the son of James Smith, both born in Harford Co., but the name of his mother was not known to informant Ralph Smith, of Darlington; he worked as a laborer and died a widower at Darlington) [Berkley Memorial Cemetery]

Smith, William V. 1869-1943 (tombstone; death certificate stated he was born February 19, 1869 and died August 12, 1943; he was the son of William W. Smith and Charlott R. Lee, all born in Harford Co.; he married Charlott A. ----, worked as a farmer and died at home in rural Darlington where he had lived for 59 years; informant was his wife) [Berkley Memorial Cemetery]

Smith, William W. August 10, 1852 – November 14, 1926 (no tombstone; death certificate stated he was the son of Winton Smith and Henrietta Cromwell, all were born in Maryland; he worked as a laborer and died a widower in Poole; informant was William V. Smith, of Darlington) [John Wesley U. M. E. Church Cemetery in Abingdon]

Smith, Willis Charles March 7, 1883 – June 9, 1944 (no tombstone; death certificate stated he was the son of Benjamin Smith, mother unknown, and husband of Sadie Frisby Smith) [Union U. M. Church Cemetery]

Smith, Yvonne Lorraine died December 15, 1990, age 46 (small metal funeral home marker with some letters and numbers missing; obituary in *The Aegis* on December 19, 1990 stated she was born in Havre de Grace, the daughter of Nellie Bishop Downing, of Forest Hill, and the late William A. Downing; she lived at Forest Hill, was formerly married, and died at Fallston General Hospital, survived by her mother, two sons, three brothers and nine sisters) [Mt. Zion U. M. Church Cemetery]

Smothers, ---- born and died May 21, 1931, lived only one-half hour (no tombstone; death certificate stated that he died at McCann's Corner, the daughter of James P. Smothers and Ida O. Dorsey, both born in Maryland; informant was her mother Ida O. Smothers) [Clark's U. M. Church Cemetery]

Smothers, ---- July 24, 1930 – July 25, 1930 (no tombstone; death certificate stated she was born and died at Bagley, the daughter of Charles Smothers and Mary Banks, both born in Harford Co.; informant was Charles Smothers, of Bel Air) [Clark's U. M. Church Cemetery]

Smothers, ---- stillborn female on July 6, 1928 (no tombstone; death certificate stated she was born and died near Bagley, the daughter of Charles Smothers and Mary Banks, both born in Maryland; informant was Charles Smothers, of Bagley) [Clark's U. M. Church Cemetery]

Smothers, ---- stillborn female, premature birth, on September 1, 1925 (no tombstone; death certificate stated she was born at Rocks, the daughter of Charles Smothers and Mary Banks, both born in Harford Co.; informant was Charles Smothers, of Rocks) [Clark's U. M. Church Cemetery]

Smothers, Carrie Elizabeth December 18, 1922 – November 26, 1924 (no tombstone; death certificate stated she was born and died at Clark's Chapel, the daughter of James Smothers and Ida Dorsey, both born in Maryland; informant was James Smothers, of Bel Air) [Clark's U. M. Church Cemetery]

Smothers, Charles W. September 2, 1925 – December 3, 1989 (inscribed "Forever in our hearts;" obituary in *The Aegis* on December 20, 1989 stated Charles William Smothers died at the Harford Memorial Hospital in Havre de Grace; he was born in Darlington, the son of James P. and Olivia Smothers, and was a retired construction worker; survived by 3 sons, 5 daughters, 6 step-children, 24 grandchildren, 2 great-grandchildren, 2 brothers, 3 sisters) [Clark's U. M. Church Cemetery]

Smothers, Darlene Ida 1959-1959 [Clark's U. M. Church Cemetery]

Smothers, Donald Lee June 2, 1952 – January 3, 2005 (no tombstone; obituary in *The Aegis* on January 14, 2005 stated he was born in Havre de Grace, the son of Walter Smothers and Theresa Baysmore, stepson of Shirley Smothers, and husband of Christine Smothers; served in the U.S. Army from January 1974 to June 1992, attained the rank of sergeant first class, worked for various military contractors and died of a heart attack at Camp Doha, Kuwait; survived by his wife Christine Smothers, of Manila, Philippines, who was expecting another child when he passed away, and 4 daughters, 3 brothers, and 1 sister) [Clark's U. M. Church Cemetery]

Smothers, Donald W. May 21, 1931 – August 20, 1931 (no tombstone; death certificate stated he died at Indian Spring Farm, the son of James Smothers and Idah Dorsey, both born in Maryland; the informant was James Smothers, of Darlington) [Clark's U. M. Church Cemetery]

Smothers, Harry Wilson died October 24, 1978, age 78 (no tombstone; obituary in *The Aegis* on November 2, 1978, stated he lived in Bel Air and died at Fallston General Hospital; he was born in Harford Co., the son of Louise and James P. Smothers, and husband of Mary Smothers; he worked as a farmer's helper and caretaker for various farms in the county; survived by his wife, a daughter Christine Smothers, and two sisters in Philadelphia) [Clark's U. M. Church Cemetery]

Smothers, Ida O. March 24, 1901 – December 21, 1932 (no tombstone; death certificate stated she was the daughter of William Dorsey and Frances Benson, all born in Maryland; she married James P. Smothers and died at Indian Spring Farm; informant was her husband) [Clark's U. M. Church Cemetery]

Smothers, James B. September 14, 1921 – March 28, 1922 (no tombstone; death certificate stated he was born and died near Aberdeen, the son of James Parker Smothers and Ida Olivia Dorsey, both born in Bel Air; informant was James P. Smothers, of Aberdeen) [Clark's U. M. Church Cemetery]

Smothers, James Parker July 25, 1852 – September 20, 1939 (no tombstone; death certificate stated he was the son of John Wesley Smothers and Adaline Tasker, all born in Calvert Co., Maryland; he married Margaret ----, was a farmer at Ford's Hill, and died in Bel Air where he had lived for 30 years; informant was Mrs. Margaret

Smothers, of Bel Air) [Clark's U. M. Church Cemetery]

Smothers, James Parker November 22, 1894 – March 1, 1974 (on same tombstone with Verna Jane C. Smothers; obituary in *The Aegis* stated he lived at Street and died in Harford Memorial Hospital; he was born in Harford Co., the son of James and Louisa Parker, and husband of Verna Reeves Smothers; he was a retired farmer, formerly employed at Indian Spring Farm; a lifelong member of Clark's United Methodist Church, he served as a "trustee, senior choir official board and steward board;" he was survived by 2 brothers, 2 sisters, 4 sons, 3 daughters, 36 grandchildren and 49 great-grandchildren) [Clark's U. M. Church Cemetery]

Smothers, Louisa August 7, 1861 – April 1, 1917 (no tombstone; death certificate stated she was the daughter of William R. Dutton and Mary E. Cooper, all born in Harford Co.; she was married and died at Kalmia; informant was James P. Smothers, of Bel Air) [Clark's U. M. Church Cemetery]

Smothers, Margaret C. May 6, 1873 – April 7, 1942 (no tombstone; death certificate stated she was born in Baltimore, the daughter of Tobias Collins, born in Maryland, but her mother's name was not known to the informant Mrs. Fanny Daugherty, of Bel Air; Margaret married James Smothers and was a widow when she died in Bel Air where she had lived for three years) [Clark's U. M. Church Cemetery]

Smothers, Margaret V. March 19, 1920 – August 17, 1927 (no tombstone; death certificate stated she died at Indian Spring Farm (near Priestford), the daughter of James P. Smothers and Ida O. Dorsey, all born in Maryland; informant was Ida O. Smothers, of Darlington) [Clark's U. M. Church Cemetery]

Smothers, Mary died September 28, 1923, age about 75 (no tombstone; death certificate stated she died a widow in Havre de Grace, but parents unknown to informant Mrs. Richard Ward) [St. James United Cemetery]

Smothers, Mary B. March 21, 1904 – May 28, 1983 (on same tombstone with Lena B. Fountain; obituary in *The Aegis* on June 2, 1983 stated Mary Banks Smothers, formerly of Harford Co., died in Philadelphia, PA; she was the daughter of William and Adeline Banks, and the widow of Charles Smothers, Sr.; she was survived by her son and daughter, 2 sisters, 2 brothers, 3 grandchildren and 2 great-grandchildren) [Asbury Cemetery]

Smothers, Mary Eliza March 14, 1833 – January 26, 1897 (next to her tombstone is a field stone marked DHS) [Green Spring U. M. Church Cemetery]

Smothers, Olie died June 2, 1926, age about 36 (no tombstone; death certificate stated he was the unmarried son of William Smothers and Emily Wallace, of Havre de Grace) [St. James United Cemetery]

Smothers, Robert Sr. 1953-2017 (small metal funeral home marker) [Clark's U. M. Church Cemetery]

Smothers, Verna Jane C. August 23, 1903 – February 22, 1973 (on same tombstone with James Parker Smothers; obituary in *The Aegis* stated Verna Jane Smothers, wife of James P., of Indian Spring Farm, Darlington, died at her home; she was the daughter of Edward and Callie Reeves, and was survived by 6 brothers, 2 sisters, 35 grandchildren and 31 great-grandchildren) [Clark's U. M. Church Cemetery]

Smothers, William H. February 13, 1894 – September 24, 1915 (no tombstone; death certificate stated he was the widowed son of William Smothers, of Harford Co., and Elenora Sears, of New Jersey; he accidentally drowned; informant was Olie Smothers, of Havre de Grace) [St. James United Cemetery]

Smothers, Wilson Edward May 11, 1925 – March 18, 1926 (no tombstone; death certificate stated he was born and died near Forest Hill, the son of Harry W. Smothers, born in Maryland, and Blanche Fells, born in Pennsylvania; informant was Harry Smothers, of Pylesville) [Clark's U. M. Church Cemetery]

Snead, Ida Harris died November 3, 1982, age 86 (no tombstone; obituary in *The Aegis* on November 11, 1982 stated Ida B. Snead died at the Brevin Nursing Home in Havre de Grace and was the widow of Sidney Snead and the daughter of Lawson and Susan Harris; she was survived by one niece and one nephew, but their names were not given in the obituary) [Gravel Hill Cemetery]

Snell (no names and no dates when copied in 1987; marker not found in 2018) [St. James United Cemetery]

Snowden, ---- stillborn female on December 24, 1919 (no tombstone; death certificate stated she was the daughter of Samuel Snowden and Mary Webster, all born in Maryland and lived in Darlington; informant was her father) [Berkley Memorial Cemetery]

Snowden, ---- stillborn male on February 7, 1933 (no tombstone; death certificate stated he was born in Berkley, the son of James C. Snowden and Helen Smith, both born in Darlington; informant was his father) [Berkley Memorial Cemetery]

Snowden, Albert Sidney May 12, 1910 – March 20, 1912 (no tombstone; death certificate stated he was born in Poole and was the illegitimate son of Bertha Snowden, both born in Maryland, but the name of his father was not known to informant John Morgan, of Poole) [Berkley Memorial Cemetery]

Snowden, Benjamin Harrison October 15, 1878 – November 24, 1944 (no tombstone; death certificate stated he was the son of Mary Snowden, both born in Maryland, but his father's name was not known to informant A. Snowden, of Harford Furnace, Bel Air RFD #2; he married Eliza A. ---- (born 1889) and was a farm hand at Harford Furnace where he had lived 27 years) [Asbury Cemetery]

Snowden, Chapman September 2, 1871 – May 11, 1931 [Mt. Calvary U. A. M. E. Church Cemetery]

Snowden, George Henry 1926-1976, SP3, U.S. Army [Berkley Memorial Cemetery]

Snowden, Gilphin October 15, 1868 – June 8, 1940 (no tombstone; death certificate stated he was born in Harford Co., the son of George and Mary Snowden, both were born in Maryland; he was married, worked as a farm laborer, lived in rural Aberdeen and died at Harford Memorial Hospital in Havre de Grace; informant was his wife, Mary Snowden, of RFD Aberdeen) [Mt. Calvary U. A. M. E. Church Cemetery]

Snowden, Hannah April 1, 1859 – August 10, 1912 (no tombstone; death certificate stated she was a widow and was employed in a boarding house in Bel Air; her parents were George Smith and Eliza Richardson; all were born in Maryland; informant was James Smith, of Monkton) [Hendon Hill Cemetery]

Snowden, James T. August 3, 1921 – March 31, 1924 (no tombstone; death certificate stated he was born in Maryland, the illegitimate son of Emma Snowden who was born in Maryland and lived at Dublin; his father was unknown; informant was Thomas Snowden, of RFD #1, Street) [Cedars Chapel Cemetery]

Snowden, Louisa January 5, 1845 – September 27, 1926 (no tombstone; death certificate stated she was married, but parents unknown to informant Gilpin Snowden, of Havre de Grace) [St. James United Cemetery]

Snowden, Lydia A. June 3, 1867 – February 10, 1929 (no tombstone; death certificate stated she was born in Maryland, married, and died in Calvary, the daughter of Isaac Dorsey and Henrietta Rice, whose birth places were not known to the informant Thomas Snowden, of Street RFD) [Clark's U. M. Church Cemetery]

Snowden, Mary A. November 24, 1888 – May 23, 1927 (no tombstone; death certificate stated she was the daughter of George H. Webster and Mary J. Kenly, all born in Maryland; she married and died at home in Darlington; informant was Samuel Snowden, of Darlington) [Berkley Memorial Cemetery]

Snowden, Mary Hemore – see Mary Hemore [Green Spring U. M. Church Cemetery]

Snowden, Mary Jane died April 10, 1919, age about 78 (no tombstone; death certificate stated she was born in Maryland, but the names and birth places of her parents were not known to informant Mrs. Eliza Snowden, of Bel Air RFD; she died a widow at Harford Furnace) [Mt. Calvary U. A. M. E. Church Cemetery]

Snowden, Samuel C. August 18, 1915 – September 24, 1935 (no tombstone; death certificate stated he was the son of Samuel I. Snowden and Mary A. Webster, all born in Harford Co.; he was single, worked as a farm laborer and died in Darlington; informant was J. Carroll Snowden, of Darlington) [Berkley Memorial Cemetery]

Snowden, Thomas H. died March 13, 1932, age about 72 (no tombstone; death certificate stated he was the son of Jessie Snowden and Caroline Gibson, all born in Maryland; he was a widower and a farmer in Dublin; informant was Emma Snowden, of Street RFD) [Clark's U. M. Church Cemetery]

Sodoli, Ioni Marie 1957-2017 (small metal funeral home marker) [Berkley Memorial Cemetery]

Soloman, Mary H. March 1, 1938 – March 10, 1975 [tombstone; Pennington Funeral Home records stated Mary Henrietta Solomon was born in Alabama, the daughter of Edward Fredrick Harris and Mary Edwards Daily, and the wife of Isaiah Solomon; she died in an auto accident on I-83 in Baltimore County; informant was her mother who lived in Havre de Grace [St. James United Cemetery]

Sorrell, Cresswell October 30, 1901 – November 3, 1918 (no tombstone; death certificate stated he was the son of Willie Sorrell, mother unknown, born in Maryland; he was single, worked as a boot black and died in Havre de Grace; informant was Eve(?) Christy, of Havre de Grace) [Skinner Cemetery]

Sorrell, William August 1, 1879 – August 6, 1916 (no tombstone; death certificate stated he was the son of Edward Sorrell, born in Harford Co., and Fannie Skinner, born in Havre de Grace; he was single, worked as a laborer and died in Havre de Grace; informant was Emma Christy) [Skinner Cemetery]

Spates, Myrtle L., "Mother" June 6, 1926 – July 2, 2009 (on same tombstone with Carolyn J. Brown, daughter, and the tombstone is inscribed with a poem titled "Just One Heart") [St. James United Cemetery]

Spearman, John January 5, 1896 – December 25, 1930 (no tombstone; death certificate stated he was the son of Marshall and Rosie Spearman, all born in North Carolina; he worked as a chef and died in Havre de Grace Hospital; informant was Mrs. R. A. Ellicott, of Baltimore) [Mt. Calvary U. A. M. E. Church Cemetery]

Speller, Randolf 1945-1984 [St. James United Cemetery]

Spellman, John R. died January 26, 1914, age about 39 (no tombstone; death certificate stated he was born in Massachusetts, the son of James Spellman, born in Virginia, and Rachel Miller, born in Maryland; he was a laborer at Darlington and was single at the time of his death; informant was Jacob R. Dorsey, of Darlington) [Gravel Hill Cemetery]

Spencer, ---- stillborn female died March 26, 1913 (no tombstone; death certificate stated she was the daughter of Daniel J. Spencer and Maria Boone, of Harford Co., who lived in Fallston) [Hendon Hill Cemetery]

Spencer, Annie July 10, 1865 – July 29, 1914 (no tombstone; death certificate stated she was the daughter of John Lisby and Nellie Coale, all born in Harford Co.; she was married, died at home in Perryman and was buried in "Sidney Park Cemetery;" informant was Benjamin Hoke) [Union U. M. Church Cemetery]

Spencer, Charles March 15, 1865 – March 20, 1930 (no tombstone; death certificate stated he was the widowed son of Christianna McGaw; father unknown to informant Daniel Webster) [Union U. M. Church Cemetery]

Spencer, Charles R. December 20, 1883 – March 31, 1948 (no tombstone; death certificate stated he was the son of George Spencer and Mary Ruff, all born in Maryland; he was single and worked as a laborer in Fallston; informant was Daniel Spencer, of Fallston) [Tabernacle Mount Zion U. M. Church Cemetery]

Spencer, Helen B. August 12, 1912 – July 16, 1982 (on same tombstone with Rev. Herman D. Spencer; obituary in *The Aegis* on July 22, 1982 gave her full name as Helen Bradley Spencer) [Tabernacle Mount Zion U. M. Church Cemetery]

Spencer, Herman D. (Rev.) October 27, 1914 – March 5, 1992 (on same tombstone with Helen B. Spencer; obituary in *The Aegis* on March 18, 1992 stated The Rev. Herman Daniel Spencer was born in Harford County, the son of Daniel Spencer and Mariah Boone, served in the Navy in World War II, retired from the federal government, and after being ordained he served in Baltimore City and County and moved to Florida in 1984; formerly of Fallston, he died at Ocala, FL and was survived by his wife Daisy T. Spencer, four sons, one daughter, seven step-children, five grandchildren and many step-grandchildren and great-grandchildren) [Tabernacle Mount Zion U. M. Church Cemetery]

Spencer, Joseph A. April – (blank) 1874 – August 17, 1929 (no tombstone; death certificate stated he was the son of Thomas Osborn and Delia Spencer, all born in Maryland; he was married and worked as a laborer for a merchant in Bel Air; informant was Mrs. Delia Osborn) [Asbury Cemetery]

Spencer, Mable E. September 28, 1898 – February 22, 1920 (no tombstone; death certificate stated she was the daughter of George Spencer and Mary M. Ruff, all born in Harford Co.; she died at Bagley; informant was Daniel Spencer, of Fallston) [Tabernacle Mount Zion U. M. Church Cemetery]

Spencer, Mable Viola October 8, 1916 – August 30, 1917 (no tombstone; death certificate stated she was the daughter of Daniel J. Spencer and Maria Boone, all born in Harford Co.; she died at home at Laurel Brook (near Fallston); informant was her father) [Tabernacle Mount Zion U. M. Church Cemetery]

Spencer, Mariah May 22, 1890 – October 28, 1918 (no tombstone; death certificate stated she was the daughter of William Boone and Caroline Bond, all born in Harford Co.; she married and lived and died in Fallston; informant was Charles Spencer, of Bagley) [Tabernacle Mount Zion U. M. Church Cemetery]

Spencer, Mark Lovell died February 4, 1981, age 19 (no tombstone; obituary in *The Aegis* on February 12, 1981 stated he was the son of Agnes Ridgley, of Havre de Grace, and died at Kings Mountain, N. C., survived by his mother, father, stepfather, grandmother, 4 brothers and 2 sisters) [Berkley Memorial Cemetery]

Spencer, Mary April 12, 1861 – August 21, 1926 (no tombstone; death certificate stated she was the daughter of William A. Rough, both born in Harford Co., and Mary Bond, born in St. Mary's Co.; she died a widow in Fallston; informant was Daniel Spencer, of Hyde P. O.) [Tabernacle Mount Zion U. M. Church Cemetery]

Spencer, Mary A. died April 15, 1910, age 69 years, 4 months and 7 days (no tombstone; death certificate stated she was the daughter of Aaron Johnson and Elizabeth Talbot, all born in Maryland, and she married Daniel Spencer and she died at Mountain; informant was her son Aaron Spencer; place of burial not given [probably Mt. Zion U. M. Church Cemetery]

Spencer, Millie (Mrs.) (no tombstone; death notice in *The Aegis* on June 26, 1896 stated she died last week at the home of Daniel Spencer and was buried "at the Mountain Church" on June 22, 1896) [John Wesley U. M. E. Church Cemetery in Abingdon]

Spicer, Cecelia H. October 5, 1936 – December 31, 2008 (tombstone with photo) [St. James United Cemetery]

Spriggs, ---- stillborn female on January 30, 1919 (no tombstone; death certificate stated she died at Allibone, the daughter of Harrison Spriggs and Roberta Clark, both in Harford Co.; informant was Harrison Spriggs, of Bel Air) [Clark's U. M. Church Cemetery]

Spriggs, Henry died February 7, 1889, age 61 (tombstone laying flat on the ground) [Clark's U. M. Church Cemetery]

Spriggs, Joseph H. died December 30, 1900, age 42 years, 5 months and 29 days (inscribed "Resting in Peace / But the Shepherd replies this one is mine / Some day the silver cords shall break / I will follow my Shepherd") [Asbury Cemetery]

Spriggs, Nellie November 30, 1871 – August 2, 1912 (no tombstone; death certificate stated she was born in Harford Co., the daughter of Louis Spriggs and Christina Sciler, both born in Baltimore Co.; she married, worked as a cook and was divorced by the time of her death at home in Darlington; informant was Mary Smith, of Darlington) [Berkley Memorial Cemetery]

Spriggs, William Henry September 7, 1853 – April 4, 1912 (no tombstone; death certificate stated he was the son of Lewis Spriggs and Christina Scyler, all born in Maryland; he married, worked as a farmer and died at hom in Dublin; informant was Stewart Smith, of Darlington) [Berkley Memorial Cemetery]

Spruill, Andrea M. Henson "Sissy, Beloved Wife and Mother" September 11, 1947 – March 16, 2000 [St. James United Cemetery]

Stafford, Roxie S. died April 11, 1976 (copied in 1987, but not found in 2018) [St. James United Cemetery]

Stallworth, Gladys October 21, 1947 – December 31, 1947 (no tombstone; death certificate stated she was the daughter of Howard Stallworth, of Gulfport, MS, and Kattie M Brown, of Ashville, NC; she died in Harford Memorial Hospital; informant was her father, of Aberdeen) [Union U. M. Church Cemetery]

Stamps, Mamie 1930-2003 (small metal funeral home marker) [St. James United Cemetery

Stamps, Patricia January 1939 – November 1960 (tombstone; obituary in *The Havre de Grace Record* on November 10, 1960 stated Mrs. Patricia Ann Stamps, of 224 N. Main St., Port Deposit, wife of William Charles Stamps and daughter of Mrs. Hannah Taylor and the late Leroy Taylor, and her infant son (name not given, but researcher Christopher T. Smithson stated his name was Carlos, as noted on a hospital plaque, and they are buried together), both died in Harford Memorial Hospital in Havre de Grace on November 8, 1960; death certificate stated Patricia Ann Stamps was born January 13, 1939, the daughter of LeRoy Taylor and Hannah Smith, and died of a post partum hemorrhage; she was married, but her husband's name was not given only because the certificate did not have a space for it) [Berkley Memorial Cemetery]

Standiford, B. Hill 1984-2014 (small metal funeral home marker) [Asbury Cemetery]

Stansbury, ---- female born and died on July 13, 1936 (no tombstone; death certificate stated she was the daughter of Charles Albert Stansbury and Helen Elisabeth Bond) [Union U. M. Church Cemetery]

Stansbury, ---- stillborn child "sex unknown" on May 11, 1918 (no tombstone; death certificate stated the parents were Charles Stansbury and Marry Christie, of Aberdeen) [Union U. M. Church Cemetery]

Stansbury, ---- stillborn female died on December 8, 1926 (no tombstone; death certificate stated she was born in Havre de Grace, the daughter of James Stansbury and Carrie Brown, both born in Maryland; informant was James W. Stansbury, of Perryman) [Green Spring U. M. Church Cemetery]

Stansbury, Anna Maria 1817 – July 25, 1876 [Old Union Chapel M. E. Church Cemetery]

Stansbury, Annie Milkey Frisby died January 1, 1940, age about 55 (no tombstone; death certificate stated she was the wife of Robert Stansbury and the daughter of John Gould and Molly Gould) [Union U. M. Church Cemetery]

Stansbury, Archer May 2, 1900 – March 7, 1935 (no tombstone; death certificate stated he was the husband of Lillian Stansbury and the son of James Stansbury and Elizabeth Johnson; informant was Mrs. Elizabeth Peaco, of Havre de Grace, and he was buried in "Swan Creek Cem.") [Union U. M. Church Cemetery]

Stansbury, Benjamin Franklin December 24, 1894 – November 2, 1913 (no tombstone; death certificate stated he was the son of John W. Stansbury and Minnie Pitt, all born in Maryland) [Union U. M. Church Cemetery]

Stansbury, Bernice V. 1929-1943 (on same tombstone with Ruth J. Stansbury) [Union U. M. Church Cemetery]

Stansbury, Bertha Mae died June 25, 1990, age 83 (no tombstone; James Dorsey Card File, African American Obituaries, maintained at the Historical Society of Harford County, has a card with obituary from an unidentified newspaper stating she was a native of Harford County, the daughter of Henry and Cora Harris and widow of Ollie Stansbury; she lived in Aberdeen and died at Harford Memorial Hospital, survived by a daughter, three grandchildren, six great-grandchildren and three great-great-grandchildren) [Union U. M. Church Cemetery]

Stansbury, Carrie 1900-1982 [Union U. M. Church Cemetery]

Stansbury, Charles A. February 22, 1904 – March 16, 1958 [Union U. M. Church Cemetery]

Stansbury, Charles Henry January 8, 1885 – February 21, 1948 (no tombstone; death certificate stated he was the son of Solomon Stansbury, but his mother was unknown; he married Mary C. Stansbury and died at home on Swan Creek, Old Post Road, Aberdeen, Rural Route 2) [Union U. M. Church Cemetery]

Stansbury, Charles Jacob Franklyn February 20, 1870 – April 6, 1937 (no tombstone; death certificate stated he was the son of Philip S. Stansbury and Elizabeth A. Smith, and husband of Mary Elizabeth Stansbury) [Union U. M. Church Cemetery]

Stansbury, Charles R. December 26, 1919 – March 6, 2011 [St. James United Cemetery]

Stansbury, Charles R. Jr. May 17, 1948 – September 6, 2011 [St. James United Cemetery]

Stansbury, Charles S. December 13, 1882 – June 16, 1947 (no tombstone; death certificate stated he was the son of William H. Stansbury and Delia Tildon, and widower of Ida Christy) [Union U. M. Church Cemetery]

Stansbury, Clarence E. August 31, 1921 – April 13, 1924 (but (no tombstone; death certificate stated he was the son of Orie Stansbury and Emma Skinner, all born in Maryland; informant was his father, of Havre de Grace) [Skinner Cemetery]

Stansbury, Clayton C. February 3, 1893 – July 24, 1962 (on same tombstone with Mary L. Stansbury) [Union U. M. Church Cemetery]

Stansbury, Daniel Reese July 5, 1874 – March 30, 1915 (no tombstone; death certificate stated he was single and son of John Quincy Stansbury and Eliza Jane Lisby, all born in Harford Co.) [Union U. M. Church Cemetery]

Stansbury, Delia S. died July 8, 1906, age 67 (no tombstone; death certificate stated she was the daughter of

Benjamin Tilden and Sophia Williams, all born in Harford Co.; she lived in Michaelsville and died a widow; informant was her son-in-law W. Elijah Hall; her place of burial was not indicated, but it was probably in Old Union Chapel Cemetery at Michaelsville; possibly reinterred later in Union Chapel Cemetery near Aberdeen) [Union U. M. Church Cemetery]

Stansbury, Douglas E. April 20, 1910 – March 17, 1980 (on same tombstone with Gladys L. Stansbury inscribed "Forever In Our Hearts;" obituary in *The Aegis* on March 27, 1980 stated Douglas Edward Stansbury, husband of Gladys Warfield Stansbury of Bush Chapel Road, died at Harford Memorial Hospital; he was born in Perryman and was employed by the Henry Tarring & Sons Hardware and Furniture Store in Aberdeen until his retirement) [Union U. M. Church Cemetery]

Stansbury, Eliza December 26, 1846 – September 15, 1927 (no tombstone; death certificate stated she died a widow and was the daughter of Billie Livezey, both born in Maryland, but her mother was unknown to informant Isaac C. Stansbury, of Perryman) [Union U. M. Church Cemetery]

Stansbury, Eliza died December 30, 1902, age 60 (no tombstone; death certificate stated she was the wife of Isaac Stansbury and was burned and died at home near Cole P. O.; she had worked as a servant and had no children; her place of burial was not indicated, but it was probably in the Old Union Chapel Cemetery at Michaelsville; possibly reinterred in Union Chapel Cemetery near Aberdeen) [Union U. M. Church Cemetery]

Stansbury, Ellen died August 28 1908, age 7 months (no tombstone; death certificate stated she was born on Spesutia Island, the daughter of Charles H. Stansbury, born at Mile Square, and Mary Cristy, born on Spesutia Island, and she died at home in Boothby Hill; her place of burial was not indicated, but probably in Old Union Chapel Cemetery at Michaelsville; possibly reinterred later in Union Chapel Cemetery near Aberdeen) [Union U. M. Church Cemetery]

Stansbury, Emma November 8, 1872 – March 22, 1913 (no tombstone; death certificate stated she was born in Harford Co., the daughter of William Mitchell, born in Virginia, and Annie Brooks, born in Talbot Co., MD; she was married and a cook and washerwoman near Aberdeen; informant was William Mitchell, of Aberdeen) [Mt. Calvary U. A. M. E. Church Cemetery]

Stansbury, Ethel M. 1926-2002 (no tombstone; small metal funeral home marker) [Union U. M. Church Cemetery]

Stansbury, Eunice Lloyd November 20, 1938 – March 13, 1986 (on same tombstone with LeRoy Stansbury and Ruth W. Stansbury) [Union U. M. Church Cemetery]

Stansbury, Florence M. August 5, 1884 – January 12, 1952 [Union U. M. Church Cemetery]

Stansbury, Florence S. August 29, 1929 – January 3, 2002 (on same tombstone with Marcus Stansbury, Sr.) [St. James United Cemetery]

Stansbury, Florence V. May 17, 1883 – March 19, 1972 [Berkley Memorial Cemetery]

Stansbury, Frazier Pitt born about 1917 – October 8, 1948 (no tombstone; death certificate stated he was the son of Lev Stansbury and Minnie Hill, and was struck by a car on Route 7 near Abingdon) [Union U. M. Church Cemetery]

Stansbury, George H. March 4, 1864 – February 25, 1925 (no tombstone; death certificate stated he was the married son of Eliza Stansbury and Peter H. Boardley; informant was Susie Stansbury) [Union U. M. Church Cemetery]

Stansbury, George T. 1922-1996 (inscribed "A True Servant To His Fellow Man") [Union U. M. Church Cemetery]

Stansbury, Gladys L. August 3, 1908 – February 18, 1990 (on same tombstone with Douglas E. Stansbury inscribed "Forever In Our Hearts") [Union U. M. Church Cemetery]

Stansbury, Grace H. died August 8, 1911, age 7 months (no tombstone; death certificate stated she was the daughter of Charles Stansbury and Mary Christy, all born in Harford Co.; she died at home in Aberdeen and was buried in "Sidney Park Cemetery;" informant was J. W. Kennedy, of Aberdeen) [Union U. M. Church Cemetery]

Stansbury, Grace R. April 7, 1929 – October 22, 1933 (no tombstone; death certificate stated she was the daughter of Charles A. Stansbury and Helen E. Bond, and died from being accidentally burned out in the field while burning brush on Boothby Hill Road near Aberdeen) [Union U. M. Church Cemetery]

Stansbury, Grant S. September 15, 1891 – November 15, 1936 (no tombstone; death certificate stated he was the husband of Annie Stansbury and son of James H. Stansbury and Marian Ringgold) [Union U. M. Church Cemetery]

Stansbury, Harriet March 17, 1871 – January 23, 1916 (no tombstone; death certificate stated she was the daughter of William H. Stansbury and Rebecca Warfield, all born in Maryland; she was single, worked as a cook, died at home in Aberdeen and was buried in "Sydney Park Cemetery;" informant was Robert Stansbury, of Aberdeen) [Union U. M. Church Cemetery]

Stansbury, Harriet M. 1861-1951 (tombstone inscription, but death certificate stated Harriet Marie Stansbury was born December 25, 1868 and died January 7, 1951)

Stansbury, Helen Peaco January 25, 1908 – June 7, 1947 (no tombstone; death certificate stated she was the daughter of James T. Peaco and Annie Giles, and wife of Douglas Stansbury) [Union U. M. Church Cemetery]

Stansbury, Ida December 24, 1884 – July 8, 1946 (no tombstone; death certificate stated she was the daughter of William Christy and Martha Christy, and wife of Charles Stansbury) [Union U. M. Church Cemetery]

Stansbury, Irene Bell died November 7, 1913, age 16 (no tombstone; death certificate stated she was the daughter of Charles Stansbury and Mary Cristy, all born in Harford Co.; she died at home near Aberdeen and was buried in "Sydney Park Cemetery;" informant was Solomon J. Stansbury, of Aberdeen) [Union U. M. Church Cemetery]

Stansbury, Isaac August 15, 1853 – September 21, 1923 (no tombstone; death certificate stated he was born in Maryland, the son of Abraham Stansbury, but his mother was unknown) [Union U. M. Church Cemetery]

Stansbury, Isaac Charles May 18, 1913 – June 20, 1913 (no tombstone; death certificate stated he was the son of Charles Stansbury and Mary Christy, and all were born in Harford Co.; he died at home near Michaelsville and was buried in "Sidney Park Cemetery;" informant was Charles Stansbury, of Aberdeen) [Union U. M. Church Cemetery]

Stansbury, James H. February 2, 1875 – February 24, 1931 (no tombstone; death certificate stated he was married and son of Elsie Stansbury and James Michael; informant was Clara Stansbury) [Union U. M. Church Cemetery]

Stansbury, John September 23, 1914 – March 23, 1915 (no tombstone; death certificate stated he was the son of Charlie Stansbury and Mary Cristie, all born in Harford Co.; he died at home near Robin Hood (community located between Aberdeen and Havre de Grace) and was buried in "Sidney Park Cemetery;" informant was Charlie Stansbury, of Aberdeen) [Union U. M. Church Cemetery]

Stansbury, John E. February 6, 1939 – April 16, 1958, Maryland, A3C, 814 Supply Sq., Air Force [Gravel Hill Cemetery]

Stansbury, John Edward died September 22, 1901, age 9 months (no tombstone; death certificate stated he died at Swan Creek, but the names of his parents were not completed on the certificate and his place of burial was not indicated [possibly Union U. M. Church Cemetery]

Stansbury, John Louis July 11, 1927 – July 24, 1984, Cpl., U.S. Army, World War II [St. James United Cemetery]

Stansbury, John W. 1868-1948 (on same tombstone with Mary J. Stansbury; death certificate stated he was born September 3, 1868 and died January 5, 1948, and was the son of Isaac Stansbury and Eliza Curtis, and husband of Mary J. Plitt, of Carsins Run) [Union U. M. Church Cemetery]

Stansbury, John Z. August 2, 1868 – April 24, 1927 (no tombstone; death certificate stated he was married and the son of Abram Stansbury and Mary Brown; informant was Isaac C. Stansbury) [Union U. M. Church Cemetery]

Stansbury, Larry Sr. 1949-2009 (small metal funeral home marker) [St. James United Cemetery]

Stansbury, LeRoy June 11, 1931 – February 26, 1999 (inscribed "U.S. Army Vet, Always In Our Hearts") [Union U. M. Church Cemetery]

Stansbury, LeRoy October 11, 1910 – May 23, 1971 (on same tombstone with Eunice Lloyd Stansbury and Ruth W. Stansbury) [Union U. M. Church Cemetery]

Stansbury, Leve H. October 24, 1886 – July 24, 1920 (no tombstone; death certificate stated he was the unmarried son of Philip Stansbury and Elizabeth Smith, all born in Maryland; he worked as a day laborer and died in Havre de Grace; informant was Ella Williams, of Aberdeen) [Union U. M. Church Cemetery]

Stansbury, Louise Virginia September 14, 1911 – March 21, 1936 (no tombstone; death certificate stated she was the wife of Orie Stansbury and daughter of Louis Monk and Hattie Wright) [Union U. M. Church Cemetery]

Stansbury, Marcus Sr. May 14, 1920 -   (on same tombstone with Florence S. Stansbury) [St. James United Cemetery]

Stansbury, Marion V. April 16, 1873 – March 12, 1941 (no tombstone; death certificate stated she was widow of James Stansbury and daughter of James Tucker and Hatumale(?) Ringgold) [Union U. M. Church Cemetery]

Stansbury, Mary died September 7, 1904, age 70 (no tombstone; death certificate stated she was born in Havre de Grace and died in Aberdeen, but the names of her parents was not completed on the certificate, and she was married, but her husband's name was not given; her place of burial was not indicated [possibly in Union U. M. Church Cemetery]

Stansbury, Mary February 17, 1871 – July 2, 1933 (no tombstone; death certificate stated she was born in Wilmington, DE and was divorced from James Stansbury; her parents were unknown, and she died at the Alms House with burial in "Swan Creek Cem.") [Union U. M. Church Cemetery]

Stansbury, Mary A. January 20, 1885 – November 23, 1938 (no tombstone; death certificate stated she was the wife of Robert Stansbury and the daughter of Samuel and Mary A. Harts) [Union U. M. Church Cemetery]

Stansbury, Mary A. January 28, 1909 – February 3, 1979 (tombstone; Pennington Funeral Home records stated Mary Amilia Stansbury was the daughter of James H. Stansbury and Marian V. Ringgold, and the sister of Hazel V. Jones) [Union U. M. Church Cemetery]

Stansbury, Mary J. 1872-1955 (on same tombstone with John W. Stansbury) [Union U. M. Church Cemetery]

Stansbury, Mary L. March 27, 1895 – February 2, 1993 (on same tombstone with Clayton C. Stansbury, but her date of death is not inscribed; James Dorsey Card File, African American Obituaries, maintained at the Historical Society of Harford County, has a card with obituary from an unidentified newspaper dated February 5, 1993 stating Mary Louise Vessels Stansbury she was born in King and Queen County, VA, the daughter of John Thomas Vessels and Mary Jane Chapman; she was raised in Virginia before moving to Baltimore where she met and married Clayton C. Stansbury, Sr.; they moved to Havre de Grace and they had been married 47 years at the time of his death in 1962; she died in Harford Memorial Hospital, survived by one daughter, three sons, five grandchildren and a great-grandson; also see a brief article with photo in *Harford Historical Bulletin* No. 20 in 1984) [Union U. M. Church Cemetery]

Stansbury, Monroe July 20, 1903 – June 21, 1927 (no tombstone; death certificate stated he was not married and the son of James Stansbury and Marian Ringgold) [Union U. M. Church Cemetery]

Stansbury, Olivia F. 1900-1968 [Union U. M. Church Cemetery]

Stansbury, Orie Louis April 5, 1947 – January 12, 1948 (no tombstone; death certificate stated he was born in Havre de Grace, son of Charles Ralph Stansbury, born in Maryland, and Ruth Wittington, born in Virginia, and died at Harford Memorial Hospital; informant was his father who lived at 319 Freedom St., Havre de Grace) [Skinner Cemetery]

Stansbury, Peter March 1, 1854 – January 14, 1917 (no tombstone; death certificate stated he was not married and was the son of Steven Stansbury and Maria Izer, all born in Maryland) [Union U. M. Church Cemetery]

Stansbury, Philip S. died April 20, 1913, age about 64 (no tombstone; death certificate stated he died a widower and was the son of Stephen Stansbury, both born in Harford Co., but his mother was not known to informant William Wilmore, of Perryman) [Union U. M. Church Cemetery]

Stansbury, Prince A. 1902-1960 [Union U. M. Church Cemetery]

Stansbury, Robert March 1, 1916 – December 1, 1917 (no tombstone; death certificate stated he was the son of Charlie Stansbury and Mary Christy, all were born in Maryland; he died at home in Aberdeen and was buried in "Sidney Park Cemetery;" informant was his father) [Union U. M. Church Cemetery]

Stansbury, Robert A. 1854 – February 26, 1913 (no tombstone; death certificate stated he was a widower and the son of Abram Stansbury and Mary Brown, all born in Maryland) [Union U. M. Church Cemetery]

Stansbury, Ruth J. 1932-1972 (on same tombstone with Bernice V. Stansbury) [Union U. M. Church Cemetery]

Stansbury, Ruth V., "Loving Wife and Mother" March 12, 1921 – July 14, 1998 [St. James United Cemetery]

Stansbury, Ruth W. January 3, 1912 – April 27, 1997 (on same tombstone with LeRoy Stansbury and Eunice Lloyd Stansbury) [Union U. M. Church Cemetery]

Stansbury, Solomon November 2, 1853 – March 17, 1939 (no tombstone; death certificate stated he was the son of Abraham Stansbury and Mary Ann Brown, and widower of Henney Stansbury, and died in 1868, age 70, but his *Havre de Grace Republican* obituary stated "Sol" was 86 which is approximate to his age being about 25 in the 1880 Harford County Census) [Union U. M. Church Cemetery]

Stansbury, Solomon E. February 12, 1901 – died between April 22, 1940 at 11:30 p.m. and April 23, 1940 at 12:30 a.m. (no tombstone; death certificate stated he was the son of Charles H. Stansbury and Mary Christy and he died in a house fire on Edmund Street Extended in Aberdeen)

Stansbury, Vernon April 24, 1894 – August 13, 1969, Maryland, Pvt., 154 Depot Brigade, World War I [St. James United Cemetery]Stanton, Gloria Faith Myrteen, "Loving Wife & Mother" October 25, 1943 – July 13, 2000 [Berkley Memorial Cemetery]

Starks, Gerald February 20, 1926 – October 21, 2012, TN, U.S. Navy [Berkley Memorial Cemetery]

Starks, James died September 11, 1918, age about 19 (no tombstone; death certificate stated he was born in Virginia and was a jockey who died from an accidental injury in Havre de Grace; informant was William Garth, of Charlottesville, VA) [St. James United Cemetery]

Steele, Lillian C. December 13, 1938 – September 22, 2007 [St. James United Cemetery]

Stephenson, Alice March 2, 1882 – March 11, 1915 (no tombstone; death certificate stated she was the daughter of Henry Thompson, birth place unknown, and Clara Stansbury, of Harford Co.; she died a widow at Gravelly Hill; informant was Clara Turner, of Gravelly Hill) [Gravel Hill Cemetery]

Sterrett, Arthur A., "Husband" 1876-1962 (on same tombstone with Fannie A. Sterrett) [Asbury Cemetery]

Sterrett, Fannie A., "Wife" (no dates; on same tombstone with Arthur A. Sterrett) [Asbury Cemetery]

Stevens, Doris V., "Beloved Wife, Mother and Grandmother" February 22, 1923 – June 4, 1995 [Union U. M. Church Cemetery]

Stevens, Mary Martha January 31, 1878 – January 3, 1938 (no tombstone; death certificate stated she was the wife of Joseph Stevens and the daughter of Hampton Monk and Lotta Ringold; she was buried in "Swan Creek Cemetery") [Union U. M. Church Cemetery]

Stevens, William M., "Beloved Father" July 27, 1921 – December 15, 2012, SFC, U.S. Army, World War II, Korea, Bronze Star (tombstone; funeral notice and photo in *The Aegis* on December 19, 2012 stated William Mitchell Stevens, of Aberdeen, died at Lorien Riverside Nursing Home) [Union U. M. Church Cemetery]

Stevenson, Amanda Jane April 5, 1880 – October 23, 1945 (no tombstone; death certificate stated she was born in Perryman, the daughter of Henry Williams and Olivia Norton, both born in Maryland; she married John Stevenson, lived in Magnolia, died at Harford Memorial Hospital in Havre de Grace and was buried in Magnolia

Cemetery; informant was her daughter Eva Tolliver, of Magnolia) [Foster's Hill Cemetery]

Stevenson, Augustus died April 13, 1901, age 82 (inscribed "At Rest") [Asbury Cemetery]

Stevenson, James Edward died September 18, 1987, age 86 (no tombstone; obituary in *The Aegis* on September 24, 1987 stated he was the son of John and Amanda Stevenson of Harford County, lived in Joppa and died at Franklin Square Hospital, survived by a daughter, two granddaughters, three sisters and a brother; interment was in "Ebenezer Baptist Church Cemetery") [Foster's Hill Cemetery]

Stevenson, Sylvester May 23, 1909 – July 5, 1938 (no tombstone; death certificate stated he was the son of John Stevenson and Amanda Williams, and they all were born in Harford Co.; he married Mary ----, worked as a laborer in Magnolia, was injured in an automobile accident near Joppa, died in Havre de Grace and was buried in "Magnolia Cemetery;" informant was Mrs. Mary Stevenson, of Magnolia) [Foster's Hill Cemetery]

Stevenson, William H. January 22, 1907 – July 14, 1937 (no tombstone; death certificate stated he was born in Harford Co., son of John Stevens *(sic)* and Amanda Williams, both born in Maryland; he was single, worked as a laborer in Joppa and died unexpectedly at home on "New Phil Road, Joppa;" he was buried in "Magnolia Cemetery;" informant was Amanda Williams) [Foster's Hill Cemetery]

Steveson, Mary December 25, 1872 – June 2, 1932 (no tombstone; death certificate stated she was the daughter of William Bond and Martha Adams, all born in Harford Co.; she was the widow of Charlie Steveson and died at Aberdeen RFD #1; informant was Mrs. Jennie Prigg, of Darlington) [Green Spring U. M. Church Cemetery]

Stewart, ---- stillborn female died on April 12, 1923 (no tombstone; death certificate stated she was the daughter of Howard Stewart and Mary Kell, and they were all born in Maryland; informant was her father, of Forest Hill) [Fairview A. M. E. Church Cemetery]

Stewart, Anthony 1959-2011 (small metal funeral home marker; funeral notice and photo in *The Aegis* on June 1, 2011 stated Anthony Jose Stewart, of Darlington, died on May 27, 2011 at Sinai Hospital in Baltimore; services held at St. James U. A. M. E. Church near Darlington) [Clark's U. M. Church Cemetery]

Stewart, Daisy April 19, 1887 – October 18, 1945 (no tombstone; death certificate stated she was born in Maryland, the daughter of Jacob Bradford, born in Harford Co., and Mary J. Bond, born in Germantown, PA; she married Howard Stewart (age 64 in 1945) and died at Rocks where they had lived for 5 years; informant was Lillie Stewart, of Rocks) [Clark's U. M. Church Cemetery]

Stewart, Edmond III died October 8, 1982, age 14 (no tombstone; obituary in *The Aegis* on October 14, 1982 stated "Eddie" was the son of Edmond Stewart, Jr., of Aberdeen, and Cynthia Taylor, of Edgewood, and was student of Aberdeen High School and a member of the school band; he died at the University of Maryland Hospital in Baltimore, survived by his parents, grandparents Mr. and Mrs. Edmond Stewart, with whom he resided, and two sisters, Kimberly Stewart and Leslie Taylor) [Union U. M. Church Cemetery]

Stewart, Edmond Sr. March 17, 1922 – April 9, 1984, MSgt., U.S. Army, World War II (tombstone; obituary in *The Aegis* stated he was born in Oveida, FL and resided in Maryland after being stationed at Aberdeen Proving Ground in 1945; after serving in France and Germany during World War II he worked in the auto shop at Bainbridge Naval Training Center and he later operated the Stewart Brothers Body Shop and the Stewart Used Car Shop in Aberdeen; he died at Harford Memorial Hospital in Havre de Grace, survived by his wife Iva Gordon Stewart, two daughters, two sons, and six grandchildren) [St. James United Cemetery]

Stewart, Elijah died November 9, 1880, age 75 (inscribed "Call not back the dear departed, Anchored safe when storms are o'er, On the border land we left them, Soon to meet and part no more") [Clark's U. M. Church Cemetery]

Stewart, Emily died July 2, 1927, age 56 (no tombstone; death certificate stated she died in 1873, but it then stated she was age 56 when she died in 1927 which would put her birth in 1871, not 1873; her parents were John Stewart and Eliza Carroll, both were born in Maryland; she was single and died at Rocks; informant was Julia A. Stewart, of Rocks) [Clark's U. M. Church Cemetery]

Stewart, Emory 1918-1979 (small metal funeral home marker) [Fairview A. M. E. Church Cemetery]

Stewart, Frank B. died October 5, 1968, age 55 (obituary in *The Aegis* on October 10, 1968 stated he was born in Harford Co., the son of Mary Kell Stewart and the late Howard Stewart; he lived at Aberdeen Route 1 and was employed by the City of Aberdeen; he was survived by his mother, a son, three daughters, a brother, six sisters, and sixteen grandchildren) [Fairview A. M. E. Church Cemetery]

Stewart, Frisbie died August 9, 1928 and about 75 (no tombstone; death certificate stated he was the son of ---- (unknown) Stewart and Sophia Boyer, all born in Maryland; he was married, worked as a farm laborer and died in Fountain Green; informant was Laura Stewart, of Bel Air) [Mt. Calvary U. A. M. E. Church Cemetery]

Stewart, Georgianna, wife of William E. Stewart (no dates on tombstone; inscribed "In Memory of") [Clark's U. M. Church Cemetery]

Stewart, Grace W. 1918-2005 (small metal funeral home marker) [St. James United Cemetery]

Stewart, John F. "died March 9, 1902, in his 47 year" (inscribed "A beautiful sleep;" death certificate stated John H. Stewart died March 9, 1903, age 47; he was the son of William H. Stewart and Elizabeth Flint, married (wife not named) and worked as a laborer in Perryman) [Old Union Chapel M. E. Church Cemetery]

Stewart, Lawrence F. July 23, 1904 – December 21, 1918 (no tombstone; death certificate stated he was single, worked as a laborer and died at Kalmia; he was the son of Howard Stewart and Julia ---- (blank), and all were born in Harford Co.; informant was Julia Stewart, of Bel Air) [Clark's U. M. Church Cemetery]

Stewart, Mary C. 1913-2014 (small metal funeral home marker) [Clark's U. M. Church Cemetery]

Stewart, Mary Rebecca, "Mother" May 10, 1881 – November 24, 1977 [Fairview A. M. E. Church Cemetery]

Stewart, Nathaniel Jr. died April 27, 1968, age 3 (no tombstone; obituary in *The Aegis* on May 2, 1968 stated he was the son of Mr. & Mrs. Nathaniel Stewart, Sr., of 553 Girard St., Havre de Grace, and he died at Johns Hopkins Hospital, survived by his parents, one brother, one sister, his maternal grandmother Elaine Jones and his great-grandparents Mr. & Mrs. J. Lee Jones) [St. James United Cemetery]

Stewart, Nathaniel C. 1935-2015 (small metal funeral home marker) [Berkley Memorial Cemetery]

Stewart, Robert Frank died February 18, 1989, age 93 (no tombstone; obituary in *The Aegis* on February 23, 1989 stated he was born in Harford County, the son of Frank Collins and Belle Stewart, lived in Aberdeen, served in the Army in World War I and died at Perry Point VAMC; no heirs were named; military records stated he was born in Perryman on September 23, 1895, was inducted into the service on June 19, 1918, served in the 154 Depot Brigade and 808 Pioneer Inf., was overseas from August 31, 1918 to June 22, 1919, fought at Meuse-Argonne, and was honorably discharged on June 28, 1919) [Union U. M. Church Cemetery]

Stewart, Sadie Belle died March 7, 1901, age 7 years, 4 months and 18 days (no tombstone; death certificate stated she was the daughter of Frank Collins and Isabelle Stewart; died at Michaelsville; her place of burial was not indicated, but probably in the Old Union Chapel Cemetery at Michaelsville; possibly reinterred later in Union Chapel Cemetery near Aberdeen) [Union U. M. Church Cemetery]

Stewart, Sarah A. December 28, 1919 – March 12, 1991 ("Sarah Steward" owned a lot in section 39 some time after 1951, yet her name "Sarah A. Stewart" is inscribed on the same tombstone with Mary E. Turner in section 31; obituary in *The Aegis* on March 20, 1991 stated Sarah Ann Stewart was a native of Harford County, the daughter of James E. Anderson and Sarah McComas; she lived in Aberdeen, worked as a dietetic aide in the food service area of the Perry Point VAMC and died at Harford Memorial Hospital in Havre de Grace; she was survived by a son, three daughters, 17 grandchildren, 11 great-grandchildren and 1 great-grandchild; Mrs. Stewart's husband was not mentioned) [Mt. Calvary U. A. M. E. Church Cemetery]

Stewart, Virginia Lee died March 27, 1988, age 48 (no tombstone; obituary in *The Record* on April 13, 1988 stated she was born in Pennsylvania, worked for the Cecil County Board of Education and was cafeteria manager at Bainbridge Elementary School; she lived in Havre de Grace and died at Franklin Square Hospital, survived by her mother Helen M. Stewart Calm, a son Zachary G. Stewart, 4 sisters and 3 brothers; her stepfather was the late Robert Calm) [St. James United Cemetery]

Stewart, William A. April 30, 1928 – July 17, 1995, Sgt, U.S. Army, Korea [Clark's U. M. Church Cemetery]

Stewart, Zachariah May 10, 1882 – April 2, 1917 (no tombstone; death certificate stated he was the married son of John Stewart, but his mother was unknown; he worked as a hotel cook in Havre de Grace; informant was Mrs. Eliza White) [St. James United Cemetery]

Stewart, Zachary G. "My Pooh-Bear" September 19, 1964 – October 23, 1997 (inscribed "In Memory Of" with the image of a fisherman; obituary in *The Aegis* on October 29, 1997 stated Zachary Gerard Stewart was born in Havre de Grace, the son of Ellsworth Stokes, of Aberdeen, and the late Virginia Lee Stewart who died March 27, 1988; he lived in Abingdon, worked as a cab driver for Montville Cab Co. in Havre de Grace and died at Fallston General Hospital, survived by his father, wife Susanna Ayala, grandmother Helen Marie Cain, mother-in-law Susanne Ayala, three uncles, four aunts, a brother, a brother-in-law and a sister-in-law) [St. James United Cemetery]

Stinson, Karen F. August 28, 1958 – August 30, 1958 [St. James United Cemetery]

Stock, Terry 1910-1978 [St. James United Cemetery]

Stokes, ---- stillborn male on May 5, 1918 (no tombstone; death certificate stated he was born in Maryland, the son of Winfield Stokes, born at Gravelly Hill, and Florence Jones, born in Maryland; he died in Havre de Grace; informant was Ida Jones, of Havre de Grace) [Gravel Hill Cemetery]

Stokes, Albert (no dates recorded in 1987, not listed in 2002, and not found in 2018, but this was likely the Albert Stokes born circa 1856-1859 who married Rachael Gibson in 1877 and died in the 1920s since he did not appear in the 1930 Harford County Census) [Gravel Hill Cemetery]

Stokes, Albert December 28, 1893 – September 25, 1946 (no tombstone; death certificate stated he was the son of Mary B. Stokes and Tuesday Thomas, and husband of Dorothy S. Stokes) [Union U. M. Church Cemetery]

Stokes, Baby stillborn male on April 9, 1920 (no tombstone; death certificate stated he was the son of Earnest Stokes, of Rollinsville, MD, and Effie Brown, of Perryman, MD) [St. James United Cemetery]

Stokes, Dennis J. December 14, 1953 – May 19, 1982, Sgt., U.S. Marine Corps [St. James United Cemetery]

Stokes, Diana V. 1946-1995 (name and dates handwritten on a flat cement slab; James Dorsey Card File, African American Obituaries, maintained at the Historical Society of Harford County, has a card with obituary from an unidentified newspaper stating Diana Virginia Stansbury Stokes was a native of Havre de Grace and the daughter of Charles and Ruth Stansbury; she married Walter Stokes, worked for Sewell Plastics in Havre de Grace for 16 years and then as a nurse's aide for Sunshine Services; she died at University Hospital in Baltimore on January 17, 1995, survived by her husband, parents, a daughter, two sons, five brothers and two grand-daughters) [St. James United Cemetery]

Stokes, Dorothy Ann died January 21, 1974, age not given (no tombstone; obituary in *The Aegis* stated she was born on Spesutia Island, a daughter of the late Charlie and Mary Stansbury, and lived at 300 Superior Street in Havre de Grace (husband's name was not mentioned); she died at Harford Memorial Hospital, survived by 4 sons, 3 daughters, 1 sister, 29 grandchildren and 2 great-grandchildren) [Union U. M. Church Cemetery]

Stokes Effie P. December 25, 1901 – April 19, 1920 (no tombstone; death certificate stated she was the married daughter of Solomon Brown and Mary Kell; she died in Havre de Grace Hospital; informant was Ernest Stokes, of Havre de Grace [Union U. M. Church Cemetery]

Stokes, Ernestine M., "Mother" 1929-1976 [St. James United Cemetery]

Stokes, Floyd R. 1939-2003 (small metal funeral home marker) [St. James United Cemetery]

Stokes, Margaret D. January 19, 1904 – August 12, 1923 (no tombstone; death certificate stated she was the married daughter of Charles Haycock and Emma Crown; informant was Ernest Stokes, of Havre de Grace) [St. James United Cemetery]

Stokes, Mary Lee 1957-2000 (small metal funeral home marker) [Community Baptist Church Cemetery]

Stokes, Mary Nettie 1929-2000 (small metal funeral home marker; obituary in *The Aegis* on July 26, 2000 stated she was born May 14, 1929 in Reidsville, NC, the daughter of the late Chalmus and Martha Broadnax, and they came to Maryland when she was 12 years old; she was the wife of the late Henry Lee Stokes, of Joppa, and died at Fallston General Hospital on July 29, 2000, survived by 8 children and several grandchildren and great-grandchildren) [Community Baptist Church Cemetery]

Stokes, Quinto A. 1989-2013 (small metal funeral home marker) [Berkley Memorial Cemetery]

Stokes, Sydney died October 25, 1917, age about 38 (no tombstone; death certificate stated he was the son of Albert Stokes and Rachael Gibson, all born in Maryland; he was married, was a laborer and died in Havre de Grace; informant was his father, of Havre de Grace RFD) [Gravel Hill Cemetery]

Stokes, William E. Jr., "Chico" September 19, 1941 – September 20, 1999 (tombstone inscribed with an image of a boxing glove) [St. James United Cemetery]

Stokes, Zanie (copied in 1987, not listed in 2002 and not found in 2018) [Gravel Hill Cemetery]

Storather, Frank Jr. October 15, 1918 – February 19, 1919 (no tombstone; death certificate stated he was the son of Frank Storather, of Virginia, and Ester Barnes, of Havre de Grace) [St. James United Cemetery]

Stout, Edith April 22, 1881 – January 7, 1913 (no tombstone; death certificate stated she was the daughter of Lloyd Green and Eliza Harris, all were born in Harford Co.; she was married at the time of her death at home near Havre de Grace; informant was Eliza Harris) [Green Spring U. M. Church Cemetery]

Stout, John Boyden, "Beloved Son & Brother" December 20, 1941 – November 16, 1973 (tombstone; obituary in *The Aegis* stated he lived at 134 S. Archer Street in Bel Air, was injured in an automobile accident and died at Franklin Square Hospital in Baltimore, survived by his father John W. Stout, of Ohio, his stepfather Louis Hickman, Sr., a brother Louis Hickman, Jr., and five sisters) [Berkley Memorial Cemetery]

Stowe, Frances M. Ellis February 6, 1931 – September 26, 2002 (inscribed "As the love seeks the heights so are souls rise home to God to forever in his care" and these names were inscribed at the bottom: Lawrence, Lemuel, Patricia, Darene and Porlia) [St. James United Cemetery]

Strange, Stacy W. February 10, 1969 – October 10, 1987, U.S. Army, Co. D, 232 Medical Battalion (inscribed "One Day At A Time" and also a white wooden cross about 3 feet in height) [Union U. M. Church Cemetery]

Strothers, Albert September 9, 1920 – July 14, 1995 ("In Loving Memory") [Berkley Memorial Cemetery]

Stump, Frederick R. Sr. July 19, 1930 – October 25, 2005, Cpl., U.S. Army, Korea (tombstone; obituary and photo in *The Aegis* stated Frederick Roland "Jack" Stump, Sr. was born in Darlington, son of Roland Harris Stump and Irene Presberry, and married Jean Brooks in 1953; during his 37-year career with the federal government, including service in the Korean War, he worked at Bainbridge Naval Training Center, Perry Point VAMC, Edgewood Arsenal and Aberdeen Proving Ground; he was very active in Hosanna AME Church and was treasurer for 40 years and president of the choirs for 20 years; he died at the Lorien Nursing and Rehabilitation Center in Belcamp, survived by his wife, one daughter, one son, two granddaughters, one godson, one adopted son, two sisters, and one brother) [Berkley Memorial Cemetery]

Stump, Harold Robert died April 6, 1991, age 67 (no tombstone; obituary in *The Aegis* on April 10, 1991 stated he was born in Harford Co., the son of the late Roland Stump and Irene Presberry, and he was an engineer and a boiler plant operator at Aberdeen Proving Ground; he lived in Bel Air and died at Fallston General Hospital, survived by wife Carrie Dorsey Stump, three brothers, three sisters, and a niece) [Berkley Memorial Cemetery]

Stump, Irene P. 1901-1976 (on same tombstone with Roland H. Stump inscribed "Family" at the top) [Berkley Memorial Cemetery]

Stump, Jean M. 1929-2015 (small metal funeral home marker; funeral notice and photo in *The Aegis* stated she lived in Bel Air and died October 13, 2015 at Franklin Square Medical Center) [Berkley Memorial Cemetery]

Stump, John L August 24, 1925 – July 13, 2001, STM1, U.S. Navy, World War II (tombstone; obituary and photo in *The Aegis* on July 18, 2001 stated John Luther "Bill" Stump was born in Darlington, the son of Roland H. Stump and Irene Presberry, and was the husband of Courtney Henrietta Brooks Stump; he lived in Darlington, retired from Aberdeen Proving Ground in 1986 and died at Harford Memorial Hospital, survived by his wife, two sons, four grandchildren, two brothers, two sisters and seven sisters-in-law; he was preceded in death by his parents, a brother Harold and a sister Esther Thompson) [Clark's U. M. Church Cemetery]

Stump, Roland H. 1902-1963 (on same tombstone with Irene P. Stump inscribed "Family" at the top) [Berkley

Memorial Cemetery]

Stump, Theresa J. May 30, 1876 – July 21, 1929 (no tombstone; death certificate stated she was the daughter of Thomas Ashton and Annie M. Cornish, all born in Maryland; she married and died at home in Darlington; informant was John W. Stump, of Darlington) [Berkley Memorial Cemetery]

Summons, Emma Skinner July 16, 1878 – March 21, 1946 (no tombstone; death certificate stated she was the daughter of John Skinner and Frances? Skinner *(sic)*, and the wife of William F. Summons, of Havre de Grace) [St. James United Cemetery]

Summons, Henry died May 28, 1928, age about 68 (no tombstone; death certificate stated he was the widowed son of Frank Summons, but mother was unknown to informant Ella Williams) [Union U. M. Church Cemetery]

Sumpter, Baby Boy May 16, 1947 – May 17, 1947 (no tombstone; death certificate stated he was the son of Fortune Sumpter and Mary Snell, of South Carolina, and died in Havre de Grace) [St. James United Cemetery]

Sumpter, Frank Lee 1945-2013 (small metal funeral home marker) [St. James United Cemetery]

Sumpter, Hattie V. November 22, 1919 – March 25, 2002 (on same tombstone with J. Wesley Sumpter inscribed "Together Forever") [Berkley Memorial Cemetery]

Sumpter, J. Wesley June 6, 1915 – October 20, 1902 (on same tombstone with Hattie V. Sumpter inscribed "Together Forever") [Berkley Memorial Cemetery]

Sumpter, Mary Ellen April 17, 1930 – August 17, 1997 (no tombstone; The James Dorsey Card File, African American Obituaries, maintained at the Historical Society of Harford County, has a card with obituary from an unidentified newspaper on August 27, 1987 stating she was born in Sumter, SC., the first child born to Maxine Miller Snell and the late Robert Snell; in the late 1940s she moved to Havre de Grace, married (husband's name not given), worked at Harford Memorial Hospital and Citizens Nursing Home, and died at Bel Air Nursing and Rehabilitation Center, survived by her mother, two sons, two daughters, a sister, a half-brother, seven grandchildren, four great-grandchildren and two nephews) [St. James United Cemetery]

Sumpter, Mary M. 1927-1997 (small metal funeral home marker; also handwritten on a flat cement slab) [St. James United Cemetery]

Swan, ---- (no tombstone, but Kurtz Funeral Home records stated Aleck Swan's child was buried in a "P im cherry" coffin on May 23, 1881 from near John Emerich's) [West Liberty Church Cemetery]

Swann, Anna M., "Mom Mae" May 6, 1910 – February 17, 1991 [William C. Rice Memorial Cemetery, St. James U. M. Church]

Swann, Bessie Viola 1912-1966 (small metal funeral home marker) [William C. Rice Memorial Cemetery, St. James U. M. Church]

Swann, Cornelia D. February 23, 1913 – July 21, 1991 (on same tombstone with James F. Swann; obituary in *The Aegis* on July 24, 1991 stated Cornelia Greene Swann was born in the area of Sharon, near Jarrettsville, the daughter of Charles Greene and Ida Harris; she had worked as a domestic and was the widow of James F. Swann; she died at home and was survived by two sisters, two brothers, and nieces and nephews) [William C. Rice Memorial Cemetery, St. James U. M. Church]

Swann, Edward Leon died August 6, 1975, age 70 (no tombstone; obituary in *The Aegis* stated he was the husband of the late Bessie V. Swann, lived in Jarrettsville, and was a retired truck driver; he died at Street and was survived by several nieces and nephews) [William C. Rice Memorial Cemetery, St. James U. M. Church]

Swann, Georganna 1871-   (inscribed "At Rest" on same tombstone with William W. Swann, but no death year was inscribed; death certificate stated she was born on February 12, 1873 at Federal Hill, the daughter of John Smith, born in Maryland, and Catherine E. Jamison, born in Harford Co. and died at home at Federal Hill on October 16, 1936, the widow of William Walter Swann; informant was Oscar Swann, of Rocks) [William C. Rice Memorial Cemetery, St. James U. M. Church]

Swann, Harry Oscar 1906-1951 (inscribed "In Memory Of") [William C. Rice Memorial Cemetery, St. James U. M. Church]

Swann, Helen L. (Rev.) March 10, 1930 – October 18, 1994 (on same tombstone with William F. Swann) [William C. Rice Memorial Cemetery, St. James U. M. Church]

Swann, James Emory December 2, 1911 – January 23, 1912 (no tombstone; death certificate stated he was the son of William E. Swan *(sic)* and Julia J. Thomas, all they all were born in Harford Co.; he died at Rocks and his father was informant) [William C. Rice Memorial Cemetery, St. James U. M. Church]

Swann, James F. March 14, 1913 – December 30, 1988 (on same tombstone with Cornelia D. Swann) [William C. Rice Memorial Cemetery, St. James U. M. Church]

Swann, Julia J. neé Thomas died November 15, 1971, age 81 (no tombstone; obituary in *The Aegis* stated she was the widow of William Swann; formerly of Jarrettsville, she died in Plainsfield, NJ, survived by a daughter, two grandchildren, one brother and three sisters) [William C. Rice Memorial Cemetery, St. James U. M. Church]

Swann, Steven A. February 7, 1955 – March 27, 2016 (inscribed "Forever In Our Hearts") [William C. Rice Memorial Cemetery, St. James U. M. Church]

Swann, William Emory June 13, 1891 – June 21, 1931 (no tombstone; death certificate stated he was the son of William Walter Swann and Georganna Smith, all born in Harford Co.; he was a married farmer and died at home at Jarrettsville; informant was Julia J. Swann) [William C. Rice Memorial Cemetery, St. James U. M. Church]

Swann, William F. July 18, 1929 – September 24, 1990 (on same tombstone with Helen L. Swann)

Swann, William W. 1870-1929 (inscribed "At Rest" on same tombstone with Georganna Swann) [William C. Rice Memorial Cemetery, St. James U. M. Church]

Swift, ---- (tombstone not found in 2018, but J. C. Taylor Marble Co. records stated "William Swift's children's tombstone was put up May 16th 1883 in Lagrange burying ground") [Chestnut Grove A. M. E. Church Cemetery, formerly LaGrange Cemetery at Rocks]

Syckles, Annie Ringgold died May 9, 1992, age 95 (no tombstone; "Annie Sickle" owned a lot in section 39 some time after 1951; James Dorsey Card File, African American Obituaries, maintained at the Historical Society of Harford County, has a card with obituary from an unidentified newspaper dated May 12, 1992 stating she was a native of Aberdeen, the daughter of Emory Ringgold and Susan Hollingsworth, and the widow of James Syckles; she died at Harford Memorial Hospital in Havre de Grace, survived by two sons, one sister, five grandchildren and three great-grandchildren) [Mt. Calvary U. A. M. E. Church Cemetery]

Talbot, Benjamin F. 1866 – October 16, 1928 (no tombstone; death certificate stated he was born in Baltimore Co., the son of Benjamin Talbot and Matilda McCamron or McCamson(?), whose birth places were unknown to informant Robert Bishop, of Joppa; he was married, worked as a laborer, died at Mountain and was buried in "Mt. Colored Cem.") [Mt. Zion U. M. Church Cemetery]

Talbot, Mary Jane died May 8, 1907, age 33 years, 4 months (no tombstone; death certificate stated she was the wife of Winfield Talbot and the daughter of Isaac Banks (mother's name not given); she died at Fulford and on the back of death certificate it is written "Asbury") [Asbury Cemetery]

Tancemore, Clifton Evins May 1, 1932 – November 7, 1977 (tombstone; obituary in *The Aegis* stated he was born in Philadelphia, son of Dorothy Tancemore, with whom he resided, and the late Wilmer Tancemore; he lived at 627 Trimble Road in Joppa, worked at Sportsman Sales and died at Franklin Square Hospital in Baltimore; he was survived by his mother, a son Anthony Bowman and a daughter Patricia Bowman, both of Philadelphia, three brothers Wilmer Tancemore, Jr., Jesse Tancemore and John Drake, and a sister Helen Green) [Mt. Zion U. M. Church Cemetery]

Tancemore, Dorothy O., "Mother" January 13, 1911 – February 9, 1991 [Mt. Zion U. M. Church Cemetery]

Tancemore, Ernest Lee August 7, 1929 – September 17, 1976 (tombstone; obituary in *The Aegis* on September 23, 1976 stated he was the son of Dorothy Tancemore, of Joppa, and late Wilmer Tancemore; married Mildred ---- and lived and died in Fredericksburg, VA; survived by his wife and mother, son Ernest Lee Tancemore, Jr., daughter Barbara Parker, three brothers, one sister and seven grandchildren) [Mt. Zion U. M. Church Cemetery]

Tancemore, Jesse B. December 25, 1930 – January 15, 1986 [Mt. Zion U. M. Church Cemetery]

Tancemore, Wilmer B. December 19, 1892 – November 3, 1970, Maryland, PFC, U.S. Army, World War I (tombstone; obituary in *The Aegis* stated he was the husband of Dorothy O. Tancemore, lived at 627 Trimble Road in Joppa and died at the Perry Point Veterans Hospital; he was survived by his wife, two sons in Joppa and two sons and one daughter in Philadelphia) [Mt. Zion U. M. Church Cemetery]

Tancemore, Wilmer Louis died September 20, 1988, age 61 (no tombstone; obituary in *The Aegis* on September 29, 1988 stated he was born in Philadelphia, the son of Dorothy (Bishop) Tancemore, of Edgewood, and the late Wilmer Tancemore; he worked at the Philadelphia Navy Yard at age 17, joined the Navy, was known to many as "Low Down Brown" and his last job was for Amtrak; he married Loretta Robinson, lived in Philadelphia and was survived by his wife and mother, 2 sons Louis and Gregory Tancemore, 1 granddaughter and 1 sister) [Mt. Zion U. M. Church Cemetery]

Tann, Roxanne Guary, "Wife, Mother and Daughter" March 7, 1959 – June 5, 2001 [Berkley Memorial Cemetery]

Tasco, Adelaide E. 1928-2014 (small metal funeral home marker; funeral notice and photo in *The Aegis* on February 12, 2014 stated she died at home in Darlington on February 4, 2014, age 85) [Berkley Memorial Cemetery]

Tasco, Laura May June 20, 1924 – October 3, 1924 (no tombstone; death certificate stated she was the daughter of Murrell Tasco and Myrtle Lee, all born in Maryland, and they lived at Aldino near Aberdeen; informant was her father Murrell Tasco, of Aberdeen) [Green Spring U. M. Church Cemetery]

Tasco, Rebecca died April 1, 1910, age 65 [St. James United Cemetery]

Tasco, William S. September 15, 1920 – January 15, 1989, TEC5, U.S. Army, World War II [Berkley Memorial Cemetery]

Tasker, Anna Bell August 9, 1916 – December 28, 1919 (no tombstone; death certificate stated she was the daughter of William Tasker and Annie Pinkney, died at Benson and was buried in "The Mountain Colored Cemetery;" informant was Mrs. Annie Tasker, of Fallston) [Mt. Zion U. M. Church Cemetery]

Tasker, Annie M. died December 21, 1920, age 39 years, 1 month (no tombstone; death certificate stated she was the daughter of James Pinkney and Cornelia Giles, all born in Harford Co.; she was married, worked as a domestic, died in Benson and was buried in "Mountain Colored Cemetery;" informant was Sarah Bradley, of Benson) [Mt. Zion U. M. Church Cemetery]

Tasker, Berna died November 30, 1972, age 19 (no tombstone; obituary in *The Aegis* on December 7, 1972 stated she was the daughter of Merle and Lucille Tasker, of 204 Pulaski Hwy., Joppa, and died at home, survived by her parents, four brothers, three sisters, one uncle Mason Dorsey, of Bel Air, and one son Avon Tasker) [Tabernacle Mount Zion U. M. Church Cemetery]

Tasker, Lucille S. December 8, 1939 – November 2, 1989 (tombstone; obituary in *The Aegis* on November 8, 1989 stated Lucille C. Tasker died November 2, 1989, age 48) [Tabernacle Mount Zion U. M. Church Cemetery]

Tasker, Philip Henry "Harry" died June 28, 1957, age 89 (no tombstone; obituary in *The Democratic Ledger* on July 4, 1957 stated he was a former post office employee in Havre de Grace and died at Harford Memorial Hospital, survived by a son Merrill Tasker and a daughter Mrs. Helen Cook) [St. James United Cemetery]

Tasker, Phoeba June 1, 1919 – December 16, 1920 (no tombstone; death certificate stated Phoeba "Taska" was the daughter of William "Tasker" and Annie Pinkney, and they were all born in Harford Co.; she died in Benson and was buried at "Mountain Colored Church;" informant was her father, William "Taska," of Fallston) [Mt. Zion U. M. Church Cemetery]

Tasker, Sarah Jane November 10, 1839 – May 23, 1917 (no tombstone; death certificate stated she was the daughter of Charles and Sarah Young, all born in Calvert Co., MD; she was married, did ironing and washing work, and died in Bel Air; the informant was Andrew Whittington) [Clark's U. M. Church Cemetery]

Tasker, William H. died August 25, 1896, age 75 [St. James United Cemetery]

Tasky (Tasker?), Georgeanna July – (blank), 1854 – October 20, 1922, age 66 *(sic)* (no tombstone; death certificate stated she was the daughter of Henry Scott and Eliza Huston, all were born in Maryland; she was a cook and died a widow in Bel Air; informant was John Scott, of Bel Air) [Asbury Cemetery]

Tatum, Roger L. Jr. 1965-2018 (small metal funeral home marker) [St. James United Cemetery]

Taylor, Adela 1880-1956 (copied in 1986 and not found in 2018, but this was most probably Adeline Taylor who was the wife of Samuel Taylor, 1877-1926) [Hendon Hill Cemetery]

Taylor, Adele M. (Mrs.) died July --, 1965, no age given (no tombstone; obituary in *The Aegis* on July 29, 1965 stated she died "recently," was the widow of Osborne Moore *(sic)* and her maiden name was Brown) [Tabernacle Mount Zion U. M. Church Cemetery]

Taylor, Albert Clinton died February 7, 1989, age 72 (no tombstone; obituary in *The Aegis* on February 16, 1989 stated he was the son of Samuel Taylor and Adeline Rebecca Jackson; he served in the Army during World War II, married (wife's name was not given), resided in Bel Air, worked for the Army Chemical Center for more than 20 years and retired from *The Aegis* after 23 years; he died at the home of his daughter Barbara J. Taylor in Edgewood and was also survived by a son Robert, 8 grandchildren, 4 great-grandchildren and 1 sister) [Tabernacle Mount Zion U. M. Church Cemetery]

Taylor, Albert Clinton Jr. December 25, 1963 – September 13, 2000 (no tombstone; obituary in *The Aegis* on September 20, 2000 stated he was born in Harford Memorial Hospital in Havre de Grace, son of Shirley Johnson, of Fallston, and the late Albert C. Taylor; he lived in Edgewood and died at Fallston General Hospital; he was survived by his mother, 9 brothers, 5 sisters, 4 uncles, 7 aunts, and a host of other relatives and friends) [Clark's U. M. Church Cemetery]

Taylor, Bessie March 30, 1985 (copied in 1987, but not found in 2018) [St. James United Cemetery]

Taylor, C. W. died 1949 (on same tombstone with W. H. Taylor; not recorded in 1987 and 2002, but this could be G. W. Taylor and possibly the Georgianna W. Taylor listed in 1987) [Gravel Hill Cemetery]

Taylor, Caria Miles "CM" May 1, 1907 – January 30, 1981, Pvt., U.S. Army, World War II (tombstone; obituary in *The Aegis* on February 5, 1981 stated he was born in Elizabeth City, N. C., the son of the late Joel Taylor and Etta Dueos, and the husband of Gladys Wilson Taylor; he lived in Bel Air and died at Perry Point VA Medical Center in Perryville, survived by his wife, a daughter, 2 grandchildren, 2 great-grandchildren, 5 brothers, and 2 sisters) [Berkley Memorial Cemetery]

Taylor, Charles A. October 18, 1863 – October 8, 1919 (no tombstone; death certificate stated he was born in Pennsylvania, the married son of Charles Taylor, of Maryland, but his mother was unknown to the informant Mrs. Sarah Taylor, of Havre de Grace) [St. James United Cemetery]

Taylor, Charles Henry December 14, 1862 – February 4, 1928 (no tombstone; death certificate stated he was the son of James Taylor and Rachel Stewart, all born in Maryland; he was single, worked as a laborer and died in Havre de Grace; informant was Miss Sarah E. Taylor, of Aberdeen) [Mt. Calvary U. A. M. E. Church Cemetery]

Taylor, Christind February 26, 1915 – July 27, 1915 (no tombstone; death certificate stated she was born at Gravelly Hill, the daughter of Isaac Taylor and Stella Bond, both born in Harford Co.; informant was Charles Bond, of Havre de Grace) [Gravel Hill Cemetery]

Taylor, Clara V. November 16, 1884 – November 24, 1912 (no tombstone; death certificate stated she was the married daughter of William Chase, both born in Harford Co., but her mother was not known to informant Alfred Taylor, of near Perryman) [Union U. M. Church Cemetery]

Taylor, Coley November 9, 1908 – April 19, 1938 (no tombstone; death certificate stated he was the son of Sam Taylor and Adeline Jackson, all born in Bel Air, and he worked as a laborer near Bel Air, was single, and died at Harford Memorial Hospital in Havre de Grace) [Hendon Hill Cemetery]

Taylor, E. B. 1910-1940 [Gravel Hill Cemetery]

Taylor, Elinore Rice November 16, 1876 – December 15, 1930 (no tombstone; death certificate stated she was the married daughter of George Webster and Eliza Gibson; informant was Mrs. John Taylor, of Perryman) [Union U. M. Church Cemetery]

Taylor, Eliza died December 17, 1931, age about 99 (no tombstone; death certificate she was the daughter of Eliza Hall, father unknown, and the widow of Charles Taylor; informant was Nelson Taylor, of Havre de Grace) [St. James United Cemetery]

Taylor, Ella Scott January 12, 1889 – November 8, 1892 (inscribed "At Rest") [Asbury Cemetery]

Taylor, Elsie Jane April 15, 1915 – August 12, 1915 (no tombstone; death certificate stated she was the daughter of Albert Taylor and Florence Holland, all born in Maryland) [Union U. M. Church Cemetery]

Taylor, Ethel James February 7, 1898 – March 6, 1970 [Berkley Memorial Cemetery]

Taylor, Evelyn (copied in 1987, not listed in 2002, and not found in 2018) [Gravel Hill Cemetery]

Taylor, George A. March 12, 1890 – November 30, 1914 (no tombstone; death certificate stated he was the unmarried son of Charles Taylor and Sarah Brown, of Havre de Grace) [St. James United Cemetery]

Taylor, Georgianna W. (copied in 1987, not listed in 2002, and not found in 2018) [Gravel Hill Cemetery]

Taylor, Gladys G. December 3, 1903 – October 23, 1995 (tombstone; obituary in *The Aegis* on November 1, 1995 stated Gladys Genevieve Wilson Taylor was self-employed and owned a beauty shop at Bond and Alice Ann Streets in Bel Air; she retired in 1980s, remained at home until 1990 and entered the Bel Forest Nursing Center in Forest Hill where she died, survived by a daughter Helen J. Scott, a brother-in-law, sister-in-law, granddaughter, grandsons, great-grandson and close friend Beatrice Whittington) [Berkley Memorial Cemetery]

Taylor, Hallie Elizabeth September 22, 1930 – April 8, 1932 (no tombstone; death certificate stated she was born in Havre de Grace and was the daughter of Freddie Fields, born in Virginia, and Elizabeth Taylor, born in Bel Air; informant was Mrs. Hallie Robinson, of Bel Air) [Hendon Hill Cemetery]

Taylor, Hannah 1900-   (on same tombstone with Leroy Taylor) [Berkley Memorial Cemetery]

Taylor, Harry C. December 10, 1888 – June 13, 1924 (no tombstone; death certificate stated he was the son of William Taylor and Susan Hopkins, all born in Maryland; he was married and a laborer in Havre de Grace; informant was Adeline Brown, of Havre de Grace) [Asbury Cemetery]

Taylor, Helen J. February 8, 1909 – October 21, 1930 (no tombstone; death certificate stated she wae the unmarried daughter of Charles Taylor and Sarah? Taylor, of Havre de Grace) [St. James United Cemetery]

Taylor, Henry January 22, 1896 – February 16, 1927 (no tombstone; death certificate stated he was unmarried and died in Darlington, parents unknown to the Stone & Webster Co.) [St. James United Cemetery]

Taylor, Howard April 12, 1913 – June 12, 1913 (no tombstone; death certificate stated he was the son of William Taylor and Leano(?) Smothers, of Havre de Grace; informant was Charles Taylor, of Havre de Grace) [St. James United Cemetery]

Taylor, I. 1893-1934 [Gravel Hill Cemetery]

Taylor, Infant stillborn female on February 25, 1922? (no tombstone) [St. James United Cemetery]

Taylor, Isaac Roland Jr. September 28, 1932 – August 14, 2008 (on same tombstone with Mary Frances Taylor with a verse from Colossians 3:14 on the front and 1 Corinthians 13:4-8 on the back; and there is also a separate marker commemorating his service in Korea with the U.S. Army) [Gravel Hill Cemetery]

Taylor, J. Edward "Ned" March 4, 1838 – January 3, 1915 (no tombstone; death certificate stated he was married and he and his mother Charity Foreman were born in Harford Co., but his father was unknown to informant Margaret Taylor; an article in *The Aegis* on January 5, 1940 titled "Happenings of Twenty-Five Years Ago As Reported In The Aegis" stated Ned Taylor was the chief hostler at the Eagle Hotel in Bel Air for upwards of 60 years until it closed; death notice in *The Aegis* on January 8, 1915 also gave a glowing account of his excellent qualities) [Hendon Hill Cemetery]

Taylor, James E. January 12, 1902 – August 26, 1937 (no tombstone; death certificate stated he was the son of John Taylor and Martha Rumsey, all born in Maryland; he married Dorothy ----, worked as a laborer, lived at 225 Freedom Alley, Havre de Grace, and died in Harford Memorial Hospital; informant was Mrs. Dorothy Taylor, of Havre de Grace) [Mt. Calvary U. A. M. E. Church Cemetery]

Taylor, James Edrie, "Loving Brother" April 20, 1965 – May 3, 2001 [St. James United Cemetery]

Taylor, James W. 1923-2000 (small metal funeral home marker) [William C. Rice Memorial Cemetery, St. James U. M. Church]

Taylor, Jane or Annie Jane April 15, 1826 – October 7, 1935 (no tombstone; death certificate stated she was born in Havre de Grace and died at home at 131 Alice Ann St. in Bel Air, aged 109 years, 5 months and 22 days; she was the widow of Jasper *(sic)* Taylor, but names and birth places of her parents were not known to informant, Mrs. Adeline Taylor, who lived at the same address; obituary in *The Havre de Grace Republican* on October 12, 1935 stated "Aunt Jane" died at the County Home and "claimed to be over one hundred years of age, but her exact age cannot be determined." She was employed as a cook for the Evans family for 30 years and her husband Japhet Taylor was a Union Army veteran in the Civil War. *The Aegis* on October 11, 1935 stated, "She was said to be 109 years old." Civil War records stated Annie Taylor, widow of Japhet C. Taylor, filed for pension in 1909; her full name must have been Annie Jane Taylor and known as Jane or Annie) [Hendon Hill Cemetery]

Taylor, Japhet C. died November 25, 1908, age 70 (death certificate; no tombstone, but probably buried here beside his wife; military pension for Annie Taylor in 1909 stated she was the widow of "Japhet C. Taylor alias Jabez Taylor" who was a private in Co. A., 24th U. S. C. T.; obituary of Jane Taylor in 1935 stated she was widow of Japhet Taylor, Civil War veteran; so, Annie and Jane were the same person) [probably Hendon Hill Cemetery]

Taylor, Jarrett died March 21, 1900, age 63 (inscribed "Husband" on very top of marker and at the bottom "I have fought a good fight. I have finished my course. I have kept the faith;" obituary in *The Aegis* on March 23, 1900 stated he died at his home near High Point and he was the brother of Uncle "Ned" Taylor; a funeral notice on March 30, 1990 stated he was buried at Hendon Hill, survived by a widow, six sons and 4 daughters, and also stated "his example could be well copied by members of his race;" however, no death certificate was found for him in Harford County) [Hendon Hill Cemetery]

Taylor, Jiane 1935-1985 (copied in 1987, but not found in 2018) [St. James United Cemetery]

Taylor, John H. April 6, 1856 – March 28, 1916 (no tombstone; death certificate stated he was born in Baltimore, the son of Edward Taylor, of Baltimore, but mother's name unknown; he was a laborer at Gravelly Hill near Havre de Grace; informant was Mrs. John H. Taylor; his death notice in the *Havre de Grace Republican* on 1 Apr 1916 reported he died in City Hospital in Baltimore from injuries sustained when a large tree limb fell on him while cutting down trees; funeral services were conducted at Gravelly Hill Church) [Gravel Hill Cemetery]

Taylor, John R. January 1, 1871 – January 20, 1915 (no tombstone; death certificate stated he was the son of James E. Taylor, both born in Harford Co., but his mother's name was not known to informant Mrs. John R. Taylor, of Aberdeen; he worked as a laborer near Aberdeen) [Mt. Calvary U. A. M. E. Church Cemetery]

Taylor, Laura F. June 4, 1898 – February 27, 1911 (no tombstone; death certificate stated she was single and the daughter of Samuel Taylor and Adaline Jackson, of Bel Air, and they were all born in Harford Co., informant was Adaline Taylor, of Bel Air) [Hendon Hill Cemetery]

Taylor, Leroy (copied in 1987, not listed in 2002, and not found in 2018) [Gravel Hill Cemetery]

Taylor, Leroy 1899-1960 (on same tombstone with Hannah Taylor) [Berkley Memorial Cemetery]

Taylor, Margaret A. August 27, 1845 – April 28, 1915 (no tombstone; death certificate stated she was a widow who lived in Bel Air, her mother was Amelia Brown and they were both born in Harford Co., but her father was unknown to informant, Blanch A. Hill, of Bel Air) [Hendon Hill Cemetery]

Taylor, Margaret I., "Loving Mother" January 5, 1932 – July 20, 2001 [St. James United Cemetery]

Taylor, Martha January 12, 1886 – September 7, 1937 (no tombstone; death certificate stated she was born in Harford Co., the daughter of James Rumsey and Ellen McGaw, both born in Maryland; she married John Taylor and died at home at 225 Freedom Alley, Havre de Grace; informant was Mrs. Pearl Milburn, of Havre de Grace) [Mt. Calvary U. A. M. E. Church Cemetery]

Taylor, Mary Dean Jackson died March 2, 1973, age 49 (no tombstone; obituary in *The Aegis* stated Mrs. Mary

Dean Jackson Taylor, wife of James Taylor, 22 N. Bond St., Bel Air, was born in Bel Air, the daughter of the late Samuel Jackson and Mable Smith; she was a member of Ames M. E. Church and was survived by her husband, 7 sisters, 2 brothers, 1 uncle and 2 aunts) [Hendon Hill Cemetery]

Taylor, Mary Ellen, wife of Jarrett Taylor, died February 2, 1882 in her 70th(?) year (tombstone was broken into four pieces, partly illegible) [Hendon Hill Cemetery]

Taylor, Mary Frances January 1, 1939 – December 1, 2012 (on same tombstone with Isaac Roland Taylor; her death notice in *The Aegis* on December 5, 2012 contained her picture and stated she died at home in Havre de Grace and was buried in St. James A. M. E. Cemetery - Gravel Hill) [Gravel Hill Cemetery]

Taylor, Mary Jane March 28, 1861 – February 19, 1915 (no tombstone; death certificate stated she was a widow and the daughter of Margaret Monk, both born in Maryland, but her father was not known to informant Edith Taylor, of Perryman) [Union U. M. Church Cemetery]

Taylor, Ned – see J. Edward Taylor [Hendon Hill Cemetery]

Taylor, Paul Augustus 1929-1976, PFC, U.S. Army, Korea (obituary in *The Aegis* stated he was born July 9, 1929 in Harford Co., was an Army veteran of World War II and Korea, was employed at Kirk Army Hospital, lived in Aberdeen and died on July 15, 1976 at Johns Hopkins Hospital in Baltimore; he was survived by his wife Mary E. Taylor, his mother Mrs. Harriet Taylor, 3 sons, 1 daughter and 3 sisters) [Gravel Hill Cemetery]

Taylor, Robert September 4, 1890 – August 2, 1916 (no tombstone; death certificate stated he was the son of William Taylor and Susan Taylor, all born in Maryland; he was single and worked as a laborer at Churchville; informant was Susan Taylor, of Belcamp RFD) [Asbury Cemetery]

Taylor, Rufus L. December 4, 1923 – November 29, 2003, PFC, U.S. Army, World War II (on the same tombstone with Ruthia M. Taylor) [Berkley Memorial Cemetery]

Taylor, Russell (copied in 1987, not listed in 2002, and not found in 2018) [Gravel Hill Cemetery]

Taylor, Ruthia M., "Beloved Wife" September 20, 1928 -   (on same tombstone with Rufus L. Taylor) [Berkley Memorial Cemetery]

Taylor, Samuel July 20, 1877 – July 2, 1926 (no tombstone; death certificate stated he was married and was a waiter in Bel Air; his parents were J. Taylor and Jane Preston and they were all born in Maryland; informant was Adeline Taylor, of Bel Air) [Hendon Hill Cemetery]

Taylor, Sarah Florence September 7, 1891 – August 9, 1915 (no tombstone; death certificate stated she was the married daughter of William Holland and Harriett Stansbury, all born in Maryland) [Union U. M. Church Cemetery]

Taylor, Sarah I. White, "Mother" June 11, 1930 – August 20, 1993 [St. James United Cemetery]

Taylor, Sarah J. November 20, 1868 – May 14, 1942 (no tombstone; death certificate stated she was the daughter of Jacob H. Brown and Harriett Johnson, and widow of Charles Taylor) [St. James United Cemetery]

Taylor, Stamps (no dates when copied in 1987, but not found in 2018) [Berkley Memorial Cemetery]

Taylor, Susan died June 15, 1917, age 49 (no tombstone; death certificate stated she was born in Harford Co., the daughter of Samuel Johnson, but her mother's name was unknown to informant Lewis Taylor, of Bel Air; she was a widow and worked as a cook in Bel Air) [Asbury Cemetery]

Taylor, Tom (copied in 1987, not listed in 2002, and not found in 2018) [Gravel Hill Cemetery]

Taylor, Victoria, Mary Smothers' Son's Wife 1912-1976 [Clark's U. M. Church Cemetery]

Taylor, W. A. 1895-1944 (tombstone copyist in 1987 listed him as William A. Taylor) [Gravel Hill Cemetery]

Taylor, W. H. died 1949 (on same tombstone with C. W. Taylor; death certificate stated William Henry Taylor was born August 8, 1878 in Harford Co., the son of John Taylor and Harriett Wells; he was a farm laborer and died a widow in rural Havre de Grace; informant was Leroy Taylor) [Gravel Hill Cemetery]

Taylor, William A. – see W. A. Taylor [Gravel Hill Cemetery]

Taylor, William H. died January 12, 1927, age about 46 (no tombstone; death certificate stated he was the son of William Taylor and F. Jeannette Taylor, all born in Maryland; he was divorced, worked as a railroad porter and died in Havre de Grace; informant was Robert Garrison, of Havre de Grace) [Gravel Hill Cemetery]

Taylor, William Henry – see W. H. Taylor [Gravel Hill Cemetery]

Taylor, William Oscar April 11, 1896 – February 7, 1946 (no tombstone; death certificate stated he was born in Harford Co., son of William Henry Taylor and Georgia Warfield, both born in Maryland; he married Florence ---- (born 1894), worked for the Sun Shipyard in Chester, PA, and had been living in rural Havre de Grace for the past 7 months; informant was Mrs. Emma T. Royster, of Havre de Grace]

Taylor, William T. April 13, 1890 – April 13, 1913 (no tombstone; death certificate stated he was the son of William Taylor and Susan Hopkins, all born in Maryland; he was married, worked as a farm hand and died in Perryman; informant was John Taylor, of Aberdeen) [Asbury Cemetery]

Tazwell, Effie E., "Mother" November 7, 1895 – April 26, 1987 (inscribed "In God's Hands") [Union U. M. Church Cemetery]

Tazwell, Howard B. 1892-1978 (on same tombstone with Mary F. Tazwell and a separate marker is inscribed "Pvt., U.S. Army, World War II") [Union U. M. Church Cemetery]

Tazwell, Mary F., "His Wife" 1886-1956 (on same tombstone with Howard B. Tazwell) [Union U. M. Church Cemetery]

Teel, Florine Burch September 5, 1888 – July 28, 1924 (no tombstone; death certificate stated she was born in Maryland, the unmarried daughter of Louis Teel, born in North Carolina, and Frances Evans, born in Maryland; informant was her father; she died in "Monkton, Harford Co.") [Union U. M. Church Cemetery]

Teel, Frances Ann February 18, 1846 – April 11, 1927 (no tombstone; death certificate stated she was married and the daughter of Jesse Smith and Rebecca Evans; informant was Lewis Teel) [Union U. M. Church Cemetery]

Terrell, Ida B. 1908-1979 (on same tombstone with John M. Terrell; obituary in *The Aegis* on September 6, 1979 stated Ida Bell Terrell, wife of John Terrell, of Havre de Grace, died in Johns Hopkins Hospital on September 3, 1979, age 71; she was the daughter of James and Bertha Bishop and was survived by son James E. Watson, daughter Helen Presbury, sister Hilda Bisnop, 6 grandchildren and 6 great-grandchildren; she was very active in St. James A.M.E. Church in Havre de Grace) [St. James United Cemetery]

Terrell, Janice A. July 22, 1958 – August 7, 1958 (on same tombstone with Bertha C. Bishop when copied in 1987, but inexplicably not found in 2018) [St. James United Cemetery]

Terrell, John W. 1912-1982 (inscribed "In Loving Memory" and his obituary in *The Aegis* on September 16, 1982 stated he died in Harford Memorial Hospital, survived by a daughter Helen Presberry, a step-son James Watkins, 2 sisters, 6 grandchildren and 10 great-grandchildren; mistakenly reported as interred in Berkley Memorial Cemetery [actually on same tombstone with Ida B. Terrell in St. James United Cemetery]

Terry, Catherine C. August 23, 1924 – February 2, 1993 (buried in section 16; on the same tombstone with Vernon C. Terry inscribed "married August 24, 1946" and "In God's Care" and at the bottom of the tombstone are the names Vernon, Ronald, Stephanie, Regina, Anthony and Maria; The James Dorsey Card File, African American Obituaries, maintained at the Historical Society of Harford County, has a card with obituary and photo from *The Aegis* on February 24, 1993 stating she was a native of Aberdeen, the daughter of Lilly M. Cole and the late Robert James Cole; she was employed as a federal civil servant in Washington, D.C. and at Aberdeen Proving Ground, and also helped develop Terry's Real Estate and became the office manager; she died at Harford Memorial Hospital in Havre de Grace, survived by her mother, her husband of 46 years Vernon Carroll Terry, three daughters, three sons, two sisters, three brothers, two sons-in-law, one daughter-in-law, 8 grandchildren and a host of nieces, nephews, cousins and friends) [Mt. Calvary U. A. M. E. Church Cemetery]

Terry, Vernon C. June 21, 1923 – October 1, 1995 (on same tombstone with Catherine C. Terry) [Mt. Calvary U. A. M. E. Church Cemetery]

Thigpen, Carrie V., "Mother" 1875-1950 (tombstone inscription, but death certificate stated she was born in Perryman on October 18, 1881, married (husband not named) and died on July 10, 1950 at 841 Erie St., Havre de Grace, where she lived for 40 years; informant was Clayton Stansbury) [Union U. M. Church Cemetery]

Thomas, ---- (no tombstone, but Kurtz Funeral Home records stated George Thomas' child was buried in an "im cherry" coffin on March 13, 1880 from W. Rampley's tenant house near G. Church (Good Will Church) [West Liberty Church Cemetery]

Thomas, Albert Jr. December 28, 1956 – September --, 1976 (inscribed "We taught him how to live. He taught us how to die;" obituary in *The Aegis* stated he was the son of Albert Thomas, Sr. and Reba Edwards and was born in Baltimore and died in City Hospital on September 19, 1976; he was survived by his parents, two brothers, two sisters, his grandmother Lillian Wainwright, of Joppa, and his grandfather George Thomas, of Baltimore) [John Wesley U. M. E. Church Cemetery in Abingdon]

Thomas, Asbury 1884-1957 (copied in 1987, not found in 2018) [Mt. Calvary U. A. M. E. Church Cemetery]

Thomas, Carol A. (Rev.) 1951-2015 (small metal funeral home marker) [St. James United Cemetery]

Thomas, Charles E. February 8, 1919 – December 3, 1975, Pvt, U.S. Army, World War II [William C. Rice Memorial Cemetery, St. James U. M. Church]

Thomas, Charles H. (Son) 1900-1966 (on ame tombstone with mother Ella; obituary in *The Aegis*, February 10, 1966, stated he died January 16, 1966, age 65, at 122 Alice Ann St. in Bel Air and was the son of the late John Wesley and Ella Thomas) [Hendon Hill Cemetery]

Thomas, Charles H. Jr. September 22, 1967 – August 28, 2016 (tombstone, with photo, inscribed "This world has lost the most wonderful, loving, caring, compassionate, kindest, funniest, giving person that anyone could ever know. 'Junie' we will love you always.") [John Wesley U. M. E. Church Cemetery in Abingdon]

Thomas, Charles H. Sr. April 19, 1942 – March 11, 2016 (tombstone with photo, inscribed "Loving husband, fantastic father, dedicated teacher. Your family & friends will always miss you Forever;" obituary in *The Aegis* stated he was born in Bellevue, MD, the son of Morris Alpheus Thomas and Etta Serina White, and was the husband of 37 years to the late Marlene Bertha Hoes; he was an educator in Baltimore City for 2 years and in Harford County for 36 years; he lived in Abingdon and died at Sinai Hospital in Baltimore, survived by a son, 3 sisters, 13 nieces, 11 grand-nieces and grand-nephews) [John Wesley U. M. E. Church Cemetery in Abingdon]

Thomas, Clifton 1904-1979 (copied in 1987, but not found in 2018; obituary in *The Aegis* on June 28, 1979 stated he was born in Saluda, SC, the son of Mr. & Mrs. Luther Thomas, and married Lillian Chase who predeceased him; he retired in 1953 as a coal miner, lived at 439 Edmund St. in Aberdeen and died on June 18, 1979 at Harford Memorial Hospital in Havre de Grace; he was survived by a son, two daughters, one brother, one sister, eight grandchildren and twelve great-grandchildren) [Mt. Calvary U. A. M. E. Church Cemetery]

Thomas, Dolly B. Govans April 17, 1929 – January 14, 1993 [Chestnut Grove A. M. E. Church Cemetery, formerly LaGrange Cemetery at Rocks]

Thomas, Ella G. April 10, 1922 – August 6, 1980 (on same tombstone with Louis A. Thomas; obituary in *The Aegis* stated Ella Gibson Thomas was born in Bel Air, the daughter of John Gibson and Sarah Whittington; she married Louis A. Thomas, Sr., lived in Bel Air and died at the John L. Deaton Home in Baltimore, survived by her husband, 7 daughters, 1 son and 11 grandchildren; James Dorsey Card File, African American Obituaries, maintained at the Historical Society of Harford County, has a card with her Tittle Funeral Home card) [Clark's U. M. Church Cemetery]

Thomas, Ella Wright "Mother" 1876-1961 (on same tombstone with son Charles H.) [Hendon Hill Cemetery]

Thomas, Emma White April 14, 1904 – May 14, 1983 (no tombstone; The James Dorsey Card File, African American Obituaries, maintained at the Historical Society of Harford County, has a card with part of her obituary abstracted from an unidentified newspaper) [Clark's U. M. Church Cemetery]

Thomas, Frances E. 1884-1970 (on same tombstone with Rev. Henry Thomas inscribed "I Have Kept The Faith. 2 Tim. 4-7;" obituary of Frances Effie Thomas in *The Aegis* on October 1, 1970 stated she was the daughter of Rufus Gore and Rose Terry and the wife of Rev. Henry Thomas, of 212 N. Stokes St. in Havre de Grace; she died on September 26, 1970 at the Citizens Nursing Home and was survived by her husband, 3 sons, 3 daughters, 1 brother, 17 grandchildren and 9 great-grandchildren) [St. James United Cemetery]

Thomas, George E. 1900-1977 (on same tombstone with Maude E. Thomas; obituary in *The Aegis* stated George Edward Thomas was born in Creswell, the son of William Henry Thomas and Mary Barrett, and he married Maude Beasley; he worked as a supply clerk at Aberdeen Proving Ground and retired after 28 years service; he lived in Abingdon and died at Harford Memorial Hospital, survived by his wife, 1 son, 4 daughters, 20 grandchildren and 13 great-grandchildren) [John Wesley U. M. E. Church Cemetery in Abingdon]

Thomas, George Edward March 15, 1844 – September 27, 1923 (no tombstone; death certificate stated he was married, worked as a day laborer in farm and garden, died at Federal Hill and was buried in "Federal Hill Church Cem.;" his place of birth and his parents' names and places of death were not known to informant, his daughter, Julia J. Swann, of Jarrettsville, who also stated he was born on March 15, but she did not know the year, and he was about 79 years old) [William C. Rice Memorial Cemetery, St. James U. M. Church]

Thomas, Gladys A. March 26, 1918 – January 5, 1985 (tombstone; obituary in *The Aegis* on January 10, 1985 stated she was born in Peach Bottom Township, the daughter of the late Joseph F. and Margaret Dorsey Bay, lived at Delta RD #1, PA, died at Fallston General Hospital and was the widow of Charles E. Thomas; she was survived by 2 sons, 2 sisters, 1 brother and 7 grandchildren) [William C. Rice Memorial Cemetery, St. James U. M. Church]

Thomas, Hannah Ellen April 15, 1887 – April 14, 1912 (no tombstone; death certificate stated she was the daughter of George Hall and Mary Whims, all born in Maryland; she died at home in Aberdeen and was buried in Sydney Park Cemetery; informant was John Washington, of Aberdeen) [Union U. M. Church Cemetery]

Thomas, Henry died December 30, 1901, age 80 (no tombstone; death certificate stated he was a laborer and died a widower at Cole, leaving 2 children; his parents were unknown and his place of burial was not indicated, but probably in Old Union Chapel Cemetery at Michaelsville; possibly reinterred later in Union Chapel Cemetery near Aberdeen) [Union U. M. Church Cemetery]

Thomas, Henry (Rev.) 1883-1977 (on same tombstone with Frances E. Thomas inscribed "I Have Kept The Faith. 2 Tim. 4-7") [St. James United Cemetery]

Thomas, John V. June 18, 1923 – February 3, 1982, PFC, U.S. Army, World War II (tombstone; obituary in *The Aegis* on February 11, 1982 stated he was born in Van Bibber, the son of Maude B. Thomas and the late George E. Thomas; he married Irene Gilbert, retired as a truck driver from Edgewood Arsenal and died at Fallston General Hospital, survived by his wife and mother, a son, a daughter, a step-daughter, 3 grandchildren and 5 brothers) [Tabernacle Mount Zion U. M. Church Cemetery]

Thomas, Leslie E. December 1, 1906 – June 26, 1954 (copied in 1987, but not found in 2018) [Mt. Calvary U. A. M. E. Church Cemetery]

Thomas, Louis A. July 31, 1916 – August 9, 1988 (on same tombstone with Ella G. Thomas) [Clark's U. M. Church Cemetery]

Thomas, Margaret Ann January 1, 1871 – December 29, 1930 (no tombstone; death certificate stated she was the widowed daughter of Joshua Jones and Eliza Berry; informant was Julia Swann, of Rocks, MD]St. James United Cemetery]

Thomas, Marlene B., "Beloved Wife & Mother" November 6, 1944 – May 19, 2005 (tombstone; obituary in *The Aegis* on May 25, 2005 state she was born in Abingdon, the daughter of Charles Hoes and Hattie Lillian Lee, and married Charles H. Thomas, Sr.; she lived in Abingdon, became a teacher, an assistant principal and finally an assistant supervisor for the Harford County Board of Education; she died at the Upper Chesapeake Medical Center (in Bel Air), survived by her husband, a son, and two brothers; her husband's 2016 obituary stated her middle name was Bertha) [John Wesley U. M. E. Church Cemetery in Abingdon]

Thomas, Mary March 9, 1851 – February 9, 1915 (no tombstone; death certificate stated she was the daughter of Abraham Hill and Annie Maxfield, all born in Maryland; she was a widow, worked as a cook, died at home in Perryman and was buried in Sydney Park Cemetery; informant was Frank Hill, of Aberdeen) [Union U. M. Church Cemetery]

Thomas, Mary Viola October 11, 1909 – June 23, 1912 (no tombstone; death certificate stated she was born in Chester, PA, the daughter of Robert Thomas, born in Salem, NJ, and Gertrude Allen, born in Harford Co.; she died at home near Aberdeen and was buried in "Sidney Park Cemetery;" informant was Gertrude Thomas, of Aberdeen RFD) [Union U. M. Church Cemetery]

Thomas, Maude E. 1894-1987 (on same tombstone with George E. Thomas; obituary in *The Aegis* on August 13, 1987 stated Maude Edward Thomas was born in Abingdon, the daughter of Charles Beasley and Laura Morgan, and the widow of George Edward Thomas; she lived in Edgewood and died at Harford Memorial Hospital on August 8, 1987, survived by 4 daughters, 19 grandchildren; 37 great-children and 7 great-great-grandchildren) [John Wesley U. M. E. Church Cemetery in Abingdon]

Thomas, Norman E. July 31, 1910 – August 4, 1941 (no tombstone; Kurtz Funeral Home Record Book 1937-1944, p. 198, stated he was born in Harford Co., the son of Albert Harris, birth place not known, and Mary Thomas, born in Harford Co.; he was single, worked as a general laborer and drowned in Lake Roland at Mt. Washington in Baltimore) [William C. Rice Memorial Cemetery, St. James U. M. Church]

Thomas, Oran T. (Deacon) June 3, 1948 – November 20, 2009 (inscribed "Always In Our Hearts" with his photo) [St. James United Cemetery]

Thomas, Pearl Alston November 18, 1923 – July 3, 1995 [Berkley Memorial Cemetery]

Thomas, Rosa L. died November 29, 1984, age 77 (no tombstone ; obituary in *The Aegis* on December 6, 1984 stated she lived in Jarrettsville, was the widow of Robert Carey and died at Fallston General Hospital, survived by 2 sons, 5 grandchildren, 2 step-grandchildren and 3 great-great-grandchildren) [William C. Rice Memorial Cemetery, St. James U. M. Church]

Thomas, Rufus T. 1920-2000 (on same tombstone with Thelma S. Thomas) [St. James United Cemetery]

Thomas, Thelma S. 1920-1979 (on same tombstone with Rufus T. Thomas) [St. James United Cemetery]

Thomas, William B. February 26, 1927 – March 26, 2010 (on same tombstone with Zilpha P. Thomas) [Berkley Memorial Cemetery]

Thomas, William Henry December 25, 1861 – August 7, 1933 (no tombstone; death certificate stated he was born in Richmond, VA, but his parents' names were not known to informant Webster D. Thomas, of 1229 Madison St., Baltimore; he was a widower who lived in Bel Air) [Asbury Cemetery]

Thomas, Zilpha P. January 25, 1928 -   (on same tombstone with William B. Thomas) [Berkley Memorial Cemetery]

Thompson, Carol July 25, 1882 – February 4, 1937 (no tombstone; death certificate stated "Carol" was born in Maryland, son of George Thompson, birth place unknown, and mother's name was not known to informant, his wife, Mrs. Carrie Thompson, of Churchville; he was a laborer in Churchville for 28 years) [Asbury Cemetery]

Thompson, Carrie L. May 17, 1930 – July 8, 1930 (no tombstone; death certificate stated she was the daughter of Wesley Thompson and Louise Akins, all born in Maryland; the informant was Wesley Thompson, of Street, MD) [Clark's U. M. Church Cemetery]

Thompson, Carrie Virginia 1881 – July 3, 1978 (no tombstone; obituary in *The Aegis* on July 6, 1978 stated she was born in Churchville, daughter of George H. and Mary Elizabeth Johnson and widow of James Carroll Thompson, Sr.; she died at Deaton Chronic Care Facility in Baltimore, leaving 2 daughters, 4 grandchildren, 8 great-grandchildren, 4 great-great-grandchildren) [Asbury Cemetery]

Thompson, Edward O. January 19, 1888 – December 21, 1971 [Berkley Memorial Cemetery]

Thompson, Elizabeth A. 1908-1992 (tombstone; James Dorsey Card File, African American Obituaries, that is maintained at the Historical Society of Harford County, has a card with obituary from an unidentified newspaper on December 23, 1992 stating she was a native of Darlington, the daughter of Carroll Webster and Annie James, and the widow of Willie Thompson; she died on December 19, 1992 at Harford Memorial Hospital, survived by three sons, two sisters, 10 grandchildren, 11 great-grandchildren and a great-great-grandchild) [Berkley Memorial Cemetery]

Thompson, Esther J. June 2, 1928 – August 23, 1991 (on same tombstone with William W. Thompson and Kevin F. Thompson; James Dorsey Card File, African American Obituaries, that is maintained at the Historical

Society of Harford County, has a card with obituary from an unidentified newspaper on September 4, 1991 stating Esther Stump Thompson was the daughter of Roland and Irene Stump and worked in special services at Aberdeen Proving Ground for many years; she lived in Darlington and died at University Hospital in Baltimore, survived by her husband of 38 years William Thompson, a son, three brothers and two sisters) [Berkley Memorial Cemetery]

Thompson, Gran April 4, 1888 – September 2, 1911 (no tombstone; death certificate stated she was born at Mt. Calvary, the daughter of George H. Thompson, born in Virginia, and Mary Ringold, born in Baltimore; she was single, worked as a house maid and died at home near Aberdeen; informant was Carrie A. Williams, of Aberdeen) [Green Spring U. M. Church Cemetery]

Thompson, Hannah died March 22, 1944, age about 70 (no tombstone; death certificate stated she was the daughter of William Morgan and Amelia Miller, all born in Harford Co.; she married William H. Thompson and died a widow in rural Darlington; informant was Olevia White, of Street, MD) [Berkley Memorial Cemetery]

Thompson, Hannah September 30, 1851 – December 2, 1915 (no tombstone; death certificate misspelled her name Tompson and stated she was born in Pennsylvania, the daughter of Henry Bond and Emma Clark, both born in Harford Co.; she was a widow, did "wash & iron" work, and died in Bel Air; the informant was Emma Borze, of Bel Air) [Clark's U. M. Church Cemetery]

Thompson, James October 25, 1889 – October 22, 1937 (no tombstone; death certificate stated she was born in South Carolina, the daughter of Croesus? Thompson and Joe Ann Broeker, of South Carolina; informant was Fred Myers, of Edgewood, MD) [St. James United Cemetery]

Thompson, James C. 1905-1976, "At Rest" (tombstone; obituary in *The Aegis* on July 22, 1976 stated he was the husband of Marian B. Thompson and a life-long resident of Harford Co.; he lived at Churchville and died at Harford Memorial Hospital in Havre de Grace) [Asbury Cemetery]

Thompson, James T. August 27, 1947 – March 14, 2006 (on same tombstone with Julia G. Gray inscribed "In Loving Memory of Mother and Brother") [Asbury Cemetery]

Thompson, Joshua Michael, "Our Little Pumpkin" April 29, 2002 – October 19, 2002 (flat tombstone with small dog engraved on it) [Berkley Memorial Cemetery]

Thompson, Julia May 18, 1895 – April 18, 1915 (no tombstone; death certificate stated she was born in Harford Co., the daughter of Benjamin Winder, born in Baltimore Co., and Mary A. Wye, born in Harford Co.; she died a widow at Good Will; informant was her father, of Monkton) [West Liberty Church Cemetery]

Thompson, Kevin F. December 12, 1963 -   (on same tombstone with William W. and Esther J. Thompson) [Berkley Memorial Cemetery]

Thompson, Lottie V. December 29, 1915 – December 4, 1987 (on same tombstone with Wesley G. Thompson) [Cedars Chapel Cemetery]

Thompson, Marian B. 1913-2002 (small metal funeral home marker) [Asbury Cemetery]

Thompson, Sarah E. 1913-1984 (on same tombstone with Celia Henry inscribed "Sisters") [St. James United Cemetery]

Thompson, Wesley G. December 23, 1906 – September 4, 1986 (on same tombstone with Lottie V. Thompson) [Cedars Chapel Cemetery]

Thompson, William October 25, 1844 – July 28, 1925 (no tombstone; death certificate stated he was born in Virginia, but the names of his parents was not known to informant Mrs. Hannah Thompson, of Darlington; he married, worked as a laborer and died at home in Poole) [Berkley Memorial Cemetery]

Thompson, William W. October 19, 1928 -   (on same tombstone with Esther J. and Kevin F. Thompson) [Berkley Memorial Cemetery]

Thurston, Deyron Akhil November 7, 1999 – December 19, 2001 (inscribed "In Loving Memory" and "The Chosen One") [St. James United Cemetery]

Thurston, Toni M., wife of Myron Thurston, June 22, 1955 – January 19, 1995 (tombstone incorrect; obituary in *The Aegis* on January 22, 1997 stated Toni Marie Thurston died January 19, 1997, age 41) [Tabernacle Mount Zion U. M. Church Cemetery]

Tibbs, Dorty March 15, 1922 – March 17, 1922 (no tombstone; death certificate stated she was born in Aberdeen, the daughter of Robert Smith, born in Maryland, and Madilen Tibbs, born in Baltimore; informant was Madilen Tibbs, of Aberdeen) [Mt. Calvary U. A. M. E. Church Cemetery]

Tildon, ---- stillborn male on November 8, 1923 (no tombstone; death certificate stated he was the son of Ringgold Tildon and Anna Taylor, all born in Maryland) [Union U. M. Church Cemetery]

Tildon, Annie November 1, 1869 – November 4, 1934 (no tombstone; death certificate stated she was the wife of George Franklin Tildon and daughter of Trialess Whims and Hannah Griffin) [Union U. M. Church Cemetery]

Tildon, Benjamin W., Co. D., 39th Colored Infantry (tombstone; military records state he served in Co. F., 39th Regt. Inf., U. S. C. T., from March 28, 1864 to December 4, 1865) [Union U. M. Church Cemetery]

Tildon, Bessie Fields died March 18, 1992, age 70 (no tombstone; James Dorsey Card File, African American Obituaries, that is maintained at the Historical Society of Harford County, has a card with obituary from an unidentified newspaper on March 25, 1992 stating she was born in Cecil Co., the daughter of Thomas and Myrtle Fields; she died at home in Darlington and was survived by her husband William N. Tildon, Sr., a son, a daughter, a brother, three sisters and four grandchildren) [Berkley Memorial Cemetery]

Tildon, Cecelia January 28, 1832 – August 16, 1918 (no tombstone; death certificate stated she was the married daughter of John Dallam, both born in Harford Co., but her mother was unknown to informant Fred Tildon, of Perryman) [Union U. M. Church Cemetery]

Tildon, Charles C. October 3, 1962 – January 15, 1988, SP4, U.S. Army [Berkley Memorial Cemetery]

Tildon, Cornelius R. S. February 12, 1902 – January 14, 1916 (no tombstone; death certificate stated he was the son of John C. Tildon and Mary Brown, all born near Perryman) [Union U. M. Church Cemetery]

Tildon, Edith V. October 21, 1896 – December 25, 1915 (no tombstone; death certificate stated she was the unmarried daughter of John C. Tildon and Harriet Brown, all of Harford Co.) [Union U. M. Church Cemetery]

Tildon, Frances Pitt September 7, 1896 – October 11, 1982 [Union U. M. Church Cemetery]

Tildon, Harriet Anne died March 19, 1901, age 57 (no tombstone; death certificate stated she was the daughter of Gabriel Garrettson and Mary Dallam, and the wife of William S. Tildon; she died near Michaelsville and her place of burial was not indicated, but her husband was buried here) [Union U. M. Church Cemetery]

Tildon, Henry E. October 15, 1842 – March 10, 1901 (tombstone; death certificate stated he was a native of America and son of John Tildon and Sarah Wilmer; he married Mary Jane Ringgold, worked as a laborer and died "1841-10-15" in Perryman, leaving a wife and 5 children) [Old Union Chapel M. E. Church Cemetery]

Tildon, Jennie September 8, 1885 – May 15, 1945 (no tombstone; death certificate stated she was the daughter of Philip Stansbury and Lizzie Smith, and the widow of Robert Tildon) [Union U. M. Church Cemetery]

Tildon, John C. April 28, 1868 – April 1, 1913 (no tombstone; death certificate stated he was the married son of William S. Tildon and Harriett Dallem, all born in Harford Co.) [Union U. M. Church Cemetery]

Tildon, Lucinda S. 1924-1982 [Union U. M. Church Cemetery]

Tildon, Lulu M. March 23, 1885 – October 12, 1925 (no tombstone; death certificate stated she was the married daughter of James Stansbury and Marion Ringgold, and she died when she fell from an automobile; informant was Clara Stansbury) [Union U. M. Church Cemetery]

Tildon, Mary Elizabeth February 22, 1875 – January 17, 1947 (no tombstone; death certificate stated she was born in Baltimore, but her parents' names were not known to informant, her husband, G. Frank Tilden, Sr. (age 68), of Aberdeen; she lived on W. Bel Air Ave. Ext. in rural Aberdeen for 20 years) [Asbury Cemetery]

Tildon, Mary M. May 5, 1900 – November 8, 1945 (no tombstone; death certificate stated she was the wife of Frank Tildon, Jr. and the daughter of William B. Chase and Mary Dennison) [Union U. M. Church Cemetery]

Tildon, Morgan E. Jr. January 28, 1952 – June 30, 2007 [Berkley Memorial Cemetery]

Tildon, Robert Albert died November 16, 1967, age 20 (no tombstone; obituary in *The Aegis* on November 23, 1967 stated he was the son of Morgan E. Tildon, Sr. and Lucinda Snowden, of Box 203, Aberdeen, and was killed in an automobile accident in Prince George's County; he was born in Harford County and was a student at Bowie State Teachers College) [Mt. Calvary U. A. M. E. Church Cemetery]

Tildon, Susie G. 1919-2013 (small metal funeral home marker; funeral notice and photo in *The Aegis* on March 1, 2013 stated she died at home in Aberdeen on February 22, 2013, age 94) [Clark's U. M. Church Cemetery]

Tildon, Thomas Henry August 25, 1943 – October 16, 1991, SP4, U.S. Army, Vietnam [Berkley Memorial Cemetery]

Tildon, Walter J. 1920-1975, Pvt., U.S. Army, World War II [Union U. M. Church Cemetery]

Tildon, William N. Jr. June 30, 1940 – March 8, 1995, U.S. Army [Berkley Memorial Cemetery]

Tildon, William N. Sr. 1918-1995, U.S. Navy, World War II [Berkley Memorial Cemetery]

Tildon, William Russell died September 30, 1900, age 3½ months (no tombstone; death certificate stated he was the son of John C. Tildon and Hattie S. Brown and he died at Michaelsville; place of burial was not indicated, but probably in Old Union Chapel Cemetery at Michaelsville; possibly reinterred later in Union Chapel Cemetery near Aberdeen) [Union U. M. Church Cemetery]

Tildon, William S. August 1, 1840 – December 23, 1931 ("Well Done") [Union U. M. Church Cemetery]

Tilghman, Lavinia July 29, 1895 – November 14, 1924 (no tombstone; death certificate stated she was the widowed daughter of Sydney Butler and Elizabeth Carroll, of Havre de Grace) [St. James United Cemetery]

Tilghman, William H. died August 20, 1924, age about 62 (no tombstone; death certificate stated he was the son of William H. Tilghman, but his mother was unknown to informant Mrs. Lavinia Tighman, of Havre de Grace; also stated he was a local preacher) [St. James United Cemetery]

Timbers, David 1846-1923 (tombstone; death certificate stated he died February 18, 1923, age about 61; he was born in Virginia, but his parents were unknown to informant Ida Brown) [Union U. M. Church Cemetery]

Timbers, Olivia A. died November 9, 1914, age 67 (tombstone; death certificate stated Olivia O. Timbers was born on November 4, 1847 and was the married daughter of Prince Stansbury and Anna Ayser, all born near Perryman) [Union U. M. Church Cemetery]

Tinsley, Mack October 4, 1883 – October 29, 1953 [Clark's U. M. Church Cemetery]

Tinson, Bell G. 1861-19___ (blank death date; on same tombstone with Jacob A., Ida A. and Ethel Tinson) [Union U. M. Church Cemetery]

Tinson, Ethel 1884-1920 (on same tombstone with Jacob A., Ida A. and Bell G. Tinson) [Union U. M. Church Cemetery]

Tinson, Ida A. 1886-1919 (on same tombstone with Jacob A., Bell G. and Ethel Tinson) [Union U. M. Church Cemetery]

Tinson, Jacob A. 1860-1937 (on same tombstone with Bell G., Ida A. and Ethel Tinson)

Todd, Ida Ella Scott, "Loving Wife and Mother" June 14, 1941 – November 14, 2002 (with her photo) [St. James United Cemetery]

Tolbert, Carlton E. Sr. September 12, 1933 – June 6, 2013, U. S Army [Berkley Memorial Cemetery]

Tolbert, Ruth Marie died March 20, 1994, age 48 (no tombstone; James Dorsey Card File, African American Obituaries, that is maintained at the Historical Society of Harford County, has a card with obituary and photo from an unidentified newspaper on April 6, 1994 stated she was born in Van Bibber, the daughter of Mary R. Norton and the late James Ellis Lee, Sr.; she married Felton Tolbert in 1968, worked for 12 years as a nursing assistant at Perry Point VAMC, moved to Lafayette, LA in 1981, returned to Harford County in 1991 and retired due to disability; she died at the Bel Air Convalescent Center, survived by a daughter, 4 sisters, 3 brothers and a grandson; predeceased by a brother James Ellis Lee, Jr.) [John Wesley U. M. E. Church Cemetery in Abingdon]

Toliver, Eva 1909-1994 (on the same tombstone with George Toliver, but her year of death is not inscribed; James Dorsey Card File, African American Obituaries, that is maintained at the Historical Society of Harford County, has a card with obituary and photo from an unidentified newspaper on October 26, 1994 stating Eva Viola Stevenson Toliver was born in Edgewood, the daughter of John and Amanda Stevenson, and widow of George Toliver, Sr. who had died in 1986 after 60 years of marriage; she worked at Edgewood Arsenal for 3 years and for 15 years at the White Star Restaurant until her retirement in 1973; she was a member of Ebenezer Baptist Church for 66 years, serving as secretary and usher, and died September 27, 1994 at her daughter Idella Ridgley's home in Forest Hill, survived by 4 other daughters, a sister, 33 grandchildren and 75 great-grandchildren; she was predeceased by five daughters and three sons) [Foster's Hill Cemetery]

Toliver, George Sr. (Deacon) 1905-1986 (on same tombstone with wife Eva Toliver) [Foster's Hill Cemetery]

Toliver, Helen Irene Stevenson June 17, 1903 – January 10, 1994 [Foster's Hill Cemetery]

Toliver, Oscar 1932-1950 (tombstone; *The Aegis* on May 19, 1950 reported Oscar D. Tolliver, age 19 *(sic)*, son of George and Eva Tolliver, of Joppa, was injured on May 12, 1950 in a truck accident near Carlisle, PA when his truck went out of control while descending White Mountain and he died soon after in Carlisle Hospital; services were conducted at Mt. Zion Baptist Church and interment was at Magnolia) [Foster's Hill Cemetery]

Toney, ---- stillborn female died March 28, 1922 (no tombstone; death certificate stated she was "stillborn" on March 27, 1922 and died on March 28 *(sic)* [1922; buried on March 28, 1922, the daughter of Howard Edward Toney and Leslie Smith; all were born in Maryland and lived in Bel Air) [Hendon Hill Cemetery]

Toney, Bessie J. April 22, 1885 – August 4, 1923 (no tombstone; death certificate stated she was married and performed house duties; her parents were George Toney and George Anna White; they were all born in Maryland and lived in Bel Air; informant was George A. Toney) [Hendon Hill Cemetery]

Toney, David M. December 25, 1875 – August 9, 1921 (no tombstone; death certificate stated he was the son of Joseph Toney and Urith F. Grey, all born in Maryland; he was single and worked as a laborer in Bel Air; informant was his father Joseph Toney, of Bel Air) [Tabernacle Mount Zion U. M. Church Cemetery]

Toney, Hannah Rice died January 28, 1961, age 73 (no tombstone; obituary in *The Aegis*, February 2, 1961, stated she died at Harford Memorial Hospital, the widow of Ned Toney, of Bel Air) [Hendon Hill Cemetery]

Toney, Joseph Edward "Ned" September 17, 1874 – July 26, 1949 (no tombstone; death certificate stated he was born in Harford Co., married and died at home in Bel Air; his parents were Joseph Toney and Fannie Guy; informant was Hannah Rice Toney; obituary in *The Aegis*, July 29, 1949, stated his wife was Hannah Rice Toney, and Ned was well known for his handlebar mustache and cane and for his habit of sitting on the court house steps sunning himself.) [Hendon Hill Cemetery]

Toney, Joseph M. July 29, 1847 – November 30, 1927 (no tombstone; death certificate stated he was born in Maryland, but his parents' names and places of birth were not known to informant Edward Toney, of Bel Air; he died a widower at home in Bel Air) [Tabernacle Mount Zion U. M. Church Cemetery]

Toney, Martha Jane, "Our Dear Mother," wife of Lloyd Toney Sr., died June 27, 1909, age 56 [Tabernacle Mount Zion U. M. Church Cemetery]

Toney, Walter October 5, 1899 – April 7, 1915 (no tombstone; death certificate stated he was born in Harford Co., the son of Joseph Toney, born in Baltimore Co., and Frances Guy, born in Harford Co.; informant was his father) [Tabernacle Mount Zion U. M. Church Cemetery]

Toodle, Dorothy Virginia November 29, 1927 – February 8, 1991 [Tabernacle Mount Zion U. M. Church Cemetery]

Toodle, Felix died March 20, 1978, age 73 (no tombstone; obituary in *The Aegis* on March 23, 1978 stated he lived in Fallston and died at Fallston General Hospital; he was a retired truck driver from Baltimore and Pittsburg Freight Lines; he married, but his wife was not mentioned in obituary and he was survived by 2 sons, 4 daughters, 1 sister, 2 grandchildren and 1 great-grandchild) [Tabernacle Mount Zion U. M. Church Cemetery]

Townley, Andrew J. Sr. May 16, 1905 – September 20, 1975 [Berkley Memorial Cemetery]

Townley, Bertha P. February 29, 1936 – February 3, 2008 [Berkley Memorial Cemetery]

Townsend, Albert L. 1949-1966 [Union U. M. Church Cemetery]

Townsend, Wilfred S. 1872-1922, "Rest in Peace" (copied as "Wilfred S. Towsend" in 1987, but not found in 2018; death certificate stated "Wilfred F. Townsend" was born on November 27, 1875 in Kingston, Jamaica; his father's name unknown to informant Ella Townsend, of Churchville, his mother was ---- (blank) Reed, both born in Kingston, Jamaica; he was married and died on April 13, 1922 in Churchville) [Asbury Cemetery]

Townsley, Florence V. December 6, 1870 – October 16, 1949 (no tombstone; death certificate stated she was born in Maryland, the daughter of Benjamin Temple and Elizabeth Moore; she was a widow who lived in Kingsville, Baltimore Co., and died in Harford Memorial Hospital in Havre de Grace after a 14 day stay; information was gleaned from the hospital records) [Foster's Hill Cemetery]

Travers, Franklin Jr. 1970-2006 (small metal funeral home marker) [St. James United Cemetery]

Travers, Franklin Sr. May 13, 1949 – February 25, 2011, Veteran, U.S. Army (inscribed "The Man of God Who Loved All") [St. James United Cemetery]

Traverse, Lewis H. 1886-1965 (on same tombstone with Mary F. Traverse) [Union U. M. Church Cemetery]

Traverse, Mary F. 1895-1988 (on same tombstone with Lewis H. Traverse; an article and her photo in *Harford Historical Bulletin No. 20* in 1984 stated she was known as "Mrs. Bell") [Union U. M. Church Cemetery]

Travis, Clarence Jack died September 27, 1956, age about 40 (no tombstone; Pennington Funeral Home records stated he was found dead by the B&O Railroad tracks at Havre de Grace near Corthell Mitchell's property; a card in his pocket indicated he was a resident of Philadelphia [St. James United Cemetery]

Trusty, George Calvin 1870 – January 9, 1946 (no tombstone; death certificate stated he was born in Baltimore, but his parents were unknown to informant Sarah Trusty, of Bel Air RFD; he married Sarah ---- (age 72 when he died) and worked as a laborer in rural Bel Air where they lived for 7 years) [Clark's U. M. Church Cemetery]

Tucker, Edward A. Jr. September 6, 1940 – April 3, 1995 [Fairview A. M. E. Church Cemetery]

Tucker, Edward A. Sr. 1904-1980 [Fairview A. M. E. Church Cemetery]

Tucker, Louis H. October 3, 1953 – November 12, 1991 [Fairview A. M. E. Church Cemetery]

Tucker, Macon Sr. 1816-2013 (small metal funeral home marker) [Union U. M. Church Cemetery]

Tucker, Mary E. May 18, 1917 – October 20, 1986 [Union U. M. Church Cemetery]

Turell, Herbert died December 15, 1919, age about 22 (no tombstone; death certificate stated he was born in Virginia and died in Havre de Grace, but his parents were unknown to informant Millie Cox, of Havre de Grace) [St. James United Cemetery]

Turner, ---- (no tombstone, but Kurtz Funeral Home records stated Ely Turner's daughter was buried in a cherry coffin on January 26, 1880 from Ely's home near Denbo Shop) [West Liberty Church Cemetery]

Turner, ---- (no tombstone, but Kurtz Funeral Home records stated Ely Turner's daughter was buried in a plain cherry coffin on June 18, 1880 from Ely's home near Denbo Shop) [West Liberty Church Cemetery]

Turner, ---- (no tombstone, but Kurtz Funeral Home records stated Ely Turner's daughter was buried in a plain cherry coffin on May 16, 1880 "from Martha Amose's") [West Liberty Church Cemetery]

Turner, ---- (no tombstone, but Kurtz Funeral Home records stated Ely Turner's son was buried in a plain cherry coffin on March 8, 1881 from Ely's home near Denbo Shop) [West Liberty Church Cemetery]

Turner, ---- (no tombstone, but Kurtz Funeral Home records stated Ely Turner's wife was buried in a plain cherry coffin with flat lid and oval glass on February 6, 1881 from Ely's home near Denbo Shop) [West Liberty Church Cemetery]

Turner, ---- (no tombstone, but Kurtz Funeral Home records stated George Turner's mother was buried in a plain walnut coffin on January 25, 1882 from his house near Denbo Shops) [West Liberty Church Cemetery]

Turner, ---- (owner of a lot in section 45 some time after 1951) [Mt. Calvary U. A. M. E. Church Cemetery]

Turner, ---- premature birth on May 20, 1927 (no tombstone; death certificate stated she died in Pylesville, the daughter of Roman Turner and Grace Taylor, both born in Harford Co.; informant was her father) [Fairview A. M. E. Church Cemetery]

Turner, Abraham (no tombstone; an unidentified newspaper in the vertical files of the Historical Society of Harford County stated he was one of four Union soldiers who served in the Civil War who are buried in this cemetery; he was also one of the trustees in 1881 when the church acquired more land; military records stated Abraham Turner, private in Co. F, 39th Regt, Inf., U. S. C. T., enlisted on March 28, 1864, served under Capt. Albert F. Dodge and was reported missing in action on July 30, 1864) [Gravel Hill Cemetery]

Turner, Ali 2009-2009 (small metal funeral home marker) [St. James United Cemetery]

Turner, Alice "Sister" 1890-1964 [Gravel Hill Cemetery]

Turner, Anna Grace July 25, 1928 – November 8, 2003 (no tombstone; obituary and photo in *The Aegis* on November 19, 2003 stated she was born in Pylesville, the daughter of Roman Turner and Grace Scott; she became "Mom" and "Grandmom" to all who came to know her and she was very active in the church; she lived in Aberdeen, drove a school bus for many years and died at Harford Memorial Hospital, survived by one son, two grandsons, six great-grandchildren, an adopted daughter, two sisters-in-laws, two god-daughters, and a sister) [St. James United Cemetery]

Turner, Annie E. February 12, 1886 – October 2, 1917 (no tombstone; death certificate stated she was the daughter of William E. Presbury and Mary F. Jackson, all born in Harford Co.; she was married and died at Forest Hill; informant was her father, of Forest Hill) [Fairview A. M. E. Church Cemetery]

Turner, Annie G., "Praying Mother" July 25, 1928 – November 8, 2003 (tombstone; funeral notice in *The Aegis* on November 12, 2003 stated she was born in Pylesville, resided in Aberdeen, and died at Harford Memorial Hospital in Havre de Grace) [Fairview A. M. E. Church Cemetery]

Turner, Annie M. 1866-1964 (on same tombstone with Henry E. Turner) [Fairview A. M. E. Church Cemetery]

Turner, Barbara died October 29, 1982, age 74 (no tombstone; obituary in *The Aegis* on November 4, 1982 stated she was born in Abingdon, a daughter of Alice Waters, lived in Baltimore and died at Lutheran Hospital, survived by four sisters; her husband was not mentioned) [Community Baptist Church Cemetery]

Turner, Byron K. June 16, 1972 – August 7, 2010 (inscribed "Forever In Our Hearts" and also an image of a football with number 93 inscribed on it) [St. James United Cemetery]

Turner, Caroline May 15, 1909 – May 16, 1911 (no tombstone; death certificate stated she was born in Forest Hill, the daughter of Roman Turner, born in Churchville, and Grace Taylor, birth place not stated; she died at Hickory, informant was her father, of Forest Hill) [Fairview A. M. E. Church Cemetery]

Turner, Catherine Jane died November 24, 1914, age not known (no tombstone; death certificate stated she was born in Harford Co., but informant Charles H. Johnson, of Forest Hill, only knew her father was a Barrett, yet he somehow knew her parents were born in Maryland; she was married and died at home in Forest Hill) [Fairview A. M. E. Church Cemetery]

Turner, Charles (no dates; inscribed on the same tombstone with George L. Turner, George F. Daugherty and M. Jennie Daugherty) [Green Spring U. M. Church Cemetery]

Turner, Charles (owner of a lot in section 8 some time after 1951; no tombstone; obituary in *The Aegis* on May 12, 1988 stated Charles Franklin Turner was born in Havre de Grace, "the son of George Turner, of Abingdon, and Margaret and Ike Kenly, of Aberdeen;" he lived in Aberdeen, was a self-employed handyman and died at Harford Memorial Hospital on May 8, 1988, age 48; "In addition to his parents he is survived by Mary (Prim) Turner," two sons, two step-daughters, five grandchildren, and one brother George Turner) [Mt. Calvary U. A. M. E. Church Cemetery]

Turner, Clara 1863-1940 (on same tombstone with Samuel Turner; death notice in the *Havre de Grace*

Republican on August 10, 1940 stated Mrs. Clara A. Turner, age 77, died August 6, 1940 at her home at Gravelly Hill near Havre de Grace, with services and burial at the nearby "Gravelly Hill Church"; death certificate stated Clara Augustus Turner, born November 28, 1862 *(sic)* in Harford Co., the daughter of Charles Lee and Sarah Bower, was born in Maryland, married Samuel Turner, and died August 6, 1940 at home in rural Havre de Grace; informant was Mrs. Edith Dorsey, of 220 Edward St., Chester, PA) [Gravel Hill Cemetery]

Turner, Clara 1879-1952 (on same tombstone with Henry Turner) [Mt. Zion U. M. Church Cemetery]

Turner, David August 22, 1841 – September 18, 1922 (no tombstone; death certificate stated he was born in Maryland, but his parents and the places of their birth were not known to informant Edith Cromwell, of 752 S. Stricker Street (Baltimore); he was married, not employed and died near Upper Cross Roads) [West Liberty Church Cemetery]

Turner, David Benjamin September 5, 1886 – October 31, 1916 (no tombstone; death certificate stated he was the son of David Turner and Amanda Cromwell, all born in Harford Co.; he was single, worked as a laborer and died at Upper Cross Roads; informant was his father, of Fallston) [West Liberty Church Cemetery]

Turner, Doris June 17, 1930 – February 12, 2013 (inscribed "He only takes the best;" obituary and photo in *The Aegis* on February 15, 2013 stated she was born in Baltimore, the daughter of the late Mildred Gibson, and married Roman S. Turner II; she lived in York, PA and died at Manor Care-York North, survived by two daughters, four sons, a brother, "a host of grandchildren, great-grandchildren, nieces and nephews;" she was preceded in death by a daughter and two sons) [Clark's U. M. Church Cemetery]

Turner, Edith D., wife of Harry S. Turner, 1892-1951 (tombstone; death certificate stated Edith Roberta Turner was born in Harford Co. on March 28, 1892, the daughter of George Daugherty and Janet Lee, was married and died on March 21, 1951 at home in rural Havre de Grace where she had lived all her life; informant was Mrs. Harry S. Turner; obituary in *The Democratic Ledger* on March 23, 1951 stated "Mrs. Edith Roberta Turner, 58, colored, wife of Harry Turner of Gravel Hill, died at her home about 1:30 p.m. Wednesday afternoon, just prior to the services of her brother-in-law W. Raymond Turner, which were conducted in the Gravel Hill church; she was the daughter of George and Jennie Daugherty, of Havre de Grace, and besides her husband and parents leaves one son.") [Green Spring U. M. Church Cemetery]

Turner, Edith V. 1904-1985 (on the same tombstone with Henry A. Turner; obituary in *The Democratic Record* on November 27, 1985 stated Edith Violetta Turner was born in Magnolia, the daughter of John Demby and Jessie Peters, and was the widow of Henry Turner; she lived in Joppa, died at Fallston General Hospital on November 17, 1984 and was survived by 3 sons, 3 daughters, 31 grandchildren, 42 great-grandchildren, 2 great-great-grandchildren) [Foster's Hill Cemetery]

Turner, Edward August 3, 1878 – January 10, 1937 (no tombstone; death certificate stated he was born in Lancaster Co., VA, the son of Frederick Turner and Sallie Artrall, both born in Virginia; he married Sarah E. ----, worked as a day laborer, and died at Big Woods near Bel Air; informant was Mrs. Sarah E. Turner, of Bel Air RFD #1) [Clark's U. M. Church Cemetery]

Turner, Edward died October 22, 1940, age 51 (no tombstone; death certificate stated he was born in Havre de Grave, the son of Henry Turner and Elizabeth Brown, both born in Harford Co.; he married Helen ----, worked as a laborer and lived at 829 Erie St. in Havre de Grace; while at work he fell off the roof of a building and died at Harford Memorial Hospital) [Mt. Calvary U. A. M. E. Church Cemetery]

Turner, Elinor September 14, 1861 – March 20, 1926 (no tombstone; death certificate stated she was the daughter of Eli Turner and Annie Rigsby, all born in Maryland; she was a widow and worked as a cook in Havre de Grace; informant was Roman Turner, of Pylesville) [Asbury Cemetery]

Turner, Emma J. September 2, 1890 – November 8, 1913 (no tombstone; death certificate stated she was the daughter of Emanuel Turner and Elizabeth Banks, and they all were born in Harford Co.; she was single and did housework and died in Havre de Grace; informant was George Banks, of Aberdeen) [Mt. Calvary U. A. M. E. Church Cemetery]

Turner, Eurika E. "Loving Mother" May 19, 1969 – June 5, 1990 [William C. Rice Memorial Cemetery, St. James U. M. Church]

Turner, Florence M. January 1, 1873 – April 12, 1912 (no tombstone; death certificate stated she was single, a servant in Bel Air, and the daughter of William Johnson and Katherine A. Johnson, of Bel Air; they were all born in Harford Co.; informant was Irene Turner) [Hendon Hill Cemetery]

Turner, Florence Taylor "Sister" 1894-1961 (on same tombstone with brother W. Raymond Turner) [Gravel Hill Cemetery]

Turner, George Sr. died August 1, 1992, age 58 (no tombstone; obituary in *The Aegis* on August 12, 1992 stated he was a native of Havre de Grace, the son of George W. Turner and Margaret Kenly; he initially worked for Whiting and Turner Construction Co. in 1965 and became a truck driver for Bata Shoe in 1968; for many years he was a member of the Bandeleros Motorcycle Club; he died in Havre de Grace and was survived by his parents, a son, three daughters, three step-children, step-father Isaiah Kenly, and ten grandchildren) [St. James United Cemetery]

Turner, George L. (no dates inscribed on the same tombstone with Charles Turner, George F. Daugherty and M. Jennie Daugherty; obituary in *The Aegis* in 1991 stated George Lee Turner, 22, of RFD 1, Box 300, Gravel Hill Road, Havre de Grace, died March 10, 1991 at Harford Memorial Hospital; no family information was given; he was a driver for Turf Cab Co.) [Green Spring U. M. Church Cemetery]

Turner, George Lee Jr. stillborn on February 25, 1939 (no tombstone; death certificate stated he was the son of George Lee Turner and Marie Presbury, all born in Harford Co., and lived at Havre de Grace RFD; informant was Mr. Jarry Presbury, of Havre de Grace) [Gravel Hill Cemetery]

Turner, Georgianna V. May 18, 1892 – November 8, 1988 (tombstone; obituary in *The Aegis* on November 17, 1988 stated Georgianna Virginia Turner was the daughter of Emanuel Turner and Mary Banks; in 1929 she accepted employment in the family of then Governor of New York Franklin Delano Roosevelt in Hyde Park and Campobello; she continued in his employ throughout his four terms as president, remaining in service to Eleanor Roosevelt until the first lady's death; during World War II she joined the Red Cross and was given leave from the Roosevelts to train as a professional nurse; after training she was employed as a registered nurse in Brooklyn, NY, where she remained until her health caused her to retire in 1958; she lived in Aberdeen and died at Harford Memorial Hospital in Havre de Grace; she never married and was survived by three nieces, 31 grandnieces and nephews, 44 great-grand-nieces and nephews, 21 great-great-grandnieces and nephews, and one great-great-great-grandniece and nephew) [Mt. Calvary U. A. M. E. Church Cemetery]

Turner, Grace Virginia February 12, 1887 – November 2, 1928 (no tombstone; death certificate stated she was the daughter of Edward Taylor and Margarett Scott, all born in Maryland; she was married and died near Pylesville; informant was Roman or Rodman Turner, of Pylesville; James Dorsey Card File, African American Obituaries, maintained at the Historical Society of Harford County, has a card with obituary abstraction from the *Bel Air Times* on November 11, 1928 stating Grace Turner was employed on the Todd Dairy Farm in Pylesville and was survived by a husband and six children) [Fairview A. M. E. Church Cemetery]

Turner, Harriett died March 15, 1936, age about 75 (no tombstone; death certificate stated she was the daughter of Eli Turner and Harriett Norris, all born in Harford Co.; she was single, lived near Pleasantville, died in the County Alms House in Bel Air and was buried in Fairview Cemetery; informant was Annie Turner, of Forest Hill) [Fairview A. M. E. Church Cemetery]

Turner, Harry Durbin April 10, 1911 – September 24, 1944 (no tombstone; death certificate stated he was the unmarried son of Henry Turner, born in Stewardville, MD, and Helen Durbin, born in Havre de Grace; informant was Mrs. Mary Christy, of Havre de Grace) [St. James United Cemetery]

Turner, Harry V. May 2, 1910 – December 18, 1975 (on same tombstone with Rose L. Turner) [Gravel Hill Cemetery]

Turner, Harvey E. June 16, 1923 – December 18, 1992 (tombstone; obituary in *The Aegis* on December 23, 1992 stated Harvey Edward Turner was born in Abingdon, son of Henry Albert Turner and Clara Mae Broadway, and retired from Fallston Utilities after 10 years of service; he married (wife was not named), lived in Abingdon, and died at Fallston General Hospital, survived by 2 sons, 3 daughters, 1 brother, 9 grandchildren, and 2 great-grandsons) [John Wesley U. M. E. Church Cemetery in Abingdon]

Turner, Hattie December 12, 1887 – March 23, 1949 (no tombstone; death certificate stated she was born in Maryland, the daughter of John Peevey and Rachel McCormick; she was married, lived at 721 Freedom Street in Havre de Grace, and died at Harford Memorial Hospital; informant was Raymond Turner) [Asbury Cemetery]

Turner, Hazel Marie died March 23, 1984, age 47 (no tombstone; obituary in *The Aegis* stated she was born in Baltimore, the daughter of Laura Alice Peaker Cooper, of Abingdon, and Harold Norton, of Baltimore; formerly of Abingdon, she was a postal clerk for 13 years in Chicago, where she died at Chicago Osteopathic Hospital, survived by her parents and a sister) [John Wesley U. M. E. Church Cemetery in Abingdon]

Turner, Helen J. March 17, 1892 – April 10, 1940 (no tombstone; death certificate stated she was the daughter of Thomas Durbin and Rebecca French, and the wife of William H. Turner) [St. James United Cemetery]

Turner, Henry 1869-1926 (on same tombstone with Clara Turner; death certificate stated he was born on October 31, 1869 in Maryland, died on December 26, 1926 at Van Bibber and he was married; informant was Clara Turner, of Edgewood, who did not know Henry's parents) [Mt. Zion U. M. Church Cemetery]

Turner, Henry died January 23, 1941, age about 60 (no tombstone; death certificate stated he was a barber in Havre de Grace and died a widower, his wife was Helen ---- (Durbin); informant was Harry Turner, of Havre de Grace) [St. James United Cemetery]

Turner, Henry A. 1900-1964 (on same tombstone with Edith V. Turner) [Foster's Hill Cemetery]

Turner, Henry Albert died January 15, 19--, age 55 (no tombstone; James Dorsey Card File, African American Obituaries, that is maintained at the Historical Society of Harford County, has a card with obituary from an unidentified newspaper stating he was a native of Edgewood, the son of the late Mabel Waters and James Turner, Jr.; he served in the Army from 1955 to 1958 and later worked in construction; he was survived by three daughters, a son, a sister, 2 brothers, a half-brother, a half-sister, 2 grandchildren, and friend Mary Ellen Goodwin) [John Wesley U. M. E. Church Cemetery in Abingdon]

Turner, Henry Albert July 28, 1922 – August 31, 1922 (no tombstone; death certificate stated he was the son of Henry A. Turner and Edith Peters, and all were born in Maryland and lived in Magnolia; informant was Henry Turner, of Magnolia) [Foster's Hill Cemetery]

Turner, Henry E. 1866-1923 (on same tombstone with Annie M. Turner; death certificate stated Henry Eli Turner was the son of Eli Turner and Harriet Norris, all born in Maryland; he was born on April 12, 1866, married Annie ----, worked as a farmer and died on July 17, 1923 at his home near Jarrettsville; informant was his wife Annie Turner, of Forest Hill RFD) [Fairview A. M. E. Church Cemetery]

Turner, Hortense Elizabeth March 24, 1915 – July 19, 1915 (no tombstone; death certificate stated she was born and died at Chrome Hill, the daughter of Jennett E. Turner, born in Harford Co., but the name of her father was not known to informant George W. Turner, of Sharon) [Fairview A. M. E. Church Cemetery]

Turner, Infant (male) born and died on August 30, 1916 (no tombstone; death certificate stated he was the son of Henry Turner and Helen Durbin, of Havre de Grace) [St. James United Cemetery]

Turner, James H. January 13, 1920 – October 14, 1978 (tombstone; obituary in *The Aegis* on October 19, 1978 stated James Howard Turner, Sr. was a lifelong resident of Abingdon, son of the late Henry Turner and Clara Demby; he worked many years for McGrady Construction Co. in Aberdeen and was married (wife not named)' he was hit by a truck on Route 40 near Spesutia Road and died at Harford Memorial Hospital, survived by 3 sons, 1 daughter, 2 brothers, 2 sisters, 18 grandchildren, and 1 great-grandchild) [John Wesley U. M. E. Church Cemetery in Abingdon]

Turner, James Lewis died on October 26, 1992, age 57 (no tombstone; obituary in *The Aegis* on November 1, 1992 stated he lived in Joppa, was a custodian for Harford County Public Schools and drove buses for the Day Company; he died at Harford Memorial Hospital, survived by his wife of 31 years Johnann Z. Gilbert, 3 sons, 1 granddaughter, 2 brothers, and 3 sisters) [John Wesley U. M. E. Church Cemetery in Abingdon]

Turner, James Russell February 2, 1923 – February 18, 1937 (no tombstone; death certificate stated he was the son of Alberta (Elberta?) Lewis, both born in Harford Co., but his father's name was unknown to the informant, Mrs. Sarah Turner, of Bel Air; he lived and died at Kalmia, Bel Air RFD #1, probably the result of a sledding accident, according to Dr. W. Hudson) [Clark's U. M. Church Cemetery]

Turner, John R. February 8, 1913 – January 6, 1924 (no tombstone; death certificate stated he was the son of Henry Turner and Clara Broadway, all born in Maryland and lived in Havre de Grace; he was killed by a falling tree limb and died in the hospital; he was buried in "Abingdon Cemetery;" informant was H. K. McComas, Undertaker, in Abingdon) [John Wesley U. M. E. Church Cemetery in Abingdon]

Turner, Lawrence L. died December 5, 1998, age 67 (no tombstone; obituary in *The Aegis* on December 8, 1988 stated he was born in Rocks, the son of Rodman Turner and Grace Scott, and was the husband of Leona V. Turner; he was employed at the John Archer School for 14 years and retired in 1986; he was a bass singer for the Bethlehem Travelers for the past 33 years and lived in Forest Hill, he died at Fallston General Hospital and was survived by his wife, two sons, two granddaughters, one brother and one sister) [Fairview A. M. E. Church Cemetery]

Turner, Leona V. 1924-2018 (small metal funeral home marker; her funeral notice and photo in *The Aegis* stated she lived in Street and died on July 2, 2018, age 94, "surrounded by her family") [Fairview A. M. E. Church Cemetery]

Turner, Leroy Alexander died February 10, 1975, age 72 (no tombstone; obituary in *The Aegis* stated he was the son of the late Phillip Turner and Virginia Barrett, and he retired from Edgewood Arsenal; he died at home on Shucks Road near Bel Air, survived by a niece and nephew) [Asbury Cemetery]

Turner, Mamie A., "His Wife" 1890-1956 (on same tombstone with William W. Turner) [Clark's U. M. Church Cemetery]

Turner, Martha died September 4, 1939, age about 84 (no tombstone; death certificate stated she was the daughter of Betsy Chancy and both were born at the Big Woods (between Bel Air and Schucks Corner) in Harford Co.; the name of her father was not known to informant Blanche Brown, of Bel Air; Martha married Phillip Turner and died a widow near Wheel) [Asbury Cemetery]

Turner, Martha (Mrs.) died May 20, 1915, age 72 (no tombstone; death certificate stated she was born in Texas, MD, the daughter of Peter Whittington and Susan Frye, birth places unknown; she was a widow and died in Bel Air; informant was Hattie Jeffris) [Tabernacle Mount Zion U. M. Church Cemetery]

Turner, Mary E. September 21, 1936 – March 27, 1991 (buried in section 31; on same tombstone with Sarah A. Stewart; obituary in *The Aegis* on April 3, 1991 stated Mary Elizabeth Turner was the daughter of the late Frank Stewart and Sarah Anderson, and she was formerly married; a native of Forest Hill, she lived in Aberdeen and was a dietician aide at Perry Point VAMC; she died at Harford Memorial Hospital in Havre de Grace, survived by 3 sons, 4 daughters, a brother, 2 sisters, 11 grandchildren, and 3 great-grandchildren) [Mt. Calvary U. A. M. E. Church Cemetery]

Turner, Mattie V. February 7, 1899 – February 24, 1995 [Fairview A. M. E. Church Cemetery]

Turner, Melvin B. 1910-2014 (small metal funeral home marker; funeral notice and photo in *The Aegis* stated Melvin Benson Turner died at his home in Bel Air on May 31, 2014, age 103) [Berkley Memorial Cemetery]

Turner, Minnie Presberry died 1921 (on same tombstone with William Lee Turner and Zay Wesley Turner) [Gravel Hill Cemetery]

Turner, Nettie J. 1896-1985 (copied in 1987, not listed in 2002, and not found in 2018) [Gravel Hill Cemetery]

Turner, Norman February 2, 1903 – November 2, 1962, Maryland, Pvt., Co. D, 743 Military Police Bn., World War II [Gravel Hill Cemetery]

Turner, Olivia M. 1915-2009 (small metal funeral home marker; notice and photo in *The Aegis* on August 22, 2009 stated she lived in Bel Air and died at Forest Hill Rehabilitation; *www.delmarvaobits.com.archives* reported Olivia Molly Turner was born on January 14, 1915, the daughter of David and Molly Haines, and she was married to Melvin Turner for 78 years; she was employed as a domestic worker most of her life and retired at age 80; she died on August 22, 2009, age 94, and was survived by her husband, one sister, 2 sons, 5 grandchildren, "great-grandchildren and great-great children *(sic)* too numerous to mention and a host of nieces, nephews, cousins and friends;" she was preceded in death by her parents, 16 brothers and sisters, and 2 grandchildren) [Berkley Memorial Cemetery]

Turner, Phillip March – (unknown), 1847 – December 6, 1928 (no tombstone; death certificate stated he was the son of Eli Turner and Annie Rigby, all born in Maryland; he was married and worked as a laborer in Bel Air; informant was Roman Turner, of Pylesville) [Asbury Cemetery]

Turner, Phillip A. May 3, 1871 – January 12, 1934 (no tombstone; death certificate stated he was born in Harford Co., the son of Mary Turner, but his father's name was not known to informant Mrs. Laura V. Turner, of Aberdeen; worked as a day laborer and died in Harford Memorial Hospital) [Asbury Cemetery]

Turner, R. J. (no dates and inscribed Co. F., 4th Regt, U. S. C. T.) [Green Spring U. M. Church Cemetery]

Turner, Raymond Austin died April 18, 1988, age 86 (no tombstone; obituary in *The Aegis* on April 21, 1988 stated he was he was a farmer in Joppa who died at Harford Memorial Hospital in Havre de Grace, survived by his wife Ruth (Hall) Turner, one daughter Mary E. Robinson, of Joppa, two grandsons, three great-grandchildren, and a sister Viola Turner, of New York) [Fairview A. M. E. Church Cemetery]

Turner, Raymond Wedley November 27, 1918 – March 18, 1919 (no tombstone; death certificate stated he was the son of Romulus Turner and Grace Taylor, all born in Maryland; he died at home in Forest Hill; informant was his father) [Fairview A. M. E. Church Cemetery]

Turner, Roman S. December 24, 1915 – January 31, 2002 (no tombstone; obituary and photo in *The Aegis* on February 6, 2002 stated he was born in Jarrettsville, the son of Roman Stanley Turner and Grace Scott and the husband of the ate Doris Hall Turner; they were married 53 years on April 19, 2001; he lived in York, PA, retired from Flinchbaugh Products in Red Lion, PA, and died at York Hospital, survived by his wife, three daughters, six sons, 9 grandchildren, 5 great-grandchildren, and a sister Anna Grace Turner, of Aberdeen) [Fairview A. M. E. Church Cemetery]

Turner, Roman S. II December 24, 1915 – January 31, 2002 (inscribed "Do Not Stand At My Grave And Cry") [Fairview A. M. E. Church Cemetery]

Turner, Rose L. March 9, 1915 -   (on same tombstone with Harry V. Turner) [Gravel Hill Cemetery]

Turner, Samuel 1860-1906 (on same tombstone with Clara Turner; death certificate stated he was born in Harford Co. and died on September 26, 1906, age 54 years and 5 months, at his home at Stewartsville; he worked as a laborer and his wife was Clara ---- (blank); his parents' names and their places of birth were not known to informant, his son, Harry Turner) [Gravel Hill Cemetery]

Turner, Samuel died October 22, 1917, age about 85 (no tombstone; death certificate stated he was born in Maryland, but the names of his parents and places of birth were not known to informant was William Dallam, of Belcamp RFD) [Asbury Cemetery]

Turner, W. Raymond, "Brother" 1884-1951 (on the same tombstone with his sister Florence Taylor Turner and his name is mistakenly inscribed W. Waymond Turner; obituary in *The Democratic Ledger* on March 23, 1951 stated William Raymond Turner, a trucker and helper for the Havre de Grace Distributing Company, died at Mt. Sinai Hospital in Philadelphia and had been lived with a sister Mrs. Edith Dorsey in Chester; he was a native of Gravel Hill, the son of Samuel Turner and Clara Lee; he was survived by another sister Bessie Scott of Havre de Grace) [Gravel Hill Cemetery]

Turner, Wanda J. died October 10, 1988, age 27 (no tombstone; obituary in *The Aegis* on October 28, 1988 stated she was the daughter of Ethel Mae Lee, of Edgewood, and Charles Edward Turner, of Hagerstown; she lived in Havre de Grace, was employed by the *Afro Newspaper* for several years and also worked ay Hazelton Systems, Inc; she died at Johns Hopkins Hospital and was survived by her parents, a son Brandon Turner, 2 brothers and 2 sisters) [Foster's Hill Cemetery]

Turner, William B. May 6, 1867 – September 23, 1921 (tombstone; death certificate stated he was the son of Robert J. Turner and Theodosia Washington, all born in Maryland; he was married and worked as a farmer near Level; informant was Mrs. W. B. Turner, of Level) [Green Spring U. M. Church Cemetery]

Turner, William H. - see Henry Turner and Helen J. Turner [St. James United Cemetery]

Turner, William Lee died 1939 (on same tombstone with Minnie P. Turner and William Lee Turner) [Gravel Hill Cemetery]

Turner, William W. 1888-1976 (on same tombstone with Mamie A. Turner; obituary in *The Aegis* on April 8, 1976 stated William Wesley Turner was born on February 2, 1888 in Thomas Run and later moved to Bel Air and lived in the Old Toll Gate House at the intersection of Old Toll Gate Road and Highway One (Baltimore Pike); he worked many years for the Board of Education, did janitorial work for the Town of Bel Air, and was a member of Ames Church for 50 years; his wife Mammie Turner predeceased him and he died at Fallston General Hospital on April 1, 1976, survived by 3 nephews and one niece) [Clark's U. M. Church Cemetery]

Turner, Zay Wesley 1879-1931 (on same tombstone with Minnie P. Turner and William Lee Turner) [Gravel Hill Cemetery]

Tyler, ---- stillborn female on June 20, 1932, an 8 month premature birth (no tombstone; death certificate stated she died at Kalmia, the daughter of Benjamin Tyler, born in South Carolina, and Dora Presberry, born in Maryland; informant was Edward Presberry) [Clark's U. M. Church Cemetery]

Tyler, ---- stillborn infant on March 22, 1929, sex unknown (no tombstone; death certificate stated the infant died in Bel Air and the parents were Ben Tyler, birth place not stated, and Dora Presberry, born in Harford Co.; informant was Edward Presberry, of Bel Air RFD) [Clark's U. M. Church Cemetery]

Tyler, Anna died January 1, 1889, age 64 (toppled tombstone; J. C. Taylor Marble Co. records stated "Ann M. Tyler's (col) tomb(stone) was put up Oct 21st 1889 Lagrange near Rocks") [Chestnut Grove A. M. E. Church Cemetery, formerly LaGrange Cemetery at Rocks]

Tyler, Benjamin Franklin November 7, 1892 – November 23, 1949 (no tombstone; death certificate stated he was married and a farmer in rural Forest Hill, but his parents and their places of birth were not known to the informant Dora P. Tyler) [Clark's U. M. Church Cemetery]

Tyler, Herbert H. Jr. June 23, 1924 – October 20, 2010, U.S. Army, World War II [Clark's U. M. Church Cemetery]

Unknown, ---- "At Rest" (stone marker, but no names or dates) [Mt. Zion U. M. Church Cemetery]

Unknown, ---- (baby-sized grave, copied in 1987, but not found in 2018) [Mt. Zion U. M. Church Cemetery]

Unknown, ---- (name illegible) died 18 Nov 1894, age 74 (date inscribed on top of tombstone) [Tabernacle Mount Zion U. M. Church Cemetery]

Unknown, ---- (illegible) T. C. B. inscribed on top of tombstone [Tabernacle Mount Zion U. M. Church Cemetery]

Unknown, ---- (small white cross near woods and an old metal funeral home marker with letters and numbers missing from it and scattered on ground: S C C E U T E 1 9 9 4 0 .) [Tabernacle Mount Zion U. M. Church Cemetery]

Unknown, ----. adult male died about June 5, 1918 "by drownding *(sic)* while bathing;" he was a laborer in Edgewood, but Howard K. McComas, Abingdon Undertaker, did not know his name or where he was born or the names of his parents and where they were born) [John Wesley U. M. E. Church Cemetery in Abingdon]

Unknown, ----, Agnes died January 1, 1880, age --- and 6 days (illegible when copied in 2000, but not found in 2018) [West Liberty Church Cemetery]

Unknown, ----, Aura L. (copied in 1987, but not found in 2018) [Berkley Memorial Cemetery]

Unknown,----, died August 6, 1890 (broken tombstone copied in 1986, but was not found in 2018; since the church cemetery was not established until 1893 the year 1890 appears to be in error) [Chestnut Grove A. M. E. Church Cemetery, formerly LaGrange Cemetery at Rocks]

Unknown, ----, died 1991 (small metal funeral home marker with name and birth year missing) [Clark's U. M. Church Cemetery]

Unknown, ----, died 1994 (small metal funeral home marker with name and birth year missing [Clark's U. M.

Church Cemetery]

Unknown, ----, Edward (copied in 1987, but not found in 2018) [John Wesley U. M. E. Church Cemetery in Abingdon]

Unknown, ----, Elizabeth, wife of ----, died November 1866, age 53 (copied in 1987, but not found in 2018) [Asbury Cemetery]

Unknown, ----, female baby found in a field in Aberdeen on October 1, 1945 (no tombstone; death certificate stated she was badly decomposed, possibly a new born infant) [Union U. M. Church Cemetery]

Unknown, ----, Gertie (copied in 1987, but not found in 2018) [St. James United Cemetery]

Unknown, ----, Harriet died 1889 (tombstone flat in ground, illegible when copied in 2000, but not found in 2018) [West Liberty Church Cemetery]

Unknown, ----, Harriet January 26, 1863 – February 1, 1881, wife of Ely ---- (broken tombstone copied in 2000; part of it found in 2018 was illegible) [West Liberty Church Cemetery]

Unknown, ----, Herbert, 1913-   (an old metal funeral home marker with most of the information missing from it) [Tabernacle Mount Zion U. M. Church Cemetery]

Unknown, ----, Jimmy(?) 1986 (age 79?) (handwritten on flat cement slab, very difficult to read) [Gravel Hill Cemetery]

Unknown, ----, Laura 1870-1933 (no last name on tombstone) [St. James United Cemetery]

Unknown, ----, Luranna (tombstone badly weathered laying flat on ground) [Clark's U. M. Church Cemetery]

Unknown, ----, Mahala (Aunt) died 1905, age about 100 years [Berkley Memorial Cemetery]

Unknown, ---- (no tombstone; death certificate stated a male was found east of Aberdeen on C. W. Baker's Plum Point Farm on the Chesapeake Bay on July 15, 1916; supposed to have drowned; his age and family were unknown and he was buried in "Sidney Park Cemetery" [Union U. M. Church Cemetery]

Unknown, ---- (death certificate stated a male was accidentally killed by Pennsylvania Railroad train near Aberdeen on January 24, 1931' no further information [Union U. M. Church Cemetery]

Unknown, ---- (deeath certificate stated a man was found dead with a fractured skull and left leg on the side of the State Road in Poole on March 28, 1925, age unknown but about age 35 [Berkley Memorial Cemetery]

Unknown, ----, died December 22, 1917 (death certificate stated he was among the workmen employed on the proving grounds who were killed when struck by a train at the Magnolia Station of the Philadelphia, Wilmington & Baltimore Railroad; *The Aegis*, December 28, 1917, stated the unidentified body was turned over to undertaker Walter H. Archer, at Benson, on December 24, 1917, after a coroner's inquest had been conducted, and was buried "in Tabernacle colored cemetery" on the 26th) [Tabernacle Mount Zion U. M. Church Cemetery]

Unknown, ----, Mary E. (?) (tombstone very badly weathered) [Clark's U. M. Church Cemetery]

Unknown, ----, Maya, daughter of Thomas and Rhonda, 1996 (no last name on tombstone) [Union U. M. Church Cemetery]

Unknown,-----, name missing and only numbers remaining were ---8 – 1983 (small metal funeral home marker) [Mt. Zion U. M. Church Cemetery]

Unknown, ----, Nick (copied in 1987, but not found in 2018) [St. James United Cemetery]

Unknown, ----, No Marker - Flower Only *(sic)* (noted twice in 1987, but only one was found in 2018 near the road and about four feet west of and behind the tombstone of William Joseph Dorsey) [Cedars Chapel Cemetery]

Unknown, ----, no names on four cement blocks and no names on two stones [Berkley Memorial Cemetery]

Unknown, ----, old colored woman (at Wilna) said to be 110 years old was buried at the colored church on the Mountain (*The Aegis*, May 11, 1894) [Mt. Zion U. M. Church Cemetery]

Unknown, ----, Rachel E. (copied in 1987, but not found in 2018) [Berkley Memorial Cemetery]

Unknown, ----, Samuel J. 1872-1943 (no last name on tombstone) [St. James United Cemetery]

Unknown, ----, two small wooden crosses with no names inscribed [Community Baptist Church Cemetery]

Unknown, ---- V ---- 1940-   (small metal funeral home marker with some letters missing) [Community Baptist Church Cemetery]

Unknown, ----, W. Phillip (copied in 1987, but not found in 2018) [St. James United Cemetery]

Unknown, A. E. P. (old stone foot marker copied in 1986, but not found in 2018) [Hendon Hill Cemetery]

Unknown, A. M. W. footstone [Old Union Chapel M. E. Church Cemetery]

Unknown, C W. (footstone) [Mt. Zion U. M. Church Cemetery]

Unknown, C-----, Gertrude? (flat stone, badly weathered) [St. James United Cemetery]

Unknown, C. S. (broken stone copied in 1987, but not found in 2018) [Mt. Zion U. M. Church Cemetery]

Unknown, C. L. T. (initials on a small flat marker) [St. James United Cemetery]

Unknown, E. A. H. and **D. H.** (two initials on same stone marker) [Mt. Zion U. M. Church Cemetery]

Unknown, E. O. P. (old stone foot marker copied in 1986, but not found in 2018) [Hendon Hill Cemetery]

Unknown, F. E. L. (copied in 1987, but not found in 2018) [Mt. Zion U. M. Church Cemetery]

Unknown, F. M. (foot marker) [Tabernacle Mount Zion U. M. Church Cemetery]

Unknown, G. R. (footstone) [Chestnut Grove A. M. E. Church Cemetery, formerly LaGrange Cemetery at Rocks]

Unknown, H. F. No. 1 (marker was copied in 1987, but not found in 2018) [Chestnut Grove A. M. E. Church Cemetery, formerly LaGrange Cemetery at Rocks]

Unknown, H. M. (footstone) [Chestnut Grove A. M. E. Church Cemetery, formerly LaGrange Cemetery at Rocks]

Unknown, H. R. (initials on a small flat marker) [St. James United Cemetery]

Unknown, H. T. (copied in 1987, but not found in 2018) [Mt. Zion U. M. Church Cemetery]

Unknown, J. D. (old stone foot marker copied in 1986, but not found in 2018) [Hendon Hill Cemetery]

Unknown, J. T. W. (footstone copied in 1987) [Berkley Memorial Cemetery]

Unknown, K. A. H. (small metal funeral home marker) [Mt. Zion U. M. Church Cemetery]

Unknnwn, K. E. J. (small, broken, arched tombstone roughly inscribed with initials) [Hendon Hill Cemetery]

Unknown, M. E. (footstone) [Chestnut Grove A. M. E. Church Cemetery, formerly LaGrange Cemetery at Rocks]

Unknown, M. L. T. (footstone) [Mt. Zion U. M. Church Cemetery]

Unknown, Marion? -----?----- (old, flat, rectangular, badly weathered tombstone) [Mt. Calvary U. A. M. E. Church Cemetery]

Unknown, R----, Alice Jeanne 1913-1976 (flat stone, badly weathered) [St. James United Cemetery]

Unknown, R. A. W. (footstone) [Mt. Zion U. M. Church Cemetery]

Unknown, R. H. D. and **E. J. D.** (initials inscribed on an old stone) [St. James United Cemetery]

Unknown, R. S. H. (footstone) [Mt. Zion U. M. Church Cemetery]

Unknown, R. W. (footstone) [Chestnut Grove A. M. E. Church Cemetery, formerly LaGrange Cemetery at Rocks]

Unknown, S----, Delores July 27, 1917 – December 28, __? (copied in 1992, but not found in 2018) [Union U.

M. Church Cemetery]

Unknown, S. A. A. (footstone) [Mt. Zion U. M. Church Cemetery]

Unknown, T. L. W. (footstone) [Fairview A. M. E. Church Cemetery]

Unknown, W. E. W. (footstone) [Mt. Zion U. M. Church Cemetery]

Vance, Infant December 10, 1920 – December 11, 1920 (no tombstone; death certificate stated he was son of Charles L. Peaco and Ethel Vance; informant was A. H. Peaco, of Havre de Grace) [St. James United Cemetery]

Vance, Infant stillborn male on August 4, 1922 (no tombstone; death certificate stated he was the son of Charles L. Peaco and Ethel Vance; informant was his father, of Havre de Grace) [St. James United Cemetery]

Vaughan, Jarrett A. October 5, 1989 – July 31, 2009 (inscribed "Gone But Not Forgotten") [St. James United Cemetery]

Vaughan, Raymond August 29, 1928 – September 3, 1997 (no tombstone; James Dorsey Card File, African American Obituaries, that is maintained at the Historical Society of Harford County, has a card with obituary from an unidentified newspaper on September 17, 1997 stating he was born in Ahoskie, NC, one of 14 children born to Charlie Vaughan, Sr. and Penny Thomas; he was a farmhand in North Carolina, moved to Maryland and worked for the Rose Furniture Co. in Havre de Grace, the Aberdeen Proving Ground Dietary Dept. and Meads Construction in Aberdeen; he lived in Aberdeen and died at Laurel Wood Nursing Home in Elkton, survived by five brothers and four sisters) [St. James United Cemetery]

Vaughan, Shirley Lorraine August 9, 1944 – August 7, 2010 (inscribed "I give thanks to my God upon every remembrance of you.") [Gravel Hill Cemetery]

Vaughn, Bettye 1938-2018 (temporary metal funeral home marker) [Gravel Hill Cemetery]

Vaughn, Dorris May 5, 1915 – May 10, 1927 (no tombstone; death certificate stated she was born in Maryland, the daughter of Alfred Vaughn, of South Carolina, and Eliza Burke, of Maryland, and died in Havre de Grace; informant was Regina Peters, of Baltimore; she was buried in "Cokesbury Cem." [probably John Wesley U. M. E. Church Cemetery in Abingdon]

Vaughn, Raymond 1928-1977 [Gravel Hill Cemetery]

Vaught, Charles E. November 7, 1931 – August 3, 2005 (on same tombstone with Linda J. Vaught) [Berkley Memorial Cemetery]

Vaught, Linda J. August 15, 1943 – July 19, 2008 (on same tombstone with Charles E. Vaught) [Berkley Memorial Cemetery]

Venable, Alice H., "Loving Wife, Mother and Grandmother" 1921-2016 [Berkley Memorial Cemetery]

Venable, Leslie C. Sr. 1925-2004, U.S. Navy, World War II [Berkley Memorial Cemetery]

Vernon, Stephen died September 24, 1913, age about 65 (no tombstone; death certificate stated he was born in Lexington, KY, the son of Reese Vernon, but his mother was unknown to informant Mrs. S. Featherstone, of Havre de Grace) [St. James United Cemetery]

Wade, Catherine B., "Mother" April 3, 1915 – October 20, 1991 (tombstone is also inscribed "Aunt Olevette Wamsley" at the bottom) [Mt. Calvary U. A. M. E. Church Cemetery]

Wade, Catherine M January 25, 1934 -   (on same tombstone with Cleophus M. Wade) [Fairview A. M. E. Church Cemetery]

Wade, Cleophus M. July 9, 1930 – August 19, 1993 (on same tombstone with Catherine M. Wade) [Fairview A. M. E. Church Cemetery]

Wade, Minnie M. 1954-2004 (small metal funeral home marker) [St. James United Cemetery]

Wade, Wamsley (owned a lot in section 41 some time after 1951) [Mt. Calvary U. A. M. E. Church Cemetery]

Wades, Charity Ann, mother of Harriet Ann Perry, died in June 1899, age 60(?) (illegible age; inscribed on same tombstone with Stewart Wades) [Hendon Hill Cemetery]

Wades, Stewart K., brother of Harriet Ann Perry, died in May 1901, age 42 (on the same tombstone with Charity Wades; death certificate stated "Stuart Wade" died May 13, 1901, age about 45, was born in Maryland, married Asia ----; his mother was Charity Wade, but his father's name was not given) [Hendon Hill Cemetery]

Wainwright, Dolores H. March 31, 1935 – October 26, 1936 (no tombstone; death certificate stated she was the daughter of Ernest B. Wainwright, born in Baltimore, and Hilda Barnes, born in Havre de Grace) [St. James United Cemetery]

Wainwright, Ernest B. July 28, 1884 – April 9, 1950 (no tombstone; death certificate stated he was the married son of John Wainwright and Ellen Pookom; informant was Mrs. Eva Wainwright) [St. James United Cemetery]

Wainwright, Leroy 1917-1965 (on same tombstone with Matilda Wainwright) [Berkley Memorial Cemetery]

Wainwright, Matilda 1921-1976 (on same tombstone with Leroy Wainwright) [Berkley Memorial Cemetery]

Wainwright, Oscar February 17, 1926 – April 27, 1927 (no tombstone; death certificate stated he was the son of Ernest Wainwright and Eva Brown, of Havre de Grace) [St. James United Cemetery]

Wainwright, William 1952-2016 (small metal funeral home marker) [Berkley Memorial Cemetery]

Waldon, Anderson M., "Chuck" July 17, 1950 – June 21, 2011 (inscribed "From your wife and children") [St. James United Cemetery]

Waldon, Francis Monroe Sunrise January 14, 1924 – Sunset October 20, 2014 (on same tombstone with Mary Catherine Collins Waldon with a photo of them and a separate image of a yacht; on the back of the tombstone it is inscribed "HON" and "Loving Memory, Michael T. Harris, Earl F. Waldon, Patricia J. Brown, Harris and Waldon Families;" funeral notice and photo in *The Aegis* on October 24, 2014 stated he died at home in Havre de Grace) [St. James United Cemetery]

Waldon, George A. February 23, 1893 -   [Union U. M. Church Cemetery]

Waldon, Hazel E. 1918-1984 [St. James United Cemetery]

Waldon, Jean A. June 16, 1939 – September 12, 1992 (inscribed "In Loving Memory;" James Dorsey Card File, African American Obituaries, that is maintained at the Historical Society of Harford County, has a card with obituary from an unidentified newspaper on September 19, 1990 stating Jean Alberta Waldon was born in Port Deposit, the daughter of the late Viola Carey, and married Rev. Claude D. Waldon; she lived in Port Deposit and died at Harford Memorial Hospital in Havre de Grace, survived by her husband, three sons, four brothers, five sisters, and four grandchildren) [Berkley Memorial Cemetery]

Waldon, Marie, "Baby Doll" and "Loving Wife and Mother" April 9, 1931 – February 28, 2018 (also a small metal funeral home marker showed her name as Marie F. Waldon) [St. James United Cemetery]

Waldon, Marion (owned a lot in section 24 some time after 1951) [Mt. Calvary U. A. M. E. Church Cemetery]

Waldon, Mary Bennita June 2, 1933 – August 7, 1975 (inscribed "At Rest;" Pennington Funeral Home records stated she was the unmarried daughter of George Andrew Waldon and Nellie V. Haycock, of Havre de Grace. and she was buried in "Swan Creek Cemetery, Swan Creek") [Union U. M. Church Cemetery]

Waldon, Mary Catherine Collins Sunrise September 3, 1921 – Sunset October 2, 2010 (on same tombstone with Francis Monroe Waldon with a photo of them and a separate image of a yacht) [St. James United Cemetery]

Waldon, Nellie Virginia Haycock November 20, 1898 – July 15, 1958 [Union U. M. Church Cemetery]

Waldon, Robert Lee, "Loving Husband and Father" March 26, 1929 – May 12, 2004 [St. James United Cemetery]

Waldon, Virginia E. 1921-1972 (tombstone; obituary in *The Aegis* on August 10, 1972 stated Estelle Virginia Waldon was the daughter of Mrs. Estella Dyson and the late James Dyson, and the wife of George A. Waldon, Jr., of 116 Bush Chapel Road, Aberdeen; she died at Harford Memorial Hospital in Havre de Grace on August 2, 1972 and was survived by her husband, her mother, 3 sons, 3 daughters, 6 brothers, 2 sisters, and 8 grandchildren) [Mt. Calvary U. A. M. E. Church Cemetery]

Walker, ---- died on August 6, 1918, age about 27 (no tombstone; death certificate stated he was a laborer and died in Edgewood; the names and places of birth of his parents were not known to informant Howard K. McComas, Undertaker, of Abingdon) [John Wesley U. M. E. Church Cemetery in Abingdon]

Walker, Comfort E. January 20, 1920 – September 16, 1997 [St. James United Cemetery]

Walker, Ella Alice December 26, 1934 – May 25, 2017 (small metal funeral home marker with photo) [Mt. Calvary U. A. M. E. Church Cemetery]

Walker, Henrietta, wife of Charles Walker, died 1891 (other information below ground) [Mt. Zion U. M. Church Cemetery]

Walker, John October 9, 1900 – September 13, 1955 (no tombstone; Pennington Funeral Home records stated he was born in Martinsburg, WV, the son of John Walker and "Lottie ? Walker," and was custodian at the Havre de Grace Consolidated School; informant was Mrs. John Walker, of Havre de Grace, and the funeral bill was rendered to Mrs. Catherine Johnson [St. James United Cemetery]

Walker, Lewis Jr. December 28, 1940 – July 21, 2006, Cpl., U.S. Marine Corps [St. James United Cemetery]

Walker, Mary 1880-1923 (on same tombstone with Thomas E. Walker; death certificate stated she was a housemaid and died a widow on July 30 1923, age about 46, in Edgewood; her place of birth and the names and places of birth for her parents were unknown to the undertaker Howard K. McComas, of Abingdon, and the name of informant was left blank) [John Wesley U. M. E. Church Cemetery in Abingdon]

Walker, Sarah Dougherty September 12, 1869 – February 28, 1944 (no tombstone; death certificate stated she was the daughter of George Samuel Dougherty and Sallie McLean, all born in Maryland; she was a cook in Bel Air and the widow of Edward Walker; informant was Emma Weaver, of Baltimore) [Asbury Cemetery]

Walker, Thomas E. 1867-1920 (on same tombstone with Mary Walker; death certificate stated Thomas Edward Walker was the son of William Walker and Harriet Butler, all born in Maryland; he married Mary ----, lived in Van Bibber and died on April 2, 1920, age 52 years, 11 months, 30 days; buried in "Collored Cemetery, Abingdon;" informant was Mary Walker, of Edgewood) [John Wesley U. M. E. Church Cemetery in Abingdon]

Wallace, ---- stillborn male on January 16, 1924 (no tombstone; death certificate stated he was son of William Wallace and Fannie Webster, both born in Harford Co., lived in Darlington) [Berkley Memorial Cemetery]

Wallace, Benjamin, "Beloved Husband" died February 22, 1930, age about 52 (tombstone; death certificate stated Franklin B. Wallace was born in Maryland; parents were unknown to informant Mrs. F. B. Wallace) [Union U. M. Church Cemetery]

Wallace, Chester A. February 2, 1897 – December 26, 1968 (on the same tombstone with Ruth A. Wallace; obituary in *The Aegis* on January 7, 1969 stated Chester Andrew Wallace was age 74 (actually 71), the son of Frank Wallace and Rebecca Murray, and the husband of Ruth Wallace, of Pylesville; he was born in Sunnyburn, PA, moved to Pylesville circa 1943 and died at the Harford Memorial Hospital in Havre de Grace; Harkins Funeral Home Records confirmed his 1897 birth date and the other information in obituary) [Chestnut Grove A. M. E. Church Cemetery, formerly LaGrange Cemetery at Rocks]

Wallace, Chester Leroy June 15, 1928 – April 22, 2008 (no tombstone; obituary in *The Aegis* on April 25, 2008 stated Chester Leroy Wallace, Jr., of Churchville, was born in Airville, PA, the son of Chester Wallace and Ruth Stewart, and served in the U.S. Army in the Korean War) [Chestnut Grove A. M. E. Church Cemetery, formerly LaGrange Cemetery at Rocks]

Wallace, Elizabeth E. "Mother" September 30, 1879 – January 6, 1966 (tombstone; obituary in *The Aegis* stated Elizabeth Ellen Wallace, widow of Joseph H. Wallace, died in Darlington) [Cedars Chapel Cemetery]

Wallace, Fannie 1903-1986 [Berkley Memorial Cemetery]

Wallace, Hattie 1886-1959 (on same tombstone with James Meadows and Irene Meadows) [Chestnut Grove A. M. E. Church Cemetery, formerly LaGrange Cemetery at Rocks]

Wallace, Ida December 26, 1910 – February 24, 1912 (no tombstone; death certificate stated she was the daughter of Joseph H. Wallace and Elizabeth E. Dorsey, all born in Maryland and they lived in Darlington; informant was her father) [Cedars Chapel Cemetery]

Wallace, James N. 1914-1969 (inscribed "In Loving Memory") [Cedars Chapel Cemetery]

Wallace, John E. June 26, 1912 – May 8, 1975 [Cedars Chapel Cemetery]

Wallace, Joseph July 15, 1939 – January 27, 1940 (no tombstone; death certificate stated he was the son of Sarah Wallace, both born in Harford Co., but his father was not known to informant Joseph Wallace, of RFD Darlington) [Cedars Chapel Cemetery]

Wallace, Joseph E. June 12, 1923 – September 24, 1998 (inscribed with an image of an Army half-track) [Berkley Memorial Cemetery]

Wallace, Joseph Henry May 10, 1870 – October 30, 1949 (tombstone inscribed Joseph H. Wallace died 1949; death certificate stated Joseph Henry Wallacae was born in Harford County, the son of William Wallace and Margaret Hopkins; he was married and worked as a farm laborer in Darlington; informant was Mrs. Joseph Wallace, of Darlington) [Cedars Chapel Cemetery]

Wallace, Mary L. 1936-2016 (small metal funeral home marker) [Berkley Memorial Cemetery]

Wallace, Paul stillborn on January 17, 1917 at Darlington (no tombstone; death certificate stated he was the son of Joseph H. Wallace, born in Harford Co., and Elizabeth L. Dorsey, born in York Co., PA; informant was Joseph H. Wallace, of Darlington) [Cedars Chapel Cemetery]

Wallace, Robert died December 16, 1933, age 46 (no tombstone; death certificate stated he was born in Baltimore in 1887, married Addie ----, worked as a farm laborer, lived at Rocks and died in an auto accident; his parents' names were not known by informant M. T. Bohler, of "Conowingo (State Police);" *The Aegis*, December 20, 1933, reported he was sitting at night alongside of the new State Road near Bush's Corner when he was struck by a car and killed; he had apparently stopped to rest on his homeward journey and was unable to avoid the oncoming car; he was an employee of John Walker Streett, of Clermont Mills) [Chestnut Grove A. M. E. Church Cemetery, formerly LaGrange Cemetery at Rocks]

Wallace, Rosa W. August 4, 1908 – October 5, 1996 (inscribed "Precious Lord Take My Hand") [Clark's U. M. Church Cemetery]

Wallace, Ruth A. December 25, 1902 – January 22, 2006 (on the same tombstone with Chester A. Wallace; obituary and photo in *The Aegis* on January 25, 2006 stated she was born in Kalmia, the daughter of Howard Stewart and Daisy Bradford, and was the widow of Chester Wallace; she died at home in Street, survived by 2 sons, 1 daughter, 1 sister, 10 grandchildren, 20 great-grandchildren, and was predeceased by 1 son, 1 daughter, 4 brothers, and 2 sisters) [Chestnut Grove A. M. E. Church Cemetery, formerly LaGrange Cemetery at Rocks]

Wallace, Ruth March 12, 1918 – June 5, 1921 (no tombstone; death certificate stated she was born in Darlington, the daughter of Joseph Wallace, born in Maryland, and Elizabeth Dorsey, born in Pennsylvania; informant was Joseph Wallace, of Darlington) [Cedars Chapel Cemetery]

Wallace, Wells stillborn on August 26, 1921 at Cedars (no tombstone; death certificate stated he was the son of Ernest Wells and Pauline Wallace, all born in Maryland; informant was Ernest Wells, of Street, MD) [Cedars Chapel Cemetery]

Wallace, William T. 1864 – February 6, 1930 (no tombstone; death certificate stated he died a widower in Forest Hill, but his parents were unknown to informant Thomas Kehoe) [St. James United Cemetery]

Wallace, William T. May 28, 1902 – June 6, 1931 (no tombstone; death certificate stated he was born in Darlington, the son of Joseph H. Wallace, born in Darlington, and Elizabeth Dorsey, born in York, PA; he was single, worked as a farm laborer and died in an automobile accident) [Cedars Chapel Cemetery]

Walls, Edith 1900-1981 [St. James United Cemetery]

Walls, Latasha N. 12-3-1978 – 11-3-2017 [Berkley Memorial Cemetery]

Walls, William 1923-1976 (tombstone; obituary in *The Aegis* on October 28, 1976 stated he was born May 9, 1923 in Cheraw, SC, son of the late Wilbert and Sally Walls, and he moved to Harford Co. in 1943; he lived at 560 Lewis St. in Havre de Grace, and died at Johns Hopkins Hospital on October 20, 1976, survived by his son Mose Walls, Jr. *(sic)*, two brothers Hubbard and Tom, four sisters, two grandchildren, and 25 nieces and nephews) [St. James United Cemetery]

Walls, Zeb W. March 3, 1910 – August 22, 1963, Maryland, Pvt., 1322 Service Unit, World War II [Berkley Memorial Cemetery]

Waltier, Howard Davis June 16, 1891 – April 26, 1916 (no tombstone; death certificate stated he was the unmarried son of William Waltier and Caroline Davis; informant was Amanda Waltier, of Havre de Grace) [St. James United Cemetery]

Walton, ---- premature female birth on September 9, 1914 (no tombstone; death certificate stated she was the daughter of Robert Kirkwood Walton and Julia Adalbert Buchanan, all born in Harford Co.; informant was her father, of Black Horse) [William C. Rice Memorial Cemetery, St. James U. M. Church]

Walton, Annie M. January 5, 1851 – June 4, 1916 (no tombstone; death certificate stated she was the daughter of Samuel and Annie Gilbert, all born in Harford Co.; she was a widow and died in Bel Air; informant was George Willis James, of Bel Air) [Mt. Zion U. M. Church Cemetery]

Walton, Charles Earl stillborn on May 4, 1923 (no tombstone; death certificate stated he was born and died at Pylesville, the son of Herbert C. Walton, born at Pylesville, and Edna A. Peaco, born in York Co., PA; informant was his father) [Chestnut Grove A. M. E. Church Cemetery, formerly LaGrange Cemetery at Rocks]

Walton, Clarence Edward November 30, 1921 – December 23, 2002 (no tombstone; obituary in *The Delta Star* on January 3, 2013 stated he was born in Pylesville, the son of Herbert Walton and Edna Peco, lived at Street and was the husband of the late Iris M. Walton) [Chestnut Grove A. M. E. Church Cemetery, formerly LaGrange Cemetery at Rocks]

Walton, Claudia Elizabeth May 16, 1946 – September 1, 1993 (no tombstone; James Dorsey Card File, African American Obituaries, that is maintained at the Historical Society of Harford County, has a funeral card for her from the Howard K. McComas III Funeral Home) [Tabernacle Mount Zion U. M. Church Cemetery]

Walton, David died on October 10, 1910, age 50 (on same tombstone with Frank Anna Walton) [John Wesley U. M. E. Church Cemetery in Abingdon]

Walton, Earl W. Jr. January 12, 1951 – January 1, 1997 (no tombstone; obituary in *The Aegis* on January 8, 1997 stated Earl Wilson Walton, Jr. was the son of Earl and Mary Jane Walton, of Bel Air, married Rev. Velma Dennison in 1982, and became an Elder in the church; he had worked for Amtrak rail services until he retired on disability; he was survived by his wife, his parents, two stepdaughters, a brother, a sister and many other relatives) [Chestnut Grove A. M. E. Church Cemetery, formerly LaGrange Cemetery at Rocks]

Walton, Earl W. Sr. 1925-2006 (tombstone; his obituaries in *The Aegis* on June 14 and 21, 2006 stated Earl Wilson Walton, Sr. was born September 25, 1925 in Pylesville, the son of Herbert and Edna Walton; he married Mary Jane Ellis on August 5, 1950, was called "Jimmy" by those who knew him fondly, and died at Upper Chesapeake Medical Center in Bel Air) [Chestnut Grove A. M. E. Church Cemetery, formerly LaGrange Cemetery at Rocks]

Walton, Edna A. 1900-1981 (on same tombstone with Herbert C. Walton; obituary in *The Aegis* on July 30, 1981 stated she was born in Delta, PA, the daughter of Joseph Peaco and Laura Murray; she died in Harford Memorial Hospital on July 15, 1981 and was the wife of Herbert C. Walton, of Street, whose obituary stated Edna died on July 22, 1981) [Chestnut Grove A. M. E. Church Cemetery, formerly LaGrange Cemetery at Rocks]

Walton, Elwood W. 1913-1950 (on same tombstone with Robert K., J. Aldalbert and William W. Walton) [William C. Rice Memorial Cemetery, St. James U. M. Church]

Walton, Fannie Viola July 29, 1897 – December 12, 1897 (no tombstone; death certificate stated she was the daughter of James Bond and Rachel Johnson, and all were born in Maryland; she was married and lived at

Rocks; informant was Sarah J. Walton, of The Rocks) [Fairview A. M. E. Church Cemetery]

Walton, Frank Anna died on May 7, 1905, age 53 (on same tombstone with David Walton) [John Wesley U. M. E. Church Cemetery in Abingdon]

Walton, Herbert C. 1898-1982 (on the same tombstone with Edna A. Walton; obituary in *The Aegis* on February 4, 1982 stated he was a lifelong resident of Harford County and died on January 27, 1982 at Fallston General Hospital; he was the husband of the late Edna C. Walton, of Street, MD, and was survived by 4 children, 11 grandchildren and 9 great-grandchildren; James Dorsey Card File, African American Obituaries, that is maintained at the Historical Society of Harford County, has a card stating he was born on January 25, 1898) [Chestnut Grove A. M. E. Church Cemetery, formerly LaGrange Cemetery at Rocks]

Walton, Iris M. May 31, 1922 – June 22, 2006 (tombstone; obituary in *The Aegis* on June 28, 2006 stated she was born in Winston-Salem, NC, the daughter of Richard Simpson and Ethel Hopkins, lived in Street, was married to Clarence E. Walton for 37 years, and died in Bel Air at the Bel Air Health and Rehabilitation Center; she was survived by a daughter, a sister, three grandchildren, five great-grandchildren, and five great-great-grandchildren) [Chestnut Grove A. M. E. Church Cemetery, formerly LaGrange Cemetery at Rocks]

Walton, J. Aldalbert 1895-1977 (on same tombstone with Robert K., Elwood W. and William W. Walton) [William C. Rice Memorial Cemetery, St. James U. M. Church]

Walton, Lawrence E. November 30, 1921 -   (Chestnut Grove A. M. E. Church Cemetery, formerly LaGrange Cemetery at Rocks]

Walton, Mary Alice June 5, 1920 – May 12, 1967 (tombstone; obituary in *The Aegis* on May 18, 1967 stated Mrs. Alice Davis Walton, wife of Clarence Walton, of Street, died on May 12, 1967 and she was the daughter of Glasgow Davis and the late Edna Davis) [Chestnut Grove A. M. E. Church Cemetery, formerly LaGrange Cemetery at Rocks]

Walton, Robert K. 1890-1973 (on same tombstone with Elwood W., J. Aldalbert and William W. Walton) [William C. Rice Memorial Cemetery, St. James U. M. Church]

Walton, William U. 1930-1945 (on the same tombstone with Elwood W., J. Aldalbert and Robert K. Walton; Kurtz Funeral Home Record Book 1944-1949, p. 91, stated William Upton Walton was born on September 11, 1930 in New Park, PA, the son of Robert Walton, born in Sharon, and Adalbret Buchanan, born in Jarrettsville; he was a school boy who died on January 8, 1945 at University Hospital in Baltimore) [William C. Rice Memorial Cemetery, St. James U. M. Church]

Walton, William Upton died April 13, 1918, age 66 (no tombstone; death certificate stated he was the son of ---- Walton and Ann Berry, all born in Harford Co.; he was married, was a farmer and died near Federal Hill; informant was his wife Sarah, of Rocks RFD) [William C. Rice Memorial Cemetery, St. James U. M. Church]

Wamsley, Aunt Olevette – see Catherine B. Wade [Mt. Calvary U. A. M. E. Church Cemetery]

Wann, Sarah C., "Sister" died June 12, 1907, age 51 (on same obelisk with E. Merryman Hall and Ruth E. Hall) [Mt. Zion U. M. Church Cemetery]

Ward, Ada Bernice, "Beloved Wife" September 29, 1929 – December 18, 1991 (tombstone also inscribed "I lived my life one day at a time") [Mt. Calvary U. A. M. E. Church Cemetery]

Ward, Flemington (no tombstone, but Kurtz Funeral Home records stated he was buried in an "im cherry" coffin on July 26, 1881 from near J. R. Rutledge's tenant house) [West Liberty Church Cemetery]

Ward, Joseph L. August 25, 1938 – January 25, 2003, MSG, U.S. Army, Vietnam [Mt. Calvary U. A. M. E. Church Cemetery]

Ward, Richard November 10, 1888 – April 30, 1934 (no tombstone; death certificate stated he was born in Calvert Co, MD, the son of Charles Ward, but mother unknown; he married Mamie ---- and died in Havre de Grace; informant was Brewster Ward, of Havre de Grace) [St. James United Cemetery]

Ward, Rosco April 8, 1898 – March 18, 1922 (no tombstone; death certificate stated he was the married son of Richard Ward and Mary Mooney, of Havre de Grace) [St. James United Cemetery]

Warfield, Aaron August 31, 1865 – September 26, 1913 (no tombstone; death certificate misspelled his name Warefield, but stated his father was Joseph Warfield) [St. James United Cemetery]

Warfield, Adea Anna May 28, 1912 – October 27, 1912 (no tombstone; death certificate stated she was the daughter of George Whims and Maddie Warfield, all born in Harford Co.) [Union U. M. Church Cemetery]

Warfield, Alberta died February 1, 1899, age 1 year, 6 months and 18 days (no tombstone; death certificate state she was the daughter of William H. and Amanda Warfield and died at home near Cole P. O.; place of burial was not indicated, but probably in the Old Union Chapel Cemetery at Michaelsville; possibly reinterred later in Union Chapel Cemetery near Aberdeen) [Union U. M. Church Cemetery]

Warfield, Alonzo April 26, 1948 – February 5, 2000 (tombstone; obituary in *The Aegis* on February 11, 2000 stated Alonzo Charles Warfield was the son of Charles H. and Katie C. Warfield; he lived in Perryman, worked at Aberdeen Proving Ground for 20 years and died at Harford Memorial Hospital, survived by his mother, a sister, a niece, two nephews, five aunts, two uncles and a host of cousins) [Union U. M. Church Cemetery]

Warfield, Amanda March 20, 1852 – December 23, 1917 (no tombstone; death certificate stated she was the married daughter of Charles Hill and Susan Johnson; informant was William A Warfield, of Aberdeen RFD; buried in "New Cemetery") [probably Swan Creek Cemetery that later became Union U. M. Church Cemetery]

Warfield, Amanda February 19, 1917 – April 11, 1918 (no tombstone; death certificate stated she was the daughter of James H. Warfield and Garia Shippard, all born in Harford Co.) [Union U. M. Church Cemetery]

Warfield, Baby (Brown) stillborn male on February 8, 1931 (no tombstone; death certificate stated he was born at the Havre de Grace Hospital, the son of Albert Brown, born in Florida, and "Alice Bowman (Warfield on birth)," born in South Carolina) [Union U. M. Church Cemetery]

Warfield, Barbara Lee September 30, 1959 – September 10, 1989 [Mt. Calvary U. A. M. E. Church Cemetery]

Warfield, Bernice Irene, "Mother" June 26, 1919 – June 25, 1970 (tombstone; obituary in *The Aegis* stated she was the daughter of the late David Warfield and Mollie Harris, and married Hannibal Warfield; they lived at 46 Monroe St. in Aberdeen and she died at Harford Memorial Hospital in Havre de Grace, survived by her husband, four sons, four daughters, four brothers, three sisters, and four grandchildren) [Berkley Memorial Cemetery]

Warfield, Carvel J. March 12, 1926 – April 1, 1981, U.S. Navy, World War II (tombstone; he is buried in section 2; obituary in *The Aegis* on April 9, 1981 stated Carvel Jerome Warfield was a lifelong resident of Havre de Grace, the son of Lula Warfield Boddy and the late Orin Warfield; he married Pinkey Reaves, resided at 402 Battery Drive and died at Harford Memorial Hospital; he was a member of the Elks and served as vice president of the Havre de Grace NAACP, but no mention was made of his military service; he was survived by his wife, his mother, five sisters and two grandchildren) [Mt. Calvary U. A. M. E. Church Cemetery]

Warfield, Charles (owned lots in section 6 some time after 1951) [Mt. Calvary U. A. M. E. Church Cemetery]

Warfield, Charles F. III 1951-1986 (inscribed "In Loving Memory;" obituary in *The Aegis* on April 9, 1986 stated Charles Franklin "Frankie" Warfield III was born in Havre de Grace, the son of Mr. & Mrs. Charles F. Warfield, of Aberdeen; he served in the Army from December 1972 to August 1975 and was a heavy equipment operator; he died at home in Aberdeen, survived by his parents, a son, two daughters, three brothers and four sisters) [Mt. Calvary U. A. M. E. Church Cemetery]

Warfield, Charles Franklin April 13, 1921 – January 9, 1967, Maryland, Pvt., Co. E, 370th Inf., 29th Inf. Div., World War II [Union U. M. Church Cemetery]

Warfield, Charles H. Jr. October 21, 1914 – November 3, 1958, Maryland, TEC5, 214 Port Co., TC, World War II [Union U. M. Church Cemetery]

Warfield, Clara December 13, 1908 – June 21, 1933 (no tombstone; death certificate stated she was the wife of Charles Warfield and the daughter of Joshua Williams and Mary Carey) [Union U. M. Church Cemetery]

Warfield, Clinton O. 1946-1976, SP4, U.S. Army, Vietnam [Union U. M. Church Cemetery]

Warfield, Darlene Elizabeth Govans died July 10, 1990, age 46 (no tombstone; obituary in *The Aegis* on July 18, 1990 stating she was born in Baltimore, the daughter of Clarence W. and Jessie R. Govans; she was active in the church and died at her home in Jarrettsville, survived by her parents, husband Ridgley Warfield, son Brian Warfield, twin daughters Christine Warfield and Tina Warfield, and two sisters Theresa Moses and Yvonne Williams) [William C. Rice Memorial Cemetery, St. James U. M. Church]

Warfield, Darnell M. August 27, 1985 – November 9, 1985 (on same tombstone with Lisa L. Nunley) [Mt. Calvary U. A. M. E. Church Cemetery]

Warfield, E. Geraldine June 28, 1933 – March 6, 1994 (inscribed "In Loving Memory;" obituary and photo in *The Aegis* on March 16, 1994 stated Emma Geraldine Warfield was born and raised at Chase in Baltimore Co., daughter of Rose and Raymond Cooper; she moved to Harford County in the 1940s and married Charles Warfield, Jr. in 1950; she was known for her stylish hats and cooking talent; she lived in Aberdeen and was survived by 3 sons, 3 daughters, 3 brothers, 3 sisters, 24 grandchildren and 8 great-grandchildren, and was preceded in death by one son and one daughter) [Mt. Calvary U. A. M. E. Church Cemetery]

Warfield, Earnest Kennard March 7, 1932 – May 4, 1933 (no tombstone; death certificate stated he was the son of Charles Warfield and Clara Williams) [Union U. M. Church Cemetery]

Warfield, Effie H. 1909-1999 (on same tombstone with William H. Warfield) [Union U. M. Church Cemetery]

Warfield, Eliza Taylor (no dates recorded in 1987 and listed in 2002 as "E. Warfield, died 1920," but tombstone not found in 2018 and no death certificate found in Harford County) [Gravel Hill Cemetery]

Warfield, Estella V. 10-6-24 7-20-90 (dates handwritten on a small flat cement slab; obituary in *The Aegis* on August 15, 1990 stated Estella Virginia Reed "Tootsie" Warfield was a native of Perryman and the daughter of John E. Reed and Beulah Jones, and widow of Moses N. Warfield; during World War II she worked at Aberdeen Proving Ground and formerly worked for the Anger family; she lived in Havre de Grace and died at Harford Memorial Hospital, survived by companion Aaron Watters, 6 daughters, 3 sons, 4 sisters, 23 grandchildren, 17 great-grandchildren, and 2 great-great-grandchildren) [Union U. M. Church Cemetery]

Warfield, Garrow 1870-1963 [Union U. M. Church Cemetery]

Warfield, George A. June 21, 1867 – August 16, 1923 (no tombstone; death certificate stated he was the married son of George Warfield and Amanda Johnson, all born in Maryland; informant was Sarah Prigg, of Perryman) [Union U. M. Church Cemetery]

Warfield, George H. June 16, 1843 – August 9, 1920 (no tombstone; death certificate stated he was born in Maryland and died a widower, but his parents were unknown to informant William A. Warfield, of Aberdeen) [Union U. M. Church Cemetery]

Warfield, Hannibal L. December 22, 1905 – April 14, 1980 (tombstone; obituary in *The Aegis* stated he was born in Perryman, the son of George Whims and Madie Warfield, lived on Second St. in Aberdeen, married Bernice Haines, who predeceased him, retired from Post Engineers at Aberdeen Proving Ground in 1967, and died at Harford Memorial Hospital, survived by 5 sons, 5 daughters, 12 grandchildren and 5 great-grandchildren) [Union U. M. Church Cemetery]

Warfield, Jamar William died June 10, 1981 (no tombstone; obituary in *The Aegis* stated he was the infant son of Reginald McDonald and Theresa Warfield, of Aberdeen, and he died at Johns Hopkins Hospital, survived by parents, two sisters, and grandparents William and Marie Warfield)

Warfield, James April 1, 1844 – April 25, 1912 (no tombstone; death certificate stated he was a widower and the son of Henry Warfield, both born in Maryland, but his mother was not known to informant W. S. Tilden, of Perryman) [Union U. M. Church Cemetery]

Warfield, James David December 17, 1916 – April 22, 1922 (no tombstone; death certificate stated he was the son of Charles H. Warfield and Alverta Johnson, all born in Maryland) [Union U. M. Church Cemetery]

Warfield, James E. July 31, 1930 – August 20, 1930 (no tombstone; death certificate stated he was the son of Gideon Warfield and Ida Christy; he was premature and lived only 20 days) [Union U. M. Church Cemetery]

Warfield, James H., "Father" 1867-1948 (tombstone; death certificate stated James Henry Warfield was born February 11, 1867 and died January 29, 1948; he was the son of Mose Warfield and Schalett(?) Monk, and husband of Garrow Shippard, and died on Bush Chapel Road) [Union U. M. Church Cemetery]

Warfield, James O. June 9, 1953 – March 14, 2011, U.S. Army (tombstone; funeral notice and photo in *The Aegis* on March 18, 2011 stated James Oliver Warfield, of Port Deposit, died at Lorien at Riverside Nursing Home in Belcamp [Mt. Calvary U. A. M. E. Church Cemetery]

Warfield, Madie P. 1888-1977 (tombstone; obituary in *The Aegis* on March 3, 1977 stated Madie Pauline Warfield was born in Perryman on April 28, 1888, the daughter of James Henry Warfield and Garrow Sheppard; she lived in Perryman and died at the Brevin Convalescent Home in Havre de Grace, survived by a son Hannibal L. Warfield, a brother Moses Warfield, two sisters Gladys Stansbury and Hilda Batson, and 25 grandchildren) [Union U. M. Church Cemetery]

Warfield, Maggie R. 1913-1996 (on same tombstone with Walter R. Warfield; obituary and photo in *The Aegis* on October 9, 1996 stated Maggie Ringgold Warfield was born July 6, 1913 in the "Old Baltimore" area of Harford County, now occupied by Aberdeen Proving Ground, and was the daughter of Ollie and Gladys Ringgold; in 1940 she married the late Walter Ray Warfield and in 1989 Harford County and the Town of Aberdeen proclaimed June 16th as Maggie Warfield Day; she retired from the First National Bank of Maryland in Aberdeen after more than 50 years service and died at Harford Memorial Hospital on September 28, 1996, survived by a son, two brothers, two sisters, and a granddaughter) [Union U. M. Church Cemetery]

Warfield, Marie V. April 25, 1930 – August 30, 1986 (inscribed "In Loving Memory;" obituary in *The Aegis* on September 11, 1986 stated she was born in Havre de Grace, the daughter of John and Mary Hill, and was the wife of William Warfield; she lived in Aberdeen and died at Harford Memorial Hospital in Havre de Grace, survived by seven daughters) [Berkley Memorial Cemetery]

Warfield, Mary Alean November 27, 1927 -   (on same tombstone with Moses Nathaniel Warfield) [Union U. M. Church Cemetery]

Warfield, Mary L. August 16, 1911 – October 12, 1914 (no tombstone; death certificate stated she was the daughter of Charles H. Warfield and Susan A. Johnson, all born in Harford Co.) [Union U. M. Church Cemetery]

Warfield, Monroe November 23, 1927 – November 25, 1927 (no tombstone; death certificate stated he was the son of George W. Whims and Madie P. Warfield, and an "accident of birth") [Union U. M. Church Cemetery]

Warfield, Moses Jr. January 18, 1941 – January 21, 1941 (no tombstone; death certificate stated he was the son of Moses Warfield, Sr. and Estella Reed) [Union U. M. Church Cemetery]

Warfield, Moses Nathaniel May 12, 1913 – December 9, 1989 (on same tombstone with Mary Alean Warfield) [Union U. M. Church Cemetery]

Warfield, Pinkney L. 1946-2018 (small metal funeral home marker) [St. James United Cemetery]

Warfield, Rickey N. April 1, 1959 – September 16, 1960 [Union U. M. Church Cemetery]

Warfield, Rita Doris 1925-1989 (tombstone; obituary in *The Aegis* on September 13, 1989 stated she was born in Havre de Grace, the daughter of Richard Jackson and Elizabeth Williams, and was the wife of Robert E. Warfield; she lived in Aberdeen and died at Harford Memorial Hospital in Havre de Grace, survived by her husband, one daughter, one brother, and one sister) [Union U. M. Church Cemetery]

Warfield, Robert E. December 28, 1919 – December 28, 1991, Sgt., U.S. Army, World War II [Union U. M. Church Cemetery]

Warfield, Rosie – see E. A. Martin [Union U. M. Church Cemetery]

Warfield, Sarah V. April 5, 1872 – February 16, 1930 (no tombstone; death certificate stated she was the unmarried daughter of Henry Warfield and Susan Johnson; informant was William Christy) [Union U. M. Church Cemetery]

Warfield, Steven Sr. 1961-2013 (small metal funeral home marker) [Berkley Memorial Cemetery]

Warfield, Susie A. 1887-1982 (on same tombstone with Walter L. Warfield; obituary in *The Aegis* on May 20, 1982 stated she was born in Michaelsville, the daughter of Mary P. Stansbury, and was the widow of Walter Lee

Warfield; she lived and died in Aberdeen on May 16, 1982, age 95, survived by a daughter-in-law Maggie R. Warfield, a brother James Stansbury, a sister Mabel Stansbury, a grandson and a great-granddaughter) [Union U. M. Church Cemetery]

Warfield, Walter L. 1878-1940 (on same tombstone with Susie A. Warfield; death certificate stated he was the son of Addie Warfield, father unknown, and the husband of Susie A. Warfield) [Union U. M. Church Cemetery]

Warfield, Walter R. 1908-1958 (on same tombstone with Maggie R. Warfield; obituary in *The Aegis* on January 30, 1958 stated Walter Ray Warfield, of Aberdeen, was the son of Walter and Susie Warfield, was employed at Aberdeen Proving Ground as an ammunition handling foreman and previously worked for J. Smith Michael; he died at home on January 24, 1958, survived by his wife, a son and his mother) [Union U. M. Church Cemetery]

Warfield, William H. 1907-1975 (on same tombstone with Effie H. Warfield; obituary in *The Aegis* stated William Horace Warfield was born May 30, 1907 in Harford County, the son of Charles Henry Warfield and Susie Alberta Robinson, and married Effie Hollingsworth; he lived at 500 Mitchell Lane in Aberdeen, retired from Post Engineers at Aberdeen Proving Ground, and died on January 10, 1975 at Harford Memorial Hospital in Havre de Grace, survived by his wife, a daughter, a brother, three grandchildren, and a great-grandchild) [Union U. M. Church Cemetery]

Warfield, William O. died April 3, 1935, age about 55 (no tombstone; death certificate stated he was the son of Addie Warfield, father unknown, and the husband of the late Rosie Martin) [Union U. M. Church Cemetery]

Warfield, William Oliver "Bunk" March 22, 1928 – August 9, 2010 (small metal funeral home marker inscribed William O. Warfield 1928-2010; obituary and photo in *The Aegis* on August 25, 1990 stated he was born in Perryman, the son of Charles Warfield and Clara Williams, and after the death of his mother he was raised by his grandmother Garrow Warfield; after serving in the Army during the Korean War he married Marie V. Hill; in his younger days he played guitar in a band, worked 39 years at Aberdeen Proving Ground and 11 years for the Harford County Public School System; he died in Havre de Grace, survived by 7 daughters, a brother Charles "BD" Warfield, 14 grandchildren, and 37 great-grandchildren [Berkley Memorial Cemetery]

Warren, Gary July 8, 1917 – November 19, 1952 (no tombstone; Pennington Funeral Home records stated he was born in South Carolina, the son of Robert Warren and Essie Arnold, and died at home near Havre de Grace [St. James United Cemetery]

Warren, John H. died July 28, 1915, age about 43 (no tombstone; death certificate stated he was the married son of Henry Warren, both born in Harford Co., but his mother was unknown to informant Ralph Mitchell, of Short Lane, Aberdeen) [Union U. M. Church Cemetery]

Warren, Maria died January 19, 1912, age 52 (no tombstone; death certificate stated she was the daughter of ---- and Annie Reeves, and they were all born in North Carolina; she was married and lived and died in Bel Air; informant was William Warren, of Bel Air) [Asbury Cemetery]

Warren, Mary A. June 15, 1841 – January 18, 1927 (no tombstone; death certificate stated she was born in Maryland, but the names of her parents and their places of birth were not known to informant Maggie Frisby, of Bel Air; she died a widow in Bel Air) [Mt. Calvary U. A. M. E. Church Cemetery]

Warren, William – see William Worin [Asbury Cemetery]

Washington, ---- stillborn female on December 24, 1925, premature birth (no tombstone; death certificate stated she was the daughter of Roy Washington and Helen Thomas, all born in Maryland; she died at Edgewood RFD; informant was her father) [John Wesley U. M. E. Church Cemetery in Abingdon]

Washington, ---- stillborn male on May 18, 1934 (no tombstone; death certificate stated he was born in Creswell, the son of Roy McKinley Washington, born in Abingdon, and Mary Helen Thomas, born in Creswell and buried at "John Wesley;" informant was his father) [John Wesley U. M. E. Church Cemetery in Abingdon]

Washington, Albert died March 14, 1916, age 31 (no tombstone; death certificate stated he was born in Maryland, the son of William Washington, born in Virginia, and Edith Washington, birth place unknown to informant Lillie Harris, of Abingdon; he was single and worked as a laborer in Abingdon) [John Wesley U. M. E. Church Cemetery in Abingdon]

Washington, Alex Jr., "Our Beloved Baby Boy" February 12, 2002 – December 10, 2002 [Community Baptist Church Cemetery]

Washington, Amelia died March 2, 1907, age 75 (no tombstone; death certificate stated she was the daughter of Isaac Washington and Fannie Prigg, all born in Harford Co., she was single, died at Berkley, but place of burial not given [probably Berkley Memorial Cemetery]

Washington, Annie Marie, wife of Isaac Washington, died June 28, 1892, age 75 (on same obelisk with Isaac Washington) [Green Spring U. M. Church Cemetery]

Washington, Augustus died April 16, 1876, age not given (no tombstone; his death notice stated in *The Aegis* on April 21, 1876 stated he was formerly the hostler at the Eagle Hotel in Bel Air; place of burial not given [possibly Hendon Hill Cemetery]

Washington, Beulah Corina June 4, 1900 – February 24, 1920 (no tombstone; death certificate stated she was the daughter of John Briley and Ada Jamison, all born in Maryland; she was married, died at Creswell and was buried in "Colored Cemetery, Abingdon;" informant was John Washington, of Bel Air) [John Wesley U. M. E. Church Cemetery in Abingdon]

Washington, Catherine L. died July 23, 1982, age 88 (no tombstone; obituary in *The Aegis* on August 5, 1982 stated she had lived in Bel Air and died at Key Nursing Home in Baltimore; her husbands were not mentioned, but she was survived by two sons, Rev. Nathaniel Washington and Rev. Daniel R. Collins, and a daughter Florence Collins) [Clark's U. M. Church Cemetery]

Washington, Debra M. August 2, 1956 – January 16, 1978 (tombstone; obituary in *The Aegis* stated Debra Margaret Washington was born in Bel Air, the daughter of Mary Washington, of Bel Air, and Leon Pounds, of Churchville; she was formerly employed as a maintenance worker with the Harford County Department of Public Works and died suddenly at Kirk Army Hospital; she was survived by her parents, a sister, Carla Washington, of Bel Air, and two brothers, Marshall Pounds, Jr. and Jeffrey Pounds, both of Churchville) [John Wesley U. M. E. Church Cemetery in Abingdon]

Washington, Edward A. died August 3, 1968, age not given (no tombstone; obituary in *The Aegis* on August 8, 1968 stated he was born in Aberdeen, the son of the late John and Jeannette Washington, and the husband of the late Ethel Kelly Washington; he worked and lived at the Old Bay Farm in Havre de Grace for a number of years and died at the Devine Nursing Home in Elkton, survived by a brother Robert Cecil Hoke and one step-son Walter Garrison; Pennington Funeral Home records contained very little information, but stated the informant was William S. James, of Old Bay Farm) [Asbury Cemetery]

Washington, Elisha April 14, 1853 – July 24, 1929 (no tombstone; death certificate stated he was the son of Isaac Washington and Fannie Washington, all born in Maryland; he married, worked as a laborer and died at home near Darlington; informant was Fannie E. Smith) [Berkley Memorial Cemetery]

Washington, Eliza 1882 – February 5, 1950 (no tombstone; death certificate stated she was the daughter of Hazard Harris, but her mother was not known to informant Isaac Washington, of Darlington; she married and died in rural Fallston; her usual residence was Darlington) [Berkley Memorial Cemetery]

Washington, Ella M. January 3, 1874 – August 17, 1929 (no tombstone; death certificate stated she was born in Maryland, the daughter of Lloyd Stewart, but his father's birth place was unknown and the name of his mother was unknown to informant Isaac Washington, of Darlington; she married and died at home in Castleton) [Berkley Memorial Cemetery]

Washington, Ethel Kelly 1893-1955 [Asbury Cemetery]

Washington, Ethel May 18, 1918 – January 21, 1933 (no tombstone; death certificate stated she was the daughter of John Washington and Beulah C. Briley, all born in Maryland; she was a school girl who died at home in Van Bibber and was buried at "John Wesley;" informant was her father) [John Wesley U. M. E. Church Cemetery in Abingdon]

Washington, Georgia October 23, 1925 – November 14, 2017 (no tombstone; obituary and photo in *The Aegis* and *www.mccomasfuneralhome.com/obituaries* stated she was born in Uniontown, AL, the daughter of Haywood

Green and Emmaline Key, and widow of Sam Houston Washington, Sr. (married 53 years); she was a member of John Wesley U. M. E. Church and died in Abingdon, survived by 4 sons, 1 daughter, a sister, 7 grandchildren, 15 great-grandchildren, and 8 great-great-grandchildren) [John Wesley U. M. E. Church Cemetery in Abingdon]

Washington, Gladys V. October 31, 1912 – December 20, 2001 (tombstone; obituary in *The Aegis* on December 28, 2001 stated Gladys Virginia Washington was born in Philadelphia, the daughter of Nicholas and Etta Johnson, and wife of the late McKinley Washington; with her husband she operated a restaurant and grocery store in Baltimore and in the early 1950s they moved to Harford Co. where she became a private duty nurse and they were also produce growers and distributors; after West Liberty Church in Fallston closed she joined St. James United Methodist Church and served on the board of trustees; she died at home in Fallston and was buried in Clarks United Methodist Church, survived by four cousins, Cleo Cole, Sarah Gaskins, Julia Drivers and Marie Brown) [Clark's U. M. Church Cemetery]

Washington, Hannah October – (blank), 1830 – January 13, 1915 (inscribed "Faithful Mammy in the Family of J. A. Hunter. And her children shall rise up and call her blessed." obituary in *The Aegis*, January 15, 1915, stated Mrs. Washington was aged 84, having belonged before the war to the Robinson family of Shepherdstown, WV and over 30 years ago she entered the Hunter family where she has raised all the children. She was universally known in this community as Mammy and died at the home of Mr. & Mrs. J. Abell Hunter in Bel Air; death certificate stated she died January 13, 1915, age 84 years and 3 months, in Bel Air; she was a widow and was employed as a nurse and maid; her parents were John and Clarissa Con, both born in Virginia; informant was Mrs. J. A. Hunter and she did not know Hannah's day of birth) [Hendon Hill Cemetery]

Washington, Henry May 23, 1880 – December 16, 1923 (no tombstone; death certificate stated he was the son of William Washington and Elsie Henson, all born in Maryland; he was married, worked as a railroad laborer and died in Abingdon; informant was Dill Harris, of Abingdon) [John Wesley U. M. E. Church Cemetery in Abingdon]

Washington, Howard Thomas February 23, 1925 – February 24, 1925 (no tombstone; death certificate stated he was premature and lived one hour at home in Stepney; his parents were Roy Washington and Helen Thomas, all born in Maryland; informant was Roy Washington, of Aberdeen RFD) [Asbury Cemetery]

Washington, Isaac died August 22, 1893, age 81, "At Rest" (on same obelisk with Annie M. Washington) [Green Spring U. M. Church Cemetery]

Washington, James Henry March 16, 1920 – May 5, 1920 (no tombstone; death certificate stated he was the son of Roy Washington and Helen Thomas, all born in Maryland, and he died at Belcamp; informant was Helen Thomas, of Aberdeen RFD) [Asbury Cemetery]

Washington, John March 15, 1872 – December 5, 1929 (no tombstone; death certificate stated he was the married son of John H. Washington and Jannette Bowser; informant was Ida Washington) [Union U. M. Church Cemetery]

Washington, John Albert died on November 26, 1983, age 61 (no tombstone; obituary in *The Aegis* on December 1, 1983 stated he was born in Abingdon, the son of the late Roy M. Washington, St. and Mary Helen Washington Waldon; he was a World War II veteran, worked as a mechanic and died at Pimlico Manor Nursing Home in Baltimore, survived by a brother and a sister) [John Wesley U. M. E. Church Cemetery in Joppa]

Washington, Laura B. May 8, 1886 – September 4, 1920 (no tombstone; death certificate stated she was the daughter of Joshua Brittain and Elizabeth Wiles, all born in Maryland; she was married and died in Abingdon; informant was Henry Washington, of Abingdon) [John Wesley U. M. E. Church Cemetery in Abingdon]

Washington, Lavarn, "Kitty – Mum – Nann" December 17, 1940 – March 29, 2001 (tombstone with photo) [St. James United Cemetery]

Washington, Lloyd U. May 27, 1900 – May 3, 1993 (on same tombstone with Lulu J. Washington) [Berkley Memorial Cemetery]

Washington, Lulu J. January 16, 1917 -   (on same tombstone with Lloyd U. Washington) [Berkley Memorial Cemetery]

Washington, Maria December 10, 1839 – October 26, 1919 (no tombstone; death certificate stated she was the daughter of Isaac Washington and Annie M. Smith, all born in Maryland; she was a widow who lived at Level; informant was Howard Washington, of Havre de Grace) [Green Spring U. M. Church Cemetery]

Washington, Mary E. May 28, 1924 – May 28, 1924 (no tombstone; death certificate stated she was a premature birth and lived 2 hours; her parents were Roy Washington and Helen Thomas, and both were born in Maryland and lived near Aberdeen; informant was her father) [Asbury Cemetery]

Washington, Maud (adopted name) September 15, 1911 – March 15, 1912 (no tombstone; death certificate stated she was the daughter of Cecelia Anderson who did not know the father's name; they were both born in Maryland and Maud died in Abingdon; informant was her mother, of Belcamp) [John Wesley U. M. E. Church Cemetery in Abingdon]

Washington, McKinley December 12, 1908 – December 8, 1995 [Clark's U. M. Church Cemetery]

Washington, Michael D. (Rev.) "Beloved Son and Brother" February 10, 1964 – October 20, 2012 (inscribed "ΑΦΑ"; obituary in *The Aegis* on October 24, 2012 stated Reverend Michael Darnell Washington, formerly of Forest Hill, died at his home in Hartly, DE and was the son of the late Walter and Gladys Fisher; he earned his Master's of Divinity degree in 1998 and was pastor of Emmanuel AME Church in Hartly, DE at the time of his death; "he leaves to cherish his memory" his second mother Mary B. Berry and other family) [Chestnut Grove A. M. E. Church Cemetery, formerly LaGrange Cemetery at Rocks]

Washington, Rachael E., wife of Hampton, died May 6, 1899, aged 69 years, 2 months and 3 days [Berkley Memorial Cemetery]

Washington, Raymond Thomas October 4, 1932 – March 10, 1933 (no tombstone; death certificate stated he was the son of Roy McKinley Washington and Mary Helen Thomas, all born in Maryland, and lived at Harford Furnace; informant was his father) [John Wesley U. M. E. Church Cemetery in Abingdon]

Washington, Sam H. Jr. March 25, 1925 – August 8, 1998 (tombstone; obituary in *The Aegis* on August 12, 1998 stated Sam Houston Washington, Sr. was born in Uniontown, AL, the son of Benjamin and Melnie Washington, and served in the Army during World War II; he worked as a fitness instructor for the government and was the first minority to be a police officer in Aberdeen; he lived in Abingdon and died at Fallston General Hospital, survived by his wife Georgia Mae Green Washington, 4 sons, 1 daughter, 2 brothers, 3 sisters, 7 grandchildren and 5 great-grandchildren) [John Wesley U. M. E. Church Cemetery in Abingdon]

Washington, Sedonia T. August 10, 1893 – June 2, 1915 (no tombstone; death certificate stated she was the married daughter of William C. Christy and Martha R. Johnson, all born near Perryman) [Union U. M. Church Cemetery]

Washington, Tyric 2007-2007 (small metal funeral home marker) [St. James United Cemetery]

Waters (marker contained no other information) [Asbury Cemetery]

Waters, --- "stillborn June 26, 1925, stillborn June 27, 1925" (no tombstone; death certificate inexplicably listed two different dates and stated she was born at Mountain, daughter of Joseph Johnson, born in Fallston, and Evelyn Watters, born in Mountain; she died in Bel Air; informant was Mrs. Harriet Waters, of Mountain) [Mt. Zion U. M. Church Cemetery]

Waters, ---- August 22, 1916 – September 3, 1916, a premature birth, lived 13 days (no tombstone; death certificate stated he died at Dublin and was the son of Walter Waters and Margaret Kenly, all born in Maryland; informant was Walter Waters, of Street RFD) [Clark's U. M. Church Cemetery]

Waters, ---- died June 9, 1904, age 2 days (no tombstone; death certificate stated she was the daughter of Jacob and Nettie Waters, all born in Maryland, and she died at home at Mountain two days after a difficult birth; informant was Dr. Keyser, of Franklinville, MD; place of burial not given [probably Mt. Zion U. M. Church Cemetery]

Waters, Alice V. October 9, 1884 – December 19, 1958 (no tombstone; death certificate stated she was born in Maryland, was widowed, and the daughter of John Waters, mother unknown; she died at home in rural Edgewood; informant was Harry Watters *(sic)*, of Edgewood) [Foster's Hill Cemetery]

Waters, Charles died in his 86th year and was buried on April 22, 1890 (C. W. footstone; no tombstone; *The Aegis* on May 2, 1890 stated he was employed by Col. John Carroll Walsh on his farm *The Mound* near Jerusalem and was "buried at the colored M. E. Church, on the Mountain") [Mt. Zion U. M. Church Cemetery]

Waters, Charles H. January 22, 1933 – December 15, 1986, U.S. Army, Korea (tombstone; obituary in *The Aegis* on December 2, 1986 stated he served in the U.S. Army for two years, was self-employed and lived in Aberdeen; he was survived by his wife Karen Waters, of Baltimore, his mother Mrs. Jeannette Waters, of Bel Air, one sister and three brothers) [Mt. Zion U. M. Church Cemetery]

Waters, Ella M. March 6, 1876 – February 2, 1929 (no tombstone; death certificate stated she was a married housewife and died in Bel Air; her parents were Noah Westcott and Agustus Sprigs; they were all born in Maryland; informant was William Waters, 21 Howard St., Bel Air) [Hendon Hill Cemetery]

Waters, George died June 17, 1857, age 30 [Mt. Zion U. M. Church Cemetery]

Waters, Georgianna March 22, 1925 – January 27, 1926 (no tombstone; death certificate stated she was the daughter of Samuel Waters and Lelia Berry, and they all were born in Maryland and lived at Aberdeen RFD; informant was her father Samuel Waters) [Asbury Cemetery]

Waters, Harriet Henrietta 1852 – August 10, 1934 (no tombstone; death certificate stated Harriet Henrietta Watters was the daughter of James Pinkney and Harriett Richardson, all were born in Maryland; she married John Waters and died a widow in Joppa where she had lived all her life; informant was John Waters, of Joppa; she was buried at "Mountain") [Mt. Zion U. M. Church Cemetery]

Waters, J. Edward April 10, 1842 – March 24, 1925 (no tombstone; death certificate stated he was the son of Dorsey Waters and ---- Jones, all born in Maryland; he was married, worked as a farmer, and died at McCann's Corner; informant was Walter Waters, of Street, MD) [Clark's U. M. Church Cemetery]

Waters, Jacob died September 17, 1975, age 92 (obituary in *The Aegis* stated he was born in Harford County, worked as a farmer and died at Provident Hospital in Baltimore, survived by a niece([name not given) in Philadelphia) [Mt. Zion U. M. Church Cemetery]

Waters, James January 27, 1921 – March 27, 1921, a premature birth, lived 2 months (no tombstone; death certificate stated he died at McCann's Corner and was the son of Walter Waters and Margaret Kenly, all born in Maryland; informant was Walter Waters, of Street, MD) [Clark's U. M. Church Cemetery]]

Waters, Jeannette E. 1909-2002 (her photo on the tombstone that is inscribed "In Loving Memory Mom" and "In God's Care") [Mt. Zion U. M. Church Cemetery]

Waters, John W. May 11, 1851 – December 14, 1927 (no tombstone; death certificate stated he was the son of Abraham Waters and Mary ---- (blank), all born in Harford Co.; he was married, worked as a laborer, died in Joppa and was buried in "Mt. Colored Cem.;" informant was John W. Waters, Jr., of Joppa) [Mt. Zion U. M. Church Cemetery]

Waters, Joseph August 1, 1916 – June 23, 1931 (no tombstone; death certificate stated he was the son of Samuel Waters and Lena Berry, all born in Maryland; he died in the Havre de Grace Hospital; informant was Mrs. Martha Waters, of Aberdeen) [Asbury Cemetery]

Waters, Lena 1893-1927 (tombstone inscription, but death certificate stated "Leila Waters" was born August 6, 1892, daughter of Walker Berry, both born in Maryland, and her mother's name was not known to informant Samuel Watters *(sic)*, of Aberdeen RFD; she died on August 5, 1927 at Havre de Grace Hospital and was married at the time of her death) [Asbury Cemetery]

Waters, Leslie Edward May 1, 1912 – October 6, 1912 (no tombstone; death certificate stated he was born in Harford Co., the son of William Waters, born in Harford Co., and Ella Westcott, born in Maryland, and they lived in Bel Air; informant was Carvel Westcott, of Bel Air) [Hendon Hill Cemetery]

Waters, Lloyd died February 25, 1937, age about 75 (no tombstone; death certificate stated he was born in Maryland, but his parents were unknown to informant Hilin(?) Waters, of Bel Air; he married Mary ----, worked as a laborer, died in Bel Air where he had lived all his life and was buried at "Mountain A.M.E.") [Mt. Zion U. M. Church Cemetery]

Waters, Louisa died January 12, 19— (illegible), age 59 [St. James United Cemetery]

Waters, Lula V., "Mother" August 15, 1902 – November 20, 1984 (tombstone; obituary in *The Aegis* on November 29, 1983 stated she was born in Van Bibber, the daughter of the late Grover Bond and Alice Waters, and lived in Joppa; she died at Lutheran Hospital in Baltimore, survived by a daughter Viola Bray, 3 sisters, 7 grandchildren, and 14 great-grandchildren) [Community Baptist Church Cemetery]

Waters, Priscilla died April 5, 1918 (tombstone; death certificate stated she died April 6, 1918, age not known, but was an adult and buried in "colored cemetery, Havre de Grace") [St. James United Cemetery]

Waters, Ruth Ann died ---- 1875, age ---- (tombstone illegible) [Mt. Zion U. M. Church Cemetery]

Waters, Samuel E. May 8, 1879 – January 26, 1963 [Asbury Cemetery]

Waters, Sarah died November 8, 1899, age 56 (inscribed "In Memory of") [Mt. Zion U. M. Church Cemetery]

Waters, William "Bill" December 11, 1901 – March 22, 1970 (tombstone; obituary in *The Aegis* on March 26, 1970 stated he was the husband of Jeannette Waters, of Bel Air, and died at Harbor View Nursing Home in Baltimore, survived by his wife, a daughter, five sons, one brother, five sisters, and eighteen grandchildren) [Mt. Zion U. M. Church Cemetery]

Waters, William E. "Chick" April 19, 1931 – July 20, 1970 (tombstone; obituary in *The Aegis* stated he was the son of Jeannette Waters and the late William Edward Waters, Sr., and husband of Marion Waters, of Bel Air; he was survived by his wife, daughter, 2 sons, 4 brothers, 1 sister, and 5 aunts) [Mt. Zion U. M. Church Cemetery]

Watkins, James E. June 11, 1905 – September 1, 1931 (copied in 1987, but not found in 2018) [St. James United Cemetery]

Watkins, John A. Jr. March 30, 1939 – January 4, 1990 (wooden marker shaped like a shield) [St. James United Cemetery]

Watson, Patti J. February 14, 1953 – July 1, 2000 (on same tombstone with Mattie V. Peaker) [Mt. Zion U. M. Church Cemetery]

Watters, Beulah Sarah Elizabeth died October 26, 1997, age 71 (no tombstone; obituary and photo in *The Aegis* on October 29, 1997 stated she was born in Joppa, the daughter of William Henry Bradley and Eliza Meldonna Peaker, and the widow of John Ellison Watters; she was a member of American Legion Post 55 (no military service mentioned, so probably a member of the Auxiliary) and of Tabernacle-Mt. Zion Church in Joppa; she died at Franklin Square Hospital, survived by 2 sons, 1 daughter, 5 grandchildren and 5 great-grandchildren) [Mt. Zion U. M. Church Cemetery]

Watters, Brenda Elaine, "Loving Daughter of Briley and Catherine Garrison" April 13, 1945 – December 25, 1984 (tombstone; obituary in *The Aegis* on January 3, 1985 stated she was born in Baltimore Co., daughter of the late Briley Oswald Garrison and Catherine Wells, and wife of Richard Orville Watters, Sr., of Joppa; she died at Fallston General Hospital, survived by her husband, a son, 3 sisters and 3 brothers) [Foster's Hill Cemetery]

Watters, Carvel L. died November 9, 1987, age 72 (no tombstone; obituary in *The Aegis* on November 12, 1987 stated he retired from the Osborne's Cleaners, formerly in Bel Air, and died at Citizens Nursing Home in Havre de Grace, survived by his brother Charles, of Joppa) [Asbury Cemetery]

Watters, Charles June 13, 1913 – March 23, 1914 (no tombstone; death certificate stated he was the son of Henry B. Wilson and Alice Watters, all born in Harford Co.; he died in Van Bibber; informant was Alice Watters, of Edgewood) [Mt. Zion U. M. Church Cemetery]

Watters, Claudia E. May 16, 1946 – August 28, 1993 [Tabernacle Mount Zion U. M. Church Cemetery]

Watters, Dorothy May February 7, 1940 – December 25, 1940 (no tombstone; death certificate stated she was the daughter of John Bond and Sarah Watters, all born in Harford Co.; informant was her mother Sarah Watters, of Street RFD, where they had lived for the past nine months) [Clark's U. M. Church Cemetery]

Watters, Edith Victoria died November 15, 1970, age 44 (no tombstone; obituary in *The Aegis* on December 10, 1970 state she was the daughter of Victor and Luella Watters; she lived at 4214 Hazel Avenue in Overlea and died at Franklin Square Hospital in Baltimore; she was survived by a sister Mrs. Alice Riley and a brother Charles Watters) [Hendon Hill Cemetery]

Watters, Ella May May 23, 1934 – October 16, 1934 (no tombstone; death certificate stated she was born in Bel Air and died at Rocks; her parents were Charles Watters, born in Bel Air, and Louise Davis, born in Virginia; informant was Charles Watters, of Rocks; Kurtz Funeral Home Records stated she died at Tattle Farm at Rocks; informant was her father) [Hendon Hill Cemetery]

Watters, Emma A. 1922-1969 (on same tombstone with Emma Akins and Mary V. Akins when copied in 1987, but not found in 2018) [Clark's U. M. Church Cemetery]

Watters, Ethel died February 17, 1923, age about 3 years (no tombstone; death certificate stated she was the daughter of Annie Watters, both born in Maryland, but the name of her father was unknown to informant C. Sheridan, of Bel Air; she died in a house fire in Fallston) [Tabernacle Mount Zion U. M. Church Cemetery]

Watters, Eva died July 24, 1969, age 74 (no tombstone; obituary in *The Aegis* on July 31, 1969 state she lived at Street and died at the Elkton Hospital, survived by two sisters, Sarah Barnes and Agnes Speight, and one brother Marvin Webster) [Cedars Chapel Cemetery]

Watters, Fletcher 1906-1983 (copied in 1987, but not found in 2018) [Mt. Zion U. M. Church Cemetery]

Watters, Harold died February 17, 1923, age 14 months (no tombstone; death certificate stated he was the daughter of Annie Watters, both born in Maryland, but the name of her father was unknown to informant C. Sheridan, of Bel Air; she died in a house fire in Fallston) [Tabernacle Mount Zion U. M. Church Cemetery]

Watters, Harry P. March 3, 1900 – January 28, 1964 [John Wesley U. M. E. Church Cemetery in Abingdon]

Watters, Hazel V. died March 5, 1907, age 2 years, 6 months (no tombstone; death certificate stated she was the daughter of William H. Watters and Ella Westcott, all born in Harford Co.; she died at Bynum and"Hendon Hill was written on the back of death certificate) [Hendon Hill Cemetery]

Watters, Ida Virginia January 7, 1913 – February 14, 1924 (no tombstone; death certificate stated she was the daughter of John W. Watters, Jr. and Annie E. Bailey, all born in Harford Co.; she was buried in "The Mountain Colored Cemetery;" informant was her father, of The Mountain near Joppa) [Mt. Zion U. M. Church Cemetery]

Watters, Irene M. February 14, 1911 – December 17, 1970 (tombstone; obituary in *The Aegis* stated Irene Margaret Watters, of Singer Road, Abingdon, died suddenly at home, survived by two daughters, one brother, Joseph Preston, of Baltimore, and four grandchildren) [John Wesley U. M. E. Church Cemetery in Abingdon]

Watters, James Edward died March 9, 1999, age 75 (obituary in *The Aegis* on March 12, 1999 stated he was the son of Samuel Watters and Lea Berry and lived in Havre de Grace with wife Constance A. Stansbury Watters; he worked as a mechanic for Wilson Motors, later Ken's Kar Klinic. and died at Harford Memorial Hospital, survived by his wife, 2 sons, 7 grandchildren, 2 brothers and 4 sisters) [Union U. M. Church Cemetery]

Watters, James H. 1942-1998 ("Lived Life to the Fullest") [Tabernacle Mount Zion U. M. Church Cemetery]

Watters, James S. died March 30, 1912, age unknown, but about 45 years (no tombstone; death certificate spelled his last name "Waters" and stated he was the son of William Henry Waters and Julia Goings, all born in Harford Co.; he was married, worked as a day laborer and farm hand, and died in Fallston; informant was "W. Henry Waters, his X mark, second father") [Tabernacle Mount Zion U. M. Church Cemetery]

Watters, John C. February 14, 1840 – October 18, 1918 (no tombstone; death certificate stated he was the son of John Watters and Harriett Bond, all born in Maryland; he worked as a laborer and was a widower who died in Abingdon; informant was Alice Watters, of Abingdon) [Mt. Zion U. M. Church Cemetery]

Watters, John Ellison April 20, 1911 – January 13, 1988, U.S. Army, World War II (tombstone; obituary in *The Aegis* on January 21, 1988 stated he was born in Joppa, the son of the late Wesley Watters and Annie Bailey, and married Beulah Bradley; he served in the U.S. Army during World War II and retired from Edgewood Arsenal in 1963 as a supervisor in the custodial department; he died January 14 *(sic)*, 1988, age 76, and was survived by his wife, two sons, 1 daughter, 4 grandchildren and 3 great-grandchildren) [Mt. Zion U. M. Church Cemetery]

Watters, John W. May 18, 1909 – June 1, 1933 (no tombstone; death certificate stated he was born in Bel Air, worked as a day laborer and his wife was Mildred Watters; his parents were William H. Watters and Ella W. Westcott, born in Harford Co.; informant was Mr. Pearl Watters) [Hendon Hill Cemetery]

Watters, Julia Goings December 20, 1840 – May 22, 1909 (no tombstone; death certificate stated Julia Goings Waters *(sic)* was born on Gunpowder Neck, daughter of Isaac Goings, mother unknown; she married Henry Waters, lived in Fallston, and died on May 22, 1909, age 68 years, 5 months, 2 days; informant was her husband Henry Waters; place of burial not indicated [probably Tabernacle Cemetery or Hendon Hill Cemetery]

Watters, Louise died February 17, 1923, age about 4 months (no tombstone; death certificate stated she was the daughter of Annie Watters, both born in Maryland, but the name of her father was unknown to informant C. Sheridan, of Bel Air; she died in a house fire in Fallston) [Tabernacle Mount Zion U. M. Church Cemetery]

Watters, Mabel E. died March 23, 2006, age 69 (no tombstone; obituary in *The Aegis* on March 29, 2006 stated she was born in Riverhead, NY, the daughter of Mabel Elizabeth Parrish Brown, of Joppa, and the late John Melvin Brown; she died at the Upper Chesapeake Medical Center in Bel Air, survived by her husband of 53 years, Charles W. Watters, Jr., 3 sons, 3 daughters, 3 brothers, 2 sisters. 14 grandchildren and 19 great-grandchildren) [Community Baptist Church Cemetery]

Watters, Mable I., "Mother" April 1, 1919 – October 13, 1967 [Community Baptist Church Cemetery]

Watters, Marion Henrietta died November 26, 1996, age 87 (no tombstone; obituary in *The Aegis* on December 4, 1996 stated she was born in Abingdon, the daughter of the late Grover Watters and Alice Bond, and had worked as a salad girl at the Edgewood Diner; she died at Union Hospital in Elkton, survived by a son William Edward Watters, a daughter Thelma Elizabeth Coleman, a sister Mary R. Norton, 6 grandchildren and 8 great-grandchildren) [Community Baptist Church Cemetery]

Watters, Martha September 18, 1912 – August 10, 1950 (copied in 1987, but not found in 2018, most likely one of those that was toppled over; death certificate stated Martha L. Watters was born in Maryland, the daughter of Sam Watters and Leila Baeir; she was single, did house work, lived at Aberdeen RFD #1 and died August 11, 1950 at Harford Memorial Hospital; informant was Samuel Watters at same address) [Asbury Cemetery]

Watters, Mary E. August 6, 1864 – April 29, 1932 (no tombstone; death certificate stated she was the daughter of Henry Peca and Lydia Dorsey, all born in Harford Co.; she was married, died at home near Bel Air and was buried in "Mountain Colored Cemetery;" informant was Ida Spencer, of 1009 Harlan Ave., Baltimore) [Mt. Zion U. M. Church Cemetery]

Watters, Milton Charles died December 1, 1971, age 59 (no tombstone; obituary in *The Aegis* stated he was the son of the late Samuel Edward Watters and Lena Berry, and the husband of Mary E. Allender, of 401 Webb Lane, Havre de Grace; he was born in Harford Co., associated for years with the F. O. Mitchell & Bro. Co. in Perryman and died at the Harford Memorial Hospital, survived by his wife, one son, two daughters, four brothers and four sisters) [Asbury Cemetery]

Watters, Otho M. September 1, 1907 – November 5, 1981, U.S. Army, World War II (tombstone; obituary in *The Aegis* on November 10, 1981 stated he was born in Bel Air, the son of the late Ella and William Watters; after serving in the Army he worked for General Motors in Detroit until three months ago when he relocated to Joppa and died at Perry Point VA Hospital, survived by a sister Mable Tittle and brothers Richard, Charles and Carvel Watters) [Asbury Cemetery]

Watters, Pearl April 19, 1894 – June 24, 1964, Maryland, Pvt., 2nd Co., 154 Depot Brigade, World War I [Asbury Cemetery]

Watters, Richard Orville Sr. died December 1, 1988, age 45 (obituary in *The Aegis* on December 8, 1988 stated he was born in Havre de Grace, the son of John Ellison Watters, Sr. and Beulah Bradley; he was formerly employed by the Paper Dry Wall Co. in Emmorton and died at Park Manor Nursing Home in Baltimore; wife was not mentioned but he was survived by his mother, a son Richard A. Watters, one brother John W. Watters and one sister Elsie M. Allen) [Mt. Zion U. M. Church Cemetery]

Watters, Robert A. October 17, 1931 – June 2, 1968 (tombstone and another marker at foot of grave inscribed "Robert Watters, 1930-1968, Wife & C. M. C.") [John Wesley U. M. E. Church Cemetery in Abingdon]

Watters, Stella Lodlow December 19, 1894 – April 14, 1924 (no tombstone; death certificate stated she was the daughter of Daniel Johnson and Mary E. Johnson, all born in Maryland, and she was married and lived in Churchville; informant was William E. Johnson, of Bel Air RFD) [Asbury Cemetery]

Watters, Victor E. May 19, 1896 – March 4, 1981, PFC, U.S. Army, World War I (tombstone; obituary in *The Aegis* on March 12, 1981 stated he lived on Hazel Ave. in Overlea (Baltimore County), retired from Edgewood Arsenal, and was the husband of the late Luella Watters; his military records stated Victor Ellsworth Watters was born in Bel Air where he was inducted into the service on August 23, 1918, served in the 154th Dep. Brig. and Hq. Co. 811 Pion. Inf., was overseas from October 20, 1918 to July 23, 1919, and was honorably discharged on July 29, 1919) [Asbury Cemetery]

Watters, Walter June 10, 1869 – December 11, 1939 (no tombstone; death certificate stated he was the son of Edward and Mary Watters, all born in Harford Co.; he married Margaret ----, worked as a road laborer until November 1937, and died at home near Dublin; informant was his widow, Mrs. Walter Watters, of Street RFD) [Clark's U. M. Church Cemetery]

Watters, William H. May 3, 1883 – September 26, 1934 (no tombstone; death certificate stated he was born in Harford Co., worked as a farmer at Rocks and was the widower of Ella Watters; his parents were Joshua Watters and Lettie Peters, both born in Harford Co.; informant was Mrs. Mable Tittle, of Rocks) [Hendon Hill Cemetery]

Watts, Mary June 15, 1857 – March 19, 1925 (no tombstone; death certificate stated she was the daughter of Henry Saunders and Margaret Washington, all born in Maryland; she died a widow at Aberdeen RFD; informant was Rev. S. N. Saunders, of Aberdeen RFD)

Waxwood, Judia died June 19, 1920, age about 90 (no tombstone; death certificate stated she was the daughter of Jane Ash, both born in Maryland, but her father's name was not known to informant Charles Waxwood, of Havre de Grace; she was a widow and died at Level) [Green Spring U. M. Church Cemetery]

Wayman, Christy 1883-1936 [St. James United Cemetery]

Weaver, Albert J. 1930-2008 (small metal funeral home marker) [St. James United Cemetery]

Weaver, Mathew died March 22, 1913, age about 40 (no tombstone; death certificate stated he was born in Virginia and worked as a laborer near Aberdeen; names and birth places of his parents were not known to informant J. H. Kennedy, of Aberdeen) [Mt. Calvary U. A. M. E. Church Cemetery]

Webb, George July 7, 1878 – April 7, 1939 (no tombstone; death certificate stated he was the son of Russell Webb and Frances Ray, all born in North Carolina) [Union U. M. Church Cemetery]

Webb, Queenie 1933-1977 (copied in 1987, but not found in 2018; obituary in *The Aegis* on February 24, 1977 stated Queen Lou Webb was born on November 12, 1933, daughter of the late George Kinsey Banks and Mary M. Banks, and was the wife of Alison Webb; she lived in Havre de Grace and died in Tennessee, survived by her husband, four sons, two daughters, six sisters, three brothers, three half-sisters, and two grandchildren) [St. James United Cemetery]

Webster or Peck, Matilda died on February 23, 1911, age about 62, "exact age unknown" (no tombstone; death certificate stated she was born in Lancaster Co., PA, and was a "grase widow" who lived and died at Dublin; her parents were not known to the informant Dr. Ephraim Hopkins, of Darlington, who listed her name as "Matilda Webster or Peck" on the death certificate) [Clark's U. M. Church Cemetery]

Webster, ---- stillborn male on December 30, 1923 (no tombstone; death certificate stated he was the son of Winfield Webster and Ruth Gordon, all born in Harford Co. and they lived in Darlington; informant was John Gordon, of Darlington) [Berkley Memorial Cemetery]

Webster, ---- stillborn male on March 3, 1933 (no tombstone; death certificate stated he was born at Cedar, the son of Elmer Johnson and Hazel Webster, both born in Maryland; informant was Rachel Webster, of Street, MD) [Clark's U. M. Church Cemetery]

Webster, Agnes 1918-1979 [St. James United Cemetery]

Webster, Alexander died November 27, 1975, age 84 (no tombstone; obituary in *The Aegis* on December 4,

1975 stated he was the son of Philip and Mary Webster, and husband of the late Mary Awkard Webster, and he died at the Fallston Nursing Home) [Berkley Memorial Cemetery]

Webster, Alfonso 1890-1978, Pvt., U.S. Army, World War I (tombstone; military records state he was born in Perryman on September 19, 1890 and was inducted into the service on June 19, 1918; he served with the 45 Co 154 Dep Brig, was overseas from August 26, 1918 to February 16, 1919 in Meuse-Argonne and Bonhomme Sector and was honorably discharged on February 28, 1919) [Union U. M. Church Cemetery]

Webster, Alice V. August 22, 1942 – January 11, 1999 [John Wesley U. M. E. Church Cemetery in Abingdon]

Webster, Anna L. April 9, 1927 – August 10, 2011 (on same tombstone with John C. Webster inscribed Together Forever") [Berkley Memorial Cemetery]

Webster, Anna M. G. May 13, 1925 – October 27, 1925 (no tombstone; death certificate stated she was the daughter of Marvin Webster and Rachel Hopkins, all born in Maryland and they lived in Poole; informant was her father) [Berkley Memorial Cemetery]

Webster, Annie E. August 2, 1847 – June 4, 1915 (no tombstone; death certificate stated she was the daughter of Bendick Bradford and Jane James, all born in Maryland; she married and died at home in Berkley; informant was John Webster, of Berkley) [Berkley Memorial Cemetery]

Webster, Annie E. December 13, 1910 – November 26, 1922 (death certificate stated Annie M. Webster (name should have been written as Annie E. Webster) was the daughter of Carroll M. Webster and Annie James, all born in Maryland, and she was a school girl in Berkley; informant was Carroll M. James (name should have been written as Carroll M. Webster), of Berkley; the name of Annie E. Webster was inscribed, but without dates, at the bottom of the tombstone of Carroll M. Webster) [Berkley Memorial Cemetery]

Webster, Annie E., "Mother" February 1, 1888 – May 28, 1981 [Berkley Memorial Cemetery]

Webster, Annie R. February 20, 1918 – November 29, 1918 (no tombstone; death certificate stated she was the daughter of James Webster and Frances Monk, all born in Maryland) [Union U. M. Church Cemetery]

Webster, Anthony E. 1956-2018 (small metal funeral home marker) [Berkley Memorial Cemetery]

Webster, Arnold A. October 8, 1900 – October 11, 1981, Pvt., U.S. Army, World War II [Berkley Memorial Cemetery]

Webster, Beatrice V. 1927-   (on same tombstone with Robert L. Webster) [Berkley Memorial Cemetery]

Webster, Benjamin January 7, 1889 – August 16, 1917 (no tombstone; death certificate stated he was the son of Elisha Webster and Jane Webster, and all were born in Berkley; he was single, worked as a laborer and died at home near Lapidum; informant was his father) [Berkley Memorial Cemetery]

Webster, Bertrum W. July 20, 1920 – April 7, 1967, Maryland, TEC5, 89 Aviation Sq., AAF, World War II [Berkley Memorial Cemetery]

Webster, Carroll Hall 1913-1938 (on same tombstone with Carroll M. Webster) [Berkley Memorial Cemetery]

Webster, Carroll M. 1888-1945 (on same tombstone with Annie Webster and Carroll Hall Webster and also inscribed Annie E., Harry E., Eugene L. and Edward M.; death certificate stated Carroll Webster was born October 1, 1888 and October 27, 1945, the son of Moses C. Webster and Georgia C. Valentine, all born in Harford Co.; he married Annie ----, worked as a crop farmer and died at home in rural Darlington; informant was Mrs. Annie C. Webster) [Berkley Memorial Cemetery]

Webster, Charles died August 27, 1938, age about 79 (no tombstone; death certificate stated he was the son of Thomas Webster and Rachel Smith, all born in Darlington; he married, worked as a laborer in rural Darlington and died a widower at Harford Memorial Hospital; informant was H. S. Bailey, Undertaker, Darlington) [Berkley Memorial Cemetery]

Webster, Charles H. 1893-1930 (on same tombstone with Phillip Webster and Mary W. Webster) [Berkley Memorial Cemetery]

Webster, Clara died February 5, 1907, age 14 years (no tombstone; death certificate stated she was the daughter of Elisha and Jane Webster and she was a school girl who died in Castleton; her place of burial was not indicated, but it was undoubtedly in this cemetery since her father and mother are buried here) [Berkley Memorial Cemetery]

Webster, Daniel L. September 19, 1894 – April 9, 1975, Pvt., U.S. Army, World War I (tombstone inscription, but no military record was found in Maryland; obituary in *The Aegis* on April 17, 1975 stated he was born in Perryman and was a former hotel proprietor in Atlantic City, NJ; he lived at 515 Baltimore St. in Aberdeen and was the husband of the late Rebecca Webster; his parents were Daniel Webster and Mary Williams and he died at Perry Point VAMC, survived by two brothers and a sister) [Union U. M. Church Cemetery]

Webster, Daniel Robert died June 2, 1966, age 77 (obituary in *The Aegis* on June 9, 1966 stated he was the son of Phillip W. Webster and Mary Akins, lived in Street and died at Montebello State Hospital in Baltimore, survived by wife Mary A. Webster and brothers Alexander and Herman) [Berkley Memorial Cemetery]

Webster, Daniel September 25, 1865 – January 3, 1933 (no tombstone; death certificate stated he was the husband of Sadie Webster and the son of George Webster and Eliza Gibson) [Union U. M. Church Cemetery]

Webster, Della April 6, 1865 – February 19, 1951 (no tombstone; death certificate stated she was born in Harford Co., daughter of William Smith and Rachel Corn; she married and died a widow at home in rural Darlington; informant was Edward Dorsey) [Berkley Memorial Cemetery]

Webster, Dora November 18, 1890 – November 6, 1915 (no tombstone; death certificate stated she was the daughter of Moses Webster and Georgia Presberry, all born in Maryland; she married and died in Darlington; informant was Elisha Webster, of Berkley) [Berkley Memorial Cemetery]

Webster, Edward June 6, 1882 – January 13, 1919 (no tombstone; death certificate stated he was the son of Charles H. Webster and Sarah A. Berry, all born in Maryland; he married, worked as a laborer and died at home in Glenville; informant was Logan Webster, of Bel Air) [Berkley Memorial Cemetery]

Webster, Edward M. February 25, 1920 – February 26, 1930 (death certificate stated he was the son of Carroll Webster and Annie James, all born in Maryland; he was a school boy and died at home in Berkley; informant was his father; his name was inscribed, but without dates, at the bottom of the tombstone of Carroll M. Webster) [Berkley Memorial Cemetery]

Webster, Elisha October 10, 1865 – March 16, 1931 (no tombstone; death certificate stated he was the son of William Webster and Annie Prigg, all born in Castleton; he married Janie ----, worked as a farm laborer and died at home in Castleton; informant was his wife Jane Webster) [Berkley Memorial Cemetery]

Webster, Eliza died March 5, 1917, age about 80 (no tombstone; death certificate stated she had died a widow and was the daughter of Thomas Gibson, both born in Harford Co., but the name of her mother was not known to informant Hattie Whims, of Perryman) [Union U. M. Church Cemetery]

Webster, Ernest S. (Rev.) March 30, 1919 – April 17, 1993 [Berkley Memorial Cemetery]

Webster, Ester C. August 3, 1925 – September 16, 1925 (no tombstone; death certificate stated she was the daughter of Stanton Webster and Sarah Aikens (probably meant Syrena Akins), and they all were born in Maryland; informant was Herbert Aikens, of Darlington) [Green Spring U. M. Church Cemetery]

Webster, Eugene Lee August 13, 1926 – August 17, 1926 (death certificate stated he was the son of Carroll Webster and Annie James, all born in Maryland; he died at home in Berkley; the name of Eugene L. Webster was inscribed at the bottom of the tombstone of Carroll M. Webster) [Berkley Memorial Cemetery]

Webster, Geneva A. 1901-1981 (on same tombstone with John H. Webster) [Cedars Chapel Cemetery]

Webster, George died May 14, 1916, age about 48 (no tombstone; death certificate stated he was single and the son of George Webster and Eliza Gibson, all born in Harford County; he was shot and killed in Havre de Grace) [Union U. M. Church Cemetery]

Webster, George W. 1893-1979 [Union U. M. Church Cemetery]

Webster, Gertrude February 11, 1899 – September 28, 1916 (no tombstone; death certificate stated she was the daughter of Elisha Webster and Janie Webster, all born in Maryland; she was single, did general housework and died at home in Berkley; informant was her father) [Berkley Memorial Cemetery]

Webster, Grace Lee, "Beloved Mother" July 11, 1926 – August 9, 1992 (tombstone with a faded photo; James Dorsey Card File, African American Obituaries, that is maintained at the Historical Society of Harford County, has a card with obituary from an unidentified newspaper on August 19, 1992 and another card with obituary and a photo on September 23, 1992, with slightly differing information, stating she was born in West Virginia, grew up in Harford County and worked for many years at Edgewood; she was the daughter of Beulah P. Higgins and the late Clark D. Higgins, and lived in Darlington or Street (both places were mentioned); she died at the home of her mother at Rocks, survived by her husband Earnest Webster, Sr., a daughter, 4 sons, 2 step-daughters, her mother, 2 brothers, 7 sisters, 23 grandchildren and a great-grandson) [Fairview A. M. E. Church Cemetery]

Webster, Harriet (no dates stated when copied in 1987, but not found in 2018) [St. James United Cemetery]

Webster, Harry E. January 12, 1923 – August 22, 1923 (death certificate stated he was the son of Carroll M. Webster and Annie James, all were born in Maryland, and he died at home in Berkley; his name was inscribed at the bottom of the tombstone of Carroll M. Webster) [Berkley Memorial Cemetery]

Webster, Henry premature birth on September 24, 1928 (no tombstone; death certificate stated he was the son of Stanton Webster and Syrena Akins, of Darlington, all born in Harford Co.) [Green Spring U. M. Church Cemetery]

Webster, Homer December 27, 1921 – February 23, 1923 (no tombstone; death certificate stated he was the son of Homer Caldwell and Emma Webster, of Havre de Grace) [St. James United Cemetery]

Webster, Howard August 28, 1929 – September 22, 2006 (on same tombstone with Samuel S. Webster and Winifred H. Webster and inscribed "In Loving Memory") [Berkley Memorial Cemetery]

Webster, I. Della (inscribed "In Loving Memory of Mother Who Passed Away February 19, 1951" and "Peaceful Rest" and "Daughter Viola and Great Grandson Frederick") [Berkley Memorial Cemetery]

Webster, Jacob W. 1855-1921 [Union U. M. Church Cemetery]

Webster, James E. 1853-1921 [Union U. M. Church Cemetery]

Webster, James E. September 5, 1957 – December 16, 1995, SFC, U.S. Army (tombstone; James Dorsey Card File, African American Obituaries, maintained at the Historical Society of Harford County, has a card with obituary from an unidentified newspaper on December 20, 1995 stating James Ernest Webster was born in Havre de Grace, the son of Ernest Stanton Webster, of Darlington, and Freda Lorraine Dorsey Barnes, of Edgewood; he was the manager for Wal-Mart in Abingdon and retired from the Maryland National Guard in Towson; he lived in Edgewood and died at Fallston General Hospital, survived by his parents, a son, two brothers and two sisters) [John Wesley U. M. E. Church Cemetery in Abingdon]

Webster, James Z. 1891-1964 (on same tombstone with Rosia Mary Webster) [Union U. M. Church Cemetery]

Webster, Jane – see Sarah Jane Webster [Berkley Memorial Cemetery]

Webster, Jerome C. November 22, 1952 – November 26, 2003 (inscribed "Forever In Our Hearts") [Berkley Memorial Cemetery]

Webster, John A. 1882-1960 [Berkley Memorial Cemetery]

Webster, John C. August 9, 1927 – February 5, 2014 (on same tombstone with Anna L. Webster inscribed "Together Forever") [Berkley Memorial Cemetery]

Webster, John H. 1905-1996 (on same tombstone with Geneva A. Webster; obituary in *The Aegis* on April 17, 1996 stated John Henry Webster was the son of Ella Poulston and John Henry Barnes and was preceded in death by his wife Geneva Ashton in 1981; he began his Christian training as Cedars Chapel which later became St. James UAME Church of which he was a charter member and served for more than 70 years as trustee, treasurer and past president of the Cemetery Committee; he did construction work on the Conowingo Dam and later at the Lockjoint Pipe Company in Perryman from which he retired, and he then became a professional junk collector; he lived in Darlington and died at Harford Memorial Hospital in Havre de Grace on April 7, 1996, survived by two nephews, one cousin and several great-nieces and great-nephews) [Cedars Chapel Cemetery]

Webster, John R. October 9, 1956 – April 21, 1988 [Mt. Calvary U. A. M. E. Church Cemetery]

Webster, John T. February 10, 1855 – April 10, 1927 (no tombstone; death certificate stated he was the son of George W. Webster and Eliza Gibson, all born in Maryland; died a widower) [Union U. M. Church Cemetery]

Webster, John T. September 9, 1913 – November 24, 1960, Maryland, PFC, QM Det, 1321 SVC Comd Unit, World War II (Pennington Funeral Home records stated he was born in Havre de Grace, the son of David Webster and ---- (mother not named), and married Cora Hawkins; he worked as a laborer at a news stand, lived at 327 Strawberry Alley, died at the Loch Raven Veterans Administration Hospital in Baltimore, and was buried at "Gravely Hill" near Havre de Grace; informant was Cora H. Webster) [Gravel Hill Cemetery]

Webster, Joni (owner of a lot in section 6 some time after 1951) [Mt. Calvary U. A. M. E. Church Cemetery]

Webster, Lloyd B. February 28, 1910 – March 7, 1968, New Jersey, Pvt., 1866 Eng. Avn. Bn., World War II [Berkley Memorial Cemetery]

Webster, Logan A. December 1, 1884 – October 11, 1919 (no tombstone; death certificate stated he was the son of Charles H. Webster and Sarah Berry, all born in Maryland; he married, worked as a laborer and died at home in Bel Air; informant was Della J.Webster, of Bel Air) [Berkley Memorial Cemetery]

Webster, Mabel P. July 23, 1876 – October 25, 1948 (no tombstone; death certificate stated she was the daughter of Robert Presberry and Jane Howard, all born in Harford Co.; she married Joseph Webster and died a widow in Darlington; informant was Mrs. Irene Stump) [Berkley Memorial Cemetery]

Webster, Martha L., "Mother" 1876-1956 [St. James United Cemetery]

Webster, Marvin E. 1898-1978 (on same tombstone with Rachel Webster; obituary in *The Aegis* on February 23, 1978 stated Marvin Elwood Webster, of near Darlington, died February 14, 1978 at Harford Memorial Hospital in Havre de Grace; he was born at Cedars, the son of Walter Watters and Ella Webster Poulston, and married Rachel Ann Hopkins; he was a Trustee of Hosanna AME Church and Vice-President of the Berkley Cemetery Committee; he was survived by his wife of 59 years, 3 sons, a step-daughter, a brother, 2 half-sisters, 24 grandchildren, 33 great-grandchildren and a great-great-granddaughter) [Berkley Memorial Cemetery]

Webster, Mary died March 1, 1901, age 29 (no tombstone; death certificate stated she was the daughter of Charles Williams and Frances Stansbury, and the wife of Daniel Webster; she worked as a cook and died at Michaelsville, leaving a husband and eight children; place of burial was not indicated, but probably in the Old Union Chapel Cemetery at Michaelsville; possibly reinterred in Union Chapel Cemetery near Aberdeen) [Union U. M. Church Cemetery]

Webster, Mary J. August 10, 1858 – July 28, 1923 (no tombstone; death certificate stated she was the daughter of William Kenly and Mary Aikens, all born in Maryland; she was a widow who lived and diedn in Darlington; informant was Olevia McLain, of Street, MD) [Cedars Chapel Cemetery]

Webster, Mary L. 1917-2008 (small metal funeral home marker) [Berkley Memorial Cemetery]

Webster, Mary W. 1868-   (on same tombstone with Charles H. Webster and Phillip Webster) [Berkley Memorial Cemetery]

Webster, Phillip 1838-1915 (on same tombstone with Charles H. Webster and Mary W. Webster; death certificate stated he was born in Maryland on May 2, 1879 and died on May 22, 1915, the son of Moses Webster, also born in Maryland, but his mother's name and place of birth were not known to informant, Mary Webster, of Havre de Grace; he was married, worked as a laborer and died in Darlington) [Berkley Memorial Cemetery]

Webster, Rachel 1898-   (on same tombstone with Marvin E. Webster) [Berkley Memorial Cemetery]

Webster, Ralph September 14, 1914 – November 13, 1915 (no tombstone; death certificate stated he was the son of Benjamin Webster and Dora Webster, all born in Maryland; he died at home in Berkley; informant was Elisha Webster) [Berkley Memorial Cemetery]

Webster, Robert June 1, 1895 – June 6, 1915 (no tombstone; death certificate stated he was the son of Daniel Webster and Mamie Williams, all born in Harford Co.) [Union U. M. Church Cemetery]

Webster, Robert F. October 29, 1942 – February 15, 1975, AO3, U.S. Navy [Berkley Memorial Cemetery]

Webster, Robert L. 1923-1999 (on same tombstone with Beatrice V. Webster inscribed "Together Forever") [Berkley Memorial Cemetery]

Webster, Rosia Mary 1913-1991 (on same tombstone with James Z. Webster; James Dorsey Card File, African American Obituaries, that is maintained at the Historical Society of Harford County, has a card with obituary from an unidentified newspaper on May 8, 1991 stating she was a native of Perryman, the daughter of Raymond Buchanan and Ada Brown; her husband Albert C. Webster died in 1983; she worked for a commercial laundry business at Aberdeen Proving Ground; she lived in Aberdeen and died at Franklin Square Hospital, survived by 3 sons, 1 daughter, 2 sisters. 19 grandchildren, and 23 great-grandchildren) [Union U. M. Church Cemetery]

Webster, Sabina died February 11, 1913, age 85 (no tombstone; death certificate stated she was born in Maryland, but the names of her parents and their places of birth were not known to informant Moses Webster, of Castleton; she died a widow in Castleton) [Berkley Memorial Cemetery]

Webster, Samuel S. July 10, 1950 – July 3, 2002 (on same tombstone with Winifred H. Webster and Howard Webster and inscribed "In Loving Memory") [Berkley Memorial Cemetery]

Webster, Sarah A. December 19, 1860 – April 7, 1935 (no tombstone; death certificate stated she was the daughter of Alexander Berry and Ann Peaco, all were born in Harford Co.; she married Charles Webster and died at home in Darlington; informant was Charles A. Webster) [Berkley Memorial Cemetery]

Webster, Sarah Jane March 10, 1872 – May 16, 1941 (no tombstone; death certificate stated she was the daughter of Abraham Webster and Mary Prigg, all were born in Harford Co.; she married Elisha Webster and died a widow in Darlington; informant was Marcus Webster) [Berkley Memorial Cemetery]

Webster, Serinna C., "Mother" October 29, 1904 – January 7, 1990 [Berkley Memorial Cemetery]

Webster, Stanton June 30, 1896 – June 12, 1949 (no tombstone; death certificate stated he was born in Harford Co., son of Annie Webster; his father was not known to informant Mrs. Stanton Webster; at the time of his death he was a farm laborer in Darlington where he was struck by a car on Route 1; he died at Harford Memorial Hospital; World War I registration card in 1917 stated Edward Wilson was his father and at that time "Staunton" was employed at Joseph Good's store in Havre de Grace) [Green Spring U. M. Church Cemetery]

Webster, Susan B. January 12, 1916 – October 4, 1916 (no tombstone; death certificate stated she was the daughter of David Webster and Martha Bond, all born in Maryland and lived in Havre de Grace; informant was Mrs. Martha Webster, of Havre de Grace) [Cedars Chapel Cemetery]

Webster, Timothy Roland, "Loving Son" February 10, 1961 – March 13, 1990 [Berkley Memorial Cemetery]

Webster, Virginia H. 1906-1950 (on same tombstone with Eben P. Hill) [Berkley Memorial Cemetery]

Webster, William died December 14, 1912, age 39 (no tombstone; death certificate stated he was the son of Alfred Webster and Ann James, all born in Maryland; he married, worked as a laborer and died in Darlington; informant was Hannah Webster, of Darlington) [Berkley Memorial Cemetery]

Webster, William died June 8, 1914, age about 85 (no tombstone; death certificate stated he was the son of Moses Webster, both born in Maryland; his mother's name was unknown to informant Elisha Webster, of Berkley; he worked as a laborer and died a widower in Berkley) [Berkley Memorial Cemetery]

Webster, Winfield June 7, 1895 – August 29, 1959, Maryland, Pvt., Co. H., 811 Pioneer Infantry, World War I (tombstone; military records stated he lived at Stafford and was inducted into the service on August 23, 1918, served overseas from October 20, 1918 to July 13, 1919 and was honorably discharged on July 19, 1919) [Berkley Memorial Cemetery]

Webster, Winifred H. November 26, 1923 – September 13, 1959 (on same tombstone with Samuel S. Webster and Howard Webster and inscribed "In Loving Memory") [Berkley Memorial Cemetery]

Weddle, Walter Jr. April 1, 1933 – March 6, 2015, U.S. Army, Vietnam [Mt. Calvary U. A. M. E. Church Cemetery]

Weeks, Bertha Freize May 15, 1873 – March 19, 1941 (no tombstone; death certificate stated she was the daughter of Henry Richardson, born in Oakington, MD, and Mary Richardson born in Virginia; she was the widow of William Weeks and died in Harford Memorial Hospital) [St. James United Cemetery]

Weeks, Harriet Ann March 13, 1855 – August 21, 1942 (no tombstone; death certificate stated she was the daughter of Solomon Haycock, born in Mexico, and Mary Ann Dennison, born in Perryman; she died in Havre de Grace, the widow of George W. Weeks; informant was Mrs. Mamie Holmes) [St. James United Cemetery]

Weeks, William T. January 28, 1880 – June 27, 1939 (no tombstone; death certificate misspelled his name Wiecks; he was the son of George Weeks and Harriett Haycock; his widow was Bertha whose name was spelled Weeks in 1941; informant was Mrs. Hattie Haycock, of Havre de Grace) [St. James United Cemetery]

Weems, Howard October 7, 1870 – January 15, 1935 (no tombstone; death certificate stated he was the son of Charles Weems and Anna Griffin, all born in Maryland, and the husband of Maggie Whims who predeceased him) [Union U. M. Church Cemetery]

Welch, Isaac died April 19, 1907, age 68 (no tombstone; death certificate stated he was the son of Edward Welch and Violet Kell, and was the husband of Susan Welch; he worked as a farm and died at Michaelsville; informant was Susan G. Holland, his niece; place of burial was not indicated, but probably in Old Union Chapel Cemetery at Michaelsville; possibly reinterred later in Union Chapel Cemetery near Aberdeen) [Union U. M. Church Cemetery]

Welch, Joseph E., "Husband" died November 15, 1911, age 40 [Union U. M. Church Cemetery]

Wells, ---- stillborn male on July 27, 1924 (no tombstone; death certificate stated he died at Cedars, the son of Jessie L. Wells and Elinor Hall, all born in Maryland; informant was Jessie L. Wells, of Street, MD) [Clark's U. M. Church Cemetery]

Wells, ---- stillborn male on July 6, 1927 (no tombstone; the death certificate stated he was born and died at Cedars, the son of Leon Wells and Elonora Hall, both born in Maryland; informant was Leon Wells, of Street, MD) [Fairview A. M. E. Church Cemetery]

Wells, ---- stillborn male on June 24, 1922 (no tombstone; death certificate stated he was the son of James E. Wells and Pauline Wallace, all born in Maryland; informant was his father, of Street, MD) [Cedars Chapel Cemetery]

Wells, ---- stillborn male on March 15, 1926 (no tombstone; death certificate stated he died at Poole, the son of Jessie L. Wells and Elinora Hall, all born in Maryland; informant was Jesse L. Wells, of Street, MD) [Clark's U. M. Church Cemetery]

Wells, ---- stillborn male on May 15, 1925 (no tombstone; death certificate stated he died at McCann's Corner, the son of Jessie L. Wells and Martha Hall, all born in Maryland; informant was Leon Wells, of Street, MD) [Clark's U. M. Church Cemetery]

Wells, Anna May May 28, 1932 – October 21, 1932 (no tombstone; death certificate stated she was born at Forest Hill, the daughter of Jesse L. Wells and Irene Thompson, both born in Street; informant was Jesse L. Wells, of Forest Hill) [Clark's U. M. Church Cemetery]

Wells, Carrie April 19, 1931 – May 6, 1931 (no tombstone; death certificate stated she died at Hickory, the daughter of Leon Wells and Marie Thompson, all born in Maryland; informant was Leon Wells, of Forest Hill) [Clark's U. M. Church Cemetery]

Wells, Cassie died November 24, 1884, age 83 ("At Rest") [Gravel Hill Cemetery]

Wells, Charles E. stillborn on November 27, 1939 (no tombstone; death certificate stated he was born and died at Street, the son of Maurice McClain and Edith Wells, both born in Maryland; informant was Mary Webster, of Route 1, Street) [Clark's U. M. Church Cemetery]

Wells, Elonora August 15, 1900 – July 6, 1927 (no tombstone; the death certificate stated she was the daughter of William A. Hall and Louise A. Gover, all born in Maryland; she was married and died in childbirth at Cedars; informant was Leon Wells, of Street, MD) [Fairview A. M. E. Church Cemetery]

Wells, Henrietta 1894-1969 (tombstone adjoins Rev. Isaac Wells with the Wells Family marker in between) [Community Baptist Church Cemetery]

Wells, Henry 1865 – February 21, 1933, age about 58 (no tombstone; death certificate stated he was the son of Carvel Wells and Mary Williams, all born in Maryland; he was married and was a farmer in Dublin; informant was Mrs. Martha Wells, of Street, MD) [Clark's U. M. Church Cemetery]

Wells, Infant stillborn female on January 8, 1922 (no tombstone; death certificate stated she was the daughter of Theodore Wells, born in Kentucky, and Mildred Harvey, born in Delaware) [St. James United Cemetery]

Wells, Isaac (Rev.) 1884-1908 (tombstone adjoins Henrietta Wells with the Wells Family marker in between) [Community Baptist Church Cemetery]

Wells, James E. 1900-1951 [Clark's U. M. Church Cemetery]

Wells, Laura died February 26, 1923, age 58 (tombstone; death certificate stated she was born in 1863 (exact date not given), the daughter of George Wells and Amanda Presco, and all were born in Maryland; he never married and lived and worked as a cook in Churchville; informant was Jane Chambers of Bel Air RFD) [Asbury Cemetery]

Wells, Mae C. 1878-1961 (on the same tombstone with parents John H. and Harriet E. Cromwell and brother G. Ernest Cromwell and sister Elizabeth V. Cromwell) [West Liberty Church Cemetery]

Wells, Malcolm Dennis "Mac" September 12, 1956 – November 4, 2014 (inscribed "I fought a good fight, I have finished my course, I have kept my faith" and also with his image riding on a motorcycle) [Berkley Memorial Cemetery]

Wells, Martha J. March 16, 1864 – February 10, 1927 (no tombstone; death certificate stated she died a widow in Poole, the daughter of Jessie Snowden, both born in Maryland, but the name of her mother was not known to the informant Ernest Wells, of Street, MD) [Clark's U. M. Church Cemetery]

Wells, Pauline H. February 20, 1904 – September 3, 1970 (tombstone; Harkins Funeral Home Records stated she was born in Darlington, daughter of Joseph H. Wallace and Elizabeth Dorsey, and died a widow at Mt. Sinai Nursing Home in Baltimore; informant was her daughter Mrs. Edith Presberry, of Darlington) [Clark's U. M. Church Cemetery]

Welsh, Alice R. died July 27, 1906, age 19 (inscribed "In Memory of" and "Gone but not forgotten. At Rest.") [Asbury Cemetery]

Welsh, Booker Washington August 18, 1916 – March 24, 1997 [Union U. M. Church Cemetery]

Welsh, Daniel K. 1888-1975 [Union U. M. Church Cemetery]

Welsh, John W. March 29, 1866 – June 19, 1951 (no tombstone; death certificate stated he was born in Edgewood, the son of Garrett Welsh and Harriott ? *(sic)*, worked as a fisherman, lived at 618 Concord St., Havre de Grace, and died a widower in Perryman; informant was Mrs. Hattie Christy, of Perryman) [Union U. M. Church Cemetery]

Welsh, Josephine Gordon January 2, 1920 – May 6, 2005 (on same tombstone with Booker Washington Welsh) [Union U. M. Church Cemetery]

Welsh, May P. December 31, 1895 – March 14, 1917 (no tombstone; death certificate stated she was the married daughter of Jacob Johnson and Katy Brown; informant was Robert Welsh, of Edgewood; she died in Perryman and was initially buried in Michaelsville, but later reinterred in Aberdeen [Union U. M. E. Church Cemetery]

Welsh, Minnie February 10, 1880 – September 27, 1938 (no tombstone; death certificate stated she was born in Cecil Co., was the wife of John W. Welsh and the daughter of George Brown, but her mother was unknown; she was buried in "Swan Creek Cemetery") [Union U. M. Church Cemetery]

Welsh, Myrtle Eliza March 21, 1915 – June 3, 1916 (no tombstone; death certificate stated she was the daughter of Robert Welsh and Mary Johnson, all born in Maryland; she died at home in Edgewood and undertaker Howard K. McComas stated she was buried at "Brick Church Magnolia" (probably meant the black church in

Magnolia); informant was Louisa Welsh, of Edgewood) [Foster's Hill Cemetery]

Wescott, Bertha J., "His Wife" 1886-1960 (on same tombstone with Carvel A. Wescott) [Mt. Zion U. M. Church Cemetery]

Wescott, Carvel A. 1890-1962 (on same tombstone with Bertha J. Wescott) [Mt. Zion U. M. Church Cemetery]

Wesley, James, son of Shelton S. Wesley, June 15, 1906 – January 27, 1931 [Asbury Cemetery]

West, Dorothy M. 1930-2017 (small metal funeral home marker) [St. James United Cemetery]

West, Isaiah C. 1926-2016 (small metal funeral home marker) [St. James United Cemetery]

Westcott, Augusta died in late March 1909 (no tombstone; obituary in *The Aegis*, April 2, 1909, stated she was an aged woman who was for many years in the employ of the late Daniel Scott and was "one of the old fashioned servants, who are now so rare, and are fast disappearing") [Hendon Hill Cemetery]

Westzel (?), Irene B., "Mother" 1881-1955 (copied in 1992, but not found in 2018) [Union U. M. Church Cemetery]

Wharton, James stillborn on August 22, 1944 (no tombstone; death certificate stated he was the son of James Wharton and Elsie Ames) [Union U. M. Church Cemetery]

Wheeler, Carol Anne December 1, 1963 -   (on same tombstone with Gregory M. Wheeler and Dale M. Harris) [John Wesley U. M. E. Church Cemetery in Abingdon]

Wheeler, Gregory Michael April 4, 1983 – May 2, 2002 (on same tombstone with Carol Anne Wheeler and Dale M. Harris and under his name is the inscription "Beloved Son") [John Wesley U. M. E. Church Cemetery in Abingdon]

Whims, Frank June 21, 1879 – October 24, 1949 (no tombstone; death certificate stated he was born in Maryland, the son of T. Whims and "unknown" mother; he was single, worked as a day laborer, lived in Havre de Grace and died at Harford Memorial Hospital; informant was Frank Tildon, Sr.) [Union U. M. Church Cemetery]

Whims, Harriet died November 16, 1895 (inscribed "Well Done Good And Faithful Servant") [Union U. M. Church Cemetery]

Whims, Hattie C. October 22, 1861 – July 27, 1930 (no tombstone; death certificate stated she was the daughter of George Webster and Eliza Gibson and she died a widow in Aberdeen; informant was George W. Whims) [Union U. M. Church Cemetery]

Whims, Hetty January 1, 1828 – May 1, 1913 (no tombstone; death certificate stated she was a widow and the daughter of Asbury Sly and Rilla Whims, all born in Maryland) [Union U. M. Church Cemetery]

Whims, Louis died April 18, 1923, age 63 (no tombstone; death certificate stated he was the son of Trilas Whims, and both were born in Harford Co., but his mother was unknown; he was married and informant Mrs. Hattie Whims, of Aberdeen) [Union U. M. Church Cemetery]

Whims, Myrtle D. January 14, 1923 – January 26, 1923 (no tombstone; death certificate stated she was born near Aberdeen, the daughter of George Chase and Edna Whims) [Union U. M. Church Cemetery]

Whims, William October 18, 1919 – October 19, 1919 (no tombstone; death certificate stated he was born and died near Aberdeen, the son of William H. Williams and Edna Whims, both born in Maryland; informant was Aquilla Brown, of Aberdeen) [Mt. Calvary U. A. M. E. Church Cemetery]

White, ---- August 28, 1912 – October 8, 1912, an unnamed female (no tombstone; death certificate stated she died in Poole, the daughter of Edward Hall and Florence White, all born in Maryland; informant was Wesley White, of Darlington) [Clark's U. M. Church Cemetery]

White, ---- stillborn female on December 3, 1919 (no tombstone; death certificate stated she died at Hopewell, the daughter of Wesley White and "Charolloth Gray," both born in Maryland; she died at Hopewell; informant was Wesley White, of Aberdeen) [Clark's U. M. Church Cemetery]

White, ---- stillborn female on October 18, 1916 (no tombstone; death certificate stated she died at Poole and was the illegitimate child of Laura Gretta White who was born in Maryland, but her father's name was not known to the informant Mans(?) Price, of Street, MD) [Clark's U. M. Church Cemetery]

White, ---- stillborn male on December 10, 1921, a 7 month premature birth (no tombstone; death certificate stated he was the son of George Edward White and Irma Catherine Williams, all born in Maryland; informant was her father George Edward White, of Kalmia) [Clark's U. M. Church Cemetery]

White, Annie, wife of William White, August 26, 1855 – March 26, 1915 (no tombstone; death certificate stated Annie E. White was married and employed in washing and ironing in Bel Air and died March 26, 1915, age 58 years and 7 months; her parents were William A. Ruff and Mary C. Barnes, and all were born in Maryland; informant was Mary Matilda Spencer, of Fallston; obituary in *The Aegis*, April 2, 1915, stated she died at her home in Bel Air at age 59) [Hendon Hill Cemetery]

White, Arthur E. June 15, 1913 – October 27, 1913 (no tombstone; death certificate stated he was the son of Ulyse White and Bertie Rice, of Havre de Grace) [St. James United Cemetery]

White, Avon December 20, 1911 – March 10, 1912 (no tombstone; death certificate stated he was the son of Hulus White and Bertie Rice, of Havre de Grace) [St. James United Cemetery]

White, Bertie Wescott died May 8, 1940, age 68 (no tombstone; death certificate stated she was born in Bel Air, date unknown, daughter of William Dorsey, born in Baltimore Co., and Letenore(?) Watters, born at Mountain, Harford Co.; married William White informant was Rev. Arthur Collins, of Dover, DE) [Hendon Hill Cemetery]

White, Calvin D. October 12, 1918, New Jersey, Pvt., 153 Depot Brigade [St. James United Cemetery]

White, Charlotte, "Mother" 1892-1954 (on same tombstone with Wesley White) [Clark's U. M. Church Cemetery]

White, Elijah 1871-1957 [Clark's U. M. Church Cemetery]

White, Eliza died November 21, 1927, age about 86 (no tombstone; death certificate stated she was the widowed daughter of Gideon Bosley, but her mother was unknown to informant Mrs. Alec Whitfield, of Havre de Grace) [St. James United Cemetery]

White, Ella N. April 11, 1898 – January 28, 1986 [Clark's U. M. Church Cemetery

White, Florence E. May 20, 1887 – September 27, 1912 (no tombstone; death certificate stated she was born in Harford Co., the daughter of George White and Emily Poole, both born in Maryland; she was single, a servant, and died at Poole; the informant was Wesley White, of Street, MD) [Clark's U. M. Church Cemetery]

White, Frank 1880-1923 "At Rest" [St. James United Cemetery]

White, George September 14, 1857 – January 12, 1922 (no tombstone; death certificate stated he was born in Maryland, the son of George White, birth place not known, and Maria Barnes, born in Maryland; he was married, worked as a day laborer and died near Aberdeen; the informant was Louisa White, of Aberdeen) [Clark's U. M. Church Cemetery]

White, George W. January 20, 1844 – April 5, 1939 (no tombstone; death certificate stated he was born in Harford Co., the son of William H. White and Julia Johns, both born in Maryland; he married Ida ---- (age 81 in 1939), worked as farm laborer, died at home in Joppa where he had lived all his life and was buried in "Mountain Cem.;" informant was his wife) [Mt. Zion U. M. Church Cemetery]

White, Hamilton H. April 6, 1925 – September 20, 1925(no tombstone; death certificate stated he died at Cedars, the son of Edward White and Erma Williams, all born in Maryland; the informant was Edward White, of Street RFD) [Clark's U. M. Church Cemetery]

White, Hannah E. November 7, 1879 – August 10, 1917 (no tombstone; death certificate stated she was the daughter of Hazzard Harris and Cassie Cox, all born in Maryland; she was married and died at Poole; informant was Elisha White, of Street, MD) [Clark's U. M. Church Cemetery]

White, Isaac Andrew October 24, 1913 – November 5, 1913 (no tombstone; death certificate stated he died at

Poole, the son of Westley White and Charlotte Grey, all born in Maryland; informant was Westley White, of Darlington) [Clark's U. M. Church Cemetery]

White, Laura Gretta January 30, 1901 – October 18, 1916 (no tombstone; death certificate stated she died in child birth at Poole and was the daughter of George White and Emily White, all born in Maryland; informant was Manc(?) Price, of Street RFD) [Clark's U. M. Church Cemetery]

White, Lewis A. died March 20, 1966, age 74 (no tombstone; obituary in *The Aegis* on March 24, 1966 stated he was a retired employee of Edgewood Arsenal, lived in Bel Air and died at University Hospital in Baltimore, survived by his wife, 4 children, 3 stepdaughters, a sister, 18 grandchildren, 4 nieces and a nephew (no names were given for his family members); he was buried in Mountain Memorial Cemetery on Singer Road in Joppa) [Mt. Zion U. M. Church Cemetery]

White, Marie P., "Mother" 1879-1932 (inscribed "At Rest;" death certificate stated she was born March 12, 1882 and died August 27, 1932, the daughter of Emma White, born in Prince George's Co., but the name of her father and his birth place were not known to the informant, her husband, Elisha White, of Street; she died at Dublin) [Clark's U. M. Church Cemetery]

White, Mary A. February 24, 1898 – September 8, 1920 (no tombstone; death certificate stated she was born in Harford Co., the daughter of James E. Brooks and Laura J. Thompson, both born in Maryland; she married and died at Kalmia; informant was Laura J. Brooks, of Bel Air) [Clark's U. M. Church Cemetery]

White, Natalia Moné November 26, 1998 – December 18, 1998 (inscribed on back: "Our Little Angel") [St. James United Cemetery]

White, Ralph W. September 11, 1918 – February 20, 1919 (no tombstone; death certificate stated he was the son of Morris Dorsey and Marie White, all born in Maryland; he died at Dublin and the informant was Marie White, of Street RFD) [Clark's U. M. Church Cemetery]

White, Rosita October 12, 1826 – October 12, 1912 (no tombstone; death certificate stated she was the widowed daughter of John Steward, but her mother was unknown to informant Jessie White, of Havre de Grace) [St. James United Cemetery]

White, Vernon Avery September 29, 1961 – July 29, 2011 [St. James United Cemetery]

White, Wesley, "Father" 1886-1954 (on same tombstone with Charlotte) [Clark's U. M. Church Cemetery]

White, William December 25, 1855 – November 22, 1945 (no tombstone; death certificate stated he was a widower, born in Maryland and had worked as a laborer in Bel Air where he had lived for 60 years; his wife was Bertie W. White, but his parents were unknown to informant, Col. J. L.G. Lee, of Bel Air; obituary in *The Aegis*, November 23, 1945, stated he was employed many years by John L. G. Lee in Bel Air) [Hendon Hill Cemetery]

Whitehead, Sarah C. H. 1935-2010 (small metal funeral home marker) [Berkley Memorial Cemetery]

Whitfield (tombstone with no names and no dates) [St. James United Cemetery]

Whitfield, Baby Girl born and died on October 20, 1964 (no tombstone; Pennington Funeral Home records stated she was the daughter of Eddie T. Warfield and Claudin Williams, of Aberdeen, and died in Harford Memorial Hospital in Havre de Grace) [St. James United Cemetery]

Whitfield, Eddie 1920-1993 (handwritten on a flat cement slab) [St. James United Cemetery]

Whitfield, Loretta March 20, 1870 – August 16, 1933 (no tombstone; death certificate stated she was the daughter of Zachariah Brown and Cassie White, and wife of Alexander Whitfield) [St. James United Cemetery]

Whitfield, Olethia R. 1931-2000 (on same tombstone with Edna F. Cain) [Berkley Memorial Cemetery]

Whitting, Hannah R. August 12, 1894 – October 28, 1957 (no tombstone; Harkins Funeral Home Records stated she was born in Harford Co., the daughter of Elisha Hewitt and Hannah Smith, and she was married, but her husband's name was not given (although records show it was Joseph Whitting); she lived at 111 Lincoln St., York, PA and died at York Hospital; informant was her sister Mrs. Georgia Bason, of 111 Lincoln St., York, PA) [Chestnut Grove A. M. E. Church Cemetery, formerly LaGrange Cemetery at Rocks]

Whitting, Joseph 1882-1958 (small metal funeral home marker stated his middle initial was L., but Harkins Funeral Home Records stated it was C. and he was born August 16, 1882 in Gloucester, VA, the son of Isaac Whitting and Julia Lancaster; he died a widower at Pleasant Acres on April 19, 1958 and informant was Georgia Bason of York, PA) [Chestnut Grove A. M. E. Church Cemetery, formerly LaGrange Cemetery at Rocks]

Whittington, ---- stillborn male on December 31, 1918 (no tombstone; death certificate stated he was the son of James E. Whitington *(sic)* and Ida Gibson, all born in Harford Co.) [Union U. M. Church Cemetery]

Whittington, ---- male died at birth on December 11, 1915 because of a "delonged and difficult birth, breech presentation" (no tombstone; death certificate stated he died at Bel Air and was the son of Thomas Andrew Whittington and Louisa Dorsey, both born in Maryland; informant was Andrew Whittington, of Bel Air) [Clark's U. M. Church Cemetery]

Whittington, Addie Ellen died September 8, 1990, age 76 (obituary in *The Aegis* on September 12, 1990 stated she was a native of Joppa, the daughter of Grover Bond and Mary Smart and widow of John Robert Whittington; she attended McComas Institute and was a member of New Hope Baptist Church in Bel Air; she died at Fallston General Hospital, survived by a daughter, 2 brothers, a sister, 5 grandchildren, 7 great-grandchildren, 3 great-great-grandchildren) [Mt. Zion U. M. Church Cemetery]

Whittington, Agnes V. June 18, 1923 – August 19, 1923 (no tombstone; death certificate stated she was the daughter of James Whittington and Ida Dickson, all born in Maryland; informant was James E. Whittington, of Bel Air) [Asbury Cemetery]

Whittington, Alan G. June 10, 1959 – May 22, 1983 (obituary in *The Aegis* stated he served in the U.S. Army; survived by parents Charles and Frances Whittington, 3 brothers and 4 sisters) [Berkley Memorial Cemetery]

Whittington, Alfred October 28, 1924 – February 3, 1977 (no tombstone; obituary in *The Aegis* on February 10, 1977 stated he was the son of the late James Edward Whittington and Ida Virginia Gibson, and died at Long Island, NY, survived by 2 daughters, 2 sisters and 2 brothers) [Asbury Cemetery]

Whittington, Alfreda J. died May 21, 1987, age 42 (no tombstone; obituary in *The Aegis* on June 4, 1987 stated she was born in Havre de Grace and was the daughter of Charlotte Couplin and Alfred J. Whittington; she was a widow and was survived by her mother and stepfather Harry Couplin, plus 3 sons, 1 daughter, 7 grandchildren, and 1 sister) [Tabernacle Mount Zion U. M. Church Cemetery]

Whittington, Baby 1964 (copied in 1987, but not found in 2018) [Berkley Memorial Cemetery]

Whittington, Betsy J. died May 9, 1918, no age given (no tombstone; death certificate stated she was born in Harford Co., the daughter of Samuel Christy and Margaret Daugherty, both born in Maryland; she worked as a servant and was a widow who died at Kalmia from burns because of an accidental fire; informant was John Christy, of Bel Air) [Clark's U. M. Church Cemetery]

Whittington, Chester M. 1917 – November 29, 1977 (no tombstone; obituary in *The Aegis* on December 8, 1977 stated Chester Monroe "Pete" Whittington was born and died in Bel Air, the son of James Whittington and Ida Gibson; he was employed at the Commercial and Savings Bank of Bel Air, was a member of Ames United Methodist Church and American Legion Post 55; was survived by a brother and two sisters) [Asbury Cemetery]

Whittington, Corrina G. 1911-2002 (tombstone only has her year of birth inscribed; obituary in *The Aegis* on December 11, 2001 stated she died on December 6, 2002, age 91, at Mariner Health in Bel Air; she was born in Poole, the daughter of Lewis Gwynn and Carrie Elsie Bell, and widow of James Alfred Whittington; she was secretary and chaplain of Clark's United Methodist Church for many years and served on the usher board for more than 50 years; she was survived by 2 sons, 6 grandchildren, 7 great-grandchildren, and 3 great-great-grandchildren; obituary noted that "She was truly a child of God.") [Clark's U. M. Church Cemetery]

Whittington, Dorothy S. died December 16, 1979, age 68 (obituary in *The Aegis* on January 3, 1980 stated she was the daughter of Samuel and Mary Snowden and the wife of Glasco Whittington; she lived in Darlington, died at Fallston General Hospital and was survived by her husband, 3 sons, 2 daughters, 14 grandchildren, 13 great-grandchildren, 1 brother and 3 sisters) [Berkley Memorial Cemetery]

Whittington, Elizabeth J. 1911-1989 (on same tombstone with Lawrence M. Whittington; obituary in *The*

Aegis in 1989 stated she died on June 22, 1989, age 77, at Fallston General Hospital; she was the daughter of Samuel Ridgley Johnson and Blanche Ruff, and the wife of Lawrence M. Whittington to whom she had been married for 54 years; she was financial secretary for Clark's United Methodist Church and treasurer of the United Methodist Women; James Dorsey Card File, African American Obituaries, that is maintained at the Historical Society of Harford County, has a card from the Howard K. McComas III Funeral Home stating she was born on November 19, 1911 and died on June 22, 1989) [Clark's U. M. Church Cemetery]

Whittington, Ella Jane January 13, 1869 – May 28, 1931 (no tombstone; death certificate initially stated she was born January 13, 1869, the daughter of Robert Tasker and Sarah J. Young, all born in Maryland; she was a widow who died near Bel Air and the informant was Andrew Whittington, of Bel Air; James Dorsey Card File, African American Obituaries, that is maintained at the Historical Society of Harford County, has a card with her obituary abstraction from an unidentified newspaper stating Ella Whittington was aged 69 years, lived in Bel Air, was the widow of Alfred Whittington and was survived by ten children) [Clark's U. M. Church Cemetery]

Whittington, Glasco died November 12, 1992, age 87 (obituary in *The Aegis* on November 18, 1992 stated he was a Harford County native and son of James and Ida Whittington; he married (wife's name not given in obituary), lived in Aberdeen and died at Harford Memorial Hospital in Havre de Grace, survived by 3 sons, 1 daughter, 2 sisters, and many grandchildren, great-grandchildren and great-great-grandchildren, and numerous other relatives) [Berkley Memorial Cemetery]

Whittington, Ida Elizabeth February 7, 1890 – May 6, 1926 (no tombstone; death certificate stated she was the daughter of Samuel Wilson and Elizabeth Banks, all born in Maryland; she was married, lived at Churchville and died in child birth; informant was James Whittington, of Bel Air) [Asbury Cemetery]

Whittington, J. Alfred March 17, 1875 – May 4, 1931 (no tombstone; death certificate initially stated he was born March 17, 1860, but was later changed to 1875; he was the daughter of James E. Whittington and Susan Thomas, all born in Maryland; he was married, worked as a farmer and died in Bel Air; informant was Ella Whittington, of Bel Air) [Clark's U. M. Church Cemetery]

Whittington, James Duglas November 5, 1910 – October 5, 1911 (no tombstone; death certificate stated he was the son of James E. Whittington and Ida Gibson, of Forest Hill, all born in Harford Co.) [Asbury Cemetery]

Whittington, James Glasco June 14, 1957 – June 8, 2005 (obituary and photo in *The Aegis* on June 17, 2005 stated he was born in Darlington, the son of Glasco Whittington and the late Dorothy C. Snowden, and he married Lavoris Inez Smith on July 26, 1982; he served in the Army for 27 years and was later employed by the Harford County Department of Public Works; he lived in Aberdeen and died at Harford Memorial Hospital in Havre de Grace, survived by his wife, 2 daughters, 1 son, 3 grandchildren with one more on the way, 3 godchildren, 1 sister, 1 brother, and a host of aunts, uncles, nieces, nephews and friends; no tombstone; a small metal funeral home marker states "James Whittington, Sr., 1957-2005") [Berkley Memorial Cemetery]

Whittington, James Leon Jr. February 19, 1963 – December 20, 1990 [Clark's U. M. Church Cemetery]

Whittington, John F. June 30, 1883 – May 8, 1942 (no tombstone; death certificate stated he was born in Calvert Co., the son of James Whittington, born in Maryland, but his mother's name was not known to the informant Lawrence Whittington, of Bel Air; John married Ora H. ---- and he lived near Bel Air for 50 years; he was a widower at the time of his death) [Clark's U. M. Church Cemetery]

Whittington, John Robert January 19, 1892 – October 13, 1974 (obituary in *The Aegis* stated he was born in Harford County, the son of Alfred Whittington and Ella Tasco, and was employed by the families of the late Phillip H. Close, of Bel Air, and the late William W. Finney, of Churchville; he lived in Bel Air and died at Johns Hopkins Hospital in Baltimore, survived by his wife Addie, 2 daughters, 2 brothers, 2 sisters, 4 grandchildren, 11 great-grandchildren, and 2 great-great-grandchildren) [Mt. Zion U. M. Church Cemetery]

Whittington, Lawrence M. 1909-2001 (on same tombstone with Elizabeth J. Whittington; obituary and photo in *The Aegis* on August 10, 2001 stated he was born in Bel Air, the son of Alfred Whittington and Ella Cascoe, and husband of the late Elizabeth Johnson Whittington; he worked for 25 years at the old Hub Department Store in Bel Air and also owned a farm on Thomas Run Road; he died on August 4, 2001 at this home in Bel Air, survived by two daughters) [Clark's U. M. Church Cemetery]

Whittington, Lee December 25, 1922 – July 12, 1933 (no tombstone; death certificate stated he was the son of Andrew Whittington and Louisa Dorsey, all were born in Maryland; he lived at Bel Air RFD, sustained severe burns from a kitchen fire and died at Havre de Grace Hospital; the informant was his father Andrew Whittington, of Bel Air) [Clark's U. M. Church Cemetery]

Whittington, Mary Ada February 8, 1916 – February 10, 1920 (no tombstone; death certificate stated she was the daughter of James Whittington and Ida Gibson, all born in Harford Co., and lived near Churchville; informant was James E. Whittington, of Aberdeen) [Asbury Cemetery]

Whittington, Mary Cornelia died February 6, 19--, age 56 (year missing from *The Aegis* obituary clippings, but it was after 1992; she was the daughter of Glasco and the late Dorothy S. Whittington and lived in Aberdeen, died at Harford Memorial Hospital and was survived by her father, 6 children, 6 grandchildren, 3 brothers, 1 sister, and many nieces, nephews and cousins) [Berkley Memorial Cemetery]

Whittington, Ora H. December 25, 1872 – September 12, 1934 (no tombstone; death certificate stated she was the daughter of Robert Tasker and Sarah J. Young, all born in Calvert Co.; she married John F. Whittington and died in Bel Air; informant was Andrew Whittington, of Bel Air) [Clark's U. M. Church Cemetery]

Whittington, Phillip M. Jr. died March 8, 2014, age 38 (funeral notice and photo in *The Aegis* on March 12, 2014 stated he died at home in Edgewood, but it gave no family information; no tombstone; a small metal funeral home marker states "Phillip Whittington Jr., 1974-2014") [Berkley Memorial Cemetery]

Whittington, Robert L. August 2, 1920 – August 19, 1972, Maryland, Cpl., 166 Fort Co., TC, World War II (tombstone; obituary in *The Aegis*, August 24, 1972, stated Robert Whittington, Jr. died at Fort Howard VA Hospital (Baltimore Co.) and was the son of Robert Whittington, who survived him, and the late Sarah Whittington, of Bel Air) [Hendon Hill Cemetery]

Whittington, Robert Roy Jr. July 10, 1921 – September 12, 1921 (no tombstone; death certificate stated he was the son of Robert Whittington and Sallie Wilson, all were born in Maryland; the informant was his father Robert Whittington, of Bel Air) [Clark's U. M. Church Cemetery]

Whittington, Rosie 1903-1989 [Clark's U. M. Church Cemetery]

Whittington, Sarah Jane May 6, 1926 – May 8, 1926 (no tombstone; death certificate stated she was premature and lived 2 days; she was the daughter of James and Ida V. Whittington, of Churchville; informant was James Whittington, of Churchville) [Asbury Cemetery]

Whittington, Thomas A. 1889-1985 (Masonic symbol) (on same tombstone with Veola H. Whittington; obituary in *The Aegis* on September 5, 1985 stated Thomas Andrew Whittington, of Bel Air, died on August 30, 1985 at Fallston General Hospital; he worked for Ed Wheeler's Lumber Yard for 39 years and was married to Veola Hopewell for 49 years; he was a 32nd degree Mason, served as the second president of Harford County's Colored P.T.A., and directed the choir at the Ames United Methodist Church; he followed the sports teams of Central Consolidated High School where he was called an unofficial mascot; also, another source, a church memorial service, stated he was the son of Alfred and Ella Whittington) [Clark's U. M. Church Cemetery]

Whittington, Thomas A. Jr., "Beloved Husband and Father" July 11, 1919 – May 21, 1993 (tombstone; obituary in *The Aegis* on May 26, 1993 stated Thomas Andrew Whittington, Jr., of Bel Air, died at Fallston General Hospital; he was the son of Thomas A. Whittington, Sr. and Louise Dorsey and was married to Beatrice Marie ---- for 46 years; he served in World War II, was a 32nd degree Mason, and retired from the Oscar Mayer Co. in Philadelphia; he was survived by his wife, son Coulbourn L. Whittington, four grandchildren and a great-grandchild) [Clark's U. M. Church Cemetery]

Whittington, Veola H. 1898-1986 (on same tombstone with Thomas A. Whittington; obituary in *The Aegis* on May 15, 1986 stated she was born in Washington Co., MD, daughter of George and Laura Hopewell, and died on May 6, 1986 in Bel Air, widow of T. Andrew Whittington; she was a teacher and a member of Ames United Methodist Church for 50 years; a church memorial service stated she was born on April 27, 1898, the daughter of Laura and George Henry Hopewell, and came to Harford County in 1926) [Clark's U. M. Church Cemetery]

Whittington Viola died April 30, 1901, age 1 year and 1 month (no tombstone; place of burial was not shown on death certificate (name misspelled Whitington), but she was most likely buried here because her mother and father are; she was born in Maryland and died at Forest Hill, the daughter of Alfred Whittington and Ella Tasker, both born in Calvert Co.; informants were her mother Ella Whittington, and Dr. F. Lee Hughes, of Gibson) [Clark's U. M. Church Cemetery]

Whittington, Wilson Ronald January 30, 1926 – April 10, 1926 (no tombstone; death certificate stated he was born and died in Bel Air, the son of Laura Whittington; father unknown; informant was Cay(?) Taylor) [Hendon Hill Cemetery]

Whye, James M. 1910-1988 [Berkley Memorial Cemetery]

Whyte, Erma K. P. 1904-1983 (on same tombstone with George W. Whyte) [Clark's U. M. Church Cemetery]

Whyte, George E. 1894-1965 (on same tombstone with Erma K. P. Whyte) [Clark's U. M. Church Cemetery]

Wiggins, James Alfred January 26, 1867 – February 12, 1964 (no tombstone; obituary and photo in *The Aegis* on February 20, 1964 stated he was born on the property of the late Judge Preston near Emmorton and was the son of Jessie and Harriet Wiggins; he worked for a time overseas in England and returned to the U.S. and was a trainer of trotting horses for a wealthy New Jersey family; he later bought a farm at Old Fields near Kalmia in Harford County; he married in Philadelphia, but his wife (not named) lived a short time; in1926 he was employed by Grover C. Greer who owned Cool Spring Farm in the Thomas Run Valley; when the Greers sold the farm and moved to Inwood in Bel Air in 1931 Wiggins, as he was fondly called, sold his farm and came to live with them; "James A. Wiggins, Genial Gentleman" died at the Bar Wil Ba Convalescent Home in Baltimore, survived by two nephews Howard W. Jackson and Edward P. Jackson, and one niece Mrs. Sarah House) [Tabernacle Mount Zion U. M. Church Cemetery]

Wiggins, Samuel circa 1878 – January 7, 1897 (no tombstone; *The Aegis* on January 15, 1897 reported that Samuel Wiggins, aged about 19, started a fight with Oscar Banks, age about 24, and it was determined that a blow to the chest caused his heart to stop and he died; he was removed to his parents' home near Churchville and was buried "at McComas Chapel on the Mountain," which refers to the cemetery adjoining McComas Institute near Joppa) [Mt. Zion U. M. Church Cemetery]

Wiggins, Tyrone L. 1960-2011 (small metal funeral home marker) [Berkley Memorial Cemetery]

Williams, ---- January 15, 1913 – February 9, 1913 (no tombstone; death certificate stated he was born in Harford Co., the son of Elsworth Williams, born in Harford Co., and Daisy Lavender, born in Virginia; they lived near Aberdeen and his father was informant) [Mt. Calvary U. A. M. E. Church Cemetery]

Williams, ---- stillborn female died on April 22, 1916 at Gibson (no tombstone; death certificate stated she was the daughter of Dennis Williams and Margaret Kell and all were born in Harford Co.; informant was Dennis Williams, of Bel Air) [Clark's U. M. Church Cemetery]

Williams, ---- stillborn female on May 16, 1925 (no tombstone; death certificate stated she was the daughter of Harry E. Williams, of Maryland, and Mary E. Simmons, of North Carolina) [St. James United Cemetery]

Williams, Adeline January 3, 1890 – June 15, 1925 (no tombstone; death certificate stated she was the daughter of John Pevey and Rachel McComas, all born in Maryland, and she was married at the time of her death near Forest Hill; informant was Garfield Pevey, of Churchville) [Asbury Cemetery]

Williams, Annie Green October 31, 1924 – January 27, 1977 (no tombstone; obituary in *The Aegis* stated Annie Green Williams was born in Havre de Grace, the daughter of Theodore R. and Alice P. Green, of Havre de Grace; she died at Harford Memorial Hospital, survived by her parents, a son Freddie Williams, Jr., a brother Robert Green, a sister Gwendolyn Jones, and three grandsons) [St. James United Cemetery]

Williams, Annie Sophin *(sic)* September 17, 1838 – July 19, 1915 (no tombstone; death certificate stated she was a widow and the daughter of Jacob H. Simms and Henrietta Johnson, all born in Maryland) [Union U. M. Church Cemetery]

Williams, Arthur died April 5, 1928, age about 30 (no tombstone; death certificate stated he was a laborer at Stepney who was shot to death; his place of birth and the names of his parents were not known to informant Mr. J. B. Ray, of Aberdeen) [Mt. Calvary U. A. M. E. Church Cemetery]

Williams, Ashton O. died December 16, 1991, age 69 (no tombstone; obituary in *The Aegis* on December 25, 1991 stated he was born in Wilmington, DE, the son of Samuel O. and Christiana M. Williams, and married C. Marie Stiffler in 1957, worked as an electrician for 20 years for Martin-Marietta and retired from Armco Steel Corp. in Baltimore; he was a World War II Army veteran and active in the church, and died at home in Fallston, survived by his wife, two sons David and Mark Williams, a sister Hazel M. Beale, and three grandchildren, and he was custodial father of Esther Showalter and Mary Ruth Putnam) [Union U. M. Church Cemetery]

Williams, Bernice B. August 8, 1920 – July 12, 1975 (on same tombstone with Thomas A. Williams; obituary in *The Aegis* stated M. Bernice Brown Williams was born in Bel Air, the daughter of the late Mitchell Brown and Mattie Brown, and was one of the first to graduate from the then Bel Air Colored High School and received a degree from Bowie State College in 1942; she taught at all levels and at her death was a specialist in Exceptional Education at North Harford High School; she was also active in various educational associations and in the NAACP; she died at Franklin Square Hospital, survived by her husband Thomas A. Williams, Sr., son Thomas Jr., two brothers, one cousin and several nieces and nephews) [Clark's U. M. Church Cemetery]

Williams, Bernice J. October 9, 1908 – January 5, 1988 (on same tombstone with Percy V. Williams; obituary and photo in *The Record* on January 13, 1988 stated Bernice Johnson Williams was the wife of Harford County School Board President Percy V. Williams and she died while visiting relatives in Anne Arundel County; Bernice had been married for 49 years; she was born in Eastport, MD, the daughter of Vandella Williams, and taught at the Havre de Grace Colored High School – later renamed Havre de Grace Consolidated High School – for more than 33 years and in 1964 then Superintendent of Schools Charles W. Willis appointed her to a committee to develop a plan to desegregate the county schools; she retired from teaching in 1969 after 38 years) [Union U. M. Church Cemetery]

Williams, Beverly died October 21, 1988, age not given (no tombstone; obituary in *The Aegis* on October 27, 1988 stated she died at Greater Baltimore Medical Center and was the infant daughter of Beverly Ione (Jones) and Thomas Williams, Jr., and granddaughter of Thomas Sr.) [Clark's U. M. Church Cemetery]

Williams, Burton 1926-2010 (small metal funeral home marker) [Mt. Calvary U. A. M. E. Church Cemetery]

Williams, Carrie died April 19, 1913, age about 26 (no tombstone; death certificate stated she was the married daughter of Charles Haywood and Susie Jones, all born in Harford Co.) [Union U. M. Church Cemetery]

Williams, Catharine October – (blank), 1834 – July 5, 1912 (no tombstone; death certificate stated she was the daughter of Seymore Collins and Catharine Collins and all were born in Anne Arundel Co.; she was married and died when struck by lightning at Kalmia; the informant was W. R. Williams, of Bel Air; her death notice in *The Aegis* on July 11, 1912 stated a severe electrical storm passed through Kalmia and it appears she was struck by lightning since one of her shoes was badly torn; "Kate" was honored with an immense funeral) [Clark's U. M. Church Cemetery]

Williams, Charles C. 1905-1988 [Clark's U. M. Church Cemetery]

Williams, Charles E. died July 15, 1900, age 3 months and 15 days (no tombstone; death certificate stated he was the son of Joshua E. and Mary Williams and died at Michaelsville; place of burial was not indicated, but probably in Old Union Chapel Cemetery at Michaelsville; possibly reinterred later in Union Chapel Cemetery near Aberdeen) [Union U. M. Church Cemetery]

Williams, Charles E. November 9, 1923 – June 9, 1965 (on same tombstone with Margaret D. Williams) [Foster's Hill Cemetery]

Williams, Charles Garland July 27, 1913 – February 12, 1920 (no tombstone; death certificate stated he was the son of Seymour Williams and Helen Collins, all born in Harford Co.; he died at Chestnut Hill and was buried at "Clarks Chaple;" informant was Edward Williams, of Bel Air) [Clark's U. M. Church Cemetery]

Williams, Charles T. died February 15, 1905, age 85 years and 5 days (no tombstone; death certificate stated he was the son of Sophia Williams, both born in Harford Co., father was not known to informant William S. Tildon, his half-brother; he died in Michaelsville and his place of burial was not indicated, but probably in Old Union Chapel Cemetery at Michaelsville; possibly reinterred later in Union Chapel Cemetery near Aberdeen) [Union U. M. Church Cemetery]

Williams, Claudette A., "Wife, Daughter, Mother, Sister and Aunt" January 21, 1955 – May 22, 2005 (tombstone inscribed with her photo) [St. James United Cemetery]

Williams, Clestine Marie Bond May 8, 1975 – September 27, 2000 (no tombstone; obituary in *The Aegis* on October 4, 2000 stated she was born in Havre de Grace, the daughter of Clarence Monroe Bond and Anne Marie Bond; lived in Edgewood, worked in a restaurant, and died at Fallston General Hospital, survived by her husband of four years David Jenkins Williams, her parents Clarence Monroe Bond, of Edgewood, and Anne Marie Bond, of Baltimore, sons Edward Joseph and Darian Williams, and her grandfather Edgar Wyckle, of Salisbury) [Mt. Calvary U. A. M. E. Church Cemetery]

Williams, Daisy G. July 9, 1899 – February 20, 1914 (no tombstone; death certificate stated she was the daughter of Richard Williams, both born in Harford Co., and Mary Z. Bradford, born in Maryland; she was crippled and suffered from "imbecility and deficiency, confined to bed during her life, refusal of food;" informant was Richard Williams of Bel Air RFD) [Clark's U. M. Church Cemetery]

Williams, Daniel T. died February 3, 1919, age 42 (no tombstone; death certificate stated he was the son of Edward Williams and Katharine Collins, all born in Harford Co.; he was single, worked as a laborer, and died at Hickory; informant was Edward Williams, of Bel Air) [Clark's U. M. Church Cemetery]

Williams, Danny J. 1928 – September 8, 2014 (on same tombstone with Robert T. Williams, but only his year of birth is inscribed; funeral notice and photo in *The Aegis* stated Danny "Jake' Williams, age 86, died at home in Havre de Grace) [Berkley Memorial Cemetery]

Williams, Dora Olevia, daughter of Alice Williams, March 29, 1892 – August 23, 1907 (inscribed "At Rest") [Clark's U. M. Church Cemetery]

Williams, Edward June 20, 1840 – March 28, 1935 (no tombstone; death certificate stated he was the son of Edward Williams and Mary Wells, all born in Harford Co.; he married Catherine ----, lived outside Bel Air and was a widower when he died in Bel Air where he had lived for 15 years; informant was Mrs. Alice Jackson, of Bel Air) [Clark's U. M. Church Cemetery]

Williams, Eliza March 16, 1843 – September 16, 1920 (no tombstone; death certificate stated she was a widow and worked as "day labor" in Bel Air; she and father Charles Anderson were born in Maryland, but her mother was unknown to informant Benjamin Williams, of Bel Air) [Hendon Hill Cemetery]

Williams, Elizabeth October 9, 1855 – May 9, 1914 (no tombstone; death certificate stated she was married and the daughter of Jacob Lisby and Semelia Clark, all born in Maryland; informant was Solomon Williams, of Perryman) [Union U. M. Church Cemetery]

Williams, Ella December 15, 1880 – May 27, 1938 (no tombstone; death certificate stated she was the wife of J. E. Williams and the daughter of Philip Stansbury and Elizabeth Smith) [Union U. M. Church Cemetery]

Williams, Ellen July 19, 1870 – April 20, 1936 (no tombstone; death certificate stated she was the widow of Henry Williams and the daughter of Harold Gibson and Nellie Garrison) [Union U. M. Church Cemetery]

Williams, Elmer August 25, 1915 – May 16, 1935 (no tombstone; death certificate stated he was the son of John Williams, both born in Maryland, and his mother's name was not known to the informant John Williams, of Bel Air, but she was born in Maryland; he was single, lived outside of Bel Air and died at Havre de Grace Hospital) [Clark's U. M. Church Cemetery]

Williams, Ernestine D. – see Tina Christon Williams [Mt. Zion U. M. Church Cemetery]

Williams, Eva Biggs March 3, 1945 – October 1, 2002 (no tombstone; an incomplete obituary in *The Aegis* on October 4, 2002 stated she was born in Havre de Grace, the daughter of Daniel W. Biggs and the late Gertrude E. Biggs; she lived in Havre de Grace and died at Bayview Medical Center in Baltimore; the newspaper noted, "A full obituary will run next week.") [St. James United Cemetery]

Williams, Evelyn L. December 22, 1935 – March 19, 1998 (tombstone; obituary and photo in *The Aegis* on April 1, 1998 stated Evelyn Malloy Williams was born in Havre de Grace, the eldest of four children born to Eugene Malloy and Eva Galloway and was the wife of Frank "Pam" Williams; she died at home in Aberdeen, survived by two sons, Keith Malloy and Frank Williams, Jr., three daughters, Barbara Malloy, Patricia Williams and Julia Williams two brothers, Eugene Malloy and Alfred Malloy, 15 grandchildren and 8 great-grandchildren) [Berkley Memorial Cemetery]

Williams, Evelyn Roberta died March 19, 1996, age 72 (no tombstone; obituary in *The Aegis* on March 27, 1996 stated "Mouse" was the third child of 13 children born to George Willard Rumsey and Dora Miles, and she was the widow of Roosevelt Williams; she retired after 25 years with Bata Shoe Company and died at Fallston General Hospital, survived by two sisters, one brother, two aunts "and many other relatives") [Clark's U. M. Church Cemetery]

Williams, Fletcher, son of Belle Lee, died May 11, 1897, age 22 [Hendon Hill Cemetery]

Williams, Frances (no tombstone; death certificate stated she was born July 1, 1898 in Pylesville, daughter of Thomas Ross Williams, born in Harford Co., and Mary E. Saul(?), born in Pylesville, died on February 14, 1914; informant was her father) [Chestnut Grove A. M. E. Church Cemetery, formerly LaGrange Cemetery at Rocks]

Williams, Frank Sr. September 18, 1924 – December 6, 2004 (tombstone; obituary and photo in *The Aegis* on December 15, 2004 stated Frank "Pam" Williams, Sr. was born in Williamstown, NC, the son of George and Lafayette Williams; he married Evelyn Malloy on March 9, 1957 and worked as a poultry and produce salesman, also worked for the city of Aberdeen several years, and retired from the Harford County School System; he died at the home of his son in Clarksville, TN, survived by three sons, two daughters, three brothers-in-law, one sister-in-law, 25 grandchildren "and host of great-great-grandchildren, nieces, nephews cousins and friends" and was predeceased by his wife and two daughters) [Berkley Memorial Cemetery]

Williams, George Carvel March 13, 1907 – July 28, 1941 (no tombstone; death certificate stated he was the son of Joshua Williams, born near Perryman, and Mary M. Carey, born near Chester, PA; he was single and was stabbed and murdered near Perryman) [Union U. M. Church Cemetery]

Williams, George E. September 12, 1872 – October 15, 1938 (no tombstone; death certificate stated he was the son of Edward Williams, both born in Harford Co, and Catherine Collins, born at West River, MD, and lived near Bel Air; he married Harriet ----, worked as a laborer near Bel Air, and died at Harford Memorial Hospital in Havre de Grace; informant was his wife) [Clark's U. M. Church Cemetery]

Williams, Georgianna B. 1908-1990 (tombstone; James Dorsey Card File, African American Obituaries, that is maintained at the Historical Society of Harford County, has a card from the Howard K. McComas III Funeral Home stating she was bornNovember 18, 1908 and died May 25, 1990) [Clark's U. M. Church Cemetery]

Williams, Gladys Irene July 24, 1919 – February 25, 2019 (obituary and photo on the Lisa Scott Funeral Home website stated she was born in Perryman, the sixth of twelve children born to Vandellia and Hattie Williams; she was an educator for 42 years and was a pioneer in desegregation of schools, restaurants and other places where Blacks were denied participation; of her many accomplishments she was a lifelong member of Union United Methodist Church, co-organizer of Harford County's first Black Girl Scout Troop, and a 50-year member of the local and state Women's International League for Peace and Freedom) [Berkley Memorial Cemetery]

Williams, Glen (owner of a lot in section 41 some time after 1951) [Mt. Calvary U. A. M. E. Church Cemetery]

Williams, Harriet 1872-1950 (small broken plastic cross laying on ground) [Clark's U. M. Church Cemetery]

Williams, Harry Edward died August 15, 1975, age 76 (no tombstone; obituary in *The Aegis* stated he was the son of Perry Williams and Ella Bradley, lived at 552 Revolution St., Havre de Grace, was a retired laborer and died at Harford Memorial Hospital, survived by 2 sons, four daughters and 1 brother; his wife was not mentioned) [St. James United Cemetery]

Williams, Harry Franklin died suddenly on July 25, 1967, age not given (no tombstone; obituary in *The Aegis* on August 3, 1967 stated he was a long time resident of Bel Air and the only survivor was a nephew Edward Jardon) [Clark's U. M. Church Cemetery]

Williams, Hattie E. 1888-1954 (same tombstone with Vandellia A. Williams) [Union U. M. Church Cemetery]

Williams, Helen died December 27, 1975, age not given (no tombstone; obituary in *The Aegis* stated she was born in Perryman, the daughter of the late George Henry and Ellen Williams; she lived at 433 Battery Drive in Havre de Grace and died at Harford Memorial Hospital, survived by a sister Ellen Holtz and a niece Effie Kell with whom she made her home) [Union U. M. Church Cemetery]

Williams, Helen died February 15, 1920, age 27 years, 10 months (no tombstone; death certificate stated her father was unknown and mistakenly completed the certificate by stating the birth place of the father was Helen Cohen *(sic)* and the maiden name of the mother was Emma Cohns *(sic)*; she was married, died at Chestnut Hill and buried at "Clarks Chapple;" informant was Seymore Williams, of Bel Air) [Clark's U. M. Church Cemetery]

Williams, Henrietta July 16, 1852 – August 1, 1917 (no tombstone; death certificate stated she was the unmarried daughter of John C. Williams and Margaret Reed, of Harford Co.) [Union U. M. Church Cemetery]

Williams, Henry August 14, 1844 – November 19, 1915 (no tombstone; death certificate stated he was born in Maryland, died a widower and was the son of Henry Williams, born in Maryland, but his mother was not known to informant Jos. Williams, of Atlantic City, NJ) [Union U. M. Church Cemetery]

Williams, Henry W. 1899-1955 (on same tombstone with Minnie A. Williams; James Dorsey Card File, African American Obituaries, that is maintained at the Historical Society of Harford County, has a death notice from an unidentified newspaper stating Henry Williams, of Motor Sales Co. in Bel Air, died at University Hospital on April 28, 19--- (undated) and burial was at Clark's Chapel on April 30) [Clark's U. M. Church Cemetery]

Williams, Herbert A. March 26, 1891 – December 7, 1958, Maryland, Pvt., 401 Labor Bn. QMC, World War I [Mt. Zion U. M. Church Cemetery]

Williams, Isaac Clay May 20, 1841 – August 7, 1912 (inscribed with this verse: "Blessed Are The Dead Which Die In The Lord From Henceforth Yea Said The Spirit That They Rest From Their Labor And Their Work Do Follow Them") [Union U. M. Church Cemetery]

Williams, James 1910-1952 [St. James United Cemetery]

Williams, James A. Sr. Sunrise September 16, 1911 – Sunset May 19, 1975 (on same tombstone with Ruth E. Williams) [Clark's U. M. Church Cemetery]

Williams, James H. November 15, 1912 – May 18, 2000, S2, U.S. Navy, World War II [Berkley Memorial Cemetery]

Williams, Jane (no tombstone; death certificate stated she was born in Harford Co., the daughter of William Dutton, birth place unknown, and Callie Maxfield, born in Harford Co.; she was married at the time of her death at Pylesville on January 21, 1914, age 41; informant was Ross Williams, of Pylesville) [Chestnut Grove A. M. E. Church Cemetery, formerly LaGrange Cemetery at Rocks]

Williams, John June 27, 1875 – July 9, 1920 (no tombstone; death certificate stated he was the unmarried son of John Williams and Lizzie Williams, all born in Maryland) [Union U. M. Church Cemetery]

Williams, John March 10, 1861 – February 13, 1928 (no tombstone; death certificate stated he was born in Alabama and died a widower; parents unknown to informant Perry Williams) [St. James United Cemetery]

Williams, John November 20, 1930 – February 2, 1932 (no tombstone; death certificate stated he was the son of Dorothy Williams, of Havre de Grace, but his father was unknown) [St. James United Cemetery]

Williams, John Richard January 10, 1861 – October 24, 1939 (no tombstone; death certificate stated he was born in Harford Co, the son of Richard Williams, born in Prince George's Co., MD, and Delia Hollis, born in Harford Co.; he married Mary ----, worked as road laborer, and died in rural Darlington, leaving a widow; informant was Walter Williams, of Street, MD) [Clark's U. M. Church Cemetery]

Williams, John Thomas May 22, 1857 – October 18, 1923 (no tombstone; death certificate stated he was the son of ---- (blank) Williams and Jane Gilbert, all born in Maryland; he was married and worked as a farm laborer; informant was Seymor Williams, of Forest Hill) [Clark's U. M. Church Cemetery]

Williams, John W. April 4, 1870 – June 7, 1936 (no tombstone; death certificate stated he was the son of William H. William, both born in Perryman, but his mother was unknown to informant Amanda Stephens, of Joppa; he died a widower in Perryman with burial at "Magnolia") [Foster's Hill Cemetery]

Williams, Kate died July 1, 1982, age 92 (no tombstone; obituary in *The Aegis* on July 8, 1992 stating she was a native of Aberdeen, the daughter of George Frisby and Harriet Green, and the widow of Joseph Williams; she worked as a domestic employee and a child care provider and died at Bon Secours Hospital in Baltimore, survived by a nephew and great-nephew) [Mt. Calvary U. A. M. E. Church Cemetery]

Williams, Laura Frances November 21, 1871 – October 12, 1935 (no tombstone; death certificate stated she was the daughter of George Dorsey and Emiline Duckett, all born in Maryland; she married George Williams and died a widow near Aberdeen, but her residence was shown as 504 M Street, NW, Washington, D.C., which was the address of informant Mrs. Lydia Green) [Mt. Calvary U. A. M. E. Church Cemetery]

Williams, Lawrence W. died December 12, 1970, age not given (no tombstone; obituary in *The Aegis* stated he was the husband of Mabel Williams, of Philadelphia, and he lived with his brother Walter Williams on Old Post Road in Aberdeen; Lawrence died at Harford Memorial Hospital, survived by his wife, brother, son Larry Williams and daughter Charlotte Williams) [Berkley Memorial Cemetery]

Williams, Lizzette Christy died July 6, 1982, age 83 (no tombstone; obituary in *The Aegis* on July 15, 1982 stated she was born on Spesutia Island, the daughter of Robert and Sarah S. Christy, and was the widow of Otho B. Williams; she lived in Havre de Grace, was active in the church and died at Citizens Nursing Home, survived by an aunt Abbie Christy Mortimer) [Union U. M. Church Cemetery]

Williams, Lydia E., "Mother" September 5, 1903 – January 1, 1983 (tombstone; obituary in *The Aegis* on January 6, 1983 stated she was born in Harford Co. and the widow of Herbert Williams; she worked with the PTA for the Bel Air, Havre de Grace, and Central Consolidated Schools; later moved to Washington, DC and died at Providence Hospital, survived by a son, a daughter, four sisters, a brother, and several grandchildren) [Mt. Zion U. M. Church Cemetery]

Williams, Madeline 1885-1980 (tombstone; obituary in *The Aegis* on December 11, 1980 stated Madeline Peaco Williams, daughter of Sarah E. Peaco and Melcar Harris, was the widow of Irvin Williams; she died at home in Havre de Grace on November 26, 1980, age 82 *(sic)*, but no surviving family members were mentioned) [St. James United Cemetery]

Williams, Margaret D. October 12, 1931 – July 24, 1979 (on same tombstone with Charles E. Williams; obituary in *The Aegis* on July 26, 1979 stated Margaret Ann Demby Williams was the daughter of the late Charles Medford Demby and Jennie Belle Turner, and she lived in Joppa, died at Fallston General Hospital and was survived by a son Tyrone Edward Williams, a daughter Melvyna Williams, 5 brothers, 3 sisters, 5 grandchildren, and was predeceased by her husband Charles Edward Williams) [Foster's Hill Cemetery]

Williams, Mary A. 1905-1945 (inscribed "She Fought A Good Fight") [Union U. M. Church Cemetery]

Williams, Mary Ella, "Mother" April 2, 1905 – September 7, 1970 (tombstone; obituary in *The Aegis* stated she was the daughter of John B. Simons, of Havre de Grace, and the late Essie Simons; she lived at 27 Fenway Street in Aberdeen (married Harry E. Williams, Sr. who was not mentioned in obituary) and died at Harford Memorial Hospital in Havre de Grace, survived by her father, two sons, four daughters, 26 grandchildren, 2 great-grandchildren and 1 brother) [St. James United Cemetery]

Williams, Mary F. died July 31, 1904, age 39 years and 8 months (no tombstone; death certificate stated she was the daughter of Andrew H. Williams and Amanda Lisby, all born in Harford Co., and the wife of John W. Williams; she worked as a cook and died at Michaelsville; place of burial was not indicated, but probably in Old Union Chapel Cemetery at Michaelsville; possibly reinterred later in Union Chapel Cemetery near Aberdeen) [Union U. M. Church Cemetery]

Williams, Mary Jane September 27, 1905 – September 24, 1945 (no tombstone; death certificate stated she was daughter of Daniel Johnson and Sarah Horce(?), and wife of Otto B. Williams) [Union U. M. Church Cemetery]

Williams, Mary October 9, 1863 – November 5, 1941 (no tombstone; death certificate stated she was born in Pennsylvania, the daughter of Isaac Carey and Mary E. Turner, both born in Virginia, and she was the wife of Joshua E. Williams) [Union U. M. Church Cemetery]

Williams, Mary Zew 1872-1932 (on same tombstone with William R.) [Clark's U. M. Church Cemetery]

Williams, Minnie A. 1899-1998 (on same tombstone with Henry W. Williams; obituary and photo in *The Aegis* on October 2, 1998 stated Minnie A. Ruff Williams was born September 8, 1899, the daughter of Steven and Emily Ruff; she married William H. "Henry" Williams on September 22, 1924 and he predeceased her; Minnie was a beautician at Gladys Taylor's Beauty Shop in Bel Air and also worked at Chevrolet Motor Sales; she died in Bel Air on September 25, 1998, age 99, survived by two nieces, one nephew, one niece-in-law, a great niece, and a devoted friend Viola Jones Scott) [Clark's U. M. Church Cemetery]

Williams, Mollie March 3, 1863 – July 13, 1937 (no tombstone; death certificate stated she was the widow of William Williams and the daughter of Trylus Whims, mother unknown) [Union U. M. Church Cemetery]

Williams, Otis January 15, 1927 – May 11, 1932 (no tombstone; death certificate stated he was born in Delaware, the son of Rupert Williams, born in Wilmington, NC and Mamie Evert, of Roberts Point, NC, and he died in Havre de Grace; informant was his father, of Seaford, DE, usual residence) [St. James United Cemetery]

Williams, Otto B. died June 12, 1981, age 89 (no tombstone; obituary in *The Aegis* on June 18, 1981 stated he was born in Abingdon and grew up on a farm in a family of ten children; he worked as a laborer for the Pennsylvania Railroad for more than 30 years and retired about 10 years ago; he lived in Aberdeen, married Lizette Christy and was a lay leader for more than 50 years at Union United Methodist Church and was recording steward for over 40 years; he died at Harford Memorial Hospital and was survived by his wife and a brother Vandella) [Union U. M. Church Cemetery]

Williams, Pearl September 23, 1904 – October 18, 1917 (no tombstone; death certificate initially stated her name was Pauline Whims, but that was lined out and Pearl Williams was written over it; yet, her parents were Howard Whims and Frances Andre, of Havre de Grace) [St. James United Cemetery]

Williams, Percy died September 6, 1942 [St. James United Cemetery]

Williams, Percy V. April 10, 1914 -   (on same tombstone with Bernice J. Williams; his death of date was not inscribed, but he died on 14 Nov 2009 and his middle name was Vandella; he served in World War II and had a distinguished career as an educator and supervisor in Harford County; his photo and a brief sketch of his career have been published in *Havre de Grace: Its Historic Past, Its Charming Present and Its Promising Future*, by Jack L. Shagena, Jr. and Henry C. Peden, Jr., 2018, p. 419) [Union U. M. Church Cemetery]

Williams, Philip I. died June 12, 1905, age 47 [St. James United Cemetery]

Williams, R. Jane died November 26, 1908, age 23 (no tombstone; death certificate stated she was the daughter of William Benson and Olivia Green, all born in Maryland; she married Asbury Williams, worked as a servant and died at Bynum; informant was her father; on the back of death certificate is written "Clarks Chapel") [Clark's U. M. Church Cemetery]

Williams, Rachel Collins July 4, 1862 – April 21, 1937 (no tombstone; death certificate stated she was born on the Nelson property in Harford Co., the daughter of Thomas Collins and Annie Preston, both born in Harford Co., and died a widow in Bel Air; informant was Mrs. Mamie Turner) [Clark's U. M. Church Cemetery]

Williams, Ramsey M. 1900-1965 [Clark's U. M. Church Cemetery]

Williams, Raymond Webster July 9, 1914 – November 14, 1914 (no tombstone; death certificate stated he was the son of Joshua E. Williams and Mary M. Carey, all born in Maryland) [Union U. M. Church Cemetery]

Williams, Robert Joseph May 28, 1939 – July 1, 1939 (no tombstone; death certificate stated he was born in Loreley, MD, the son of Osborne Davis, born in Virginia, and Bessie Williams, born in Loreley; their residence was Loreley-Fullerton R.D., Baltimore County, but he died near Van Bibber (Harford County); informant was Margaret Williams, of Loreley) [Clark's U. M. Church Cemetery]

Williams, Robert T. 1951-1971 (on same tombstone with Danny J. Williams; obituary in *The Aegis* stated he was the son of Danny J. and Delores M. Williams, 506 Revolution St., Havre de Grace; he was recently employed at the Bata Shoe Co. and died on June 10, 1971, survived by his parents, a brother James L. Williams, four sisters Jada M., Barbara A., Maxine E. and Susan D. Williams, his grandmother Mrs. Emma Jane Lehman, and 8 uncles and 8 eights) [Berkley Memorial Cemetery]

Williams, Roosevelt "Skeet" died March 20, 1992, age 68 (no tombstone; James Dorsey Card File, African American Obituaries, that is maintained at the Historical Society of Harford County, has a card with her obituary from an unidentified newspaper on April 1, 1992 stating he was born in Harford Co., the son of John and Drussella Williams; he was a retired cement finisher and died at home in Bel Air, survived by his wife Evelyn Williams and three sisters) [Clark's U. M. Church Cemetery]

Williams, Russell E, July 24, 1916 – October 15, 1961, Maryland, Cpl., Co. A, 811 Engineers AVN Battalion, World War II [Union U. M. Church Cemetery]

Williams, Ruth E. Batty Sunrise February 8, 1913 – Sunset October 11, 1973 (on same tombstone with James A. Williams) [Clark's U. M. Church Cemetery]

Williams, Sadie December 20, 1880 – April 7, 1935 (no tombstone; death certificate stated she was the daughter of Richard Hawkins and Caroline Floyd, all born in Harford Co.; she was the widow of Robert Williams and lived and died at 616 S. Union Ave. in Havre de Grace; informant was Roy Williams who lived at the same address) [Gravel Hill Cemetery]

Williams, Solomon W. February 22, 1857 – June 26, 1915 (no tombstone; death certificate stated he was a widower and son of Solomon Williams and Maria Pitt, all born in Maryland) [Union U. M. Church Cemetery]

Williams, Sydney A. died January 6, 1916, age 52 (no tombstone; death certificate stated she was born in 1854, date unknown, married, and lived in Fallston; her parents were Sydney *(sic)* Miller and Fannie Moore and they were all born in Maryland; informant was Augustus Boone) [Hendon Hill Cemetery]

Williams, Thomas A. October 11, 1919 – December 3, 1994 (on same tombstone with Bernice B. Williams, but his date of death is not inscribed; obituary and photo in *The Aegis* on December 7, 1994 stated he was born in Harford County, the son of Seymore Williams and Helen Cohen, and married the late Bernice Brown; he served in the Navy during World War II and later worked for Dr. H. P. White in Bel Air; he died at Fallston General Hospital, survived by a son Thomas A. Williams, Jr., two brothers-in-law, and two grandchildren) [Clark's U. M. Church Cemetery]

Williams, Tina Christon 1945-1964 (tombstone; obituary in *The Aegis* on August 20, 1964 stated her name was Ernestine D. Williams and she was the wife of Douglas Williams; she died on August 17, 1964 as the result of an automobile accident and was survived by her husband and her parents Clarence and Mary Christon, and a daughter Tanya Williams) [Mt. Zion U. M. Church Cemetery]

Williams, Vandella January 4, 1913 – January 14, 1913 (no tombstone; death certificate stated he was the son of Vandella Williams and Hattie Brown, all born in Maryland) [Union U. M. Church Cemetery]

Williams, Vandellia A. 1887-1988 (on same tombstone with Hattie E. Williams, but his year of death has not been inscribed; his photo appeared in *The Record* on May 6, 1987 and obituary in *The Record* on January 6, 1988; an article and photo in the files of the Historical Society of Harford County stated Vandellia Armatage Williams was born in Perryman, the son of Solomon Williams who was one of the founders of Union Chapel M. E. Church in Michaelsville in 1849; Vandellia was a founder of the Harford County Colored PTA in 1929 and he served 40 years as Sunday School superintendent and 75 years on Union Chapel's administrative board; Vandellia and wife Harriet ("Hattie") had 10 children and 17 grandchildren) [Union U. M. Church Cemetery]

Williams, William January 17, 1868   May 3, 1927 (no tombstone; death certificate stated he was married and the son of Harrison Williams, but mother was unknown to informant Mary Williams) [Union U. M. Church Cemetery]

Williams, William F. July 24, 1903 – January 29, 1935 (no tombstone; death certificate stated he was the son of Joshua E. Williams and Mary M. Carey, and was divorced) [Union U. M. Church Cemetery]

Williams, William H. September 18, 1917 – April 27, 1960, Maryland, TEC4, Truck Co TC, World War II [Clark's U. M. Church Cemetery]

Williams, William Henry August 7, 1897 – August 7, 1986 (no tombstone; obituary in *The Record* on August 30, 1986 stated he was born in Harford County, the son of William and Molly Williams, served in the Army in World War II, lived in Havre de Grace, worked at Aberdeen Proving Ground for 30 years and died at the Perry Point VAMC on his 89th birthday, survived by his wife Virginia Williams, five step-children, and a sister Effie Tazwell) [Union U. M. Church Cemetery]

Williams, William R. 1872-1926 (on same tombstone with Mary Zew Williams; death certificate stated he was born on April 4, 1871 and he was the son of Edward Williams and Katherine Collins, all were born in Maryland; he was married, worked as a farmer, and died at Forest Hill; informant was Mrs. W. Richard Williams, of Forest Hill) [Clark's U. M. Church Cemetery]

Williams-Johnson, Pamela – see Pamela Johnson [Berkley Memorial Cemetery]

Williamson, ---- stillborn female died on April 18, 1939 (no tombstone; death certificate stated she was born and died in Harford Memorial Hospital in Havre de Grace, the daughter of Roman Williamson and Gertrude Wells, both born in Maryland and lived at Street; informant was her father) [Clark's U. M. Church Cemetery]

Williamson, ---- stillborn female on December 25, 1935 (no tombstone; death certificate stated she was born and died in Havre de Grace Hospital, the daughter of Roman P. Williamson, born in Glenville, and Gertrude Wells, born in Street; informant was her father) [Clark's U. M. Church Cemetery]

Williamson, ---- stillborn male died on March 1, 1921 (no tombstone; death certificate stated he was born in Dublin, son of Roman Williamson and Gertrude Wells, all born in Maryland; informant was her father Roman Williamson, of Street, MD) [Clark's U. M. Church Cemetery]

Williamson, Claratta T. June 3, 1922 – August 25, 1988 (on same tombstone with Herman M. Williamson and her name is inscribed Claratta T. Thompson, but obituary in *The Aegis* on September 15, 1988 gave her name as Clara Thompson Williamson; she was born in McDonald, NC, the daughter of Ora Jackson and the late Lionel Thompson; married Rev. Herman M. Williamson and was a retired LPN at the Perry Point VAMC with 27 years of service; they lived in Aberdeen and she "died recently" and was survived by her husband, her mother, three daughters, two sons, and five grandchildren) [Berkley Memorial Cemetery]

Williamson, Dennis L. May 14, 1927 – October 13, 1994, U.S. Army, U.S. Air Force, World War II [Berkley Memorial Cemetery]

Williamson, Gertrude July 30, 1902 – April 19, 1939 (no tombstone; death certificate stated she was the daughter of Henry Wells and Martha Snowden, all born near Street; she married Roman Williamson, lived near Street, and died from a hemorrhage after delivering an infant in Harford Memorial Hospital in Havre de Grace; informant was her husband) [Clark's U. M. Church Cemetery]

Williamson, Henry February 15, 1867 – February 15, 1945 (no tombstone; death certificate stated he was the son of Henry Williamson, both born in Calvert Co., and Kate Gray, born on the Eastern Shore of Maryland; he was married, worked as a farm laborer, lived on Route 1, Bel Air, and died at Harford Memorial Hospital in Havre de Grace; informant was Nellie Turner) [Clark's U. M. Church Cemetery]

Williamson, Herman M. (Rev. Dr.) August 21, 1919 – October 4, 2008 (on same tombstone with Claratta T. Williamson and a circular metal emblem with the words "Department of the Army, United States of America" is mounted on a rod at the head of his grave) [Berkley Memorial Cemetery]

Williamson, Louisa died April 24, 1931, age about 77 (no tombstone; death certificate stated she was the daughter of John Butler and Sophia Cain, all born in Maryland; she was a widow and died at Kalmia; informant was Caroline Curtis, of Bel Air) [Clark's U. M. Church Cemetery]

Williamson, Mary E. June 3, 1859 – December 25, 1921 (no tombstone; death certificate stated she was the daughter of Henry and Louisa Smith, all born in Maryland; she worked as a servant, was a widow, and died at Muttonburg; informant was Roman Williamson, of Bel Air) [Clark's U. M. Church Cemetery]

Williamson, Mary Turner January 11, 1867 – November 29, 1922 (no tombstone; death certificate stated she was the daughter of Robert J. Turner and Talitha Washington, all born in Maryland; she was married and died at Level; informant was Talitha Turner, of Havre de Grace) [Green Spring U. M. Church Cemetery]

Williamson, Myrtle E. June 21, 1902 – March 22, 1924 (no tombstone; death certificate stated she was the daughter of James Preston and Ora McCall, all born in Maryland; she was married and died at Berkley; informant was William Williamson, of Berkley) [Clark's U. M. Church Cemetery]

Williamson, Roman P., "Father" April 4, 1899 – February 19, 1976 (tombstone; obituary in *The Aegis* stated he was born at Hopewell, Harford Co., the son of William and Clara E. Williamson, and was a retired maintenance worker at Edgewood Arsenal; he lived with his daughter and son-in-law Edith and David Gordon, in Darlington, and died at Harford Memorial Hospital, survived by two other daughters, two sons, nine grandchildren and twelve great-grandchildren) [Berkley Memorial Cemetery]

Williamson, Thomas B. February 2, 1900 – December 12, 1936 (no tombstone; death certificate stated was born in Harford Co., the son of William Williamson and Elizabeth Smith, both born in Calvert Co.; he was single, worked as a laborer for public works for 10 years, and died at home in Darlington; informant was Roman Williamson, of Route #1, Street, MD) [Clark's U. M. Church Cemetery]

Williamson, Thomas Clarence died suddenly at birth on September 28, 1932 (no tombstone; death certificate stated he was the son of Roman Williamson and Gertrude Wells and all were born in Maryland; he died at McCann's Corner; informant was Roman Williamson, of Street, MD) [Clark's U. M. Church Cemetery]

Willis, Anna M., "Wife and Mother" September 4, 1942 – January 2, 2017 (on same tombstone with Michael D. Willis) [Berkley Memorial Cemetery]

Willis, Jack September 5, 1895 – September 18, 1960, Ohio, Cpl., Co. B, 365 Infantry, World War I [Union U. M. Church Cemetery]

Willis, Josephine 1868-1967 [Union U. M. Church Cemetery]

Willis, Mary Ruth died July 7, 1944, a 21-week premature birth, lived only 10 minutes (no tombstone; death certificate stated she was born and died in Bel Air, the daughter of Clarence K. Willis, born in Pennsylvania, and Westaka Minerva Jones, born in Bel Air; she was buried in "Mountain Cemetery, Harford Co.") [Mt. Zion U. M. Church Cemetery]

Willis, Michael D., "Son" October 29, 1970 – July 9, 2016 (on same tombstone with Anna M. Willis) [Berkley Memorial Cemetery]

Willis, Phillip Lewis November 11, 1928 – August 27, 1972, Maryland, STM1, U.S. Navy [Berkley Memorial Cemetery]

Wilmer, Ida M. (no dates on field stone; see Isaac Harrison Wilmer) [Foster's Hill Cemetery]

Wilmer, Isaac Harrison December 2, 1863 – May 6, 1942 (no tombstone; death certificate stated he was the son of Samuel Wilmer, both born in Maryland, but his mother was unknown to informant Ida Wilmer, of Magnolia; he married Ida ----, worked for the B & O Railroad and died in Magnolia, where he had lived for 6 years. *Ed. Note*: A descendant, Frances Scroggins Johnson, of Baltimore, stated Ida's maiden name was Garrison and Ida was age 35 in the 1910 census and Isaac Wilmer (Wilmore) was age 50.) [Foster's Hill Cemetery]

Wilmore, Annie E. died February 2, 1925, age about 50 (no tombstone; death certificate stated she was the widowed daughter of William Kenly and Milky Griffith; informant was Mrs. Susie Kell) [Union U. M. Church Cemetery]

Wilmore, Annie G. March 19, 1871 – April 24, 1949 (no tombstone; death certificate stated she was the daughter of John W. Williams and Susie Ann Kenly and died a widow at home at 847 Erie St. in Havre de Grace) [Union U. M. Church Cemetery]

Wilmore, Irwin McKinley July 22, 1895 – June 18, 1912 (no tombstone; death certificate stated he was the son of Isaac Wilmore and Ida May Jones, all born in Maryland; he died in Abingdon and was a school boy at the time; informant was his father) [John Wesley U. M. E. Church Cemetery in Abingdon]

Wilmore, James A. March 4, 1840 – March 20, 1915 (death certificate stated he was born in Harford Co. and was the married son of Joseph Wilmore and Mary A. Christy, both born in Maryland; informant was George Wilmore, of Perryman RFD; "Father" and "At Rest" and the dates 1841-1915 are inscribed on same tombstone with Sara Wilmore) [Union U. M. Church Cemetery]

Wilmore, Mary E. November 8, 1878 – October 5, 1924 (no tombstone; death certificate stated she was born in Harford Co., the daughter of Isaac Hamilton and Melinda Cooper, both born in Maryland; she was married when she died on Swan Creek near Aberdeen; informant was Isaac Wilmore, of Aberdeen RFD) [Asbury Cemetery]

Wilmore, Patience J. January 5, 1884 – March 30, 1943 (no tombstone; death certificate stated she was the wife of James E. Wilmore and daughter of Charles H. Prigg and Sarah Holland) [Union U. M. Church Cemetery]

Wilmore, Sara 1841-1920 (on same tombstone with James Wilmore inscribed "At Rest") [Union U. M. Church Cemetery]

Wilmore, William P. September 25, 1871 – September 9, 1924 (no tombstone; death certificate stated he was the married son of James H. Wilmore and Sarah L. Lewis; informant was Mrs. W. P. Wilmore, of Havre de Grace) [Union U. M. Church Cemetery]

Wilsan, Annabell E. 1896-1961 [Berkley Memorial Cemetery]

Wilson, ---- stillborn male on January 11, 1933 (no tombstone; death certificate stated he was the son of John W. and Annabelle Wilson, all born in Harford Co., and they lived in Darlington) [Berkley Memorial Cemetery]

Wilson, Alexander August 23, 1899 – June 16, 1913 (no tombstone; death certificate stated he was the son of William Wilson, both born in Maryland, but the name of his mother was not known to informant which was someone in the Havre de Grace Hospital) [Mt. Calvary U. A. M. E. Church Cemetery]

Wilson, Bernard S. 1931-1987, PFC, U.S. Army, Korea[Cedars Chapel Cemetery]

Wilson, Cassie died March 1, 1918, age about 57 (no tombstone; death certificate stated she had died a widow and was the daughter of Lloyd Hill and Charlotte Warfield, all born in Maryland; informant was Arthur Wilson, of Perryman) [Union U. M. Church Cemetery]

Wilson, Daisy Priscilla. "Mother, Grandmother and Sister" Sunrise December 11, 1922 – Sunset May 3, 2010 (inscribed "Loving Memory of") [Clark's U. M. Church Cemetery]

Wilson, Eddie 1891 – November 24, 1944 (no tombstone; death certificate stated he was the widowed son of Gideon Wilson and Lucy Hardwick, all born in Georgia; informant was Pearl Gibbs, of Havre de Grace) [St. James United Cemetery]

Wilson, Estella February 4, 1900 – August 23, 1926 (no tombstone; death certificate stated she was the daughter of Charles Wilson and Oscinnia Jones, all born in Maryland; she was a school teacher at Level; informant was Oscinnia Jones Cottman, of Cold Springs, NY) [Green Spring U. M. Church Cemetery]

Wilson, Ethel October 22, 1900 – October 23, 1953 (no tombstone; death certificate and Pennington Funeral Home records stated she was born in Havre de Grace and was the wife of John Wilson; her residence was at Hempstead, Nassau Co., Long Island, Floral Park, NY, and she appears to have been a member of Emanuel Baptist Church in Elmont, NY; buried in "Swan Creek Cem." near Aberdeen) [Union U. M. Church Cemetery]

Wilson, Frances Jane, wife of William H. Wilson, died December 27, 1893, age 45 (inscribed "Gone But Not Forgotten") [Gravel Hill Cemetery]

Wilson, George (owned a lot in section 40 some time after 1951) [Mt. Calvary U. A. M. E. Church Cemetery]

Wilson, Gracie Arlene, "Beloved Mother and Grandmother" May 17, 1940 -   [Berkley Memorial Cemetery]

Wilson, Hannah J. 1849-1919 (on same tombstone with Steven H. Wilson; death certificate stated she was born on August 24, 1849, the daughter of George and Sarah Presbury, all born in Harford Co.; she married and died on February 4, 1919 in Darlington and the informant was Benjamin Wilson) [Berkley Memorial Cemetery]

Wilson, Hannah March 10, 1863 – March 12, 1933 (no tombstone; death certificate stated she was the widow of Levie Wilson and died at home on Bond St. in Bel Air; her parents were unknown to informant Robert Whittington, of Bel Air; James Dorsey Card File, African American Obituaries, that is maintained at the Historical Society of Harford County, has a card with obituary from the *Bel Air Times* on March 17, 1933 stating she was the widow of Levin Wilson and died March 13, 1933, age 72, survived by three daughters and seven grandchildren) [Hendon Hill Cemetery]

Wilson, Harry A. August 18, 1888 – February 16, 1983, PFC, U.S. Army, World War I (tombstone; military records stated Harry Anderson Wilson, of Perryman, was inducted into military service on August 23, 1918, served in Co. H., 811 Pion Inf., was overseas from October 10, 1918 to July 13, 1919 and was honorably discharged on July 19, 1919; obituary in *The Aegis* on February 24, 1983 stated he was born in Perryman, lived in Aberdeen, served during World War I and died at Perry Point VA Medical Center, survived by his wife Agnes Banks Wilson) [Berkley Memorial Cemetery]

Wilson, Hattie V. November 12, 1874 – March 2, 1920 (no tombstone; death certificate stated she was the daughter of Sylvester Jones and Mary Washington, all born in Maryland; she was married and lived near Level; informant was Charles Wilson, of Havre de Grace) [Green Spring U. M. Church Cemetery]

Wilson, Henrietta December 20, 1885 – June 2, 1911 (no tombstone; death certificate stated she was single and a servant in Bel Air, and the daughter of Lev Wilson and Hannah Barrett, also of Bel Air; informant was Hannah Wilson) [Hendon Hill Cemetery]

Wilson, Henry November 28, 1854 – April 12, 1928 [Green Spring U. M. Church Cemetery]

Wilson, Henry B. May 31, 1921 – April 16, 1923 (no tombstone; death certificate stated he was son of Henry B. Wilson and Hattie Turner, all born in Maryland; he died in Abingdon and was buried in "Mountain Cemetery;" informant was his mother Hattie Wilson, of Edgewood) [Mt. Zion U. M. Church Cemetery]

Wilson, Howard died July 22, 1906, age 35 [Mt. Zion U. M. Church Cemetery]

Wilson, John Archer died July 14, 1935, age 65 (no tombstone; death certificate stated he was born in Harford Co., the son of John L. Wilson, born in Towson, MD, and Emiline Green, born in Harford Co.; he married Sarah Parrott, worked as a farm laborer, lived at Kalmia all his life, and was a widower; he was killed in an automobile accident on Conowingo Road about 5 miles from Bel Air; informant was Mrs. Charlotte Griffin, of White Plains, NY) [Clark's U. M. Church Cemetery]

Wilson, John Joseph died March 1, 1975, age not given (obituary in *The Aegis* on March 6, 1975 stated he was the son of the late Stephen and Hannah Jane Wilson, but his wife was not named; he lived in Darlington, worked for and retired from the Philadelphia Electric Co. at Conowingo and died at Harford Memorial Hospital in Havre de Grace, survived by three sons, three daughters, two sisters, six grandchildren and ten great-grandchildren) [Berkley Memorial Cemetery]

Wilson, Lewis H. April 30, 1930 – May 3, 1923 (no tombstone; death certificate stated he was the son of John J. Wilson, both born in Maryland, and Annabelle Williams, born in Pennsylvania; he die at home in Darlington and informant was his father) [Berkley Memorial Cemetery]

Wilson, Lillian B. February 6, 1902 – August 1, 1930 [Berkley Memorial Cemetery]

Wilson, Maggie May (no tombstone; death certificate stated she was born December 24, 1892, the daughter of Charles Rice and Jane Dutton, all born in Maryland; she married and lived and died at Rocks on January 12, 1916 due to childbirth complications and pneumonia; informant was Arthur Wilson, of Rocks) [Chestnut Grove A. M. E. Church Cemetery, formerly LaGrange Cemetery at Rocks]

Wilson, Margaret S. September 22, 1918 – April 28, 1995 (inscribed "In Our Hearts Forever") [Clark's U. M. Church Cemetery]

Wilson, Marshall L. November 7, 1943 *(sic)* – January 28, 1997, U.S. Army, Korea (*Ed. Note:* His year of birth was apparently engraved incorrectly since he would have been too young to serve in the Korean War, 1951-1955; therefore, his year of birth was probably 1934, not 1943.) [Berkley Memorial Cemetery]

Wilson, Mary died February 8, 1936, age about 67 (no tombstone; death certificate stated she was born in Darlington, was unmarried, and died in Havre de Grace Hospital; parents unknown to informant Ollie Carr, of Havre de Grace) [St. James United Cemetery]

Wilson, Priscilla P. June 27, 1865 – March 3, 1911 (no tombstone; death certificate stated she was the daughter of George Presbury and Sallie Ruff, all born in Harford Co.; she married and died at home in Darlington; informant was Henry Wilson, of Darlington) [Berkley Memorial Cemetery]

Wilson, Raymond Leroy April 4, 1923 – October 18, 1924 (no tombstone; death certificate stated he was son of Henry B. Wilson and Hattie Turner, all born in Maryland; he died in Abingdon and was buried in "Mountain Cemetery;" informant was his mother Hattie Wilson, of Edgewood) [Mt. Zion U. M. Church Cemetery]

Wilson, Samuel died November 4, 1913, age 78 (no tombstone; death certificate stated he was the son of Henry

Wilson and Ruth Dutton, all born in Harford Co.; he married, worked as a farmer and died at home in Castleton; informant was Wesley Wilson, of Darlington) [Berkley Memorial Cemetery]

Wilson, Sarah Jane August 10, 1868 – October 22, 1934 (no tombstone; death certificate stated she was born in Maryland, the daughter of Ely Parrott, born in Virginia, and Hannah Chambers, born in Maryland; she was the widow of Arch Wilson and died at Kalmia, Bel Air RFD; informant was William H. Parrott, of Bel Air RFD) [Clark's U. M. Church Cemetery]

Wilson, Shamekia C. 1980-2012 (small metal funeral home marker) [Community Baptist Church Cemetery]

Wilson, Steven H. February 3, 1843 – May 8, 1924 (inscribed 1843-1924 on same tombstone with Hannah J. Wilson; death certificate stated he was the son of Sham Wilson, both born in Maryland, but his mother's name was not known to informant Mary Wilson Hutchins, of 1226 W. Dolph St. W., Philadelphia, PA; he married, worked as a farmer and died at home near Darlington; military records stated Stephen H. Wilson was a corporal in Co. F, 4th Regt. Inf., U. S. C. T., from August 4, 1863 to May 4, 1866) [Berkley Memorial Cemetery]

Wilson, Syied Tyreik-Duriel, "Loving Son, Brother & Uncle" October 22, 1991 – July 12, 2016 (photo and "The biggest heart, The biggest smile, The waviest waves and one of the realist") [Berkley Memorial Cemetery]

Wilson, Viola E. March 22, 1926 – August 30, 1952 [Berkley Memorial Cemetery]

Wilson, Viola V. September 20, 1906 – January 23, 1992 [Berkley Memorial Cemetery]

Winder, Rose Ann 1941-2017 [Mt. Calvary U. A. M. E. Church Cemetery]

Winfield, George Francis June 15, 1877 – December 23, 1944 (no tombstone; death certificate stated he was son of Peter Winfield and Margaret Tinson, and died in a house fire) [Union U. M. Church Cemetery]

Wing, Clara V. July 28, 1917 – October 5, 1918 (no tombstone; death certificate stated she was the daughter of Rufus Wing and Rebecca Hill, of Havre de Grace) [St. James United Cemetery]

Wing, Edna May January 6, 1935 – February 25, 1935 (no tombstone; death certificate stated she was the daughter of Richard Wing and Ruth Brown, of Havre de Grace) [St. James United Cemetery]

Wing, Martha April 17, 1930 – June 25, 2006 (on same tombstone with Roland H. Wing) [St. James United Cemetery]

Wing, Roland H. December 21, 1923 – February 12, 1992 (on same tombstone with Martha Wing and also on a marker with same dates: Roland H. Wing, Sr., PFC, U.S. Army, World War II) [St. James United Cemetery]

Wing, Roland H. Jr. 1950-2017 (small metal funeral home marker) [St. James United Cemetery]

Wing, Rufus 1883-1958 (on same tombstone with Verle Wing) [St. James United Cemetery]

Wing, Verle 1882-1968 (on same tombstone with Rufus Wing) [St. James United Cemetery]

Wise, Daniel Winslow died April 30, 1950, age about 62 (no tombstone; death certificate stated he was born in Harrisburg, PA, the unmarried son of Samuel Wise and Mary E. Skinner; informant was Paul Wise, of Havre de Grace) [St. James United Cemetery]

Wise, Earline March 2, 1933 – June 14, 1949 (no tombstone; death certificate stated she was born in Mississippi, the daughter of Sylvester Jorden and Neomi Culpepper; she lived at 66 Battle Street in Edgewood and died in Bel Air; she was shot to death by her husband "at Negro High School, Bel Air;" informant was Chester McNutt, 66 Battle St., Edgewood; burial in "John Wesley Cemetery, Magnolia" [Foster's Hill Cemetery]

Wise, Frankanna May 28, 1868 – July 1, 1928 (no tombstone; death certificate stated she was the married daughter of Israel Robinson and Eliza Stansbury; informant was Daniel Wise) [Union U. M. Church Cemetery]

Wise, I. Henry October 29, 1876 – June 20, 1924 (no tombstone; death certificate stated he was the son of Daniel Wise and Mary Ellen Skinner, all born in Maryland; informant was his father) [Skinner Cemetery]

Wise, James February 6, 1915 – April 25, 1919 (no tombstone; death certificate stated he was the son of Thomas Wise and Florence Pinion and was buried in St. James A. M. E. Cemetery) [actually Skinner Cemetery]

Wise, Mabel July 13, 1913 – September 28, 1913 (no tombstone; death certificate stated she was the daughter of

Thomas Wise and Florence Pinion and was buried in St. James A. M. E. Cemetery [actually Skinner Cemetery]

Wise, Mary Ellen died December 21, 1926, age about 60 (but (no tombstone; death certificate stated she was the daughter of Jack Skinner and Frances Legar, of Havre de Grace) [Skinner Cemetery]

Wise, Milton April 2, 1913 – October 4, 1913 (no tombstone; death certificate stated he was the son of Thomas Wise and Susie Pinion and was buried in St. James A. M. E. Cemetery) [actually Skinner Cemetery]

Wise, Paul D. 1895-1964 [Berkley Memorial Cemetery]

Wise, William L. June 20, 1929 – June 14, 1949 (no tombstone; death certificate stated he was born in North Carolina, the son of Clarence E. Wise and Lena White; he lived at 628 N. Bond St. in Baltimore, worked as a laborer and died in Bel Air; he shot himself to death at "Negro High School, Bel Air;" informant was Hester Holmes, 18B Hartman St., Edgewood; burial in "John Wesley Cemetery, Magnolia" [Foster's Hill Cemetery]

Wise, William Lee Jr. March 8, 1949 – April 11, 1949 (no tombstone; death certificate stated he was born in Havre de Grace, son of William Wise, born in North Carolina, and Earlene Culpepper, born in Mississippi, and he died in Edgewood; informant was William L. Wise, of 628 N. Bond St., Baltimore; burial in "Magnolia Methodist Cemetery, Magnolia") [Foster's Hill Cemetery]

Witherspoon, Baby 1968-1968 (copied in 1987, but not found in 2018) [Berkley Memorial Cemetery]

Witherspoon, Christine May 25, 1922 – June 10, 2000 (on same tombstone with Julius Witherspoon) [St. James United Cemetery]

Witherspoon, Connie 1945-2018 (small metal funeral home marker) [St. James United Cemetery]

Witherspoon, Jeniful, "Jim" November 6, 1952 – July 2, 1997 (tombstone; James Dorsey Card File, African American Obituaries, that is maintained at the Historical Society of Harford County, has an obituary from an unidentified newspaper on July 7, 1997 stating he was born in Havre de Grace, moved to Baltimore, lived in Cedonia, retired from the Social Security Administration, died at Joseph Richey Hospital, and was survived by his mother Christine Witherspoon, of Aberdeen, three brothers and two sisters) [St. James United Cemetery]

Witherspoon, Julius June 1, 1923 - October 19, 1978 (on same tombstone with Christine Witherspoon and his military service, PFC, U.S. Army, World War II, is on a separate grave marker) [St. James United Cemetery]

Witherspoon, Selena 1924-2011 [St. James United Cemetery]

Wood, John 1902 – December 2, 1926 (no tombstone; death certificate stated he was born in North Carolina, not married, and died in Darlington at the Stone & Webster Co. Hospital; parents unknown to informant Dr. V. H. Michael) [St. James United Cemetery]

Woodard, Hauson T., "Tank" December 13, 1984 – May 8, 2011 (inscribed "Gone But Not Forgotten" with an image of a motorcycle and a separate photo of him) [St. James United Cemetery]

Wooden, Donna E. Jackson, "A Loving Mother" June 8, 1959 – March 19, 1997 (tombstone; James Dorsey Card File, African American Obituaries, maintained at the Historical Society of Harford County, has a card with obituary from an unidentified newspaper on March 26, 1997 stating Donna Elaine Wooden was born in Queens, NY, the daughter of Herbert Roosevelt Dews, of Abingdon, and the late Constance Mareva Perkins Dews; she lived in Bel Air, was a psychologist and worked for the Family Preservation Initiative of Baltimore, and died in Abingdon; survived by her father, two daughters, a brother, and two sisters) [St. James United Cemetery]

Woods, Paul Jr. July 15, 1921 – August 21, 1987, SP3, U.S. Army, WW II, Korea [St. James United Cemetery]

Woods, Sarah V. 1935-1991 (tombstone; James Dorsey Card File, African American Obituaries, that is maintained at the Historical Society of Harford County, has a card with obituary from an unidentified newspaper on September 18, 1991 stating Sarah Virginia Woods was born in Aberdeen, the daughter of the late Jacob A. Giles and Eva Kenly, and she was a custodian at the Hillsdale Elementary School for more than 20 years and retired from the Harford County Board of Education; she lived in Aberdeen and died at Harford Memorial Hospital, survived by two brothers and three sisters) [Union U. M. Church Cemetery]

Woolfolk, Jesse (Rev.) 1898-1968 (tombstone; obituary in *The Aegis* on February 8, 1968 stated he was born in

Spotsylvania, VA, the son of Samuel and Genniareather Woolfolk; he retired from the Aberdeen Proving Ground in July, 1967, was a Mason, and was pastor of the New Hope Baptist Church in Bel Air; he lived at 517 Girard Street in Havre de Grace and died at Harford Memorial Church on February 2, 1968, survived by a sister and three brothers) [Union U. M. Church Cemetery]

Worin, William died January 7, 1918, age 79 (no tombstone; death certificate stated he was born in Virginia, but his parents were unknown to informant Mary C. Hemore, of Havre de Grace; he was married, worked as day laborer and lived and died in Havre de Grace) [Asbury Cemetery]

Worthington, Charles Wilmer July 15, 1894 – April 18, 1935 (no tombstone; death certificate stated he was born in Harford Co., the son of Ezekiel Worthington, born in Pennsylvania, and Annie Bonds, born in Harford Co.; he married Annie ----, worked as a day laborer for 20 years, lived near Aberdeen, was struck by a B&O train in Aberdeen and died in Havre de Grace Hospital; informant was Mrs. Emma Warfield, of Aberdeen) [Mt. Calvary U. A. M. E. Church Cemetery]

Worthington, Jaida 2004-2005 (small metal funeral home marker) [St. James United Cemetery]

Wright, Bessie 1920-1979 (copied in 1987, but not found in 2018) [St. James United Cemetery]

Wright, Florence October 23, 1905 – October 25, 1905 (no tombstone; death certificate stated she was the daughter of William Wright, born in Pennsylvania, and Lizzie Pitt, born in Harford Co.; she died at home near Cole P. O., but place of burial was not given; probably Old Union Chapel Cemetery at Michaelsville [possibly reinterred in Union U. M. Church Cemetery near Aberdeen]

Wright, Jesse September 16, 1857 – March 8, 1926? (no tombstone) [St. James United Cemetery]

Wright, Josephine 1889-1926 (tombstone; death certificate stated she was born on February 15, 1889 and died on November 29, 1926 in Havre de Grace, married daughter of John Burk, of Pennsylvania, and Mary Ellen Young, of Maryland; informant was Edward Wright, of Havre de Grace) [St. James United Cemetery]

Wright, Mary E. January 1, 1870 – October 11, 1912 (no tombstone; death certificate stated she was the daughter of Stephen Peaker and Eliza Bishop, and they were all born in Harford Co.; she was married, worked as a servant and died in Bel Air; informant was Charlott Johnson, of Bel Air) [John Wesley U. M. E. Church Cemetery in Abingdon]

Wyche, Mary C. 1937-1998 (on the same tombstone with Otis G. Wyche; however, the dates are wrong; obituary in *The Aegis* on June 16, 1999 stated Mary Cornelia Wyche was born on November 4, 1932, daughter of William Govan(s) and Laura Rebecca Blaney, married Grant Otis Wyche and died June 11, 1999, age 66 *(sic)* in Bel Air) [Chestnut Grove A. M. E. Church Cemetery, formerly LaGrange Cemetery at Rocks]

Wyche, Otis G. 1925-2001 (on the same tombstone with Mary C. Wyche; obituary in *The Aegis* on July 6, 2001 stated Otis Grant Wyche was born in Portsmouth, VA, the son of Grant Otis and Pinkie Wyche, married Mary Govans, served in U.S. Navy in World War II and died at Upper Chesapeake Medical Center in Bel Air on July 3, 2001, age 87 *(sic)*) [Chestnut Grove A. M. E. Church Cemetery, formerly LaGrange Cemetery at Rocks]

York, Harret died March 31, 1919, age 71 (no tombstone; death certificate stated "Harret" was a widow and the daughter of Charles Stewart, both born in Maryland, but her mother was unknown to informant Sharlett R. Holland, of Aberdeen RFD #3) [Union U. M. Church Cemetery]

York, John W. died January 7, 1892, age 63 (inscribed "In Memory Of" and "Blessed are the dead who die in the Lord") [Old Union Chapel M. E. Church Cemetery]

Young (name inscribed on two small stone markers about 8 inches square and placed flat on the ground at the head and foot of the grave site) [Asbury Cemetery]

Young, Alexander died August 15, 1938, age about 70 (no tombstone; death certificate stated he was born in Harford Co., but informant Howard Bonte, of Aberdeen RFD, did not know his parents' names; he was single and worked as a farm laborer at Level for 69 years) [Green Spring U. M. Church Cemetery]

Young, Caroline died November 28, 1901, age 43 (no tombstone; death certificate stated she was born in Harford Co., the daughter of Benjamin Johnson and Charlotte James, and wife of Robert Young; she died in Bel

Air and on back of death certificate it is written "Mountain") [Mt. Zion U. M. Church Cemetery]

Young, Dupree March 6, 1896 – October 20, 1967, Maryland, Pvt., Co. A, 408 Res Lab Bn, QMC, World War I (tombstone; however, published Maryland records do not list his name) [Union U. M. Church Cemetery]

Young, Evelyn Marie Presbury August 11, 1929 – June 10, 1996 [Fairview A. M. E. Church Cemetery]

Young, Henry died November 12, 1860, age 23 years, 1 month and 5 days (inscribed "May he rest in peace" when copied in 1987, but marker not found in 2018) [Asbury Cemetery]

Young, Joseph March – (blank), 1884 – August 30, 1946 (no tombstone; Kurtz Funeral Home Record Book 1944-1949, p. 120, stated he was born at Hereford, Baltimore Co., the son of John Young, but his mother and their birth places were unknown to informant Helen Winston, 2535 N. Howard St., Baltimore; he was divorced and died at home in Jarrettsville) [Fairview A. M. E. Church Cemetery]

Young, Rutledge A. April 10, 1908 – September 17, 1977, Pvt., U.S. Army, World War II (tombstone; obituary in *The Aegis* on September 22, 1977 stated he was born in Lauren, SC, son of the late Nancy Young and husband of the late Mary J. Young; a veteran of World War II he was a cook, grew up in the Bel Air area and died at the Veterans Administration Hospital in Baltimore on September 17, 1977, age 69) [Asbury Cemetery]

Heritage Books by Henry C. Peden, Jr.:

A Closer Look at St. John's Parish Registers [Baltimore County, Maryland], 1701–1801

A Collection of Maryland Church Records

A Guide to Genealogical Research in Maryland: 5th Edition, Revised and Enlarged

*Abstracts of Marriages and Deaths in
Harford County, Maryland, Newspapers, 1837–1871*

Abstracts of the Ledgers and Accounts of the Bush Store and Rock Run Store, 1759–1771

Abstracts of the Orphans Court Proceedings of Harford County, 1778–1800

Abstracts of Wills, Harford County, Maryland, 1800–1805

African American Cemeteries in Harford County, Maryland

Anne Arundel County, Maryland, Marriage References 1658–1800
Henry C. Peden, Jr. and Veronica Clarke Peden

Baltimore City [Maryland] Deaths and Burials, 1834–1840

Baltimore County, Maryland, Overseers of Roads, 1693–1793

Bastardy Cases in Baltimore County, Maryland, 1673–1783

Bastardy Cases in Harford County, Maryland, 1774–1844

More Bastardy Cases in Harford County, Maryland, 1773–1893

Bible and Family Records of Harford County, Maryland, Families: Volume V

*Biographical Dictionary of Harford County, Maryland, 1774–1974:
Over 1,200 Sketches of Prominent Citizens during the First 200 years of the County's History
with Seventeen Appendices Listing Public Officials from 1774 to 2020*
Henry C. Peden, Jr. and William O. Carr

Cecil County, Maryland Marriage References, 1674–1824
Henry C. Peden, Jr. and Veronica Clarke Peden

Children of Harford County: Indentures and Guardianships, 1801–1830

Colonial Delaware Soldiers and Sailors, 1638–1776

*Colonial Families of the Eastern Shore of Maryland
Volumes 5, 6, 7, 8, 9, 11, 12, 13, 14, 16, and 19*
Henry C. Peden, Jr. and F. Edward Wright

Colonial Families of the Eastern Shore of Maryland: Volume 21 and Volume 23

Colonial Maryland Soldiers and Sailors, 1634–1734

Colonial Tavern Keepers of Maryland and Delaware, 1634–1776

Dorchester County, Maryland, Marriage References, 1669–1800
Henry C. Peden, Jr. and Veronica Clarke Peden

Dr. John Archer's First Medical Ledger, 1767–1769, Annotated Abstracts

Early Anglican Records of Cecil County

*Early Harford Countians, Individuals Living in
Harford County, Maryland in Its Formative Years
Volume 1: A to K, Volume 2: L to Z, and Volume 3: Supplement*

Family Cemeteries and Grave Sites in Harford County, Maryland

First Presbyterian Church Records, Baltimore, Maryland, 1840–1879

Frederick County, Maryland, Marriage References and Family Relationships, 1748–1800
Henry C. Peden, Jr. and Veronica Clarke Peden

Genealogical Gleanings from Harford County, Maryland, Medical Records, 1772–1852
Winner of the Norris Harris Prize from MHS for
the best genealogical reference book in 2016!

Harford County Taxpayers in 1870, 1872 and 1883

Harford County, Maryland Death Records, 1849–1899

Harford County, Maryland Deponents, 1775–1835

Harford County, Maryland Divorces and Separations, 1823–1923

Harford County, Maryland, Death Certificates, 1898–1918: An Annotated Index

Harford County, Maryland, Divorce Cases, 1827–1912: An Annotated Index

Harford County, Maryland, Inventories, 1774–1804

Harford County, Maryland, Marriage References and Family Relationships, 1774–1824
Henry C. Peden, Jr. and Veronica Clarke Peden

Harford County, Maryland, Marriage References and Family Relationships, 1825–1850

Harford County, Maryland, Marriage References and Family Relationships, 1851–1860
Henry C. Peden, Jr. and Veronica Clarke Peden

Harford County, Maryland, Marriage References and Family Relationships, 1861–1870
Henry C. Peden, Jr. and Veronica Clarke Peden

Harford County, Maryland, Marriage References and Family Relationships, 1871–1875

Harford County, Maryland, Marriage References and Family Relationships, 1876–1880

Harford (Maryland) Homicides: Cases of Murder and Attempted Murder: Committed by Men and Women Who Were "Seduced by the Instigation of the Devil" in Harford County, Maryland During the 18th and 19th Centuries

Harford (Maryland) Suicides: Cases of Self-killings and Attempted Suicides Committed by Men and Women Who Suffered from an "Aberration of the Mind" in Harford County, Maryland, 1817–1947

Harford (Old Brick Baptist) Church, Harford County, Maryland, Records and Members (1742–1974), Tombstones, Burials (1775–2009) and Family Relationships

Heirs and Legatees of Harford County, Maryland, 1774–1802

Heirs and Legatees of Harford County, Maryland, 1802–1846

Inhabitants of Baltimore County, Maryland, 1763–1774

Inhabitants of Cecil County, Maryland 1774–1800

Inhabitants of Cecil County, Maryland, 1649–1774

Inhabitants of Harford County, Maryland, 1791–1800

Inhabitants of Kent County, Maryland, 1637–1787

Insolvent Debtors in 19th Century Harford County, Maryland: A Legal and Genealogical Digest

Joseph A. Pennington & Co., Havre De Grace, Maryland, Funeral Home Records: Volume II, 1877–1882, 1893–1900

Kent County, Maryland Marriage References, 1642–1800
Henry C. Peden, Jr. and Veronica Clarke Peden

Marriages and Deaths from Baltimore Newspapers, 1817–1824

Maryland Bible Records, Volume 1: Baltimore and Harford Counties

Maryland Bible Records, Volume 2: Baltimore and Harford Counties

Maryland Bible Records, Volume 3: Carroll County

Maryland Bible Records, Volume 4: Eastern Shore

Maryland Bible Records, Volume 5: Harford, Baltimore and Carroll Counties

Maryland Bible Records, Volume 7: Baltimore, Harford and Frederick Counties

Maryland Deponents, 1634–1799

Maryland Deponents: Volume 3, 1634–1776

Maryland Prisoners Languishing in Goal, Volume 1: 1635–1765

Maryland Prisoners Languishing in Goal, Volume 2: 1766–1800

Maryland Public Service Records, 1775–1783: A Compendium of Men and Women of Maryland Who Rendered Aid in Support of the American Cause against Great Britain during the Revolutionary War

Marylanders and Delawareans in the French and Indian War, 1756–1763

Marylanders to Carolina: Migration of Marylanders to North Carolina and South Carolina prior to 1800

Marylanders to Kentucky, 1775–1825

Marylanders to Ohio and Indiana, Migration Prior to 1835

Marylanders to Tennessee

Methodist Records of Baltimore City, Maryland: Volume 1, 1799–1829

Methodist Records of Baltimore City, Maryland: Volume 2, 1830–1839

Methodist Records of Baltimore City, Maryland: Volume 3, 1840–1850 (East City Station)

More Maryland Deponents, 1716–1799

*More Marylanders to Carolina:
Migration of Marylanders to North Carolina and South Carolina prior to 1800*

More Marylanders to Kentucky, 1778–1828

More Marylanders to Ohio and Indiana: Migrations Prior to 1835

Orphans and Indentured Children of Baltimore County, Maryland, 1777–1797

Outpensioners of Harford County, Maryland, 1856–1896

Presbyterian Records of Baltimore City, Maryland, 1765–1840

Quaker Records of Baltimore and Harford Counties, Maryland, 1801–1825

Quaker Records of Northern Maryland, 1716–1800

Quaker Records of Southern Maryland, 1658–1800

Revolutionary Patriots of Anne Arundel County, Maryland, 1775–1783

Revolutionary Patriots of Baltimore Town and Baltimore County, 1775–1783

Revolutionary Patriots of Calvert and St. Mary's Counties, Maryland, 1775–1783

Revolutionary Patriots of Caroline County, Maryland, 1775–1783

Revolutionary Patriots of Cecil County, Maryland, 1775–1783

Revolutionary Patriots of Charles County, Maryland, 1775–1783

Revolutionary Patriots of Delaware, 1775–1783

Revolutionary Patriots of Dorchester County, Maryland, 1775–1783

Revolutionary Patriots of Frederick County, Maryland, 1775–1783

Revolutionary Patriots of Harford County, Maryland, 1775–1783

Revolutionary Patriots of Kent and Queen Anne's Counties, 1775–1783

Revolutionary Patriots of Lancaster County, Pennsylvania, 1775–1783

Revolutionary Patriots of Maryland, 1775–1783: A Supplement

Revolutionary Patriots of Maryland, 1775–1783: Second Supplement

Revolutionary Patriots of Montgomery County, Maryland, 1776–1783

Revolutionary Patriots of Prince George's County, Maryland, 1775–1783

Revolutionary Patriots of Talbot County, Maryland, 1775–1783

Revolutionary Patriots of Washington County, Maryland, 1776–1783

Revolutionary Patriots of Worcester and Somerset Counties, Maryland, 1775–1783

*St. George's (Old Spesutia) Parish
Harford County, Maryland Church and Cemetery Records, 1820–1920*

St. John's and St. George's Parish Registers, 1696–1851

Survey Field Book of David and William Clark in Harford County, Maryland, 1770–1812

Talbot County, Maryland Marriage References, 1662–1800
Henry C. Peden, Jr. and Veronica Clarke Peden

The Crenshaws of Kentucky, 1800–1995

The Delaware Militia in the War of 1812

*Union Chapel United Methodist Church Cemetery Tombstone Inscriptions,
Wilna, Harford County, Maryland*

www.ingramcontent.com/pod-product-compliance
Lightning Source LLC
Chambersburg PA
CBHW080533300426
44111CB00017B/2697